BALI
HANDBOOK

"Statoë's

→ Kapal"

No good.

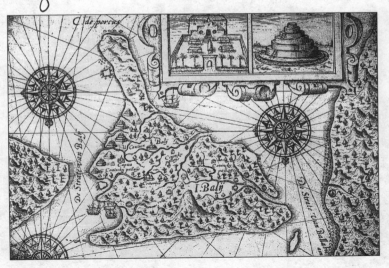

drawn by Francis Valentine; published by the Vereenigde Oost-Indische Compagnie in 1725

BALI
HANDBOOK

SECOND EDITION

BILL DALTON

MOON
PUBLICATIONS INC.

BALI HANDBOOK
SECOND EDITION

Published by
Moon Publications, Inc.
P.O. Box 3040
Chico, California 95927-3040, USA

Printed by
Colorcraft Ltd., Hong Kong

ISBN: 1-56691-073-0
ISSN: 1088-0933

Editors: Michael Raymond Greer, Kevin Jeys
Assisting Editors: Matt Orendorff, Patricia Reilly, Mike Sigalas
Copy Editor: Nicole Revere
Production & Design: Carey Wilson
Cartographers: Bob Race, Brian Bardwell, Chris Folks, Rob Warner
Index: Diane Wurzel

Front cover illustration: Willem Gerard Hofker's "Festival Day," from the collection of the Agung Rai Fine
Art Gallery, Peliatan, Ubud, Bali

All photos by Bill Dalton unless otherwise noted.

Distributed in the USA and Canada by Publishers Group West
Printed in Hong Kong

Please send all comments,
corrections, additions,
amendments, and critiques to:

**BALI HANDBOOK
MOON PUBLICATIONS, INC.
P.O. BOX 3040
CHICO, CA 95927-3040, USA
e-mail: travel@moon.com
or
bdalton@ttci.net**

Printing History
1st edition — December 1989
Reprinted — February 1992
2nd edition — July 1997

Dedicated to my daughters
Sri and Ari

CONTENTS

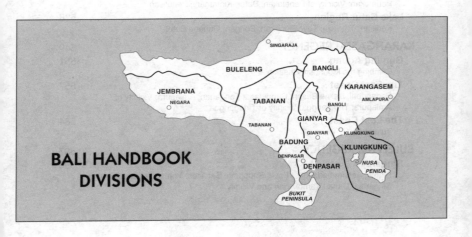

BALI HANDBOOK
DIVISIONS

MAPS

MAP SYMBOLS

WATER	MAIN ROAD	■	POINT OF INTEREST
TEMPLE (PURA)	SECONDARY ROAD	•	ACCOMMODATION
MOSQUE (MESJID)	UNPAVED ROAD	○	CITY
GAS STATION	PATH/TRAIL	○	TOWN VILLAGE
AIRPORT/AIRSTRIP	BRIDGE	▲	MOUNTAIN
	DISTRICT BOUNDARY	★	SIGHTSEEING ATTRACTION
	REGENCY BOUNDARY		

CHARTS AND SPECIAL TOPICS

ABBREVIATIONS

ABRI—Angkatan Bersenjata Republik Indonesia
    (Armed Forces of the Republic of Indonesia)

a/c—air-conditioned, air-conditioning

d—double occupancy

IDD—International Direct Dial

MAS—Malaysian Airlines System

PKI—Partai Komunis Indonesia (Communist
    Party of Indonesia)

Rp—rupiah

s—single occupancy

SESRI—Sekolah Seni Rupa Indonesia (High
    School of Fine Arts)

SMKI—Sekolah Menengah Karawitan Indonesia
    (government-run academy of instrumental and
    performing arts in Batubulan)

STSI—Sekolah Tinggi Seni Indonesia (the
    government-run performing arts academy in
    Denpasar)

YHA—Youth Hostel Association

ACKNOWLEDGMENTS

SCORES OF PEOPLE HAVE CONTRIBUTED their talents and insights into this much-expanded second edition of *Bali Handbook.* For all their support and encouragement I give sincere thanks. My gratitude first goes to my editors Kevin Jeys and Mike Greer who worked so hard and skillfully to make this the best and most comprehensive textual survey to Bali yet published. Thanks also to Dave Hurst, our art director, who chose the photographs, and Bob Race, our in-house illustrator, who created all the line and tonal art for my guide. Chris Folks and Rob Warner deserve high praise for turning out such fine maps. I am also grateful to Sue Booth, Moon's publicist, for her diligent efforts in launching *Bali Handbook,* second edition.

Special thanks also to the constant support provided by all of Bali's regency tourist offices, in particular the staff at the Denpasar Government Tourist Office in Denpasar. Finally, this guide would not have the depth nor the ring of firsthand authenticity were it not for the hundreds of readers who have sent in information and tips over the years since *Indonesia Handbook* was first published in the mid-1970s and *Bali Handbook* was published in 1990.

LET US HEAR FROM YOU

Although I do everything in my power to make the information in *Bali Handbook* as accurate and current as possible, the task can be daunting. You can help. Please let me know if prices have gone up, if services have been discontinued or are now unacceptable, if certain suggestions are misleading, if you can offer shortcuts, warnings, transport tips, or information on new guesthouses or closed restaurants. If you come across a special place we do not mention, fill me in so I can pass your recommendation on to other users of the guide. A questionnaire in the back of this guide will help me find out about who you are and learn about what improvements might be made for the third edition.

We also value highly letters from resident expatriates, hikers, and outdoor enthusiasts. Letters from Balinese themselves, with their impressions of *Bali Handbook* and their insider's view of Bali, are particularly welcome. Correspondence from hotels and restaurants, including complete address, fax number, and guest commentaries, are also welcome (letters written in Indonesian are quite acceptable). If you can correct, improve, or add to a map, or are able to suggest a new and useful map, send it in.

Amateur and professional photographers are also invited to submit photographs for consideration. All photos must be specifically identified if they're to be of any use. Photographers will be acknowledged in the book's photo credits, and receive a free copy of the edition in which their work first appears. By submitting photos, it's understood the photograther is granting Moon Publications the nonexclusive right to publish the photo(s) under the above terms. The publisher cannot, in most cases, return photographs.

This guide is updated at every reprint and completely revised every two years, so your contributions will eventually be shared with thousands of other travelers to Bali. Address letters to:

Bali Handbook
c/o Moon Publications, Inc.
P.O. Box 3040
Chico, CA 95927-3040

or e-mail us at
travel@moon.com

BOB RACE

INTRODUCTION

This tiny island of nearly three million Hindus, surrounded by a sea of 190 million Muslims, is one of the smallest yet most visited of Indonesia's main islands. More than 500,000 visitors arrive each year on this beautiful isle that exactly fits the Western definition of a tropical paradise, famous for its charming people, lovely scenery, and the sophisticated artistry of its distinctly Indonesian-Hindu civilization. Earlier versions of this Hindu culture once flourished over large areas of Java and portions of the other islands, but it's now found almost exclusively on Bali. Today Bali is less a western Pacific paradise than an Asian hotbox—overpopulated, overdeveloped, underfed, and prone to eruptions, both volcanic and political.

THE LAND

Lying less than two kilometers off Java's eastern tip, Bali is the westernmost island of the chain that contains the Lesser Sundas. Its northern coast faces the Bali Sea, the eastern coast lies 24 kilometers west of the Indonesian island of Lombok in Nusatenggara, and the southern coast faces the Indian Ocean.

Compared with some of the Indonesian archipelago's giants, Bali is quite small, with an area of only 5,632 square kilometers, about the size of the U.S. state of Delaware. The mushroom-shaped island measures 90 kilometers along its north-south axis, and 135 kilometers from east to west. The neck of the island at its narrowest is only 18 kilometers wide.

A geographic extension of Java, Bali shares much the same topography, climate, flora, and fauna as the mother island. Roughly 18% of Bali's arable land is covered in rice fields, 27% in dry fields, 23% in forests, 17% in commercial gardens, and 12% in valleys, with the remaining acreage covered by urban and suburban areas. Most of the population lives in the rural villages of the southern half of the island. The island's largest expanses of forests are found in the thinly populated west and around the six volcanoes ranging from Gunung Agung to Gunung Patas.

Bali's dry months (May-Sept.) prevent the development of true tropical rainforests or fetid malarial swamps. It is an island blessed with a

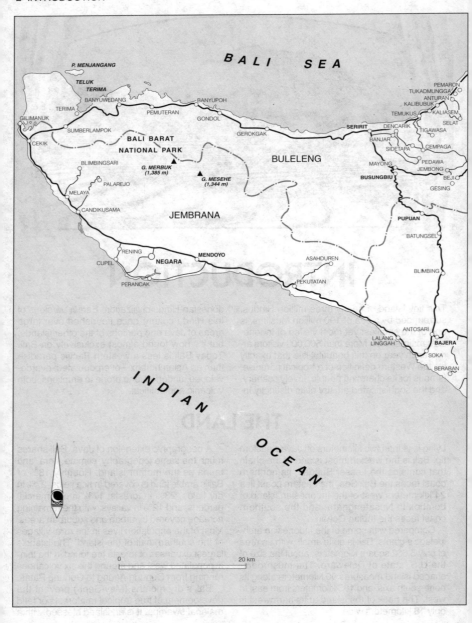

BALI SEA

P. MENJANGANG

TELUK
TERIMA

PEMARON
TUKADMUNGGA
ANTURAN
KALIBUBUK
KALIASEM
TEMUKUS
SELAT
DENCARIK
TIGAWASA
CEMPAGA

BANYUWEDANG

TERIMA

BANYUPOH

SERIRIT

BANJAR
SIDETAPA

GILIMANUK

PEMUTERAN

GONDOL

SUMBERLAMPOK

GEROKGAK

CEKIK

BALI BARAT
NATIONAL PARK

BULELENG

PEDAWA
JEMBONG
BEJI

MAYONG

BLIMBINGSARI

BUSUNGBIU

G. MERBUK
(1,385 m)

G. MESEHE
(1,344 m)

GESING

PALAREJO

PUPUAN

MELAYA

JEMBRANA

BATUNGSEL

CANDIKUSAMA

RENING

BLIMBING

NEGARA

MENDOYO

CUPEL

ASAHDUREN

PERANCAK

PEKUTATAN

INDIAN

LALANG
LINGGAH

ANTOSARI

BAJERA

OCEAN

SOKA

BERABAN

0   20 km

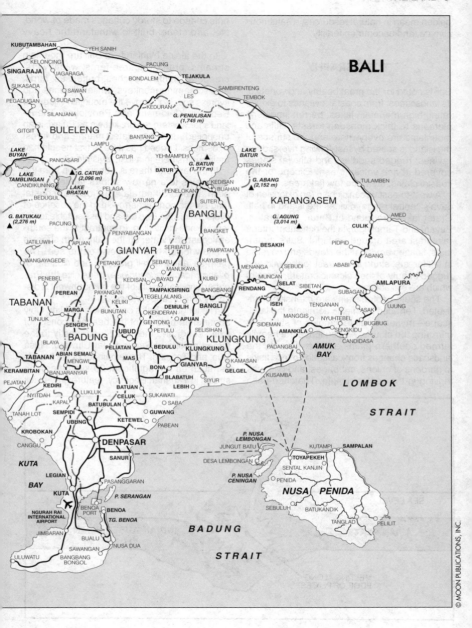

BALI

KUBUTAMBAHAN
YEH SANIH
KELONCING
PACUNG
SINGARAJA
JAGARAGA
BONDALEM
TEJAKULA
SUKASADA
SAWAN
SAMBIRENTENG
PEGADUGAN
SUDAJI
LES
TEMBOK
SILANJANA
KEDURAN
GITGIT
BULELENG
LAMPU
G. PENULISAN
▲ (1,745 m)
SONGAN
LAKE
BUYAN
BANTANG
YEHMAMPEH
G. BATUR
BATUR
LAKE
BATUR
PANCASARI
CATUR
G. CATUR
(2,096 m)
TERUNYAN
TULAMBEN
LAKE
TAMBLINGAN
CANDIKUNING
LAKE
BRATAN
PELAGA
KATUNG
PENELOKAN
KEDISAN
BUAHAN
G. ABANG
(2,152 m)
BEDUGUL
SUTER
KARANGASEM
AMED
G. BATUKAU
▲ (2,276 m)
PACUNG
PENYABANGAN
BANGLI
BANGKET
G. AGUNG
(3,014 m)
CULIK
JATILUWIH
APUAN
SERIBATU
BESAKIH
PIDPID
ABANG
WANGAYAGEDE
GIANYAR
PETANG
SEBATU
PAMPATAN
KAYUBIHI
MENANGA
SEBUDI
ABABI
PENEBEL
KEDISAN
MANUKAYA
KUBU
MUNCAN
AMLAPURA
TABANAN
PEREAN
PAYANGAN
BAYAD
TAMPAKSIRING
BANGBANG
RENDANG
SELAT
SIBETAN
SUBAGAN
MARGA
KELIKI
TEGELLALANG
DEMULIH
BANGLI
ISEH
TENGANAN
ASAK
UJUNG
TUNJUK
BUNUTAN
OKENDERAN
APUAN
SIDEMAN
MANGGIS
NYUHTEBEL
BUGBUG
SENGEH
GENTONG
SELISIHAN
SENGKIDU
BLAYA
BADUNG
UBUD
PETULU
KLUNGKUNG
AMANKILA
CANDIDASA
ABIAN SEMAL
PELIATAN
BEDULU
PADANGBAI
AMUK
BAY
KERAMBITAN
MENGWI
MAS
BONA
GIANYAR
KAMASAN
BANJARANYAR
BLABATUH
GELGEL
TABANAN
BATUAN
LEBIH
SIYUR
KUSAMBA
LOMBOK
PEJATAN
KEDIRI
LUKLUK
CELUK
SUKAWATI
NYITDAH
KAPAL
SABA
STRAIT
TANAH LOT
SEMPIDI
BATUBULAN
GUWANG
UBUNG
KETEWEL
PABEAN
KROBOKAN
DENPASAR
CANGGU
SANUR
P. NUSA
LEMBONGAN
KUTAMPI
SAMPALAN
KUTA
JUNGUT BATU
TOYAPEKEH
BAY
LEGIAN
PASANGGARAN
DESA LEMBONGAN
SENTAL KANJIN
BAY
KUTA
P. SERANGAN
P. NUSA
CENINGAN
PENIDA
NGURAH RAI
INTERNATIONAL
AIRPORT
BENOA
PORT
BENOA
NUSA
PENIDA
SEBULUH
BATUKANDIK
JIMBARAN
TG. BENOA
BADUNG
BUALU
NUSA DUA
TANGLAD
PELILIT
ULUWATU
SAWANGAN
STRAIT
BANGBANG
BONGOL

golden mean in natural resources, a salubrious climate, and uncommon fertility.

TOPOGRAPHY

Bali is noted for the great beauty and variety of its landscapes, from coastal lowlands to exhilarating high mountain lakes, barren limestone plateaus to thick monsoon forests. Hills and mountains are everywhere and the surface of the island is scored by fast-flowing rivers, deep ravines, rugged saddles, and alluvial slopes covered in rich volcanic ash. Except for the coastal plains, there are few flat areas.

A west-to-east volcanic chain (an extension of Java's central range) divides the island in half. Crater lakes are found at Batur, and Bratan, Buyan, and Tamblingan in the rich submontane rainforest area around Bedugul. Bali's mountains, floating amongst the clouds and covered in tall forests, stand in contrast to the wild and rugged beauty of the volcanic craters, some of which are still active.

The south-central plains are intensively cultivated. Terraced rice fields dominate the landscape—myriad small rectangles of still water mirroring the clouds. As you leave the heavily farmed southern plains and head north, the landscape changes from cascades of rice fields to gardens of onions, cabbages, and papayas thriving in the cooler climate. Thatched-palm huts change to sturdy cottages made of wood, tile, and stone, built to withstand the heavy rains.

In the alpine highlands of Bali are mountain streams, prehistoric tree-ferns, wildflowers, creepers, orchids, leeches, butterflies, birds, and screaming monkeys, while tall pines and cypress soar high above the mountain villages of Bedugul, Kintamani, and Penelokan. The island's far western region, known as Pulaki, is an unspoiled, underpopulated marine and forest wilderness. Legend has it Bali's first people had their origins here in a lost, invisible city.

In the far north there is a sharp drop from the mountains to a narrow strip of fertile coastal plain around Singaraja. The lowland coastal fringe of the north is narrow, and the absence of rivers makes the land dry and less suitable for intensive rice cultivation. In contrast to the southern coast, the water off the calm north shore is shallow for up to a kilometer out to sea. The palm savannahs, tall grasses, and clusters of *pilang (Acacia leucophloea)* trees give the Prapat Agung Peninsula of the far northwest a distinctly African appearance.

The length of Bali's coastline is 460 km. Only about eight percent of the beaches consist of white sand, and they are found mostly in the famed resorts of Sanur, Kuta, Uluwatu, Nusa Dua, and Tanjung. The remainder of the beaches, such as a magnificent 30-kilometer-long stretch in Tabanan Regency, feature gray-black

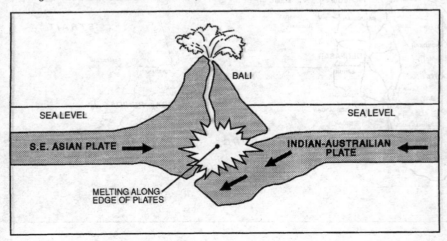

Terraced rice fields dominate Bali's landscape.

volcanic couscous-like sand and are almost deserted—like being on another planet.

The coast from Sanur extending down through Benoa Bay is long and sheltered, lined with 1,400 hectares of natural mangrove forests and mudflats. Because so many of the original mangrove stands suffered from the effects of saltmaking, shrimp ponds, coral collecting, and the charcoal industry, a major reforestation project has been underway along this coastal strip since 1992.

Bali's six volcanic peaks, all exceeding 2,000 meters, trap rain clouds that swell the rivers rushing down from the highlands through deep, narrow gorges overgrown with lush tropical vegetation. Running parallel to each other north to south, irrigating the rice fields on the lower slopes, are Bali's two major rivers, the Pakrisan ("Kris River") and the Petanu ("Cursed River"), their history steeped in myths and legends. Both are regarded as holy; it is on their banks where most of the archaeological remains of Bali's ancient kingdoms have been found.

The astonishingly rich coastal plains of the south have given rise to Bali's unique civilization. Until recent times, the entire southern drainage of the island has been politically divided into eight small but powerful rajadoms. These partitioned, pie-shaped realms of south Bali were always aligned north to south along the ravines rather than east to west—travel on Bali has always been hampered by deeply cut longitudinal ravines. Even today, because of the island's difficult topography, most highways carry traffic north and south.

Bali lies over two major tectonic plates—the rigid Sunda plate to the north and the Indo-Australian plate to the south—that grind over one another, producing frequent geologic instability. One of the worst natural catastrophes of this century was the 1917 earthquake in which a series of tremors devastated the eastern and southern regions of the island, followed by a major eruption of Gunung Batur. When the tremors came to an end, 1,500 people had died and 2,431 temples and 64,000 homes had been destroyed.

Another extremely destructive eruption of 1,717-meter-high Batur occurred in 1963. In August 1994, after lying dormant for 20 years, the volcano began to erupt again, venting more than 600 times a day and shooting hot ashes and smoke into the sky for months. Bali's highest and most revered mountain, Gunung Agung, which also erupted in 1963, destroying villages and covering fertile rice fields with rivers of lava and showers of ash and debris.

The Periphery

The climate and landforms on the island's fringes and Bali's offshore islands differ drastically from the lush lowland plains. The far eastern peninsula of Karangasem, surrounding Gunung Seraya, is arid and hot, the land difficult to cultivate. In the far south, the tableland of the Bukit Peninsula, with its scarce water and bushy thickets, is Mediterranean in appearance. The western and southern shores of this barren plateau are lined with rugged, 150-meter-high limestone cliffs and deep caves.

The islands of Nusa Lembongan, Nusa Ceningan, and Nusa Penida in the deep strait between Bali and Lombok are as dry and inhospitable as the Bukit. On these austere islands of limestone hills, poor rocky soil, scrubby vegetation, and open grassland, the inhabitants live in coral-walled villages and eke out a subsistence living growing maize, beans, and cassava. The reefs and clear waters of these sister islands make for spectacular diving.

Spatial Orientation

Geographically, Bali is divided by its chain of mountains into two halves, Bali Selatan ("South Bali") and Bali Utara ("North Bali"). The Balinese of North Bali call South Bali "Bali Tengah" (literally, "Central Bali"), which refers to all the regencies in Bali except Buleleng.

Among the chain of volcanic mountains traversing the island from west to east is Gunung Agung (elev. 3,014 meters), Gunung Batukau (2,276 meters), Gunung Abang (2,152 meters), and Gunung Batur (1,717 meters). Legend tells of Shiva dividing the sacred Hindu mountain Mahameru and placing the two halves on Bali: Gunung Batur to symbolize the female element, towering Gunung Agung symbolizing the male.

These lofty mountains play an important role in the lives of the Balinese and are accorded awesome respect and veneration. On top of the peaks dwell the divine spirits who bring prosperity and good fortune to the people; the mountain lakes and rivers are the source of the land's fertility; and their eruptions, though often destructive, have enriched the soil immeasurably.

The Balinese have even devised their own mountain-oriented system of spatial orientation. Directions are given either toward the mountains *(kaja)* or toward the sea *(kelod)*. *Kaja* is usually associated with holiness, the source of life-giving water. The highest of the island's mountains, sacred Gunung Agung, is known as the "Navel of the World," the focal point from whence the world springs. Since their sacred mountains are "north" and the sea "south," these are the cardinal points for the Balinese. Their villages, their houses, and even their beds are

aligned in these directions. Temples are oriented on the same axis, with the most sacred courtyards and shrines in the *kaja* end of the temple. In the family compound the orientation persists: the *kelod* end of the home is where the pigs are kept and garbage is thrown; the *kaja* end lies closest the mountains.

Even for the people who actually live north of the mountains, the direction toward the mountains is *kaja*. Many villages, such as Sayan west of Ubud, are divided into two sections, a "north" Sayan (or Sayan Kaja) closest to the mountains and a "south" Sayan (Sayan Kelod) closest to the sea.

You cannot translate *kelod* and *kaja* into English or Bahasa Indonesia. People in the north and south who say *"kaja"* will point in opposite directions. But in Bahasa Indonesia or in English, those saying *"utara"* (north) or *"selatan"* (south) will point in the same direction.

It's said the Balinese are one of the few island peoples who don't turn their eyes toward the sea, but gaze instead upward toward the mountains. They believe everything high and mighty like the mountains is magical, healthy, and divine, whereas the ocean is the domain of the underworld, the source of threatening, impure, and harmful forces: fanged demons, monsters, sharks, poisonous sea snakes. The Balinese are thus very cautious when they're around or in the sea. Few Balinese know how to swim. Only during low tide do small children venture from shore to catch tropical fish trapped in shallow tidepools. Balinese women may sometimes wade a short distance out but they always come splashing fearfully back to shore, holding up their *sarung* before the incoming tide. Not surprisingly, the Balinese dwell in the intermediary region—the rich farmlands between the mountains and the sea—between, as it were, heaven and hell.

The Balinese seem to have an innate and infallible sense of direction. No matter where they are—even in California—they always sleep with their heads facing toward Bali's mountains. The impure, baser parts of the body, such as the feet, face *kelod,* toward the sea. To do otherwise would offend the gods.

If s/he is unable to achieve proper orientation, a Balinese will feel uncomfortable and out of balance. S/he will almost invariably turn a map so the top is oriented toward *kaja,* facing the mountains which afford the most obvious landmark. When giving directions, a Balinese will not say "left" or "right" but *"kauh"* or *"kan-gin," as in "the* banjar is fifty meters to the *kauh* of the marketplace." If you ask a *bemo* driver where he's going, he'll say "toward the *kelod"* (south, toward the sea). Because this system of orientation only has relevance on Bali, a Balinese can easily become lost when abroad or on another Indonesian island.

CLIMATE

Bali, lying just eight degrees south of the equator, basks in the even and warm climate of the tropics—eternal summer, nice sea breezes, and a monotonously high humidity of around 75%. There are basically two seasons. The "rainy season" *(musim hujan)* lasts from October to April, with December and January the wettest months. The "dry season" *(musim panas)* runs from May to September, with August the driest month. July is the coolest month, and February, March, and April are the hottest months of the year. The highest humidity occurs in February.

Rainfall can occur in the dry season from time to time, which keeps this small island a verdant paradise. Even in the rainy season the sun shines somewhere on Bali everyday. Rain most often arrives in the late afternoon and at night and can last for several hours. Just as common are short, sharp tropical showers which can quickly give way to blinding sunshine. Rainfall is usually not heavy and continuous; only one or two days per year does it rain all day long.

When the monsoons are at their peak there are strong winds, though because of its proximity to the equator, Bali avoids the terrors of typhoons and cyclones. Bali is subject to the northeast and southwest monsoons, with most of the rain arriving from the northeast. Because of the monsoon climate, you can sense the wind coming from just one direction.

Bali's high mountains attract rain; the southwest monsoons dump their loads on the southern plain, where rainfall averages over 2,000 millimeters per year. The mountains could average 3,000 millimeters of rain annually. The south and west receive an average of 200 rainy days

per year, while the arid narrow strip in the north gets only 50-80. This is why northern farmers, who live in the rain shadow of the mountain ranges, cultivate maize, dry rice, manioc, beans, and copra. In the higher and cooler regions, coffee, cabbage, tobacco, and peanuts are grown.

Temperatures

With each day the same length and with the surrounding seas exerting a moderating influence, the average temperature on Bali at sea level is a lovely 26° C throughout the year. Only in January and February does the heat ever get unbearable. In the windy, cloudy Balinese winter (July and August), when southeasterlies blow up from the cool Australian interior, the east coast can even get decidedly chilly.

Since nowhere on Bali is more than 40 kilometers from the sea, there's usually a light sea breeze to cool you down. The island's crisp mountainous regions are five to 10° cooler than the lowlands and are wet the year through. Indeed, May, June, July, and August in the highlands can get downright cold (18-20° C).

Day Length

Bali's location near the equator assures that the lengths of day and night remain relatively uniform. The shortest day, in late June, and the longest day, in late December, have only about an hour's difference between them. A mother will indicate to her child when to return home from the market by simply pointing to the place in the sky where the sun will be. Since the sun's position in the sky changes only a fraction from one day to the next, this homespun method is a way to make appointments and keep time with uncanny accuracy.

Best Time to Visit

It's recommended visitors come during the dry season months May through September because during this "winter" period the weather is more reliably pleasant, with months of uninterrupted tropical sunshine. But this is also, of course, the tourist season. Since you're competing for accommodations, goods, and services with many more tourists, prices are higher. There is also a greater need to make reservations for flights and rooms at least a month before your arrival. The most expensive period of all is the two weeks on either side of Christmas and New Years, when Australians are on holiday and domestic tourists flood in from Java.

ENVIRONMENTAL DAMAGE

Bali has big ecological problems, its extraordinary culture and unparalleled natural environment coming under increasing stress. As far back as the 1930s the filmmaker Andreas Roosevelt suggested the island be turned into a sort of Hindu theme park, insulated from contamination by the modern world. He wanted Bali maintained as a living cultural museum to remind the rest of us what we had lost. Roosevelt's well-meaning but absurd proposal obviously never was taken seriously.

The devastation of the Balinese environment over the last 20 years is shocking. With virtually no enforceable environmental protection laws, no environmental monitoring, few waste disposal programs or facilities, and great social inequality in the face of undisciplined growth and development, Bali desperately needs a master plan for sustainable long-range development. The present situation poses an extreme danger for the present inhabitants as well as for generations to come.

The lack of planning and ineffective environmental regulations are a far greater threat than any cultural influences from abroad. Motivated solely by economics, the Balinese are doing it to themselves at least as much as we're doing it to them. Although you do see occasional signs of a new environmental consciousness, restaurants still throw their waste into roadside drains, households dispose of garbage in irrigation canals, and rubbish piles spill down into streams where people bathe.

A walk down Kuta Beach reveals sand full of bottle caps, cigarette butts, and plastic wrappers. No attention is given to preventing leakage of toxic liquids from rubbish dumps. Fishermen plunder the coastal waters of coral, fish, and shells. Small plastic bags of tropical fish are sold to dealers for Rp500, who in turn sell the fish to buyers in the cities for Rp5000-7500 a bag. The same fishermen could rent out their boats at Rp10,000 per hour to tourists who come to view the island's beautiful tropical fish.

Tourism

Although tourism increases employment, raises incomes, brings valuable foreign exchange to the island, and has helped improve the standard of living of vast numbers of Balinese, it's also a big part of the environmental problem. This is especially true now that, due to the unregulated spread of alcohol licenses and discos, "beach" tourism has become dominant over "cultural" tourism.

In the 1990s the illegal mining of building materials—limestone, sand, rock—for hotel construction and airport extensions is out of hand, particularly in the Badung area. Typically, small violators are punished while the major criminals are left alone to go on wreaking havoc. Because of the extensive harvesting of coral for the tourist industry, many reefs around Bali have been totally destroyed. To prevent further erosion of beachfront, long, ugly concrete jetties have been built in Nusa Dua and Candidasa.

The construction of a monumental gold statue of Garuda on the Nusa Dua Peninsula, an Rp80 million monstrosity rivaling the Statue of Liberty, is underway. Other depredations include a gigantic statue of Garuda in the main Tuban intersection and the huge Nirwana Hotel Resort in Tabanan Regency. The cause of reigning in unchecked tourism development is not helped by Bali's present governor, Ida Bagus Oka, who seems to have the tendency to blithely rubberstamp any project that originates in Jakarta.

Deforestation, Erosion, Water Depletion

Because of Bali's dense population and high carrying capacity, the destruction wrought by deforestation is not surprising. Today about 19% of Bali consists of forests, and efforts are underway to reforest (reboasasi) 39,000 hectares to bring that percentage up to the perceived ideal of 30%.

Commercial tree plantations—coconut palms, eucalyptus, teak—are found only in the 77,000-hectare Bali Barat National Park, the one area that Bali's original flora has been left intact and secure. Buffer areas around the park have been established by the government to protect it from exploitation by firewood cutters.

The problem of erosion was recognized as far back as the 1930s, when the Dutch observed that growing population pressure had shrunk the

TANAH LOT—R.I.P.

Although a prosperous agricultural region, Tabanan has always cast an envious eye on Kuta and Ubud and since the mid-80s has sought to increase its earnings from tourism. Toward this end, in 1992 the district head made a secret deal with giant, Jakarta-based business conglomerate BAKRI to build a mammoth hotelpolis overlooking the world-famous seaside temple of Tanah Lot. The temple is considered one of the six most important religious sites in all of Bali because of its charisma and unreal location on a small island offshore.

The 121-hectare estate will eventually contain luxury villas, a five-star hotel, resort condominiums, 18-hole golf course, sports center, and private beachfront. Permits were issued and by 1993 the project started without the environmental impact report (AMDAL) required by law. When news of the private deal surfaced, there was a major uproar. Even the usually circumspect Bali Post dilligently published excerpts from the public debates stirred by the project before its supporters were intimidated and backed off.

The overwhelming majority of Balinese favored canceling the project, though it enjoyed the support of Bali's Jakarta-appointed governor, Ida Bagus Oka. In a biting editorial, the governor paternalistically chastised the critics and urged everyone to accept the inevitable march of modernization. This resulted in an even larger and more vociferous demonstration in which participants demanded his resignation. But ground was broken in March of 1994 and the resort was opened in August of 1995. You can see advertisements regularly appearing in Asian in-flight magazines. Tourism has arrived in Tabanan Regency—Big Time.

island's forest cover to 13% of its previous total area and that the spread of ravines from runoff threatened cultivated land. In 1934 the Dutch prohibited any further clearing of riverbanks and encouraged the cultivation of bamboo thickets, *arenga* sugar palms, and other perennials.

Under the weight of its population, Bali's infrastructure is strained to the breaking point. To satisfy the requirements of the populous Badung Regency, water from the Ayung River is being taken from Peraupan with the result that farmers in the Krobokan area are forced to wait much longer to get water to their fields. A study commissioned by Gajah Mada University predicted that by the year 2000 the average water needs of Bali will reach 73% of the total water supply.

The Scourge of Plastic

Plastic is a big problem. In Old Bali scavenging dogs controlled the buildup of organic garbage, but starting with the widespread use of plastics in the 1960s you saw for the first time in Bali's history rubbish piles (banana leaves degrade, plastic doesn't). Today, plastics are everywhere. Even homestays serve water in plastic cups and bottles. After a storm the beaches of Bali are full of plastic litter; plastic clogs rice field irrigation canals. Plastic refuse in drains is a haven for mosquitoes and their noxious diseases.

The population practices a mixed bag of waste disposal—it's either buried, burned, or recycled. Javanese collectors pick up plastic and sell it to recyclers who truck it to Surabaya. Governor Oka's wife has publicly encouraged people to burn their plastic rather than recycle it, and Indonesia's environmental minister's wife has urged that every woman take to market cloth bags rather than depend on plastic sacks.

What's to Be Done

There is a nascent environmental movement on the island. The menu at Ubud's Mumbul Restaurant states "Save Bali! Don't use plastic bottles!" Restaurants are starting to serve beverages in glass bottles only. Water purifiers are becoming popular. To their credit, about 25% of Bali's forest is protected in four nature reserves, the largest of which is 196-square-kilometer **Bali Barat National Park.**

A number of emerging environmental groups are determined to save the island from further pollution. The **Wisnu Foundation,** a nonprofit Indonesia-based organization founded on Bali in 1993, has begun an integrated waste management pilot program in Pupuan, involving a composting project to deal with wet garbage from hotels. The foundation sells organic compost—no rocks, no weeds, no smell—at Rp400 per kilo. All proceeds are reinvested into current and planned recycling projects. Another group, the Bali Sustainable Development Project, has exerted pressure on the restaurants of Ubud to use recyclable bottles rather than plastic water bottles.

FLORA

Many plants we assiduously and lovingly cultivate as pot plants in the West—poinsettia, dracaena, coleus, begonias—grow in riotous profusion along the roadsides of Bali and have to be hacked back with machetes. Due to difference in altitude, rainfall, temperatures, and humidity, there's a wide variation in the types of plants in bloom from month to month on Bali.

Along Bali's roads and crowding its markets are stands selling all manner of fruits of strange colors, shapes, and sizes. All the usual varieties known in tropical Asia are grown on Bali, plus about 20 or so grown nowhere else, such as the enormous grapefruit-like pomelo (jeruk Bali). For a description of Bali's fruits, instructions on how to eat them, their Balinese names, and when they come into season, see "Fruits" under "Food and Entertainment" in the On the Road chapter.

FLOWERS

Flower fragrances are especially adored by the Balinese and their gods. Fresh flowers are required offerings in almost all temple rituals and ceremonies, a way of providing a pleasing environment for spirits and ancestors during their frequent visits to Earth. The Balinese also use flowers to decorate themselves ; statues of gods and goddesses are adorned with flowers; legong dancers wear crowns of blossoms; each time a Balinese prays s/he holds a flower between the fingers. Before a bemo driver sets out for the day his wife or daughter prepares for him a floral offering, or canang. Indeed, flowers are so much in demand here that it's rare to see flowering trees in full bloom.

The majority of the delightful flowers you see are not native to Bali but have been introduced from around the world, either imported in recent years or centuries ago by Indian or Arab traders. With the Chinese grafting everything and people bringing plants back and forth from Hawaii, it's difficult to tell anymore what's native to Bali and what's not.

The variety is astounding: the hardy, colorful bougainvillea (bunga kertas), climbing over walls

and balconies; the common gardenia (jempiring) and hydrangea (pacah seribu); poinsettias; the rose (maya); the spiked tumbak raja; the star-shaped, lavender manori; the jasmine (menuh), a symbol of holiness; the common marigold (mitir). The malu-malu, a sort of creeping mimosa, is known as the "sensitive plant" because its leaves fold compactly at the slightest touch—thus its Balinese name, meaning "shy."

The trumpet-shaped red or orange hibiscus (pucuk), which adorns the ears of temple statues, come in all shapes and sizes. The large-leafed, floating water lily or lotus (Nelubium nelumbo) can be detected from a distance because of its fragrant smell and beautiful colors. The Balinese believe it to be the flower of the goddesses in heaven; this aqueous plant has a high religious value on Bali and is also used as a traditional medicine.

There's a great variety of flowering trees and shrubs: the acacia; ornamental kenyeri (oleanders); the bright orange African tulip trees; the spectacular flame tree merak; the pure white cempaka, a large type of magnolia, with a strong long-lasting delicious fragrance; clusters of sweet-smelling white, pink, and red frangipani (bangan jepun) blossoms; the stunning flamboyant (flamboyan); the Singapore rhododendron; the bright orange didap, used in cremation processions; the datura or "Handkerchief Tree" with its drooping white or pink flowers; the firecracker hibiscus; the kecubung, keduk-duk, sabita—the list goes on.

The best place to see flowers is in the front yards and living fences of private homes; ask the proprietor or concierge to take you on a botanical tour of your hotel or homestay garden. The Nusa Dua hotels and Hotel Tanjung Sari and the Bali Hyatt in Sanur are famous for their brilliant year-round floral displays. Village markets all have flower stalls that sell flowers for offerings. Also visit the big nurseries of Niti Mandala, near Renon, in East Denpasar.

The Lila Graha Botanical Gardens in Candikuning offers a well-presented collection of orchids and exotics. Behind the Candikuning market are dozens of stalls selling such dazzling flowers as gardenias, roses, canna lilies, heliconia, marigolds, and cock's combs at very good prices. The grounds of the Bali Handara Country Club, also in the Bedugul area, are definitely worth visiting. By the side of the road from Mengwi up to Candikuning flowers grow everywhere. Also visit the orchid nursery near Blahbatuh in Gianyar Regency; commercial orchid nurseries are also found on the road from Denpasar to Sanur.

If you can find it in a hotel or supermarket bookstore, get a copy of Fred and Margaret Eiseman's well-researched *Flowers of Bali* containing 35 color photos of Bali's native flowers. In 1995, Thames and Hudson published *Balinese Gardens,* written by William Warren, Adrian Vickers, and Anthony Whitten, with photographs by Luca Invernezzi Tettoni, which beautifully illustrates numerous examples of contemporary and traditional Bali gardens.

TREES

Offerings are frequently made to trees, especially in southern Bali. Selected, representative trees are adorned with ceremonial parasols and dressed in traditional black-and-white checkered cloth *(kain poleng),* scarf *(saput),* and headband *(udeng)*—the same dress Balinese men wear to temple. The Balinese believe that in large trees dwell a host of spirits and demons; one often sees offerings placed on the ground before them, shrines constructed in their branches high above the ground. Legend has it that temples have even been founded next to important, spiritually charged trees. There are small, sacred reserves of trees all over the island, such as the Monkey Forest of Ubud and the majestic grove of dipterocarps at Sangeh.

Myriad uses are found for trees. Tree-trunk hollows are used as signal logs to call people to prayer, much like church bells in the West. The sacred milkwood *(pule),* sought after by woodworkers, is used to make the fearsome Rangda masks. In October, *kasia* trees, with huge clusters of bright yellow flowers, beautify the main road between Sanur and Tanjung Bungkak. Venerable tamarind trees line kilometer after kilometer of roads in northern Bali east of Singaraja; you can also see these huge shade trees on Jl. Suropati alongside Puputan Square in Denpasar.

Plantations of clove *(cingke)* trees grace the highland road from Penulisan, winding down the mountains to the northern coast. Acacia trees and other members of the mimosa family line long stretches of the Bypass Highway; planters are also reforesting the ocean side of this highway with five species of mangrove. In southern Bali, thick tangles of mangrove turn shallow tidal flats into valuable solid ground.

The stately, solitary *kepuh* tree, a member of the *kapok* family, populates Balinese cemeteries. It's believed that on moonlit nights its eerie-looking branches are infested with evil birds and demons, its branches festooned with the entrails of the dead, its roots winding in and out of skulls and bones. The *kepuh* is sacred to Durga, Goddess of Death.

Leaves from the *dadap* tree are used for *ngotonin,* the birthday celebration for children, and in the *beakawonan* wedding ceremony. Tiger's claws *(tjangin),* a species of *Erythrina,* has scarlet flowers which grow in clusters, protected by "claws" or spines which cover the tree's entire surface. These trees are planted by farmers along irrigation canals or used as fences to keep animals and humans out of *sawah.* To be pricked by its thorns is excruciatingly painful; the thorns are capable of penetrating rubber thongs.

Bali's most famous trees are the massive banyans *(beringan)* which hang over roads and temple gates, spreading their feathery branches and hundreds of vine-like trailers. Left unchecked, these creepers will take root and spread a canopy over an entire hectare. When the aerial roots of this sacred tree are cut to make room for a road, the workers need to be protected by prayers invoked by a priest. Considered holy and immortal, this member of the fig family is most often found inside temples or near the main *puri* of a village. There's a special atmosphere under the shady pillars of a gnarled old banyan, where often a small shrine is placed in the gloom. The largest blooming banyan in the world—virtually a forest—is found in Bongkasa, a few kilometers west of Ubud.

The Palms

Twelve varieties of the coconut palm *(nyuh)* exist on Bali. The palm provides tools, food, drink, and habitation; every part of the tree is used by the Balinese. So essential is the coconut tree in everyday life that the Balinese make special offerings to it once a year. The farmer knocks the tree three times to waken it, prayers for a plentiful harvest are said, then the tree and offerings are sprinkled with holy water. Coconut palms are individually owned, often by a different person than the owner of the land. The coconuts on the tree are the property of the tree's owner, but a coconut that falls belongs to the person who picks it up. A good tree produces about 50-100 mature nuts per year for 50 years.

One of the world's biggest seeds, the coconut provides copra, and its milk and grated meat are important ingredients in many Balinese dishes. Young coconuts, always available on request, make a sweet and refreshing drink, and their soft jelly-like meat is a real treat. White coconut oil is the only oil used for cooking on Bali. Frothy palm beer, *tuak,* is also derived from this tree.

The strong, hard, pest-resistant wood of the tree makes outstanding building timber. The woody husk is excellent fuel for cooking fires, the black husk fiber *(duk)* is utilized as an abrasive dish cleaner, and for brushes, rope, brooms, and as a roofing material. The Balinese use the small leaves of the central branch to fashion containers.

Whole coconut leaves *(don nyuh)* are the primary material in woven mats *(tikar)* used for sitting or as temporary walls or roofing. Any Balinese can fashion a coconut leaf into a small *tikar* in 15 minutes. Many of the intricate and beautiful offerings made by Balinese women are fashioned from the young leaves of this useful palm. The yellow coconuts of the dwarf coconut tree provide a receptacle for holy water.

Other indispensable palms are the sugar, *sago,* and *lontar.* The Balinese use the toffee-like leaves of the sugar palm to make offerings, particularly the magnificent *lamak* banners that adorn gateways during the twice-yearly Galungan celebration. From the *sago,* with its huge

dark green fronds, is extracted *ijuk,* the black thatching fiber. The palm also provides the Balinese with a handsome dark-grained wood, *jakuh,* utilized for making tool handles. As elsewhere in eastern Indonesia, the pith of the tree is processed into *sago* flour.

The *lontar* provides the raw materials for making many everyday articles. *Lontar* leaves, after being dried and pressed, are bound into book pages and inscribed with elegant Sanskrit-like Balinese characters *(tulisan Bali).* Bali's most important historical chronicles have been written on *lontar* leaves.

BAMBOO

Thirteen species of this giant grass grow on Bali. Bamboo *(tiing)* has countless uses: it can be eaten, fed to cattle, made into paper, rice steamers, clothespins, crab traps, boxes, flutes, ladders, firecrackers, fishing poles, and unbelievably strong twine. Lengths of bamboo tubing are used as haunting resonators in xylophonic instruments, and sometimes whole orchestras consist of bamboo key instruments which produce a unique, mellow, liquid sound.

Sections of tubing make a perfect cup for imbibing *tuak.* Long, flat strips of bamboo tubing are fashioned into mats, baskets, and walls. Tables, chairs, and other furniture are made of attractive spotted bamboo *(tiing tutul).* Bamboo irrigation water pipes, often several kilometers long, arc over Balinese roads. Halved bamboo stalks are used as clappers in the rice fields to scare away birds. Ingenious and melodious musical windmills are also made of bamboo.

The **Environmental Bamboo Foundation,** Box 196, Ubud 80571, tel. (0361) 974027, fax 974029, based in an experimental community in Nyuhkuning three kilometers south of Ubud, is promoting this remarkable and ancient plant—one of the fastest growing on earth—as a viable replacement for deforested or ecologically blighted lands.

FAUNA

Bali is home to 32 species of mammals, including a wildcat, two species each of civet (the *musang*, or palm civet , which resembles a mongoose), two species of monkey, *sambar,* barking deer, mouse deer, wild ox *(banteng),* and a miniature squirrel.

In the early 1900s, a writer reported that his camp in west Bali was trampled by a herd of feral elephants, but by the 1920s it was difficult to meet anyone who'd ever seen an elephant on the island. By that time the Balinese tiger, the smallest of eight subspecies of tiger, was very rarely sighted, and the last known animal was shot in 1937. Today only five sad stuffed specimens are left behind.

A visit to the 76,000-hectare Bali Barat National Park (BBNP), covering most of the heavily forested interior of western Bali, is obligatory for animal and bird lovers. The park is effec-tively protected against exploitation and development and is well-patrolled by rangers based at the park headquarters of Cekik and Labuhan Lalang. Here you can see *rusa* deer, wild boar, and fairly tame long-tailed macaques and leaf monkeys sitting high in the trees chewing on leaves. The 165-hectare offshore island of Menjangan has a population of around 50 barking deer.

The Wallace Line

Bali is the physical end of what was once mainland Asia. Observing that a great contrast exists between the animal life of Bali and that of the islands to the east, the great 19th-century English naturalist **Sir Alfred Russel Wallace** suggested that the treacherous, 24-km-wide strait separating Bali from the neighboring island of Lombok is an important divide, a biologically impassable

HANGING OUT WITH THE MONKEYS

Monkeys, considered descendents of General Hanuman in Hindu mythology, occupy a semi-divine status on Bali and are allowed to proliferate around some of Bali's most sacred temples. The best places to watch monkeys (and people) are the monkey forests of Ubud and Sangeh. Feeding time brings the monkeys down out of the trees around 1000 and 1600 when they are fed potatoes. Talk to one of the feeders—some have been caring for monkeys for the past 15 years. They have given the monkeys names and know the quirks of most individuals in the troop.

Even though signs often say Don't Feed The Monkeys, vendors sell peanuts and bananas at the gates. Gate price for peanuts is Rp1000, *warung* price is Rp100. It's the same story for bananas. The secret for enjoying the monkeys without getting hurt or robbed is to sit very quietly and let them come to you.

Before you arrive, put away all extra food, zip purses shut, and lock down cameras. The monkeys will search you. Take off any jewelery and paraphernalia that you don't need—they'll gladly take possession of earrings, necklaces, watches, even hearing aids. Then either hand the food to them or simply lay it in the palm of your hand. Always look out for the dominant male; he should be given food first to avoid fighting. Don't feed the subadults or you may get bitten by their mother. Never show your teeth when smiling at the animals as it's regarded as an aggressive gesture.

If you take these precautions, you can spend long stretches with the monkeys. They'll perch on your lap, drape a warm furry arm on your shoulder while they munch, and watch everything. They don't care to be petted at all. Unwary tourists can get scratched or bitten by treating these creatures as pets, which is easy to do because they appear friendly. They are wild animals with all the dignity, free will, and unpredictability that implies.

Whatever you do, don't leave a pet monkey behind as a burden to a Balinese family who of course can't say no. The mothers are killed in order to get the babies to sell. The animals are kept on a short chain out in the weather with no protection, given no water, and teased until they become mean. The creatures will eventually die, sick from the cold. Only one out of 10 survive.

line cleaving Asia from Australia. "In just two hours," he suggested, "you can pass from one great division of the earth to the other, differing as essentially in their animal life as Europe does from America."

During the last ice age, Wallace theorized, the sea level around the Greater Sundas fell enough to enable animals to travel overland from the Asian mainland, fanning out through the archipelago until they reached the deep trench of the Lombok Strait and could go no farther. While the Selat Bali ("Bali Strait") separating Bali from Java has a maximum depth of 60 meters, the ocean depths between Bali and Lombok exceed 1,300 meters.

Wallace's book, *The Malay Archipelago,* published in 1869 contemporary and parallel with Charles Darwin's work, advanced a theory of evolution based on Wallace's examination of the flora and fauna of the region. His imagined line dividing the Asian and Australian regions on either side of the Lombok Strait has since become known as the Wallace Line.

The differences between Bali and Lombok are obvious. Bali is lush, equatorial, smothered in the luxuriant vegetation of tropical Asia, while Lombok is wind-blown and dry like the Australian plains. Bali, Java, and islands west are characterized by the monkeys, squirrels, rabbits, tigers, elephants, bears, sheep, oxen, horses, orangutans, and pythons found in the dense tropical forests and jungles of Asia. On the islands east of Bali begin the parrots and other peculiar bird species, marsupials like wombats and kangaroos, the platypus, and giant lizards of the Australian region. Some "leakage" occurs, i.e., monkeys are found in Sumba.

DOMESTIC ANIMALS

A cousin to the wild boar, Bali's famous pigs are weighted to collapse with their loads of pork, their backbones sagging as if broken and their enormously heavy pink bellies dragging through the dust. Pigs are the property of the woman of the house and any money she earns from them belongs to her. A great Balinese delicacy not to be missed is suckling pig (*be guling* in Balinese, *babi guling* in Indonesian) roasted on a spit.

The ducks of Bali, kept as family pets, rank among the island's most prominent citizens. Squads of them are taken from the family *kampung* by the herders each day to feed in the rice fields, marching in formation under flags on long poles from which they never stray. In the irrigation channels between the rows of plants these comics act like up-tailed, web-footed vacuum cleaners, loosening old roots, nosing through the mud grubbing for worms, snails, frogs, insect pests, and leftover grains of rice. At day's end, the chattering flock gathers around the duck herder's pole to be taken home again. Ducks are much better behaved and more complacent than bothersome chickens, well-suited for the communal living of the Balinese domestic compound. Duck meat, as in the strongly spiced dish *bebek betutu,* makes for some of the finest eating on the island.

The Balinese goose-swan, the nearest thing on the island to a true swan, is the sacred mount of Dewi Saraswati, the goddess of learning and the arts. They make excellent watch geese. Fighting cocks can be seen preening in bamboo cages on the sides of Bali's roads. Compared to their Western cousins, these birds are wild and supernatural, able to fly up to and perch on rooftops. The flesh of pugilist rooster tastes and has the texture of lizard hide. Loops of sound seem to follow flocks of pigeons circling the sky; each is hung with small bells on its feet and bamboo whistles on its tail feathers. Turtle doves and other pet birds are hoisted in their cages high on bamboo poles to enjoy the view and provide fluting and cooing music for the villagers below.

Cattle, hung with sweet melodic wooden bells, leap from banks with the lithe grace of an antelope. These amiable, beautiful creatures with long eyelashes, delicate features, dew eyes, manicured velvet coats, slender necks, trim bodies, slim legs, and short tails look more like fawns than cattle. Like most cows in the tropics, they give no milk. Unlike the Hindus of India the Balinese don't consider cattle as sacred; they are bred for their meat and exported to other islands. Nevertheless, cows live a privileged life on Bali, lovingly bathed in village streams, billeted in cozy hay-strewn mangers, let loose on village lawns to feed. The largest cattle markets in Bali are in Beringkit, 20 kilometers south of Mengwi, and in Bebandem (Karangasem), a scene out of medieval Bali.

Domesticated water buffalo *(kerbau)* with thick curving horns are used for plowing the rice fields. A special event in Jembrana Regency is the Makepung buffalo races in which two *kerbau* pull a jockey in a wheeled carriage. The animals are specially bred and trained, a process that has produced a healthier strain of cattle more resistant to the diseases prevalent in other Balinese cattle. The same district has developed Magembeng, in which cows carry big wooden musical bells *(gembeng)* around their necks. As they walk, their slow and graceful swaying causes the instruments to sound and form haunting music. The cows take part in competitions in which posture, beauty in the head and tail, and the precision and softness of their music is fastidiously evaluated.

Balinese cats are scrawny, unbelievably loud and raucous creatures with truncated tails and unpleasant dispositions. Scavengers like dogs, they are omnivorous and eat among other things ants and mangoes. Bali's miserable *anjing* (dogs) abound—mangy, flea-bitten bags of skin, bones, and open sores. There are an estimated 600,000 on the island. The mongrelized Balinese dog has a short pointed muzzle, a piggy tail, weighs about 30 pounds, births one litter per year, and is an expert at survival. Colin McPhee, in his *A House in Bali,* wrote of Bali's infamous dogs, "grey, starved and tottering, on walls, in doorways, the dogs infested the villages. They were so anemic they could hardly drag themselves off the road. We drove along, knocking them to one side with a thud."

Little has changed since those words were written in 1945. In the West dogs bark too, but somehow their barking isn't as stubborn or as irritating as that of the dogs of Bali. Most dogs are ill-kept pets; the tens of thousands of strays who roam the island are not destroyed because of the Hindu/Buddhist taboo against killing living things.

The traditional island belief is that dogs contain the souls of reincarnated thieves. They do serve a useful purpose by scaring away both corporeal intruders and the evil spirits which haunt the Balinese. They provide a free morning wakeup call. They clean up the trash, and seldom actually bite anyone. Though few are rabid, none are wo/man's best friend. Look upon them as rats, or pigeons with teeth, and you'll have no problem with them.

BIRDS

There's been a dramatic drop in the local bird population over the last 20 years. Although many of the more obvious and colorful species, particularly birds of prey, have been all but eliminated, species still number about three hundred. These include beautiful wild fowl; an iridescent blue kingfisher; the dollarbird of western Bali's open woodlands; the acrobatic ash-colored drongo; the olive-beaked sunbird, which feeds on flowers; the black-naped oriole, with its completely black abdomen; the white-breasted wood swallow with triangular wings; and the streaked weaver, which builds delicate nests in colonies in the long grass of open country.

Specialized seabirds inhabit Bali's south coast. The white-bellied sea eagle and white-tailed tropic bird nest and breed in the stunning vertical limestone cliffs and offshore islets of the Bukit Peninsula and Nusa Penida. At low tide, a prime viewing area for waterbirds is the long, sheltered coast of mudflats and mangrove swamp from Sanur to Benoa Bay. Here you'll find large flocks of plovers, sandpipers, and other wading birds feeding on the mudflats at low tide. Along the shores of the Bay of Gilimanuk on Bali's western tip are the large brown and white brown booby, the great crested tern, and the common tern.

Inland, around the canals and ponds, are congregations of stately Javan pond herons and white egrets. North of Ubud in Petulu, between 1600 to 1800 in the afternoon, you can see thousands of short-billed egrets, cattle egrets, and snow-white little egrets arriving to roost for the night in the palms. In the main rice-growing country of central Bali keep a lookout for grain-feeding munias, sparrows, and white-bellied swiftlets. During the breeding season these tireless little birds build intricately woven nests in the tall grass and bushes. Farther north, around the volcanic lakes of Bratan, Buyan, and Tamblingan, are trails leading into dense submontane rainforests where you can view forest birds like cuckoos, barbets, and babblers. Australian brown honeyeaters are also found in this terrain, flitting about in low bushes and feeding on flowers. Only one species of honeyeaters crossed the Wallace Line, the sole exception to the rule.

The extremely rare Bali starling, or Roth-schild's or Bali mynah *(Leocopsar rothchildi)*, is the only vertebrate animal indigenous to Bali. The bird is snow-white, with black on its tail and the tips of its wings and a bright blue patch around its eyes. Don't confuse it with the black-winged starling, which has a yellow skin patch around its eyes. When the bird's population plummeted due to loss of habitat, a group of U.S. zoos saved the starling by shipping individuals to the Surabaya Zoo; they were then reintroduced into the island's northwest corner. The *jalak Bali* has been recorded along 85 kilometers of coastline from Singaraja to Gilimanuk. The best watching post is at Teluk Kelor on the north coast of the Prapat Agung Peninsula where a handful of starlings come down from the hills to roost near the beach. There's a Bali Starling Project Research Station two kilometers north of the guardpost at Sumber Klampok.

Birdwatching

The best place to see birds in the wild is Bali Barat National Park in western Bali, home to at least 160 different species. Bali Bird Park in Singapadu is a two-hectare aviary housing more than 1,000 rare and beautiful birds from both Indonesia and all over the world—breathtaking Australian cockatoos, magnificent South American macaws, Irianese birds of paradise, and the Bali starling. The many shady rest stops, waterfalls, and ponds ornamented with lotus and water lilies serve as a splendid backdrop for this striking collection. Some of the settings are spectacular, re-creating desert, savannah, and soaring, mist-shrouded rainforest (in 1996 a reptile park was opened as part of the complex). Many of the tamer species roam freely, and everywhere is birdsong.

Another way to get close to birds is to join one of Victor Mason's "Bird Walks" in the fertile countryside of Ubud, an incredible and entertaining stroll into the natural untouched flora and fauna of Bali's heartland. Here you're bound to see 30 or so different species, including such Indonesian endemics as the Java kingfisher, the barwinged prinia, the black-winged starling, and the Java sparrow. Ask about the **Bali Bird Club** (Box 3400, Denpasar 80001, Bali, tel. 0361-95009) organized by Victor.

REPTILES, AMPHIBIANS, INSECTS

The island is home to the rarely spotted lethal, luminous green viper *(lelipis gedong)* identified by the red in its tail. Bali's other snake, the *ular sawah,* is brown and nonpoisonous.

There are also crooning frogs, lucinea spiders which build their webs along paths (if they bite you, your head aches for three days), fireflies, butterflies, crickets, poisonous scorpions (rare), and huge black, harmless beetles that thud off your hotel walls trying to find a way out. Children catch dragonflies on long, glue-tipped bamboo poles, then thread them like *sate* on strings to take home and deep-fry in oil for a crispy, protein-rich delicacy. Cicadas are the multitudinous unseen chorus to all Balinese nights. Bats can be seen at Goa Lawah cave east of Klungkung; they also emerge all over Bali at dusk to feed.

What do you call an Indonesian lizard with a loud voice? A gecko blaster. The lovable gecko—*cicak* in Indonesian—is about 15 cm long, has a scaleless alabaster body and beady eyes, screeches *"tsk-tsk,"* and scampers upside down on any surface with the use of vibrations from its pudgy toes. The bottoms of their feet resemble the gills of fish. It's believed that if a gecko chirps while someone is talking it means that person is telling the truth. Geckos make cheap pets because you don't have to feed them—they eat each other.

A nontoxic lizard called *alu-alu,* reaching one meter in length, waits on riverbanks to snatch passing ducks. To "witness man's bravery with live crocodiles and snakes" pay a vist to the Ayung Reptile Park near Sanur. Performances given twice daily (0900 and 1700), plus there's a collection of reptiles from all over the Indonesian archipelago.

The tokay lizard, often heard but rarely seen, emits a wonderfully ear-curling, indescribable rachet windup sound followed by a series of *"BO"* croaks never forgotten once heard. Each time the tokay croaks, the sound gets a little softer, deeper, and slower, as his wind runs out. The Balinese believe that anyone who hears a lizard moan nine times will receive good luck. They can croak up to 30 times—at the drop of a hat gamblers will bet on how many. Up to 45 cm long, with deep orange spots, they can eat mice and baby birds. Tokays defecate black cigar-shaped droppings from the same spot on the ceiling everyday and can only be discouraged by attaching or hoisting mothballs up to the spot.

SEALIFE

Hire boats at Labuhan Lalang for snorkeling and diving in the marine reserve of Bali Barat National Park in the northwest. The wonderful sealife of the coral reefs off Menjangan Island is one of Bali's premier dive sites. A unique species of lobster is caught in these waters, as well as a wide range of colorful coral fish, including parrot fish, damsels, angels, wrasses, butterfly fish, puffer fish, groupers, and moray eels.

To the east, about 10 kilometers before Singaraja, is the coastal resort of Lovina Beach, where dozens of motorized *prahu* go out to view schools of dolphins in their feeding grounds. These shallow, calm waters teem with a wide variety of small reef fish, crustaceans, sponges, and hard coral. In deeper waters are planktoneating whale sharks. Two other popular dolphin-viewing and dive locales are Candidasa and Padangbai in Karangasem. An indispensable reference for marine study is Kal Muller's *Underwater Indonesia: A Guide to the World's Greatest Diving*.

ENDANGERED SPECIES

It's a common sight to see men and boys walking the back roads of Bali carrying small caliber rifles and air guns for the purpose of shooting birds for food or sport. Because it's illegal to shoot birds without a license, if you see this say *"Jangan membawa senapan tanpa ijin!"* ("Don't carry a gun without a license!").

Among Indonesia's endangered wild creatures are its sea turtles. The much-publicized turtle-breeding ground off the island of Serangan in southeastern Bali is a cover-up; at least 25,000 turtles per year are caught in Indonesia's seas and slaughtered for Bali's major festivals, in which turtle meat and turtle soup are entrenched ceremonial requirements. Really big festivals require the consumption of as many as 50 of these magnificent wild creatures. This is an issue which has the international conservation community incensed. To appreciate the magnitude of the problem, visit Pegok village in the eastern suburbs of Denpasar, where you can see the sad spectacle of dozens of turtles lined up for butchering, immobilized with their front flippers tied together in front of their beaks. Before you buy turtle products or order turtle *sate* at one of Bali's restaurants, remember that sight. One good sign is that the number of tourist shops in south Bali selling stuffed sea turtles and turtle-shell products has dwindled considerably.

HISTORY

PREHISTORY

For tens of thousands of years small bands of hunter-gatherers must have lived and foraged in Bali's jungles and scavenged the tidal pools of the island, yet few artifacts dating from the Stone Age have turned up. Paleolithic implements (stones roughly flaked on one side) have been found near Sembiran in northern Bali, and there is also evidence in the form of rectangular stone adzes, blades, axes, hoes, and picks used by a Neolithic people who inhabited Bali.

The most significant find has been the remains of a Neolithic settlement and a burial site of 100 Mongoloid adults and children uncovered at Cekik, south of Gilimanuk. These were a coastal people who swam the strait or walked across to Bali via a land bridge from East Java and Bali in their migration east through the islands from Indochina. Bali was already well populated by the time the Bronze Age began around 300 B.C.

The Bronze Age

Early Metal Age remains include such stray finds as clay utensils, stone mounds, and bells shaped like two bowls. The people who fashioned these items lived in villages and buried their dead in pottery jars or stone sarcophagi, complete with such funeral gifts as arm and foot rings, beads, highly polished stone tools, and bronze and iron implements and ornaments. The metal objects relate strongly to the Bronze Age designs of the Dongson culture of Indochina. See specimens at the Bali Museum in Denpasar and at Lembaga Purbakala in Pejeng.

The Moon of Pejeng, a deep-rimmed, hourglass-shaped kettle-gong—misnamed a "drum"—is one of the most remarkable archaeological artifacts discovered in Bali and a masterpiece of the Balinese Bronze Age. The gong hangs in a roofed shrine in the most sacred courtyard of the old imperial temple of Pura Panataran Sasih in Pejeng. The gong resembles other Dongson culture gong designs found throughout Indochina, Indonesia, Nusatenggara, and as far east as the Kai Islands of Maluku. But the Balinese gong of Pejeng, nearly 187 cm long with a sounding surface 160 cm in diameter, is the largest of its kind. The Balinese consider the object charged with awesome magical power; some say it's an earplug of the moon goddess Ratih.

By the Bronze Age, Bali's population practiced both wet- and dry-rice cultivation, worked the fields with stone tools and water buffalo,

An edict written in Old Balinese on a bronze plate (prastasis) dating from before A.D. 914, dealing with the foundation of a monastery near Bangli. It's preserved in the Pura Kehen of Bangli.

BALINESE MEGALITHIC SARCOPHAGI

Denpasar's Bali Museum houses a collection of historic and cultural objects, some dating back to the Neolithic (2600-600 B.C.) and Megalithic (300 B.C.) periods. The sarcophagus above dates from 200 B.C. Some sarcophagi contained skeletons in the squatting position. The diagram here shows how corpses were fitted into the tight space. Another broader, longer type contained full-length skeletons. All types, hewn from single blocks of stone, were decorated with hideous or comic knobs or engraved facial features. The 53 separate sarcophagi found at 37 different sites around Bali were for prominent community members. When an intact sarcophagus was discovered in recent years at Puyangan in south-central Bali, the villagers had to perform the act of burning it since there is no rest for the dead without a cremation.

raised pigs and poultry, and developed a sophisticated megalithic culture which made use of menhirs, stone chairs, and stepped pyramids. Village meetings took place around large stone seats taken from riverbeds; these seats are the precursors of today's meeting pavilions (bale agung). When the island became Indianized in later centuries, the menhirs hewn to memorialize dead ancestors eventually evolved into Hinduistic stone portrait statues. It's believed the Balinese cili motif, representing the rice goddess Dewi Sri, may have originated from a fertility cult existing during Bali's Bronze Age.

Early Historical References

Prehistory, the preliterate part of any people's past, ended for Bali with its earliest contacts with the far more advanced cultures of India and China, the leading powers in Far Eastern trade during the first centuries A.D. But since Bali was neither on the direct trade route between India and China nor a stopover on the way to the spice islands of Maluku, it attracted little notice. During the Chinese Tang dynasty a reference was made to Dwa-pa-tan, a country "east of Kaling" (Central Java) featuring "characters written on leaves, the dead burned on a pile, adorned with gold, and with gold in their mouths, and all kinds of scents." Chinese annals of the 5th and 6th centuries mention a Hinduized state called P'o-li, which might have referred to Bali. Additionally, there's a short mention in the Buddhist text Manjusri Mulakalpa some time before A.D. 920 to the effect that a country called Bali was among those peopled by barbarians.

Early Indic Influences

The Hindu religion and culture was brought to Indonesia about 2,000 years ago, probably by Indian traders from Gujerati who were attracted to the islands by their riches in gold, spices, and sandalwood. Inscriptions in Indian script from the 5th century A.D. reveal Indianized kingdoms then extant in West Java and East Borneo. By the 7th century A.D., 1,000 students were studying Buddhist and Shivaite teachings in what was then the Sumatran Hindu empire of Sriwijaya, from where priests and monks could have spread their teachings to Bali, probably at the invitation of local princes.

Remnants of ancient hermitages and monasteries can be seen today at Gunung Kawi and Goa Gadjah, both in Gianyar. Holy men trained here empowered and consecrated Balinese princes by bestowing upon them the status of god-kings and giving them a place in the Indic family tree. Balinese script is derived from the Palava script of South India.

JAVANESE INFLUENCE

Over 400 years ago most of East Java was exactly like Bali is today. Prior to 1815 Bali had a greater population density than Java, suggesting its Hindu-Balinese civilization was even more successful than Java's. When Sir Stamford Raffles wrote his *History Of Java* in the early 19th century, he had to turn to Bali for what remained of the once-great literature of classical Java. Even today Bali provides scholars with clues about India's past religious life, clues which long ago vanished in India itself.

The Warmadewa Dynasty

Bali first came under the influence of Indic Javanese kings in the 6th to 8th centuries. The island was conquered by the first documented king of Central Java, Sanjaya, in 732; stone and copper inscriptions in Old Balinese have been found that date from A.D. 882.

From the 10th to the 12th centuries, the Balinese Warmadewa family established a dynastic link with Java. Court decrees were thereafter issued in the Old Javanese language of Kawi and Balinese sculpture, bronzes, and other artistic styles, bathing places, and rock-cut temples began to resemble those in East Java. The Sanur pillar (A.D. 914), partly written in Sanskrit, supports the theory that portions of the island were already Indianized in the 10th century.

Bali's way of life was well defined by the early part of the 10th century. By then, the Balinese were engaged in sophisticated wet-rice cultivation, livestock breeding, stone- and woodcarving, metalworking, roof thatching, canoe building,

even cockfighting. The Balinese of the time were locked into feudal genealogical and territorial bondage. They were subjects of an autocratic Hinduized ruler—one of a number of regional Balinese princes—who himself acknowleged the sovereignty of a Javanese overlord.

Airlangga

The marriage of Balinese Prince Udayana of the Warmadewa dynasty to east Javanese Princess Mahendradatta in A.D. 989 led to even closer cooperation between Java and Bali. Airlangga (991-1046) was born to the royal couple around 1001. As a young man, the prince was sent to Java for his education. There, Airlangga married a princess and became a local chief in the kingdom of his uncle Dharma Wangsa. Shortly after Airlangga's arrival, Wangsa was attacked by the forces of Sriwijaya and murdered. Airlangga ascended to the throne, becoming one of the most glorious monarchs in Java's history. The dynasty he put in place—more centralized and less Indianized than any up to that time—lasted for more than 300 years. As befits an Indic hero, Airlangga ultimately renounced the kingdom he'd made great and died a hermit under the guidance of his spiritual adviser.

A fascinating legend relates how Airlangga's kingdom was nearly destroyed by a plague supposedly brought by the dreadful witch Rangda, queen of evil spirits. According to some historians, Rangda was Airlangga's own mother, Mahendradatta, whom her husband had sent into the jungle for practicing black magic. Other theorists maintain Rangda sought revenge against Airlangga because he did not side with her when his father took a second wife. Out of the mythical struggle between the magic of the witch and that of the great king arose the legend of Calon Arang, depicted today in Bali's *barong* dance. Rangda, who died relatively early in life, is thought to be buried in a tomb near Kutri. In Balinese myth she is forever associated with witchcraft.

Balinization

For a long time Airlangga was forgotten in Java, whereas in his native Bali he has always been much revered. With the royal compound established near Batuan, his court's language became the common language of Bali. Another feature of these early times was the practice on

Bali of both Hinduism and Buddhism (with a strong Tantric element) side by side.

This early period of Balinese history has long been perceived as an age of darkness, but based on an analysis of royal charters *(prasasti)* this is incorrect. Village communities started to take part in masked dances, dramas, and puppet performances staged by the royal courts. Tantric magical beliefs and rites surfaced, building upon and infusing the native animism. This period was the origin of the contemporary Balinese preoccupation with *leyak* (witches) and such supernaturally charged characters as Rangda in the tale of Calon Arang. Artistically, the style of the cliff *candi* of Gunung Kawi was largely derived from East Javanese 11th-century architecture. The early monuments of Bali from this era, exemplifed by the ghostly Gunung Kawi tombs, have fascinated religious, social, and cultural anthropologists the world over.

Division of the Kingdom

After the division of Airlangga's empire under his sons, Bali's next indigenous ruler was Anak Wungsu, who became one of the island's greatest kings. He and his predecessors are specifically connected by their monuments with the remarkably rich stretch of land between the Petanu and Pakerisan Rivers in south-central Bali.

According to Javanese court records, in 1284 the mysterious last king of the East Javanese Singosari dynasty, Kertanagara (1268-92), sent a military force against Bali. During this expedition, the last descendant of the Warmadewa dynasty was taken prisoner, and Bali again became a vassal state of Java—yet another fluctuation in the turbulent relationship between the two islands. When Kertanagara was assasinated in 1292, the fierce Balinese took advantage of the confusion to rebel against their Javanese overlords.

Majapahit Conquest

The fall of the Singosari Empire after Kertanagara's 1292 assassination was followed by the rise of the new dynasty of Majapahit. Gajah Mada, the grand vizier or *patih* of King Radjasanegara, was sent to Bali in 1343 to subjugate the semidemonic king of the Balinese Pejeng dynasty, Dalem Bedulu, who refused to recognize Majapahit supremacy. A haunting myth tells of how the demon-king exchanged his human head for that of a wild boar, and how Gajah Mada tricked him so he could see the pig-head. The effect was devastating—Bedulu literally burned up in indignation.

After Gajah Mada conquered Bali, East Javanese influences spread from purely political and religious spheres into the arts and architecture. Bali became an outpost in a mighty empire—Indonesia's greatest—which encompassed nearly the entire archipelago.

The Javanese court chronicler, Prapanca, relates how all the "vile, long-haired Balinese princes were wiped out . . . now all the barbarian Balinese customs are consistent with Javanese ones." This, of course, was not true, as elements of Old Balinese culture—prestige stratification, endogamous patrilineages, a developed witch-cult, and tight-knit irrigation societies—survive intact to the present day.

A young Brahman nobleman, Mpu Kapakisan, was appointed king of Bali by Gajah Mada, and a colony of Javanese settlers was dispatched. The Balinese frequently revolted against the mighty Majapahit, but the uprisings were put down in memorable battles. Military figures *(aryas)* became rulers of Bali, and to them the present Balinese aristocracy 'Wong Majapahit' traces its origins.

The first four vassal rulers under the Javanese resided at a royal court in Samprangan near Gianyar. During Hayam Wuruk's rule in the late 14th century a dissenting vassal, I Dewa Ketut Tegal Besung, fell out with his elder brother—he'd married his sister to a horse—and established a princely court in Gelgel near Klungkung. Bali was conquered at the peak of Majapahit's artistic flowering, and thus Gelgel soon became an artistic power center, exerting a powerful influence over Bali's subsequent cultural development. Hinduistic concepts filtered down to the villagers via the electrifying medium of the shadow play.

Historically speaking, Bali today is still a fossil of Java during Majapahit's golden age, a living museum of many elements of the old Indo-Javanese civilization. Through it's isolation Bali kept its culture whole.

The Decline of the Majapahit Empire

Civil wars, revolts, and internal decay spread in Majapahit's colonies, and soon the great empire went into decline. Muslim missionaries became influential in Java, converting princes who, attracted to the economic benefits of Islam, declared themselves sultans and repudiated their allegiance to Majapahit. This gradual Islamization quickened the pace of deterioration in Majapahit; eventually, peaceful religious propaganda turned to armed force. When the empire crumbled under the military and economic invasion of Islam at the dawn of the 16th century, the cream of Majapahit's scholars, jurists, dancers, painters, craftsmen, intellectuals, and literati migrated to isolated parts of East Java, and to Bali. Priests took with them all the kingdom's sacred books and historical records. Because of the lack of good harbors and the small volume of trade, Islam never succeeded in taking a firm hold in Bali's coastal areas. Only in Bali's extreme west, in Jembrana, did part of the population accept Islam. The regency to this day is home to Bali's largest Muslim population.

Nirartha, a great Hindu sage from Kediri in east Java, arrived in Bali in the 15th century, establishing a hermitage *(griya)* in Mas. There he became famous for his teachings, attracting many disciples. Nirartha created the system of village-level *adat,* a microcosm of the larger order of the universe. He also conceived of the open-roofed shrine *(padmasana)* found in every Balinese household and temple courtyard. Nirartha's descendents now form one of Bali's four most important Brahmana classes.

Over the years, as descendants of Majapahit consolidated their power on the island, a Bali-Hindu civilization evolved like nowhere else in the archipelago. Only the Bali Aga, aboriginal mountain Balinese, resisted the Hindu inroads. Easternmost Java remained Hindu until the end of the 16th century; the Blambangan region in far eastern Java lost its independence only during the 17th century. Bali then became the last refuge of Hindu culture in Asia, a splendid historical anachronism.

The Gelgel Period

In the 14th century a Javanese settlement was established at Samprangan, at the foot of Gunung Agung. The capital was then moved to the south coast at Gelgel in Klungkung Regency. Gelgel did not wield direct political power over the other courts but became the passive and much respected nucleus around which the other kingdoms revolved. Its powerful succession of rulers were distinguished by the semidivine title of Dewa Agung ("Grand Lord") and were no less than the titular leaders of Bali.

Here, for two centuries, successive kings of Bali resided, developing unique Bali-Hindu customs and institutions and welding together the traditions of East Java and old Bali. Complex death rituals, offerings, and high ceremonial language were all probably introduced during this period. The greatest ruler of Bali's Gelgel dynasty, Dalem Batu Renggong, expanded the island's influence east by conquering and colonizing Lombok and Sumbawa, and the Blambangan Peninsula of East Java.

Whole colonies of court artisans, carvers, men of letters, painters, architects, and gold- and silversmiths created the lavish trappings of royalty. Theater associations and orchestras sprang up, folk art flourished. The arts were indistinguishable from the life of the courts and the religious activity of the people. Art was never executed for its own sake but presented as an offering or prayer in service to the community and the gods. A woodcarver carved the eaves on a royal *bale* from an almost client-like obligation to his lord, an architect designed a stone altar in the temple as an act of faith in his religion. Gratuity for the craft, product, labor, or service was given in the form of rice, privileges, and/or political patronage.

During Dalem Batu Renggong's rule, the *saka* calendar of Hindu Java and 30-week Balinese *wuku* calendar were combined into the intricate schedule of religious ceremonies that exists today. Cremations, until the Gelgel period the privilege of the nobility, began to be practiced by the common people. The Dewa Agung also constructed nine great temples throughout the land, with Pura Besakih serving as the island's "mother temple." Numerous present-day Balinese temples—Gunung Kawi, Pura Penulisan—are actually memorial shrines to ancient rulers and their families.

Around the mid-17th century, the dynasty moved north to Klungkung. Countless microrevolts erupted among Bali's seven principalities, sparked by conflicts over status relationships, prestige, and pressure from upwardly mobile commoners. A state of constant war prevailed throughout the 18th and 19th centuries and ended only when the various kingdoms were forced to integrate into the Netherlands East Indies in the early 20th century.

Gelgel remained the island's center of political power, if only in name, until its final defeat at the hands of the Dutch. The Balinese consider this dynasty their great classical period. Even after the Dutch conquests of 1906 and 1908, the local regents of the Gelgel and Klungkung districts retained their autonomy into the 1950s, when finally the Indonesian republican government stripped them of their lands and feudal authority.

Yet seven of the secondary principalities of Batu Renggong's time survive as administrative districts today: Badung, Gianyar, Bangli, Tabanan, Karangasem, Buleleng, and Jembrana, all based on the seven kingdoms that emerged from the 17th-century Gelgel dynasty. The metropolitan area of Denpasar, Bali's largest urban area and government center, was declared a regency in the early 1990s.

THE EUROPEAN ERA

Early Contacts

Bali remained obscure in the West for so long because of its lack of spices, fragrant woods, ivory, and natural harbors, and because of its natural orientation toward the deep straits and treacherous tidal currents and reefs of the south rather than the tranquil Java Sea. These factors tended to isolate Bali from the elaborate international trade which swirled around it.

Bali was therefore allowed to evolve uninterrupted artistic and social traditions far more independently than other settlements in the region. But the island soon attracted notice because of its position at the beginning of the Lesser Sunda Islands. In the early 16th century, navigators started labeling the small island east of Java Major "Java Minor." Not long thereafter the name "Bally" began to appear on maps.

The English buccaneer Sir Francis Drake paid a call in 1580. In 1585 the Portuguese attempted to establish a trading station in south Bali, but their ship was wrecked off Bukit. Finally, in 1597, a small fleet of Dutch war yachts, headed by Cornelius de Houtman, landed on Bali. He and his crew of 89 men were all that

were left after a 14-month trading journey that began in Holland with 249 men.

Bali was the high point of de Houtman's journey, an island attractive and hospitable. The Dutchmen made great friends with the king, who, according to written accounts of the time, was "a good-natured fat man who had 200 wives, drove a chariot drawn by two white buffaloes, and owned 50 dwarves whose bodies had been distorted to resemble *kris* handles." After a lengthy stay and many postponements, de Houtman announced a sailing date. Reluctant crew members disappeared up to the moment of departure. Upon their return to Holland the Dutchmen's reports of the new "paradise" created such a sensation that in 1601 the trader Heemskerk was sent to Bali weighted down with gifts for the king.

Early Dutch Incursions

In 1602 the Dutch trading company Vereenigde Oost Indische Compagnie (VOC) was formed by a group of merchants. Maintaining its own private army, the VOC's goal was the unlimited exploitation of the East Indies. At first Bali offered little of commercial value, and for more than 250 years after its discovery the island was more or less left alone while the company concentrated its efforts on capturing control of the cash crops and spice trade of Java and the Moluccas.

Bali did not grow cloves or nutmeg—spices needed by the Europeans to make their meats more palatable—so there was little on the island to exploit. Bali's imports were gold, rubies, and opium; its exports mercenaries who fought in various wars in Java, and thousands of highly prized male and female slaves sold to Batavia, the Dutch capital in West Java. The massive eruption of Gunung Tambora on Sumbawa in 1830 brought so much devastation to Bali it forced curtailment of the slave trade. The rajas of south Bali, finding their wealth and power drying up, turned to rice, coconut oil, cattle, pigs, dried meat, hides, tobacco, and coffee. This new mercantile orientation attracted traders, including the English.

The Dutch versus the English

During the Napoleonic Wars, when the East Indies were occupied briefly by the English, a

THE WHITE RAJA OF BALI: MADS LANGE

The year was 1839. The Dutch had not yet succeeded in penetrating the fertile rice-growing districts of southern Bali, where a glorious and carefully guarded Hindu theater state had flourished undisturbed for a thousand years. In that year, after he had been run off the neighboring island of Lombok by an English rival, the flamboyant Danish merchant-adventurer Mads Johansen Lange (1806-56) set up a fortified "factory" (trading post) on Bali's southern peninsula near the fishing village of Kuta. The Balinese were eager for trade contacts, but at the time foreigners were strictly confined to the edge of the island in places like Kuta, a political freeport and no man's land where outcasts and opponents could find refuge. Lange's busy emporium became a vital link between inter-Asian trade and the inland Balinese economy. Although his sojourn on Bali lasted only 10 years, it was to change Balinese history.

Although a few Chinese and Buginese monsoon traders had settled near the main harbors of the island in the 19th century, mostly serving as intermediaries in the slave trade, Mads Lange established the first large trading post. Surrounded by an imposing wall with an elaborate gateway, the huge complex contained warehouses, a *pasar*, comfortable residences, and an open dining pavilion with a billiard table where foreign guests—merchants, ship captains, early tourists, Indologists, botanists, linguists—were sumptuously entertained. Lange lived there with his Chinese and Balinese concubines, his Dalmation dogs, and his retinue of servants.

In the evenings cosmopolitan parties were held there, from where the Kuta villagers could hear Danish folk music and bawdy songs sung and played by Lange and his friends on flutes, violins, and a piano. Half the races of Europe were represented at the trader's hospitable table. The Balinese gentry, *sarung*ed and parasoled, were also often invited to the gay parties and treated with the utmost care and deference. Relations with the dirt-poor Kuta villagers, however, were not as cordial. Once, when one of Lange's servants struck a Balinese, his factory was surrounded by a howling mob who wanted to burn it to the ground. Deftly, the trader bought the peace with 200 guilders and two balls of opium.

Lange himself came to play a crucial role in early colonial expansion. He fell under the protection of the highest-ranking raja of south Bali, Gusti Ngurah Gde Kesiman of Badung, who made Lange a *perbekel* (district official). Not only was he a powerful commercial broker who gained great profit from trade, but Lange also served as an indispensable link between the Dutch and southern Balinese rulers. In 1844, the Dane was appointed Dutch agent and official middleman, maintaining many personal relationships with the quarrelsome Balinese princes. He served as a channel of information between the vastly different worlds of East and West, able to solve most problems by simply buying protection and goodwill. Lange was also an adept mediator between conflicting parties, acting as a human buffer and diplomat between Dutch colonial interests and internal Balinese court politics. To avoid conflicts between oafish Europeans and the Balinese natives, no one but Lange and his brother Hans were allowed into the island's interior.

Although Kuta at the time was the gateway to the island's rich inland economy of coffee, tobacco, and other cash crops which Lange brokered, his major business derived from a monopoly on the sale of Chinese *kepeng*, which became the island's dominant monetary unit. Lange would buy the round coins cheap and sell them on Bali at 100% profit, or else trade them for rice. Large quantities of these coins were sent from China to Singapore, from where Lange would import them to Bali along with opium, iron, arms, and textiles. Working through Chinese agents, Lange maintained a system of storehouses on neighboring islands where his fleet of 12 ships would gather raw produce to resupply stocks on Bali. Numerous European ships called at Kuta to buy rice, coconut oil, animals, hides, cotton, tobacco, coffee, and other goods. He maintained two slaughterhouses, killing oxen to supply dried beef for the Dutch garrisons on Java. His close relationship with the local ruling elite allowed him to expand his trade and commercial contacts without competition or political risks. Lange became an immensely rich and powerful man. But with the launching of several large-scale military expeditions by the Dutch against Bali in 1846, 1848, and 1849, Lange's world was about to come tumbling down, leaving him brokenhearted.

At one point during a Dutch attack on Klungkung in 1849, Lange's trading station at Kuta was threatened. Filled with plunder, it was much coveted by the rajas of Mengwi and Gianyar. With opposing armies poised to attack near Klungkung, Lange averted a bloody disaster by dramatically riding out to meet the Dutch troops marching inland from Padangbai. He mediated a temporary peace by arranging an extravagant ceremonial meeting at his factory between the Dutch commander and the southern rajas, attended by 30,000 followers of the rajas in case something went wrong. For his reward, Lange received from the old raja one of Bali's highest titles, *punggawa besar.* Through this meeting, Lange's local patron and descendants were able to dominate southern Balinese politics until the final *puputan* of 1906-08, by which time nearly the whole of the Indonesian archipelago had come under Dutch colonial rule.

Because of new technology and commercial pressure the fortunes of Lange's factory soon began to decline. The Dutch naval blockade of Bali (1848-49) and the continual warfare of the 1840s had seriously disrupted trade. The rice-growing hinterlands had suffered the ravages of war and a plague of rats, while accompanying smallpox epidemics and water shortages contributed to the chaos. In addition, Kuta harbor was inadequate for the steamships which were used increasingly after 1850 in the inter-Asiatic trade. Finally, new commercial rivals entered the picture when the northern harbor of Buleleng and Ampenan on Lombok began to attract the bulk of Balinese exports. All these factors conspired to cause Lange losses from which he never recovered. It was said of him that there was more of the bold Viking than the prudent trader in his nature. He was soon put out of business.

Bankrupt and dispirited, Lange died mysteriously in 1856 just before he was to return to Denmark. Historians believe he may have been poisoned by a member of a competing dynastic group seeking revenge. His brother and nephew tried in vain to continue the factory, but Raja Kesiman's death in 1863 left the establishment completely vulnerable. After several years nothing remained of the once-prosperous compound except for high stone walls. Remnants of the compound survived into the 1950s but today all has vanished. Descendants of his Chinese and Balinese wives went on to make names for themselves in Singapore, Malaysia, and Sarawak. Today, Lange's grave behind Kuta's *pasar malam,* a nearby alleyway named Gang Tuan Langa, and descendants of his Dalmation dogs are the only physical traces left of this remarkable Dane's mercantile adventure on Bali.

British military mission was sent to Bali. Sir Stamford Raffles, who would establish the colony of Singapore in 1819, visited Bali in 1814. Rumors circulated the English were about to take possession of Bali, intent on building a second Singapore. The Dutch, believing the English sought to obtain control over the archipelago's rice trade, began their own colonial adventure in Bali. From 1839 to 1844, the Dutch East Indies Trading Company (Nederlandsche Handels Maatschappij, or NHM), which had taken over operations from the bankrupt VOC, ran an agency, or "factory," in Kuta. In 1837 The Hague decided the NHM would function as a political outpost on Bali and Lombok. The aim was to obtain exclusive contracts and acknowledgments of sovereignty, binding the rajas of Badung, Klungkung, Karangasem, and Buleleng to Batavia.

But because the NHM was not allowed to sell opium or weapons, the enterprise was economically a failure. Ultimately the Dutch began involving themselves directly in Balinese internal affairs. They fomented discontent among the lesser, increasingly independent rajas in order to gain concessions from the highest-ranking raja, the Dewa Agung of Klungkung.

Direct Action

In 1846, after the shipwreck of a Dutch vessel on the Badung shores and its looting by the local population, the Dutch envoy threatened the raja with reprisals. There were also several cases of looting—an ancient and accepted right of island peoples—of ships washed up on the northern coasts. When the Dutch resident went to Buleleng to investigate these cases and exchange contracts, he received a hostile and humiliating reception.

At the end of June 1846, the first Dutch punitive military expedition was launched against Buleleng—23 warships and some 3,000 men. With rifles and mortars, the soldiers fought all day against a Balinese force estimated at 50,000, armed with just spears and *kris*. Four hundred Balinese were killed and the royal palace at Singaraja was destroyed.

Within a few days a new treaty of submission was signed, the raja forced to pay 400,000 guilders, and a Dutch garrison stationed at Buleleng. Political tension increased all over the island, convincing the Dutch that further military intervention was necessary. In June 1848, after their treaties were violated and resistance continued, another Dutch expedition was launched. Opposed by a young prince named Gusti Ketut Jilantik, today an Indonesian military hero, this incursion ended in disaster for the Dutch. Lured into pursuing the Balinese force to the inland fortress of Jagaraga, the Dutch troops were encircled and soundly defeated.

The Balinese suddenly became the nightmare of the mid-19th century Dutch colonial state. There was no alternative but to show the Balinese, the English, and all their enemies that this rout was simply an aberration, and that the Dutch were still the dominant power in the Indies. So in April 1849, 5,000 infantrymen, 3,000 mercenaries, and a fleet of 60 vessels with 300 marines set out to settle once and for all this Balinese business. Shipping out of Java, this was one of the largest Dutch military expeditions ever organized in the archipelago. After just two days of fighting and the loss of Jilantik, Buleleng and the fortress of Jagaraga were defeated.

The army of 20,000 men under the raja of Buleleng sued for peace. In May of that year Karangasem and Klungkung were likewise subjugated, the first time Dutch forces entered southern Bali. Gradually, over the next five years, political authority passed from the native rulers of north Bali into the hands of Dutch *controleurs.* Buleleng and Jembrana were placed under the direct administration of the Netherlands East Indies government in 1882. The Balinese ruling neighboring Lombok fared no better. In 1894 the Lombok War was initiated with the landing of Dutch forces, who were promptly thrown into the sea. Heavy artillery and reinforcements arrived and the well-trained Netherlands colonial army swept over the whole island, capturing the Balinese capital of Cakranegara, killing the crown prince, and exiling his father.

THE TWENTIETH CENTURY

The Conquest of South Bali

At the time of Holland's final conquest of Bali in 1906, the island was administered by autonomous lords and their officials. Each of its nine warring principalities—Klungkung, Karangasem, Mengwi, Badung, Bangli, Tabanan, Gianyar, Buleleng, and Jembrana—was separated by sharply demarcated borders and each competed for the loyalty, support, and deference of the population.

In May 1904 the small Chinese steamer *Sri Koemala* was wrecked and looted off Sanur. The owners held the Dutch government directly responsible. The Dutch, in turn, demanded the raja of Badung pay damages and punish the looters. The raja, with the support of bordering states, refused. The dickering between the Dutch and the raja dragged on for two years, with the deadlock finally used as a pretense for the Dutch to throw a complete naval blockade around southern Bali.

On 15 September 1906, the Dutch anchored a large war fleet off Sanur and landed an expeditionary force of 2,000 men. Opposed on the beach at dawn the next day by Balinese attacking with golden spears, the Dutch started their final advance on Denpasar, trundling their cannons behind them. By 19 September they reached the town's outskirts. The naval bombardment commenced early the next morning, firing the king's palace and the houses of the princes.

The royal families of Badung were in a state of frenzy. Hopelessly outgunned but unwilling to face the humiliation of surrender, the raja invited anyone who wished to follow him in a *puputan,* a "fight to the end." After ordering everything of value destroyed, the raja, his nobles, generals, ministers, courtiers, retainers, and all his relatives—men, women, and children—dressed in their most splendid ceremonial attire. They then formed a fantastic procession on great gilded palanquins of state and marched down the main avenue of Denpasar to face the Dutch rifles.

Hurriedly, interpreters were sent out by the Dutch to stop them, but they continued. Suddenly the procession stopped. The raja dismounted the palanquin, gave a signal to one of his priests, and was stabbed in the heart. Immediately, the Balinese began killing each other. The Dutch soldiers, startled by a stray shot, fired volley after volley into the crowd. As if in a trance, men and boys and loinclothed women with loose hair savagely attacked the Dutch, while court ladies contemptuously flung gold coins and jewels at the stunned soldiers.

This fight to the death resulted in 3,600 Balinese dead and the annihilation of the entire royal family. The wives and followers of the king crawled upon his body to die; the heaps of dead became mounds. Some Balinese went among the fallen, killing the wounded with gold *kris* while priests sprinkled holy water on the dead and dying. Another mad rush, led by the 12-year-old brother of the raja, were all mowed down.

The way to the burning palace was now free, over hundreds of mangled, bloodied corpses. The Dutch lost only one sergeant, stabbed to death by a woman. Only one small Balinese boy survived the massacre. Later that day, the army faced another *puputan* led by the raja of Pemecutan. Dutch troops then ranged through the countryside, slaughtering the aristocracy and looting and leveling palaces.

It was not yet over. On 23 September 1906, the Dutch marched on Tabanan, the regency west of Badung. The raja offered to surrender on condition that he be allowed to retain his title and certain rights to his land. The resident, unable to answer until he consulted the colonial government, took him into custody. The following day the raja cut his own throat with a blunt *sirih* knife.

Two years later the only remaining independent raja at Klungkung, the Dewa Agung, launched another *puputan,* killing himself and his entire family. The rajas of Karangasem and Gianyar to the east, who had formerly pledged their loyalty to the Dutch, were allowed to retain their titles and land. Any remaining royalty who opposed the Dutch were exiled and their properties confiscated.

The Dutch now controlled the entire island, and the glorious Bali-Hindu theater-state, so jealously guarded and preserved for more than a thousand years, came to a bitter end. The puputan is commemorated today with a plaque in front of the Bali Museum in Denpasar depicting men, women, and children marching to their deaths.

Early Twentieth-Century Dutch Administration

In contrast to its violent and bloody campaigns to subdue the island, the Dutch colonial administration after Bali's conquest can only be described as benign, even enlightened. Newspaper accounts of the massacres of 1906 and 1908 shocked church groups, the Dutch people, parliament, and governments around the world. Protests poured into the colonial office. The Dutch colonial administration was then shamed into treating the Balinese with a patriarchal, soft, hands-off policy unprecedented in the Indies, instituting reforms, engineering roadways, establishing schools and hospitals. The island soon took on the appearance more of a trusteeship than a colony. The army stayed on until 1914, when Balinese resistance was considered sufficiently controlled and its duties were taken over by a police force.

Governance of the island was then reorganized along the same hierarchical lines employed by the rajas. In 1929, the former kingdoms of Bali were restored to their hereditary rulers as *zelf-besturen* (self-governing territories) in a grandiose ceremony at Besakih. In this system of indirect rule, those who had been loyal to the Dutch, such as the raja of Karangasem, retained their autocratic rights over the people of their regencies. These puppet regents were made responsible to the colonial government for the conduct of their subjects and for the payment of taxes. The Dutch *controleur* was looked upon as an "elder brother," and his orders were called "recommendations."

The Dutch Legacy

The Balinese became the darlings of the Dutch authorities. Indeed, the Dutch administration took a patronizing attitude toward the people and their culture, allowing the Balinese to continue using their own language and practice their own *adat.* Although the remaining pro-Dutch princes were deprived of political powers, they maintained much of their influence and importance as patrons of the arts. We must also be forever thankful to the Dutch for keeping the missionaries out of Bali; it was more convenient for them to control the people through their liaisons with local leaders and let religion take its own course. So little did Dutch colonialism affect Bali that even up until the 1970s, before the building of the international airport, a rural Balinese village was probably very similar to a Javanese village of the 17th century.

Foreign visitors and tourists were vigorously discouraged from visiting Bali. A small group of dedicated Dutch officials safeguarded Bali's culture, which enjoyed a rebirth during the first three decades of Dutch rule. One can still see in the highlands above Singaraja and in Denpasar steepled homes with double doors, wrought-iron grillwork gates, and hanging porcelain lamps, remnants of Dutch efforts to Hollandize Bali.

The occupying Dutch were not, however, totally humanitarian. Although no rubber or tea plantations were established, as in many parts of Java, the Dutch took over the highly profitable opium monopoly. Starting on 1 January 1908, any Balinese over the age of 18 was allowed to legally purchase opium from one of 100 official suppliers set up around the island. Realizing a profit margin of over 90%, within one year opium sales accounted for 75% of the island's administrative budget. Only a small portion of the money ever benefited the Balinese directly. In 1910 alone, while the Dutch earned one million florins from opium, they spent less than 20,000 florins on schools. By the late 1930s, because of the combined clamor from Indonesian organizations and the Dutch Ethicists, the Dutch opium monopoly served only a few old die-hard Chinese addicts.

Discovery by the Western World

Over the decades following the conquest and occupation of the south, a select group of tourists, expatriates, actors, and celebrities adopted Bali as their private paradise, building ornate villas in Ubud and Sanur. These early sojourners would arrive on Bali by steamship at Singaraja, then motor south to Denpasar, invariably staying at the Bali Hotel.

The publication in 1926 of a remarkable book of photographs, Gregor Krause's *Bali: Volk, Land, Tanze, Feste, Tempel,* mesmerized all of Europe. Krause's priceless photos, taken while he was a government doctor on Bali between 1912 and 1914, revealed a culture which had remained unchanged through the centuries. In the early 1930s a few documentary films, such as *The Island of Demons* from Germany

and *Goona Goona,* out of the U.S.A., were distributed in America and Europe, bringing this isolated cultural outpost to the attention of the world. Bali by this time had also gained an underground reputation as a homosexual paradise; in 1935, a nightclub opened in Manhattan called the Sins of Bali.

The influence of such foreign artists as Walter Spies, Rudolph Bonnet, and Le Mayeur during the 1930s made a significant impact on the development of modern Balinese painting. An elite circle of foreign anthropologists, ethnologists, intellectuals, and musicians—Margaret Mead and Buckminster Fuller among them—were also drawn to Bali, devoting themselves to studying its culture.

Among the classic works produced in the 1930s is *The Island of Bali,* by the Mexican illustrator and writer Miguel Covarrubias. It was also during this period that the German novelist Vicki Baum visited the island, writing her vivid *Tale of Bali* in 1937, depicting the European conquest from the Balinese point of view. Dutch colonial officials and distinguished European scholars began to build a body of published work on Bali, anthropological literature with no parallel anywhere else in the world.

The Japanese Invasion

In the early 1940s the Balinese were rudely shaken out of the political isolation and benign lethargy which typified the latter years of Dutch rule. On 10 January 1942 the Japanese invaded the Dutch East Indies, landing troops on Celebes and Borneo. Denpasar's airfield was taken on 20 February, cutting communications with Australia and the Indies. Bali was used as a Japanese base for the invasion of Java on 26 February. On 8 March 1942 the Dutch surrendered with hardly a fight.

During the ensuing three years of Japanese occupation, while the rest of the eastern islands were subject to the oppressive arrogant control of the Japanese Navy, the occupier's treatment of the Balinese was comparatively indulgent. Nevertheless, Bali's population suffered critical food and medical supply shortages, while the island's transport system was almost totally disrupted.

With his oratorical power and dominating, charismatic style, an ex-engineer named Sukarno

(1901-1970) had emerged as Indonesia's most forceful nationalistic political personality during the 1930s. Sukarno cut deals with the Dutch to avoid being sent into exile; later, the Japanese used him to help them govern more effectively. During the Japanese occupation Sukarno seized every opportunity to educate the masses, inculcating in them nationalistic fervor.

In spite of their arbitrary cruelty and oppression, the Japanese offered an extraordinary and unprecedented opportunity for independence. The Japanese indoctrinated and politicized the Balinese, trained and armed paramilitary youth groups, and generally encouraged consciousness of what it means to be an Indonesian.

In April 1945, with the war turning against them, the Japanese even sent Sukarno and other independence figures on a speaking tour to promote nationalism. But the most useful contribution the Japanese made to Indonesia, in the end, was to lose the war.

Revolution
On 17 August 1945, 11 days after the atomic bomb was dropped on Hiroshima, Sukarno proclaimed Indonesia's independence in Jakarta. Before the Dutch could return to restore order, Balinese militants moved to sieze weapons from the Japanese. The subsequent war of independence against the Dutch lasted for more than four years.

On 20 November 1946, the Battle of Marga was fought in Tabanan in central Bali. Colonel I Gusti Ngurah Rai, 29 years old, led his 95 guerrillas in a last-ditch battle in which all were killed by aerial bombardment—a reenactment of the *puputans* of 40 years earlier. Today you see Ngurah Rai's name commemorated on street signs all over the island; Bali's international airport is named in his honor.

Although Balinese resistance was broken, the Indonesians eventually won the war. In 1946 the Dutch made Bali the headquarters of their federal "Republic of East Indonesia" (NIT), which they backed as a rival to the revolutionary republic based on Java. Their plan was to one day merge the island into a pro-Dutch federation. The Dutch tried to build support among the people by promising to revitalize Bali's devastated economy. But the Dutch lost their chance at dividing the islands when they broke their treaty with the new

government and launched a direct attack on republic headquarters in Yogyakarta in central Java. After this "police action" proved ineffectual, Holland formally transferred the former Netherlands East Indies—including Bali—to Indonesian authorities in 1949. The Dutch left behind their most precious legacy—a wildly diverse Indonesian nation welded into a unitary state.

The New Republic
Following the exit of the Dutch came constant bickering between the military, secessionists, communists, conservatives, and religious fanatics. The new country experimented with a democratic constitution; cabinets turned over every six months. To stop the chaos, President Sukarno declared in 1956 his policy of "Guided Democracy," involving the creation of a National Council made up of members handpicked by himself. Sukarno declared the age-old Indonesian tradition of *mufakat,* or decision through consensus, would best suit Indonesia as a method of decision-making. Politcal parties and legislative bodies were abolished. On Bali, the old power arrangements continued, with the various principalities converted into *kabupaten* and the rajas or members of their families assuming the office of *bupati* (mayor).

In the years following the establishment of Sukarno's extralegal "Guided Democracy," Bali came to distrust the arrogant, incompetent, and corrupt centralized regime. Jakarta, in turn, resented the special treatment Bali had received from the Dutch; many in the government also felt the Balinese had cooperated all too willingly with their former colonial masters. Though Sukarno was half Balinese, he showed little empathy for the Balinese and their plight. In the late colonial period, the island had been one of the best-administered regions in the archipelago, but under the new republic it became one of the most neglected and dependent. By 1962, the island was relying on injections of 300 tons of rice per month from the powers in Jakarta. A clique of corrupt Sukarnoists and new Balinese capitalists, both civilian and military, lorded it over the landless peasants, aggressively jockeying for state patronage and competing with each other for wealth and power at the expense of the natives. Village administration, local *adat,* and large public rituals were redefined and appropriated by Indonesian government institutions to enhance state authority.

Bad government led to the disintegration of the island's economy. Government offices were filled with bungling bureaucrats who insisted on bribes before performing even the most routine services. Sukarno meanwhile treated Bali like his own private playground. He and his entourage visited the island constantly, demanding special dance performances be staged, abducting Balinese women for sexual favors, commandeering without payment vehicles, paintings, and whatever else seized their fancy. Advance squads of soldiers would sweep in to shoot dogs and pigs so parties of devout Muslim visitors would not be revolted by sight of the unclean creatures.

What did the Sukarno era leave behind? A former Dutch resthouse at Tampaksiring converted to one of Sukarno's private palaces, the eyesore of the Bali Beach Hotel at Sanur, and the establishment of Bali's only tertiary institute, the Udayana University of Denpasar.

The 1965 Coup and its Aftermath

In the waning days of Sukarno's reign, conflict increased between the high-caste capitalist class and communists pursuing a more militant role in land reform and harvest-sharing policies. Bali's governor, Anak Agung Bagus Suteja, increased the participation of the Indonesian Communist Party (PKI) and other leftists in the island's administration and legislative bodies. The PKI's aggressive policy toward land reform understandably had tremendous appeal to landless peasants and poor tenant farmers. Land was seized unilaterally from rich landowners; landlord-employed thugs destroyed sharecroppers' crops and razed their huts. Government offices were burned, scuffles and armed attacks broke out, religious ceremonies were disrupted. A full-scale civil war, drawn along class lines, was underway.

A series of ominous natural catastrophes also weighed in: rat and mouse plagues, insect infestations, crop failures, and, finally, the violent eruption of Gunung Agung.

The mountain exploded during the holiest of Balinese ceremonies, Eka Dasa Rudra, a purification rite in which harmony and balance in people and nature are restored in all 11 directions. The ceremony, held only once every 100 years, was precipitously held some 10 years early at the behest of Sukarno, apparaenty to impress a convention of travel agents. Midway through the opulent proceedings, Gunung Agung began to shower the whole area with ash and smoke, finally exploding in its most violent eruption in 600 years. Earthquakes toppled temples, hot ash ignited thatched roofs, volcanic debris rained upon the earth. As the molten lava moved toward them, Hindu priests prayed frantically, hoping to appease the angry gods, assuring worshippers they had nothing to fear.

In the end, 1600 Balinese were killed, 86,000 left homeless, and 100,000 hectares removed from production. A layer of hot choking dust lay over the whole island for a week, covering fields, houses, and streets. One-quarter of Bali was turned into black lava desert. The catastrophe was attribted to the wrath of the god Shiva in his most evil aspect as Rudra. This disaster ultimately became a damning judgment on the entire Sukarno era.

Because empty land for evacuees was not available on Bali, the consequences of overpopulation became acute for the first time in the island's history. No longer could farmers move temporarily to another part of the island, later returning to a land covered in fresh, fertile ash. Thousands had to be resettled in Sulawesi.

The failure of crops, the uprooting of many villages, and the forced evacuation of masses of people contributed substantially to the communal clashes and massacres of tens of thousands of Balinese during the purge of Indonesian communists in 1966. Internal refugees poured into Denpasar and Singaraja where, together with large numbers of unemployed urban poor, formed a restive, disaffected underclass ripe for mobilization by communist mass organizations.

Finally, all hell broke loose. On the night of 30 September 1965, six high-ranking army leaders were kidnapped, tortured, and killed in Jakarta, allegedly by communist conspirators. The attempted coup d'etat, suppressed skillfully within days by a previously little-known general named Suharto, led directly to an archipelago-wide bloodbath.

The Indonesian Communist Party was immediately banned, and Sukarno was forced to delegate wide powers to Suharto. Mass arrests followed. On 8 October fanatical Muslim youths attacked and burned the communist party headquarters in Jakarta, initiating a bloody wave of anti-communist reprisals that rolled over Java and Bali, leaving whole villages devastated and in many cases obliterated. The killings on Bali started in earnest in December 1965 and soon began to take on the dimensions of a mass purgation, an "essential" exorcism of the island. Devout Balinese murdered godless communists whom they believed mocked their religion and threatened their pious way of life. In the witch hunt for "communists" old scores were settled and many noncommunists wiped out. Wealthy businessmen took advantage of the chaos to murder their Chinese and Balinese competitors.

On Java the people had to be egged on to kill the communists; on Bali they had to be restrained. The "trance killings" reached a fever pitch in 1966, when whole groups of Balinese were rounded up and slashed, clubbed, and chopped to death by communal consent. The killers included small boys, encouraged in some cases by Hindu priests. The purge on Bali became so indiscriminate commandos finally had to step in to restore order. From then on the killing was coordinated by the military and police, working with civilian authorities to make sure only the "right" people were executed. Dressed in ceremonial white attire, the victims were led to the killing fields dispassionately, almost politely, without hatred. Of a population of two million, it is estimated as many as 50,000 were killed. The horrific bloodletting is rarely referred to today.

Suharto's pro-Western "New Order" ushered in a long period of relative stability and rampant capitalist development. In 1979, the Eka Dasa Rudra cleansing ceremony was held again and completed without incident. Suharto's attendance at the ceremony was an attempt to place Bali's religion and culture firmly in the national psyche, an indispensable part of the pan-Indonesian culture.

GOVERNMENT

Indonesia is easily the most broken-up country in the world, and its sheer expanse and diversity make it awesomely difficult to govern. On the state crest are the old Sanskrit words Bhinneka Tunggal Ika, "We are many but we are one." This line is played hard by Indonesia's leaders, who try to bring unity to the country by invoking nationalistic ceremonies claiming a mystical, divine mandate to rule; and pushing a national fitness program of *senam pagi* (morning exercise), practiced every morning in even the most remote hill villages. The Indonesian language is another effective unifying force.

To bring all the diverse people of this sprawling island nation together within the political and geographic entity called Indonesia will always be the greatest single problem facing its leaders. Along with such typical fundamental problems of a developing Third World nation as overpopulation, unemployment, and lack of an industrial base and technical expertise, the widely dispersed group of 17,000 islands suffers from an unevenly distributed population and unequal distribution of natural wealth. In addition, it's a massive job trying to usher a feudal agrarian society into the 20th century.

The country's gigantic conservatism, the low-key Indonesian temperament, an almost feudal deference to established authority, the docile resignation of the masses, and the help of the army keep the government in power. Indonesians are most concerned that the government satisfies them—food in their bellies, a roof over their heads, clothes to cover them.

Bali is an Indonesian province. Administratively, Indonesia is divided into 27 provinces, each headed by a governor nominated by a provincial legislature and approved and appointed by the central government. Akin to the U.S. states, each province has its own provincial capital. The provinces are further divided into regencies, subdistricts, and municipalities.

Pancasila

The concept of Pancasila ("Five Principles"), authored by Sukarno during the Japanese occupation, is the basis of civilized rule. The government urges all Indonesians to accept this state ideology as their fundamental political philosophy, crucial to national unity. Displayed on practically every government building, the emblem of the five *sila*, or principles, are: 1) belief in one supreme God; 2) a just and civilized humanity; 3) nationalism, the unity of Indonesia; 4) democracy, guided by the wisdom of unanimity arising from discussion *(musjawarah)* and mutual assistance *(gotong royong);* 5) social justice, the equality of political rights, and the rights of citizenship, as well as social and cultural equality.

Since 1985, all social, political, and religious organizations have been required to adopt the Pancasila principles as their basic platform. Rather than hard and fast guidelines, each regime tends to interpret these five concepts in a way that will further its social and political goals.

THE NEW ORDER

Jakartan Centralism

The government is centered on Java and is also intensely Java-centered. The Dutch established their colonial bureaucracy to hold together the great Dutch East Indies on Java, and as a result it is Java that has emerged as the most industrialized and modernized island of Indonesia. Indonesia's is not a truly representative government; the Javanese are in effect the new colonialists of the archipelago. An elite of perhaps 2,000 Javanese men manipulate Indonesian politics. With only a dozen or so exceptions, they all speak English, drive new Japanese cars, live in Jakarta, and are ethnic Javanese. This is why government development agencies and Javanese business interests could prevail in the development of a mammoth 121-hectare tourist resort near Tanah Lot in Tabanan, against the wishes of local Balinese opposed to the exploitation of the island's oldest and most sacred sea temple.

The Armed Forces

Indonesia's armed forces were founded in 1945 during the revolution against the Dutch. From that time to the present, the army has been the most powerful of all the services. Under the direct control of the president and the ministry of defense, the armed forces consist of the army (Angkatan Darat), navy (Angkatan Laut), air force (Angkatan Udara), and police (Polisi Negara). A central command (ABRI) coordinates all four services. Armed forces personnel numbers 284,000, with another 800,000 in reserve. The military's arsenal includes F-16 fighter planes and A-4 Sky Hawks; work is progressing on ballistic missiles.

The military is the nation's only credible political power. The service provides the country with its president, half its ambassadors, and two-thirds its regional governors. Half of Indonesia's cabinet ministers are retired military officers who retain strong loyalties to the military. The interests of the armed forces are formally represented in the MPR by a bloc of 100 reserved seats. From its inception, retired military men have secured up to 80% of the leadership posts in Golkar.

The army considers itself a sociopolitical force, a role enshrined in the doctrine of *dwifungsi,* or dual function, which calls for its extensive participation in politics and government. *Dwifungsi* ensures that military personnel permeate civilian life through a network of watchdogs running parallel to the whole civilian bureaucracy, prodding their civilian counterparts when necessary. A typical military officer's career consists of serving alternating stints in both regional and combat commands at the end of which he "retires" into the civil bureaucracy.

THE STATE ORGANS

According to the text of the country's 1945 constitution, still in effect, the nation is a republic, with sovereignty residing in the people. Functions of the government include executive, legislative, and judicial, but there is no specific separation of powers, no system of checks and balances. The constitution provides for a strong president who serves a term of five years. Apparently, this highest government executive may be reelected indefinitely; it's up to the president to accept or reject another term. Suharto was overwhelmingly reelected to serve a sixth five-

year term in March 1993. Only Cuba's Fidel Castro has served longer as a head of state.

Suharto's cabinet, officially called Development Cabinet VI, is responsible only to him. With a current membership of 41, the new cabinet is the world's largest, after China's. Previous cabinets promulgated policies to improve agriculture, as the president has always had a soft spot for farmers. The present cabinet, however, is intent on turning Indonesia into a modern industrial state. The man most responsible for the realignment of the president's priorities is Minister of Research and Technology B.J. Habibie. This German-trained aeronautical engineer has turned to politics to advance his vision of a modern Indonesia that can take its place beside the tigers of Southeast Asia. Habibie is equally committed to developing a qualified, skilled workforce to implement Indonesia's ambitious technological programs. Bali's principal contribution to the Indonesian economy is not as an industrial or manufacturing center, but as a tourist center.

The president himself is directly responsible only to the **Majellis Permusyawaratan Rakyat (MPR),** the People's Consultative Assembly. This "super parliament" consists of 1,000 farmers, workers, students, businesspeople, clergy, intellectuals, and military types—a heterogeneous body meant to represent a wide cross-section of society. The MPR meets every five years to select a president and endorse the general policy guidelines for the president's next five-year term.

Just because Indonesia has a parliament, doesn't mean it's a democracy. Although empowered by the constitution with the highest authority of state, in reality the MPR is a classic rubber-stamp body that rarely meets and never decides important issues. Members must pass an ideological screening administered by the military, and the president has the final right to approve MPR appointees. At least 60% of the body works for the government party; nearly 200 are admirals, generals, or air marshals.

The 500-member **Dewan Perwakilan Rakyat (DPR),** or the House of Representatives, is a legislative body that sits at least once a year. Only 400 members are elected; the remaining 100 seats are reserved for armed forces personnel. DPR representatives are not known for their candor and outspokenness. Every statute passed by the DPR requires the approval of the president.

The judiciary cannot impeach, nor can it rule on the constitutionality of the decrees or legislation passed by the other branches of government. The number of sitting supreme court judges varies in number from 15 and 20; they preside over 300 subordinate courts scattered across the country. The court faces a maddeningly complex set of social and cultural issues relating to differing *adat* and the incongruities of a Dutch-based legal system. Adequate qualified staffing is a major problem bedeviling the scope and speed of settlements.

Political Parties and the Electoral Process

The government **Golkar party,** founded in 1964 as a counterbalance to growing PKI influence, enjoys the full backing of the army and the bureaucracy. This all-powerful government political machine, with almost unlimited resources, dominates all levels of government. Golkar represents the armed forces, the bureaucracy, farmers, women's organizations, students, and many other "functional groups" *(golongan karya).* Golkar always wins.

All parties must adopt Pancasila as its sole political philosophy. Golkar screens the candidates for the only other currently allowed two major parties, often installing a particularly unpopular character to further tilt the election in its favor.

Although political campaigns have an exciting, carnival-like, grassroots atmosphere, Indonesia's electoral process is actually heavily managed and controlled. Little effort is expended in educating the people to inform them of their political choices. Indonesians have a vote but not a say. The whole process is designed to demonstrate the government's legitimacy to its people and the world, while avoiding as much as possible any real contest among competing political parties.

Voting is not compulsory, but government officials in provincial districts apply pressure on village heads to get out the vote for Golkar. Campaigns are limited to 25 days, with a one week "quiet period" just prior to the election. Golkar issues the permits required to hold political rallies, where criticisms of government policies and discussion of religious or racial issues are forbidden.

Voters select parties, not individuals. The voting occurs in small polling stations in workplaces and residential areas where political loyalties are closely monitored. Civil servants vote at their offices and must ask permission from their superiors if they intend to vote for a party other than Golkar.

LOCAL ADMINISTRATION

On Bali, all traditional political concepts are based on Hinduism. Each of Bali's regencies is headed by a *bupati,* and each is separated into smaller *kecamatan* headed by a *camat,* the executive officer of the *bupati.* Under the *camat* are the village headmen, *perbekel,* who govern an area comprising several small communities.

There are 564 incorporated villages under a *perbekel,* as well as 1,456 *desa adat* (common villages). The smallest political unit is the *banjar,* an individual community ward consisting of 200-300 male householders and administered by a *klian* (*banjar* head). The sprawling seacoast village of Sanur, for example, has 22 *banjar.*

Gotong Royong

Gotong royong means joint responsibility and mutual cooperation of the whole community, all working together to achieve common ends. With origins in much earlier times, this is an all-important institution in Indonesian village life. Bali consists of hundreds of villages, and the tradition of *gotong royong* is the real grassroots base of political rule.

Whenever fire, flood, earthquake, or volcanic eruption strikes, when pipelines break down or a dam needs building or repairing, the principle of *gotong royong* goes into effect. If a rice field must be harvested, all have a right and duty to help, receiving a share of the crop as compensation. If a temple is to be built, all villagers will join in building it, or else contribute money in lieu of labor. Men usually work with their own tools and without pay. Sometimes neighboring villagers are expected to help. If a village follows this communal organization, no household will be without land to farm, work to subsist, food to eat. Anyone in trouble will receive help.

A number of ancient Balinese customs—three-day cycling markets, *subak* organizations, unpaid labor required by feudal lords—have their origins in an Indianized Bali preceding Javanese contact, so the practice of mutual cooperation and ritual corvée was already well established on Bali before *gotong royong* became an all-important principle in modern Indonesian political life. *Gotong royong* as it works on Bali revolves around thousands of *perbekel* and *klian* who coordinate *gotong royong* programs and carry out government policies. *Perbekel* rule by assigning friends and assistants to tasks, a sort of administration by relationships. Loyalties to family, village, and friends are more important than self-advancement. The central government greatly stresses this village socialism—it makes the government's job much easier, enabling the country to almost run itself.

When the local government feels it can bring economic benefits to an area, it sends men out to the villages to explain the advantages, asking the help of the local *banjar*. In this way, with the villagers supplying the labor and the government the equipment and materials, real progress and a higher standard of living can be achieved.

By channeling agricultural production campaigns through the local *subak* and *banjar*, the government can ensure that the nine regencies of Bali develop harmoniously in all sectors. Under government supervision, vineyards are planted along the arid northwest coast, old coconut and coffee trees are replaced with more productive varieties, high-yield rice strains are promoted, fisheries and other small marine industries are established, and tourism and transportation infrastructures are constantly improved upon.

CIVIL LIBERTIES

Indonesia's military bureaucratic state can best be described as an open patriarchal dictatorship. Don't think Big Brother is always watching. The Javanese are a softer civilization than the North Koreans or Saudis. There's authoritarianism, but not mind control. A citizen or visitor is actually quite inept if he can't arrange to pay, cajole, or otherwise work a way through this system.

The rule of formal, court-upheld law doesn't exist here. Customary law *(adat)* and the regulations of the *banjar* cover even criminal and civil cases and are the most powerful social forces of all. Regulations can be stretched more in Indonesia than in the West; problems can often be worked out before they come to a confrontation. Because *adat* affords so much latitude and reinterpretation, the amount of personal liberty in practice is astonishingly high. Government controls actually felt by the Balinese are extremely limited compared to places like the U.S., where government regulations, laws, and taxes touch every individual every day. Though demonstrators are sometimes confronted with the military, protest marches continue and activist organizations exist. Balinese pro-democracy student groups agitate for human rights and environmental issues. The most recent passionate public protest occurred in 1994, opposing a monstrous 400-billion-rupiah, 125-meter-high statue of Garuda in Nusa Dua.

Dissension and Censorship

Although the Indonesian constitution guarantees freedom of the press and speech, censorship is taken for granted in Indonesia. Accompanying the economic deregulation of 1988 was a tendency toward *keterbukaan,* or openness in Indonesian society. Some public political protest was allowed to occur and there was some freedom of the press. But the result was like removing the lid from a pressure cooker. Demonstrations erupted all over the archipelago from hospital workers demanding a minimum wage of US$3.70 per day, to conservative Muslims damning American diplomats bringing the drug XTC into Indonesia.

On Bali in 1994 were vociferous demonstrations, provincial parliamentary debates, and passionate letters written to oppose the US$200 million Bali Nirwana Resort near Tanah Lot, threatening the sanctity and cosmological significance of the ancient temple. This was the first time many Balinese mustered the courage to protest government decrees since the orgiastic communist massacres of 1965-66. Not only was there a placard-waving, shouting demonstration of 500 students at Udayana University in the capital city of Denpasar, but it was actually reported by the island's newspaper, the *Bali Post*. This was such a momentous occurrence, the edition sold out within an unprecedented eight hours of its release. Subsequent editions of the *Post* dutifully reported the ongoing debate. It seemed everyone on Bali was against the project—with the exception of Jakarta-appointed Governor Ida Bagus Oka. In a fiery editorial retort, the governor paternally admonished citizens to shut up and accept the inevitable. The result was an even larger student demonstration, demanding the governor resign. This so aggravated the police and military, they charged into the crowd and beat stragglers with rattan canes.

Everyone in Bali knows the governor's nickname—Ida Bagus "O.K." This refers to his proclivity for rubber-stamping any project that originates in Jakarta. A few cosmetic concessions were granted. The local business owners of Tanah Lot, with their modest streetstalls and simple cafes, were uneasy about the project, aware they would be swallowed up. Glumly they watched as the bulldozers arrived in March 1994 to begin shaving off the topsoil for the cement underpinnings of the mammoth project. The resort opened on schedule in August 1995.

This time, the *Bali Post* was thoroughly browbeaten, the whole publishing industry under seige. In Indonesian political culture, freedom of the press is regarded as less important than stability and harmony. There is rarely an exchange of opinions, only a one-way monologue from the government down to the people. In the past 10 years, the New Order regime has banned the publication of over 120 books and periodicals. Pages critical of Indonesia are often blacked out in such imported weeklies as the *Far Eastern Economic Review, Time,* and *Newsweek.* Moon Publications' *Indonesia Handbook* has been unavailable for sale in Indonesia for over 20 years.

Java versus Bali

Bali is a Hindu enclave deep within the largest Muslim country in the world. Most of the fabulous wealth derived from Bali's tourist industry finds its way back to corporate shareholders in the capital of Jakarta on the neighboring island of Java. This results in a smoldering animosity between the two islands, one only somewhat assuaged when the Indonesian House of Representatives passed the country's first Tourism Bill in 1991. This statute allows residents of areas set aside for tourism to become owners and managers of their own resorts by forming small private companies or cooperatives.

The animosity between Java and Bali is heightened by Java's image of Bali as a spoiled child of tourism and itself as a spurned and neglected older sibling. The relationship between the two islands, though separated only by a narrow straight, is quite complex. Most Balinese attribute their ancestry to Java but believe the Javanese blew it when they converted to Islam in the 13th-16th centuries, at the pinnacle of their Golden Age. The Javanese, in turn, claim the Balinese sold out their culture for tourism. This sentiment is tinged with envy: Bali has been the cornerstone of the country's tourism industry for the past decade, receiving as much investment in tourism as the rest of Indonesia combined.

Javanese domestic tourists who flock to Bali seldom deign to wear traditional clothing when attending Balinese temple festivals and ceremonies or even wear scarves, a simple sign of respect when visiting a Hindu temple. This is an obvious sign to the local people that the visitors do not acknowledge or respect their religion. This, and other historical and cultural differences, add up to a belief that Islamic Javanese business interests are prone to running roughshod over Balinese sensibilities—since Muslims, it is believed, do not recognize or respect Hinduism anyway. The Balinese at times find it necessary to assert their autonomy to protect, for example, their sacred sites. In 1993, when the national government wanted to make Besakih a national monument along the lines of Borobudur, the local Hindu community raised such a clamor the idea was dropped.

Another trend exacerbating the situation is the influx of economic migrants from Java. For several decades these refugees from overpopulated Java have poured into southern Bali to work in road construction or in the hotel, restaurant, and building industries. Kampung Java have sprung up at building sites all over the island, supplying the labor forces used in every new project. At the same time, Javanese ruling and business elites build more and more vacation homes on the island. This rapid migration has left little time for adaptation and compromise. Furthermore, the Javanese-controlled government continues to encourage the transmigration of Balinese families to other, less-populated islands of Indonesia. These policies raise fears among the Balinese that their island is being literally usurped by the Javanese.

The government denies any strain between the two peoples, as the task of governing the world's largest archipelago, with its multitudinous differing religions, customs, languages, and local societal systems, necessitates maintaining an appearance of generosity. Nevertheless, the fact is: majority rules. Local Balinese who've made a career in the government or military have a vested interest in preserving the status quo, repressing dissent, and furthering integration into the national agenda.

ECONOMY

With a per capita income of more than US$500 per annum, Bali today is one of Indonesia's most prosperous islands. The standard of living is much lower on Java, where the "minimum wage" is only about Rp1000 per day. On Bali it's Rp3500 or Rp4500 per day for day laborers—Rp5000 and up in Singaraja, Rp7500 in Ubud and Kuta. Only 10% of the island's villages are without electricity. The number of new Mercedes 300 and BMW 5 series cars is striking—proportionally far more than in the States (well, excepting Palm Beach or Beverly Hills). The ones who have it really have it.

Rice-growing and export—about 100,000 tons annually—still dominates the economy, but tourism is catching up fast, employing an ever greater proportion of the population. In 1990, only 50% of the population was employed in agriculture. Of Bali's 550,000 hectares of arable land, 18% is covered in irrigated rice fields (sawah), 27% in nonirrigated dry fields (tegelan), 23% in state-owned forested lands, and 17% in cash-crops gardens (kebun). Rice cultivation is most widespread in the south and east.

Alfred Russel Wallace reported 100 years ago that Bali was so well cultivated there was little room for indigenous vegetation. Besides rice, the Balinese grow tea, tobacco, cacao, copra, groundnuts, cassava, indigo, maize, onions, and legumes. Coffee is another major export crop, shipped primarily to Japan, the Netherlands, and the U.S.A.

Indonesia produces 85% of the world's vanilla, and Bali grows more than any other island in Indonesia, about 30 tons per year. Soybeans, chili peppers, and tropical fruits are also cultivated. In the Bedugal area, cauliflower and broccoli are grown to supply the tourist industry in the south. Vineyards have been established in Buleleng Regency along the dry northwest coast. Pigs, cattle, cotton, sea vegetables, canned fish, kapok, and copra are other principal exports.

In the days when barter was the major means of exchange, the man who owned many rice fields was considered very wealthy. Today, rice lands are steadily giving way to urban growth. Real estate and tourist development and the cash economies of the tourist and souvenir industries have become powerful agents of change in the egalitarian Balinese village. Now the Balinese want money—not bartered goods or labor—to buy consumer items, Hondas, cosmetics, electronics.

RICE-GROWING

Bali is one of the few places on Earth made visually stunning by its main economic activity. The cascading terraces of rice fields are the most striking feature of the landscape, claiming even slopes that look too formidable to be of any possible use. The island is one big sculpture. Every terrace is manicured and polished, every field and niche carved and tailored by hand. Some plots are so small, they hold just four rice plants each. The Balinese have lovingly carved their own world in a series of geometric steps that climb up the volcanic slopes to the mountains where the gods live. Fringed by coconut palms, deep ravines force their way through this checkerboard pattern to the sea.

On Bali rice-growing is both an art and a science. Because of the island's superb drainage pattern, the high volcanic ash content, and Bali's equable climate, conditions for traditional sawah cultivation here are perhaps the most ideal in all Indonesia. However, rainfall in the

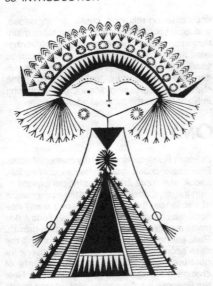

Made from palm leaf, this abstract female head with a large fanlike headdress is dedicated to the rice goddess Dewi Sri and dates from pre-Hindu rice cults. The figure is a symbol of wealth, fertility, and good fortune; it can also be found on cakes, baked clay, or made from old Chinese coins. The art of cutting and folding young coconut or palm leaves in intricate designs, both for impressive large-scale ornamentation and small-scale temple flower offerings like the above, is thought to be a pure Balinese art form, with no trace of borrowing from outside cultures.

lowlands is insufficient to grow wet rice, and Bali's steep and narrow ravines are not easy to dam. To remedy these problems, the Balinese have devised ingenious cathements to collect rainwater and channel water. Thousands of tiny waterfalls spill a precious allotment of water onto tiers of paddy from high mountain lakes to coastal rice fields. This complex irrigation system, continuously maintained, groomed, and plowed, has been developed over many centuries. With a remarkable system of hand-built aqueducts, small dams, and underground canals, the island's terracing and irrigation practices are even more elaborate, sophisticated, and seasonally predictable than

those on Java. Water is sometimes carried by tunnels through solid rock hillsides; water needs high on the ridges often require tunnels two or three kilometers long, some dug eight or nine centuries ago.

About 70% of the population are rice farmers and it's due to their expertise that the Balinese have been able to support such a refined civilization and theatrical, picturesque religion. The discipline required to share water and resources has also created a remarkably cooperative way of life. Rugged individualists cannot exist in communities where every farmer is utterly dependent on the cooperation of neighbors.

Rice land is not cheap, about Rp3.5 million per *are* (100 square meters). The main expanse of the island's rice-growing lands lies south of the mountains, in south-central Bali. These well-irrigated slopes produce three crops of high-quality rice every 14 months, with an annual yield of up to six tons per hectare. It's claimed this extraordinary harvest is equaled only by the "golden triangle" of Thailand and a small area of the Philippines. Specialized vocabularies deal with every aspect of rice farming, and a huge amount of time, energy, and money go into petitioning the gods so the rice farmer's work may yield good results.

A computer program called "Bali Notebook" now models the hydrology and rice ecology of Bali. Based on historical data, it calculates the likely effects of changes in rainfall, water flow, planting schedules, fertilizer use, crop yield, and pest damage to help establish a permanent water-management system for the island.

IR36 versus *Padi Bali*

In 1969, a new "miracle" breed of rice, IR36, was introduced, a high-yield, disease- and insect-resistant variety developed by the Indonesian Department of Agriculture. By 1985 the new variety accounted for 90% of all rice grown on Bali, having replaced about 20 venerable old indigenous varieties, *padi bali* or *beras bali,* now grown mainly in the Pujung area. The growing time (90 days versus 180 days) and the yield (six tons versus four tons per hectare) make the new variety the government favorite. Yet many Balinese prefer the superior-tasting, lower-yielding, higher-priced *padi bali*. One can easily tell the difference between the diminutive IR36 and the magnificent, organically grown native plant, which stands as high as a human (120 cm).

Agricultural officials note that in 1970, even with all its land under intense cultivation, Bali still had to import 10,000 tons of rice annually. After adopting IR36, Bali began exporting thousands of tons each year. With the new variety has come drastic changes in the organization and technology of working rice. The large quantities of chemical fertilizers, herbicides, and pesticides needed to pamper IR36 degrades the quality of the soil. Because growing the new variety is not as labor-intensive, employment has been reduced by at least 18%. Since the grains of the new variety fall off rather too easily, rice is no longer carried back to the village for threshing as needed.

It used to be common along Bali's roads to see bales of *padi bali* gracefully balanced on women's heads or bobbing at the ends of bamboo poles. No more. A number of traditional harvest festivals and ceremonies have also withered away. Women pounding rice in wooden troughs are giving way to thousands of mechanical rice mills. Since the new strain is considered "foreign," the Balinese feel it's no longer necessary to use the traditional handheld knife *(anggapan)* so as not to offend the rice goddess. Balinese now use sickles *(arit)* which shatter the new breed's fragile stalks easily. Still, small patches of *padi bali* are maintained, cut with *anggapan* to placate Dewi Sri.

Subak

Bali's well-defined dry season makes irrigation necessary, but the island's mountainous nature makes it difficult. Since a farmer is unable to build and maintain elaborate irrigation systems, only through cooperation with neighbors have the Balinese become famed as Indonesia's most efficient rice-growers. The *subak* is a communal association consisting of growers, tenants, and sharecroppers who work adjacent holdings averaging 50-100 hectares. Acting as a sort of local "water board," this intra-village civil engineering organization's main function is to control the distribution of irrigation water and organize joint work projects to build and maintain dams, canals, tunnels, aqueducts, and waterlocks. In existence in Bali since at least A.D. 896, there are today around 1,200 of these irrigation cooperatives, each with several hundred members. All must abide by the same rules. Each member is allotted work in proportion to the amount of water s/he receives; a *pekaseh* arbitrates any disputes. All government programs to improve rice production are channeled through the *subak* by a staff of field agents who live right in the main rice-growing areas.

Though it's the bedrock unit of the Balinese community, the *subak* will buckle under to policies adopted by the central government. In 1994, after the government rezoned the land around Tanah Lot to clear the area of rice fields, the regency cut off all water supplies to the local *subak*. The villagers were eventually forced to

relocate to make way for the massive 121-hectare Nirwana Resort. Even a venerable social institution like the *subak* subordinates itself to the imperatives of tourist development.

Rice Rituals

The divine rice plant is the source of all life and wealth, a gift of the gods. Rice rituals differ depending upon place, time, and situation, but all over Bali huge importance is placed on the growing of the island's single most important food crop. As in other areas of Balinese life, women prepare the offerings, designed to gain the goodwill of the deities who provide water and other favorable conditions for a successful harvest.

Before each planting season, the head of the local *subak* undertakes a trip to the mountain lake of Bratan to ask Batara Wisnu ("Provider of Water") for his assistance. A few drops of water from the lake are symbolically splashed in each rice field before planting begins.

Just as rite-of-passage ceremonies mark stages in a person's life, prayers and rituals accompany every cycle of growth in the life of the rice plant: germination of the seedbed, the planting, the plant's first birthday (42 days), ripening, Dewi Sri's "pregnancy," harvest, and at last a thanksgiving ceremony *(ngusaba nini)* in which a handsome meter-high cone of cooked white rice is offered up to Dewi Sri in the *subak* temple.

Small bamboo shrines, resembling Thai spirit houses, stand at the corners of every *sawah* to hold the offerings dedicated to such agricultural deities as Ibu Pertiwi ("Mother Earth"), Surya (the sun-god), Batara Wisnu, and Dewi Sri, the lissome and beautiful rice goddess. Dewi Sri's deified effigy, fashioned from rice stalks, is found everywhere in the rice fields until the harvest is completed, when it's moved to an elevated place in granaries *(lumbung)* located in the backyard of almost every Balinese domestic courtyard. To discourage the evil spirits who are accountable for seed loss by birds and mice, offerings of flowers, rice, and eggs are laid before the shrine; cockfights may also be held to satisfy the spirits' bloodlust.

Stages of Growth

There are no particular seasons for growing rice. Traveling over the island at any time of year it's possible to see all phases in progress.

In fields side by side you'll see the stubble of newly harvested fields; the glimmering mirrors of flooded, newly prepared fields; the jade of freshly replanted shoots; the swaying green or robust gold of a mature crop; the burning of the stalks; the plowing of fields interspersed with bright green seedbeds. *Sawah* are at their most beautiful when flooded, just before the young rice is transplanted. The smell of a healthy young *sawah* is akin to the odor of a healthy aquarium.

To prepare the fields for planting, the farmer first rakes and breaks up the bare, dry ground and stubble of the *sawah;* this is called *ngendag* ("opening up"). After hoeing, the field is flooded, then smoothed with a wooden sledge *(lampit)* pulled by one or two cows (buffaloes lack the necessary stamina) until the whole field is turned into a muddy, watery ooze. The dikes *(pundukan)* must be continuously cleared of vegetation that would steal needed water from the *sawah*.

Next, if one is planting *padi bali,* a corner of the rice field is walled off and a seedling nursery is begun with already germinated seeds. With the new high-yield dwarf varieties, the seeds are simply broadcast by hand. Seedlings grow for 25 days in the seedbed *(ngabut)*. Several days before they are transplanted, the fields are again flooded and smoothed, then fertilized with urea and TSP. The more intensively and diligently the field is worked, the higher the yield.

The transplanting in the larger field next to the seedbed is a group effort, the shoots thrust one by one into the watery mud, spaced one hand's breadth apart and lined up in rows. As the rice grows and the ears fatten on the heads, the rice is said to be pregnant; at this time the fields must be vigilantly guarded from mice and birds. Fluttering plastic strips, rags, bamboo clappers, whips, whirring, clacking contraptions—even human scarecrows—are found all over the fields.

Traditional Harvest Methods

After four months (six months for *padi bali*), the deep green of the nearly ripe crop appears, turning a golden yellow when fully mature. Although only men plant the rice, harvesting *(gampung)* is carried out by both men and women. This is a time when the usual quiet of the rice fields is replaced with the lively chatter and upbeat singing of happy throngs of workers—a time of great excitement in a Balinese village. Working under great bamboo hats, every able-bodied villager joins in the work, including children. Harvest is an opportunity to meet future sweethearts.

During a harvest the village streets are almost deserted, the *banjar* empty—everyone is out in the fields. Offerings are made first, the rice goddess thanked for her bounty. So as not to frighten the goddess, women cut off the ears of *padi bali* with a small knife concealed in their palms.

Behind the women as they progress across the field come the children, gathering whatever rice has inadvertently been left behind. These leftovers become the harvest of the children, which they can take home for themselves.

Each handful of *padi bali* stalks is gathered into a sheaf of 10, handed to a man whose job it is to form the wonderful round bales *(suwun)*. Ten sheafs comprise a 10- to 12-kg bale, which is tied with a bamboo string, turned upside down, and hung on the ends of bamboo poles to be carried back to the village in a sort of half-walking, half-running gait, or transported home on the heads of women.

The modern, faster-growing hybrid IR36 is cut by sickles and threshed right in the fields, as it's brittle and tends to fall off the stalk if carried too far. After the harvest, the straw left in the fields is burned, enveloping the whole region in suffocating smoke. After several crops of *padi bali*, soybeans or some other legume are planted to rejuvenate the soil.

Threshing, Winnowing, Storing, Milling

Traditionally, bundles of rice are taken from the granary and husked a little at a time, just enough for one day's cooking, or sold as the family needs cash. The rice stalks must first be threshed, which frees the grains from the stalk. Then, because the Balinese prefer white rice, the grain is pounded to separate the husk from the inner kernel, usually in a hollowed wooden trough by women using metal-tipped, two-meter-long bamboo poles they rhythmically change from hand to hand. The sound of several women engaged in this task is an ancient form of percussion; some musicologists theorize the hypnotic cadence produced is the origin of most forms of Balinese xylophonic music.

After the pounding loosens the chaff *(nebuk)*, the rice is winnowed *(njidi)*, the grains thrown up and caught on large split bamboo trays while the chaff falls to the ground or is carried away on the wind. The rice is then milled in one of the 1,500 or so gas- or diesel-powered mills found all over Bali. Mills purchase the rice outright, mill it, then sell the processed rice *(beras)* in 100-kilo sacks. Farmers can have their rice milled for around Rp100 per kg. The coarse bran, germ, and husk byproduct is used as food for pigs.

Rice is the farmer's savings account. In Dutch times, farmers sold their crops for cash to the Denpasar rice mills, the money often squandered long before the next harvest. Now, after the harvest, rice is stored in the *banjar* granary, or tied in bundles *sepingan,* to the top of tall poles. You still sometimes see these bundles of rice drying in the sun, particularly in the uplands. The Indonesian government subsidizes the price of rice, known as the "mother price," so that all citizens are at least able to eat. Both government, military, and private-sector employees are paid partly in coupons that can be redeemed for rice.

MARINE INDUSTRIES

Harvesting products from the sea is vital to the lives of many Balinese. The people of the east coast burn coral to make lime, process sea salt, and fish. The Balinese are not known as great seafarers like the Polynesians, nor do they have a history as long-range maritime traders like the Makassarese. Seldom did they trade farther than Lombok or Java. Bali's lack of good, sheltered anchorages and its inhospitable, unprotected coastline studded with jagged coral reefs and high cliffs were not conducive to the development of maritime skills. Most inland Balinese look upon the sea with fear and misgivings, but there is a quite vibrant local fishing industry which tourists rarely see. The island's largest fishing center is at Pengambengan, 10 kilometers southwest of Negara. The second most important fishing center, and the easiest to visit, are the four fishing villages along Jimbaran Bay just south of Ngurah Rai Airport on the west side of the narrow isthmus separating southern Bali and the Bukit Peninsula. The best time to visit Jimbaran Bay is at the peak of the dry season (May-Sept.); get there soon after sunrise, as the beach is deserted by midmorning. The scene is even more frenetic at Kedonganan, directly east of the airport, where up to 50 trucks line up in front of the T.P.I. fishing cooperative office waiting to haul off each day's catch.

Bali's fish harvest is around 60,000 tons per year. Roughly 70% are sardines, 20% tuna and mackerel, 10% sharks and coral fish. The export of fresh tuna to Japan and the United States alone brings in US$10 million. Most fish are canned in the plant at Suwung near Benoa, which produces 15-20 tons daily, most exported to Java.

Seaweed Farming

The Balinese have collected seaweed for hundreds of years, though government-supported commercial production only began in 1980. The most successful cultivation site is the narrow strait between the islets of Nusa Lembongan and Nusa Ceningan, and on the north coast of Nusa Penida. About 1,000 families are engaged in seaweed production on Nusa Penida, while 35 families work at the Cape Geger project.

To farm seaweed, stakes are first driven into the sandy ocean bottom near shore, then plastic ropes are tied between the stakes to form a rectangle 2.5 by five meters square; 50 of these rectangles make up a 625-square-meter area; 16 squares occupy a hectare. All cultivation and harvesting take place underwater.

It takes a family of five to maintain one-quarter of a hectare, producing about 20 tons of dried seaweed per year. The collected seaweed is used in food, sauces, soups, condiments, and agar-agar, a thickening agent used in cooking. The harvest is sent first to Surabaya, then exported to France, Denmark, Japan, and Singapore for processing. Bali exports approximately 400 tons of seaweed per year. The government does all it can to promote this highly exportable, profitable, labor-intensive, nonpolluting, nonseasonal industry.

Saltworks

Next to lombok (chili peppers), salt is the favorite condiment of the grain-eating Balinese. In the southern part of the island a vigorous family-run cottage industry produces clean, unrefined natural salt from seawater.

The island's salt-making capital is Suwung. Another salt-producing area is the broad tidal flats of Jimbaran. The glistening, volcanic black-sand beach at Kusamba, three kilometers northeast of Klungkung, is a third salt center.

All three locations use different methods to produce salt, though the principle is the same: large amounts of seawater are deposited onto land and allowed to dry under the sun; the residue is scooped up, leached, and the outflow allowed to evaporate, leaving gritty salt crystals which are then purified. The Jimbaran saltworks employs an evaporator, a large, loosely woven bamboo basket extruding a long, white, dripping stalactite around which forms a cake of salt. Saltmakers produce an average of about 25 kg per day.

Saltmakers at each site claim that the salt from the other locations is crude and bitter, but it's generally believed Jimbaran salt is the highest quality. Because of its complex beneficial minerals and bio-electronic properties, sea salt balances alkalinity/acidity levels, renews energy, restores good digestion, rejuvenates the body's biosystems, and relieves allergies and skin diseases.

SMALL INDUSTRY

Garments/Textiles

One of the best places in Southeast Asia to buy fashionable clothes and beachware is in Sanur and along the road running between Kuta and Legian. European and American designers have teamed up with nimble-fingered Balinese garment workers to open hundreds of fashion boutiques selling the latest in continental and industrial fashion designs, as well as every type of batik imaginable, including Malaysian imports.

The garment industry of Denpasar, Kuta, and Sanur comprises over 150 establishments employing about 8,000 people. Garment exports total over US$90 million. Two of Bali's largest textile factories lie along the main tourist artery between Denpasar and Mas. Government-owned Patal, opened in 1965, makes polyester and rayon yarn for Central Javanese batik. The raw materials are brought in by truck from Java;

about 200,000 kg of finished product is returned to Java each month. The other factory, Balitex, is owned by the provincial government of Bali, its 60 looms producing about 30,000 meters of good-quality cotton and rayon cloth each month. Most of the cloth is sold to garment makers in the Kuta-Sanur-Denpasar tourist grid. The factory also maintains a wholesale/retail shop on the premises.

Several other, smaller textile weaving factories *(pertenunan)* are found in Gianyar, where there are also a number of large display rooms. Weaving factories in Singaraja specialize in reproducing ancient, finely detailed silk *ikat* and distinctive handwoven *sarung* and *kain.*

The Balinese make very little *batik* themselves, importing for resale *batik* from Java. But they do produce a very striking and distinctive tie-dyed cloth called *endek,* actually more popular with the native Balinese than with tourists. Scores of factories all over Gianyar, Denpasar, and Singaraja manufacture this unique fabric. *Endek, ikat,* colorfast *sarung,* and gold-threaded *songket* are created and sold in Poh Bergong village about 10 kilometers south of Singaraja on the way to Beratan.

Other Small Industries

The Bukit Peninsula is home to a number of important industries. One is the conversion of coral into quicklime *(pamor),* used in the making of mortar. A very high temperature is required to slake lime; you can always locate a lime kiln by its great clouds of choking, polluting fumes.

During the early 1980s the offshore tidal environment and reef fauna of Kuta, Sanur, and Candidasa were totally degraded by indiscriminate coral gathering. Now regulations prohibit coral harvesting less than three kilometers from shore. Fortunately, lime output has started to fall off as more builders switch to superior cement.

Limestone quarrying on the Bukit to produce blocks and bricks is concentrated south of Pecatu. You can see many old quarries on the main road to Uluwatu Temple. Long crowbars *(linggis)* are used to pry the limestone loose from the cliffs, and the blocks are sawed where they fall.

Baked red bricks and roof tiles are made in wooden molds by hand in the northern part of the island wherever there are clay deposits, which is just about everywhere. This enterprise is a curious sight, the brick- or tilemaker's shed completely surrounded by a deep moat dug right out of the clay topsoil. The island's brickmaking center lies just south of Mambal on the road north from Denpasar to the Monkey Forest, where half the population is involved in this lively industry.

Bali's prefab clay, concrete, and ceramic center is at Kapal, between Tabanan and Denpasar. Kapal is also famous as a manufacturing center for Bali's rice cookers—the weird and wonderful *dang-dang* many tourists mistake for hats—as well as numerous other sheet metal products. A growing market is the export of traditional Balinese wooden house frames and parquet floors, particularly to Australia and the United States.

TOURISM

Bali is the Hawaii of the East. Of the four million tourists who came to Indonesia in 1994, more than 750,000 flew straight to Bali. The number of foreign and domestic tourists arriving in Bali is now approaching 1.5 million a year. The growth in visitors, which stands at about 10% per year, is expected to continue through the late 1990s. Bali already has a full half of all the hotels in Indonesia.

Bali makes a valuable study in the effects of mass tourism on the social and cultural patterns of an indigenous population. Every generation of visitors arrives to "discover" Bali, pronounce it a paradise, then once home mourn that it's lost forever. Visitors are so enthralled with the legend surrounding Bali, many arrive thinking that Indonesia is a part of Bali rather than the other way round.

Able to survive Islam, war, coups, and occupations, Bali has been less successful in withstanding the tidal waves of tourists. Commercialism has crept into every aspect of Balinese life. You now have to go deep into the interior, up to the mountain villages, to find people still adhering to the old traditions.

Who Are Those Guys?

Two types of foreign visitors arrive on Bali: those who come to relax on holiday, and those who come to experience the culture, to "discover" Bali. Demographically, the highest percentage is in the 25-35 range with an average length of stay of about 12 days. Singapore sends the greatest number of visitors, followed by Japan, Malaysia, Australia, Taiwan, the Netherlands, the United States, the United Kingdom, Germany, France, Hong Kong, and South Korea.

The "international class" stay in culture-neuter luxury resorts concentrated in an unseen, unfelt quarantine zone along the southern coastline. With snapshots of volcanoes and rice terraces in their cameras and souvenirs in their hands, they shuttle in air-conditioned buses with tinted windows to talky, fake trance dances, truncated *wayang* performances, and staged cremations. They return south at dusk to Nusa Dua and Sanur to watch yet more dances by torchlight while eating continental dinners. These tourists have almost no impact on the values of Bali, leaving the Balinese culture more or less intact.

Then there are the yuppies, the travelers, and the college students. These so-called "cultural tourists" have come to Bali to experience the gentle climate, relatively low prices, good surfing beaches, and general ambience that have made this island a popular hangout for young people for more than 15 years. They stay in inexpensive homestays or beach inns in Kuta, Legian, Seminyak, and Candidasa, romp in the surf off Uluwatu, roar around the island on rented motorcycles or Suzukis, and trip out on magic mushroom omelettes while listening to rock tapes.

The Germans, Americans, Dutch, and English you see year-round, with the French, Spanish, and Italians arriving only in July and August, and the Australians in December and January. Australians come to disco and pub crawl at Third World prices. Australians are more tourists than travelers nowadays; the days are long gone when you could travel overland from Down Under to the U.K. cheaper than you could fly. The Australians are usually in their twenties and seldom venture from the southern resorts. At least 75% are on package tours. The Australians, Asian in temperament, are generally well liked for their easygoing attitude, though Balinese guides quickly grow bored working for them. They have to stay on their toes with the French and Germans, who ask more demanding questions. They come for the culture, while Australians come for the beach.

Then there are the domestic tourists. The summer months (the Balinese winter) and Christmas holiday season are incredibly busy, with throngs of tourists from Hong Kong and Singapore and rich Chinese from Surabaya arriving by the thousands to rent cars and drive insanely around the island. During these times it's difficult to even *walk* around Kuta, Legian, and Ubud, and every hotel along the beachfront is booked solid.

History of Tourism

Ever since two members of van de Houtman's crew jumped ship in 1597, Bali's utterly unique, highly developed culture has been endlessly fascinating to Westerners, the paradigm of tropical beauty and exotic adventure.

The Dutch steamship line KPM began calling at the northern Bali port of Buleleng in the late 19th century, though its cargos consisted mostly of pigs, copra, and coffee rather than tourists. Following quickly upon the *puputan* of 1906, Bali's first tourist was Dutch parliamentarian H. Van Kol, who reached Bali at his own expense and toured the island with a senior Dutch official. Upon his return to Holland, he wrote of his travels on Bali in a book called *Out of Our Colonies.* By 1914 KPM was producing brochures rhapsodizing about Bali as an enchanted Garden of Eden.

Next came a classic book of photos of wild dances, corrupt kings, and bare bodies, published in Germany in 1921 by Gregor Krause. As early as the 1920s, the island drew a steady stream of affluent, intrepid, genteel world vagabonds; these visitors perplexed the Dutch, who looked upon their tour of duty on quiet Bali as a boresome necessity.

In the 1930s the documentaries *Isle of the Demons* and *Goona-Goona* depicted Bali as a paradise on earth. The celebrated anthropologist Margaret Mead arrived to extol the island, getting things very wrong in her studies of the Balinese children. The aristocratic Balinist and painter Walter Spies wrote and photographed the proud bronzed Balinese trance dancers and noble dusky peasantry; it later came to light that Spies was attracted to the island for its young boys.

Bali's first hotel, KPM's Bali Hotel in Denpasar, catered to the rich and famous, including Charlie Chaplin. In the introduction to his 1930 book *The Last Paradise,* the American dilettante Hickman Powell wrote, "This nation of artists is faced with the Western invasion, and I cannot stand idly by and watch their destruction." In the early 1930s other hotels began to open, and the first souvenir shop was established on Sanur Beach in 1935. Miguel Covarrubias, author of the 1937 classic *Island of Bali,* lamented the arrival of the tourist hordes. The "absence of beggers," he wrote, "is now threatened by tourists who lure boys and girls with dimes to take their pictures. Lately, in places frequented by tourists, people are beginning to ask for money as a return for a service."

After the war, Bali was celebrated in songs and movies, which generated a small increase in visitors. Facilities were still few, the infrastructure nonexistent. Still, by the late 1940s, Cassandros Like, the curator of the American Museum of Natural History lamented that tourism had just about ruined Bali. At least, he wrote "the Second World War put a halt to the tourist trade to Bali so that the corruption and dissolution of the culture could be given a respite."

In 1953, Bob Hope's vapid movie *The Road to Bali* depicted an island of maidens in grass skirts, unknown here. The mythical "Bali Hai" in James Michener's book *Tales of the South Pacific* was actually located thousands of miles from the island. Nevertheless, these fictions instilled in the popular mind the idea of Bali as synonymous with tropical beauty and exotic adventure.

The political upheaval of the Sukarno regime years was not conducive to Western tourism, but it was during the turbulent '60s that the first international-class luxury hotel was erected on the island. With Japanese war reparations money the ugly, garish multistoried Bali Beach Hotel of Sanur was built in 1963. In that same year an international conference of travel agents convened on Bali.

The anti-communist slaughter of 1966-67 caused only a temporary blip in the inexorable growth of tourism. In 1966 Bali's Ngurah Rai airport was enlarged for wide-bodied jets.

Since the Bali Beach Hotel couldn't accommodate everybody, traditional style "bungalow" or "cottage" accommodations with thatched roofs and open pavilions rose along the southern beaches. Restaurants, art shops, and travel agencies appeared. In the mid-1970s Australian surfies and hippies discovered Kuta/Legian. Aussie surfing magazines glorified the beautiful beaches, dangerous waves, and laid-back, low-cost lifestyle. In Kuta, enterprising villagers opened pension-style "homestays," cheap restaurants, shops, moneychanging facilities, telecommunication offices, and vehicle rental outlets. Kuta's family-owned enterprises sank revenues back into the local economy, directly benefiting the villagers until their average per capita income was four times the Balinese average.

As early as 1972 it was widely recognized that developments in Kuta and Sanur were badly planned. The government established the Bali Tourism Development Corporation (BTDC) to more closely monitor and supervise future projects. Bali was earmarked for intense development, with an enclave-type complex planned for Nusa Dua, formerly a fishing village and coconut plantation on the east side of the Bukit Peninsula.

The backlash began in the early 1980s in the quiet traditional village of Ubud in the Bali uplands. Locals began to curse the tourists for disrupting ceremonies and dressing inappropriately. The people fought to preserve Ubud's natural beauty and ensure that the increasing numbers of visitors did not degrade their customs and culture. This effort eventually fizzled, as Ubud continued to grow pell-mell, the town drowning beneath waves of tourists and eventually exploding into a small city.

A swinging singles scene of Australians and Europeans formed in the Kuta/Legian/Seminyak region in the late 1980s. These were the boom years. Indonesia kick-started mass tourism in the 1990s with a big "Visit Indonesia Year" campaign. Families bought stereos, television sets, and cars with the money they made from tourists, even sold off rice fields to buy motorbikes to rent, hoping to live off the bounty of the tourist industry indefinitely. A new class of Balinese nouveau riche created jealousy and envy in the community. Business was so good, the Balinese were totally unprepared for the abrupt drop in tourism sparked by the 1993 war in the Persian Gulf. Hotels and restaurants stood empty and the few visitors were hounded mercilessly by the street peddlers who now outnumbered tourists 20 to 1. Suddenly everyone realized just how dependent they were on the tourist dollar.

The provincial government cleaned up the really disagreeable peddlers and vendors, confiscating their goods if they ventured into a designated hassle-free zone on Kuta Beach.

A ban was placed on the construction of all international-class hotels within a designated "green belt," and a Rp500,000,000 hotel in Tampaksiring was even razed by bulldozers. The airport was upgraded and handled an estimated 2.5 million air travelers in 1995. Twelve international airlines currently fly into Bali, with 77 international flights each week. There are now at least 35 star-rated hotels on Bali, nine in the Nusa Dua area alone. It is estimated the Ngurah Rai Airport will process 10 million visitors annually by the year 2000.

The Nusa Dua and Other Experiments

In 1974 the government concocted the Nusa Dua Experiment, calling for the construction of luxury hotels along the east coast of the arid, thinly populated Bukit Peninsula. By offering foreign investors 50-year leases with maximum incentives and tax holidays, it was hoped the Nusa Dua resort would accommodate and contain the surge in visitors. Nusa Dua constituted a major shift to elite tourism, planned as an isolated, self-contained ghetto that would allow visitors the experience of Bali but keep their interactions with the natives to a minimum. Because relatively few of the island's 2.7 million people live near the sea and few tourists want to stay anywhere else, the plan looked really good on paper. But the resort was very slow to develop. It was only in the 1980s that Nusa Dua finally came into its own; it wasn't until late in the decade that tourist projections were met.

In these Mediterranean-style, self-contained hotel resorts tourists can sun their near-naked bodies on white sandy beaches without scandalizing anyone and watch abbreviated psuedo-events performed in expensive hotel foyers. Those with a spirit of adventure may day-trip around the island in air-conditioned buses to preselected villages and tourist sites, leaving untainted the rest of Eden.

The early 1990s brought a more formal experiment in "village tourism," wherein groups of tourists move discreetly in small numbers with a minimum of intrusion, making direct, low-impact contact with the Balinese. The idea is being tried in three Balinese villages, Jatiluwih (rice-planting and fabulous views), Penglipuran (a nearly Bali Aga village in Bangli), and Sebatu (woodcarving and other art forms). Guests from the southern hotels experience something "real" by joining day or weekend excursions to these villages. This cultural tourism is really just an extension of enclave-style tourist development, consistent with the policy of limiting and canalizing tourist development to minimize its impact on Balinese society.

Tourism Yes

Tourism is Bali's biggest source of hard currency. The foreign currency brought in by tourists improves Indonesia's balance of payments, helping to correct the structural imbalance of trade between the developing and developed nations.

The government recognizes that tourism is Bali's best hope for raising living standards and bringing jobs and prosperity. Tourism has meant that many people are now able to send their children to school. A senior high school diploma (SMA) is required to enter a tourism school, and all the big hotels only want students from these schools. Work in a hotel in almost any capacity is considered an excellent job. Tour guides and drivers can do even better. They can make between US$400 and $500 per month, compared with a monthly salary of US$100-150 for Balinese high school teachers.

Many Balinese view tourism as a cure for overcrowding and poverty. Tourism provides extra income for the landless as well as for those put out of work by the "green revolution," the introduction of machines, and shrinking land holdings. Even backpackers leave money. Their priority is to travel cheaply, but the very length of their stay—often up to the two-month limit—means they usually drop more cash than the wealthy tourists who spend but four days on the island.

It's now common for whole families to work in tourism—father and son as drivers, the mother a waitress, little brother a roomboy in a hotel, the daughter a masseuse. Tourism has created a whole new middle class of hoteliers, art shop and gallery owners, and tourist agents. No one can expect the Balinese to live stuck in the middle ages. The worldliness that the heavy influx of foreign visitors has brought is undeniable. It's common to hear bell captains greet hotel guests in five different languages. Tourist brochures are routinely written in at least three languages, including Japanese.

Bali's true folk art is no longer living on borrowed time. Communities are willing to subsidize the high costs of sumptuous ceremonies and music and dance troupes, conscious that these expenditures secure the arrival of future generations of tourists. Indeed, some dances and art forms once fading away have been revived by tourist demand. The island's musical ensembles and dance troupes are as active now as at any time in Bali's history.

> *It's all too easy at this great distance to worry about the commercialism of Bali and forget the native resistance which absorbs us all. The Balinese win, and our eyes are opened. Sometimes I feel guilty recommending friends to Bali, knowing I contribute to the acculturation process. As my wife says, 'Bali is not for everybody. Those travelers who come away disenchanted were rejected by Bali.' I also know destruction is inevitable. Perhaps as Bali is diluted, it will be diluted worldwide. The spirit of Bali will spread to this island earth. And the loss of a small island will be the gain of an entire planet.*
>
> —BERT CREWS

Tourism No

The impact of tourism on Bali's environment has been horrendous. The island's affluence has given way to ugly urban sprawl in the capital of Denpasar. Even more serious is the environmental damaged caused by the plundering of offshore reefs for coral used in the construction boom of the 1980s. Live reefs are threatened by sewage, runoff, and silt. Over 1,000 hectares of agricultural land are lost every year to art shops, hotels, and housing estates. Megaresorts displace traditional landowners and tenants.

The southern region is woefully lacking in the infrastructure necessary to sustain a burgeoning population. The water table is sinking, and water is already in short supply. Electricity is barely adequate. The problem of waste disposal has reached crisis proportions. No one seems to know what to do with all the *sampah* (garbage) as the volume of nonorganic, nonbiodegradable waste grows. Profits made from tourists may soon be canceled out by the cost of maintaining the environment.

Inflation is inexorably driving up the price of land. In 1993, a restaurant owner on the Bypass paid Rp55 million for 10 *are* just to increase the bus parking space for her restaurant. Land in Kuta now runs Rp100,000 million per *are*. The Balinese themselves cannot raise the necessary capital to open big enterprises. Jakarta-based businessmen and women in partnership with transnational corporations now dominate Bali's real estate market. In 1995 *The West Australian* published a list of the major investors in five-star hotels and golf courses in Bali, revealing that numerous high-end properties are owned by President Suharto's children.

On Bali popular paintings, carvings, and antiques are mass-produced to satisfy undiscerning collectors, transforming everything from cow bones to coconut shells into souvenirs. Temples are pillaged for artifacts to sell to tourists. Religious ceremonies, dance and *gamelan* forms, and traditional crafts are all being changed and in some cases subverted to fit tourist tastes. To reach such sacred temples as Tanah Lot, Tampaksiring, Besakih, and the Monkey Forest you have to walk past tawdry commercial corridors of hard-sell souvenir and art shops. Resorts arrange helicopter rides over sacred temples. Pushy vendors infest every nice beach. T-shirts for sale are emblazoned with the message: "Fuck Off! I Don't Want a Massage, Painting, Woodcarving, or Another Hotel!"

Tengenan, once one of the most traditional pre-Hindu villages in Bali, is overrun by souvenir shops and art galleries. A proposal to create a shopping center outside the walls of the community was rejected by villagers who'd already begun selling souvenirs out of their homes. Blue jeans have replaced *sarung,* rubber thongs cover formerly bare feet, sacred religious symbols decorate hotels, kerosene burners ignite cremation pyres, and palm-leaf covers protecting offerings have been replaced by plastic flyscreens. Many Balinese young men don't care so much for work anymore, preferring instead to hang around with foreigners or make a living out of short-time romances with fair-haired, round-eyed European women.

The much-publicized wedding of Mick Jagger and Jerry Hall in Ubud in 1990 led inevitably to a Western trend of marrying on Bali. A number of beachfront hotels now specialize in wedding ceremonies for American, Dutch, and Australian couples. The service costs US$1000 and includes traditional costumes, photographer, photo album, lunch, dinner, and champagne.

Villagers still celebrate religious festivals with traditional Balinese dancing, but they also cluster around TV sets in the evening to watch Indonesian sitcoms. The expansion of hotels has limited access to the beaches for rituals. Balinese residents can now only reach the waters of Sanur via the narrow *gang,* snaking their way between the large hotels.

In Italy no one would dare enter a church or cathedral in a short-sleeved shirt or shorts, but in Bali Italians wear this sort of disrespectful clothing into Balinese temples all the time. The only bare-breasted women on Bali today are the Europeans who go topless on the beaches, ignoring government prohibitions against doing so.

Prices are getting higher, it costs money to use the toilet facilities, the whine of motorbikes is constant, the quality of paintings and carvings is declining, multilane highways and big shopping centers and even condo-type developments ("Own your own Bali Hideaway for US$200,000") are legion, brash disco music drowns out tinkling *gamelan,* money-minded vendors in the tourist ghettoes of Sanur, Kuta, Denpasar, and Lovina are a constant hassle. Tourism has brought stress, tension, corruption, congestion, pollution, urban blight, and crime. You used to be able to leave your bag in the open anywhere on the island for three days and nothing would move it but the wind. Not anymore. Revered Hindu priests wear graffiti art T-shirts and atheist foreigners can pay their way into a Bali-Hindu wedding. Cremations are held specially for tourists, advertised with signs like: "Cremation this Saturday in Bangli! Rp20,000! Book now!" You can even book a seat in advance in Melbourne.

Real Economic Effects
It's estimated that as much as 80% of all tourist receipts end up outside Bali. This revenue leakage must be measured against the much-touted claims of tourism generating huge foreign exchange earnings. Not surprisingly, the estimated $200 million brought in each year by tourists has not been entirely beneficial for the Balinese economy.

Actual improvement in the standard of living is significant but not dramatic. Much of the population is poor, in many cases desperately poor. The minimum wage is about Rp30,000 per month. Lowly hotel workers earn only Rp2000 per day, receive free lodging, and if they're lucky get one meal a day. Assistant carpenters earn about Rp5000 per day, young workers in the garment industry sew beads or sequins on clothing for as little as Rp600 per day. The vast majority of Balinese live in villages and do not directly benefit from foreign-exchange earnings. The advent of tourism has widened the gap between rich and poor. A UNESCO study demonstrated that those who benefit most from tourism are directly engaged in the industry—hotel and art shop owners and employees, guides, drivers, hotel workers, musicians, performers.

Tourism creates jobs, but not all of the type endorsed in the country's development plans. Only about 15% of the workforce is employed directly or indirectly in the tourist industry. Moreover, the low season means a dramatic drop in earnings. Neither do all the jobs go to the Balinese. The larger the hotel, the greater the tendency to employ imported labor. People from Java fill a great number of the responsible positions. Only one sector consists exclusively of Balinese—tour guides. At least it's the Balinese who interpret Bali for the tourist.

Although Bali may still seem cheap compared to the West, there's a danger that the Balinese are driving themselves out of business by overpricing. When visitors first began arriving in Bali, the exorbitant airfare was quickly absorbed in the low cost of rooms, meals, and transport. But Bali isn't that cheap anymore. Travel agents don't push Bali as much as they used to—Thailand and East Malaysia are the preferred destinations these days. Packaged trips to Phuket are very attractive and represent less flying time from Europe.

The Balinese have become greedy. Shopkeepers hardly bargain anymore; even in Ubud, their eyes are filled with contempt. Most seem to have no interest in attracting repeat customers. Drivers now routinely ask for US$65 per day; some charge as much as US$100.

There's ample evidence of overbuilding. You see lots of empty shells of buildings—white elephants—the result of bankruptcies and deals gone bad. One such example is the magnificent five-star Saba Beach Resort, as yet unfinished and now housing only the police guarding the site. Half the restaurants and shops in Candidasa are bankrupt from lack of tourists.

What's Left
The best things on Bali are still free: orange and gold tropical sunsets, an astoundingly rich culture, the smiles of the children, the sounds of the talcum-powder beaches, the coral dive sites. You can still get into temple dances and music rehearsals free. Violent crime is almost unknown. Bali's dogs aren't as frightened of Westerners as they once were and don't even bark as much as they used to. You can still live well for US$10 a day or less.

The tourism cancer is limited to the southern one-eighth of the island. If you get away from the commercial strips of Sanur, Kuta, and Legian, you can find hundreds of villages and vast areas of terraced hillsides which haven't changed since the 1930s. Many haven't changed for millennia. Traveling off the beaten track is no problem at all. You don't need directions; just head for the hills. On Bali you can still get as lost as you want.

THE PEOPLE

The Balinese are just one of Indonesia's 250 ethnic groups. Like most Indonesians they are a blend of races, with the accent on the deutero-Malayan race of Central and East Java, with traces of Polynesian and Melanesian blood, as well as Indian and Chinese. This genetic background explains the variety of racial types seen on the island. Most Balinese are small, handsome people with round, delicate features, thick black hair, long sweeping eyelashes, heart-shaped lips, and warm brown complexions, Others are darker-skinned and straight-haired like Pacific islanders, or curly-haired with flat noses like Papuans.

The Balinese are an extraordinarily creative people with a highly sensual, theatrical culture. Their cults, customs, and worship of god and nature are animist, their music warm-blooded, their art as extravagant as their nature. By West-

boatbuilder and son

ern material standards most Balinese are poor, though their poverty is masked by their exuberance, their outdoor-oriented, picturesque ritual life, and their personal openness and congeniality. Culturally, the Javanese lean more toward refinement and modesty, keeping themselves in check in life and art, while the Balinese prefer the headier, flashier sensations—laughs, terror, spicier and sweeter foods. They're more lavish and baroque in their colors and decorations; they like explosive music and fast, jerky dancing.

Demographics

The vast majority of the rural population practices the syncretic Bali-Hindu religion, known officially as Agama Hindu or Hindu Dharma. There's also a sprinkling of Muslims in the coastal towns, a Bugis settlement on Serangan Island, Buddhists in the mountains, and Christians everywhere. Several thousand Arabs and Indians, many shop owners dealing in textiles, gold, silver, etc., live in Denpasar. Ten thousand Chinese are found in the main trading centers of Denpasar, Singaraja, and Amlapura, running the majority of the businesses. Relative to the rest of Indonesia, the number of Chinese on Bali is very small.

There are also around 25,000 Western expatriates—clothes designers, exporters, artists, aid workers, consultants, English teachers. Many Western jewelry and garment makers have intermarried with the Balinese—it seems every other fashion boutique or restaurant in Kuta and Legian has an Italian or Australian somewhere in the family tree.

Population

Bali is a spectacular example of an island favored by nature. Able to sustain a total population of 2.7 million, it has easily the carrying capacity of neighboring Java. With a population density of nearly 500 persons per square kilometer, Bali is Indonesia's second most densely populated island after Java. In some of Bali's southern districts the density is even higher, as much as 1,100 per square kilometer. If the population density of the 48 contiguous United States were as great as Bali's, the U.S.A. would boast 3.6 billion people.

Present estimates are that Bali's population will increase to 4.5 million by the year 2000. The Indonesian government's answer to mounting population pressure is to move tens of thousands of Balinese to the Outer Islands in massive *transmigrasi* programs. Complete Balinese communities—with temples, *banjar*, and *subak*—now exist in Kalimantan, Sulawesi, and Sumatra. In addition, Bali's modern family-planning practices, implemented through 150 clinics in villages and hamlets all over the island, have resulted in the "Miracle of Bali"—a birth rate down from 2.3% in 1970 to 1.6% today. Road posters everywhere encourage families to produce only two children. Under the slogan "Catur Warga" ("Four Citizens"), posters show a smiling, well-fed, and transparently well-off family of mother, father, and two children, obviously thoroughly convinced of the advantages of family planning.

The Bali Aga

As you climb into upland Bali the people become harder looking, their faces less expressive, less likely to smile, reflecting the harshness of their lives. On Bali there's still a distinction between the Wong Majapahit, descendants of 16th-century migrants of East Java's fallen Majapahit Empire, and the Bali Aga, the original inhabitants of the island who retreated into the mountains where they're found to this day, indifferent to outsiders. The Bali Aga never came under the religious and despotic influence of the Javanese nobility, and thus still reflect the true, republican nature of original Balinese society. In their reclusive communities they constitute a nation within a nation.

As a people, the Bali Aga are woefully understudied, their archaic dialect dying, many of their rituals abandoned. They are known for their great austere temples—striking examples in Taro and Trunyan—and the peculiar social divisions of their communities.

There has long been an unfavorable social stigma attached to the Bali Aga; they're looked down upon by lowlanders. But as time wears on, education, intermarriage, interdependent economies, and the Indonesian language work

to blur the distinctions between the Bali Aga and *Wong Majapahit* Balinese.

THE CASTE SYSTEM

A Balinese lives in a complex social web. His first bond is determined by his descent group *(wangsa)* and caste *(kasta);* his second, more democratically, by his village, clan, and *banjar*. Before Indonesia gained independence a third bond tied the citizen to a leige lord or prince. On Bali today, it is politically correct to observe that only vestiges of the caste system remain, but anyone who lives in a village for a few weeks will learn that caste is still deeply ingrained in the social fabric.

The Javanese introduced the caste system when they established themselves in Bali in A.D. 1343, creating a colony for the Majapahit classes. With its ancestor worship, vassal princes, and deified warrior kings, this social institution has its roots in a Hindu origin myth developed in India more than 4,000 years ago in which Brahman (god) was sacrificed and cut apart to create all things in the universe. In the Hindu Rig Veda, the world's oldest liturgical text, god's mouth becomes the Brahman class, his arms the Ksatriya class, his thighs the Wesya class, and his feet the Sudra class. Just as a person needs his head, arms, thighs, and feet, so does society need all four constituent parts to function.

This Vedic myth justified a strict feudal division of society, but because Bali developed in near isolation from the rest of the Hindu world, the social stratification dictated by the caste system is more relaxed and irregular on the island than in India.

As in India, however, the forefathers of Bali's nobility were considered to possess supernatural powers, granted legitimacy and state sanction by the great priests of the day. These men were sticklers for protocol and their edicts carried the full weight of the law.

In the late 16th century, Javanese nobles systematically established kingdoms over the whole island, eventually culminating in Bali's eight rajadoms. Descendents of these nobles today go by the name Gusti and Ngurah, and still hold positions of great power and wealth, though hereditary rule is technically banned in Indonesia.

Concept and Function of Caste

Each Balinese Hindu strives to achieve liberation, the union of the soul *(atman)* with Brahman or god. Through actions and thoughts *(dharma),* the Balinese continue to incarnate until the soul is pure enough to fuse with Brahman. It's the duty of each caste to help the other castes.

Each Balinese knows his or her place and is quite willing to work within it. Duty transcends self and must be obeyed without regard to personal wishes or desires. Each caste must follow its own elaborate set of rules, and each member knows how to behave under almost any set of circumstances.

Caste is not based on occupation or profession, but on birth. But because one was born into a certain caste does not necessarily have the aptitudes, temperament, and skills typical of that caste. A Ksatriya does not cease being a Ksatriya just because s/he does not do the work of a Ksatriya. And if a Brahmana does not work as a priest or a teacher, it doesn't mean s/he is not accorded the esteem due a Brahmin.

Caste also means little in terms of wealth or community power. There is in fact a growing gap between status title and such economic indices as wealth and job. Brahmana and Ksatriyas work as tourist guides, room boys, bartenders, even *bemo* drivers, while Sudras attain high government posts and Wesya run restaurants and hotels.

Triwangsa

Meaning "Three Peoples." This is the gentry class of Bali, the highest three societal stratifications of traditional Hinduism: the Brahman, Ksatriya, and Wesya castes. These privileged classes, constituting perhaps 10% of the population, are held in great respect. Observing subtle differences in titles and a complex system of etiquette, Triwangsa are addressed in a more refined language than that used in everyday speech. Formerly Triwangsa lived in or near the *puri.*

The Dutch persuaded these three upper classes to assist them in ruling Bali, but by the early 20th century most had lost their power and social position. Having fallen on hard times, they had to levy taxes on cockfights and markets to pay for the trappings of their symbolic power.

Some Balinese families devote a life of service to a Ksatriya, or Brahmana family, for the privilege of including a grandparent as a follower *(pengiring)* in the elaborate cremation ceremony of a great raja. Allegience to a leige lord honors the palace's lifelong services to the community—as keepers of the faith, custodians of the temples, and, in the case of Brahmans, the making of holy water.

Spiritually, the nobility's most important function is that of custodian *(pangemong)* of the island's major temples. The deified ancestors of Bali's original palace families are integral members of the pantheon of gods in the village temples. In spite of all the democratizing and defeudalizing on Bali, this bond between palace and worship has not been interrupted. The tie between Balinese and leige lord is unbreakable. It is said the Balinese truly "love their lords."

Brahmana is the highest class, consisting of mostly priests, scholars, and teachers. Brahmana live in a *geria.* Only a Brahmana may become a priest *(pedanda),* receive certain burial rights, and enjoy a high level of ritual communication. Brahmana believe their high caste sets them above even the *triwangsa* aristocrats. It's always a Brahman who repairs or repaints a *rangda* or *barong* mask because only the Brahmana know how to protect themselves from the magic powers released. This intellectual class is the best source for information on religious and social matters. Brahmana men are addressed as Ida Bagus; women Ida Ayu or Dayu.

The Satram is the political, warrior, and raja, or princely, caste. Formerly Balinese royalty, this caste is primarily divided mostly among the descendents of the five royal families of Klungkung, Gianyar, Bangli, Badung, and Tabanan. Nearly every village has a *puri,* the elaborate residence of the Ksatriya.

Ksatriya names are variable, depending on the family, but male Ksatriya usually begin with Cokorda Gede, Cokorda, Anak Agung, Dewa, or Dewa Agung, while the women are called Dewa Ayu or Anak Agung Istri. In the name Dewa Gede Putu, Dewa is the title, Gede is an honorary prefix meaning "great," and Putu denotes a first born child.

Wesya is the administrative, merchant, economist class, which, on occasion, has ruled Bali's smaller principalities. There are approximately six Wesya groups; the most important is the Arya group, descended from a raja. Men's names begin with Gusti, women with I Gusti Ayu.

Sudra

About 90% of the Balinese belong to this caste. Sudra, though commoners, are not considered "untouchable" like the pariahs of India. The duty of the Sudra caste is to labor for the three upper classes. Men are addressed I, women Ni. Formerly, Sudras were not taught to read or write, and thus were dependent on the specialized knowledge of upper-class scholars to interpret religious texts and prayers.

The Sudras have their own exorcist specialists *(sungguhu)* who banish *buta* and *kala* (devils) from ceremonies. Today, most Sudra families turn to a Brahmana household for help in setting propitious dates, interpreting omens, refurbishing ceremonial paraphernalia, dedicating a *bale* or shrine, purifying a house, translating *lontar,* or reciting sacred Kawi passages for necessary ceremonies. The Sudra family is obliged to repay such assistance by paying a call and bringing food.

Caste Rules and Taboos

Caste rules are largely restricted to the observance of established etiquette. High-caste Balinese must be addressed by the proper title. Triwangsa castes should sit above lower-class folk, and may not be touched by Balinese of lower caste. People should marry only within their caste. At one time a lower-caste man who dared marry a Brahmana women was drowned in the ocean. Even in this era of *globalisasi,* intercaste marriages are still frowned upon particularly when men of lower caste marry higher caste women.

Status Changes

The Balinese are now dealing with issues that bring into question values and traditions that are deeply rooted. No one knows whether to abide by the old rules or disable them. There still seems to be a deep need to maintain overall status differences within each of the regencies. The craze in geneology writing, which last surfaced in the 19th century, has become popular among families who feel the need to position themselves in relation to other high-caste clans.

The Klungkung royal family asserts it was the original founding family against which all others must be measured. Other families claim to have located ancient *prasasti* edicts proving that they are superior. Every village contains families desparately trying to raise themselves to a higher caste by almost any means possible. You hear of spectacular status changes: i.e. the family of a *kepala desa* going from Dewa to Anak Agung to Cokorda in three generations, allegedly bribing villagers to address them in the proper way.

In Tabanan, when a group of Sudra raised themselves to Dewa, it incensed the other Dewa in the *banjar* so much it triggered pitched battles with bamboo *runcing.* The *camat* and police had to be called in to pacify the combatants. Also at work on Bali is the principle of sinking status. If a high caste man marries a low caste woman, and their male children continue to marry beneath them, over three or four generations the family loses its high caste status. This is why you're always meeting Balinese who claim to come from priests or kings of the Triwangsa aristocratic castes.

MEN AND WOMEN

Gender Roles

Although sex discrimination in daily activities is unknown in Balinese society, men's and women's tasks and roles are clearly defined and quite separate. There's a certain hardiness in Balinese women and a softness in Balinese men that seems to reflect an ease with their sexuality and gender role. Men and women both play male and female roles in Balinese dance. Both sexes wear *sarong* skirts. Though once the exclusive preserves of men, women are now becoming more involved in painting, sculpture, and woodcarving. There's an acclaimed woman's *gamelan* orchestra in Peliatan and a women's art gallery in Ubud.

Women often have independent incomes and are in charge of raising pigs and cultivating the fields. They also prepare for all the milestones in family life considered important or magical: birth, the first cutting of nails and hair, filing of teeth, the piercing of earlobes, marriage, and death.

Women prepare temple offerings and are responsible for the main work of festivals. They perform much of the backbreaking labor in the building industry.

Walking upright and graceful as queens, Balinese women can carry 30 kilogram loads that stand up to 1.5 meters tall on their heads, while men take up the rear cradling their *parang*. A young Balinese girl can train herself to carry 40 coconuts, stacks of fruit, or great water jars on her head—all this while riding a bicycle down a bumpy country road.

Men make most of the family and village decisions. Men also look after the fields and do all the chopping and food preparation at festivals. While women care for most of the animals, the handling of cocks and cockfights is the exclusive domain of men. The market is almost solely a woman's environment, a place of abundant female energy and initiative where females derive most of their earnings. Buying and selling cattle is the province of men.

The Balinese are extraordinarily welcoming, inviting visitors to take part in village life. They expect guests to adhere to their rules and customs. If you live in a village, you learn how to live communally. You know you're accepted when the villagers don't hesitate to ask for favors.

Menstrual Blood

As in many traditional Indonesian societies, strict taboos used to govern menstruation. Women could not prepare food, enter a temple or kitchen, make offerings, or attend feasts. In aristocratic families menstruating women were even sent out of the home to board in a special house or compound.

A Balinese man believed if menstrual blood ever touched his scalp he would become impotent for the rest of his life and follow his wife around like a dog. If a woman's menstrual blood fell into the hands of an enemy it could be used as a powerful weapon by practitioners of black magic. Today such practices and beliefs are on the wane.

Dress and Grooming

Most older Balinese women wear a *kain* or *sarung* and *kebaya* wrapped artfully around their slim bodies. Men wear bright *sarung* as well. Among the young girls, jeans and T-shirt are the latter day *sarung* or *kebaya*. Ceremonial dress is elaborate and employs a number of precious textiles: hip cloths *(kamben)* extending from waist to ankle, ribbon-like belts *(sabuk)*, and tightly bound chest cloths *(anteng)*. Shoulder cloths *(selendang)* are only worn in the Old Balinese villages of Tenganan and Trunyan.

The custom of appearing topless was discouraged when Europeans began arriving in numbers in the 1930s. Formerly, women were always naked to the waist in public—only prostitutes wore blouses. In the 1950s, with Indonesia's new found revolutionary fervor, tourists were forbidden to snap photos of bare breasts, cameras and film were confiscated, the women themselves fined. Today Balinese women wear bras like Western women wear bikini tops.

Women have long, silky, black hair which they tie in a number of ways around the head, without use of hairpins, or interweave with scarves. Unmarried women often sport a loose lock of hair hanging down the back over one shoulder with a *gonjer* (flower) dangling in it. Hair can also be rolled inside itself in a great puff, held in place by a few separated strands.

Many Balinese women had their ears pierced when they were children. Women delouse each other and their children as a social pastime and an affirmation of familial love.

Occasionally, you see children with the traditional clipped short hair but for a single lock hanging down in front; the Balinese believe the child will become ill if this lock is cut.

MARRIAGE

Marriage is the final initiation into the Balinese community. Most Balinese consider it an important social obligation to raise a family and carry on the family name, and only a stable married man or household head may become a member of the *banjar*. A person who never marries is looked upon as an oddity; if a man dies a bachelor the Balinese say that in the next life he will feed pigs, a woman's task. If a woman dies childless, she is doomed to be suckled by a giant caterpillar.

Many Balinese marriages are still prearranged or negotiated, though young men may also "kidnap" their wives, and mixed-caste marriages are increasingly common. Marriage customs differ from caste to caste and village to village, but all

Balinese marriage practices share fundamental similarities. There are basically two ways to get married on Bali, *ngerorod* and *mapadik*.

Ngerorod

This is marriage by elopement, in which the prearranged honeymoon precedes the wedding ceremony. Since it's otherwise quite expensive to marry on Bali, *ngerorod* is becoming more and more popular. It has particular appeal to the Balinese sense of theater. Balinese love a spectacular kidnapping in which friends of the suitor capture a woman in the fields, on the road, or down by the river. Theatrics are paramount: she is expected to bite and kick her abductors in mock self-defense. These days it's more stylish and fashionable for the woman to be whisked away in a hired sedan, and more often than not she goes willingly. The couple then repairs to a friend's house stocked with provisions, offerings, and the bride's wardrobe. The woman's infuriated father sounds the alarm demanding to know what has become of his daughter. A search party is organized which eventually returns unsuccessful and exhausted.

Meanwhile, the couple is consummating the marriage before special offerings *(sesayut tabuh rah)* have the time to wilt. These offerings alone make the marriage binding by customary law. Emissaries of the groom visit the bride's father to argue the advantages of the union. Begrudgingly, the girl's father gives in, after a suitable bride price has been agreed upon. The groom's father must finance and conduct the marriage ceremony, welcoming the bride as a new daughter into the family. The actual public wedding, within 42 days of the staged kidnapping, is only an official confirmation of their union. They are already married in the eyes of the gods.

Mapadik

This is marriage by consent, in which an upper-class couple conducts a formal courtship. Since daughters were once regarded as property useful for attaining a family's social and political goals, high-caste families tried to wed a son to the daughter of a friend or relative so a blood bond would unite the resources of both families.

Under no circumstances may a woman "marry down," i.e., take a commoner. The preferred marriage is through a parallel patricousin,

the father's brother's daughter. It has been noted that Triwangsa couples often get along so well because they are all first cousins.

Traditionally, the man or his father journeys three times to the bride's house with food and *sirih*. When the bride's family visits, the groom's father is obliged to give them food, *sirih* is chewed (an ancient, ritualistic means of coming to agreement), and presents are exchanged. The groom then regularly visits the home of his prospective bride, presenting gifts and performing services for his future father-in-law.

The groom's family arranges and pays for the wedding, the date set well in advance on a propitious day. Wedding guests are often entertained by professional storytellers and musicians. Enormously detailed rules govern dining and seating arrangements. Sometimes the bride's family is not even invited.

The actual ceremony varies. It could be very simple and short, presided over by a common temple *pemangku,* or it may be elaborate, expensive, and go on all day. Both the bride and groom dress in bright *songket,* with brocades of gold thread, and the woman's hair is decorated with glittering gold flowers.

Usually the bride and groom offer food to one another, then simulate such domestic duties such as washing, cooking rice, and cutting bamboo. Prayers are intoned, then the couple eats together in public, feeding each other. This is an important symbolic act, as in former times only married men and women were allowed to eat food together in public. The priest then performs a ritual purification and blesses the couple. Neither rice nor flowers are thrown. Today there could very well be a Western-style buffet reception held afterward where speeches are offered by members of the two families.

Married Life

After the wedding, the new bride leaves her old ties behind and formally becomes a member of the husband's kin group and caste, serving the new family's gods. The couple resides in the house of the husband's parents for the first few years; relations with her own family may be severed.

The wife owns all her clothes, jewelry, household utensils, pigs, and chickens, and often has her own income from the sale of market goods.

Inheritance is invariably passed along the male line; the man owns the house, the rice fields, the cattle, and his tools, and is in charge of handling the money.

Polygamy amongst the aristocracy was once widespread but is now quite rare. At one time the wife of a prince could hold varying levels of status in a *puri*, depending upon her caste and whether she ranked as first, second, third, or fourth wife. The prince usually did not even appear at his wedding ceremony with a low-caste bride; she was ceremonially married to his *kris*, or a tree.

A man may be awarded a divorce by the village authorities if his wife is lazy, quarrelsome, adulterous, or sterile, while a woman may divorce her husband by simply leaving his home if he is cruel, under an occult power, or impotent.

CHILDREN

The Balinese have a love affair with kids. Having come recently from the other world, a baby is looked upon as a god. The smaller the child, the closer s/he is to heaven. At home a child is seldom disciplined, but rather cajoled into obedience as an equal. A child is given responsibilities which contribute to self-sufficiency and maturity. Children are never beaten: it's believed such treatment will damage or drive the soul from the body.

Rarely are Balinese infants left alone, nor are they allowed to cry. If you're pushing a crying child in a stroller down the street, Balinese will stop you to inform you your child is crying, and you'll be expected to do something about it immediately.

Balinese children always seem happy, though calm. They have an innate gentility, and are quite well-behaved. In the most frenetic village festivals seldom do you hear a child cry, or see children squabble, fight, or throw tantrums. Nothing is hidden from children; they listen attentively to adult conversations.

A boy, especially the first son, usually takes up the trade of his father, whether it be caring for cattle or running a souvenir or electronics shop. There's lots of pressure on boys and men to make money. Daughters are very important to the family—for ceremonies, cleaning house, for carrying offerings. Small girls learn from their mothers how to make offerings, weave, cook, and thresh rice, and never question their many religious duties.

Why do you see so many Balinese kids who look like they're ditching school? Balinese children attend classes in three separate shifts—0700-1000, 1000-1300, and 1300-1600. White and gray uniforms are worn by high school students, white and dark blue by secondary school students, white and red by those in primary school.

Naming

The full name of every Balinese not only indicates his or her caste but also his or her sequence of birth. The first born is called Wayan (Gede or Putu in the upper castes), the second child Made (or Nengah or Kadek), then Nyoman, and the fourth Ketut. With a fifth child the rotation starts over again. Today, with Bali's vigorous family-planning program, one meets fewer and fewer Nyomans and Ketuts.

Children also receive a formal, personal name. Thus, a Balinese called Cokorda Made Sita is the second-born son in the Sita family, belonging to the Ksatriya caste.

To make the naming system more complicated, parents' names change at the birth of each child. Identifying people by their descendants rather than by their ancestors reflects the direction of time flow from the present to the future rather than from the past to the present.

Transitional Events

Throughout a child's life various rituals are performed on propitious dates chosen with great care. Some life-cycle ceremonies take place even before birth: for example, a ceremony is held to appease evil spirits as soon as it's learned a woman is pregnant. This is designed to ensure the child's good health and well-being. A father may be prohibited from killing animals or cutting his hair until the child is safely born.

When the umbilical cord falls off, another purification ceremony takes place, and yet a third when the child is named three months after birth. The latter ceremony is called *nelubulanin*. A puppet shadow play may be staged, and at the end of the performance the child sprinkled with holy water and the name announced by the *dalang*.

The afterbirth *(ari-ari),* which protects a person from sickness throughout entire life, is buried by the doorway of the house in a coconut shell. For 42 days after birth the mother is considered unclean *(kesebelan)* and ritual actions must be undertaken to purify her. Twelve days after birth, offerings are made at home; additional offerings are taken to a *balian,* consulted to determine who's been reincarnated in the new infant. Preferably the *balian* is unknown to the family, avoiding the possibility of cheating with foreknowledge of family history. The *balian* goes into trance and speaks with the voice (or voices) of the person(s) who inhabit the infant. The spirits state why they've chosen to come back and announce any conditions attached.

The birth of boy and girl twins is considered a calamity, an evil omen. It's thought the twins have committed incest in the womb, and rigorous purification ceremonies are required. Traditionally, they should be separated at birth, brought up by different families, and married to one another when they come of age.

Since the Balinese detest actions characteristic of animals, children are not allowed to crawl. An infant may not even touch the impure soil until the age of three months, carried everywhere on the hip of a parent or older brother or sister. It is believed the earth is too strong to risk the vunerable infant coming into contact with it.

At 105 days old, the child is bedecked with gold and silver bracelets on wrists and ankles, and an elaborate ceremony is performed as the infant first makes contact with the earth. At this time, the personalities of the previous owners of the child's soul are supposed to remove themselves to allow the new being to continue life unencumbered by memories of what went before.

For a child's first birthday—at 210 days, the length of a Balinese year—a small banquet is arranged and a Brahman priest blesses the child, rings bells, sprinkles holy water, recites *Kawi* litanies, and places small offerings before Sanghyang Rare Kumara, the god of small children. This rite is considered so critical to the child's future well-being that poorer families often pitch in to share the high costs. At this time, the child receives a magic name, held secret from the personal name uttered in daily use. From then on, the child is considered an adult.

Once able to walk, a child falls into the care of other children, allowed to roam freely through the village in small, self-sufficient kid republics. A girl's first menstruation *(nyacal)* is an important rite of passage. Since she is believed unclean *(sebel),* she enters into partial seclusion until the day when her period is at an end, emerging in gold brocades, jewels, and flowers. A *pedanda* performs the purification blessing and recites magic prayers *(maweda).*

Only one major ritual remains, the filing of teeth—a sort of Balinese bar mitzvah, the passage into puberty—celebrated by both males and females.

Toothfiling

Called *mapandes* in High Balinese, *matatah* in Common Balinese. The reason for filing is to control evil human characteristics *(sad ripu):* greed, lust, anger, confusion, stupidity, jealousy, ill-will, and intoxication by either passion or drunkenness. This important life-cycle event usually occurs when a Balinese boy or girl reaches puberty—at a girl's first menstruation, when a boy's voice changes. If not then, it must definitely take place before marriage; sometimes filing is incorporated into the marriage ceremony. After filing, a father's duties to his female children are generally regarded as complete.

Before a cremation the teeth of a cadaver may be filed. Why? Pointed teeth are likened to those of ferocious witches, demons, wild animals, savages, or, almost as bad, dogs. A person's canine teeth, regarded by the Balinese as animalistic fangs *(caling),* are filed flat so the child may become fully human, able to reign in the emotions. It's believed a Balinese may be denied entrance into heaven if the teeth are not filed because s/he might be mistaken for a wild creature. In the old days the teeth of adolescents were also blackened with betel nut to distinguish them from the white teeth of animals.

Mapandes is a costly affair; invitations must be issued, musicians hired, the fees of the *pedanda* paid, elaborate offerings carried out, and a banquet prepared for guests and villagers. Because of the great expense, it may be delayed until enough money has been saved. A number of families may participate in a mass

Toothfiling represents the evening out of the extreme and kasar (rough) aspects of one's personality as one enters adulthood. Toothfiling also rids the person of the six evil animal passions that Balinese believe everyone possesses to some degree: laziness (alus), love of sensual pleasures (raga), love of luxury and splendor (dewasa), love of worldly goods (tresna), indifference (nidra), and irresoluteness (baja). Though representatives from each caste are in the toothfiling ceremony, a girl of the lower caste will be asked to lie on a platform at a lower level than her upper-caste sisters, and she wears less lavish ceremonial clothing. The most important event of adolescence, Balinese endure it with not a sound of complaint. After the filing, youths of all castes can go on to lead healthy, well-adjusted lives as a part of Bali's tightly knit family, clan, community, and society.

toothfiling in order to share costs, or it may be held simultaneously with some other costly ceremony such as a cremation or wedding. The *banjar* often determines that financial help should be extended to the lower castes to enable them to participate. To view the maximum pomp and ritual, attend a toothfiling ceremony sponsored by a Brahman family, where as many as 14 people may participate and expenses could top Rp35 million.

Filing is scheduled on an auspicious day and performed by a specialist Brahman priest on a special platform. For the occasion makeshift bamboo shrines with gay, colorful offerings of rice, sweet cakes, flowers, and fruits are erected within the compound. All attendees dress in traditional clothing, and the customary white cardboard box of snacks and bottle of sweetened tea is handed to all who enter.

Having spent the previous two or three nights praying while confined in *bale* built for the occasion within the high-caste family's compound, from two to 100 initiates are assembled, dressed in white and yellow to signify holiness. Girls wear precious *kemban* (breast cloth), the finest the family can afford, with garments as ornate as those of *legong* dancers. Boys wear a *songket* from the armpits to the knees, a *kris* protruding from a yellow sash in the back.

The ceremony begins with the *pedanda* sprinkling holy water and blessing the group with mantras. Offerings are placed before the gods of sexual love. The initiates lie down on the richly draped bamboo platform wide-eyed and fright-

ened, clutching their pillows as close relatives ring around. Incense is lit, mouthwash placed at the ready, files and whetstones blessed to cleanse them and render the operation painless. Magic symbols *(aksara)* are inscribed on the teeth.

The "dentist" *(sangging)* first places a small cylinder of sugarcane in the corners of the mouth to prop the jaws open and prevent gagging. The front two upper canines are filed so they're even with the upper incisors; it's important to effect an even line of short teeth. The actual filing requires about five to 10 minutes. A mirror is provided to allow the patient to observe the progress of the ritual. Filings are spit into a yellow coconut. Tears may roll down their cheeks, but the filees seldom cry out.

Sometimes members of the family sing a *kekawin* about Arjuna, the brave young hero of the Mahabharata epic, to bolster the spirts of their loved ones, someone else may recite Kawi translated into vernacular Balinese. To lighten the atmosphere, the *sangging* may joke with the filee as he files.

After consulting with his girlfriend, wife, or mother, a boy may decide he still possesses too much animality and lie back down on the bed for more filing. Occasionally, there are requests for just a few token, symbolic strokes of the file.

When the filing is finished, the astringent betel pepper leaf *(base)* is rubbed on the ends of the teeth, then the *pedanda* places various other soothing, healing tinctures on the end of the initiate's tongues. The coconut shell receptacle of filing debris and saliva is then buried behind the ancestral shrine lest it be occupied by evil spirits.

VILLAGE LIFE

Ninety percent of Bali's population is rural, living in hundreds of hamlets and villages all over the island. Traditionally, the social organization of the island is based on the village, each completely self-sufficient, providing for all the needs and functions of the individual from birth through cremation. Not just a collection of family compounds, the rural community was and is a whole series of interlocking corporations, a living organism, a microcosm of the cosmic order.

Housewives walking lazily down the street, lounging in courtyards, men gossiping in *warung*, children playing—it's a scene unchanged after generations of Dutch rule, harsh Japanese wartime occupation, turbulent Indonesian revolution and independence, and now the age of mass tourism.

Village Layout

Pre-Hindu villages were linear in layout, with meeting houses and longhouses running down the spine of the village. The rustic village of Belantih on the slopes of Gunung Batur, with its long, flat avenues, is an example of Bali's prehistoric village layout. With the Hindu influx 500 years ago, Aboriginal longhouses were replaced by courtyard homes.

Though there are enormous variations, a Balinese village usually consists of walled family compounds lining tree-shaded dirt lanes. Even in big towns like Bangli, Amlapura, and Ubud, this traditional layout is still evident.

People live virtually outdoors. The street outside each courtyard dwelling is actually the village living room/lounge area. The land in back of and/or in between the compounds is planted with banana, papaya, coconut, and breadfruit trees. Nearby woods provide bamboo, rattan, pandanus, and wood. Under the coconut groves sloe-eyed midget cattle graze; in a nearby stream is the village bathing place. Since all land belongs ultimately to the gods, who lease it to the Balinese so they may live, the concept of absolute land ownership is unknown here.

Where the two main streets of the village intersect is a miniature *alun-alun*, the village banyan tree, and the *pasar*, surrounded by such important public buildings as the village temple of origin *(pura desa)*, the cockfight pavilion *(wantilan)*, the *puri* of the local raja or his descendants, and the *bale banjar*, usually with a blaring TV or table tennis. Also in the village center is the signal-drum tower *(kulkul)*. A series of quick, frantic beats means an emergency like a fire, while slow, doleful rhythmic beats denote a more ordinary community event, like a funeral. The *kulkul* is a pre-Hindu tradition. One finds slit drums all across the societies of the Pacific, the origin of some components of Bali's population.

Different castes or professions live in various *banjar* in the village. For example, Banjar Satria is where the aristocracy lives; Banjar Pande the neighborhood of the smiths. On the edge of the village is the *pura dalem* and the cemetery, an eerie overgrown field with ramshackle bamboo altars.

The Family Compound

While the village is open and communal, the Balinese home is hidden and private. High thatch-covered mud walls run along the roads, broken at intervals by high pillared porticos with thick, carved wooden doors, each the entrance to a family compound, invariably guarded by a barking dog or two. The thick, mud walls of the enclosure define and protect the family; they would feel insecure without them.

A central ramp runs up the flight of steps so motorcycles can be ridden into the walled enclosure. These cells of unbroken, interlocking, single domestic courtyard homes are open only in the back, where the rubbish is thrown and pigs root. Behind the main gate is a thin wall *(aling-aling)* which affords privacy and prevents evil spirits from entering; it's difficult for the beasties to turn corners.

Just as the layout of the village reflects the grand order, so too does the layout of the family compound. The Balinese believe each part of the house corresponds to a part of the human anatomy: the head is the family shrine, the sexual organs are the gates, the arms are the bedrooms and the social parlor, the navel is the courtyard, the legs and feet are the kitchen and granary, and the anus is the backyard garbage pit. In each corner of the yard are temples dedicated to guardian spirits.

Because sons generally take their brides home, several generations—up to 10 separate families—share the compound, each maintaining separate hearths and properties. Open-sided raised pavilions for sleeping, playing, and working all face inward, forming a circle around the inner courtyard. Near the center of the yard is the family open-air "living room." Separate enclosures and huts are assigned to cooking and washing. Just outside the compound, off in the corner, is the pigsty, where the next festival's main course is fattened up.

Daily Rhythm

The passage of days is marked by a succession of sounds. Everyone rises at first light with the raucous crowing of the fighting cocks. The women begin the day cooking, tending children, cleaning, preparing offerings. They bring water from the village well or stream, then briskly sweep the compound yard with twig brooms. Small palm-leaf packets *(ketipat)* of boiled rice and condiments are prepared for the men to take to the fields.

Trays in hand, the women and girls make the rounds to the various yard shrines, distributing offerings *(ngedjot)*. Perpetually hungry dogs follow, gobbling up grains of moldy rice as soon as they're placed on the ground. The offerings are intended to protect the homestead against evil spirits, which might very well be embodied in the scabrous dogs.

Most Balinese eat their first rice meal late in the morning, or the women buy small palm-leaf packets of cakes and sweetmeats that are washed down with coffee. During the rice harvest women often take food to the men in the fields. Before the heat sets in, everyone except the old are out of the compound going about their daily routines. The school day starts at 0630, when throngs of children gather on the road carrying brooms and buckets to clean the

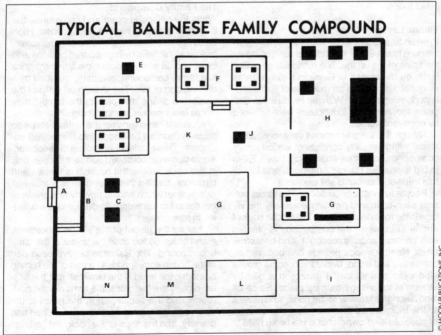

TYPICAL BALINESE FAMILY COMPOUND

schoolyard. Bell-shaped baskets, in which the game cocks are kept, are lined up on the street.

On market days the streets of the village are crowded with women from nearby villages, baskets poised on their heads. The markets teem with great stacks of pots, piles of produce, herds of farm animals. Since raising pigs and chickens is one of the main sources of income for women,

on market days it's not uncommon to see a woman carrying a food stand on her head, walking her pig to market at the end of a piece of twine.

As the sun tops the palms, family members take their morning wash at the village spring or river. The middle of the day is a time for resting, or talking with friends in the shade of the village banyan tree. As the afternoon cools, activity

TYPICAL BALINESE FAMILY COMPOUND

A) **candi bentar**—entrance gate

B) **aling-aling**—a small wall inside the doorway to stop entry of devils and evil spirits. Chinese derivation.

C) **apit-lawang**—house shrines, at entrance of compound

D) **bale tiang sangah**—social pavilion and guest bale. Generally contains benches or mats where guests can sit cross-legged.

E) **tugu**—a small shrine, west of the uma meten, where offerings are laid at the beginning of each work day

F) **uma-meten**—the windowless, locked sleeping quarters for the head of the family and his wife, built on the side nearest the holy mountain on a platform of bricks or sandstone. Supported by eight pillars and four walls, it's often topped by a thick roof of thatch. There are usually only beds inside. It is also the treasure-house of the compound where heirlooms, cassette recorders, jewelry, motorcycles, etc., are kept. In more prosperous households the platform of the meten extends into a veranda-like platform with additional beds. Hung on the walls are photographs of President Suharto and the family in formal attire, etc. After the shrine area, the most important building in the compound.

G) **bale sikepat** and **bale sekenam**—guest pavilions for relatives and children; also where souvenirs are made, for weaving looms, and crafts- and implement-making activities. These vary in size and number according to each family's needs.

H) **sanggah kemulan**—the family counterpart of the formal village temple in the more well-to-

do families, usually walled in and consisting of shrines with grass thatch and an altar for offerings. These shrines are dedicated to the ancestral spirits, to the holy mountains (Gunung Batur and Gunung Agung), to the interpreter of the gods, etc. In the compound of noblemen, the sanggah section is as elaborate as a temple and is called a pamerjan; in the poorest families they're just small bamboo god-houses on top of split bamboo.

I) **lumbung**—rice granary, the size an indication of the wealth of the family. These are tall structures with steep thatched roofs, four wooden pillars with rat-stopping discs attached. Always on the south side of kampung, alongside the kitchen, at a lower level and west of the sleeping quarters.

J) **pengijeng**—a small shrine dedicated to the Spirit of the Jewel.

K) **natar**—interior courtyard. In the old days this included a cleared area behind the granary where rice was threshed, but now with the new strains of miracle rice, the threshing is done in the fields.

L) **paon**—the dark, hot kitchen, often just a flimsy bamboo structure with woven palm-leaf walls, a smooth, hard dirt floor, a simple roof of coarse thatch supported by posts. At one end a raised bamboo platform serves as the kitchen table, a mud stone at the other. The dirt floor keeps food inside the clay pots hot for hours, and is smooth and easy to clean. The paon is always located on the south side of the compound.

M) **pigsty**

N) **chicken coop**

picks up. The men return home and after a refreshing bath they gather, clutching or stroking their prized fighting cocks in tight groups outside their favorite *warung,* or squatting in front of the temple so their cocks may be amused by passersby.

The last meal of the day is usually the same food served at lunch, this time eaten cold shortly after sunset. The cool of the evening is the time to put on clean clothes and saunter through the night market, or meet beneath the lamplit foodstalls on the main road of the village. The roads in the early evening always provide a lively scene: *gamelan* recitals, young boys strumming guitars in doorways, men squatting under thatch huts sipping *tuak,* children playing on the warm asphalt. If you wander the streets after 2100 or 2200 don't expect to see too many locals—they all seem to disappear shortly after dark. The Balinese believe the hours of the night are the time for evil spirts to wander and tempt the nightwalkers.

Warung

The *warung* is the testing ground for a boy's first love, a refuge for inebriates, and the equivalent of a smoking room for the village gents. There are both long-established *warung* and those that materialize overnight for temple festivals, market days, cockfights, and dance performances. It's where one fully indulges one's sweet tooth or partakes of *brem* or *arak.*

These remarkably well-stocked makeshift foodstall/cafes feature several hard wooden benches, the back support built into the structure. The *warung* is a simple affair of bamboo walls and thatch roof. A platform bed is often attached for lounging, napping, gossiping, eating. The food is cooked and water boiled in the back. Shutters fold down at night, securing the contents.

Farmers stop here before going to the fields or to work repairing roads; in the late morning they stop in again. The *warung* is the men's club of Bali. The enterprise is often run by coquettish teenagers looking for a boyfriend or husband. If the girl is particularly beautiful, boys will come from the surrounding villages just to buy things from her. A male will order hot tea or coffee so he can flirt longer. Some boys come with a new motorcycle ("smoking ass," *yit mekudus*) or a new watch to impress her.

Late night *warung,* lit invitingly by hissing gas lamps, are popular with *bemo* drivers, small traders, truck drivers, and insomniac sufferers. Caste, age, social status dissapear in the proletarian atmosphere of the *warung.* They're great sources of gossip, and unfettered and spirited conversation is the order of the day.

The *Pasar*

Markets are a necessity in a society where refrigeration and corner stores are not yet widespread. Markets are a refreshing slice of real Bali, away from the suntan oil, laser disc movies, and pineapple *lasi.* The village housewife still makes her way to the public market before dawn, often her only outing of the day. Markets are the women's clubs of Bali, where goods and gossip are exchanged.

Pasar are usually located on the busiest intersection in the center of the village to the south of either the main village temple *(pura puseh)* or the *puri.* In the more traditional villages, the *pasar* is spread under the shade of a huge *waringin* tree. A small village *pasar* may be just a row of makeshift stalls on a dusty lane off the main road.

Traditionally, *pasar* are held on the *pasar* day of the Balinese three-day week, rotating between different villages, but these roving portable stands and mats are nearly extinct. Now villagers favor larger district markets. The 20th century city *pasar,* as typified by Denpasar's crowded Market and Pasar Badung, is housed in a huge, square, multistoried cement block where the stench is unbearable and rubbish piles are everywhere.

The *Mandi*

An indispensable feature of a village, the *mandi,* or bathing place, is located in a tidal lagoon, in a river at the bottom of a ravine, or in an artesian spring pouring from rock cliffs or hillsides around which villagers build walled enclosures. Bamboo or pipe spouts carry the water onto the heads of the bathers. Nearby will probably be a small shrine built into a rocky face, dedicated to the guardian diety of spring water, Dewa Wisnu.

The *mandi* is a soothing day's end activity for the water-loving Balinese. Women gossip while doing the laundry, tired farmers soak aching bones, children cavort and scream. Here the village meets and enjoys itself. It's polite to avert your gaze from bathing villagers, especially women. The island's most famous *mandi*—Tampaksiring, Air Sanih, Goa Gajah, Toyabungkah—are known to cure certain maladies, including paralysis, skin diseases, and impotence.

THE *BANJAR*

The *banjar* is the village council—the community extension of the house and family. Each Balinese village is divided into one or more *banjar,* a cooperative association of neighbors who assist each other in the preparation and financing of costly events. Each *banjar* swears separate allegiances to certain temples, palaces, and holidays.

More than any other factor, the *banjar* has kept intact the Balinese way of life through the decline of the local *adat* princes and chieftains. *banjar* captured most of the administrative power the *desa* lost to the princes after the Dutch invasion, when land was divided among the people. Its importance persists even in the modern Indonesian state. The *banjar* today is the basic governmental unit of the village and is of immense help to the government in disseminating information and policy. Problems with family planning and development programs have occurred because civil officials from government agencies have sometimes miscalculated the social, ritual, and administrative power of the *banjar.*

Under the fast-paced veneer of Kuta and Legian, the network of *banjar*-based village life remains intact and inviolate. Westerners have yet to stir by the time all the *banjar*-prescribed *sajen-sajen* (offerings) have been made. Even the bustling metropolis of Denpasar is rigidly divided into its many constituent *banjar.*

Every adult belongs both to a *desa* and a *banjar.* Each household pays a subscription fee to its *banjar.* When a man marries, membership is compulsory; otherwise he's considered a moral and spiritual outcast, denied even the right to burial in the village cemetery. Some *banjar* obligations may be considered even more important than family ties. Each member exists less as an individual than as one thread in the social fabric of the *banjar.*

The *banjar* serves simultaneously as town council, tribunal, department of public works and welfare, and department of environment and sanitation. It's a cross between a masonic lodge, a town planning committee, and a church congregation. It galvanizes the community to prepare for and participate in major feasts, rites, and dance performances; it votes in a democratic manner on road and temple construction; lays you beneath the ground.

A man usually marries within his *banjar* and only takes on full status in the *banjar* when he has sired a child. Summoned by the beating of the *kulkul* drum, attendance of all household heads is required at regular evening meetings; absentees are fined. Since all decisions must be unanimous, new ideas take a long time to gain acceptance; in the meantime discussions proceed peacefully.

The *banjar* is a community of equals; before the *banjar* all castes are equal. The leader of the *banjar,* the *klian,* is elected by its members and approved through a medium by the gods. The *klian* is unpaid but for small gifts like extra rice, a small percentage of collected fines, or an interest in a *banjar* commercial venture. He may also be rewarded with rice fields close to an irrigation source.

It's common for the *banjar* to sponsor youth groups *(sekehe teruna)* with their own pavilions in the village common. Ceremonies and regular meetings every fortnight prepare young people for the responsibilities of full *banjar* membership.

The local youth may initiate programs of their own, meeting, say, every Sunday morning to clean the streets and temples. Young teen Balinese surfboard carriers on the Bukit Peninsula have created a *banjar*-style organization to fix prices and network among themselves.

Banjar Property and Duties

The *banjar* often owns its own rice fields, which are worked communally to provide food for banquets and to bring in cash revenues for the communal treasury. The family house is built upon *banjar* land. The *banjar* also maintains its own temple *(pemaksan),* spiritually its most important piece of property. The *banjar*'s meeting hall or clubhouse *(bale banjar)* is an open pavilion with a large porch. Men often gather here during the evenings to fondle their fighting cocks, drink *tuak,* chat, gamble, and play cards. Each member takes a turn as cook or waiter. At night the bamboo platforms become long beds where villagers sleep, sardine-like, safe in the company of their fellows. Male villagers may spend more time in the *banjar* pavilion than at home.

With its own orchestra and dance troupe, *banjar* members practice *gamelan* or watch play rehearsals. The *banjar's* dancing properties— headdresses, masks, luxurious costumes—are stored in a nearby fireproof building called the *gedong.* The *bale* is provided with a kitchen fully stocked with pots, pans, knives, axes, and chopping blocks all available on loan to members who require them.

The *banjar* runs its own communal bank from which the villagers may borrow to buy farm equipment, cattle, or other necessities. All members are required to help one another with materials and labor. All labor is shared and work usually performed in pairs or groups. If members don't sign up for work assignments, a fine is imposed. The *banjar* supports and maintains village temples, ditches, markets, roads, and bathing places; handles taxation, cockfighting, divorces, and duck-herding; and helps to arrange and finance weddings, family celebrations, temple festivals, cremations, and community feasts. The *banjar* advises villagers on matters of religion, marriage, and morals, all regulated carefully by elected members. It's also responsible for the village graveyard, guaranteeing that the correct funerary rites are carried out, that corpses are disposed of properly.

The *banjar* can function as a vigilante committee to forcibly expel undesirables from a village. Its role as village police force accounts for Bali's extremely low crime rate; the island averages only one armed robbery per year. The *banjar* operates its own school for the arts, training new generations in a line that extends back through the centuries.

No other political system has yet broken through the patriarchal shield of the *banjar,* though increasingly its cohesiveness is weakened by consumerism, modern lifestyles, and the tourist industry. Many members now send a monetary contribution in lieu of their presence.

LANGUAGE

Most young Balinese speak at least three languages fluently. Among themselves they speak ordinary Balinese, a difficult tongue which few Westerners ever master. To strangers and in the presence of Brahmana they converse in high Balinese. Nearly all the Balinese speak the official national language of Indonesia, Bahasa Indonesia, a language similar to Malay.

American-style English is the most widely spoken foreign language on Bali, particularly by those involved in the tourist industry. There are proportionally more English-speakers on Bali than in anywhere else in Indonesia.

You can in fact embarrass an Indonesian working in an international-class hotel by failing to address him in English, thereby implying he lacks necessary language skills. An increasing number of Balinese tourist guides, travel agents, and hotel staff also speak rudimentary French, Italian, Spanish, Dutch, or German.

Although contemporary Balinese is written in Roman letters, the cleft-like characters of the traditional alphabet are related to Sanskrit-derived *Kawi* of Central Java. Balinese is a very difficult language to master because of its many subtle pronunciations. Serious students of the language should obtain *A Basic Balinese Vocabulary* and the handy *Bali Pocket Dictionary*, both compiled by Rev. N. Shadeg, S.V.D. The *Kamus Bahasa Bali* Bali-Indonesia and Indonesia-Bali dictionary by Sri Reshi Anandakusuma is available in Bali for around Rp10,000.

Balinese

There are four different Balinese languages, each used by a distinct social class, each with a vocabulary of its own. Although each level shares numerous common nouns, many verbs referring to human activities and nouns designating human body parts differ.

The language of the Sudra caste is of ancient Malayo-Austronesian-Polynesian origin, utilizing many vernacular words from the aboriginal dialects of the eastern islands, particularly Lombok and Sumbawa. This coarse, low Balinese is the oldest language on the island; traces can still be found on the isolated island of Nusa Penida.

The high Balinese dialects of the Triwangsa classes are largely Javanese in origin, using a great many Sanskrit words derived from the court languages spoken widely on Java from the 10th century. This highly refined sub-language *(basa alus)* of about 1,000 words consists almost entirely of honorific levels of speech. Reflecting the rigid Hindu caste system once in force here, another form, *basa singgih*, is used when speaking to high priests or when alluding to sacred objects or ceremonies.

A person of lower caste must use a posh high language— *basa madia,* the "Language of Courtesy"—when speaking to a member of a higher caste, al-

THE BALINESE LANGUAGE

A mixture of both Austronesian/Polynesian and Sanskrit vocabularies and phrases, Balinese is essentially a spoken language without as many fixed rules of grammar and syntax as Western languages. Until the 20th century, Balinese was written only in the Javanese script, although today it is related more directly to the languages of eastern Indonesia (Sumbawa and the Sasaks of Lombok) than it is to Javanese. Balinese has three speech levels: High Balinese is the polite form or court language, Middle Balinese is used when caste is not stressed but deference is still desired, and Low Balinese is the vernacular spoken by the common people. When Balinese first meet, they will initially talk in High Balinese, then during the conversation the speech level is adjusted to coincide with the rank and caste of the people talking. If he starts his conversation in Low Balinese and finds out later that the person being addressed is of a higher caste, it will cause a Balinese acute embarrassment. If a teacher wants to discipline a troublesome student who is the descendant of a prince, she must scold him in the High Language. A low-caste government official speaking to a high-caste friend selling dance tickets uses polite Balinese.

though today not many Sudra are conversant in this high Balinese. The lower caste individual should, in turn, be replied to in low Balinese *basa sor,* the rough everyday tongue spoken in the marketplace. If a conversation begins in low Balinese and one later finds that the person addressed is of higher caste, acute embarrassment can occur. This is why Balinese initiate a conversation in the highest form of Balinese when speaking to strangers whose caste they do not know. In time, a Balinese will ask "Where do you sit?" (i.e., "What is your caste?") so s/he can adjust to the level of speech appropriate to the rank of the person addressed.

Common Balinese *(basa lumrah)* is used when speaking to people of the same level, as well as friends and family. There is also a sacred Sanskrit vocabulary employed only by high Balinese priests in their rituals, mantras, and formulas, as well as other vocabularies used in anger, to insult someone, or when referring to animals.

BAHASA INDONESIA

Such is the diversity of tongues in Indonesia (200 indigenous speech forms, each with its own regional dialect) that often the inhabitants of the same island don't speak the same native language. On the tiny island of Alor there are some 70 dialects, on Sulawesi 62 languages have been identified, and Irian Jaya is home to an astounding 10% of the world's languages.

One language, Bahasa Indonesia, is taught in all schools to all students from age five; it's estimated about 70% of Indonesia's population is literate in Bahasa Indonesia. This language is the only cultural element unifying the entire ethnically splintered population.

First used as a political tool in 1927 with the cry "One Nation, One Country, One Language," it's the only language used in radio and TV broadcasting, in official and popular publications, in advertisements, and on traffic signs. Taught in Balinese schools, Indonesian is widely spoken by the educated, in government offices, and in communities with mixed ethnic groups. All films shown in Indonesia are required by law to be dubbed in standardized, modern Indonesian.

Most of the country's regional languages change forms and endings to show deference to the person addressed, but Bahasa Indonesia does not. Thus, Indonesian has been a powerful force for the democratization and unification of the myriad races and classes of Indonesia. Together with the decline of the caste system, Bahasa Indonesia language works to increasingly blur the formerly distinct levels of Balinese speech.

Characteristics of Bahasa Indonesia

Although Indonesian derives from Old Malay, a trader's language used throughout the archipelago since at least the 12th century, the proliferation of acronyms and infusion of foreign words makes Indonesian reading material barely comprehensible to Malaysians, though known for the economy of its vocabulary and for its simple, even child-like phrases. Bahasa Indonesia is actually an elaborate, subtle, and ambiguous speech form for expressing complex thought.

Initially, this nontonal language is sublimely easy to learn. It's written in the familiar Roman alphabet, words are pronounced the way they're spelled, the morphology is simple. Nouns and verbs lack cases, genders, declensions, confusing conjugations, not even the verb "to be." Perhaps the most difficult aspect of the language is its use of prefixes and affixes to turn roots into nouns and verbs.

Indonesian is a poetic language. *Matahari* means sun, or literally "eye of the day"; *rumput laut* means "sea hair" or seaweed; *merah muda,* for pink translates literally as "young red." It's also very picturesque—*bunga uang* means bank interest, from *bunga* for flower and *uang* for money; *seperti cari ketiak ular* (searching for the armpit of a snake) means looking for something that is nonexistent or impossible to find. Words you may have already run across include *amok* (blind terror), *sarong* (the Malay skirt), and *bambu* (bamboo).

Indonesian has a tremendous amount of dialectical variation, and each ethnic group speaks its own accented form. The Javanese speak it very slowly and monotonously, the Sundanese use a singsong manner, while the Irianese employ an archaic form taught by missionaries. All dialects are mutually intelligible.

TEN POINTERS FOR LEARNING BAHASA INDONESIA

1) First learn the number, time, and calendar systems, and how to spell your name in Indonesian. Mastering these will spare you frustration and save you money. Next, learn how to greet people. The formality of welcoming people is of paramount importance to Balinese. Also master the forms of polite speech, a social skill carrying much weight in Bali.

2) Avoid Balinese who try to speak to you in English. They are your most formidable obstacle to learning Indonesian. The fastest way to learn another language is never to speak your own.

3) Concentrate at first on just listening and speaking. It takes only a few weeks to learn the sound system properly. You must hear Indonesian spoken and speak it every chance you get. Listen and constantly repeat words and phrases, impressing them on your memory. Take the word *menandatangani*, a bit of a stumbler, meaning "to sign something." Have Indonesians teach you how to pronounce it. The more times you use it, the quicker you'll learn to pronounce it correctly and the quicker it will become a part of your vocabulary. Only after you've learned the pronunciation should you take on written language.

4) Don't worry about making grammatical errors or common mistakes. Self-consciousness is a big block to learning. You *have* to make mistakes to learn. Children are quite willing to be wrong and that's why they're able to learn a foreign language so quickly. They don't care if speech comes out grammatically correct. Speaking "perfect" Indonesian is of little concern to the Balinese, who will always give you the benefit of the doubt. And you still get points for trying!

5) Although at first you may not have a substantial vocabulary, try to use the words you *do* know skillfully. You'll be flabbergasted at what you can say with a vocabulary of only 200 or so words. It seems you can get along for weeks with just variations of *makan, tidur, mandi, terlambat, sebentar lagi, sekarang, belum,* and *sudah* (eat, sleep, wash, too late, in a little while, now, already, and not yet). Infinite combinations of sentences are possible! After one month of diligent work you'll be speaking the *pasar melayu* or market talk—all you'll need for bargaining, getting around, and meeting and relating to people.

6) After awhile you'll reach a point where you actually speak without having to stop and think. The plateau you want to reach is to ask questions in Indonesian and quickly integrate the answers. The most important phrases toward this end are "What is this called in Indonesian?" *("Apa namanya ini di Bahasa Indonesia?")* and "How do you say this in Indonesian?" *("Bagaimana anda menyebutnya?")*

7) *Warung,* bus stops, markets, kiosks, and offices are the best classrooms in the land. While waiting for a friend, a bus, a *wayang* show or movie to begin, or for a shop or restaurant to open, head toward any foodstall or group of bystanders and start up a conversation. Educated Indonesians in any gathering will make themselves known, and they delight in teaching you. You'll find them very patient, repeating and writing words out, teaching you sayings and idioms, and breaking sentences down for you. Indonesians are also very encouraging, crying *"Wah, pintar sekali!"* ("Wow, very smart!") the moment you utter just a few intelligible words. These daily, regular Indonesian lessons with the people are the equal of a US$1500 Berlitz Total Immersion Course.

8) For a reference book and vocabulary builder, all you really need is a good dictionary. Never go anywhere without it and never stop asking questions. Listen to the radio and TV, translate songs, labels, posters, signs, newspapers, tickets, and handouts.

9) Force yourself to speak in complete sentences. Don't be lazy and speak pidgin Indonesian! Start out with a proper opening and always include a subject, object, predicate. Speak whole phrases, not expletives or one or two word sentences. This will result in a more polished use of the language.

10) If you are determined to learn Balinese, use Bahasa Indonesia as your learning medium. Always ask for the Indonesian—not the English—when questioning a Balinese word.

LEARNING INDONESIAN

Learning Indonesian is the miracle drug that helps minimize culture shock, enabling you to settle into Bali more quickly. Using a phrasebook is alright, as long as you realize you're not really using the language. You're simply holding up verbal signs "Where is the toilet?" God forbid you get back an answer not in the phrasebook. In truth, the most important sentence in the phrasebook is "I don't speak the language." Then you can ask your questions. If you don't profess your ignorance, you're likely to receive an outpouring of verbiage impossible to comprehend. To really learn the language requires six months of intensive work.

On Bali many Balinese in regular contact with tourists obligingly speak an abbreviated, simplified, form of Indonesian, a sort of "Tourist Indonesian" involving much gesticulating and use of body language. Listeners sensitive to your very limited vocabulary and struggles to find the right word will begin to use the same words as you, accommodating you by adopting *your* method of expression.

Dictionaries

The best dictionary for the truly serious Indonesianist is the brilliantly compiled *An Indonesian-English Dictionary*. Covering modern Indonesian in its entirety, this dictionary has become the standard work used by English speakers since the first edition was published in 1961. The companion volume is the 660-page *An English-Indonesian Dictionary*. Both available from Cornell University Press, Ithaca, NY, tel. (607) 277-2338. Another useful dictionary is *Contemporary Indonesian Dictionary* by A. Ed. Schmidgall-Tellings and Alan M. Stevens, specifically listing words not provided in the E & S tomes. Softcover versions of all three dictionaries are available in Indonesia for around Rp50,000.

The best available pocket dictionary is *Selected Indonesian Vocabulary for the Foreign Executive* by Helen and Russel Johnson, which lists the root word in alphabetical order according to prefix. A pocket-size dictionary available in North America is *Van Goor's Concise Indonesian Dictionary, English-Indonesian and Indonesian-English* by A.L.N. Kramer Sr. Order from Charles E. Tuttle Co., Box 410, Rutland, VT 05701-0410, tel. (802) 773-8930; ask when the new edition is due.

Also beginning to appear in Indonesia are handheld pocket-sized electronic dictionaries; type in an Indonesian word and immediately the English translation of the word is displayed. It's got a Japanese brand name, Wiz, and it costs around Rp190,000.

Phrasebooks

If staying for a month or less, a good phrasebook will serve you well. Allegedly designed with the traveler in mind, the handy, bilingual (though it doesn't contain "truck") Periplus *Pocket Dictionary* has 2,000 Indonesian words most commonly used in asking directions, bargaining, simple conversation, and other everyday situations. Brief spelling and pronunciation guide included.

Everyday Indonesian: A Basic Introduction to the Indonesian Language & Culture by Thomas Oey contains relatively new written and spoken words and phrases divided into the usual phrasebook categories. Very helpful and widely available on Bali.

A very competent phrasebook available only in the U.S. is *Say It In Indonesian* by John Wolff. Order it from Dover Publications, 31 E. 2nd St., Mineola, NY 11501, tel. (516) 294-7000. Compiled by a professional linguist; very thorough. A slightly less expensive alternative is *Indonesia Phrasebook* by Lonely Planet Publications. Memorizing this little booklet will serve you well for a 30 days or less stay. Also try the Bahasa Indonesia section in the back of this guide.

Books and Magazines

Children's school readers, available in bookshops all over Bali for Rp1200-2500, are well suited for foreigners. The Indonesian is idiomatic and has everyday applications; they also contain valuable information about Indonesian culture and history. Some you can almost read by following the pictures.

A cheap, endlessly reprinted, and competent study book available in bookstores and tourist kiosks all over Bali is A.M. Almatsier's *How to Master the Indonesian Language*. Almatsier's *The Easy Way to Master the Indonesian Language* costs Rp8000, and is just as widely available. This book provides a step-by-step method of learning Indonesian, designed especially for the long-term resident. Chapters cover everyday situations frequently encountered—Basic Colloquial Expressions, To the Supermarket, Sports, and the like.

The Indonesian language courses at U.C. Berkeley use the classic *Beginning Indonesian Through Self Instruction* by John U. Wolff, Dede Oetomo, and Daniel Fietkeiwicz. *Indonesian: A Complete Course for Beginner* by J.B. Kwee is a difficult course but one that will provide you with a sound working knowledge of formal spoken and written Indonesian. *Bahasa Indonesia: Introduction to the Indonesian Language and Culture* by Yohanni Johns is a standard introductory text used in universities around the world. This excellent, in-depth, two-volume set is completely self-contained, providing clear explanations of basic grammar. Extensive notes on usage and etiquette.

The intelligently produced school reader *Pelangi* is an excellent resource to learn intermediate-level Indonesian. Order the magazine through USQ Press, Box 58, Darling Heights 4350, Toowoomba, tel. (076) 31-2852, fax 31-1758.

Indonesian Language Tapes and CDs

"Language/30 Indonesian" tapes provide an excellent introductory, self-taught language program which will put you in tune with the language in about six hours. Based on a U.S. Army speed learning method, this concise course stresses only conversationally useful words and phrases. Two cassettes of guided greetings, introductions, requests, and general conversation for use at hotels, restaurants, businesses, and entertainment venues, using only natives speaking flawless Indonesian. Contact Educational Services Corp., 1725 K St. NW, no. 408, Washington, D.C. 20006, tel. (202) 298-8424.

The standard tapes for audio Indonesian language training in the English-speaking world are "Indonesian Conversations" and "Beginning Indonesian Through Self-Instruction," an extensive set of 60-minute study tapes duplicated from professionally recorded masters. This expensive course (US$441 for the complete 83-tape set) is accompanied by text supplementing the oral training. To order, call Tape Sales, Rm Gll Noyes Lodge, Cornell University, Ithaca, NY 14853, tel. (607) 255-3827.

Based on their phrasebook, Lonely Planet's "Indonesian CD Audio Pack" records an Australian couple's travels from Australia to Indonesia. The approach is unique because the CD program takes you through a number of real life situations.

Language Programs

A program offering individual and group instruction is located on Bali at the **Centre for Foreign Languages (SUA Bali)** in Kemenuh, seven km from Ubud. Dra. I.A.A. Mas and other skilled instructors are fluent in German, English, and Dutch. The standard fee for a two-week intensive course, including accommodations, is US$650. Offering a variety of opportunities for foreign visitors to learn elementary or advanced Indonesian in a village setting, individual courses can also be designed for specific needs.

One of Bali's leading language learning schools is **IALF Bali Language Centre,** Jl. Kapten Agung 19, Denpasar, tel. (0361) 221782, 221785, or 225243, offering accelerated learning programs five evenings a week for four weeks. Call for an appointment for an individual placement test. The **Bali Language Training & Cultural Centre** in the Mastapa Garden Hotel, Jl. Legian 139, Kuta (tel. 0361-751660, fax 755098, or write P.O. Box 3013, Denpasar), presents regular 12-week or intensive four-week Indonesian language classes that cost US$515. Tea breaks with Balinese cakes, free cultural excursion, special menus for BLTC students, open-air classrooms. The school is located in one of the nicest family-run hotels in Bali, a Garden of Eden in the Fires of Hell.

BODY LANGUAGE

Such aggressive gestures and postures as crossing your arms over your chest or standing with your hands on your hips while talking, particularly in front of older people, are regarded as insulting. These are the traditional postures of defiance and anger in *wayang* theater.

Anger is not shown openly. Loud voices are particularly offensive. In their efforts to make themselves understood, many Westerners speak with exaggerated slowness, raise their voices, or wave their arms about. To Balinese all these gestures may convey anger. The more important and vehement the subject under discussion, the quieter a Balinese is likely to become.

The feet are considered the lowliest part of the body, and it's offensive to sit with the soles of your feet pointing at people. It's also impolite to use your toes or the tip of your shoe for pointing, as when indicating something displayed on the ground in the *pasar*.

To beckon someone with a crooked index finger is rude. If you need to call to someone—e.g., a passing taxi driver—extend your right hand and make a motion using the cupped fingers turned downward. Neither should you point with your forefinger; instead use your right thumb for pointing.

Since Asians consider the left hand unclean, never use it to touch someone or to give and receive things. If you should use your left hand, say *"Ma'af"* ("Excuse me"). When giving or receiving something from someone older, or in a high office or elevated status, extend your right arm (but not too far), bring your left arm across the front of your body, then touch your fingers to your right elbow. When passing in front of an elder or high-born person, or person of equal rank whom you don't know, bend your body slightly, particularly if that person is sitting. Avoid blowing your nose into a handkerchief (especially loudly). Make a point of asking a guest to eat or drink when food is served since he will wait until you verbally offer it by saying *"Silahkan"* ("Please"). Conversely, it's polite to wait until you are given permission before you eat or drink.

BOB RACE

RELIGION

Outside of India, Bali is the largest Hindu outpost in the world. Put in another way, it's the furthest reaches of the Hindu empire. On Bali, Hinduism has developed along lines all its own. In fact, the way in which the Balinese practice their frontier Hinduism is still their greatest art. Hinduism is at least 3,000 years old and dates from the creation of the Vedas, compilations of prayers, hymns, and other religious writings. Hinduism doesn't have a single founder or prophet. There is only one god, though its many different manifestations are named and classified in great detail.

The Balinese call their religion Agama Tirta ("Science of the Holy Water"), an interpretation of religious ideas from China, India, and Java. Agama Tirta is much closer to the earth and more animist than Hinduism proper; the two sects are as different from each other as Ethiopian Christianity is from Episcopalian Christianity. If a strict Hindu Brahman from Varanasi ever visited Bali, he'd think them savages. Although the Hindu epics are well known and form the basis of favorite Balinese dances, the deities worshipped in India are here considered too aloof and aristocratic. Often the Balinese don't even know their names. The Balinese have their own trinity of supreme gods, the Shrine of the Three Forces.

Because of the caste system, 200 million people are shunned in India. On Bali only the older people still believe in the caste system; the young ignore it. Though a bull served as the sacred mount of Shiva, Bali Hindus do not eschew beef; *bakwan* carts sell meatball noodle soup in the smallest villages, and there's a beef sausage plant in Denpasar. In India a Hindu must be cremated at once in order to enter into heaven; because of the expense, on Bali sometimes a whole village will temporarily bury its dead and later stage a mass cremation. In India widows must not remarry but on Bali they can—here, even high priests marry. In India, worship at home is all-important but on Bali group worship is preferred.

Bali Hindus are not obliged to study sacred texts, follow any set doctrine or scripture, practice celibacy or adhere to a puritan lifestyle. There are no prescribed prayers, no fixed moments of devotion. There are many paths to take that please God—singer, dancer, priest, *dalang*, carpenter, carver, actor. The worshipper need only perform daily offerings and participate actively in village and temple events. Since the high Brahmanic teachings are a mystery to most of the Balinese population, the emphasis has always been on frequent and visibly dramatic ceremonies and rituals rather than theology, on behavior and service rather than the fine points of belief.

On Bali there are two ways to pray: *mbakti* and *muspa*. The first is worship through devotion, the second shows respect with flowers. A Balinese with hands together at the hips is praying to Sanghyang Kala, Shiva, the Destroyer; with hands at chest level the prayer is to a dead family member; hands held in front of the forehead indicate prayer to Sanghyang Widhi, the Supreme God.

The Gods of Bali-Hinduism

All the many gods of Bali-Hinduism are merely realizations or manifestations of the holy rays from the one God, Sanghyang Widhi, the omnipotent supreme being. In this universal, all-embracing god, all deities and ancestral spirits achieve a higher unity. Sanghyang Widhi manifests himself to the Balinese in three main forms: Brahma the Creator, Vishnu the Preserver, and Shiva the Destroyer. This three-in-one embodiment is called the Trisakti, the Holy Trinity. The average Balinese does not utter prayers or make offerings directly to Sanghyang Widhi. Not one of the island's temples, altars, or shrines is dedicated to him. Instead, three-seated temple pedestals enshrine the Trisakti. Before a ceremony temple guardians will decorate the pedestal with bright wraps of colored cloth: red for Brahma, white for Shiva, black for Vishnu. These three powerfully symbolic colors predominate in all religious processions.

In the hierarchy of the divine, below Sanghyang Widhi and the Trisakti, are a multitude of manifestations named and classified in great detail. These protective spirits are closely related to nature. God in his power to create the wind is Dewa Bayu, to create rice he is Dewi Sri, to create the ocean Dewa Baruna. God's gender is indicated by Dewa (male) and Dewi (female).

Most Balinese concentrate their worship on Shiva, God's manifestation as destroyer, since it is he who is most often seen and felt by the people through suffering and sickness. The Balinese believe in taking care of the god first who can destroy you, not the god that creates or preserves you. Appeasing Shiva, as well as the local *dewa,* will bring prosperity, happiness, and liberation. Though Shiva is often manifested as Surya, the sun, the Balinese are not pagan sun-worshippers. Balinese religious scholars were livid when a full-page ad appeared in *Time* featuring a group of *kecak* dancers on the beach, with a cutline reading "Bali is still full of half-naked sun-worshippers."

Vishnu, connected with the creation of life, is particularly associated with the irrigation systems that nourish the rice fields and is the most important figure in the *kampung.* Saraswati is the goddess of learning and knowledge. Shiva's consort is Durga, goddess of death, and ruler of demons, ghosts, and witches. Each god or goddess also has a mount or vehicle for transport. Shiva rides the bull Nandi, while Vishnu flies upon Garuda, a mythical bird.

The Official Religion

With Rabindranath Tagore's visit to the island in 1927, Balinese theologians restored contacts with India and began to align their brand of Hinduism more with Hinduism proper. Monotheism has been particularly emphasized since independence, and following the 1966-67 anti-communist bloodbath Bali-Hinduism was recognized by the government as one of Indonesia's state religions. A modern Hindu organization, the Parisada Hindu Dharma Indonesia (PHDI), or Hindu Council of Religious Affairs, is Bali's highest religious body, officially sanctioned by the government to decide all spiritual matters. Similar to its Islamic counterpart Majelis Uleme Indonesia, the PHDI is more or less a rubber stamp for government policy, reflected by the large number of military figures and civil servants holding leadership posits in the organization.

Through the PHDI, however, Bali-Hinduism has achieved legal, international status. Since Bali is virtually surrounded by Muslims, some of whom are determined to turn Indonesia into an Iran-style theocratic state, the Balinese regard the government's official sanction of their religion as a means of preserving their identity and way of life. The Balinese have further legitimized their religion by aligning it with the discoveries of modern science and by formulating their own independent canon, *panca cradha.*

Other Religions

Foreign religions have not had an easy time of it on Bali—Bali-Hindus have strongly resisted new faiths. Muslim communities established a toe-hold during the Majapahit era; Gelgel Mosque, just south of Klungkung, is the most ancient on Bali, built by Muslim immigrants who served the Dewa Agung during Bali's Golden Age. Other prominent Muslim communities include Kusamba and Sarenjawa in Karangasem, Lovina in Buleleng.

Approximately 1,000 Buddhists live in the north, in the mountains to the east, and among the Chinese populations of the urban centers. Their most important temple is the Brahma Vihara Asrama in Banjar, Buleleng. Western visitors have popularized the practice of metaphysics, mostly New Agers from California. Since the 1930s Ubud has been a center for paranormal practices.

There are about 7,000 Christians on the island; the Dutch finally allowed Christian missionaries on Bali in the 1930s at the behest of the Chinese. Early Christian communities emulated Dutch Reform-style architecture and customs, but under the leadership of I.W. Mastra, the Church of Bali is now incorporating the island's rich traditions of dance, drama, and music. The new Christian churches of Bali look more like Balinese temples than Dutch churches, except that they're guarded by angels, not demons. Bibical stories are dramatized through Balinese-style dance and music, and *gamelan* orchestras celebrate church festivals. "The Mango Tree Church" relates the dramatic story of the development of the Protestant church on Bali.

Balinese Animism

Bali Hinduism is only a veneer over complex, deeper-lying, indigenous superstitions. Before a Balinese picks a leaf or flower or chops down a tree, s/he first asks permission of the spirit *(tonya)* within. The Balinese even respect such inanimate objects as books, stones, large trees, and motorcycles. Just as the Balinese treat themselves to a bath in the streams late in the afternoons, revered objects too are accorded frequent bathings and renewals.

The Balinese are scared witless of ghosts, goblins, and the like, which disguise themselves as black cats, naked women, and crows. A Balinese can tell when a domestic animal is possessed—a cow that darts away, startled; a chicken that pecks in a peculiar manner. Many Balinese can point to several people in the village who practice black magic, but would never name them for fear of incurring their wrath.

The Balinese believe souls sometimes wander from people's bodies while they sleep. This is why a Balinese will never wake up someone sharply or suddenly, fearing the soul would not be given time to return to the body. One must always wake someone gently, even in a crisis. It's also believed the soul may enter the body of an animal during the night; this is why a chicken is never slaughtered after sundown.

BUTA

While offerings for the gods—money, flowers, rice, fruits, parts of pigs—are like presents given to human beings, gifts given to *buta* are smelly, moldy, or decayed plants and food thrown contemptuously on the ground. Entrances to temples and *kampung* are constructed in such a way—with mazes, narrow lanes, dead ends, high mud walls, sliding gates, barricades, etc.—so as to confuse and bewilder evil spirts. Besides the delightful fellow at left, the "reverse" *buta* stands on its head, loiters around trees, forests, and swimming holes, and is a favorite guardian at temple gates. Other *buta* come in the form of a dirty little dwarf *(togtogsil)* with a large pointed tooth. Yet another consists of an arm or a leg with a hideous face. One popular ploy is to summon demons and spirits to a feast, then expel them with magic formulas.

One hears of lingering, mysterious illnesses from unidentified poisons, of a husband who meets an untimely death at the hands of a jealous mistress. These incidents are often attributed to malicious spirits called *kala* and *buta,* who have no other purpose than to cause misery and havoc amongst humans. They enter people's bodies, making them ill, insane, or imbecilic. Like vampires, these spirits relish sucking the blood from sleeping victims, and have been known to abduct children for a tasty snack.

Even more dangerous and unpredictable are *leyak,* the witches. The Balinese believe a witch must endure 1,000 years as an earthworm and 200,000 years as a poisonous mushroom before rebirth as a human. At least the true demons, like Rangda and *barong,* are predictable and belong to the natural order of the cosmos. Not so the dreaded *leyak.* These evil beings, who manifest themselves in the form of a monkey with golden teeth, a great rat, a baldheaded giant, a bird as large as a horse, a ball of fire, a riderless motorcycle, haunt such desolate places as dark back roads, deep forests, ravines, seashores, crossroads, and cemeteries. When the dogs begin to whine on moonless nights, the Balinese know the *leyak* are about. When these bloodthirsty creatures are not appeased with offerings, they can run rampant through the village, causing epidemics and famine. With their fire-dripping tongues, they suck the blood of unborn babies. Only the most elaborate purification ceremonies *(mecaru)* and blood sacrifices can expunge them. On these occasions a visit to Pura Dalem Penataran Ped on Nusa Penida's northeast coast is in order. This temple was built to honor Ratu Gede Mecaling, the patron saint of all *leyak.*

Spirits dominate everything the Balinese do, and they are constantly offering fruit and flowers to appease angry deities. If put in our society, a Balinese would show all the classic symptoms of paranoia and neurotic disorders, but on Bali these traits are ritualized and institutionalized. There are sun gods, totemic gods, deer gods, secretaries to the gods, mythical turtles, market deities. Clay figures of the fire god are put over kitchen hearths, bank clerks place pandanus-leaf offering trays on their desks. Before a journey offerings are made to guarantee a safe passage. Once a year coconut trees are honored by dressing them in bright skirts and scarves. Old banyan trees are venerated by the placement of offerings in altars among their aerial roots. *Ngedjot* are placed in the courtyards of every house; these offerings consist of little squares of banana leaves holding a few grains of rice, a flower, salt, and a pinch of chili pepper. No one eats until *ngedjot* are placed at the cardinal points in the family courtyard and in front of each house. Though mangy dogs eat the offerings as soon as they touch the ground, their essence has already been consumed by the spirits. Every morning this quiet drama is carried out all over Bali, from inexpensive *losmen* courtyards to the lobbies of Nusa Dua's grandest and most lavish hotels. Even the most Westernized youth, wearing a World Beat T-shirt, head engulfed in a Sony Walkman, will still take time out every morning and evening to place offerings of flowers and rice before the shrines of his ancestors.

Types of Offerings

Fire, water, and flowers are the basic components of all offerings; additional items are given according to one's profession and wealth, and the season in which they're made. No matter what the offering, it must be of the finest ingredients and ritually cleansed before being placed. The variety is mind-boggling, in countless designs and styles. Some offerings may even be as simple as a few grains of rice placed on a banana leaf. Once you know what to look for, you begin to see offerings everywhere—in rice fields, yards, trees, temples. Three-meter-long palm-leaf panels and scrolls, a captivating *cili* figure with fan-shaped headdress and long, graceful arms. Spectacular, colorful *gebogan* or *banten tegeh* are enormous towers of up to three meters, embellished with glass, paintings, roast ducks or chickens, suckling pigs, pig entrails, garlands of white *cempaka,* and fragrant yellow *jepun* blossoms. They're carried on the heads of women to the temple, blessed by the *pemangku* and sprinkled with holy water.

Gods and goddesses, who protect or threaten every act performed by a person during his or her lifetime, inhabit stone thrones and statues or simply hover in the air. Gods are often invited down to visit earth and are gorged with offerings and entertained with music and dance, but eventually they must go back home because they're too expensive to maintain. The Balinese always try to stay on the good side of all the forces. If the spirits are kept happy, the people can relax and even grow lighthearted. Children carry flowers to shrines and learn to dance at an early age to please the gods and the raja.

Feasts mark special periods in an infant's first year: three days after birth, 42 days after the first bath, 105 days after birth, and 210 days after birth—the first birthday celebration. At each stage of the agricultural cycle ceremonies are held, offerings made, and holy texts chanted. Even cockfighting was originally a temple ritual—blood spilled for the gods. During the 1965 political butchering in which 50,000 Balinese were killed, victims dressed in spotless white ceremonial attire before being led away to execution. Devils were believed to live in the communists or their sympathizers, and their deaths were necessary to cleanse the island of evil. Heaven? The Balinese believe heaven will be exactly like Bali.

PRIESTS AND PRIESTHOOD

There are two kinds of priests on Bali, the *pedanda,* or high priest, and the *pemangku,* or temple priest. Only a Brahman can become a *pedanda; pemangku* are recruited from the lower castes. There are about 20 times more *pemangku* than *pedanda.* Priests don't hold political office and their economic power is limited, yet they're the most respected members of Balinese society, their place the highest a mortal can achieve.

Balinese priests don't stand between a worshipper and god; he's there to make sure a person's prayers are properly directed so the desired results may be achieved. Before a family moves into a new house or opens a *losmen,* a priest is asked to give god's blessing. Priests purify people after an accident or illness, avert curses, and bring people out of spells and trances.

Pedanda all claim lineage from Wau Rauh himself, the highest priest of the Majapahit Empire. A *pedanda* is usually an old man, quiet, gentle, thin, clad in white with a white turban. He is cared for by his sons, his spiritual practice "subsidized." It's bad manners to ask a proud *pedanda* how much a ceremony will cost; the answer will most likely be, "no, I'm busy."

Pedanda outrank every other caste and are considered the most scholarly members of Balinese society. Belonging more to families than to temples, consecrated *pedanda* are called into service by higher-caste households to bless such ceremonies as marriages, births, and cremations, as well as for such informal celebrations as the building of a new dike or bridge. They exercise a virtual monopoly on liturgical knowledge, and with their intimate familiarity with the Balinese calendar are always consulted to determine a lucky date on which to begin any important undertaking. *Pedanda* enter into a trance state to become an empty medium through which the gods can talk to the people.

Every temple has its own *pemangku,* a lay priest who maintains the temple and officiates at everyday rituals. *Pemangku* remain in direct contact with the ancestors and can exorcise devils. Even the most indigent Balinese will make a great effort to hire the services of a *pemangku,* especially when it comes to making sure dead loved ones are properly ushered into the spiritual world.

The proud *pedanda* look down upon *pemangku,* disdainfully calling them "sweepers" (*jero sapuh*) in reference to their lowly task of sweeping temple courtyards. *Pemangku* are simple, good-natured souls who live near the temple, leading normal lives except when a temple celebration makes them the center of attention.

Pemangku are not paid any compulsory amount. Before a ceremony takes place, the family gives an offering of money to the *pemangku's* shrine of spiritual power *(taksu).* This offering *(sesari)* is generally Rp500-1000. The *pemangku* doesn't make a living as a priest, but works as a farmer or merchant.

Pemangku should not be confused with the *balian,* a witch doctor or healer, nor with bell ringers or scribe writers. A third kind of technical specialist, the *sungguhu,* is a low-caste priest whose duties are limited to propitiation of the malignant *buta* and *kala.*

Festivals

There's an unending chain of festivals, over 60 religious holidays a year. The basic tenet of the Balinese religion is the belief the island is owned by the supreme god Sanghyang Widhi and has been handed down to the people in sacred trust. Thus the Balinese seem to devote most of their waking hours to an endless series of physically and financially exhausting offerings, purifications, temple festivities, processions, dances, and cremations. Festivals are dedicated to woodcarving, the birth of a goddess, and percussion instruments; there are temple festivals, fasting and retreat ceremonies, parades to the sea, and celebrations of wealth and learning.

Get ahold of a Balinese calendar; besides offering faithful pictorial representations of simple, realistic folk scenes, they show the most propitious days for religious activities. Try to catch one of the full moon ceremonies, a traditional affair that can last for some days. Lots of praying, singing, and dancing—a wonderful opportunity to interact with the people in their own environment on a special occasion. Your hotel owner will tell you what to wear or perhaps even dress you in traditional attire. Incidentally, ceremonies concerning people take place in homes rather than temples. The temples are only used for ceremonies to gods.

TEMPLES

The temple is the most important institution on Bali and the center of religious activities. Though Bali is renowned as the "Land of Ten Thousand Temples," there are actually at least 50,000 scattered over the island. Large or small, simple or elaborately carved, they're everywhere—in houses, courtyards, marketplaces, cemeteries, and rice paddies; on beaches, barren rocks offshore, deserted hilltops, and mountain heights; deep inside caves; within the tangled roots of banyan trees. At most intersections and other dangerous places temples are erected to prevent mishaps. Even in the middle of jungle crossroads, incense burns at small shrines brightened with flowers, wrapped leaves, and gaily colored cloth.

Each village has its own shrines for community worship, and public temples may be used by anyone to pray to Sanghyang Widhi or any of his manifestations. There are mountain temples (pura bukit), sea temples (pura segara), genealogical temples, temples for the deities of markets and seeds (pura melanting), lake tem-

ples, cave temples, hospital temples, bathing temples, temples dedicated to spirits in springs, lakes, trees, and rocks. There are also private temples for those of noble descent, royal "state" temples, and temples for clans (pura dadia) who share a common geneology. Some temples commemorate the deeds of royalty. Numerous important temples—Gunung Kawi, Pura Penulisan—are actually memorial shrines to ancient rulers and their families.

Balinese temples are not dedicated to a specific god but to a collection of spirits, both good and bad, who reside in the various shrines. No one knows which spirits are visiting which shrines, so to make sure that only their beneficent aspects appear offerings are placed in all shrines.

Unlike the austere, restricted temples of other countries in Asia, the Balinese temple is open and friendly, with children, tourists, and even dogs wandering in and out. During festivals the temple grounds serve as a stage where the worshippers become actors, the priests directors, and the gods and demons invisible but critical spectators.

Once every six months in the Balinese calendar, each temple holds an odalan or anniversary celebration. Since there are tens of thousands of temples on the island, an odalan is in progress almost every day somewhere. On the occasion ancestral personages descend from heaven and the temples are alive with fervent activity. For the really big religious ceremonies and rites, temple pavilions are sometimes completely wrapped in cloths and umbel-umbel banners, studded with ceremonial umbrellas. Foods are placed on altars under the eyes of the stone deities, the gods occupying small gold, bronze, or gilded wood figurines (pratima). During festivals the temple courtyard is literally covered in gifts to the gods, with seething throngs of people beneath high tapering white and saffron-colored flags, the air thick with smoke and the clanging of gamelan. Everyone arrives beautifully dressed, presenting the deities with prayer, devotions, food, music, and cockfights to amuse them during their visit to Earth. Temple dances like the pendet and rejang welcome and delight the visiting spirits. After one to three days, thoroughly entertained and surfeited with food, the deities return to heaven.

Temple Etiquette

Anyone who's properly dressed may visit a temple. If you're wearing long pants or a long skirt, a sash will usually be required; if you're wearing shorts, you'll need a *sarong*. Tour guides provide these items, as do ticket-sellers at many of the most-visited temples. Best is to buy your own in the local market for around Rp5000. Sashes should also be worn for any temple festival you may happen upon.

All temple complexes and historical sities now charge Rp550 admission. If there's no entrance fee, you may be asked for a small contribution to help offset the cost of maintenance. It's also common to sign a guestbook. At some of the more obscure sites beware of guestbooks in which zeros have been added to all the preceding figures, making it appear donations have been substantial.

Use your camera with discretion. Don't climb onto temple buildings or walls, or stand or sit higher than a priest. If people are praying, avoid getting between them and the direction in which they're praying. Stealing is unthinkable. In 1993, 14 people were murdered on the spot after they were caught stealing from temples in the Ubud area. Non-Hindus may not enter the innermost courtyards *(jeroan)* of some temples. Tour companies are now starting to drop Brahman temples from tours at the request of temple keepers. By ancient law menstruating women are banned from temples, due to a general sanction against blood on holy soil.

Temple Types

Bali is a floating shrine, where all the homes are temples and all the temples homes. Thousands of private domestic temples—*sanggah,* or *pamerajan* for the upper castes—are dedicated to various deities and family ancestors. Each small domestic altar is very well maintained and receives fresh offerings each morning. Every house has a small shrine *(sanggah paon)* by the hearth dedicated to Bhatara Brahma, the god of fire, and yet another by the well dedicated to the god of water, Bhatara Vishnu. Temporary shrines *(sanggah crucuk)* are constructed for special purposes, such as a death in the family or before work commences on a project.

Every Balinese village features at least three obligatory temples—in the north, center, and south of town. The *pura puseh* is the "navel" temple, or temple of origin, around which the original community sprang. This temple is dedicated to the spirits of the land, to the deified village founder, and to Vishnu, the Preserver of Life. The *pura desa,* or "village temple" is concerned with everyday village matters and ritually prescribed village gatherings. Dedicated to Brahma, the creator, the *pura desa* is also an assembly hall where men meet for communal, ceremonial meals. Also called the *pura balai agung,* it's oriented to the mountains and to the east. The temple of the dead, *pura dalem,* is dedicated to Shiva the Destroyer or his consort Durga. It is also connected with ancestors. As most villages are built on a slope, the southern or *kelod* end in the lowest part of the village is where the temple of the dead and the burial ground with its mournful *kepuh* tree are located. Each faces the sea, where the powers of the netherworld dwell. The *pura dalem*'s carved walls are often decorated with explicit pornography and gruesome depictions of the fate awaiting offenders who violate taboos or fail to observe customs. Before the deceased have been completely purified by cremation, their souls rest in the death temple. The *pura dalem* is also where the sacred *barong* mask is stored. In some villages a single temple functions as both *pura puseh* and *pura desa,* with only a wall dividing them.

Agricultural temples are also important. All over Bali are *pura* dedicated to the rice goddess, Dewi Sri, divine consort of Dewa Vishnu, the Preserver. In northern Bali, where *subak* control every facet of life, the elaborate temples dedicated to Dewi Sri—called here Pura Hulun Swi—are the grandest religious edifices on the island.

Pura Ulun Danu Bratan in Candikuning and Pura Luhur on Gunung Batukau are dedicated to lake goddesses worshipped as sources of fertility. These are deemed female temples; their male counterpart is Pura Besakih on the slopes of Gunung Agung. Also widespread are the *subak* temples belonging to local irrigation societies.

Known as the "Six Great Sanctuaries," *Sadkahyangan* temples are the holiest places of worship on Bali. Owned by the whole island rather than by individual villages or clans, they're also

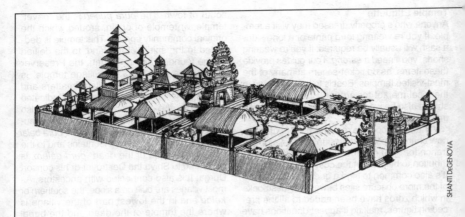

SHANTI DeGENOVA

TYPICAL BALINESE TEMPLE

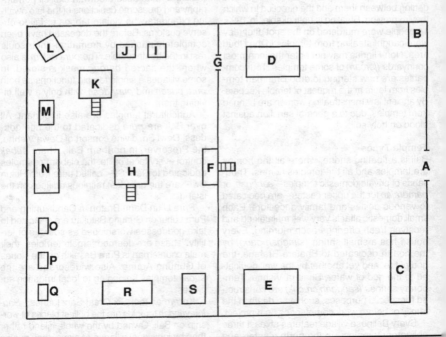

Jaba means "outside." This is the first courtyard of a Balinese temple. One enters it through the split gate (A) or *candi bentar*. It serves as an antechamber for social gatherings and ritual preparations. Contains thatched-roofed storage sheds, bale for food preparation, etc.

Jeroan means "inside." The inner courtyard of a Balinese temple, the temple proper. Here are all the shrines, altars, and *meru* towers that serve as temporary places for the gods during their visits to Bali. This enclosure, behind the closed gate *(paduraksa)*, is the "holy of the holiest."

A) *candi bentar*—The split gate, two halves of a solid, elaborately carved tower cut clean through the middle, each half separated to allow entrance into the temple. Its form is probably derived from the ancient *candi* of Java.

B) *kulkul*—a tall alarm tower with a wooden split drum, to announce happenings in the temple or to warn of danger

C) *paon*—the kitchen, where offerings are prepared

D) *bale gong*—a shed or pavilion where the gamelan is kept

E) *bale*—for pilgrims and worshippers

F) *paduraksa:* A second, closed ceremonial gateway, guarded by *raksasa*, leading to the inner courtyard *(jeroan)*. This massive monumental gate is similar in design to the *candi bentar* but is raised high off the ground on a stone platform with a narrow entrance reached by a flight of steps. Often behind the door is a stone wall which is meant to block demons from entering the *jeroan* This gate is only opened when there's a ceremony in progress.

G) side gate—always open to allow entrance to the *jeroan*

H) *paruman* (or *pepelik*)—a pavilion in the middle of the *jeroan* which serves as a communal seat for the gods

I & J) shrines for Ngrurah Alit and Ngrurah Gede, secretaries to the gods, who make sure that the proper offerings are made to the gods

K) *gedong pesimpangan*—a masonry building with (usually) locked wooden doors dedicated to the local deity, the ancestor founder of the village

L) *padmasana*—the stone throne for the sun-god Surya, almost always located in the uppermost right hand corner of the temple, its back facing the holy mountain Gunung Agung. Sometimes there's a shrine for Shiva, Vishnu, and Brahma here as well.

M) *meru*—a three-roofed shrine for Gunung Agung, the holiest and highest mountain of Bali

N) *meru*—an 11-roofed shrine dedicated to Sanghyang Widhi, the highest Balinese deity

O) *meru*—a one-roofed shrine dedicated to Gunung Batur, a sacred mountain in northern Bangli Regency

P) Maospait Shrine—dedicated to the divine settlers of Bali from the Majapahit Empire. The symbol of these totemic gods is the deer, so this shrine can be recognized by the sculpture of a deer's head or stylized antlers.

Q) *taksu*—The seat for the interpreter of the deities. The *taksu* inhabits the bodies of mediums and speaks through them to announce the wishes of the gods to the people. Sometimes the medium is an entranced dancer.

R & S) *bale piasan*—simple sheds for offerings

known as "State Temples," or by the even more pretentious designation "World Sanctuaries."

Visitors are sometimes confused to hear of as many as 12 sites listed among the "Six Great Sanctuaries," a result of regional favoritism. Most important is Besakih, the great mother temple complex on the slopes of mighty Gunung Agung. This volcano, the "Navel of the World," is Bali's holiest mountain, where all the gods and goddesses live. Others among the six include Pura Panataran Sasih in Pejeng, Pura Dasar in Gelgel, Pura Panataran Goa Lawa in Klungkung, and Pura Kehen in Bangli.

Also included—depending on who's counting—are the magnificent Uluwatu sea temple on the Bukit Peninsula, built on a long narrow cliff 76 meters above the sea; Pura Tirta Empul in Tampaksiring, famous for its sacred pool; Pura Sakenan on the island of Serangan; Yeh Jeruk in Gianyar; and Pura Batukau near the top of Gunung Batukau in Tabanan.

Temple Layout

Balinese temples are derived from the Neolithic sanctuaries of prehistoric Bali. Like the primitive stone enclosures and platforms of ancient Polynesia and Micronesia, the aboriginal prototype of the Balinese temple was a rectangle of holy ground containing sacrificial altars and crude heaps of stones. Ancient Balinese temples evincing this strong Polynesian feeling are found either in the mountains or along the coast.

Some mountain villagers still practice ceremonies echoing back to prehistory, when through shamanistic rites the spirits of fearsome nature gods would visit the megaliths. The shrines in courtyards of contemporary temples can be traced back to these rough stone pyramids. In many cases, craftsmen have added new stonework, cement altars, and fresh decorations, often hiding the original work. The terraced layout of such temples as Pura Kehen and Pura Besakih also suggest very early origins.

The Bali Aga still build distinct temples with such odd features as little bridges and separate halls for priests and other groups. See the great temples of Trunyan on Lake Batur and Taro in the mountains behind Gianyar.

Though a "typical" Balinese temple does not exist, the innumerable temples of Bali generally share a number of characteristics. In contrast to China, India, or Hinduized Java, where the temple is a roofed hall with a statue of a god as its focus of religious worship, on Bali space is emphasized over mass. A requirement for any consecrated place on Bali is that it be an open area enclosed by walls; the interior space is holy ground, as sacred as the shrines within; the temple is open to the sky, to make the shrines more accessible to the gods. A replica of a lake or mountain may be placed in a temple to save devotees the time and effort of visiting the actual sacred site.

The Balinese temple consists of two or three walled-in courtyards. *Jabaan,* the outermost yard, is used for offerings, dances of a secular or commercial nature, and by musicians. *Jaba tengah,* the middle yard is dedicated to food preparation, the making of offerings, and classical dances. *Jeroan,* the innermost yard is the locus of worship, ceremonies, and sacred dances. Elaborate stone gates lead from one courtyard to the next. All courtyards are oriented in the *kaja* direction, toward the sacred mountains, and worshippers always face *kaja* when they pray.

Temples are also divided into vertical layers of spirituality—the higher the tower, the more sacred the shrine. A distinctive Balinese structure is the pagoda-like *meru,* with as many as 11 (always an odd number) superimposed black thatch roofs. The top roof is the perch for the particular god when s/he descends. Most "seats" for deities are located at the end of the temple nearest the mountains. The last courtyard is the most sacred; to enter this inner sanctum, worshippers often must pass through an enormous gate under the threatening gaze of the fanged guardian demon Boma. In the belief that evil spirits cannot turn corners, numerous temples feature a solid brick wall just behind the entrance.

One of the most familiar Balinese architectural features is the remarkable split gateway *(candi bentar),* a tall monument cut exactly down the middle, its walls rising to an ornamental peak, always facing the sea. The large gap symbolically separates the two halves of the Indic cosmic mountain, Mahameru. An instantly recognizable emblem of Bali, this sacred structure often serves inappropriately as an entrance gate to hotels, palaces, and government offices.

Northern Bali's temples embody yet another design, which departs dramatically from those of the temples of the south. Here, richly carved stone monuments are often built on the slope of a hill, accessible by long flights of steps. Pura Meduwe Karang in Kubutambahan and Pura Beji in Sangsit are two outstanding examples of this style. These architectural extravaganzas contain many humorous relief panels in which European technology and burlesque caricatures coexist together in the spirited world of Balinese mythology.

Temple Construction

No special class of architects constructs temples. The master sculptor who designs and directs the work takes part in the backbreaking toil, assisted by a number of stone and brick masons. He sometimes works from a blueprint, but more often the temple is begun without a drawn plan. Possessing skills passed down through generations, the master builder claims to know the traditional proportions and specifications of a temple "in his belly." In traditional temple construction all units of measurement are based upon the sculptor's own body. This unscientific yet flawless technique assures that no two temples share the same dimensions.

The aesthetics of a temple are judged by its symmetry and harmony with its surroundings. Blocks of stone and baked bricks are joined without mortar and must fit together perfectly to give the structure strength. Stone surfaces are worn by rubbing them together while sluicing them with water. After the mass of stones and red brick are fitted, work begins on the extravagantly sculpted decorative motifs and reliefs.

Balinese temples are constantly being cleaned, rebuilt, and restored. Because the gray sandstone in the temples of southern Bali wears out, every temple must be completely renewed at least once every 50 years. In 1993, a small community of 250 people near the village of Mas raised 12 million rupiah to rehabilitate their banjar temple. With the growing use of ferro-concrete form construction, traditional temple building is becoming a lost art.

CREMATION

A cremation is a superb study of all the most important symbols of Balinese ceremonial life, what anthropologist James Boon calls "a vast

historical and ethnographic musing on the inevitability of death." The Balinese believe a person's sojourn on earth is but a short interlude in the long evolutionary process of the soul. Death occurs when the soul escapes from the body, but out of habit it continues to hover around the corpse. The soul cannot be freed as long as there is a body; only when the corporeal container is destroyed by the elements can the soul be liberated from all worldly ties.

Because the Balinese perceive death not as an end but as a new beginning, a cremation is a time of joyous celebration, the greatest day in a person's life. The ngaben ritual is the last and most important rite a family can perform for a loved one. Failure to free the soul by neglecting a cremation, or by incomplete or improper rites, renders the soul into a ghost who will wreak havoc on its neglectful descendants.

For hundreds of years, cremation was a privilege of the noble classes, but today it is estimated 10-30% of all Hindu Balinese cremate their dead. Except for the disappearance of suttee, the practice of widows immolating themselves on the funeral pyres of their husbands (the last occured in 1903), Balinese ngaben rites haven't changed significantly in well over 300 years. However, the quality and elaborate nature of ceremonies performed today are more determined by the underwriting of overseas film units than by the fees paid to high priests. A priest's main job is to consecrate the deceased and his effigy with holy water, cleanse the body before cremation, and write letters of introduction (ratnyadana) to open the doors of heaven for the soul. Only high Brahman priests may officiate at cremations of the high-born, and only the poor would hire a lesser-ranking pemangku.

Pre-Burial and Preparation

The signal of death in a house is a coconut-oil lamp hung from a long bamboo pole high over the roof. During the period before cremation, the soul of the deceased is thought to be agitated, longing for release, and the lamp enables the wandering spirit to find its way home in the dark.

On the first auspicious day after death, the body is prepared for purification and pre-burial. If the cremation is to take place quickly and the body to remain in the house, it may be mummified. If necessary, the teeth are filed. While prayers and mantras are recited, the corpse is rubbed with a mixture of sandalwood powder, salt, turmeric, rice-flour, and vinegar. The hands are bound and folded over on the breast in the gesture of prayer. Mirror-glass is placed on the eyelids, slivers of steel on the teeth, a gold ring in the mouth, jasmine flowers in the nostrils, and iron nails on the limbs, all to ensure a more perfect rebirth with "eyes as bright as mirrors, teeth like steel, breath as fragrant as flowers, and bones of iron." An egg is rolled over the body, and the corpse then wrapped in many meters of white cloth.

If the cremation will be postponed and it's decided the cadaver will be buried and not mummified, the corpse is carried to the graveyard accompanied by chanting relatives bearing offerings. The body is then buried, often simply wrapped in cloth and placed directly on the earth. Open mourning is forbidden; a weeping child is sent out of the cemetery. The body will lie buried until it is burned. A small bamboo altar is erected next to the grave and offerings brought to it daily for 12 days. Forty-two days after death more offerings are placed, at which time it's believed the soul has fled the body.

The expense of a cremation ceremony can be staggering. With hundreds of callers to feed, entertain, and keep supplied with cigarettes for as long as a week, a special *gamelan* ensemble required, and priest's and assistant's fees, an elaborate mass cremation can easily cost eight to 12 million rupiah. It takes RP2 million alone to take down power lines so that cremation towers can pass underneath. But for this spectacular send-off—the life goal of every Balinese—a family is prepared to make sacrifices. One of the kings of southern Bali killed in the mass suicide in Denpasar in 1906 wasn't officially cremated until 28 years after his death. Only then was the family at last able to accumulate enough wealth to give him a proper departure befitting his high rank. Among people of the lower castes, the extravagant cost has produced a tendency to forget to open the grave of long-dead relatives and perform the overdue cremation. Apparently, the risk of the deceased soul haunting the living, requiring constant appeasement with offerings, just doesn't frighten the survivors the way it used to.

The Procession

Days before the cremation, relatives "reawaken" the deceased by opening the grave. The remains are cleaned and wrapped in a white sacral cloth and taken to the cremation grounds to await the arrival of the coffin containing the effigy, which takes the place of the actual bones. Bones buried in unclean ground may never enter the family compound. On the morning of the cremation, relatives and friends visit the house to pay their respects.

When all the guests have partaken of a lavish banquet, the village *kulkul* is sounded to begin the final march to the cremation grounds. Incited by the climactic rhythms of the *gamelan*, members of the dead man's *banjar* rush into the home and lift the corpse from its stretcher and hoist it, by way of an elaborate decorated stairway *(raren),* onto a soaring decorated wood and bamboo tower *(bade)* supported on a bamboo substructure. The tall *bade* is a fantastic Christmas tree-like creation beautifully decorated with tinsel, paper ornaments, flowers, glittering mirrors, and expensive fabrics. Since height is considered holy, the higher the tower, the higher the rank of the deceased. Towers for wealthy Ksatriya may attain heights of 20 or more meters, though the pervasive power lines of the island mean the really tall towers of the past are seldom seen today.

For the more elaborate funeral, such as one for a prince, as many as three shifts of 100 men may be required to carry the heavily decorated funeral tower in a tumultuous, seething parade for two or three kilometers to the burning site. A venerable high priest may ride in a sedan chair at the top of the tower, accompanying the mummy; there may even be space provided in front for a small *angklung* orchestra.

The villagers line up, each with something to carry: holy water, ritual accessories, pyramids of food offerings piled high on their heads. A single, smoothly flowing line of colorfully dressed women leads the parade, carrying a long white cloth attached to the coffin; this "towrope" symbolizes their assistance in transporting the coffin. Men follow, carrying roasted quail and rabbits on sticks The procession moves boisterously amid clouds of dust and fireworks, in an uproar of music, yelling, and hooting, handfuls of old Chinese coins scattered at the participants' feet.

It's important the parade be bustling, crowded, and noisy—this shows the funeral has achieved large-scale public recognition. Chaos reigns especially around the tower, as relatives struggle to carry the body, each striving to prove loyalty to the deceased. The tower is spun on top of the bearers' shoulders to confuse the soul and prevent it from finding its way back to its house, where it might make mischief for the living. Since evil spirits may be following, seeking to pilfer the soul, the procession might cross a stream, because spirits hate to get their feet wet, or zigzag down the main street, to confuse the corner-impaired creatures. Finally, the near-stampede streams onto the cremation grounds.

The Burning

The cremation grounds are usually located near the temple of the dead in the cemetery just outside the village. In the center of the grounds stands an animal-shaped sarcophagus, the appropriate figure determined by the caste of the deceased: a bull for a Brahman male, a cow for a Brahman woman, a winged lion for the Ksatriya class, a mythological half-elephant, half-fish (gadjamina) for a lower-class Sudra. Once hewn of tree trunks, these coffins are now constructed of bamboo and plaster. Access is gained through a lid in the back. The entire coffin is draped with velvet or other expensive cloth and decorated with goldleaf, silk scarves, and cotton wool. Sometimes the Balinese rig the bull-shaped sarcophagus so its sexual organs become distended and red with blood when someone pulls a hidden string.

When the cremation tower reaches the burning site, a lengthy white shroud (kajang) is attached to the body. Held over everyone's heads, the corpse is led by the kajang down from the tower and placed inside the coffin. The fragile, pagodalike tower, no longer of any use, is tipped over and stripped of all valuables. A sea of fingers then passes ritual items up to be placed on the coffin. Family members huddle together to take one last look at their loved one, then a high priest climbs up on the platform to recite prayers over the body. Pots of holy water are poured over the corpse, then shattered on the ground. Hundreds of old Chinese coins are showered over the body as ransom to Yama, the Lord of the Underworld. After all the precious materials are piled on top, the high priest ignites the fuel under the pyre. In the span of a few seconds, the splendid tower—coffin, offerings, decorations—is engulfed in flames, hundreds of thousands of rupiah going up in smoke in one last wild extravagant gesture. The Balinese believe that the soul is lifted to heaven on the column of smoke.

Westerners find it curious how the Balinese treat the body of a dead relative. While the soul is regarded as all-important, the body is considered a foul, contaminated object to be dispensed with at the first opportunity. At cremations men clobber burning bodies with bamboo poles in order to break them up so they burn better. Corpses are unceremoniously prodded by relatives who make raucous jokes, mocking the body for not burning fast enough so they can all go home. As the fire subsides, the pedanda climbs the elevated platform and utters a few mantra, ringing a bell to hasten the soul's journey to heaven. The eldest son rakes the ashes to make sure all the flesh is burned.

Water is poured over the embers, and children are allowed to poke through the hot muddy ashes for coins and trinkets. The white bone ash is carefully separated from the wood ash. Sometimes the remaining, blackened bones are piled into a small mound, then placed in a clay vessel or coconut shell. Carried on a richly decorated sedan chair, the ashes will eventually be borne in another disorderly, laughing procession to the sea or to a nearby seagoing river, where they are set adrift, finally freeing the soul. A small prahu is sometimes used to carry ashes out past the reefs so they won't wash ashore.

This act represents the final purification and disposal of the material body, the ultimate purification of the triple cleansing cycle of earth, fire, and water. Later, there are private, often quite elaborate ceremonies for the care of the soul. In these rites the soul takes its rightful, honored place as one of the family ancestral deities installed in a special shrine in the family temple. Twelve to 42 days after the burning, offerings and powerful incantations are made on the soul's behalf. Wealthier families even construct a second tower at this time, nearly as elaborate as the cremation tower.

Attending a Cremation

Westerners are welcome to attend the cremation festivities, which may last several days. The Balinese don't sell tickets to their cremations, but they sell transport to the ceremonies. In tourist resorts you'll see signs announcing the event, as well as the address and telephone number of the transport agency. The local tourist office also knows when and where cremations take place. Some don't need advertising: the 1993 funeral for the last raja of Gianyar drew 50,000 people, almost two percent of the total Balinese population. Wear a sash around the waist while attending a cremation.

BALINESE ART

Art still plays an integral role in the ritual life of Bali's culture, even though the artworks are produced primarily for the tourist market. Art surrounds the Balinese from earliest childhood and is everpresent everywhere. The Balinese seem to make an art out of even the simple necessities of everyday life: fruit salad is served with flowers strewn on top, and coils of pigs' intestines are used on temple decorations.

Since the start of the 20th century, the Balinese have never allowed artistic knowledge to become centralized in a special intellectual class. Everyone down to the simplest peasant can be both an artist and an aesthetically conscious art critic. A field-laborer might chide a clumsy instrument maker for a job poorly done, and even young *dagang* (foodstall sellers) from humble families are skilled practitioners of Bali's classical dances.

While painting, sculpture, carving, and music have traditionally been the province of men, women have channeled creative energy into making lavish offerings to the gods. At almost any festival you can see spectacular pyramids of flowers, fruit, and cakes up to two meters high, fashioned with such love and adoration that they could only be meant for a higher being.

These religious obligations have also ensured that the arts be constantly practiced—the gods demand it! Feverish and backbreaking preparations go into the celebration of festivals as well as the transitional events in the life of a Balinese. In service to religion, each artist strives to make objects well-proportioned and pleasing. New shrines have to be built, reliefs renewed, new prayer offerings made, dances and dramas rehearsed, and music practiced continually in order to please gods, appease devils, and honor ancestors.

Although put at the service of religion, Balinese art does not solely serve religion. Sacred symbols decorate speeding *bemo,* jackets, menus, motorcycles, hotel doorways. Their use in such ordinary earthly objects is not looked upon as sacrilege.

An important factor contributing to the creative productivity of the Balinese is Bali's well-organized cultivation system. The astounding fertility of the island—everyone is fed, sheltered, and clothed—has given the Balinese the leisure to develop their arts for centuries.

Though the impetus to create art has always

endured, art objects have not. The Balinese have no eternally "great" art like Egypt's pyramids, Cambodia's Angkor Wat complex, or France's Chartres Cathedral. Bali's most readily available stone is soft volcanic sandstone, which crumbles easily and is eaten away by rainfall after only a few years. Earthquakes and volcanic eruptions ravage hundreds of shrines several times each decade, necessitating gigantic reconstruction projects engaging thousands of workers.

Balinese art is not made to last. Humidity wilts paper and rots cloth paintings; dogs or people eat the magnificent offerings; white ants perforate wooden sculptures, all of which must be refurbished constantly. All this rebuilding, renovating, and replacing assumes that the island's unparalleled concentration of emphemeral folk art continually evolves and perpetuates itself.

Communal Art

Whereas in the West, an artist pours a great amount of energy into establishing a distinctive style and technique to achieve personal wealth and fame, Balinese artists subordinate their ego to the needs of the community and to the requirements of the belief system. Art is an expression of their collective thought. Many paintings, carvings, and sculptures are made communally in workshops, where a master craftsman supervises a group of apprentices.

A statue or a *gamelan* composition may also frequently be the work of more than one artist, and the instructor may very well execute a portion of a pupil's painting. Though the colors and technique might be easily recognizable as the work of an individual, artists repeatedly use traditional standard themes and motifs executed in the local style. More decoration than art, the products of Bali's non-academically trained artisans still show a mastery of craftmanship.

THE HISTORICAL PERSPECTIVE

Since the 15th century, the island has been visited by traders from all over the world, all of whom have unwittingly influenced Balinese art. From every foreign culture they've come in contact with, the Balinese have absorbed what they wanted—digesting it, improving upon it, and creating what is probably Asia's most artistic civilization.

Their greatest inspiration was received from India via ancient Java. But starting in about 1596, extensive mercantile contacts with Europe, Japan, China, Indochina, Polynesia, and Arabia provided an international palette of influences. Decorative motifs, props, sculpture and painting techniques, and themes and characters for their theatrical performances were borrowed from the outside cultures. The Balinese are unabashed and uncanny copyists. Some of their paintings and stone carvings—a holdup, a plane crash, atomic bomb explosions—are copied right out of magazines or posters.

Ancient Balinese Art

As early as 300 B.C., coastal inhabitants created metal bells, lances, spiral-shaped rings, bronze implements, bracelets, and magnificent woven textiles. Although physical remnants of this culture are few, much of the spirit of these first Balinese has been passed down and is visible today in textile patterns, sculptural and dancing styles, theater forms, and rituals. In particular, the native Bali Aga of the highlands still adhere to pre-Hindu practices.

An example of a motif of pure native origin is the lovely *cili* figure of a girl shaped like an hourglass, seen everywhere in palm-leaf ornaments for temples, on cakes, standing in rice fields, and even made out of Chinese coins sewn together. The mysterious *cili* is thought to derive from the island's original rice deity, Dewi Sri.

Javanese Influence

As early as the 5th century, Bali was ruled by Javanese princes. Every political event and disturbance that occurred on Java had a ripple effect on the political life of Bali, and the art history of Bali reflects the development of art in the mother country.

Java's golden age of monumental art—A.D. 600-800—finds its counterpart in the evolution of Balinese art. Besides edicts written on old bronze plates *(prastasis)*, other physical remains of this classical period are found today in the vicinity of Pejeng and Bedulu—the area between the two rivers Petanu and Pakerisan—which has always been amazingly rich in antiquities.

The most impressive examples of Java's classic influence on Bali are the nine magnificent cut-rock tombs of **Gunung Kawi** near Tampaksiring, completed around A.D. 1080, which are strikingly similar to East Javanese monumental architecture from that period.

Under the great Airlangga's reign at the start of the 11th century, a vigorous renaissance of art occurred in East Java. The Balinese-born leader gave a new impetus to all the arts, particularly literature, reviving the old Javanese language of Kawi as Bali's official language.

The rule of the nationalistic Majapahit Empire on Java in the 14th century saw a repudiation of the classic, austere, religious, Indic elements and a resurgence of the more primitive native Javanese art styles and motifs. The powerful, erotic architecture of Candi Sukuh in East Java typifies this period.

Less than 100 years later, as Islam crept deeper and deeper into Majapahit territory, priests, poets, artists, sculptors, and painters began to migrate to Bali, bringing with them the earthy spirit of Majapahit. This influx accounts today for the extent to which classical Javanese romantic legends (the *Panji* and *Tantra* fables) have penetrated Balinese literature.

The populating of Bali by Javanese migrants also explains the extravagantly decorative motifs found in all media of Balinese art: floral patterns in the paintings, sensuous flaming motifs in the textiles, baroque temples, fast-paced music, and the bizarre realism of Balinese sculpture.

The Balinization of Javanese Arts

The collapse and subsequent dispersion of the Majapahit's cultural elite is considered the great watershed of Balinese history. The influence of its artisans and craftsmen brought to Bali a golden age of the visual arts, theater, and literature. From the 15th century onward, the descendants of the original Javanese colonial rulers founded a number of small independent regional states on Bali, free of Java's administration.

The Balinese natives adopted those Hindu practices, arts, and deities that suited their taste and rejected the rest, giving rise to today's distinctive folk art forms. Each noble house (called a *puri* or *jero,* depending upon rank) constituted a political and religious hub where the best orchestras practiced and where the finest painters,

weavers, sculptors, architects, blacksmiths, dancers, and actors lived and worked as privileged wards of the ruling princes.

These specialized artisans were paid in ritual gifts, relieved of certain social duties, or awarded tax exemptions and rice fields. Today, many of these privileged relationships remain in effect, the descendants living from the produce of the same fields, still carrying on their ancestors' handicraft or fine art.

This flourishing artists' utopia ended with the crack of Dutch rifles in 1906. From that point on, art began to radiate out from the divine cores of the *puri* and started to touch the villages. Bali, as a colony of the Netherlands East Indies empire, was soon profaned with modern technology, tourists, films, books, magazines. As a result of a drastic political reorganization, most of the princes could no longer afford to patronize the arts; palace *gamelan* were sold, royal theater groups broke up, and Balinese art became a true art of the people.

Art also became less decorative, representational, and formalized. Influenced by incoming European artists in the 1920s, Balinese artists for the first time dated and signed their paintings. They began to experiment with new styles, techniques, themes, and media. They set up sales organizations and the most outstanding among them received recognition overseas.

The 1930s are known as the "classical" period of modern Balinese art, when many of the finest and most innovative pieces of the 20th century were produced. Samples of these works may be viewed today in the Neka Museum, Neka Gallery, Agung Rai Gallery, and in the famed Puri Lukisan Museum—all in or around Ubud, Bali's traditional arts center.

Modern Influences

Over the past 40 years, the once all-important sponsorship of art by the local aristocratic families has all but ceased. Bali's past 20 years have wrought even greater changes. No longer does art occupy a traditional place and purpose within the community. No longer is it produced simply out of service to the deities. Now it's created for its own sake or just to make money.

Perhaps nowhere are artists more appreciated by their own people than on Bali, yet Balinese fine art isn't taken seriously by foreign buyers. In order to earn a living, artists have had to sacrifice quality. The "tourist corridor" up to Ubud is lined with opulent-looking galleries filled with an overwhelming range of kitschy junk, some of it good, and signs that say "You drop it, it's yours."

Inside the galleries you'll see row upon row of lookalike carvings and color-by-number images of villagers fishing, stereotypical market scenes, fantastical birds from the island's Hindu lore, predictably posed nude figures, mass-produced half-life-sized copies of dramatic masks, and "custom-made" reproductions of antiques.

On a weekend afternoon, the galleries are packed with tourists. Yet it's often deserted over at Ubud's Puri Lukisan museum—where for 35 American cents you can marvel at the bygone genius of Balinese painting. The island's two principal museums, in Ubud and Denpasar, lack the money to continue buying contemporary works. As a result, the really remarkable, high-quality pieces are bought up by discerning tourists or foreign art dealers, taken overseas, and lost to Bali forever.

PAINTING

Painting had all but died out on Java when the last Hindu civilization there emigrated to Bali in the 15th century, but on Bali painting has been practiced continuously for the last 400 years. The oldest extant paintings are two painted wooded slabs in the Pura Batu Madeg and Pura Panataran Temples in the Besakih complex; the works date from the mid-15th century.

Early traditional painters created temple hangings on cloth or manuscripts, adhering to conventional themes and standardized colors handed down through generations. Painting was intended to serve the religious needs of the community. If the painting was too innovative, it might not be qualified in the service of god and was therefore considered a failure.

Today, paintings—portable, cheap, and unique—are Bali's most exported craft. Of all Bali's art forms, painting is the most influenced by Western demand and Western aesthetics. Though still masters of technique, the majority of today's Balinese painters work for commercial gain, reasoning that it's senseless to go to the trouble of making a good painting when a bad painting will sell for just as much, just as fast. As a result, much Balinese painting, though opulent in color, has a paint-by-the-numbers sameness. Most pieces are more like colored drawings than paintings—too-hastily made, and sadly limited in subject matter, treatment, and symbolism. It takes careful, persistent searching to uncover work of skill and elegance.

Studying Painting
Watercolorists and photographers couldn't pick a more colorful subject than Bali. Art tours are common here. An Australian painter, Barbara Miller, runs an inn on the beach in remote Tabanan Regency, accommodating artists from around the world. Called **BeeBees** (fax 062 361 36021), and located just four km beyond Krambitan near the village of Tibubiyu, the seven rustic yet comfortable *lumbung*-style bungalows are the perfect retreat for painters.

Scores of painter's homestays in the Ubud area—Mimpi's, W Wayan Serathi's, I Wayan Suka's, to name a few—give lessons (look for the sign "Painter & Homestay"). Certain galleries, like **Agung Rai** in Peliatan, offer lessons to foreign artists. Or you may want to see if you can get accepted as a student in the **Balinese Art Development Center Program** on Jl. Bayusuta (in the Art Center in Abiankapas). Always try for a student discount.

Characteristics of Balinese Paintings
For a survey of the different schools of Balinese painting, refer to the accompanying special topic. Balinese painters demonstrate an accurate and instinctive knowledge of human anatomy and a tendency to use rich decorative colors. They never lack a theme, having been filled with stories and myths from childhood on. Jungle scenes show an elaborate, riotous decoration of leaves, flowers, and animals, with every leaf and tree carefully outlined, and tiny blades of grass and insects found in the farthest corners of the canvas.

The best paintings reflect the Balinese sense of divine order, with all elements well-proportioned and balanced, and everything in its proper, harmonious place. This is why Balinese paintings are seldom executed spontaneously but are carefully preplanned—the coloring, shading, boundaries, and contours penciled in first. In many of their paintings, dozens of stories happen all at once and several different perspectives are employed, as if the scene were composed from different viewpoints.

TRADITIONAL PAINTING

For centuries Java was the mother country, a fact reflected even today in the subject matter of traditional Balinese painting. The traditional styles derive for the most part from the 14th and 15th centuries when the Hindu population of East Java migrated to Bali, taking their art forms with them.

The first painters were puppet painters, a skill which evolved over time to include painting figures on cloth according to well-established iconographic rules. Known as *wayang*-style paintings because the figures resembled shadow-puppet characters, these highly formalized traditional paintings related scenes from Balinese mythology and from the classical Hindu Mahabharata and Ramayana epics.

Popular, everyday scenes from daily Balinese life were never depicted. This was a world of Hindu gods, demons, and princesses dressed in the ancient attire of Hindu Javanese times. Quaint but uninspiring, their purpose was to instill moral and ethical values by relating laws of *adat*.

Specialists in the traditional arts of religious drawing and painting were commissioned by the rajas to paste gold leaf on pieces of clothing; paint statues and artifacts in bright splashy colors; and decorate wooden cremation towers, palace altars, and pavilions. Noblemen from the courts loaned each other artists, in this way spreading art all over the island.

Types of Traditional Paintings

These early Hinduized Balinese produced three main types of paintings. The first, called *ider-ider,* were cotton scroll paintings in the shape of banners, usually two meters long and 30 cm wide, hung under the eaves of shrines during festivals.

The second type, *langse,* were large rectangular pieces of painted cloth, up to 15 meters long and four meters wide, suspended from *puri* pavilions or used as curtains to partition off areas of a temple. Both the *ider-ider* and the *langse* were religious narrative paintings characterized by a flat, stiff, formal style—a serial representation of people, gods, and demons painted according to a very strict traditional formula and lacking in all emotion.

The third type of traditional painting was the astrological calendar *(pelelintangan),* examples of which exist to this day.

With the Dutch conquest of the island in 1908, the courts lost power and ceremonial painting went into immediate decline. After that, only the wealthy princes of fertile Gianyar Regency were able to retain their rank and thus continue to patronize the arts.

Painting still finds its way onto statues, cross-beams, and building columns. Color is applied at its most frenzied on religious architecture and in ceremonial *bale,* particularly in the decoration of bedboards and shrine boxes *(prabu),* and on the long banners that beautify temple eaves during *odalan.*

Characteristics of Traditional Paintings

The painter of traditional works is governed by a strict set of rules regarding subjects, scenery, and composition. Colors are traditionally confined to red *(barak),* vermilion *(kencu),* blue *(pelung),* indigo *(tengi),* yellow *(kuning),* white *(putih),* and black *(selem),* and a little ochre for flesh tones. These colors at one time were made from organic soot, clay, minerals, fish-gelatin, and pig's bones, but now imported oil colors, acrylics, and black Chinese ink are used.

Originally, the painting surface was handwoven cotton cloth imported from Nusa Penida. Today a thin, unbleached cotton fabric is coated with rice paste until an even, matte-like surface is achieved. The cloth is then polished to a sheen with a large smooth seashell. The coating dulls even bright colors, giving the work a vintage appearance; hence the modern term for these paintings, *lukisan antik,* or "antique paintings."

The master first systematically and mechanically draws the preliminary outline of the picture. Assistants color it in, then the master gives the finishing touches. Shading to indicate perspective is traditionally not used. Profiles are rare and full-face representations rarer still. Most

SCHOOLS OF BALINESE ART

Kamasan or *Wayang*-Style

An ancient traditional painting derived from the *wayang kulit* (shadow puppet) religious myths. The best place to shop for these is in Kamasan village, south of Klungkung. Mandra is considered a living master. Prices range from Rp10,000 for a small painting up to Rp2 million for one executed by a top painter.

Ubud-Style

Basically, there are three different types, all using acrylic paints. In the Spies-style, extravagant vegetation envelopes small human beings or dancers with terraced rice paddies and steaming volcanoes in the background. The *wayang*-style are religious paintings but are more frightening, mature, and three-dimensional with a whole array of battling, howling, contorting supernatural figures. Finally, the Bonnet-style portrays large figures harvesting or winnowing rice and tying rice bundles, often working in a line across the canvas.

Batuan-Style

Tiny figures painted in black and white on paper with absolutely no unfilled space. The subject is usually a rustic scene of everyday village life with the ubiquitous Rangda and *barong* dance. Collectors of this style should visit Batuan village and see the galleries. The recognized premier practitioners are currently Budi and Bendi. Price range: Rp50,000-2 million. Batuan-style paintings have changed little since the 1930s.

Young Artists School

During the period of inactivity in the 1930s, an utterly new style emerged in Penestanan near Ubud. Later to become known as The Young Artists School, teenage artists began to produce refreshingly bold paintings using strong primary colors and simple confident lines. Encouraged by such resident artists as Arie Smit (Dutch) and Donald Friend (Australian), this style was characterized by a joyful, childlike artistry yet contained a youth's insightful view of reality.

The story goes that the style was founded one day in 1956 when Arie Smit was painting a landscape outside Ubud. A 12-year-old boy shepherding a waddle of ducks nearby watched him and began drawing village scenes and people in the dirt. Smit asked him if he would like to come to work for him and learn how to draw on paper and use colors. Permission first had to be obtained from

faces are drawn in three-quarter profile, with the eyes always shown.

All available space is covered in designs. Cloud and wind patterns, flaming ornamental borders, rocks or mountain motifs, and characters standing back-to-back are common devices used to separate the plot-related scenes. Captions are written in the fluid script of archaic Old Javanese or Kawi.

Traditional paintings are read like a comic strip, the characters and events represented in separate space cells, the scenes all taking place in a divine cosmic world with the same heroes appearing again and again in different attitudes. Important scenes are positioned in the center, peripheral events to the sides; gods are at the top, demons on the bottom. Sky and clouds are indicated by stylized, codified ornamentation.

Each god is distinguished by details of dress and aspect which set him or her apart, whether they be *halus* ("refined" heroes, deities, and princes) or *kasar* ("rough" rogues, giants, retainers). Noble, high-bred figures wear rich courtly costumes, elaborate headdresses, and jewelry. Their faces are aloof and poised with a serene smile on their lips (even during the bloodiest battles), their arms and legs are long and thin like classical dancers.

Coarse characters are denoted by their wild, bulging eyes, sinister sharp teeth, bulbous mouths and noses, hairy black scowling faces, and threatening poses. A character's attributes dictate his age, class, demeanor, position, and actions. For example, the eyes of women are downcast, those of men are proud and alert.

Although rigidly standardized and holding to an inflexible set of conventions, traditional "Kamasan-style" paintings have a balance, a quality of design similar to that of Persian miniatures, Byzantine mosaics, or illuminated manuscripts of the Middle Ages. While European religious narrative art of medieval times portrayed the boy's father, who only granted it after it was agreed that Smit pay for hiring another boy to take care of the family's ducks. Soon the talented boy, through the sale of his paintings, was able to buy a cow for his father. Within three years the group of "Young Artists" consisted of 25 boys. Smit's first and most devoted pupil, Nyoman Cakra, still lives and works in Penestanan.

The best Young Artists paintings show the same masterful sense of color and love of imaginary animals, mysterious spirits, and ordinary country life as did their artistic forebears. The striking characteristic of this school is the primitive, flat colors used—a practice which prevails to this day.

These simple and naive paintings, particularly the landscapes, are produced quickly and in large quantities. Critics have gushed that the Young Artists constitute "perhaps the most fascinating and brilliant example of peasant art to be found in the world today." Something you should know: Young Artists' pictures, ever popular with tourists, are frequently priced the same as other works of superior quality that take one to two months to paint and demonstrate a much deeper knowledge of anatomy and perspective.

Tropical Birds
In 1985, large pastel paintings of birds started appearing all over Bali. Once popular with interior and hotel designers, the birds have now fallen out of vogue, though the images are very attractive and suitable for some settings. Price ranges from Rp50,000 to Rp1 million.

Modernists
This school takes in Affandi and Aziz to Mohamed. Usually Javanese, not Balinese, artists. Price range: Rp200,000 to Rp4 million. One of the best known Modernists is the multi-media artist Abdullah Aziz from Jakarta who lives in Mas. Aziz paints pictures of Balinese boys and girls flirting; also into boat-building, music, and painting women. Fine technique.

Naked Women
A favorite subject of painters in Bali since the 1930s. Schlocky, clumsy paintings sold in galleries and on foot proliferate. No one has ever emulated the Dutch artist Hofker in the rendition of the graceful Balinese female form. Price range: Rp25,000 to Rp500,000.

episodes from the New Testament, Balinese religious art show scenes from their sacred, popular Hindu mythology.

By far the finest original examples of traditional paintings date from the 14th century's Gelgel/Klungkung dynasties. These are found on the painted ceilings of the Kerta Gosa ("Hall of Justice") in Klungkung, where you can see (with the help of binoculars) the different tiers showing all the levels of existence between heaven and hell. The most famous panels illustrate the torments of evildoers—people being torn, impaled, crushed, mutilated, eaten, and boiled alive.

All these paintings were rendered by anonymous medieval artisans lying on their backs for months on end. The kings, princes, and temple councils of other courtly centers in Gianyar, Tabanan, Sanur, Bangli, Singaraja, and Karangasem also commissioned ritual art.

Buying Traditional Paintings
Modern examples of traditional *wayang*-style cloth paintings are still created, particularly by artists living in the village of Kamasan, a few kilometers to the south of Klungkung (Klungkung Regency). These paintings make superb souvenirs because their cotton cloth can be folded easily. When you get back home, just stretch the canvas or spray or dampen it with water, then iron it carefully on the back on a low heat setting.

In the past, the Kamasan studios worked with natural paints made from slivers of bone, a mixture of plain and holy water, and powdered stone (from which the color was derived). The paint's base was worked with a pestle and mortar for an hour, and the only color that was not natural was blue. Today, the majority of artists use acrylics because few people still know how to prepare the natural paints.

Fine specimens of Kamasan paintings are seriously undervalued and masterpieces are available for Rp75,000-150,000—practically the cost of day labor and materials. As in former times, paintings are still unsigned and the artists are taught from a very early age not to express themselves in original and individual forms but in highly patterned ways.

Look before you buy. Watch the painter at work if you can, then you know they're authentic. Spend time learning about the painting you're considering. Let it grow on you. What's the story behind it? Just like the stained-glass windows in the cathedrals of Europe, which illustrate fables from the gospels, these Kamasan paintings portray a certain character or god in Balinese legend. Have the artist explain the work to you.

In the village of Krambitan, 20 km southwest of Tabanan, the painters' association Karya Dharma has revived a regional offshoot of traditional Balinese painting that thrived here during the 1930s. They produce *wayang*-style paintings but with more colors and a bolder style. For antique pieces, look in the antique shops of Klungkung and Kamasan.

For something unusual, check out Balinese traditional calendars, which depict a cross section of Balinese culture. These paintings are chiefly made for tourists but are also used to predict the future. (See the special topic "The Balinese Calendar" for more information.) There are two kinds of these old-style calendars, both of which pictorially represent the days of the month. A small size with yellow coloring made in Bedulu (near Ubud) costs only Rp15,000 or thereabouts because it's easy work. The more classic style, made in the calendar-making center of Klungkung, starts at around Rp20,000.

MODERN PAINTING

As early as the turn of the century, the art of northern Bali had come under European influence. But by 1930 Balinese painting was stagnating, the art form no longer in demand by the Balinese themselves. The palaces stopped commissioning artists, and the highly stylized, traditional hangings were no longer painted. Bali was about to undergo a tumult of suffering and chaos, but it was the period between the two great wars that brought the heaviest changes and greatest surge of creativity.

Guidebooks have repeated the outdated fairy tale that was started in the 1930s by the Dutch scholar Sutterheim and the painter Rudolph Bonnet (1895-1978). The men published articles claiming that modern Balinese art was born during the years 1933-39 when it first made contact with Western painters. This premise was put forth to further the career of Bonnet, and it reflected a strong colonial bias that colored all Dutch scholarship in the first half of this century.

This legend is only half true. Bonnet, the German artist Walter Spies (1895-1942), and others *did* demonstrate to Balinese artists that painting could be free of set formulas. Rather than paint to a single stylistic convention, the Europeans introduced by way of example the concept of the third dimension, the imaginative use of color, modern graphic elements, and a wider range of subject matter. They also provided Balinese artists with new media and materials such as Chinese ink, bristle brushes, watercolors and tempera, steel pens, and European paper.

But the Balinese were not romantics given to passionate improvisation, expressiveness, and creativity. It was as much their exposure to modern stimuli, the economic inducement of the tourist industry, and their growing knowledge of the world at large that encouraged Balinese artists to stop painting according to rules and to start re-creating their own visual experience. Tourists began to request that their canvases be stretched and framed; this tended to limit the subject matter of a picture to a single scene instead of depicting episodes taking place in a series.

The extraordinary creativity of the 1930s pulled Balinese art out of its lethargy, but all the upheaval of WW II and the postwar Indonesian struggle of independence from 1945 to 1950 put a sudden stop to artistic activity. After the wars, Balinese painting entered another low period, with much of the original creative impetus of the 1930s dissipated. Subject matter was designed to appeal to tourists; artists churned out paintings with idealized, unrealistic *legong* dancers, women presenting offerings, men working the fields, and cockfights.

The Young Artists School
Suddenly, around 1956, a new style of modernism appeared. Under the guidance and encouragement of Dutch painter Arie Smit, young boys around Penestanan and Ubud began creating naive three-dimensional paintings based on scenes from their daily life: a village street, a woman feeding hens, people working the harvest or bartering at the market, ritual and dance

festivals, birds and animals, a cremation—themes that had never been attempted before.

This movement became known as the Young Artists School, and the exuberant paintings in bright, bold, hallucinogenic colors found a ready market. Here was taking place a rekindling of artistic expression, a new realism that soon developed into a sophisticated, distinctive, naturalistic style.

A new generation of Balinese artists came to the fore—I Sobrat, Made Griya, Gusti Njoman Lempad, Ida Bagus Made, Ida Bagus Anom. Though they all had unique styles, these artists were *traditionally* talented. That is, their genius only found expression working within the general iconographic and formal framework of tradition. Their skills were still aimed at making recognizable shapes and characters that could be related to traditional stories or themes known to sell.

During this early period, pleasingly harmonized mosaics of spindly black lines washed with foreboding gray and black tones appeared. Canvases became crowded with dark fantastic forests; strange ghostlike animals; tenuous, halftone figures of villagers almost hidden amid shadowy jungle vegetation; or nightmarish visions of monsters with snakes for genitals.

Towering over the group was **Gusti Nyoman Lempad** (1862-1978) of Ubud, a master artisan, carver, architect, and painter. He was both a strong advocate of conservative Balinese culture and an avid crosscultural innovator. Choosing as his medium paper rather than larger-sized cloth, Lempad was the first in the group to experiment with the single-scene format, rather than multiple narrative frames. His works illustrated episodes from Bali's rich folklore and mythology.

In 1936, together with Spies, Bonnet, and the nobleman Tjokorde Sukawati, Lempad helped found an art association, **Pita Maha** ("Great Vitality"). The group presented exhibitions in Java and Europe and maintained a high level of quality among its members. For the first time, art began to be bought by collectors and museums. At its peak in the 1930s, Pita Maha counted more than 150 painters, sculptors, and silversmiths among its ranks. By the time Lempad died at the bibical old age of 116, the society had emancipated Balinese painting from its comatose state.

Anyone who has an interest in Lempad should see the brilliant film made of his life and the magnificent body of art and architecture he left behind. Directed by John Darling and the late Lorne Blair, it is available through Mystic Fire Video Inc., Box 1092, Cooper Station, New York, NY 10276 (tel. 800-292-9001).

Art critics have mistakenly compared Balinese painting with the eerie jungle scenes of Henri Rousseau, with the black-and-white ornamental illustrations of Aubrey Beardsley, and even with the gruesome spooky fantasies of the 15th-century Dutch painter Hieronymus Bosch. Although Balinese painting shares some similarities with the themes and techniques of these artists, it's almost certain that early Balinese artists never saw their works.

Non-Balinese Artists

Beginning in the 1930s, an influx of foreign artists fell in love with Bali and did some of their most significant work here. The famous Dutch painter **W.O.F. Nieuwenkamp** traveled and painted on Bali long before Spies, Bonnet, or anyone else. In fact, it was he who informed Bonnet about Bali.

Willem G. Hofker and Bonnet became masters at painting the female form. Bonnet worked mainly in crayon on paper and his paintings today fetch very high prices. **Theo Meier** (1908-1982), inspired by German expressionists, painted vibrant and colorful religious ceremonies.

All the works of these Europeans today command much higher prices than any Balinese artist of that era. Paintings by Spies, who died at age 47 and painted few canvases, sell for as much as US$500,000. Any of the others' work can easily fetch US$50,000.

The canvases of contemporary painters also can fetch astronomical sums. Australian **Donald Friend** (1915-1990) was a gifted writer and wrote several books which he himself illustrated. The flamboyant hilltop home of **Antonio Blanco** (b. 1926) is a shrine to erotic art and illustrated poetry. **Han Snel** (b. 1925), a Dutch soldier who refused to fight the Indonesians in their war of independence, owes much to his teacher, Theo Meier. **Arie Smit** (b. 1916) paints mainly landscapes and temples in oil or acrylic. Smit has always been prolific though now that he's nearing the age of 82 he is slowing down somewhat.

THE LIFE AND DEATH OF WALTER SPIES

Walter Spies is a legendary figure who, more than any other artist, ushered Balinese art into the 20th century. There are only a few accounts of his years in Java and Bali, but those stories which have been passed down show a man of extraordinary artistic abilities. He had talent not only for painting but for musicology, dance and choreography, archaeology, and anthropology. The man had an almost paganistic love and awe of nature and was a skilled field naturalist. Spies also worked as a photographer, filmmaker, and linguist. In contrast to a life of peace and great service, Spies was to die a violent death.

Born in 1895 in Moscow, Spies came from a wealthy family of diplomats, growing up in the grandiose atmosphere of czarist Russia. At the age of 15, the slender delicate boy was sent to a private school in Dresden. During these early years, until the war put a stop to it, Spies came under the influence of Futurism, Cubism, and Expressionism. Spies migrated to Germany in 1918. Being a German citizen, he was arrested by Russian soldiers while visiting Moscow on summer holidays. The young aristocrat was thrown into an internment camp in eastern Russia. Escaping amid the confusion at war's end, he returned to Moscow, where he was first struck by the haunting "naive" paintings of Henri Rousseau.

In July 1919, Spies's first exhibition opened in Dresden. In Berlin, he kept company with the greatest musicians of his day, designed stage sets, and assisted in the direction of silent films in the unbelievably stimulating creative environment of Berlin in the 1920s. He exhibited at the Stedelijk Museum in Holland in 1923, his penchant for expressionism and miniaturism starting to reveal itself. While in Amsterdam Spies would spend hours at the Royal Museum of the Tropics, studying the displays of the East. Perhaps because of some scandal connected with his homosexuality, in 1923 he set sail for Java, eager to leave his European life behind him.

Spies jumped ship in Jakarta and found his way to Bandung, where he played piano in a Chinese cinema which showed silent films. His next stop was Yogya, where he moved into the sultan's palace and worked as the conductor for the *kraton*'s European orchestra and taught music to European children on the side. In May 1925 he took part in a group painting exhibition in Surabaya. This exhibit first brought the mystical and impressionistic qualities of his paintings and sketches to the attention of art critics. During his stay in Yogya, Spies learned to play all the instruments of the *gamelan*. He rendered *gamelan* music on two pianos tuned to the Western scale and devised a system of notation which enabled *gamelan* players to write down their parts.

Spies first visited Bali in 1925, staying in the palace of Ubud's leading gentry family, the Sukawatis. He fell immediately under the spell of Bali. A tall gangling figure with thick yellow hair and wearing khaki pants, Spies could be seen tramping all over the island on foot. He visited Bali several more times and finally moved there permanently to spend the next 15 years of his life. Spies built his own two-story bamboo studio-house in 1928 at the confluence of two rivers in Campuan on land donated by the Sukawati family. Spies would repay his patron's kindness with paintings. Unfortunately, many works done in Spies's expressionist period of the late 1920s and early 1930s have been lost, the only surviving record being faded black-and-white photographs. During this period he also created the *kecak* dance for a German film company. Spies's reputation grew, he was sought out as the decisive authority on music, helped direct films, and collaborated on books with famous anthropologists.

By the 1930s Balinese painting was suffering from a severe lack of individual free expression. In 1936, Spies helped found an art association, Pita Maha, with the Dutch painter Rudolph Bonnet and the nobleman Tjokorde Sukawati. It was largely due to the efforts of this society that Balinese painting finally became emancipated from its comatose state. Hundreds of Balinese artists visited Spies's house, and with his encouragement they began for the first time to draw their inspiration from the scenes of everyday life—farmers, cockfights, landscapes, market scenes, animals. They learned to respect the dictates of perspective and anatomy, and they experimented with new colors. The legends and myths of Old Javanese literature, which had hitherto been drawn in such a systematic and mechanical manner, took on new forms. The innocent, yet strong and dynamic paintings of the 1930s displayed today in Ubud's Puri Lukisan are eloquent testimony to the excitement generated by Pita Maha. Members of this group eventually brought about the secularization of painting on Bali.

Famous scientists, anthropologists, artists, writers, and globetrotters visited Spies in the 1930s: Barbara Hutton, Noel Coward, Charlie Chaplin, Vicki Baum, Margaret Mead, Jane Belo, Miguel and Rose Covarrubias, Colin McPhee, Sutterheim of the Archaeological Service, Dr. Goris, and Beryl de Zoete, with whom Spies wrote *Dance and Drama in Bali*. As he had gained almost the complete trust of the Balinese, Spies also gave Dutch administrators valuable advice, accompanying them on their rounds. In 1932 he was appointed the curator of the Bali Museum in Denpasar, which testifies to the high regard in which he was held by Dutch officials of the time.

But Spies soon grew weary with the number and the quality of the visitors to his home in Campuan. In 1937, he bought a little mountain hut in Iseh in Karangasem Regency, turning his residence in Campuan over to two Germans to run as a guesthouse. But Spies still found time to remain active on the jury of the Pita Maha Association, whose membership had swelled to 150. Many of the works presented were sold abroad, bringing recognition for the artists and commissions for Spies. Around this time, he is credited with inventing the elongated style of woodcarving. Pita Maha remained active until 1942 when the disorder and hardship of war dampened all artistic expression. Painting fell into a state of torpor until the 1950s, when a school of "naive painting" in bright colors developed in the village of Penestanan under the tutelage of Arie Smit.

In the late 1930s, with the specter of war looming in Europe, the fascist elements in the Dutch government launched a witch hunt against homosexuals. Spies, along with hundreds of others in the Indies, was arrested on 31 December 1938. The Balinese were shocked at the behavior of the Dutch, and members of his *gamelan* gathered under his prison wall in Denpasar to serenade him. Spies was released from Surabaya prison eight months later, and his Dutch friends from his Yogya days were there to welcome him. Between his release and the outbreak of WW II, Spies immersed himself in the study of insects, developing a good working relationship with the director of the world-famous botanical gardens in Bogor. A few of his watercolor renderings of insects made during this period are displayed in the Museum of Natural History in Leiden. Storm clouds over Europe continued to gather.

When Hitler invaded Holland in May 1940, all German nationals in Indonesia were arrested as enemy aliens. Spies's period of internment—first in Ngawi (Java) then Kotacane (North Sumatra) was to last 20 months. Even in detention camp, the artist/musician asked his sister in Batavia for paints, brushes, symphony scores, and he kept himself busy writing, composing, and painting (only one photo of a painting survives from this period). On 18 January 1942, the *Van Imhoff*, crowded with thousands of prisoners of war, sailed from Padang to Ceylon. The next day the ship was sunk by a Japanese torpedo bomber. Walter Spies was not among the survivors.

Today, Spies's room at Hotel Campuan is faithfully preserved, and there's a memorial to him at the Denpasar Art Center, where reproductions of some of his paintings are displayed. Each February a Walter Spies Festival is staged. For a sample of the foundation's news bulletin, contact Stichting Walter Spies, Steenstraat 1, 2312 BS Leiden, Netherlands. A phonograph album recording the 1984 Walter Spies Festival, which features the music of the *gamelan gong gede*, is also available from the foundation.

The Little Mists *by Walter Spies*

Javanese, Sumatran, and Western artists have started moving into the area between Mas and Ubud, setting up shop and selling paintings to tourists—competing with the Balinese on their own turf. Each year new art styles come into vogue, then fade out. See under "Arts and Crafts" in the Ubud section (Gianyar Regency chapter) for more on individual painters working in the area.

The Academic Painters

Modern Balinese art is now expanding and developing in two different directions: the art of artisans and the art of academicians. Academically trained painters are concerned with a distinct personal style and a national identity. With formal training in the European tradition from art academies on Java and in Denpasar, they exhibit a diversity of styles. Only in subject matter, not in ingenuity and skill, do they differ from their European or American counterparts.

The captivating erotic sketches of **Nyoman Gunarsa** have been very well received. Though he has had academic training on Java, Gunarsa has also been heavily influenced by the traditional *wayang* style. His museum and gallery are just before Klungkung (if traveling from Gianyar), but he spends a lot of time on Java.

Wayan Lotra is self-taught, but paints in an academic style and has been much influenced by Hofker and Bonnet. **Abdul Aziz, Lee Man Fung,** and **Basuki Abdullah** employ Balinese and Javanese motifs and diverse techniques (including painting on *batik*), and have a tendency toward abstraction.

A growing number of Balinese artists, particularly those affiliated with government schools like STSI, are breaking away from modern traditional *(kreasi baru)* and are producing advanced and sophisticated experimental art. With the strong support of an emerging Balinese urban middle class, they have created a distinct local version of an international, cosmopolitan artistic culture that is only partly Balinese. Young artists to keep your eye on, all of whom show a strong and unique creative vision, are Made Sumadiyasa, Ngakan Rai Lanus, Ketut Budiana, Nyoman Cakra, and Ketut Soki.

The Non-Academic Painters

Non-academicians have learned their trade by serving as apprentices under established mas-

ters. These artists, though not formally trained, often display extraordinary technical skill. Their work is eclectic and can't be easily classified, but most still paint in the traditional style for the tourist market.

You need at least a rudimentary knowledge of Balinese literature to appreciate them. Subject matter includes detailed scenes from Buddhist mythology, bird-and-banana leaf panels (the current rage), and vivid depictions of the natural world. The art comes straight from the heart.

Among the most eminent are **I Made Nyana, Bendi,** and **Budi,** whose paintings cost up to US$1000. These painters work in the Batuanstyle—naturalistic, heavily shadowed figures, and miniatures of paper with little leftover space. Another extremely successful artist is **I Nyoman Meja,** whose studio is in Taman near the Nomad Restaurant (if coming from Peliatan, turn right). He asks US$2000 for one of his phantasmagoric, exquisitely executed paintings.

Women Artists

The women of Bali are freeing themselves more and more from being mere objects of paintings to being active painters themselves. There are women's *gamelan* orchestras, women carvers, and a gallery in Ubud, **Seniwati Gallery** (Jl. Sri Wedari 2 B, Banjar Taman, tel. 0361-975485, fax 975453), devoted solely to art by Balinese and Indonesian women and girls. The gallery is open 1000-1300 and 1400-1700; closed Monday and Friday.

Dewa Biang Raka studied under Bonnet, and was the only female artist among 10 pupils who used to go into the rice fields with him to paint. Now she lives like a hermit and paints monochromatic works, yet the subtle colors grow on you. Raka doesn't sell her works because she wants to know where they are and who buys them. Some paintings you may buy but may never sell.

Motherhood is a favorite theme of **Tjok. Istri Mas Astiti,** whose works often depict pregnant women with children. In her paintings, Astiti also examines the roles of women in different societies and relationships. Her moving work is reminiscent of the social realism found in the art of modern China and Vietnam.

A well-established artist in the Batuan-style is **Gusti Ayu Natih Arimini,** who paints lively pictures full of charming details and enchanting stories. **Sri Supriyatini** has gained recognition for her dark, gloomy paintings which have a rough, textured surface, almost like a bas-relief.

Javanese-born **Yannar Ernawati** is known for her expressive, surreal pictures and unusual colors. **Ni Made Suciarmi** (b. 1932) is a master of traditional Kamasan-style paintings, adapted from *wayang kulit*. Made started her career mixing paints for her uncle during the renovation of the original Gerta Gosa masterpiece in Klungkung in 1938. One of her high quality one-by one-and-a-half-meter paintings costs around a million rupiah. Even her students charge this much!

Information

A visit to the following artists is recommended to familiarize the visitor planning a purchase: Han Snel in Siti Bungalows (Ubud), Antonio Blanco (Campuan), Ida Bagus Tilem (Mas). Ida Bagus Made (Tebesaya) is still crazy, still the best of the old masters. He doesn't care about fame or money so you won't find his paintings in galleries, only in museums. He won't sell his work but if he likes you he may give it to you. Also visit **Nyoman Sumertha** and **Nyoman Ada** in Peliatan, one km east of Ubud.

Founded in 1979, the **Taman Werdi Budaya** or Denpasar Art Center is on Jl. Nusa Indah in Abiankapas, on the road to Sanur. It's a center for painting, mask, and woodcarving exhibits where Balinese and Indonesian artists are featured. Each year from mid-June to mid-July the Center also hosts a summer art festival with painting expositions.

An event worth attending is the **Walter Spies Festival** put on by Yayasan Walter Spies each February at Denpasar Art Center; get the foundation's newsletter by writing Stichting Walter Spies, Steenstraat 1, 2312 BS Leiden, Netherlands.

For a thorough discussion of the traditional Kamasan painting style, see "Kamasan and Vicinity" under "Vicinity of Klungkung" in the Klungkung Regency chapter. The following books are definitive references to Balinese painting: *The Sukarno Collection of Paintings* (Jakarta, 1959), a catalog of great Indonesian paintings in the collection of the late President Sukarno;

Perceptions of Paradise: Images of Bali in the Arts, published by the Neka Gallery (1993) with text and photographs by Garrett Kam; *Willem G. Hofker, Painter of Bali,* a helpful treatise; and *Walter Spies and Balinese Art* by Rhodius and Darling (Amsterdam, 1980), an excellent introduction to the man and his extraordinary life and work.

Indonesian Art by Joseph Fisher is a catalog produced for the "Year of Indonesia" traveling exhibit of 1991. It includes a section on Balinese painters. *Balinese Painting* by A.A. Djelentik (Oxford University Press, 1986) is a tiny book that tries to wrap up the whole subject. Good try. For more information about the origin of Klungkung-style paintings, refer to Idanna Pucci's exhaustive study of the Gerta Gosa paintings called *The Epic of Life* (Van der March, 1985).

Mystic Fire Video (225 Lafayette St., Suite 1206, New York, NY 10012, tel. 212-941-0999) sells a 60-minute color video called *Lempad of Bali* (1979) directed by Lorne Blair. This film captures some of the strength and genius of this remarkable artist who was known throughout Europe in the 1920s for his religious and erotic art.

Museums

You'll soon learn that many galleries call themselves museums but are really display rooms selling paintings. The real museums are well known. Preeminent among them is the **Bali Museum** in Denpasar (east side of Puputan Square), which contains many masterpieces tracing the development of Balinese painting. This venerable museum, the ultimate repository of Balinese culture, also frequently exhibits contemporary artists.

To familiarize yourself with high-quality historical works, visit the **Puri Lukisan Museum** in Ubud. Founded in 1954 by Tjokorda Sukawati and Rudolph Bonnet, this "Palace of Art" houses a permanent collection of many early treasures of modern Balinese sculpture and painting—from impressionism to abstract expressionism. Displayed in chronological order, the museum gives the viewer an idea of the stylistic trends in Balinese art over the past 25 years. One wing is devoted to new work, where it's possible to meet the artists.

Framing and Shipping

If you don't want the frame to the painting you're buying, you can often buy it without the frame, but bear in mind that frames here are real bargains compared to prices in the West. All Balinese frames are different; sometimes they're plain with no carving, sometimes they have very ornate carving. But for the most part, Balinese framing is heavily carved—not the austere sort of thing that would go well in a minimalist New York apartment.

When visiting galleries, be aware that the frame could add substantially to the price of your purchase. The most elaborate ones cost around Rp15,000 per meter—works of art in themselves. For the lower-cost paintings, you might find that the frame may cost you more than the painting. The price of the frame also depends on the wood used and who carved it.

The gallery will (or should) break down your frame into four pieces, roll it up safely in cardboard, and package it for carrying or shipping. Up to 10 paintings can be rolled into one mailing tube without damage (frames should be packaged separately). Stationery stores in Denpasar sell plastic or cardboard tubes. Some galleries will even package and ship for you, either through an air-frieght company or via surface post through the Indonesian post office (which takes a lot longer but is safe and cheaper).

Gati is a first-class frame maker who works off Jl. Raya Kuta. If you're coming from Ubud, take a left on the street just before Neka Gallery in Padangtegal (one km east of Ubud's center). Gati's house is on on the left. His asking price is Rp7500 per meter. For more detailed information on shipping crafts, see "Information and Services" in the Introduction.

SHOPPING FOR PAINTINGS

Paintings are sold in souvenir stalls, art markets, cooperative galleries, and pushed by hawkers on foot everywhere you turn. Finding *good* paintings, however, is hard work. It helps to understand that artists are now working mostly for a European market and the tourists' demand for paintings "suitable for framing" has changed the technique and content of their painting style. Balinese artists only started to sign their paintings when Westerners started to ask them to about 50 years ago. Now almost all paintings are signed with the artist's name and the village where he or she lives.

Producing copies is one of the main occupations of the artist or his or her assistants. If a particular painting sells well, umpteen copies are spawned. This explains why all over the island you'll find similar paintings portraying hackneyed tourist cliches of a tropical paradise—glowing sunsets, smoking volcanoes, sloe-eyed nymphs bathing. The worst, sold by peddlers on Kuta Beach, possess all the banality of velvet paintings in cocktail lounges.

The competition between all the small galleries and painters' studios has become so intense now that shop owners are contracting with travel agents and tour operators, paying Rp3-4 million up front for the delivery of busloads of tourists. This drives the price of the paintings up, since so many people have to be taken care of—the agent, the bus owner, the guide, the driver. But a tourist who only has a week in Bali and has the money to burn will buy expensive paintings, even for US$3000-4000, no problem. This is how such high-class galleries like Agung Rai, Rudana, and Agung Raka in Gianyar Regency have grown so fast.

To avoid getting fleeced, do your homework. Visit a number of galleries to learn about the different painting styles. Some have whole rooms dedicated to a distinct style so you can get a good sense of each. Don't be put off by the schlocky quality of the majority of the art on display. It's strictly for mass tourist consumption. Finding the best art takes persistence, and when you *do* find good art it costs a bundle.

If you see something you like in one of the big commercial galleries, you may be able to look up the artist in his or her home/studio, probably nearby. Many of Bali's finest painters live around the villages of Ubud, Batuan, Penestanan, Blahbatuh, and Sukawati—all major centers of Balinese painting in south-central Bali. Go to the village indicated on the painting and ask around in your primitive Indonesian. Many painters are even listed in the phone book. It could be 1000% cheaper if you buy directly from the artist, avoiding business with Ubud's countless galleries. Art shops customarily pay only 20-30% of the sale price to the artist. You also won't have to pay a commission (10-50%) to a guide or driver, which is tacked on to the price of a painting.

However, be aware that high quality paintings by well-known artists may be sold for the same price in the painter's home as they sell for in the galleries. This is because the painters do not want to undercut the galleries where their work is displayed and thus make a bad reputation for themselves. They want the galleries to continue to buy from them. They will sell a good painting to a gallery for Rp500,000, and the gallery in turn charges a million for it.

Naturally, the less successful painters are more likely to sell their paintings cheaper than the shops sell them for because they need the money faster. A painting of good souvenir quality costs about US$200. Ubud is the best place to shop for paintings in this class—the so-called Ubud-style—characterized by men and women naked from the waist up harvesting, planting, dancing, with leafy Spies-like trees and minute birds and insects filling all space.

The cost of higher quality paintings, if you can find them, is roughly US$500 per square meter, the price depending on the markup the owner of the gallery puts on a piece. Van Glerum's in The Hague and Christie's in Amsterdam hold Indonesian painting auctions twice a year, in which some canvases sell for tens of thousands of dollars.

As far as prices are concerned, "classes" of artists don't really mean much. It's the experience that counts. An older artist has a more accomplished stroke than a younger one. Now only the most established, prominent painters have their own studios. Lesser-known, younger artists can only exhibit in one of the hundreds of commercial art shops all over the island, or hit the road and peddle their paintings directly to tourists.

Some Buying Tips

Buy only something you really like. Ask yourself: "Do I want to look at this painting for the next 10 years?" Taste obviously plays an immense role in your purchasing decision. By no means should you take advice solely from a gallerist. Ask the locals and ask other tourists. Look at a lot of paintings.

Decide how much you have to spend. This will narrow your scope. With practice, you can tell the difference between a great artist and a mediocre one. Before you buy, decide where the painting is going to go in your house so it doesn't get stuffed in an attic forever.

If you've decided to invest in a fine piece of art, then start reading reference books (see "News, Travel, and Entertainment Media" under the Information and Services section in the On the Road chapter) and visit art galleries. Go to a gallery where paintings are clearly priced. Fixed prices are fairer to the purchaser; the artist also knows what price his work is being sold for. (You can still bargain a little, by the way.)

Galleries

Hundreds of large and small galleries are found all over Bali. Smaller galleries are more apt to bargain than big galleries. Walk up and down the roads of Ubud, Pengosekan, and Peliatan, an area smothered in art shops and galleries. With few exceptions, their interminable labyrinths are filled with a bewildering, conflicting, super-kitsch, haphazard collection of paintings from virtually every school encompassing widely differing styles and big gulfs in quality. In many cases, there are so many paintings that they're stacked up in piles on the floor. In addition to these commercial galleries, many painters have small galleries attached to their studios.

For an overview of the full range of Balinese painting, visit the **Neka Museum** (one km west of Ubud in Campuan), which displays the whole gamut of styles, prices, and sizes. This private museum, the first of its kind on Bali, is distinct from the Neka Gallery in Padangtegal (near Ubud). The owner/proprietor of both, Suteja Neka, is an important force in Balinese painting and has published several books on the subject (see Booklist). The first gallery owner to actively collect the art of expatriate painters, Neka is an excellent source of information and always has time to talk to visitors.

The museum, which should more aptly be called a gallery, is made up of Balinese-style buildings set in an exquisite garden. One room contains just the Balinese masters and early modernists such as Lempad and Togog; another contains just foreign artists who've worked in Bali like Smit, Spies, and Bonnet; another holds Indonesian academic artists who've painted in Bali; and yet another is filled with Western masters such as Blanco, Meier, Snel, and Friend. At the entrance, buy *Perceptions of Paradise* (Rp65,000) by Neka Gallery, as well as postcards of the famous works inside.

The superb, spacious, and expensive **Agung Rai Gallery** is in Peliatan (two km east of Ubud). Assembled by a self-made visionary collector of every school of Balinese art and an expert in the evolution of Balinese painting, Agung Rai's collection is accommodated in six separate display halls. Ask to visit the permanent collection and his private museum in Peliatan. The gallery sponsors well-attended painting classes on a regular basis. In 1995, the **Agung Rai Museum** complex opened in Peliatan. The three-hectare site consists of a spacious building for the permanent collection, another large structure for visiting exhibitions, an art school for children, a library, and an international artists colony.

Also don't miss the **Rudana Gallery** north of Mas and about one km south of Teges (south of Peliatan). The gallery displays a large collection of traditional, naive, and modern paintings in a sprawling complex of rooms. Also pay a visit to the **Sanggraha Kriya Astra Arts Centre** in Tohpati outside of Denpasar on the road to Ubud, where a wide range of good quality paintings are for sale at fair prices.

ARTS AND CRAFTS

The Balinese arts and crafts industry is a veritable engine of productivity. It is roughly divided into art for religion, art for tourists, and art for export to every corner of the world. Government-supported institutes work to create new craft products, promote art education, and revive dying artforms. Bali's primary schools offer pupils the opportunity to study painting, carving, dancing, etc., at least four hours per week.

With its thousands of art shops and hundreds of thousands of visiting tourists, Bali is also a major entrepôt of arts and crafts from all over the Indonesian archipelago—from giant Sasak water vases and Leti ancestor statues, to Batak magic wands, Sumbawanese basketware and Rotinese *ikat*. Imports—can also be found. Thai jackets, paintings from Europe—can also be found. The sheer glut of goods, in fact, makes shopping in Bali an overwhelming experience at first. There are so many handicrafts around that after awhile you may burn out and not even notice them anymore. You are haggled to buy-buy-buy on the beach, on the street, in restaurants, in stalls or stores, even seated on the porch of your lodging.

A woodcarving is one of the best value and unique purchases you can make, as carving is the Balinese creative art par excellence. Both wood and stone carvings are imaginative, inventive, and reflect superb technical skill. But bear in mind if you intend to send a wood or stone carving home, the cost of packaging and shipping can easily exceed the cost of the article. If you pack an article in unaccompanied baggage on the plane, make sure it gets a "fragile" sticker on it at baggage check-in.

Information

For more information on Balinese crafts, write **Impact Publications** (9104-N. Manassas Drive, Manassas Park, VA 22111, tel. 703-361-7300) for a copy of their *Shopping and Traveling in Exotic Indonesia* which outlines the best of the island's shopping. Also on the very handy **Pathfinder Map** (Silvio Santosa, 1985), for sale in Ubud bookshops, you can find the locations of craft villages around Ubud. Lonely Planet's 4th edition *Bali & Lombok: TSK* (1992) has a comprehensive photo essay of Balinese arts and crafts.

Studying Arts and Crafts

Since the Balinese are so dedicated to the arts and making beautiful things so ingrained in their society, Bali is an ideal place for Western artists to work and co-exist. Bali has long been considered the perfect working environment for an artist—a place preeminently conducive to creativity.

The following institutes accept paying Western students: **SESRI** (Sekolah Seni Rupa Indonesia), the School for the Visual Arts in Denpasar; **Fakultas Teknik** (Jurusan Seni Rupa) under the Technical Faculty at Udayana University in Denpasar; and **Sekolah Teknik** under the department of sculpture (Jurusan Ukir) at the Technical College in Guwang.

Expect to pay from Rp5000 to Rp10,000 per lesson, depending on the reputation of your teacher. It also helps to get a letter of recommendation from Wayan Paksa of Siti Homestay in Peliatan (Br. Kalah, tel. 0361-975599). Wayan can also help you obtain a cultural/study visa.

Shopping for Crafts

The most important thing to remember when buying crafts is to take your time. It doesn't take long to learn to distinguish quality. Leisurely browsing isn't always possible if you take part in guided tours because the bus stops at preselected showrooms and galleries, but if you're by yourself, you have all the time in the world.

All art shops accept traveler's checks and major currencies, most accept credit cards, and some even take American Express. A surcharge of five percent is added to your bill if you use a credit card. Rate of exchange offered by shops for traveler's checks is invariably worse than that given by moneychangers.

Much shopping on Bali still entails bargaining, a traditional and very acceptable way of doing business. Much to the relief of many Westerners, you may not bargain in fixed price shops. How can you tell a fixed-price shop? If it's a hotel gift shop, it's fixed price. And, generally speaking, if it's an a/c store with glass doors and/or windows and the wares have price tags, it's fixed price. But even if there's a sign reading *Harga Pasti* (fixed price) or "Sorry—Fixed but very Reasonable Price," and the clerk says all prices are fixed, always give it a try. Cut the asked price in half, then you may end up with a 25% discount. This technique used to work better but now the Balinese have responded by quadrupling their prices to ensure adequate profits.

Effective bargaining requires knowledge of the correct price. For a high-priced purchase like a big wooden statue or a leather jacket, do your research first and buy in a reputable outlet. Check out the price first in a fixed-price shop, to give you a good idea of what you should be paying, then hit the streets to see how well you can do. Bargaining is not arguing. Executed with good humor, it provides both buyer and seller with a mutually acceptable price. Prices may seem absolute, but they may not be. It may take you an hour or even repeated visits to clinch a sale. A few minutes spent in bargaining will usually obtain a 20-30%—sometimes 50%—reduction in the price. For more on bargaining, see the "Money" section of the Introduction.

The best time to go shopping is in the evening when it's considerably cooler. In some hotel gift shops, prices are given in rupiah; in others prices are quoted in U.S. dollars. Always pay in rupiah, which almost always works out cheaper (if you're getting a good rate of exchange). Also, Legian is cheaper than Kuta. In fact, the further north you travel on Jl. Legian (if starting from Bemo Corner), the cheaper it gets.

During certain seasons, prices are more favorable. French tourists start raining down on Bali in July and August, and Aussies overrun the island during the Christmas holidays and January school break. But from March to June, crafts can be one-fourth to one-half the usual price. During these four months, a small Garuda carving, which goes for Rp45,000 in the high season, is down to Rp10,000; full-length dresses in Ubud sell for only Rp15,000 (other months: Rp35,000); Rp75,000 paintings are only Rp25,000; small wall-hangings just Rp5000.

To cut down on costs, avoid taking your guide and/or driver or agent into a gallery or art shop. Why? They'll almost always expect the gallery owner to give them a commission. The majority have made arrangements with the owner beforehand and will always steer you into only those shops paying them commissions. This is why guides are always so eager to take you shopping. Visit the home of the artist instead, saving yourself the percentage (10-50%) of the

---

SELLERS' FAVORITE LINES

"Special price only for you."

"Very cheap. No profit for me!"

"For good luck . . ."

"Okay, you pay for fabric only . . ."

"Please come to my stand or my boss very mad." (A favorite of winsome 14- and 15-year-old girls.)

THE CRAFT VILLAGES OF BALI

For handicrafts at their cheapest, and for the widest range, go to these craft villages. Certain villages are known for certain crafts, and each has several outlets selling the specialized craft the village is known for. Frequently, crafts are made on the premises and visitors are allowed to observe and photograph. Some of the villages, like Bona and Batubulan, will stage dance and musical performances while you're shopping. Take a break and take in a little culture. The following is an alphabetical list of Balinese crafts centers:

Bangli: The unspoiled *pasar* sells terra-cotta vessels, soft pandan leaf mats, cattle bone carvings, incense, and household utensils.

Batuan: Especially crowded, you'll find "Batuan-style" paintings and carved and painted wooden panels.

Batubulan: Sandstone carving center. Visit a stonecarver and watch him and his apprentices work. You'll also find antique shops.

Bedugul: Orchids and other flowering plants, bamboo, fresh fruit and vegetables.

Bona: A center for the plaiting industry. Shops here sell large, heavy bamboo chairs and tables, *lontar* mats, delicate split bamboo mats, baskets, sandals, bags, fans, bamboo birds and flowers, and coconut shells fashioned into bowls and spoons.

Celuk: Silverwork, particularly delicate filigree jewelry. Prices are better in family workshops in the back lanes. Shops also sell textiles, woodcarving, and tortoise-shell carvings.

Denpasar: Pasar Kumbasari's morning market sells farm and fish produce, dry goods, spices, clothing, and housewares. Cheap garden tools, rice cookers, horse-bells, woks, woven mats, and traditional implements can also be bought here. Also visit the city's textile street, Jl. Sulawesi, running beside Pasar Kumbasari. Denpasar's gold street is Jl. Kartini, which leads into Jl. Sulawesi. Just outside of Denpasar in Tohpati, the Government Handicraft Center sells gift items, silver, leather, textiles, and woodcarvings at fixed prices.

Gianyar: The handloom weaving (*batik* and *endek*) center of Bali, Gianyar is an excellent place to shop for textiles at good prices. Buy direct from the factories themselves.

Goa Gajah: basketry, leatherwork, horn and bone carvings.

Kamasan: Eggs, hats, bags, and all manner of goods painted in the typical *wayang*-style of Kamasan. Buy directly from the masters. Also traditional astrological calenders, silver bowls, gold jewelry, and other metal working.

Kemenuh: Very active woodcarving area.

Kintamani: Aggressive street hawkers sell ebony woodcarvings and bone and horn spoons.

Klungkung: Oranamental jewelry, *kris,* wood and horn handicrafts, and fine woven *songket* cloths. Buy 22-carat gold jewelry at Notina.

Kramas: A village of weavers of Balinese weft *ikat.* Buy directly from the factories.

Kuta: Some of the finest clothing and garment shops in all of Asia, especially for Euro-designs and beachwear. Stylish boutiques sell leather, kid's clothes, handicrafts, and jewelry. Also audio cassettes, shoes, straw hats, shells, furniture, home furnishings and accessories.

Mas: A major woodcarving and painting center with numerous galleries to explore, a must for wood sculpture collectors.

Pejatan (20 km west of Denpasar): Distinctive terra-cotta figurines and tiles.

Puaya: Leather *wayang kulit* puppets.

Pujung: Woodcarving center.

Sanur: Check out the rambling antique furniture shops on Jl. Bypass running between Sanur and Nusa Dua. Scores of shops carry glazed ceramics, gold and silverwork, and Balinese *ikat* fabrics along Sanur's Jl. Danau Tamblingan.

Singapadu: The maskmaking center of Bali. A few craftsmen take Western students.

Sukawati: Bali's largest and most accessible market for religious paraphernalia such as umbrellas, *prada* cloths, dance costumes, offering vessels, and magic marrows. Also good *wayang kulit,* wind chimes, split bamboo basketry, and everything imaginable that's woven out of lantana or bamboo. Visit both the old market and the newer Sukawati Art Center

Tampaksiring: Coconut, cattle bone, and buckhorn carvings.

Tegalalang: Soft-wood carving center for small animal tables, brightly painted flowers and fruit, and other artifacts. Pieces may split and crack after they've arrived in the temperate climate of North America, as the wood is improperly cured.

Tenganan: Rare, unique, and expensive *gringsing* handwoven textiles made by the double-*ikat*

method, tightly woven grass baskets, *tingklik* musical instruments, and *lontar* (palm leaf) manuscripts and calenders.

Ubud and Peliatan: These twin towns are art centers with literally hundreds of galleries large and small, stocking the most comprehensive collection of paintings in Bali. For paintings, also scout the neighboring hamlets of Campuan, Penestanan, Sanggingan, Sebatu, and Pengosekan. Every school of Balinese painting is represented here. Small shops sell woodcarving, silver, anqitues and clothes. Ubud's open market sells aromatic oils, grasses, and tropical potpourris in tiny kiosks in the back.

cost which must go toward the commission. Often paintings that sell for US$2500 in the art shops on Ubud's main road the artist sells himself for US$300-400 in his home studio just down the path in the *kampung behind* the art shops. You can find the artist's home through persistent inquiry, or in the phone book or by using directory assistance (tel. 108).

Don't buy big-ticket items from street peddlers and hawkers. You're just fresh meat to these shrewd professionals, and if the item is shoddy, misrepresented, or if you want to trade it for another you have no guarantees and no recourse. Just tell them you already have it. Stick to shops your friends have recommended. You have to trust the seller.

Where to Buy

Most of the big art shops are found on the main tourist corridor between Denpasar and Ubud. This crowded road, for a stretch of 25 km, is dotted with hundreds of boutiques and art shops selling every type and quality of souvenir, painting, carving, antique, jewelry, handicraft, readyto-wear clothing, and woven cloth. The bigger the gravel parking lot, the more likely it is the shop caters to tour groups and the prices will be ridiculous.

Tour buses tend to visit only those places which can accommodate the large a/c buses. If a shop doesn't pay to get the buses to stop, it is destined to pine away into oblivion. These showrooms are increasingly located behind or beyond the craft villages. Vendors on motorcycles, offering carvings and paintings in US dol-

lars, follow and descend upon the buses everywhere they stop.

In price, quality, and variety, the Ubud area offers some of the island's best shopping. Shops lie close together and you can wander up and down Monkey Forest Road in a leisurely fashion. Another extremely dense concentration is Jl. Legian in Kuta/Legian, and the roads running from Jl. Legian to the beach. In the traditional village of Tenganan on the eastern part of the island, arts and crafts products are possibly the best that Bali has to offer. The crafts are not expensive, and it's a great six-kilometer walk through thick forests to get there from Candidasa.

Hotel gift shops usually carry a good selection of the island's crafts but at high prices. The cheapest and most hassle-free tourist shops are in Candidasa on the east coast. Here you can buy a *sarung,* for example, for as little as Rp6000. Other places for the same *sarung* you'll hear "Rp20,000 but for you I make special price Rp15,000."

The **Sanggraha Kriya Asta** (Government Handicraft Center, P.O. Box 254, Denpasar, tel. 0351-222942) in Tohpati, is just 10 minutes by *bemo* from Denpasar on the road to Ubud. This fixed-price art cooperative is made up of five roomy buildings, each containing an important craft—silver and goldwork, paintings, stone- and woodcarvings, textiles, and clothing. The center has always been a good place to visit to determine a fair price for bargaining purposes, but lately their prices have gone up. Though they have a large selection and the quality of the goods are high, the silver, woodcarving, and clothing are now more than double what you would pay in Ubud. Kriya Asta doesn't give commissions to guides and their mobiles are still cheap. Open daily 0830-1700, Saturday 0830-1630, closed Sunday. Free transportation provided.

Don't forget the supermarkets/department stores, where you can come across surprisingly reasonable items: In Kuta, visit **Gelael Dewata,** Jl. Raya Kuta next to the gas station on the way to Denpasar, and **Alas Arum,** Seminyak, close to Jl. Dhyana Pura; in **Sanur,** head to **Gelael Dewata** on Jl. Bypass; in **Denpasar** you'll find **Tiara Dewata,** Jl. M.J. Soetoyo, and **Hero,** Jl. Dewi Sartika; and **Tragia** right in the middle of Nusa Dua in the Galleria.

Matahari Dept. Store, in the eastern part of Denpasar (ask directions, everybody knows where it is), consists of three amazing floors selling everything under the Balinese sun—fashion clothes, cheap well-made nonethnic Western clothes, stationery, household furnishings, sporting goods, untold racks of T-shirts. It even has a supermarket and a KFC in the basement.

Mega is a six-shop art shop chain. The main one is at Jl. Gajah Mada 36 (tel. 0361-224592) with branches in the outskirts of Denpasar on the road to Gianyar (Jl. Gianyar, Km 5.7, tel. 0361-228855); in Kuta at Jl. Raya Kuta 137 (tel. 0361-751626) and at the Pertamina Cottages Arcade (tel. 0361-751161); in Sanur in the Bali Hyatt Hotel arcade (tel. 0361-288271); in Nusa Dua in the Bali Hilton International Arcade No. 15 (tel. 0361-71102). Mega stores have a great variety of items, and prices aren't too outrageous. Depending on the location (Bali Hilton is much more expensive than the one in Denpasar), silver bracelets cost US$12, three sorts of *wayang* puppets US$10-20; also textiles, *kris,* etc. The branch at the Km 5.7 mark in Denpasar's outskirts is a *huge* emporium of arts and crafts.

Art Markets

If you have only two or three days on Bali, you may not have time to batter your way down Kuta's Jl. Legian in the heat and traffic going into all the shops. In this case, the art markets of Bali offer an excellent overview of all the available crafts and souvenirs.

Every major tourist center and medium-size town has an art market. One of the best is **Pasar Badung** by the river in the center of Denpasar. Different commodities—cookware, *batik,* bamboo basketry, fabrics—are all offered in the market. Bargaining is an absolute must at this huge multistoried market; it helps to have a working knowledge of Indonesian.

More tourist-oriented **Kumbasari Shopping Center,** a giant market just west of Pasar Badung across the river, is choked with hundreds of small shops selling ready-to-wear, house furnishings, knickknacks, woodcarvings, textiles, jewelry, and other crafts. Prices are unbeatable. Sanur also has an art market on Jl. Segara on the beach, but prices are substantially higher.

The mother of all art markets on Bali is the **Pasar Seni,** in Sukawati on the main road from Denpasar to Ubud. A big two-story building with shops and stalls inside and out, this is one-stop shopping at its best. Very comprehensive and diverse range of basketware, place mats, sarongs, local fabrics, *ikat,* woodcarvings including carved fruit, the usual *barong* T-shirts, and lots of ethnic kitsch—all at the lowest possible prices. Offer no more than one-third of the opening bid. Two roadside shops here sell authentic dancers' costumes and hats, rhinestone-studded gold leather angel wings, and other paraphrenalia, but not cheap.

In addition, small village markets usually have small stalls that sell traditional implements to the Balinese; English is not spoken. Souvenir stalls have also sprouted up around all the most popular tourist sites: Tanah Lot, Tampaksiring, Goa Gadjah, Goa Lawah, Besakih, Tirtagangga, etc.

Don't miss the fascinating, one-of-a-kind, old-style Asian market in Klungkung, just past the stoplight (coming from Denpasar) in the middle of the block on your right. Different sections—to the left is bamboo, ready-made clothing, *sarung,* and more. Good prices. One of Bali's best kept secrets.

Shipping Crafts

If you have bought quite a bit of stuff and want to ship it back home, sea mail (surface post) via the Indonesian postal service is the cheapest way to go. It will take a trip into Denpasar, Kuta, Singaraja, or Ubud to the *paket pos* office, an hour of your time, and will cost around Rp4500 per kilo. Overseas-bound packages may be posted, insured, and registered *(tercatat)*.

For a large quantity of goods, use one of the numerous air and sea freight forwarding services, concentrated in all the major tourist centers. These professionals assure secure packing and can arrange all the paperwork and permits to ensure your shipment's safe arrival. They also provide pick up service. Cost depends on the weight of the goods and the destination. Beware of all the ludicrous add-on costs like the "Archaeology Certificate" and the "Container Freight Station" charge which could double a US$300 ocean freight bill (150 kg). For more on shipping parcels overseas, refer to "Information and Services" in the On the Road chapter.

WOODCARVING

There are two main types of woodcarving. Traditional carvings, in the form of intricate bas-relief tableaux and plaques, are used mainly for decorating doors, walls and columns. Small, highly standardized wooden statues of deities and mythical heroes are also produced, designed for use in public buildings. The second type is contemporary woodcarving, first developed in the 1930s. Themes usually include highly stylized human or animal figures, often grotesque, almost psychotic—expressing so well the Balinese fear of the supernatural. These symbolic carvings evidence a very strong, sensual feeling for nature.

For the most part, a purely souvenir variety of modern woodcarving is turned out now. Twenty or thirty talented and innovative artists have evolved their own distinctive styles, and—just as in Balinese painting—their successful creations are often assembly-line produced. Fortunately, the technical skill remains high. A dozen or so places in Mas, Kemenuh, and Sumampan, the principal woodcarving centers, sell high-quality carvings for as much as US$3500 apiece.

Some "galleries," like Ida Bagus Marka in Kemenuh, are actually large complexes of adjoining rooms containing carvings in all sizes, themes, and colors—from Rp30,000 to Rp10 million. But regardless of commercial orientation, all carvings share certain characteristics

and techniques uniquely Balinese. Even the copyists work strictly within the self-imposed parameters of an established style. Virtually all woodcarvers and maskmakers accept special orders. Bring a photo or a picture of the piece you'd like copied.

History

In the times of Bali's old feudal kingdoms, woodcarving served as temple decoration and as the *bale* of the rajas. Wood was also utilized in such everyday household features as carved beams, columns, doors for houses, and implements like musical instruments, tool handles, bottle-stoppers, and hilts of *kris*. All these functional carvings were painted in bright colors, lacquer, or gold leaf; seldom was the wood left raw.

The 1930s, with the ever-increasing influx of tourists, saw a dramatic change in the perspective of Balinese wood sculptors. Shops, street corners, hotel lobbies, marketplaces, the airport, and harbors suddenly blossomed with objets d'art of an unequivocally commercial mold, produced to sell. In contrast to the traditional polychrome, mythological religious carvings, more realistic statues of peasants toiling, nude girls bathing and deer grazing appeared, themes that found a very ready market among the tourists. This mercenary impulse gave the art a terrific boost. An export market soon developed, which found Balinese statues turning up in Jakarta, Singapore, Paris.

One of the most striking milestones in modern Balinese sculpture was the emergence of the fluid form of figure sculpture with elongated arms and face, resembling the thinness of a Giacometti statue or a long-necked Modigliani. This style was born one day in 1930 when the artist I **Tegelan** of Belaluan was asked by Walter Spies to carve two statues from a long piece of wood. Several days later the carver returned with a single statue of a girl with an exaggeratedly lengthened torso. I Tegelan told the delighted Spies he refused to cut such a beautiful piece of wood in two. With Spies's encouragement and support, the abstract style soon caught on, and its appeal to carvers and tourists alike continues to this day.

During the highly creative 1930s, other techniques also developed. Competition gave rise to much experimentation. In the villages of Peliatan and Nyuhkuning (near Ubud), sculptors delicately carved animals and birds with either astounding realism or in caricature, distorting the features of a subject to heighten its special character. Often the Balinese artist mischievously sculpted a creature's face to resemble someone in the community—a stingy old man would be portrayed as a detestable beetle; a fat, ill-tempered woman as a waddling querulous duck.

One sculptor, **I Tjokot,** cleverly chiseled great whorls of demons, divinities, and other mythological characters out of thick tree branches, crafting his sculptures into benches, lamp supports, and trays. It's still easy to recognize I Tjokot's abiding earmark, most often hollowed-out tree stumps over one meter high. A few of this master's original works may be seen in Ubud's Puri Lukisan.

Another outstanding carver of modern times was **Ida Bagus Njana** of Mas, who created phantasmagoric abstract sculptures of human beings and surrealistic knotty "natural" sculptures out of gnarly tree trunks. Only small incisions on the surface indicated contours, the wavy grain of the wood contributing to the motion of the figure. Ida Bagus was also the progenitor of the fat statues of toads, elephants, and corpulent sleeping women you now see everywhere. Several of his carvings may be seen in Ubud's Museum. His son, **Ida Bagus Tilem** of Mas, is a talented sculptor in his own right and enjoys an international reputation.

Contemporary Woodcarving

Traditional-style pieces are still carved. These exotic, utterly imaginary compositions still hold a basic fascination for tourists: mythological characters like the great god Vishnu riding on the back of Garuda, a menacing demon brandishing a *kris,* and other immortal deities, villains, and legendary beasts from the *Ramayana.*

If you bargain, Balinese religious statues go for as low as Rp10,000. These free-standing sculptures once served as protective figures for households or as resting places for honored gods during prayer offerings and other ceremonies. Dressed in classical attire and profusely ornamented, you'll find Hanuman wrestling a serpent, a dancing Sita, and painted woodcarvings of a mythic bird to hang from your ceiling. Called "The Bird of Life," this motif is used in cremation ceremonies as the bearer of a deceased person's soul to heaven.

In Kuta, the starting price for large mythological statuary is Rp100,000, but the price will come down to Rp50,000 or less in the place where it's sculpted. The villages of Pujung, Jati, and Tegalalang, on the road from Ubud to Gunung Batur, are great places to wander around and meet carvers. Sebatu is another really active family-oriented woodcarving center (check out the huge elephants at Sedana Yogya by Iwy. Genjur). Nearly the whole population of these communities, including the children, are busy turning chunks of hibiscus, *sawo,* and *belalu* into technicolor sculptures of trees, fruit, flowers, flying angels, cartoon figures, or whatever. Prices are very reasonable (don't forget to take cash), and you'll see pieces hard to find in the high-priced factories of Mas and Kemenuh. If you want something made to order, it isn't a problem and will usually take about two weeks.

Some of Bali's best woodcarvers also come from the villages of Singakerta and Pengosekan, both walkable from Ubud. The best *kodok* work on the island can be found in these two villages. Batuan (near Ubud) is the place to shop for carved wood panels.

Buddha statues, still very much in vogue, come in two sizes: big ones Rp15,000, small ones Rp7000; old men and *pedanda,* Rp10,000; a grandmother and grandfather pair, Rp20,000. The *singa* (lion) motif is also seen widely. A unique collectible are *lontar,* the fan-like leaves of a species of palm tree. For hundreds of years sacred texts have been meticulously inscribed on these dried strips of palm, shaped like rulers. These masterpieces of illustrative art and calligraphy provide the only record of ancient Balinese culture, history, and literature.

Chess sets of carved teakwood (or bone) are also quite distinctive. Balinese *wayang golek* (puppets in-the-round) are larger than Javanese ones. First price is around Rp25,000, but you can get them down to Rp15,000 apiece. For carved chopsticks, some foot peddlers on Kuta ask as much as Rp8000 a pair, although you can get them as low as Rp3000-4000 a pair. They are beautifully carved with owl-head, abstract, or *garuda* designs. Whole box sets of 12 pairs go for only Rp15,000 first price. Don't pay more than Rp2000 a pair for low-end ones.

One abiding product is whole carved banana, durian, or coconut palm trees, colossally heavy and hanging with wooden fruit. It takes about a month to produce one of these two-meter-tall trees. The wood used is *Albizzia falcata,* which is easy to work with and readily available. Also found are giant wooden replicas of the "high offerings" which disassemble and fit solidly back together again. Fruits like rambutan and jackfruit come alive under the carver's skillful hands. The center for this type of carving is Tegallalang (Gianyar).

For something different, the more ancestral woodcarvings of the un-Javanized Bali Aga people of the uplands have a more primitive feel than those produced in the Hinduized portions of the island. To see traditional *gamelan* instrument makers carve ornate stands and frames for instruments, visit the workshop of Pak Gabeleran in Blahbatuh, and the *gong kembar* factory near the village of Tihingan, 10 km southwest of Klungkung.

Techniques

Woodcarving is a skill requiring more precision and sureness than that of carving stone. The carver starts with a virgin block of wood which he hacks down to roughly the same size as the piece to be carved. Using very simple tools, the carver lightly taps the highly sharpened instruments. Unlike the technique used in the West, he does not use hand pressure except for really close work.

Fine-grained hardwoods such as teak *(jati),* and strong fruit trees such as jackfruit *(nangka),* the compact *sawo* (a beautiful dark red wood), shiny ebony *(ebon),* tamarind, hibiscus, frangipani, and *kayu jepun* are the most popular carving woods.

The texture of the grain determines the nature of the piece to be carved. Dark ebony, particularly pieces with striped grain, are best suited for vertical shapes or faces. Rarer are pieces made of unpolished ebony (sanded and brushed only) where you can make out the grain in the wood. The blackest ebony might be used to depict a subject of great dignity. Satinwood, a light striped, beige-colored wood native to Bali, may inspire pieces of a softer theme. The grain often follows a skin pattern or veins in the arms of the statue.

Traditionally, if the statue is not to be gilded or painted it is made smooth with pumice and given a high polish by rubbing it with bamboo. These finished carvings were once treated and stained with oils to achieve a pleasing subtle gloss, but now Balinese artisans find that neutral or black shoe polish produces much the same result with half the effort.

Walking down the lanes of the carving villages, you can hear the gentle hammering, sanding, and spontaneous chatter of the woodcarvers. They sit crosslegged on the floor surrounded by piles of freshly carved wood chips and rough, uncut blocks as chickens peck their way around the tools. The sweet aroma of clove cigarettes and coffee fills the air.

Carvers are paid by the day (Rp5000-10,000), polishers earn about Rp100,000 per month. Top-class carvers earn 60% of the selling price. These master carvers usually do not jealously guard their creations but share ideas willingly with sons and assistants. They invite apprentices to study carving under them. These pupils eventually turn out accomplished pieces patterned after their teacher's style.

Studying Woodcarving

Students can get a lot out of learning woodcarving under masters like Muka and Anom in Mas. These teachers charge Rp10,000 per day for a lesson, and if you go every day, you can learn to carve your own mask in about three weeks. The carver guides and supervises your work.

Most students buy their own knives so they can continue carving at home. Because of all the carving activity on the island, Bali is one of the best places in Indonesia to buy a set of carving knives—chisels, gouges, scrapers, mallets in every shape and size. A complete 30-piece set, made from flat steel, costs Rp30,000-35,000. The steel in better sets (up to Rp190,000) comes from ground-down automobile springs or concrete reinforcing rods and keeps its edge better than stainless steel. The better sets include 18 tools, two wooden mallets, and three finishing knives. Ask around the carving villages or buy them where Muka buys his.

Buying Woodcarvings

Look for a carving that radiates a vitality, that possesses an inner life of its own. Some figurine carving is unique with faces of painstaking detail. Always bargain; high, fixed prices are intended for the tour bus participants who don't have time to bargain. If the price is reasonable, buy it. In Candidasa, where prices are low, Rangda masks cost as little as Rp25,000 (but start at Rp50,000). In carving centers like Mas and Kemenuh, carved banana trees cost Rp75,000, or you can walk down the road and find the same tree for Rp35,000 (starting price).

Explore Denpasar's **Art Centre** (Taman Werdi Budaya, Jl. Nusa Indah in Abiankapas, a suburb of Denpasar) before making any purchases. Here you'll see a wide range of carving. Also visit the row of antique shops in Klungkung (east of the Kerta Gosa), and the **Arts of Asia Gallery,** Jl. Raya Tuban, Denpasar, tel. 752860 (see Darwiko).

For a souvenir style carving, head to Denpasar's **Kumbasari Shopping Center,** a rabbit warren of shops bristling with carvings—most the tall, thin, Lempad-inspired type. Decent statues run in the Rp35,000-45,000 range. **Mahartha,** Jl. Ir. Soetami 8, Kemenuh, is a very talented family woodcarver in the neighborhood of Mas who speaks English, Dutch, and a little French.

The gallery of **Ida Bagus Tilem,** one of the great Balinese carvers, is located in Mas. Many of his carvings are not for sale, and the ones for sale are very expensive. **I Wayan Sila** sells beautiful carvings for a reasonable price. While in Mas, check out the **Tantra Gallery** too.

In Gianyar, Dutch priest Pater Maurice runs a carving school where you can see the finest carved teakwood panels, some several meters in length. They are priced by the cubic meter. Smaller ones are also for sale.

If the seller claims that an article is made of pure sandalwood from Nusatenggara Timur, there's a 99% chance it is some cheap imitation like coffeewood, even if it *smells* like sandalwood. Also beware of bargain prices for "ebony" carvings. True ebony is expensive, very dense, heavy, and has a glossy, reddish-brown striped surface. If the statue is painted, it's difficult to detect defects in the wood. Check for cracks and make sure all attached parts—like wings, crowns, and feet—are properly fitted. Have the carver explain any discoloration. To prevent the wood from cracking and shrinking in more tem-perate Western climes, some dealers have drilled a large cavity within the statue to allow moisture to escape. The bottoms of truly old statuary have not been touched.

MASKMAKING

Balinese masks *(topeng)* are seen most often in the scores of regular dance performances in special tourist venues all over southern Bali, as well as in resturants and hotels. For ritual purposes, the Balinese use masks most often when celebrating temple birthdays. With over 20,000 temples on Bali, each with a different birthday every 210 days, there is ample opportunity to see *topeng* in action. Masks are also displayed "officially" in processions and trance rituals.

Sacred masks must be made from crocodile wood *(pule),* a tree that grows in cemeteries, the domain of the goddess Rangda. The whole tree isn't cut down. When the *pule* tree produces a knot, the maskmaker asks the spirit of the tree to be allowed to take the knot for a mask.

The most difficult part of the carving is removing the back, which usually takes a day and a half. Carving out the nose and getting around the knots can also be very time-consuming. The sand-papering of the average mask lasts about four hours. A plain natural wooden mask only takes around five days to treat because it is protected with just three layers of neutral shoe polish. On a painted mask, however, up to 80 coats (maximum number of coats in one day is four) are applied. This is really arduous work because the piece is held between the feet. For paint, calcified pigbone is used. It's pulverized for 12 hours to make a powder, then mixed with Chinese lacquer.

Finally, real hair and gold leaf may be used to embellish the mask. Once the mask is finished and before it is used by a dancer for the first time, a traditional ceremony is performed by a priest to remove the carver's spirit from the mask, enabling the dancer's spirit to enter.

A very good introduction to Balinese *wayang topeng* can be found in *Masks of Bali* (Chronicle Books, 1992) by Judy Slattum (photographs by Paul Schraub). This beautiful picture book includes 50 stunning photographs of Balinese

BALINESE *TOPENG* MASKS

Only first-class artisans carve the masks used in Bali's theater performances. Maskmaking is a thriving business in and around Mas and Singapadu, the two maskmaking centers of Bali, where scores of maskmakers work. They don't lack for business; overseas orders are regularly placed for 50-200 masks at a time. Inside these shops a petrified world of surprisingly human faces stare eerily from the walls. The best actors make the best salesmen as they strap on the masks and act out realistically the appropriate personality. When a Western actor puts on a mask he pretends he is another person, but when a Balinese dancer puts on a mask he totally identifies with the personality being depicted. In a word, he *becomes* that person.

Balinese masks are elaborately decorated with real hair, fang-like teeth, bright colors, bulging eyes, and hinged jaws. Of the 30-odd *topeng* masks—from dashing lords to bucktoothed clowns, some are full-faced, which prevents speaking, and some are half-faced, which allows speaking. The carver must not only possess great skill but also a meditative turn of mind and a profound scholarly knowledge. The expressiveness of the face is paramount; the *topeng* maker must be familiar with all the typical movements that the performer of each *topeng* makes so that his character can be portrayed by the mask's expression. Colors also indicate personality—red or black masks depict a powerful rival with full face and large features, while the more refined white masks are usually reserved for a king and his queen. It is the eyes which must radiate the soul of the character; only one mask in perhaps 50 can achieve this power. Some sacred masks are so powerful that they are sometimes brought to the homes of the sick and have been credited with miraculous cures. A carver's connection with a revered mask brings him great status in the community.

The traditional maskmaker is not just a woodworker but someone who creates works of art. The traditional *tapel*-making process is arduous. First the wood is picked for the particular mask, a strong, low-density, lightly colored wood of the balsam family called *pule (Alstonia scholaris)*. The green wood, which gives off an offensive odor, has to be seasoned for several months before work can begin. The carver sits cross-legged on a mat holding the mask with the feet and, making confident, swift strokes, first carves an outline of the face, then begins work on such facial details as hair, curls, wrinkles, frowns, scowls, and leering grimaces. To mark the positions of the features, the carver uses a pencil and a sliver of bamboo. A full day is spent sanding the mask to satin-smoothness with sandpaper and the split ends of bamboo. At ear level on each side of the mask holes are then punched for the head strap. Traditionally, paints were made from calcified deer bones (nowadays pig jaw bones), charcoal, clay, and gold leaf, then mixed with a binder *(ancur)* made from fish gelatin. Sometimes up to 30 coats of paint are meticulously applied, then mother-of-pearl teeth, goatskin, eyebrows and moustaches, and real pig's fangs finish the mask off and bring it to life. To see traditional masks being made the old-fashioned way, visit the workshop of I Wayang Tangguh in Singapadu.

masks, the first mask history, explanations on the process of making ritual masks, and the specific types and functions of making Balinese masks. Anyone who is shopping for a mask, or who already owns one, can find in this book the type of character it represents and for which rituals it is used. For more complete information on Balinese *wayang topeng,* see under "The Performing Arts" section of this chapter.

Notable Maskcarvers

I Wayan Tangguh and Cokorde Raka Tisnu are perhaps the most accomplished traditional maskmakers working on Bali. I Wayan Tedun of Singapadu and I Wayan Muka and I.B. Anom of Mas also do good work. Prices for top quality masks run from Rp75,000 to Rp150,000, depending on the style, the wood and paint used, etc.

Oka Trevelyan Mask Makers was created by David Trevelyan, a Canadian artist, and Ida Bagus Oka, a master carver from Mas. The result of this remarkable fusion of talents from two different cultures is Tlingit Indian-style masks found in the northwestern United States. Visit their showroom in Mas in front of Anom's.

Besides Mas, the village of Puaya near Sukawati is a maskmaking center. Many shops along Ubud's Monkey Forest Road and Kuta's Jl. Legian sell attractive masks. Also, visit the Bali Museum to see a fine collection of Balinese *topeng,* and in the Mangkunegaran Palace of Yogya is a very complete collection of famous *topeng* from Bali.

STONECARVING

The Balinese seem unable to tolerate unadorned stone. With fanged, bulging-eyed statues guarding every gate and shrine, and walls, benches and pedestals of traffic signs carved in stone, stone-carving is so ubiquitous on Bali, you may begin to take it for granted. Superbly crafted stonework is also much in evidence in Bali's hotel properties—from humble homestays to luxurious five-star resorts.

An art patronized almost exclusively by the Balinese themselves, the carvings on Bali's communal public buildings—temple walls, drum towers, gateways, public baths, hotels, court-houses—are exuberantly ornamental, a riot of swirling spirals, arabesques, intricate volutes, swastikas, leaves, rivers, tendrils, flowers, and trees.

Balinese temples are never really finished, guaranteeing that stonecarving will continue as a living art. Stonecarving has been unaffected by tourist consumerism because stone is too dear to ship home. This doesn't mean you can't slip a 10 kg stone statue in your flight bag, but be careful as the stone used, though unexpectedly light, is also fragile and easily crumbles.

Temple stonecarving reflects the creative assimilation which has been at work on Bali for 2,000 years. Elements of Chinese and Dutch decorative art, such as winged lions and floral patterns, have crept into stonecarvings, and on their temples and in many of the interior altars lightbulbs have been embedded into the intricate stone masonry, even though there's no electricity in these buildings!

The stonecarving style of southern Bali, typified by the temple architecture found in Denpasar, Tabanan, Gianyar, Bangli, and Klungkung, is more subdued than that of the north. The baroque, flame-like entranceways of northern temples stand tall and slender; their reliefs are more lavish and depict more lighthearted and comic scenes than those of the south. Since the north was occupied by the Dutch a full 60 years before the south, you'll find in Buleleng Regency's stone art more images from European magazines and movies. This is where the Balinese sense of humor and ribaldry really shows. Panels are filled with buzzing airplanes, bobbing sailing ships, car holdups by two-gunned masked bandits, bicycles made of flowers, grinning monkeys, Dutchmen drinking beer, long-bearded Arabs, and automobile breakdowns. New influences taken in without destroying the integrity of the old is a trademark of Balinese history.

Carving Material

The material for stonecarving is a soft, ashy, light gray volcanic sandstone *(paras)* quarried from the banks of rivers. When freshly dug from the river and still soft, it's roughly cut and shaped with adzes, then transported to the temple site. At first as malleable as plastic, the stone grows harder, more durable and darker with time.

The extreme softness of "new" *paras,* which feels almost like dried mud, accounts for the over-lavish adornment of Balinese art in stone. These flaming motifs combined with the Balinese love of loud colors, gives some of their temples the appearance of a carnival ride. The most outrageously painted temples in northern Bali are in the villages of Jagaraga, Bebetin, and Ringdikit. In the north, sandstone is more durable than in the south, and thus temple sculpture is considerably more flamboyant. Eaten away by rain and weathering, the soft volcanic tuff of southern Bali requires carvings be replaced or refurbished at least every five years. Statues only a decade old may appear to date from the Majapahit invasion.

To see a *paras* quarry, where rock is cut from cliffs with long knives, visit Blayu and Kukuh on the way to Marga. Climb down the hill from the stacks of *paras* water filters, cornerstones, and blocks on the road.

Motifs and Themes

There are as many carving styles as there are carvers. Because the Balinese believe constant maintenance of their stone temples is a moral obligation, stone sculpture survives today as the only Balinese art with a religious function.

Stone statuary were never intended as holy objects of worship, but rather were looked upon as pure embellishment or dwelling-places for invisible spirits invited down from heaven.

Stone figures *(pratimas)* often portray religious personages—best described as "pictures in stone." One seldom sees stone representations of such deities as Vishnu, Shiva, or Sanghyang Widhi. Demons, *raksasa,* giants, and evil spirits are the preferred subject matter. In the *pura dalem* (Temple of Death), the witch-queen Rangda is often enshrined, immobile and threatening, in her own niche.

Numerous steadfast rules must be followed when carving the final decoration for a temple. Over the entrance must always hang the face of a coarse, leering monster *(Kala* or *Bhoma)* with wicked lolling tongue, splayed hands, tusklike teeth, the lower jaws missing. It prevents evil characters from slipping into the sacred grounds. Two guardian demons almost always flank the steps to the gateway or stand guard to either side (as they do at both ends of Balinese

bridges) as well. Esoteric religious symbols and grotesque mythological creatures such as one-eyed birds and heads of elephants glare out from temple friezes or adorn temple corners in mass profusion.

All around the base run carved borders *(patra),* frame panels portraying in stone scenes from Balinese literature: animal heroes from the *Tantri* tales, episodes from *Arjuna Wiwaha* in which heavenly nymphs attempt to seduce Arjuna while he's meditating, battle scenes from the Hindu epic poems, a pop-eye above upper canine teeth, magic birds, snorting devils, twisting serpents, and a host of other supernatural, fanciful creatures.

Besides the profusion of carved vines, leaves, and tendrils which entwine the temple, many other symbols and mythical characters populate the confines, peering out from moss-covered walls. The *padmasana* (lotus seat) is a small stone pillar resting on an image of a turtle and crowned with an empty stone throne. Found in temples all over Bali, the *padmasana* represents the entire cosmos. Swastikas adorn walls, and the lotus—the symbolic flower of the Hindu cosmos—is seen in the most common motifs. You will also spy, if you look closely enough, erotic, pornographic scenes of earthly, sensual pleasures. The master sculptors know all the themes and variations of these stone designs by heart, or as the Balinese say, "in the belly."

Where to Buy

The shops lining the main street of **Batubulan,** a small village northeast of Denpasar on the way to Gianyar, sell most of their carvings to locals. Bargain vigorously. These workshops will carefully pack stone sculpture in wooden frames with shredded paper so it's ready for shipping. The height of the figures vary from 20 cm to two meters. The average height of a small figure is one meter, weight around 10 kg, and cost around Rp40,000 (after bargaining).

Another stonecarving center is **Karang,** north of Batubulan. Open dawn to dusk, visitors are welcome to visit the workshop of the master carver where you'll see long rows of young apprentices working in small groups chiseling and chipping away at demons, turtles, ogres, nudes, frogs, and all the characters from the Balinese scriptures. For something different, **Wayan**

Cemul, who lives just up the lane from Han Snel in Ubud, makes nontraditional, wild and wonderful *paras* sculptures.

CLOTHING

Bali has come a long way since the days when Kuta's bamboo and gaslight *losmen* sold *barong* T-shirts and *batik* drawstring cotton trousers to hippie world travelers. In the last five years especially, Kuta, Legian, and Seminyak have become major centers for shops and boutiques selling chic and sophisticated Euro-fashions.

Southern Bali is now one of the best places in Southeast Asia to buy the latest continental, smart city clothes, industrial-fashion designs, and contemporary beachwear. Many internationally recognized European designers—Milo, Itang Yunasz—have teamed up with Balinese designers and nimble-fingered Balinese garment workers. You'll also find collections from such high-end imported labels as Gigli, Gaultier, Doc Martens, Palladium.

Literally hundreds of clothes shops line Kuta/Legian's main road (Jl. Legian), as well as the roads running between Kuta/Legian and the beach. Fashions made for domestic and foreign tourists may also be bought at boutiques in the major hotels. These shops tend to stock a

---

THE THIRTEEN BEST FASHION SHOPS IN SOUTHERN BALI

The area code for south-central Bali is 0361.

Asse, Jl. Pantai Kuta 24 A. An international-style boutique on the cutting edge of Kuta fashion with imported labels like Gigli, Palladium, Gaultier. Also very striking silks by Italian designer Milo.

Biasa, Jl. Raya Seminyak 39 (tel. 752945). Features superb Indian tie-dye chiffons and silks and earth-color garments, stunning patchwork shirts for men. Nice atmosphere.

Jonathon Silver, Jl. Legian (tel. 751584 or 753092). An elegant shop selling high-quality silver jewelery.

Kuta Kids, near corner of Jl. Raya Legian and Jl. Pantai Kuta. An old and trusted shop selling bright kids clothing in polka dots, stripes, and star patterns.

Rags, Jl. Raya Basang Kasa 28 A, Kuta (tel. 751556). A smart shop selling unisex padded jackets, painted *batik* T-shirts, hand-printed shawls, most in neutral colors and Euro-styles.

Rama Collection, Jl. Legian Kelod 400 (tel. 751570). Carries very attractive plaited briefcases, backpacks, traveling bags, purses, and totes made out of leather, *ikat,* canvas, and fabric.

The Range, Jl. Seminyak, Kuta (tel. 261155). Specializes in resort-style clothing and international

men's and women's fashions in silks, tie-dye chiffon, and high-quality cotton.

Salasa, Jl. Raya Legian 431. A small boutique selling stylish men's shirts, silk chiffon scarves, shawls, string bags, baskets, gifts, etc.

Tete, Jl. Legian Kaja 473, Kuta. The top of chic wear for both men and women. High prices. For uptown glamorous dresses.

Vertigo, Jl. Raya Seminyak 24, Kuta (tel. 754355 or 754354). Attractive shirts for men, and women's clothes in soft voiles and muslin in neutral colors.

Whitesands, Jl. Poppies 1 (opposite TJs Restaurant). Fashion, gifts, home furnishings, and accessories.

Wira, Jl. Imam Bonjol (tel. 751727 or 751737). A huge collection of fashionable *batik,* macrame knits, sari silks, sarongs, embroidered clothing, bags, baskets, and many other arts and crafts at very good prices. Located on the way into Denpasar on the left, just out of Kuta.

Baik Baik, Jl. Legian (tel. 51622), opposite the start of Jl. Melasti. A stylish boutique which carries casual *batik* clothes. Asih Migliavacca, owner and designer, is fond of combining intricate traditional patterns with modern ones. Beautiful Hawaiian-style shirts start at Rp30,000, long-sleeved floral evening blouses are Rp200,000.

lot of high-fashion *batik* clothing. Designers on Bali shy away from the wildly mixed colors favored by the Balinese and limit combinations to varying shades of one or two colors in a single pattern. Smaller shops and markets offer better bargains in simpler styles.

Be careful when buying unbelievably inexpensive pants, blouses, shirts, T-shirts, and jackets for sale in the shops along the main drags of the beach resorts or sold by peddlers on the beach. These garments are often overruns, defects, and seconds. This is why you find so many flaws in the workmanship—button holes not lined up, mismatched dye lots, bad stitching, wrong size, sleeves too long or too short, label wrong (says large when it's really small). Much of the material is cheap rayon. Check every piece.

Several shops sell sequined bodices, tops, hats, and purses. Have a good giggle but be careful of buying loud and radical clothing you will probably never wear back home. Also be wary of those flimsy white and black plastic zippers. Bikinis cost as much as Rp20,000 (!) but you can get them for Rp4000 apiece. Balinese G-strings are flimsy but lots of fun. For classier one or two-piece swimsuits and after-swim wear, try Kuta's **No Shit** (Jl. Bakung Sari), **Bali Balance** on Jl. Buni Sari, **The Curl** and **Blue Groove** on Jl. Legian.

For children's clothes, try **Kuta Kids** on Jl. Legian near Bemo Corner in Kuta, and **Bali Balance,** Jl. Bumi Sari, Kuta; for men's and ladies' fashions, **Rag's Warehouse,** Jl. Basangkasa 28 A, Seminyak, tel. (0361) 751556; for shirts and shorts, **Mr. Bali** has several shops in Kuta and Legian; for sportswear and footwear, try **Tao, Kingkong,** and **Kartini** in Legian; and **Bali Barrel, Ulu's Shop,** and **The Surf Shop** for surfwear.

Silk articles are not that great a bargain anymore. Silk shirts, blouses, and skirts cost Rp75,000-150,000 here, whereas in the U.S. you find these garments for only US$29-50. A wonderful shop for creative and expensive silk articles (men's shirts Rp150,000, women's shirts Rp75,000) is **Biasa,** Jl. Raya Seminyak 39 (tel. 0361-752945). Other great deals (but not beachwear) can be found in the giant supermarkets of Denpasar like MA, Matahari, New Dewata Ayu, and the Tiara Dewata. At Libi, you'll see a whole line of dresses for Rp20,000-30,000. Fixed prices.

Tailoring

Remember you can have a skirt, pants, shirt, or dress made to fit by a tailor or seamstress, so you shouldn't pay more than the amount you'd pay him or her (plus material) for the same garment at a market stall or art shop. Also you get the best price because you're dealing directly with the person making your garment. Stay clear of tourist ghettoes: a tailor in Kuta charges Rp10,000 for a shirt while in Ubud only Rp5000.

Tailors on Bali do good work, take only two to three days to complete a job, charge very reasonable prices (average US$2-7.50), and are very clever at copying from an already sewn piece or from a photo in a fashion magazine or catalog. Give a false deadline to avoid a delay. They may charge you Rp1000 or so extra for "fast work" (two days). More elaborate designs cost more and take more time.

Bring a shirt, skirt, or pair of trousers which fit you very well. From any of these garments the tailor will make a paper pattern. Always specify the buttons to be used and whether you desire double stitching (you do). Check out their previous work.

Prices for typical materials like print *batik* for a shirt, cotton for dresses or trousers are extra. Two-and-a-half meters of cloth to make a long-sleeved shirt, for example, costs Rp5000-10,000. You'll find a good selection of materials on Jl. Sulawesi in Denpasar.

Locate a good tailor on Jl. Legian (between Kuta and Legian); in Denpasar there are few tailors along Jl. Gajah Mada who do sew for less. Or you can get the name of a good tailor or seamstress from a fabric shop. If it's a retail outlet that offers alterations, look for a sewing machine on site; it's a good sign because you work directly with the tailor and avoid the middleman.

TEXTILES

Balinese produce and sell textiles to satisfy tourist demand as well as to dress pleasingly before the gods in temple ceremonies and rites of passage. Textiles are an integral part of every ritual or ceremony, from a toothfiling to a cremation, and incorporate powerful motifs and symbols. Color also plays a big role; it enables the Balinese to communicate with deities within the context of a religious event. A priest dresses in white, the color of purity and *shunye* (the Cosmic Void), which allows him to communicate directly with sacred beings. Shiva's color, yellow, is worn by worshippers at almost any ceremony.

Dressing stylishly in sumptuous clothes is also a mark of social standing. You can often tell an aristocrat by the silk brocade she wears or the gold thread lining the *sarung* of a Brahman man.

Two of Bali's largest textile factories lie along the main tourist artery between Denpasar and Batubulan, Gianyar, and Mas. **PATAL** is one km east of the Tohpati junction of the Nusa Dua Bypass road, and **BALITEX** is one km west of the Tohpati junction between Tohpati and Denpasar. BALITEX operates a shop on the premises selling both wholesale and retail. Several other, smaller textile factories are in Gianyar, a favorite tourist stop, where also exist a number of textile showrooms. Visit one of the garment factories to watch aisles of prepubescent teenagers dribbling wax designs over cloth, then dipping the shirts into cisterns filled with hot, bubbling, frothing dye. It takes an average of six hours to weave a *sarung*.

Ikat

Bali is a major outlet for *ikat*-woven blankets, *kain,* sarongs, and scarves from Nusatenggara. In this unique Indonesian craft, the threads are dyed *prior to* the material being woven. With their primitive designs and subdued blue, white, red, brown, and black colors, these striking cloths have always held a fascination for tourists.

You find *ikat* in almost all of Bali's textile shops, which stock both handwoven *ikat* in silk and cotton, as well as ready-to-wear *ikat* clothing. Many shops also offer custom tailoring—they'll make anything you want out of *ikat!* Because of the small supply and large demand, *ikat* on Bali costs Rp150,000 and up for small blankets.

A chain specializing in *ikat* is **Nogo** with shops at Jl. D. Tamblingan 98 (tel. 0361-288765), Jl. D. Tamblingan 208 (tel. 0361-288832) in Sanur, and Jl. Legian, Kuta (tel. 0361-754335). The owner, Lily Coskuner, who studied design in Germany, uses handwoven fabrics in her clothing which includes quilted kimono-style jackets (Rp150,000 and up), slacks (Rp75,000), and shirtwaist dresses (Rp150,000). Very fine ethnic cloths are also available at **Polos,** Jl. Legian;

Arts of Asia, Jl. Raya Tuban (tel. 0361-752860); **Andung Art,** Jl. Legian Kaja 494A (tel. 0361-757710); and **Ikat Art,** Jl. Bakung Sari 12 (tel. 0361-752684).

In the Klungkung area, you might be able to still find traditional gold-embroidered *songket* and amazingly elaborate *ikat* for which Klungkung was once famous (now rare). Some villagers on Nusa Penida Island, in Klungkung Regency, weave a red, brown, or yellow-patterned *ikat* cloth which may be seen in a few shops in Sampalan, Toyapekeh (on Nusa Penida), and in Klungkung's souvenir shops.

Endek

The very distinctive tie-dyed woven cloth called *endek* is more popular with the native Balinese than with tourists. Worn all over the island for any occasion, *endek* is perhaps Bali's most visible craft. Scores of factories all around Gianyar and Denpasar, as well as Singaraja, manufacture this unique fabric.

Using only wooden, hand-operated looms, *endek* is woven by the usual weft-*ikat* method; i.e., portions of the cloth are tied and wrapped before immersion in a dye bath. The overall effect ranges from an irregular, wavy, diffused look to the most primitive patterns. You also see triangular, zigzagging, and diamond designs, or unusual outlines of animals or masks. The fuzzy irregularities of this native cloth are hypnotic. The mottled patterns even appear to change color and shape in different angles of light. Factories, which number from six to 100 employees, can produce *endek* with up to six colors. It takes a weaver one day to complete approximately one meter.

The Balinese adore *endek,* wearing it on both formal and informal occasions. Men like *sarung* made of *endek* cloth, women wrap *kain* made of *endek* tightly around the hips (with no drapes). Colors range from dark blue and brown to vibrant greens, oranges, and reds. The cost is about Rp4000 per meter for printed *endek,* depending on the amount of colors used and intricacy of design. Colors do not bleed, and the weave is durable. The price for true *endek* is Rp12,000-15,000 per meter. Pay a call at **Pertenunan AAA** in Denpasar (Jl. Veteran 9), and **Pertenunan Setia Cap Cili** (Jl. Ciungwanara 7) and **Cap Togog** (Jl. Astina Utara 11, two km before town) in Gianyar. A small *endek* factory is also located in **Sideman** (Karangasem Regency). All factories have showrooms, and photography is allowed in the workshops.

Batik

Beautiful handmade *batik* textiles are among the most popular craft products sold on Bali for tourists. Every *batik* pattern imaginable is available. You even see Balinese-made *batik* clothing on Java now because it has gained popularity with the great number of Javanese tourists who visit Bali.

The *batik* available on Bali includes block prints and hand-painted *batik*. Intricate hand-drawn designs *(batik tulis)* are more expensive than simpler designs created with stamp blocks *(batik cap)*. The colors on block-printed *batik* are soft and only printed on one side, while the colors on *batik tulis* (true *batik*) are much richer and equally vibrant on both sides of the cloth. Each of these styles can be printed on any quality of cotton. Usually *batik* is displayed in three or four rows with the finest quality items on the top row. One can definitely feel the difference between the fineness of a top row piece and a bottom row piece. Prices vary from Rp8000 for a simple block- or machine-printed *batik sarung*, up to Rp450,000 for silk *batik*.

Although every Balinese wears *batik*, few produce *batik* cloth on a large scale. Each day women wrap a length of *batik* around their waist like a skirt, and men wear *batik* with a plaited tail that almost touches the ground in front (usually only to religious events).

Batik Shops and Factories

Batik cloth can be bought in the markets, especially Denpasar's main market and in nearby fabric shops on Jl. Sulawesi, dealing in both *batik tulis* and *batik cap*. Expect to bargain; they'll start off asking Rp20,000 for a printed *batik* sarong but you should end up paying no more than Rp8000-10,000.

Phalam, Jl. W.R. Supratman in Tohpati, tel. (0361) 225215, has a fine *batik* collection and ready-made clothing. One of the few shops in Bali specializing in *batik* made on Bali. Items are not cheap: Rp300,000 for fine *batik tulis;* there are also *cap batik* varieties. Try for at least a 30% discount.

In addition, all the big Javanese textile chains are represented in or around Denpasar: **Batik Keris,** Galleria Nusa Dua, tel. (0361) 771303 or 771304 (also branches at both the international and domestic terminals at the airport); **Batik Semar,** Jl. Thamrin 33-35, tel. (0361) 435937; **Danar Hadi,** Jl. Legin Raya 133, Kuta, tel. (0361) 752164 or 754368; **Batik Shanti,** Galleria Nusa Dua B 6/2, tel. (0361) 71308. **Pekalongan Perus Batik Shop,** Jl. Gianyar, tel. (0361) 225833 and Jl. Bypass, tel. 224364; **Batik Surya Kencana,** Banjar Sasih, Batubulan, tel. (0361) 298361. All have showrooms and accept traveler's checks and credit cards.

Kain Prada

These are lustrous fabrics woven of cotton or sometimes silk decorated with silver, gold thread, or paint. Pure gold leaf or gold dust, and increasingly more affordable bronze dust, can also be used, adhered by a unique process onto the fabric by using a natural glue *(ancur)* obtained from bones. These dazzling, boldly patterned textiles, that almost blind you with their shine, are worn only during festivals or by dancers in theatrical performances. A gilded ceremonial cloth two meters long could take three weeks to a month to weave, depending on the intricacy of the design.

Since *kain prada* was initially brought to Java by Indian traders, then later carried to Bali, stylized Hindu motifs like sacred lotus blossoms and Indianized swastikas, as well as temple relief designs and ancient woodwork patterns, still decorate the borders. The old courts of Klungkung and Karangasem were the most important cen-

kain prada

ters of *prada* production. *Prada* fabrics used for wall decorations feature entire scenes from the Mahabarata or Ramayana painstakingly painted on, giving them a mural-like appearance. Both kinds of *prada* are not washable, so clean by dusting, then let them air in the sun.

Gringsing

Certainly one of the rarest weaving techniques in the world is practiced in Tenganan, a traditional native Balinese village in eastern Bali, about five hours by bus from Denpasar. Here the amazingly difficult *gringsing* (flaming cloth) cloths are made by an elaborate process of dyeing. Both the warp and weft threads are carefully bound and then dyed in predetermined places, creating patterns which are made to fit harmoniously together into a finished design once the piece is completely woven on a backstrap loom.

The geometric, repetitive patterns must interlock in exactly the same place in order for the fabric to have any aesthetic value or meaning. Stars, flowers, and crosses fill the body while rhombuses and chains of keys run lengthwise through the long, narrow cloth. The colors used are muted earth tones derived from vegetable dyes like indigo and turmeric bark. *Gringsing* are worn as sashes in everyday wear but on festival days women dress from head to toe in *gringsing*. The cloth protects and preserves the wearer from harm. No rite of passage may be carried out without the obligatory wearing of a *kain gringsing*.

Though other forms of *ikat* were probably imported from India, *gringsing* weaving is thought to have originated only in Tenganan. To support this theory, nowhere else in Indonesia is this intensely time-consuming and jealously guarded "double-*ikat*" process practiced, and less than 15 women still know how to weave it. A woman may labor for three years on a single piece of *gringsing*. A large *kain* may easily cost a million rupiah. Strictly for collectors.

Songket

Silk brocades with interweaving patterns of gold and silver thread, *songket* is the ceremonial dress of the Balinese, to be worn on religious occasions or to one's wedding. Tapestry-like, with motifs of lotus flowers, leaves, birds, butterflies, and *wayang* figures, *songket* fabrics are woven on small backstrap looms. Usually only the

wealthy can afford a real *songket*, woven with pure gold thread—gorgeous works of art. *Songket* can't be washed, so when wet from sweat, it's hung up to dry in the sun.

The whole *kain songket* is purchased in two pieces which are then sewn together. Men wear the *songket saput*, a narrow length of cloth worn over the *sarung*, and the *songket udeng*, a head band, on formal occasions and religious ceremonies. Beware of shiny ersatz *songket* from Singapore, with the gold painted on, which looks like the real thing from a distance.

Northern-style *songket* is made in Banjar Bratan, a southern suburb of Singaraja, and the Klungkung-style is made at Banjar Jero Agung in Gelgel, two km south of Klungkung; other *songket* cottage industries are found in Batuan (northeast of Sukawati), in Sideman (Karangasem Regency), and particularly Blayu in southwestern Bali (between Mengwi and Marga). Balinese *songket* is also sold in art shops of Kuta, Sanur, Denpasar, and Ubud.

Other Textiles

Plangi ("rainbow") is a multicolored tie-and-dye process of decorating cotton and silk pieces, an art practiced on Bali and Lombok. Each fabric is knotted in certain places very tightly with string, then dipped into dyes. When the knots are untied a picturesque pattern appears, leaving uncolored patches where the dye did not penetrate.

Black and white checkered **poleng** cloths appear everywhere on Bali, especially as a covering for guardian statues in temples. The checkered pattern symbolizes the changeable world, which is made up of pairs of opposites—night and day, good and evil, man and woman, positive and negative, yin and yang—the duality of earthly existence. Their use is to sanctify a tree, a weird-shaped stone, or a statue so it becomes an object of worship. The cloth is restricted to the lower deities and never would be wrapped around Shiva's shrine as high gods are considered to dwell beyond the temporal realm.

Chinese **kebaya** (women's blouses) have rich hand-embroidered edges and a swooping décolletage. It's difficult to find the real fine oldies anymore for under Rp100,000 (in Kuta, Rp200,000 and up). **Kamben** are scarves worn around the breast by women on grand occasions and holidays. Some *kamben* are thought to possess magic protective qualities to stave off evil; others are worn only for certain dances.

PLAITING AND WEAVING

Usually Bali's more elaborate arts—rich jewelry, sumptuous textiles, engaging sculptures—grab the attention of the shopper. But among Bali's least recognized, oldest, and most perishable artforms are the imaginative and beautiful weaving and plaiting of natural fibers into utilitarian implements and decorations.

To the Balinese, making these throwaway offerings is a labor of love *(bakti yoga)*, floral and pastry testaments to their devotion to their temple. Over 10,000 varieties of offerings are used in religious ceremonies. The whole culture seems to revolve around the decorative arts. During festivals, the Balinese decorate columns, statues, and shrines in checkered cloths, palm leaf flowers, and bright tasseled umbrellas. The roads at festival time are graced with long lines of intricate bunting, woven *penjor* poles, and open pavilions are festooned with twirling *busing* (young palm).

Lamak

The purest example of Balinese art is the ancient mosaic-like *lamak,* woven from strips of palm leaf, bamboo, or yellow blades of sugar or coconut palm pinned together to form fancy borders, rosettes, and treelike or anthropomorphic designs.

There are infinite varieties of *lamak* patterns. Perhaps the most popular is the figure of a girl with an hourglass figure, a central motif on many *lamak,* believed to predate the arrival of Hinduism on Bali. These abstract figures *(cili)* with rounded breasts and long thin arms appear in the rice fields when the rice seeds first sprout. Scholars believe *cili* derive from the goddess of the earth and fertility, Dewi Sri, the focal point of many rituals.

These dried palm-leaf decorative strips last only for a day; after hanging on an altar or rice granary, they're wilted by night. *Lamak*-making is one of the few arts that women are allowed to do; it's not a woman's place to pursue *gamelan,* painting, or carving.

Bamboo and Rattan

There are many different species of bamboo—from a dark brown to a spotted variety. Bamboo furniture is lightweight and cheap, but it's a bulky hassle to ship. The bamboo furniture center is **Belega** village (near Blahbatu, Gianyar Regency) where tables, chairs, and other pieces are made out of attractive spotted bamboo *(tiing tutul)*. The dozen or so family-run workshops here also carry bamboo hats, ceremonial umbrellas, mats, purses, bags, and lamp shades.

Rattan wickerwork, made from an immense climbing palm with stems 10 meters long, is more expensive. In southern Bali, an outstanding shop for rattan and bamboo plaited articles is **Rama Collection,** Jl. Legian Kelod 400, tel. (0361) 751570; nice belts Rp15,000, Javanese sisal/palm purses Rp35,000.

Sukawati is the place for all-purpose bamboo basketry. Prices (Rp3000-30,000) depend on the size (from 10 cm up to almost a meter), strength, and closeness of the weave. Baskets with lids make excellent, sturdy shipping containers for fabrics and other unbreakables. The Sukawati basket retailers also carry a full range of the famous crushproof *ata* baskets of E. Bali as well as captivating bamboo wind chimes. Another outstanding wind chime shop, **Kubu Ku Windchime,** is in the outskirts of Ubud just up the path from the Monkey Forest. The different sections of Denpasar's Pasar Badung (Jl. Gajah Mada) have a great variety and low prices for every type of woven article.

METALLURGY

The earliest and most remarkable specimen of metallurgy present on Bali is the famous pre-Hindu bronze kettle gong, the largest of its type in the world, in the towerlike shrine in the back of Pura Panataran Sasih in Pejeng. This mysterious hourglass-shaped artifact, nearly two meters high and adorned with eight stylized heads, survives from Indonesia's Bronze Age, which began around 300 B.C. It is not clear if the Balinese possessed the sophistication to forge the gong themselves, or if it was imported from Indochina.

The Balinese, as recently as the 1950s, excelled in working precious and semiprecious metals into many more instruments and accessories than they do today. At one time the coppersmiths and copper casters of Banjar Budaga (near Klungkung) forged or cast brass bells, incense holders, and lamps which were used as ritual objects by all classes of priests. They also fashioned handsome gold and silver plates, vases, knives, and scissors for cutting *sirih.* Now, only the ornate rings, bracelets, earplugs, ear pendants, and flowers for dancers' hair made from hammered and chiselled gold are still crafted. Nowadays metalworking is a common occupation, for the most part a craft of souvenir and jewelry makers.

Blacksmiths

Working as the king's armorers and as the vital source of agricultural tools and metallic musical instruments in pre-industrial Bali, the village blacksmiths were of very high social standing, free from the confines of the Hindu caste system. As a sign of deference, even the haughty Brahmanas were obliged to speak in High Balinese when speaking to a smith in his workshop. Royalty often made gifts of rice fields to honor smiths in their service. Blacksmiths had their own temples and burial grounds.

Traditional blacksmiths *(pande wesi)*—using bellows, tongs, anvils, charcoal fires from coconut-husks—still can be found on Bali. To see traditional *gamelan* instrument makers in action, visit the workshop of **Pak Gabeleran** in Blahbatuh where bronze is forged into xylophonic keys or pots. Ornate instrument stands are carved here as well. **Tihingan village,** five km north of the main Gianyar-Klungkung road, is another instrument-making center. Balinese musicians from all over the island come to these foundries to buy their musical instruments.

The art of stained-glass and iron-mongering is kept alive by **Mondirama** in Padangtegal just before Ubud (if coming from Peliatan). Dolf, the owner, designs all his own glass and iron pieces. The glass manufactured at the shop is burned (oxidized) to achieve 130 colors. This method was used in medieval times. Artisans who restore European cathedrals have to use this method to match the ancient colors. Mondirama is the only factory of its kind in Indonesia. There's another one in Bandung, but they import glass

from the U.S., which makes their products expensive.

One of the largest and most complete stores for bronze decorative objects in Indonesia is the **Golden Buffalo House of Bronze,** on Monkey Forest Road in Ubud, tel. (0361) 96328, fax 752013, and at Jl. Legian Tengah 412 in Kuta, tel. (0361) 755936, fax 752013. They can create any kind of motif by designing a piece after one in their catalog or by creating a sample.

KRIS

As on Java, the traditional *kris* dagger not only represents the pinnacle of the art of metallurgy but also served at one time as the most important symbol of rank and power for Balinese men. In the not-so-distant past, so much of a man's worth was represented by his *kris* it could even attend his own wedding in place of himself, or a judge could send his *kris* to attend a trial if he were ill.

Now worn more as an accessory to a ritual or as pure ornament, you'll still see men of nobility wear their *kris* to official ceremonial occasions such as inaugurations, purifications, cremations, and weddings.

Jewel-encrusted, spiritually charged *kris,* called *kris sakti,* were passed down through the generations and were an intrinsic part of the aristocratic male's heirloom, looked upon as a family deity *(batara kawitan)* and a gift from the gods in which the cumulative strength of all the ancestors still resided. Smiths spent months in perfecting the ruby-studded *kris* handles of a king. The economic status of a man was determined by the elaborateness of his *kris,* and much of a man's wealth was invested in the jewels and gold decorating it. The precious stones, jewels, and ivory of a kris can be pawned in case of need, but never the heirloom blade. Less fancy *kris,* with more pragmatic wooden handles for a better grip, were used in hand-to-hand combat.

A *kris* can guard the bearer against evil, disaster, or illness and can bring luck, happiness, and prosperity. It is said that a *balian,* through consultations and trances, can talk to a venerable *kris* and learn its past history. Famous, bloodthirsty *kris* have made men run amok, burned down buildings, killed enemies by being pointed at them, or acted as powerful amulets against misfortune.

Kris-makers *(pande)* belonged to a privileged guild who worshipped the volatile, fiery Batur volcano. Since they knew how to work the two magic elements of iron and fire, they were regarded as powerful sorcerers. New *kris* were brought to life by a priest who blessed them in a magic rite. Today, it's still considered necessary that certain old *kris* are "kept alive" with offerings *(sajen)* of incense, fruits, rice, and frangipani because if a *kris* turns rusty and becomes neglected, it's spiritual power dies.

Components of a *Kris*

Although the Balinese *kris* is generally larger and more ornate than the Javanese form, they have basically the same shape. The most sacred and important part is the blade, which can either be straight and simple or shaped like the mythical *naga,* the body forming the blade and widening as it nears the hilt to form the head of the serpent. This vicious, flame-like blade is full of barbs, indentations, and curlicues wrought in a number of styles.

The unusual watery rivulets *(pamor,* which means "metal-alloy") on the blade—silvery metal against blue-black iron—was achieved by endlessly beating alternating layers of meteoric nickel and iron layers. The extraordinary moiré-like damascene pattern, which is thought to give the *kris* its mystical power, is obtained by blackening the iron layers with a mixture of lemon juice and antimony.

Hilts were either made of gold set with jewels, or else of ivory, ebony, or other precious woods. The sheath not only protected the *kris* from physical or psychic damage but also insulated the powerful vibrations emanating from the sinister-looking blade itself, which could bring great harm to anyone who came too near. The sheaths of elaborate *kris* were made of a rare wood such as *kayu katimoho.* Particularly in high demand was the incredibly mottled *kayu pelet (Cattimarus)* which had to be imported from Java. In the old days a raja would pay as much as 50 Dutch guilders for a fine piece of *pelet* used in the crosspiece *(wrangka)* or for use in the *kris* grip *(gagang kris).*

Of less value were sheaths made of *kayu ke-* *muning (Murraya exotica),* aromatic *kayu cendana* (sandalwood), and *kayu jati* (teakwood). Sheaths were covered with a wrapper of silver or gold, chased all the way with flower and plant motifs. The handle was shaped like a demon or a god and set with rose diamonds and rubies.

The most famous *kris* were taken as Dutch war booty from the corpses of the kings of southern Bali in the great mass-suicide in Denpasar in 1906. These splendid bejeweled specimens may now be seen in the National Museum of Jakarta.

GOLD, SILVER, GEMSTONES, AND JEWELRY

In Balinese life, gold is more coveted than rupiah; women can tell a man's wealth by the size of his *kalong* (gold necklace). Though the traditional center for gold and silver jewelry-making is Denpasar, the art has now also taken hold elsewhere on the island.

Dozens of gold- and silversmiths work in Banjar Pande Mas in Kamasan, four km south of Klungkung. Once working under the auspices of the old Gelgel court, these smiths produce large, delicately ornamented silver and gold betel nut bowls, chased gold *kris* handles, offering platters, and vessels for holy water. A market still exists for these ceremonial objects, which are necessary for sacrificial and exorcistic rituals, luckily guaranteeing the survival of the craft. Younger men work beside the older masters and learn the patterns and techniques by imitation and repetition.

When buying expensive gold and silver ready-made articles, it's best to find an honest, reliable, reasonable, fixed-price shop and buy from them. Though you'll pay average prices, at least you won't get cheated. For custom work, ferret out a *kampung* artisan whose workshop is just a dirt floor, crude wood benches, and a tree trunk with a metal spike for an anvil. If he has a ring mandrel, all the better. At virtually any workshop/salesroom combo, you'll be able to observe a silver-working demonstration.

Ask your hotel proprietor or other unbiased Balinese who does good work and request to see samples of the work. The price depends on the weight, the design, the stone, or all three.

Another approach is to buy unworked silver or gold elsewhere in Asia (at cheaper prices) and trade it for jewelry, or give the jeweler coins with high silver content in exchange for hand-done, made-to-order rings, brooches, necklaces. You can bring rare stones for setting—you have your choice of some very striking backgrounds.

Besides the souvenir and gift shops of the big hotel lobbies in Sanur, Nusa Dua, and Kuta, jewelry is made and sold in the village of **Celuk** (beyond Batubulan). For starters, **Bali Sun Sri** (Jl. Raya Celuk, Sukawati, tel. 0361-298275 or 298730) has a large collection of jewelry, gemstones, and precious stones. Since Celuk is the first stop for tour buses after the completion of the *barong* dances in Batubulan, get there before 1000 to miss the crowds. No problem using plastic.

Kuta Beach is another center for gold and silver jewelry; try Jonathon, Jl. Legian (tel. 0361-751584). Also check out the shops along Jl. Raya (Pasar Ubud, Mirah, Ganesha Bookshop) and Monkey Forest Road (Bali Rosa, Purpa) in Ubud, and Kunang-Kunang in Campuan. Tampaksiring is well known for its wooden jewelry, carved tusk and bone, and coconut shell ornaments. Tampaksiring's real carving center is **Manukaya,** north of the Tirta Empul holy springs.

Gold

For jewelry, the ratio is three grams of gold to one gram of copper. For traditional and modern Balinese-style jewelry, shop in the gold center of Bali—the 15 or so gold shops *(toko mas)* around the busy intersection of Denpasar's Jl. Sulawesi and Jl. Hasannudin. One of the best is **Kenanga,** Jl. Hasannudin 43 A (tel. 0361-225725). These shops—and others like them in almost any Balinese town—sell mostly traditional earplugs, gold chains, zodiac signs, pendants, and big gold rings which Balinese men like to wear. Here in these Jl. Sulawesi shops you'll at least be given a fair fixed price much faster than you will in way-overpriced Celuk where you have to bargain like mad for a fair price.

Gold is cheaper in Asia than in the West, costing usually only around Rp25,000 per gram which is equal to about US$340 per ounce as compared to $380 per ounce worldwide. For a seven gram ring you'll pay Rp175,000 for the gold and Rp50,000 for the filigree work. The ring will take two weeks to complete, and most shops will even deliver it to your hotel. Draw your design, or select a ring from the shop's showcases and modify it. Tell them to have it finished a week before you really need it. Allow two weeks (maximum) for completion. Take one of their business cards and call back in a week to see how the work is progressing. Check the work carefully as a ring or an armband can break easily, stones fall from mountings, etc.

For a custom order, go to the two reliable goldsmiths in Denpasar (Melasti and Kenanga) in the row of gold shops on Jl. Hasannudin. Another *tukang mas* (goldsmith), capable of good work, is at **Zamrud** on Jl. Sulawesi, which is opposite the line of gold shops in Denpasar. **Singaraja** is also a great place to shop for 14-24 carat gold; friendly shops all over town.

Gianyar has a few *toko mas.*

Silver

Balinese silver is on average 92.5% pure (they mix every 50 grams of silver with two grams of copper). The larger pieces such as flat silver trays, bowls, tableware, and teapots are plated and not pure. The Balinese import most all their silver, almost always hand-construct their jewelry, and rarely use casting techniques.

Balinese silver-filigree necklaces, bracelets, and rings are very light, delicate, and highly decorated. A technique called granulation is employed whereby small pellets of silver are heated until soft enough to adhere to the piece. For the ready-to-wear, cash-and-carry pieces, it is usually cheaper in Yogya and West Sumatra, although Bali's silversmiths tend to be more inventive.

On Bali, the first asking price in a local market or by a peddler is not necessarily lower than that of the exclusive shop. Both start out at equally escalated prices. You should get them to come down at least 40%, and in some cases as much as 60%. They may ask Rp150,000 for four pairs of heavy silver earrings, but in the end you might be able to get them for around Rp100,000. In the workshops east of Celuk, simple silver stud earrings cost as little as Rp2000.

Celuk is generally spoiled by the tour buses; they'll take only only Rp5000 or Rp10,000 off their first price. A fairly honest shop in Celuk is **Gala Silver,** only a half kilometer from the main road. Here they teach small children silvermaking. Cakra is a nice man, speaks good English (he once worked for a travel agency), and he'll give you a demo of the silvermaking process. He sells earrings and rings, depending on the workmanship, for Rp30,000-35,000.

Silver items in the back lanes of **Beraton** (one km south of Singaraja) are very reasonable. This is the place to have something made—it works out to only about Rp600 per gram. Unknown to many, here you can buy a heavy silver identity bracelet for Rp35,000; in Celuk the same bracelet goes for Rp100,000. Rings cost Rp15,000 with your own stone set in it (in Celuk, the same ring would cost Rp35,000).

Gemstones and Semi-Precious Stones

Gemstones are not native to Bali; most come from Hong Kong. A new phenomenon are the gem shops opening in Kuta, Nusa Dua, and Sanur. Know your stuff. Visit a jeweler in your home country. Buy a book on stones, gems, and jewelry. Pearls on Bali cost about Rp100,000 per gram, or three grams for about Rp250,000. Look for a nice lustre and round shape.

Bali Opal Center (Jl. Raya Tuban 2 D, Tuban, tel. 0361-752761) sells beautiful amethyst (kecubung) for US$29 per carat—a faceted 43 carat stone costs US$1260. The darker the opal, the older and more valuable it is. White opal (kalimaya) costs US$735 for a 45 carat stone, black opal from Java is US$8800 for a 9.79 carat stone, milky white opal from Banten (West Java) is US$650. Also sold are chameleon opal, amber (miklak) bracelets (US$15-25).

The Uluwatu parking lot is a center for the sale of agate (akik) artifacts and stones: turtles, cats, frogs, ducks, eggs, Buddha heads, bracelets, ashtrays. Their first price of Rp10,000 can be reduced by as much as Rp5000. Also bead bracelets and necklaces, multicolored woven belts (Rp7500-10,000), and shells by the tableful.

Rare and beautiful coral plants, with their rich chainlike floral patterns seemingly printed inside the stone, make intricate jewel-like decorative ornaments. The colors of these 100-year-old fossils vary from soft to warm. Kuta's **Citra Batu Alam** has Bali's widest choice of coral gemstones (they also specialize in jasper and opal)

where you may choose any desirable shape and matching ring, pendant, earrings, or buckle.

CERAMICS AND POTTERY

Ceramic firing techniques never developed into an advanced craft on Bali. Up until the early 1970s, precious green Sung dynasty plates would still occasionally turn up. On some Balinese temple walls dating from the last century, valuable ceramic bowls and saucers of European origin have been embedded in plaster (visit Puri Anyar in Krambitan village, Tabanan). Even "Kitchen Ming" chinaware plates, once used in common trading and bartering, are now becoming scarce, only available on Kuta Beach at exorbitant prices.

For modern ceramics, check out **Sari Bumi** on Jl. D. Tamblingan opposite Batu Jimbar in Sanur. Started by New Zealander Brent Heslin, these functional, high-fired glazed ceramics include salt and papper shakers, ashtrays, small vases, etc. All the major hotels carry his stuff. Also check out Nacha in Legian for housewares, tea and dinner sets, vases, lamps, etc.

A distinguished ceramics designer, **Kay It,** lived and worked in Tabanan. Born of a Chinese-Balinese family of shopkeepers, It was one of Indonesia's most promising modern impressionistic artists until he died suddenly at the age of 39. It's tall totem poles and other ceramics on the landscaped grounds of the Bali Hyatt in Sanur remind one of the ancient Incan and Aztec designs. It's works can also be viewed in the Neka Gallery and Puri Lukisan in Ubud, and his influence can still be seen in the designs of many small ceramics available in Bali's markets: ashtrays, candleholders in the cili style, and tiles for wall hangings.

Pottery and Terra-cotta

Although bamboo and pandanus containers largely take the place of pottery, the Balinese do produce artful and pragmatic terra-cotta articles and various clay vessels, embellished with patterns by artisans using the same tools and methods as woodcarvers. Found in almost any village market on Bali, the pottery is brittle and great care must be taken in transporting it.

Kapal, 10 km to the west of Denpasar, is another pottery center where the island's distinctive red pottery is produced—vases, flasks, lamp bases, ashtrays, clay figurines, standing yard sculpture and statuary, lamp bases, concrete shrines. Be sure to see the ceramic lanterns and traditional slitted clay coin banks in the shape of pigs, horses, dogs, etc.

Other pottery *gerabah* (sellers) can be found in **Ubung,** northwest of Denpasar. In **Dulung** village, 3.5 km past Krobokan beyond Seminyak (at T-junction, turn left), is a ceramics center which produces delightful ashtrays, tissue and toothpick holders, and condiment sets in dark green, blue, sandy *(abu).* Orders take about one month.

Pejaten near Tabanan is a village devoted almost exclusively to producing pottery and terracotta. Visitors are welcome in the many co-op workshops, which turn out glazed ornamental roof tiles, soap dishes, stand-alone figurines, and wonderful clay animals with dull matte finish, celadon, or glossy glazes. A shop in Candidasa (Tanteri's, on main road) and in Ubud (opposite Ubud Bookstore) sells Pejaten work.

SHELLS AND TRINKETS

Hole-in-the-middle 100- to 250-year-old Chinese coins *(kepeng),* with Chinese characters on one side ("Year of the Corn") and Pali script on the other, are ideal for setting, hanging, or for casting I Ching. In Kuta, they cost Rp300 each (in quantity); inland, Rp100 each. In Dutch times, about 700 *kepeng* could buy one Dutch guilder. Since traders purchased them at 1,400 per Dutch guilder in China, a 100% profit was realized. Since the 17th century, export of coins was so great a drain on Chinese coinage that the Chinese government attempted in vain to stop their export. Literally thousands of bags of these crude bronze or lead coins were shipped from China to Bali, recounted, then put on strings 200 at a time to be used as an island-wide currency.

Puka shells are small, round, white shells found along the shores of Pacific Basin countries. Look for necklaces with all shells the same size. On Kuta you pay Rp5000 for a small puka necklace, but at the surfers' hangout, Uluwatu's souvenir *warung,* really long chains sell for as lit-

tle as Rp2500. Turtle Island (Serangan) sells perhaps Bali's most gorgeous seashells.

Akar bahar bracelets are in the shape of a serpent. Shape them further with heat, then tie with wire. Or shape them while still wet, then dry in the sun. Polish with ash until smooth and shiny. Some say they have a therapeutic effect, giving relief from rheumatism and arthritis. These seaweed bracelets (actually a sea-tree) grow on your wrist from the heat and perspiration; it *lives.*

The bone-and-ivory carving center is in the *kampung* of **Manukaya** near Tampaksiring on the main road between Denpasar and Kintamani. But don't believe the vendors if they claim their work is ivory. It's a 98% chance it is bleached, hourglass-shaped, cow thighbone. Ivory, which is imported from Flores, does not have the flat white color of these wares; look for the rhombus effect on real ivory.

Prices for bone carvings range from Rp3000 to Rp25,000, depending upon their size and intricacy. Ivory and deer horn carving can also be purchased. Full carved tusks run US$600-5000, depending on the size. Ivory figurines (12-15 cm tall) cost Rp200,00-500,000.

Beads
Usually made of glass, beads are also found in stone, clay, bone, ivory, wood, shell, seed, amber, metal, and plastic and come from India, China, the Middle East, and Europe. A note of caution: For hundreds of years beads have been copied, making the task of dating and determining their origin difficult. New glass beads have a rougher surface than old ones which are silky smooth. Also the holes of ancient glass beads tend to be larger and more irregular, and they weigh a lot more than plastic beads.

A half dozen shops in southern Bali resorts specialize in beadwork. **Ishmala Beadworks,** Jl. Golden Village I No. 16 (tel. 0361-752401), is in Seminyak, 100 meters past Jl. Dhyana Pura. Open 1000-1600. Also check out **David Shop,** Jl. Legian Tengah 471 (tel. 0361-752003), which sells strands for around Rp30,000. In "downtown" Legian, **H. Shata Shop,** Jl. Raya Legian 588, specializes in earrings (three pairs for Rp5000).

But the best and rarest beads are found in **Andung Art,** Jl. Legian Kaja 494A (tel. 0361-757710) and **Ikat Art,** Jl. Bakung Sari 12 (tel. 0361-752684). For opals, don't neglect to visit

Bali Opal Centre, Jl. Raya Tuban 2 D (tel. 0361-752761, fax 751930).

ANTIQUES

Ground zero for antiques is the Kuta/Legian/Seminyak area where lots of shops are stuffed with dusty, dirty artifacts and stacks of repros. Look for the grotesque, primitive statues out front. Not all pieces are Balinese; many originate in Nusatenggara and other areas of eastern Indonesia.

Take your time. You may have to lower your sights and buy a clever, well-made reproduction rather than a true antique. Perhaps the only true antique left on the island is Victor Mason's polyphone at the Begger's Bush in Ubud.

Before buying antiques, increase your knowledge as much as possible by referring to the reference books in the booklist and visiting the Bali Museum of Denpasar and the Puri Lukisan of Ubud. Tribal artists don't experiment, but adhere to a rigid iconographical framework. If it's Dayak carvings you're after, study the art books and museum catalogs first. If the piece doesn't conform to the norm, it's suspect.

Probably no place on earth—with the possible exception of Kathmandu—contains a greater density of beautiful "artifakes." These wonderful repros (*antik baru,* or "new antiques") may be far superior to some of the ugly originals you come across. And the repros cost far less.

If you ask for a true antique, you have to always assume you'll be cheated. Be an investigator first and a buyer second. Looking old and being old are not the same. Pay attention to how the patina—the wear and tear, dirt and dust of an art object—was created. A *tukang patina* craftsmen (seldom the salesperson) specializes in creating a convincing patina. The seller will deceive you by standing the piece up in the ground, letting it rust in the elements, layering it with dust, grime, etc. Be on the lookout for other irregularities that don't make sense. With a magnifying glass, study the scratches on the surface of old metal objects. The scratches should be of various lengths, depths, shapes, and angles. Scratches of equal length and depth are indications of fakery because they have been uniformly buffed, sanded, and polished. The same

applies to woodcarvings as even grooves caused by erosion can be carved.

Often you can tell they were made on Bali because the carvers can't seem to suppress a Balinese style or incorporate typical Balinese motifs. Also, successful fakes are apt to appear in a number of outlets within a relatively short time, so always look around first to see if your "original" shows up anywhere else. You can ask a dealer directly how old a piece is, but he will often whisper the little white lie "This piece is not so old but it is also not so new." Dealers of questionable repute will also tell yarns about a piece. The more elaborate the tale, the less likely it is true. If it's a big ticket item and you're skeptical, ask for a written guarantee stating the conditions of the purchase. This won't really protect you, but it may make the dealer think twice before ripping you off. Always get a photocopy of the documentation (with certification number) for any statue or antiquity to have ready for a customs official at the airport or docks in case he asks.

Leave the really old stuff. A law, *Cagar Budaya,* was passed in 1993 to prevent the hemmorrhage of antique treasures from Bali. The law states that any object over 50 years old is considered "antique" and must be turned over to the government. The only exceptions are those objects—like old *kris* and carved stones—still being venerated.

Furniture

Furniture-making is not really a part of the Balinese artistic repertoire. Today, repro furniture is the one of the fastest-growing industries on the island. Because of tourist demand and the large number of tourists concentrated on Bali, the island has become a frenetic furniture emporium. Agents comb the countryside and villages of Java looking for unusual pieces, buying them up for a song. The furniture is often made of *jati* (teak) and usually is in decrepit shape. Once fully restored in Bali, the same pieces sell for as much as 10 times the original price in the antique shops of Batubulan, Legian, and Krobokan.

Still, the prices for these beautiful, unique, and authentic antiques are a fraction of what they would cost in the West: antique easy chairs Rp300,000, Madurese carved storage boxes

Rp500,000, rustic married cabinets Rp500,000 (married means old wood joined with new wood), wooden benches Rp350,000, Javanese partitions with Islamic motifs Rp400,000, carved prows of traditional boats, wooden buckets Rp75,000, small tea tables Rp125,000, rare and ornate colonial chairs Rp300,000, reclining lounge chairs Rp250,000.

But the supply is not inexhaustable and it's going fast. Presently as many as 100 containers a month leave Bali and Java for the living rooms of Milan, Stockholm, and San Francisco (as many as 500 containers a month of repro-furniture). Some types of furniture have disappeared altogether. Don't even bother looking for Dutch-Chinese *(peranakan)* furniture with traces of original pigment. Indonesia was cleaned out of these pieces decades ago.

Choose your piece very carefully as there's a lot of junk out there and prices for the good stuff vary considerably. Beware of parts of the piece which are not original and be sure the add-ons match properly. Make sure, for example, that the dealer doesn't replace old teak with cheap, green wood, then use a dark stain so that you can't discern the difference until it's too late. Termites will devour the cheap wood (they won't go near the old teak) and the piece will crack and split once it's been shipped to a cold temperate climate.

Also examine the finishes the dealer uses; most often they slap on dark, unevenly applied shellac which makes a real antique look like a piece of repro-rubbish. If you like the design, buy it plain and finish it yourself or hire a Balinese carpenter at Rp9000 per hour and supervise the work.

Most dealers don't bargain because they can easily get the prices they ask. Wait until you see something you like and (if reasonable) pay the price asked—quickly.

Ethnographica

Bali is also fast becoming an international center for primitive art. The competition for the art of the Outer Islands is intense—many pieces were plundered by Indonesian Army officers. A great number of souvenir shops now sell contemporary tribal baskets, bamboo containers, amulets, statuettes, tribal body ornaments and jewelry—all newly made and well crafted.

Forget about finding something original. All the major museum-quality pieces were bought up over a century ago and now form parts of very old European collections. There are no Borobudur Buddha heads or Leti ancestor statues left.

Balinese artists are extremely adept at reproducing ethnographica from all over the archipelago—authentic-looking Asmat carvings, Borneo *hampatong* figures, Niah, Batak, or Sumba-style wooden statuary. Though not the real thing, these relatively inexpensive "antiques-to-order" are all perfectly legitimate artforms, attractive, worth every rupiah if you can buy something you like for a good price. The best reproductions are made by the ethnic groups right in the place where they live and work.

Souvenirs *not* to buy, lest customs in your country fine you and/or confiscate your articles, are items made with alligator, lizard, snake skin, ivory. Combs, barrettes, and jewelry made from tortoise shell and souvenirs made of feathers, fur, dried turtles, or butterflies can also be confiscated.

Where to Shop

Individual shops are on the main shopping streets of Sanur and Kuta. The shopping arcades of major resort hotels are another rich source of beautiful antiques at sky-high prices, but make sure what you're buying is genuine and not a repro.

There are literally hundreds of furniture shops, by far the most concentrated in southern Bali within the Mas-Jimbaran-Krobokan triangle. Wherever you see a mass jumble of old beds, decaying screens, posts, stop and dive in. Investigate the high-end big dealers and galleries first. For furniture, check out **Polos** in Legian, **Warisan** in Krobokan, **Marios** near the big Buddha baby on the Gianyar Road. Stay away from the shops on the main drag (Jl. Bypass) where the worst fly-by-night con-artists work. Buy only from reputable dealers.

One of the best of the big dealers is **Arts of Asia Gallery,** Jl. Raya Tuban, Denpasar, tel. (0361) 752860, which houses a priceless collection of old *wayang kulit,* woodcarvings, textiles *(gringsing, endek, songket),* Chinaware, and fine *kris.*

Don't neglect such first-class galleries as the **Polo Gallery** in the Four Seasons Hotel, the

Kungang-Kunang in Campuan and the **Aman-dari Gallery** in Kedewetan (both near Ubud); **Baharuddhin's** for luscious hand-dyed *ikat* from Sumba, Flores, Sawu, and Kalimantan, plus beads, baskets, and curios; **Kaliuda Art Shop,** Jl. Legian, for woodcarvings and *ikat* from Timor, Sumba and Flores.

Klungkung has a cluster of seven antique shops on Jl. Diponegoro east of the main intersection; treasures can almost always be uncovered in these cluttered, dusty shops. **Kerajinan Art Shop** can be depended upon. **Batubulan** also has a row of shops, especially strong on fine old gilded or plain carved wood panels, statues, and old Balinese art objects; also Kamasan paintings, vintage musical instruments, fans, cowbells, wooden *kulkul* bells, etc. The shops are just south of Batubulan's stonecarving workshops.

The self-appointed arbiter of taste and style, Australian-born Made Wijaya, whose other passions include anthropology, architecture, and gardening for rock stars, has fitted out his **Gallery Bebek** at the Tohpati intersection (on the way to Ubud) with an eclectic collection of contemporary furniture and objets d'art.

MISCELLANEOUS

The tape shops of Bali are quite good, with very wide-ranging selections, even better than can be found in London! For the price (Rp10,000 for Western music, Rp8000 for Indonesian), the recording quality is high. On Kuta, **Mahogony** opposite Goa in Legian, is the best shop.

For home furnishings, try the **Linda Garland Showroom,** Jl. Hyatt, Sanur. For backpacks, day packs, wait packs, sleeping bags, surfing bags, visit **Dody Production Inc.,** Jl. Hasanudin 69, Denpasar.

For as little as Rp5000, imitations of top-brand name perfumes—Anais Anais, Opium, Chanel, Paris—have been the rage on Bali for about five years now, perhaps reflecting the steady increase in European arrivals. A few drops of essence are put in alcohol and the fragrance lasts only for a few minutes. Eyeglasses are another bargain. At least six optical outlets in

southern Bali sell such exclusive international collections as Cartier, Fred, Etienne Aigner, Kenzo, Missoni, Giorgio Armani, Lacel, Sillhoute, Essilor, and Ray-Ban. One of the best known is **Optik Melawai,** Block 13, No. 2-3, Galleria Nusa Dua. Most shops can fit from your optometrist's prescription or can offer computerized fitting service. A few sell contact lenses.

Watches are cheaper in Kuta than anywhere else in Indonesia. Use your bargaining skills and know the prices. They are good for trading in Lombok and probably also on any other island. They sell for big money in India.

The craft of *jukung*-building is still alive in the villages of Jimbaran, Suwung, and the remote east coast. A *jukung,* a type of Indonesian *prahu* (outrigger canoe), is cut from a single tree trunk. A small *jukung* (known as a *petunggalan*), which measures five meters in length, 40 cm in width and 60 cm in height, takes about 40 days to construct. A *jukung* made from the best wood *(ganggangan)* can last 30 years.

Leather

You can get reasonable prices and average quality on leather products at the shops outside of Goa Gajah, or you must go into Denpasar and pay a bit more for marginally better quality, but nothing like the standards in Yogyakarta. Leather jackets, with fake wool collars, cost Rp200,000.

Wayang kulit (shadow puppets) are cut from buffalo hide with a chisel-like stylus and then painted. The two-dimensional figures, with intricate lace patterns on the body and arms, have the appearance of dolls. On Bali this form of *wayang* has been developed into a spellbinding medium for conveying the great classics, the Mahabharata and Ramayana. Puppets are made in Puaya (near Sukawati) and in Peliatan (near Ubud). You have about 150 characters to choose from.

Rama Collection (Jl. Legian Kelod 400, tel. 0361-751570) sells well-made leather purses Rp30,000, men's leather briefcases Rp65,000, traveling bags Rp85,000-115,000. **Prima,** in Legian just before Warung Kopi on the left if coming from Kuta, sells and makes shoes. Give them your favorite pair and they'll copy them for only around Rp25,000.

MUSIC

Loved by the people, music is as much a part of the environment as rivers, trees, and the snarl of *bemos*. It is often difficult to know where music ends and nature and Balinese life begin. Echoing, throbbing xylophones, drums, and clashing cymbals can be heard all hours of the day and night, blending with chirping crickets and croaking frogs. Bathers sing in rivers, rattles clack in fields, bicycle bells tingle, kites vibrate in the wind, little boys imitate the sound of gongs, pigeons circle overhead with whistles attached to their feet, and during the space of just a few kilometers one may hear the hard and feverish rehearsal of half a dozen percussion-centered *gamelan* the centerpiece in this rich and varied musical environment.

The word *gamelan* simply means "musical group" and may refer to 20 different kinds of xylophonic, percussion-type musical ensembles. There are more *gamelan* regularly performing on Bali today—over 1,500 orchestras and 100 dance troupes—than ever before. Just as the Balinese share the planting of rice and the upkeep of their temples, traditional orchestra clubs, *sekaha*, are a communal organization in which everyone shares an equal interest and pride.

History and Development

Scholars believe *gamelan* music may derive from the sound of priestly bells. Another theory holds that the percussive component of *gamelan* developed from workers using heavy pounding-poles to beat out music as they beat the husks off rice grains, perhaps lifting the trough off the ground and laying it on crossbeams to enhance the resonance. The *gamelan* is likely indigenous to Indonesia and probably consisted of bamboo instruments. The royal courts of Bali emulated the pomp and ritual of the Javanese

Majapahit Kingdom of ancient Java, and Balinese courtly music was no exception. Mention of *gamelan* orchestras have been found in chronicles dating back as far as the 14th century.

With the Dutch seizure of power in 1908, Balinese court culture began to undergo a drastic transformation. Their power and sources of revenues sharply curtailed, the *puri* ceased to function as cultural centers. By the 1930s the ceremonial glitter of the courts had faded and most of the court *gamelan* were in storage, gathering dust. Unable to afford their traditional role as patrons of the arts, many courts sold their *gamelan* to village musicians, thus passing the domination and fostering of the arts into the hands of common villagers. Whole orchestras were melted down and recast in forms that better suited the flamboyant and frolicsome tastes of the masses. From the moment the music left the courts and filtered into the villages, its development accelerated and took on a life of its own, becoming louder, faster, more earthy, and available to a much wider audience.

Today, the village *gamelan* is played with more vigor and passion than the slower, haunting Javanese-style orchestra, which remained the prerogative of the courts on Bali until well into the 20th century.

Musical Composition

Sudden changes, displaced accents, bursts of rapid, precise, highly syncopated playing, increases and decreases of volume, and a highly developed counterpoint based on simple melodies give many Westerners the impression that *gamelan* music is improvised like jazz, but this is untrue. If an orchestra musician started hammering out his own tune, he'd be immediately ostracized from the troupe. Alternately

a rebab

A Balinese *gamelan* piece usually consists of four or five movements, each divided into four phases: a solo to introduce the piece, the introductory theme, followed by central body and then the clashing, thunderous finale. Typically, compositions are named after animal actions or temperaments: "Crow Stealing Eggs," "Fighting Cats," "Toad Climbing Pawpaw," "Golden Butterfly," or "Snapping Crocodile."

Composers are selected from the orchestra's best players. In everyday life they could be waiters at a restaurant, artisans, or field laborers. It's difficult to make out who controls the orchestra so perfectly and precisely because the *gamelan* has no real conductor. Instead, the orchestra is lead by the two drummers, often the most accomplished musicians of the group. They link the instruments together, control the tempo, and underline the accents. With their knowledge of both dance and music, the drummers signal other musicians to play the proper musical gesture to accompany a specific dance. The music itself is played from memory, which is extraordinary when you consider how lengthy and complex some pieces are. The Balinese have worked out a system of notation, but the orchestration of the melody is fixed so notation is seldom used. Learning by repetition, the Balinese say when a piece

playful, blaring, with a frenetic, vibrant sound, *gamelan* is Balinese music like no other you have ever heard.

The assorted drums, gongs, and cymbals carry a wide variation of pitch and timbre. What might be called octaves are not exact octaves and may sound off-pitch or dissonant to Western ears. Instruments with a high range of notes are struck with more frequency than those with lower ranges, so there's a greater proportion of high harmonics over fundamental harmonics; half and quarter notes are employed to a considerable extent.

There are five or seven tones in Balinese music, just as in Java. The instruments are tuned when they're made to either the pentatonic (five-tone) *pelog* scale or the septatonic (seven-tone) *slendro* scale. All the instruments have fixed pitches, with the exception of the wistful, viola-like *rebab* and wailing *suling* (flutes). Each gong-like instrument is tuned to its neighbor, making the whole *gamelan* a self-contained, coherent musical unit, played as a single instrument rather than a collection. Each instrument is tuned to its partner in a slightly higher tone, producing the shimmering, tremolo, so characteristic of Balinese *gamelan*. Even on an individual instrument, the octave notes may be tuned slightly higher than the matching lower tones. Played together they produce a rich, throbbing sound.

the cengceng

is practiced long enough "it enters the musician's liver and he plays without thinking."

Musicologists marvel at the way two musicians play interlocking parts as fast as possible, beating out alternate notes at top speed and in perfect coordination, resulting in a faster performance than one player is capable of. The Balinese like their music very loud and dramatic, with sharp changes in the tempo and volume. A piece always seems to end unexpectedly—as if in mid-song. In the south, the playing style is more refined and fluid, radically different from the violent, rhapsodical style of the north.

Forms of *Gamelan* Orchestras

Strictly defined, the word *gamelan* refers to the Javanese orchestra, though it may be applied in general to any Indonesian percussion orchestra. The Balinese themselves refer to their orchestra simply as *gong*, as in *gong gede* or *gong kebyar*, and each set of instruments is given names such as "Sea of Honey" or "Floating Cloud." There's a *gong* for almost every occasion—weddings, cremations, cultural performances, birthdays. Special music accompanies long processions to the sea, or lures the gods from their celestial heights. Other melodies induce a trance, entertain the masses with musical comedy, or accompany all-night operas for the elite.

Ensemble size ranges from the huge 40 member *gamelan gong* to the mini-xylophonic quintets carried on multistoried pyres in funeral processions. In between you'll find 30-piece bronze percussion orchestras, small *angklung*, bamboo *gamelan*, orchestras entirely of lutes and mouth-harps, and small quartets playing the accompanying music for choral symphonies composed of chants and grunts. Each ensemble differs in the instruments that make it up, the scale used, and the sonority. Many types of orchestras can be pared down so that they can be played by marching bands.

Since the 1960s, credit goes to tourists for keeping alive some forms of *gamelan* which might otherwise have succumbed to the pervasive influence of modernism, though experimentation with new styles never ceases. The Western music inundating Bali is now looked upon as a stimulus rather than a threat, but youthful composers also look to older traditional Balinese forms for inspiration, and forms are always coming in and out of style. The seventone *semar pegulingan* orchestra in which some instruments are played with two hands has now become the most sought-after ensemble for the creations of contemporary Balinese composers. The archaic and rare *gong selunding* features metallophones with iron keys and very simple trough resonators.

The highly distinctive, classical *tektekan* orchestra of Krambitan in Tabanan is made up of men carrying split bamboo drums and giant cowbells around their necks. Exorcizing malignant spirits when pestilence strikes the village, this is the only orchestra of its type in Bali. The island's only all-women *gamelan*, known as *gong wanita*, is from Peliatan in Gianyar where they perform on the Tirtasari Dance Stage.

The refined *gong gede* and *gong pelegongan* prevalent in the early years of this century, essentially as temple orchestras, were superseded in the 1920s and 30s by more up-tempo *gong kebyar*, which started catching on in northern Bali in 1915. Until recently, it was the most popular and widespread type of orchestra, but has reached a state of saturation both in numbers and style.

A few older ensembles are coming back in popularity. Revived in the past five years is the spectacular *gamelan jegog* of the western Jembrana Regency which consists of mammoth tubes of bamboo, the largest measuring up to 30 cm in diameter and over two meters in length. When struck with a big, padded mallet, the sound made by the resonating *jegog* tubes can be heard over a great distance. One impetus behind this revival is the unremitting and intense competition between different musical associations. Encouraged by the provincial government which sponsors annual music festivals and competitions, these contests are like sporting events.

The Instruments

As many as 25 separate instruments make up different musical ensembles on Bali. Instruments are framed in splendidly carved, painted, and gilded stands. More elaborate and expensive frames have scenes from the Hindu epics carved along their sides. All *gamelan* instruments are sanctified; some melodies are considered so sacred they may not be played or even hummed without special ceremonies and offerings. Even before a commercial *gamelan* performance, a priest is always summoned to bless the venue, the musicians, dancers, and instruments, and to neutralize any malevolent spirits which might cause mischief.

The principal instruments of the orchestra are the metallophones of various sizes and pitches. The *gangsa*, the highest pitch, is used to play rapid, interlocking rhythms and melodies. The midrange instrument, the *calung*, plays the core melody, while the bass metallophone, the *jegogan*, punctuates the longer phrases and reinforces the basic melody. Their metal keys are suspended over bamboo resonating tubes, mellowing the harsh metallic sound. Each instrument plays an integral role in the group, which is be divided into sections: instruments to embellish the basic melody, instruments to lay down the metrical structure, and instruments to "sweeten" the melody.

Holding conical *kendang* drums in their laps and using both hands and rounded sticks, the lead drummers pour forth incredible rhythms. They can vary the tonal quality depending on whether the drum is played with the tips of the fingers, the palm of the hand, or damped with the fingers. The big *wadon,* or female drum, is played by one of the leaders. The smaller, male drum, or *lanang*, dictates the rhythm of the *gamelan;* dancers always follow the beat, or what musicologists call the "drum language," laid down by these two open-ended drums.

Other instruments include the fast, tinkling cymbals *(cengceng)* that change the tempo and carry the faster rhythms. Holding the composition together is the *kempli,* a small gong held on the lap which is steadily beaten with a stick, keeping the beat, and medium-sized suspended gongs *(kempur)* that punctuate the phrases at critical moments. The xylophonic *tingklik* provides liquid, mellow contrast to the brazen, bright notes of the metallophones. The 10 keys are made of bamboo and have no resonators. Different forms of *tingklik* are played in Bali's outer districts like Jembrana and Tenganan. The deep, luscious accents of the great bronze gongs mark off the basic line of the piece (much like a piano in Western orchestras), while the theme and the rich, rippling chords are played on sets of inverted gong-shaped bells *(reyong)* and the alto bells *(trompong)*—inverted, nipple-shaped

bronze bowls which look like small kettles and are beaten with padded sticks.

Instruments that accompany particular dances or dramas include the bamboo flute *(suling)* and the two-stringed, violinlike zither *(rebab)*. Both provide ornamentation and a lead for the melody, but are not indispensable parts of the orchestra. These specialized instruments are most often found in small chamber-like ensembles performing in prestigious restaurants and hotels. The simple flute *(suling)* is a common instrument played from the mouth or the nose. It measures approximately six cm around and 90-115 cm in length. The oldest ensembles still use a large number of *suling.* Their mournful sound accompanies the *gamelan* melody during the most poignant parts of the story. In Indonesia, where there is no set scale, this adaptable bamboo tube is crafted to fit the scale being used.

The *genggong,* a bamboo jew's harp, is one of the world's oldest instruments developed in In-

The genggong (jew's harp) is the perfect instrument for casting spells or greeting animist spirits.

donesia in the 10th or 11th century. Just two-cm-wide and 20-cm-long, it's made from a short, thin, dried rib of palm leaf with a long, vibrating tongue. The *genggong* is held in front of the mouth while a finger tugs a string attached to the other end, causing the instrument to vibrate. Both a percussion and tonal instrument, the *genggong* produces a melody and a twanging, hypnotic rhythm at the same time. The cavity of the mouth acts as the instrument's sounding board, and the harmonics are changed by opening or closing the mouth and by breath control. By "breathing" the tune, a skilled player can make this ancient instrument bleat, trill, croak, laugh, or lull you to sleep. When well played, the *genggong* can sound somewhat like the Australian aborigine's didgeridoo, a set of bagpipes, or the curious whispering voices of night insects. Like many other traditional Balinese instruments, it is tuned to the pentatonic *(slendro)* scale, making it possible to play the *genggung* in the bamboo *angklung* ensemble. It's most often heard accompanying the humorous *genggong*, or frog dance, performed at birthdays, farewells, and wedding parties.

Gamelan Instrument-Making

The finest *gamelan* made on Bali cost US$20,000-30,000. Bali's consummate *gamelan* instrument craftsmen live and work in the villages of Tihingan, Sawan, and Blahbatuh. These highly respected artisans have a profound knowledge of metallurgy, bronze-smithing, instrument-tuning, and woodworking. The tone of each bronze key is matched against a wooden tuning stick, then laboriously filed to acquire just the right pitch. Similar instruments are slightly out of tune with each other to make a shimmering, more appealing sound. Although all ensembles are tuned to roughly the same scale, there is no universally accepted reference. This is very much in keeping with the belief that each *gamelan* has its own spirit. For a Balinese, it's unthinkable to step over an instrument lest the unique spirit residing in it be offended.

The largest and most famous gong foundry *(pabrik gong)* is **I Made Gabeleran's** in Blahbatu. After melting an alloy of tin and copper with hot coconut charcoal fires stoked with bamboo plungers, Pak Gabeleran's smiths forge magnificent sets of *trompong* or cast *reyong* in molds. In the big display room, completed instruments are for sale from Rp125,000 for a small *kendang batel* to Rp800,000 for an impressive, glittering *gangsa giing*. Specialists carve the ornate wooden frames and stands for the instruments in a rear courtyard. This workshop complex, **Sidha Karya-Kerajinan Gong**, which produces five or six complete *gamelan* ensembles a year, is a must-see for the lover of *gamelan*. Turn at the *balai banjar* and you'll see the wooden logs for making stands stacked outside.

In the Northern village of **Sawan** live four generations of *gamelan*-instrument makers. Workshops here turn out *gender, gangsa, ceng-ceng*, and other instruments. Of all the instrument-makers on Bali, Widandra gives the best explanation of the entire process. Or check out the poster in the showroom with photos and explanations of the steps involved. Instruments and small, carved, gilded stands are also for sale. If you don't buy anything, please leave a donation in appreciation of Widandra's time and effort.

The Players

Gamelan players are not professionals but are drawn from all walks of life—farmers, shop owners, postal clerks, and might be from eight to 80 years of age. Some have played together for as long as 50 years, and some groups have long outlived their original members, existing unbroken for hundreds of years. Each *banjar* appoints a leader and a treasurer, and members contribute all they can to assure the success of the group. It's their responsibility to contribute money and labor, carry instruments, train new musicians, and rehearse. Members speak in the low language and no one sits higher or lower than the other. If the orchestra receives payment from a large hotel or from other commissioned performances, the money usually goes to the *gamelan* club to cover expenses, transportation, tuning, and maintaining or acquiring new instruments or costumes. Excess funds are divided among members in time for Galungan, the Balinese New Year.

Rehearsals

To achieve the rich sonic complexity and subtlety of Balinese music—without a notational system—requires long hours of rehearsal. Depending on the orchestra, rehearsals are held as infrequently as once every six months or as often as five days a week. In preparation for an upcoming festival, temple anniversary, or to provide music for a dance troupe, incessant rehearsals take place.

You have an excellent chance of happening upon a *gamelan* rehearsal, usually after sunset when villagers gather around the *bale banjar* where the orchestra is kept. Follow your ears— you can't miss the metallic, jangly energy and deep, reverberating gongs. Sit near the musicians so you can feel the power of the music. Rehearsals are casual, open-air affairs with dogs prancing across the dance floor, old men playing flutes in the background, infants suckling, and babies falling asleep amidst the clashing of drums, gongs, and cymbals. If not preparing for a performance a musician might even hand over his mallets to a spectator during a session. Entry is free.

The instruments remain in the *bale banjar* for anyone who wishes to practice. Training starts at a very early age; when the musicians take a break, a mob of little boys descend on the instruments (it's almost impossible to damage them) and start improvising a melody, often quite deftly. They learn the various parts of the composition by imitation, and the most talented youngsters in a village are singled out and sent to one of two outstanding and innovative conservatories of dance and music in Denpasar. The **SMKI** conservatory is for high school level students, while the government-sponsored **STSI**, the Music and Dance Academy in Denpasar, offers work on undergraduate through master's degrees. After mastering the related forms of music, dance, and drama, the students usually return to their villages to teach. The custom of all-male groups has now fallen by the wayside; at SMKI in Denpasar you are just as likely to see girls practicing.

Performances and Events

A great number of villages offer commercial daily or weekly performances in the *bale banjar*—outfitted with a ticket table, rows of chairs, and lighting. Foreign audiences are bused in from the resorts and pay a fee of Rp5000-6000. The performances usually start at 0930 or 1000.

Gamelan are most often owned by the *banjar,* and a village could have as many as three *banjar,* each with its own *gamelan,* though temples, as well as independent families, may also own smaller orchestras. If it's prosperous enough, the goal of every *banjar* is to own the most outstanding *gamelan* among the surrounding communities. As evening approaches on the roadways of Bali, you'll see gaudily attired musicians and their instruments piled on trucks on their way to the resorts to play.

A temple performance is one of the best places to see the *gamelan* perform. Temple anniversary ceremonies, *odalan*s, are always taking place somewhere on Bali and visitors are always welcome. Ask the local tourist office, your hotel proprietor, driver, or guide. Go in the late afternoon or early evening when spectators are arriving with their offerings. A group of interested people may also commission a performance. The fee is very reasonable (US$100-500), depending upon the size and elaborateness of the orchestra and dance troupe, and the length of the program. Go up to the head of the music club, the *ketua sekaha gong,* and make arrangements for your group to be seated in the *bale banjar* or other community space. The comraderie and interplay such an event fosters between visitors and villagers is unforgettable.

At the **Denpasar Arts Center** on Jl. Nusa Indah in Abiankapas (a 15-minute walk east of Kereneng Station) visitors can see dance and music rehearsals as well as public dances. The art center also features two magnificent open-air amphitheaters with modern lighting and hosts a Bali Arts Festival. Each year from mid-June to mid-July musical and *sendratari* competitions, as well as diverse classical and modern music performances, are held daily. If it's the high season, book your hotel early so that you don't miss it.

Overseas *Gamelan* Sets

The Balinese *gamelan* first traveled overseas in 1931 when a small troupe of dancers and musicians toured Europe. In the 1950s, another group visited Europe, the U.S., Mexico, and Australia. The inimitable quality of the Balinese *gamelan* has attracted Western composers ever since. There are hundreds of authentic, first-class Javanese and Balinese *gamelan* owned by Indonesian consulates or embassies, private nonprofit groups, and ethnomusicology departments in a number of universities in Japan, Australia, Europe, and the United States. Indonesians consider the *gamelan* as an important emissary connecting them to the world at large, although native Balinese *gamelan* are seldom played outside of Indonesia because of the high costs of transporting 30 instruments and 40-50 people.

There are Balinese ensembles in Montreal, Canada; Belfast, Northern Ireland; Munich and Freiburg, West Germany; and Melbourne, Australia. In the U.S.A. alone there are 100 groups, and in Japan at least 15 Balinese *gamelan* exist. Modeled after the Balinese *sekaha* system, orchestra members are sought from the community. These students learn to play from experienced non-Balinese tutors or from native Balinese invited as guest-teachers.

Active *gamelan* can be found at the Indonesian embassy in Washington, D.C., and the New York and Los Angeles consulates (ask for the cultural representative). Universities which maintain *gamelan* and hold performances include Brown University, California Institute of the Arts, Ohio State University, UCLA, and San Diego State.

One of the most thrilling American groups, now in its 17th year, is the nonprofit, 35-member **Gamelan Sekar Jaya** of the San Francisco Bay area (6485 Conlon Ave., El Cerrito, CA 94530, tel./fax 510-237-6849). This *gong kebyar* club is currently under the direction of I Nyoman Windha. Their repertoire includes both traditional pieces and new compositions, often accompanied by dances. Another private group is the *Giri Mekar Gong Kebyar* of Woodstock, New York. The **American Gamelan Institute** in Lebanon, New Hampshire, runs the performing ensemble Gamelan Lipur Sih. The ethnomusicology department at **Bowling State University** has a *gong kebyar* called Kusuma Sari. A handful of students at **Cornell University** regularly stage *gender wayang* performances as a part of the music department's outreach program. Denver's group, Tunas Mekar, a nonprofit 18-member community orchestra, is under the umbrella of the **Colorado New Music Association.** They perform *angklung* and *kebyar* with dancers and offer a cassette. **Dartington College of Arts,** Totnes, Devon, TQ9 6EJ, U.K. (tel. 0803-865491, fax 863569) has a *gong kebyar* set.

Studying Music

Though the wide variety of Balinese compositions are generally attractive to Western ears, some formidable obstacles face Western students. The rhythm defies Western music notation. Indeed, the whole Western concept of scales and keys, as well as the terminology, is alien to Balinese music. While a Westerner may discern two separate five-tone scales, a Balinese can recognize at least seven.

Learning to appreciate the music requires great concentration and ear training. Students are started off kindergarten style with big charts, and audible counting games accustom the class to the role of each instrument before they kneel behind the real thing. Singing their parts along with the music, Westerners must adjust to rhythms that can't be wrestled into four beats per measure.

Although the instruments appear simple, a number of tricks go into playing them. One of the most difficult to learn is the mallet technique—the knack of striking the keys with a mallet in the right hand while dampening the keys with the fingers of the left a millisecond later. This split-second timing at very high speeds sometimes takes years to master.

Decide first on the style of music you want to study. The most popular choices for Westerners are the *tingklik*, *gong kebyar*, and *gender wayang*. Michael Tenzer, author of *Balinese Music,* advises students to learn the basic melodies on the *gangsa* first, as other instruments like the *reyong* and *kendang* are too abstract for the beginner. Bring a tape recorder so that you can hear the lesson and practice later. Determining payment is awkward for a Balinese teacher because their instruction is usually given to a group and payment is made in favors or obligations rather than in coin. Ask other students what the going rate is—about Rp10,000 per lesson in 1995.

The **Center for World Music** (10715 Anaheim Drive, La Mesa, CA 91941, U.S.A., tel. 619-440-7200) presents summer music study programs in Bali each year. Courses usually last four weeks in July or August. Tuition is US$750, including on-site meals. Inexpensive camping-style accommodation in tents or nearby homes is available as well. Also look for art-oriented tour companies. **Overseas Adventure Travel** (tel.

617-876-0533) of Cambridge offers a two-week itinerary which includes a lesson in *gamelan* playing and stylized Balinese dance. More informal is the **Balinese Music Workshop** offered by Ubud's Ganesha Bookshop, Jl. Raya (opposite the post office); Rp15,000 per person every Tuesday evening 1800-1930. This is an introductory workshop and no previous musical knowledge is necessary. Participants are given a brief history and outline of the *gamelan* and then invited to choose one of their instruments to learn some basic music. Instruments include metallophones, gongs, cymbals, drums, flutes, and others. Inquire about group bookings.

It's possible for Westerners to study music at KOKAR/SMKI in Batubulan and at STSI (Indonesian Academy of Music and Dance) on Jl. Nusa Indah in Denpasar. Many of the island's best dancers, choreographers, and composers work at these renowned conservatories. The majority of the faculty speak English. If you just want to see and hear the musicians practicing, classes always take place in the mornings. Music study also makes up part of the curriculum at the **Yayasan Siddha Mahan Foundation** in Sideman (Karangasem Regency).

To seriously study Balinese music for any length of time, however, you need a permit from LIPI in Jakarta as a "guest student." Wayan, the proprietor of Siti Homestay (tel. 0361-975599) in Peliatan, can help you obtain a long-term study visa and/or academic sponsorship. Ask musicians or your hotel or homestay proprietor if they know of any music teachers who take Western students. The study locale is often just a room in a private home with a pair of instruments facing each other—yours and the teacher's.

Essential Reading

Dance and Drama in Bali (Faber and Faber Ltd., 1938) by Beryl de Zoete and Walter Spies is a recognized classic. More updated is *Balinese Music* by Michael Tenzer (Periplus, 1991), the definitive and indispensable introduction to more than a dozen different types of Balinese *gamelan*.

To learn about the location of orchestras outside of Bali and related topics, students of ethnomusicology and lovers of *gamelan* and the performing arts should subscribe to the journal *Balungan,* published by the **American Gamelan Institute** (Box 1052, Lebanon, NH 03766, U.S.A.; call or fax 603-448-8837); US$15 for two issues per year, US$20 overseas, US$30 institutions. Write or call for a sample. Volume 4, No. 2 is a special issue devoted to Bali.

Balinese Music in Context is published by the Institute of Musicology, Petergraben 27, 4051 Basel, Switzerland. They've also issued *Ritual Music from Bali* in their anthology of Southeast Asian Music series. In Volume No. 5, you'll find an inventory of all the recordings of Balinese ritual music *(gambang, selunding, gong luang* and *saron/caruk)* in their archives (copies are available). Dating from the 1930s, this is the largest collection of Balinese traditional music in the world.

Recordings

There are plentiful selections of cassette tapes of classical and modern *gamelan* music available for Rp6000-8000 in the shops of Kuta, Legian, Denpasar, and Ubud. At commercial performances a table is often set aside for the sale of *gamelan* tapes and CDs. **CMP Records,** 155 W. 72nd St., no. 704, New York, NY 10023, U.S.A., sells two volumes of Balinese music on CD. Consumers with Master/Visa may order by telephone (800 443 4727).

The **American Gamelan Institute** (A.G.I.) produces cassettes and CDs of contemporary Indonesian music, including works by Balinese composers as well as others from the West. Ask about their "Bali Cassette Collection" (10 cassettes: US$75), a wide-ranging musical survey recorded in dozens of different villages, covering a wonderful variety of musical styles and instruments: a children's group in Peliatan, *gamelan* composed of bamboo flutes or xylophones, and some of Bali's most popular modern *kebyar* compositions. Also ask about their "New Music from Bali" (US$10) with contemporary works by Astita, Rai, and Suweca. A.G.I. maintains an archive and distributes a journal, musical scores, monographs, and other educational materials.

THE PERFORMING ARTS

With over 100 troupes on the island, dance is at the very center of Balinese life and will probably be the most impressive thing you'll see and remember. In all, there are over 200 kinds of dances, though only around 20 are performed regularly, many still religious and each a composite of not only dance but drama, music, spoken poetry, opera, and song.

There are frog dances, monkey dances, bumblebee dances, epic ballets, martial dances, dances for choosing a mate, and dances to exorcize evil spirits. Dances are roughly divided into those of Hindu origin and those of animist, Old Indonesian derivation, which are usually performed in the innermost courtyard *(jeroan)* of the temple.

In the classical Hinduized dances, invariably there's a princess to rescue or a kingdom to conquer. Some are danced only by women, others only by men. Each is performed in many different styles, depending on the locale and artistic influence.

For the most part, dance and dance-dramas have come down to us remarkably well preserved because it's an art form zealously supported and well cultivated by the community. Old plays, completely rearranged and with recast choreography, are periodically revived by the Balinese and staged at the island-wide Denpasar Arts Festival.

Although Westerners lament that Bali's arts have suffered from the flood of tourism—not to mention TV, video, Hollywood films, and B-grade kung-fu movies—the arrival of tourists has actually preserved, fortified, and revitalized the island's performing arts. Again, the Balinese have shown themselves to be dynamically resilient.

Religion and Dance

Over a thousand years ago Chinese and Indian pilgrims to Bali were struck by the ritual and frenzy of the island's dances and celebrations. They named the island Wali, a Sanskrit word meaning "religious festival."

In Balinese, the word *wali* is still used to refer to stately row or circle dances offered to the

gods as opposed to *balih-balihan* dances which are performed as commercial entertainment only. In the 20th century, visitors from Charlie Chaplin and Margaret Mead to Mick Jagger and Antonin Arthaud have been transfixed by the island's elaborate temple festivals put on to entertain the Hindu gods.

Because all Balinese dances were originally religious in nature, a gift for the visiting gods, the Balinese have always attached great importance to their dances. To this day no large cremation, temple ceremony, wedding, or important social rite is complete without a dance drama or *wayang kulit* performance. Certain dances are even prohibited from being staged in public.

A fuzzy boundary is maintained between what the Balinese do for themselves and what they do for visitors. In 1992, Governor Ida Bagus Oka decreed that 11 sacred or *wali* dances may no longer be performed in hotels or at the usual commercial dance venues. This policy was a long time in coming: during President Reagan's 1986 visit, the holy *pendet* welcoming dance was cut from a 10 minutes to a pathetic two minutes at the request of the White House.

Dance and drama also serve as important mediums through which centuries-old culture, history, values, notions of religious piety, and even political philosophies flow to contemporary and future generations. Before the opening of native Malay schools in the 1920s, theater was the only way to transmit traditional values and knowledge, such as the purpose of a village's three temples, the importance of carrying out your parent's cremation, what happens if you don't meet your *banjar* obligations.

Reference

The following books give valuable insights into Balinese dance and drama: *Dance and Drama in Bali,* by Beryl de Zoete and Walter Spies; *Island of Bali,* by Miguel Covarrubias; *Music in Bali,* by Colin McPhee; *Masks of Bali,* by Judy Slattum, photos by Paul Schraub. Publishers and short annotations for the books are listed in the Booklist.

History and Development

About 1,500 years ago, Indian influences began to make their way via Java to Bali. Thus, the characters of the Hindu Mahabharata and Ramayana epic poems are today the heroes and deities of Hinduized Balinese dancing, and strong traces of 10th-century Tantric rites and magical sorcery as well as several Indian *mudra* are found in several Balinese dances.

Since the mass infusion of the Javano-Hindu culture into Bali that followed the Majapahit collapse, the Balinese have created their own dances and characters. The clowns *(bebanyolan),* for example, are a personification of the Balinese genius for assimilating new influences without destroying the integrity of the old.

The first commercial tourist performances were staged in 1928 at KPM's Bali Hotel in Denpasar and at the Kuta Beach Hotel. In the 1930s, with the decline of the aristocratic houses, dancing and musical instruments were taken over by the villages. As a result, dancing became more dynamic, fast-moving, and enthralling. Nurtured by the stability of the colonial period, musical activity in the villages flourished and dance clubs proliferated.

In the early 1930s, the Peliatan *legong* troupe was the first Balinese dance company to perform abroad. They were feted in London and New York and played at the 1931 Exposition in Paris. During the Japanese occupation (1942-45), Bali became a rest and recuperation center for Japanese soldiers; the taste of the occupiers gave rise to such dances as the *prembon* and *wiranata,* still occasionally staged today.

Under the sponsorship of the nation-building Sukarno regime, the dancers and musicians of Ubud-Peliatan were again dispatched on a world circuit tour in the 1950s. Also in the 1950s, the same troupe costarred with Bing Crosby, Bob Hope, and Dorothy Lamour in the very forgettable Hollywood film *Road to Bali.*

Starting in 1967, with Suharto's New Order regime reopening Bali's doors to foreigners, dances were staged at the newly inaugerated Bali Beach Hotel in Sanur. By the late 1960s, the number of foreign visitors had reached 30,000 per annum, and Bali was adopted as a showcase for Indonesia's efforts to promote "cultural tourism."

This development of tourism undeniably stimulated performing arts—a cultural renaissance. Even at this relatively early date, Balinese dancing represented the island's trademark for outsiders and a yardstick of artistic activity for the Balinese themselves.

Ever since the late '70s, Balinese dance troupes have regularly made world tours, but the exoticism and spectacle of a Balinese performance is no longer in itself sufficient to guarantee spellbinding success with Western audiences, who have become increasingly sophisticated over the years. According to the critics, a group of professionals on tour in 1989 was deemed "perfunctory and devoid of all feeling," falling far short of the intoxicating presentations of the 1930s and '50s.

Characteristics of Balinese Dance

On Java dance is in large part the prerogative of the courts, but on Bali it's a living, popular art form, most active in the villages. On Java a fine classical dancer is frequently a member of the sultan's retinue. On Bali, a dancer is an ordinary villager with unusual skill who performs pleasingly before the gods—for community prestige, for the entertainment of friends and family, and for tourists for money.

Balinese dance is much influenced by Javanese dance movements, which are a mirror of the Javanese *wayang kulit* theater in which all emotion is expressed through rigidly controlled gestures, the eyes unfocused, the lips closed, and the face fixed and mask-like as if the actor were a marionette. In both female and male dancing, the limbs form angles with the head sinking down so far that the neck disappears.

At other times, the eyes flicker and dance. In Balinese classical dance, all movements and limbs are very expressive—the face, fingers, wrists, neck, eyes, hips, knee, feet, ankles. Unlike in India, the majority of Balinese dance movements—a tilt of the head or twist of the fingers—are decorative and do not carry any specific meaning.

The exceptions are the pronounced gestures that convey anger or prayer; nose kissing, greetings, and impassioned speeches, which have their inherent emotional meanings; or those that obviously represent daily tasks, such as opening a curtain, holding a cloth, or weaving.

The names of a few basic gestures describe an attached meaning in metaphorical terms. These gestures are often taken from nature, usually from flowers or animals—a sudden whirl might be named after a tiger defending himself, the flutter of hands after the flight of a bird.

Sudden changes of direction and precise, jerky accentuations mark Balinese choreography. Each basic posture *(agem)* evolves into another posture through a succession of smaller, secondary gestures *(tandang)*. The transition from one series to another is marked by short steps *(angsel)*.

A typical posture is legs half bent, torso shifted to one side, elbow raised and then lowered in a gesture displaying the suppleness of the dancer's hands and fingers. The torso is always shifted in opposition to the arms—if the arms are to the left, the shifting is to the right, and vice versa.

In the celebrated, acrobatic *sanghyang dedari,* entranced little girls perform acrobatic backbends *(ngelayang)* that defy logic. Balinese dancing is nearly as preoccupied with the upper half of the body as European dancing is with the lower half. In certain dances, like the *kebyar,* the legs don't move at all.

The Balinese don't dance upward and away from the earth, but move along its surface in slow, horizontal zigzagging circles or in movements describing lines and rows. The leaps, runs, lifts, and spins so familiar in Western ballet seldom appear in classical Balinese dance. In fact, only demonic and bestial characters jump and move in a broad and brusque manner. Noble characters move with refined gestures.

Balinese dance is subtle, drawing the audience into the dancer's world. Simultaneously, it is blatantly erotic. Female postures are characterized by bent legs held close together, open feet, off-center shoulders, and spines curved to sensuously push out the buttocks. A dance teacher can often be heard reminding her students to strike provocative poses, "Tits and asses! Tits and asses!" she'll exclaim over and over.

In men's dancing, legs are arched and shoulders pulled up, with sharper gestures meant to give the impression of dynamic power, reinforced by the male's strong, broad features. While women's dancing is pure form, in men's dancing the content of the dance is more open to interpretation.

In contemporary dance, women play numerous male roles, for example, the prince Rama and Laksmana in the Ramayana story. The easiest way to recognize masculine from feminine forms is by the costuming. Male dancers or male impersonators have a short *sarung* or pants down to the middle of the calves, with a long tongue handing down between the legs.

Female dancers wear a long *sarung,* the end of which often drags a meter or more on the dance floor. Women have long hair while men wear crowns or headdresses. High, square-shaped crowns are attributes of kings, claw-shaped crowns of princes, and the lower-castes wear simple headdresses. Women wear flower crowns.

Although movement between dancers is highly synchronized, rarely in traditional dance do two dancers come in contact with each other. Mockery and stylized violence may, however, be shown on the Balinese stage, though they would never be permitted in real life.

The complete lack of emotional expression on the dancer's face can be likened to a state of trance, a frame of mind which seems to render dancers immune to fatigue. Few show any trace of exhaustion after dancing for hours on end.

Entranced dancers, considered to be in contact with the spiritual world and thereby holy, are left free to express themselves, always under the guidance of a temple priest and the protection of several strong guardians, ready to intervene should the trance get out of hand.

The Balinese dance with a mesmerizing intensity, as if they're always being startled. Like their music, Balinese dance is abrupt, dramatic. All the excitement gives Balinese dance an air of spontaneity, yet hides a mastery over a highly technical set of motions and a rigidly stylized technique.

Precise directions are laid down for *seledet* or *nyledet,* those quick eye flicks to the right and left, up and down, which convey so much expression. Eyebrows often lift and eyeballs roll sideways either slowly or extremely quickly. In the whole of Indonesia such energetic eye movements appear only in Balinese dancing; without these movements Balinese dancing would lose much of its allure.

Training

Dancing is a difficult science, requiring years of physical training and practice. A strong cadre of professionals work in the dance academies of Denpasar, but the vast majority of dancers arise from the community at large. Every Balinese is a potential artist—a bricklayer or farmer by day may transform into the glittering Rama for the *kecak* dance by night.

The postures and movements of dance stem from the work the Balinese do: they are just working gracefully and wearing beautiful clothes when they dance! Men climb coconut trees with prehensile toes, which you also see utilized in some dance steps. When a man carries coconuts or cans on a pole, it is excellent training for male dance roles, giving him rhythm and a breathing sense, enabling him to rise and fall almost imperceptibly in dance.

On the street women carry offerings, jugs of water, piles of bricks on their heads, flicking their eyes in the same way as in dance to greet each other and to watch their step along the path. Carrying everything on their heads gives Balinese women straight backs, a sure, steady step, and extraordinary grace. Life becomes dance.

Children are first exposed to dance long before they can walk. An astounding one-quarter of Bali's children learn to dance, and about as many play a musical instrument. Prospective dancers are chosen for their attractiveness, physical fitness and coordination, or aptitude for a specific dance. A pupil always learns a particular dance, such as *legong, baris,* or *janger,* but never dancing in general. Especially sought after because of the suppleness of their limbs are very young children. If a dancer is double-jointed, all the better.

A significant number of movements have to be acquired at a very early age through long and arduous training, and are impossible for the untrained. Little girls for the *legong* are chosen from four- to five-year-olds, and famous dancers in Bali are reputed to have been able to dance before they learned to walk. Many girls retire at age 12 or 13, when they are considered full grown and too big and awkward to dance.

Teachers, usually unpaid, are generally former dancers of great repute who know every fine detail of certain dances. Some pupils become so expert at such a young age that they begin *teaching* dance at age fourteen. Choreographers are frequently also dancing masters themselves. Teachers are often called upon to travel to different communities to impart the finishing touches to a well-trained troupe.

The value of a dancer rests not only on the boy's or girl's talent but also on personality, emotional intensity, and the expressiveness of the face. Dancers must have fire, and it must come from the eyes.

All members of the community—from toothless old crones to Kuta cowboys—are astute dance critics, openly and publicly evaluating a dancer's style, technique, and physical beauty. If a dancer is not pretty—even though she might be a masterful dancer—she is pressured into some other social pursuit.

Except for the sacred temple dances *(rejang, pendet),* which are learned in performance, ceremonial and secular dancing is taught by "osmosis." The master does not analyze or explain individual movements, then string them together from start to finish. Instead, he or she demonstrates for the pupils the whole dance, in its final form. Mirrors—and nowadays video camcorders—are sometimes used.

The teacher then stands behind and guides the movements of her pupils, forming and molding and prodding the dancers' bodies, leading them vigorously by the wrists, adjusting a hand here and a knee there, kneading an improperly tilted shoulder into place. Soon, by sheer repetition, the student begins to gain confidence and the dance "enters" him. Years later, famous dancers say they can still feel their teacher's hands on their arms and shoulders.

Positions of hands and fingers are pivotal criteria for judging the quality of a dancer; experts can tell immediately who a dancer's teacher is by the complexity and suppleness of her little finger. Balance is also all-important—rarely do you see a dancer trip or stumble.

Along with training their visual memories, the dancers must also learn the music to the point of being able to sing it. The music guides the dancers; teachers are constantly reminding students *Dengar musik* ("Listen to the music!"). When the teacher exhausts her knowledge, she finds the student a new master, and another until the child's talents reach their limits.

DANCE PERFORMANCES IN AND AROUND UBUD

All tickets are Rp5000 and can be purchased either from touts on the street or at the Ubud Tourist Information booth in the center of Ubud. In the case of Bone and Peliatan village performances, the ticket price includes transport. Padangtegal, the venue for many of the performances listed below, lies just outside of Ubud to the east (between Peliatan and Ubud). Peliatan is two km east of Ubud. Teges village is three km east of Ubud.

In addition to the dances listed below, there's a free *barong* and *kris* dance put on in Sidan village (east Gianyar) at 1000 each day. Ask about transport information at Ubud's Tourist Information office. The stage there is set in magnificent rice terraces.

Sunday
Kecak fire and trance dance in Padangtegal at 1900. Presented by the Trene Jenggala Troupe.

Kecak fire and trance dance in Bone Village (12 km from Ubud) at 1900. Bus leaves at 1800 from the Ubud Tourist Information booth.

Wayang kulit at Oka Kartini's in Padangtegal at 2000.

Mahabharata ballet at Ubud Palace (Puri Saren) at 1830. Presented by the Jaya Swarna Troupe of Ubud.

Women's *gamelan* with children's dance held in Peliatan at 1930. Bus leaves at 1845 from the Ubud Tourist Information booth.

Monday
Legong dance at Ubud Palace at 1930. Presented by the Sadha Budaya Troupe of Ubud.

Kecak fire and trance dance in Bone Village at 1900. Presented by the Trene Jenggala Troupe.

Ciwa ratri dance with classical *gamelan gebyug* at Pura Dalem Puri at 1930. Presented by Gurnita Wreksa.

Tuesday
Mahabharata Dance at Teges Village at 1930. Free transport from the Ubud Tourist Information booth leaving at 1845.

Ramayana ballet at Ubud Palace at 2000. Presented by the Bina Remaja Troupe of Ubud.

Spirit of Bali at Jaba Pura Desa Kutuh, Ubud, at 1930. Presented by the Semara Ratih Troupe of Ubud.

Wednesday
Wayang kulit at Oka Kartini's in Padangtegal at 2000.

Kecak fire and trance dance in Bone Village (12 km from Ubud) at 1900. Bus leaves at 1800 from the Ubud Tourist Information booth.

Legong and *barong* dance/dance drama of Sunda Upasunda at Ubud Palace at 1930. Presented by the Panca Arta Troupe of Ubud Kelod.

The Clowns *(Bebanyolan)*
No temple ceremony, wedding celebration, or dance-drama is complete without a clown or two to liven up the performance. Just as the Javanese venerate their clownish *panakawan,* the Balinese believe there is a strong connection between the comic and the divine. The laughter is a kind of offering, making the tales' morals more memorable. It also keeps the classics from becoming too ossified.

The clowns and courtiers deal with themes of topical interest and practical value. For example, to dispel some of the tension generated by insensitive tourists, clowns have even invented a caricature of a tourist. He is a disruptive, bad-mannered, wooden-nosed buffoon wearing a ridiculous trenchcoat and galoshes, with a

swinging camera on his shoulder. Immensely popular, this character helps the Balinese preserve their dignity.

By dramatizing and satirizing contemporary problems and lampooning historical chronicles and heroes, these wily bands of sacred merry-makers establish a continuity between past and present that reassures the Balinese in their attempts to cope with a bewilderingly changing world. As mass tourism and commercial development poise to destroy traditional Bali, the clowns show the people how foolish they can be. All the laughter and self-mockery serves as a catharsis.

For all these reasons, the Balinese clown is looked upon not only as an entertainer but also as a highly respected spiritual guide, filling a special role in Balinese and national culture.

Legong and barong dance at Banjar Tengah, Peliatan. Bus leaves from the Ubud Tourist Information booth at 1845.

Kecak fire and trance dance in Padangtegal at
1900. Presented by the Trene Jenggala Troupe.

Thursday
Gabor dance at Ubud Palace at 1930. Presented by
the Panca Arta Troupe of Ubud Kelod.

Kecak monkey dance at Puri Agung in Peliatan at
1930. Bus leaves the Ubud Tourist Information
booth at 1845.

Calongarang dance at Mawang Village (nine km
from Ubud) at 1930. Free transport from the
Ubud Tourist Information booth at 1830.

Ramayana at Padangtegal at 1900. Presented by
the children's troupe Sekar Alit.

Friday
Barong dance at Ubud Palace at 1830. Presented
by the Sadha Budaya Troupe of Ubud.

Kecak fire and trance dance in Bone Village (12
km from Ubud) at 1900. Free transport at 1800
from the Ubud Tourist Information booth.

Legong dance in Peliatan at 1930. Free Transport
from the Ubud Tourist Information booth at 1845.

Barong landung ballet at Padangtegal in Ubud at
1930 by the Semara Kanti Troupe.

Kecak fire and trance dance in the pura dalem in
Ubud at 1930. Presented by the Krama Desa
Adat Ubud Kaja.

Saturday
Legong dance in Ubud Palace at 1930 by the Bina
Remaja Troupe of Ubud.

Calonarang dance at Mawang Village (nine km
from Ubud) at 1930. Free transport from the
Ubud Tourist Information booth at 1830.

Legong dance in the Pura Dalem Puri, Ubud at
1930. Presented by the Gunung Sari Troupe of
Peliatan.

Political parties use clowns to address prickly issues and woo voters. During Balinese political
rallies, opponents often mimic the clown's absurd, singsong tonal alterations. In his wonderful book Subversive Laughter (Free Press,
1994), the theater historian Ron Jenkins writes,
"Claiming the margin as center, the clown is the
personification of cultural resistance."

Bebanyolan undergo rigorous physical and
intellectual training. From childhood they receive instruction in voice and dance, as well as
in the religious literature and historical chronicles
of the island. Their mastery of the old religious
texts equals that of Balinese priests. The clowns
are master linguists as well as superlative co-
medians, singing their parts in ancient Kawi,
modern Indonesian, and Balinese.

The bebanyolan improvisational skills are masterful. Not having to adhere to a rigid script, they
constantly improvise, a fact that renders their
verbal proficiency even more startling. If the play
is before a group of tourists, smart-alecky phrases in English pepper the performance.

The clowns' talents can best be appreciated
viewing the masked topeng theater, a highly
charged and still popular wayang form on Bali.
Royal characters speaking the higher literary

verse are usually accompanied by a comic servant speaking the commom idiom. Except for a
few expressions, most Balinese don't know the
old language. Consequently, the clowns play
the same role of plot commentator as Shake-
spearean fools do.

The clown, of course, falls prey to all the temp-
tations that the princely character spurns, and
when he performs a classical dance there is always something a little bit wrong or uncoordinat-
ed with each gesture, all of which sends the audience into hysterics. Few realize that this subtle
burlesque requires a higher degree of technique
and muscular control than the proper dance.

DANCE VENUES

In 1994, Dr. I Made Bandem, director of the
STSI (formerly ASTI) dance and music academy
in Denpasar, carried out a survey of the Balinese performing arts. He found and listed over
5,500 sekaha music, dance, and theater clubs
and organizations all over Bali, so you won't
have any trouble finding live dancing.

Restaurants and most hotels are not really
sympathetic environments for Balinese dance.

BOB RACE

Before dances appeared in commercial venues, theater space as such did not exist in Bali; instead, anyplace was a potential theater. Even today you can find these authentic performances in villages. There will be a row of *warung,* a few glowing gas lamps, a mob of jostling, wild-eyed kids, and *kretek* smoke thick in the air. If the village hall is too small for a masked dance-drama production, space will be cleared in a nearby field, in a dusty courtyard inside the temple, on a plastic tarp, on mats on the floor of a *wantilan,* or in the middle of a muddy crossroads with the open starry sky and the towering palm-trees as a roof. Locals erect the framework of a stage, hang a curtain backdrop, lay mats for the orchestra, and the show's ready to begin.

At spontaneous dances put on out in the villages you are more apt to see old-style, uninhibited, undiluted dance forms—dances meant for the Balinese and their gods. It's also fairly easy to view performances connected with a temple festival *(odalan)* or other local ritual event, since there are 10 per year for the average Balinese. One is going on somewhere on the island every day.

One way to find a performance is to just fall in behind one of the trucks loaded with musicians dressed in intense red, blue, or green costumes and headcloths. You will start to see these trucks careening down Bali's roads in the early evening, on the way to their engagements. Since the Balinese regard many of these events as sacred, inquire about conduct, dress, and custom beforehand.

The Audience

Balinese drama appeals to all age groups, from the tiny children lining the front rows to the wrinkled, white-haired grandmothers and haughty *pegawi.* Even the portly governor of Bali, Professor Ida Bagus Oka, has been known to don with gusto the full costume of the demon king Rawana. For teenagers, the occasion is an opportunity for flirting and mixing with the opposite sex, the boys and girls in separate knots of two or three.

The spectators themselves take part in the dramas since the stage is often the open street itself or a dirt clearing before a temple where gods and kings mingle with the commoners. Balinese spectators are extraordinarily well behaved, patient, and welcoming—the picture of polite social behavior. No one swears, shouts, or pushes.

No formal spatial separation exists between the audience and the players. Scabrous dogs stroll on and off the "stage" and small children run in and out of the legs of the actors, to no one's chagrin. During improvisations a performer may touch members of the audience or refer to them by name.

Extravagant sets and props are only seen in lavish hotel performances. In the villages, the audience fills in the stage with its own imagination. Antonin Arthaud's theory of modern theater derived from the traditional, open Balinese performing stage, modeling its negation of the spectator/actor separation.

Small children huddled together in the front rows scurry away giggling and screaming as the Queen of the Witches, Rangda, lunges at them. And when the king gestures for his clown/servant, with the whole audience waiting, the clown's raspy, bawdy voice emanates from a nearby *warung* where he is found drinking, completely ignoring the king, the dance, and the audience—which roars with laughter at such antics.

When the *kendang* players leave their instruments for a few moments, children scamper to take their places. No one shoos them away; the cacophony they produce is accepted as part of the densely textured celebration. By breaking the traditional barrier between performer and audience, the message is brought even closer to home.

The size of the crowd is the only sign of whether a drama is coming off successfully or not. Just as a choral performance in a Western church expects no response, a good dance performance will not provoke any applause because dance is looked upon more as an offering than as a performance. It's believed that always present among the spectators—invisible but keenly attentive—are the ancestors, gods, and demons.

Rehearsals

Dance groups are organized by the villagers into an association along the same lines as a musical society. The community contributes money, trains dancers, and acquires instruments. Those who can't dance or play music contribute in some other way, such as building dance platforms, taking tickets, or making costumes.

Banjar community halls are the scene of *gamelan* and dance practice several nights a week. Dancing is also taught in the mud-walled courtyard of family compounds—the proprietor of your *losmen* may even be a dance teacher—and in the forecourts of temples.

Tourist Performances

Tourism is a vigorous and generous patron of the performing arts. The income produced is a great incentive for ensembles and dance groups to preserve and expand, and the money earned keeps being recycled in ever larger and grander extravaganzas for the gods.

Currently, 18 different drama and/or dance performance genres are represented regularly for tourists; many other troupes perform on a less regular basis. Five villages present *barong*, four do *kecak* (one with a "fire dance"), six show *legong*, one presents *wayang kulit*, one *tetekan*. Get the booklet published by Dinas Pariwisata from their office at Jl. Bakung Sari 1, Kuta, or in Denpasar, to learn about the times and places.

To accommodate the dances and dramas, about a dozen permanent venues have been established in the troupes' home villages of Batubulan, Bona, Sanur, Kuta, Legian, Ubud, and Peliatan where tourists arrive by the busload. Most tourists seem to end up sooner or later in Bona, but there are excellent productions put on in Peliatan near Puri Agung, and Padangtegal in Ubud, three streets to the east of Jl. Tebesaya. Dance presentations are also put on in the big hotels of Sanur and Nusa Dua during dinner.

Just because dances are put on for tourists, it doesn't mean that they're not high quality. To the Balinese, paid dances are not "floor shows" but an integral part of their culture. This applies to performances deliberately designed to appeal to a foreign audience like the Ramayana and commercial spectacles derived from rites of exorcism like the so-called "Angel Dance" and "Fire Dance."

In a number of instances, such as in performances of the *pendet,* Balinese ritual dances

dance teacher and pupil

BOB RACE

have been adapted to pure tourist entertainment. The Balinese feel an extreme embarrassment when they attempt to separate the sacral from the profane. They partially overcome this difficulty by making a distinction between those dances performed for the divine or supernatural *(sakti)* and those performed for demons *(suci)*. But even in commercial presentations, the headdresses, masks, and *kris* are consecrated before a performance, rendering them "magic." In other words, the Balinese do not differentiate between a commercial show and a rite of exorcism.

Some of the most accomplished dancers on the island take part in these tourist performances, their participation bringing them a reliable source of income—about Rp10,00 per performance. The Balinese also feel that the dances bestow magical/mystical benefits on their villages.

Some venues, such as in Denjalan just outside of Batubulan, have presented dances almost continuously since 1936. The performance halls are big, decorated, airy, thatched buildings with brick stages and row upon row of elevated bamboo seats. A split gateway usually towers over the stage.

Tables are set up outside with attendants and vendors selling tickets for Rp5000-7500 and audio tapes for Rp6000-10,000. Programs are available in numerous languages.

As a rule, the productions are enthralling and absolutely professional. There is always a *barong,* an ambling, goofy monkey, pretty dancing girls, a king, a prince, a servant, a villain or two, and a trance fire dance. It's customary to applaud after the show.

Although the movements are the same in secular tourist dances as they are in ritual dances, the dances are not complete. The stories have been modified, the action moves uninterruptedly, and the dances are abridged to adjust to the Western attention span—usually an hour to an hour and a half. This may be a bit long for very young children and, because the music is so loud, you may want to sit a few rows back.

Take a pillow as seating may be uncomfortable. Get there early so you can sit in one of the front rows. If you don't, other tourists will stand up in front of you every few minutes to take pictures. Camera flashes during a performance are extremely distracting to other viewers, but expect a lot of them.

During the show, stroll backstage and see the actors dressing and going on and off stage. You might even be able to have your picture taken with the arch villain! After the show, you can meet and chat with the actors and musicians while they stop for a drink at an outside *warung.*

DANCE STUDY

To seriously study dance, inquire at one of the institutes in or near Denpasar which have been set up to teach, preserve, and promote Balinese artisitic traditions: SMKI (Sekolah Menengah Karawitan Indonesia) in Batubulan; KOKAR (High School of Performing Arts); STSI (Sekolah Tinggi Seni Indonesia).

For long-term study, you have to have a permit from LIPI in Jakarta as a "guest student" because you can't learn much with a 60-day entry visa. Wayan, the proprietor of Siti Homestay (Br. Kalah, tel. 0361-975599) in Peliatan (near Ubud), can help you obtain a long-term study visa.

For the short term, it's more rewarding to take up study on an informal basis in one of the villages for several weeks. A great number of Westerners study in the Ubud/Peliatan area. Saba and Batuan (Gianyar Regency) also have very strong dance traditions.

The best way to find a dance teacher is to first find a style you like by watching performances, then approach the dancer directly for lessons. Or ask your hotel or homestay proprietor if they know of any dance teachers who take Western students. The excellent teachers tend to get overrun with Westerners.

To hire an older teacher, you'll need to know Indonesian. Be sure to see one of these mature teachers in action as they lead five-year-olds through intricate stances and postures, thrusting their bodies and arms doggedly and relentlessly into position until the complicated movements are letter-perfect. You can see these seasoned taskmasters at work every Sunday and Thursday 1400-1600 in front of the Tanjung Sari Hotel in Sanur.

The average dance course lasts one to two years, and it takes at least three years more to

DANCING AS ONE

The little girl's body would be tucked into the enveloping form of Gusti Biang behind her. The child's head would fit under the teacher's chin, and that chin and the guiding palms of the teacher's hands would indicate the head movements. Arms pointed out warningly before the child's eyes would anticipate the side glances of the eyes. The whole body would be precisely fitted into the teacher's, the child's back stemming from the teacher's belly. The teacher's arms would outline the child's arms, her hands holding and manipulating the child's hands and fingers; behind the child's legs would be the teacher's legs, which would shuffle, push and firmly kick the child's legs and feet into the right positions and sequences.

The little girls, with their fragile bodies, would work till the sweat coursed down from their necks, their faces miraculously expressionless and patient in spite of angry commands from the perfectionist drummers, never answering back, never complaining, meek and slender like reeds, six hours of instruction every day.

—FROM *DANCERS OF BALI*
BY JOHN COAST

the biggest dance event is the **Bali Arts Festival** (Pesta Keseni Bali), held from June to July each year. Launched in 1979 to foster Balinese artistic creativity while at the same time stimulating tourism, this monumental, five-week-long series of presentations draws huge crowds to the 5,000-seat Werdi Budaya Art Centre of Denpasar (Jl. Nusa Indah) almost nightly.

The atmosphere is similar to the bustle of a big *odalan*—like a three-ring circus of the arts! The Balinese themselves make up the main part of the audience. Sellout audiences are the rule at the island-wide *gamelan* competitions and elaborately staged new *sendratari* productions put on by teams of Bali's top musicans and dancers. The wide variety of programs includes ancient court dramas and dances that have been revived. Unusual offerings at the 1995 festival included *bumbung gebyog, tektekan,* and *joged.* Programs are available from Denpasar's tourist office.

become proficient. SMKI will charge foreigners around Rp5000 an hour, but it's negotiable. They can perhaps arrange for you to participate in a dance lesson on a trial basis. Dance accoutrements, costumes, and paraphernalia are available from two roadside shops outside Pasar Seni in Sukawati.

At STSI, along with traditional classical Balinese dance, there are sometimes classes in Javanese dance, Indian dance, and American modern dance, ballet, and choreography. With its 30 masters—traditional dancers, musicians, and puppeteers—this school is beginning to make headway in its effort to create new choreography. Yayasan Siddha Mahan, in Sideman (Karangasem), is another center for dance and music.

Dance Festivals

SMKI often holds dance festivals, as does the Galleria in Nusa Dua; ask the tourist office. But

DANCE FORMS

Arja

This Balinese folk-opera, accompanied by flutes and metallophones, has been compared to Western-style musical comedy with overtones of grand opera. Lines are both spoken and sung, and there's a good deal of improvisation to suit the mood of the audience. Arja's basically tragic themes are derived from the classical romances of the medieval kingdoms of East Java, as well as from Chinese love plays.

Developed around 1880 as an all-male dance drama, with homely middle-aged actors taking on female roles, today the leading players are royalty such as the prince *(ratu),* important members of the court such as the prime minister *(patih),* plus their attendants *(condong).* A performance of *arja,* which seldom begins before midnight, is a momentous occasion in a village.

Being a story about the jaded nobility, the movements and steps are very stylized and courtly. The character Galuh is impeccably solemn and dull, Limbur is silly, the Desak is an outrageous comic. *Arja* drips with moaning, syrupy melodrama and sorrow. Its plots often are difficult to follow because the dialogue and songs are chiefly in Kawi.

The lovers—in spite of all the misery—are always reunited in the end and live happily evermore. The clowns punctuate the drama with their off-color jokes and slapstick comedy and translate the classical Kawi into Low Balinese for the benefit of the unlearned crowd.

Baris

The *baris* is a dignified pre-Hindu ritual dance performed at festivals and ritual feasts. While the *legong* is the representative feminine dance, the *baris* is the basic dance that shows best all the prowess and ferocity demanded of male roles. The synchronization between the dancers and the *gamelan gong* is spellbinding; as the orchestra must be precisely attuned to the warrior's changing stances, moods, and tactics. The name *baris* means "on line in military formation."

Although at one time the best *baris* performers were middle-aged men, the dance is now the domain of young boys. Originally a war dance, the *baris* was later adapted to the themes from the romantic *Arjuna Wiwaha* tale, using dramatic dialog to accompany the movements. In this version, the noble young warrior prepares for battle. There are heroic poses, expressive faces, sham battles, duels, violent music. With mercurial movements, the *baris* dancer's whole body is alive and quivering with controlled yet tense action. He goes through all the emotions—ferocity, passion, alertness, pleasure, rage, tenderness, compassion, love—of a chivalrous nobleman.

The frenetic music grows more and more violent, the dancers raising themselves trembling on their toes and scowling and cursing at the enemy. *Baris* can talk but not sing. The *kris* is drawn and the foes execute a violent stylized battle. Watching, you can see why the *baris* has been called one of the most manly and passionate dances in the world.

There are some 20 different forms, each named after an item of clothing the dancers wear or a weapon they carry. In the *baris pendet,* dancers carry an offering. One of the oldest forms, *baris gede* (or *baris upacara*) was initially used to exorcise evil from a temple or was performed at religious festivals, cremations, and feasts in un-Javanized Balinese villages.

Typical of the most masculine aspects of Balinese life, the traditional *baris gede* is staged with as many as 60 men. A modernized version, *baris pendet,* consists of heroic plays performed in a formalized dance-pantomime with dialogue and singing. This native dance can be seen in Sanur, Tabanan, Ubud, and in the mountain villages of the Batur region.

Barong

The *barong* is a dance pantomime of a fantastic dragonlike holy animal, the *barong,* in pitched battle against the machinations of the menacing witch Rangda. Charged with magic, the drama functions as a spiritual purgative for a village, but it has been mostly preempted by the tourist industry.

THE *BARONG KET* DANCE MASK

Because of their power to exorcise evil spirits, the *barong* dance masks are considered sacred *(sakti).* A purification ceremony with extravagant offerings and prayers is always held to initiate a new mask. When not in use, the mask is wrapped in a magic cloth and kept in a special bale surrounded by mountains of fruit and flowers. Sacrifices are presented before the masks and priests keep a close eye on them lest they "escape." Whenever a mask leaves the temple, a mask is followed by a colorful procession of hundreds of people.

Today at least 20 *barong* groups perform on Bali, and the dragon's appearance can vary radically from one to the next. The *barong*, a beast of unknown origin, manifests itself in many forms: as a tiger, it is *barong macan;* as a lion, *barong singha;* as a wild boar, *barong bangkal;* as an elephant, *barong gajah;* as a cow, *barong limbu.*

On the surface, the dance-drama seems to be about the momentous confrontation between good and evil. But, as de Zoete and Spies pointed out, "to express the fight between Barong and Rangda in terms of good and evil is to miss the point." The function of each character is morally ambiguous, not as clear-cut as in the Judeo-Christian world. One cannot project an ethical interpretation on the play. On Bali, the actions of Barong and Rangda have cosmic repercussions that affect all Balinese, whose role is simply to help maintain balance.

In ritual life, the *barong* personifies the guardian spirit of the village, defending mankind with white magic. Belonging to the "right" side, he is the protector of humanity treated with the utmost respect and consideration. The most powerful of all is the famous "Black Barong" of Singgi—a *kampung* near Sanur—made from the black feathers of a rare bird.

By far the most popular and holiest form is the *barong ket,* a huge and frightening lionlike creature with feathers and bells all over its body, popped-out eyes, clacking jaws, a hollow, swaying back, and a long black beard decorated with flowers. Strength is concentrated in the beard. Its body is decorated with gilded leather, spangled with glass and mirrors, its fur coat made of chicken feathers or pineapple plant fibers. Cloth strips and bells hang from its animated tail.

This awkward, shaggy creature resembles the demon-head *(bhoma)* above the entrance to Balinese temples; see a famous example at Goa Gadjah near Bedulu. The face is also a popular woodcarving motif. See the excellent collection of *barong* masks in Denpasar's Bali Museum.

Manipulated by two highly trained men who occupy the front and hindquarters of a bamboo frame, the *barong*'s paws are two pairs of human feet. The men can make the *barong* wiggle its rear end, stretch and contract like an accordian, amble around playfully and coquettishly while savagely snapping its jaws.

The men's skill can make it appear as if the *barong* is acting under its own power, taking the swaybacked beast through comic yet very complex and synchronized dance movements which cause people to laugh—but not *too* loud.

The mask of this sacred character is thought to contain awesome spiritual power; it's kept carefully guarded in a special storage building *(gedong)* with other holy props, protected with charms and swathed in magic cloth that shields its powerful vibrations. The consecrated mask is stored awaiting the occasion when it will come to life at a temple's anniversary feast, go to visit far-off temples, or be led through the village to accept offerings whenever disease, death, and witchcraft are gaining the upper hand.

Offerings are always made to it during Galungan, and the *barong* is taken out only when the *pedanda* or *pemangku* sprinkles it with holy water to prevent it from doing harm. Whenever a *barong* mask is moved for any reason, villagers will form a splendid procession to accompany the adored creature, holding a white parasol above its head to honor it. At each household doorway, the high-spirited *barong* obligingly dances and snaps its jaws to clear the air of demons.

The climax of the stage play comes when the *barong* confronts Rangda, the ugly, lolling-tongued, pendulous-breasted Supreme Witch—evil incarnate, the personification of all negative, destructive powers. The *barong*'s followers attack Rangda with real *kris* only to find their fury turned against them under Rangda's wicked spell.

In a trance-state, possessed by Rangda's power, they attempt to plunge their weapons into their own chests in a fit of suicidal violence. But in the end the power of the right side proves stronger—the *barong* makes them invulnerable so the *kris* have no effect.

Incredibly, none of the participants wound themselves. As the men convulse on the ground, a *pemangku* brings them out of trance before they can injure themselves. These magico-religious performances serve as a powerful exorcism of black magic both for the players and the onlookers.

In another version, *barong landung,* the *barong* is in human shape in the form of a giant doll. Used for dispelling evil spirits and sickness, *barong landung* characters have their origins in the legend of Jero Gede Mecaling, the fanged monster of Nusa Penida. *Barong landung* is most likely to be seen in street performances during Galungan and Independence Day and only in southern Bali and on the small offshore island of Serangan.

The ideal venue for a *barong* performance is open-air in the middle of the road, but in today's Bali a shortened, watered-down version of the "Barong And Kris Dance" is put on for tourists. The players in it are still in a trance, but not such a *deep* trance. With minimal dialogue and infused with slapstick humor, the dance is not as intense nor as long as sacral performances—lasting only an hour or so. See it in big performance halls in Batubulan where no less than three troupes present it simultaneously every morning at 0900.

Calon Arang

Though it has many variations, this dance-drama is essentially an act of exorcism against *leyak* (witches). *Calon arang* combines acting, singing, comedy, tragedy, and classic theater, combined with elements of the wistful *legong*. It is backed by a full orchestra augmented with long bamboo flutes.

Only a few *dalang* are willing to perform the shadow puppet version as they fear the consequences of inviting *leyak* to the show, a gesture that is deemed necessary. The perfect setting for this magic play is on the night of the full moon casting shadows on the temple roofs, palm trees, and on the clearing where the drama takes place.

The main character is Rangda who takes the form of an old widow, Calon Arang. Rangda is the bloody-fanged Queen of the Underworld, whose power is an ever-present danger. She claws at the air with dreadful, knife-like fingernails, her voice alternating between a piteous mutter and a deep-voiced, moaning growl. Her sawdust-filled breasts sag, her pop-eyes stare, her flame-like tongue lolls wickedly beneath a row of sharp upper incisors, and a necklace of human entrails hangs around her neck. Brandishing a magic white cloth, she rushes at children in the audience, scattering them, and scowls at babies in mother's arms.

Anthropologists see Rangda originally as a maternal figure; drama historians claim she is the personification of the witch par excellence; archaeologists contend that her origin is Shiva's wife Durga in her evil aspect; historians claim she was the legendary Queen Mahendratta of King Airlangga's 11th century East Javanese kingdom.

Rangda is not an entirely unsympathetic, evil figure, as she serves a very critical role protecting village temples from demons and helps recycle dead bodies into the Cosmos so that the dead's spirits can be reborn. People worship her ardently because she can protect them against black magic. Margaret Mead saw Rangda as the dark side of the Balinese female archetype—the supple and alluring young dancing girl metamorphosed into the horrific, angry old witch.

Calon arang is a story of revenge and penitence. Long ago in the days of great King Airlangga, an old widow, Calon Arang, lived in the jungle with her beautiful daughter, Ratna Menggali. Calon Arang wanted her daughter to marry a prince from Airlangga's court, but despite her beauty, no prince came. Becoming very angry, Calon Arang made offerings to Durga and learned the art of black magic. She sent Celuluk, the perfect manifestation of evil, to lay waste to the land and destroy the kingdom.

When Airlangga heard of the widespread epidemics and destruction, he beseeched his high priest, Mpu Paradah, to step in. The priest sent his son, Bahula, to ask for the hand of Ratna Menggali. This so pleased Calon Arang that she cured all the sick and brought the dead back to life. The plagues subsided.

But one day Calon Arang's son-in-law found a *lontar* book of Calon Arang's black magic. These he conveyed to his father, who deciphered its secret formulas. When Calon Arang discovered Mpu Paradah had learned her source of power, she became enraged and declared war upon him. Mpu Paradah was then forced to do battle with Calon Arang (Rangda). The eerie witch appears on stage amidst bloodcurdling curses and descends howling and shrieking upon the priest.

In defense, Mpu Paradah unleashes a spell and vanquishes Calon Arang. Before she dies, Calon Arang asks forgiveness. Mpu Paradah absolves her deeds and she is allowed to enter heaven. However, the lesson is not lost to the Balinese. By dramatizing Rangda's powers, it's hoped that good favor will be gained with the ever-present witch, her appetite for destruction placated.

Cekepang

Pronounced "check-a-poong," this dance is specifically eastern Balinese and rarely performed outside Karangasem Regency. Some regions of Lombok still perform it, a legacy of the days when Lombok was ruled by the rajas of Karangasem. The *cekepang* relates a story chosen from classical Hindu literature, the tale of *Arjuna Wiwaha*. The music, chanting, dance and costuming of *cekepang* are as spectacular as they are unusual. The best practitioners come from Dukuh village.

Cupak

An old Balinese dance drama, the **cupak**'s origins date back to East Java's Kediri Kingdom. Although it has the earmarks of a comic opera, the *cupak* is really an epic tale of jealousy, heroic deeds, and treachery. There are many variations. The Cupak story is also performed as a shadow play.

The chief protagonists are a gluttonous villain named Cupak and his handsome younger brother, Grantang. One day it's discovered that the beloved daughter of the king of Kediri, Mustikaning Daha, has been kidnapped. The king announces that whoever finds her may become king. Cupak and Grantang resolve to look for her, encountering many adventures along the way.

Drama Gong

This popular dance form was only created in the late 1960s. In *drama gong,* music and dance are downplayed, while acting is the most important medium. Actually no one seems to pay much attention to what's going on up on the stage as this type of play is the occasion for the Balinese to socialize. For this reason, *drama gong* is becoming even more popular than *arja*.

Gambuh

Written records describing this semi-sacral dance go back 1,000 years, making it the oldest known dance on Bali. At that time these court stories were popular at all levels of society. The *gambuh* is closest in style to Javanese dance forms.

It's said that the *gambuh,* which has undergone practically no development, is the mother of all Balinese dances—the classic technique to which all other dances owe their descent. It's believed that if a dancer masters the *gambuh,* she is able to dance any Balinese dance. A number of Bali's most popular dances—*wayang wong, cupak, calon arang, joged, topeng, legong,* and *arja*—have either been influenced by it or else are derived directly from it.

Although it's required for certain ceremonies, performances of *gambuh* are not easy to find. Only two groups stage tourist *gambuh* in Batuan (Ubud area); STSI in Denpasar has another *gambuh* troupe, and there are three or so others scattered around. Kuta is reviving an old group.

Look in the most recent *Calendar of Events* or ask about upcoming performances at the Denpasar Tourist Office. The *gambuh* is also put on for such serious occasions as a temple's *odalan,* which takes place every six months. It's often staged in a temple's middle courtyard.

The mysterious flute music, the strains of the *rebab,* the eerie singing, and the *gambuh*'s slow, stylized dance movements make it a hypnotic and dramatic dance to watch. The *gambuh* usually lasts three hours—traditional versions are even longer. The play is performed in episodes which are usually comprehensible to Westerners.

The story frequently opens with a princess and a group of her attendants who perform a beautiful dance. There is the usual collection of Balinese kings and handsome princes who act out status rivalries. The dialog is spoken by attendant-comedians in the Balinese language of the 17th century, similar to Old Javanese.

Plots derive from the *Malat* tales, the Javanese equivalent of the *Arabian Nights.* Other dramas presented are the *Panji* and *Ranggalawe*—historical dramas imported from East Java.

Janger

The *janger* started suddenly in 1925 after a company of Malay opera mimes visited the island. With its two swaying rows of seated boys and girls, it appealed immediately to the Polynesian spirit of the Balinese. It was the first time that boys and girls danced together solely for enjoyment—Bali's first social dance!

Have you noticed the habit the Balinese have of cracking finger joints practiced by virtually everybody on the island? This is how they get to flutter their fingers in such an exaggerated way in their dancing. It is rigorously enforced by dance masters, and as everybody learns to dance to some extent it permeates as a habit throughout the people. I remember children in England being told not do do this, with the warning that it causes arthritis in old age.

The Balinese, however, believe the opposite—that it protects one from arthritis. It certainly seems to be the case as although I've met a multitude of old people here, I've seen none with arthritis, whereas in England the older generation seem riddled with it. This joint cracking is not limited to the fingers either.

Everybody here seems to be a natural masseur (except those who charge for it on the beach!), and the culmination of an extensive two-hour long massage is to crack virtually every joint in the body. I got quite surprised when the masseur sent this cracking noise up my spine like a ripple.

—LYNN FRIED

The Balinese never hesitate to introduce a new dance from such mongrel sources and soon every *banjar* strove to outfit a company of *janger* dancers, whose gay costuming and acrobatic posturings often approached farce. In one group the girls even wore shorts, a moral outrage in Bali at the time.

Janger was still the rage when Covarrubias wrote his *Island of Bali* in the 1930s. Within a few years, however, its popularity was utterly eclipsed by the *arja* opera form, and later by the ubiquitous *drama gong* which originated in the mid-1960s. Nowadays, *janger* is almost completely defunct, taking place perhaps only once or twice a year, and needs a major rescue effort to revive it.

Jauk

This very demanding classical solo dance of a demon-warrior dates from the 18th century. *Jauk* has its origins in a traditional play in which all the dancers, wearing fearsome *raksasa* masks, enact episodes from the Ramayana and Mahabharata epics in the old Kawi language.

This masked pantomime is danced in the *legong* technique, similar to the *baris* in style, but more flamboyant and violent. The troupe generally appears in a group of up to six dancers, sometimes together with Rangda. You often see the *jauk* precede the *baris*, followed by perhaps a *topeng;* these are all very commonly staged together.

The *jauk* dancer's ghost-like mask is colored a violent red, or sometimes white, with thick black moustache, bulging zombie-like eyes, and an eerie smile. As his whole face is covered by a leering mask, the *jauk* dancer must convey his emotions solely through his movements and gestures.

Also characteristic of the costuming are gloves with long nails and high headdresses with colorful pompoms and tassels. The demon king's long transparent fingernails flutter incessantly to a *pelegongan* orchestra. Though of sinister appearance, the *raksasa* are usually friendly and the dance is mischievous and high-spirited.

Joged

The popular flirtation dance, the *joged* is, except for the *janger,* the only Balinese social dance. Each of the many variations of this relatively new dance—*joged bumbung, joged pingitan, joged gebyog, joged pudengan,* and *gandrung*—has been created in different areas of Bali using various styles. All have a rather weak story line based on the legend of *calon arang.*

A woman, dressed in a costume similar to a *legong* dancer's and performing traditional *legong* steps, enters a circle. After she dances for a while, she starts to make eyes at a particular boy among the onlookers, enticing him into the circle by tapping him with her fan. Some boys try to escape, but are dragged back by their friends.

Every five minutes or so she encourages a new boy and partners change, or a bolder one simply cuts in. The boy chosen must dance in his own improvised style, often quite artful and animated in itself. The object is to come as close as possible to the girl's face to catch a whiff of her perfume—a Balinese kiss—while the girl plays hard to get. Sometimes the *joged* begins with two or more women dancers, ensuring more male spectators will get their moment in the circle.

Possibly a modernized, popularized version of an ancient mating rite, the *joged* today is a recreational dance, a sort of mixer—a way for teenagers to meet and get to know each other. It is especially entertaining when a French bank clerk or an Australian abalone fisherman is tapped on the shoulder, with all his mates egging him on.

Traditionally, only men were asked to dance, but now women may dance also. The *joged* is particularly popular after the harvest or after a great religious ceremony; it is a celebratory event for all levels of Balinese society. It's an occasion when members of the community who are not usually dancers or performers may dance in public, show off, and have fun.

The *joged* is accompanied by the *pedjogedan,* a *gamelan* of the *gandrung* type. Its bamboo instruments give the dance a happy and melodious background.

Kebyar

The name of this dance means "lightening." Like the *baris,* it is a male solo exhibition dance, often an interpretation of one of the epic poems *(kekawin).* The *kebyar* is unique, however, in that it is usually performed in the sitting position.

Kebyar originated in northern Bali in the 1920s, derived from certain movements of the delicate *legong,* the heroic postures of the masculine *baris,* and one of the most ancient of Balinese dances, the *sanghyang.*

The present *kebyar* cannot be separated from its greatest practitioner, I Mario, who was responsible for the perfection of the dance. A former *jauk* dancer, Mario rearranged the *jauk* and began performing the *kebyar* in 1915.

During a performance, Mario was completely taken over by the role he played; people who met the soft-spoken young man during the day

would be amazed to find out that he was the brilliant virtuoso they had seen dancing the night before. Mario would not even recognize himself; when shown a photo of himself dancing the *kebyar,* he exclaimed, "That man is a good dancer!" At his peak, Mario was perhaps the greatest channel in the history of modern Balinese dance.

There are many different *kebyar* styles. The most popular form in south Bali is *kebyar duduk,* the "seated" *kebyar,* in which the dancer sits cross-legged through most of the dance. In *kebyar trompong,* the dancer joins the orchestra by playing a long instrument of inverted bronze bowls *(trompong)* as he dances and twirls the *trompong* sticks between his fingers.

As well as being the most strenuous of Balinese dances, it is said that no one can perform the *kebyar* without a profound knowledge of music. Frequently the *kebyar's* solo male dancers can play every instrument in the orchestra.

To attain mastery, all the fluctuating moods of the orchestra must be mirrored in the body's flexibility and in the dancer's facial expressions— whether the tones are light and lyrical, somber, frantic surprise, or ominous sorrow. The dancer must in fact *become* a sensitive musical instrument. Seated in a small square bounded on all sides by *gong kebyar* instruments, he throws himself under the absolute influence of the music, being moved, drawn, swayed, and driven by it to the most minute details of nuance and rhythm.

Typically, the dancer dresses in a long brocaded *kain* worn as a skirt around his waist, one end trailing on the stage. A gilt cloth winds around his torso; a great hibiscus flutters in his ear; in his right hand is a fan. The dance is performed from the squatting position with only the knees changing position. Moving from just the waist up, the dancer focuses the audience's attention on the agile movements of his torso and arms, and his powerful facial expressions. With darting glances, fan waving furiously, muscles tense and taut, torso languidly swaying then nervously rippling, the dancer's body fills with the music—almost to the exclusion of the performer's personality.

Good *kebyar* dancers are extremely difficult to find as they must possess mobile, supple facial features, a fine grace, plus a tremendous personal magnetism and charm.

Kecak

In this spine-tingling nocturnal choir dance, a large moving mass of bare-chested men simulate the sounds of a *gamelan* orchestra. A mesmerizing theatrical experience created by workers just in from the fields, the dance is named after the hypnotic and repetitive *Chak-ka-chak-ka-chak!* sounds the men make.

The *kecak* was initially choreographed by Walter Spies in 1931 while he was acting as a consultant for a German company making Baron von Plessen's film *Die Insel der Damonen (Isle of Demons)* shot at Bedulu. It soon became known among tourists as the "Monkey Dance" which alluded to the singers sitting in concentric circles playing the part of monkey soliders sent by Prince Rama to rescue his wife Sita. Spies took the male chorus from the exorcistic *sanghyang dedari* and added a fragment from the Ramayana to create a new and vigorous art form. The dramatic *kecak* has also borrowed some typical *kuntao* movements, a secret fighting art imported from China.

The best performances today are of a hypnotic chorus of men chanting rhythmically in perfect unison—an exhilarating, unnerving, experience. Since the participants have to enter and be brought back from a trance state, the whole enactment can take several hours. The worst performances resemble the blase emotions of an Ivy League pep rally.

Now you have to pay Rp5000-7500 to see a watered-down "tourist" version of the *kecak* in 30 minutes flat, only one component in a medley of dances. This form of *kecak* is pure show, devoid of all religious significance, and caters to the short attention span of tourists.

With at least 30 *kecak* groups, the dance is performed throughout the year all over Bali. The Bualu troupe is said to be best, and the best venue is still Bona, though the dance was first developed in Bedulu over 50 years ago. The biggest *kecak* on the island takes place at the Peliatan Palace every Thursday at 1930—200 men instead of the usual hundred.

Since the *kecak* is usually performed just before sunset, with coconut palms and vegetation all around, the moon on the rise, and the crickets starting their chorus, you feel as if you're in the countryside. It's a magical experience. Eighty to 150 loinclothed men sit in five or six concen-

tric circles, in the middle of which stands a torch defining the stage and casting flickering shadows on the courtyard or cleared arena. The members of this living theater, only partly visible, wait in silence as the audience is seated. At a signal, the group begins to sway back and forth, circling and bending, their outstretched hands and torsos rising and falling in the shadows in wave-like motions. Suddenly they throw out their arms and shake their fingers wildly as erratic shadows form and flee in the lamplight. Gradually, the rhythm of the surging mass gains speeds. Arms flutter while dancers perform a fast interlocking vocal pattern of shouts, grunts, screeches, and hisses with remarkable precision and organ-like volume. At fixed times, half the circle falls backward together in a dramatic, unearthly swoon. The individual dancers are totally swallowed up by the power of the whole.

The *kecak* usually reenacts a short episode from the Ramayana when Rama, his brother, and his wife Sita are exiled to the dark forests of Sri Lanka. The dance tells of the kidnapping of Sita by the evil demon-king Rawana and of her rescue by her husband with the help of an army of monkeys—the male chorus—led by the monkey general, Hanuman.

Sita, with her winged golden headdress, moves delicately onto the "stage," with wrists arched and fingers bent back. Rama and his brother Laksamana are more vigorous, stamping with flexed feet. When Rawana leaps to stage center, the vocal chorus simulates his flight with a long hissing sound. The moment Sita is abducted, the mass of men leap up as one. In one version, when Rama is shot with an arrow that magically turns into a snake, the circle becomes the snake surrounding him. The passion of the monkey men soars. Finally, in the battle in which good defeats evil, the grouped chorus divides in two to represent Hanuman defeating the powerful giant Rawana's army. This part made this dance play very popular in Dutch times because it held out the hope that the downtrodden masses would eventually rise up to throw out their colonial masters.

Legong

Considered the most dazzling of all Balinese dances, the *legong* represents the archetype of femininity and grace, and is one of the most familiar of Indonesia's dances outside Bali. Swathed in cocoons of gold-brocaded fabrics, with hands palpitating and eyes flashing, heavenly nymphs perform a highly abstract interpretation of a literary classic. Yet despite this superficial dramatic content, the *legong* exists almost purely for the sake of dancing. Again, the performances for tourists are far removed from the style, beauty, and technical perfection of a *legong* staged for private or religious functions.

Inquire at STSI (College of Performing Arts) where the most polished performances take place. The best exemplify Balinese classical dance par excellence; the worst offer little more than the dispassionate swaying of disinterested little girls marking time until the cameras stop flashing.

There are now at least 40 commercial *legong* troupes on Bali. Some say Peliatan is home to the finest group on the island, but only in Teges is the classical "antique" version still practiced. Probably the most beautiful presentation of the *legong* is on the grounds of Ubud's royal palace. It's very crowded, so get there early.

This dance-pantomime is so highly stylized that only the themes of the *gamelan* and the abstract movements and costumes of the dancers give a clue as to the scenes and actions taking place in the story. The *legong* is really an elaboration of the old *wayang kulit* shadow play in which humans simulate the movements and dramatic stories of marionettes. Since none of the historical records mention this form, *legong* is probably relatively modern.

The *legong* was at one time patronized by local princes and only held in the *puri,* the royal compound of a village. Prepubescent *legong* dancers were once a prince's own private property, recruited from the most agile and attractive palace children. Originally, a narrator recited

In his book, A House in Bali, *Colin McPhee described the fragile, chalk-white faces of* legong *dancers as imbued with a sexless calm—haunting, enigmatic, mysterious. Aficionados vehemently discuss the merits of particular* legong *dancers for hours.*

the literary text and chanted the dialogs and episodes in time with the orchestra while the dance was in progress, but this feature has disappeared.

The story is performed by three dancers: the *condong,* a female court attendant, and two identically dressed *legong* dancers who adopt the roles of royal persons. Although training actually begins at age five, for live performances a pair of girls from eight to 12 years old are chosen for their good looks and agile physiques. Lovely round faces are the ideal. If all three girls look alike and are the same size, all the better.

The girls are chosen before they begin menstruation because only then are they considered pure and limber enough to perform all the necessary movements. Extraordinary muscular control and great physical endurance are required. Sometimes the bodies of the little pupils have to be made supple by means of special massages. Dancers retire when their menstrual cycle begins.

When preparing for a performance, dancers are first dressed in gorgeous costumes: head to toe in silk and gold leaf with a headdress of fresh frangipani blossoms and enormous earplugs of gold. Their passionless, melancholy faces are heavily powdered, and a white dot *(priasan),* symbolizing beauty and innocence, is placed on their foreheads. Their eyebrows are shaved and replaced with a line of black paint. Their bodies are tightly girdled from chest to hips with many meters of heavy cloth and covered with rich beautiful silk bibs decorated with gold. These stiff layers of clothing help to support their backs and give them a graceful line. Although the *legong* is an erotic dance, visual sexuality must be suppressed. The purpose of the tight breast-bands is to flatten the figure. A sash of gilt cloth, a collar of bright stones and mirrors, a silver belt, and ornamental scarves complete the dancers' extravagant costuming.

The drama begins with the more simply dressed *condong* taking her place alone in the middle of the dance floor. There is a pause; suddenly a cue from the *gamelan* and she comes alive, twirling in a circle in time with the music, her arms outstretched and fingers tense, her body rising and arching and her head held high. After this introduction, the music changes tempo, and the two *legong* enter the stage forming graceful patterns and sharp turns with the *condong*. After a short dance together, the *condong* hands the two dancers each a fan and retires. The accents of the orchestra then quicken and the *legong* dancers begin one of the most glittering and highly disciplined displays of body movements in the world of dance. They fly away from each other, waggling their hips and shivering their shoulders, each enacting a separate role, only to return after executing a perfectly synchronized circle.

According to her posture and the eyes, a *legong* can be a statue, a butterfly, or a flower. The *legong*'s hand drops then suddenly flies up like a bird on the wing, her fan fluttering at almost blinding speed. Both dancers seem the double image of the other; their heads snap back and forth and even their eyes and hands flick in perfect accord.

In a love scene between Lasem and Rangkesari, the dancers come together and playfully rub noses *(ngaras)*, followed by a flutter of the shoulders to signify a thrill of pleasure from a kiss. In the 1930s, Charlie Chaplin once sent a Balinese audience into paroxysms when he mimicked the elegant poses of a *legong* dancer.

There are at least eight different stories for *legong* and thus eight different dances, always consisting of an introduction, a drama, and a farewell. The repertoire includes *legod bawa,* a traditional form; *abimanyu,* a comparatively new (1982) creation; *leko pertiwi* accompanied by a *gamelan tingklik; legong keraton kupukupu tarum* depicting butterflies flitting from flower to flower and playing together. In a newly resurrected form, *legong prabangsa,* Rangda the witch appears and self-stabbing may break out—very unusual for a *legong* performance!

The plot most often acted out is the Lasem story from *Malat,* the Balinese *Thousand and One Nights.* Derived from a historical event that happened in East Java in the 12th century, this is a drama of a princess kidnapped by a despised royal suitor. On a journey, the arrogant king of Lasem comes upon the maiden Rangkesari lost in the forest. He abducts her and locks her in his house of stone. Her anger rising, you can see Rangkesari repelling the evil king's advances by beating him with her fan, then slapping her thigh in a gesture of grief. When Rangkesari's brother, the prince of Daha, learns of her capture, he threatens to go to war unless she is freed. Rangkesari implores her abductor to free her and avoid war, but the king vows to fight to the death. On his way to do battle, a black bird of ill omen (a crow, played by the *condong*) intercepts the king and warns him of his imminent death. She beats the earth with her "wings" and swoops down upon the king to dissuade him from going to war. At this point, with the king's decision made and his *kris* drawn, the ominous battle takes place and the king is killed.

Mendet

The *mendet* is a processional dance of married women winding in and out of temple grounds, carrying offerings of *arak* and holy water to sustain the gods on their journey back to their divine home.

Oleg Tambulilingan

A modern dance specifically designed for tourists in the early 1950s by the late I Mario of Tabanan, *oleg* is often chosen to supplement a performance of the *legong.* The word *oleg* means the "swaying of a dancer," and *tambulilingan* means "bumblebee."

Symbolizing a Balinese courtship, this flirtation dance depicts two bumblebees, a male and a female, happily sucking honey in a flower garden. The female bee enters the garden first, circling the stage in tight quick steps, trailing a long silk scarf. The dancer runs the full gamut of female emotions: seductiveness, scorn, teasing, moodiness, naughtiness, gay-heartedness. The female dancer first pretends to snub the male, but he is finally able to win her love by various devices. In one sequence the female may dance in the seated position while she sensuously sways and flutters her hands. The male circles her with a manly stride, his head cocked, feeling his power over her. They come close, only to swirl apart again. The *oleg* ends with a love dance of the two bees.

Pendet

This is the basic temple dance, a religious offering, usually performed by young girls at the beginning of any temple ceremony, ritual, wedding, or toothfiling to ensure the gods are made welcome. Whereas the exhibition dances such as *legong* and *baris* require years of rigorous training, the *pendet* is taught by imitation.

The dance is first done by a *pemangku,* followed by any who feel like it: old men and women are particularly inclined to join in. Since dancers bear holy offerings for the gods, Balinese tradition holds that *pendet* dancers be unmarried women, but this custom has fallen by the wayside.

Because of the risks of desecration when it's performed out of context, *pendet* for tourists was forbidden in the '70s, replaced by the similar but more secular *penyembrama* performed by girls. Now bare-shouldered young girls copy the movements of their grandmothers, the most accomplished dancers of *pendet.*

All dancers—whether young, middle-aged, or elderly—carry in their clasped hands palm-leaf and flower offerings, or in their right hands water vessels, incense, and cakes. With their offerings they dance from shrine to shrine within the temple complex. A man also joins the dance; his function is to burn incense.

There are a number of *pendet* forms: a slow-moving, welcoming dance; a collective dance performed by six, eight, or more dancers dressed in wraps of gold brocade in rows and files; or a procession by women dressed in everyday clothes. When its purpose is to open the *legong,* the dance movements are highly synchronized and precise. At the finish, the girls throw flowers to the audience in a gesture of welcome.

Prembon

Created only in the 1940s by the raja of Gianyar, the *prembon* incorporates movements from *arja, baris, gambuh, parwa,* and particularly *topeng.* It is an excellent introduction to a whole range of different dances.

Ramayana

For years the Hindu epic Ramayana has been depicted in *wayang wong* in which live masked

Hanoman, the monkey-king from one of the scenes from the popular Ramayana ballet. The gaudy costumes and headdresses worn by the dancers are as much a part of the dance as the dancers themselves. The dancers' cumbersome, crustacean-like costuming consists of stiff and profusely decorated leather aprons and collars, gold-woven sarung, *elegant and lavish body jewelry, glittering scarves and sashes, meter upon meter of embroidered cloth wound tightly around torsos, splendid crowns of flowers. Round, protruding eyes, long fangs, and tentacle-like sharpened fingernails are characteristic of demons. Try to get backstage before a performance where you can see the dancers and actors dressing and applying their makeup.*

actors in splendid costumes enact the battle between Rama and evil King Rawana for the hand of the beautiful princess, Sita. In the mid-1970s a new dance interpretation of the Ramayana was introduced on Bali by KOKAR. It was modeled after the Ramayana Ballet conceived by a prince from Solo in an amphitheater constructed in front of the Loro Jonggrang temple in Prambanan, Central Java.

Backed by a full *gamelan gong,* this ballet is a musical blending of both classic dance movements and the hilarious comedy of monkeys and clowns. The scene opens in the forest where Rama, Laksmana, and Sita are living in exile. The two brothers are played by beautiful women, Rama with golden headgear and Laksmana with a black headdress. Their style of dancing is very refined and stately, as is becoming of royal personages.

The giant Rawana, on the other hand, is swaggering, lecherous, and gruff, a style more in keeping with a demon role. The animals are often the most picturesque and rowdy participants, stealing the show with their wondrous leaps, slides across the stage, and other miraculous feats of agility and strength. The monkey general Hanuman outwits vastly superior opponents by simply dodging and wiggling out of the way so that they collide into each other. Children and adults in the audience are indistinguishable in their glee.

Rejang

An indigenous, sacred temple dance presented as an offering to the deities who have momentarily visited a shrine, the *rejang* is performed by women ages two to 85 to propitiate ancestral spirits. The steps and gestures are absurdly simple, probably Polynesian in origin. The dancers move slowly and deliberately to the *padmasana,* holding their hip sashes and twirling their fans. Occasionally a *pedanda* or a *pemangku* leads.

Sanghyang

The Balinese have an uncommon facility and susceptibility for falling into trance states. *Sanghyang* means "holiness" or "revered one," referring to the divine spirit which temporarily inhabits the bodies of entranced dancers. The dancers, transfixed by their own movement,

have entered a supernatural world where fatigue is unknown. This is why dancers, when they come out of this dissociated state after hours of exhaustive posturing, appear to have no knowledge of what has just happened to them.

Probably derived from rituals practiced in the distant past, the various *sanghyang* dances serve the religious function of protecting a community from the forces of black magic and other dangers. *Sanghyang* were staged in time of trouble to alleviate or divert epidemics or misfortune in a village. In the Kintamani area, you can still commission one.

Sanghyang is the source dance from which a number of modern-day dances derive. In its original form, offerings are made to placate the *leyak* (witches), and benign spirits are implored to come down to Earth where they reveal themselves to humankind through the medium of the *sanghyang* dancer.

There are a number of *sanghyang* forms. *Sanghyang jaran* features a *pemangku* or boy in trance either riding a hobbyhorse or imitating the movements of a horse. He prances around a bonfire of glowing coconut husks, trotting possessed through the red-hot embers. As the trance mediums are attracted to all kinds of fire, no one in the audience may smoke. This form, accompanied by only a male *cak* chorus, can be seen five times weekly at Bona.

Staged only around Lake Batur and other mountain villages, the *sanghyang deling* consists of dancing puppets suspended on strings between two poles, the strings manipulated by children. The accompanying music is starkly primitive, consisting of only *suling, terbang,* and *kendang.*

Sanghyang dedari is a trance dance performed by little girl mediums (*dedari* means "angel") in a slow-motion version of the *legong* style, which serves as an exorcism of sickness and evil spirits. This celebrated shamanistic ritual performance is a way of contacting the gods.

Two little girls are selected from the community by the *pemangku* for their psychic abilities. Only virgin girls are considered pure enough. For weeks they are trained by means of rhythmical chanting, incense, and hypnosis to be able to fall into a deep trance. Once the two girls achieve this ability, the formal offering ceremony can begin. A child chosen to be a *sanghyang* dancer will fall into a trance in her mother's arms when she hears music or smells incense.

Though the girls have never received dance lessons, when they fall into trance they are able to execute the most intricate dance movements which ordinarily would take years of training. This fact is not a bit extraordinary to the Balinese, as they understand that it's the spirits of the male *dedara* and the female *dedari* who dance in the bodies of the little girls. Their skilled dancing is proof that a god has entered them. They become temporarily divine.

While in the temple, swaying back and forth, the girls fall into a swoon. The small dancers' limp bodies are straightened up and they are identically dressed in the costumes of *legong* dancers. Women place frangipani-flowered crowns on their heads, dress them in heavy silver anklets, bracelets, rings, and earplugs of gold.

As these deified dancers may not touch the impure earth, they are hoisted on top of the shoulders of the strongest men of the village and carried. They never open their eyes, as if asleep, yet their seated performances coincide perfectly. Balancing at first gracefully from the waist up, they soon bend and contort their bodies at unbelievable angles.

Hunting for *leyak*, a procession is formed which wends its way to a dance clearing nearby or to the death-temple where a high altar has been erected. The dancers are then set down between male and female choruses, before braziers smoking with incense. Employing the same dance movements as the *legong*, the girls sway dreamily to the inarticulate sounds of the mantras offered up to maintain the health and well-being of the village. They have also been known to recite remedies for ailing members of the community. Sometimes a full *gamelan* group accompanies the ritual.

When the chanting stops, the girls fall to the ground in a faint. The performance over, they are revived by a priest who brings them out of trance by means of incense, chants, and rhythmical movements, then blesses them with holy water. Once awake, the girls cannot remember any of the performance, nor are they able to repeat any of the motions they enacted while in trance. The *sanghyang* dancers become ordinary, giggling little girls again.

The true *sanghyang dedari* ritual dance is extremely rare; you'd be very fortunate to see one by chance. This is true even though the various genres of *sanghyang* were exempted from the governor's decree prohibiting sacred dances from being staged at hotels and public theatres. Certain villages still look upon the ritual as extremely sacred.

The "virgin" or "trance dance" offered by tour agents is but a laughable, diluted version of the real thing. A tourist rendition of the *sanghyang jaran,* the "fire dance," can be seen at Bona (near Gianyar) as part of the evening presentation. Though an intriguing and scary demonstration of firewalking by a lone performer, the "angel dance" sequence is not a true trance-dance.

Miscellaneous Dances

In vogue currently are the new genres of dance, *garle le pas* or *tari lepas* ("free dance") in Indonesian, which are non-dramatic, out-of-the-ordinary dances using new gestures and modern staging equipment. All of these new creations are presently coming out of the SMKI and STSI dance institutes.

Except for these modern dances, no attempt has been made to revamp the rather limited number of existing gestures in Balinese dance. New dances *(kreasi baru)* are being created all the time but when a new dance is created, it usually consists of a new combination of already existing gestures and movements fused with a few Western elements. There's even a modern version of *legong* now.

Some have political origins, such as the weaving dance *tari tenum,* specially requested by President Suharto on his visit to the island in the late 1960s. *Tari nelayan,* depicting men fishing, is another typical example of a contemporary *kebyar*-style dance. *Tari manuk rawa,* "long-legged bird dance," portrays the stylized mannerisms of a bird.

The *genggong,* or "frog dance," originating in Batuan, is about the life of the kings Daha and Jenggala and features a wonderful jumping frog. Because it's so unique and humorous, snippets of the *genggong* have found their way into many a hotel and restaurant program. *Jaran Teji,* choreographed by I Wayan Dibia, is a comic dance in which performers ride horses.

Be ready for such "tourist" innovations as the *cendrawasih* dance which mimics birds of paradise and *tari kedis perit* which portrays sparrows. A troupe of child mock-warrior dancers accompanies Bali's only all-women *gamelan* orchestra, *gamelan ibu-ibu,* in Peliatan.

Tektekan is not actually a dance but an exorcistic procession of men carrying bamboo slit drums and giant cowbells around their necks. This ceremony is found only in Krambitan District (Tabanan) and in only four villages—Krambitan, Kukuh, Baturiti, and Penarukan—most opulently at Krambitan's Puri Anyar. For more info, refer to Krambitan. In times of crisis under the guidance of a *pemangku,* the *tektekan* can also serve as a *wali* or religious dance.

Large-scale *sendratari* dance-dramas, incorporating a mix of traditional and modern dance and music, are the rage at the **Bali Art Festival** in June and July each year. Stemming from Java, these galas are a Balinese attempt to imitate the movies. Painstakingly staged, yet with little actual dancing, the characters don't speak but mime very theatrically. When these melodramas are shown in the villages, loudspeakers are used which sound terrible.

WAYANG TOPENG

A masked-dance theater, *wayang topeng* features a troupe of grand kings, ministers, and clowns depicting semihistorical, semilegendary stories. Excerpts of this *wayang* form can be seen at most tourist performances. Each regency of Bali features a different style of costuming, dancing, and *topeng,* which also means "mask."

As part of a large number of religious activities—processions, offerings, and prayers—*topeng* theater is most often staged during elaborate temple anniversary celebrations called *odalan.* Although the melodic accompaniment of the *gamelan* is essential, in *topeng* the emphasis is on the unfolding of the plot.

Though it's now rare on Java, *wayang topeng* stems from the ancient Javanese practice of masked dancers performing at primitive death rites. Its introduction on Bali dates from the 16th century. Today's masked plays are usually derived from the historical romances, chivalrous military adventures, court intrigues, and pas-

sionate love stories of local Balinese kings and heroes. *Topeng* has even derived elements from the ancient pre-Hindu *gambuh* dance. The lines that separate fact, legend, and magic are fuzzy: mythic struggles and religious epics unravel side by side with common tales and topical problems.

Characters

You see the whole gamut—stoic, cowardly, and simple-minded characters alongside effeminate, sweet, and cruel ones. There are even parts for bulbous or long-nosed tourists, whom everybody guffaws at, and in historical dramas the conquering Dutch colonialists are portrayed as bumbling fools. During the Japanese occupation, the clowns acting in the periphery of the epic passed on covert Resistance information to the audience.

Female roles are always played by men. Although usually a mix, a *topeng* play almost always starts out with a petulant prime minister *(patih)* who can either be a refined or gruff character. Another popular character is the prime minister who has retired but is called back into active service by his king. These high-born characters do not condescend to speak their parts. Other stories recount the exploits of a humble frog who turns into a noble prince when he is very old.

The masks of the demons and the animals both share the same characteristics—flaring nostrils, bulging eyes, extended, elaborate fangs—reflective of all the base, animalistic traits which all of us have at least in part. On the other side are the heroes who are actually incarnations of gods and goddesses. With their beautiful, refined countenances, they represent spiritual perfection.

Invariably, there is always the dottering *orang tua,* a pale-faced old man. Back bent and moustache drooping, the *orang tua* continually nods off to sleep, examines his white hair for lice, and stumbles weakly, almost falling into the audience from time to time. It's an extremely poignant performance.

Stock characters also include nobility like kings who stride and dance in the refined court style with jeweled *kris* at their backs. Since the others cannot speak through their finely crafted masks, but only pantomime, the clowns provide a running narration, interpreting royalty's gestures in Low Balinese so that the audience can follow the story.

Clumsy male clowns, Penasar and Kartala, are usually cast in the role of absurd body-servants to dignified masters. Often there are two clowns who take on opposing roles, copying their master, making jokes to the side, encouraging him in a servile manner. One, Penasar, is pompous and struts around the stage lording it over his half-witted younger brother, Kartala, who gets back at Penasar by sarcastically imitating his self-importance. The audience rolls as the two exchange barbed witticisms and bawdy jokes.

One particularly adored clown routinely rushes into the audience at the end of a performance and abducts one of the children to the other side of the curtain, where he's given cakes and sweetmeats to share with his friends. The comic character, Jero Dalam Pegek (literally, "end of the ceremony"), is an amalgam of madman, god, king—an embodiment of the sacred and the potentially subversive. His presence is associated with a myth that reminds the audience not to be deceived by appearances.

The clowns, equally at home in both the absurd and the sublime episodes, are known by the type of mask they wear. Whereas the masks of gods and kings are full and cover the entire face, the clowns wear only partial masks with their mouths and chins exposed, enabling them to sing and speak in three languages. Or they may wear no mask at all but just a painted face.

The Actors and Their Masks

In most *topeng* plays, three or four actors, normally men, take on the roles of all the characters, each with a sharply defined personality. Refined, noble characters wear full masks; clowns and servants wear half-masks allowing them to speak, narrate or expound morality.

A full set of 30-40 *topeng* masks might belong to a solitary star who could perform four or five successive dances with different masks in the *topeng pajegan*. Giving life to a grotesque, immobile face of wood requires great subtlety and skill. It is truly an inspiring spectacle to watch these actors make their masks cry, breathe, sweat, bellow, moan, bleat.

A powerful bond—*taksu*—exists between a sensitive actor and his masks. When the actor dons his mask, he is linked to the spiritual realm, blessed by the gods. His task is to transform himself, to change his voice to his character's, to infuse his performance with its spirit. Sometimes you hear the comment "It was a technically superb performance, but there was no *taksu.*"

Just before each play the performer pauses for a moment unseen and attempts to enter into the archetypal character represented by each mask During this private moment he sprinkles holy water over himself and recites sacred mantras. This is the actor's last conscious act, as the moment he comes on stage he is oblivious to all but the personality and energy of his character.

On stage, the shiny beautiful masks with big mysterious eyes seem as if suspended in air. Some kingly masks radiate such authority and power that villagers have been known to fall into a trance when seeing them for the first time, and it's believed that certain masks can even induce trances from which actors never recover. Rare and prized masks are paid awesome reverence, and offerings of incense and flowers are regularly dedicated to them.

You will never be able to try on one of these sacred *topeng,* as it would offend its spirit to be taken up by a stranger. When not in use, masks are covered neatly with a white cloth, stored in a specially made basket, and kept high up in the temple where they must "sleep together" and not be separated. After a famous actor dies, his masks are never moved from the spot where they were at his death. The oldest surviving set of masks are kept in a temple in the village of Blahbatu.

WAYANG KULIT

One of the oldest forms of dramatic entertainment, *wayang kulit* is a performance of flat leather puppets in the hands of a mystic storyteller, the *dalang,* who casts their shadows on a backlit screen. This *wayang* form exerts a powerful magnetism over Balinese of all ages. For sheer enjoyment, it's even preferred over the more spectacular *wayang topeng,* in which human beings act like puppets.

With its fluid, ethereal music and epic themes, its eerie shadows, its slapstick comedy, *wayang kulit* is an extraordinary mixture of ribaldry and mysticism. It is at the same time a morality play, a religious experience, and pure entertainment.

For the Balinese, *wayang kulit* also serves as a medium through which they learn about their classical literature, the Mahabharata and the Ramayana. Referred to as "Society's Teacher," the stories narrated are all important in Balinese education, its range of anecdotes covering all of life's situations.

Wayang kulit was popular at the court of King Airlangga of East Java in the 11th century. Through the 11th to 14th centuries, it was used by Hindu teachers on Bali to propagate their religion. Though the chants relating the stories of Rama and Arjuna were sung in ancient Sanskrit, the texts were always interpreted by storytellers into everyday Balinese idiom. All the classics of Hindu mythology were eventually adapted into this theater so as to inculcate the masses. Even though the attractions of the electronic age—TV and video—have devastated this art form over the past decade, *wayang kulit* can be seen at important stages in the life of a Balinese: weddings, toothfiling ceremonies, children's birthdays, cremations, marriages, and temple feasts.

Performances are also put on by hotels as entertainment for guests. In the presentation put on at Denpasar's Hotel Puri Pemacutan, the performance is shortened to cater to a Western audience. In the *wayang kulit* staged at Sanur's Mars Hotel, some of the characters speak English. The shadow puppet theater staged at Oka Kartini's in Ubud is the medium's only public performance; it's also the most authentic because all the characters speak High Balinese.

Be sure to take in a show if you hear of one, as they are becoming less common. Always announced in advance, shows start at around 2100. The traditional six- or seven-hour performance which takes place out in the villages is divided into three principal parts. The leading characters seldom appear before midnight, and the plot is resolved just as the sun comes up in the real world.

The *Dalang*

The mystic narrator of the *wayang kulit,* the *dalang,* is not only a skilled artist but a great spiritual teacher and philosopher, a master of eloquence and poetic embellishment. He is the true star of this shadow theater who almost singlehandedly directs the whole drama.

The *dalang* must be a captivating juggler and have surpassing endurance, able to remain seated for more than six straight hours while deftly manipulating his puppets. Each puppet may weigh up to a kilo, and he may be required to handle as many as three or four at a time.

The *dalang* is a refined classical orator and linguist who can sing episodes from the Mahabharata and Ramayana in as many as 47 different poetic measures, demonstrating an astonishing memory. He also conducts the *gender wayang* orchestra with its drums and other percussion instruments, and he is also an accomplished musician who can play each one of the instruments if need be.

Years of training in the now-defunct Kawi language and a scholar's knowledge of the rich fund of Balinese literature are also required of the *wayang kulit* master. The *dalang* is as well an ordained priest who can make offerings and divert evil, possessing a formidable *sakti*—magic power—with which he can move his audience to laughter or to tears.

Dalang are slowly becoming extinct. In the 1930s there were perhaps one thousand puppeteers on the island; now there are fewer than 20. The most famous are I Ketut Rupik of Lukluk, I Wayan Wija of Sukawati, I Wayan Dibia (a lecturer at STSI), and I Wayan Nartha.

The Staging

The translucent screen *(kelir)* is a rectangle of white cloth stretched on a bamboo frame and lit by an oil lamp *(damar)* hanging directly above the *dalang*'s head. The primitive coconut-oil or a gas-flare lamp, set behind the screen, is preferred over an electric bulb as its warm, flickering flame dramatizes, enlarges, and mystifies the motions of the puppets.

Wayang kulit can also be staged in the daytime when the usual screen is replaced by twine tied between two poles or the branches of a tree, allowing the audience to view the puppets directly. At the foot of the screen is the soft trunk of a banana tree where the pointed horn ends of the puppets are stuck when not in use. The *dalang* sits cross-legged next to a long, coffin-shaped wooden chest *(kropak)* in which are stored his puppets. Between the toes of the *dalang's* right foot is a buffalo horn tapper with which he knocks out sharp raps on the *kropak* clapper, providing sound effects, punctuating the action, signaling starts and stops, changing the tempo and moods, and cueing the musicians.

Behind the *dalang* sit the musicians, usually a virtuoso *gender* orchestra consisting of four xylophones in the case of the Mahabharata, plus a few *kendang* and kettle gongs for excerpts from the Ramayana. The musicans must play specific music—such as martial music or love music—consistent with the scene so that the music and drama mesh perfectly. After offerings are made and all is ready, the *dalang* strikes the wooden box containing the puppets, signaling the delicate tones of the *gamelan* to begin. Suddenly, a leaf-shaped shadow *(kayon)* appears. This mysterious motif, a link between the various scenes and also used to mark the beginning and end, is thought to derive either from the holy mountain Meru or the Tree of Life. When in use, the cosmic *kayon* silhouette is placed always in the center of the screen, waving in and out of focus, seeming to tremble in time with the music.

By its movements or its angle, the *kayon* prepares the mood of the episode to follow, or may represent water, fire, or wind. When the *kayon* is removed, the show begins. The *dalang* strikes the *kropak* three times in order to "awaken" the puppets. He then introduces the characters one at a time, the *wayang* figures raised and pressed flat against the *kelir*.

Though both forms share the same repertoire, the Balinese puppets have longer necks, smaller bodies, and are more naturalistically carved than Javanese *wayang*, which are made much more stylistically because Islam forbids realistic portrayal of the human or animal form.

Puppets are manipulated by three long stem-like supports of horn or bamboo, one for the body and one for each arm. With only their arms jointed, their acting consists of rhythmical fast arm gestures while the *dalang* recites their lines. Small boys love to sit in back on the *dalang's* side of the screen to marvel at his deft hands and to better appreciate the designs and colors of the puppets.

The puppets can tilt, advance, retreat, fall, pivot, dance, fight, rise, hover, come down from the sky, or fly up like a bird. For an otherworldly effect, the puppets are moved toward or away from the screen, the shadows themselves becoming sharp black outlines or blurry grays, always fading and wavering and mysterious.

Plots

On the framework of a scenario which would take only about five minutes to read in its entirety, the *dalang* unfolds a six-hour drama in which he continuously narrates, chants poetry, sings, does sound effects, and simultaneously carries on many-sided dialogues.

Throughout the presentation the *gamelan* keeps up a steady accompaniment that echoes, evokes, and amplifies the intertwined themes and actions of the poetic drama. Since many of the characters and episodes are accompanied by their own appropriate musical theme and mode of articulation, the audience is able to imagine who is talking and exactly where in the story the event is taking place, even without following the *dalang's* narration. The appearance of a certain puppet tells the audience immediately just what episode is about to be enacted.

The *dalang* must have an encyclopedic knowledge of the Hindu epics; the Mahabharata alone has 90,000 couplets, seven times longer than Homer's *Iliad* and *Odyssey* put together. Not that the whole poem needs to be presented, but he must vary the episodes enough to hold the interest of his very discerning audience.

The Mahabharata deals with the feud between two rival royal families, the Pandawas and the Korawas. It's a story of treachery, jealousy, banishment, and a battle so awful that it made "the rivers stand still, the sun pale, and the mountains tremble." In this classic, the mighty hero Bima unleashes a furious attack on the evil Korawas, who are finally exterminated.

Or the play could present the theme of the Ramayana in which Prince Rama tries to rescue his beloved Sita from the clutches of the monster-king, Rawana. Rama is helped by a great army of monkeys, led by their flamboyant and fearless leader, the white ape Hanuman. The two armies meet in a clash so terrible that millions die on both sides. The ranks of the clumsy *raksasa* are swarmed over by biting, clawing, screaming monkeys and at last give way. As in the Mahabharata, absolute virtue in the end wins out over absolute evil, without which cosmic order would be unattainable.

Modern stories have started to make their appearance on the shadow puppet stage. An example is I Wayan Dibia's experimental Balinization of Racine's *Phaedra,* complete with raunchy dirty jokes and not-so-oblique jabs at political figures.

You're also beginning to see performances in broken English, which often break up both the Westerners and the Balinese in the audience. These two-language presentations are still in their formative stages, but their supporters believe that they have the potential of becoming a cross-cultural experience for those who don't understand Balinese. I, for one, believe they taint this theatrical form in the same way that foreign films are ruined when dubbed in English.

Characters

The heroes of these plays are the models after which the Balinese pattern their behavior and judge their neighbors and colleagues. Each character, whether a hero or a villain, is sharply defined by means of his headdress, color, garments, shape of eyes, and so on. The noble characters of the Right speak in Kawi, and the gruff ogres, *raksasa,* and demons of the Left speak in the Low Balinese tongue, or even in Indonesian. Whichever language is used, it's always spoken in the appropriate speech level, style, and accent.

The comic retainers of the heroes remain the most popular and amusing of all the *wayang* personalities. While the august figures of Hindu origin wear the Indian *dhoti,* hold themselves aloof, and speak with airs, these indigenous clowns, with no apparent counterpart in the Hindu pantheon, wear the Malayo-Polynesian *sarung* and behave ludicrously, yet possess great magic and power. Two righteous clowns and two wicked clowns are always pitted against one another in a jocular bawdy rivalry. Twalen and his son Merdah, on the side of truth and goodness, are in constant and hilarious conflict with their antagonists, Sangut and Delam, flying across the screen, jabbing and knocking into each other, alternating biting insults with riotous good-natured exchanges. They parody the poetic love scenes, employ spells on their foes, change into old women, and mutter cynical jokes, as spectators hold their sides in laughter. The clowns also play a useful dramatic role by translating from Kawi into the vernacular.

The Balinese say that Twalen is actually the son of the god Tintiya Himself, but since he liked his worldly pleasures so much he renounced his right to be deified in exchange for the freedom to eat, drink, and make merry as much as he wished. Beloved, impudent, and faithful Twalen is the Sancho Panza, the Poncho, the Falstaff of Balinese theater.

Sangut

Twalen

BOB RACE

ON THE ROAD
FESTIVALS AND EVENTS

The Balinese devote most of their waking hours to an endless series of offerings, purifications, processions, dances, and dozens of other religious rites. Ceremonies and festivals guide a Balinese from birth to death and into the world thereafter. There can be few places of comparable size where ceremonial obligations hold such a sway over people's lives. There are festivals dedicated to the art of woodcarving, the birth of a goddess, percussion instruments. There are temple festivals, fasting and retreat ceremonies, parades to the sea to cleanse villages, special prayer days for the dead, nights of penance *(sivaratri)*, harvest festivals *(usaba)*, blood sacrifices, and house deity anniversaries *(odalan sangguh)*. No one who has encountered a Balinese procession will ever forget the total immersion into Balinese culture and the wonderful opportunity to interact with the people on a special occasion.

Over 90% of Balinese are Hindu, so Indic holidays dominate the festival calendar. A basic tenet of the Balinese religion is that rituals and ceremonies maintain harmony between the two equally powerful forces of good and evil, and that the proper and harmonious behavior of the people brings the supernatural forces under control. Balinese also believe that the island is owned by the supreme god Sanghyang Widhi and has been handed down to the people in a sacred trust. In return, the people show their gratitude by filling their lives with symbolic activities and worship. Time seems to be measured only by the days and weeks between festivals. Because of the heat, the Balinese stage the majority of ceremonies in the late afternoon or evening and they last until early morning. The full moon is perhaps the most favorable time to view an event on Bali because of a heightened, magic feeling when a whole month's devotion reaches its peak. The new moon or when there's just a sliver of the moon, when the sky is almost completely dark, is also very spiritual. This is a time of the spirits, of renewal, for starting over.

Travel During Festival Times

Religious holidays can cause some inconvenience for travelers. Bali's roads become clogged with cars and motorcycles during the days leading up to **Galungan,** when people leave the towns to spend the holidays in their home villages. The opposite happens during **Nyepi,** an annual spring-cleaning to drive away evil spirits. Transportation ceases and all shops and businesses shut down. Travel is expensive, complicated, and time-consuming— you might wait eight hours to catch the ferry to Java. (Note that the dates of Nyepi through 1999 are: 9 April 1997, 29 March 1998, 18 March 1999).

Religious holidays observed all over in Indonesia can also affect travel on Bali. The Islamic holiday **Idul Fitri** marks the end to the fasting of Ramadan and the beginning of Syawal, and marks the peak season for domestic tourism. As many as 25 million Indonesians leave the cities for holiday destinations like Bali. Starting at least a week prior to the holiday, this exodus strains all transportation services and accommodations. Be advised not to travel in Bali at this time. The day before and after **Proklamasi Kemerdekaan** (17 August) it may be difficult to travel because of traffic jams *lalu lintas macet.* Don't plan to travel on these days if you're on a tight schedule. Also, starting a week before Christmas, the entire island is gridlocked with foreign and domestic tourists.

Information

If you see a procession of women in traditional dress carrying small bowls or balancing offerings on their heads, or a group of men in *batik* shirts and headcloths, put on a shirt, take your camera, and mingle with the crowd—you're always welcome. If participants get in a *bemo,* get in after them; if they're walking along the road, fall in behind.

Get the ***Indonesia Calendar of Events,*** covering festivals, holidays, and events throughout the archipelago for the current year. Pick it up at Garuda offices in any of Indonesia's large cities, or at Indonesian Tourist Information or Garuda offices abroad.

Travel agents, hotel owners and managers, and houseboys can supply information about specific events during any given period.

Denpasar's tourist office at Jl. Surapati 7 (tel. 0361-234569) opposite Puputan Square, is another excellent place to inquire about any festivals taking place. Ask for the ***Bali Calendar of Events,*** which lists the major temple anniversaries *(odalan)* taking place that year. (One difficulty is that many ceremonies are scheduled only several weeks in advance.) The office is open Mon.-Thurs. 0800-1300, Friday 0800-1030, and Saturday 0800-1300. Also check your hotel bulletin board. You can always tell if a festival is going on. The tinkling of a *gamelan* emanating from inside a temple, gauntlet of hawkers lined up on the road, or village streets lined with high arching bamboo poles all point to a celebration or festival nearby.

You can also follow a calendar which indicates the festival dates. Balinese calendars are used by astrologers to read horoscopes, and by priests to fix the most propitious days for planting, getting married, holding a cremation, opening a restaurant, constructing a house, or gathering for some social function.

The Balinese Calendar

Indigenous calendars usually start the Balinese year with the vernal equinox (March on the Gregorian calendar). Major festivals seem to change not only from year to year, but from month to month within a specific year if viewed through the Gregorian calendar. Temple birthdays, a commonplace event throughout Bali, occur frequently at regular, scheduled intervals, but some ceremonies—such as the extraordinary mouse cremation at Ababi village near Tirtagangga which takes place once every 10 years—occur at far greater intervals.

The main problem with trying to keep up with Balinese holidays and festivals is they are three different yet parallel calendrical systems in use. Tacked up side by side on the wall, each calendar is referred to simultaneously to keep track of festivals in progress and to plan for upcoming events. Our familiar Gregorian calendar is used to determine political and Christian holidays, but dates for the most important celebrations and exorcisms are determined by the conjunction of dates on Bali's two distinctive, non-Western calendars.

One system is based on the Indian *saka* year which determines festival dates events in the non-Javanized parts of the island. Several major

Hindu temples still celebrate their anniversaries according to this Sanskrit-based calendar. Calculated from new moon to new moon, the *saka* calendar is divided into 12 months *(sasih)* of 29-30 days each. The *saka* calendar commenced at the founding of the Indian Saka dynasty in A.D. 78, meaning that the year 1900 in Bali began in 1978. This system most closely follows the Gregorian year in terms of length; we can synchronize this lunar calendar to the Western solar calendar by inserting a month every 30 months. When reading this calendar, the dates run vertically rather than horizontally as in the West.

The other is the *pawukon* calendar cycle, imposed on Bali by the Majapahit conquerors and based on the so-called Javano-Balinese *uku* year which has 30 weeks of seven days each totaling 210 days. Although festival dates can't be predetermined precisely, celebrations tend to fall around the same time every year. This traditional calendar, called *pelelintingan,* is used to schedule the most important island-wide rituals and feasts like Kuningan and Galungan, as well as temple birthdays *(odalan).*

The *uku* year is divided into six individually named periods of 35 days *(tumpek),* so each has five seven-day weeks. Based on the movements of the seven visible planets and the three-day market week, each frame depicts activities that are auspicious to carry out on a particular day. Particularly powerful days occur when special dates from two calendars intersect. Also significant are those days which precede the night of the full moon *(purnama),* or end a month with no moon *(tilem).* Details of the Chinese, Buddhist, Christian, and Islamic calendars are also included so that the Balinese *uku* calendar is truly international.

A computer program by Balinist Fred Eiseman enables you to input Gregorian calendar dates and output lunar month and the Balinese lunar day number. Another allows you to input the year number (e.g., 1998) and get the dates for *purnama* and *tilem* for the entire year. Enter the name of one of 45 events on the list, and another program will give you the date for that event in the year you enter. Creating this software was a tormenting task because the relationships between the different calendar systems had to be worked out. The programs will work for any date, past or future, fit on a 3.5-inch double-density disk, and are menu-driven and easy to use. Complete instructions are included. For a copy of the disk, send US$25 to Fred Eiseman, 13025 East Mountain View Rd., Scottsdale, AZ 85259, U.S.A.

THE BALINESE CALENDAR

The Balinese year has 210 days, 30 weeks *(wuku)* of seven days each, or six months of 35 days each. Every week of the year has its own name, printed in red in the upper row to the left of "wuku." In this example (November) there are the weeks 5, 12, 19, and 26, the dates running vertically downward instead of horizontally as in the Gregorian calendar. Red ink always designates special holidays. The weeks conform to our counting of the weeks, and Sunday begins the week. Truly an international calender, the outer left-hand column shows the days of the week in Indonesian, Balinese, English, Japanese, and Chinese. Not only Bali-Hindu religious events but details of events from Indonesia's other major religions are also indicated.

Inside the boxes are names for days which are based on a different counting system. For example, the top line of each square lists the Muslim month and number. Below the *ingkel* row are lists of Balinese festival days, coincidental dates, *odalan,* and special days connected with Galungan and Pagerwesi, with advice as to what to do and what not to do on certain days. In the right-hand vertical column is a list of auspicious days for certain activities. By glancing at this list, a Balinese can determine the best days for a harvest, toothfiling, cremation, wedding, house building, restaurant opening, etc. A 35-year-old photograph of the 78-year-old creator of the calendar, Ketut Bangbang Gede Rawi, is pictured in the lower right-hand corner. Bangbang has published this official Balinese calendar since 1950!

Exorcisms

No ritual or purification takes place on Bali without first placating the demons and witches. If a village has been visited by a calamity such as the birth of twins of different sexes, a murder, a bad accident, an epidemic, or a flood, a priest needs to purify the ground to avert more trouble and strengthen the spiritual force of the village.

Any dangerous transitional event, natural disaster, calendrical shift, or anniversary always calls for the appeasement of ancestors who then descend to Earth and dispose of evil forces or banish vermin from the fields. In return, they receive offerings and entertainment from the people. The more elaborate the performances and music, the less likely these benign spirits are to become bored. In this way, they will dally longer on earth, continuing to protect the people.

In a ruse to drive out demons, the Balinese New Year (Nyepi) is a day of silence—no activity is allowed anywhere on Bali. A 15-day ceremony in 1991 in Ubud to straighten out the axis of the world was so complex it took an IBM computer to run the event. The grandest and most important exorcism, taking place every 100 years, is the stupendous Eka Dasa Rudra. Involving tens of thousands of people, it is a ritual purification of the whole island.

Family Rituals and Ceremonies

The most common family ritual involves placing small woven-coconut trays filled with sticky rice, flowers, and salt at the four cardinal points of the courtyard and outside the front gate of every house. Three times a day these tiny offerings *(sesajan)* are sprinkled with holy water and offered up to the gods—perhaps the most important religious activity on Bali.

Family rites of passage—toothfilings, first birthdays, weddings, cremations—are one-time events that require a special ceremony prepared by the family. After the passage of six months on the Pawukon calendar, an infant will be named, blessed, and allowed to touch the ground for the first time in the colorful *oton* ceremony. Because these intimate events take place on favorable days determined by a priest, only the family or close relatives know about them ahead of time. *Losmen* or hotel owners frequently invite their guests to these special occasions.

Temples are only used in ceremonies relating to God, not for petty human life and interaction. Ceremonies for people take place at home and not in a temple, although offerings are made there. A deified ancestor of the family is invited to descend and take up temporary residence in a special statue *(pratima)* in a house shrine or at the village temple. Every family temple in Bali has an anniversary *odalan,* a closed affair when the family pays homage to their ancestors and to Sanghyang Widhi, the supreme god.

Festival Activities

Large celebrations, lasting for days and mobilizing thousands of people, are performed with startling efficiency. Nobody is left out; peasants as well as aristocrats take part in the preparations. Indeed, the Balinese seem the happiest when they are getting ready for a musical performance, building altars, fashioning offerings, or cooking a ritual feast. The idea is to fulfill your re-

a festival procession

ligious obligations and have a good time while you're at it.

Rules govern exactly how much food, oil, palm leaf strips, *lamak,* and symbolic money are offered. One way of pleasing the gods is to present them with prayers and offerings, so major festivals are brightened by rows of sumptuous fruit and flowers. Women prepare sweet cakes, cook glutinous rice, or cut decorative patterns from palm leaves. Men ready the temple grounds; hanging friezes, canopies, and banners, building bamboo platforms and altars, slaughtering pigs, erecting *penjor* poles, performing guard duty, and covering the genitals of statues with checkered cloths.

Another way to entertain the gods is with dance, drama, and *gamelan* music. Laughter brings joy to the gods, so each household makes a contribution to the musicians. Both the higher deities and the gods of the underworld are taken into account, one reason why Balinese festivals are so noisy, colorful, and confusing. Be patient as nothing happens to a fixed schedule. Your inquiry as to when a procession or event will take place will always be *"Sebentar lagi . . ."* ("In a little while . . .").

Fashionable dress shows respect and is also a mark of social prestige. Women don rich handspun *kain* and ornament themselves with jewels, scarves, and pounded gold in their hair. At festival times a young woman looks her best. She's allowed to wear lipstick and makeup at religious events but not in daily life when it would be considered too flirtatious. Infant girls wear flowers in their hair and bright sashes around their tiny waists. Men wear a brocaded headcloth, *kris,* and colorful *sarung.*

A large temple festival is like a stage for a lavish form of metaphysical theater, a three-ringed circus of the arts when the temple comes alive with devotees who crowd into the courtyard and parade between the shrines. Babes are carried in the arms of small children, priests recite mantras, elders translate poetry from sacred *lontar,* children fly kites, and men gather to joke and gamble with brightly colored Chinese cards or fight their cocks. Clove cigarettes and incense smoke choke the air, peanuts and rice cakes are sold, and there is spirited gossiping among neighbors and friends. For three or four days almost without break, ritual dances, festive

music, and dramas are performed as if the occasion were a gay costume party instead of a fervid act of worship. Finally, bloated with sensory pleasure, the gods are invited to return to their heavenly spheres.

Conduct

The best way to behave at family events—funerals, *selamatan,* circumcisions, weddings, prenuptial ceremonies—is to watch the Balinese and mirror them. As in our country, family events need invitations. Just because you're a tourist doesn't mean you can stroll into a family compound where something interesting is going on. You're welcome to attend any "public" ceremony or festival at a temple, and encouraged to actively participate, as long as you follow certain rules. There's always room for one more in a crowded courtyard—just nudge a few people over, roll out another mat, or pick a pillar to lean against.

Since festivals are religious occasions, traditional dress *(pakaian adat)* is expected—a sash worn around the waist, often handed out for a small fee near the entrance. Most hotel/bungalow owners are only too happy to supply you with the necessary clothing and accompany you. If you don't have a sash, wrap a *sarung* or even a towel around your waist. Wear long pants or skirt and your best shirt or blouse (no beachwear). A nice gesture is to make a simple contribution such as a couple packages of cigarettes or some pens and notebooks for the kids. Proper dress is all the more appropriate if you're invited to attend a family ceremony.

Stay in the background. Don't stand in the way of people praying and never stand or sit on a wall or platform higher than officiating priests. If you enter an area of prayer, remove your shoes and sit cross-legged on a mat or the ground. Ceremonies and religious events, particularly in the Denpasar area, charge small fees (Rp200) to enter temple compounds. Women are not allowed inside temples during their menstrual periods; photographs and tape recordings are permitted except at prayer services.

Holidays of Other Faiths

Major holidays of other religions are also national holidays on Bali. Ramadan and the Islamic holy days leading up to Idul Fitri are fervently observed by Bali's Muslim community, and Christmas is enthusiastically celebrated among Christians. At Christmas time Ubud's Puri Anyar is bedecked with colored lights, ropes of phony gold fur, giant effigies of Mickey Mouse, and large plastic snowflakes.

MAIN EVENTS

Odalan

Since the island has an estimated 20,000 temples, *odalan* is one of the most frequently seen ceremonies. The congregation of every active temple on Bali schedules its temple's anniversary celebration on certain auspicious days during the *uku* year, and all villagers are invited to attend. On the pragmatic side *odalan* provides an opportunity for temple repair and renewal.

Because they follow a fixed calendar, an *odalan* is always taking place at a temple somewhere. Even if you're only in Bali for two or three days you have an excellent chance of attending one. Many *odalan* take place on the night of a full moon, *purnama*. The Denpasar Tourist Office, tel. (0361) 234569, and a branch in Kuta Jl. Bakung Sari 1 have a *Calendar of Events* pamphlet which lists all the times and places for the major *odalan* in southern Bali for the current year.

The lavishness of the *odalan* depends on the importance of the temple and the wealth of the sponsoring *banjar*. Some temple birthdays are small and inconspicuous, others are gigantic and last a week. During the preparations of a large public temple like the Pura Kehen in Bangli, village men and women clean, decorate, build altars and awnings, erect flagpoles, and fashion ornate offerings of woven palm leaf, fruit, rice, cookies, and flowers.

Draped in fine *sarung*, sashes, and head-dresses, hibiscus and frangipani blossoms woven into their hair, women balance lofty pyramids of beautiful and delicate offerings on their heads in long, colorful parades. All afternoon the splendid towers arrive at the temple gates, some accompanied by marching bands. Inside, the men sit around the compound proudly wearing *kris*. White-robed priests sprinkle holy water over each family's offerings, the blessing punctuated by the chiming of tiny silver bells—an invitation to the deities to descend. For several hours the gods feast on the essence of each

offering. Afterward, the Balinese take home the material remains. In this way both the gods and the Balinese are blessed with prosperity.

During the three-day celebration the temple is alive with the atmosphere of a country fair—snack-stalls, cockfights, chanting *pemangku*, shimmering gongs, *batik* vendors, toys, balloons, sizzling *sate*, noisy games of chance, and *balian* selling cure-alls. From midnight to dawn, dances, dramas, and *wayang kulit* are performed. The whole affair is happy and casual, a social occasion as well as a religious rite.

Occasionally, a group of identically clad older women dance the slow, stately *pendet*, a dance dedicated to the deities of each shrine. The *odalan* at Pura Luhur Batukau features a tiger manifesting itself in a dancing human. Sometimes other *odalan* feature a procession to the sea. Before returning home, the priests recite prayers, politely requesting the visiting deities to depart in hopes that they have been well treated during their visit and will return to heaven pleased.

Galungan

The most important regularly held holiday on Bali, Galungan celebrates the creation of the world by the supreme god and the victory of goodness or virtue *(dharma)* over evil *(adharma)*. Observed in the 11th week of the 210-day *uku* year by Balinese all over Indonesia, Galungan is the start of a 42-day holy period. The celebration probably has its origins in an ancient pre-Hindu harvest festival—it's still forbidden to begin planting during this period. In Bali-Hindu legend, Galungan is a celebration of the defeat of the legendary demon-king Mayadanawa by the people (represented by the god Indra).

Preparations begin seven days in advance when Bali's roads are draped with *penjor*, tall, curved bamboo poles adorned with unhusked rice and flowers. Placed in front of each door as a symbol of thanks to Sanghyang Widhi for his gifts of life and prosperity, they dip toward the center of the street. The sight of long lines of *penjor* gracing Balinese villages alone are worth a trip to Bali.

In the days before the holiday, town and village markets overflow with bright-colored rice cakes *(jajan)*, turtles and pigs are slaughtered to make *lawar*, green bananas ripen in huge clay pots, temples are spruced up to receive the ancestral spirits, and the whole island is decked out in *lamak* scrolls, delicate palm-leaf cut-outs, and other festive decorations.

On Galungan day, starting at dawn, people dressed in their finest clothes and jewelry bear elaborate offerings to their temples of origin, while ancestral spirits and deities descend to earth to be honored. Like Christmas in the West, but without the tawdry commercialism, it's a day of prayers and feasting when schools are closed and commerce comes to a standstill. On the day after Galungan, Manis Galungan ("Sweet Galungan"), there are great family reunions and visits to friends and neighbors.

Kuningan

Following the fixed 210-day *uku* cycle, Kuningan is held 10 days after Galungan, bringing the holiday period to a close. Kuningan, the second most important day on the Hindu-Balinese calendar, is observed throughout Bali with new offerings made and religious services held. The name Kuningan is derived from the special offerings of yellow rice (*kuning* means "yellow") made at this time in honor of the souls of ancestors and saints. It could be termed a sort of Balinese "All Saints' Day."

The holy springs at Tirta Empul in Tampaksiring are jammed as pilgrims bathe to purify themselves. Big temple festivals are also held at Pura Bukit Jati, Pura Dalem Tenggaling, and Banjar Taman Bali in Bangli; Pura Panti Timbrah and Desa Pakesebali in Klungkung; Pura Sada in Kapal; Pura Sakenen on Serangan Island; and Pura Taman Pulo Mas in Ubud. The day after Kuningan (always on a Sunday), Kuningan Manis is a family day when the playing fields, parks, markets, and beaches are filled with people.

Melasti (also Malis or Makiis)

Three or four days before the New Year (Nyepi), the paraphernalia and *pratima* images of deified ancestors from thousands of temples all over Bali are carried in long, joyous processions to the beach or to a nearby holy spring where they are sanctified with water. By late afternoon, thousands of Balinese have reached the shore, raising a din of clashing *gamelan*. White-turbaned priests tinkle prayer bells as the palan-

quins holding the icons are rushed, swirling, into the marigold-strewn surf. After the symbolic washing, men in deep trances lop off the heads of young pigs and are wrestled away, swinging at their captors with bloody swords. This is no show; it is an awesome display of a living religion.

One day before Nyepi, purification ceremonies conducted by priests are held at all the main crossroads in Bali's villages and towns. Offerings of *brem* and the flesh of domestic animals are placed there to tempt the lurking *bhuta* and *kala* into the open. Toward evening on the same day, the last day of the old year, the whole island starts making as much noise as is humanly possible, cleansing the land of malevolent spirits.

Children, especially little boys, set off continuous explosions, lighting small amounts of kerosene in big bamboo tubes. They blow whistles, set firecrackers, and bang gongs, homemade cymbals, pots and pans, trash cans, corrugated roofing, and petroleum drums. Any noisemaker they can lay their hands on will suffice to create pandemonium in all corners of the family compound and down every alleyway.

Priests stay up the whole night chanting magical formulas to exorcize the hordes of malevolent spirits from the old year. In Denpasar, thousands of boys gather at Puputan Square for a parade through the streets carrying flaming torches and weird bamboo and paper monsters and demons *(ogoh-ogoh)* to make sure that all the malingering spirits are aroused. The next day, Nyepi, all is deathly silent.

Nyepi

The Balinese New Year in the lunar *(saka)* calendar, this holy day almost always occurs during the spring equinox toward the end of March or beginning of April. Nyepi is a day of silent retreat, prayer, and quiet meditation—a Day the World Stood Still. It feels like Bali 30 years ago—no electricity, no cars, no tourists—as the people sleep so do the dogs. The new year must begin with complete nothingness because all existence originates from nothingness. The purpose of this behavior is to suppress passion, teach control of excesses, and practice *semadhi*. No transportation is taken, no work done, no lamps burned, and no sexual or other sensory pleasures are indulged in. Meals are prepared in advance as no fires may be lit, only small candles inside the home are permitted. You may not read, smoke, cook, or eat, and for 24 hours no one leaves the house compound.

To see that stillness is preserved, male members of the local *banjar* keep silent watch at points along the roads and in the alleys. Only those with special written exemptions are allowed on the roads or into other public areas. If guests must leave for the airport, the hotel has to submit the names of those leaving to the *banjar*. Streets are patrolled and if the occupant of a stopped car isn't on the list, there could be a problem.

Restaurants, offices, and shops are closed, traffic lights are shut off, and even Denpasar's streets are deserted. Bali's ports are closed down because no ships or ferries are in operation. To find their way around grounds, hotel staff carry shaded flashlights pointed downward. Why all this? The Balinese hope that the demons and evil spirits aroused by the noise the night before will be deluded into thinking that Bali is completely devoid of life, prompting them to leave the island.

Tumpek Anniversaries

Ceremonies dedicated to a class of useful or revered objects take place about once every 35 days. Refer to a Balinese Puwukon calendar to find out when. For **Tumpek Kandang,** prayers are offered up in thanks to useful domestic animals, particularly the island's soft golden-brown cattle, which are scrubbed, dressed in a *kain,* showered in uncooked rice, and have their horns decorated with *lamak.* Bali's enormous sway-backed pigs are wrapped in white cloth and fed a special concoction of boiled banana stem or tree leaves mixed with rice *(oot halus).* Chickens, ducks, and water-buffaloes are also honored.

Tumpek Wariga is the Balinese Arbor Day. Palm trees, fruit trees, and gardens are thanked with offerings for providing humans with a source of food and income. Coconut trees are even dressed in *kamben,* the same skirtlike cloth worn by people going to the temple to pray. Another *tumpek,* known as **Soma Ribeg,** is devoted to the goddess of rice and fertility. The implements and equipment used in rice farming are honored and the milling or selling of rice is forbidden.

On **Tumpek Krulut,** all theatrical costumes, masks, accessories, and musical instruments are decorated with coconut-leaf offerings, cleansed, and blessed in order to restore them to their original condition. Theatrical groups from all over the island give banquets (though there are no performances) and hold big ceremonies. Homage to *wayang kulit* is paid on Tumpek Ringgit when sacred heirloom puppets are taken from their storage boxes, sprinkled with holy water or rice, then solemnly reconsecrated. Weapons of war, sharp implements, and all metal tools including cars, trucks, and motorcycles are blessed during **Tumpek Landep.** On this day most sacred to blacksmiths, *kris* are bathed, leaf offerings are hung from handlebars and steering wheels, radiator grills are decorated with garlands, and hoods are dressed in bright *batik.*

Pagerwesi

A day of offerings for Batara Guru, a Hindu god from the creation myth, Pagerwesi is held a few weeks before Galungan to assure protection of the family, the village, and the world at large. Pagerwesi means "iron fence," symbolizing the fortification around you to keep out greed and evil during the ceaseless battle between good and evil. The family asks for spiritual strength in confronting life's trying cycles and suffering. Offerings are brought to the cemetery for the uncremated dead and *penjor* poles are erected. This holiday is most closely observed in Buleleng Regency, where it's nearly as important as Galungan.

Hari Raya Saraswati

This island-wide holiday commemorates Batari Dewi Saraswati, the wife of Brahma and the beautiful goddess of learning and the creative arts. On this day it is not permissible to read or write. It is a day of thanks for bringing education to the world, a day when all books are taken out and dusted, then given as an offering to be blessed by the goddess. Special attention is paid to sacred *lontar,* the Balinese bible. Early in the morning, students by the hundreds attend special ceremonies conducted by *pedanda* at Denpasar's Pura Jaganatha where they pray for success in school.

Eka Dasa Rudra

With some 30 ceremonies lasting as long as 11 weeks and attended by up to 200,000 people, this is the island's largest and most important religious celebration, though no one alive had seen the ceremony before the last time it was held. According to tradition, the festival should occur once every hundred years, but in recent history it has been necessary to hold the festival more frequently. The one in 1963 was a portend of things to come beginning just before mighty Gunung Agung erupted, killing more than 2,000 people. The last Eka Dasa Rudra took place during Feb.-May 1979. The purpose of the festival is to restore a balance in the world between the forces of good and evil. The Balinese explain that they do not do this for themselves or for Hindus of the world, they do it for us all. The ceremony begins with images of the gods borne in a three-day procession to the sea where they are symbolically washed. Men in an outrigger sacrifice a water buffalo calf to sea demons by pushing it into the surf, its horns encased in gold, silver bracelets on its legs, and a heavy stone tied around its neck. A stylized war dance, *baris,* as well as the ancient *gambuh,* are often staged.

In culminating event, worshippers pack into trucks hired by the *banjar* to converge on Bali's mother temple, Besakih. Rivers of Balinese carrying offerings arrive here for the climactic Taur sacrifices. Addressing their prayers to the 11 directions of Balinese space (*eka dasa* means "eleven"), two dozen priests make offerings, bestow gifts, and sacrifice scores of animals—from an eagle to a snake—to appease Rudra, the demonic manifestation of Bali's supreme being. In the 1993 follow-up ceremonies to the cycle, 125 *pedanda* high priests took part, and the sacrifices included 18 seven-month old water buffaloes, goats, deer, geese, and dogs, as well as 15,000 various offerings of other types.

NONRELIGIOUS EVENTS AND HOLIDAYS

The Bali Marathon

With nearly 2,000 runners, this run around the Nusa Dua area is divided into two categories, a 10 km run and a half marathon of 21 km. The first Bali Marathons were popular mainly with Japanese and Indonesian runners, but in the most recent (there have been eight so far) there has been an increase in international interest, with participants from the Netherlands, Australia, and New Zealand competing.

International Kite Festival

The International Kite Festival is held at Tohpati north of Sanur, usually in August when there's lots of wind but no rain. Kite enthusiasts from Germany, the U.S.A., and Japan take part, launching extraordinary kites of every shape and size: fantastic windsock kites, fighter kites, hexagonal kites, and fish kites. Write Tracy Borders of Roman Associates Inc., 1159 Verdemar Dr., Almeda, CA 94502. Also get ahold of *Kite Lines* magazine, who has an issue devoted to Southeast Asia.

Surfing Competition

With the opening of the first **Bali Surfing Club International Pro-Am** contest in 1980, Bali joined the international surfing community. Once a year around July, the competition opens in true Balinese fashion with 40 local dancers. The event is attended by Bali's governor and foreign ambassadors, while champion surfers from Hawaii, California, and Australia serve as judges. The contest is held at Uluwatu or Padang Padang on the Bukit Peninsula north of Kuta.

Bull Races

At Negara in Jembrana Regency, bull races are held between July and October. Trained bulls are dressed in silk banners, their horns painted, and big wooden bells placed around their necks. Each team is judged by speed and style, and a lot of gambling takes place. Like Roman chariots the beasts and their drivers come thundering and kicking up mud all the way to the finish line. Jockeys whip and shout and twist the bulls' tails to gain speed. This festival is staged to please the god of harvest, and the winning bulls are used for stud.

Proklamasi Kemerdekaan

August 17 each year marks the anniversary of Indonesian independence from Holland, declared in 1945 but not actually won until late 1949. The biggest Indonesian national holiday, it's celebrated differently on each island. On

Bali, the national colors are draped over streets and public buildings, and there's an official ceremony in Denpasar's *alun-alun,* followed by speeches, games, public entertainment, performances, and parades of schoolchildren. The tradition is that children and youth organizations take part in the parades and marches, and the older generation look on.

Bali also has its own "National Memorial Day" which commemorates the Battle of Marga in which a whole regiment of guerrilla fighters was killed in the Marga rice fields (45 km northwest of Denpasar) by Dutch ground forces and aerial bombardment after the end of WW II on 20 November 1946. A Hero's Ceremony is held each 20 November when the "Long March" led by Lt. Col. Ngurah Rai to General Agung is reenacted by *pemuda,* scouts, and soldiers, the older veterans looking on. This eight-hour march to Denpasar lasts from evening until early morning. See under "North of Tabanan" in the Tabanan Regency chapter.

Bersih Desa
Once enacted to remove evil spirits from the village, Bersih Desa has lost most of its ritualistic significance. The ceremony takes place at the rice harvesting, and in some Balinese communities it expresses gratitude to the fertility figure Dewi Sri, the rice-goddess. Houses and gardens are cleaned, fences whitewashed, and village roads and paths are repaired.

Kartini Day
Raden Kartini (1879-1903) was Indonesia's first women's emancipationist. The daughter of the regent of Jepara, Kartini had a formal Dutch high-school education and was offered a Dutch scholarship, but instead of continuing her education, she was given in marriage and died in childbirth at age 24. Kartini's collection of published *Letters,* written to close Dutch friends at the turn of the century, is now a modern classic. Celebrated on 21 April, the day is marked with parades, lectures, and social activities attended by women, schoolgirls, university teachers, female workers, and members of women's organizations, all wearing traditional dress. Like Mother's Day, mothers aren't allowed to work. Kids and fathers do the cooking, washing, housecleaning, and other chores.

Bali Arts Festival
The rich Bali Arts Festival begins with a parade leading from Denpasar's Puputan Square to the Werdi Budaya Art Centre on Jl. Nusa Indah. Usually from June to July each year, the program might include a speech contest, pop song and modern dance competition, music and drama contests, *sendratari, jegog,* and *bumbung gebyog* production. There could also be a Wayang Festival featuring master *dalang* from Solo and Yogya, the audience almost entirely composed of Javanese. In 1994, a Festival Cak was organized in which groups were invited to show the various vocal patterns used in the form. An Arja Festival was also held.

Parties
In addition to disco nights, ladies nights, and various entertainment offered by the hotels, discos, and clubs of Kuta and Legian, the Warisan Resto in Krobokan holds their annual New Year's Eve Ball, transforming this Italian bistro into a grand ballroom.

COCKFIGHTING

If cocks have been keeping you awake ever since you arrived in Indonesia, this is your chance to see them killing each other. In the past, the gambling connected with cockfighting frequently brought economic ruin to many families, a man addicted to the habit sometimes wagering a whole month's income on the outcome of a match. Cock-crazy rajas in the early part of this century lost whole fortunes, palaces, and even wives by playing the cocks. Because of the gambling, the Dutch forbade the sport (in 1926). They found it equally as difficult to suppress them as the provincial government does today. Given the fact that 90% of Indonesians are Muslim, a religion which prohibits gambling, it's no wonder that the central government in Jakarta banned public cockfights on Bali in 1981 to prevent moral decay and the squandering of valuable cash resources.

Though unofficial, unauthorized cockfights *(tajen)* are illegal, fighting is still allowed at religious events *(tabuh rah).* In essence, the cocks are sacrifices to the devil. Hungry evil spirits *(bhuta* and *kala)* are especially fond of the blood of fighting cocks because their temperaments are similar. The Balinese the blood offering satisfies the spirits and assures a good harvest. In these purification rites, called *tabuh rah* (pouring blood), cockfights are not only allowed, they're *required*. The fights usually coincide with temple ceremonies, and the village council must alert the police. Three to five rounds are allowed in which betting is legal; all other rounds and bets are illegal. If you're lucky enough to see a match at a temple, it may last for three days.

By charging admission, cockfighting is also a means by which a village raises money for road repairs or various festivals. Like a lottery, every male member of the *banjar* has to contribute a cock; he is fined if he doesn't. Ten to 25% of all winnings go to the *banjar*, the rest is contributed to the cost of the festival. Unrestricted cockfighting also takes place during the great purification offering of *mecaru* prior to the Day of Silence (Nyepi). It is believed that blood spilt over the impure earth will cleanse it. On this occasion, thousands of cocks fight and die all day long everywhere on Bali.

Fresh blood may also be needed to dedicate a new accommodation or tourist restaurant. In these cases, the Balinese don't even ask the police because they know they'll be denied permission. Some may try to pay the authorities with money or a carton of cigarettes to look the other way.

Social Function

The atmosphere of cockfights is not bloodthirsty and warlike. It is ritualized, rechanneled violence where no one gets hurt (except the cocks)—like playing with fire and not getting burned. All the villagers know each other, and the procedure is well understood. Matches are governed by an unbelievably complex set of rules listed in sacred *lontar* books, dictating the length of rounds, the settlement of disputes, gambling etiquette, and the classification of cocks by color, body shape, neck ruff, and other characteristics. Winning bets are collected after each match, and the chief judge *(juru dalem),* a man of unsullied reputation, has the last word in all disputes.

No one congratulates the winner, sympathizes with the loser, argues or disputes the outcome. The fights move unsentimentally and dis-

passionately, each a self-contained world enclosed by raucous laughter and chatter. Predominantly a male-bonding event, there are few more graphic studies of Balinese values and behavior than cockfights. The drama, gesticulating, and hysteria of this nearly impenetrable crowd is fascinating to watch. Raffles wrote in his *History of Java:* "The Balinese are strangers to the vices of drunkenness, libertinism, and conjugal infidelity: their predominant passions are gaming and cockfighting. In these amusements, when at peace with their neighboring states, all the vehemence and energy of their character and spirit is called forth and exhausted." This is true today as much as it was when that observation was recorded in 1817.

The Balinese are amused at the attitude of Westerners who find their cockfights cruel. A rooster is just as dead in the cooking pot as it is on the ground of a cockfighting arena. In religious celebrations the losers provide food for festival banquets and many a prize rooster has found its way into a delicious curry dish.

Care and Training

Fighting cocks are given loving care—regularly massaged, bathed, bounced on the ground, and trained every day. Their feathers, combs, earlobes, and wattles are trimmed so that none provide a beak-hold for the opponent bird. The owner prepares a diet of specially selected grains and a mixture of chopped, grilled meat, and jackfruit, which is believed to thicken the blood—preventing serious bleeding if injury results—and to make the bird lean and little subject to fatigue. Its sexual energies are directed only toward fighting, so the cock leads a celibate life except when breeding new fighters. The offspring of a champion cock are prized and considerably more expensive than those of less proven blood lines.

All over rural Bali special rock ledges are built outside homes and beside roads to hold bell-shaped cock cages. The cages are shifted about during the day to expose the cocks to the right proportions of light and shade, and so that they are amused by the passersby and do not get lonely. The exposure also accustoms them to the raucous street noise and activity of people so they aren't disturbed where it really counts—in the ring.

Pet, mascot, child, dream, income, the bird is carried around the courtyard and to the village *warung* or *banjar* clubhouse, taking as much attention as a new wife. Each is given a name, and in the Balinese language the word for cock has the same double meaning as it has in English, giving rise to the same stale locker-room jokes. The Indonesian word for cock *(sabung)* can also mean champion, warrior, or hero; scholars have even speculated that Balinese men look upon their fighting cocks as detachable, self-operating penises with a life of their own. You'll see them with their birds, endlessly inspecting, stroking, and fondling their muscles, ruffling their feathers, pulling their combs, tenderly bathing them, letting them exercise, and pairing cocks for impromptu sparring without spurs. Young men are just as passionate about the sport as old men, but the extent of their enthusiasm depends on their environment. Youths in the countryside, where there are no TVs and discos, are naturally more into cockfighting than urban youth.

The Arena

Since many cockfights are illegal, matches today are held in secret down back lanes of most villages and towns, usually in the mornings. Guards are posted to make sure participants are not discovered by the police. It's easy for visitors to jostle their way into the noisy, sweating circle, and usually no admission is charged. Though women may enter religious events where cockfights are held, you see only men at *real* cockfights. It is not a place where a woman likes to be seen—these birds are men's business only.

When police raid cockfights, there's a frenzied scramble to escape, a cat and mouse game in which everyone scatters in all directions. If caught, offenders are fined Rp2000 and may even be jailed for a night. Less risky are "private" cockfights which families stage right inside their living compounds to exorcise malevolent spirits. (The Balinese also stage cricket fights but these matches are not easy to find.)

Legal cockfights are held in an open shed or pavilion called a *wantilan,* usually outside the temple, measuring about 15 square meters, and surrounded by tiered seating. Cockfights are also staged in the *banjst* meeting hall, or simply in a flat, roped-off area enclosed by rough benches.

Some cockfights even take place inside the temple itself, but this is rare. Whatever the venue, the courtyard is never swept before a cockfight.

Preliminaries

An auspicious day must be decided on to hold a cockfight. The men arrive at the *wantilan* carrying a floppy, openwork satchel of fresh coconut leaves woven around the body of their cock, its tail sticking out so as not to damage its ornamental feathers. Reeking of *kretek* smoke, the arena is packed with men 20 deep, fused into a single body.

Expert handlers are hired to manage the cocks. Specialist blade-affixers, *pemasang taji,* carry leather or wooden cases where—like surgeon's knives—the lethal, razor-sharp polished steel daggers are kept. The blades are bound tightly to the natural spur of the cock's strongest leg; if they are not properly fastened, the cock will be seriously handicapped. Some of these razor-sharp gaffs are wavy-bladed like miniature *kris* and can reach lengths of up to 15 cm; the finest cost Rp20,000 apiece.

Before a fight, the owners exchange cocks to ascertain if they are equal in size and strength. Squatting on their haunches, the men incite the cocks to fury by setting them close to each other in the center of the arena. The birds are teased by their handlers, tails pulled, feathers ruffled, palm-wine spit or red pepper shoved down their throats, and swung close to each other—all to arouse their fighting spirit.

Betting

The betting process begins when parties crowd into the ring to find out which pairs of birds seem to really want to fight each other. Owners wander around the arena with their cocks held high, looking for a suitable opponent eager to fight. Just by looking at a cock, a Balinese can tell if it's a winner, and if it's worth placing money on. They look at the coloration, size of their bodies and legs, and the size and strength of their feet.

Birds of equal size and spirit are carefully matched, then lined up for a whole series of fights. It's a chaotic scene, extraordinarily stimulating and exciting. The handlers of the first two cocks meet in the center of the ring with the referee *(saya)* and cash is handed over for the central bet. The *juru dalem* signals the amount of the central bet (always even money) to the official timekeeper, which triggers the start of frantic side betting *(koh kesasi).* Pandemonium results as members of the audience exchange codified hand and finger signals placing uneven bets on the favorite and the underdog. The colors of each cock are shouted across the arena; backers confirm their bets first with eye contact, then with intricate finger, palm, and lip movements. If agreed by both parties, a handicap is imposed on an obviously stronger, larger bird by tying the blade at a disadvantageous angle.

It's really a tight money game. Some have a good cock but not enough money to fight him, betting just Rp1000. Others risk as high as Rp100,000, but most bets average Rp5000 (or in the *desa,* less). A whole village has been known to put up as much as a million rupiah on its favorite cock.

No bets are recorded; if a man doesn't honor his bet, he won't be allowed in the *wantilan* again. The only records kept are of money owed to the *banjar* (usually 10% but sometimes 25% of the take). Bets are paid at once with IOUs seldom accepted. After the brokers have squabbled, the bets have been placed, and the opponents are ready, the fight is blessed by a lay priest, the *pemangku.* Offerings to the *bhuta* and *kala* spirits are made in the center of the ring and rice wine poured on the ground. The referee and timekeeper go to their places and the fight starts with a loud gong. An intense stillness descends on the arena.

The Fight

Squatting down, the handlers face each other, firmly holding the excited birds who are pecking and glaring at each other. The cocks are let go as the whole audience moans together. After the first contact, often resulting in the wounding of one cock, they are separated and a series of rounds determines the outcome. Rounds are measured by water-clocks *(ganji),* half a coconut shell with a hole the size of a penny. The timer places it in a bucket of water, and the round *(ceng)* is declared over when the shell sinks (typically around 10 seconds).

Each fight is limited to three rounds but the bouts seldom last that long. The match can very well be finished in five to 10 seconds; with ruffs aflare and feathers flying, the death blow is frequently delivered in the air. The cocks show amazing ferocity even when crippled, and the best cocks can only fight five or 10 times before they are killed or seriously wounded. If a wounded cock cannot be revived and his opponent can stand upright for one *ceng,* the fight is over. If both cocks are still fighting after three rounds, it's a draw (very rare). If one of the cocks runs off, he is disqualified. After a blur of feathers and wings the cocks might suddenly face each other, then one will just keel over dead, the winning bird still flapping its wings, crowing, and pecking vengefully at the corpse.

Sometimes handlers take blood from the wound of a defeated cock and smear it over their bird's beak, giving it a taste of victory. A badly wounded cock can often be revived by artificial respiration or special massages to fight again and win, or kept as a pet out of respect and sentimentality. The losing bird is always given a final chance, and special trainers stand by to tend to injuries between rounds. If his bird is down and out, the owner picks it up and gives it a few seconds to see if it can stand up by itself. If it can't, it's mortally wounded and that's it. If both cocks refuse to continue, the umpire puts them both under a wicker dome basket. One almost always kills the other within the confined space. The winning bird is held aloft as bettors claim their money. The loser is brought straight to a man whose job it is to cut off the bird's leg, take the spur from that leg, and jam it straight into the bird's heart. The owner of the winning cock takes the limp body of the dead rooster home for cooking (a defeated bird is considered tastier than normal). The breast is torn from the body and made into pretty feather dusters.

After another couple of minutes of betting, the next fight starts. As the crescendo of male voices rises it sounds like a gaggle of geese or the speaking in tongues at a revival meeting. When the gong sounds another pair of cocks go at it, and all is silent. Even in these days of illegal, clandestine gaming, the fights may continue until nightfall. It's been observed that much of the Balinese character comes to the surface in the fighting ring because it is not just the cocks who are fighting, it's also men. The great ethnographer and Balinist Clifford Geertz called these bouts of mortal fury "so pure, so absolute, and in their own way so beautiful, as to become abstract—a Platonic concept of hate."

BOB RACE

SPORTS

ON LAND

If you like to play competitive sports, volleyball is popular in many villages and they don't mind you joining a game. You can find a volleyball game just about anytime of day. The Chinese card game *cekian* is also very popular. Aerobics and workout classes have become the rage in some Balinese villages. You can even see Madonna's influence in the leotards with rawhide lacing up the legs. From July through September, kite-flying competitions take place in the rice paddies outside of Sanur. See "Sports" under "Sanur" for more information. If you're into corporate games, there's even a jungle skirmish using paintball pellets; contact **Bali Splat Mas** in Sanur (tel. 0361-289073).

Beggar's Bush Bar and Restaurant, tel. (0361) 975-009, in Campuan, just outside Ubud, is the Bali chapter's headquarters of the Asia-wide **Hash House Harriers** running club. All runs start from here, as your host, Victor Mason, who runs barefoot with his two dogs, steps larger than life out of a Somerset Maugham short story. Victor, who is an author, ornithologist, and long-time Bali resident, also leads **Bali Bird Walks,** taking you through the beautiful countryside around Ubud where you'll see many brilliant birds such as the striking turquoise Java kingfisher and the scarlet-headed flowerpecker. The four-hour walk, suitable for all ages, costs Rp64,000 including binoculars, refreshments, and a well-prepared lunch at the Begger's Bush afterwards. Don't forget shorts, T-shirt, hat, walking shoes, camera, and sunscreen. Walks begin Tuesday, Friday, Saturday, and Sunday mornings at 0915. If Victor isn't there, the walk will be led by several of his very able assistants.

For **trekking** enthusiasts, Sobek offers a three-hour jungle trek with knowledgeable guides that takes you into the wilderness areas around Bedugul. The walk begins high above the twin lakes of Tamblingan and Buyan. You trek through canopied forests, past the unique Danau Dalam Tamblingan temple and enormous creeper-clad trees, then back to your waiting transport. The day ends in a restaurant overlooking picturesque rice terraces. You can do this walk by yourself for much less than the Rp108,000 Sobek charges by just handling your own transport to Lake Tamblingan and hiring a local guide. Take long cotton trousers, a hat, walking shoes, a change of clothes, sunscreen, and your camera.

You can hire forestry guides in west Bali for crosscountry and jungle walks in **Bali Barat National Park.** Inquire at the PHPA Headquarters in Labuhan Lalang. The entrance fee is Rp2000 per person per day, plus Rp2000 per vehicle to park in Labuhan Lalang's parking lot for a day. A guide costs Rp15,000. For all fees and a guide, count on about Rp20,000 per day. A typical walk lasts from 1000 to 1500. If you intend to say overnight, bring a sleeping bag, mosquito netting, and all food and beverages. You can rent camping equipment from the park forestry office at Labuhan Lalang. For more information on walks, see "Getting Around" in the On the Road chapter.

Mountain Climbing

Climbing **Gunung Batur** (1,717 meters) in Bangli District is one of Bali's most heavenly experiences. The sunrise from the top is awesome. To find information on climbing Batur, in the village of Toyabungkah at the base of the volcano look for the sign **CV. Jero Wijaya Tourist Service,** P.O. Box 1, Kintamani 80652, Indonesia, run by I Made Suarsana. He can explain the geologic history of the mountain, show you some excellent maps of the area, and arrange guides to the top. The guide fee includes eggs and bananas cooked in the steaming fissures at the summit, but your guide should be discouraged from engaging in this environmentally polluting practice.

I Wayan Pineh, who works in Surya Homestay in Kedisan, is one of the most experienced professional guides in the whole Batur area. Wayan specializes in leading tourists to the peak and guarantees satisfaction. From the moment he knocks on your door at 0330 until you get back at 0900, He is good-natured and fun. Don't let the weather fool you; if he says it will be clear at the top, you can bet the farm it will be. Wayan also cooks the best volcano eggs and bananas, and he'll take you to see black lava and the bat cave.

The climb up Bali's highest (3,014 meters) and holiest mountain, **Gunung Agung** in Karangasem District of east Bali, is the most arduous of any on the island. The oval crater at the top is 500 meters across and the highest point is on the western edge overlooking Besakih. The shortest and most popular routes are from Selat via Sebudi and from Besakih Temple itself. Refer to the Gunung Agung section of the Karangasem Regency chapter for more information on tackling this imposing peak.

Bicycle Touring

Sobek does a bike tour, "The Batur Trail," which costs Rp115,000. It begins with a drive up to the Kintamani area at 1,700 meters above sea level by a air-conditioned van. After brunch you ride back down a less-trafficked road, an easy-going two-and-a-half-hour trip with one hill that you can ride up in the van or on your bike. Back roads take you through dense rainforests and groves of giant bamboo, and past picture-postcard terraces and sleepy mountain villages. The price includes all transport, mountain bikes, helmets, gloves, breakfast, drinks, and buffet lunch in Ubud. For more experienced cyclists, Sobek offers an off-road tour of twisting mountain tracks, steep-sided gorges, rocky river beds, and rice terrace paths. This two-hour trip takes in superb scenery around the Was River north of Ubud. The price of Rp142,000 includes transport, equipment, refreshment, and lunch. For both tours take along voucher or payment, shorts, a T-shirt, running shoes, sunglasses, sunblock, and camera.

Iskander Wawo-Runtu in Sanur does mountain bike tours from his upland farm in Pupuan down to the sea. You can join the group for a portion of the day, or stay overnight at his house in Pupuan and do a two-day trip. You'll see beautiful rice fields, forests, rivers, steep ravines, and remote villages. Your choice of selected off-road routes for different skill levels. From the starting point in Batungsel village at 1000, the route may take any direction. The price of Iskander's tour includes well-equipped, tough mountain bikes, two guides, and transport to and from your hotel. Hotel pick-up time in Sanur is 0800, drop-off around 1800. Cost: Rp138,000 per person for a minimum of five people per trip. Contact **Meru Bicycle Day Trips** at the Tanjung Sari, Private Bungalows, Jl. D. Tamblingan 41, Sanur (tel. 0361-288441, fax 287930), or at Cafe Batu Jimbar on Jl. D. Tamblingan, tel. 0361-87374. For more on bicycle touring, see the "Getting Around" section of the On the Road chapter.

Tennis

To avoid the heat, tennis time on Bali is 0500 or in the cool evenings. Two girls in *sarung*, stationing themselves at each end of the net, are your ballgirls. Although there are some fine players among them, the Balinese on the whole have a happy-go-lucky attitude toward the game. Seldom rushing the net, they leave you to knock yourself out red-faced from exertion. Learn instead to just play a steady, nonaggressive game on the red-clay courts of the island. For many tourists, this is their only chance to meet Indonesians on equal ground, and vice versa. Tennis courts are found at the Bali Beach Hotel and the Bali Hyatt in Sanur; Pertamina Cottages in Tuban (near Kuta); Hotel Tjampuan in Ubud; and the Bali Golf and Country Club in Pancasari (near Bedugul). You can find tennis courts as part of the resort complex of virtually every hotel in Nusa Dua, and in dozens of other top-end hotels around Bali. In Denpasar, courts are located at Jl. M.T. Haryono, Jl. Kamboja, Putung Karangasem, and in Tanjung Bungkak.

Bungee-Jumping

Australian-based **A.J. Hacket Company** invites you to experience the wonder and excitement of jumping off a 44-meter-high tower tied to a giant rubber band. The platform, manufactured in Australia, overlooks one of southern Bali's most spectacular beachfronts. A professional crew will take you through the preparations, then it's up to you. Or as a spectator, sit back and relax, take a swim, have a drink at the pool bar or a snack, and just watch the jumpers. You can also ride the lift to the viewing platform without jumping, and take in Bali from a new perspective—views stretch from the northern volcanoes to the surfing beach of Ulu Watu. On a clear day you can see Java. The jump only is Rp101,000 including hotel pickup, T-shirt, jump certificate, and comprehensive insurance. Second jump is Rp58,000. Photos and videos of the unimaginable event are extra. Right on the beach at the Double Six Club, Jl. 66, Legian, tel. (0361) 730666, fax 730466. Open 1000 until sunset.

Two other companies have emerged: **Adrenalin** is located to the south on the Kuta-Legian line, and **Bungee-Bali** (tel. 0361-758362 or 941102) offers Bali's highest and only waterfall jump.

Paragliding

Based at windy Bukit Peninsula's Bali Cliff Resort, the qualified professionals of **Waterworld**, tel. (0361) 771992, offer instruction and tandem glides for those wanting to try it first. One of the best locations on the island to take off. No cliff-jumping involved, just a gentle breeze to lift you off the ground. It's easier than it looks, and on a clear day you'll see Bali from a new perspective.

Third World toy

Golf

Five in the morning is golf time; get two hours of exercise and breakfast under your belt by 0800. The finest course in Asia and one of the world's top 50 is the **Bali Golf and Country Club** in Pancasari near Bedugul just north of Lake Bratan. Judged fifth in the world for technical design and service, this 18-hole championship course features tall trees and flowers in riotous colors separating its grand, panoramic fairways. For reservations and information, call tel. (0361) 71791 or 288944, fax 71797. Other courses are the **Bali Golf and Country Club** on Nusa Dua, tel. (0361) 771791 or 771793, and at the **Grand Bali Beach Hotel,** tel. (0361) 288511, in Sanur. All courses have caddies available for hire. You might get a discount by contacting **Bali Discount Golf** (tel. 0361-286044); they provide transfers, greens fees (18 holes), club hire (full set), caddy, and golf cart (Nusa Dua only).

Pony Rides

It's a long, pretty drive down bumpy country roads to the Pony Tour facility deep in Tabanan Regency for this full-day guided circular tour. Horses allow you access to an area only three kilometers west of Tanah Lot, yet almost totally unaffected by tourist development. After a safety talk you'll get a five minute riding lesson to assess your experience and find a suitable mount. You may be led or ride unassisted. Helmets are available as are ponchos if it rains and a fanny pack to carry valuables.

The word "pony" is used because it sounds safer, but these are actually retired racing horses from Java and Sumba. A variety of heights are on hand—from small ponies to larger horses. These aren't your ordinary, trail-weary steeds, they are well cared for and cost as much as seven million rupiah. Like Indonesians, they are small but very strong and highly spirited—miniature versions of classic Arabian stallions. After the horses are fitted with English saddles and snaffle bits, you head out a narrow path through stunning rice fields, bushland, and across rivers. The guides are absolutely first-rate. Ketut, looking like an American Indian chief and always in control, is a magnificent guide and horseman. He'll explain rice growing techniques and you'll get a wonderful tour of a traditional Balinese compound with an explana-

tion of each building. Later you'll ride along the beach, the perfect place to learn. You'll get the quickest cantering lesson you've ever had and see displays of horsemanship that would measure up to any seasoned cowboy or rodeo star.

On returning to the stables, mediocre Balinese food is served cold and there are too many flies; better to eat a pack lunch on the beach instead of near the stables. Nevertheless, this is one of the most glamorous and exciting activities you can do on Bali, an unforgettable day for anyone who loves horses and the Balinese culture.

The Rp115,000 price includes transport, lunch, and refreshments. You're picked up in an air-conditioned van at your hotel in Kuta or Legian at 0830, Sanur and Nusa Dua at 0800; also pickups from Ubud, returning around 1500. Bring long pants, a strong pair of shoes (no thongs), sun hat, sunblock, and a bathing suit and towel if you want to swim in the ocean. Changing rooms are available at the stables. Sign up at the **Mesari Beach Inn,** Jl. Dhyana Pura in Legian, or call P.T. Bali Jaran Jaran Kencana, Loji Garden Hotel, Legian, tel. (0361) 751672 or 751746, fax 751746. Office hours 0800-1600; after office hours tel. 751672 or 751572. Also ask about the Sunset Pony Tour.

SURFING

Bali's surf is world class, with power and speed comparable to Hawaii. Surfers who have experienced waves from Santa Cruz to Baja claim that Bali's surf is superior to any along the United States' West Coast. Drawn by the surf, thousands of Californians, Japanese, Australians, and Brazilians arrive each year to test themselves on Bali's famous tubular waves. International and professional surfers train on Bali for the prize money on the contest circuit around the Pacific. Bali's Annual Surf Championships are held at Suluban, not far from Jimbaran, but the logistics of the Bukit Peninsula make it difficult to hold big events like the Quicksilver Pro contest.

Venturing into the surf beginning around 1972, a breed of hip young Balinese surfers evolved, wearing neo-primitive neck pendants, talking about their boards, and calling you "Mate" or "Hey, Spunky!" Their fluid movements, control, robust natures, and easy-going lifestyle make

WHERE TO SURF

Kuta Beach

Kuta and Legian offer some excellent recreational waves of up to two meters, fanned and given shape by the offshore winds for at least nine months of the year. During the summer (Dec.-Feb.) the weather is inconsistent, from clear and calm to cyclone and back in five hours. Watch out for hardpacked sand, sneaky undertows, and cross-currents, and heed the danger signs posted on the beach. Around Kuta there's a wide range of boards for rent (Rp2500 per day, Rp10,000 per week) and for sale against *losmen* walls. Buy wax for your board at Sunshine Surfboard Shop, Jl. Legian near Legian.

Kuta is so popular that there could be as many as 200 surfers out on a good day, with a particularly heavy local component. It's difficult to escape the crowds even if you paddle way out. Best is to take a *jukung* out (Rp3000 roundtrip); the surf is safer; the boat boys will advise where it's all happening. Kuta Reef, which surrounds the end of the runway approximately one-half km offshore, creates fast left-handers which sometimes attain three meters without boiling or sucking dry over the shallow coral reef. Another left-hander, usually bigger than Kuta Reef, breaks just off the channel in front of the Pertamina Cottages. Because of its easy takeoff, this is an ideal wave for beginners. South of

the airstrip you'll find some big right-handers during high tide (pick a windless day); take a *prahu* (Rp10,000 return). For an easygoing right-hander, check out the Canggu lava ledge on the northern extremity of the bay; take Legian Road north to Krobokan, then at the intersection turn left down to the beach.

Uluwatu

Lying on the southerly tip facing the menacing Indian Ocean, in the driest part of the island, the Balinese consider Uluwatu ruled by "left" black magic energy. With its impressive cliffs, remote beaches, endless sunshine, and heaps of bikini girls, this is one of the premier surfing spots on the planet. From the road at the top of the cliffs where the *bemo* drops you off, boys will carry your surfboard and equipment the three kilometers down to the gorge for around Rp1000. Or a motorcycle will take you most of the way down; park it by the gorge. Climb down into the large sea cave at the bottom of the cliff which opens to the ocean, the only way to paddle out to the waves.

Since it sits on the extremity of the bay, Ulu picks up bigger swells than Sanur or Kuta. Get there early for the morning session when it's not uncommon that sets of 10 waves continue for two or three

the Balinese skillful and ardent surfers. Usually the majority, with their own surf clubs, they can be found in numbers at nearly all beaches. They also tend to be hotheaded if surfing etiquette or territory is breached. Drop in on them and they could get physical. They'll be quick to remind you that this is their country, their waves, so don't bring your home beach mentality with you.

Surfing Seasons

Considered a mecca for warm water surfing, Bali gets the full force of ocean swells breaking over shallow coral reefs. Winds blow away from the land, bringing trade winds which give shape and consistency to the waves. Bali offers good surf all year long, but the best, most consistent swells are from June to August. It's the best known surfing locale in Indonesia.

The island experiences a hot, wet season (Nov.-Feb.) and a long, cooler dry season

(March-Oct.). During the dry, winds for the most part are from the northwest and often accompanied by rain squalls, creating large waves on the Nusa Dua-Sanur side of the island. When the winds get too strong, though, Nusa Dua is usually blown out. Also during the dry season, the northeast tradewinds make respectable offshore breaks at Uluwatu, G'Land, and Nusa Lembongan Island. The months in-between have variable conditions and winds. Bali's worst wind for surfing is a southerly. The Nusa Dua headland, for example, will divide the flow on both the Uluwatu and Nusa Dua sides. Tides also play a big role in the type, duration, and size of swells. The best tides come in during the full and new lunar phases.

Sudden, powerful cyclones in the Indian Ocean dramatically increase the size of swells. The waters around Bali have the advantage of being warm year-round; in the wet season the hours. When the offshore winds are coming in, it's almost impossible to take off on some of Ulu's two- and three-meter waves. Thatched *warung* in a row above the cave sell drinks, food, snacks, and beds for the night. From here you can survey what the other surfers are doing and decide which of the six different breaks you want to take on—the Peak, the Race Track, the Bommie, the Outside Corner, etc. If they haven't all been slaughtered by the time you get there, giant sea turtles and dugongs can sometimes be seen in the water.

Padang Padang

Uluwatu's status as the number one surfing spot has since been challenged by Padang Padang, a shallow reef break just two km down the coast on the southern tip of Bali. *Surfer Magazine* has called Padang Padang "one of the 10 best surf spots in the world." The hollow left-handers here are some of the most consistent in the world, which is essential for competition. Since Padang Padang receives swells from storms generated deep in the Indian Ocean, the tides can swell from a half-meter low to extraordinary highs of six to eight meters in a matter of hours. Very risky below mid-tide. From Uluwatu, take the narrow track along the cliff, then climb down to the beach, or ask for the car/bike track down to the beach. Imposing coastal scenery.

Sanur

Easily reached by *bemo*, Sanur lies on the east coast opposite Kuta Beach. The break in front of the Bali Beach Hotel maintains fast, good-sized, hollow right reef breaks at four or five meters; beware of the strong current. When the wind turns onshore at Kuta, it turns offshore at Sanur. Best in the wet season (Oct-April). Depending on swell size and direction, Sanur can be surfed at any tide. When it's on, this is a world-class wave. Lots of locals. At high tide in front of the Sanur Beach market there's a very sharp, fast, short left-hander. For bigger waves, hire one of the sailboats to take you out to the channel (Rp4000) in front of the Bali Hyatt, but in a high wind and rips the spot can be lethal.

Nusa Lembongan and Medewi

Another superb surfing spot is Nusa Lembongan, a small island off the east coast near the island of Nusa Penida. Take a *prahu* from Sanur (at least three daily, two- or three-hours' passage) for Rp5000 per person, or a group can charter one for Rp30,000. Stay in Wayan's Bungalows in front of the old shipwreck. There are three main breaks in this vicinity. Also check out Medewi, near Negara, about 75 km on the main road west of Denpasar. Several *losmen* to stay in.

average temperatures are in the 80s F, but a vest or spring suit is needed during the dry when temperatures can drop into the 70s at exposed locations. The dry season is best because there's less humidity and evenings are cool.

Surfing Locales

The best surfing spots are crowded during the dry season, but since there are so many the experienced wave rider is always able to find his own retreat. Pride of place goes to Uluwatu and nearby Padang Padang on the Bukit Peninsula, which get swells churned in storms in the Indian Ocean during the wet season. For more detailed info, look up each surf spot in the travel chapters.

Uluwatu, famous for its left break, is ringed by high cliffs which surfers must climb down to reach a large sea cave. This is the only way to paddle out to breaks with names like The Race Track, the Peak, The Bommie, The Inside Corner, the Outside Corner—about seven breaks in all. If the current is too strong to reach the cave or the reef in front, make for the beach. Get here from Kuta by *bemo* (30 minutes), then walk about three km. Or get a motorbike, which will take you most of the way in. **Padang Padang,** north of Uluwatu toward Kuta, can be reached by walking a cliff path from Uluwatu, then climbing down to the beach, or by car or motorcycle from Kuta. The very shallow, hollow left here is treacherous because of the cliffs. It's not for beginners, and don't surf if there are too many surfers. Very popular is **Bingin,** near Padang Padang, a hollow left best at medium to low tides.

Kuta and Legian beaches are not an episode out of Baywatch. With a vicious undertow, the inviting appearance of the waves at **Kuta Beach** can be deceptive. An average of 40 people still drown each year off Kuta and Legian. Always stay within the clearly marked red and yellow flags. Lifeguards constantly patrol the beach during daylight. **Kuta Reef,** a long stretch of coral about one km out to sea, is best known for its left-hand break. Most riders take an outrigger to this reef, then get picked up again at a specified time. When the wind turns offshore at Kuta, surfers evacuate for Sanur on the other side of the island where the wind is onshore.

Sanur's famous hollow right-hand break is considered by many the best on the island—when it's working, which is only about 25 days a year. Sanur is sheltered from most waves so the swell needs to be big to get in here. When it does, the walls line up down the reef for long, fast rides. It's imperative that you pull out before the final dredgeout or you'll be driven against the reef. **Nusa Dua** offers a consistent right-hander through the wet season, though consistency means big crowds. Hire a boat for the return trip because the best waves are far offshore. On the way out are lefts and rights but the outside rights are the main attraction—steep takeoffs and fast bowling walls. This high quality wave is known as the Sunset of Bali. In this same area, just in front of Club Med, is a very fast, difficult right-hander known as Sri Lanka.

Surfing is a big attraction at **Nusa Lembongan,** a small isle off the southeast coast. Three of the most superb though deadly breaks in the world can be found off the west side of the island. This uncrowded surf is reasonably accessible from Sanur, just two hours by motorized boat. You can stay in very inexpensive and comfortable beach inns strung out in the small fishing/surfing village of Jungut Batu. The adjacent, larger island of **Nusa Penida** to the east, has abundant surf but dangerous coral. Other locales include **Tanjung Sari, Serangan, Canggu** near the village of Krobokan, **Medewi** about 75 km west of Denpasar, and **Padangbai** on the east coast. The jetties at **Candidasa** were built to protect the beach and create a nice environment to swim in, but the surf is located out to sea. Nearly all of these surfing spots have *warung* where you can do the dharma bum thing: eat, drink, nap, even stay overnight in makeshift thatch shelters.

Transport

Surfers usually charter *bemo* to their favorite beaches. From Kuta, it costs a group of four

around Rp15,000 to have the *bemo* drop you off in Uluwatu and pick you up three hours later. A motorcycle (Rp12,000 and up per day) can travel the more difficult tracks to remote beaches, although in the wet season the tracks become muddy and slippery. Get a strong board strap (with foam padding) or sew a strap to your board cover so it can be carried on a motorcycle.

Safety

Although a visit to Bali is one of the world's best surfing holidays, don't take on too much at once. Familiarize yourself with the coral reef breaks, and ease into it, taking on more formidable breaks gradually. For protection against the merciless Balinese sun, always wear sunscreen and a T-shirt. In case of broken bones, cuts, or infections from live coral reefs, get yourself to the **Nusa Dua Clinic** on Jl. Pratama 81 A-B, tel. (0361) 771324, or the new emergency annex at Denpasar's **Sanglah Hospital** on Jl. Bali 5, tel. (0361) 235546. All the top-class hotels have resident physicians who are familiar with surfing injuries. Watch when paddling across shallow reefs; the reef-dwelling sea urchin is a brownish sphere covered in 20- to 25-cm-long spines. With a needle, remove the spines very carefully without breaking them. Urinate on the wound or place it in thick mud to relieve the pain. Hot water or methylated spirit baths help too. Surfers may also be called upon to give mouth-to-mouth resuscitation. A well-equipped first-aid kit, including elastoplast and needles to remove sea-urchin spines, is a must. Refer to the Health section later in this chapter

What to Bring

Bring a snorkel, fins, mask, wetsuit vest, small daypack, surfboard repair kit, silver tape, at least five blocks of wax, and the widest, waffle-bottom running shoes you can find. For most of your surfwear and accessories, shop at **Rip Curl** on Jl. Legian Kelod, tel. (0361) 754455, but expect high prices compared to Australia or the U.S.A. Bring your own board as most of the ones available in Bali are pretty ratty by the time they're old enough to be hired out. Better ones are available at higher prices (Rp7000-10,000 per day). California and Australian-style short boards are okay for the breaks at Kuta Beach, but you'll need at least a seven-foot board for the bigger waves at

Uluwatu and Padang Padang. For fast waves, like Uluwatu's, a semi- to full-gun design is recommended. If you don't have a good travel cover, use bubble plastic. Take special care in packing detachable fins in your luggage or consider taking along extras. You can't count on replacing them here. Hardsole wetsuit booties are critical when walking across coral reefs at low tide. A wetsuit vest gives warmth in cold winds and protects against falls on coral.

Garuda's baggage allowance is 20 kg (44 pounds) in economy class (based on weight, not the number of pieces). A surfboard is considered part of this allowance and will be transported at no extra cost as long as the entire weight (including surfboard) does not exceed 20 kg. Garuda personnel often look the other way, but don't push it.

Surf Tours

A few outfits in Benoa, Sanur, and Nusa Dua specialize in surfing excursions on private boats to premier surfing spots around Bali and Indonesia's southeastern Islands. A weeklong safari to Lombok and Sumbawa is organized by Mainski Inn on Nusa Lembongan. They'll take you to some wonderful breaks that can't be reached by land. Contact **Offshore Adventure,** P.O. Box 636, Epping 2121, N.S.W., Australia, tel./fax 02-868-1265. About US$100 per person per day, all expenses paid.

SNORKELING AND SCUBA DIVING

Bali is a scuba, spearfishing, and snorkeling center, famous among divers for marinelife, superb visibility, and sensational dropoffs. Six hundred km of coastline and numerous offshore islands offer a wide range of snorkeling and diving locations. Your options include one of many operators offering snorkeling and diving trips or join an all-inclusive package that sails to dive sites around Bali and islands to the east. If it's not monsoon season (Oct.-April), count on warm tropical waters around 80° F.

Snorkeling is an excellent and safe activity for children. Abundant marinelife can be enjoyed on the reefs off Sanur, Nusa Dua, Lovina, and Padangbai—all accessible by boat. Snorkeling can be enjoyed anywhere there's scuba diving—if an area has good coral reefs, there will be snorkeling gear for rent. Scuba diving is more expensive, frequently requiring land or sea transport to the best dive locations. The best diving on Bali is from around five to twenty meters, though during the wet season storms may reduce visibility. Drift diving was made popular on Bali because techniques were needed to accommodate the deep currents surrounding the island. Divers usually suit up on the beach in front of the dive master's favorite restaurant (where he'll receive a kickback later on). Most operators take divers (two people per boat) to the dive site in outriggers *(jukung)* fitted with small outboard motors. Passengers often get soaked, no matter how skilled the boatmen, and sometimes you have to clear the boat off a fringing reef.

Costs

Price depends on the number of people in your group and where you start. Dives are not much less than you'd pay in the U.S., Europe, or Australia, they're quite reasonable considering the personalized nature of the tours and the amenities: two tanks, weightbelt, wetsuits, refreshment, and experienced dive masters. Also lunch, transport to the site, excellent Balinese-style accommodations, even porters to and from the beach. Operators will pick you up at Kuta, Legian, or Sanur for free. But from the Ubud or Tanah Lot areas, there's an extra charge of Rp15,000. Shop around and carefully examine an operator's "Diving Menu." There could be as much as a Rp46,000 difference in price. One way to save money is to arrange your own transportation to the site and rent directly from the dive shop there, or bring your own equipment: a mask, snorkel, and fins rent for Rp6000, marine gloves Rp4000, B.C.D. Rp10,000, regulators Rp10,000, wetsuits Rp6000, underwater torch Rp15,000, motor marine camera Rp30,000. Rental gear varies in quality, but some outfits use top-class Bauer compressors and Scubapro equipment.

Typical prices from any of the southern resorts like Sanur: one dive in Sanur/Nusa Dua Rp128,000, Padangbai Rp153,000, Tulamben/Amed Rp162,000, Nusa Lembongan/ Ceningan/ Penida Rp195,000, night dive Rp128,000, extra dive Rp34,500, overnight dive (room and board) Rp218,500, beginner dive Rp230,000 full day,

Rp175,000 half-day. For certification: PADI/CMAS course (if over 15 years old) Rp805,000, two-day Advance Open Water Course Rp655,000.

Dive Operators

Bali is one of the best places to learn how to dive. Even though the island is not the best dive locale in Indonesia, it does have the greatest concentration of dive operators. Most are in and around Sanur, and most hotels have dive desks or can put you in touch with an operator who not only sell half-day trips to Nusa Dua and Sanur, but also fully equipped, all-inclusive safaris lasting from three to 14 days. Agencies can also can arrange for parasailing, jet skis, paddle canoes, waterskiing, and banana boats.

Baruna Water Sports, tel. (0361) 753820 or 751223, the oldest and largest dive operator on Bali, handles about 35,000 guests each year. Baruna has the only privately owned decompression chamber on Bali, state-of-the-art compressors, dozens of boats, and 35 guides. The company is under the ownership of a 55-year-old German with over 6,000 dives under his belt. They have sales counters at the Bali Beach Hotel, tel. (0361) 288511, ext. 764, and Bali Hyatt Hotel, tel. (0361) 288271, ext 93, in Sanur, and at the Bali Sol Hotel, tel. (0361) 71350, and Putri Bali Hotel, tel. (0361) 71020, ext. 7737, in Nusa Dua.

Other operators in the Sanur/Nusa Dua area include: **Dive & Dives,** Jl. Bypass 23, Sanur, tel. (0361) 288052 or 289309, offers a four-day PADI open water course for Rp600,000. Request an English or Japanese instructor. They run a well-stocked shop with US Divers, Scubapro, Sea Quest, and TUSA equipment, as well as rentals and service. **Oceania Dive Center** is efficient, well managed, and very enthusiastic. Their office is easy to find, only 200 meters before the first traffic light if coming from Kuta at Jl. Bypass no. 78XX in Sanur, tel. (0361) 288652 or 288892, fax 288652. All divers insured to Rp50 million. Oceania is Bali's only dive outfit selling expensive, good quality scuba gear, and the rental equipment is reliable.

Bali Marine Sports, Jl. Bypass, Blanjong, Sanur, tel. (0361) 287872, 288776, or 289308, fax 287872, P.O. Box 672, Denpasar. **Barrakuda Bali Dive,** Jl. Pratama 34 A, Nusa Dua, tel. (0361) 772130, ext. 731, fax 772131.

In other areas try: **Bali Diving Perdana,** Jl. Danau Poso Gang Tunjung 30, tel. (0361) 286493, fax 288871, which offers an introductory scuba diving program. Lessons start in a freshwater pool or their protected saltwater basin, then go out for the real thing. They also have the full range of tours to Tulemben, Menjangan, and other sites. **Ena Dive Centre** offers special PADI international dive courses in both English and Japanese. Head office is at Jl. Pangembak 7, Denpasar, tel. (0361) 287945 or 287134. Besides the specialized dive outfits listed, a number of boats make day trips which include snorkeling. Call the agency representing the sailing ketch *Golden Hawk* to join a cruise over to Nusa Lembongan for Rp177,500 per person (capacity 30 people). You anchor in a small bay and go snorkeling (and skin diving with a day's notice). Climb a small hill and see the sun setting over Bali.

Information

Balinese dive guides don't have literature, the best operators employ guides proficient in both English and Japanese. Bring your own information or learn Indonesian. You don't want just a floating babysitter, but someone who can point things out like turtle-sand mantras. For Pulau Menjangan, you'll need interpretive material. Anyone really serious about diving in Bali, as well in the rest of Indonesia, should get ahold of the latest Periplus Travel Guide *Underwater Indonesia* by Kal Muller. This excellent dive guide contains color photos, essays on reef ecology, local geography, history, charts of site conditions, and maps.

Safety

Bring your scuba certification—whether PADI, BSAC, NAUI, SSI, or FAUI. Bali's dive operators will not take you out without an internationally recognized certificate. If you want to learn how to dive, dozens of companies specialize in PADI and introductory one-day courses using fully qualified teachers and divers. Although virtually every piece of equipment you could possibly need is available on Bali, hardcore divers might consider taking along their own masks and regulators. Before diving, your instructor will make an offering to the gods of the sea. Always go with a dive master or guide who knows the area, and who's made the dive before. Make sure your guide is paying attention to your safety. Don't let him take you somewhere beyond your skill level, and make sure you don't get bad air.

Dive Sites

Despite the explosion of tourism since the 1960s, Bali still has at least 10 very attractive sites, each offering different skill levels. Only at Sanur and Nusa Dua do you have to be experienced. Always try to dive with others of the same skill level. It's not very satisfying for anyone when amateurs dive with experts, which can happen if it suits the needs of the dive operator. For more information about individual dive sites, refer to the travel chapters.

Padangbai, 90 km northeast of Sanur, is a favorite scuba spot where you can dive from the beach or a boat offshore. Dives are from three to 20 meters, and the current can be very strong. This underwater wonderland is populated by fish of every size, shape, and color, including harmless reef sharks. Dive along the coast or take a *prahu* to the spectacular reefs offshore or around **Pulau Kambing.** Ideal for the open water diver course, there are several isolated bays nearby with white beaches, numerous inexpensive accommodations, and restaurants. When diving off the islands near the east coast in the Candidasa area, for example, the waters can be very cold so you'll need a wetsuit.

Balina Beach, a resort between Padangbai and Candidasa in east Bali, employs an impressive team of five professional dive guides, a dive master, and a PADI open water instructor. Rates start at Rp80,000 for two dives on **Pulau Kambing,** which has fascinating Blue Hole, large turtles, napoleon fish, pelagic tuna, and reef sharks between three and 40 meters. Tours are available in English, Dutch, or German. Room rates for the Nelayan Village Cottages: Rp70,000-90,000.

Five specialized dive *losmen* have sprung up southeast of Amed. These small northeastern resorts rent snorkeling equipment and arrange for transport and boats. This "lost coast" has beautiful, solitary, stony black beaches. Enter the water down a sandy slope followed by a dropoff (three to 33 meters) with fully grown anenome, gorgonia, sponges, and fish of all sizes.

Sambirenteng, a village on the northeast coast between Tulamben and Tejakula, is a new dive site about 100 km from Kuta. One of the best dive *losmen* on Bali, a long coral reef 15 meters from the hotel is terraced down to 35 meters. Since this entire area is under protection, the stock of fish is enormous. The German-run Alam Anda dive complex, tel. (0361) 752296, issues CMAS certificates and offers dive tours for only Rp50,000, using high grade equipment in top condition. Kadek, the Bali-

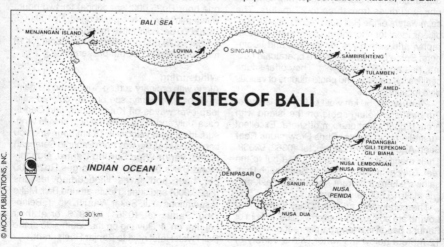

DIVE SITES OF BALI

nese dive master, is outstanding. Stay in one of six spacious bungalows (capacity five persons) for Rp90,000. Twenty-five km to the northwest, **Tulamben,** is a superb dive site. The main attraction is the wreck of an American merchantman one and a half km to the east. Sunk during WW II, it's now completely overgrown with anemone, gorgonia, sponges, and corals, making for dramatic and adventurous diving to depths of 10-40 meters. Ideal for divers of all levels. Stay at Paradise Palm Beach Bungalows (Rp25,000 d) with a restaurant and excellent snorkeling right out front.

Remote **Pulau Menjangan,** an island surrounded by coral reefs off the northwest coast, is in the middle of a 6,600-hectare marine reserve. Offering outstanding unspoiled diving, these deep waters abound in dolphins, black marlin, whales, yellowtails, and 10-meter toothless whale sharks. Full of gorgonians and black coral trees, the wall is similar to the one at Bunaken (North Sulawesi). To get to these reefs you must hire a boat at Rp42,000 per hour (four persons maximum). If you're alone, it's the same price, so wait for other people to go in with you. Day trips to Menjangan are possible but the long distances make it more practical to stay at nearby Pemuteran or Lovina.

Lovina Beach, on the north coast west of Singaraja, offers sloping underwater topography, and dives from three to 27 meters. The calm waters of the Bali Sea create pool-like conditions ideal for snorkeling, underwater photography, and safe dives for families and beginners. **Spice Dive,** the only dive operator in Lovina, has an office in Arya's. They offer scuba certification courses and photo albums of various dive locations.

Pemuteran, 50 km west of Lovina, is one of the best snorkeling spots on the island with great dropoffs just one km offshore. Excellent Australian dive master Chris Brown runs **Reef Seen Aquatics Dive Centre,** tel. (0362) 92339. Their modified dive *prahu* take you out to the reef. Stay at first-rate Pondok Sari Beach Bungalows where they rent snorkeling mask and fins at Rp15,000 for five hours.

The coral reefs at **Nusa Dua, Sanur,** and **Lovina** are popular snorkeling locales. In front of Sanur's beach is a long barrier reef only two to 12 meters below the water with a variety of corals, sponges, and tens of thousands of fish. Nusa Dua is known for its beautiful white beach and a variety of stunning corals, fish, and sponges; dives between three and 20 meters are the most rewarding.

Nusa Penida dive sites can be reached in two hours by boat from Sanur. Dives vary in depth from three to 40 meters and offer white sandy bottoms, cool crystal-clear water, and a tremendous assortment of colorful fish. **Nusa Lembongan,** one of two small islands off Nusa Penida, has also become a mecca for divers. The beach slopes gently out to the reef, and the best diving is from five to 20 meters where you'll see famous underwater sea grottoes. No dive operators yet in the main resort/fishing village of Jungut Batu.

OTHER WATER SPORTS

If you're really into water sports, stay in Nusa Dua, Sanur, or Tanjung Benoa, Candidasa on the coast, or Bedugul in the mountains of Tabanan Regency. Dozens of sea sport agencies line Sanur's main street, offering waterskiing, jet skiing, parasailing, windsurfing, and chartered sailboats. Sample prices: jet ski for 15 minutes Rp40,000; parasail for Rp20,000 per round; water-ski for 15 minutes Rp20,000; windsurf for one hour Rp25,000; speedboat for two hours with a minimum of two passengers Rp100,000, Rp20,000 per hour with a maximum of four; paddle cat Rp20,000 per hour; banana boat for 15 minutes at Rp20,000 per passenger.

Windsurfing
Along with ordinary surfing, windsurfing is gaining great popularity; see brightly colored sails leap over waves off Kuta, Sanur, and Candidasa. July and August are the best time to windsurf. Ideal wind velocity is 15 km/hour, and you can windsurf all the way from Sanur to Serangan Island. **Sanur Wind Surfing Centre,** probably offers Bali's best service, charges Rp25,000 per hour and gives windsurfing lessons (Rp30,000) and surfing tours around Bali. Make reservations at Jl. Sekar Waru II, No. 1, Belanjong, Sanur, tel. (0361) 288976, or at their counter on Jl. Duyung on the south side of the Bali Hyatt Hotel next to Banjar Restaurant.

Swimming

The safest areas to swim are the coral lagoons abutting Sanur, Nusa Dua, and Candidasa. Kuta and Legian boast excellent bodysurfing with crystal-clear water and top-to-bottom tubes. For your own safety, swim only between the red and yellow flags, never after sunset, and don't swim deeper than your body length. The undertow off Kuta/Legian is extremely treacherous and unpredictable. One of Bali's nicest, least known beaches for swimming is at the airport end of Kuta in Tuban. Virtually all of the luxury-class hotels, and a growing number of small, moderately priced hotels, have swimming pools, open to nonguests for Rp2000-3000.

Waterbom Park

Six hundred meters of slides and other aquatic thrills make up this beautifully landscaped three-and-a-half-hectare park. Two twisting, looping jungle rides, an adventurous run on a two-seat tube raft, 250-meter-long circular lazy river rapids and cascading waterfall, water race tracks where you can reach speeds of 50 kph, children's area, large pleasure pool with underwater music, underwater volleyball, and a swim-up bar. The water here is chlorinated by a state-of-the-art saltwater system, and the park offers a tranquil environment undernearth a large, shady, coconut grove with no vendors. Food ranges from croissants and gourmet sandwiches on fresh bread to homemade ice cream and an honest burger. There's swimgear and accessories shops, changing rooms, showers, lockers, and towel rental. The staff keeps a careful eye out for young children. Located on Jl. Kartika Plaza in Tuban, open 0900-1800, tel. (0361) 755676. Adults Rp15,000, children (five to 12) Rp8000, children under five years free. Season passes and group rates available.

Penyu Dewata, Box 666, Sanur, tel. (0361) 89211 or 89212, is a nine-hectare water park in Padang Galak in the delta of the Ayung River. The olympic-size pools are cleaned regularly, certified lifeguards are on hand, and there's a cafeteria, lockers, and changing rooms. Children can take lessons from qualified and experienced instructors.

Game Fishing

For years local Balinese fishermen trolled "feathers," brightly colored lures of plastic or rope, baiting the Spanish mackerel that populated Bali's waters. Farther out, *jukung* plied the waters off Nusa Penida for prized red snapper. With the rise of the Japanese market in the late 1980s, fleets of fishing boats based themselves at Benoa, which also became Bali's sport fishing base.

There are dozens of operators to take tourists game fishing. One of the best tours is onboard the **Simone II,** a high-tech, high speed, American designed vessel powered by twin 300-hp motors. It's equipped with game rods from 20 to 80 pounds, a tower overlooking the large aft deck, a shower, toilet, fridge, microwave oven, and a "V" berth.

Passengers are picked up at their hotel at 0800; the *Simone* departs Benoa around 0830 for the fishing grounds. These waters harbor several species of dolphin, whales, sharks, and giant manta rays near Nusa Penida. The predominant species are the yellowfin tuna, blue an, dogtooth, Spanish mackerel, wahoo, and mahimahi. Off the coast of Candidasa and the south coast of Lombok are the game angler targets—sailfish and black marlin. Below the 100-meter-high cliffs at Nusa Penida is the habitat of large tuna. The area off the southwestern coast is known for big yellowfin tuna. Releasing rare billfish is encouraged, preserving these species and bringing enjoyment to other anglers. At the end of a hard day's angling a delicious buffet lunch is served, unless a catch results in instant sashimi.

Trawling and coral fishing is offered by the **Sea Rover** for Rp690,000 per day (maximum four persons). Departing Benoa Harbor at 0900, returning at 1600, the price includes return hotel transport, an experienced crew, ice cold beer, soft drinks, or mineral water, delicious box lunch, fishing equipment, and bait. The *Rover* sails down Bali's coast, following the birds to the best fishing spots. For more information on both the *Simone III* and the *Sea Rover,* contact P.T. Tour Devco Benoa, tel. (0361) 231591, fax 231592. Book at least a day ahead; for extensions, book one week ahead.

A one-day fishing tour is offered by the **Ena Dive Center.** Pick-up is at your hotel at 0800, then climb aboard a specially built outrigger with trawling and deep sea fishing gear for the trip to Nusa Penida. Off Nusa Lembongan you can also enjoy snorkeling in unspoiled coral gardens. Rp138,000 per passenger, four passenger minimum. For reservations, call tel. (0361) 287945 or 286446, fax 287945, or visit their office at Jl. Tirta Ening 26 Sanur, Box 3798, Denpasar. **Bali Marine Sports,** Jl. Bypass, Blanjong, Sanur, tel. (0361) 287872, 288776, or 289308, offers a "sea tour with fishing" to Lembongan, designed along the same lines. The *White Marlin* fishing boat can be chartered for eight hours to Nusa Lembongan and Nusa Penida: for deep sea excursions Rp805,000, coral fishing Rp172,500, troll fishing Rp218,500. Reserve a place by contacting **Bali Camar Yacht Charter,** tel. (0361) 720591 or 771956, fax 720592.

Glass-Bottom Boat Tours

The *Sea Rover* departs at 1030 from Benoa Harbor, returning at 1300. For Rp35,000, the tour includes onboard tour guide, soft drink, delicious lunch box, equipment, coral viewing, snorkeling, a visit to Turtle Island, and transport back to your hotel. Children under 10 are half price. You dive on a rugged, colorful reef, teeming with tropical fish. Contact **P.T. Tourdevco,** Benoa Harbor, tel. (0361) 231591, fax 231592, or their home office at Jl. Segara Werdi 6, Tanjung Benoa, tel. (0361) 72535. Other outfits, like **Bali Marine Sports,** Jl. Bypass, Sanur, tel. (0361) 287872, 288776, or 289308, fax 287872, charge only Rp25,000 per person, with a minimum three people, for a one hour tour. A variation on the glass-bottom theme is the **Beluga Submarine Tour.** Experience exotic underwater scenes from the comfort of a sophisticated submarine. With the help of specially designed floodlights, you'll be able to observe tropical fish, delicate corals, and unusual plantlife. For more information and reservations, call **P.T. Submarine Safaris Asia,** Jl. Segara Kidul 3, Tanjung Benoa, Bali, tel. (0361) 80361. The *Island Princess* sails on Monday, Wednesday, and Saturday and is one of the cheapest excursions available. For only Rp113,000 you get hotel pickup at 0800, morning and afternoon tea or coffee, fresh fruit, a flame-grilled barbecue, snorkeling, game fishing (trolling), and a bus tour of Nusa Penida Island. Book where you pick up their brochure, or call direct to **Island Explorer Cruises,** Jl. Sekar Waru 8, Sanur, tel. (0361) 289856.

Dolphin Watching

The two principle sites for commercial outings are off Candidasa (Karangasem) on the east coast and Lovina (Buleleng) on the north coast. However, you have a fairly good chance of seeing dolphins anytime you go out on a boat in Bali's waters. On average five or six boats follow the dolphins, then turn off their motors to experience the dolphins flipping, diving, and blowing. In a split second they're gone. You may go out and not see one dolphin—it's hit or miss. Kids sell tickets on the beach for Rp6000-15,000 including breakfast and drinks. Book the day before and give them your room number. They'll wake you up 15 minutes before departure.

Sobek Whitewater Rafting

Run by Sobek Adventures, with 18 years in the business, this fast, exciting, yet safe two-hour trip on the stunning Ayung River is a blast. Not only is the Ayung Bali's longest river but it flows year-round. The nine-km run is expensive, but rafting is one of the best ways to see things you normally can't, namely one of Bali's last original rainforests. This excursion is just dangerous enough to be scary but it's not life-threatening. There are 21 rapids in all, but none hairier than Class II. You'll raft under a large, pounding waterfall, ram into stone walls, take on water, and piroutte with your skilled captain. If you're with a young group, there's lots of splashing, passenger dunking, and raft bumping, so if you want a sedate experience choose a group of older thrill-seekers.

The trip is a botanist's delight and the safest means to enjoy nature really close up. Sadly, you won't see much wildlife. First you'll descend a twisting hillside track to the river where you receive a stern safety lecture about water safety, rafting commands, and what to do if the raft capsizes. It's all very safe with high-standard bright yellow helmets, paddles, and life jackets required—plus Rp58,000,000 insurance coverage.

The service and facilities are international standard. Each Avon self-bailing raft holds four to six people, depending on size. The captains are well trained and extremely capable but also know how to have fun. They have pulleys, throwbags, and first-aid kits and know how to use them. Ask for the Batak, Jungle Johnson—the most experienced. In spite of the first sharp bend, the overall run is ideal for children because the river is shallow. If the raft turns over you can just stand up. Two snapshots of your gasping, screaming group are provided. Copies are available at the end of the trip for Rp3500 apiece.

The cost is Rp145,000 (you may be able to get a 10% discount from Cafe Wayan in Ubud). Book where you see the red raft brochures on hotel and restaurant countertops, or phone one of their English-speaking guides at (0361) 287059. Their headquarters is at Jl. Bypass Ngurah Rai 56 X, Sanur. At no extra charge Sobek will pick you or your group up in an a/c van at your hotel almost anywhere on Bali. A new private road leads to the rafting base in the mountain village of Begawan.

Bring a voucher or payment, shorts or bathing suit, loose-fitting T-shirt, towel, Teva-type sandals or rubber-soled river shoes, hat, sunblock, a change of clothes (changing rooms and showers available), and a camera (they have a dry bag). Near the village of Kedewetan at the end of the trip, a big Indonesian-style, all-you-can-eat buffet, catered by Ubud's Cafe Wayan, is waiting for you. First-class dining! Without lunch the cost is Rp135,000. Sobek also offers **Class IV Wild Whitewater** on the West Bali River, leaving Kuta at 0700 and arriving back at 1700. This trip is Rp150,000 because it takes longer to get there. Limited space so confirm your booking in advance.

Other Rafting Outfits

As a result of Sobek's wild success, a whole slew of rafting companies has opened up. Of-fering tours to the island's first Class IV river, is **Bali Safari Rafting**, Jl. Hayam Wuruk 88 A, Denpasar 80235, tel. (0361) 221315 or 221-316, fax 232-268. For those who enjoy the spills and thrills of whitewater rapids, the full day excursion includes transfers, lunch, and experienced guides for Rp149,000. The run down the Telaga Waja River starts from Muncan, 17 km from Klungkung. Be prepared for a quieter, yet faster wilderness ride than the Ayung River. You'll paddle through a spectacular waterfall and plunge five meters from the Bajing Dam into churning whitewater. Also check out **Bali International Rafting,** with offices in Kuta at Jl. Raya Kuta 16 M, tel. (0361) 757052, 757053, or 757054, fax 752956; **Ayung River Rafting,** Jl. Diponegoro 150 B, tel. (0361) 238759 or 224236, fax 224236; **Arha Bali Rafting,** Jl. Muding Indah II/4, Krobokan, tel./fax (0361) 427446, who advertise the longest (12 km) whitewater adventure on Bali on a Class II-III river for Rp149,000.

Kayaking

Sobek offers a kayaking tour using small, inflatable, new-designer kayaks that can't roll—completely safe for beginners. Tour an excellent section of river through tropical rainforest and vine-hung gorges. The price of Rp100,000 includes world-class guides, splash-proof camera bags, a great meal at the end, and hotel pick up in Nusa Dua (1100-1115), Kuta (1130-1145), Sanur (1145-1200), and Ubud (1245-0100).

HEALTH

Traveling in Bali today can be medically safe—if you take precautionary steps regarding transport, food, drink, and hygiene. If you work it right, you could even return in better health than before you left. The truth is that the traveler is much more likely to get hurt or killed riding a motorcycle on Bali, which snuffs out about three tourists per month, than to contract some hideous tropical disease.

For example, a common injury is the "Bali Kiss," a dreaded motorcycle burn on the inside of the calf. Drink lots of bottled water right away, then apply an antiseptic cream with lidocaine or benzocaine. After two days, start applying aloe vera or papaya compresses. To prevent this injury, wear long pants. Flying bugs are another hazard—wear sunglasses to protect your eyes while riding a motorcycle at dusk.

Start out on your trip as healthy as possible. Amp up your immune system. The most common ailments afflicting travelers and tourists are diarrhea ("Bali Belly"), parasitic diseases, and gastrointestinal infections. Thank god the island is free of rabies; its population of scavenging dogs is enormous.

Take common-sense precautions but avoid paranoia ("How were these dishes washed? Was this tea boiled long enough?")—it will spoil your trip. Even in upscale hotels, hygienic techniques aren't always followed, so if it's your turn to get sick, you'll get sick. But once you have your first bout with diarrhea or prickly heat, it seldom recurs.

Staying Healthy in Asia, Africa, and Latin America, produced by Volunteers in Asia, is packed with important information that's basic enough for the short-term traveler, yet complete enough for someone living in Bali. It's a very compact and well organized little book. Your own doctor won't be able to supply you with this hard-to-get information because he doesn't have it. Order a copy through Moon Publications, tel. (800) 345-5473.

Prevention

If you take care with personal hygiene, use caution in what you eat and drink, and get plenty of rest, you'll be safe from most health problems while traveling in Bali. Most illnesses travelers suffer are resistance diseases, a result of their health running down, poor eating, unrestrained self-indulgence, or overexposure to heat and sun.

Upon arrival, you owe it to yourself to become acclimated to the tropical environment: maintain adequate fluid and salt intakes, avoid fatigue, dress light. Jet lag may change your sleeping patterns and eating habits, so at first, plan extra rest. To avoid undergoing dental treatment in Indonesia, go for a complete dental checkup before your trip.

Knowing what and where the risks are and how to avoid them is your very best protection. What's wrong with walking barefoot in the tropics? Several different types of infectives that can enter the body through the skin, such as cutaneous larva migrans, thrive here. An Indonesian's left hand is unclean because it's used to clean himself, with water, after using the toilet. Vendors selling bottled drinks on the beach and on the streets use the straws again and again. Throw the straw away or bend it before giving the bottle back so it can't be used again.

On Bali, scruffy cats roam everywhere. They hang around restaurants, *warung,* and family-style hotels. Pregnant women, or those who are planning to be so, should avoid contact with these animals and their excretions because of the risk of toxoplasmosis infection. This parasitical disease can cause abortion or early birth, or the unborn child could contract congenital toxoplasmosis, possibly resulting in death or serious central nerve system disorders.

If you're staying in a budget hotel in the Kintamani area or down on Lake Batur, don't leave food open in your room but seal it in solid containers—rats can even chew through backpack canvas. If you're going to one of Bali's monkey temples, remember monkeys are wild animals. Don't take any food with you, and don't hide food in your pockets because monkeys can smell it. Their eye teeth are very sharp. When feeding them, always look out for the dominant male. He should be given food first to avoid fighting. Never show your teeth while smiling at monkeys—this is regarded as an aggressive gesture. Don't touch their young or they may savage you.

Street lighting is generally very poor at night. Watch out for drainage ditches. You hear tales of tourists falling two meters into ditches. A flashlight must be carried at all times; you need it also to protect you against cars, motorcycles, and other pedestrians.

Another common threat to health is the treacherously slippery tiles found gracing the floors of Bali's hotels—on bathrooms, steps, stairways, verandas. Even when not wet they are slick and dangerous. When wet, they can be life-threatening. Don't wear hard-soled leather or plastic shoes on them; soft-soled rubber sandals or bare feet offer a little better traction.

Travel Insurance

Check whether your health insurance entitles you to reimbursement of medical and evacuation expenses incurred overseas. If not, get special health or travel insurance to cover your trip for as little as US$3 per day. Short-term insurance, covering medical emergencies, loss of possessions, flight cancellation penalties, is sold by **STA Travel,** other student travel organizations, and **Cigna Travel Guard** (tel. 800-826-1300), International SOS Assistance (tel. 800-523-8930), and **Access America** (tel. 800-284-8300).

Be sure to get a policy which includes access to one of the medical evacuation services available on Bali—AEA (Asian Emergency Assistance), International SOS Assistance, and WAI (World Access International). Read very carefully the policy small print for exclusions. Evidently, insurance companies have been taken to the cleaners by people involved in accidents who obtained an easy-to-get Balinese license and drove a motorcycle for the first time on Bali.

IMMUNIZATION AND SERIOUS DISEASES

Get the latest World Immunization Chart of IAMAT (International Association for Medical Assistance to Travelers, 417 Centre St., Lewiston, NY 14092), which indicates the immunizations currently recommended for travel to Indonesia (double-check with the Indonesian Embassy). Another good place to check in the U.S. is the Centers for Disease Control in Atlanta (tel. 404-639-3311). Get your immunizations through your doctor or local health center.

Tetanus, polio, and yellow fever are not a big threat; immunizing against them is only necessary if you're going to the Outer Islands of Indonesia. Among travelers who stay in tourist accommodations and avoid potentially contaminated food and water, the risk of cholera is very small. Among all the foreign tourists flocking to Bali, it appears that only the Japanese appear to be coming down with cholera (150 people in 1995). Cholera vaccine is only about 40% effective anyway. Typhoid and paratyphoid vaccinations are also optional.

Malaria

The malarial season in Indonesia lasts all year and the whole country is affected below 1,200 meters altitude. Risk is low on Bali, especially if you sleep in a room with screened windows, keep well-covered after dusk, and use insect repellents and electric anti-mosquito mats. Take along chloroquine or chloroquine-substitute to prevent malaria. The mainstay of state-of-the-art protection is Larium, taken once weekly. A doctor's prescription of 20 tablets costs a devilish US$77, or US$3.85 per tablet! Don't use Fansidar; it's dangerous.

Hepatitis

One must exercise all the same precautions against this disease as one does in preventing dysentery and diarrhea. Unsanitary eating utensils and unwashed salads and fruits are prime suspects. Hepatitis is a debilitating liver disease which turns the skin and whites of the eyes yellow, the feces whitish, and the urine deep orange or brown. These symptoms—as well as sleepiness, chills, nausea, headaches, weakness, depression, and a dramatically diminished appetite—appear around three weeks after infection.

See a doctor immediately. Don't drink alcohol, eat fatty foods, use tobacco, or take antibiotics while under treatment. Get plenty of rest and drinks lots of fluids. Though it doesn't prevent the disease, a gammaglobulin injection will give you about six months' protection against the worst symptoms of hepatitis only; this shot, however, only gives protection against infectious type A

MEDICAL KIT

The kit's contents listed below will prepare you for almost any common problem. Most of the following supplies can be bought in Bali after your arrival, so don't pack too many medicines. You can also get prescriptions easier and cheaper in Bali than the West. Generic names are used whenever possible. Tablets are always more convenient than liquids when traveling; keep your medicines in small hard-to-break plastic bottles. Label each with a full description of its purpose and dosage.

Pepto-Bismol
In case of stomach trouble, use Pepto-Bismol or antacids. Sodium bicarbonate will also neutralize acidity.

Tinactin or Micatin
Available in the U.S. without a prescription (Desenex also works well). Used to treat prickly heat, jock itch, athlete's foot, ringworm. Native herbal skin treatments include Cap Pagoda Cream for tropical ulcers.

Analgesics
Aspirin to relieve minor pain, for lowering temperatures, and for symptomatic relief of colds and respiratory infections. Codeine is more powerful for the relief of pain and coughs.

Antihistamines
Eases and soothes the debilitating symptoms of allergies, hay fever, colds, vomiting, irritating skin conditions, insect bites, and rashes. Also effective for jellyfish stings.

Motion Sickness
For motion sickness and nausea, one to two antihistamine tablets such as meclizine (Antivert) are recommended. Nonprescription Dramamine can help prevent and relieve the discomfort. Paspertin (metoclopramid hydrochloride) relaxes the stomach.

Clove Oil
For toothaches. Cotton wool soaked in strong Balinese *arak* serves the same function in relieving tooth and gum pain.

Antidiarrhetics
Highly concentrated tincture of opium or less-concentrated camphorated tincture of opium are superb remedies against diarrhea; paregoric or charcoal tablets are also effective. Brand-name drugs include Stop Trot in Britain, Kaopectate in the United States. The active ingredients in both of these is powdered psyllium husks; these may be mixed with water, juice, or soda for a similar effect in stopping diarrhea.

More powerful medications such as Lomotil or Imodium (Streptotriad in U.K.) should be used sparingly. Lomotil, a prescription drug, also helps to ease abdominal cramps, nausea, chills, and low-grade fever that are frequently byproducts of diarrhea. Any anti-diarrhea drug is contraindicated if the diarrhea is persistent with high fever, blood in stools, jaundice, or drowsiness.

Laxative
Metamucil, a mild laxative with natural dietary fiber, aids digestion and combats constipation, but is bulky to carry. A natural fiber laxative in pill form would be better.

Antibiotics
Carry one of the many different varieties for skin or urinary-tract infections. From the cheapest to most expensive: tetracycline, penicillin G tablets, penicillin V tablets, ampicillin or amoxicillin capsules, and broad-spectrum cephalexin capsules.

Topical Eye Antibiotics
Very useful for treatment of eye irritations and conjunctivitis. Avoid penicillin products as you are more likely to become allergic to them if they are used on the skin. Good antibiotic eye creams include those that contain bacitracin, neomycin, or polymixin.

Antiseptics
Handy for minor cuts and scrapes, Savlon is a great antiseptic cream available in the U.K. (Cetavlon in the rest of the world). Antibiotic Cicatran Cream or Betadine work well for cuts and mosquito bites gone septic. Sepsstupf from Germany heals small cuts by morning. Bacitracin is a very good bacterial ointment available in Indonesia. Outstanding

ointments to use against tropical ulcers are F.G. Ointment (Meiji), and Neosporin or Polysporin.

Anti-Insect

Roll-ons and sprays like Off! are available on Bali. Pharmacies on Bali sell Minyak Sereh mosquito repellent (contains citronella) which works well but doesn't last as long as Off! Many people swear by Avon's Skin So Soft lotion (available only from Avon representatives); mosquitoes seem to dislike the scent. Use Kwell (not available in Indonesia) or Pyrinate shampoo to combat head lice and scabies.

Sunblocks

Expensive in Indonesia, so bring your own. Paba or zinc oxide, an opaque ointment, is widely available. Reapply after heavy sweating or swimming. If you do burn, benzocaine and calamine lotion ease the pain. Hat and sunglasses are critically important items to carry in the tropics. Use a lip salve like Chap Stick or Carmex. Comfrey cream also works well.

Vitamins

Vitamin tablets are fiendishly expensive and of dubious pedigree in Indonesia. The country's fruits and vegetables should instead provide all the vitamins you need. Because of the lack of dairy products, take iron and calcium. An iron supplement is especially important for women. If you feel rundown or have trouble with menstruation, take one ferrous sulfate tablet (200 mg) per day or eat liver in *nasi padang* restaurants until you feel better. If you eat too much rice, you'll lack Vitamin B; take Vitamin B12 and B6 because they work as catalysts for each other.

First Aid

Assorted Band-Aids are light, take up little room, and make fantastic gifts out in the villages. More practical, however, are the ectoplast strips which can be cut to any variety of sizes and shapes. Bring a roll of sterile cotton gauze and a roll of adhesive surgical tape, an elastic bandage for strains and sprains, and moleskin felt padding with adhesive backing for prevention of blisters (adhesive tape can be used as a substitute)

Also pack disinfectant, soap, thermometer in a hard case, tweezers, scissors, safety pins, needles, a sterile razor blade, and plastic dropper bottles. For rinsing out cuts or tooth and gum infections, use sodium bicarbonate, which is like a toothpaste, soap, and deodorant all in one. Rinsing with hydrogen peroxide three times a day is equally effective.

Others

Bring antifungal powder; calamine lotion to soothe itching; and eyedrops for infections (choloromycetin available in N. America, Albucid in the U.K.—both in liquid or ointment). Meat tenderizer works very well for stings of all kinds. Skin cleanser, birth control pills, cotton tipped swabs, dandruff medication, foot powder, laxative, rubbing alcohol, Hyland's Calms Forte sleeping pills, and nasal spray (phenylephrine HCL, one-half percent, or xylomethaciline solution) or nasal decongestant for sinuses and stuffed noses. Tampons in plastic (not paper); they are difficult to find in Bali so take enough. Also protein pills (concentrated soybean), particularly if doing a lot of walking. Bring dry powder to dust infections because wet ointments draw flies and you'll go through many dressings.

hepatitis and not serum hepatitis. Consider getting it if you're going beyond Bali.

FOOD AND DRINK

Food- and water-borne infections are one of the greatest threats to the traveler in the tropics. Bacterial infections (typhoid, paratyphoid, cholera, salmonella, shigella), infectious hepatitis, and such lovely parasitic infections as guineaworm, bilharzia, bacillary or amoebic dysentery, worms, and giardia can all be transmitted by contaminated food and water.

In restaurants unboiled water is still used for washing dishes and cooking certain foods, but an increasing number of restaurants in Kuta, Legian, Ubud, Lovina, and Candidasa brag about the fact that the ice used in their juices and cocktails is made from purified water and that they don't use unboiled water (or MSG) in their cooking.

As dairy products are often made with untreated water and unpasteurized milk, they are outstanding media for the breeding of many pathogenic bacteria. It's advisable not to drink local fresh milk or eat ice cream sold by street vendors. Stick to dairy products labeled as pasteurized. Diamond, Peters, and Campina are quality brand-name ice cream products sold on Bali. Hotel ice creams should be safe.

Powdered whole milk (Dancow brand), cartons of long-life milk, or sweetened condensed milk (Indomilk) are safe for kids or morning coffee, but don't mix with tap water! A great many restaurants on Bali specialize in delicious homemade yogurt. Being relatively more acidic, yogurt is safer, and in fact is a remedy against upset stomach.

All vegetables and fruit eaten raw should be thoroughly washed, rinsed, or peeled before eating. Vegetables used in raw salads may have contaminating organisms remaining on the vegetable surface. Lettuce and cabbage are particularly difficult to clean. Salad dressings (particularly mayonnaise-based ones) may be a potential source of bacterial infection, especially after sitting out. Avoid sandwiches made with mayonnaise.

Seafood should be eaten while fresh; shellfish should never be exposed to the hot sun and should always be thoroughly cooked. All meat should be well cooked or you stand the chance of being infested by worms. Cold meats, in particular, provide an excellent medium for the multiplication of bacteria in the heat and humidity of Bali. If you have to eat meat, stick to well-cooked meals served hot. Stay away from rare meats and cold buffets.

Contaminated Water

One of the biggest culprits in transmitting such diseases as cholera, typhoid fever, bacillary dysentery, and giardiasis, well water and tap water must be considered unsafe to drink on Bali because of poor sewage disposal and improperly treated water supplies. Ice served in restaurants is okay. To assure cleanliness and safety, all ice production is controlled by the provincial government.

Hot beverages carry fewer disease-causing organisms than cold beverages. Beer, non-carbonated plastic bottled water, or plain soda water are about the only non-sweet beverages available to drink. Though it contains a load of sugar, Fanta is safe for kids to drink, hydrates the body, and has no caffeine. Fruit juices in cardboard boxes are fine but invariably oversweet.

The freezing of water does not kill the organisms within, nor does the alcohol in a drink. Consider only plastic bottled water (Agua) safe. Non-

carbonated glass-bottled drinks may or may not be safe. Use carbonated, bottled, or boiled water instead of tap water for brushing your teeth.

Diarrhea

Traveler's diarrhea constitutes 90% of health problems for the traveler. Diarrhea often begins within a few days of arrival in a tropical climate because travelers are exposed to organisms they're not used to. Many stomach troubles like diarrhea are often a result of sudden changes of climate, food, and water, rather than poor hygiene during food preparation. This is equally true for travelers from Bali visiting the West.

People frequently refer to acute diarrhea as dysentery, but this is a misnomer. Diarrhea is much more common than dysentery. Diarrhea is generally a self-limiting disease lasting only a few days. Dysentery, on the other hand, is a serious, highly contagious disease characterized by blood or mucus in the stool. If you have severe diarrhea that lasts more than two to three days, accompanied by fever, headache, black-colored stools, or painful stomach cramps, you may have amoebic or bacillary dysentery. Seek medical attention as this disease can cause severe damage to your intestines and general health.

Take antibiotics to treat diarrhea, not to prevent it. Don't overconsume fruits, especially during December and January. Even the Balinese get the infamous "Bali Belly" during this epidemic season. Avoid all obvious sources of contaminated food and drink. Before you consider eating in a *warung* or restaurant, look closely at the faces and hands of the cooks and people who will be serving you. They also eat the food they sell. If their faces reflect ill health, their fingernails are dirty, and their establishment is unkempt and unsanitary, walk on by.

If diarrhea does strike, you will lose a considerable amount of fluid and salt. These *must* be replenished by immediately drinking lots of fluids (but not alcohol or strong coffee) to avoid dehydration. The best liquid is an oral rehydration solution, available in pharmacies, which contains the necessary salts. Take in clear fluids such as water, weak tea, juice, clear soup or broth (no milk), or soda that has stood awhile and gone flat.

Gradually add such plain foods as biscuits, boiled rice, bread, boiled eggs, adding other solid foods until you recover. Balinese, if they eat at all, drink *jamu* and eat the young *jambu* fruit and plain rice. Bananas are also good because they're bland and contain the binding agent pectin. Papaya contains digestive enzymes, so it's easily digested. Avoid fatty or spicy foods and stick to bland foods while under treatment. Add milk products last.

An over-the-counter drug sold in Bali which clears up diarrhea is Diatabs. One ounce of Pepto-Bismol liquid taken every 30 minutes provides symptomatic relief for most people with diarrhea. If your immune system can handle it, a well-tried and effective remedy is codeine-phosphate, available only by prescription.

For even stronger stuff, Lomotil comes in the form of minuscule white tablets. The A-Bomb of diarrheatic medicines, Lomotil shouldn't be used for more than a day or two since it only relieves the symptoms and has the potential of locking in the infection. It usually completely stops bowel movements for two or more days. Imodium is one of the best non-antibiotic treatments for diarrhea. Milder than Lomotil, it allows you at least to go on functioning, but is counter-indicated if the patient is severely dehydrated or has a high fever.

EXHAUSTION AND HEAT EXPOSURE

Bali can be hot, particularly from February to May, and travelers need to adjust to a climate that is extreme by temperate zone standards, possibly producing fatigue and loss of appetite for the new arrival. Even after two weeks, it doesn't seem to get any easier. For some, acclimating to the enervating heat and humidity can take months.

First, slow down the pace. Don't exert yourself. No one else does. Don't go on extended walks at your normal pace between 1000 and 1600. Persuade yourself to follow the Balinese custom of *tidur siang* (napping) sometime between 1200 and 1600, the hottest part of the day, or at least lie low during this time.

It's not uncommon for a Balinese to take a *mandi* up to three times a day to stay cool. Balinese women put rice powder on their faces to protect their skin from the sun and to keep their complexions from turning dark. Travel in very

hot areas only at dawn or dusk. Walk slow in the shade, fast in the sun. Prevent travel exhaustion by breaking up cross-island trips with stopovers.

Adapt yourself to exposure to the sun gradually; you'll be able to stay out in it more and more. It's healthy to be out in the sun's torrid heat for a while during the day; it has a purifying, acclimatizing effect. Use sunblock, zinc oxide, or coconut oil as protection against the sun. Small children should be especially careful. Wear loose cotton clothing, light in color and weight. Wear a hat. If you carry an umbrella, you'll always be walking in the shade.

Apply sunblock to your feet and bald spots on your head. Protect your nose and lips with zinc cream. Drink increased amounts of water with fresh lemon and lime juice, and make sure there's salt in your diet. Restrict alcohol and smoking. Avoid rich, fatty foods and stick to a light diet of rice, vegetables, and fish. Don't eat too much fruit as this can cause stomachaches and diarrhea.

Heatstroke Prevention

Heatstroke is caused by the breakdown of the body's cooling mechanism. Symptoms are a marked increase in body temperature to over 40° C (105° F) accompanied by flushed red skin, extreme lethargy, reduction in perspiration, and sometimes nausea, muscle cramps, or vomiting. Avoid heatstroke by drinking plenty of fluids, taking in enough salt, wearing light clothing, and moderating your intake of alcohol. Though rare, heatstroke could be an emergency. The victim should be taken to a cool room, doused with cold water, covered with a wet sheet, the body fanned and sponged until the temperature drops to at least 39° C (102° F), at which point the sponging should stop. Keep the patient at rest.

Salt

When your body sweats under the tropical sun you lose salt, so more should be added to your diet. Initial jet lag and fatigue might simply be caused by salt deprivation. Loss of body fluids as a result of diarrhea or dysentery also calls for increased salt consumption. Salt tablets are not really necessary, but after heavy physical exercise you might add a little extra salt to your food.

SUGGESTED MEDICAL TREATMENTS

Cuts, Bites, and Abrasions

Since bacteria breed so quickly in the Balinese climate, the tiniest cut or sore could soon become an ugly, festering tropical ulcer requiring prolonged antibiotic treatment. Most tropical ulcers and sores are due to mosquito bites or breaking in a new pair of sandals. Make sure your room has screens and use mosquito coils or the electric "mosquito mat" device. Wear long sleeves and trousers at sundown, and apply insect repellent after dark. Wear only broken-in footware, cover your legs, and wear protection when walking through tall grass or on coral reefs.

Whenever the skin is broken, it requires much more attention and time to heal than in colder climates. First, clean the opening with soap and water, apply some antiseptic, and cover it with a Band-Aid. Re-clean the cut and change the bandage every day, more often if it gets damp or wet. If it's a large cut or wound, use a nonstick sterile gauze dressing. Use transparent tape if you don't have surgical tape. If you can't have it sutured, at least try to join the skin's edges or use butterfly plastic strips.

As long as you have open wounds, avoid the beach. Swimming in the sea is also best avoided. If you can't resist the beautiful beaches, wash the wound after leaving the ocean and apply a new dressing. If an infection sets in (inflammation, itching, and pain after two days), soak the wound in hot water for 15 minutes, cover with a sterile dressing, then apply topical antibiotics.

Injuries from Sea Creatures

The comfortable water temperature, clear visibility, and spectacular dropoffs make Bali a popular dive destination. While swimming in the ocean, always wear enclosed shoes or flippers covering the whole foot. Never walk in bare feet on coral as stonefish inflict nasty injuries and live coral also abrades the skin by cutting or poisoning. For coral cuts, wash out the coral with fresh water and soap within the first hour after the injury. Once the wound is clean, prevent infection by keeping it covered for five to seven days and changing the dressing daily.

Avoid *all* contact with cone shells in Bali's reefs and shallow waters as these inject a dangerous venom. Handle only with forceps. Don't ever put live cone shells in your pocket. Single urchin spikes

need to be removed carefully. Urinate on the blisters, burst them, then keep them dry and covered. Multiple small spikes cannot be removed but will come out in time. To destroy the toxin and relive the pain, soak the injured area in hot water or vinegar for 10-15 minutes.

Off Menjangan Island in western Bali's Bali Barat National Park are tiny stinging jellyfish which leave welts on your arms and torso. Wash the area off gently with alcohol or whiskey. Heat is not recommended. Apply a meat tenderizer paste and the irritation and rash will be gone in 10-15 minutes.

Ear Infections

You'll meet heaps of people who've come down with ear infections, nearly always from snorkeling and/or swimming in the ocean or in an unchlorinated pool such as the one at Tirtagangga or in spring-fed hotel pools. In most cases, the infections are severe, keeping one out of the water for weeks. Take an antibiotic orally every six hours until the infection has been absent for two days. Also take a systemic decongestant to reduce swelling around the opening of the ear's eustachian tube. A hot water bottle applied to the ear, aspirin, and warm olive oil inserted into the ear reduce the pain.

Food Poisoning

Food poisoning lasts about three days. Little can be done for this awful illness. Prevent it by avoiding raw foods not adequately refrigerated, including shellfish, salads, mayonnaise, and custard-filled pastries served under unsanitary conditions. Treatment consists of lots of bed rest and plenty of clear, slightly sweetened fluids to rehydrate yourself.

Fungal Infections

These include athlete's foot and ringworm. Avoid them by using only your own towel, wearing flip-flops to bathe, wearing only open sandals, and not wearing nylon or other synthetic garments. Get rid of athlete's foot by exposing the area to air and sunlight as much as possible, and repeated applications of Tea Tree Oil.

Ringworm is not really a worm but a fungal infection which produces a red-ringed patch, usually on the trunk of the body, accompanied by itching, pain, and scaling. When cured it leaves a small red spot. Within a year, new skin appears. Dab on a Chinese medicine called Three-Leg-Brand Ringworm Cure. One application is enough. Go into a Chinese apothecary and point at the fungus—they'll know what you need. Or use a benzoic acid compound. Tinaderm, available in the UK, is a cream applied at night. From the U.S. try Micatin, a broad spectrum antifungal.

Selsun dandruff shampoo can also be used in the treatment of fungal infections. First wet the area, rub shampoo on like soap, leave for five to 10 minutes, then rinse off with water. Treat fungus in this manner two to three times. In Bali, buy the wide-spectrum antifungal Mycolog. You need the cream or lotion, and powder in case infected areas get soaked with sweat. In the case of vaginal infections, fungus is caused by a bacterial imbalance. Yogurt is a bacterial culture, so yogurt on a tampon neutralizes the fungus and soothes the itch.

Infections and Skin Ailments

In a tropical climate, be more careful about personal hygiene. Bacteria thrive in hot, humid areas, causing an increase in the variety of infections. Bacteria can enter the body through wounds or insect bites, especially those which have been scratched. Extra care should be taken when drying yourself, particularly around the ears and crotch area after bathing or swimming, so rashes won't develop.

Phisohex is effective for cleaning rashes and sores. A highly effective lotion called Caladine can be bought in Indonesia and is also highly recommended. Corn starch, baby powder, or arrowroot powder help keep the skin dry, preventing rashes which tend to develop if you're always splashing yourself with water in toilets.

Cutaneous larva migrans is caused most frequently by the larval form of dog and cat hookworms and is picked up by direct skin contact with contaminated soil. These larvae penetrate the skin. They don't grow to maturity but travel a tortuous path just under the skin, leaving a tiny trail behind them, progressing about two to five cm a day. The presence of the larvae often produces severe itching at the site.

Giardia

Giardia is an intestinal parasite found in contaminated water. Symptoms include nausea, stomach cramps, bloated stomach, gas, and watery diarrhea. The incubation period is several weeks after exposure to the parasite. Symptoms may vanish for a few days, then reappear. The disgusting-tasting drug Flagyl, to be taken only under a doctor's supervision, is the standard antidote.

Prickly Heat

This intensely irritating skin rash is quite frequently encountered in the tropics, usually soon after arrival. Red pimples or blisters break out on areas of the body that are always moist from sweating—under a tight-fitting belt, on the scalp, in the armpits or crotch area, or behind the knees. Your chances of getting it can be lessened by wearing loose-fitting cotton clothing and by avoiding synthetic materials that don't "breathe."

To treat prickly heat, splash cold water on the rash to cool it, dab it dry, then apply a dusting of powder like talcum powder. Calamine lotion can also be soothing. In severe cases, when the rash keeps you awake at night, use an antiseptic powder and even an antihistamine. To keep it from acting up, cut down on your use of soap.

Headaches and Body Aches

Balinese think it ludicrous that Westerners take aspirin for a headache when the only sensible thing to do is to get a massage. All over the island skilled masseuses can be hired to mercilessly pinch you for an hour (Rp5,000-15,000; in hotels Rp40,000-60,000). During a massage *(pincet),* the Balinese use exotic body lotions such as *boreh,* composed of rice paste, scented wood, hibiscus seeds, clove root, eucalyptus oil, etc.—which causes the skin to feel cold or hot, whatever is needed. *Boreh* is smeared across the brow to ease headaches; it's also said to ameliorate fatique and sprains.

Plants

Don't be too quick to blame insects when you return from a hike with your hand or leg swollen or tingling with a rash. A great variety of plants harbor toxic chemicals in their leaves or sprout nasty nettles. Merely brushing against them results in nagging skin irritations. Some people are more sensitive than others. Exercise caution with garden and house plants, particularly when children are around; some are poisonous if eaten. Carry an antihistamine cream to soothe severe skin irritations.

(continues on next page)

SUGGESTED MEDICAL TREATMENTS

(continued)

Venereal Disease

Indonesia's population is at high risk for the AIDS infection because most favorable conditions which facilitate transmission exist here—high-risk sexual behavior, poverty, a high prevalence of sexually transmitted diseases, a tourist industry, and seaports visited by AIDS-infected sailors from other countries. It's estimated that there are 16,000 people in Indonesia infected with the virus. By the year 2000, 5,000 will have full-blown AIDS and 50,000 will be infected.

There are no available statistics for Bali.

Everyone should take precautions (use condoms, avoid dirty or shared hypodermic needles, etc.) to avoid this deadly disease. However, *Kondoms* (Rp500, in supermarkets and pharmacies) sold in Indonesia are not to be trusted, so travel with your own supply.

Being a seafaring nation, gonorrhea has spread to most ports of the archipelago. Syphilis (blisters, sores, rashes around the genitals) is much less common. If you get gonorrhea, it's only serious if ignored or not recognized. Don't try treating it yourself; you should have a full lab test in a private clinic or public hospital. You need two injections plus a full course of ampicillin. A hospital will charge you around Rp25,000 for this routine and simple treatment.

Worms

Worm *(cacing)* infestations are common in warm countries like Indonesia where rainfall is plentiful and domesticated animal populations are large.

Hookworm eggs are passed into the soil in human or animal feces. Eggs hatch in the soil and the larval form enters the bloodstream when the skin comes in contact with the contaminated soil. Severe itching and burning may occur at the site where the parasite enters the body (often the area between the toes).

Roundworm infection may occur when you eat vegetables that have been fertilized with human feces. The eggs hatch in the stomach, then the larvae enter the blood and may migrate to infect other organs of the body. Only mild symptoms may be evident after some time, or the worms may cause abdominal discomfort, distended stomach, diarrhea, and sometimes a generalized rash.

Pinworm infestations are common in rural areas. Their eggs are often swallowed, then hatch in the stomach. From there they enter the intestines and ultimately to the anus where they lay sticky, white eggs. Pinworms (also called threadworms), about half a centimeter long, are easy to detect in the area around the anus where there will probably be itching.

Roundworms, hookworms, and pinworms are common infections which are easily spread, so all members of a traveling group should simultaneously take worm medicine. To prevent worms, wear footwear and eat clean, well-cooked food. One extremely effective nonprescription antiworm medicine available over-the-counter in Indonesia is Combantrin (one two-pill treatment, Rp2500). To find out if you have worms, labratory stool exams are available in the hospital at Sanglah in Denpasar (Jl. Bali 5, tel. 0361-235456).

If trekking into the Bali Barat National Park or climbing one of Bali's volcanoes, take along ordinary sea salt. A mixture of salt and water also serves as a mild antiseptic. If you have a sore throat, gargle with this solution.

WESTERN-STYLE MEDICAL TREATMENT

Pharmacies

There are plenty of pharmacies *(apotik)* in Bali's tourist and urban centers. The majority of the island's international-standard hotels have pharmacies, and the state-owned pharmaceutical company **Kimia Farma** has an big retail outlet in Denpasar (Jl. Diponegoro 125, tel. 0361-227811).

On Jl. Raya in Ubud, near Ganesha Bookstore, is a very good pharmacy (tel. 0361-974214). Indonesian pharmacies carry the most common prescribed and over-the-counter brand names like Anusol, and Benadryl. As in the West, the more potent medications require a prescription.

Because brand names for many drugs might be different, it helps to know your medicine's generic name. If you can't read the Indonesian on the container, have the pharmacist explain the proper dosage, which might be different from what you're accustomed to. Ask to read the leaflet (usually in English) that comes in the medication's packaging to make sure it's what you need. American drug companies have manufacturing subsidiaries in Indonesia, mostly in Jakarta, so many U.S. drugs are available at prices only slightly less expensive than in the U.S.A.

The **Temuku Health Food Shop & Bakery,** in the Krakatoa Business Center at Jl. Raya Seminyak (tel. 0361-730849), carries a whole range of vitamins, homeopathic remedies and creams, as well as organic whole foods and health teas.

Doctors

Doctors' offices are open in the evening, from around 1700 to 2000; to avoid a long wait, get there 15 minutes before opening and sign up on the list. The charge is Rp5000-15,000 per visit, depending on the doctor's specialty. Drugs (if needed) are usually the more expensive cost. If it's a hospital or clinic, drugs are dispensed from a pharmacy right on the premises for an additional cost.

To make up for their dearth of diagnostic skill, doctors tend to prescribe a standard recipe of antibiotics, antihistamines, tranquilizers, and vitamins for periods of three days or longer. They figure this recipe covers just about anything that could go wrong with you. And whatever problem you have, the Indonesian doctor is going to stick a needle in you. Make sure that he uses a new syringe, even if you have to buy it yourself at a pharmacy.

If you're systemically ill, insist on a blood or stool test if you suspect it's dysentery because they seldom order one. Perhaps as effective as taking pills and succumbing to injections is to choose a natural treatment of *jamu* (see above). Recommended doctors: Dr. Hendra Santoso (children), Jl. Suli 42, Denpasar, tel. (0361) 234794; Dr. Otong Wirawan, Jl. Br. Semawang, Denpasar, tel. (0361) 287482. Ask around to see if any foreign-trained physicians are serving as house doctors in the four- and five-star hotels of Sanur and Nusa Dua.

The proprietor of your hotel or homestay can come up with the name of a reliable and reasonably priced *dokter* or two. Specialists are found in the Bali telephone directory under "Medical Practitioners." If you feel that language will

be a problem, get the names of English-, German-, or French-speaking doctors from your respective country's consulate (see "Foreign Consulates in Bali" under "Information and Services" later in this chapter).

Specialists

Routine dental care such as cleaning and fillings can be performed by dentists *(dokter gigi)* in Denpasar. Recommended dentists: Drg. Gede Winasa Kesama, Jl. Diponegoro 115 A, Denpasar, tel. (0361) 233907, appointments 0900-1400; Drg. Retno W. Agung, Jl. Bypass, Sanur, tel. (0361) 288501; Drg. Ritje Rihartinah, Jl. Pratama 81 A, Nusa Dua Clinic, tel. (0361) 71324; Drg. Rudita, Jl. M.H. Thamrin, tel. (0361) 226255. For emergency dental treatment, contact Dr. Indra Guizot, Jl. Patimura 19, tel. (0361) 222445 or 226445. You can also locate a good *dokter gigi* through your consulate (see "Foreign Consulates in Bali" under "Information and Services" later in this chapter).

If you need complicated root-canal therapy, surgery, or bridge construction and repair, you will often be referred to specialists in Singapore. No certified orthodontists work in Bali. Dental floss is hard to find, so bring an ample supply. It's wise to attend to all your dental needs before arriving in Indonesia. Also take an extra pair of glasses or contact lenses, as well as contact lens cleaning and storage fluids. Acquiring new glasses is cheap and fast in Bali, but no need to go through the time and trouble.

Hospitals

If you get really sick or injured, fly home for treatment. If you want to remain in Indonesia, Jakarta offers Indonesia's best medical services. Your first choice for emergencies should be **St. Carolus Hospital,** Jl. Salemba Raya 41, Menteng (tel. 021-858 0091) or **Pertamina,** Jl. Kyai Maja 43, Kebayoran Baru (tel. 021-707211). Particularly good for cardiac cases is **Dr. Cipto Mangunkusumo ICCU,** Jl. Diponegoro 69, Menteng (tel. 021-334636). **Sumber Waras,** Jl. Kyai Tapa, Grogol (tel. 021-596011) also has a sound reputation, as does **RS Pondok Indah,** Jl. Metro Dua, Kava UE (tel. 021-769 7525). Closer to Bali is the **Catholic Hospital St. Vicentius a Laulo** (tel. 021-7562) in Surabaya (East Java).

Despite Bali's being Indonesia's top tourist destination, the general hospital in Denpasar, **Sanglah** (Jl. Bali 5, tel. 0361-235456), offers inconsistent medical services. The new Japanese-built emergency unit, **Unit Gawat Darurat,** has very sophisticated, high-tech equipment.

For really quality care, private clinics are your best bet because they offer doctors on-call 24 hours, radiology, pharmacies, laboratories, as well as ambulance service. **Manuaba Clinic,** Jl. Cokroaminoto 28, Denpasar (tel. 0361-426393) gets high marks; they have a branch clinic on Jl. Raya Kuta-Tuban (tel. 0361-754748).

In Kuta visit **Kuta Clinic,** Jl. Raya Kuta 10 X (tel. 0361-753268). In Nusa Dua is **Nusa Dua Clinic,** Jl. Pratama 81 A-B (tel. 0361-771324); see Dr. Ritje Rihatinah. In Ubud, go to **Darma Usadha,** Jl. Abangan Tjampuhan (open 24 hours), tel. (0361) 975235. In Ubud, go to **Darma Usadha,** Jl. Abangan Tjampuhan, tel. (0361) 975235. Open 24 hours.

Bali's regency *(kabupaten)* capitals also have hospitals: in Klungkung (Klungkung Regency) at Jl. Flamboyan 40-42 (tel. 0366-21172), in Singaraja (Buleleng Regency) at Jl. Jen. A. Yani 108 (tel. 0362-22396), in Gianyar (Gianyar Regency) at Jl. Ciung Wanara (tel. 0361-93049), in Bangli (Bangli Regency) at Jl. Kusumayudha 27 (tel. 0366-91043), in Amlapura (Karangasem Regency) at Jl. Ngurah Rai (tel. 0366-21011). In smaller district seats, it might be necessary to ask the assistance of the local Department of Health—ask for Dinas Kesehatan Kabupaten. In remote areas, the only treatment available is at small, crowded, poorly outfitted government health centers *(puskemas)* who employ medicos who are overworked, underqualified, and trained only in first-aid. The equipment can be pretty rustic. A doctor will not be in attendance.

If you've been struck by a *bemo,* a *puskemas* won't take you. Only a *rumah sakit* (hospital) will accept emergency cases (the stitching used more resembles thick twine than suturing thread). Mental hospitals are found only in Bangli and in Denpasar (Wong Aya). A multilingual Dutch psychiatrist, Dr. Robert Riverger, works in Denpasar (tel. 0361-434543).

Rescue and Medical Evacuation Services
The **AEA** (Asian Emergency Assistance) can often work with an accident victim's or sick person's insurance carrier. If not covered by insurance, have your foreign consulate on Bali contact your relatives back home. AEA has an office in the Denpasar side of Sanur and can offer 24 hour medical advice (tel. 0361-231443 or 227271).

Don't even entertain the thought of being rescued if you are swept out to sea off the extremely dangerous beaches of southern Bali. The Indonesians have only one rusty helicopter for marine rescue operations, and most of the time it's down. The ocean undertows are deceptively strong and every year as many as 40 swimmers are carried out and lost. No one seems to be aware of how treacherous these waters can be.

Note: Always swim within the safety zones demarcated by the red and yellow flags!

FOLK MEDICINE

Herbal Medicines
Found in the markets of Bali, traditional medicines are said to cure anything from nosebleeds to fainting spells. Spices are an important ingredient in these Balinese folk remedies, and families still grow their own medicinal plants and grind their own medicinal pastes on flat stones in the corner of the *bale.* Headaches are cured by spraying the head with a mixture of crushed ginger and mashed bedbugs; a heated or irritated condition is cured with a cooling medicine.

Other formulas include plain soft-boiled rice porridge *(bubur),* used to remedy diarrhea, and the leaves of the tall *punyan kolor* tree are laid on the site of a dog bite in order to "draw the blood out" and relieve pain. The palm spirit *arak* is popularly used for both external and internal maladies. If a person eats the leaves of the papaya tree, it's believed that mosquitoes will not bite him as his blood "turns bitter." *Kayu sepang* is for stomachaches and headaches. Wearing garlic around your neck or ear is believed to ward off evil spirits. Sacred pools (Tampaksiring), hot springs (Toya Bungkah), and natural spas (Yeh Panas) are said to have magic or curative powers.

If symptoms persist after seeking help from family members, neighbors, and doctors, the patient then employs the magico-medico skills of indigenous healers, the *balian.* It's believed that—

like landslides or being struck by lightning—there's a supernatural cause. Ritual neglect, the wrath of ancestors, or witchcraft has led to the "faulty illness," and it's now outside the expertise of Western-style medicine to effect a cure. Even a sick child is not innocent—he's suffering for some crime he committed in a past life.

Jamu

These are over-the-counter herbal medicines derived from the forests of Indonesia—hidden pharmacies of potent medicines in the form of plants, grasses, minerals, fungi, roots, barks, twigs, dried flowers, and parts of mammals, birds, reptiles. They come in the form of pills, capsules, powders, beans, peas, flat seeds, or can look like tea leaves.

Jamu shops are found in Denpasar (one is opposite Pasar Badung on Jl. Sulawesi, others include Toko Jaya Abadi and Toko Sentosa on Jl. Gajah Mada) with row upon row of small packages and little jars and bottles lining the shelves. You need no doctor's prescription. Explain your problem to the vendor and he'll know what you'll need. Follow the dosage directions on the packet or bottle. Jamu is cheap, about Rp500-750 per packet. The "super" is served with an egg, two kinds of wine, a cup of sweet tea, and a piece of candy afterwards, all for Rp3000-4000.

There are hundreds of different jamu, one for seemingly every conceivable malady. Women over 40 drink a special jamu to keep themselves from getting too thin. Jelok temu is given to year-old babies for strength. Jantung fortifies the heart. Lular paste, made from rice mixed with pulverized bark and flowers, slows the wrinkling and aging process. Mangir is a yellow powder put on the skin to make it clear, fragrant, refined. Ginjal is for an inflamed appendix. Kumis kucing (cat whiskers) is for urinary tract infections. Beras kencur peps you up all day.

Other jamu treat colds, tightness or dizziness in the head, runny nose, bronchitis, flu, and even "starry eyes." There are anticough herbs and others for sore bones, backaches, and listlessness. Men's tonics increase strength, and an aphrodisiacal jamu increases sex appeal and fertility. They've even got a jamu for men who do extreme physical labor, as well as special herbs ("Magic Formula No. 125") for hard-working

mothers with many children that will make their husbands more considerate.

Balian

A great number of Bali's rural people put their faith in the balian, the Balinese folk doctor. For the villager he's cheap and on the spot—they'll go to him before a hospital or clinic. The balian receives a voluntary consultation fee, or he may accept payment in commodities, food, or labor. He also derives income from the sale of his herbs and potions. In the balian's home there's a sitting room just like at a doctor's office where patients are willing to wait hours if the balian is busy.

Long-established opponents of Western medicine, these barefoot doctors have used locally made remedies and treatments for hundreds of years. Though most of the balian's medicines have never been laboratory tested, many have a sound scientific basis in modern medicine. Most have inherited their practices from older male relatives, while others come to their calling after a visionary dream.

Some combine practical folk medicine (barks, herbs, roots, other curative substances) with religious magic learned from detailed and lengthy lontar usada books. It's claimed some balian tulang can set bones so well that a broken leg can heal in two weeks. Balian apun (masseuse) have developed massage into a high science, even for orthopedic problems and headcolds.

Both revered and feared, it's believed that certain balian are men of supernatural powers who have the power and specialist knowledge necessary for diagnosis and treatment of illnesses not curable by ordinary means. The better known of these spirit mediums (balian taksu) attract clientele from all over the island. At times, they prescribe treatments while in a state of trance.

Other balian are inspired diviners (balian tenung) who embody the souls of dead people who "speak in tongues" through them. They also use horoscopes and offerings to practice both "right" and "left" magic, love-magic using prayers, medicinal recipes, as well as amulets, talismans, a ring, or some other magical object or figurative diagram (rarajahan) to exorcize evil spirits from houses. Balian kebal specialize in imbuing their clients with strength (kemasukan kekuatan) in order to protect them from their enemies.

Balian mediate between the natural or human world and that of the supernatural. Mantras and supplicatory prayers are sometimes employed to negotiate or entreat malignant forces to vacate the body. They dispense holy water and oil in order to heal illnesses by faith or achieve success in a university exam. If a baby is sick too often, the *balian* may simply change his name, or place a slice of onion on her fontanelle to prevent entry by a *leyak.*

Among the *balians* are shamans who claim to be able to cure people who have been secretly poisoned or purge them of spells cast on them by less powerful *balian. Balian* can also improve a client's sex appeal. A "diamond blown onto the lips" by a *balian* will give his customer an irresistible smile and fascination for the opposite sex.

Don't confuse the *balian* with *pedanda* (high-caste Brahman priests) and *pemangku* (lay priests), as their social and religious function lies somewhere in between. The term *balian* actually applies to a variety of healing practitioners. Some are total quacks. The Ubud area has always attracted talented natural healing practitioners from the West—in a sense, Western *balian*—who conduct regular workshops and sabbaticals.

COMFORT

On Bali, the battle never ends against fried food, sugar, fat, and meat in food, noxious cigarette smoke, noise, heat and humidity, insecticide spray cans, and over-air-conditioned rooms. Do what Balinese do to maintain comfort: notice that while relaxing they wear *sarung* and *kain,* ideal for this climate. Synthetic fabrics are too hot and sticky, so just wear drip-dry, loose-fitting, light-colored cotton or rayon clothes.

Choose a room with a split-level air-conditioner so that the noise stays outside. In other situations, it can be too cool. All performances on Bali, as well as many restaurants and bathrooms, are open-air, so in the uplands (Ubud area) from July to September always take along a light jacket. If your room is damp, clammy, and dark, get in the habit of in the mornings airing out all your bedding on a line in the sterilizing sun; the Balinese do.

SPECIAL TOILET VOCABULARY

bak mandi—cement bathtub that holds bathing water

mandi—to bathe, or the bath itself

kamar mandi—bathroom, consisting of just the bath or a bath-and-toilet combination

WC—toilet, whether Western- or Asian-style (pronounced WAY-say)

gayung—plastic or tin can dipper for use in the toilet and cleaning yourself

Di mana WC nya?—Where is the toilet?

Mahu buang air kecil?—Do you want to urinate?

Mahu buang air besar?—Do you want to have a bowel movement?

Permisi, bolehkah menumpang mandi?— Excuse me, may I use the bath?

Like the Balinese, take a *mandi* as frequently as you need to stay cool and grunge free. The verb is *mandi,* to bathe. The place where you go to bathe is called a *tempat mandi,* which could be a river, a well, or a *kamar mandi* (bathroom). In almost any hotel you may pay Rp2000-6000 (including towel) to enter the swimming pool without being a hotel guest.

Beards can be quite itchy in the heat (and scare Indonesian children). Bring your inner body temperature up to the outside temperature by drinking water or hot tea. Sugary, ice-cold sodas just make you thirstier. If the food is too spicy hot *(pedas)* drink hot water; it will sting at first, but the spiciness will go away faster.

In Kuta, Legian, or Ubud, you'll find half a dozen beauty salons where you can indulge yourself with a manicure, hand massage, or pedicure for around Rp10,000. Exercise classes and health salons are popping up all over Bali now. To experience the nimbleness and strength of Balinese women, get your hair plaited on Kuta Beach (Rp5000 is the correct price, Japanese pay Rp20,000).

Spas: Bali's spas offer a dazzling and sophisticated menu of holistic healing therapies—aromatherapy, massage, herbal wraps, thermal mud treatments, saltwater jacuzzis. To take advantage of this New Age trend, hotels in the Nusa Dua area have incorporated "spa" in the name of their health clubs. In Tabanan Regency in the small village of Penatahan, the natural hot springs of Yeh Panas have been developed into a modern, open-air spa, set in manicured gardens—Bali's leading natural spa facility.

Massage

To improve circulation and muscle tone, try a massage. Get a personal recommendation for a masseuse through your homestay, beach inn, or hotel reception—the best are old, blind women. For example, Pak Guru Rasin renders superb traditional massages for Rp8000 at BeeBee's in Tibubiyu (Tabanana). The staff of almost any hotel knows a professional masseuse or two.

One also encounters scores of practitioners on the beaches of Kuta, Legian, and Sanur where mature women with distinctive hats and T-shirts stroll the beach with bottles of coconut oil mixed with herbs. They generally have numbers on their hats or preposterous nicknames like "Hot Dog," or "Go-Go." Men are very seldom seen performing massage on the beach.

Prices vary from masseuse to masseuse depending on how business is and how much they think you're willing to pay—anywhere from Rp7000 to Rp15,000 for 30-45 minutes. Bargain. Always be sure of the price first; otherwise you could be ripped off. If you find a good one, stick with her. Don't worry—she'll stick to you too.

The incredibly strong hands of these women gently knead your body from head to toe, rubbing in *boreh*, which consists of coconut oil, flowers, aromatic roots, cloves, nutmeg, *kunyit* (turmeric, for coloring), and *lulur*—a yellow paste from Java made from mashed *don kolor* leaves—part of the beauty care of royal families. When rubbed in vigorously, this concoction tin-

gles and refreshes the skin when you're hot or gives it heat after you've been out in the rain. You come out smelling like a flower. Balinese masseuse are also adept at skin rolling and "percussion"—hands, palms together, chopping over a particular area.

The culmination is the cracking of virtually every joint in your body. Massages may last from a half hour to an hour and a half, depending upon how wrapped up you get in conversation. Try to concentrate while being hit on to buy bikinis, watches, and woodcarvings from an unending line of vendors.

Anti-Mosquito Aids

On Bali, mosquitoes are only bad at dusk on the coast. In cheap hotels, keep what mosquitoes there are off you by moving your bed under a fan or by using mosquito coils *(obat nyamuk),* which are quite effective, slightly nauseating, and available anywhere for Rp800 for a box of five. Far superior are electrically powered (Baygon brand) anti-mosquito mats, much easier to take and not nearly as toxic. The whole setup—device, cord, small sealed packages of tabs—costs around Rp12,000.

Before stepping out at night, apply Autan spray or citronella oil to the skin. Also extremely effective is Minyak Angin (Eagle Brand Medicated Oil), which can be purchased at any Chinese apothecary. If unprotected while sleeping at night, use a mosquito net *(kelambu),* which can be bought for around Rp20,000 in any supermarket.

A repugnant habit of the hotel staff is the spraying of insecticide (Baygon) all over your room and under your bed before you go to sleep at night. This problem is easily remedied by simply telling the person armed with the sprayer, *"Tak usah, terimah kasih"* ("Thank you, but it's not necessary").

CONDUCT AND SAFETY

If traveling in Bali for the first time, spend some extra money and begin your stay in a nice, comfortable hotel to lessen the initial impact. Once you meet other Western travelers, you'll become part of the traveling community and won't feel so alone. Traveling in the out-areas, you need to get accustomed to the lack of privacy. If staying in a budget hotel, you immediately have to adjust to the noise level. The *kampung* of Bali are noisy—dogs howl, roosters crow, cassettes blare, women quarrel, horns blow, and motorbikes whine. Your only defense is to rise when the cocks crow and get into the daily rhythm of the island. Use your imagaination, energy, daring, and style to avoid following well-worn tourist ruts. Staying a week in accommodations in or near a *kampung* will give you a faint glimpse of what it's like to be Balinese.

Travelers should also be prepared to forego an occasional night's sleep. Make of the night, the day. Many forms of entertainment, *wayang*, prayers, and religious festivals run all night long. The Balinese often stay up the whole night of a full moon simply for the cool temperatures and the magic still to be found on Bali.

When trying to get someone's attention, use common "call names." For someone older or of higher social standing than you, *Pak* is short for the Indonesia word *bapak* or father. When calling an older woman, *Bu* is short for the Indonesian word *ibu* or mother. When addressing a young woman, *Geg* is short for the Balinese word *egeg*, or "pretty," and when addressing a young man, *Gus* is short for *bagus*, "good."

Don't say thank you for everything that's done for you. It sounds ridiculous because Indonesians seldom say thank you. Don't show any sentimental attachment to animals; this is Asia. Balinese treatment of their fellow creatures reflects the revulsion they have for all forms of animality. Balinese children jump with glee while dogs die horribly from a rifle shot or drowning.

Polite conversation will be initiated by the usual exchange of greetings. When meeting strangers it's polite to introduce yourself without waiting for someone else to do the introductions. Shake hands when greeting people; both men and women will offer their hands. The inevitable questions will follow about what country you're from, whether you are married, how many children you have, and where you bought the *sarung* you're wearing. If you take a business card, spell out the person's name phonetically on the back, being sure to divide their name into syllables and put in the correct accent. An especially gracious gesture on Bali is to give the Hindu greeting *"Om swasti astu"* while holding your hands together in the traditional Hindu blessing. After a conversation with a Balinese, it's polite to ask permission to leave.

Remote villagers have not become used to the presence of Westerners *(orang asing)* and can stare unmercifully for long periods of time. If this occurs, it may help to say *"Jangan melihat saya."* ("Don't stare or look at me.") This usually is enough to make them too embarrassed to continue. Children will yell out "Hello Mister!" and "Hello Miss!" and other calls from the lexicon of tourist greetings. You can answer *"Pergi ke mana?"* ("Where are you going?") or *"Dimana jalan kaki?"* ("Where is the footpath?") and watch their surprise. Pass your cigarettes around, and if you've been into town bring back biscuits for the kids.

The Balinese Character

The Balinese are easygoing, courteous, gentle, and kind if you are kind. But don't think that because the Balinese smile a lot and are friendly they make good, long-lasting friends. The villages are tight-knit, almost impossible for non-Balinese to penetrate, and are very business and family oriented. Westerners dislike hierarchy, are suspicious of authorities, and believe in egalitarianism. Balinese, on the other hand, are submissive to authority. Loyalty to family, clan, village, and friends is most important.

Balinese are more direct than the Javanese who are taught as little children to lie, as in "If you stop crying, there's an ice cream man in front of the house." They want to tell you only what they think you want to hear. The Balinese though are more straightforward. In business dealings they come more quickly to the point. On Bali, every driver uses the horn; on Java, no one does. The Balinese also work harder than the Javanese, are easier to train, and complete their jobs. They make better houseboys, waiters, porters, and drivers. After all, they've been dealing with Westerners and their myriad idiosyncrasies since the 1930s.

The Balinese have a strong propensity for jealousy *(irihati)* or envy of other Balinese and Indonesians, especially in the upper classes. They gossip, slander, and make snide remarks behind the backs of other people in their compound or village. A *banjar* can be a veritable hotbed of gossip—some mischievous, some vicious.

But the Balinese are very adept at hiding jealousy, envy, and anger. When Balinese men drink, they might lose their temper and become excitable over perceived insults or discourtesies, particularly if they lose face. Otherwise, they're passive. Anger is not shown openly. Loud voices are considered vulgar, and the more vehement the discussion, the quieter a Balinese is likely to become. In a quarrel with a Balinese, Westerners are assertive, confrontational, and openly angry. Westerners think they are being frank and down-to-earth, but Balinese find them rude and offensive. Watch what happens at Denpasar airport when 17 pushy real estates agents from Los Angeles learn that Garuda has overbooked and their seats given away. The angrier they become, the more withdrawn and soft-spoken the Balinese become. He will continue to smile, maintain a calm appearance, and withdraw from the quarrel, choosing to deal with the issue later through a third person. Under intolerable stress, the normal Balinese reaction is retreat deeper into one's self, seeming no longer to inhabit their bodies and cutting themselves off from the outside world.

After a fatal car accident, relatives of the deceased can be seen sleeping at the accident site. Or as a village court decides what to do with a thief, he'll nod off. If you've been away and come back to find your *ibu* or houseboy asleep in the afternoon, you know that something has been lost, broken, or stolen. When pushed beyond this temporary catatonic state, a Balinese may "run amok," an extreme cultural reaction to overpowering stress. Balinese rarely show anger but when they do, they erupt without warning like a volcano. An estimated 50,000 people died on Bali in 1966-67 during an orgy of killing which followed an alleged communist coup. Essential reading on the subject is *The Balinese People: A Reinvestigation of the Balinese Character* (Jensen and Suryani: 1993). Co-authored by a Balinese, this insightful book takes a refreshing look at the Balinese character from their perspective.

Individual versus the Group

There's no place for the individual in this society like in the West. Bali is a crowded island, and its people live in very close proximity. As exemplified in the Balinese *banjar* and *subak* organizations, it's the individual's duty to obey the will of the group and the group leader. Loyalty to family, *banjar,* and village are more important than self-advancement.

Emphasis is placed on mutual togetherness, and on physical and emotional closeness to others of the same sex. The Balinese seek the security and support of others. Individuals aren't admired and may eventually be ostracized from the *banjar* if they don't fulfill their community obligations. Community members feel at one with the group, self-identity deriving from group identity. Balinese consider the man or woman who stands alone as unnatural and a little absurd.

Many Balinese are accustomed to sharing their beds with family members and may feel lonely or frightened when sleeping alone. A family member who brings disgrace to the family, even through no fault of their own, will be cast out in order to maintain family dignity.

Sex and Intimacy

Balinese of the opposite sex are not openly affectionate to one another. At public gatherings men always sit to one side of the courtyard and women on the other—gossiping, praying, smoking, gambling, or whatever. Though considered homosexual behavior in Western societies, Balinese males and females frequently touch, link arms, or hold hands with their peers in a social setting. The whole island seems to share this quite unaffected and casual intimacy, considered a mark of friendship and sociability, not sexuality.

On Bali it's okay for men to touch other men in public. Balinese sometimes perceive Western men as unfriendly when they don't allow them-

TRAVELING WITH CHILDREN

Bali is a great place to take the kids. The Balinese are extremely fond of children (not so in Flores where they touch, pinch, and even throw stones). Western children really get into the Balinese culture and feel its spirituality and understand its unique legacy to the world very quickly. There's always plenty to occupy them, and they'll be healthy and safe. It's also cheap to take them because you pay only two-thirds the airfare for your child (if under 12). The long, disorienting flight from Europe or the States is the worst part of the whole trip.

If you say you're over 20 years old, and don't have any children, the Balinese pity you. In fact, to answer with an outright "No!" is too blunt; say instead *belum* (not yet) or *di hotelnya* (back at the hotel).

With young children, you've got to be patient, creative and flexible. Don't be on the move all the time. Accommodate your children's needs, or they won't have any fun and neither will you. Establish rituals around mealtimes, clean up, family meetings, study plans, and nighttime story to provide structure.

Have your kids always wash their hands thoroughly before eating or after going to the toilet. Bring sterilizing airplane wipes or alcohol anti-bacterial wipes for this purpose. Don't let them run around barefoot because worms and other parasites from infected excrement enter through the feet. Carry baby wipes for those times when soap and water aren't available. Loose cotton pajamas covering most of the body or a tucked-in mosquito net keep a child from getting bitten by mosquitoes during the night.

Bring an infant analgesic, medicine dropper, thermometer, sunblock, and hat. Take a car seat if you're going to be there a long time. Also bring a good child's motorcycle or bicycle helmet. Some transport is freaky because there are usually no seatbelts, so pay extra and get a Kijang with seatbelts. All medicines and baby accessories (Vaseline, baby wipes, baby powder) are available in the tourist-oriented shopping centers of Bali. Buy Dial or Fisher-Price liquid soap.

If you're into herbal medicine, homeopathy, vitamins, bring it all with you. Your kid probably won't get sick, but if she does, take her to a *puskemas* (local clinic). There's an excellent pediatrician in Gianyar, but many of the doctors have big egos and don't like it when you question them. They also

have a tendency to used hypodermic needles too much. Sometimes the serum shots are bootlegged, outdated, or not fully certified. (See "Health" section for more tips.)

Be prepared to fix food—mashed eggs, bananas, fruits—in your hotel room for infants who are eating solid food. Baby food is becoming increasingly available in Kuta, Sanur, Lovina, and Ubud. Yogurt, good bread, noodle soups, rice porridge *(bubur)*, fruit juices, and boiled vegetables can be ordered in restaurants or your hotel kitchen. Cartons of long-life milk, which lasts at least 24 hours after opening, and plastic bottles of sterilized water (Rp800-1500) are for sale in stores everywhere. Teach them how to drink soda water if you don't want them to drink sugared soda.

Bring a submersible heater to heat water, then submerge the baby food jar in it to warm it. Handling baby bottles is a major league hassle. One doesn't dare rinse nipples and bottles out under tap water, and it could be tough to arrange for kitchen privileges. One could ask for a thermos of hot water and steep nipples in that and use bottles with disposable liners. A better bet is to breastfeed, which will meet with enthusiastic approval and support from Balinese mothers. If a toddler is still using a bottle, you might want to cut them off before your trip. Breastfeed during takeoffs or landings to equalize pressure on both sides of the eardrum.

If you use disposable diapers you might want to know that they are for sale only in Bali's modern shopping centers, and prices are a bit high (Rp20,000 for 20). Native kids don't use anything when they defecate, just water. If you use cloth diapers, bring enough to last you as it takes several days for the laundry to come back. Take lots of self-sealing plastic bags to carry powdered formulas, baby food, cereals, and shampoo; also dirty diapers, wet laundry, and trash.

Bring just one change of clothes as clothes here are really cheap. But don't forget scissors, spoons, portable plastic changing pad, blanket. Practice *mandi*-ing with them because they sometimes freak when there isn't a bathtub. Don't take too many toys with you. Let your kid discover the simplicity and allure of Third World toys.

Cribs and high chairs are difficult to find, only available in the big hotels. Indonesians don't use them, and if you find them, their design leaves something to be desired. Balinese children sleep with their parents and infants are fed in their mother's lap. A kiddie papoose-style backpack is a definite plus. Your child can see, but is safely away from traffic, monkeys, and merchandise. Or learn how to use a *sarung* as a baby carrier, even when riding a motorcycle locally.

If you go to see the monkeys, make sure there are no cookies, crackers, or other goodies in your kiddie pack or diaper bag. Don't take a stroller to Bali. There are only a few places with sidewalks, and road edges tend to be broken and bumpy. The traffic is also fast and erratic—you would run a real risk of getting the stroller (and child!) clipped by a car, scooter, or motorbike.

The Balinese are naturally gifted, gentle babysitters—one sees 20-year-old boys play with kids. Sitters can easily be arranged in the tourist resorts; ask your hotel proprietor. They cost around Rp5000 per day, more if you have more than two kids. Or maybe one of the girls at the homestay you're in will babysit. It's also easy to get a long-term babysitter *(pembantu)* for around Rp70,000 per month. Just put the word out. Sometimes they come with the house you rent or lease.

The Balinese are very receptive to Western children, so if you're traveling with your child—especially a fair-complexioned male child—the problem is not finding a free babysitter for the day. The problem is getting your child *back* from the babysitter and the whole *kampung* that have adopted him. Be ready to answer all kinds of questions such as how old the child is, whether boy or girl, how many teeth.

You can just leave older kids all day at your hotel to roam the grounds, with specific instructions and prohibitions left with the hotel staff. Kids must have a place to run around and let loose, so before moving into a hotel, check out the free space and if there are children's activities. Is it a child-friendly environment? Are there gardens, a swimming pool, a coconut grove, or a beach nearby?

One idea is to leave your kid at the Crackpot *batik*-making studio on the Monkey Forest Road in Ubud all day, or at a well-supervised agency for low-water snorkeling, or hire some kid to take them for a hike, or sign them up for a pony tour, or raft trip. Ideas are endless. In Ubud, children wearing plain clothes practice dance at the *puri* on Sunday and Tuesday afternoons at 1500. It's free, fun, and fascinating to watch. Foreign kids may join in. At the Padangtegal stage every Thursday at 1900, a Ramayana ballet is put on by the children's troupe Sekar Alit.

A great number of homestays are ideal environments for children. For example, **Madra Homestay** (Br. Kalah, Peliatan, Ubud, tel. 0361-975749), long a center for the Balinese arts such as music, dance, and painting, is a wonderful place for small children because of the friendly family and natural surroundings near beautiful rice fields, next to a babbling stream, with frogs and crickets serenading you. Pak Madra's wife, Ibu Wayan Kondri, and other family members have won the hearts of many friends from around the world with their warmth and good humor. Although the rooms are very basic, the setting and atmosphere of this homestay is quite special.

---

selves to be touched, while Westerners perceive Balinese men as effeminate when they do. Touching very seldom occurs between people of the opposite sex, especially lovers. To do so would bring shame and embarrassment to the families of those involved. Out of respect, Westerners should never kiss or show affection in public. All this doesn't mean that the Balinese are puritans. They love to tell bawdy off-color jokes, children are adept at making ribald puns, and the men aren't a bit shy about courting Western women.

Hygiene

Inside *mandi* (bathroom) consist of just a cement tub for bathing, or a bath and toilet com-

bination. Don't jump into the bath water; it's for throwing over you. The floor gets wet, but that's okay. Balinese are surprised and amused when they see Westerners trying to keep their bathroom floors dry. Most outdoor bathing places have concealing walls and separate areas for men and women. The Balinese bathe at least twice daily—early in the morning, and after school or work.

It's okay to bathe with your respective gender. They'll probably laugh. Bring your own towel, soap, and shampoo. Both sexes are very discreet about showing their private parts and it's extremely bad manners to stare at bathers even if the bathing place is open. It is grossly impolite to take photos of bathers, covered or not.

Bathing places should be avoided from around 1700 on to let Balinese bath in peace. In many locales, the Balinese wait until the last tourist bus has gone because they don't like being photographed while bathing.

The left hand is used in the toilet and the right is kept clean for eating, shaking hands, and sprinkling holy water or wafting incense. Men needing to urinate in a crowded place just squat down in a ditch with knees spread for cover. Avoid blowing your nose into a handkerchief in front of others.

Anything low to the ground or touching it is considered soiled, including babies until they are six months old. Clothing is looked upon as unclean, particularly the clothes of women who have recently given birth or clothing which might have been tainted with menstrual blood. It's inconceivable for a Balinese to walk under a line hung with drying clothes.

Dress and Grooming

Be neat, clean, and fairly careful about what you wear. Shorts, tank tops, braless jerseys, or strapless tops in small villages could be insulting, something only fieldworkers and laborers do. This clothing can be worn in the beach resorts of southern Bali, but upland towns such as Ubud and Bangli are not surfing beaches and conservative dress is in order. Old, faded, or torn clothes, bare shoulders and knees, or excessively native dress is also considered bad form. Wear a collared shirt, skirt, or trousers, and shoes when a visiting a government office such as *kantor imigrasi* (immigration office), applying for a driver's license, visiting a sacred area, or attending a ceremony. Take your shoes off before entering a private residence.

A *sarung* tied above the breasts is only acceptable on the way to the beach or on the way to bathe. The Balinese are not bothered by nude or semi-nude bathing, but the ruling Javanese are—it's illegal on Bali's beaches. However, it's impossible to arrest scores of barebreasted Italian and French women.

Religion

Ninety percent of Balinese are Hindu; their temples are roofless, open to the air, and very informal. Guests *(tamu)* may enter a temple any time as long as they are properly dressed and follow some simple but strict rules meant to preserve the temple's sanctity. Since the early 1970s signs in English have been posted in front of temples and government offices showing graphic examples of appropriate and inappropriate dress.

When entering temples, traditional *adat* dress is required: the legs must be covered; if you don't have a *sarung* then you may rent one to wrap around shorts or short dresses; if wearing long pants, sashes should be worn around the waist. Smile when you pay the token fee (Rp550) which goes to the upkeep of the temple. Except when praying or attending a ceremony, temple courtyards are not for sitting in, and don't use your flash during ceremonies or praying.

Menstruating women are believed to be "impure" *(sebel)* and may not enter temples or participate in any religious activity. If a Balinese woman enters a temple during her period and makes an offering, she could be severely fined. This does not reflect a sexist attitude but is based on the prohibition of unsanctified blood on sacred ground.

When ceremonies involving revered objects are underway, sit on the ground or move to the back of the temple. Keep out of the way and don't move in front of worshippers. It's forbidden to climb up on temple walls (to take a better photograph, for example) or to put oneself on a higher level than that of a priest. It's also considered sacreligious to step over or stand with one's head above a revered *barong* mask or other sacred object in a temple. Clothes should never be hung to dry on temple walls including those surrounding domestic shrines.

The Balinese aren't offended easily, but they do have their own opinions on religion. If you're an atheist, don't tell everybody—the Balinese will react with confusion, disbelief, even scorn, thinking you're a godless communist. For them, it would be like discovering that a person was alive without a heartbeat.

Table Manners

A Balinese will always offer to share his meal when a visitor arrives at his house, office, or park bench, and he will usually excuse himself for eating in front of you at a *warung*. If you're offered food or drink in someone's home it is polite to accept or at least ask for a glass of hot tea. A guest may not start to eat or drink until invited to do so by the host with *"Silakan"* ("Please begin to eat") or *"Minimlah"* ("Please drink"), sometimes 20 minutes later! Take a small helping the first time because your host will be offended if you don't eat a second. It's polite to keep pace with your host. If you empty your plate, it means you want more. If you are the host, ask your Indonesian guest to eat or drink when food is served since he will wait until you offer it. Many Balinese don't use utensils at home but eat the traditional way with the fingers of the right hand. Never eat with the left hand—it's used instead of toilet paper. When you're done eating ask the host or hostess for permission *(permisi)* to leave.

Indonesians are not accustomed to eating uncooked food such as salads, cold meats, and dairy products, but fruit is often served after a meal. Westerners rarely eat the insides of cattle, pigs, or chickens, but on Bali every part of an animal is eaten except its eyes. Families don't usually talk during meals; conversation starts after. If you have to pick your teeth cover your mouth with your hands—only animals show their fangs.

Body Language

Aggressive gestures and postures such as crossing your arms or standing with your hands on hips while talking, particularly with older people, is regarded as insulting since this is the traditional posture of defiance and anger in *wayang* theater. In an exchange with someone older or in a high office, extend your right arm (but not too far) and bring your left arm across the front of your body touching your fingers to your right elbow. Also show respect by bowing from the waist when passing an older person, a priest or reverend, or a person of equal age whom you don't know—particularly if that person is sitting. Turn your body slightly sideways, extend your right hand, and walk by half bent over.

Next to sex organs, feet are considered the lowliest and most profane body parts. It's a serious offense to sit with the soles of your feet pointing at people (such as propping them up on a table). It's also terribly impolite to use your toes for pointing as when indicating something displayed on the ground in the *pasar*. Also, to beckon anybody with the crooked index finger is

rude. If you need to call to someone, extend your right hand and make a motion using the cupped fingers turned downward. Neither should you point with your forefinger, but use instead your right thumb. The left hand is considered unclean, never use it to touch someone or to exchange things. If you should use your left hand, say *"Ma'af"* ("Excuse me").

Don't pat children on the head. In fact, never touch anybody's head as the Balinese see the head as sacred, the seat of the soul. Pillows shouldn't be used for sitting because they are meant for the head. A barber will ask permission before he cuts your hair, and a hotel receptionist will apologize before placing a flower behind your ear.

HASSLES

Even though Bali is one of the world's least policed territories, violent crimes are practically unheard of. Singapore, with about the same population, has five times the crime and five times the police. The secret to the low crime rate is the stabilizing influence of the *banjar* (village council). When crimes do take place the Balinese almost exclusively blame the Javanese or the Sasaks. As evidence, they point to the fact that after an arrest it turns out the criminals came from either Java or Lombok. Other oft-accused scapegoats are Bali Aga thieves from Kintamani in the mountains of Bali.

Beware of over-friendly strangers speaking slick English peppered with American or Australian slang. They are usually trouble, so don't be decieved by their Western-style dress or manners. Never get pushed into paying for something without bargaining first, and don't make donations without verifying the existence of the object or the authenticity of the cause. The Balinese sometimes confuse generosity with abundance, taking advantage of your good nature and desire to be friendly. They borrow things—surfboards, sunglasses, cassettes, guitars, books, and "forget to return them" *(pinjam lagi, terus hilang)*. With the disarming smile of a little girl, they are skilled at coaxing you into doing things you don't really want to. If you want someone to leave you alone, just say simply *"Bukan adat kami."* "It's not our custom."

Vendors

In the tourist locales street vendors can be unbelievably pushy. Be polite at first, expressing your disinterest while looking them in the eye. They're just trying to make a living like everyone else, and if you ask the price they'll think you're interested and hound you mercilessly until you buy. If the vendor persists, make a stand, stating firmly and unequivocally that you don't want the item. Repeat this in Indonesian or in English, and look them straight in the eye (don't look at the item they're selling) until they back off. This usually works. If it doesn't, say vehemently *"Silahkan pergi!"* ("Please go away!"). Another effective technique to use with a nagging crafts seller is to make an offer so ridiculously low he gives you up for a lost cause (but be careful, he could accept it!). Be wary of predatory guides who offer to show you around arts and crafts shops. They expect a commission from the owners.

Dealing with the Bureaucrats

Tourists who break the law make it hard for those who follow the rules, so give your fellow travelers a break. But don't always assume you need permission to do something or go somewhere. The more questions you ask, the more questions will be asked of you. Humility goes a long way when dealing with Indonesian bureaucrats. If you get into any hassles with annoying cops, customs agents, or *imigrasi* officials, just act meek, friendly, and innocent. In most cases, they just want you to show respect and acknowledge that they're real. If there's a problem, bypass petty officials if you can and go right to the top. Often, people in authority are more intelligent, reasonable, and understanding, and you'll eventually have to go to them anyway.

Drugs

The ultimate hassle in Bali is getting busted for selling or using drugs, an offense the Indonesians take very seriously. You'll be offered marijuana and hash along Jl. Legian in Kuta and Legian, but half the time you'll get ripped off and may risk being turned in by a police informer, hotel owner, or passerby. Indonesian authorities believe that foreign tourists have established a narcotic network on Bali. About the only "legal" drugs are the magic mushrooms *(oong)* served in omelettes and fruit juices in some of the restaurants of Kuta.

It's no longer easy to bribe your way out of a drug bust. Nine year sentences for drug dealers is the norm, and there are always Westerners stranded in jail for drug convictions, abandoned by country and friends.

Beggars

In the sacred *lontar* it states that the Balinese must give to beggars. They are accepted members of society, but only if they are crippled, retarded, or have some other health problem. You're not obliged to give money to strong, healthy people.

The beggars you see in Kuta and Legian are usually mountain people from the Kintamani area. Traditionally they grow corn, potatoes, and *salak,* which they sell or barter in the rice-growing towns. However, many have turned to begging because they make a better living off dumb tourists. They put on a sad face and dress themselves and their small children in rags. Don't fall for it. The more you give, the less motivation healthy individuals and their children will have to earn an honest living. Never give money to children as it creates an endless cycle of dependence and diminishes their self-worth. Encourage Balinese pride by saying *"Tidak boleh!"* ("You may not!") to begging children. Instead of money, offer a look through your binoculars, pens, notebooks, or color postcards (in Kuta or Legian or you'll be mobbed). If an adult Balinese does a favor, a little *uang rokok* (literally, "cigarette money" or pocket change) may be appropriate. A small child who hikes all the way up Mt. Batur before sunrise to sell cokes, or fetches coffee and a newspaper is not begging. A small gratuity is definitely in order.

A Note for Women Travelers

Though Bali is a much easier place than Islamic Indonesia for a solitary woman traveler, there are still difficulties. A young, statuesque woman with blonde hair and blue eyes could face even more problems. Balinese "Kuta Cowboys" (i.e. beach bums) flaunt their Western girlfriends or marry Western women and become prosperous. Others now see it as their hope for the future. A single woman will never receive so many marriage proposals in her life.

Women are much more likely to get raped in the U.S., Europe, or Australia than on Bali, but you can expect men to pay you a lot of unwanted attention. To cut down on the attention, choose your clothes with care and do nothing to invite advances. Except when going to one of Bali's southern beaches, it's not a good idea to wear short shorts or skirts, braless tanktops, or strapless tops. Don't ask a man to accompany you to the beach at night for protection. He might misinterpret this as an invitation to have sex, because Balinese men don't realize American and Australian women fear they might be raped, robbed, or murdered if they go to the beach alone.

It's almost incomprehensible to Balinese men that a woman can live and travel alone. Women in Bali are afraid of living alone. They need their families to perform religious rites for their ancestors. Strong obligation to care for family members also keeps them at home. Men feel a particularly strong obligation to care for their households and ancestors. So here comes an unmarried, unaccompanied woman—she must want to be cared for and protected. Balinese men have an innate charm and graciousness, and when you ask a question, you're likely to get a sensitive answer. They feel they are responding naturally and instinctively to what women really want.

For years Australian men have gotten a big kick out of telling naive Balinese men that all Western women like dirty talk and sex, and if they say no they mean yes. They encourage the Balinese men to keep pushing because all Western women want it. Then they laugh about what fools they've made of the Balinese. As a result, men will ask if you're married, have a boyfriend, or if you've ever slept with a Balinese man. Answer very directly and even become rude to get rid of them—whatever it takes. The polite way is to say *"Saya senang sendiri"* ("I prefer to be alone") or *"Saya mau lihat-lihat se-orang saja"* ("I'd like to look around by myself"). As a last resort, take off your sunglasses, turn your face away expressionless, and say emphatically "No!" If they ever acted this way to Balinese women, they'd be knifed.

Some drivers say such filthy things that eventually women don't feel safe getting into taxis. If you want more comfort and convenience than a *bemo* provides, hire a car, but avoid situations

where intimacy might develop with your driver. Never take one driver for long-terms or overnight, don't sit in the front seat with him, and don't eat meals with him. Give him money for his own food if necessary. Another way to discourage sexual harrasment is to say you're married and your husband is waiting in the next village. Wear a wedding ring to back it up. Confidence is important. Don't give out your room number to men, and don't hug a Balinese man as it will invariably be misunderstood. You can also join other travelers for out-of-town trips. It might be best for some single women to join a group tour. But try to avoid turning every comment made by a Balinese man into a sexual innuendo. Don't become livid at your roomboys when they always ask "Where are you going?" In Indonesian culture, this is a courteous inquiry along the lines of "How are you?" Politeness is not a sexual advance so keep an informed and balanced point of view.

THEFT

Although muggings and other violent crimes are rare on Bali, stealing is a problem, particularly in resort areas with lots of tourists. Budget travelers are more vulnerable to theft than affluent tourists who take planes, taxis, and rent cars. Since travelers carry their money and valuables on their persons, they are prime targets for thieves. Suspicion and wariness demand constant effort. Not agreeable states of mind, they do prevent thefts, which would be more unpleasant.

The best measure against theft is to travel without jewelry, a watch, or camera. Balinese are proud and consider temptation an affront. The less you travel with, the less there is to steal, and less resentment is aroused. See what happens to your bargaining position if you flash money or jewelry. Lock up valuables or keep them out of sight. Travelers also rip off other travelers, so exercise caution around Westerners too. Never carry a lot of cash, perhaps only US$50 to see you through that day or week. Whether it's English pounds, U.S. dollars or Australian dollars, keep your money in small denomination traveler's cheques, cashable at banks, shops, and restaurants all over Bali. Even if you go to a

> *Please warn your readers about the night bus to Denpasar from Malang (East Java). The place to be extra cautious is where the bus loads onto the ferry. Three young men entered the bus and took the seats next to me and across the aisle and when I went to the restroom, got into my bag and removed the compact camera and presumably passed it to a confederate. I thought I had locked the main compartment of the dufflebag with a small padlock but they got the zipper undone anyway and I didn't realize it until after we left the bus. Several thoughts: 1. Don't take a camera. 2. Carry everything with you at all times. 3. Buy a hard case that can be securely locked. At first I rejected the idea of a Zero case as advertising that you are wealthy but they assume any tourist is wealthy anyway.*
>
> —JOHN S. LAYNARD

moneychanger twice a week to cash traveler's cheques, it's better than losing all your cash.

Discouraging Theft

All imaginable precautions should quickly become second nature to you. Always lock your hotel room. If you're traveling in budget places it's even better to bring your own lock and key to prevent inside jobs by houseboys or maids. Quick and quiet, thieves will enter your room through a window while you sleep and steal the camera from the hook above your head or the backpack from underneath your bed. Some *losmen* owners practice extraordinary security, checking at night to see if your door is locked properly. It's an eerie sight to see your doorknob slowly turn, but it might just be your landlord.

Ask to keep your valuables with the proprietor at a homestay, or at the front desk at small hotels for safekeeping. Many hotels now have safe deposit boxes *(tempat simpan uang)*, the more expensive ones even have them inside

the rooms. When you go inside supermarkets or department stores you can usually check your bag and your valuables in a storage bin *(tempat pinitipan barang)*. If you have the slightest doubt about security, spend the extra money on a more expensive, safer hotel with bars on the windows, a *penjaga* (guard), constant supervision by family members or the manager, and a high fence or stone wall with barbed wire or broken glass on top. The general public *must* be prevented from entering the inner compound, and your window shouldn't face an alley or side street, but toward the interior of the hotel. Don't leave bags on floors where they can be hooked with a line or pole and pulled to the window, and don't set anything valuable near an open window or on a curbside table while dining al fresco. Also don't leave valuables in a vehicle—leave the glove compartment open to show you don't have anything of value—and never leave a camera bag unattended in the back, even if you're in the vehicle with the back doors locked. Bags can be stolen when you stop and talk to boys crowding around your vehicle trying to distract you.

Pickpockets

If your mind is not on your money, you'll be vulnerable to pickpockets. Don't put your wallet in your back pocket—instead keep money deep inside your front trouser pockets. Be wary of minor accidents—being shoved or bumped, or having your foot stepped on. Don't be taken in by distractions, and be very watchful while attending crowded festivals. One big advantage of traveling with someone is that you're less likely to get robbed; you can keep an eye on each other and your gear.

As a general rule, don't let anyone touch you. On Kuta don't let the kids selling bracelets, wrist bands, or watches near you. They might try to pick your pocket, moneybelt, or fanny pack—working in tandem, one shows you the wares while the another shows you how a moneybelt "works" by putting it around you, holding the belt just above your wallet. No matter how cute or friendly they appear, just walk around them. If it's your first time in Asia, it's always better to buy in a shop and not from street peddlers.

Be cautious on Bali's *bemo* where travelers get ripped off by young pickpockets dressed as schoolkids. Working in groups, one or two act as a diversion while an accomplice steals. A large package, basket, or painting serves as cover. On the *bemo* which ply the tourist corridor between the capital and the hinterland, don't freak out if a pickpocket probes your jeans or shoulder bag for money. Take the strange fingers out, point, and announce to everyone, *"Pencopet!"* ("Pickpocket!"). Probably no one will do anything, but the thief won't stick around after that. Sit in the "traveler's seat" in the back of the *bemo* with your right or left side next to the cab. This will make your pockets and bags more difficult to get into. Keep your backpack against the cab with your eye on it, pockets facing the wall. If you see a suspicious situation shaping up, just get out and flag down another *bemo*—why take chances?

Wallets, Shoulder Bags, Passports

The whole concept of the wallet-in-the-hip-pocket must be discarded while in Bali. Pickpockets know exactly how to get at them, and at purses and shoulderbags. Avoid zippered shoulder bags because the zipper doesn't always close all the way, leaving room for a hand to reach inside. Instead, use a latch or snap which fastens the bag and can be locked, or a bag with a small opening which you have to pry apart yourself. The less you open your bag in public, the better.

Snatch thieves work in pairs on a motorbike. One sitting in back grabbing your shoulder bag or moneybelt, dragging you with it if you don't let go, and the other driving. Be wary of approaching motorbikes. Some travelers bear scratch marks from thieves who try to tear off necklaces and watches. Don't put valuables in a camera case; thieves have caught on to this practice. Cheap styrofoam coolers are better for storing valuables because they don't look like they contain valuables.

When moving around the island, leave your address book, traveler's check serial numbers, passport number, photographs, heavy money, air tickets, and other hard-to-replace papers in the bottom of your backpack. You're less likely to lose your backpack, and valuables can be taken out in the privacy of your room as you need them. Your backpack offers the most security because it either remains in your room or on your back, making it difficult for a thief to get into it without being detected. Keep only those possessions you can live without in side pockets or on the top layer of unlocked rucksacks or daypacks.

Lost Air Tickets/Passports

Write down your airline ticket number, flight number, issuing agent, date of issue, and method of payment. This information will make your ticket easier to refund in case of loss, but you still have to pay US$10 or more to the airline to replace it. The airline wants to be sure tickets haven't been used, so they can only be refunded at least three months after their expiration date.

Don't put your passport and money in the same place. If they're stolen, you've lost everything. Report passport loss immediately to the nearest police station and ask for a letter of reported theft/loss. Without this letter, a replacement passport to give you an extension from the *imigrasi* could be difficult. New passports or letters of travel can be obtained through consulates and embassies, most likely in Jakarta. Indonesia's major trading partners (Australia, Japan, U.S.A., the Netherlands) maintain consulates on Bali, many in Sanur (see "Information and Services," later in this chapter).

Moneybelts

An underpaid policeman can end up being your only friend in the case of a stolen or lost moneybelt. He might console you, feed you, then start up a collection to get you back safely to "your friends." This happened to me once in Padangpai after my moneybelt was stolen aboard the ferry from Lombok.

Designed to go *under* your clothes, moneybelts are highly recommended for Indonesia. If you hang a compact pouch on a leather strap around your neck, dangling under your shirt, it can be yanked off in crowds. A tight moneybelt fastened around your waist next to your skin is better. Keep your traveler's cheques, passport, and other documents in plastic covers inside so they don't become soiled with sweat, thus illegible or troublesome to use. On extended trips around the island, wrap a cloth or handkerchief around your belt so your skin doesn't get irritated because of the wet canvas. Select a moneybelt with the buckle in front so it doesn't gouge into your back when you're carrying your backpack.

Highly durable, water-repellent, cotton-blend, field-tested moneybelts with heavy-duty zippers are available for only $8.95 plus $1.25 shipping direct from Moon Publications, P.O. Box 3040, Chico, CA 95927, U.S.A. (tel. 800-345-5473). Another very secure and un-detectable way to carry large-denomination bills is a thick leather belt with a zipper along the inside which opens to a long, narrow, interior compartment. These cost around US$15 in Europe (not easy to find in the U.S.A. or Australia).

FOOD AND ENTERTAINMENT

INDONESIAN FOOD

Indonesia has one of the world's great cuisines, its influences originating from all corners of the globe. Located at the crossroads of the ancient world, astride the great trade routes between the Middle East and Asia, wave after wave of traders, adventurers, pirates, and immigrants have, since the Middle Ages, been drawn by the riches of these Spice Islands. Thus, nature and history have conspired to give Indonesia a cuisine as varied and highly seasoned as its thousands of islands and its hundreds of ethnic groups.

From India came curries, cucumber, eggplant, Indian mustard, cowpeas. The Chinese brought the wok and stir-frying, Chinese mustard, and vegetables such as brassica and Chinese cabbage. From Arabia came typical Middle Eastern gastronomic techniques and dishes such as kebab and flavorful goat stews. Peanuts, avocado, pineapple, guava, papaya, tomato, squash, pumpkin, cacao, soybean, and cauliflower have all been introduced by Europeans. During their occupation of Indonesia in WW II, the Japanese inroduced rice paddy fish and improved methods of planting rice. Yogurt and milk were introduced by Westerners in the 1970s due to the Balinese repugnance for dairy products. More recent additions have surfaced due to tourist demand: cheeses, ham, good meat, pickles, and locally grown citrus fruits.

Just a few years ago the only chicken one could find was the skinny, sinewy *kampung* variety, but today there are juicy drumsticks, Javanese-style fried chicken, *ayam suharti, syam chichi, ayam timbungan* with curry, as well as such exotics as California fried chicken. In Denpasar, new eateries on the Kuta-end of Jl. Imam Bonjol serve *ayam taliwang,* a superb chicken receipe from Lombok. Beef consumption is lim-ited, particularly on Bali, because cows and buffaloes are needed as draught animals in the rice-growing lowlands. Pork is produced and avidly consumed by the Balinese, the urban Chinese, and the non-Malay population. Goats, the Muslim staff of life, are the favorite animal protein of Bali's Indian population. Other main sources of protein are fish, poultry, and eggs. The soybean, the yellow vegetable cow of Indonesia, provides such hearty organic foods as *tahu* (tofu, or soybean cake) and high-protein *tempeh* (fermented soybean cake).

National Indonesian Dishes

From a few hundred in the early 1980s to several thousand today, restaurants have proliferated on Bali. Consequently, all Indonesian national dishes are available in Bali's restaurants. Anything with the word *nasi* in front of it means that it's prepared or served with rice. An old standby in any Padang- or Javanese-style restaurant from one end of Indonesia to the other is **nasi campur,** a heap of steamed rice topped with vegetables, meat, pickles, and *krupuk*—an excellent value for Rp1500-3000. A criticism of the Padang-style restaurant is that the ingredients are fresh only in the mornings and that the meat tends not be "tourist quality," i.e., it is stringy, fatty, and tough. Very popular with tourists and Indonesians alike is **nasi goreng,** a soft and crunchy fried rice dish offered by many restaurants as standard fare. **Mie goreng** means noodles fried in coconut oil with eggs, meat, or seafood, plus tomato, cucumber, shrimp paste, spices, and chilies. Both *nasi goreng* and *mie goreng* are common Indonesian breakfast dishes. If *istimewa* ("special") is written after either dish, it means it comes with fried egg on top.

Javanese-style **sate** is widely available on Bali. On Java, *sate* are marinated mini-kebabs of chicken, beef, or mutton impaled on skewers of coconut palm, grilled over an open charcoal fire, then dipped into a spicy peanut sauce. The Balinese make their *sate* by mixing minced meat laden with freshly grated coconut, prawn paste, garlic, chilies, lemon leaves, and salt to make a sticky dough-like mixture. Wrapped around a thick vein of bamboo or sugarcane, it is then charcoal-grilled and served with either a mild or peppery sauce. Pork, shrimp, bowel *(usus, jerohan),* egg, dog meat, and turtle meat *sate,* absent on Java, are popular on Bali.

A frequently encountered Indonesian dish acquired from the Dutch and found mostly in Bali's hotel restaurants is **rijstaffel** ("rice table"), a sort of Indonesian smorgasbord. In colonial days, a ceremonial *rijstaffel* could embrace as many as 35 courses. Today, five to 10 courses is more the norm. The total meal offers a variety of dishes, some sweet, others spicy, all to be eaten with boiled rice and condiments. The Balinese-style *rijstaffel* is made up of well-spiced regional fish, vegetable, and meat dishes and black rice pudding for dessert. The dishes are served in handmade pots, often accompanied by a haunting *tingklik* orchestra.

The *rijstaffel* presented at the Tanjung Sari Hotel in Sanur for Saturday and Sunday lunch is nothing short of spectacular. Many other big hotels serve their own versions of this popular dish, for example the Kartika Plaza (tel. 0361-751067) in Kuta and the Pesona Bali (tel. 0361-753914) in Seminyak for Rp30,000. The Beluga Restaurant (tel. 0361-71146) on Tg. Jl. Segara Windu, Tanjung Benoa, serves *rijstaffel* in the original style on antique plates by young Indonesian girls.

Gado-gado is a healthy Javanese salad combining potatoes and other vegetables. Peanut butter-loving Americans are particularly fond of this dish because it's served with a good quantity of rich, spicy peanut sauce on top. Luckily for vegetarians, it is available in almost every tourist restaurant on Bali at a very reasonable Rp1000-3000.

Another widespread, nourishing dish is the Chinese **cap cai,** a kind of Indonesian meat and/or vegetable chop suey. **Soto** means that thick *santen* (coconut cream) is added to a soup; this is also a breakfast dish. **Sop** is a watered down meat and vegetable stew.

Krupuk is a big, crispy, tangy, oversized cracker made from fish flakes, crab meat, shrimp paste, or fruit mixed with rice, dough, or sago flour. After being dried to look like thin, hard, colored plastic, when fried in oil the *krupuk* unfolds and blossoms. Since bread is seldom eaten, being too expensive and not to their taste, Balinese eat *krupuk* instead. **Emping** is another type of cracker made from *melinjo* which you crush *krupuk*-like over your food. When hungry, grab one of these delicious and nutritious crackers. It'll tide you over until you can get a proper meal.

BALINESE FOOD

It isn't easy to find genuine Balinese food. Sure, the hotel restaurants have a token *babi guling* on their menus but the dish is so modified to suit sensitive Western palates as to render it unrecognizable. Though Balinese food ranks behind Java's in subtlety, variety, and creativity, it is still an unusual and respectable Asian cuisine. Unfortunately, it doesn't travel well. In the entire length and breadth of Jakarta there is not a single Balinese restaurant. Even on such important ritual occasions as weddings or family rites of passage, the Balinese themselves serve a majority of Javanese or Chinese dishes and not Balinese. Since dining out is not a social custom on Bali, the visitor is not likely to experience real Balinese cooking unless invited into a Balinese home. About the only place to consistently experience the real thing are the night markets and *warung.* In your homestay, talk your way into your hostess's kitchen and sample some homemade Balinese meals. Every household prepares dishes in different ways. The most delectable, subtle foods—even banquet foods—are prepared with two burners, one wok, and a steamer pot. Balinese food is so hard to find because it's usually only prepared for hundreds of people on special occasions. Since coconut oil goes bad very quickly and refrigeration is limited, preparations for such perishable, difficult feast dishes as *mebat* and *lawar* are begun early in the morning, labored on through the dawn, and eaten fresh later in the morning.

The two or three meals the Balinese eat each day are almost identical—lots of boiled white rice supplemented by tiny fish, vegetables, peanuts, cucumbers, chilis, and minute portions of spiced meat, egg, or *tempeh.* In inland areas, dried and salted fish is more common.

In poorer areas, the rice is mixed with corn, cassava, or sweet potatoes. There are no courses. In a sense, there are no mealtimes. Food is prepared when hunger comes in the morning and is left in pots under protective baskets on the kitchen table to partake of whenever desired. Except during ceremonial feasting, the Balinese are very modest eaters. A glass of warm water or tea accompanies the frugal meal, which is often eaten cold.

Balinese cuisine is to be eaten with the fingers so that none of the delectably spicy flavors are compromised by the taste of aluminum. The Balinese always eat with the right hand, taking three fingers full of rice, dabbing it into spiced side condiments like *sambal,* then popping it into their mouth with a quick flex of the thumb. Eating is almost the only activity the Balinese prefer to do alone. It's bad manners to speak to a Balinese while he's eating. Having helped himself to some rice, and mixing it all up with his fingers on a banana leaf or a plate, a Balinese will go off by himself and sit in silence and with great haste scarf his food, gulp a glass of water, and then after a cooling *kretek* cigarette be on his way.

For those who would like to learn more about Balinese cooking, the 120-page *The Food of Bali* (Periplus Editions), edited by Wendy Hutton with recipes and photographs by Master Chef Heinz von Holzen, contains such recipes as suckling pig, *lawar,* various *sate, sambal,* leaf-wrapped fish, and rice desserts. The book costs Rp30,000 at hotel bookstores.

Ingredients

The Balinese will eat almost anything that crawls, flies, swims, or walks: worms, frogs, flying foxes, snakes, porcupines, anteaters, lizards, wild boars, centipedes, grubs, crickets, flying ants, bee larvae, birds (bones and all), crayfish. Dog is reputed to be an aphrodisiac rendering a man hot and strong through the night. It's also believed that dog meat is good for asthma. A Balinese kid will take you dragonfly-catching using a long thin wand *(tempilan)* with a sticky end that catches the gossamer wings. After catching

them, they take the wings off, fry the bodies in coconut oil until crisp, then eat them with spices and vegetables. Dragonfly larvae *(belauk)* are harvested in footprints in the rice fields, then fried, boiled, or grilled wrapped in banana leaves and eaten with rice and *sambal.* A Balinese family will smoke live bees out of a beehive, break the hive up, then soak it in water for about an hour. A mild spicy sauce is then stirred in and the resulting pulpy mass, complete with grubs, is parcelled out in banana leaves and grilled. Very tasty. Rice field eels *(belut),* which look like baby snakes, are caught at night, usually by feeling them with bare toes squirming in the mud. After cleaning, they're cooked over glowing embers and the next day served up crisp and salty. They're eaten whole, head and all—a bit chewy but good. Frogs are another source of protein from the flooded rice fields, caught by young children at night in a special hourglass-shaped bamboo trap.

Rice: All traditional Balinese food is designed to complement or be complemented by rice, a plentiful crop grown on the country's terraced paddies. Rice is so important to the Balinese that their word for "to eat" and "to eat rice" is the same *(ngajengang).* The Balinese ardently worship a rice-goddess Dewi Sri of pre-Hindu origin, and a complex series of rituals accompanies each of the plant's growing cycles, just as if the rice were people. There are dozens of words to describe the various stages of growth of rice and the variety of ways it's cooked.

Ordinary uncooked white rice is called *beras.* Steamed rice is *nasi kuskus,* steamed in a special cone-shaped bamboo cooker called a *pengukusan* (which tourists often mistake for field hats). Rice is cooked just once daily, in the mornings. As it sours quickly in the tropical climate, what has not been eaten by nightfall is fed to the pigs. For the Balinese, the whiter the uncooked rice, the tastier it is when cooked (although all the nutrients have been taken out). Turmeric *(kunyit)* is often added in the cooking to give rice a yellow coloring. Not only is rice the basic ingredient of every meal, but it's used to make rice wine *(brem)* and a giddy variety of colorful sweet cakes *(jajan)* used in temple offerings.

There are a number of varieties of rice grown on Bali. When buying white rice *(beras putih),* try the old-fashioned, short-grained paddy rice,

RECIPE FOR *BABI GULING*

To make **babi guling** (*guling* means "to turn"), which is stuffed suckling pig roasted on a spit: Kill pig. Pour boiling water over it and scrape the skin with a coconut shell. Open mouth and scrape tongue also. Cut open belly wide enough for the hand and remove viscera. Wash inside of pig well with cold water. Stuff to taste with *lombok* (red chili pepper), garlic, red onions, *kunyit* (turmeric), *jahe* (ginger), salt, *tinke* (nuts resembling ginger), *cokoh* (aromatic roots of ginger), *merica* (black pepper), *saladam* (aromatic leaves), and *ketumbah* (peppercorn).

Chop all these ingredients fine and mix them with coconut oil. Stuff the pig and put a piece of coconut bark inside as well. Sew belly up. Run pointed stick through the mouth and anus. One end of the stick must be crooked to serve as a crank. Coat the pig in crushed turmeric mixed with water to give the skin a brown color. Make a big wood fire and place the pig to one side of it, not over it, on a spit supported with forked branches. Turn the pig constantly and fan the fire to direct smoke and flame away. You want the heat to be concentrated on the head and tail and not on the middle so that the stomach skin doesn't crack. Roast for two hours to make pork juicy and tender. Skin should be brittle and covered with a golden-brown glaze. Eat.

BOB RACE

beras asli or *beras bali*, which is considered more flavorful than the newer long-grained rice and other "improved" dwarf varieties. One can easily distinguish *beras bali* from the new high-tech rice. Its grains are oval-shaped, while the dwarf grains are long and needle-like. *Beras bali* is also three times more expensive. Red rice *(gaga)* and black glutinous rice *(injin)* are also grown, but are scarcer and more expensive.

Vegetables and Greens: Bali's abundant vegetation and relatively few edible animals have led its inhabitants to adopt a semi-vegetarian diet. Bali is blessed with over 100 vegetables *(jukut)*, including such exotics as acacia leaves *(tuwi)*, bean pods *(buah pete)*, spinach-like greens *(bayem)*, edible ferns *(paku)*, sweet potato leaves *(kesela pohon)*, tasty banana plant flowers *(pusuh biu)*, and tender shoots of banana leaves *(kekalan)*. Leaves of bamboo, mangoes, peanut *(don kacang)*, and papaya *(don gedang)* are also used in cooking. Raw greens, as in our green salads, are seldom eaten. When the housewife needs instant vegetables or herbs to round out her dinner, she forages leaves from plants, shrubs, or trees in her backyard, washes and then boils them up with grated coconut and such spices as MSG and *basa genep*. Periodically, rice fields are dried out for a season, and other crops such as sweet potatoes *(ubi)*, peanuts *(kacang tanah)*, maize *(jagung)*, lima beans *(kekare)*, sugarcane *(tubu)*, and various types of beans *(kacang)* are planted. Cassava (ubi kayu) is grown on the dry Bukit Peninsula. Bangkuwang, a root vegetable similar in texture to the Chinese water chestnut, is eaten raw or with rujak. The Balinese leek, bawang pere, is a frequent ingredient in the Chinese dish cap cay. The onion family is also well represented. Tuwung butuh is a solanaceous vegetable which means "bull testicles." Because of its climate, the mountains around Bedugul on Lake Bratan grow the island's widest variety of temperate-zone type vegetables—cabbages, tomatoes, string beans, mustard leaf, cauliflowers, peppers, white potato, eggplants, avocados, carrots, celery, cabbage. Visit Bedugul's market at Candi Kuning to behold great piles of giant European vegetables.

Spices and Condiments: The Balinese consider Western food flat and tasteless. Their own food tends to be peppery and served with such potent spices as mashed onions, garlic, fermented fish paste, and scalding red peppers. The most ramshackle warung can bring forth an array of exquisite dishes with flavors, textures, and aromas that you never dreamed existed: tingling ginger sautes, rich and creamy peanut sauces, and spice-laden chili sambal toppings that will fire the palate. Surprisingly, one seldom comes across the spices—nutmeg, pepper, mace, and cloves—that gave the "Spice Islands" their name and spurred Columbus to accidently discover America. The job of having the proper spices on hand is made easier for the Balinese housewife with the purchase of a bag of basa genep, mixed spices, which contains a good portion of the 40 or so spices used in Balinese cooking. Spices are ground into a paste in back of the family compound, using a black stone mortar (batu basa) and cone-shaped pestle (cantok); buy a set in Denpasar's market for Rp10,000.

A crucial spice in Balinese cooking is sra, a ground and putrid shrimp paste which has been dried and mixed with seawater, then allowed to ferment for months. Having the consistency of toothpaste, sra is fried first to bring out its flavor; a pea-sized amount is enough to give a racy, briny dimension to a whole dish. Sra has no substitute. Some standard spices include a gritty sea salt (uyah), black (mica selem) and white (mica putih) pepper, candlenuts (tingkih), tiny, mild, pear-shaped red onions (bawang barak),

ginger (jahe), coriander seeds (ketumbah), sour tamarind (celagi), and garlic (kesuna). Aromatic roots and leaves, MSG (monosodium glutamate, or pitsin in Balinese), and citrus juice (lemo) are added for extra flavoring. Laos powder (isen) is another exotic Indonesian spice. Bright orange-yellow turmeric (kunyit), a root of the ginger family that resembles a small carrot, is frequently used in Balinese festival dishes to produce yellow-colored rice.

Coconuts (nyuh), an essential ingredient in Balinese cooking, add richness to many native recipes, especially curries and sauces. Frying is done exclusively in coconut oil. At least 12 varieties of nyuh, either green or yellow, are found on Bali. When they are old and dried out, they turn gray. Able to produce fruit for 50 years, the coconut provides the Balinese with vessels, clothing, soap, cosmetics, housing materials, food, and drink. Coconut milk is made by shredding the meat of the old coconut, kneading, sieving, then blending it with water. As it cooks, the coconut milk thickens; with the addition of flour or corn starch it becomes a thick, white, rich cream (santen). Balinese-style sate is often kneaded into coconut cream. The sweet, creamy contents of the young coconut (kuwud) also makes a refreshing drink. Any boy or man can shape a spout and spoon of the coconut husk to allow you to drink from the nut or scrape out the pulpy meat.

Chilies (tabia), the elongated pods of the Capsicum pepper family, turn from green to red when ripe. Usually the larger the size, the milder the chili. The largest sizes are used principally to decorate offerings, but the smallest (tabia kerinyi) are highly flammable! Chili bushes grow easily inside the family kampung, and chilies are plucked as needed. Chilies are de rigueur in any kind of sambal, and thin slices of chili go into the spicy-hot, salty, and popular Balinese soybean sauce called kecap (pronounced "KECH-ap") which has nothing to do with tomato-based catsup as we know it. In restaurants there are almost always two kinds of kecap, sweet (kecap manis) and sour (kecap asin). Indonesian-made Western-style tomato ketchup is only available in Bali's restaurants. There are many kinds of hot chili sauces (sambal) and spiced chili pastes. Almost every dish has its own kind of sambal, and every Balinese family makes its own a little differently. But don't get the idea that all Balinese food is hot. Many dishes are quite palatable to the Westerner. Peanut sauces made with chilies and unsweetened coconut cream top the Indonesian delicacies most enjoyed by Westerners. When in doubt as to whether the dish is spicy hot or not, ask *"Pedas atau tidak?"* ("Hot or not?"). If the dish is too hot, don't try to douse the fire with a glass of cold water, cold beer, or a carbonated drink, which only exacerbates the problem. Instead, eat some boiled rice, cucumber, a banana, or some bread. To make a dish less fiery hot, squeeze a little lemon with some salt over it. Or drink hot tea or warm water which will sting at first, then bring relief.

Typical Balinese Dishes

In virtually every hotel—from majestic to humble—you can order a "Balinese Special Feast" with only 24 hours notice. Though a Westernized, toned down version, it will give you a taste of Balinese/Indonesian food. *Tum* is ground beef and spices wrapped in banana leaf and steamed. *Be tambus* is boiled fish served with a thick spicy sauce and sliced tomatoes. Above all, don't miss roast steamed duck *(bebek betutu)* stuffed with spices and vegetables, wrapped in banana or betel nut leaf, then smoked to perfection for three or four hours in a ground oven or rice steamer. Though *bebek betutu* is a big hit with most Westerners, some complain it has too many bones. The Balinese like to snap all the tiny bones off at the end and suck out the succulent marrow *(sum-sum)*. The best steamed duck is cooked in Peliatan.

Most of Indonesia is Muslim, and the eating of pork is forbidden by the Islamic religion. Thus pigs are absent on Java but run all over Hindu Bali where they are bred and cooked magnificently. Bali's famous delicacy, *babi guling,* is a whole pig stuffed with tapioca leaves, red chilies and onions, garlic, green peppers, turmeric, ginger, aromatic leaves, candlenuts, and whole peppercorns. The pig (weighing four to six kg) is then stitched together, skewered, and roasted *(guling* means "to turn") very slowly on a spit over a low coal fire for three hours. Brushed with crushed turmeric, the flesh turns juicy and tender, the skin brittle and covered with a golden-brown glaze.

Although tourists are told it's roast suckling pig, the pig is usually way past the suckling stage. If your homestay does the cooking, one small pig serves four or five. Although a ceremonial meal, you can find *babi guling* in many markets and specialty street stalls at any time of the year. Sample it in the traditional way with rice, spicy sausage made from the innards, stuffing, crackling, pork *lawar,* boiled jackfruit, and vegetables.

Very possibly the best *babi guling* in Bali is served in several crowded *warung* on the main road to Candidasa in the Banjar Tegas compound next to Terminal Gianyar in Gianyar Town. These *warung,* which don't normally open before 1000 or 1100, roast more than a dozen animals a day and the food is always fresh and delicious. Try a glass of the refreshing native brew, *tuak,* while you're at it.

Warung and Roadside Stalls

Along Bali's road sides are small eating stalls—consisting of a dirt floor or bamboo platform, a palm-leaf or plastic canopy, and a bench or two—which dispense quick meals as cheap and nutritious as anywhere in the world. These roadside foodstalls and cafes offer a mixed fare of coffee, tea, cakes, biscuits, rice cakes, peanuts, and homemade spirits. They may even serve complete meals, usually served cold on a banana leaf. *Warung* that serve only coffee *(kopi)* and biscuits *(kue)* cater particularly to the menfolk who stop there to gossip, read the newspaper, or listen to the radio before returning home. Sit with the farmers and sip a glass of foaming *tuak* while sampling some rice treats wrapped in banana leaf *(nasi bungkus).* If you want a dish served heated, say *"Yang masih panas."* Temple festivals and village markets are the best places to find these flimsy, makeshift eateries where you can sample such truly native Balinese snacks and treats as *rujak, babi guling,* original paddy rice, fruits, vegetable mixes, spicy sauces, boiled corn-on-the-cob, roasted and steamed bean pods, crunchy baby peanuts which look like corn kernels, and high-protein sweet potatoes served with coconut, palm sugar, and *kecap.*

Serving as meeting places for young and old, *warung* also make excellent language labs for learning Indonesian. These coffee shops also

a typical warung

sell domestic supplies such as kerosene, lamps, batteries, cigarettes, needles, buttons, medicine, dried fish, and salt. Even the smallest country villages have five or six *warung.* At night the *warung* could be the only well-lit place in the whole village.

Pushcarts and Mobile Kitchens
The Balinese snack at all hours of the night and day. Even the streets of the tourist centers (except Nusa Dua) are filled with vendors selling cheap food for the thousands of Indonesians working in the shops, cleaning hotels and restaurants, and driving taxis. Food is prepared from the freshest ingredients right before your eyes at one-quarter the price you'd pay in a restaurant. Just sit on the curb to eat and join in conversation with the Indonesians beside you. As they push their carts along, these vendors make distinctive sounds with their voices or with implements that signal their specialty: noodle soups, *nasi* and *mie goreng, bakso* (beef meatball), *sate,* Arabian pancakes *(martabak), tahu gunting, rujak,* poisonous-looking iced syrups, steamed sweetmeats, beans, sticky cakes, fruits, peanuts.

Whole kitchens also dangle from shoulder poles. These sellers set up at street corners and even along the beaches dispensing leaf or newspaper cones full of soggy, newly steamed peanuts, boiled peanuts *(kacang cina malablab),* peanuts fried in oil *(kacang cina magoreng),* fried without the skin *(kacang cina kapri),* or

roasted (kacang cina manyanyah). The Balinese are addicted to small, green beans called *kacang ijo,* which are also available around the clock, fried, boiled, or roasted.

Balinese Festival Foods
Balinese banquet food is as sophisticated as any of the world's great cuisines. Women cook the daily meal, but only men may prepare the festival dishes. Great banquet chefs admired all over Bali are in demand at the more important feasts. On these occasions the assembled guests sit in long rows while members of the *banjar* weave amongst them, setting before each a small square banana leaf on which they place all the principal dishes: a pyramid of pure white rice topped with fried beans *(botor),* crushed peanuts, crispy baked grated coconut, dried *kunyit,* and various delicacies. Five principal banquet delicacies are prepared on special family occasions and important religious holidays like Galungan.

Mebat centers on turtle; for even a small amount of *mebat,* one wild sea turtle must be killed—in inland areas, they use pork instead. *Lawar,* one of the dishes that make up a *mebat* ritual feast, is a mixture of uncooked grated coconut, young jackfruit, tree leaves, sauce, long slivers of meat, and the obligatory spices, all of which is pounded and chopped to the consistency of lawnmower mulch. Pig's blood is mixed with *lawar* only if requested because it goes bad in an hour. Ask for either the "red" (mixed with blood) or the "white" (not yet mixed with blood). The best and cheapest *lawar* is sold at open-air *warung* set up at festivals, cockfights, and other village events. *Sayur urap,* similar to *lawar,* is vegetables, corn, and beans mixed with tamarind leaves *(celagi)* and grated coconut to create a creamed vegetable dish (best in Klungkung). *Sate,* another ritual food, is made from pork, chicken, duck, or turtle. Savory *leklat* (or *sate lembat)* is diced turtle meat with a spiced paste kneaded in *santen,* then roasted until crisp over coals.

Sea turtle *(penyu)* is a specialty of the Denpasar area. Turtle meat spoils easily, so a meal containing turtle meat must be cooked and eaten within 24 hours. Sacrificed in the wee hours of the morning, the shell, flippers, and head are severed from the body, and for some hours afterwards the jaws snap hideously and the entrails twitch violently on the beach. The blood of the turtle is collected and diluted with lime juice to prevent coagulation. The skin and meat are chopped very finely and prepared with spices, coconut, and even raw blood (in dishes like *kiman, lawar,* and *gecok).* At the rate these endangered wild creatures are being slaughtered, turtle-based dishes will soon disappear. To see how depressing it can get, visit Pegok, a suburb of Denpasar. Tourists shouldn't contribute to the slaughter.

Communal meals for a family or village feast often take at least a full day of preparation, sometimes starting late at night and carrying on until morning. If you really want to experience the old Balinese way of presenting a royal banquet, attend Puri Krambitan's "Puri Night" in the village of Krambitan in Tabanan Regency.

Variation in texture is an integral aspect of the classical meal—mushiness *(lawar)* and juiciness (pork) is always accompanied by crunchiness (pigskin) and dryness *(krupuk).* To guarantee the freshness of the meat and sauces in Bali's tropical climate, the men are awakened in the middle of the night to slaughter the turtles and pigs. Food containing coconut, a central ingredient of so many Balinese dishes, must be eaten the same day. At about 0400 on the morning of the ceremony the men will gather, each carrying a large heavy chopping knife *(berang).* While sitting cross-legged on bamboo mats on the floor of the *bale banjar,* the men are busy

cooking, scraping coconuts, chopping meat, stirring big black pots, preparing mountains of spices, and constructing altars and sheds. The women make offerings, carry water, and cut out *lamak* decorations. The many chefs return home soon after dawn to their families carrying their portions which are immediately devoured with relish by all.

INTERNATIONAL AND TOURIST FOOD

Except in Denpasar, the restaurant business is largely based on tourism, unlike Jakarta where restaurants are also patronized by locals. A non-tourist restaurant in Bali's capital city will naturally have plenty of Indonesians sitting in it. Since Indonesians are fastidious eaters, you can bet it's good. If you want really authentic Indonesian food, stick to the streets or eat in *warung* or night markets, both of which are found even in tourist areas. Just go around to the back or to the sides of any hotel where all the service people eat.

The only restaurants where you can make reservations and use your plastic are expensive four- and five-star hotels. No matter what the class, many restaurants offer free transport though they may not advertise the fact. Always call ahead to ask. If you're eating in tourist restaurants all the time, you need to allow about Rp15,000-20,000 per day for two people. Don't take it for granted that the bill is correct. If it is incorrect, it will never be in your favor. Double-check the prices and add the bill up again. The higher-priced the restaurant is, the more likely a service charge and tax, varying from 10% to 21%, will be added to your bill. Hotel restaurants and restaurants at tourist sites invariably add these charges. If it's not added, please don't tip! It's not expected and it should not be introduced on Bali. If you feel it's called for, Rp1000 is the absolute maximum you should give.

Public Restaurants

There are hundreds of first-rate restaurants in Denpasar, Sanur, Kuta, Legian, Candidasa, and Lovina Beach. In both public and hotel restaurants of southern Bali every sort of international cuisine can be found: Japanese, French, Italian, Swiss, Mexican (in the Kuta area), Spanish,

Moroccan. When groups of Japanese enter a restaurant, they play Japanese music; when Americans enter, they play American music.

Some are fantastic people-watching venues and also serve first-class Indonesian cuisine. Although the competition in the tourist areas like Kuta and Sanur make for a higher standard of food, the setting could be drab and noisy, the service slow, their tables set under bright neon lights. The multitude look, sound, and smell alike and offer identical menus at identical prices. Ask your hotel's front desk or the homestay owner where you should eat. Indonesians love to eat and they'll pinpoint the best places.

When ordering food, many restaurants provide slips of paper on which to write down your order and the price; this is a good idea because it prevents misunderstandings. If you don't write your order down precisely, half the time they'll get it wrong. If there is no paper or pen, verify your order with the waiter before it goes to the kitchen. All waiters speak at least some English, and many can get by in Japanese, French, even Italian. Don't assume that your waiter knows what goes into a dish; ask the cook instead. If you're allergic to MSG, tell your waiter *"Saya tidak mau aji-no-moto."* If you don't, half the time you'll get MSG in your food. The Chinese, in particular, use a lot of MSG.

Also be prepared for the proper sequence to be backwards, i.e., main course, then soup, then salad. Often some members of your party may not receive their food until everyone else has finished. Typically, what finished cooking first is served first. The only way to control the order in which the food arrives is to order one item at a time.

One of the hardest things to take, especially in restaurants with good reputations, is the inconsistency. For example, one time your order of *gado-gado* is what it is supposed to be: a warm fresh vegetable salad with a mild peanut sauce. Another time it's an overcooked pile of sauteed cabbage topped with a greasy, bland peanut-flavored gravy. You never know what ingredients you'll find in your dish, what color the dish will be, or how big the portion. Also hard to predict is the amount of fat and meat, especially chicken, that goes *nasi goreng* and *mie goreng*. One way to avoid the unpredictable fare is to just stick with simple dishes like grilled fish with rice and veg-

etables or soup without MSG. *Nasi campur* is a safe bet if you personally pick what goes into this "mixed rice" dish.

Tourist Restaurants

A tourist restaurant is characterized by menus in English featuring Western-style dishes. As is the case anywhere, the number of people who patronize the establishment is an indication of its quality. Restaurants and painting galleries, particularly those along the tourist corridors, pay tour bus companies and travel agencies to stop at their establishments on their tours around the island. Your guide and driver, or the owners of the tour company, receive a commission for each person they deliver to their doorstep.

One should be wary of the species of tourist restaurant that serve Balinese/Indonesia/Chinese buffet luncheons. Popular tourist sites and heavily trafficked tourist routes seem to breed these restaurants. Since they have you and the rest of the people on your bus captive, you have no recourse but to eat the awful, tasteless, high-priced food. The restaurant is only saved by the view. Though many of these roadside restaurants have truly inspiring and romantic garden settings or are situated in breezy open-sided pavilions, they tone down or eliminate many of the "funny-tasting" Indonesian spices in order to make the food more palatable to Westerners. On the other hand, buffets targeted to the traveler and put on by certain tourist restaurants of Kuta, Legian, and particularly Lovina, can be extraordinary good values. Read the advertised menu items carefully—soy sauce and napkins are not worthy of being included!

The biannual magazine *Menu's: The Restaurant Guide of Bali* (Box 2179, Kuta) is a collection of menus from some of the best restaurants of Bali. Available for Rp2000 at most bookstores, kiosks, and hotel reception desks, it comes with a convenient restaurant locator map, index, and food list vocabulary in Indonesian. Each of the restaurants included have been personally researched and recommended by at least five people based on quality, atmosphere, cleanliness, service, and originality. Another honest source of information for the gourmand is *Eating Bali: The Complete Restaurant Guide* by Mark Beshara (Times Books International), which humorously evaluates over 200 restaurants in the island's six tourist areas. Restaurants are graded on their food, service, atmosphere, sanitation, and price. Includes maps, photos, plus a list of 59 restaurants to avoid. The information in this book, published in 1990, is only about 70% accurate.

Hotel Restaurants

The hotel restaurants of Bali are capable of truly gourmet fare. In the big resort hotels the price of all-you-can-eat breakfasts and dinner buffets, from Rp15,000 to Rp30,000, is kept reasonable so the restaurant can compete with outside dining establishments. They run on a very thin margin and thus are quite a good value.

At elegant hotel restaurants you start the day off at extravagant breakfast buffets with assorted local and imported fresh fruit, followed by ham, steak, eggs, croissants, toast, yogurt, coffee or tea. Almost all the star-hotels put on gigantic dinner buffets in which a different cuisine is featured every night of the week. Known as "food entertainment," hotels present a variety in order to hold the interest and loyalty of hotel guests.

When hotel restaurants are good, they are very good, serving such international cuisine as marinated dolphinfish, barbecued prawns, lobster-stuffed red chili peppers, avocados overflowing with shrimp, mango zabaglione, pineapple flambéed with Grand Marnier sauce, and huge river crabs with claws the size of lobsters crammed with extraordinarily delicious sweet fluffy white meat; all are accompanied by fine imported European and Australian wines. Some hotels offer hot and cold breakfast and dinner buffets of 50-odd dishes.

In all but the very cheapest and most expensive hotels, breakfast is included in the price of the room. The lady who runs your homestay will probably give you fresh fruit, a bottomless pot of good tea, a thermos of hot water for coffee, and a dish of homemade *jajan* (cookies to the Americans, biscuits to the Brits). Unless you say otherwise you'll be served coffee and tea in glasses filled one-third with sugar and sweet condensed milk. In the higher cost hotels (US$20-30 and up), you can save the cost of breakfast (usually charged extra) if you travel with a heating element and make your coffee or tea and eat baked goods and fruit (bought the

day before) in your hotel room each morning. You can cut down on your food costs if you buy snacks, drinks, and groceries at a nearby supermarket, then prepare some of your food in your hotel room or front veranda. Higher-priced hotels frequently have refrigerators in the rooms.

Ethnic Restaurants

For those who crave a dish cooked in the style of their home country, you will not be disappointed on Bali. The choice of international cuisine is unlimited—Bali offers everything from Moroccan couscous and Mexican enchiladas to Polish borchst and Swiss fondue.

Not all ethnic restaurants are good—some fall down on the job of re-creating their cuisine on Bali. Really authentic versions of Italian and French food, for example, are difficult to achieve when using local ingredients. If it's a pizza or home-style steak you're looking for, don't be too critical. Fried bread is many restaurants' version of toast. Salads, as a rule, are not their forte. Balinese banana pancakes don't contain any leavening, only flour and egg, and taste like extra thick crepes. Despite its Hindu origins, neither is Bali the place to eat great homemade curries. "Maharaja Curry" bears about as much resemblance to curry as Westminster Abbey does to the Taj Mahal. Dozens of restaurants serve Mexican dishes, but be forewarned that tacos are sometimes nothing more than Chinese stir-fried vegetables on a big cracker—no relation to a real taco. Nachos and guacamole are served with *krupuk* instead of corn chips. When in doubt, always order food from the restaurant's Indonesian menu—*that* they know how to cook well. And you'll have ample opportunity to try Javanese cooking on Bali, which is perhaps more to the liking of the Western palate.

Chinese restaurants are generally more expensive than tourist eating places but offer more variety and culinary sophistication. Visit Chinese restaurants in a group so that a wide variety of tasty dishes can be sampled. The Chinese are a little fussy about their meat intake, taking only small, gourmet-cooked portions, so if you feel that Indonesian or Balinese food is short on vegetables head for a Chinese restaurant, which usually serves an abundance of fresh vegetables with their dishes. A typical Chinese-style restaurant now charges about

Rp10,000-15,000 per person minimum for a large meal, including beer.

Vegetarian

Bali is not Yogyakarta—the vegetarian capital of Indonesia—but in the countryside you come across amazingly nutritious and tasty vegetarian dishes. All over Bali you can enjoy *bubur sayur bayam* (rice porridge with coconut shavings, coconut cream, chili sauce, and peanut plant leaves) for as little as Rp200. The little old ladies who sell it come out from 0600 to 0700, then again from 1400 to 1700. There is health food in restaurants in Kuta, Legian, Sanur, and Ubud. It's common for restaurants to include many vegetarian items on their menus. Look for Chinese-style dishes in particular. You can, in fact, pick almost anything from a menu and get the vegetarian version by saying (though writing it out is always better) *tanpa daging* or *kurang daging* (without meat) after the name of the item. Example: *Nasi goreng tanpa daging* is "nasi goreng without sugar." Also *teh tanpa gula* means "tea without sugar." The majority of restaurants have tofu *(tahu)* and *tempe* in the kitchen, so just say *"Saya mau cap cay tanpa daging. Sayur-sayuran saja. Boleh pakai tahu atau tempe"* ("I want chop suey without meat. Vegetables only. Please add tofu or tempe"). When ordering *nasi campur,* go up and point to what you want to make sure you don't get meat. Don't leave it up to them. Don't hesitate to ask for more vegetables (*tambah lagi* means "add more").

Seafood

Though surrounded by sea, the Balinese themselves are not big on seafood; the catch goes either to the island's canneries or to the local tourist restaurants. Kuta and Sanur's Chinese restaurants serve the best seafood on the island.

You should try exotic fish and shellfish dishes, which are probably more affordable on Bali than in your own country. Fish and shellfish dinners average Rp10,000-15,000, about half the Singapore price and about one-third the American or European price. The flipping wet fish is usually brought to you on a platter for your inspection, then it is charbroiled and presented to you cooked, tantalizingly tender, spiked with scallions and slices of lime. You can often get a better price if you bargain before you even enter the restaurant. Select the fish you want, then offer 30% less than the price they quote you. You'll probably get it at around 15% less. Remember: The more fish you buy, the better price you should get.

Lobster is supposedly the delicacy of the island; it costs about US$5 per 100 gram. This means a full lobster dinner with bottle of beer will set you back US$15-20. The Nusa Dua hotels are the most expensive at about US$6 or US$7 per 100 gram. A better deal is fresh grilled red snapper, which is firm, fleshy, and tasty.

Fast Food

A relatively new phenomenon are Bali's fast-food restaurants. In spite of a wonderful native cuisine, you see popping up such outlets as Burger King (two locales in Kuta), Kentucky Fried Chicken (outlets in Kuta, Legian, Sanur, and Denpasar), McDonald's, Pizza Hut, and Church's Texas Fried Chicken. There are also two Swenson's and one Pioneer Chicken. For the most part, these Western franchises cater to Jakartans and other Indonesian "outsiders" who like to eat "modern."

Night Markets

Open-air *pasar malam* in Bali's large towns offer a collection of smoky, ramshackle *warung* where some of the best food for the money can be had. A trip into town to eat at the night market—whether in Kuta, Ubud, Bangli, Gianyar, Singaraja, or Amlapura—makes for a great night out. The visitor will discover an array of European, Arabian, Chinese, Indian, and local Indonesian cuisines.

These collections of makeshift foodstalls—poor-men's restaurants—are aglow with hissing gas lamps, covered by plastic canopies, and provided with wooden benches or stools. Pure Indonesian and occasionally Balinese cuisine, including such delicious snacks as *krupuk, pisang goreng,* and fried *tempeh,* are eaten with a cheap aluminum spoon amid much banter from your fellow diners. You're assured of a genuine and lively atmosphere. If you're sitting in one foodstall, it doesn't mean you can't also order from ones nearby. Choose one with the friendliest atmosphere, then walk around to neighboring *warung* and order different food treats. If you gesture to where you're sitting, each vendor will deliver your dish to you. If you don't speak Bahasa Indonesia, simply point to anything that looks good.

Excellent *pasar malam* are often in the perimeters of markets and bus stations. One of the largest is in Denpasar, behind the parking lot of the multistoried Kumbasari Shopping Complex; other night markets are at the Suci Bus Station and the Sports Stadium (corner of Jl. Supratman and Jl. Melati). At night along Jl. Teuku Umar, tent restaurants open up. Very popular with the locals are such dishes as *ayam chi-chi,* grilled fried chicken with *lalab* (Sundanese salad).

Day Markets
If you prefer to do your own cooking, buy household and kitchen utensils in the markets along Jl. Gajah Mada in Denpasar, then visit the native markets for your grocery staples.

While the cattle market *(pasar ternak)* is the domain of the men, the everyday village market is the world of women—haggling, gossiping, cooking, working. Markets in most villages, even the size of Ubud, take place every three days where you'll see a cornucopia of grains, beans, seeds, greens, fruit, and pastes of all colors and textures, as well as typical *pasar,* and snacks such as *klepon, pisang rai, bubur sumsum.* Stands in the markets serve up soups, vegetables, curries, betel nut wrapped in palm leaf. Great care is taken to make the food attractive so as to catch the shopper's eye: flowers are strewn over fruit, dishes are brightly garnished, and green leaves are spread under vegetables. Get there by 0600 with the housewives and *pembantus* (house-servants) because the best and freshest produce and the best prices go to the quick and audacious. There are at least three price levels: the lowest to those in the same *kampung,* a higher price to fellow Balinese, and highest of all to the Javanese and other foreigners who pay a "newcomer's tax" on local goods and services (don't feel ripped off, it's a negligible amount). Treat bargaining as entertainment, an enjoyable means of communication.

Supermarkets
At a number of Western-style, air-conditioned supermarkets around the island you can score such imported and expensive items as peanut butter, jams, cereal, liquor, Australian T-bone steaks, New Zealand lamb legs, U.S. sirloins (local meat is too lean and tough), frozen meat, and fresh seafood from lobster to snapper. Most are laid out like mini-shopping malls. Some even offer discounted goods, giveaways, and special promotions. Kuta's Galael Dewata (with a branch on Jl. Bypass in Sanur) has the best deli and wine selections (bottles of wine start at Rp20,000). There's even a market in Seminyak near the road down to the Oberoi that's open 24-hours called K-Markt. It carries deli items like fresh and processed cheeses, fresh baked breads, dairy products, cereals, biscuits, and beverages. If you're buying biscuits, nuts, and snacks, get the Indonesian product, which is fresh, delicious, and cheap. Especially good are the locally produced butter cookies and shortbreads. All imported fruit is expensive, but if you want oranges or stone fruit you have no choice in the matter.

DRINKS

Drinking water will keep the price of your meals down. Thirsty foreigners are provided, in most cases, with boiled water or tea from their hotel or homestay, so you don't have to be paranoid about drinking unclean water. At a restaurant or shop, order *air putih* (boiled drinking water) or cold plastic-bottled drinking water. Aqua is the best known brand. Big plastic containers (19 liters) cost around Rp5000 or six-liter ones are Rp2800 (Rp400 per liter). The most common size container is 1,500 miligram; buy these at big grocery stores for Rp800 rather than at your corner *warung* for as much as Rp1200.

The Balinese themselves often prefer to take warm or cold tea with meals, just as refreshing without milk or sugar. Tea helps stimulate the appetite and digestion and will keep you awake after a heavy lunch. If you don't want your tea (or coffee) filled with 50% sugar, say *teh pahit* or *tea tawar* (unsugared tea) which you shouldn't be charged for; plain iced tea *(teh es pahit)* should cost only Rp500 or so. Another way to avoid over-sugared drinks is to opt for soda water *(botol soda)* or beer *(bir).*

Powerful Balinese coffee, a crop grown in the highlands as far back as 1880, is served pitch-black (fresh milk not usually available), sweet, thick, and rich, with the grounds still floating on top. This black, unfiltered coffee, made by pouring hot water on top of coffee powder, can be hard on the stomach. Don't drink more than two cups a day as it's like chewing coffee beans. In most restaurants and *warung,* coffee costs Rp1000-2000 for a tall glass. Stir well to get the grinds to sink. Condensed milk is often the only kind of milk available and is so sweet you don't have to add sugar. If you need to wake up, try spiking your morning coffee with *arak* or drinking hot ginger tea.

In Kuta, Legian, and Seminyak's cosmopolitan cafes you can sample not only Bali coffee but gourmet Colombian, Brazilian, and other imported coffees as well, including frothy, piping hot cappucino. Some cafes cater to certain cliques like the rather self-conscious Cafe Luna in Seminyak, a hangout for European and North American jewelry and clothes makers and designers.

Since there are so many natural fruit juice drinks around, both hot and cold, many derived from fruits found nowhere else in the world, it's insane to drink Fanta with ice juice *(es jus).* Such exotic hippie trail items as fruit-flavored *lasi* goes for Rp1200. Half a dozen juice bars are available in 50 exotic iced-fruit juice blends (papaya-lemon, avocado-pineapple, etc.).

On the carts lining Bali's streets and at festivals are tubs of a poisonous hue bobbing with ice. These contain delicious (though overly sweetened) drinks like citrus juices *(air jeruk), es zirzak,* or bright pink drinks of sugar water and fruit flavoring. Sari Temulawak, is a safe, refreshing, not-too-sweet ginger drink popular with Balinese, costs only Rp500 (Rp800 with ice), and is available at *warung* and restaurants. The usual Western soft drinks like Fanta, Sprite, 7-UP, or Coca-Cola are available everywhere and cost Rp800 in a *warung* and up to Rp1500 in a restaurant.

Because fresh milk is unsafe to drink in the tropics, stores all over the island sell sealed cartons of milk (with straw attached), treated to last up to 24 hours after opening. Canned, sweet condensed milk is also available. Coconut milk is a form of sterile water containing potassium and is a superb source of glucose which can help you rehydrate. On a hot day it's not too difficult to persuade someone to clip down a young coconut or two with a bamboo pole knife. Fresh ones are green, old ones are yellow. Its water *(yeh nyuh),* mixed with ice and sugar water, makes a delicious, thirst-quenching drink.

ALCOHOLIC DRINKS

Beer, Wine, and Hard Stuff
Heineken of Holland taught Indonesians how to brew Bali's ubiquitous Bintang lager beer (620-milliliter or 22-ounce bottles), the best accompaniment to the island's hot, spicy food. Some visitors feel that Anker beer is better, derived from the south-Netherlands and Bavarian breweries. Indonesia also produces the lesser known San Miquel beer. Irish whiskey and Guinness Stout are served in the bars and restaurants of Kuta, Sanur, and Denpasar. The one beverage some Western visitors really crave is a decent bottle of wine for a decent price. Australian wine can be had for around Rp2000 per glass.

High quality mixed drinks and cocktails can be ordered at any hotel or public bar for Rp5000-12,000. The skill of the bartender depends on the place, but as a rule Balinese bartenders use fresh ingredients and follow the recipes exactly without resorting to those obnoxious bottled or artificial mixers found in the West. In other words, a margarita is truly a margarita—built from the bottom up by bartenders trained at bartending school in Ubud (only Mexican restaurants carry good tequila).

Native Alcoholic Drinks
The fancy cocktails and other recreational drinks concocted in the tourist restaurants and hotel bars are totally alien to village Bali, where mellow, homemade, mildly alcoholic native brews are preferred. These are produced in home breweries all over the island: *arak* (insidiously strong distilled rice spirit or "palm whiskey"), *tuak* (sweet palm beer or "palm toddy"), and *brem* (rice wine)—all cheap, plentiful, refreshing, potent. Most villages have special drinking clubs of men (never women) who meet after sundown and sit around on coconut-leaf mats exchanging news and getting stoned. Thousands of Bali's *warung* and certain stalls in the night markets sell palm or rice toddy. As the day wears on, the brews get stronger and the morning price of Rp2000-3000 per bottle may rise Rp500 or so.

Tuak is fermented palm tree juice, the same tipple that is enjoyed everywhere in tropical Africa, Central America, and Asia. Imparting a slow-motion high, *tuak* is made by cutting the flower of an immature coconut tree *(punyan nyuh)*, then allowing the sugar water to ferment for about a month. *Tuak* is sold by the large beer bottle *(botol bir)* and can be bought at many *warung*. Depending upon how long the brew has been allowed to "spoil," there are two kinds of *tuak*, sweet *(nguda)* and old *(wayah)*. *Tuak manis* is newer, musty-smelling, and may cause flatulence; more popular *tuak wayah* is older, more sour, earthier, and has a higher alcoholic content (the same as beer, around five percent).

Brem is a wine to be gently sipped like sherry; it's subtle, gentle flavor gives little warning of the warm-hearted kick that follows. Made from black glutinous rice *(injin)*, yeast, and water, old *brem* (more than three days old) is sour and has more alcohol content (nine percent), while new *brem* (under three days old) has an extreme sweet taste and seven percent alcohol content. Want to visit a *brem* brewery? Ask for Perusahaan Brem Bali Cap Dewi Sri in Sanur.

Colorless, sugarless *arak* is simply distilled *tuak* or *brem*, a cheap (Rp3500 per large beer bottle) and powerful drink (20-50% alcohol, depending on the quality). The best is sold at Talibeng market, between Klungkung and Sideman. Balinese and some tourists drink *arak* over ice and fruit juice or *brem* to take the edge off the *arak*. *Arak* is an important ingredient in temple offerings.

FRUITS

Discovering the local fruits, delicately crisp and bursting with juices, is one of the delights of Bali. Many of Indonesia's fruits are found nowhere else on Earth. There are pineapples *(nanas)*, melons, guavas, passion fruits (from Kintamani), tangerines, grapefruits, lemons, limes, lychees, grapes, vitamin-rich breadfruit *(campedak)*, papayas, sweet *jeruk bali* (like a grapefruit, pink ones are best). Also try Bali's large, cheap, delicious oranges *(juwuk)*. A serving of fruit is the customary dessert for most Balinese; fruit vendors and stands are found at almost every step along the busy streets of Bali's towns and vil-

Fruits on Bali come in all shapes, sizes, colors, and—for many of us—exotic names that give little clue to their edible qualities. The greenish zirzak (soursop in English) is a large fruit covered with scattered, rather soft, short spine-like projections. Eaten raw, it has a thick, sweet pulp and contains numerous hard black seeds. The genus also produces other edible fruits, such as the custard apple (the sweetsop) and the anona (bullocks-heart).

lages. The local markets offer an even greater variety. All fresh fruit and vegetables should be peeled and washed before eating. Stands selling fruits and/or juice stay open after most other *warung* close down, so you can find fruit to snack on until late at night. Along Jl. Legian in Kuta you see fresh fruit stands selling fruit for sky-high prices, and ladies on the beach sell beautifully cut-up pineapples (Rp500 per slice). Prices vary widely depending on supply and demand and how far you are from the growing area. *Salak*, for example run Rp1000 per kg in the dry Karangasem area but at scalper's prices down on Kuta (Rp500 for two or three).

The largest of all fruit (up to 90 cm long) is the jackfruit *(nangka)*. *Sayur nangka muda* (young jackfruit) is used in cooking and taste like artichoke hearts. The very best mangoes come from the Singaraja area, the sweetest within the sound of the sea. A cousin, the mangosteen *(manggis)*, is hailed by some as the most perfect of fruits. Its outside is round and purple, its inside is like an orange, but creamy, cool, and melts on the tongue. The mangosteen was enjoyed and lauded by Queen Victoria. Named for its prickles or *duri*, the smelly, infamous durian (family *Ster-*

culiuceae), spiked like a gladiator's weapon, tastes simultaneously like onions and caramel fluff. It's a fruit much enjoyed by those who are not put off by its evil aroma. Believed to be an aphrodisiac, an old Malay expression goes, "When the durians are down, the sarungs are up." The fruit is named for its prickles or duri. Grown from Bangli to Kintamani, when they're in season you'll see them piled in stands along the road. Durian on Bali can cost as much as Rp8000 for select large ones, but it's often difficult to find a good one (sellers seem almost eager to sell you unripe ones!).

The lychee-like rambutan has a prickly rind of a pale rose color. Within, it holds a dark green transparent jelly, somewhat like a grape in taste, but far more luscious. Don't be alarmed by the rambutan's hairy exterior—this is an easy fruit to love. Gently squeeze open the fruit and enjoy the sweet, translucent flesh inside. Salak (best from Rendang) is called the snake-fruit because of the remarkable pattern of its skin; carefully peel and enjoy. It's similar in taste to an apple. The amazing array continues: the succulent zirzak, the tiny, delicious belimbing (starfruit), and the bell-shaped jambu air ("water apple," genus Eugenia) which, though tasteless, is an effective thirst-quencher. There are sweet, gooey, sumptuous fruits like the ceroring. The sabo is shaped like a potato but tastes like a ripe, honey-flavored peach or pear. The unbelievably juicy sweet-sour zirzak, meaning "sour sack" in Dutch (sakaya in Balinese), is unforgettable.

Bananas

The pride of place among Balinese fruits goes to the cheap and ubiquitous banana (biyu). Steamed, deep-fried, or boiled, they are sold everywhere. Bali has, in fact, over 20 varieties in all shapes, flavors, textures, sizes, from the tiny finger-like biyu susu to the biyu raja ("king banana") which comes closest to the size and shape of bananas as we know them in the West. Some bananas are big and fat and red-skinned; others have edible skins. There are seedless ones and ones with big black seeds (biyu batu), wild species, and some varieties that are only edible when cooked. One of the sweetest is the small "milk banana" (biyu susu), with its thin skin, incomparable taste, and perfect size. Biyu gadang are green yet ripe and ready to eat.

Bananas are used frequently as pig food and also to season meats and stews for humans. Plantains are sometimes cut into very small cubes to resemble nasi goreng and prepared in the same way as fried rice. Banana stems boiled with spices (ares) is a widespread side dish. Banana leaves also make handy food wrappers, plates, and umbrellas, functions being usurped by ugly, nonbiodegradable plastic. In the past 10 years rubbish piles have accumulated on Bali for the first time—banana leaves rot away; plastic doesn't.

DESSERTS

The Balinese love their sweetmeats and you'll see them everywhere: lentil pastes, coconut cakes, gaily colored rice pastries, crunchy peanut cookies, sticky banana cakes, mung-bean soups, and other bizarre munchies. Warung offer a great variety of sweets and snacks kept in big glass jars. Help yourself and let the owner know afterwards how many you ate of each item (prices are standard, usually Rp100-200 for each).

Lak-lak, bendu, giling-giling, culek, and batun cluki are traditional Balinese sweets served with grated coconut and grated sugar. Another local favorite is tape (tapioca) with jaje uli, enjoyed with durian and coffee. Try Balinese dodol, a mixture of flour and pure cane sugar. Considered a delicacy, it's prepared by stirring the concoction constantly for two hours over medium heat.

Scores of desserts are derived from rice. Lontong, used in gado-gado, is rice cooked in banana leaves and tastes somewhat like cold Cream of Wheat. After cooking rice, what sticks to the bottom of the pot turns brown, crunchy, and sticky. This rice—also considered a dessert—is coveted by the children of an Indonesian family as much as cake icing is in an American family. Ketan is rice pudding cooked in coconut milk and sugar syrup. Among the most popular, most filling, and heartiest native desserts is black rice pudding with coconut milk and melted brown palm sugar on top. Sumping is banana wrapped in rice dough, then steamed in a rice cooker. Irresistible godoh biyu (pisang goreng elsewhere in Indonesia) are peeled bananas dipped in manioc batter, then fried to a golden brown.

Special holiday desserts are also made of rice flour or glutinous rice; over 70 different types of rice cakes (jaja), cookies, and sweets of every color and shape imaginable (including plant, animal, and human forms). Specially made rice cakes, colored with gaudy artificial dyes, are a required component of the magnificent "high offerings," skewered on a central banana plant stem up to two meters high. Meant for divine consumption, these are carried to temples in processions by identically dressed women. See masses of commercial rice cakes in certain sections of the market, like molten rivers of bright colors cascading over the stalls.

Another variety of jajan, made from more natural ingredients such as squash, beans, or manioc flour, is meant for human consumption. Served still warm, these sweets are a common Balinese breakfast available early in the morning from foodstalls and street vendors. At breakfast time, women walk down the lanes of Bali's villages carrying a huge selection of jajan on trays on their heads.

Two kinds of sugar are used for desserts, the white, super-refined gula pasir (same as white sugar available in the West) and the more natural dark brown sugar, gula barak, made from the sugar palm (gula merah, in Indonesian). A syrup derived from gula barak is a favorite topping for rice cakes, fruit, and such ice dishes as es cendol, which is palm sugar, coconut milk, jackfruit and other fruits on a bed of cendol (a sweet green pudding made from rice flour and mung beans).

Es campur is the Indonesian equivalent of the banana split, and many travelers become real aficionados of this dessert. Es campur are made differently all over Indonesia but a typical one consists of sweetened water, milk, fruit syrup, gelatin, cubes of sweet bread, tape (cassava root or tapioca), gage uli, and other nameless brightly colored coagulated pulpy substances. They run anywhere from Rp500-900. The es kacang that you find on Java is not found here; on Bali it's a strange mixture of other fruits and little doodads.

In the "tourist dessert" category, ice cream comes in all the usual flavors plus durian, sweet corn, coconut cream, and lychee fruit. Or you can stick with such Indonesian brands as Peters. Kuta's restaurants are known for apple pie with vanilla ice cream.

NIGHTLIFE AND ENTERTAINMENT

Western-style nightlife is overwhelmingly concentrated in the resorts of southern Bali where you'll find throbbing discos and bars packed wall-to-wall with gyrating bodies. The variety of nightlife possibilities is enormous and encompasses all musical tastes and age groups. Nightlife doesn't really begin until very late. The revelers of Kuta, Legian, and Seminyak sleep late, spend a leisurely day on the beach, return to their hotel rooms, go back for the sunset at 1900, wash up, then go out to eat at 2000 or 2100. Visitors don't even begin partying until at least 2300 or midnight. If this is what you want to get out of Bali, then you must get into this daily rhythm.

For evening entertainment, the Balinese themselves prefer to saunter up and down the street chatting with friends and neighbors for evening entertainment. TV, radio programs, and movies are enormously popular. The Balinese never attend the dance shows that are presented for tourists. Most traditional music and dance is associated with religious ceremonies. These are not likely to begin until well after dark, and may go on until dawn. Troupes of traveling players also present popular entertainment such as drama gong. For information on Balinese dance and music performances, refer to the Introduction. For info on the nightclubs and discos of Kuta, Legian, Seminyak, Tuban, Nusa Dua, Sanur, Denpasar, and Ubud, refer to the "Nightlife" sections in those chapters. Also check out the latest issue of the bimonthly Bali Echo for ads and articles.

Karaoke Bars

Some of these bars can be quite elegant and sophisticated, others can be divey and working class, or slightly sleazy massage parlors along the Bypass. Some have Ladies' Nights; others boast soundproof rooms, computerized automatic selection, competitions, Asian delicacies, or hire escorts who urge clients to sing. Asians are their most enthusiastic patrons and on most musical menus you'll find popular Japanese,

Taiwanese, Chinese, Korean, and Indonesian top-40 hits. Most close at 0200.

Movies

Most towns have small movie houses *(bioskop)*, but most young people seize movie nights as an opportunity to stand outside the theater to talk rather than to see the movie itself. Movies are most apt to be of the swashbuckling kung-fu epic variety from Hong Kong. For current Western movies, a great number of restaurant/bars in Kuta, Legian, Seminyak, Ubud, Candidasa, and Lovina show films to tourists starting at around 1900 most evenings.

ACCOMMODATIONS

Bali—which has more than half the hotels in all of Indonesia—offers the best and widest range of accommodation of any region of Indonesia, from international five-star hotels with extravagant suites costing US$600 per day to simple, homey, family-run inns with a thin mattress for a bed and a single hanging light bulb for less than five dollars per night.

Elsewhere in Indonesia, someone is always inviting you home to meet their family. But this is not the case on Bali where accommodations are so cheap and plentiful. Families are not permitted to put you up as long as there's a hotel or homestay in the same village. At the low end of the price scale, Bali offers some of the best value accommodations in all of Asia.

There is a full range of accommodations to fit every budget—from lowly *losmen* to five-star hotels. Hotel associations are cracking down on the heretofore loose use of the term, and now won't let just anyone call themselves a "hotel" without meeting certain standards. If the front desk clerk speaks English to you, and the tarif as well as all the prices in the hotel gift shop are given in dollars, you're probably in a hotel. They'll take either rupiah or dollars at a bad rate.

In general, in the smaller, family-run homestays of 10-15 rooms you come into more contact with the Balinese way of life than in the large, efficient yet impersonal hotel properties with their huge wings and tower blocks of rooms, run more like luxurious high-rise apartment buildings.

Among the 4,000 hotels on the island you'll find Japanese hotels, Aussie hotels, five-star properties, bamboo and thatch hippy hotels, surfing hotels, dive *losmen,* hotels that cater to families, hotels that cater only to package tourists, hotels that cater to honeymooners and singles, hotels specifically designed for long-term stays.

You can even stay in a colonial-era hotel, the newly remodeled and modernized Natour Bali Hotel of Denpasar, which retains much of its distinct glamor and charm. Another historical art-deco relic, dating from the Sukarno era, is the grand old Bali Beach Hotel of Sanur.

Many hotels are using their money to build new units rather than repair the old, and Bali is so furiously building hotels in towns and villages all over the island now that at times it feels like you're vacationing on a construction site. Building freezes are periodically announced, yet for unexplained reasons, they're only partially enforced.

Finding a Good Place

Other travelers are the best sources of information. The same person who tells you that a hotel, cottage, or homestay in this book no longer exists will also be able to tell you where another good one is.

The local police set the price of accommodations and are also charged with collecting the tax. With the intensity of competition, particularly among the budget class of accommodations, prices are very reasonable. But no matter what class place you're staying in, bargain. Tell the manager or front desk clerk that the hotel is out of your budget *("Taripnya terlalu mahal untuk saya.")*. The manager might be amenable to giving you a discount "if you promise not to tell the other guests."

If you intend to be in a particular area for awhile, the best is to just grab any halfway decent place for the night and spend an hour or so the next morning hunting for accommodations which better fit your tastes and budget. There's a tremendous range in the quality and price of the rooms, in the variety of the services, furnishings, and amenities offered, and in locations. It's incredible how different in atmosphere two hotels in the same price range can be, even hotels very close to each other like the Nelayan Village and Puri Buitan in Balina.

For a complete night's sleep, don't choose hotels near schools, bars, discos, or main streets. Also don't stay in hotels where prostitutes or Indonesians stay. Ask what you're going to get for breakfast; sometimes the breakfasts included in the price are really skimpy. It's also important to determine if you're going to be charged service and government tax, which can be as high as 21%! Make sure the place is clean, as your room may be frequented by other guests like cockroaches and rats.

The police are more likely to help you if you stay in a registered homestay, hotel, or *losmen*. They have a reputation to protect. All *melati* and *bintang* class hotels are registered, but with unregistered hotels, sometimes your name and passport number will not be recorded. In the cheaper homestays, always keep your valuables with the proprietor for safekeeping.

You can often tell the nationalities that frequent an accommodation by checking out its library to see what languages the books and magazines are written in. If you search around and find a hotel that suits you, take the room immediately, pay a day in advance, and get the key.

Smoker's Rooms

When Westerners stay in places that accept Indonesians and other Asian guests, they find that they have different habits—such as talking, laughing, and playing the radio far into the night. Asians are also more likely to smoke, and many of the rooms at places catering to them stink of cigarette smoke. Rooms in homestays and inns, which cater almost exclusively to travelers, usually don't smell of smoke.

The whole concept of nonsmoking rooms is only now just beginning to catch on in Indonesia. For example, it's almost impossible to find a room that doesn't reek of tobacco smoke in some of the beachfront hotels of Kuta like the Sahid Jaya. Repulsive! If you're booked into a hotel frequented by Asian guests, always choose the "cottage" block, a part of the hotel which is apt to more frequented by Europeans or North Americans, who generally smoke less than Asians.

Baggage Storage

Virtually any hotel, no matter what the class, will offer to store your luggage in special storage rooms while you're traveling around Bali or to other islands of Indonesia. In lower-priced homestays, the owner will even store your gear in the family quarters with the tacit understanding that you'll stay there again upon your return.

Seasons and Bookings

The low season is Jan.-June, when even Bali's expensive hotels will give as much as 50% off. But during the high season (July, August, and December), accommodations are booked solid in all the main tourist areas and you'll have to head for the hills to find a night's lodging. During this time, hoteliers don't need your business to survive, are not inclined to bargain, and charge 10-15% more. Lovina's accommodations, for example, all increase by Rp5000-10,000 during this time.

Make reservations ahead of time during such national religious holidays as Leberan, the high tourist season, and during Christmas and New Years. There's a "shoulder season" (16 Sept.-9 Oct. and 16 Jan.-31 Jan.) when reservations are not as necessary but wise.

Don't neglect to take full advantage of fax. Most moderately priced-and-up accommodations now have fax machines. It's an easy matter to fax ahead and make all your bookings; you also eliminate any travel agent fees. If you're in Java, Kuala Lumpur, Australia, or the U.S.A. you customarily receive a speedy reply from Bali within 48 hours.

Arriving

At Denpasar airport there are accommodations service desks in both the domestic and international arrival lounges. These dispense excellent information and the staff will even call a hotel of your choice and order transportation which is usually free, though you could end up paying for it. To the Four Seasons, it can cost Rp40,000. Find out who pays before you commit.

As you emerge from either the domestic and international terminals at Bali's airport, drivers or their assistants will be waiting there to escort guests to the hotel of their choice. They'll be holding up hotel signs; if you have already decided to stay at a certain hotel, take advantage of the free ride.

TOP SEVEN
BUDGET ACCOMMODATIONS

1. Pension Dua Dara, Kuta
2. Two Brothers Inn, Denpasar
3. Dutha Seaside Cottages, Candidasa
4. Nusa Lembongan Bungalows, Jungut Batu, Nusa Lembongan
5. Rona's Accommodations, Ubud
6. The Blue Yogi, Pujung
7. Puri Rena, Yeh Sanih

Hotel touts are another excellent source of recommendations. When arriving at the airport, you'll be approached by locals with offers of a room. These could be quite good, newly opened, and eager to please. If you're approached by hotel reps, all competing for your patronage, this is an excellent time to ask for a discount. Many homestay owners (like Pande in Peliatan) even meet overland travelers at Denpasar's Kereneng Bus Station, though most (around 25) wait for travelers to arrive at Batubulan station.

Accommodations at Tourist Sites
Most travelers do not look upon actual tourist destinations as viable places to stay, but they can be. At night, after all the tourists have gone home, the tourist site is turned back over to the Balinese and it becomes a unique place to stay—a small, self-contained scene where you can really get to know the locals who run the shops and *warung*. Examples of these out-of-the-way sites which have accommodations are: Yeh Pulu, Tirtagangga, Pemuteran, the Ahmed area, Medowe, and to some extent Tanah Lot.

Don't be afraid to follow a sign and venture down narrow back roads in search of places to stay. At the north end of Candidasa is a very elegant and comfortable hotel called Puri Bagus. It's located at the end of a nondescript road that feels like it leads to nowhere. In Toyabungkah on the shores of Lake Batur you'll find accommodations as low as Rp5000 s—some of the best deals on Bali—with breakfast, mountain view, and fewer hassles than tourist-trap Penelokan above the lake.

Hotels in Ubud, Denpasar, Bangli, and Klungkung are situated in the palaces *(puri)* of Brahmin families, with individual *bale* converted to Western tastes with full bathrooms, Western toilets, and front verandas. Charging between US$35 and US$60, these traditional-style hotels have great personality and charm. **A tip:** Don't wait until too late in the day to arrive at popular places like Ahmed, Tulemben, and Padangbai as most of the best accommodations—no matter *what* the class—fill up by noontime. Get there as early as you can.

Also, don't settle for low standards in high-priced accommodations. For example, the Bali Intan of Kuta is expensive, and everything's got a surcharge—use of the telephones, room service, taxes on drinks and meals. House movies never come on when they say they're going to come on. The rate of US$120 per night is simply not worth it. You would never pay this for a hotel back at home—for just a plain room, nothing special. *Much* better values are the so-called "Beach Inns," "Homestays," "Cottages," and "Bungalows" that are everywhere and five to 10 times cheaper. Read on.

***Losmen,* Inns, Beach Inns, Homestays**
These are small enterprises of only 10-15 rooms. The nicest places are found down the back lanes on the wings of such resorts as Kuta, Candidasa, Lovina and Ubud where it starts to get quiet and shady; these tend to be lower-priced and more relaxing. But these locales don't have a monopoly on the best homestays. Some excellent ones can be found in the villages of Peliatan, Penestanan, in the vicinity of Amlapura, Singaraja, and even in the capital of Denpasar itself.

In these small budget accommodations, you're under the charge of an *ibu* (literally "mother," your hostess, the "lady of the house") who will probably speak an abbreviated, easily understood "tourist" dialect of Indonesian. Your gear is safe as there's always some family member around, and barking dogs go into a frenzy whenever a stranger enters the confines of the family home. In remote places like Toyabungkah (Batur) and Lovina (on Bali's north coast) you'll find rooms as low as Rp5000 s, but usually the tarif is Rp8000-10,000 s, Rp12,000-15,000 d.

Rooms are set in a row, an ideal way of meeting other travelers and swapping information while having meals or drinks throughout the day or night. When not out sightseeing, you spend much of your time outdoors, breakfasting on the covered veranda furnished with a small table and two bamboo chairs often facing a garden or courtyard. Room service depends on the particular accommodations or on the *ibu.* Tea or coffee is often available free throughout the day. Laundry service is available with a price list posted.

Most of these bargain accommodations are built in Balinese style with separate bungalows or rooms surrounding a family courtyard. There's electricity, shower, and a private *mandi* and toilet inside your room. The room itself is usually a spartan affair—four thin walls, table, chair, bed with *batik* cover, *batik* curtains, perhaps a wardrobe—but what do you want for five bucks a night? Each guest is issued one bed sheet—or you can use your sarong. The better places will be well screened, but few budget accommodations provide mosquito nets, so bring your own or use an electric mosquito coil.

Be prepared. Roosters, babies crying, children playing, and loud music all begin promptly at 0600, and Bali's apocalyptic dogs will serenade you asleep at night, so if you've got a full day ahead of you make sure you turn in early. Houseboys are very conscientious about waking you up to catch a *bemo,* bus, or plane, and these places are less strict than hotels about enforcing the out-by-noontime rule.

Budget accommodations are run by a family or a group of friendly, unsophisticated young boys under the supervision of an absentee owner or manager. In many of the "beach inns" of Kuta, Legian, Tulamben, Lovina, and Ubud, there's not a family member in sight. The houseboys who run the place are overworked and underpaid and give the rooms occasional perfunctory cleanings which are mostly symbolic.

Because you may live right inside the family compound and participate in the life of the family, homestays can be the finer experience and preferable over luxury-class hotels in the tourist enclaves of Nusa Dua or Sanur for immersing yourself in the life and culture of the people. You get to relate to the Balinese in the family context rather than relating to them while they're driving you around or serving you in restaurants.

You learn how to make offerings from the mother, flutes from the father, kites from the small ones, and how to cook *lawar* from the grandmother. The grandfather will take you out for a drink or two of *tuak* at the local *warung,* and the daughter will show you the shortest way to the dance hall or how to sew a *kain* into a skirt. They may well give you snacks to sample, transportation advice, and descriptions of good walks in the area.

Your *losmen* owner can also find you the best dance, painting, or *wayang kulit* teachers, take you to a wedding, *odalan,* toothfiling, or some other special ceremony. In fact, many travelers choose their homestay for the extras provided; e.g., the family teaches dancing or silversmithing or gives Bahasa Indonesia lessons, lends bicycles, offers a bigger or better breakfast, or has an outstanding paperback library.

Almost all accommodations charging under US$10 include breakfast in the price. Breakfast is a very flexible term but usually includes a cup of strong hot Bali coffee or tea with sugar, toast, egg, freshly picked bananas or a bowl of fruit salad, though some places just give tea or coffee. The best places offer a different breakfast each morning, rotating between omelettes, fruit salad, pancake, toast, or sometimes all four!

The least expensive accommodations ordinarily provide a tank of cold water for bathing and a squat toilet (no toilet seat). Forget airconditioning. If there are nights that are temperature-perfect, Bali has them. Some homestays have native-style, open-air sleeping pavilions *(bale);* these are really cool and comfortable as the *atap* roof and open sides are conducive to napping or spending the night.

Bungalows, Cottages, Guesthouses, and *Pondok Wisata*

"Cottages" and "Bungalows" usually consist of one- or two-room freestanding buildings, with each room having its own bath. The asking price for these is far higher than for the average *losmen,* but they are far nicer. If it's the low season, you may be able to bargain as low as Rp15,000-20,000 per person per night for a really nice "cottage" with a shower. Often these accommodations have a decent restaurant, comfortable beds, ceiling fans, and plumbing that works. Some even have lovely garden bathrooms.

When found as a part of the name, such as "Siti Bungalows," these are all different twists on the same-grade accommodations. Usually built in Bali-style, these places have nicely furnished rooms complete with all the amenities—but not the price—of proper hotels. They charge $20-30 per day for rooms with red brick walls, traditional *atap* roofs or brownish-red roof tiles, verandas, tile floors. Inside you'll find bamboo furniture, fresh flowers, private bath with European shower, hot water, ceramic Western-style toilet, and wooden beds. To accommodate a family, Rp5000-10,000 is charged for an extra bed.

Some mountain guesthouses, like the Lila Graha of Candikuning (near Bedugal), look like Swiss chalets. In Ubud, they are usually located overlooking rice paddies. The majority of these moderately priced accommodations sell tours like horseback riding, rafting, and birdwalks and will phone to have the operator pick you up in the morning and drop you off in the afternoon. A *pondok wisata* is a house where the owner lets out rooms for a moderate price. The owner often stays there too. No meals usually.

Youth Hostels and Campgrounds
There's only one legitimate youth hostel on Bali, the **Bali International Hostel** on Jl. Mertasari 19, Banjar Suwung Kangin, Sidakarya, Denpasar Selatan (tel./fax 0361-63912). But unless you feel a dogged loyalty to always staying at a YH, better deals can be found elsewhere. Campgrounds are rare on this small, densely populated island. The only place to camp is in the **Bali Barat National Park** in west Bali. Don't underestimate either the terrain or the chill. Take rain gear because precipitation is always a possibility, even in the dry season. In the backcountry areas of this reserve, it may be necessary to pack in water.

Melati-Class Hotels
In Indonesia there are two types of hotels: the *melati* (jasmine) class and the *bintang* (star) class. There are three classifications of *melati:* one jasmine, two jasmine, and three jasmine. The one-star to five-star hotels are higher standard, with the five-star hotel the highest.

Medium-priced *melati* class have all the modcons including a/c, hot water, adjoining bath, a coffee shop, restaurant, and almost always a swimming pool. *Melati* may even offer International Direct Dialing (IDD) from your room, often provide vehicles for rent, and take small groups of guests on a personalized tour (ask the manager). They do not however offer the range of sports facilities and activities the luxury class hotels do.

Melati class are just as comfortable and cost—as a rule—only US$20-25, or US$30-35 per day if it has a swimming pool. You can even find some very comparable accommodations, like Oka Kartini's in Ubud, that charge as little as $15-20 per day *with* pool. You tend to get a bigger bang for your rupiah in hotels outside of Kuta, Nusa Dua, and Sanur. For example, check out at the Puri Bagus and Rama Ocean View in Candidasa, and the Baruna Cottages in Lovina.

It's rare that any accommodation, like *melati* class, charging over US$10-15 per day, won't include breakfast in the price of the room. Starting at around 0700, meals can either be served in the rooms or in attached restaurants. In the venerable Hotel Tjampuan of Campuan (near Ubud) room service is summoned by sounding a gong in the form of a demon using a penis-shaped cudgel. If you have to get an early start, order breakfast at almost any time, even at 0500 in the

TOP FIFTEEN SMALL HOTELS

1. Puri Joma, Tanjung
2. Mastapa Garden Cottage, Kuta
3. Orchid Garden Cottage, Legian
4. Puri Buitan, Balina
5. Nirwana Cottages, Candidasa
6. The Watergarden, Candidasa
7. Puri Bagus Beach Hotel, Candidasa
8. Murni's House, Campuan
9. Vienna Beach, Amed
10. Paradise Palm Beach Bungalows, Tulamben
11. Oka Kartini's, Ubud
12. BeeBee's Bungalows, Tibubiyu
13. Puri Lumbung Cottage, Mundok
14. Baruna Beach Cottages, Lovina
15. Pondok Sari, Pemuteran (West Buleleng)

morning. However, the earlier the hour, the least likely you'll be served a hot breakfast.

If your plane leaves at 1800, try to bargain for a "day rate." There's usually no extra charge for children under 12 occupying the same room as their parents if no extra beds are required. More and more often now a 15.5% government tax and service charge is added to your bill. No matter what class hotel you're staying in, you usually have to vacate the room by noon the next day or you'll be asked to pay for an additional day.

International-Standard or *Berbintang* Hotels

Bali unquestionably has Indonesia's swankiest international-class hotels. A "star system" *(berbintang)* is used whereby hotels are assigned a certain number of stars to denote their class. Five-star is the highest rating, one-star is the lowest. Prices range from US$120 to US$170; suites are US$200-2500. About half the guests are European, about 15% Indonesian, 12% Australian, 12% North American, and the remainder Japanese, Singaporean, and Taiwanese.

All of these luxury hotels have the capacity and facilities to cater to all nationalities and tastes. They have huge vaulted lobbies, closed-circuit color TV in the rooms, in-house video programming, fridges and minibars, round-the-clock room service, International Direct Dialing (IDD), business centers, fax machines, laundry and dry-cleaning services, safe deposit boxes.

On their extensive grounds are Chinese, Italian, Asian, and Indonesian restaurants, pizzerias, piano lounges, discos, 24-hour coffee shops, shopping arcades, house clinics. Also offered are floodlit tennis courts staffed by professional coaches, fully equipped aerobics and fitness rooms, jogging tracks, game and video rooms, and children's playgrounds.

On their private beaches you can enjoy a smorgasbord of water activities: surfing, parasailing, sailing, windsurfing, outrigger sailing, and waterskiing. There are free-form swimming pools with sunken bars, poolside cafes, jacuzzis, and saunas. Their poolside areas transform into open-air theaters, restaurants, and *pasar malam* at night. In spite of their central location, these huge hotel properties offer tranquility because they're huge and have extensive grounds, and guarded gateways keep the public out.

In this class of hotel you may arrange guided tours and sporting adventures (scuba diving, snorkeling). They'll order you transport, post your letters, reconform your flights (Rp5000), and charge it all to whatever credit card you carry. Baggage may be carried to your room on a battery-powered cart along the winding garden walkways. Shuttle service into the nearest shopping center is frequent, and transfers to and from the airport are often free. In any "starred" establishment, you can count on a 21% government tax and service charge being added to your lodging and food bill.

Most of the major international-class hotels are concentrated in Denpasar, Nusa Dua, Kuta, and Sanur—the tourist triangle of Bali. First-class hotels are also starting to appear in Ubud, the upland art center of Bali. Some call the unbelievably posh hotels of Nusa Dua, with their extravagant, groomed lawns and artificial Bali-style facades, the ultimate vacation getaway. Others call Nusa Dua a tourist ghetto where pampered tourists reside and where the Balinese not employed there are not even allowed to enter.

Though Nusa Dua is scarcely Bali, its greatest value is that it offers an escape from the cacophony of Kuta and Sanur. However, the negative of Nusa Dua's—and Bali's—luxury hotels is that they have a pervasive atmosphere of administrative overkill and often feel sterile, soulless, and cut off from Bali.

The Aman and Four Season Resorts

Off the map. Hotelier Adrian Zecha's Aman hotels—the Amandari of Kedawatan, the Amankila in Bugbug in east Bali, and the Aman Nusa in Nusa Dua—are in a class by themselves. Architecturally speaking, these are Bali's top hotels—the ultimate in luxurious living. All are situated on high points (the architect is fond of grand vistas) and every detail has been integrated so it all fits together—even down to the ashtrays and napkins. The Amans' combination of natural and modern materials create a refined sensual indulgence unequaled in any other resort of Bali. Of course, at US$600 a night, they ought to. Only the Four Seasons of Jimbaran and the Oberoi of Seminyak can hold a candle to them.

Each Aman resort is set in a different environment—coastal, mountain, and cosmopolitan. The Amanusa, on a promontory over the fairway of the Nusa Dua golf course, is so magnificent that it feels as if it has lost its human scale. The Amankila was built in the proper proportions. Soaring dramatically 100 meters above the beach, with its white collanades and enormous open public places, its architecture is reminiscent of an opulent palace by the sea. The smaller Amandari near Ubud is a re-creation of the stark integrity of a traditional Balinese village—but without the mud, pigs, and screaming children. Its smaller proportions make it more introspective and intimate than the other Amans.

None of the Amans advertise; their fame is spread by word of mouth, and bookings are essential during the high season. All share the same philosophy. There are no TVs in the rooms. The guests are instead encouraged to relax in an atmosphere of understated elegance. There's no check-in; guests just discreetly slip their American Express Gold Card to the concierge. Also there's no signing for food or laundry (in deference to guests, who shouldn't be bothered with such mundane annoyances).

The Aman resorts don't have twin-bedrooms; couples have to take two double-bed bungalows. This is why some guests prefer the Four Seasons, which does have twin-bedrooms. Four Seasons villas also have private plunge pools, but at Aman you have to pay extra for units with their own pool. Four Seasons are generally more guest-related, hands-on hotels than the Amans. They offer more hotel-type amenities like business services, color TVs, and stereos in every room. You can watch HBO, CNN, and Monday night football back home. Four Seasons staff are dressed to the hilt; there's a captain's table each night, and cocktail parties every Monday night in a special guest dining room. Amans, on the other hand, are more elegantly au natural.

Long-Term Accommodations
Because of the competition between the accommodations and the huge concentration of tourists, Bali offers the best long-term residence opportunities in Indonesia for the money. A bonus is that you are not the object of constant scrutiny as you would be on almost any other island of Indonesia. On Bali there are so many tourists that no one even takes notice of you—except the street vendors or if you're in a re-

mote village. On Bali you can go about your business anonymously.

Rental homes can be found through a legal service with several offices in Ubud. Westerners and Japanese either lease land for 20-35 years, build a structure, make improvements on the property, then hand it back to the Balinese owner at the end of the lease, or they lease already built residences. Around Seminyak and Petitingit on the coast west of Kuta are hundreds of homes that have been built by Westerners. These can be thatch-roofed bungalows built for Rp20-25 million (US$12,000) or elaborate US$100,000 multistoried structures.

A popular inland locale for long-term residents is the Ubud area, particularly around Penestanan (rice paddies, views, country life) and Peliatan (for its appeal to students of culture). Another way to settle into Bali is to negotiate for a room or section of a house "under contract." If you're studying dance, music, painting, or puppetry for several months, this is the way to go.

Talk to people in your hotel and they might know someone with a house for rent. Look for *rumah disewakan* signs along the road up to Tanjung in the Bukit Peninsula and in north Bali (around Yeh Sanih) where houses still rent for around Rp200,000 per month. If you're spending Rp5 million per year for a two-bedroom house with kitchen and veranda, you're doing real good. A cook and housekeeper cost about Rp100,000 per month extra.

Or just find a nice homestay, guesthouse, or hotel and ask for a special long-term rate; you could arrange for a nice bungalow with room service for as little as US$10 per night. For extended vacations, there are a whole string of isolated hotels on the south coast at Petitenget, Canggu, and Berawa. An excellent choice for families, small groups, and honeymoon couples is **Serendipity** (Jl. Padma Utara, Legian, Kuta, P.O. Box 41, tel. 0361-751331, fax 753333), which offers complete, fully equipped, spacious, and very private two-story homes.

If you're looking for a long-term rental, advertise in the *Bali Advertiser*, Jl. Tanjung Mekar 28 D, Kuta (tel./fax 0361-755392). Distributed in Kuta-Legian, Denpasar, Nusa Dua, Sanur, Ubud, Lovina, and Candidasa, for commercial ads brought into their office, a 25% discount and faster service is offered.

Private Villa Rental

Private Villas Ltd. offers short term rental of about 30 private villas in Bali. Most of these leisure homes are owned by affluent foreigners who occupy them for only a short period of time each year and have agreed to rent them through Private Villas on a weekly or monthly basis to reputable tenants from overseas. You can choose from cozy hideaways for just two persons to large, prestigious estates, accommodating up to 12 or more guests in comfort.

Rental prices range from US$1750 to US$10,500 per week (US$250-US$1500 per day) depending on the season, the number of bedrooms, and the facilities of each villa. All costs for household staff, electricity, water, and tax are included. Your only additional expenses are for food and drinks. The most expensive property, a magnificent two-hectare beachfront estate renting for US$1500 per day in the high season (US$1000 per day in the regular season and US$800 per day in the low season) features a main building of 11,000 square feet, three bedrooms, a large swimming pool, archery range and tennis court, veggie and herb garden, seaview sauna, and the use of a game fishing boat. This spectacular residence is serviced by 14 full-time household staff, including an Italian chef.

However, even the least expensive villa (US$250 per day in the shoulder season) has two comfortable bedrooms with a private bathroom, dining and living areas spacious enough to entertain visitors, a fully equipped kitchen, and a beautiful garden with a private pool. Serviced by two staff, it's located less than 600 meters from the beach.

Although private villa rental is not cheap, the total cost of a villa holiday always turns out to be surprisingly reasonable compared to staying in hotels. Villa guests experience substantial savings on food and beverage, as they pay only low supermarket prices for anything prepared for them by the household staff. A few U.S. dollars per head for food per day is still a lot of money on Bali, and even French champagne can be bought for just US$20 per bottle. The total extra costs per day, therefore, will probably be less than the price for an appetizer in a hotel restuarant. Extra costs are usually less than 10% of the accommodations costs in contrast to hotel holidays where the extras can more than double your bill.

No units are rented less than a week. A security deposit of US$1000 plus US$100 per day deposit against telephone use (refundable eight weeks after you leave) is required. Bookings should be made through Private Villas Ltd., tel. (0361) 703060, fax 701577, e-mail info@villanet.com. Mailing address: P.O. Box 1166, Tuban, Bali. On the Web, find Private Villas Ltd. at http://ww.balivillas.com. For the high season, book a year ahead.

Mandi

The verb *bermandi* means to bathe or wash; the noun *mandi* means the place where you bathe or wash. Western-style toilets and showers with running, piped-in water are becoming more and more widespread, even in the cheapest accommodations. A *mandi* could be an ornate, tiled washroom with jacuzzi in a high-priced "star" hotel, or an open-air, roofless, shoulder-high cement bathing enclosure in a domestic courtyard of a homestay near the coast where you can shower in the warm sun in complete privacy.

Some of the dive *losmen* on the north and east coast offer rooms with an inside *mandi* equipped with a large water tank. Bobbing in the middle of the water is a plastic or metal scoop with which you throw water over yourself, elephant-fashion. Don't climb in the tank and bathe, which fouls it. Instead, soap yourself down and rinse yourself off while standing on the *mandi* floor. The water is warm to cool; you'll welcome its refreshing tingle after spending a day in the tropical sun.

In mountain towns like Kintamani, Penelokan, and Bedugul, or in those places that are supplied with water from underground wells, the water could be icy cold. In these cases, wait until the hottest part of the day to bathe or talk the proprietor into boiling some water for you. It'll be provided in buckets. There may be an extra charge of Rp2000 or so.

WC

Pronounced "WAY-say." This abbreviation stands for "water closet," the basic European designation for toilet. Other Indonesian phrases for toilet are either *kamar mandi*, or *kamar kecil* ("little room"). The toilet can be either Western-style or Asian-style. Sometimes, but increasingly rarely, the WC is located in the *mandi* room itself. More often it's a separate, darkened enclosure. If you just need to urinate, it's quite socially acceptable to use the floor of the *mandi*; just rinse the floor down afterwards with a couple of scoops of *mandi* water. In places that have Western-style toilets, toilet paper most of the time will be provided, but if you're attached, bring some in case it isn't.

Once in a while you can still run into an Indonesian-style WC which consists of two footpads and a drainage hole made of molded cement. One squats on the pads and afterwards cleans oneself and the hole by splashing water from a nearby can or plastic dipper. Fill the can either from the *mandi* water or a faucet beside the toilet for that purpose. For urine, throw in two or three scoops; for feces throw in five or six scoops or until the water is clear.

The Asian-style WC is rapidly giving way all over Bali to Western-style sit-down toilets, which is a shame because there's not a more comfortable, orthopedically sound, and physiologically natural position in which to relieve yourself than squatting on your haunches. Also, using water is a more hygienic cleaning method than smearing yourself with toilet paper. In fact, not only is toilet paper expensive and hard to find, but Indonesia's squat toilets are not designed to flush paper products. Westerners, who are reluctant to do as the Romans, often clog up WCs with their copious and inappropriate use of toilet paper.

GETTING THERE

Air routes and fares into Indonesia change constantly. As soon as the *Official Airlines Guide* is published, it's out of date. Check the latest and cheapest means of getting to Bali in the Sunday travel section of a major metropolitan newspaper near you. Also check the Yellow Pages and adventure-travel media.

The International Air Traffic Association (IATA) is a cartel of air carriers that fixes high fares for all participating carriers—you'll pay the same inflated rate no matter which of these airlines you use. Avoid paying full IATA fares by buying your tickets from travel agencies and consolidators. The latter discount agencies often offer gray-market tickets at low rates that cannot be advertised. To know what fares, features, and restrictions you're trying to beat, check first with Garuda, the Indonesian national air carrier.

Before paying for your ticket, inquire about restrictions, refunds, cancellation fees, and stopovers. Technically, to obtain an Indonesian entry stamp you need a ticket out of Indonesia. In reality, however, immigration officials never ask to see a ticket out. Travelers under 26 should inquire about student discounts. Children four to 12 could also receive substantial discounts.

A good deal could be an Advance Purchase Excursion (APEX) fare, which must be reserved and paid for two to three weeks before departure. There's a substantial penalty for cancellation, and no stopovers are allowed. Since APEX tickets require rigid departure and return dates, purchase one-way tickets only. Rates are lower in the off-season, February to November. Always ask about special promotional fares.

Consider buying a one-way ticket from Europe or the U.S. direct to Bangkok, Hong Kong, or Singapore; from these points it's relatively inexpensive to continue on to Bali. Discounted roundtrip flights from London to Bangkok cost £400 and from Los Angeles to Bangkok around US$750. From Bangkok you can travel down to Penang, from where it's an easy hop on a boat or plane to Medan, North Sumatra.

It doesn't usually pay to join a package from Europe, U.S., or Australia because accommodations in Bali are so inexpensive. However, Garuda Orient Holidays, a subsidiary of Garuda Indonesia Airlines, is an exception. They offer some airfare and hotel combos for little more than the cost of airfare alone (see "From the U.S.A.," below). If you plan to make a number of stops in Indonesia, investigate Garuda's Airpass, which allows you to make three flights on any of 35 routes flown by Garuda or Merpati for just US$300 extra. See the "Getting Around" section for details.

Gateways
You can fly into Bali from all over the world. The three main international air gateways are Jakar-

THE CHEAPEST

Readers should be aware of **Air Broker's Intl. Inc.** (323 Geary St., Suite 411, San Francisco, CA 94102, tel. 800-883-3273 or 415-397-1383, fax 415-397-4767), which sells more round-the-world tickets than any other consolidator on planet earth. They are also the largest non-Indonesian consolidator of Garuda tickets in the U.S.A., selling the Los Angeles-Denpasar-Jakarta ticket for an unbelievable US$880 roundtrip.

ta, Denpasar, and Medan. By far the largest number of flights arrive in Jakarta's international Sukarno/Hatta Airport, 20 km west of Jakarta in Cengkareng.

Unbelievably, except on expensive cruise ships, slow passenger ferries, or private yachts, it's difficult to reach the world's largest island nation by water. You'll find only two regular maritime entry points. Ferries depart Penang, Malaysia for Medan, and a daily ferry connects Singapore with Palau Batam in the Riau Archipelago; from there you can board another ferry to Pekanbaru, East Sumatra, or Jakarta.

Ocean liners and cruise ships of Holland American Lines, Spice Island Cruises, and Lindblad Travel call at remote Indonesian ports at luxury prices. These upscale tour companies offer fly/cruise arrangements whereby you're flown to Surabaya, Bali, or Medan to meet your cruise vessel. See your travel agent.

All flights to Bali arrive at **Ngurah Rai Airport,** which is actually referred to as "Denpasar" though it is 11 km south of Denpasar and three km south of Kuta at Tuban.

Circle-Pacific and Round-the-World Tickets

Using a combination of airlines out of the U.S.—Air New Zealand, Qantas, MAS, Singapore Airlines—travelers can spend up to a year circling the Pacific and Southeast Asia. For Qantas and Air New Zealand, you're looking at around US$2449 roundtrip, 14-day advance purchase, with four stopovers. Additional stopovers are US$75-200 extra. Most require that you use all your tickets within 12 months, some give only six months. To

save money, either ask your travel agent to do business through a consolidator offering flights to Asia, or call a consolidator directly. The cheapest fares entail midweek departures.

Air Brokers International, Inc., 323 Geary St., Ste. 411, San Francisco, CA 94102, U.S.A., tel. (800) 883-3273 or (415) 397-1383, fax 397-4767, sells more round-the-world tickets than any other U.S. consolidator.

Bali is often included as a stopover on many round-the-world tickets. The variations possible in round-the-world itineraries depend on the ticketing alternative the traveler selects. The best and most expensive is the full-fare, full-service ticket. You can go where you like on almost any airline and take six months or a year doing it. The main drawback is you have to zig-zag around the world in one direction only, booking individual flights as you go without the privilege of switching carriers. Plus, all your flights may not be available when you want them. You sacrifice some flexibility but save some cash by buying a round-the-world package offered by an individual airline or specific group of airlines. It's cheaper still to string together several discount tickets, acquired in such bargain centers as London, Bangkok, or Hong Kong.

Ticket packages vary considerably in price, length of validity, and number of stopovers permitted. If your round-the-world ticket doesn't offer a stop in Bali, try to land as close as possible—Singapore or Bangkok—then hop down to the archipelago.

Singapore Airlines sells a US$2570 economy ticket with stops in at least three cities; six-month validity, 14-day advance purchase. The airline offers daily flights east from New York to Bali via European cities and Singapore; and west to Bali via Singapore. Qantas offers a US$3000 ticket on a 21-day advance purchase.

Arriving by Air

In the luggage pick-up areas in both the domestic and international terminals at Bali's **Ngurah Rai Airport** there are well-staffed hotel booking counters. Have the clerks (all speak English) try to arrange free transport for you to a hotel of your choice (usually only higher-priced hotels are represented here, US$50 and up). The two terminals are only about a five minute walk from each other.

In the International Terminal you have to clear customs first. Curiously, in spite of the large number of tourists visiting Bali, the customs officers are among the most officious and demanding in all of Indonesia. Get in a long line where they are under more pressure to process you faster.

After customs there are a number of quick and honest moneychangers, both inside and outside the terminal, where you might as well change money because the rates only vary a few points from what you can get anywhere else on the island. There are also tourist information booths with a fairly good amount of literature.

After changing money, look for your hotel vehicle for a free ride. If you've booked ahead the driver will usually be there to greet you, holding up a sign with your name on it. For a taxi, go up to the taxi window, buy your ticket, and then present it in the taxi line. Fixed tarifs to various parts of the island are: Kuta Rp8000-10,000 (depending upon which part), Legian (7 km) Rp11,500, Seminyak (9 km) Rp12,500, Denpasar (14 km) Rp15,000, Ubung Station (17 km) Rp16,000, Sanur (18 km) Rp17,500, Nusa Dua Rp17,500, Jimbaran (10 km) Rp11,500, Tanjung Benoa (20 km) Rp18,500, Krobokan (17 km) Rp15,000, Batubulan Station (22 km) Rp21,000.

If going to Ubud, instead of paying the exorbitant fare, just get a taxi to Batubulan (Rp21,000), then board a blue Izuzu the rest of the way to Ubud for another Rp6000. If you want a cheaper metered taxi to anywhere, you can push your cart to the end of the sidewalk only about 100 meters from the entrance of the airport. Lug your stuff past the toll booths to the first street on the left and then flag down a metered yellow taxi, an even cheaper *bemo*, or hitch anything (someone will stop). Yellow taxis are not allowed to pick up passengers at the airport, but they are allowed to drop passengers off.

REACHING BALI FROM WITHIN INDONESIA

Bali is accessible from a number of different islands and directions. If you're landing in Jakarta, you can travel overland all the way to Denpasar on a comfortable, air-conditioned, long-distance night bus—a 24-hour trip—for around Rp65,000 (Rp25,000 economy class). Regular and efficient ferries leave from Ketapang, East Java to Gilimanuk, far-western Bali, and from Lembar, Lombok, to Padangbai, east Bali.

Express buses to Denpasar are available from Bandung, Yogyakarta, Semarang, Surabaya, Malang, and many other Javanese cities. A reliable traveler's transport service is **Perama,** with offices at Jl. Pembangunan 2 (tel. 021-345-3636) in Jakarta and Jl. Prawirotaman 29 (tel. 0274-72853) in Yogyakarta. Perama sells a bus ticket from Jakarta to Denpasar for Rp60,000 and from Yogyakarta to Denpasar (15 hours) for Rp45,000.

All buses from Java terminate at Denpasar's Ubung bus station from where you can take a *bemo* to other stations in Denpasar, or connect with other *bemo* to go anywhere on the island. If you want to go to Lovina in northern Bali's Buleleng District, buy a ticket to Gilimanuk in far west Bali from where you can catch a *bemo* to Lovina.

By Sea
Pelni, Indonesia's national shipping concern, operates 20 passenger/cargo ships, each of which navigates a different interisland loop every two weeks. For the latest timetables and routes—which change about every 90 days—check with one of the Pelni offices before you go. On Bali, Pelni's port is Benoa just west of Sanur. The ships offer four classes, from deck class or economy—where you sleep in a huge common room—to first class private cabins with inside bathroom, a/c, and TV.

It's important to book ahead. The main Pelni office is at Jl. Gajah Mada 14 (tel. 021-343307, fax 381-0341). Ticket offices: Jl. Angkasa 18, Jakarta (tel. 021-421-7406); Jl. Pelabuhan, Benoa Harbor, Bali (tel. 0361-228962); Jl. Industri 1, Ampenan (tel. 0364-37212, fax 31604); Jl. Kol Sugiono 5, Medan (tel. 061-518899); Jl. Pahlawan 3, Kupang, West Timor (tel. 0391-21944).

By Air
Four major domestic airlines (Garuda, Merpati, Bouraq, and Sempati) and a number of military, timber and oil, and private air-transport companies service every corner of the archipelago. Always shop around to get the best

fares. Sample one-way fares to Bali: from Jakarta, Rp220,000; from Kupang, Rp192,000; from Medan, Rp400,000. Don't forget to add Rp4500-7500 per departure for domestic airport tax.

FROM MALAYSIA

From Penang
Malaysia is a good place to buy cheap air tickets. Refer to the *Straits Times* for ads. Popular with travelers is the low-priced hop from Penang across the Strait of Malacca to Medan in North Sumatra, from where you can work your way through western Indonesia to Bali. The MAS flight leaves Penang daily, takes just 20 minutes, and costs around M$54 one-way, M$108 roundtrip.

An excellent high-speed ferry service operates between Penang and Medan every Tuesday and Friday at 0800, returning from Medan to Penang the same day at 1330. First-class fare is M$100 one-way, M$180 roundtrip; economy class is M$90 one-way, M$160 roundtrip. Children two to 12 fly half price. Free refreshments and snacks and free transfer from the port of Belawan to Medan city center are included. Belawan customs doesn't seem to check tickets out. In Penang, buy ferry tickets at the KPLFS office, PPC Shopping Complex, Jl. Pusara King Edward, 10300 Penang, tel. (04) 625630 or 625631, fax 625508. In Medan, call (061) 514888 or 518340. Travel agencies and hotels along Chulia Street in Penang sell tickets.

From Kuala Lumpur
Malaysia's capital is a real travel bargain center. It's now just as cheap flying to Bali from Kuala Lumpur as from Singapore. The flight to Medan with MAS or Garuda is around M$78 one-way, M$156 roundtrip. MAS now flies from Kuala Lumpur to Surabaya, from where it's a short flight or overland trip to Bali.

Student Travel Australia (STA), sixth floor, UBN Tower Letter Box 32, 10 Jalan P. Ramlee, 50250 Kuala Lumpur, Malaysia, sells a Kuala Lumpur-Denpasar MAS or Garuda ticket for about half the price of other agencies. On the same street as STA in Kuala Lumpur are other cheap ticketing agencies.

FROM SINGAPORE

By Air
Singapore is a popular and convenient departure point for Denpasar, Bali. Remember that 30-day excursion fares are usually cheaper than regular fares. Check travel agencies for the cheapest fares. Many advertise in the *Straits Times*.

Airmaster Travel Center, 36-B Prinsep St., Room 1, Singapore 0718, tel. 338-3942 or 337-6838, sells a Singapore-Jakarta-Denpasar ticket and a Singapore-Denpasar ticket with a stopover in Yogyakarta. Ask about their 30-day excursion fares. Price varies depending on airline and length of stay.

Student discount tickets (ID card required) are available from Singapore to Denpasar. Check with **Student Travel Australia (STA),** 02-17 Orchard Parade Hotel, 1 Tanglin Rd., Singapore 1024, tel. 734-5681, fax 737-2591.

Airline Offices
Cathay Pacific, Ocean Bldg., Collyer Quay, tel. 533-1333; **Garuda,** Gold Hill Sq., 101 Thomson Rd., 13-03, Singapore 1130, tel. 250-5666; **KLM,** Mandarin Hotel, 333 Orchard Rd., tel. 737-7211; **MAS,** Singapore Shopping Centre, 190 Clemenceau Ave., tel. 336-6777; **Qantas,** Mandarin Hotel, 333 Orchard Rd., tel. 737-3744; **Singapore International Airlines,** SIA Bldg., 77 Robinson Rd., tel. 223-8888.

By Sea
Travelers can enter the Riau Archipelago, three hours south of Singapore, on their own and visa-free by taking a ferry (S$20, 40 minutes from Singapore to Palau Batam or Palau Bintan). Launches leave every couple hours from Finger Pier, Prince Edward Rd., Singapore. A speed boat also runs directly from Singapore to Tanjung Pinang for S$45 (two and a half hours).

From Tanjung Pinang, a Pelni ship sails to Jakarta every other Sunday. The Pelni office is at 50 Telok Blangah Rd. No. 02-02, Citiport Centre, Singapore 0409, tel. 272-6811, 271-5159, or 271-8685. These ships provide the cheapest way of getting to Jakarta from Singapore (about S$35 total). However, they leave early in the morning and require at least one night in Tanjung Pinang. If you plan to arrive in Tanjung Pinang from Singapore on Saturday, you'll encounter another problem. The Pelni office—Ketapang 8, tel. 2151—closes at 1300 Saturday, and the direct ferry from Singapore to Tanjung Pinang (S$46) won't get you there in time to buy your Pelni ticket for the following day. Solution: Take the smaller, faster boat from Singapore to Palau Batam (45 minutes). Go through customs in Sekupang and catch a taxi across the islands to Kabil. From Kabil, speedboats leave constantly for Tanjung Pinang (crossing time 30 minutes); when you arrive catch a minibus (Rp200) to the Pelni office. Once in Jakarta, you can either fly or head overland to Bali.

FROM OTHER ASIAN NATIONS

From the Philippines
Garuda operates a 2,179-km-flight from Manila to Jakarta on Wednesday and Saturday for US$570 roundtrip; minimum stay five days, maximum 180 days. For good tickets check **YSTAPHIL,** 4227 Tomas Claudio St., Manila, Philippines, tel. (02) 832-0680.

From Thailand
Near the Malaysia Hotel in Bangkok are a number of travel agencies selling cheap tickets. Fares and departure dates fluctuate, and getting a straight answer to a seemingly simple question is like trying to bite the wind. Walk around and compare prices. Student and off-season discounts are available, as are package deals offering no-frills indirect flights. **K Travel Service,** 21/33 Soi Ngam Dupli, Bangkok 10120, tel. (2) 286-1468, has a good reputation among travelers. Several other agencies are found along Sukhumvit Road. STA in Viengtai Hotel is expensive but honest.

From Japan and Korea
Tokyo is a better place to buy air tickets than is generally realized. The city's many resident *gaijin* (foreigners) are required by Japanese immigration to periodically leave the country and reenter. This requirement has created a ready market for cheap excursion fares. Many discount travel agencies specializing in overseas flights advertise in English-language media like the *Japan Times* and *Tokyo Journal.* Tokyo's

a big place, so it's best to phone around and compare prices.

The following agencies are worth checking: **Council Travel,** Sanno Grand Bldg., Room 102, 14-2 Nagata-cho, 2-chome, Chiyoda-ko, Tokyo 100, tel. (03) 3581-7581; **STA,** seventh floor, Nukariya Bldg., 1-16-20 Minami-Ikebukuro, Toshima-Ku, tel. 5391-2889, fax 5391-2923; **A.B.C. Air Bank Co.,** tel. 233-1177; **Asahi International Travel,** tel. 584-5732; **E.H.L.,** tel. 351-2131; **M.I.C.,** tel. 370-6577; **N.L.C.,** tel. 988-7801. The only nonstop flight from Tokyo to Bali is offered by Garuda on DC-10 widebody jets for US$1021 one-way coach fare; US$1752 one-way first class.

Few discounters are found in Korea. The travel agent in the **USO Club** outside the gates of the Yongsan U.S. Army Garrison is worth a try: 104 Kalwol-dong, Yongsan-gu, Seoul, tel. (2) 792-3063 or 792-3028. He sells mostly roundtrip tickets to Asian destinations for GIs and dependents. Also try the **Korean International Student Exchange Society** (KISES), YMCA Bldg., Room 505, Chongno 2-ga, Seoul. Tickets to Jakarta sometimes sell for as little as US$550.

From Hong Kong
Hong Kong is as cheap as Bangkok and Penang for air tickets in Southeast Asia, with direct flights available to Jakarta and Denpasar. Return flights are even better bargains. The discounted fare to Denpasar is around HK$3000 roundtrip (roughly US$400). Many discount travel agencies advertise in English-language morning newspapers like the *Hong Kong Standard, South China Morning Post,* and the monthly magazine, *Business Traveler.*

The following agencies are consistently good: **Phoenix Travel Service** at Tjim Tja Soi in Kowloon, tel. 2722-7378 (talk to Rocky); **STB,** 26 Des Voeux Rd., Central Bldg., 26/F, tel. 2810-7272; **Time Travel,** Chungking Mansions, 16th floor, A Block, tel. 2366-6222; **Hong Kong Student Travel Bureau,** Room 1021, 10th floor, Star House, Tsimshatsui, tel. 2730-3269. Ask agents about the Cathay Pacific roundtrip flight to Denpasar.

From Taiwan
For discount travel agencies in Taiwan, see the notice board at the Taipei Hostel near the Lai Lai

Sheraton Hotel. Travelers tend to gravitate toward **Jenny Su Travel Service,** 27 Chungshan N. Rd., 10th floor, section 3, Taipei, tel. (02) 595-1646.

FROM AUSTRALIA

From Australia, even economy-class tickets are expensive. Qantas and Garuda offer frequent service to Bali from Adelaide, Brisbane, Cairns, Darwin, Melbourne, Perth, Port Hedland, and Sydney. Only Garuda offers the Darwin, while only Qantas flies from Brisbane. Flight time from Melbourne to Bali is about six hours, from Sydney to Bali about five and a half hours.

Qantas and Garuda offer precisely the same fares and flight restrictions to Bali (A$753 one-way, A$915 roundtrip), with seven-day minimum stay, maximum 45 days. During the Dec.-Feb. high season, flights from Australia to Bali are heavily booked; reserve your place at least three months ahead.

Fly to Bali from Perth for A$596 one-way, A$937 roundtrip (peak); A$504 one-way, A$787 roundtrip (low). Flight time is three and a half hours. Perth-Denpasar-Jakarta flights leave twice weekly. If you have an International Student ID card, check out STA flights from Perth to Bali. Student and under-26 fares are about 10% cheaper.

The cheapest indirect flight to Bali is on **Royal Brunei,** which flies from Darwin (A$902) or Brisbane (A$1054 roundtrip) via Brunei once a week. You arrive in Bali the same day you take off. They also fly from Perth (A$876 roundtrip) twice a week, but you have to overnight in Brunei.

Many travelers fly from Darwin to Kupang, West Timor, then island-hop to Bali. From Kupang, regular flights to Denpasar cost A$190 one-way. From Darwin, Merpati flies to Kupang twice weekly for A$330 one-way, A$407 roundtrip in low season. This flight leaves each Saturday morning and takes two hours; return flights leave Friday. Upon arrival in Kupang you'll receive a 60-day entry stamp.

Ansett International flies to Bali from Sydney, Melbourne, and Darwin twice weekly; from Brisbane to Bali once weekly; and from Perth to Bali three times weekly. Fares from Brisbane and Adelaide are the same as from Melbourne

and Sydney. You'll find scant difference between the fares offered by all the airlines—Ansett, Qantas, Garuda—which service Bali.

Airline Offices
Air New Zealand, 5 Elizabeth St. (corner of Queens and Customs Streets), Sydney, tel. 02-9223-4666; **Ansett,** 501 Swanston St., 16th floor, Melbourne, tel. 03-962-3333; **Garuda,** 175 Clarence St., Sydney, tel. 02-334-9900 (Australian-wide telephone is 008-800873); **Merpati,** 12 Westlane Arcade, Darwin, tel. 08-941-1030; **Qantas,** International Square, Jamison St., Sydney, tel. 02-957-0111 or 9236-3636 (Australia-wide telephone is 131767); **Singapore Airlines,** 17 Bridge St., Sydney, tel. 02-9236-0111.

Discount Ticket Agents
Anywhere Travel, 345 Anzac Parade, Kingsford, Sydney, tel. 02-663-0411; **STA Travel,** 732 Harris St., Ultimo, Sydney, tel. 02-9281-9866 or 9212-1255, and 256 Flinder St., Melbourne, tel. 03-9347-4711 (other offices in Cairns, Townsville, Canberra, and Adelaide); **Discount Travel Specialists,** Shop 53, Forest Chase, Perth, tel. 09-221-1400; **Topdeck Travel,** 45 Grenfell St., Adelaide, tel. 08-8410-1110.

Package Holidays and Group Tours
Numerous package tours from Sydney and Melbourne to Bali are available for around A$800. Even though you pay for places and services unseen, the prices on a twin-share all-inclusive package are unbeatable: Sydney to Bali, A$900 (peak), A$750 (low) for eight days, and from A$1150 for 15 days. This includes airfare, transfers, accommodations, continental breakfast in a three-star hotel, and a token sightseeing tour or two. Each extra night costs only A$20 per person. Children are usually charged two-thirds the adult airfare.

Certain restrictions may apply. Departure and return schedules are usually unchangeable. The tour packages issue hotel vouchers, which you exchange for accommodations in either Sanur, Kuta, Nusa Dua, or Ubud. Other packages offer accommodations in Jimbaran, Lovina, and Candidasa. Vouchers are sometimes also issued for dining or for rental of bicycles or motorcycles. The final price depends on how long you stay, the class of hotel you choose, and when you go. Low-season fares are in force from February to March and from 16 October to 30 November; shoulder season is 16-31 January, April-May, and 1 July to 15 October; high season is 1 December to 15 January.

Package tour prices can be so good that some travelers take advantage of the cheap airfares offered and ignore the vouchers. Don't sign on for too many extensions and additional sightseeing tours because these can be purchased much cheaper in Bali. Look for deals in the travel sections of Australia's big-city newspapers. Find a flexible agent who can arrange for you to use vouchers in a selection of hotels so your movement won't be too restricted.

Australia is the place to take advantage of some unique adventure and sports tours to Bali offered by specialist tour operators. **Surf Travel Company,** with offices at 12 Cronulla Plaza, Cronulla Beach, Sydney (tel. 02-527-4722), and at Kirra Surf Centre, corner of Gold Coast Highway and Coolangatta Road, Kirra, Queensland (tel. 075-5599-2818), sells surfing packages to Bali including accommodations, meals, and transport. **Pro Dive,** Royal Arcade, Shop 620, Pitt St., Sydney (tel. 02-9264-9499), specializes in dive packages to Bali including airfare, accommodations, diving equipment, and transport to dive sites.

FROM NEW ZEALAND

Both Air New Zealand and Garuda offer twice-weekly direct flights between Auckland and Denpasar for NZ$1358 (low season) and NZ$1518 (high season). Fourteen-day advance purchase is required, and you must stay a minimum of five days and a maximum of 35 days. Add at least NZ$350 if you fly from Christchurch or Wellington.

Airline Offices
Air New Zealand reservations in Auckland is 09-357-3000; **Ansett,** 50 Grafton Rd., Auckland, tel. 09-307-5378; **Garuda,** 120 Albert St., Auckland, tel. 09-366-1855 (reservations in Auckland 09-366-1855 or 366-1862); **Qantas,** Qantas House, 154 Queen St., Auckland, tel. 09-303-2506; **Singapore Airlines,** West Plaza Building (corner of Albert and Customs Streets), Lower Ground Floor, Auckland, tel. 09-379-3209.

FROM THE U.S.A.

Airlines serving Bali from the U.S. include Garuda Indonesia, Hong Kong Airlines, Singapore Airlines, Japan Airlines, China Airlines, Malaysia Airlines, and KLM. An hour or so spent calling toll-free numbers (see below) will provide the most up-to-date info on current airfares, timetables, and connections.

The travel sections of the *Los Angeles Times, New York Times, Chicago Tribune,* and *San Francisco Examiner* are full of ads for cut-rate transpacific flights. Other good sources are *Great Expeditions Magazine,* 242 W. Milbrook, Suite 102-A, Raleigh, NC 27609, tel. (800) 743-3639, fax (919) 847-0780; and **ITN,** 520 Calvados Ave., Sacramento, CA 95815.

If you work through travel agents, have them contact a knowledgeable Asian consolidator for the best fares. If you plan to travel in the high season (June-Sept., December, and the Chinese New Year), you'll need to book months in advance. If you're planning extended travel in Asia, buy an open ticket valid for one year.

Tickets from the U.S. west coast to Hong Kong or Singapore average US$1150 one-way or US$1400 roundtrip. From these points board another flight to Jakarta or Bali. Some incredibly cheap tickets are available between Los Angeles, San Francisco, Seattle, and Singapore with stops in Hawaii, Japan, Korea, Taiwan, Hong Kong, and Bangkok.

The real bargain fares into Bali depart from Los Angeles. For as little as US$1000 in the off-season, **Malaysia Airlines** flies from Los Angeles to either Tokyo or Taipei (two-hour layover), then flies to Kuala Lumpur and Denpasar. One free stopover is allowed each way, and the total travel time to Bali is 24 hours.

Singapore Airlines flies to Bali from New York via Frankfurt or Amsterdam for US$1375 (low season) and $1575 (high season); flying time is 26 hours. SIA also flies to Bali from Los Angeles with a two-hour stopover in Singapore for US$1150 roundtrip low season, $1275 high season. **China Airlines** offers daily flights from Los Angeles to Bali via Taiwan.

Continental flies from Los Angeles to Denpasar four times weekly for US$1450 roundtrip, via Honolulu and Guam. The low-season fare is

US$1350 roundtrip, for departures before May 31. You're allowed one stopover, for up to six months. **American Airlines** and **United Airlines** both offer regular flights from major cities to Los Angeles and New York, with connections to Bali.

KLM flies from New York to Jakarta via Amsterdam; one-way fare is US$1234 coach, US$2059 first class. **Icelandic Airways,** tel. (800) 223-5500, connects New York with Luxembourg for US$159; from there you can catch a cut-rate European charter to Asia. **Malaysia Airlines** flies five times weekly from Los Angeles to Bali via Tokyo and Kuala Lumpur. **Thai International** offers four flights weekly from Los Angeles to Bali via Bangkok and Seoul.

Garuda Indonesia

Garuda offers direct flights four times a week between Los Angeles and Bali, via Hawaii (18 hours). The usual fare is US$1050 (low season), US$1225 (high season) from Los Angeles to Bali. This is the same fare as from Los Angeles to Jakarta. From New York, the ticket to Bali via Los Angeles is US$1350 (low season) and US$1575 (high season).

Garuda doesn't give discounts on tickets you buy from them. You get one "free" stopover in Bali on the flight from Los Angeles to Jakarta. Ask about Garuda's Visit Indonesia Pass, which allows you to visit three cities in Indonesia for US$300. Each additional city costs US$100, to a maximum of 10 cities. For more information, call (800) 247-8380, or fax (213) 389-1568.

North American Garuda Offices: 3457 Wilshire Blvd., Los Angeles, CA 90010, tel. (800) 342-7832 inside California or (800) 826-2829 outside California; 360 Post St., Ste. 804, San Francisco, CA 94108, tel. (415) 788-2626; 51 E. 42nd St., Ste. 616, New York, NY 10017, tel. (800) 248-2829 outside New York or (212) 370-0707 inside eastern region; 1600 Kapiolani Blvd., Ste. 632, Honolulu, HI 96814, tel. (808) 947-9500; 1040 W. Georgia St., Vancouver, B.C., Canada V6E 4H1, tel. (604) 681-3699.

Garuda Orient Holidays: Some airfare and hotel combos offered by Garuda cost little more than the airfare alone. For US$1279 in the high season, US$1099 in the low season, you can buy a roundtrip package from Los Angeles to Denpasar with five nights in Kuta, including transfers and sightseeing tours. Inquire also

about their eight-day and 15-day packages that include airfare from Los Angeles, all transfers, and five nights in Ubud for only US$1500. Hard to beat. The price depends largely on the rating of the hotel you stay in. For more information call (800) 247-8380 from the U.S. and Canada.

From Hawaii

Asia Travel Service, tel. (808) 926-0550 interisland or (800) 884-0550, sells tickets to Bali or Jakarta for US$799. Also check out **Panda Travel,** tel. (808) 734-1961, fax 732-4136. **Emerson Travel** offers a seven-day tour of Bali for US$950, including five nights in a hotel, daily breakfast, airfare, transfers, and day tours. A tour to Yogyakarta is optional. Emerson also sells tickets to Jakarta, Bali, Yogyakarta, Solo, and Surabaya for US$799.

Budget U.S. Ticket Agencies

Overseas Tours, 475 El Camino Real, Ste. 206, Millbrae, CA 94030, tel. (800) 323-8777 in California or (800) 227-5988 outside California, claims to match any advertised ticket price to the Orient. Overseas represents 20 scheduled airlines, 300 tours, and 500 hotels in Asia.

Travel agencies owned by Indonesians or with strong connections to Indonesia are well placed to offer bargains. Such companies include **Canatours Inc.,** 427 Bernard St., Los Angeles, CA 90012, tel. (800) 345-2262 outside California or (213) 223-1111 in California, fax (213) 223-1048; and **Royal Express Tours and Travel,** 731 S. Atlantic Blvd., Monterey Park, CA 91754, tel. (818) 289-8520.

Also with great prices to Asia are **Adventure Center,** 1311 63rd St., Ste. 200, Emeryville, CA 94608, tel. (510) 654-1879; and **Community Travel Service,** 5299 College Ave., Oakland, CA 94618, tel. (510) 653-0990, fax 653-9071. The latter sells Japan Airlines roundtrip tickets for US$952 with stops in Tokyo.

Air Courier Association, 191 University Blvd., Suite 300, Denver, CO 80206, tel. (303) 279-3600, sells deeply discounted flights to Bali, as does the **Educational Travel Center,** 438 N. Frances St., Madison, WI 53703, tel. (800) 747-5551.

Air Brokers International, Inc., 323 Geary St., Ste. 411, San Francisco, CA 94102, tel. (800) 883-3273 or (415) 397-1383, fax (415)

397-4767, sells a Los Angeles-Denpasar-Jakarta ticket for as low as US$875 roundtrip (low season) and US$1050 roundtrip (high season).

Council Travel Services, 2511 Channing Way, Berkeley, CA 94701, tel. (415) 848-8604, and 205 E. 42nd St., New York, NY 10017, tel. (800) 743-1823, is a well-known student discounter; nonstudents may also use its services.

Pan Express Travel, 209 Post St., Ste. 921, San Francisco, CA 94108, tel. (415) 989-8282, sells a US$830 roundtrip ticket for a San Francisco-Honolulu-Denpasar-Yogyakarta-Jakarta flight.

Student Travel Network is a budget student ticket agency with offices worldwide. **STA,** 48 E. 11th St., New York, NY 10013, tel. (800) 777-0112, and 5900 Wilshire Blvd., Ste. 2100, Los Angeles, CA 90036, tel. (213) 937-1150, sells Garuda tickets from anywhere in North America to Bali. Prices aren't the absolute cheapest but the service is dependable.

Airline Toll-Free Numbers
American Airlines, tel. (800) 433-7300; **Cathay Pacific,** tel. (800) 233-2742; **China Airlines,** tel. (800) 227-5118; **Continental Airlines,** tel. (800) 231-0856; **Garuda Indonesia,** tel. (800) 342-7832; **KLM,** tel. (800) 374-7747; **Malaysia Airlines,** tel. (800) 421-8641; **Singapore Airlines,** tel. (800) 742-3333; **Thai International,** tel. (800) 426-5204; **United Airlines,** tel. (800) 538-2929.

FROM CANADA

With persistence, some good bargains are available from Toronto, Montreal, and Vancouver. Look for cheap flights at travel agencies specializing in Southeast Asia and in the *Toronto Globe and Mail.*

Discount agents offer low-season roundtrip fares of C$1400 on Air Canada flights that connect with Garuda in Los Angeles. High-season fare is C$1600.

Another approach is to try to find a cheap flight to Bangkok, then travel overland to Bali. Consolidators in Canada sell roundtrip tickets on **Canadian Airlines** (tel. 800-776-3000) to Bangkok via Vancouver and Hong Kong for as low as US$750 in the low season, US$850 peak season. Flying time is 21 hours. Also check out

Cathay Pacific flights out of Vancouver, connecting with Garuda in Los Angeles or Honolulu. Their low season fares are as little as C$1200, high season C$1425.

Probably the best bucket shop in Canada is **Adventure Centre,** 17 Hayden St., Toronto, Ontario M4Y 2P2, tel. (800) 661-7265, with offices in Calgary, Edmonton, Toronto, and Vancouver. Also an excellent choice is Nouvelles Frontieres, 1001 Sherbrook East, Ste. 720, Montreal, H2L 1L3, tel. (514) 526-8444; another branch is in Quebec City.

Travel Cuts, the Canadian student travel bureau, sells consistently inexpensive fares: C$850 one-way (C$1340 roundtrip) to Jakarta. Travel Cuts main office is located at 187 College St., Toronto, Ontario M5T 1P7, tel. (416) 979-2406. **Pan Express Travel,** 6 Wellesley St., Ste. 303, Toronto M41 186, tel. (416) 964-6888, is worth checking out as well.

FROM THE NETHERLANDS

You can fly from Amsterdam to Indonesia at very reasonable prices—sometimes even cheaper than flying from Sydney to Singapore. One of the cheapest flights from Holland is with Czechoslovakian Airlines—a 20-hour Amsterdam-Prague-Abu Dhabi-Bombay-Singapore-Jakarta jaunt.

To find the cheapest flights, check the Saturday editions of Holland's main national newspapers. The best is *Volkakrant.* Many small ticketing offices are found in Amsterdam's Chinese quarter (where you might find a Cathay Pacific flight for 1200-1300 guilders). Ask if the agent is a member of ANVR, a union of travel agents which requires its members to join a fund that guarantees your ticket in case anything goes wrong.

The problem of leaving from Holland lies not in the reasonableness of the fares but in being able to actually get a seat on an aircraft during the July-August busy season, when 150,000 Netherlanders fly to Indonesia. You can always buy a First Class ticket on KLM, but it may be hard to find a cheap Garuda, KLM, MAS, SIA, or Thai discount ticket.

If you absolutely must get to Indonesia during this time, try to get a flight to Frankfurt and then connect with a Lufthansa flight to Indonesia for around 1600 guilders. Or you might try to get on an expensive economy seat on an Air France flight out of Paris.

KLM and Garuda operate a weekly B747 joint service between Amsterdam and Bali. The fare to Denpasar is 4075 guilders one-way, 7416 guilders roundtrip. Garuda APEX fares from Amsterdam to Bali: 1593 guilders one-way, 2950 guilders roundtrip (minimum seven days, maximum 180 days, valid only until 31 May). Garuda's office is at Singel 540, 1017 AZ Amsterdam, tel. (020) 272-626.

Cheaper flights might be found through **NBBS** (the official Dutch student travel agency), Rokin 38, tel. 624-0989, or at Leidsestraat 53, tel. 638-1736. Another good outfit is **Amber Reisbureau,** Da Costastraat 77, 1053 ZG Amsterdam, tel. (020) 685-1155; 100% reliable. Also worth a try is **ILC Reizen,** NZ Voorburgwal 256, tel. 620-5121.

FROM LONDON

London is famous for low airfares to the Orient—the best place in Europe to buy air tickets. In fact, you won't be able to find anything *but* budget airfares, thanks to the city's many discount ticket outlets called "bucket shops." Each shop may or may not have its own advance-purchase requirements and cancellation penalties, so inquire.

The weekly *Time Out,* available at London newsstands, contains ads for many bargain airfares and bucket shops. The *Sunday Times* and the *News and Travel Magazine* may also prove useful.

Cheap tickets may not be available at peak periods, when airlines can fill their planes at higher prices. During the summer high season, discount airfares to Bali run about £700, but plummet to about £530-580 other times of the year.

Compare prices with those of Brunei Airlines which are lately coming in as the cheapest low-season airlines from London to Bali (about £700 in the high season). Also investigate Aeroflot flights to Jakarta for £500 year-round, and Thai International's flights.

Start inquiries at London's **Garuda** office. To Bali, Garuda offers a fare of £708 one-way or £1159 roundtrip, minimum stay seven days, maximum 180 days. Garuda is the only airline out of

London which flies direct to Bali (21 hours). The flights leave three times weekly, stopping en route in Zurich, Abu Dhabi, and Jakarta.

Also check Qantas and Singapore Airlines, both offering nonstop flights to Bali via Singapore; they lay over just an hour in Singapore, then fly straight to Bali (17 hours total).

When buying a ticket through a bucket shop, don't pay more than a deposit before receiving the ticket—these agencies have a high rate of closure. Make sure the shop you use belongs to the Association of British Travel Agents (ABTA); its members guarantee a refund in case the individual shop goes broke.

An appealing option is to fly London-Singapore, for which fares are deeply discounted (around £600 roundtrip). Then—after a trip into Malaysia—buy a roundtrip Singapore-Jakarta ticket.

Or try for a good fare from London to Australia (around £500) with a stopover in Bali. A roundtrip ticket from London to Sydney with a stopover in Singapore and Bali will run around £1000. Various low-cost London-Australia and London-New Zealand flights are available for about £500-800 roundtrip, with inexpensive stopovers in either Singapore or Bali. The fewer the stopovers, the cheaper the ticket.

Travel Agents

A reliable and competent travel agent for cut-rate tickets is **Trailfinders,** 42-50 Earls Court Rd., London, tel. 0171-938-3366; 194 Kensington High St., London W8 7RG, tel. 0171-938-3939; take the tube to High St., Kensington.

The largest budget agency for those under 26 is **Student Travel Australia** (STA), located at 86 Old Brompton Rd., London NW1 2SX, tel. 0171-937-9962, and 38 Store St., London WC1, tel. 0171-361-6262. Branches in Birmingham, Cambridge, Canterbury, Cardiff, Coventry, Durham, Glasgow, Leeds, Manchester, and Nottingham.

Also worth a look are **Council Travel,** 28 A Poland St., London W1V 3DB, tel. 0171-437-7767; and **Travel Bug,** 597 Cheetham Hill Rd., Manchester M85EJ, tel. 0161-721-4000. Another specialist in low-cost flights is **Campus Travel,** 52 Grosvenor Gardens, London SW1 OAG, tel. 0171-730-8111; branches in Birmingham, Brighton, Bristol, Cambridge, Edinburgh, Manchester, and campuses and YHA offices all over the U.K.

Airline Offices
Aeroflot, 70 Piccadilly, London W1V 9HH, tel. 0171-355-2233; **Garuda Indonesia,** 35 Duke St., London W1M 5DF, tel. 0171-486-3011; **Malaysia Airlines,** 61 Picadilly, London W1V 9HL, tel. 0181-740-2626; **Qantas,** 182 The Strand, London WC2R 1ET, tel. 0345-747767; **Royal Brunei Airlines,** 49 Cromwell Rd., London SW7 2ED, tel. 0171-584-6660; **Singapore Airlines,** 143-147 Regent St., London W1R 7LB, tel. 0181-747-0007; **Thai International,** 41 Albemarle St., London W1X 4LE, tel. 0171-491-7953.

FROM IRELAND

No direct or nonstop flights serve Bali from Ireland, but agents can put you on an Aer Lingus flight to London, connecting you with a Garuda, Thai International Airways, SIA, or Qantas flight to Bali. From Dublin to Denpasar, the best peak-season fare (July-Aug.) available presently is with Thai Airways via London and Bangkok for IR£665. Garuda charges around IR£775 for the Dublin-Denpasar flight in the high season and about IR£150 less in the low season. From Belfast, get a flight first to London with British Airways, then board a connecting flight to Bali. Roundtrip fares start at around IR£765 in the high season, IR£650 in the low season.

Long-Haul Ticket Agencies
Best discount agency for students is **USIT,** Aston Quay, O'Connell Bridge, Dublin 2, tel. 01-679-8833; Fountain Centre, College St., Belfast BT1 6ET, tel. 01232-324-073; 10-11 Market Parade, Patrick St., Cork, tel. 021-270-900. Also check out **Apex Travel,** 59 Dame St., Dublin 2, tel. 01-672-5933; **Flight Finders International,** 13 Baggot St., Lower, Dublin 2, tel. 01-676-8326; and **Inflight Travel,** 92-94 York Rd., Belfast, tel. 01232-740-187.

Airline Offices
Aer Lingus, 41 Upper O'Connell St., Dublin 1; 42 Grafton St., Dublin 2, tel. 01-844-4777; 46 Castle St., Belfast BT1 1AB, tel. 01232-245-151; 2 Academy St., Cork, tel. 021-327-155; **British Airways,** Dublin reservations, tel. (800) 626747; 9 Fountain Center, College St., Belfast BT1 6ET, tel. 0345-222-111.

FROM OTHER POINTS IN EUROPE

It's not difficult to find low fares from Amsterdam, Athens, Basel, Brussels, Frankfurt, Paris, Rome, Vienna, or Zurich. Indeed, Indonesia-bound traffic has become so frantic that European countries now offer unbelievably cheap package deals.

In Germany, the fare from Frankfurt to Denpasar is DM3902 roundtrip, DM2828 one-way excursion fare. Recommended is **SRS Studenten Reise Service,** Marienstrasse 23 (U-Bahn and S-Bahn: Friedrichstrasse), for discounts to students up to age 34. Travel agencies offering cheap tickets advertise in the travel section of such publications as *Zitty*. Also try **Alternativ Tours,** Wilmersdorfer Strasse 94, U-Bahn Adenauerplatz, tel. (069) 881-2089, a well-known and trustworthy consolidator.

In Austria, the biggest student travel agency is **Osterreichisches Komitee fur Internationalen Studentenaustausch** (Okista), with head offices at 9 Garnisongasse 7, Vienna, tel. (0222) 401-480. Open Mon.-Fri. 0900-1730, Saturday 0930-1200. Try other Okista offices at 9 Turkenstrasse 4-6 and at 4 Karlsgasse 3, tel. 505-0128 in Vienna.

In Switzerland, get a recent issue of the best Swiss travelers' publication, *Globetrotter-Magazin*, which lists loads of cheap airlines. The **SSR** offices are also outlets for cheap Bali-bound tickets: try first the head office at Rue Vignier, Geneva, tel. (022) 29-97-33; open Mon.-Fri. 0900-1730. Another good ticket agency offering budget fares to Asia is **Globetrotter.**

In Belgium, try the student travel agency **Acotra,** Rue de la Madeleine 51, tel. (02) 512-8607; or **Connections Travel Shop,** Rue du Marche-au-Charbon 13, tel. 512-060, both in Brussels. **Nouvelles Frontieres** of Italy and France offers cheap airfares to the Far East; the Rome-Jakarta ticket costs only 950,000 lira roundtrip. In Rome, the student travel center **CTS,** Via Genova 16 (off Via Nazionale), tel. (06) 46-791, has some great fares to Southeast Asia. In Paris, investigate **Selectour Voyages,** 29 Rue de la Huchette, tel. (01) 43-29-64-00, open weekdays 0945-1830; and **Council Travel,** 31 Rue Saint Augustine, tel. 42-66-20-87, open Mon.-Fri. 0930-1830, Saturday 1000-1400.

GETTING AROUND

Major points of interest on this 70 km long by 45 km wide island are easily accessible within a day's journey of Kuta, Sanur, Ubud, Nusa Dua, or Denpasar, using a variety of transport. The shortest distance by road between the island's north and south and between the eastern and western tips is only around 200 km. Tourists congregate in the bottom eighth of the island while most of Bali's 5,000 square kilometers of back country remain rural, traditional, and nearly unspoiled.

Next to walking, the best ways to travel are by the *bemo* and minibuses, which can't be beat for speed, mobility, economy, and firsthand contact with the people. On public minibuses, you can get from one end of the island to the other for less than Rp5000. Those visitors with limited time or who desire maximum flexibility may want to hire a car or minibus which you can hire with a driver or drive yourself. There are also taxis and motorcycles for rent. Alternatively, if you want a quick introduction to the island, join one of the many guided tour groups.

Due to the enormous growth of tourism, everyone speaks some English along the tourist routes, and you can get by quite adequately without Bahasa Indonesia. But even though more and more Balinese are learning English each year, if you venture into the rugged back roads of the island it might be difficult to even find people who speak passable Indonesian. Refer to the appendix for Indonesian phrases which will help you get around in the countryside of Bali.

There are dozens of ways to get around. In Kuta, you can flag down a taxi, *bemo,* or hop on the back of a motorcycle on just about any streetcorner. If you have a quick errand to run, just borrow a kid's bicycle for a few minutes. Small sailing craft *(jukung)* are popular with marine enthusiasts for exploring near the shore and inside a reef. *Dokar,* horse-drawn carts holding three to six passengers, are an expensive way to jog through Denpasar (Rp2000 for a one- to two-km ride). Settle the price before climbing in. Unfortunately, these picturesque contraptions are on the verge of extinction.

Ojek

A handy method of motorcycle transport is *honda sikap* or *ojek,* in which you pay a driver for the privilege of riding on the back of his motorcycle to your destination. Though relatively expensive, this is one of the quickest and most convenient ways to travel short distances on Bali. This service is offered, for example, in Penelokan down to Lake Batur, from the north coast highway to Banjar hot springs or the Buddhist temple, and from the main Gianyar-Amlapura road up to the village of Tenganan.

But anywhere you see motorcycles and their riders gather, such as the start of country roads or at intersections, *ojek* service is for the asking. How do you tell if it's a professional *ojek* driver? He will have an extra helmet dangling from the back seat of his bike.

If you're really stuck, approach a motorcycle or scooter owner for a ride *anywhere,* even though they don't obviously give people rides for money. Or simply flag down a passing motorbike on the road—who knows, you may get the ride for free. Normally, the 20-km ride from say Sanur to Kuta costs about Rp8000. An *ojek* ride from Kuta to Denpasar is Rp5000.

Best Time to Travel

Adopt the Indonesian concept of *jam karet* ("rubber time"). Times of departures are stretched or contracted depending on the whim of the driver or how full or empty the vehicle is. So don't be in a hurry—no one else is! The best times of the day to travel are in the very early mornings and late afternoons when it's cooler and when the widest variety of transport is available, leaving the middle of the day free to rest and eat.

During important religious holidays such as Galungan, tens of thousands of Balinese hit the road to visit relatives and temples. During these times the roads are hectic. The best time to visit climate-wise is in the cooler dry season (May-Sept.) when skies are clear, there is less rain, and coastal breezes cool the air.

The best time to travel to avoid tourists is during the non-tourist season (roughly January through June). During this time, public transport after sundown slows to a crawl. Plan accordingly. In July and August, Europeans start raining down on the island. After Christmas the Australians leave and from then on it gets more and more quiet until May when Australians on school holidays start to arrive again.

Road Conditions

Traffic conditions worsen from day to day. It has become a horror to drive a car, let alone a motorcycle, between Denpasar and Kuta and Sanur, east to about as far as Klungkung, west as far as Tabanan, and north on the roads up to Ubud.

In most other locales on the island, the traffic is relatively light. There are stretches of dirt roads, particularly in the mountains, but by far most roads are paved (even in the northeast) and consist of just a single lane. The signing is casual and erratic; double white lines on the road only mean that someone has put paint on the road. Only the Bypass Highway from Tohpati to Nusa Dua is a proper highway with shoulders; most other roads do not have shoulders, so be very careful because vehicles can stop in the middle of the road. This means that large oncoming vehicles force you completely off the road. Three vehicles overtaking at once is not unusual if the road might allow it (ignoring oncoming traffic). Speed limits are liberally interpreted.

The most dangerous are those infernal buses and Javanese trucks, particularly at night. They don't give a damn about who is in front of them. The number of trucks is incredible! At one point in 1994, 200 trucks a day were carrying loads of sand from Klungkung to Tuban. The drive to Ubud is sometimes bumper-to-bumper trucks, vans, cars, and motorbikes. They've widened the main roads, and the Bypass has been extended from Tohpati cutting north and west to come out on the main road to Tabanan in Ubung. The Bypass in Sanur has been divided on either side by concrete blocks to form local lanes a la Jakarta.

A new coastal road which starts north of the Gelalel Supermarket in Kuta heads straight across to Tanah Lot and beyond. It was finished in 1996 when the massive Nirwana Resort at Tanah Lot was finally completed. Although many buildings were destroyed in the process, this road relieves a lot of traffic congestion in southern Bali. Now it takes only 20 minutes to drive from Tanah Lot to the airport! Another new road is being built to the northeast to Kusamba.

Traffic development always comes first; traffic rules come later. With thousands of trucks, vans, and local buses spewing out diesel, it has become quite smoggy in southern Bali now, yet more emphasis is placed on road rules than vehicular environmental standards.

In the main towns a motorcycle culture has developed. Hundreds of leisure bikes mark the prestige of young men who spend their afternoons and evenings riding from one meeting place to another to see their friends and be seen by everyone else. Most of these bikes are low-power, low noise bikes, but there are also high-powered bikes with mufflers rigged to produce maximum noise. Their owners like to roar arond the main streets in the wee hours of the morning. The dogs and roosters have to yell at triple volume in order to communicate.

When a festival is taking place, a town like Ubud can be brought to a standstill under continuous ritual parades. Also, the day before and the day after Hari Proklamasi Kemerdekaan (Independence Day, 17 August) may be difficult traveling through Bali's big towns because of *lalu lintas macet* (traffic jams). If you're bound to a tight schedule, don't plan major travel by land on those times.

Another problem is parking. The traffic jams around the Penelokan/Batur area can be as long as three km in the peak tourist season, with no place to park except at expensive restaurants up the road. Normally, however, one may park in designated parking areas for a small fee, or just anywhere, even at the base of the Batur volcano—but never leave anything valuable in the car.

Contracts

With all charters, it's important that there be no misunderstandings. When chartering a bicycle for a day or two, since the amount is so low, you can just make a verbal agreement. But with a boat or vehicle you hire for two or more days in which a large amount of money is involved (Rp40,000 and up per day), it's always best to write out an informal contract on a piece of paper or on the back of their business card. Have him write out the particulars in *his* handwriting: date, your name, the beginning and ending date of the charter period, and then have him or her initial it. Write this contract in English as there will always be people around who can translate it back to Indonesian. This will save you lots of misunderstandings that frequently and almost inevitably occur between tourists and Balinese service providers. With tour agencies or operators there is not so much of a need to draft a contract because the terms of the agreement are often spelled out in the tour agency's literature.

Hitching

Hitching on Bali is some of the best in Indonesia. Just stand out in the highway and hitch whatever comes by, including public transport. Even if you have to pay, it won't be that much. Just give what you feel is a fair price, plus a little more. You may also get rides with tourists, mail and delivery trucks, aid workers, or motorcyclists.

The Balinese find it difficult to understand the concept of a Westerner (i.e., rich person) asking for a free ride, but don't let their curious stares discourage you. More often than not, they will pull over since it's the custom to flag down rides for which you pay a fare.

HIKING AND TREKKING

The best way to see Bali is to get out and walk and just get lost. The Balinese themselves don't like to walk—anything over 500 meters is considered *jahu* (far)—but for Westerners it's the best way to totally immerse yourself in the culture because the roads *are* its culture. Bali's roads are also its sidewalks, playgrounds, work areas, kitchens, living rooms, laundry rooms, and the principal village meeting places, though increasing traffic is discouraging these uses. Footpaths can also be used by motorcycles during peak hours.

The start of trailheads are always accessible by public *bemo* or *ojek*. Take a *bemo* to the end of a country road, then set off on a narrow half-hidden pathway and follow it inland perhaps 15 km. You won't lose your way if you know what *Ke mana?* means ("Where?"). People will correct you if you make a wrong turn. It's easier than you think finding your way through cultivated rice fields which act like giant steps. Be careful to always remain on the narrow borders of the fields and not to tread in the paddies themselves.

If you veer ever so slightly from the well-trod paths, it's just like walking into someone's living room. You may end up spending the night in places about as outlandish as you want to be in—no cold drinks, police, shops, or transport connections. Children pop up and yell out a sing-song "Hello," and you could come across infants who start screaming, cattle who start stampeding in terror, and dogs who'll howl mercilessly at the sight of your white face.

Take only two changes of clothes: a shirt and shorts, of decent length, which can be washed and dried in the sun, and a sash and *sarung* for swimming or as a coverup when entering temples. You don't need boots, which are too hot, sweaty, and smelly, unless you're climbing Gunung Agung. Sturdy strap sandals (Tevas) will protect your feet, allow you to ford streams without removing footwear, and walk along irrigation ditches and paths between rice fields. They can also be worn on semi-formal occasions.

Ubud is surrounded by some of the most superb walking and running country to be found anywhere in the world. When you're hiking, especially through any of the more remote villages—such as the ones along the back road from Ubud to Kintamani or in the Putung or Tegalalang areas—there's no need to take a tent and sleeping bag. Sleep on the village *bale banjar,* which is specifically meant to accommodate strangers. The Balinese don't like you over in the trees or in the dark jungle with all the spirits. They want you out where they can see you. The next morning, give a small donation to the *banjar.*

Leeches, which only occur in the deepest of Bali's forests, can be picked off as you see them. Another possible hazard are vicious red tree ants which can inflict painful bites, especially en masse. Tiger's claws *(tjangin)* is a cactus-like plant that can puncture a hiker's skin with razor-sharp needles. There are also prickly brambles and stinging nettles which produce large red welts on the skin, so don't venture from well-marked forest trails, especially at high-altitudes.

Bali is dissected by innumerable steep and treacherous ravines, especially if you're walking from east to west (or vice versa). These gaping valleys were formed by streams cutting deep into the island's volcanic tuff. Don't try to make your way down into these poorly-lit chasms as the way is often just a damp, mossy, difficult path cut into the rock face, across a rickety bamboo bridge, or straight down into the river itself. Instead, make your way back out to the main road and follow it until you reach a more substantial bridge.

Don't worry. If you get lost, just head for smoke or the sound of habitation, or just stay put. Someone will sooner or later come within shouting distance and lead you to the nearest *desa* or to a more trafficked path or at least be able to point you in the right direction.

Mountain climbing on Bali requires no special skills or equipment. All you need is a flashlight, warm jacket, sturdy shoes, and water. Although there are few facilities and the trails are ill-maintained and in some cases trashy, most of the best hikes can be done in one day. An exception to this is of course 3,142-meter-high Gunung Agung, which is not to be taken lightly. Climbing mountains is best in the dry season.

For long climbs, start very early on a night near the full moon. This will enable you to climb when the day is at its coolest, you can see the trail, reach the top before the sun comes up, and get back down before dark. Always go with a companion and let either the *post hansip* (village guard) or your hotel proprietor know where you'll be climbing and when you expect to return.

Trekking Specialists
Several agencies based in Bali specialize in personalized walking tours to memorable locations off the beaten track. **Santa Bali Tours & Travel** has an office in the Grand Bali Beach Hotel in Sanur. Their "Ubud Hinterland Track" tour, for example, gives you a chance to observe Balinese life in villages around Ubud which are inaccessible by car. You'll also visit some talented painters and woodcarvers. Depart 0800, return 1600, price US$27.50. For reservations, call (0361) 287628, ext. 1356, or 288057, ext. 1295, fax 236508 or 286825.

Ibu Rai Trekking, Jl. Monkey Forest Rd. 72, P.O. Box 153, Ubud 80571 (tel. 0361-975066 or 975579, fax 96472). Four times a week a car picks hikers up at 0800 from Ibu Rai Restaurant and takes them to Banjar Sala village outside Ubud. The walk consists of easy segments through rice fields, across streams and little bridges, then some climbing up through river valleys and forests. You'll visit the ancient temple of Pura Taman in Umakuta village, arriving back in Ubud around 1330. The cost is US$12 (lunch included). The guides are well informed and English-speaking.

BICYCLING

If you stay well clear of the main population centers, and know the best roads, long-distance cycling on Bali can be very satisfying and exhilarating. For most of the island's 2.7 million people, still the most common means of transport is the bicycle. A bicycle is a consistently good icebreaker and conversation piece in making you welcomed by the Balinese. It puts you in contact with the sights, sounds, and smells of the villages. It's a great way to enjoy the beautiful landscape and meet friendly people.

Although the ride up is a grueling challenge, as you wheel effortlessly down the slope of a volcano for 40 kilometers, your heart goes out to the poor sightseers trapped inside their air-conditioned tour buses. You'll be able to hear the rustling of the wind through the paddies, the laughter of the children, the thumping of women pounding rice. A chorus of "Hello turis!" and "Hello Mister!" rains down upon you at every village and schoolyard.

Although the main thoroughfares are heavily trafficked, the island is crisscrossed with an extensive network of narrow, pockmarked secondary roads with relatively light, though constantly increasing, four-wheel traffic. These byways reach every corner of the island; Nelles Verlag's Bali map will guide you off the main roads. Being Indonesia's foremost tourist island, good maps are available and the signposting is adequate. Unexpected vignettes greet you at every turn.

Count on covering about 15 km an hour in flat country. Your most formidable challenges are the hills, the heat, and riding on the left-hand side of the road. Traffic (cars, trucks, buses) is hectic and extremely unstructured. It can be rather dangerous at times to pedal around town amidst the *oplet,* trucks, and Toyota carryalls.

One idea is to put your bike into a vehicle you've rented and take it far into the country or high into the mountains. The person you rented it from will show you how to break it down by using the quick releases on the wheels and loosening the brake cable. Take the wheels off and it will easily fit into the back of a *kijang.* When you get to your destination, park your vehicle in a safe place where someone can look after it, then just set off.

Don't carry a lot of gear; you can do a bicycle tour here with just a couple of changes of clothes because the distance between local accommodations is always less than a day's ride. There's no need for cooking equipment because cheap roadside *warung* are frequent. If using a bicycle for short errands, the carrier racks *(bagase)* over the rear fenders of the local bikes are quite adequate for carrying your shoulder bag or knapsack, fastened with a couple of shock cords.

Be sure to wear a helmet whenever you're riding. Carry enough plastic Aqua (drinking water) containers, as dehydration can be a serious danger in the tropical heat. If you're taking on a volcano, you need to drink at least two liters a day. Whenever the cycling gets too difficult, just flag down a passing *bemo* or bus and throw your bike on the roof. It'll usually cost you just one additional passenger's fare.

Be sure to bring your bike inside accommodations at night; ripoffs are common and you could easily pay up to Rp150,000-250,000 for a lost rented bike. Many local bikes are equipped with a claw-like key lock which locks around the wheel and guards against petty theft but not against the determined bicycle thief.

Bringing Your Own Bike

If you're an ardent cyclist, or intend to cover some distance, you should consider taking your own bike. Airlines are surprisingly lenient about accepting bikes as luggage. If you only have one other checked piece of luggage, boxed bicycles may be checked on Garuda's domestic and international flights at no extra charge; if they want to play by the rules there could be a US$100 extra charge. Qantas offers a similar service.

For serious touring, a thoroughly robust 100% reliable touring or mountain bike with low gear-

ing for the steep grades is recommended. High-tech 10- or 21-speed parts and tools will prove difficult to obtain in Bali, so bring your own. Also bring at least one spare tube and tire, as well as a pump and a couple of extra spokes. Avoid bikes with skinny one-inch and $1^1/_8$-inch tires; 1.25 inch or $1^3/_8$-inch are stronger and more shock-absorbing.

Bring the best-quality, strongest back panniers because they will take a lot of punishment. Tires and tubes are available in Denpasar's bike shops in all the usual sizes. A critical accessory is a horn or loud bell. A heavy-duty hacksaw-proof steel cable lock or a solid U-lock (like a Kryptonite or Citadel) offer maximum security.

Renting and Buying a Bicycle

Bali has hundreds of bicycle rental places—either full-blown rental shops or the owner of the homestay's son will rent you his bike. Bicycles can also be rented at the various hotels and homestays. The dilemma is finding a machine that works, particularly one suited for an extended tour of the island.

Check out your bike carefully before you rent it. Take it on the road for half a day. Most are inadequate, dilapidated one-speed junkers with uncomfortable seats and without reflectors, lights, or good brakes. These sorry specimens (called *kumbang*) rent for only Rp2500-3500 per day, cheaper by the week or month (about Rp2000 per day). The fewer the bikes they have left, the higher the rental fee. Ten-speed bikes are now widely available and rent for Rp6000-8000 per day. Twenty-one speed mountain bikes (Rp8,000-10,000 per day), enabling you to tackle almost anything, are the latest rage.

Ask your *losmen* proprietor which rental places carry the newest bikes. Try getting the owner to deduct the costs of improving the bike. For example, instead of paying the full amount in cash, ask if you can buy a new padded seat (Rp10,000-15,000) to replace the old one and discount it from your rental fee.

Another approach, especially if you'll be here for several months, is to offer to purchase a new or new used bike and improve it if the bike shop will agree to buy it back when you leave for 20-25% less than what you initially paid. You can buy a used, sturdy English-made three-speed for around Rp200,000, spend another

Rp30,000-35,000 upgrading it, then when you leave a month later re-sell it to the same shop for perhaps Rp150,000. This works out to a very reasonable per day rental cost—and for a good, well-equipped bike!

Bicycle Check

Volcanoes offer unbelievably steep climbs and dizzying descents. Never go into the mountains without good brakes. Both front and rear brakes must be able to stop your bike alone while riding downhill in case one of the brakes fails. Brake shoes (karet rem, Rp500 a pair) should be symmetrically positioned and show plenty of rubber. The best test is whether or not either brake can stop your bike and hold it while you push forward with all your might.

Before renting or buying, turn the bicycle upside down and spin the wheels to see if the rims have any deep rust spots which could cause the wheel to buckle under stress. Observe the wheel as it passes by the brake shoe; if it wobbles noticeably, have it trued. Also, examine carefully for loose or broken spokes.

Don't rent or buy bikes with bald or soft tires (ban); the shop will promptly pump them up for you—but so will you every day after that. A bell (bel) and light (lampu) are essential. Spin the wheel with the generator (dinamo) engaged to make sure that the light works. A back reflector (stopan) is another important safety feature.

Lightly oil all moving parts before setting out each day, and check that all nuts and bearings are tight (seat, brake cables, hubs, etc.). Make sure that the gears change smoothly; there should be no grating sound from the gears and the chain while cycling. Handlebars should be one to two inches below the level of the saddle.

If your bicycle seat (sadal sepon) is uncomfortable, so will you be during your whole tour. Buy a new soft, padded seat or at least a tie-on foam seat cover (Rp10,000) at any good bike shop. Adjust the seat so you can straighten your legs and touch both your feet on the ground, with one or two inches of clearance between your crotch and the crossbar.

Repairs

Since bicycles are used so much in everyday life by the Balinese themselves, makeshift, bamboo-roofed, dirt-floored bicycle repair lean-tos are found in even the smallest villages or on the corner of a busy town street. Sometimes the tukang sepeda (bicycle repairman) will allow you to borrow tools to work on your own bike. Always offer a drink or cigarettes in return.

If the repairman is to do the work, labor charges are low. Fixing a flat tire, using only rubber from an old inner tube, a pot of glue, and an old hammer with which to bang on the patch, costs only Rp2000-3000 (Rp1000 in the country). Replacing the front and back brake shoes and adjusting the brakes will run Rp4000-5000.

Suggested Itineraries

In the south, from Kuta (if the tide is out) ride west along the hard-packed sand to Seseh, then cut inland through serene rice fields and villages before looping back to Kuta. From Nusa Dua ride up to the Bukit Peninsula along a beautiful country road to the sea temple of Uluwatu. Take almost any track off this road to reach high cliffs and panoramic views over the ocean, then climb down steep trails used by surfers and local fishermen to deserted beaches. Leave your bike in the back of a local warung for safekeeping.

From Sanur, battle the heavy traffic to Tohpati, then turn down one of the smaller roads to black-sand beaches and crashing surf. In the east, the wonderfully scenic ride from Amlapura to Rendang via Selat and Muncan is on a road with light traffic. From Ubud in south-central Bali, make the climb up to Gunung Batur. Get an early start, bring lots of water, have lunch at the top, then coast at speeds of up to 40 kph all the way back down. On the way, visit the wood-carving villages Pujung, Tagalalang, Jati, and Peliatan.

MOTORCYCLES

Motorcycles are widely available for rent at the beach resorts and inland tourist centers. They are the easiest to rent in Kuta, Legian, and Seminyak. Though motorbikes may appear to be the best transport, they often prove more trouble and expense than they're worth. Intrusiveness in quiet villages, pollution, and breakdowns all go against them.

You also have to worry about gasoline (Rp750 and up per liter), oil money, as well as parking

ing and clutch and gas tank under the seat; just insist upon one and one will show up sooner or later. There're even a few tanks around like the four-stroke 225cc Merzy model by Kawasaki, as well as popular Vespa motor scooters. The latest craze, obnoxious trail or dirt bikes, are able to command up to Rp150,000 per week in the mistaken belief that these machines are better able to handle Bali's backcountry roads.

The cost of hiring a motorcycle depends on your bargaining skills, which season it is, and how badly the owner wants money. The more powerful and newer the machine, the higher the rate; the longer the rental period, the lower the rate. The usual price for a 75cc, 100cc, or 125cc motorbike in the off-season is from Rp10,000 to Rp12,000 per day or Rp50,000 to Rp75,000 per week. Rental charges rise when the Europeans and Australians arrive in numbers in July-Aug. and Dec.-January. During this busy season, it climbs to Rp15,000 or even Rp18,000 per day or as much Rp100,000 per week, paid in advance. Many renters give one free day for each week you rent the bike. Gas is your expense.

In Kuta and Sanur you'll be approached by guys offering to rent their bikes. Restaurants, shops, and travel agencies in all the tourist enclaves will also advertise motorbikes for rent. Ask around. Start making inquiries with your homestay owner or hotel bartender, houseboy, or driver. (Three Brothers Inn in Legian is a good place to rent bikes.) If you rent direct from an owner, you won't have to pay a commission to a go-between or rental agent. Also consider renting from a motorbike repair shop. Their bikes may be in better condition than private rentals. They are also better able to keep up with the maintenance and can service their machines if anything goes wrong.

Be wary of being overcharged for a faulty bike. Anyone renting a motorcycle for a week or more should first test drive it for a day at the day rate, looking for any bugs that may appear. If anything is remiss, take it back to the owner and ask him to fix it before you clinch the deal for a longer period. Some of these flaws could be either very irritating, dangerous, or both. Check the lights, battery, oil, cables, clutch, turn signals, horn, and especially the tires. Pay extra for safety. Do everything you can to give yourself that added margin of safety. You'll need it.

fees (Rp100-200) at nearly every tourist site and even in front of popular restaurants and nightclubs. The law about wearing a helmet (usually a plastic bowl with a flimsy safety strap) seems almost forgotten, but the possibility of serious injury in an accident becomes much more serious without one.

Still, motorcycles provide one of the cheapest and most convenient ways to get around the island. Within 30 minutes, the machine can catapult you into the remote countryside where you are the only Westerner for kilometers around. You can travel all the way from Kuta to Singaraja in just one day on a motorcycle, though that's rushing it. You can stop anywhere at anytime.

The ideal season for motorcycling is the dry season (May-Sept.). If you already have an International Driver's License with a motorcycle endorsement, you're covered. If you don't, you'll need a special Balinese driver's license (see "Driving Practicalities," below). Before setting off, be sure to ask for the bike's registration papers (STNK) in case you get stopped randomly by the cops.

Average size engines are 100 and 110cc. You certainly don't need anything gnarlier because you can't open it up on these roads anyway. All the familiar Japanese brands are available, for the most part conventional one-stroke shift bikes. A bit more difficult to find but easier to drive are the fully automatic 70cc and 80cc models (Indonesians call them *bebek*) with automatic start-

MOTORCYCLE SAFETY

Driving a motorcycle on Bali is dangerous and requires lightning reflexes. Even experienced bikies get shattered nerves after just a week of riding on Bali, where trucks and huge tourist buses drive right down the center of the road, and chickens, ducks, pigs, pedestrians, children, and unexpected potholes are everywhere. You've also got unposted roadworks, slippery surfaces, lumbering oxcarts, dogs asleep in the road, suicidal drivers who ignore stop signs, great mounds of gravel dumped right in the middle of the road, cars traveling at night without headlights, and motorbikes carrying wobbling 10-meter-long bamboo poles! Everything you can do to increase your safety margin is to your advantage. Some basic safety rules:

- Wear a good helmet, long pants, shoes, shirt, goggles or glasses, and a windbreaker for the higher elevations because temperatures drop considerably. Helmets are required. Cheap, flimsy helmets usually come with the bike. If you're going to do a lot of riding, consider buying your own in Denpasar. A good one costs around Rp100,000 but you can sell it when you leave.

- Drive slowly and carefully on the narrow roads; this way you also see more. These roads are full of the unexpected where things happen very quickly. To be assured of safety, go only about 40-45 km per hour. The Balinese themselves drive on their roads extremely slowly. Slow down on curves.

- While on the open highway, make a lot of noise. Use your horn continuously when approaching animals or people on the road who may not see you coming. Better to be loud and obnoxious than to kill or be killed.

- Avoid riding at night when it gets pitch dark and is particularly hazardous. Bicycles seldom have rear-fender reflectors. Unless you have goggles or a face shield, for half an hour before and after sundown a dense cloud of insects batters you in the face. At nighttime bats even fly into your face!

Get into your motorcycle bubble and make the bubble very big. Lessen the likelihood of an accident by driving with your light on in the daytime to let everyone know you're coming. Remember to drive on the *left* side of the road and obey international traffic signs. Wear clothing and good shoes to protect your skin if you fall off and to keep you warm and dry if you're going over the central mountains. Don't forget sunblock. One of the biggest dangers to motorcyclists are Bali's black dogs wandering invisibly into the street at night and jamming up the machine's front wheel. (See the accompanying special topic "Motorbike Safety.")

Be aware of the White-Boy-on-a-Motorcycle phenomenon. It doesn't matter that you're doing everything the Balinese do—like driving pell-mell across a crowded intersection—the cop is likely to flag you over, confiscate your registration, and ask you to come to the police station the next morning to pick it up. This is just graft and prejudice. Just ignore the cop's gesture and keep going, or refuse to pay it without a hearing, or accept a reprimand with a Rp10,000 "fee."

BUSES, *BEMO,* AND ISUZUS

Cheapest public transport on Bali are full-size buses. These rare local beasts, such as the ones from Gilimanuk or Amlapura, can be excruciatingly slow (28 stops in one hour!) but excellent for drinking in and experiencing Balinese village life. Nowadays, the biggest buses on the island are used by tour operators and are always painted white. In 1994, 10 French tourists died and 17 required emergency evacuation from Bali when a bus rolled over and down a 200 meter slope at Kintamani.

However, and somewhat sadly, these big lumbering, crowded public buses are giving way everywhere to the blue Isuzu vans. Hundreds of Isuzus head to every district of the island from Denpasar's main terminals. They are more expensive, faster, and offer better views than regular *bemo umum* (public *bemo*) or smaller minibuses.

Multitudes of *bemo umum* run along the roadways of Bali at a steady rate and, when approaching the cities, in constant streams. Fares range from Rp500 to Rp5000. Both kinds of *bemo* leave when they're full. Frequency of service slows down in the afternoons. *Bemo* hold a sacred place in Balinese traffic because they can stop anywhere anytime without signaling, including at curves and intersections. Potholes here can also assume mindboggling proportions.

Every town and village on Bali has a *bemo* station, sometimes a 10 meter space under the only shady tree. Larger towns and cities have several *bemo* terminals serving destinations in different directions. To go from one end of Bali to another, it's often necessary to go through at least two of Denpasar's bus/*bemo* terminals. The most important terminal on the whole island for public transport to the main tourist points is Terminal Batubulan, 10 km northeast of Denpasar.

Bus/*Bemo* Stations

There are at least five main bus/*bemo* stations in Denpasar, with more opening up every year. Smaller minibuses (also called Colts) also leave from these stations. **Terminal Ubung** (on Jl. Cokroaminoto, the main road northwest of Denpasar) is for Isuzu and *bemo* to the west and north: Tabanan Rp1000, Mengwi Rp1000, Kediri Rp1000, Negara Rp2500, Tanah Lot Rp1500, Sangeh Rp1200, Gunung Batukau Rp1500, Gilimanuk Rp5000, and Singaraja Rp5000.

Terminal Kereneng (east of Denpasar off Jl. Hayam Wuruk) serves mainly as a central drop-off point between Denpasar's bus/*bemo* terminals. From here to Terminal Batubulan it costs Rp500. **Terminal Batubulan** (east of town just before the village of Batubulan on the road to Gianyar) is the hub for points east and north: Sanur Rp800, Mas Rp1000, Ubud Rp1500, Tampaksiring Rp1200, Gianyar Rp1500, Klungkung Rp1500, Candidasa Rp3000, Amlapura and Tirtagangga Rp3500, Padangbai (where ferries leave for Lombok) Rp3000, Amlapura Rp2000; also Bangli Rp1000, Ubud Rp2000, Bedugul Rp3000, Tampaksiring and Penelokan Rp3000, Kintamani and Singaraja Rp5000.

Isuzus from **Terminal Suci** (near the intersection of Jl. Hasanudin and Jl. Diponegoro) to Benoa cost Rp800 (be ready for traffic jams); intercity buses also leave from Suci. Buses from **Terminal Tegal** (southwest of Denpasar, near the intersection of Jl. Imam Bonjol and Gunung Wilis, on the road to Kuta) take you to points south like Kuta Rp900, Legian Rp1000, the airport and Tuban Rp1000, Nusa Dua Rp1000, and Terminal Kereneng Rp500. Finally, **Wan-**

gaya Bemo Station has blue minibuses to all northerly directions in Badung, including Carangsari, Peteng, and Sangeh.

Shuttle Buses

Shuttle services specifically organized to cater to tourists and travelers now operate to all the most popular tourist destinations on Bali. Along the main drags of tourist resorts you'll find signboards advertising rates, destinations, and departure times. The service is generally overpriced (i.e., Candidasa to Singaraja Rp8000, Singaraja to Ubud Rp7500, Kuta to Ubud via Sanur Rp8000, etc.) but undeniably convenient.

Shuttle buses are sometimes just as crowded as the public Isuzu buses. At other times there may be only one or two other passengers. They depart at regular intervals on a fixed schedule traveling a standard route; from Kuta to Ubud they run at least six times daily, to Bedugul and Lovina at least three times daily.

There are shuttles from Sanur to Nusa Lembongan Island for Rp17,500 (leaving 1030 and 1615), from Ubud to Nusa Lembongan for Rp22,500 (leaving 0700, 1000, 1600), and from Lovina to Nusa Lembongan for Rp35,000 (leaving 0700, 1300). There are even shuttles running from Kuta to Gili Trawangan on Lombok for around Rp25,000, which includes bus transfer to Padangbai (east Bali), ferry across the Lombok Strait, bus transfer on Lombok from Lembar to Bangsal and again ferry to Gili Trawangan. They also operate buses to Sumbawa farther east.

The most efficient, widely available transport service is **Perama.** Pick up one of their brochures which gives the addresses and phone numbers of their offices in Kuta (tel. 0361-287594), Ubud (tel. 0361-96316), Candidasa (tel. 0366-41114 or 41115), Lovina (tel. 0362-41161), Padangbai (tel. 0366-41419), Kintamani, Bedugul (tel. 0361-21191), and Lombok. They are on-time, fast, usually quite comfortable, radio-linked, and part of a vast and well-organized network. Their head office in Kuta is Jl. Legian 20 (tel. 0361-751551 or 751875, fax 751551). In Ubud, one of their agents is Rona's, Jl. Tebesaya 23 (tel. 0361-975120). Always try to book the day before. Show your old ticket or your member's card for a 10% discount.

Shuttle buses pick you up at your hotel, go direct to the hotel or destination of your choice, and make few stops in between. Sure, you can do it for a few dollars cheaper, but it will be much more complicated and time-consuming. If you want to go from Lovina to Ubud, for example, you'd have to take a *bemo* into Singaraja, from there an Isuzu to Denpasar, change to a *bemo* to Batubulan Terminal, then board another Isuzu to Ubud. It will take you five hours as opposed to two and a half hours on a shuttle. Public transport from Ubud to Denpasar is also complicated. First to Batubulan, then another *bemo* across town to Kereneng, then Tegal, then Kuta—in all four *bemo* and approximately two hours. The shuttle takes only one and a half hours and costs around Rp8000.

Another type of shuttle service operates from Bali's starred hotels to the nearest shopping center, town, or the airport. Seats must be reserved, both outbound and inbound, in order to make sure you have a seat. Convenient pickup spots, such as in front of The Bounty on Kuta Beach, are arranged. These courtesy shuttles leave as often as 12 times per day, sometimes from 0500 right up until 2000.

Bemo

Very convenient are *bemo,* small, Indonesian-made, canopied camper-like trucks designed to carry up to 12 people which sputter to every corner of the island as well as around the town centers. The game of chicken has reached state-of-the-art in Indonesia, so the *bemo* drivers drive like maniacs. There used to be even scarier, smaller, cheaper three-wheeled *bemo* called *bemo roda tiga,* but these have been put out of business.

Nowadays *bemo* can also mean any public vehicle smaller than a full-size bus which takes paying passengers. Even the long blue Isuzu vans, which can hold up to 20 people, are now loosely called *bemo.* One unique feature of the smaller variety is that they can stop on a dime to pick up and drop off passengers and goods at any point along the road.

Disadvantages of these four-wheeled vehicles are that they are invariably crowded, may pose security risks (see "Warning," below), have uncertain departure times, become scarce at around 1700 (depending on where you are), and usually stop running altogether shortly after sundown.

As evening approaches, you need to start thinking about getting back to where you came from or else you might get hung up and be forced to charter a *bemo* at an exorbitant cost. Always allow plenty of daylight for your return trip. For example, if you want to get back to Ubud, make sure you get the last Isuzu that leaves Amlapura at around 1600.

The public transportation system on Bali is now so extensive and efficient that you can go virtually anywhere worth going to by *bemo* on day trips from Denpasar, Ubud, or Singaraja. In the terminals, driver's assistants often usher you physically by the arm to the *bemo.* This they do to everyone—don't be offended.

Enter the vehicle from the side. Be prepared to step over sacks of rice, trussed chickens, and bundles of copra. The prime seat for sightseeing is beside the driver, where up to two passengers may sit. When someone vacates this shotgun seat, hop up front and grab it; the scenery is better and it's cooler than in the back.

Many *bemo* and Isuzus have internal buzzers which you use when you near your destination. Otherwise, tap lightly on the window or shout STOP! The drivers and assistants know where to let you off in order to make with your next *bemo* connection.

Destinations are usually posted on front or side signboards on the vehicle. There could be many different spellings for the same place. If the *bemo* is coming from the north or east, the sign will say Denpasar, but it will actually mean it is headed for Batubulan; most of them don't enter Denpasar proper.

If there's no direct service from one village to another, you may have to do it in stages. For example, if you want to go from Ubud to Gianyar, get to the Sakah intersection first (Rp500), then flag down another *bemo* the rest of the way (Rp1000), or just hitchhike whatever comes by. It's always cheaper to go direct to a destination than to do it in segments.

Chartering a *Bemo*

A whole *bemo* can be chartered between five or six people in the off-season for as little as Rp40,000-45,000 per day (from 0800 to sunset). In the tourist season, the same *bemo* might cost Rp50,000-65,000. But no need to pay for insurance or for a driver's license. You also get to use the driver and sometimes even an assistant, *free*. They know their way around, particularly if you need to do errands in the city. They can also be useful translating from Balinese into Indonesian, or for carrying things.

Smaller, older *bemo* are cheaper to hire than larger, newer ones. You can easily find *bemo* and minibuses for rent because touts and drivers are always asking if you want transport. Or you can simply go to a station and ask around. Try to deal directly with the drivers *(sopir)* and not an intermediary. Because there aren't as many idle *bemo* in the mornings, you can bargain for a less expensive rate in the afternoon when you are better able to play one *bemo* driver off against another. Make it clear who pays for gas; if you pay, then you should get a lower rate.

A small group may also hire a *bemo* for one-way trips direct to your destination. This saves hassles and actually costs less than if you were to hire a car, although the cost of a metered taxi could be quite competitive with a *bemo*. You can stop and shop, take photos, eat, take a walk—it's all included in the day price of the *bemo*.

How do you know what to pay for one-way trips? Since ordinary *bemo* carry an average of 12 people, simply multiply 12 by the normal single fare for the route to come up with a ballpark figure that initiates the bargaining. For example, since a *bemo* from just outside the airport to Kuta is normally Rp500 per passenger, Rp6000 is roughly what a group of 12 would pay. Any stops you make along the way—even for a mere two minutes to buy a Coke—are inevitably charged extra. The price you pay also depends on how far you want to go.

If you're concerned about getting back from an outing, consider asking the *bemo* to wait at your destination. You may have to pay for the petrol for the return trip anyways, and the waiting surcharge isn't that much. In some cases, if you don't arrange to have the *bemo* wait, you might have trouble finding another for the return trip, especially if it's late in the afternoon or if it's from a remote place.

Warning

On Bali, thefts on *bemo* do occur. Once confined to the Denpasar area, "robber *bemo*" occasionally cruise the roads looking for unwary travelers. Once onboard, several aggressive pickpockets crowd around to intimidate, distract, or confuse the traveler while compatriots rifle through his gear and pockets. They often use a painting or a parcel to hide their treachery. Be particularly on guard on the Denpasar-Ubud route. Bonafide *bemo* have yellow-black license plates instead of the black-white ones of private vehicles. Watch for this as it's a way to distinguish real *bemo* from private robber ones.

Public Transport
Costs and Overcharging

For public transport, a rough guide would be about Rp75-100 per kilometer. Within the city limits of Denpasar, Singaraja, Amlapura, and all other towns, *bemo* rides should cost no more than Rp500. From terminal to terminal, the fare is also Rp500—no matter what the city. *Bemo* prices for short distances in the country outside of Denpasar are always cheaper (for example, Rp300 compared to Rp500 for two to four km).

Operated by hundreds of independent contractors, you may also be overcharged in Denpasar and Kuta where the *bemo* drivers and their assistants are some of the most *kasar* on Bali and refuse to haggle (the fare from Denpasar to Kuta should be no more than Rp1000). They take full advantage of your ignorance, so you must constantly exercise your bargaining powers. Catch them at it, then have a laugh together over it.

If it turns ugly, then you have to take other measures. For example, a reader reported that a *bemo* driver tried to charge her Rp10,000 for a Rp900 ride. She warned him that she would report him to the special office which issues *bemo* licenses, and they were scared to death. If they try to overcharge you a preposterous amount, suggest that you go to the police station *(stasiun polisi)* to settle the matter.

The tourist office has a list or can make a list of *bemo* fares. After awhile you develop a sense of what you should pay, a feeling that a Rp500 *bemo* ride is really worth only Rp300. When you're traveling with a large backpack or bicycle on a *bemo* or minibus, you're expected to pay another full adult fare. This is only fair as your baggage does take up another place and they lose out on a fare.

Know what the correct price is on the public *bemo* by asking other passengers the standard fare *(harga biasa),* watch what other passengers are paying and then pay the same, or confirm the correct fare with your *losmen* owner or officials at bus/*bemo* terminals. Public transport costs are also posted on the bulletin boards of tourist information centers like the one near Ubud's main intersection.

If you pay too little, you'll be told in no uncertain terms. Sometimes the Balinese passengers are helpful regarding telling you the regular price; other times there are knowing smiles and a certain collusion with the *bemo* driver since everyone knows that tourists are rich and can afford to pay more.

Driver's assistants never seem to have the correct change. Always have the exact change ready because you don't want to show your money to pickpockets. Pay at the end of the journey. Don't get out of the *bemo* or cab without receiving your correct change first. Oh, and don't get *into* an empty *bemo* without making it clear that you don't want to charter!

On big religious holidays *bemo* drivers frequently raise the price. Also, there's often a day price and a night price; the night price is sometimes double the day price. Ordinarily it costs Rp500 between Kuta and Legian, but at night it could be as much as Rp1000. The later it is, the less bargaining power you have and the more expensive the fare will be.

VEHICLES FOR RENT

Hundreds of hotels, restaurants, travel agencies, and freelancers in all the tourist areas rent four-wheeled vehicles, priced according to the type, age, and condition of vehicle. There are basically two types of arrangements: hiring a car with a driver or driving the car yourself. In both kinds of rental, the price includes unlimited mileage and the cost of gas is your responsibility.

Drawbacks are the vehicle's environmental impact, the barrier that the vehicle places between you and the Balinese, that you may cut an outing short because you're paying as much as US$35 per day, your weakened bargaining position if you arrive at a hotel or a shop in a rented vehicle, parking difficulties, and the need to return the vehicle to the place you rented it from. You also may not take a rental car across to

Java unless you have prior written permission from the owner. You may, however, park your car in Gilimanuk and pay a guard Rp10,000 to keep his eye on it.

Be flexible. It may well be easier just to rent, especially for a short distance, one of the small, ubiquitous *bemo,* particularly if there are no other cars or taxis around. Most *bemo* drivers are quite willing to go anywhere on the island for the same amount they normally make hauling passengers.

Normally vehicles rent for Rp45,000-60,000 per day, but discounts are given for longer rentals. It's possible to rent a vehicle for a month for as low as Rp25,000 per day or Rp750,000 per month, and you may even be able to negotiate one for longer for even less. Another tack is to ask for one day's free rent for every week you rent or one week's free rent for every month your rent. You also have to pay for insurance (around Rp75,000 per month) which the owner of the vehicle can arrange (see below).

Suzuki Jimneys normally rent for Rp30,000-40,000 per day if you rent them for one to three days, cheaper if you rent for four to seven days, cheaper still for 15-30 days. These compact cars with low gear ratio, high wheel base, low gas mileage, and small size are very popular, though at times they can feel a bit cramped and vulnerable—a top heavy tin can with a souped up motorcycle engine. More expensive and safer are Kijangs (Rp60,000 and up per day) and Panthers (diesel, Rp70,000 and up per day). If you head off the beaten track up country roads, hire a Land Cruiser (Rp100,000 per day), most easily obtained through a travel agent.

New air-conditioned Suzuki four-wheel-drive jeeps can be had for Rp50,000-55,000 per day. If you want to cover long distances, a four-wheel drive vehicle or a gutsy Katana is the way to go. Japanese compacts like Mazda sedans go for Rp50,000-65,000 per day, depending on condition. A jeeplike, a/c Toyota Kijang, with enough room to hold five to six people plus luggage, costs at least Rp60,000 per day for one to three days, Rp57,000 for four to seven days, Rp55,000 for eight to 14 days, Rp52,000 for 15-30 days.

Families may consider renting a Mercedes Benz RV for about US$150 per day. This is a traveling, full a/c, deluxe, self-contained motor home equipped with a 220 volt generator, water tank, comfortable beds, bathroom, small washing machine, spin dryer, entertainment center, sink, bed linen, stove, oven, kitchen utensils, chemical toilet, hot water shower, microwave, toaster oven, refrigerator. Sleeps six adults. Comes with driver and guide who sleep outside for added security. You can take it out of Bali. Contact Nirwana Cottages in Candidasa (tel. 0361-36136, fax 35543).

Rental Agencies

There are at least 200 rental agencies on Bali. You'll see signs all over advertising cars for rent with rates posted. The Kuta/Legian/Tuban Beach area has the largest selection of rental places. It's cheaper to rent a car here than in Candidasa, Lovina, or Ubud. Shop or call around to get the best rate. Rent a car in the south for a good daily rate, then drive it all over the island. Also, if you're going to be on Bali for a time, hire a vehicle at a high rate for a day or two, then use it to find a vehicle for a lower rate.

The big guys, Hertz and Avis, are here but are so expensive they're not even worth considering. Instead, stick with locally based agencies. Your first choice should be **Bali Car Rental** (Jl. Bypass, P.O. Box 3382, Sanur, tel. 0361-288550 or 288359, fax 288778). Though your corner rental shop may rent self-drive Jimneys for Rp35,000 per day, Bali Car Rental rents them for Rp55,000 per day but offers a number of advantages. One is that the cars are delivered on request to your hotel, villa, or to the airport. Another is good insurance coverage. While most rental agencies carry insurance liability up to Rp1 million, this outfit insures up to Rp10 million, which covers not only what you do to other people but injuries you do to yourself. And they actually make good on the claims. The longer your rent, the deeper the discount they give: 15% for four to six days, 20% for seven to nine days, 22% for 10-13 days, 25% for 14-20 days, 27% for 21 days or more. The owner, Andre Reich, also rents Toyota Kijang for US$40 per day, Mitsubishi L300 Microbus for US$50, Toyota Crown for US$55, and Volvo 264 GL for US$65. The vehicles are not new but technically in good condition.

Andre Reich has been in the business for 24 years—the first to establish a rental agency on Bali. He also has offices in Yogya and Ujung Pandang, which means that you can rent a car in Bali and drive it to Yogya or Ujung Pandang and vice versa—the only car rental service that allows you to leave the island in your car. His office in Yogya is in front of Adisucipto Airport, P.O. Box 30 YKAP YOGYAKARTA, tel. (0274) 62548.

Another reliable agency on Bali is **Giri Putra Car Rental**, Jl. Raya Kuta 504, Kuta (tel. 0361-751349 or 753470), which has a wide range of a/c Suzuki jeeps and Toyota Kijang, plus such luxury cars as Mercedes Benz, Honda Accords, and BMWs. Some of Kuta and Legian's moneychangers have terrific deals too.

Driving Safely in Bali

Driving your rental car is the fastest and most convenient transport on Bali. This option also allows for the most freedom; you establish your own itinerary and decide how much time to spend at each site. Though obviously safer than motorcycles, cars must be driven with great caution. If you collide with a horse cart, with the help of the police you'll have to negotiate a settlement with the owner more or less on the spot. Because the traffic is fast, erratic, and left-hand drive, driving is hair-raising unless you come from a left-hand drive country already. Toot your horn constantly to warn people and other vehicles of your approach. It's better to be an asshole than to hit or be hit by someone.

An experienced driver for Rp15,000-20,000 per day extra might be the best investment you will ever make. He will know how better to handle the normally polite Balinese who seem to become possessed by demons with no regard for safety whenever they get behind the wheel. Add to this the lack of traffic discipline, indeterminable traffic rules, inadequate infrastructure, and atrocious traffic caused by the introduction of 15,000 new vehicles every month.

Before clinching a deal, always take it for a test drive before committing yourself. Make sure the vehicle's emergency brake operates properly, check kilometer distances when following directions, and make sure the odometer works. Check the oil right off as the vehicle is often given to you empty of oil. Also check tread on tires (Bali's roads can be rocky and potholed) and make sure the horn, wipers, and lights work. It's got a cassette player, but does it work? Ditto for the air conditioning. It's really scary not having seat belts; no rental vehicles come equipped with them even though you need them on Bali more than anywhere in the world.

If you're going to tackle Bali's mountains by car, do it in the daylight hours when it's safer and when you can enjoy the scenery more. Honk your horn before the dangerous turns to let other drivers know you're coming. As a rule, try to avoid driving at night because many bicycles, food carts, and horse-drawn conveyances don't have any lights front or rear to warn you of their approach, not to speak of big piles of sand in the middle of the road and trucks with high beams heading straight for you.

Hiring a Driver

Along with doing without all the headaches involved in driving your own vehicle, there are other distinct advantages to hiring a driver. Comparison shop to find a driver who can also serve as guide, i.e., provide some cultural/historic context to what you're viewing. A good driver will also know of all the secret shortcuts in the back alleys of Kuta and Legian.

In some cases, depending upon where you are or who you rent the vehicle from, it can cost just as much to hire a vehicle with driver as it costs to hire a vehicle without. This might be the case, for instance, in hiring a vehicle from your homestay owner who may have his eldest son do the driving just to keep you safe and protect his investment.

As a rule, however, count on it costing as much as Rp15,000-20,000 per day extra to have the services of a driver. For overnight tours, it will cost you another Rp20,000-40,000 because the custom is that you pay for the driver's meals and accommodations. Or give him this as part of his per diem and let him cover his expenses himself. Hotels often have quarters and special meals set aside for drivers.

One expense you won't have is the daily cost of insurance as this is usually assumed by the rental agency when they rent out a car with driver. In the very least, you'd be required to carry less insurance than if you drive it yourself. Another advantage is that a driver will be responsible if anything mechanical goes wrong or if there's a traffic violation or accident. Also a driver can guard your belongings inside the vehicle while you're not there. In the Kintamani area, the locals may even disconnect your fuel

pump in order to convince you that you need a mechanic.

A word of caution. A driver will probably get a commission for delivering you to a posh restaurant, gallery, or art shop. Don't give in to all his suggestions, especially commercial ones. He also may think you are not able to eat anywhere but in a fancy overlook restaurant where you may end up paying an enormous amount (Rp25,000 and up per person). Suggest instead that you eat lunch in a local *warung*.

DRIVING PRACTICALITIES

Driver's License

To drive a car on Bali a valid Indonesian Driver's License (SIM) or an International Driver's License (IDL), carried as a supplement to your national driver's license, is compulsory. You may get by with your national driver's license with your picture on it, but not always. Since you can't get an IDL on Bali, get one at your local automobile association (AAA in the U.S.A., US$8, valid for a year) before your trip.

If your IDL isn't stamped for motorcycle operation, then you'll need a Balinese Driver's License. Not only is it fairly expensive to get a license but it's also a hassle (takes a whole morning!). Technically, you have to be 21 to get a license for a car but only 17 to drive a motorcycle (though they don't enforce it). The license is not good anywhere else in Indonesia.

Your *losmen* owner or motorcycle owner can often take you through the assembly-line process of getting a license at the police station (Jl. Seruni, about a 15-minute walk from Kereneng, open Mon.-Sat. 0800-1200). Wear long pants and shoes. Applicants should also bring their passport, three passport photos, and their national driver's license.

The license costs Rp52,500. Answers to the written multiple-choice test are: BCCACACCC-CCCACBCABABAA. If you don't know an answer, you can always ask the attendant what the question means and she'll swiftly tell you the answer. You'll also take a driver's test (a figure-eight on a little kiddie circle, dodging tin cans), get fingerprinted, and pay Rp2500 for forms.

If you fail either test, you're allowed two more tries, and start paying all over again. On the

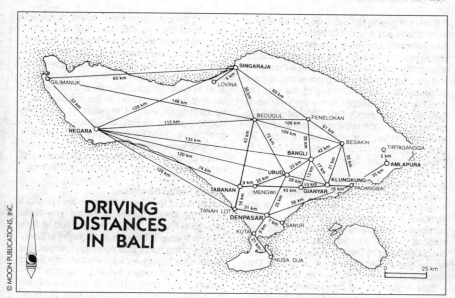

© MOON PUBLICATIONS, INC.

DRIVING DISTANCES IN BALI

books, the fine for driving a car lacking the required equipment or driving without a license is a hefty Rp250,000, and to enforce it there are occasional roadblocks put up by police looking for some additional income.

Traffic Regulations

On an island where red lights are for decorative purposes only and the rule of the jungle states that the biggest vehicles have the right of way, one way the police have of encouraging people to drive safely is by mounting grisly wrecks of cars high on pedestals along dangerous sections of Bali's highways. In a more orthodox attempt to cut down on road fatalities, Indonesia's Traffic Act was enacted in 1992. The result was that many motorists now actually apply for driver's licenses and papers to fully document their vehicle ownership.

Though these new traffic regulations have stimulated drivers to be more disciplined on the road, they have also prompted people to settle traffic violations with the police on the spot rather than in court. This practice of receiving *hadiah* (gifts) constitutes a normal portion of income for lower-rank policeman.

Naturally, foreigners who are stopped for violations are asked considerably higher *hadiah* than Indonesians. Thankfully, in the interest of promoting tourism, foreigners are rarely stopped. Since the system is intrinsically unfair, if you are waved to the side of the road, just pretend that you don't see the wave. If you are stopped, don't speak Indonesian, plead ignorance, and profess that you don't know what the police officer is talking about. If you can't get out of it, try paying just Rp10,000 (the minimum fine).

Insurance

The cost, whatever you end up paying per day, should include third party insurance and unlimited kilometers. Always ask that the per day vehicle rental rate includes insurance. Vehicular insurance costs anywhere from Rp10,000 to Rp17,000 per day extra, or about Rp80,000 per week. Most car rental companies carry coverage of one million rupiah with Rp100,000 deductible. Insurance covers damage, theft, and third-party liability, which will guarantee that the family of anyone you kill will get around US$700.

Agents won't necessarily tell you about or voluntarily include insurance—you have to request it. If you are paying Rp25,000-35,000 for a Suzuki, chances are it is not covered. If you don't take insurance, the rental agency may have you you sign a waiver indemnifying them of any responsibility in an accident involving a third party.

If you hire a vehicle with a driver, insurance is automatically included in the rental fee. This could work out cheaper in the long run as insurance can cost up to Rp17,000 per day. Motorcycle insurance is priced according to engine size and length of rental time, i.e., Rp14,000 for a 110-125cc for one week; Rp17,500 for 135-225cc for one week.

Gasoline and Air

Called benzine or premium in Indonesian, petrol in Australia. Government-run Pertamina stations are found on all the main roads and intersections of the island. In the south, the main stations are just outside of Kuta, on the road out of Denpasar at Tohpati, at Tanjung Bungkak on the Sanur-Denpasar road, at Suci in Denpasar, and at Ubung on the road to Tabanan.

Gas at stations will cost around Rp750 per liter; air in your tires around Rp500 (sometimes using a bicycle pump). Some stations, for example at Tanjung Bungkak and Kuta, have Super 98 (high octane) gas. Always check gas prices at the pump because you could get ripped off for Rp10,000 or more. The attendants sometimes charge you for gas you never receive.

Roadside fuel vendors are also found all over rural Bali. Recognizable by the signs Solar (diesel) and Premium (gas), these mom-and-pop kiosks sell fuel out of 44-gallon drums for as low as Rp600 per liter. They fill your tank using a plastic pitcher and funnel. Rumor has it that they water down the gas, which causes your engine to sputter. Keep your gas tank full; sometimes, particularly at night, petrol supplies become scarce and/or high priced.

Repairs

Roadside repair shops (bengkel), found in virtually every village, consist of a tarpolin-covered patch of oil-soaked dirt beneath a plastic tarp. Your squatting teenage mechanic, equipped with no more than an old hammer, screwdriver, pliers, and wrench, is able to disassemble an entire engine in the blink of an eye, leaving parts scattered everywhere. After soaking the nuts, bolts, and screws in gasoline (siphoned from your tank), he is able to put everything back in place in a matter of minutes.

Prices are very reasonable. Complete motorcycle or car tuneups and engine adjustments run around Rp10,000-15,000 (less in the countryside). For a motorcycle, a flat tire at a tire-patching shop (pres ban dalem) in the country costs Rp3500 to fix, but in Denpasar it's more like Rp5000. In Kuta it's Rp7500. One type of car repair place is called Bengkel Ketok Magic in which the mechanic/magician takes your vehicle behind a tall gate, performs some rituals, and lo and behold drives your vehicle out as good as new!

Roads Not to Be Missed

Get ahold of the Nelles Bali map and pick out one of the island's hundreds of small back roads and go exploring. You'd be surprised at how many are paved. These lead through traditional villages going about their everyday routines and rituals. One beautiful road is from Ubud's Bemo Corner to Tegalalangan, looping around to Tampaksiring, then coming back via Petulu. It's worth the airfare to Bali just to see this road, but hurry as some of the tour buses are doing it now. Another scenic country road is from Luwus to Petang/Sangeh. Feels like a million miles away from Kuta. On the way, visit the traditional market at Abiansemal just before Sangeh.

The highest road on Bali is the road to the north coast through Kintamani which at one point is 1,646 meters above sea level. But if heading for the north coast, the road through Bedugul is faster, in better condition, and more scenic than the one through Kintamani. Another approach to the north coast is the stunning, little-known road from Antosari (about 42 km west of Tabanan) north to Pupuan. From Pupuan, the road twists down to Seririt on the north coast. This route passes perhaps the most spectacular rice field landscapes on the island, right through aromatic vanilla, clove, and coffee plantations.

TAXIS

Hotel Taxis

There are several kinds of taxis. First there are sedans and vans without meters (private cars) that serve hotels. Usually parked in a line or in a parking lot outside the hotel, the concierge or the taxi desk calls them when needed. These are the most expensive: from a Nusa Dua hotel like the Putri Bali to Kuta, this type of taxi charges Rp25,000 for up to five people. They can command so much because they have you captive. By contrast, on the return trip from Kuta to Nusa Dua, it will cost as little as Rp6000 in a metered taxi.

But if you want to go someplace cheap or fast, just walk outside the hotel gate to the nearest big street or intersection. There you can assume that virtually any car, truck, motorbike, or van that passes you is a taxi. Employees driving company vehicles on their way to and from hotels and other businesses will pick up tourists as a way to make a couple of thousand extra rupiah to supplement their meager wages.

Airport Taxis
Cousins to hotel taxis are the taxis which await arrivals at the airport. You must first buy a ticket from the taxi counter, then you're assigned a taxi. The rates are all expensive and fixed: Kuta Rp8000, Legian Rp11,500, Denpasar Rp15,000, Sanur Rp17,000, Nusa Dua Rp17,500, Ubud Rp47,500.

Save money by walking 150 meters out of the domestic airport building to the intersection just outside the airport gate. Here you can catch cheaper public *bemo* into Kuta for only Rp500 (plus Rp500 for a big suitcase or rucksack); they run until around 2000. Use the baggage cart right to the edge of the walkway, then just leave it and carry your gear the rest of the way to the intersection.

Yellow taxis aren't allowed to pick up passengers inside the airport, but you can catch them on their way out (after dropping off their fare) if you wait outside the gate. Here a group of four can hire a taxi all the way to Ubud for as little as Rp28,000, which is less than the official fare and is the same as the minibus shuttle (Rp8000 each).

Taksi Kuning
The best deals, however, are metered radio taxis which cruise the roads all over southern Bali. There are now 300 *taksi kunung* concentrated in southern Bali, although they can travel outside of southern Bali. The most popular outfit is **Praja Taxi** (Jl. Bypass Ngurah Rai, Blan-

jong, Sanur, tel. 0361-289090 or 289191) or **Praja Bali Taxi,** (Jl. Bypass Nusa Dua 4, tel. 0361-701621). Their Japanese cars are blue and yellow with a taxi sign on the roof. Just wait a couple of minutes and one will come by. Lines of them also wait at certain places outside the big tourist hotels of Kuta, Nusa Dua, and Sanur.

These *taksi kuning* (yellow taxis) are very reasonably priced. Minimum fare at flagfall is Rp900; most trips within Kuta/Legian are around Rp2000-4000. The fare from Kuta to Sanur is Rp5000-6000. From the Puri Ratih Hotel or the Bali Intan in Seminyak, the fare is only Rp6000 into Denpasar. An unmetered taxi driver will charge you at least Rp10,000 for this same trip. If you want to tip your driver for extra service or friendliness, give them only Rp500 per Rp2000 fare and they'll be very happy.

The best thing about *taksi kuning* is that you don't have to hassle with the pushy, rude, and aggressive drivers of the cars and vans which line the main streets of the tourist centers. *Taksi kuning* are quite comfortable for up to three adults. Most of the drivers are friendly but usually speak little English. If you can speak Indonesian or if they can speak English, the drivers can be a rich source of local information and tips.

The drivers will almost always ask for the higher, unmetered fixed fare first, but always ask him to switch on his meter. When they say "it's up to you" it means that it could be really expensive and sometimes it could even get nasty. Also don't let them charge you the "air conditioning rate." There is only one, metered rate. When it's raining, and between 1900 and 2100 in the evening, taxis are very busy and you may have to wait awhile. After midnight you usually have to agree to a fixed fare in order to find a taxi willing to take you.

Taxis are very useful for short distances, say between Legian and the airport (around Rp5000), but even for long-distance travel around Bali *taksi kuning* are worth serious consideration. Let's say that you go from Kuta via Sanur, let the car wait in Sanur an hour or two, then drive to your destination in Ubud. If you use it for six hours altogether, the fare should be about Rp8000-10,000 per hour by the meter. This is a vast improvement over *bemo*. These street robbers normally charge at least double the price of the metered taxis and have been known to ask for five or eight times the appropriate fare.

Yellow taxis should be patronized to keep rapacious private taxis from proliferating. They are so cheap in fact that jealous unauthorized, unofficial taxis beat the hoods of their cars and sometimes even hit the drivers when they try to pick up fares along Jl. Legian and at Bemo Corner in central Kuta. Moreover, taxis often don't dare to wait for fares in front of the Double Six and Gado-Gado nightclubs because they are chased away by *bemo* drivers who demand two or three times more for their service than a taxi would charge.

BOATS AND FERRIES

Bali has five harbors. Once the hub of Dutch shipping companies, the northern port of **Buleleng** along the waterfront in Singaraja is the oldest. Now this old, crumbling, picturesque port is no longer used by big ships because of its exposure to tropical storms. To the west, the newer port of **Celukanbawang** offers more protection and is Bali's principal port, but its new jetty, port buildings, and sailors' canteen seem nearly deserted. Check here for Bugis schooners heading for Sulawesi or East Kalimantan.

The port of **Benoa,** across the bay off the end of the airport runway, is a small boat harbor where foreign yachts moor. Take a canoe out and ask around for a ride or if they need another crew member. The government-owned Pelni ships *Kambua, Kerinci,* and *Umsini,* which visit Bali on their various circuits, call at this port. The Pelni office is in Benoa, tel. (0361) 228962.

Padangbai, on the east coast, handles marine traffic between Bali and the eastern islands.

This small village, with its cheap accommodations and charming restaurants, is a pleasant place to stay a few days. From the port, board a ferry for Lembar on the neighboring island of Lombok to the east. Padangbai is also where cruise ships drop anchor when they call.

Finally, on the island's westernmost point is the port of **Gilimanuk** which receives vehicles, passengers, and cargo on ferries from Ketapang, East Java. See the Buleleng chapter for schedules and fares. If you take the last ferry across from Java, you arrive in Bali at first light to see the whole island come to life: mists lifting over tiered pagodas, ducks off to the fields under flags of herders, women yawning in doorways, pots boiling on early morning fires, lines of shadowy people going off to market.

Jukung

This sailfish-shaped craft may be hired to take passengers to offshore reefs to surf or snorkel, to take people from one of Bali's offshore islands to another offshore island or to islands like Serangan, a short way from Desa Suwungan off Jl. Bypass. Swift and graceful, they are used primarily by the Balinese for fishing.

These Balinese *prahu* are about five meters in length and one-half meter wide and can hold two to three passengers (takes two people to handle one). There are two models, the *penunggalan* and the *pemelasan,* both of which are propelled by paddle or sail. Larger models, called *gede* or *mesin,* utilize outboard motors.

Small and narrow enough to be hauled up on the beach, *jukung* are equipped with a single outrigger for stabilization. The bow is in the shape of the mythological *gajamina* (elephantfish) with a long double trunk and big bloodshot eyes that supposedly see in the night.

The traditionally designed, narrow, single- or double-outrigger jukung *comes in three sizes. Up to five meters long and only one meter wide, the plank-built* jukung *is light enough to be hauled up on the beach. The outriggers, necessary for stability, are made of bamboo; when not in use they are removed from their supports and stored in the shade. The smallest size native* jukung, *called a* penunggalan, *is propelled by paddle and can accommodate only one person. Tourists usually rent the* pemelasan, *which accommodates two people; these are usually propelled by single-masted, colorful "Bir Bintang" sails. Motorized* jukung mesin *(motorized outrigger) are also available for rent.*

BOB RACE

TOURS

You'll save money, your experience will be less structured, and your mobility increased if you take on the island independently. An organized tour, however, enables you to quickly see what Bali has to offer. Then you may decide to go back and experience in depth what you enjoyed most. In nearly every case, it's possible to do some independent touring before and after your tour.

Contact the Indonesian embassy or consulate in your home country for tour companies specializing in Bali. In Indonesia, any of the regional tourist offices can help you select the right tour company (see "Information and Services," later in this chapter).

There's a wide range of guided tour activities to choose from: volcano-climbing, bicycling, skin diving, snorkeling, sunbathing, hiking, shopping, attending festivals, visiting temples, exploring the island's archaeological remains, or systematically visiting Bali's arts and crafts centers. On cultural tours, if silverware, woodcarving, and souvenir shops aren't your interest, don't let the guide stop in too many. These stops serve only to fatten the pockets of the guides and drivers.

Tour agencies lining the streets and lanes of Kuta, Legian, Candidasa, Ubud, and Lovina offer fixed-departure tours for a set price, usually for six to 12 people. The Denpasar and each regency government tourist office, as well as the tour desks at larger hotels, are always ready to advise you about specialized tours.

The success of a tour depends largely on the experience and knowledge of the guide leading it. Tours are conducted by English-speaking guides unless tour participants request guides speaking other foreign languages (French, German, Japanese, Chinese). Tours often start from the agency's head office, though many also pick up participants at their hotels, homestays, or in front of well-known landmarks.

The price depends primarily on the type of transport used, the number of people in your group, and the length of your tour. Most only run if there are at least four people, so if one operator can't run the tour you want when you want it, just check out the next place. Most take in sights along the way and the tour lasts all day. Tour participants may alter/modify the tour by pitching in and paying extra. For example, from Penelokan down to the crater floor costs an extra Rp5000 per person on the Kintamani Volcano Tour.

TOUR GUIDES

Independent Tour Guides

There are two kinds of guides. Freelance, unofficial guides or touts, pushing tourist-oriented businesses and hanging around Bali's airport, the bus/*bemo* stations, and ferry terminals. Though they can be quite forward and persistent at times, you don't necessarily have to be paranoid about these men or boys who volunteer their services. They could actually save you a lot of trouble, footwork, and even money if you learn how to work with them and if you are able to sense the good ones from the bad.

Be open. Guides could lead you to a new accommodation that's really eager to please, may offer discounts to a hotel that wants to attract new clientele, or could help you get transport or performance tickets. Their fee, tacked to the base price—if not ridiculously high—might be worth it.

The same thing goes for self-appointed, multilingual guides who attach themselves to you at the base of volcanoes and at entrances to temples and museums. These contacts could lead to fresh insights and even exciting experiences. Local guides are a part of the color of a new place. These characters seem to have friends everywhere, might work for a tour company on the side, and have an uncle who will sell you *wayang* puppets for a special price.

Then there are the officially sanctioned guides who supposedly have been professionally trained. These 300 "registered" guides, belonging to the Bali Guide Association, speak either English, Japanese, German, French, or Mandarin in addition to Indonesian and their own regional tongue. Their services cost more than volunteer guides. You'll meet one of these certified guides if you join a local tour. The most talented know the best stopovers for snacks or modern amenities, can take you to places seldom visited, explain landmarks, put you in touch with the local people.

But the government regulation as to who can qualify as a registered guide is highly restrictive. Only people with money can afford to register, and thus they jack up the prices to cover their official fees. Moreover, not all these registered guides get high marks. Some demand fees from art shops and restaurants for delivering tourists; others pocket expenses that were promised as part of your tour price.

Sometimes it's better to employ a nonprofessional, family-style guide, particularly if you're coming for only 10 days or so, don't want to be in a group tour cocoon, and would like to expedite matters so as not to have to find out everything on your own without getting ripped off. The price freelancers charge often winds up being cheaper than most tour agencies. A good place to start inquiring about a personalized guide is with your homestay or hotel owner.

One of Bali's best known guides is also one of its best dancers. Cokorda Istri Ratih Iryani (Jl. Nangka 93, Denpasar, tel. 0361-91245) exemplifies a grassroots guide service. After getting input from you, she'll give you an overview of what you might like to do and how you might like to go about doing it. She'll tell you which performances to avoid and which to see; she'll arrange for a car and, if necessary, a driver who speaks Japanese. Ratih can get you discounts at hotels, arrange overnight trips, introduce you to highly regarded dancers, healers, and sculptors.

Local Tour Operators

There are pages of travel/tour operators listed in the most current Bali phone book under Travel Bureaus. The most ubiquitous agency—the traveler's agency—is **Perama Tourist Service,** Jl. Legian Kuta (tel. 0361-751551, 751875, or 751170, fax 751170) with offices in Ubud, Candidasa, Padangbai, Lovina, Kintamani, Bedugul, and Sanur. Get ahold of their latest brochure listing all their addresses and phone numbers. Perama now have large, new coaches heading for all parts of Bali. In Ubud, pick-up is at major hotels and locations, especially along Monkey Forest Road. Perama also offers land-sea adventures and cultural tours to Lombok and beyond using modified Bugis *pinisi* schooners.

Established in 1988 by an experienced Balinese group, **Nagasari Tours and Travel** (102 Jl. Danau Tamblingan, Sanur, Bali 80227, tel. 0361-288096, fax 289285, e-mail nagasari@dps. mega.net.id) provides services, in Bali and throughout Indonesia, ranging from economy itineraries to deluxe packages, but always with the same emphasis on originality and efficiency. For special-interest groups of for individual travelers,

Nagasari can arrange for natural history, cultural, spiritual, or just plain relaxing vacations. Rates are competitive and service is excellent.

Established in 1984, experienced and professional **Nusa Dua Bali Tours and Travel,** Jl. Bypass, 300 B, Box 3419, Denpasar 80034, tel. (0361) 51-223, fax 52-779, organizes both packaged programs and first-class tours. The company features competitive rates, excellent service, and a consistently high standard of accommodations and guides. Nusa Dua has cut its teeth in the business by catering to demanding and discriminating European clients.

Natrabu has more than 34 years of experience in leading tours. Its U.S. headquarters can be reached at (800) 628-7228 (U.S. and Canada), fax (415) 362-0531. Award-winning **Vayatours Inc.,** tel. (800) 999-8292 (U.S. and Canada), fax (213) 487-0838, one of Indonesia's largest tour companies, staffs a sales office in North America at 6420 Wilshire Blvd., Suite 420, Los Angeles, CA 90048, tel. (213) 655-3851.

A reliable operator is **PT Bali Avia Ltd.,** P.O. Box 1094, Ngurah Rai Airport, Tuban 80361 (tel. 0361-751257, 755840, or 752282, fax 752282 or 75333. They offer the "Sasak Traditional Tour," which takes in the sights and culture of the Sasaks of Lombok, as well as tours to Borobudur, Yogya, Torajaland, and Mt. Bromo in East Java.

Tunas Indonesia Tours & Travel, Jl. D. Tamblingan 107, Sanur (tel. 0361-288450 or 288581) and in the Hotel Bali Beach in Sanur (tel. 0361-288056), specialize in wildlife and adventure tours to Komodo, Baluran (East Java), Kalimantan. They also do daily air-conditioned coach tours of Bali.

Grand Komodo, Jl. Bypass, Sanur, Bali (tel. 0361-287166, fax 287165), sells three and four-day packages to Sumbawa and Komodo with scheduled departures. Also ask them about other adventure packages to Irian Jaya (Baliem Valley), Flores (Gunung Kelimutu), and Lombok (climbing Gunung Rinjani). Tours start at about US$275, including accommodations with all meals, transfers, and English-speaking guide. Price doesn't include airfare and laundry.

Other reputable, locally based companies: **PT Motive Bali Tours & Travel,** Jl. Bypass 21, Sanur (tel. 0361-289018 or 286248, fax 289018); **PT Gloria Bali Jaya Tours,** Jl. Raya Krobokan (tel. 0361-730272 or 730273, fax 730273); **Nagasari Tours & Travel,** Jl. D. Tamblingan 102, Sanur (tel. 0361-288096, fax 289285); **Media Tour,** Jl. Kartika, P.O. Box 1008, Tuban (tel. 0361-753556, fax 753555). Catering to demanding Europeans, the most efficient Bali-based operator I ever worked with is **PT Nusa Dua Bali Tours & Travel,** Jl. Bypass 300 B, P.O. Box 419, Denpasar 80001, tel. (0361) 751223, fax 752779.

Elderhostel Indonesia is an organization serving the travel needs of mature adults. It leads various three-week study tours in Java, Bali, and Sulawesi. The emphasis varies depending on the location, but academics are always stressed. Contact address in Bali is Agung Dewaputra, Elderhostel Indonesia, Puri Kapal, Peliatan, Ubud (tel. 0361-975180, fax 975162).

Another educational outing is the "Bali Archaeological Tour" offered by **Santa Bali Tours & Travel,** Grand Bali Beach Hotel, Sanur (tel. 0361-287628 or 288057, fax 236508), which takes in sites including Pura Durga Kutri, the Royal Temple of Bedulu Kingdom, Gunung Kawi, and Pejeng, which departs at 0830 and returns at 1630, for US$37.50 (lunch included).

The art lover, dancer, and spirit quester should get in touch with **Bali Living Arts,** 8600 East Alameda No. 17106, Denver, CO 80231, which caters to such specialized clientele that the result is a smaller, more focused, and more spontaneous group experience. You get 18 days of yoga on secluded atoll beaches, study of Balinese culture and language, participation in a full moon ceremony, an inner-island cruise, snorkeling, hiking, relaxation. Trip leader is Marya Mann, gypsy yogini, Ph.D. artist, dreamweaver, and world dancer. Call (303) 355-3278 or (800) 641-Bali, or fax (303) 757-8287.

Overseas-Based Tour Operators

The Big Three Indonesian companies represented in North America are: **PT Garuda Orient Holidays** (tel. 800-665-2254 in the U.S. and Canada, fax 604-736-7154), the tour arm of the Indonesian national carrier Garuda Indonesian Airlines; **Natrabu** (tel. 800-628-7228 in the U.S. and Canada, fax 415-362-0531), an Indonesian travel agency with more than 33 years experience; and **Vayatour** (tel. 800-999-8292 in the U.S. and Canada, fax 213-487-0838), one of

Indonesia's largest tour companies. All sell tour and accommodation packages on Bali. Call the Indonesian Tourist Promotion Office (tel. 213-387-2078, fax 380-4876) in Los Angeles for a complete list.

Since they believe that Bali is too commercialized, **Danu Enterprises** is taking their clients to more and more out of the way places. The founders, American Judy Slattum and Balinese I Made Surya, have conducted high quality, personalized tours since 1980. The instructor of their Yoga tour to Bali, Ann Barros, teaches the *Iyengar* tradition. Their new "Healing Arts" tour to Bali has been especially popular, and their "Discover the Back Roads" of Bali is designed for trekkers and water-sport enthusiasts. This trip includes in-depth seminars in Balinese history, language, culture, and religion with Made, the founder of Bali's mountain climbing club. The price US$2850 includes the 14-day tour, roundtrip air on Singapore Airlines, two meals a day, accommodations in small, locally owned bungalows, and five days in Bali's only Hindu ashram. For more details, contact Danu at P.O. Box 156, Capitola, CA 95010 or call/fax (408) 476-0543. A first-class outfit. Their office in Bali is at Jl. Kepundung, Gang XII No. 1, Denpasar 80231.

Backroads (1516 5th St., Suite PR, Berkeley, CA 94710-1740, tel. 800-462-2848 in the U.S. or 510-527-1555) sells a nine-day walking vacation that takes in Lake Bratan, the lower flanks of Gunung Agung, a rafting expedition on the Ayung River, performances, open-air markets, local arts and craft shops, swimming, snorkeling, scuba diving, first-class meals and accommodations, and the services of highly trained professional guides. Backroads also offers cyclists two to 17 day excursions with daily mileage options, maps, catered meals, directions, and van support (see "Bicycling," under "Getting Around").

Naropa Institute (2130 Arapahoe Ave., Boulder, CO 80302, tel. 303-444-0202), America's only Buddhist university, sponsors a Study Abroad program in Bali which runs from mid-January to mid-March, combining classes in meditation, Balinese *gamelan* and the Indonesian language, discussion groups on Bali's arts and culture, field trips, attendance at performances and ceremonies, and independent research projects. A 50-minute video on the US$3800 program is available.

Passport to Indonesia Inc., 2731 Tucker Lane, Los Alamitos, CA 90720, tel. (800) 303-9646, offers personalized tours for independent travelers as well as walking and cultural tours of Bali. **Archaeological Tours,** 271 Madison Ave., Ste. 904, New York, NY 10016, tel. (212) 986-3054, specializes in high-end cultural and educational tours.

In Britain, **Bales,** Bales House, Junction Rd., Dorking, Surrey RH4 3HB, tel. 01306-885991, sells tours to Bali from around £1000. Also check out **Earthwatch Europe,** Belsyre Ct., 57 Woodstock Rd., Oxford OX2 6Hu, tel. 01865-311600, which hosts ethnological tours of south-central Bali. **Hayes & Jarvis,** Hayes House, 152 King St., London W6 OQU, tel. 0181-746-5050, gives holiday tours to Bali. **Thomas Cook Holidays,** P.O. Box 36, Thorpe Wood, Peterborough PE3 6SB, tel. 01733-332255, offers hotel-based holiday tours to south Bali and the Ubud area.

Warning

Most operators are reliable, but watch the budget-priced, fly-by-night outfits. They will tell you anything: that you'll get all your cold drinks free, that all entrance fees are included, and even promise you lunch—but then you'll end up paying for everything! Exploiting your ignorance of the island's upcountry attractions, drivers or guides may try to pocket all these expenses and not report it to their superiors. For example, your tour leader might not offer to take you inside Klungkung's Kerta Gosa, telling you that the beautiful detailed paintings can be appreciated from the outside. Not so.

These outfits could also keep you waiting until about 1500 or 1430 before they take time to stop for lunch; then they'll take you into a tourist restaurant where you have to pay Rp7500 for a simple *nasi goreng.* Just tell them that you want to go out to a *warung* instead, and take all your friends with you! Don't forget that you are the clients; they should respond to what you want from your tour. You can bargain with the guide and driver to modify the tour, pay extra (which they can pocket) to take you way out of the way. Be creative.

SAMPLE LOCAL TOURS

Full-day excursions (seven to 10 hours) range from Rp25,000 to Rp55,000. The most expensive are offered by international starred hotel establishments which charge up to Rp200,000 per day, with prices always in U.S. dollars. Stick to tours recommended by your friends and people you trust.

Look for the unusual. Trips to the south emphasize the shoreline and beachlife, trips to the center the historic classical monuments, trips to the north vault the volcanic mountain range to the coast of north Bali, and trips to the east and west tend to cover the more isolated parts of the island. Often a *kris*, fire, or tourist trance dance in Batubulan or Bona is thrown in, and the bus could stop at one too many temples on the way—unless you request otherwise. You can get templed-out real fast after your third or so temple, no matter how unique or beautiful it is.

Here are some samples of typical day tours that can easily be arranged by most hotels and travel agents. The Volcano Tour, in one form or the other, passes through Batubulan, Celuk, Batuan, Mas, Ubud, Bedulu, Tampaksiring, and Penelokan to Kintamani. For those who are staying for just a short while, this one is a good introduction to the natural beauty of the island, and you'll be exposed to a wide range of arts and crafts. One-day tours out of Ubud, for example, run Rp15,000-25,000 per person.

The Besakih Tour passes through Batubulan and Celuk, then usually continues east to Klungkung. From here the tour heads north through Bukit Jambul to Besakih. The Tanah Lot Tour follows the main road to the northwest from Denpasar, then branches off at Kediri through the rural countryside to reach the coast opposite the small islet on which the temple of Tanah Lot is situated. The Bedugul Tour heads northwest from Denpasar to the regional capital of Tabanan, then passes through rising rice country to the lakeside resort of Bedugul. The City Tour takes in the Art Centre, The Bali Museum, and Denpasar market.

Also offered are two-night, three-day budget group tours in the Rp250,000 range. The first day you visit Celuk, Mas, Ubud, Bedulu, Klungkung, Kusamba, Tenganan, Bukit Jam-bul, Besakih, Bangli, Penelokan. The second day Kintamani, Penulisan, Kumbutambahan, Air Sanih, Singaraja, Lovina Beach. The third day Gitgit, Bedugal, Mengwi, Tanah Lot, Sangeh, then return to your hotel. Book three days in advance. Donations and accommodations not included in the price. A group can easily design other tours to anyplace in Bali.

BALI BY AIR

Something different and extravagant, this tour offers stunning views over rice fields, rivers, seaweed farms, coastline, jungle, and volcanoes poking through halos of white clouds. **Bali Avia** uses a new Bell 206B Jet Ranger helicopter to take two to four passengers on an aerial tour of Ubud, Bangli, Gunung Agung, Bali's eastern coast, Lake Bratan, Bedugul, Tanah Lot, Kuta, Besakih Temple, and Gunung Batur. Departures are from the helipad of Hotel Bali Beach at 0930 and 1030 daily (minimum two passengers). Cost is US$174 or US$375 for a half-hour flight. Call Bali Avia (tel. 0361-751257 or 752282) or Motive Bali (tel. 0361-89435, fax 89435). Other helicoptors used are Bell 412, Bell 212, BO 105, Piper Navajo, and Skyvans. Great photo ops. Free pick up and drop off.

Wakalouka Land Cruises, Jl. Imam Bonjol 335 X (tel. 0361-227085 or 227067, fax 227067 or 426972), offers an unusual "Journey to the Secret Soul of Bali" which takes participants by Land Rover through grassy tracks and terraced rice fields to see a traditional *gubuk* farmhouse made of mud bricks, learn about fragrant spices, visit a mineral hot springs and an ancient quarry, and relax with a delicious lunch at the Wakalouka Rainforest Camp deep in a forest of giant bamboos. You are picked up at 0800 by Land Rover and returned to your hotel in an a/c minibus at around 1600. The price of US$83 includes all transfers, lunch, soft drinks, wine, and beer.

BALI BY SEA

Cruises
The trouble with cruises is that passengers are able to stop for only three or four hours at some ports. The luxury and service, however, are un-

deniable. **Swan Hellenic,** 77 New Oxford St., London WC1A 1PP, tel. 0171-800-2300, organizes upmarket cruises to Bali. **Orient Lines** 38 Park St., London W1Y 3PF, tel. 0171-409-2500, calls at eastern Bali's port of Padangbai.

Royal Cruise Line offers the "Golden Odyssey," departing Bangkok for Semarang, Yogyakarta, and Bali on its way to Hong Kong. **Pearl Cruises** offers "Bangkok, Bali and Beyond," with an itinerary including Jakarta, Semarang, and Bali. **Royal Viking** offers the "Jewels of the Orient" cruise aboard the *Royal Viking Star,* which departs Singapore and Bangkok for Bali. The *Sea Goddess* also calls on several Indonesian ports.

After the style of the defunct Lindblad Explorer, **P & O**'s four luxury catamaran ships ply regularly between Lombok, Komodo, Sumba, and Flores. Their four-star *Bali Sea Dancer* boasts first-class facilities and eminently qualified lecturers. Based in Bali, she does a three-day cruise to Badas, Sumbawa, and then on to Komodo National Park before returning to Bali. Small by cruise ship standards, they carry only 150 passengers housed in compact, a/c cabins. Each stop includes day trips, cultural tours, shopping opportunities, and a chance to explore marinelife with a dive master. The night's five-course dinners, with an excellent and reasonably priced wine list, are accompanied by live music, dancing, and an occasional show. The ship has a well-stocked lounge bar, swimming pool, library, gym, and a hospital. For the three-day cruise, prices start at US$450 per person. For details, contact P & O Spice Island Cruises, Jl. Padang Galak 25, Sanur, Denpasar (tel. 0361-286283, fax 286284), or check with a travel agent.

PT Wisata Tirta Baruna, Jl. Bypass Ngurah Rai 300 B, P.O. Box 419, Denpasar 80001, Bali (tel. 0361-53820 or 51223, fax 53809 or 52779), sails to Indonesia's eastern islands from the port of Benoa. The first port of call are the Gilis off western Lombok, then Sumbawa Besar, Bima, Sabolan Island (West Flores), Komodo, and Sumba from where passengers fly back to Bali. Passengers who want to participate in the westward cruise (same content as above, but in the opposite direction from Sumba to Bali) must fly from Bali to Sumba to join the cruise. Cost is US$1498 d on A deck, US$1348 d on C deck. Price includes all meals, shore excursions,

ground transfers, and airfare, but excludes beverages, alcohol, laundry, telephone calls, tips, and 15% service and tax. They have sales counters in many of southern Bali's most exclusive hotels; their cruises are approximately one-third the price of P & O-owned Spice Island Cruises.

A Dutch company outfits magnificent Indonesian *pinisi,* which have not changed designs since the 18th century to modern safety specifications. Their eight-day cruise takes in Flores, Sumbawa, Komodo, Lombok, and Bali. Longer tours of two and a half weeks to a month follow Russel's footsteps and sail the whole length of Sulawesi, all of Maluku, Irian Jaya—truly an oceangoing company. The scenery is excellent, and the traditional Indonesian food prepared by an Indonesian chef is better quality than at most Indonesian restaurants and *warung.* Contact Sea Trek, Keizersgracht 463, 1017 DK, Amsterdam (tel. 31-20-62-72078, fax 31-20-42-20153), or PT Oceana Tirta Wisata, Jl. Bypass 78 XX, Sanur 80228, Bali (tel. 0361-288892, fax 288652).

Boat Tours

The oldest continually operating ship in the world—older than the Statue of Liberty—is the 115-year-old gaff-rigged ketch *Golden Hawk* which takes passengers daily to Nusa Lembongan. She carries eight sails and is 63 meters long. Hotel pickup, food and drink, snorkel gear, and glass-bottom boat trips are included for US$85 price. Children half-price. Reserve tickets by calling Tour Devco, tel. (0361) 231591 or 231592, book through your hotel, or direct to Golden Hawk Cruises, Jl. Danau Poso 20 A, Sanur, Bali (tel./fax 0361-287431).

Another tall ship, the 115-meter-long 1902 Dutch clipper *Adelaar,* sleeps 18 passengers and a crew of five. When not away on charter, it operates day cruises to Nusa Lembongan for US$77 and US$55 (budget cruise, alcoholic drinks not included). For information, phone Enno Schulze at (0361) 261190.

All the following boats can be arranged through Tour Devco (tel. 0361-231591 or 231592): *Helsal III,* a legendary racing yacht that at one time held every racing record on Australia's east coast, gives day tours for up to 15 guests. For US$66, your day includes a trip to Nusa Lembongan, pick up and return transport, fresh buffet lunch, boat transfers to island, complimentary teas, cocktails, and Aqua, snorkeling and sailing tuition, toilet and shower facilities. The 176-meter-long, powerful *Island Explorer* gives leisurely day tours. On the way, try your hand at game fishing. Famous for its flame-grilled barbecue with crisp salads and fresh tropical fruit. *Ocean Lady II* offers day (US$69) and overnight (US$165 per person) tours to Nusa Lembongan. This 47-foot sloop sails from Benoa Harbor at 0900, returns at 1700. Price includes all food and drink, coral viewing, and island exploring. Call (0361) 287739. The *Anne Judith II,* a 65-foot timber ketch, comfortable and roomy, offers two and three-day tours. The *Kriez An Ael,* a 20-meter French-built yacht, offers three- and five-day itinerary for six to seven guests in four cabins.

The *Simone III* is a specialized Blackwatch game-fishing boat with state-of-the-art electronics and a speed of up to 25 knots. Range of heavy and light fishing tackle for fishing tuna, wahoo, mahi-mahi, mackerel, and marlin. Day cruises start at US$660, maximum six persons. Call Camar Yacht Charter, tel. (0361) 231591, 231592, or 287446, fax 231592 or 287446.

Catamaran Tours

Most cruises make the passage over to Nusa Lembongan, an island 24 km to the southeast of Bali, which takes two-and-a-half hours. The vessels anchor in a quiet bay. Explore inland, visit local villages and seaweed farms, swim and snorkel, sunbathe and beachcomb. The cruise almost always includes a hot buffet lunch and ice cold drinks. At around 1500, the boat sails back to Bali into a tropical sunset, arriving in Benoa at 1700 or 1730 for free transport back to your hotel.

The *Wakalouka* is a 23-meter luxury catamaran which sails from Benoa Harbor every morning at 0900 for a two-hour cruise. At the exclusive Waka Nusa Resort, enjoy a sumptuous barbecue buffet lunch with many Balinese specialties, view the amazing coral formations offshore from the glass-bottomed boat or while snorkeling, swim in the floating pool, play volleyball and deck games, visit the aviary, or just laze and enjoy the sun and fresh air. Return at sunset (1800). Cost (including hotel transfers, unlimited soft drinks) US$70, children five to 15 half-price. Contact PT Tour Devco, tel. (0361) 231591 or 231592.

Quicksilver, a modern, spacious catamaran with three air-conditioned decks for over 300 people, sails daily to Nusa Penida. Popular with Asian groups. International buffet lunch, ride on submersible coral viewer, and excursions to village, seaweed farm, etc. on Nusa Lembongan, 25 km from Benoa Harbor. All for US$85 per person. Reserve a place by calling (0361) 771997 or 771977.

Moggy is a sailing catamaran with a relaxed atmosphere that sleeps eight. Day and extended charter. Call Surf Travel Company or B.B.S. at (0361) 261051 or 261052. Use the same number to charter the *Mimpi Manis,* a traditional Indonesian *pinisi* which cruises to Nusa Lembongan.

Bali Hai II is a 34-meter luxury catamaran for 300 people, featuring several decks, air-conditioned interior, lavish international buffet luncheon, two bars. Day tours (starting at 0930) to Nusa Lembongan, rides in semi-submersible coral viewer, snorkeling instruction from a moored pontoon (all equipment provided), a ride on a glass-bottom boat, unlimited water sausage rides, and shore excursions—all for US$75. An introductory scuba diving course ($40) is optional. Returns at 1600. Children under 15 half-fare. The sunset dinner cruise, departing at 1800 (two and a half hours) with disco, laser disk *karaoke,* Batak singers, is US$35. Book through a travel agent or call (0361) 234331, fax 234334.

Hobie Cat Tours

Run by two Frenchmen, **Aloha Sailing Tours** (tel. 0361-701888, ext. 7605), offers a different kind of sailing experience for adventurers who enjoy sailing, surfing, and fishing from a small fleet of Hobie Cats. The seven-day tours take place off the coast of North Bali, an area of beautiful bays and reefs, untouched beaches, hot springs, temples, good fishing spots, consistent wind conditions. The price of US$600 includes sailing an average of six hours each day, a stop at a different *losmen* each night, food and refreshments, and an assistant boat to keep an eye on everyone.

Chartered Yachts from Bali

Indonesia maintains one of the largest fleets of schooners in the world. Itineraries in the archipelago are only limited by your time, imagination, and money. The charter companies on Bali will pick you up at your hotel for an early morning departure from Benoa Port. The crews prepare delicious meals of fresh seafood, and amenities include private cabins with a/c, stereo, snorkeling gear, fishing tackle, hot showers, and shaded decks. Yachts are fully equipped to meet international safety standards, and they employ fully licensed, usually Western-trained captains and Indonesian pilots.

Australian-owned **Rasa Yachts** (tel. 0361-88756), the largest and longest established yacht charter business in Bali, operates three big, safe, luxury yachts on day trips or extended cruises. Maximum 12 passengers per yacht at US$79 per person per day, all inclusive.

A sturdy, 24-ton, 14-meter-long steel-hulled sailing yacht, the **Wyeema**, can be chartered for safe and comfortable sailing adventures. Marvel at the unpeopled islands, deserted beaches, and magnificent diving on reefs discovered on previous sailing safaris by Captain Bruce Collins. Their specialty is a seven-day, six-night package to Komodo (Bali, Komodo, Sape, Bima, then a flight back to Bali). This package may be extended to 12 days and 11 nights. Book at Jl. Pemamoran 12, Taman Sari, Sanur (tel. 0361-287593).

The **Sirius,** a 20-meter-long pleasure schooner built in 1935, fully restored and renovated with every modern convenience, is also available for extended charter throughout the Indonesian archipelago. Capacity is eight people. To reserve, call (0361) 262824.

MOVING ON

BY BUS

Bali is not just a destination but an important and convenient jumping-off point for the less spoilt islands to the east as well as Java to the west. It's easy to shop for the best deal because most bus companies are on just two streets: Jl. Hasanudin (near Jl. Sumatra) and Jl. Diponegoro.

Most transport outfits are listed in Bali's telephone directory. A number also have offices at Ubung Station selling tickets to Java and points west. The quality of the service is similar, so just pick an agent with a convenient departure time. There are dozens of ticketing agents in Kuta, Legian, Ubud, Candidasa, Lovina, and Sanur who can sell you a ticket.

There are plenty of buses going to Surabaya and Malang. Take note that Java is one hour behind Bali. For Surabaya, *bis malam* leave Ubung at 1900, 2000, and 2100 and arrive early in the morning. Start with **Jawa Indah**, Jl. Diponeogoro 14 (tel. 0361-227329), which charges Rp21,000 including a meal halfway through the 11-hour trip. Their full a/c bus with toilet leaves at 0600 and 1800. There are at least 10 buses per day, depending on the season. If you leave in the cool of the evening (last bus at 2100), you miss the scenery.

If you take a Simpatik bus to Surabaya, it costs Rp15,000 (toilet, video, breakfast, water, and snacks) and arrives at 0530 Java-time at Bratang Station which is where all the night buses arrive. For **Yogya/Solo,** long-distance a/c buses cost Rp38,500. The Damri bus leaves around 1730 and takes 14 hours; other buses leave Ubung at 1430 or 2000 and arrive at around 1700. Two meals (*nasi campur* and drinks) are usually included in the fare.

For **Jakarta,** take the punishing a/c express bus from Ubung at 0600 or 0730 for Rp45,000 and taking at least 35 hours. It arrives (two out of three times) at Jakarta's Pulau Gadung Station by 0930 the next day (Rp58,000). Note that you can't travel direct from Singaraja to Jakarta. You have to spend a day in Surabaya waiting for a connection.

If you need to catch a nonchangeable, nonrefundable flight out of Singapore, book your bus seat ahead of time. If you try to do it in stages, the bus to Surabaya could be four hours late, and then you may sit at the ferry slip at Gilimanuk in western Bali for five hours before the crossing. In the evening the beast could break down several times or the main road could be closed. Allow three days to get to Jakarta.

Another option is to get to the Gilimanuk ferry terminal, then take the ferry across to Ketapang on the Java side. Here buses will be waiting to take you to Banyuwangi's Terminal Blambangan where you can catch buses straight to Surabaya or else travel via the southern route to Malang (six hours). Or you can take a bus from Bali straight to Malang for around Rp25,000 (10 hours), leaving at 1830 or 2000. Long-distance buses now travel all the way to Sumbawa Besar on Sumbawa and Medan in northern Sumatra. Either destination takes about a week!

Bus Traveling Tips

In the busy season, it's best to buy your ticket the day before and choose the best seat—seats can get booked days in advance. In the slow season, just show up at the time of departure and you'll probably get on. Buying your ticket from a travel agent costs about five percent more than purchasing it directly from the bus company. The exception is buying through the bus company's official ticketing agent, where the price is the same.

Look for a bus with comfortable reclining airline seats, pillows, and an inside toilet. The prime (and most hair-raising!) place to sit is beside or close to the driver. The worst is in the rear. However, the seats in the rear recline, because there's no one behind you.

BY AIR

Numerous direct flights leave the domestic terminal of Bali's Ngurah Rai Airport (tel. 0361-751011) daily for Surabaya, Yogya, and Jakarta on Java, as well as to such Outer Island cities as Mataram on Lombok and Ujung Pandang in South Sulawesi.

You'll find ticket agents all over Kuta, Legian, and Sanur. These discounters also sell tickets to Singapore, Hong Kong, Bangkok, Darwin, Sydney, and London. Confirm your reservation at a Garuda ticket office (below) at least three days before departure. Or call the reservation/reconfirmation office at (0361) 35169/27825 (hunting system) or 751178. Office hours: Mon.-Fri. 0730-2100, Saturday, Sunday, and holidays 0900-1700.

If you want to order an air ticket, do so from a ticket agent or hotel courtesy desk anywhere, but allow about 48 hours for your money to be sent to Denpasar and the ticket to return via shuttle

bus or courier service. Reconfirming reservations usually costs Rp6000 or so if done through a local travel agency, or you can phone the air offices in Denpasar yourself for less (they speak English). If you pay for a ticket with a credit card, add three percent bank's fee.

Don't forget that holders of an International Student Card (ISC) receive as much as a 25% discount. Garuda, Merpati, Sempati, and Bouraq all charge about the same for the Denpasar-Jakarta flight. It's cheaper and faster to fly from Bali to Ujung Pandang than it is to fly from Surabaya to Ujung Pandang. Also Bali is the best place from which to fly into Nusatenggara and the string of islands to the southeast.

If you're heading into Nusatenggara, your flight almost always stops in Mataram on Lombok first. On the flight east, there are great views over Gunung Rinjani and Gunung Tambora if you sit on the left-hand side of the plane. On the flight to Maumere (Flores), you stop also in Bima (East Sumbawa) where they have to chase the goats off the runway in order for the plane to take off.

Sample domestic airfares: Ambon Rp328,000, Balikpapan Rp306,000, Biak (Irian Jaya) Rp525,000, Ende (Flores) Rp223,800, Jakarta Rp222,900, Kupang (Timor) Rp227,100, Malang Rp94,000, Manado (North Sulawesi) Rp374,000, Maumere (Rp207,300), Medan Rp457,000, Palembang Rp351,400, Pontianak (Rp414,100), Semerang Rp160,000, Surabaya (East Java) Rp94,000, Solo Rp122,500, Ujung Pandang Rp157,800, Waingapu (Sumba) Rp184,200), Yogyakarta (Rp122,600).

The Garuda flight to Los Angeles from Bali or Jakarta takes about 13 hours to Honolulu, then another five hours to Los Angeles. This plane is often about an hour late, both ways. On the way to the states, you may no longer deplane at Biak and visit the Baliem Valley because the big new combis don't need to refuel and can make it now all the way to Hawaii. Now a Garuda "Visit Indonesia Decade Pass" or "Indonesia Airpass" in which you are allowed to visit any three cities within Indonesia for an extra US$300, is the only economical way to reach Irian Jaya. Each additional stop is US$100.

Flight information at Ngurah Rai International Airport in Tuban is tel. 751174. Note that during December and January, flights out of Bali can be booked solid with many people on stand-by. Due to Garuda's habit of overbooking flights, be at the airport counter at least two hours early on international departures; otherwise, your seats could be given to people on the waiting list.

From Denpasar's Stasiun Tegal, take a *bemo* to the airport, Rp1000. From Kuta to the airport, minibus and *bemo* drivers first ask Rp25,000 for a charter. Just laugh at them—Rp3000-5000 is the going rate. Make sure they drop you at the right terminal, domestic or international, depending on your destination. Another way is to walk to Kuta's Pertamina station, near the Kentucky Fried Chicken, turn right and flag down a *bemo*, Rp500.

Domestic airport tax is Rp7500; international departure tax is Rp21,000. Porters don't wait to ask whether you would like your baggage carried—they just grab it and then demand Rp500 apiece. Baggage storage is available for Rp3300 per day. The new international terminal has color TVs, gift shops, news agencies, a spacious departure hall, lounges, comfortable seating, etc. Brace yourself for high prices: Rp31,500 for Fujichrome (three times the Kuta price) and Rp2500 for water (five times the correct price). Better to just change excess rupiah back into home-country currency at the bank windows.

Garuda Visit Indonesia Decade Pass

You may have trouble with a Garuda VIDP flight if your ticket is canceled and you have to get rerouting. Most Merpati offices won't touch it, even if a rerouting would be the same price. This is because the ticket was issued abroad. In fact, any international ticket they won't reroute. So, if they make you buy a new ticket, go to the biggest Garuda/Merpati office you can find, get the reroute done, and ask for an "XO"—a single rebate on the ticket you had to buy.

"Garuda Indonesia City Check-In"

Check-in and seat assignment facilities for Garuda's international and domestic flights are available at all the off-airport offices mentioned in the chart "Garuda Offices." Passengers may check in for their flight and obtain boarding passes at any of the locations between 24 and four hours prior to scheduled flight departure time. Baggage must still be checked in at the

---

GARUDA OFFICES

The following offices are open Mon.-Fri. 0730-1645, Saturday, Sunday, and holidays 0900-1300.

Denpasar: Jl. Melati 61, tel. (0361) 225245 or 751178, near Kereneng Bus Station, sales and booking tel. (0361) 222028 or 222788

Kuta: Hotel Kuta Beach, tel. (0361) 751179

Sanur: Hotel Bali Beach, tel. (0361) 88243 or 87920

Nusa Dua: Hotel Nusa Indah, tel. (0361) 71864 or 71572, ext. 560 or 561, and Nusa Dua Galleria, tel. (0361) 771444 or 771864, ext. 727

Ngurah Rai Airport: Terminal International, tel. (0361) 751178 or 751011, ext. 1453

Don't bother calling the Garuda office at the Kuta Beach Hotel in Kuta as it's constantly busy; also get there early in the morning before the line gets too long.

---

airport, but this may be done at a special counter reserved for GICC passengers. Any international departure taxes must also be paid at the airport. For GICC passengers, the airport reporting time for international flights is 90 minutes prior to scheduled departure time and 45 minutes for domestic flights. City check-in locations are open seven days a week 0800-1700 on weekdays and 0900-1300 on weekends and holidays.

Airline Offices

The majority of foreign airlines have their offices in the Grand Bali Beach Hotel in Sanur. Their hours are generally Mon.-Fri. 0830-1630 (with an hour off for lunch) as well as Saturday mornings until around noon. (See also the chart "Garuda Offices.")

Ansett, tel. (0361) 289637

Cathay Pacific, tel. (0361) 288576

China Airlines, tel. (0361) 287840 or 288511, fax 287841

Continental, tel. (0361) 287774 or 288511, fax 287775

KLM, tel. (0361) 287576 or 287577, fax
  287460 or 288511

Korean Air, tel. (0361) 289402 or 288511

Lufthansa, tel. (0361) 287069 or 288511

Malaysia Airlines, tel. (0361) 288716 or
  288511

Qantas, tel. (0361) 288332 or 288511

Singapore Airlines, tel. (0361) 287960

Thai, tel. (0361) 288141 or 288511

Other foreign airlines may be found in these
separate locations:

Bouraq, Jl. Jend. Sudirman 19 A (tel. 0361-
  223564 or 234947), in front of Udayana
  University offers flights at very competitive
  prices to Nusatenggara, Sulawesi, and
  Kalimantan.

Merpati Jl. Melati 57 (tel. 0361-228842), near
  the Garuda office or on Jl. Ngurah Rai
  Tuban (tel. 0361-751375).

Sempati Air (tel. 0361-288824 or 281117) an
  efficient up-and-coming domestic airlines is
  open 24 hours a day and has its main
  office on Jl. Airport Tuban.

UTA is at Jl. Bypass I Gusti 87 X, Ngurah Rai
  (tel. 0361-289225, 289226, or 289227).

BY SEA

If traveling alone to Bali's offshore islands, Nusa
Lembongan and Nusa Penida, take one of the
long, motorized outrigger ferries that depart either from Kusamba, Padangbai, or Sanur. Ask
for *stasiun bot*. Boats leave only at 0800 or 0900
(Rp15,000).

  Benoa Harbor in southern Bali is a favorite
port for visiting yachties. Inquire around for a
lift on a private yacht in exchange for work.
There may be a lot of competition from other
travelers. Also check the bulletin board at Poppies in Kuta for advertisements for crew. Another place to check for possible rides on Makassarese schooners is Bali's main deep-water harbor at Celukanbawang in Buleleng Regency.

Pelni, Indonesia's National Shipping Company, operates 20 passenger-cargo ships, each
of which does a different inter-island loop around
the archipelago every two weeks. For the latest
timetables and routes, which change about once
every 90 days, check with the Pelni office (tel.
0361-228962) at Benoa just west of Sanur. The
ships offer four classes from economy where
you sleep in a huge common room to first class
with inside bathroom, a/c, TV, two-to-a-cabin. It's
important to book ahead.

Lombok by Boat

Take a minibus from Batubulan to Padangbai
(Rp2000) on the east coast of Bali. From
Padangbai, the three-and-a-half-hour ferry departs for Lembar on Lombok every two hours,
except at midnight. The standard fare is
Rp4000. Be warned: every day there are
changes in the schedule and if you want to
catch the 0800 ferry and have to take the 1000
ferry instead, you probably won't make it to the
Gili Islands in one day.

  Another way to get to Lombok is by the
Mabua Express a high-speed jetfoil from Benoa
Harbor. The two-deck hydrofoil leaves Benoa
at 0800 and 1430, arriving in Lembar Harbor
(Lombok) at 1030 and 1700 respectively. Punc-
tuality depends upon weather and sea conditions. Here you'll find a bar, TV/video screens,
and reclining lounge seats. Fares are Rp50,000
Diamond Class for the upper deck, Rp32,500
Emerald Class, and Rp25,000 Economy Class.
Children's rate is 50% of adult rate. Capacity is
248 passengers. For more info and to order
free pick-up service, call (0361) 772521 or
261212 24 hours.

  Yet another way is to join **Perama Travel**'s
very reasonably priced "Land-Sea Adventure"
which sells seven-day tours of Lombok, the
Gilis, Sumbawa, Rinca, and Flores. Or just fly independently from Bali to Lombok for Rp47,000
in 25 minutes. Heading east from Bali, island
hop all the way to Timor. Or charter a boat
roundtrip to Komodo for Rp560,000 with your
own cook and guide as a Swiss tourist who
wrote me did.

MONEY

Bills

The Indonesian monetary unit is called the rupiah, issued in notes of Rp100, Rp500, Rp1000, Rp5000, Rp10,000, Rp20,000, and a new Rp50,000 hologram note, which will help eliminate the huge stacks of Rp10,000 bills it used to take to pay for large purchases. The demand for these is heavy.

Bills are all roughly the same size but different colors. Be careful with the old Rp10,000 notes which still circulate; they are maddeningly similar to current Rp5000 notes. If you don't recognize the difference, this is a real quick way to lose a couple of bucks. The new Rp10,000 note is cobalt, so no problem there. Likewise, the new Rp50,000 note looks deceptively like the Rp1000 note—same color and almost the same size. Put these in a different place.

If heading into the countryside of Bali, take small denomination notes (Rp10,000 or less) because it's nearly impossible for rural people to make change for Rp10,000 notes or higher. Keep on hand lots of small denominational rupiah notes because taxi drivers and small vendors will invariably be "out of change" and you'll need small change for public WCs and snacks.

Coins

Different-sized coins are valued at Rp25, Rp50, and Rp100. A Rp500 coin also exists, but it's not frequently seen; it's useful for some public phones. Study the coins until you're familiar with them. You'll sometimes see worthless Rp5 and Rp10 coins. Just keep them as souvenirs.

Attitudes

To swagger with your money in Bali is against your best interest. To the man in the street, a dollar's worth of rupiah has the same emotional impact as US$10 has to us; US$2000 is enough to sustain a rural Balinese family of four for a year.

In Indonesia a price is put on everything "extra"—a better seat on the minibus, a fan in your room, an egg on top of your *nasi goreng,* an application form at a government office. Someone who carries a 7-UP halfway up a mountain on their head will sell it for twice the price you can buy it cold in the city.

EXPENSES

First Rule: Don't ask how much Indonesian currency is worth in "real money" (your home-country money). It's just as real as German or Australian currency. Don't make the mistake of always translating Indonesian prices into U.S. or European currency, then feeling relieved and grateful for the cheap price. Instead, think in rupiah. It doesn't cost "just" 50 American cents, it costs a thousand damn rupiah!

Second Rule: It's not even worth going to Bali if you're constantly obsessed with getting the cheapest price. Bali is cheap by any foreign standard, but instead of paying Rp3500 for a great meal many travelers pay Rp500-1000 at the same restaurant for a simple plate of fried rice. Why travel and save US$50 if you only eat rice the whole time?

Third Rule: A common practice of hotels is to give their prices in U.S. dollars, and they expect you to pay with U.S. dollar traveler's checks. However, because the dollar is consistently

With a hole in the middle and worn thin by many years of trading, bronze or lead Chinese kepeng are commonly used in offerings, cremations, and ceremonies. During Dutch times, it took 700 of them to make a ringgit and 10,000 kepeng equaled one timbang or "weight." If a man had to pay two timbang in tax, he had to set aside enough husked rice to balance 20,000 kepeng on a scale. Be careful: fake kepeng are being mass-produced.

HOW MUCH DO THINGS COST, ANYWAY?

Coconut oil: Rp2000 per large Bir Bintang bottle

A six-month old cow: US$300; a one-and-a-half-year-old cow: US$600

Electricity for a two-bedroom house in the city for small family: Rp14,000

Cost of a plumber: Rp7000 per day; a carpenter: Rp6000 per day

Average monthly wage: Rp100,000; minimum wage: Rp30,000 per month.

Cost of a tailer to sew a shirt: Rp5000 (a famous tailor, double the price)

Cost of a major ceremony like *galungan* for a small family: Rp60,000 (mostly for the slaughtering of a pig, Rp50,000)

A visit to the dentist (two fillings): Rp10,000 per visit; to the doctor's office: Rp5000

Schoolbooks for grammar school: Rp25,000; for high school: Rp50,000

Rent for a student's room with a bathroom: Rp15,000 per day

Enrollment for public high school: Rp7000 per month; private high school: Rp12,000

School uniforms (each of the three grades): Rp25,000 plus plastic shoes for school Rp6000

Fees per semester at Bali's UNUD University: Rp500,000

climbing against the rupiah, the price in rupiah is nearly always considerably lower.

For example, a hotel might ask US$50 d per night. At the exchange rate of Rp2300 per US$1, you will pay the equivalent Rp115,000 if you pay in dollars. Yet the price in rupiah may be only Rp95,000! Always compute the hotel's dollar price in rupiah before deciding which currency to pay your bills in.

Fourth Rule: Always carry enough small change and bills to pay *bemo* drivers and market sellers. You could settle with a driver on a price of Rp4000 for the charter of a *bemo*, but if you pay with a Rp10,000 note he could very well give

you back less money than he owes you. If you complain, he might give you another Rp1000, then drive away quickly. Similarly, people might try to give you less than the correct change at restaurants, moneychangers, and some hotels.

Daily Expenses

How much money you spend per day depends upon your tastes, the level of comfort you desire, where you want to go, how you get there, and what season you're traveling in. There are two tourist seasons: Balinese winter (July and August) and the Christmas holidays. Prices go up a little bit in December, but it's a short season—only two weeks. The peak tourist season lasts from around 15 July to 15 August when prices really escalate. Budget accommodations sometimes *double* their tariffs this time.

Bali was once the cheapest place to eat and sleep comfortably in Asia. Since the Gulf War in 1991, however, prices have risen significantly. Budget accommodations shot up from Rp10,000 d to Rp20,000 d, and petrol prices also rose steeply. Many of the expensive hotels had to charge extra because they paid so much in advertising during the "Visit Indonesia Year 1991" and all the smaller hotels followed suit. They also had to compensate for the tremendous downturn in tourism because of the war during the first quarter of 1991.

Though Yogyakarta is cheaper than Bali for budget traveling, Bali is still very much a bargain. If you stick to such budget traveler's resorts as Lovina, Padangbai, and Lalang Linggah, prices for food and accommodations are unbelievably cheap due to the intense competition. On the other hand, if you're on the move around the island, buying tickets on shuttle buses and using taxis, count on living on at least US$15-20 per day.

Roadside foodstalls all over the area charge only around 50 U.S. cents or less for a very filling vegetarian meal, as little as US$2 for comfortable rooms, and around Rp75 per kilometer for *bemo* rides. As far as tourist resorts go, Candidasa has the lowest prices, but even in a swank restaurant like Poppies in Kuta, you'd be making an absolute glutton of yourself if you spent over US$15 for two.

Although there are hundreds of villages where you can live for US$5 per day or less, you are discouraged from doing so by local authorities because you'd be taking business away from hotels and restaurants. Most tourists and travelers stay within the Sanur-Denpasar-Kuta axis, where prices are blown out of proportion. The rest of the island is less expensive.

The most expensive places to stay are the tourist resorts of Sanur and Nusa Dua, where prices for food and accommodations are the highest on the island. In Sanur, you'll need US$30-40 per day minimum; in Nusa Dua, more on the order of US$90-120. Yet you can save lots simply by leaving your hotel grounds. Within a kilometer of Nusa Dua in Bualu you're able to enjoy a decent *warung* meal for only 50 cents.

Entrance Fees

Guards *(penjaga)* and attendants *(juru kunci)* frequently make you pay a fee of around Rp550 to enter an historical site, temple, or museum, plus another Rp200-500 to enter the parking lot and another Rp500-1000 for your camera. At numerous high-traffic tourist sites like Goa Gajah, Besakih, and Tanah Lot, a video camera has to pay an entrance fee too.

Gatekeepers may also ask for an additional fee for renting a scarf each time you enter a temple, so it's best just to buy your own for Rp1000-1500 at almost any clothing boutique or market, such as Pasar Sukawati. It will pay for itself very quickly. Sometimes the scarf is included in the entry charge. To enter the Bali Barat National Park of West Bali, you're required to pay an insurance premium of Rp50 on top of the admission price.

Don't pay an entrance or parking fee without getting an official receipt, unless only a "donation" is requested; then around Rp200 is appropriate. If you can spare it, give something—in many cases the attendants make their living from tourists. If you spend a whole day at an *odalan,* give Rp5000 when a donation is asked for. It's a trifle when you consider what you get, yet very acceptable and appreciated.

If the *juru kunci* shows you the visitor's book with sums like Rp10,000 after people's names, someone has ingeniously written in some extra zeros. Don't fall for this trick. Put a dash after your contribution so zeros can't be added. When viewing a family compound, always give the money donation to the oldest woman because the oldest man will gamble it away and the young men will squander it.

Tipping

A few annoying Western customs, like tipping, have caught on. Never tip waiters in restaurants, bartenders, reception people in small hotels, hairdressers, medical personnel, or tailors. Only tip taxi drivers and porters for unusually good service or extra-heavy bags.

Don't contribute to this cancer! Tipping in the Western sense is not part of Balinese culture. When you *do* give a tip—for your houseboy or cook—it is always unexpected and thus has more impact. Save tipping only for those instances when it's really deserved.

In the places where you're *supposed* to tip for individual services, a 10% service charge (plus 11% government tax) is added to your bill. Expect these charges to be added in the big tourist hotels of Nusa Dua, Sanur, and Kuta. As in Europe, only high-priced hotels and leading restaurants add the charge. Airport porters expect a payment (not a tip) of Rp500 *per bag;* this is posted.

Hired drivers *(sopir)* and guides *(petunjuk)* may be tipped Rp5000-10,000 per day—but only if you're pleased with their performance. Although bribery in the civil bureaucracy exists, it's unlikely that travelers or tourists will ever need to resort to it. In most cases you won't even know if you've just paid a bribe because it's deftly institutionalized and masked behind some official fee or charge.

CHANGING MONEY

United States dollars, accepted all over Indonesia since WW II, are still the most useful foreign currency to carry through these islands. The dollar has the most fixed rate of exchange because the rupiah is based on it. Though the dollar will probably have the most favorable exchange rate, it's possible to cash other well-known currencies like Australian dollars, German marks, Netherlands florins, French and Swiss francs. Canadian and New Zealand dollars are a bit more difficult.

Cash

Traveler's checks and cash in U.S. currency can be changed at almost any moneychanger or bank, although changing other currencies can sometimes pose a problem. The smaller towns of Bali may not have banks or, if they do, they may not accept your particular currency. They may turn their noses up at the good old British pound, but they'll usually accept crisp US$100 bills. No passport is usually required to change cash.

Change money in Kuta's or Denpasar's banks, which offer the best rates. Large denomination U.S. notes or traveler's checks (100-dollar bills as opposed to twenties) fetch a higher rate of exchange. Obviously, this only really matters if you're going to be changing large amounts.

Indonesian banks, even on Bali, refuse to touch foreign banknotes which are soiled, worn, or physically damaged. If you do a good job taping them with transparent tape, you'll probably get away with passing damaged notes off. Banks also won't exchange foreign coins.

Indonesian paper currency tends to stay in circulation longer, so Indonesian banknotes start to take on the appearance of filthy scraps of torn cloth. This worn money won't be accepted, so don't allow it to be passed on to you. If it is, the only place you can change it is at a bank.

Exchange Rates

Exchange rates depend on the bank and even on *the branch* of the bank. In some cases, the headquarters bank changes money but their city branches do not. You'll need your passport and tourist entry card for each transaction.

In order to encourage tourism and because of the intense competition between moneychangers, the best rates on Bali are in the tourist areas. In the far reaches of the island, such as Amlapura and Gilimanuk, the exchange rates tend not to be as good or there could be no banks at all.

Avoid, if you can, exchanging money at hotel front desks, where you'll get at least 10% below the rate offered by state banks. The more expensive the hotel, the worse the rate. The three moneychangers at Bali's Ngurah Rai Airport offer very competitive rates. So good in fact that you might as well change several hundred dollars as soon as you land on Bali, to save you time and trouble changing money later.

APPROXIMATE EXCHANGE RATES

British pound	Rp3649
Australian dollar	Rp1856
U.S. dollar	Rp2342
Singapore dollar	Rp1665
Malaysian ringgit	Rp939
Deutschmark	Rp1586
Dutch guilder	Rp1414
Swiss franc	Rp1962
French franc	Rp463
Hong Kong dollar	Rp303
Japanese yen	Rp21.63
Canadian dollar	Rp1715

Moneychangers

Moneychangers generally do not charge a fee for their services, so you can change money as often as you want without it costing you. Anyplace tourists congregate will be choked with moneychangers. Though their rates vary, they offer quicker service and usually give a better exchange rate than banks. They also don't open as early but stay open much later than banks. Banks seldom post exchange rates, but moneychangers always do.

Rates fluctuate daily. Check out more than one moneychanger and compare the rates of the currency you have. Rates may differ by Rp5 or so, i.e., 25 cents on US$100. You could try for a better rate, but you could wear out several cents' worth of shoe soles finding it. Pay more attention to finding a place where they don't try to forget the last Rp300 or give you Rp500 instead of Rp5000 and see if you notice.

Count your money to see if it's correct.

Reconversion

Technically, when leaving the country a limit of Rp50,000 may be exchanged for foreign currencies. Reconvert *before* you clear security at the airport as once past the security check you can't go back. The rate is quite acceptable. The shops and coffee shops beyond the security point sometimes accept dollars at so-so rates. Early on, keep your international departure tax (Rp20,000) tucked away for use when exiting Bali.

When entering Indonesia, you're also supposed to carry no more than Rp50,000. But actually, you needn't bring any Indonesian money to Bali since there are several moneychangers at Bali airport. You'll pay more than three times as much for rupiah in Germany than you would have paid when changing traveler's checks upon arrival.

TRAVELER'S CHECKS AND CREDIT CARDS

There's no black market in Indonesia, so for safety's sake bring only a portion of your funds in cash. Though rates are often better for traveler's checks than for cash, always carry some US$5, US$10, and US$20 dollar bills in case you need quick money and banks or moneychangers are closed.

The bulk of your traveling funds should be in the form of a widely accepted brand of traveler's checks. American Express (Amex), Bank of America, First National City Bank, Barclays, Wells Fargo, and Thomas Cook Traveler's Checks are accepted all over Indonesia.

All the above companies have branches in Bali in case you lose your checks. Amex, the most popular traveler's checks, has an office c/o Pacto (tel. 0361-288449) in the Jabaan Shopping Arcade of the Bali Beach Hotel in Sanur. Open Mon.-Fri. 0800-1600, Saturday 0800-1200, closed Sunday. This office sells traveler's checks, has a poste restante service, emergency card and traveler's check replacement service (within 24 hours), but does not do travel/tour services. Another Amex representative is c/o Pan Indonesia Bank, Jl. Legian, Kuta (tel. 0361-751058).

Bank Bumi Daya, Bank Expor Impor, Bank Rakyat Indonesia, and Bank Negara Indonesia (BNI) take most Australian and the better-known traveler's checks. Use the Indonesian phrase *trapel cek* for traveler's checks. *Cek jalanan turis* is also widely understood.

Upon presentation of your passport, it usually takes no more than 20 minutes to cash traveler's checks at a bank. If clerks in a bank won't accept your brand of checks, it might help to ask for the bank manager. Major hotels, department stores, and many pricey shops will also take traveler's checks, though at lousy rates.

Credit Cards
Indonesia is still very much a cash-oriented society, so Visa, MasterCard, and Amex credit cards can only be utilized in Bali's major tourist and business centers equipped to process a charge. Middle-range to upscale hotels, tourist-oriented souvenir shops, the big art shops along the tourist corridor, domestic and international airlines offices, and the more expensive restaurants will accept them. As a general rule, most air-conditioned businesses with glass windows will accept plastic.

Travel agencies will usually accept them, which is convenient because you can pay for a car rental or a tour through them. Not all retail outlets accept the American Express card, but Garuda now accepts it. The Amex representative on Bali is in Galleria Nusa Dua, Shop A 5 Unit 1-3-5, Nusa Dua (tel. 0361-773334).

Diner's Club (c/o Bank BDNI, Jl. Diponegoro 45, Denpasar, tel. 0361-238041 or 238042) is gaining strength. If you have problems with your Visa card, contact the "Card Centre," Lippo Bank, B/R Ketut Winaya, Jl. Thamrin 77, Denpasar (tel. 0361-422176).

Most merchants can't authorize your limit; you can only purchase goods equal to a total value of Rp250,000. Also, it's common for Indonesians to add a two to five percent "commission" if you use your credit card. Try to bargain this commission away. Your passport and your credit card are needed for all transactions. Be sure to verify the total amount charged.

Ask the retailer or service provider to convert the total amount into dollars and cents, then write the amount on the charge slip. This way, in spite of currency ups and downs, you'll know exactly what is owed your credit card company. Take a list of your credit card numbers and phone numbers to call so you can cancel your credit cards if you lose them. Leave a duplicate list with a friend back home.

Always keep the customer copy because charge slips could be altered and used to defraud you by adding extra zeros. Don't discard the slips until the charges have been paid. Later, if you discover that you have been cheated by a merchant who switched or misrepresented merchandise, write your credit card company, which may be able to satisfactorily resolve the problem. Always keep your credit cards within sight when making a purchase.

Cash Advances Against Credit Cards
You can also use your Visa, MasterCard, or Amex (but not Diner's Club) cards to get cash advances (normally up to US$500) from moneychangers, but they charge a steep six percent commission. Banks that give cash advances against credit cards vary widely in their commission. Make sure you know the rate of commission before you make the transaction. Bank Duta—perhaps the best bank in Indonesia—is always prompt and hassle free; in other banks the clerks may suffer apoplexy if you hand over your Visa card for cash.

Dutch PostChecks
Dutch tourists or people with a Dutch giro-account at the state Postbank are lucky because they may use PostChecks to get up to Rp200,000 per check at most Indonesian post offices. It takes about a month for the money to be deducted from their accounts.

PostChecks are cheaper than traveler's checks. Because there's no such thing as a Dutch guilder traveler's check, the Dutch have to change guilders to dollars, buy traveler's checks, then cash them. That's three transactions, which comes out to more than a five percent commission.

PostChecks are insured against loss, and are also usable in Malaysia, Thailand, Hong Kong, and Japan. The Dutch may also use their Postgiro credit cards (the same cards they use in Holland) to draw cash, but these can only be used at the main post office of a city or town.

Wire Transfers/Remittance Orders
Take enough money with you in the first place (US$2000 for two to five months of budget travel should suffice) so you won't have to go through the trouble of having money wired, a service which costs up to US$15. Additionally, you might be charged another US$25 per wire on the L.A. end! Cash against your credit card is a faster, less expensive way to go—even after paying the six percent charge.

Travelers caught short have also found that it may take several weeks to get money remitted by wire from Australia, North America, or Europe. If you're really stuck, an Amex "Money-gram" or telex is a faster way to transfer money than ordinary telegrams. Before you go, get your bank's telex number. A slower way is to wire home and ask for an international money order.

BARGAINING

Bargaining is a long-established custom in Indonesia, so always be ready to bargain—even for drugstore medicine, hospitalization, entrance charges to small museums or temple sites (unless fees are posted)—no matter what type of establishment it is, even "fixed-price" shops. Bargaining is most critical in open markets, with anyone who quotes you a ridiculous price, and with beach or street vendors of tourist souvenirs that natives themselves seldom buy.

Bargaining is not the rule at foodstalls or restaurants, but always ask for a lower rate for your hotel room—no matter what class hotel—especially if it has many empty rooms or if it's the off-tourist-season. Bargain for transportation on *bemo* and buses only if you know you're being overcharged. Prices for tailors and hairdressers are standardized and fixed, but bargain with your mechanic, tire-fixer, or with someone who gives you a lift on the back of a motorcycle.

Buying and bargaining in Indonesia can be good-humored or it can be infuriating. At its best, it can be a social vehicle by which one requests and receives favors, a method by which one solidifies one's status in the local economy. It's a game won by technique and strategy, not by anger or threats. It's an invaluable skill developed through getting burned many times.

The price is always made in consideration of the merchant's need on that day, his assessment of the potential buyer, how much he or she likes you, plus the sporting spirit of the exchange. An item in fact has *many* prices, each reflecting the correct price for a particular customer from the *tukang*'s (shopkeeper's) point of view.

It's really challenging to try to get the same price as the locals. There's a second (higher) price for out-of-town Indonesians, and still a third and higher price for Chinese, *orang besar* ("big

BARGAINING TECHNIQUES AND STRATEGIES

Try to find the price range of the item first; don't ever assume a price or take a (perhaps biased) bystander's word for it. Before you go out shopping, spot-check prices in your hotel shop. If a smaller hotel, ask your hotel proprietor, houseboy, driver, or someone not involved with the shop what the *correct* price for the item in question is. The Balinese themselves are always swapping price information as a way of keeping down costs.

Don't stop and buy at the very first stall, vendor, or shop you come across. Compare prices first, learn about the quality and the differences. Do all your heavy buying your last week in Bali when you are the most knowledgeable and experienced.

Start by asking the seller his price. He will be apt to start out too high. Laugh heartily and in a friendly way, as if he were sharing a wonderful joke with you. Keep things light, smile a lot, and keep on saying *terlalu mahal* (too expensive).

Then bring him down to earth by counter-offering with a reasonable price so the remainder of the exchange is more realistic. When the seller smiles, it means he knows that you know the items value. Sometimes, in the hope that you'll be over-generous, Indonesians are fond of replying "It's up to you" when you ask "How much?"

For luxury items like carvings, jewelry, textiles, or paintings, start at 50-60% of the asking price, then inch up. For services like transportation, start out with 50% the asking price. Sundries like canned goods, soap, toilet paper, and cigarettes are usually bought at a set price from small convenience stores or hotel kiosks.

A rule of thumb is to cut their first offer and then go up begrudgingly in small increments. For example, the merchant might ask Rp200,000 for an *ikat* blanket. You counter with Rp130,000, knowing that the final price should be around Rp160,000. The merchant will then come back with Rp190,000. From here on you go back and forth two or three times until you "meet" at around Rp170,000 or so. Don't feel bad about offering less than what they ask. Remember: On Bali this is a sporting event.

When the merchant reaches his final price and won't budge, try for some "extras." Throw in an inexpensive item and say that you will accept his offer if he includes this small item. Try getting him to accept your credit card *without* charging you a com-

mission. Or try to persuade him to absorb packing and delivery to your shipper in the final price, or perhaps to at least share some of the freight and insurance costs.

Your position is strongest when you appear not to care. As a last resort, try "the walk away" because feigned disinterest will make for many a good deal. This is almost always necessary with *bemo* and *honda sikap* drivers (*before* climbing in) but is just as effective in shops. Just smile, shrug your shoulders, and walk slowly away with cocked ears. Often the driver or seller will call you back, agreeing to your last bid.

In the very least, "the walk away" will give you a true assessment of what price the seller is willing to let the item in question go for. Sometimes you'll find that your own judgement is wrong and, after asking in other shops, you'll return to the original shop to buy the item!

Remain flexible. There's a vast difference between the opportunistic tourist-oriented stores, markets, and street sellers, and those businesses that offer goods and services mostly to Balinese. You tend not to get overcharged as much in the country as in the city.

If you buy more than one item, you should qualify for a "bulk-purchase" discount of at least a portion of the price off each item. On a large bulk purchase or on a multiple luxury purchase, many thousands of rupiah should be taken off the retail total, or at least the bill rounded to an amount lower than the total.

Another strategy is not to show interest in the item you want. Don't hover around or fondle it; try not to give a clue of your *true* interest. If you show enthusiasm for it, the seller knows you want it and will be less flexible. Instead, include the item with other articles you want to buy, almost as if it's an afterthrought. Throw it in at the last minute before clinching your negotiations. "Oh, how much for this too?"

Another trick is to bid for goods early in the day just as the shop opens for business. Balinese believe that making a sale right off will give them luck the rest of the day, so they are usually willing to take a lower price just to get the day off to a good start. The expression "morning price" means a special price given in the morning to stimulate sales (there's even a verb, *penglaris*).

If you have a Balinese friend bargain for food in the market—or even negotiate for boat or vehicle charters—they can probably get better prices than you. Expat residents always send their cooks and houseboys to the market to do the shopping.

Also try asking for the *harga biasa* (normal price), *harga penduduk* (the price for the locals), or *harga belajar* (student's price). This saves face.

There is much more incentive for the budget traveler to learn the language than for the more affluent traveler. One can save lots of money and make friends easier if they know how to bargain in Bahasa Indonesia. If you speak Indonesian, natives assume you already know the prices and usually won't charge you as much or will give in to your price more quickly.

If you think it's going to cause an argument, just give that little bit extra. The vendor may not be overcharging you and it's just not worth the ill will. In certain places you can reduce the price, but Balinese work very hard and must maintain a profit margin. Some travelers are just too stubborn and aggressive and won't pay that extra Rp200. Here they've traveled halfway around the world to become livid over a lousy dime. The Balinese won't make a million; he's got a family of six to feed.

It's bad form to continue bargaining after an amount has been agreed upon or a deal has been struck.

Ask for a receipt listing the specific items and the prices you paid as proof that you made the purchase in case the item is not shipped or for clearing both outgoing and incoming customs. Observe the wrapping process closely—there have been instances of merchants substituting an inferior product for the one actually purchased.

man"), Jakartans, Indonesians from other islands, and foreigners like you. The Japanese tourist, thought to be the most ignorant and richest of all, gets overcharged constantly. You pay according to your station in life. If you say you're poor, they laugh. If you're so poor, how come you're on Bali?

Admittedly, being overcharged gets very tiresome after a while. Though it's only a matter of pennies, the practice eventually manages to annoy every Westerner, as a matter of principle. The best bargaining is done with your feet, by going back to the good places. The Chinese are seasoned businesspeople and will probably be the easiest to deal with. They are knowledgeable about what they sell, can quickly make offers, give accurate shipping information, and make sound business decisions.

Bargaining isn't a one-way process at all. Balinese enjoy it and respect you more if you bargain. It's a pleasurable way merchants have to relate to you. It should be leisurely, lighthearted, and friendly. It's a theatrical event in which you play the role of "the buyer." Never get angry, and don't feel bad about offering less than what they ask.

Bargaining can be a prolonged exchange lasting days and even weeks. Take your time; the more patient you are, the less you're likely to pay. Get to know the seller and his family, build a personal relationship, go back again and again, have tea, and keep it civil. He or she might be in a better mood or need the money more in a few hours, days, or weeks.

Finally, *never* pass up an item you really want—even if you have to pay an inflated price for it—because chances are you will not run across the same item again, or will be unable to obtain it. When you get back home, the money you spent will seem a paltry amount anyway.

Fixed Price

Shops only offering fixed prices (*harga pas*) are a growing trend now and offer a shopping environment where Western shoppers will feel immediately comfortable. In these shops, the price is unbargainable with no discounts or reductions. This is most often the case in high-priced hotels and tourist shops. It is always the case in supermarkets and department stores.

If you see a price posted or attached to an item, it's a fixed-price shop. If no "fixed price" sign is posted or prices are not attached to merchandise, there's room to haggle. All the verbally stated prices are merely starting points from which you should receive anything from a 10 to 60% discount.

INFORMATION AND SERVICES

Tourist Offices

The most convenient for Denpasar is the **Badung Tourist Office** (Jl. Surapati 7) on the *alun-alun* (Puputan Square), which provides outstanding information in fluent English and free brochures. Office hours are Mon.-Sat. 0800-1300, except Friday, which is 0800-1030. From Monday to Thursday 0700-1530, and on Friday 0800-1030, you may telephone this office for information at (0361) 234569, or telephone 166 only.

The **Bali Government Tourist Office** (Dinas Pariwisata Pemerintah Propinsi Daierah Tingkat I Bali), the headquarters office for the whole island, is out of town a bit in the Renon Civic Center (Jl. S. Parman, Niti Mandala, tel. 0361-222387 or 226313). Open Mon.-Thurs. 0730-1430, Friday 0730-1200. Chances are that this office has a wider selection of literature, though the office downtown dispenses better oral information.

There's also a tourist information desk at Ngurah Rai Airport in the international terminal, and a hotel information desk in the domestic terminal. In Kuta, a **Government Tourist Information Centre** is on Jl. Bena Sari (tel. 0361-751419), open 0700-1400, closed Saturday and Sunday. In Ubud, Bina Wisata Ubud is next to the village head's office. Each regency also has a tourist office (see below), but in several of them—such as in Gianyar town—the staff speaks no English.

Around Bali, the tourist offices of the other regencies are: **Diparda Tingkat II Tabanan,** Jl. Gunung Agung, Tabanan 82151 (tel. 0361-811602); **Diparda Tingkat II Gianyar,** J. Ngurah Rai 21, Gianyar 80551 (tel. 0361-93401); **Diparda Tingkat II Klungkung,** Jl. Surapati 3, Klungkung 80751 (tel. 0366-21448); **Diparda Tingkat II Bangli,** d/a Kantor Dinas Perkebunan Tk. II Bangli, Jl. Brigjen. Ngurah Rai, Bangli 80613 (tel. 0366-91537); **Diparda Tingkat II Karangasem,** Jl. Ngurah Rai 31, Amlapura 80817 (tel. 0363-21002 or 21003); **Diparda Tingkat II Jembrana,** Jl. Dr. Setiabudhi 1, Negara 82251 (tel. 0365-41060); **Diparda Tingkat II Buleleng,** d/a Gedung Sasana Budaya, Jl. Veteran 23, Singaraja 81117 (tel. 0362-61141).

Look for the *Bali Tourist Guide* (free from hotels) and the *Bali Path Finder* (Rp10,000) and *Ubud Post (Napi Orti),* issued by the Ubud Tourist Office in Ubud. The pamphlet *Calendar of Events* lists all of Bali's major religious holidays and annual cultural events. Indonesian embassies and consulates overseas as well as Garuda offices around the world dispense promotional literature, but publications go out of print quickly and may not see a reprint.

Immigration

The *Kantor Imigrasi* (Immigration Office) is in the Renon Complex, Niti Mandala, Denpasar, tel. (0361) 227828; another office is near the airport on Jl. Ngurah Rai, Tuban, tel. (0361) 751038. Both are open Mon.-Thurs. 0700-1300, Friday 0700-1100, Saturday 0700-1200. Follow the dress code chart on the wall. If you don't dress properly, these bureaucrats won't even talk to you. T-shirts, halter tops, and bathing suits don't cut it.

Always apply for an extension three or four days prior to the expiration of your entry stamp or else you'll be held up at the airport and may even miss your flight. This applies even if you're one day over your two-month allowable period. Valid reasons for going over are a medical emergency, a missed flight, or a flight or ship you must board just a few days away. A letter or ticket confirming your departure date makes the extension easier to get.

Legal Services

There are now several, private, one-stop visa services on Bali that do the legal paperwork necessary for visa extensions and renewals: **CV Jasa Bali,** Jl. Legian Kaja 486 (tel./fax 0361-757008), and Wayan's **CV Jasa Werda Dwi Karya, Biro Jasa** (tel. 0361-975599). Wayan's office is just 100 meters from his Siti Homestay in Peliatan (near Ubud) in Gianyar. They both can help you obtain a social/cultural/business visa as well as provide legal services and notary assistance.

Business Services

The best business services on Bali for sending and receiving faxes, making international phone calls (IDD), for secretarial service, translations, courier service, and even real estate are: **Ary's Wisata Travel Service** on Ubud's main street; **Cafe Krakatoa** (tel. 0361-752849) in Legian; and **Ra Business and Communication Center** (tel. 0361-281253) in Sanur.

Police Stations
Badung, Jl. Diponegoro 10 (tel. 0361-234928) and Jl. A. Yani, Denpasar (tel. 0361-225456); **Bangli,** Jl. Nusantara, Bangli (tel. 0366-971072); **Bualu,** Jl. Bypass Nusa Dua (tel. 0361-772110); **Buleleng,** Jl. Pramuka, Singaraja (tel. 0362-241510); **Gianyar,** Jl. Ngurah Rai, Gianyar Town (tel. 0361-973110); **Jembrana,** Jl. Pahlawan, Negara (tel. 0365-110); **Karangasem,** Jl. Bhayangkara (tel. 0366-110); **Klungkung,** Jl. Untung Surapati (tel. 0366-221115); **Kuta,** Jl. Bypass Tuban, Tuban (tel. 0361-751598); **Sanur,** Jl. Bypass Ngruah Rai, Sanur (tel. 0361-288597).

Emergency Numbers
Ambulance, tel. 118; **police,** tel. 110; **fire,** tel. 113; **Search and Rescue,** tel. (0361) 751111.

Foreign Consulates in Bali
Netherlands, Jl. Imam Bonjol 599, Denpasar (tel. 0361-751904 or 751497, fax 752777); **France,** Jl. Raya Sesetan 46 D, Banjar Pesanggaran, Denpasar (tel. 0361-233555); **Japan,** Jl. Moh. Yamin 9, Renon, Denpasar (tel. 0361-231308 or 234808); **Germany,** Jl. Pantai Karang 17, Sanur (tel. 0361-288535); **Italy,** Jl. Padang Galak, Sanur (tel. 0361-288996 or 288896).

Switzerland/Austria, c/o Swiss Restaurant, Jl. Pura Bagus Taruna, Legian (tel. 0361-751735); **Sweden/Finland,** Segara Village Hotel, Sanur (tel. 0361-288407 or 288408); **U.S.A.,** Jl. Sanur Ayu 5, Sanur (tel. 0361-288478); **Denmark/Norway,** Jl. Jayagiri, Gang VIII/10, Denpasar (tel. 0361-235098 or 233053); **Australia,** Jl. Prof. Moh. Yamin Kav. 51, P.O. Box 243, Renon, Denpasar (tel. 0361-235092 or 235093, fax 231990).

Alcoholics Anonymous Meetings
Ten to 20% of the traveling public may appreciate learning that AA Meetings are held in Legian at the Dhyana Pura Hotel Coffee Shop (tel. 0361-751442 or 751443) on Tuesday at 0800, Wednesday at 2000, and Friday at 1800. In Ubud, meetings are held at Mumbul's Restaurant on Thursday at 2000. In Gianyar, meetings are held on Sunday at 1630 in the Waterfall Restaurant en route to Gianyar town.

Religious Services
Most churches and mosques are in the Denpasar area: Catholic Church, Jl. Kepundung; Protestant Maranatha, Jl. Surapati; Seventh Day Adventist, Jl. Surapati; Evangelical Church, Jl. Melati; Raya Mosque, Jl. Hasanudin; Annur Mosque, Jl. Diponegoro; Taqwa Mosque, Jl. Supratman; Al-Hassan Mosque, Bali Beach Hotel, Sanur.

Catholic Mass: Bali Beach Hotel on Saturday at 0500-0600 (Legong Room); Bali Hyatt Hotel, Saturday at 1800-1900 (Hibiscus Room); Church of St. Francis Xavier, Kuta/Tuban, Sunday at 0800; Bali Solo Hotel, Sunday 1700 (Conference Hall I); Nusa Dua Beach Hotel, Sunday at 1800 (Garuda Room).

Protestant Service: Bali Beach Hotel in Sanur on Sunday 1830-1930. Inter-denominational Service: Nusa Dua Beach Hotel (Garuda Room) at 1730 in Nusa Dua.

Ecclesiastical Service: Jl. Raya Tuban, Sunday at 1830-1930, in Tuban; Legian Church on Gang Menuh (off Jl. Legian), Sunday at 1700 in Kuta; Bali Beach Hotel, Sanur, Sunday at 1830-1930.

Pentecostal: Jl. Kresna 19, Denpasar, Sunday at 2000; Jl. Raya Kuta, Sunday at 1800 and 2000 (tel. 0361-751504); Bali Sol (Conference Hall) in Nusa Dua at 1700.

Marriage Services
Some hotels in south Bali specialize in marrying Westerners for about US$1000, which includes the priest for the ceremony, blessings, witnesses, lunch and dinner for four, traditional Balinese wedding attire *(pakaian adat),* travel to Tanah Lot for photographs, other photo ops, a photo album, and champagne. **Bolare Beach Bungalows** (P.O. Box 256, Denpasar 80001, tel./fax 0361-35464) next to the Dewata Beach Resort in Petitingit is only one of many hotels offering this unique service which some have unkindly dubbed "masquerade tourism."

Laundry
Laundry is twice as cheap as in the West. Your accommodations will almost always offer a laundry

service. There are no laundromats on Bali. In a homestay or *losmen,* there is often an *ibu* or one of the houseboys who does the washing. The charge depends on the article. Sometimes they don't even charge, but in those cases give a tip. Guests may also wash their clothes in the sinks or in the courtyard's *mandi.* Buy laundry soap, Rp400 per packet, at any grocery. An inexpensive nylon clothesline or length of rope, plus a few clothes pegs, are smart items to take to Indonesia.

If you're staying in an upmarket hotel, try to find a laundry service outside your hotel as starred hotels could easily charge you US$15-20 to wash and press an average load of laundry. The tax alone may account for a fifth of the cost. In Kuta, Poppies Lane II has several laundries that wash your clothes at a much more reasonable rate: Rp1000 for a shirt, Rp500 for a T-shirt, Rp2000 for a pair of pants, Rp500 for a pair of socks.

Big hotels offer drycleaning; every room has a price list. Don't ever put valuable garments, such as an expensive silk shirt, into the hands of *any* laundry service—they may ruin it. If it's a small, budget hotel doing your laundry, you need at least one good sunny day for them to complete the job. Better allow two or three days. Bigger, more expensive hotels have laundry facilities and can even offer 12-hour express laundry service for a surcharge.

Babysitting
Though a housegirl receives a wage of about Rp35,000 per month, you have to give more for a babysitter who is trained in first aid and childcare. Informally ask her. Expect to pay around Rp85,000 per month for a full-time babysitter, and even more if she's able to speak English. For more on babysitting, see the special topic "Traveling with Children."

POSTAL SERVICES

Incoming Mail
Most travelers use the poste restante service to pick up mail in Bali. Since Bali's main post office is inconveniently located on Jl. Raya Puputan (open Mon.-Sat. 0800-2000, closed Sunday, tel. 0361-223565) in the administrative district of Denpasar (Renon), have your mail sent to any of the island's branch post of-

fices. In Sanur, one is located in Banjar Taman, in Singaraja on Jl. Gajah Mada.

Ida's Postal Agent on Jl. Legian in Kuta, tel. (0361) 751574, sells stamps, postcards, phrasebooks, aerograms, stationery, and offers postal service, registered post, and free poste restante. Just show your ID, that's all. Less convenient is Kuta's main post office at Jl. Raya Tuban. The poste restante at Ubud's post office (Jl. Jembawan 1) is a free-for-all and none too reliable. Letters can go astray. Have letters sent to a hotel if you can.

Since letters are frequently missorted (such as under "P" when they should be under "B"), all mail should be addressed to you with your last name in caps and underlined, using only your first and middle initials. You might be able to locate a missorted letter under your first name. Tell people back home to put your name first, then poste restante, Kantor Pos, the town name, Regency name, Bali, and lastly Republik Indonesia. A fee of Rp50 is charged to pick up a letter at any of Bali's poste restante windows.

Sending Letters
In the post office, go to the window with a scale first; your letter has to be weighed and given a stamp value. Sometimes you then have to take it to another window for stamps. Go up to the clump of people and push your letter as far as possible through the barred window to gain the attention of the postal clerk. Then try to squeeze your money into some gap between all the other hands. These are acceptable manners at Indonesian post offices.

The glue on Indonesian stamps is weak. After getting stamps, take them over to the glue stands and reglue them. Stamps can also be purchased at shops selling postcards, and most of the larger hotels sell stamps and collect letters for mailing, as well as handle faxes.

For international mail, always use the express service *(kilat),* which takes only five to seven days to the Americas, Europe, or Australia. Airmail costs for postcards are Rp1000 to the U.S., Rp800 to Europe, and Rp800 to Australia. An airmail letter costs Rp1550 to the U.S., but handy and fast aerograms are only Rp750.

Bring strong envelopes with you to Bali to make sure your exposed film or letter arrives safely. Register anything of value. The charge for registering a letter *(surat tercatat)* is about equal to postage, but the chances will greatly improve—though not be guaranteed—that your letter will reach its destination. Letters bound for overseas or domestic delivery may be registered at any post office branch.

SHIPPING ARTS AND CRAFTS

Art shops will usually wrap your purchases in layers of newspaper, binding the whole in plastic twine with a convenient carrying handle, an arrangement that would never withstand the rigors of surface post. To better protect your wares for shipping overseas, the best padding is foam carpet backing available from carpet stores. Also look for sturdy bamboo or rattan baskets from Sukawati, which run Rp3000-5000 for large ones. Found in dozens of shapes and sizes, these baskets have lids and hold up to 10 (the limit for overseas parcels) tightly packed kilos. Their interlocking construction can withstand almost any kind of punishment except crushing or penetration by sharp objects. Fabrics are the most damage-proof craft to send back home. Cheap colorful Chinese *tali,* plastic twine, is used to bind them. Some of the big art shops along the tourist corridor to Ubud buy bulky and heavy crafts—even some stone sculpture—by surface post.

Shipping Companies

Bali has specialized air express companies at Kuta, Legian, Seminyak, Sanur, and Ngurah Rai International Airport, so if you're buying crafts in the Outer Islands wait until you get to Bali to air or sea freight them. Some companies are more competent than others, and different companies can charge wildly varying prices. Look around and query every exporter you meet. Dealers can't be trusted to recommend reliable shippers as they invariably send you to their brother-in-laws (nepotism is rampant in Bali). In any case, be patient. Don't be surprised if it takes longer than they promised. The shipper will tell you what you want to hear.

These companies take care of everything: domestic and international air cargo, freight forwarding, container and warehouse service, packing and surface shipping, insurance, customs clearance, DHL (door to door) worldwide

express service, postal agent. Shipping is expensive, charging for one square meter a total of US$270, which includes US$35 for packing (crating), US$25 for documents, US$25 for handling, US$20 for transport. Everything is trucked overland first to Surabaya. A 20-cubic-foot container costs US$2000-3000 to ship anywhere in the world.

If you pack it yourself, you might get the price down. Also, check on the "unaccompanied baggage" rates on your flight home, which may be cheaper than air freight. Some airlines only allow you 20 kg of "free" luggage. Garuda usually won't let you check in more than two large pieces of luggage; for a third piece you'll be charged. For example, it costs US$110 for an extra bag from Denpasar to Los Angeles. Have them paste "fragile" stickers on any parcels containing breakables.

Several good shippers in Ubud: **CV. Ary's Jasa Wisata** (Ary's tourist Service Centre), Jl. Raya Ubud 80571 (tel. 0361-975162 or 975523, fax 975162); PT Bali Purnama Cargo, Jl. Jembawan (tel. 0361-975033), near the post office. Quality problems? **PT Bali Surya Agung Cargo & Buying Agents** (tel. 0361-975547, fax 974361) can help you find it, buy it, get the right quality, and get it shipped. Wir sprechen Deutsch.

Other cargo agents: C.V. Bali Great, Jl. Raya Kuta 93, Kuta (tel. 0361-755649, fax 756761); **Alpha Sigma CV,** Jl. Raya Imam Bonjol 98, Denpasar 80361 (tel. 0361-227768 or 227760); **Bali Delta Express CV,** Jl. Kartini 58, Denpasar 80112 (tel. 0361-223340 or 224430); **Bali International Cargo CV,** Jl. Raya Sanur 2, Sanur (tel. 0361-288563).

PT Bayu Pesona Cargo, Tegehe, Batubulan, Gianyar (tel./fax 0361-298067), just up the road from the *bemo* terminal, offers worldwide packing and shipping service by air, sea, or land, international air and sea freight, domestic door-to-door service, household and office moving, and exhibition freight forwarding. Prices are very competitive.

Also receiving good reports for reliability are **PT Golden Bali Express,** Jl. Hayam Wuruk 162 A, Denpasar (tel. 0361-238174, fax 235303), with branch offices in Kuta (tel. 0361-751771) and at the airport (tel. 0361-751011, ext. 4114); and **PT Orient Pacific Express,** Jl. Diponegoro 155, Denpasar (tel. 0361-234791, fax 234366). **Aero Sea Cargo,** Jl. Dhyana Pura 2, Seminyak (tel. 0361-753531), offers two safe ways of packing. Their hanging system, with each item hung on a frame before going into the container, is the best way to pack ready-to-wear garments. Their cardbox system is suitable for more durable goods like furniture and garments.

UPS, Jl. Raya Sesetan 118, Denpasar (tel. 0361-232720), offers package and document delivery with electronic tracking capability to over 180 countries. Rates: 15 kg to San Francisco costs US$312, five kg to San Francisco US$170, 15 kg to Copenhagen US$356, five kg to Copengagen US$195, letter to New Zealand US$20, letter to Frankfurt US$24, letter to Sydney US$26.

Another nifty service is **VIP**—"Very Important Package"—offering same-day door-to-door service or overnight door-to-door service anywhere in Indonesia. You can easily check the location and status of your package anytime. VIP will pick up your package until 1900, or you can drop it off at their office at Jl. Diponegoro 196 (tel. 0361-240033, 231329, or 756879, fax 756879) until 2200.

Paket Pos

Seamail or surface post *(paket pos)* is the cheapest way of all to send goods home. It will cost you a trip into Denpasar, two hours of your time, and average out to about US$3 per kilo. The most efficient *paket pos* (parcel post) office is in Denpasar where overseas-bound packages may be posted, insured, and registered. Customs inspectors will open the parcel to make sure you're not smuggling out antiquities, so don't bother sealing it up.

Packers will be on hand to package your goods securely for Rp5000-6000. Get there as soon as it opens at 0800 because the postal inspectors, who must inspect every parcel, may go home at 1300.

Sample seamail rates from Bali to U.S.: up to one kg, Rp7250; over one kg but less than three, Rp12,350; over three kg but less than five, Rp17,550; over five kg but less than 10, Rp28,900. To Europe: up to one kg, Rp8000; over one kg but less than three, Rp10,250; over three kg but less than five, Rp13,050; over five kg but less than 10, Rp17,750.

When sending packages, always max out your parcel to 10 kg because you're paying for the five- to 10-kg rate anyway. Likewise, on the three- to five-kg rate, max out to five kilos. In case of loss or damage, put your name and address on a slip of paper inside the parcel as well as outside. International seamail can take up to six months, but it usually takes six to eight weeks.

If you have a lot to send back, try surface instead of a more expensive shipping company. The postal agent on Jl. Legian on Kuta offers parcel service with the same rates as official government rates, but they charge Rp10,000-15,000 for packaging. Kuta's main post office does not have *paket pos* service for parcels over one kilo.

COMMUNICATIONS

Both domestic and international calls can routinely be made from any hotel with an in-house phone system. Pay phones can now be found virtually all over Bali—look for a three-meter-tall blue sign with a picture of a phone on its end and an arrow pointing down to the phone. Finding a working one with a phone directory could be difficult.

Take note that in 1993 all phone numbers in southern Bali were changed to accommodate the demand for more phones. Nearly all numbers in this part of Bali now have six digits. In the Denpasar/Sanur area, this was achieved by adding a "2" in front of the old number, but there have been some variations to this: Kuta numbers, for instance, added a "7." All the changes have been made, and there are currently recorded messages in English and Indonesian for misdialed numbers.

Local calls (Rp100 for three minutes) from public telephones are fairly easy to place, though it's a hassle collecting the heavy Rp100 coins. There are two handy public telephones outside of Ngurah Rai Airport's international terminal which are normally in working order. The number for directory assistance is 108; use the Alpha-Bravo system in spelling out proper names. The number for the police all over Bali is 110 (like 911 in the U.S.A.). All operators speak at least rudimentary English.

AREA CODES AND OTHER USEFUL NUMBERS

Bali Area Codes

South and central Bali, which includes regencies of Badung, Denpasar, Gianyar, and southern Tabanan: 0361

Klungkung and Karangasem Regencies and southern Bangli Regency of eastern Bali: 0366

Buleleng Regency and northern Bangli and Tabanan Regencies: 0362

Jembrana Regency: 0365

Useful Local Numbers

Local and long-distance directory assistance: 106

Local and long-distance operator: 100

International directory assistance: 102

International operator: 101

International Calls from Bali

Dial 00 + IDD (International Direct Dialing) country code + area code (minus the first "0") + your telephone credit card number

International Calls to Bali

Dial the international access code (Australia 0011, Canada 011, U.K. 00, U.S.A. 011, etc.) + 62 (Indonesia's country code) + Indonesia's area code (minus the first "0") + telephone number

---

If you're in southern Bali, calls to Tabanan, Gianyar, Badung, Ubud, and Denpasar Regencies are considered local "city" calls, while calls to Bali's more distant regencies like Karangasem, Singaraja, Buleleng, and Jembrana are considered long-distance *(interlokal)*.

Depending upon their size and class, hotels charge from Rp250 to Rp3000 for local calls made from your room. From 0600 to 0900, long-distance calls from hotels are usually Rp1000 for three minutes; from 0900 to 1400, business hours, Rp1750 for three minutes; from 1400 to 2000, Rp1000 for three minutes; and from 2000 to 0600 a 50% discount (Rp500) applies.

But the rate is arbitrary; hotels could charge you anywhere from Rp1000 to Rp5000 for each long-distance call. For example, an *interlokal*

call made from the Kartika Plaza Hotel in Kuta to Singaraja costs Rp4700 for three minutes, and a call made from Candidasa's Puri Bagus to Legian is Rp3000. The Booklet "International Direct Dialing and Other Telephone Charges," found near the phone in hotel rooms, gives a breakdown of the hotel's rates.

For calls outside of Bali to other cities in Indonesia, dial long distance by first dialing the city code number, for example, Malang 0341, Banda Aceh 0851, then the local number. The archipelago is divided into five zones, and calls are priced according to zone. The rate ranges from Rp4000 to Rp12,000 per minute.

If you're doing a lot of calling, an Indonesian telephone credit card, or *kartu telpon,* can be bought in Denpasar's supermarkets as well as at many hotels. Look for the sign Kartu Telpon Dijual Disini. These very convenient cards can be used all over Indonesia at telephones that accept them—in hotel lobbies, train stations, and airports. You choose how many units you want— 140 units is Rp11,000, 500 units is Rp30,000. A call to Amsterdam is 140 units. Keep your card away from magnetic fields.

International Telecommunications

International calls are handled by Indosat, a state-owned enterprise that uses an international satellite and microwave system linked with 127 countries. Since the early '90s, Bali has experienced an explosion in sophisticated communications technology which has brought the world much closer. Nowadays Balinese aren't as likely to gather in the *balai banjar;* they'll just call up their friends and chat. Now if your phone doesn't work and you call the telephone company, somebody actually comes to fix it. Sound quality has improved considerably, too.

Presently foreign visitors may avail themselves of a wide network of **Warung Telekomunikasi** (Wartel), or privately owned telephone offices, some technically more together than others. Sometimes only two of four booths operate properly, and out of 45 minutes spent in one, six of eight Westerners trying to make calls may have initial difficulties. Though the person in charge may repeatedly ask if you want to cancel, it pays to persevere.

For International Direct Dialing (IDD), do it from your hotel room or go to one of Bali's many

Wartel. Dial the country code (U.S. 01, Australia 61, etc.), then the area code and the local number. You'll be charged according to the country zone you dial. To get AT&T service on a call to the U.S.A., dial first the access code 0080110, then give your telephone credit card number, then the telephone number you want. When you get back home, the charge will appear on your telephone bill.

Although it's a thrill dialing direct in minutes to a friend in New York from your Nusa Dua hotel room overlooking the pool, hotels routinely levy preposterous surcharges for in-room international calls—as much as Rp35,000 for a three minute call. It'll cost US$2.50 for the calling card service charge, plus US$4.07 for the first minute, then US$1.63 for each additional minute. In other words, a 15 minute call to New York will cost around US$26.89 (14 x 1.63 + 4.07 = 26.89). Calls to the U.K. can be made for Rp31,000 for three minutes.

Instead, take a *bemo* to the nearest Wartel, some open 24 hours a day seven days a week. There's a Wartel within five minutes walk from the Ngurah Rai Airport's domestic terminal building, going toward the road where you get *bemo* to Kuta. In Kuta, a Wartel, open til 2100, is on Jl. Bakung Sari on the top floor of a two-story building which also has a Korean restaurant on the top floor. This office is about 10 minute's walk from the corner of Jl. Ngurah Rai.

In Ubud, a Wartel is on the main road between the *pasar* and the Kantor Pos, open til 2000. Another is near Nomad's Restaurant. There's also an office in Padangbai, open til 2000, and a 24-hour, seven days a week Wartel in Amlapura. *Bemo* going into Amlapura drive past it on the way to the *pasar*/terminal, but not on leaving the town.

Collect (reverse-charge) calls are only accepted now between Indonesia and Europe, America, and Australia. Remember it's at least 10% cheaper to dial direct than to have an operator assist you. Person-to-person calls are almost twice as expensive as station-to-station calls, with reduced rates on Sunday. The collect call fee for a long-distance call is Rp2500, and the cancellation fee is Rp1000.

Home Country Direct is a service whereby you merely lift the receiver on a special phone, press a button next to the country you want to dial (20 different countries participating), and speak directly to an operator in your home country. One phone is outside the airport's international terminal, others are found in Kuta, Ubud, and in Sanur's Bali Beach Hotel. It's marvelous to be able to talk to a U.S., British, or German operator, give her your credit card number, and be connected in 30 seconds.

Other High-Tech Services

Shops offering photocopies at Rp20 per copy are found in Denpasar, Kuta, Sanur, Ubud, Singaraja, Lovina, and Candidasa. Telegrams can be sent from Bali's *kantor telekomunikasi* (telephone offices) run by the government's telephone system monopoly, Permuntel. Fax machines are available in major hotels which boast "business centers" like the Kartika Plaza in Kuta and the Bali Hyatt in Sanur. Wartel centers also send faxes for Rp10,000 or receive faxes for Rp1000. Computers are popping up everywhere in Bali now. Your hotel may offer computer connected services.

TIME

There are three time zones in Indonesia. Bali shares the same time zone as Nusatenggara, but the neighboring island of Java is one hour behind Bali. West Indonesia standard time (Sumatra, Java) is Greenwich mean time plus seven hours; central Indonesia standard time (Kalimantan, Bali, Nusatenggara) is GMT plus eight hours; east Indonesia standard time (Maluku, Irian Jaya) is GMT plus nine hours.

What this means is (daylight saving time excluded) that at 0500 in the morning in London, it's 1200 in Jakarta, 1300 in Denpasar and Lombok, and 1400 in Ambon and Jayapura. What time is it elsewhere when it's 1200 on Bali? It would be 0400 in London, 1100 in Singapore, 1400 in Sydney, 2000 in San Francisco, and 2300 in New York.

Since Bali is only eight degrees south of the equator, days and nights are about the same length. On Bali, about midpoint in the archipelago, the sun rises 90 minutes before it does in West Sumatra. There is full daylight before 0630 and total nightfall at 1830 when the sun drops out of the sky like a lead balloon.

Nighttime is lively on Bali. You have to admire the Balinese ability to go without sleep, such as during an all-night *wayang*. Even as little children, they start to practice staying awake. Consequently, the best time of the day for people-watching is after sunset.

Business Hours

Business hours are flexible, depending on numerous variables. The workweek on Bali can seem convoluted because of the country's attempt to accommodate two separate religious schemes, meshing the Islamic calendar with the Gregorian. Consequently, banks, offices, and schools close early on Friday for the Islamic Sabbath, but Sunday is also observed as a day of rest. Saturday, meanwhile, is a partial work day, so the Balinese workweek consists of four full days and two partial days. During major Islamic holidays such as the monthlong Muslim fast, restaurants on overwhelmingly Hindu Bali are unaffected.

Always get an early start for bureaucratic offices, before the lines get long and the day grows hot. Generally speaking, government offices open at 0800 Mon.-Sat., closing at 1500 or 1600 Mon.-Thurs., 1100 or 1130 on Friday, and 1400 on Saturday. Banks are open Mon.-Fri. 0800-1200, Saturday 0800-1100. Bank branches in hotels often remain open into the afternoon, and moneychangers in the tourist centers and the bank windows at the airport stay open until up to 2100.

Shops operate from 0900 to 1800 or later, six days a week. Shopping arcades and the new Balinese "supermarkets" frequently remain open until 2100. Expect businesses to take midday lunch breaks of an hour or more, during which time no one answers the phone, even in Denpasar.

ELECTRICITY

Because of the power generated by a heat conversion plant at Bondalem (near Tejakula), power is fairly reliable, with about 75% of Bali's villages supplied with electricity. Current may be 110V, 50 cycles AC, but most areas have by now completely changed over to 220-240V, 50 cycles AC. Some residences and hotels may even have both 110 and 220. Always check to make sure which current is installed before plugging in expensive electrical appliances.

One almost pines for the days of the oil lamps, which used to blend in so well with the environment. But the amount of electricity in some village *kampung* can be absolutely minimal—solitary, dim, 25-watt bulbs, which you can replace with higher-wattage bulbs. In the larger towns, humming fluorescent lamps are all too prevalent. The lack of street lighting can make for hazardous walking at night. Ubud, Kuta, and Candidasa's back lanes may be pitch dark and run alongside treacherous open drainage ditches. Always carry a flashlight.

PHOTOGRAPHY

Ever since Gregor Krause's photos stunned Europe in 1912, Bali has been photographed by some of the world's best professional photographers. With its lush landscapes, colorful markets, spectacular temple sites, long colorful processions, and above all its friendly people, Bali is an endlessly photogenic island with thousands of subjects popping up constantly.

Get up with the Balinese at sunrise to catch the best village scenes in clear, crisp colors—women carrying loads on their heads to market, children bathing in streams, fishermen casting their nets. Light diffusion on the equator differs from that in the temperate zones, so be aware of intense sunlight and haze from around 1000 to 1500, which causes color film to flatten and wash out. A polarizing filter will cut down on this, while a lens hood will reduce reflection or direct sunlight on the lens.

When photographing performances, even in the dim, flickering, phantasmagoric light of a *kecak* dance, the latest low-lux camcorders can produce quite acceptable recordings. But with so many amateur filmmakers present at these dances, it's difficult to get a good shooting position. Your best bet is to use a tripod from one of the elevated back rows; this way, you'll have an unobstructed shot, and you won't block the view of others. If you have a handheld camera, try to get a seat in the front row, where you can follow the action with a wide-angle lens.

For those sunset shots on Kuta Beach or Tanah Lot, switching to the manual sunshine setting rather than the automatic white-balance will get you deeper, richer, more exotic colors. Or take your light exposure reading off the sky rather than the bright sun, then shoot directly into the sunset. If you use a camcorder, use the wide-angle mode and a tripod to keep the scene steady. When photographing monkeys in the shade of the forest at Ubud's Monkey Forest or at Sangeh, you'll need a strong flash. Remember also that the lush tropical green of *sawah* or jungle usually photographs better if backlit by the sun.

Equipment

For recreational photography, leave your cumbersome changeable-lens, 35mm SLRs at home. If you're struggling with two bags full of photo equipment, you'll only worry about your gear. Instead, take a new generation, 35mm, fully automatic subcompact.

For camera repair, try **Prima Photo** on Jl. Thamrin in Denpasar. **Camera Service & Repair,** Pertokoan Terminal Tegal Sari No. 27 (no telephone), on Jl. Imam Bonjol, has a better reputation—at prices much lower than in the West. This shop is in the same complex/terminal where you catch *bemo* to Kuta.

Film

Color film on Bali is cheaper than in Europe or North America and is widely available. With the suffocatingly humid climate, make sure it has been stored in an air-conditioned environment. The most popular 35mm brand is Fuji, in a full range of ASA/DIN ratings. Although a 36-exposure Kodachrome 64 slide film is for sale at a cost of around Rp15,000 for film and processing, the processing is unreliable unless it is sent to Jakarta or Australia.

By contrast, a 36-exposure roll of Fujicolor print film (100 ASA) costs around Rp7000, 200 ASA is Rp8000. Batteries are also less expensive here: a six-volt lithium battery is Rp25,000, while in the U.S.A. it's US$17. You'll find good selections of film at dozens of photo shops on Kuta, Legian, Sanur, and Denpasar, and at most of the high-priced hotels.

Bali Foto Centre (Jl. Raya Kuta 121, tel. 0361-751329 or 751373) in Kuta carries more than 50 film brands, kept in an air-conditioned showcase, including such leading world brands

as Agfa, Polaroid, a range of black-and-white films, as well as film in larger formats (9mm), Super 8 movie film, and videotapes. Prices tend to be higher than back home.

Printing

Any one of the dozens of photo shops in Kuta, Legian, Nusa Dua, Sanur, or Denpasar can develop and print color film in just two hours or less. Slide film takes five to seven days, movie film seven. The quality is generally good. At around Rp350 per print, color print costs are lower than in most Western countries. This equals to about Rp8500 for 24 exposures, Rp12,600 for 35 exposures. Most of the hotels of south Bali offer Kodak and Fuji film development and printing service. If reception calls, someone from a photo shop comes around and picks up your film and then delivers your prints three hours later in a mini-album. Most hotels sell film too.

An alternative to printing on Bali is to just store your exposed film, which can keep up to two months before processing if kept in a cool, dark place, or send your exposed film via airmail to processing centers back home. Kodak mailers sell for around US$10-13 for both film and mailer in U.S. camera shops or through the mail-order houses of New York. By using mailers, all your processed slide film will be waiting for you when you get back home.

Etiquette for Photographers

The Balinese are polite, congenial, and usually willing to have you record them and their ceremonies on film. Although there are no religious prohibitions against taking photos of people in prayer, it's extremely impolite to photograph people bathing in streams or bathing places.

As a courtesy before taking a photo, first ask permission with the word *permisi* or an expressive hand gesture making your intention clear. Please respect refusals. Being pushy will make it not only unpleasant for you but also for photographers who follow. The discreet use of a telephoto lens obviates having to ask permission.

Be aware of the sacredness of many of the ceremonies you may witness; act accordingly when using a flash or maneuvering for shots. Although a powerful flash is sometimes the only means by which to capture the nighttime dances of Bali, it is distracting to the audience and mars the performance.

Unless there happens to be a festival taking place inside, ask first before photographing the interiors of temples. It's highly unlikely that permission will be refused. A modest fee may be charged for a camera and a higher one for a movie or video camera. This fee may apply to the exterior, interior, and even surrounding grounds.

EDUCATION AND MUSEUMS

Study Opportunities

The **School for International Training** sponsors a college semester in Bali intended for students interested in artistic and cultural traditions and in how change affects traditional societies. An important component of this 15-week-long program is independent study, as well as language instruction, classes in life and culture, and fieldwork methodology. For information, write the Admissions Office, College Semester Abroad, School for International Training, Kipling Rd., Brattleboro, VT 05302-0676 (tel. 802-257-7751).

Bali Language Training & Cultural Centre, sponsored by the Mastapa Garden Hotel of Kuta Beach (Jl. Legian 139, P.O. Box 3013, Denpasar, tel. 0361-751660, fax 755098), offers courses in Balinese painting, carving, dancing, music, *batik,* and the Indonesian language. Regular classes are 72 hours per week for 12 weeks; the intensive is 40 hours per week for four weeks. Fees run US$15 for enrollment, US$700 for the regular course, US$500 for the intensive course. Price includes field trips.

The Arts of Bali is a nine-seminar course on Balinese culture, literature, painting, music, dancing, archaeology, and sculpture presented by Ki Mantle Hood, Seminar Director (2816 Deerfield Dr., Ellicott City, MD 21043, fax 410-313 8500), in collaboration with the Sekolah Tinggi Seni Indonesia of Denpasar, Bali. Incidentally, the SSTI Press publishes a Journal of Balinese Arts called *Mudra: Jurnal Seni Budaya.*

Each summer, **The Society of Balinese Studies** (SBS, or Perhimpunan Pengajian Budaya Bali) holds an international interdisciplinary conference covering a wide range of topics on Baliology. Conference fees are Rp20,000 per day or Rp50,000 for three days for Indonesians, US$20 per day or US$50 for three days for non-Indonesians. The exchange of views is about as frank and open as you'll ever get in an Indonesian academic setting. Keep your eye out in the BACN newsletter (see below) for upcoming SBS conferences.

Museums

One of the first things you should do is visit the **Bali Museum** at Puputan Square, Denpasar, for an introduction to the archaeology, crafts, building styles, and the folk, traditional, modern, and theatrical arts of Bali. **Museum Puri Lukisan** in Ubud houses a collection of modern Balinese paintings and some sculptures from the 1920s. The **Neka Museum** (also a gallery) in Campuan (near Ubud) houses a collection of some of Bali's best contemporary paintings.

Also visit the **Museum Le Mayeur** in Sanur, which contains the works of the Belgian painter Le Mayeur, who arrived on Bali in 1932 and lived there for 26 years. The **Pejeng Archaeological Museum,** one km north of Bedulu on the road to Tampaksiring, contains megalithic and Bronze Age artifacts found on Bali.

The **Agung Rai Museum of Art** (tel. 0361-974228, fax 974229, e-mail armaubud@den-pasar.wasantara.net.id) in Peliatan, near Ubud in Gianyar District, is a dynamic new enterprise consisting of a whole complex of ventures including a hotel, restaurant, conference venue, cafe/nightclub, galleries, a painting school, *gamelan* orchestra, and a bookshop well-stocked with books on Balinese arts and culture. ARMA is also in the process of establishing a reference library of published works, unpublished manuscripts, and audio-video materials. It will not be a lending library but function more as a reading room.

In the Netherlands, the **Royal Tropical Institute** (Koninklijk Instituut Voor de Tropen) occupies a large, beautiful old building at 63 Mauritskade, Amsterdam 1092 (tel. 020-924949). Specializing in the tropical areas of the world, this institute is involved in economic-development programs in Indonesia. They often have special exhibits on Bali. The best museum in Indonesia for Baliana, besides the Bali Museum in Denpasar, is the **National Museum** in Jakarta.

NEWS, TRAVEL, AND ENTERTAINMENT MEDIA

Television and Radio
Televisi Republik Indonesia (TVRI) is a government-operated nationwide TV network which covers most of Indonesia via domestic satellite and microwave stations (Bali's microwave is on the Bukit Peninsula). Television broadcasts six hours daily. Programming consists of pro-government Indonesian-language local and national news, educational and religious programs, sports and special events, Indonesian music and dramas, nationalistic documentaries and reports, and about one and a half hours of English-language cartoons and old syndicated American re-runs. Don't miss the English-language news broadcast—with a Balinese perspective—each day at 1800.

Since 1991, Bali has had a second television channel, **Surya Cipta Televisi** (SCTV), which formerly was broadcast only in Surabaya (East Java) and Bandung (West Java). SCTV broadcasts news and current affairs from overseas, western films and serials such as *Spencer for Hire,* popular sports such as Italian and English League Soccer, and music programs like *American Top-10.* As many of its programs are in English, SCTV also appeals to tourists.

Despite the fact that transnational television networks may officially air their programs in Indonesia, the **CNN** signal is scrambled now as a result of government censorship. Only those who can afford the decoder and exorbitant cable rates can get it. These include the international-standard "starred" hotels of Bali.

Radio Republik Indonesia (RRI) still keeps much of the population informed and entertained. RRI broadcasts news and commentary in English about an hour each day (early morning and evening) and contemporary Indonesian pop music. Besides the government radio station, there are local commercial stations in Denpasar, including a great "soft and easy" FM station (at 89.7 Mhz) with a "Flashback to the 60s" program, "American Top 40" (Sunday 0400-0700) hosted by American DJ Shadoe Stevens, a classics hour with Beethoven's "Emperior's Concerto," a jazz hour with Billie Holiday, Ella Fitzgerald, and company, and a "Bali in a Week" cultural program (Sunday 0900-1000)—they do it all.

Libraries
Pusat Dokumentasi Kebudayaan Bali (PUS-DOK), on Jl. Ir. Juanda (tel. 0361-228593) near the Governor's office in Renon, Denpasar, collects and preserves documentation in any form that concerns Bali and the Balinese. The Gedong Kirtya in Singaraja is incorporated within the Pusat Dokumentasi. Their collection of thousands of *lontar,* transcriptions of *lontar,* and books is especially valuable. A printed bibliography is available, but no card catalog.

The **Mitchell Library** in Sydney, Australia, has one of the world's largest collections of books on Indonesia, while Melbourne (Australia) has **The Centre for Southeast Asian Studies** at Monash University. The library at Australian National University, GPO Box 4, Canberra ACT 2601 Australia (fax 06-249-0734), actively acquires material on or about Indonesia and Bali.

The **Wason Collection** of the Olin Library (Room 107) on the campus of Cornell University in Ithaca, New York, U.S.A., is the finest and largest library of Indonesiana in the world. Cornell University also publishes studies, bibliographies, and dictionaries. Their Indonesia magazine is an outstanding journal for scholars of Indonesian culture and history with at least one article in every issue devoted to Bali. Write Southeast Asia Program Publications, Distribution Office, Cornell University, East Hill Plaza, Ithaca, NY 14850, tel. (607) 255-8038.

In the Netherlands, the **Koninklijk Instituut Voor de Tropen** (Royal Tropical Institute), 63 Mauritskade, 1092 AD Amsterdam (tel. 20-5688-711, fax 20-6654-423), has a very fine and very large collection of books and old photos on Indonesia and Bali. Another huge, famous prewar collection of books and periodicals on Indonesia and Bali is housed at the University of Leiden (Witte Singel) in the **Koninklijk Instituut voor Taal-, Land-en Volkenkunde** (KITLV).

Newspapers and Magazines
The *Bali Post* is a twice-monthly newspaper with a 20,000 circulation. It features columns about Balinese culture and schedules of events happening all over the island. If you can read Indonesian, Bali's oldest existing newspaper is

an excellent source of information covering local happenings in literally hundreds of isolated hamlets. Since it relies on amateur news-gatherers in the villages themselves, the lead stories have a charming local flavor: reports on village awards, competitions, personalities, enterprises. The *Bali Post* is also an interpreter of the ongoing dialogue between tourists and the Balinese. Buy it at any bookstore and in the gift shops and news agencies of the big hotels. It used to have a one- or two-page "English Corner," but this was eliminated in 1994.

Bali Echo Visitor's Guide, published six times yearly by PT Wijaya Grandmedia (Jl. Hayam Wuruk 173, Denpasar, tel. 0361-228333 or 228888, fax 228888), is a slick, very readable, tourist-oriented magazine for sale in hotels, bookstores, and restaurants for Rp5000. It contains the latest "in" spots, restaurants, ex-pat events; its articles are well written, opinionated, and practical. Even the infomercials and ads—aimed mostly to upscale visitors—are informative and useful.

English-language dailies published in Jakarta include *The Indonesian Times* (morning), *The Indonesian Observer* (afternoon), the *Jakarta Post,* and the English-language *Surabaya Post* (published in East Java). All are available on Bali, cost around Rp600, have limited, one-sided world coverage, and contain occasional articles on Bali. Newsstands at the large hotels sell overseas editions of the *Asian Wall Street Journal, London Times, Bangkok Post,* Singapore's *Straits Times,* and *Time* and *Newsweek* magazines (Rp5000). Tragia Supermarket in Galleria Nusa Dua is a great place to pick up foreign newspapers and magazines.

The best daily newspaper for bringing international news from the leading news organizations, with regular business, financial, and sports features, is the *International Herald Tribune* available in the tourist centers of Bali for Rp4500. For a 12-month subscription (Rp843,150) delivered to your address on Bali, write NV Indoprom Co. Ltd., Arthaloka Bldg., Ground Floor, Jl. Jend. Sudirman, Jakarta Pusat (tel. 62-21-809-1928, fax 62-21-809-2679).

Specialty Publications

Specialized magazines for the business community are the weeklies *Review Indonesia* and *Asiaweek.* Both magazines are excellent sources of the latest news highlights from Indonesia, with an emphasis on the economy, and both are available for around Rp5000 from newsstands in the metropolitan and tourist areas of Indonesia.

If you're looking for a job or want to rent or sell your house or land, one of the best advertising vehicles is *Bali Advertiser,* Jl. Tanjung Mekar 28 D, Kuta (tel./fax 0361-755392). Distributed in Kuta-Legian, Denpasar, Nusa Dua, Sanur, Ubud, Lovina, and Candidasa, they publish personal ads and notices for all clubs, groups, and other nonprofit organizations free. For commercial ads brought into their office a 25% discount and faster service is offered.

Bali Pathfinder is a walking guide and map for sale for Rp10,000 in hotels and newsstands, particularly around the Ubud area. The guiding philosophy of this 166-page booklet is that tourists should be treated like guests in the hopes that they'll *act* like guests. A new feature of the booklet is vouchers which can be redeemed at photo shops, restaurants, and swimming pools (Rp1000 instead of Rp2500), so you can quickly recoup its purchase price in savings.

Inside Indonesia is a hard-hitting, incisive, illustrated, independent magazine published in Australia containing brilliant insights into Indonesian politics, lifestyles, culture, new technologies, environment, foreign policy, human rights, dissent, and the business community, as well as book reviews and listings of new resources. Equally valuable to the traveler and to the scholar, *Inside Indonesia* monitors Indonesia's political landscape like no other publication. Every issue has at least two stories about Bali, usually addressing the powerful impact of tourism on the island. For a subscription (28 issues for AUS$50 in Australia, AUS$78 overseas), write Box 190, Northcote, Victoria 3070, Australia, tel. (03) 481-1581, fax 416-2746.

An extremely informative periodical for Balinists, scholars, and artists is the *Bali Arts & Culture News* edited by the renowned scholar Fredrik E. DeBoer. This newsletter is aimed at facilitating the free flow of news and information among those interested in the arts and culture of Bali. Though a subscription is free (write to BACN, Wesleyan University, Middletown, CT 06457 U.S.A., tel. 203-347-3417, fax 343-3965), those receiving it are expected to report news of interest to readers from time to time or else contribute toward the cost of postage and handling. For those with access to the Internet, the address is fdeboer@eagle.wesleyan.edu.

John MacDougall is the publisher of *Indonesia Publications* which sponsors a number of periodicals such as the *Indonesia News Service*, which digests current news stories about Indonesia and Bali from leading magazines and newspapers. Subscriptions to this 12-page bulletin, issued four times a year, cost US$6 in the U.S., US$9 in Europe, and US$10 in Asia and Africa. John is also the publisher of *Antara Kita*, the quarterly official English-language bulletin of the Indonesian Studies Committee of the Association for Asian Studies. The subscription is US$6 surface in the U.S.A. and Canada, US$8 elsewhere in the Western Hemisphere, US$9 in Europe, and US$10 in Asia. E-mail subscriptions are available for US$5, anywhere. Address: 7538 Newberry Lane, Lanham-Seabrook, MD 20706, tel. (301) 552-3251, fax 552-4465, e-mail apakabar@access.digex.net.

American Gamelan Institute, Box 1052, Lebanon, NH 03766 U.S.A. (tel./fax 603-448-8837), produces cassettes and CDs of Balinese music. Their "Bali Cassette Collection" is an essential survey for teachers, students, and enthusiasts, representing many major styles of Balinese music. Ten cassettes: US$75. They also publish the periodical *Balungan* on Indonesian performing arts and their international counterparts for US$15 for two issues, US$20 for overseas, US$30 for institutions. Vol. 4, No. 2 is a special issue on Bali: US$7.50.

Leading Book and Guidebook Publishers

Refer to the backmatter for a definitive reading list of books on Bali. One of the most prolific and inspired publishers of books on the society, culture, art, ancient history, language, and natural history of the whole Malay Archipelago is **Periplus Editions,** 1655 Scenic Ave., Berkeley, CA 94709, tel. (510) 540-0146, fax 540-1057. Distributed in the U.S. by Passport Books/NTC, 4255 W. Tougy Ave., Lincolnwood (Chicago), IL 60646. Their Singapore office is at Periplus Pte Ltd, Farrer Road, P.O. Box 115, Singapore 9128. Periplus has published a number of excellent reference books on or about Bali.

The most active publisher of both reprints and new titles on Indonesia is **Oxford University Press** (Walton St., Oxford OX2 6DP, London, England; their American office is at 16-00 Pollitt Dr., Fair Lawn, NJ 07410 U.S.A.). OUP carries at least 40 titles on Indonesia in its famous, well-written, and attractive "Oxford in Asia" series.

Of a more scholarly persuasion are the publications of the **Cornell Modern Indonesia Project** (102 West Ave., Ithaca, NY 14850). Ask for a complete list of publications. Another estimable publishing house occasionally publishing books on Bali is the **University of Hawaii Press** (2840 Kolowalu St., Honolulu, HI 96822).

E.J. Brill (Postbus 9000, 2300 PA Leiden, the Netherlands, Holland, tel. 071-312624) publishes Dutch-, English-, German-, and French-language reprints of old out-of-print classics on Indonesia and Bali.

The **KITLV Press,** Royal Institute of Linguistics and Anthropology, Reuvensplaats 2, P.O. Box 9515, 2300 RA Leiden, The Netherlands (tel. 071-27-23-72, fax 31-71-27-26-38), also publishes some intriguing titles on Bali. Ask for a copy of their latest catalog.

AMS Press, Inc. (56 East 13th St., New York, NY 10003) publishes a fascinating selection of reprints of arcane classics on Indonesia and Bali. Ask for their Southeast Asia mail-order catalog. In Australia, a publisher to keep your eye on for material on or about Bali is **Allen & Unwin,** P.O. Box 8500, St. Leonards, New South Wales 2065, tel. (02) 901-4088, fax 906-2218.

The **Instituut Indoneisische Cursussen** (Rappenburg 8-10, 2311 EV Leiden, The Netherlands) has issued a catalog of interest to readers interested in purchasing books relating to Bali. **Antiquarian Booksellers Gemilang,** P.O. Box 47, 1120 AA Landsmeer, The Netherlands, and **Tamarind Books,** P.O. Box 49217, Greensboro, NC 27419, U.S.A. (tel. 910-852-1905, fax 852-0750), also sell many items of interest to Balinists in English, Dutch, and Indonesian in their mail-order catalog.

Bookstores

On the road in Asia you'll always meet people with books to trade, so bring some of your best paperbacks and hard-to-get magazines for trading. On Bali, prices for imported books, paperbacks, and magazines are high. Kuta Beach Road and Jl. Legian in Kuta, as well as Jl. D. Tamblingan in Sanur, have some of the island's best new and used bookstores where you'll find ample reading material.

Denpasar's supermarkets are the best place to buy new foreign-language publications on Bali. Probably the best selection of new books is in **Gramedia Bookstore** in the basement of the Matahari Shopping Center, and **Gunung Agung Bookstore** in Libi. Hotel bookshops also have newsstands with surprisingly good selections. Prices are high: *Wildlife of Indonesia,* by Elizabeth MacKinnon, published in Indonesia, costs Rp84,500.

Many small hotels have an informal policy allowing guests to take a book if they donate a book to the hotel library, and nonguests may take a book if they donate two books. In non-hotel bookshops along Jl. Legian, most of what's available are used, dog-eared paperbacks. The cheapest, which could be five years old, run about US$1; most are about US$1.50-2, but some cost up to Rp7000-8000. However, the system does work for the buyer to some degree. Once the book is finished, it can be returned and half the purchase price either returned or deducted from the cost of the next book.

In Singapore, **Select Books Pte. Ltd.,** 19 Tanglin Rd. No. 03-15, Tanglin Shopping Centre, third floor, Singapore 1024 (tel. 65-732-1515, fax 736-0855), is a bookseller, library supplier, distributor, and publisher with one of the world's largest retail selections of books on Southeast Asia currently in print. They always have books on Bali.

Also in Singapore, the huge **Toppan Bookstore** in the Orchard Plaza Shopping Centre on Orchard Road, and **MPH Bookstore** at 71-77 Stanford Rd. both have very respectable Indonesian collections as well. These big Singaporean chain bookstores may very well have a wider selection of books on Indonesia than many bookshops in Indonesia itself.

Ge Nabrink Antiquarian Booksellers, Korte Korsjespoortsteeg 8, 1012 TC Amsterdam, The Netherlands (tel. 020-622-3058, fax 31-20-62457), has a huge stock of 100,000 used books, pamphlets, wonderful old b/w prints, photographs, and folios on Indonesia and Bali on four floors near the center of Amsterdam. This Indonesiana store is divided into different categories, such as scientific, literary, and anthropology. Prices and quality are high.

Film
Ring of Fire documents an extraordinary 10-year voyage of two British filmmakers, brothers Lorne and Lawrence Blair. As much a spiritual travelogue as a harrowing physical journey, this avant-garde series is made up of four volumes, each an hour long. The volume called "East of Krakatoa" is about Bali and contains some mesmerizing footage on the Balinese *kris* dance. The set is available for US$99.50 from Mystic Fire Video, Inc., 225 Lafayette St., Suite 1206, New York, NY 10012, tel. (800) 727-8433 (credit card orders). Total running time: 232 minutes. These videos describe a Bali of 25 years ago. They have also produced *Lempad of Bali* (color, 60 minutes, 1979, US$29.95), which portrays the great Balinese painter known throughout Europe for his remarkable religious and erotic art.

The paradise myth of Bali is exposed in the blistering Australian film ***Done Bali.*** While there have been many films which expound the Western image of Bali as an idyllic, creative, tropical holiday destination, this film looks behind the myth—to the island's traumatic past and its current, fragile state as it moves into the future. Using rare archival film footage and interviews with locals, anthropologists, historians, business leaders, and academics, *Done Bali* examines a range of social and historical tragedies that have rocked the island "paradise" and her inhabitants. For more information, contact SBS, tel. (02) 430-3783.

Mitra Tourism Development Division, Jl. Ciputat Raya 64, Pondok Pinang, Jakarta 12310, tel. 769-6004, produces videos on such popular tourist performances and attractions as "Bali," "The Topeng," "The Kecak," "The Barong & Kris Dance," "Drama Gong," "The Bedugal Tour," "The Besakih Tour," "The Legong Dance," and "The Baris and Rejang Dance." Tapes sell at the Ngurah Airport for Rp50,000 apiece.

Documentary Educational Resources, 1001 Morse St., Watertown, MA 02172 U.S.A., sells films and videos on Bali such as films on the trance dances of the late Jero Tapakan. Write for their new price list.

Film on Indonesia, a catalog, has been compiled by Toby Alice Volkman; send US$5 (which includes shipping). Write to Yale Southeast Asia Studies, Yale University, P.O. Box 208206, New Haven, CT 06520-8206. This is a valuable, informative, and very readable resource for teachers and students of Indonesian studies, anthropology, ethnographic film.

Anthropological film archives at universities in the States or in Australia may have copies of Margaret Mead's *Island of Bali;* the strong, primitive feeling of this 1930s film no longer exists on Bali.

The Lincoln Center for the Performing Arts in New York has a very fine collection of books, manuscripts, and artifacts on Asian dance, including audio recordings of Javanese and Balinese dance masters, photos, and other documents provided by the Claire Holt Collection on Indonesian dance.

Music

Recordings of Balinese music have been made since 1928 when some 78s were produced by the Odeon and Beka companies from Europe. In the backmatter of the visually sumptuous large-format book *Bali: The Ultimate Island* by Lueras and Lloyd (1987) you'll find an exhaustive discography and cassetography compiled by Andy Toth of postwar LP records and cassettes, as well as a Bali Filmography (1926-1986) compiled by John Darling.

The **American Gamelan Institute** (tel./fax 603-448-8837, Box 5036, Hanover, NH 03755) produces a journal as well as videos, cassettes, and CDs featuring Indonesian music. Recent productions include four CDs for US$50.

Trans Asian Press (Hoffmannlaan 641, 5011 VP Tilburg, The Netherlands, tel./fax 013-555994) is a multi-media company specializing in Southeast Asia with an accent on Indonesia; inquire about their delightful "Bali: Eternal Circle 1" music tape. Their office in Indonesia is at Jl. H. Agus Salim 67 A, Yogyakarta, tel. (0274) 74876.

Consultants

MAP International (Box 56, Nusa Dua, Bali 80361) provides traditional dancers, both locally and abroad, for embassies or cultural events. They also help TV crews with permits, locations, and other similar needs. Contact the Entertainment Division, Box 63532, 2502 JM Den Haag, Netherlands, tel./fax 31-70-3694416.

Maps

The best folded maps available of Bali are produced by Nelles Verlag GmbH, Schleibheimer Str. 371 b, D 80935 Munich 45, Germany, tel. (089) 351-5084 or 351-5085, fax 354-2544. This beautiful map features vivid color printing, topographic features in realistic relief, and major city plans in margin inserts. Widely available in bookstores with good travel sections in the U.S. for US$7.95, they're cheaper in Indonesia (around Rp12,000). Periplus Editions (address above) also publishes a map to Bali.

Another high-quality folded map of Bali is put out by **APA Maps** (scale 1:180,000) and is available for Rp8000 at any well-stocked bookstore or gift shop on Bali. In the U.S. it's distributed by Prentice-Hall, but you can buy it for US$6.95 at any travel bookstore or general bookstore with a good travel section. This beautiful map has color printing, topographic features in realistic relief, and major town plans—Denpasar, Sanur, Kuta, and Ubud—in close-up margin inserts, as well as a special map of southern Bali. The map is almost too detailed, with place-names labeled so small they are difficult to read.

Tourist offices in Bali sometimes stock maps of Indonesia and Bali, but you can't always rely on their accuracy or up-to-dateness. Airline offices, travel agencies, and hotels display big wall maps—the best local area maps available. Small hotels frequently even publish their own maps so their guests won't get lost and will also be able to find their way to the owner's sister's restaurant, prominently labeled on the map.

PT Pembina (Jl. Pajaitan 45, Jakarta, tel. 813886) publishes a regional map of Bali, complete with distance chart, found at most bookstores. The most extensive stock of Southeast Asia maps for sale in Australia are at **Angus and Robertsons,** 107 Elizabeth St., Melbourne; Sydney's **Angus and Robertsons** on Pitt St.; **Dymock's** on George St., Sydney.

VISAS AND OFFICIALDOM

TYPES OF VISAS

In some cases, tourists to Bali needn't obtain a tourist visa in advance (see "The 'Entry Stamp' Tourist Pass," below). If you are required to obtain a tourist visa, or are interested in obtaining one of the other types of visas, it's a good idea to apply at least six months in advance in your home country. Some visas allow extensions and multiple entries, at the discretion of authorities in any of Indonesia's 74 immigration offices in provincial and district capitals. The prices for all the different types of visas are standardized. If Indonesia, you'll find the prices posted on the walls of the immigration offices; in addition to the appropriate fee, bring with you a little knowledge of Indonesian, good manners, and a friendly attitude. Wear clean clothes (no tank tops, shorts, or T-shirts), and don't try to bribe an official.

The "Entry Stamp" Tourist Pass

Provided they enter and exit Bali or Indonesia through specific air- and seaports (see "Official Points of Entry and Departure," below), tourists from certain listed countries do not need to obtain a tourist visa prior to arrival. The listed countries are: Argentina, Australia, Austria, Belgium, Brazil, Brunei, Canada, Chile, Denmark, Egypt, Finland, France, Germany, Greece, Hungary, Iceland, Ireland, Italy, Japan, Kuwait, Liechtenstein, Luxembourg, Malaysia, Maldives, Malta, Mexico, Monaco, Morocco, Netherlands, New Zealand, Norway, Philippines, Saudi Arabia, Singapore, Spain, Sweden, Switzerland, Taiwan, Thailand, Turkey, United Arab Emirates, United Kingdom, United States, Yugoslavia, and Venezuela.

Upon arriving, tourists from those countries will receive a tourist pass or entry stamp in their passport, allowing them to stay up to two months anywhere in Indonesia (except certain off-limits areas of Irian Jaya and East Timor). Don't lose the white arrival/departure card that comes with your entry stamp; if you do lose it, go to the nearest immigration office promptly and get a replacement. Don't wait until your day of departure at the airport to inform immigration officials that it's lost.

A tourist receiving an entry stamp upon arrival must also have an onward ticket by plane or boat out of Indonesia, or a letter from an air carrier, ship line, or travel agency confirming the purchase of those tickets. Also note that if you already have an entry stamp, it's not easy to change the status of your visa. This usually must be done outside of Indonesia.

The tourist pass can be extended only if you are ill, injured, or have missed your flight. In such cases, apply for an extension three or four days prior to the expiration of your entry stamp, if possible. Otherwise you'll be delayed at the airport and may miss your rescheduled flight. Officials take the two-month time limit very seriously, allowing not even one day's slack. If you want to stay longer, you must leave Indonesia, then reenter for another two months (see "Reentry," below).

Alternate Tourist Visa

Visitors from countries other than those listed above, or visitors planning on entering the country at an unofficial point of entry, can obtain a tourist visa before their arrival from any Indonesian embassy or consulate; two photos are required and a small fee is charged. These visas are valid for 30 days. Many travelers fly into Kupang (Timor Barat) and travel via land and sea to Bali, a great opportunity to see the eastern islands along the way. If you arrive in Kupang without a return air ticket to Australia, the Indonesian authorities want to see that you hold at least AUS$1000. At some other points of entry, *imigrasi* (immigration) officials don't even bother to ask if you have an onward ticket or enough money to sustain yourself. This is often the case in Biak (Irian Jaya) and Batam (Riau).

Visitor's Visa

This type of visa (also called a "social visa") isn't granted as often as it once was. You must either have a legitimate reason to enter the country (e.g., to visit relatives, to study Balinese dance), or be involved in an accredited STSI or SMKI art course. Visit both the Immigration Office and the Education and Culture Department

(Departmen Pendidikan dan Kebudayaan) in Renon, Denpasar, to find out what's required.

You should apply at least six months in advance in your home country, and will need to show a letter of invitation or provide the name of an influential sponsor or guarantor in Indonesia. This sponsor/guarantor might include a government official, a high-ranking military officer, a respected non-Chinese business owner, or even a well-established, well-connected West-

ern expatriate. Basically, the person you name will be held responsible for you in case something goes wrong.

Visitor's visas are normally given for a four- or five-week initial stay. They can be extended up to five times for one or more month's duration each time, for a total of six months. (Don't stay the full six months or the government will hit you with the dreaded "foreign fiscal tax"; see "General Rules and Regulations," below.) Ex-

SELECTED INDONESIAN CONSULATES ABROAD

Australia

Indonesian Consulate General, Beulah Park S.A., Adelaide 5067, tel. (08) 318-108

Consulate of The Republic of Indonesia, 22, Coronation Drive, Stuart Park, Darwin-NT 0801, tel. (089) 819-352

Consulate of The Republic of Indonesia, third floor, 52 Albert Road, South Melbourne, Victoria 3205, tel. (03) 690-7811

Indonesian Consulate, Judd Street South Perth, Western Australia 6151, tel. (09) 367-1178

Indonesian Consulate General, 236-238 Marcubra Road, Marcubra, New South Wales 2035, tel. (02) 344-9933

Belgium

Indonesian Consulate General, Suikerul 5 Bus No. 9, 2000 Antwerp, tel. (031) 3225-6136

Canada

Indonesian Consulate, 425 University Avenue, ninth floor, Toronto Ontario M5G 1T6, tel. (416) 591-6461

Indonesian Consulate, 1455 W. Georgia Street, second floor, Vancouver, B.C. V6G 2T3, tel. (604) 682-8855

France

Consulate D'Indonesie, 25 Boulevard Carmagnole, 13008 Marseille, tel. 9171-3435

Germany

Indonesian Consulate General, Eplanade 7-9, 0-1100 Berlin, tel. (030) 472-2002

Indonesian Consulate General, Berliner Alle 2, Post Fach 9140, Düsseldorf, tel. (0211) 353-081

Indonesian Consulate General, Bebelallee 15, 2000 Hamburg 60, tel. (040) 512-071

Indonesian Consulate, Widermayer Strasse 24d-8000, Muenchen 22, tel. (089) 294-609

Hong Kong

Indonesian Consulate General, 127-129 Leighton Road, 6-8 Koswick St. Entrance, tel. (5) 2890-4421

Malaysia

Indonesian Consulate, 467 Jalan Burma, P.O. Box 502, 10350 Penang, tel. (04) 374-686

Spain

Indonesian Consulate General, Rambia Estudios 119, Apartado 18, Barcelona-2, tel. 317-1900

United States of America

Indonesian Consulate General, Two Illinois Center, 233 North Michigan Ave. Suite 1422, Chicago, IL 60601, tel. (312) 938-0101

Indonesian Consulate, Pri Tower 733 Bishop Street, P.O. Box 3379 Honolulu, HI 96842, tel. (808) 524-4300

Indonesian Consulate General, 3457 Wilshire Blvd., Los Angeles, CA 90010, tel. (213) 383-5126

Indonesian Consulate General, 5 East 68th Street, New York, NY 10021, tel. (212) 879-0600

Consulate of The Republic of Indonesia, 1111 Columbus Avenue, San Francisco, CA 94133, tel. (415) 474-9571

There are jails in Denpasar and Singaraja, but from what I can gather your description of humane treatment is a little rosy. There is an Immigration Detention Centre in Denpasar, called "quarantine" amongst the staff there. They do treat you very well there, but the quantity of food provided leaves a lot to be desired. Lunch at 10am, dinner at 5pm, but no breakfast, so you've got 17 hours to wait between feeds from one day to the next. Of course you can pay to get extra food, cups of coffee, etc. I spent four days there for one month's overstay while they claimed they were referring to a higher authority— their euphemism for waiting until the haggling over price with my husband was complete. They behaved to me as if I didn't know what was going on!

While I was there a Frenchman was transferred in on his way home from the real jail, which I gather was not such a pleasant experience. He had been detained for five months, two months awaiting trial and three months sentence—for overstay. I don't know how long his overstay had been but I think his main problem was language. (How can one stay in Indonesia long enough to overstay without knowing what "Dari mana?" means?). Presumably he threw their system into confusion as he didn't understand when they were asking for money, and so they had to process him according to the law.

There was also a Dutchman on his way home after four years for narcotics offences, and a Chinese man who has been in the detention centre since 1960—something to do with not having any papers and the Chinese didn't want him back! He seems quite well settled there though, his room is well furnished and he always seemed to have cigarettes and extra food. It baffles me how he still has money after so long.

—ELAINE ROGERS

to present a completed application along with an institute's or teacher's extension-request letter or a sponsor's ID-card copy (as applicable). You'll also need a good measure of serenity. Even a saint would lose patience with the *imigrasi* people. Typically, you might be asked to wait a few minutes to see an official. An hour later, you're told that the man will be in his meeting until 1400 (the time the office closes). Then comes the oft-heard "come back tomorrow." Finally, it turns out you never had to see that official in the first place.

Apply for your extension early because it might take as little as two days or as long as three weeks to be granted, and you might have to go back to the immigration office four or more times. *Imigrasi* also appreciates it if you bring an Indonesian friend; they *hate* to speak English.

After three months, it gets more difficult to stay longer. You may need to be fingerprinted and fill out additional forms. Also, your sponsor may have to write new letters. When you have used up your six-month limit, the words "Final Extension" are stamped in your passport.

It's generally easier for Europeans to get visitor's visa extensions than it is for North Americans or Australians. Australians are processed with the most prejudice because their country makes it difficult for Indonesians to enter Australia and remain for any length of time. Dutch travelers are given a lot of slack because of historical ties between the two countries; Indonesians go out of their way to show the Dutch that they hold no grudge. Dutch travelers even have a better chance if the *imigrasi* officer speaks Dutch.

tensions are granted at the sole discretion of *imigrasi* personnel and often involve a two-day bureaucratic hassle. Each extension costs Rp10,000, and the first extension costs an additional Rp30,000 "landing fee" (some European nationalities excluded). Have lots of room in your passport as each extension takes up a full page. To apply for an extension, you'll need

302 ON THE ROAD

Business Visa

A business visa, available at Indonesian embassies and consulates (see the special topic "Selected Indonesian Consulates Abroad"), allows a stay of up to 30 days and can be extended to three months. It's for single entry and costs US$5.50. Submit forms in duplicate with two photos, plus a letter in duplicate from a business firm or employer stating the purpose of your visit and providing financial guarantees. If you're a writer, journalist, photographer, or filmmaker don't say so.

Under certain circumstances, this type of visa might be easier to obtain than a visitor's visa. A business manager or owner must vouch for the fact that you are carrying out some service for him or her on Bali. Some foreigners, in order to export handicrafts and textiles, start up a company with an Indonesian, then "the company" sponsors them. Still, whether you get a Business Visa or not depends on the *imigrasi* department and the Department of Labor (Departmen Tenaga Kerja, or simply Depnaker) in Denpasar's Renon complex. Unfortunately, it seems too many tourists have rubbed these two departments the wrong way; the workers can be defensively arrogant. The 1994 license revocation of a rafting company run by an Australian had the expat business community of Bali running scared for a while, but things have since calmed down.

Anybody with too high a profile gets cut back a couple of notches periodically. Businesses co-owned or sponsored by Balinese or Indonesians are favored. For a businessperson who can tie up his or her affairs in less than eight weeks, it makes more sense to enter Bali with a tourist pass and maintain a low profile.

Restrictions on Certain Nationals

Citizens of Israel and Portugal may not enter Indonesia on their passports. Business travelers from Eastern European countries are given a one-month, nonextendable visa allowing them to travel freely within the country. Visitors from Hong Kong can get 30-day visas for group travel (minimum five people) from the Indonesian Consulate in Hong Kong. They must enter and exit Indonesia in Medan, Jakarta, or Denpasar (Bali), and all tour details such as accommodation and travel must be arranged through a travel agent.

Also note that during 1994-95 there was a crackdown on foreign residents in Bali. Next time you visit the immigration office in Denpasar, take a look at the statistics for EPO's granted. (EPO stands for "exit permit only"—granted for residents who don't intend to return.) The figures took a sharp upturn starting in mid-1994, from tens to hundreds.

General Rules and Regulations

All visitors must possess a passport valid for at least six months after their arrival date in Indonesia. Immigration officials reserve the right to deny entry to any visitor who, in their opinion, is not properly dressed or groomed (long hair is okay), lacks the proper funds, or "may endanger the country's security, peace, and stability or the public health and morals." These unfortunate undesirables will receive a transit visa upon arrival that allows them to hang out at the airport until the first available flight out.

If you stay longer than three months in Indonesia on *any* visa, you must "register as an alien," pay Rp1500 (plus Rp400 for two forms), and be fingerprinted. After residing in Indonesia six months, any foreign resident wishing to leave the country must obtain an exit permit and pay a "foreign fiscal tax" of Rp250,000. This tax constitutes an advance payment of income tax. Only the diplomatic corps, members of international aid organizations, airline personnel, and government-sponsored persons are exempt.

Finally, note that as in most Third World countries, if a Western man marries an Indonesian woman he is granted no special residency status; he must leave the country every two months and return each time as a tourist when he'll receive the usual entry stamp. This is not the case when a Western woman marries a Balinese man. She is able to obtain a residency visa, subject to renewal every six months or so.

Information and Assistance

For help with immigration problems or requests, go to the main immigration office in the Renon Complex, Niti Mandala, Denpasar (tel. 0361-227828). Another immigration office—convenient for visitors who stay in Kuta, Nusa Dua, or Jimbaran—is near the airport on Jl. Raya I Gusti Ngurah Rai, Tuban (tel. 0361-751038). Both of-

FOREIGN EMBASSIES IN JAKARTA

The area code in Jakarta is 021.

Australia: Embassy of Australial, Jl. Thamrin 15, tel. 323109

Canada: Embassy of Canada, Wisma Metropolitan I, 5th Floor, Jl. Jen. Sudirman, Kav. 29, tel. 510709 or 514022

Denmark: Royal Danish Embassy, Jl. Abdul Musi 34, tel. 346615

West Germany: Embassy of West Germany, Jl. Thamrin 1, tel. 323908, 324292, or 324357

Great Britain: Her Britannic Majesty's Embassy, Jl. Thamrin 75, tel. 330904

Japan: Embassy of Japan, Jl. Thamrin 24, tel. 324308, 324948, or 325396

Malaysia: Embassy of Malaysia, Jl. Imam Bonjol 17, tel. 332170, 336438, or 332864

Netherlands: Embassy of the Kingdom of Netherlands, Jl. Rasun Said, Kav. S-3, 12950, tel. 511515

New Zealand: New Zealand Embassy, Jl. Diponegoro 41, tel. 330552, 330620, or 330680

Singapore: Embassy of the Republic of Singapore, Jl. Proklamasi 23, tel. 348761 or 347783

Sweden: Embassy of the Kingdom of Sweden, Jl. Taman Cut Mutiah 12, tel. 333061

United States of America: Embassy of the USA, Jl. Merdeka Selatan 5, tel. 360360

---

tension. Wayan has gotten visas for about 25 people so far and charges Rp600,000-700,000 for six months—a bargain compared to leaving the country twice. His office is just 100 meters from Wayan's Siti Homestay in Peliatan, Gianyar (tel. 0361-975599).

OFFICIAL POINTS OF ENTRY AND DEPARTURE

Entikong in West Kalimantan is the only land gateway into Indonesia. Official air and sea entry points into the country change frequently. Only the following are officially designated as international ports of entry and departure by air:

Medan, North Sumatra: Polonia Airport

Padang, West Sumatra: Tabing Airport

Pekanbaru, East Sumatra: Simpang Tiga Airport

Riau, East Sumatra: Hang Nadim (Batam); Batubesar Airport

Jakarta: Soekarno-Hatta Airport

Badung, West Java: Husein Sastrangegara Airport

Surabaya, West Java: Juanda Airport

Bali: Ngurah Rai Airport

Lombok: Mataram's Selaparang Airport

Timor: Kupang's Eltari Airport

Sulawesi: Manado's Sam Ratulangi Airport

Kalimantan: Balikpapan's Sepinggan Airport; Pontianak's Supadio Airport

Maluku: Ambon's Pattimura Airport

Irian Jaya: Frans Kaisiepo Airport, Biak

Arrivals and departures by sea must be through the following seaports:

Medan, North Sumatra: port of Belawan

Bengkulu, Bengkulu Province: port of Padangbai

Riau, East Sumatra: Batam Island's ports of Batu Ampar and Sekupang; Bintan Island's port of Tanjung Pinang

Jakarta: port of Tanjung Priok

---

fices are open Mon-Thurs. 0700-1300, Friday 0700-1100, Saturday 0700-1200. You may also go to any one of Indonesia's 74 other immigration offices. If you don't dress properly (follow dress code chart on wall), these bureaucrats won't even talk to you. T-shirts, halter tops, and bathing suits don't cut it.

Wayan's **CV Jasa Werda Dwi Karya, Biro Jasa** can make your life a lot easier. This privately owned enterprise can help you obtain a social/cultural/business visa and provides legal services and notary assistance. If you try to get a visa by yourself, you may have to make as many as nine visits to *imigrasi* to get just one ex-

Semarang, Central Java: port of Tanjung Mas

Surabaya, East Java: port of Tanjung Perak

Bali: Benoa (south Bali); Padangbai (east Bali)

Manado, North Sulawesi: port of Bitung (east of Manado)

Ambon, Central Maluku: Yos Sudarso (Ambon Harbor).

If you enter Indonesia at any point not listed above, you're required to have a proper visa obtained beforehand, and you will be permitted to remain in the country for just 30 days. If you enter Indonesia overland from PNG, or take a boat from the southern Philippines to East Kalimantan, you are entering Indonesia illegally. If caught, Indonesian immigration officials may jail or deport you.

OVERSTAYS AND REENTRY

It's possible to get a short extension on your visa in order to meet a ship or plane. *Imigrasi* routinely grants a three-day overstay, particularly if you're leaving by ship. For a longer overstay, the only legitimate excuse is that you've lost your passport or are in the hospital or can bring a note from a doctor or hospital verifying a medical problem.

If you know you're going to overstay your visa—even for a lousy day—go to the immigration office and obtain an official extension. Don't try to talk your way through the immigration checkpoint at the airport when leaving the country; the officers there are stickier than expected and will require you to straighten it out at the *imigrasi* office. They really make your squirm and sweat, you may have to pay a fine (bargain!), and you might even miss your flight.

If your booked flight is scheduled to leave during the week after your visa expires, you should be able to get an extension from the *imigrasi* office for the waiting time. It will probably require a letter from your travel agency explaining the situation. Show up with a confirmed ticket out and a reason why you can't get an earlier flight.

Reentry

If you use up your two-month maximum stay on an entry stamp but want to spend more time in Bali, one oft-used solution is to leave the country, return, and get a new entry stamp or visa in your passport. You must obtain a visa if your place of arrival is not an official entry point. Most people in this situation spend the US$350-400 or so on a roundtrip ticket from Bali to Singapore, spend a few days in Singapore shopping and catching the latest movies, then fly straight back to Bali. A cheaper alternative is to leave Indonesia at certain points as close as possible to neighboring countries from where you can reenter. The following are the most convenient, least expensive routes out:

- By speedboat (twice weekly, Rp130,000 roundtrip) or air from **Medan** (North Sumatra) to **Penang** (West Malaysia).

- By air from **Pekanbaru** (East Sumatra) to **Melaka** (West Malaysia), then by taxi to **Kuala Lumpur.** See "From Pekanbaru to Singapore by Boat," below.

- By air from **Jakarta** to **Singapore** (US$140 roundtrip on Sempati Airlines). To fly to Tanjung Pinang is more expensive than the direct flight to Singapore.

- By air from **Pontianak** (West Kalimantan) to **Kucing** (East Malaysia) (Rp208,000 roundtrip, leaving once weekly on Friday). Returning at Pontianak's airport you get an entry stamp.

- By road from **Pontianak** (West Kalimantan) to **Kucing** (Sarawak, East Malaysia). Four daily buses cross the land border separating the two countries; Rp22,000.

- By air or by boat from **Tarakan** (East Kalimantan) to **Nunukan** and **Tawau** (Sabah, East Malaysia). The boat connection operates three times weekly and costs Rp68,000 roundtrip; this boat is sometimes on, sometimes off. You need a visa before reentering Indonesia because no entry stamp is issued on arrival in Tarakan, Indonesian Borneo.

- By air from **Kupang** (Timor) to **Darwin** (Australia).

- By ferry from **Melaka** (Peninsular Malaysia) and **Dumai** (East Sumatra). The problem with this reentry is that you need a visa and have to go to Kuala Lumpur to get one.

CUSTOMS REGULATIONS

Indonesian Customs

Customs procedures have become more informal with the installation of green and red routes at international airports. Tourists with nothing to declare use the green route, which involves no baggage inspection. The customs and immigration people at Bali's **Ngurah Rai International Airport** are usually mellow and respectful, but it all depends on the time of day, the official's mood, who's watching, the crush of the line behind you, and your nationality. The officials are mostly concerned with moving the tourists through as quickly as possible.

Duty-free items that may be imported are: 200 cigarettes or 50 cigars and two pounds of tobacco; cameras (no limit) and reasonable amounts of film; two liters of liquor; a reasonable amount of perfume for personal use. Weapons and ammunition, narcotics, anything that can be considered pornographic (such as a scorching copy of *Playboy*), books with Chinese characters in them, and Chinese medicines are forbidden entry.

Technically, photographic equipment, computers, radios, typewriters, cassette recorders, TV sets, cordless telephones, and transceivers should be listed on your passport, declared to customs, and taken out upon departure, but officials don't seem to care. All movie films, videocassettes, laser discs, records, and computer software should first be screened by the Film Censor Board. Books and printed matter using Indonesian languages are supposed to be cleared by the Minister of Culture, but seldom are.

Except for drugs and weapons, customs officials are pretty relaxed about enforcement. If you need or if you carry prescription medication, carry a letter from your doctor. The import of pets, plants, and fresh fruit is also controlled. Pet owners must present a certificate from a veterinarian vouching for their pet's good health. Dog and cat owners must carry proof that Fido and Kitty have been inoculated against rabies within six months prior to arrival.

Home Country Customs

Importation into other countries of organic souvenirs bought in Indonesia may be prohibited. One reader reported that when she tried to take some *wayang* puppets into Australia, they were quarantined. Anything purchased with feathers or furs or made in part with organic matter or parts of endangered species will most likely be confiscated. If you don't declare these items, you may be fined.

WHAT TO TAKE

Documents

You'll need a passport to enter Bali, exchange traveler's checks, pick up mail at poste restante or at American Express, to sign in at a hotel, or whenever police ask to see it, which they hardly ever do. Take extra passport photos with you, then have 30-40 more printed cheaply from the negative on Bali. These are useful when filling out applications, applying for a *surat jalan,* and to give out as mementos.

It's advisable to travel with a copy of both your birth certificate and passport. These should be kept separate from the originals in case you lose your passport or for repatriation purposes.

If you're traveling with your spouse, a copy of your marriage license is necessary if you have to enter a hospital or undergo some legal or immigration difficulties. Also make a list of your passport number, traveler's check numbers, credit card numbers, vital contact addresses, and any other pertinent information. Make two copies; carry one with your luggage, leave the other with a friend or family member back home. It would also be wise to jot down your plane ticket numbers, place and date of issue, and type of payment. This information is invaluable if your ticket is lost or stolen, and could save you enormous hassles. Bring a credit card in

MISCELLANEOUS CHECKLIST

breathable moneybelt

sleeping bag liner or washable top cotton sheet for sleeping in

light canteen or plastic bottle for liquids

bathing suit

handkerchiefs (it's hot!)

rubber sandals

cheap butane lighter and/or candles in case of power outages

high-standard English/Indonesian, Indonesian/English Dictionary and phrasebook

guidebooks

maps and maps case

calculator for moneychanging

name tags for luggage (when storing, flying, etc.)

bicycle padlock and bicycle-locking chain if you bring your own bike or know you'll rent one on Bali

luggage locks

flashlight or penlight to keep you from falling in open drainage ditches, a good way to chip a tooth or bruise a shinbone. Buy an aluminum Chinese-made flashlight in a shop for only Rp2500

alarm clock or alarm wristwatch for catching early morning buses, trains, boats, planes

(although most Balinese accommodations provide reliable wake-up service)

tampons are only available in the tourist centers at prices about 20% higher than in the West. Buy ones with applicators that are wrapped in plastic such as O.B. The others such as the all-paper Tampax get moist and swell up in the humidity and can't be used in Bali!

dental floss (difficult to find in Bali)

camera and film

electric converter and adapter plugs (if traveling with electronics)

razor and blades or rechargable electric razor

an efficient, hand-held fan

medicine and/or first-aid kit

sunblock (at least 19 SPF) and aloe vera for sunburns

insect repellent

a portable, light mosquito net with plenty of hoops

string to hang mosquito net on and to dry laundry on

collapsible umbrella (or buy one there)

sunglasses and sun hat/rain hat

prescription glasses (take one spare pair)

a roll of toilet paper (if you use it)

case you need cash, which you can get at some banks at a six percent commission.

If you wear glasses or contacts or take medication on a regular basis, carry a copy of the prescription. Have your doctor make out prescriptions using scientific names that are understood internationally. Bausch and Lomb and Barnes Hind contact lenses along with cleaning solutions are sold by competent optometrists in larger cities and major tourist areas. Unless you are entering Indonesia from an infected area, you won't be asked for your International World Health Certificate.

Indonesia only has a few official youth hostels so you really don't need an International Youth Hostel Association (IYHA) card here. If you want to stay in a hostel, just pay the few dollars extra. However, an International Student Identification Card (ISIC) could be useful for getting dis-

counts of up to 25% on rail and flight tickets out of Bali, as well as discounts on entrance fees to museums. Counterfeit ones sell in touristy places in Southeast Asia, but be careful of poor forgeries. Indonesian officials wary of fakes. They may require additional identification and that you are no older than 26 before giving you a discount. To apply, write: CIEE Student Travel, 205 East 42nd St., New York, NY 10017, tel. (212) 661-1414. Make sure to include your date of birth, citizenship, and name of school or university where you are a full-time student.

Do obtain an International Driver's License, valid for a year, from your local automobile association. You never know when you'll want to rent a car or van. An Indonesian license on Bali costs Rp52,000 whereas an IDL in the States costs only US$8. Get an IDL with a motorcyle endorsement if you plan to rent a motorcycle on Bali.

goggles or diving mask for underwater sports, and bicycle and motorcycle rentals. A heavy-duty pair of sunglasses can substitute.

binoculars for nature observation or when taking ships between islands

cassette recorder for recording dances, singing, and theatrical performances

pushpins, thumbtacks, or heavy duty tape for pinning up sarung or towel over windows because of too much light, posting notes to people, etc.

fannypack

sewing kit and scissors

toiletries: your portable washroom can be either assembled before departure or after arrival as many brand-name toiletries are available on Bali. Nail file and stainless-steel razors are useful.

can opener, Swiss Army knife (with bottle opener, can opener, corkscrew, scissors, tweezers)

bags: a fishnet bag or large open cloth bag can double as a knapsack for excursions or to carry souvenirs, suntan oil, towels, etc. Plastic bags hold food, carry soiled clothes, protect clothes from rain while backpacking

a small, sturdy theft-proof day pack that folds up into your larger pack and/or a soft, empty plastic duffel with which to carry purchases back home in a small canvas bag for storing cassettes, spare glasses, breakables and other small things you don't want crushed (stuff socks and underwear in as cushioning)

a good pair of foamy earplugs (a life-or-death item, particularly if you're traveling on a budget)

small notebook and ballpoint pens, pencils

light scarf to wear when entering Balinese temples. Rent them at temple gates (Rp200) or buy one (Rp1000-2500).

sarung can be used to carry things in, as a cover to cover a dirty mattress, as sunshade, as a towel, or for warmth—a super useful item.

black-and-white passport photos

reading matter (even used books are expensive in Bali)

snacks and eyeshade for the plane ride to Indonesia

Don't leave home without a small electronic organizer or conventional address book in which to record the names of new friends and to refer to when you write home. Your business card or name card is highly prized by Indonesians. Bringing a stack of them will save you from continually writing out your address. However, be prepared to receive mail asking for money, favors, and gifts.

Packing

A top-loading duffel bag with a strong shoulder strap is very convenient and will expand to hold a vast amount of gear. Choose a sturdy, well-designed duffel or backpack with heavy-duty zippers, noncorrosive Fastex, and Dacron thread. If it's a backpack, make sure it has a hip belt and semi-rigid frame so it's more comfortable.

Fill your pack only one-half or two-thirds full; you'll find yourself gradually replacing all your drab Western clothes with the colorful, fashionable garments sold in the boutiques of Kuta, Legian, Sanur, and Ubud. Ideally, wear one set of clothes on the plane and buy locally made clothes after you arrive. In truth, you don't need to take anything but money. All the tourist resorts of this prosperous, crowded island boast transport companies, travel agencies, restaurants, air-conditioned hotels, laser disc bars, photo shops, pharmacies, supermarkets, and grocery stores that cater to Bali's growing affluent middle class. Be sure to include an empty, fold-up canvas bag to carry home extra things you buy.

Garuda allows you to check in two pieces of luggage, but will charge you extra for a third. Always put an identifying badge or mark on your luggage; this will prevent someone from picking it up and will also keep you from picking up someone else's. It's also wise to put an identifying badge inside each piece of your luggage in case the ones on the outside get lost.

If you want to camp in Bali Barat National Park, pack a light tent, compass, inflatable pillow, poncho, and portable one-burner kerosene stove (kerosene is available). All other camping gear you can buy in Denpasar and is of acceptable quality. Local outfitters also rent tents, sleeping bags, and other equipment, or these may be supplied by your guide (see Bali Barat section of "Buleleng" chapter). Keep in mind Bali is generally too hot for your standard sleeping bag. If you're going to be staying in budget accommodations or doing some hard traveling, bring a sleeping bag liner or make a light sleeping bag by running a seam down a folded cotton bedsheet. It's a more attractive alternative to sleeping on grimy mattresses and mats.

Men's Clothing
Take only clothes that are lightweight, easily rinsed, brushed, and renovated. In a tropical climate, cotton is very comfortable (nylon doesn't breathe in the heat) and dries quickly in the humidity. However, 100% cotton needs ironing, so bring along a few half-cotton, half-synthetic (rayon is good), wrinkle-free garments for special occasions and visits to bureaucratic offices. Denim is too hot for Indonesia and takes too long to dry; perhaps bring one pair if you're going to do high-altitude trekking or cycling. Looser corduroys or light summer trousers are better suited for this climate. It's generally considered inappropriate for men to wear short shorts for anything except the roughest manual work, long-distance cycling, hash runs, or for going to and from the bathroom or beach.

Bali is too hot for Western-style sportcoats. Buy a light *batik* sportcoat or an attractive long-sleeved *batik* shirt for dressing up—quite acceptable and very chic in Indonesia. Choose patterned or dark-colored fabrics that won't show wear or soil as quickly. Take along a light sweater or sweatshirt for the cool of the evenings or for higher elevations such as Kintamani and Bedugul. These also serve as protection against sunburn and insects. Also take a water-resistant, wind-proof jacket. It packs light and keeps you warm when worn over a sweater. Keep in mind the temperature drops about 3° F for every 325 meters in elevation, and heavy cloud cover at Bali's mountain climes can bring on an even a sharper fall in temperature.

Also recommended is a cloth baseball cap or khaki fisherman-style hat with a brim, deep enough to stay on your head in heavy winds, and to protect you from rain or the intensity of the sun. Don't forget to spray it with water repellent. It may be frumpy looking, but it will do the job. A helmet is a life-saving investment for cy-

clists and motorcyclists; choose one with a plastic shield to protect your face from rain, sleet, and insects. Bring one with you; the ones available on Bali are dangerously flimsy.

Women's Clothing
Women should take a few long-sleeved blouses and longish skirts. Skimpy clothing, backless dresses, and shorts can be offensive in Bali's small back-road villages, on formal occasions, and particularly if worn in the island's temples or to religious festivals. Your bikini is acceptable provided it's worn only at the swimming pool or to the beach. Take one wrinkle-proof dress that is easy to wash and dress up or down with. Dresses of double-knit cotton T-shirt material are excellent. If you prefer to complete your travel wardrobe on arrival, the clothes shops and boutiques of Kuta and Legian have a wide selection of contemporary and economically priced dresses, jackets, skirts, blouses, pants, and beachwear. Always closely scrutinize the quality of the fabric and workmanship.

As an alternative to possibly poorly sewn ready-made clothes, commission one of Bali's hundreds of seamstresses to sew a dress (Rp15,000-30,000) or skirt (Rp7500-10,000). Your hotel or a clothes shop can recommend a dressmaker. Just give them one of your best-fitting garments or a photograph from which they will make a paper pattern.

If you lighten your hair, bring enough lightener with you to last your entire trip. Only black and a few brown shades can be found on Bali. Also bring deodorant and antiperspirant. The only decent products here are FA or Purol powder; the rest are ineffective.

Footwear
A good pair of hiking or walking shoes can add hours of sightseeing or hiking to your day. However, don't leave home with brand-new footwear; they should already be broken-in and comfortable. Change frayed laces before leaving so you don't have to take a spare set along. Also very useful is a pair of Teva sandals or a good quality imitation. You can wear them anywhere—for everyday traveling, hiking, to the beach, for snorkeling, coral walking, dancing, motorcycle riding, or even to the immigration office. Perfect for Indonesia! Teva-type sandals are sold all

THE INDONESIAN WOMAN'S NATIONAL DRESS

Provided you wear the garment properly on the right occasions, the Balinese will take it as a compliment if you wear traditional Balinese dress. Get expert local advice before sallying forth in your *sarung, kain,* and *kebaya.*

The *sarung* is a simple, oblong (2.5 by 1.5 meters) rectangle of *batik* cotton cloth. It is worn wrapped around the waist and falls in a single fold in front and is sometimes held in place by a tight sash *(selendang).* When worn for religious celebrations, a line of identically dressed women walk to temple wearing their *sarung,* their finest brocade and *batik,* and flowers and gold ornaments in their hair.

Dyed in brilliant colors and delicate designs, the *sarung* on the slim and graceful bodies of the dark-complexioned Balinese is respectable and pretty, but worn on some of the robust figures of Westerners it can look ludicrous. A *sarung,* for both men and women, is comfortable in the heat (except when on the move) and has a multitude of uses: a sunshade, baby carrier, sheet at night when it's cool, or to cover a dirty bed. A towel is bulky to carry, so learn to substitute an absorbent cotton *sarung,* then air dry it in the sun.

A *kain* is a length of cloth measuring approximately 2.25 by one meter, made of cambric-based *batik* and worn as a wraparound, ankle-length skirt. The *kain,* when interwoven with silk or metallic threads, is called a *songket.*

The Balinese *kebaya* (*left*) is a short blouse of a fine flower-sprigged plain cotton, muslin, silk, synthetic fabric, brocade, lam, or organdy, with cutwork embroidery and a closed front. The bottom edge falls to the hipbone and is even all around. It may be worn with an unpleated Balinese *kain, songket,* or skirt-wrapping. A matching scarf is tied over the *kebaya* around the waist.

White, red, and gold flowers decorate the loose, twisted tail of hair falling from one side of a small knot worn by unmarried women. Married women wear their hair twisted and double-looped, long on one side, and also decorated with flowers.

over Kuta Beach at lower prices than the West, but they're not as well made. Dress shoes come in handy for weddings, meetings with officials, formal visits, but are not recommended for the average traveler. Rubber sandals (flip flops) almost always come with your hotel or homestay room, but they are invariably too small for Westerners, so bring your own.

Don't expect to buy footwear on Bali. Good-quality European-sized footwear is not so easy to find. The international chain, Bata, in Denpasar sells inexpensive shoes in leather, canvas, or plastic, but a U.S. men's 12 and a women's 9 are about the largest sizes they make.

Gifts

Small trinkets from home make great gifts for a foreign host. Colorful foreign stamps are the least expensive, simplest, and lightest gifts to carry and tell a lot about your country. Indonesian kids love coins, stickers, balloons, and soap bubbles. Rather than candy, give pens, pencils, notebooks (schoolkids often have to pay for their own school supplies). Small boxes of raisins are also appreciated. Teenagers love designer T-shirts, or ones with imaginative, artistic, screen-printed designs and mottoes. One of the best gifts for older kids is a soccerball or volleyball. These sports are very popular; most villages have set-up goalposts and a net of sorts. They also enjoy tapes of music from your country.

For adults, big fluffy heavy-duty cotton towels, as well as wool headcoverings for babies, are much appreciated by the Balinese. For a young boy or man, a stainless steel pocketknife is an excellent way of saying "thank you." Avoid giving cigars; most Indonesians don't like them. Small items such as cigarette lighters, tiny camper's can openers, gift catalogs (like Sears), large safety pins, multicolored paper clips, and packaged flower seeds also make interesting gifts. Postcards of your country or hometown, your business card, color photographs of yourself, your family, and especially of your children are highly prized. Balinese also delight in photos of your home and kitchen.

BOB RACE

DENPASAR REGENCY

Once part of Badung Regency, in 1992 the Denpasar area split off and became Bali's ninth *kabupaten.* In addition to the island's capital, Denpasar Regency encompasses Sanur, Benoa Port, and Serangan Island, leaving Badung more pencil-shaped than ever.

DENPASAR

Denpasar is the largest and busiest city on the island. An old trading center, its name means "east of the market." It's the headquarters for the government, the media, the island's principal banks, airline offices, and hospitals. Bali's two universities, Udayana and Warmadewa, are also based here. The city's local name is Badung, its old name, and you'll hear "Badung" sung out by *bemo* drivers all over Bali. Though it's been the capital of Bali since 1958, it's no longer the administrative center of Badung Regency. In 1992, Greater Denpasar and Sanur split off from Badung and formed their own administrative entity—Denpasar.

A hot, dusty, cacophonous, former Brahman-class city, Denpasar has grown fifteen-fold over the past 10 years and is now home to 367,000 people. Its citizenry consists of Badung's landed gentry, the priest class, and the new Balinese techno and bureaucratic elites, as well as Indonesians drawn from other islands to this economic magnet. Denpasar is one of Indonesia's most fully integrated and tolerant cities, with separate *kampung* of Bugis, Arabs, Indians, Chinese, Madurese, and Javanese. Without doubt it's the richest, most important city in eastern Indonesia.

Unless you've got business here, the city has few charms, other than those quiet back alleyways where people are quite friendly. The most important government offices are located in a tree-shaded administrative complex of handsome reddish brick and gray stone. Industry is low-tech and non-polluting. Denpasar is actually best at night, when it's not so hot and the individual *kampung* resume their normal rhythms.

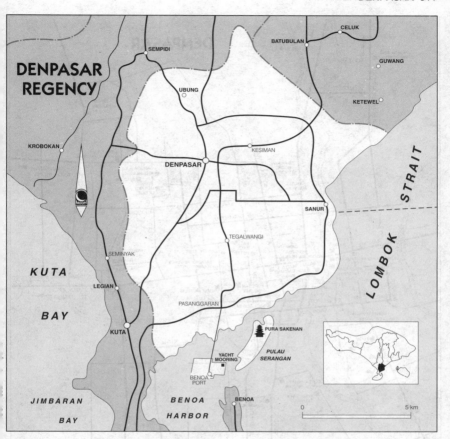

It seems the whole population is either directly or indirectly involved in the tourist industry, and you can easily engage people in conversation.

Denpasar's main one-way east-to-west shopping street, Jl. Gajah Mada, is crammed with chauffeured cars, noisome putt-putting *bemo,* roaring motorcycles, and smelly, spewing buses. The city's limited attractions include a spacious *alun-alun,* tourist information offices, the island's main bus stations and best-stocked markets, some good Chinese restaurants, a spirited night market, dance and drama academies, a major art center, first-class museum, and five big cinemas heralding the coming of the next kung fu epic.

SIGHTS

A great place for families to hang out in the evenings is the huge, well-kept park in the middle of town, **Puputan Square,** named for the bloody 1906 extermination of the island's ruling class by the Dutch. An heroic-style monument facing Jl. Surapati commemorates this tragic event. Note the woman with the *kris* in one hand and jewels in the other. Eyewitnesses of the time reported that female members of the court tauntingly flung their jewelry at the Dutch troops before being mowed down by rifle fire.

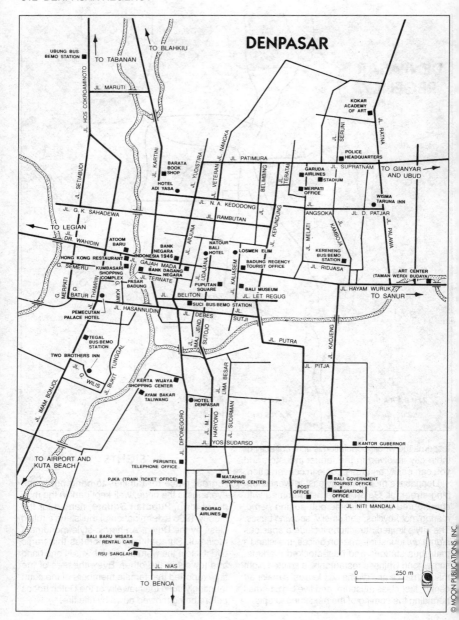

© MOON PUBLICATIONS, INC.

On every side of Taman Puputan are the traditional symbols of the power elite. North of the square is the **Governor's Residence,** built in Javanese *pendopo* style. Facing the Bali Museum is the stolid, modern military headquarters complex. Just south of the square in the middle of the city's busiest intersection is a five-meter-high, four-faced, eight-armed statue—*Mukha,* representing Batara Guru, "God of the Four Directions," who is even-handedly blessing all the cardinal points simultaneously.

The Bali Museum

The largest collection of Baliana in the world is located on the east side of Taman Puputan on Jl. Mayor Wishnu just south of the tourist office. The Bali Museum was established in 1910 by the conquering Dutch, who sought to collect and preserve artifacts they felt were disappearing overseas or succumbing to the elements. In 1917, an eruption of Gunung Batur and subsequent earthquakes destroyed hundreds of Denpasar's buildings, including the museum. Rebuilt in 1925, it was used as a storehouse for artifacts and temporary exhibits until 1932, when it was established as an ethnographic museum. The German painter Walter Spies helped assemble many of its original treasures from private collections and donations.

The grand, well-kept complex consists of a series of attractive, grassy courtyards containing all the archetypes of Balinese architecture—*bale agung, candi bentar, kulkul.* The main structure, with its many pillars, is built in the manner of Puri Kanginan in the eastern regency of Karangasem. Standing next to it is a reproduction of Singaraja Palace on the north coast. With rich ornamentation both inside and out, the museum's architecture combines the two principal edifices of Bali, the temple *(pura)* and the palace *(puri).*

The museum's four buildings contain a splendid collection of Balinese art—Neolithic stone implements, a hoard of Buddhist clay seals excavated near Pejeng, Balinese folk crafts, carved and painted woodwork, cricket-fighting cages, dance costumes, textiles, masks, weaving looms and fabrics, agricultural tools, musical instruments, furniture, scale models of ceremonial events, ethnographic exhibits. The first pavilion is a two-story building containing high-quality, early traditional, Kamasan-style paintings; classical Balinese calendars; modern Batuan and Ubud-style paintings; and work of the Academic and Young Artists (or Naive) schools. Another pavilion displays carved media—wood, stone, clay, and bone—including sculpted windows, doors, pillars, ceiling beams, friezes, old guardian figures, demons, and specimens of Bali's extraordinarily earthy and vigorous folk art. The building, dedicated to prehistoric artifacts, displays Bronze Age implements, including the famous Gilimanuk bronze spearhead, the largest ever discovered in Southeast Asia. Also see ritual objects, priestly accoutrements, and a veranda lined with old stone statues. One building is devoted entirely to masks, weapons, and costumes of the performing arts, including rare *barong* pig masks and primitive dance masks from remote villages. There's also an incredible display of *topeng.*

A good part of the displays are annotated with English explanations, and clear maps in the central building show all the important prehistoric and historical sites of Bali. The museum also has a library and a shop selling postcards and books in English. However, there's no ground plan of the museum nor is a guide available to show visitors around. Open Tues.-Thurs. 0800-1700, Friday 0800-1530, closed Monday. Admission Rp500. Wear long pants.

Temples

Just east of the big *alun-alun* on Jl. Mayor Wishnu, next to the museum, is a Hindu temple, **Pura Jagatnatha,** built in 1953. In the afternoon, people from the surrounding *kampung* come here to pray; the temple's especially busy during the full moon. On a towered throne of white coral sits a bright, gold statue of Ida Batara Sanghyang Widhi in his typical pose. This is the supreme god of Balinese Hinduism. The *padmasana* rests on the back of the sacred turtle, clasped by two *naga* on plinths carved with scenes from the Mahabharata and Ramayana. The central courtyard is surrounded by a moat containing gigantic carp.

Also visit **Puri Pemecutan** near Tegal bus station on the corner of Jl. Thamrin and Jl. Hasannudin, built in 1907 to replace the original palace of the raja destroyed by Dutch artillery. Pemecutan, which shares the complex with Pemecutan Palace Hotel, houses old weapons and a renowned *gamelan mas* which survived from the original *puri.* Don't miss the handsome, four-tiered *kulkul* diagonally opposite the palace with its eight small *raksasa* statues. Chinese porcelain plates decorate the topmost tier.

Another unique and archaeologically important temple is **Pura Masopahit,** located in a small alley in the middle of the city off Jl. Sutomo. Enter through a door in the alley. This temple, one of the oldest on Bali, has its origins in the great 14th- and 15th-century Javanese Majapahit Empire when Hinduism was first introduced to Bali. The massive statues of Batara Bayu and Garuda guard the split gateway. On the imposing facade is a pantheon of carved demons and deities, including Yama and Indra. Heavily damaged in the 1917 quake, the earliest, now-restored buildings are in the back. Look for the terra-cotta statues.

Pura Melanting, in the midst of Pasar Badung, is a market temple where vendors make offerings on their way to their stalls. Northeast of Denpasar on Jl. Ratna (near the Sekolah Menengah Musik), off to the left and just before the signpost to Kesiman, is old **Dalem Pura Tastasan** with a monolithic altar and *batu hitam.*

ACCOMMODATIONS

Unless they have business in the city, most tourists and travelers prefer the cheaper accommodations and more agreeable surroundings in the nearby beach resort areas of Kuta, Legian, or Sanur. Most of those who use Denpasar's 100 or so hotels are Indonesian businessmen, tour groups, and domestic tourists. Book ahead during high seasons.

Budget
For the budget traveler, **Wisma Taruna Inn,** Jl. Gadung 31, tel. (0361) 226913, lies on a quiet back street, two km from the city center (Rp200 by *bemo* or a 20-minute walk). From downtown Denpasar, walk up Jl. Hayam Wuruk and turn left at the Arya Hotel, approximately 100 meters down on the right. Rates Rp5000 s, Rp10,000 d (without breakfast); in the off-season even lower. Rent motorcycles and bicycles here. Other amenities include laundry service, beverages, and food. Friendly houseboys. This hostel is only a 10-minute walk from the Kereneng bus terminal, which provides transport to all of eastern Bali.

The **Bali International Hostel,** Jl. Mertasari 19, Banjar Suwung Kangin, Sidakarya, Den-

pasar Selatan, tel./fax (0361) 63912, opened in 1993 and caters to young people and student groups. Be sure to book ahead. Rp10,000 for fan-cooled rooms, Rp15,000 a/c. Each room holds two to four beds; restaurant; clean and safe; lockers provided. Get a taxi as it's a bit out of town, just two km from beach. Tours and sporting activities can be arranged.

Catering exclusively to travelers is **Two Brothers Inn** off the main road (Jl. Imam Bonjol) to Kuta Beach. It's only a five-minute walk from the Tegal *bemo* terminal and a 10-minute fast walk from downtown. Go down the lane (Gang VII/5) to the right of Banjar Tegal Gede. One of the cheapest *losmen* in Denpasar (Rp10,000 to 15,000 d without *mandi*), the Two Brothers is clean and safe, with electricity, sitting toilets, showers, fragrant flowers, free tea and coffee. It's also quiet, except for the dog chorus at night. Excellent value; please don't try to bargain. Try local meals in nearby *warung* and a small restaurant 200 meters away; ask proprietor Ibu Anom for the best eateries. From Two Brothers you can easily walk or take a *bemo* into town (Rp350), or just stroll down the lane in your swim gear with your towel over your shoulder and thumb a *bemo* (Rp800) to Kuta Beach.

If Two Brothers is full, try the noisier 31-room **Hotel Tamansari,** Jl. Imam Bonjol 45, tel. (0361) 226724, for Rp10,000-15,500. Some rooms have Indonesian-style *kamar mandi;* some have a fan. The pool is a surprising addition to a budget hotel. Also with a pool, and near the Two Brothers toward the city, is **Hotel Dharma Wisata,** Jl. Imam Bonjol 83, tel. (0361) 222186; Rp15,000 d for rooms with their own *mandi.* The place is cool, clean, efficient, and has a pool.

Quite central and cheap is **Hotel Adi Yasa,** Jl. Nakula 23, tel. (0361) 22679, asking Rp8500 s, Rp15,000 d with bathroom and breakfast. The 22 rooms, which may be hot and muggy and badly need refurbishing, all face a pleasant, central garden. Request a fan. When getting off the long-distance bus at around 0500, this is a convenient transit place to stay as it's only 1.5 km from Ubung station. Another way to hit it is from Kumbasari Market on Jl. Gajah Mada; walk up Jl. Kartini until you reach Jl. Nakula (the third right); Adi Yasa is about 100 meters down the street on the left, set in from the road.

Good reports about **Nakula Familiar Inn,** Jl. Nakula 4, tel. (0361) 226446, across the street and 40 meters west of Adi Yasa's in the direction of Jl. Kartini. Some of the new, clean, upbeat rooms (Rp16,000 d) feature balconies, fresh curtains, and big bathrooms. All rooms surround an outside dining area and courtyard. Another reasonable place is the family-run **Penginapan Tambora**, Jl. Gunung Tambora 6, tel. (0361) 226352; Rp15,000-25,000 s or d, Rp1500 extra for a fan. **Penginapan Mertapura**, Jl. Belimbing 22, tel. (0361) 225036, charges Rp15,000 s, Rp20,000 d. Can be noisy, as it faces the street.

A centrally located *losmen* catering primarily to Indonesian businessmen is **Hotel Ratu**, Jl. Yos Sudarso 4, Sanglah, tel. (0361) 226922. Central location, yet cushioned somehow from city noise. Rooms cost Rp12,500 s, Rp15,000 d without fan; Rp15,000 s, Rp20,000 d with fan. All prices include tax and service. Rooms are clean, with showers but no hot water. Breakfast not included.

On Jl. Diponegoro near the Matahari Shopping Center are many low-cost *losmen* popular with Indonesians, including **Hotel Damai, Hotel Dewi, Hotel Artha**, and **Diponegoro Inn. Hotel Chandra Garden**, Jl. Diponegoro 114, tel. (0361) 226425, has some a/c rooms; it's central, close to shopping centers, and includes a restaurant and bar. Rates (Rp27,500 s or d for rooms with fan) include tax and breakfast. **Hotel Viking**, Jl. Diponegoro 120, tel. (0361) 235153 or 223992, has budget rooms for Rp35,000 s or d, Rp60,000 a/c. Farther south on Jl. Diponegoro are **Hotel Rai** and **Hotel Oka. Hotel Diregapura**, Jl. Diponegoro 128, tel. (0361) 226924, offers 20 economy rooms for Rp10,000 s, Rp15,000 d. Nice garden. **Losmen Marhaen**, on Gang VII/4 off Jl. Diponegoro, tel. (0361) 223781, is a good deal for the money: Rp12,000 s, Rp14,000 d with fan. Only 12 small rooms, but each includes private *mandi* and is reasonably clean and quiet.

Moderate
The **Sari Inn**, Jl. Mayjen Sutoyo, tel. (0361) 222437, has 15 large, comfortable rooms with *mandi,* fan, and tea—very reasonable for Rp15,500 s, Rp20,000 d. An inexpensive *rumah makan* is 200 meters away. Call the inn from the airport and the owner will pick you up for Rp10,000. Seventeen-room **Losmen Elim**, Puri Oka, Jl. Kaliasem 3, tel. (0361) 224631, charges Rp15,000 s, Rp25,000 d; Rp50,000 for a/c front rooms. Breakfast extra, no hot water, all the hot

tea you can drink. **Hotel Denpasar**, Jl. Diponegoro 103 (Box 111, Denpasar), tel. (0361) 28336, features Bali-style cottages for Rp30,000 s, Rp45,000 d with a/c, private *mandi,* hot water, and a restaurant. Hotel Denpasar also offers a number of spartan, lower-priced fan-cooled rooms. Located in the south of the city on the road to Suwung. In the heart of Denpasar, **Hotel Puri Alit**, Jl. Sutomo 26 (Box 102, Denpasar), tel. (0361) 228831, fax 288766, has 22 rooms. With fan Rp16,000 s, Rp20,000 d; with a/c Rp30,000 s, Rp35,000 d. Private bath, tub, shower. For reservations, call the head office at Jl. Hang Tuah 41, Sanur, tel. (0361) 288560, fax 288766. Part of the Alit chain; if you like it here check out **Alit's Beach Bungalows** in Sanur and **Alit Kuta Bungalows** in Kuta.

Luxury
Recently renovated **Pemecutan Palace Hotel**, Jl. Thamrin 2 (Box 489), tel. (0361) 223491, has 45 rather ordinary rooms ranging from Rp30,000 s to Rp45,000 d, most with a/c and phones; no hot water. The restaurant serves Chinese, Indonesian, and Western food. Amenities include laundry and a car rental service. Quiet, despite its central location. The hotel is housed in a rebuilt palace—the royal occupants were annihilated in the 1906 *puputan*. Today, you may observe the day-by-day activities and rituals that still take place in the extensive courtyards of the *puri*. The singing birds add a nice touch. Ask to see the old *meriam* (cannon), an 1840 gift to the raja by the Dutch.

For more spacious surroundings, away from the hustle and bustle, stay in nearby Tohpati at **Hotel Tohpati Bali**, Jl. Bypass Ngurah Rai 15, tel. (0361) 236273, fax 232404, northeast of Denpasar. Luxury facilities—cottages surrounded by tropical trees and flowers, pool and sunken bar, piano bar, restaurants, shops, fitness center, putting green, tennis courts, and a contracted beach in Sanur with "every water sport available."

Centrally located at Jl. Veteran 3, just a short walk from Jl. Gajah Mada and the Bali Museum, is the closest thing to first-class accommodations in Denpasar—the venerable three-star, 73-room **Natour Bali Hotel** on Jl. Veteran 3 (Box 3003, Denpasar), tel. (0361) 225681, fax 235347. Built by a Dutch shipping company in 1927, this was Bali's first tourist hotel, and though it's becoming rather frayed, it still retains vestiges of its charming past with a palm-shaded lobby, antique black fans, art-deco lamps, dark wood finishings, and shady walkways. Here stayed the early Western anthropologists and writers who arrived to study Bali. The hotel charges Rp92,400 for rooms with a/c, ceiling fans, private bathrooms, hot water, TV, video, and a sound system. Suites are Rp150,150. Other amenities include gift shop, bar, and the Puri Agung Restaurant.

A new luxury convenience hotel, the **Sanno Denpasar Hotel Bali,** Jl. Hayam Wuruk 200 (tel. 0361-238185, fax 238186), has opened in Renon, five minutes' drive from Sanur Beach. Rates: Rp125,000 s, Rp150,000 d (plus 21%).

FOOD

With its sizable population of bureaucrats, businessmen, laborers, and service personnel, Denpasar offers an abundance of well-established *warung, rumah makan,* and restaurants serving Indonesian specialties at very reasonable prices. The city's densest concentration of Indonesian-style eating establishments is on Jl. Teuku Umar, which eventually joins Jl. Imam Bonjol, the road to Kuta.

Food Markets

For an instant introduction to Indonesian cuisine, visit the colorful open-air *pasar malam* in the parking lot 150 meters behind the multistoried Kumbasari Shopping Complex, just off Jl. Gajah Mada by the river. Open 1800-2400. Dozens of stalls under plastic covers serve Chinese noodle soups, fried rice, *sate,* excellent *martabak, babi guling, nasi campur, pangsit mie,* chocolate donuts, and hot drinks. Try steaming *kue putu* smothered in coconut shavings. At night the *pasar malam* is a splendid place to visit, with hundreds of milling people of all ages, races, and islands. Other *pasar malam* include the Kereneng bus station (the Asoka Night Market), serving excellent *babi guling* (only Rp1500) and other native dishes; opposite Tegal station (where you catch minivans to Kuta); and on Jl. Diponegoro near the Kertha Wijaya Shopping Center. All are good, cheap, entertaining night eateries that are so inexpensive only a glutton could possibly spend more than Rp6000.

Virtually all of Denpasar's six big shopping centers feature good quality, cheap, and genuine bakeries and cafeteria-style food marts with a wide range of Indonesian, Chinese, Muslim, and Western meals Rp2000-5000. The huge **Tiara Dewata Food Centre** on Jl. Mayjen Sutoyo, serves 150 different kinds of foods—a cheap, clean, lively place with meals starting at Rp1000.

Nasi Campur

Near Hotel Adi Yasa, on Jl. Judistira at Tapakgangsul, clean and simple **Rumah Makan Wardani,** tel. (0361) 224398, serves a delicious Balinese-style *nasi campur* for only Rp3000. Wonderful vegetables; open 0800-1600. A superb *nasi campur* served in the **Food Centre** of the Tiara Dewata, Jl. Mayjend Sutoyo 55, tel. (0361) 235733, costs about Rp3000. There are at least four restaurants on Jl. Diponegoro and several on Jl. Gajah Mada serving *nasi padang.* The **Minang Indah** *padang* restaurant next to the Amsterdam Bakery at Jl. Diponegoro 122, tel. (0361) 235035, is outstanding. Next door, at no. 124 A, tel. (0361) 223534, **RM Siang Malam,** lets patrons pick out *padang*-style dishes from the many stacked in the window. Open 24 hours.

Specialty Foodstalls and Restaurants

A simple *warung* on Jl. Kartini opposite the cinema serves fantastic crab soup (Rp2000) with green vegetables and egg plus a plate of rice. It also specializes in excellent shelled fried crab. Closed on Monday. A bottle of the ginger Sari Temulawak caps the meal; Rp1000 with ice.

For American food, go to the **Coffee House,** Jl. Gajah Mada 124 A, tel. (0361) 222579, next door to the Hong Kong Restaurant. They have a good breakfast for Rp2500-4750 (with cinnamon toast), pizza (Rp3000), BLTs (Rp3500). Clean, padded chairs, *batik* napkins. Open daily 0800-2130. **Libi** department store, Jl. Teuku Umar 104-110, tel. (0361) 232007 or 221438, has a fast-food Texas barbecue chicken restaurant (tel. 226560), open everyday 1000-2200; Rp1500 per piece.

A jump in elegance is the **Puri Agung Restaurant** in the Bali Hotel, Jl. Veteran 1, tel. (0361) 225681, which features a memorable *rijstaffel* (Rp10,500) as well as fixed-priced and a la carte meals. For inexpensive but first-class and not too spicy Indonesian/East Javanese food in a clean environment, eat at **Rumah Makan Betty** at Jl. Sumatra 56, tel. (0361) 224502—a simple, spacious, glassed-in, cafeteria-style place, popular with locals and expats, and one of Denpasar's best restaurants. The *nasi campur* and *bubur ayam* are good values; some vegetarian dishes. Open daily 0700-2100. Next door is a fine *mie pangsit* noodle shop.

For East Javanese specialities, try the excellent **Kikel Sapi** on Jl. Sumatra downtown. Tasty *gado-gado, gule,* and *rawon.* So crowded at night you may have to share a table. Open 0800-1600. Find Sunda-style fish at **Pondok Melati** in the government office district. **Ayam Bakar Taliwang** on Jl. Tengku Umar, tel. (0361) 228789, open 1000-2000, serves complete dinners of extra fat and juicy Sasak-style Taliwang chicken, with rice, *sambal,* vegetables, and delicious *es kelapa muda* (Rp1000). Outstanding fish *sate* with hot sauce. Particularly popular with high-placed government people. Another above-average chicken place is **Ayam Goreng Nyonya Suharti,** Jl. Gatot Subroto Ubung, tel. (0361) 234815—delicious Javanese-style roast chicken.

Balinese Food

Genuine Balinese food is not easy to find. Tasty Balinese *babi guling* and *lawar* for about Rp3000 per portion at **Warung Nasi Bali,** Jl. Hayam Wuruk 69 A, tel. (0361) 223889, an easy walk from the Kereneng bus station. Head out to Jl. Hayam Wuruk and turn east; it's on the left, about 300 meters before Jl. Nusa Indah. Open 0730-1800. Clean **Kakman Restaurant** on Jl. Tengku Umar 135 (halfway to Kuta), tel. (0361) 227188, also specializes in Balinese food. Try the Klungkung vegetables and the *urab.* Moderate prices. The atmosphere of a Balinese household with *bale bali;* patronized mostly by Chinese businessmen.

Asian Restaurants

Denpasar has some of the best Chinese restaurants on the island, several located on Jl. Gajah Mada. **Hawaii,** tel. (0361) 435135, on the second floor of the Kumbasari complex, offers a tourist menu with items like banana-and-cheese pancakes (Rp2800), club sandwiches (Rp3500), and traditional Chinese dishes. Be aware of the additional 10% government tax. The unpretentious but excellent and central **Atoom Baru,** Jl. Gajah Mada 106-108, tel. (0361) 426678, offers tasty *nasi goreng* for Rp3500, *cap cai,* a classic fishball soup, and delicious fish and veg-

etables with tomato sauce. A long-standing local favorite. The few flies landing on your table makes it all the more authentic. Also try the popular, fancier, and slightly overpriced **Hong Kong Restaurant,** Jl. Gajah Mada 99, tel. (0361) 434845, across the road from the Atoom Baru and right in front of Kumbasari Market. Dinners start at about Rp10,000; each dish can be ordered in different sizes. Specialties include stewed seafood and bean curd in a clay pot, Sichuan hot and sour soup, fried fresh carp, *nasi goreng* (Rp4000), and medium lobster (Rp50,000). Nice air-conditioned atmosphere; good for groups.

The **Akasaka** on Jl. Teuku Umar, Simpang Enam Square, tel. (0361) 238551 or 238552, is known for fine Japanese food. The restaurant's bar and *karaoke* music room, with a big-screen and twirling disco lights, are very popular with locals. Music programs in English, Japanese, Korean, and Chinese. Every second night is ladies night. Open 1900-0200. The only real nightclub in Denpasar, the Akasaka hosts live rock-and-roll bands in the basement.

Baked Goods and Desserts

There are dozens of bakeries in Denpasar providing fast food for people on their way to work. The biggest is **Amsterdam Bakery,** Jl. Diponegoro 122, tel. (0361) 235035—also a steak house, ice cream parlor, and restaurant. On Jl. Sumatra (no. 34A) is **Toko Roti Matahari,** tel. (0361) 234447, with bread, cheese and raisin rolls, donuts, muffins, and ice cream. The city's new shopping centers also feature bakeries; **Tiara Dewata** on Jl. Mayjen and **Sutoyo** are especially good.

EVENTS AND EXHIBITS

Dances and musical performances take place throughout the year. Keep your eyes and ears open. There are many tourist dance venues in southern Bali within easy reach of Denpasar, especially at Sanur's pricier hotels and restaurants. For cheaper, longer, and more traditional dances, see the celebrations and festivities in the villages.

The best way to follow religious ceremonies and festivals is to obtain a calender of events at one of Denpasar's tourist offices. In Denpasar itself, full moon ceremonies occur at Pura Jagatnatha (next to the Bali Museum) with its white coral lotus-throne shrine to Sanghyang Widi. You may watch if you wear the traditional Balinese *sarung.*

For Western films, go to **Wisata 21 Cineplex,** Jl. M.H. Thamrin, tel. (0361) 423023. This movie theater features five full-screen cinemas with three shows daily. Air conditioning, stereo surround sound, plush seats, cafeteria.

The Art Center

Also called **Taman Werdi Budaya,** the Art Center is on Jl. Nusa Indah in Abiankapas, a suburb of Denpasar in the direction of Sanur, only a 15-minute walk east of Kereneng station. Set in a restful garden with lotus ponds amid richly carved baroque Balinese buildings, the Taman Werdi Budaya houses exhibits of modern painting, masks, and woodcarving. Both Balinese and Indonesian artists are featured. You'll find a car park, museum, and small, fixed-price handicraft shops.

Visitors can view dance and music rehearsals in two open-air amphitheaters with modern lighting. Dances are also regularly staged for the public, including works incorporating modern Balinese choreography. In the *kecak* performance, staged each night 1830-1930 (Rp5000), traditional flickering oil lamps are still used. Eerie and powerful.

The Art Center also hosts a summer art festival each year from mid-June to mid-July, with competitions for costumes, dance, drama, *sendratari* performances, music, woodcarving, metalworking, and food. Every year is different, with each of Bali's regencies sending its best teams. Also see art events, crafts exhibits, and an extravagant production of the Ramayana Ballet. If it's the high season, be sure to book your hotel in advance. These entertaining and exciting cultural shows draw tens of thousands of visitors from around the world.

The Balinese Art Development Center Program, Jl. Bayusuta (in the Art Center), is open 0800-1700 daily except Monday. This tertiary-level institute offers work on the undergraduate through master's degree levels. Besides staging dances, plays, and pop concerts, it houses permanent exhibits offering handicrafts, paintings, carvings, and silver. Student discounts available.

STSI and SMKI

More advanced students attend Sekolah Tinggi Seni Indonesia (formerly ASTI), the Institute of Arts and Dance on Jl. Nusa Indah near the Art Center in Abiankapas, tel. (0361) 272361. Classes are 0700-1300 daily except Sunday. STSI director Made Bandem is responsible for a virtual renaissance in the Balinese arts. Tourism revenue is recycled into larger and grander ceremonies for the gods that, inevitably, include Balinese theater, music, song, and dance, and thus contribute to the development and preservation of Balinese art.

SMKI is the Conservatory of Instrumental Arts and Dance (tel. 0361-975180, fax 975162), for high school students in Batubulan. Opened in 1960; all Balinese dances are studied here. Visitors are welcome in the mornings to watch teachers train their pupils.

Hotel and Commercial Performances

In Sanur (nine km southeast of Denpasar), the Ramayana, *joged,* and *legong* are frequently staged at such big hotels as the Bali Hyatt just about every night of the week starting about 1900. Performances last 45 minutes to an hour and are often accompanied by buffet dinner. Cost: Rp25,000-30,000. *Wayang kulit* is performed every Monday, Wednesday, and Saturday 1900-2000 for Rp6000 in the Laghawa Beach Inn.

A high-quality, dynamic *barong* is put on especially for tourists at Batubulan, a suburb northeast of Denpasar, on one of three open-air stages every morning, 0900-1000. Jammed with hundreds of Europeans, and suffocating with peddlers, admission is Rp5000. In the afternoon, 1630-1730, is a *kecak* fire dance. At Tanjung Bungkah, between Denpasar and Sanur, a *kecak* and fire dance has been staged 1930-2030 regularly since 1972, admission Rp5000. While here, see the small but colorful *pura dalem* temple.

SHOPPING

Denpasar is where the Balinese shop for staples and necessities. Small shops and businesses are generally open 0830-1400, close for several hours, then reopen in the evening around 1700, then close again around 2100. On Sunday, everyone goes home at 1200 or 1300. The best way to shop in Denpasar is on foot. Denpasar's shopping street and business center is Jl. Gajah Mada, where anything—cassette tapes, textiles, medicine, stationery, tacky souvenirs, electronics, shoes—is available. The chance of being overcharged here is just as great as in Kuta or Sanur. Downtown is not the only place to shop. Other shopping streets include Jl. Thamrin for textiles, tailors, souvenirs, and leather wear, and Jl. Diponegoro for clothes and books. The big, bustling shopping centers, a few kilometers from the downtown, are open from 0900 or 1000 until 2000. The tourist corridor between Kuta and Ubud is choked with art shops carrying every conceivable native craft.

Downtown Markets

One of Denpasar's main attractions is the massive, multistoried, visually fascinating central market, **Pasar Badung** on Jl. Gajah Mada alongside the river. With droves of people and amazing colors, this market is especially strong in plaited ware and inexpensive trinkets. Good cheap eateries. As you enter the market, kids will offer to carry your merchandise for Rp1000. Lines of *dokar* wait to take shoppers and their goods home.

Different goods are sold in different sections. The cool, dark, basement level houses a huge, bustling fruit and vegetable market, as well as meat and fish markets. The first floor is devoted to hardware, flower offerings, and spices. The top floor features textiles, *songket, sarung* from Java, dance and ceremonial accoutrements, kitchen utensils, hardware, tinware, brassware, bags, inexpensive clothes, basketry, a giddy variety of things made from palm leaves, and a great view over the city.

West of Pasar Badung, just across the river, is the giant **Kumbasari Shopping Complex,** a rabbit's warren of small wholesale and retail shops selling clothes, bedcovers, *batik,* paintings, Mas-style carvings, Celuk silver, and scads of junk. Cinemas cap the complex. This is the closest Denpasar gets to an art market. Opens at 0800.

Shopping Centers

To satiate the increasingly urbane appetites of Bali's growing middle class, there's been an alarming proliferation of huge, air-conditioned, well-scrubbed, Western-style shopping centers. At last count the city had seven. Each contains a comprehensive supermarket, bookstore, department store, food center, and playground, as well as beauty salons, music stores, cosmetic counters, and sports, houseware, and hardware departments. Kitchen utensils like stainless steel pots, glassware, and wooden spoons are a real bargain, cheaper than in the *pasar.* The guitars are better quality than those sold in Bandung. If buying foreign-brand items like high-pressure kerosene lamps (Rp40,000) or staplers, remember spare parts. Also buy conventional, Western-style, ready-to-wear clothing, children's clothes, and all types of consumer articles: electronics, office and art supplies, housewares, crafts, and jewelry. All offer free parking with security guards and luggage counters *(tempat titipan)* where you can check in your valuables.

The three-storied **MA Department Store,** Jl. Diponegoro 50, tel. (0361) 222178, fax 36562, is on the street that extends past RM Beringin Jaya. Particularly strong on fashion apparel and accessories. All plastic accepted.

The **Matahari,** on Jl. Dewi Sartika, is owned by a Christian Chinese, Darmawan, who is trying to imitate Kmart in the States. **Tiara Dewata,** on Jl. Mayjend, Sutoyo, tel. (0361) 235733, has Bali's largest supermarket, a swimming pool (Rp1500 adult, Rp1000 child; bring towel), and children's amusement park with bumper cars and other assorted rides. Also check out **Libi** on Jl. Teuku Umar, tel. (0361) 232007, and **Matahari** on Jl. Dewi Sartika. **Hero,** Jl. Teuku Umar, offers superb fruit and vegetable sections, including fresh herbs and American seedless grapes. The seafood, meat, and dairy departments are the best on the island, and the range of baby products, cosmetics, and basic pharmaceuticals is excellent. A mammoth new shopping center, **New Dewata Ayu,** opposite the old favorite Matahari, opened in 1994. Smaller centers include **Supernova** on Jl. Raya Kuta, tel. (0361) 751186.

Other Markets

A morning market, **Pasar Kereneng,** is also a major terminal for buses to central and east Bali. Fruits and vegetables are sold here, as well as a limited selection of woodcarvings, paintings, and crockery. Denpasar's *pasar malam,* just south of the Kumbasari market, is clogged with vendors selling cheap clothes, jewelry, shoes, and *batik.*

The **Taman Werdi Budaya Bali** arts complex, in Abiankapas on the east side of Denpasar, houses exhibits of modern painting, woodcarvings, shadow puppet exhibits, and displays of giant *barong landung* puppets; regularly scheduled dances. Open Tues.-Sun. 0800-1700.

Sanggraha Kriya Asta Handicrafts Centre
You'll find this art center in Tophati's northeast suburbs, seven km east of Denpasar where the Bypass Highway from Nusa Dua joins the main road from Denpasar to Batubulan (P.O. Box 254, Denpasar, tel. 0361-222-942). This art cooperative, supervised by the Department of Industry, displays samples of nearly all the crafts produced on Bali today: woodcarvings, paintings, *batik,* dresses, shirts, silverwork. Prices about double what you'd pay in the art shops of Ubud, triple what you'd pay in a good art market. The quality, except for such items as mobiles, just isn't there.

Consisting of five spacious buildings, each devoted to a major craft, this art cooperative provides a good idea of what's out there—from high quality *batik sarung* for Rp35,000 to a pair of wooden earrings at Rp2000. All prices fixed. Open daily 0800-1700, Saturday 0900-1700, Sunday closed. Call for free transportation in the Denpasar, Kuta, and Sanur areas; the center will give you a lift if you spend Rp100,000 or more.

Next door to the handicrafts centre is a big Mega shop—better to spend time at Mega than at Sanggraha Kriya Asta. See "Craft Shops," below.

Pasar Satriya
Located by the temple Pura Satriya, on the corner of Jl. Veteran and Jl. Nakula, this small art dealer's wholesale market sells woodcarvings, paintings, and other crafts, plus produce and good Bali-style takeout food. Look in on the only bird market on Bali—the **Satriya Bird Market** (Pasar Burung) at Jl. Veteran 64, where 40 shops sell parrots, cockatoos, partridges, and parakeets, as well as tropical fish and aquariums.

Craft Shops
C.V. Nuratni, Jl. Gianyar 15, tel. (0361) 235613, is a large and well-known art shop on the road from Denpasar to Tohpati. Painted 2.5-meter-high Tegalalang Garudas go for Rp3 million; small ones are Rp31,500. Carved wooden ducks full of carved fruit, Rp735,000; a realistic banana tree for Rp630,000. Nuratni is an exporter and also accepts credit cards, traveler's checks, and personal checks. Prices not marked. Purchase unique clothing by a Japanese designer in the **Bali Baru Wisata** gallery at Jl. Sumba 26, tel. (0361) 2223998 or 31784.

Peek in at **Mega Art Shop,** Jl. Gajah Mada 36, tel. (0361) 225120, for its wide range of Balinese arts—jewelry, leather, puppets, paintings, ceramics, and fine textiles, including reasonably priced framed weavings from Timor for Rp230,000-287,000, and Sumbu *ikats* for Rp115,000-287,000. Ten percent cash discount. Visit only to see incredibly delicate, museum-quality antique gold artifacts from Flores. Open 0730-1700. An even larger **Mega,** tel. (0361) 228855 or 224570, is at Jl. Raya Gianyar Km 5.7 on the outskirts of Denpasar in Tohpati. Ask to see the owner's private collection of *kris* and *ikat* (not for sale). While there, check out the **Popiler,** tel. (0361) 235162, next door, open until 1800. There are now six stores in this trustworthy chain, including one downtown at Jl. Gajah Mada 36. Even if you buy some jewelry and then decide you don't like it, you can return it and staff will gladly allow you to exchange it for an item of equal value.

Fabrics and Textiles
Jalan Sulawesi is the fabrics street, especially for Indian or Muslim-style fabrics. Several well-stocked shops, including **Dua Lima** and **Toko Murah,** carry everything from gingham to velvet, nylon net to the finest cotton. Fair prices. At Jl. Sulawesi 58, tel. (0361) 225421, **Meubal Yani** carries *bantal guling* (Dutch wife) for only Rp6000.

Indonesians themselves shop for clothes at **Galuh Tenun and Batik Bali,** tel. (0361) 98304, in Batubulan on the main road out of Denpasar on the right. Here you can buy a *sarung* for as little as Rp4000. Enough of the staff speak English so you can make yourself understood. For high quality *batik sarung* and *batik,* try **Winotosastro** on Jl. Hayam Wuruk 102 on the road to Sanur. Silk is the specialty of the **Duta Silk House** in Duta Plaza, Denpasar. **Panca Mulia Textiles,** Jl. Gajah Mada 78, is a great place to buy *sarung* and three-meter-long *kain,* mostly traditional designs, Rp10,000-15,000.

Ikat

Toko Pelangi at Jl. Gajah Mada 54 specializes in fine *ikat* from Bali, Sumba, and Savu. **Sekana House,** Jl. Diponegoro VII/4, tel. (0361) 235776, offers traditional antique *ikat.* **Surya Jaya,** Jl. Gajah Mada 62, sells convincing copies of *ikat* for curtains, bedspreads, and the like.

Antiques

Alit's, on the east end of Jl. Thamrin, tel. (0361) 436645, and the **Meteor Shop,** Jl. Kartini 32, are known for their antiques as well as carved chess sets and sandalwood fans. Check out the **Pelangi Art Shop,** Jl. Soko 48, tel. (0361) 222689; another branch on Poppies Lane in Kuta, tel. (0361) 755646.

Mario Antiques in Batubulan proffers a lot of junk—also some gems. The nicest pieces of furniture come from wealthy families, and they don't part with them cheaply. You really have to know what you're doing in this place. A half kilometer past the market on the left.

Gold and Silver

On Jl. Sulawesi beside the household market, a number of silver shops sell 22-24 carat pieces. Some offer wholesale prices competitive with Hong Kong and Singapore. Try **Solomon Silver,** no. 66. tel. (0361) 224920. As is the case throughout Indonesia, you buy gold jewelry by the weight; the actual workmanship is free. Worth investigating is **Zamrud's** on Jl. Sulawesi, which carries and makes fine jewelry.

A very specific place for gold is the row of gold shops on Jl. Hasannudin. At any of them, you may also have gold articles made (a gold ring costing $500 in the States can be made here for about $200). The **Kenanga Gold Shop** at no. 43 A, tel. (0361) 225725, has a fine selection. If you change your mind after your purchase, you may return the item and get your money back, less 10%. Take a peek in **Melati,** no. 41 F, tel. (0361) 237065, and the **99 Gold Shop,** no. 31 D, tel. (0361) 237169, while you're in the neighborhood.

Bookstores

The best bookstore for Westerners, and one of Bali's largest, is **Gramedia,** tel. (0361) 221026, in the basement of the Duta Plaza Shopping Center on Jl. Dewi Sartika. English-language paperbacks, guidebooks, maps, coffee table books, magazines. Open daily 0930-2000. **PT Gunung Agung,** in the Libi Shopping Center at Jl. Teuku Umar 110, tel. (0361) 263387, is also excellent. **C.V. Garuda Wisnu,** Jl. Teuku Umar 90 X, tel. (0361) 238010, and the bookstore at the **Tiara Dewata Shopping Centre** on Jl. Mayjend Sutoyo, tel. (0361) 225733, are also very good. **Toko Buku Muda,** Jl. Gajah Mada 18, tel. (0361) 224297, sells books as well as office and art supplies, sports equipment, and typewriters. The best Indonesian-language bookstores are **Garuda Wishnu,** Jl. Teuku Umar 90 K, and **Barata,** Jl. Kartini 107/156, tel. (0361) 223746.

Odds and Ends

Purchase flowers at the **Lely Flower House,** Jl. Nangka 41, tel. (0361) 224514, or **Rose Flower Shop,** Jl. Hasanuddin 28, tel. (0361) 222239. The furniture center is around the Sanur Bypass area and Batubulan. In the city, try **Harapan Meubel,** Jl. Sumatra 6, tel. (0361) 224106. Drop by **Pelangi** on Jl. Thamrin 27-37, tel. (0361) 428303, for kitchen supplies, including stainless steel items at bargain prices. A wide variety of less expensive kitchen and cooking appliances are sold in the specialty shops along **Jl. Diponegoro.** One well-stocked shop is **Telaga Mas Jaya,** Jl. Diponegoro 28, tel. (0361) 227544. Find wide selections of watches at **Toko An,** Jl. Gajah Mada, tel. (0361) 424193; **Toko Bali Joy,** Jl. Sumatra 57, tel. (0361) 223535; **Bandung Toko,** Jl. Kartini 29, tel. (0361) 224347; and **Toko Mujur,** Jl. Gajah Mada 69, tel. (0361) 222904. Buy arts and crafts supplies at **C.V. Garuda Wisnu,** Jl. Teuku Umar 90 X, tel. (0361) 238010, and in the **Libi Department Store** on Jl. Teuku Umar. Sporting goods available at **U.D. Bali Dirgantara,** Jl. Dr. Wahidin 47 B, tel. (0361) 420234; **Bali Sport,** Jl. Teuku Umar 117, tel. (0361) 238033; and **Ruci Sport,** Jl. Teuku Umar 65 B, tel. (0361) 234206.

International Optical, Jl. Gajah Mada 133, tel./fax (0361) 426294, carries a wide range of glasses. Other eyefolks include **Optik Kimia Farma,** Jl. Diponegoro 125, tel. (0361) 227811; **Moses Optical,** Jl. Diponegoro 66, tel. (0361) 226257; and **National Optical,** Jl. Sulawesi 134, tel. (0361) 222934. Buy cassette tapes at **C.V. Dasa Dewa,** Jl. Diponegoro 98 D, tel. (0361) 236278. Other music shops: **Dynamics Music,** Jl. Imam Bonjol, tel. (0361) 225472; and **Vini, Vidi,**

Vici on Jl. Supratman, tel. (0361) 227219. **Toko Bhineka Jaya,** tel. (0361) 224016, the largest distributor of coffee on Bali, is across from Alus on Jl. Gajah Mada. Robusta and Arabica and many other blends sell for Rp4500-10,000 per kg.

Pembina Ilmu, Jl. Durian 3, tel. (0361) 232677, specializes in medical, scientific, geological, and geographic supplies and instruments at pretty good prices compared to those in Europe and the U.S.A. A good place to take or buy something for a kid. You'll find leather luggage, shoulder bags, and duffel bags on the second floor of the **Kumbasari Market. Gung Wahade** is a tattoo parlor on Jl. Bukit Tunggal on the way to Stasiun Tegal. For graphic arts and printing needs, **Tata Grafika Percetakan,** Jl. Ir. I.B. Oka, Gang Kujang 3, tel. (0361) 224355, does good work. Buy electronic goods like Walkmans, cassette recorders, and radios from one of the many shops along Jl. Diponegoro. Or try **Toko Palapa Agung** on Jl. Sumatra 8, tel. (0361) 225721; **Toko Osaka,** tel. (0361) 234665, also on Jl. Sumatra; **Toko Agung Plaza,** Jl. Veteran 44, tel. (0361) 223216; and **Toko Surya,** Jl. Gajah Mada 128, tel. (0361) 422254.

SERVICES

Tourist Services

The **Denpasar Regency Tourist Office,** Jl. Surapati 7, is a five-minute walk from the Bali Museum. Open 0700-1530, Friday until 1030, Saturday until 1230, closed Sunday. This is the best, friendliest, and most convenient source of information in the regency and all of Bali. Pick up a map of Denpasar, a calendar of events, and ask about an *odalan* or other events taking place in the countryside. Telephone the office at (0361) 234569 (from a foreign country dial 0361-166 for information). You can temporarily store your backpack here during office hours.

Tourism headquarters for the whole island is the **Bali Government Tourist Office** on Jl. S. Parman, tel. (0361) 222387, a 10-minute walk behind the post office in Denpasar's government complex. Present yourself at the reception desk and fill in the request form. More an administrative office than one geared for tourists. Open Mon.-Thurs. 0700-1400, Friday until 1100, Saturday until 1230. Find a **Department of Tourism Regional Office,** tel. (0361) 25649, on Jl. Raya Puputan.

The **immigration office** is on Jl. Panjaitan, off Jl. Puputan Raya, tel. (0361) 227828. If staying in or near Kuta, *kantor imigrasi* at the airport on Jl. Ngurah Rai (near the post office) is more convenient. Open Mon.-Thurs. 0700-1400, Friday until 1100, Saturday 0700-1230, Sunday closed. Always visit government offices early in the morning and dress neatly.

Consulates: Australian, Jl. Moh. Yamin Kav 51, Renon, tel. (0361) 235002, fax 31990; Danish and Norwegian, Jl. Jayagiri VIII/10, tel. (0361) 235098 or 233053; French, Jl. Raya Sesetan 46 D, Banjar Pesanggaran, tel. (0361) 233555; Dutch, Jl. Imam Bonjol 599, tel. (0361) 751904 or 51497, fax 52777; **German,** Jl. Pantai Karang, tel. (0361) 288826; **Japanese,** Jl. Moh. Yamin 9, Renon, tel. (0361) 231308 or 34808.

Medical Services

The most modern government hospital is **RSU Sanglah,** Jl. Kesehatan Selatan 1, tel. (0361) 235456, ext. 11. Another hospital, **Wangaya,** is on Jl. Kartini, tel. (0361) 222141. **Surya Husada Clinic,** Jl. Pulau Serangan 1-3, tel. (0361) 223786, in Sanglah near the government hospital, is the best private hospital. Though it charges twice the prices of the public hospitals, the service is better, and the staff is better trained and speaks English. Open around the clock. Another 24-hour clinic is **Manuaba Clinic,** Jl. Cokroaminoto 28, tel. (0361) 426393.

For **emergencies,** call an ambulance at tel. 118 or 27911. A physician with experience treating tourists is **Dr. Tjokorda Gde Subamia,** Rapco Station, tel. (0361) 234139. **Dr. Gst Putu Panteri** is in charge of a psychiatric clinic on Jl. Raya Denpasar, tel. (0361) 423301.

The city's largest pharmacy is **Kimia Farma,** Jl. Diponegoro 125, tel. (0361) 227812, just up from the Matahari Shopping Centre where Jl. Diponegoro meets Jl. Teuku Umar. It's also the busiest and has the longest wait; get there early in the morning. Open 24 hours. Another **Kimia Farma** pharmacy is in front of Sanglah hospital, tel. (0361) 223877. At smaller pharmacies you get faster service. A handy apothecary is **Toko Obat Jaya Abadi,** Jl. Gajah Mada 71-73, tel. (0361) 263026, which specializes in Indonesian and Chinese medicines. Also try **Apotik Sehat,** Jl. Diponegoro 205, tel. (0361) 225158, and **Apotik Kresna Farma** on Jl. Thamrin, tel. (0361) 422133. A small, inviting *jamu* opposite

Pasar Badung on Jl. Sulawesi has an outstanding selection. There are many others. **Toko Jaya Abadi** on Jl. Gajah Mada sells *jamu* and traditional Chinese medicines. A wonderful traditional Chinese apothecary, **Toko Sentosa**, on Jl. Gajah Mada, tel. (0361) 222812, carries everything from ginseng root to Ho Shou Wu.

Dentists working in Denpasar hold to a surprisingly high standard. Emergency treatment is administered by **Dr. Indra Guizot**, Jl. Patimura 19, tel. (0361) 226834, appointments 1000-2100.

Beauty Salons, Tailors, Massage, and Fitness

The **Pantes Beauty Salon**, Jl. Gajah Mada 59, tel. (0361) 222984, gives perms for Rp25,000 and haircuts for Rp7500. The latter includes sideburn, ear, neck, and mustache trims, generous dose of talcum powder, and a glass of iced tea. A full range of body treatments, hair styling, and facials are available at **Topstar** in the Kertha Wijaya Shopping Centre, Jl. Diponegoro 98, tel. (0361) 221768; **Paul and Irene Boutique**, Jl. Melati 55, tel. (0361) 225717; and **Mustika Ayu Salon**, Jl. Danau Buyan 10, tel. (0361) 289080.

If you're in need of a **tailor**, see Alus at Gajah Mada 77, tel. (0361) 224522, or Hadi Tailor on Jl. Sumatera, tel. (0361) 223260. It's only a one to three day wait for the finished product.

The best of the city's masseuses are specially trained blind men. **Mitra Jaya**, Jl. Imam Bonjol 58, tel. (0361) 232071, charges about Rp8000 for an hour and a half session. The **LG Club Sehatku**, Jl. D. Tamblingan 23, tel. (0361) 287880, in Sanur does shiatsu.

The **Bali Fitness Centre** is at Jl. Diponegoro 98, tel. (0361) 232853, Pusa Pertokoan Kerta Wijaya, Block B 15/16, tel. (0361) 232853; find the **Mahajaya Fitness Centre** in Kompleks Pertokoan Mahajaya, Jl. Cokrominoto 63, in Ubung, tel. (0361) 432079.

Photo Shops, Communications, Bank, and Postal Services

Tati Photo, Denpasar's leading photographic supplies store sells cameras and equipment, prints and enlarges photos and slides, repairs cameras, and snaps passport photos in both black-and-white and color. Find the place at Jl. Sumatra 10-14, on the corner of Jl. Sumatra and Jl. Thamrin, tel. (0361) 264203. Photo services also available from **Prima Photo,** Jl. Thamrin 41, tel. (0361) 425031, and **Diamond Photo Studio,** Jl. Thamrin 5, tel. (0361) 426903.

The **telephone and telegraph office** is at Jl. Teuku Umar 6, tel. (0361) 222021, at the intersection of Jl. Diponegoro. Make international, collect, and calling-card calls, send and receive faxes and telexes. Open 24 hours. Send telegraphs and faxes Mon.-Sat. 0800-1900, Sunday 0800-1200.

Wartel (Warung Telekomunikasi) telecommunication centers are found in several locations—Jl. Segara Perempatan, tel. (0361) 288864, and Jl. Besakih, tel. (0361) 235067. Telephone, fax, or telex a message to anywhere in the world. Usually open 0800-1600.

The **central post office,** tel. (0361) 223565, 223568, 226581, or 226584, is on Jl. Raya Puputan in Renon, which is difficult, though possible by *bemo,* to reach. Best bet is to hire an *ojek* from Kereneng Station for about Rp2000. Open Mon.-Thurs. 0800-1400, Friday 0800-1100, Saturday 0800-1100. They don't forward mail, though they say they will. Although they have poste restante service here 0800-2100, you're better off with the poste restante centers in Ubud, Sanur, or Kuta. Even better is to have mail sent directly to your hotel. Other major Denpasar post offices are at Jl. Kamboja 6, outside Kereneng *bemo* station, open Mon.-Thurs. 0800-1200 and 1300-2100, Friday 0800-1200 and 1330-2100, Saturday 0800-2000, Sunday 0800-2100; on Jl. Teuku Umar across from the telephone office, open daily 0800-2100; and at Sanglah near the Udayana University on Jl. Diponegoro on the road to Benoa.

To send parcels, go to the *paket pos* building at Jl. Diponegoro 146, tel. (0361) 227727. Open Mon.-Fri. 0800-2000, Friday and Saturday until 1100. From Ubung terminal, take a *bemo* to the corner of Jl. Sudirman and Jl. Niti Mandala Renon, then walk 500 meters to the west. This is a good place to have parcels sent, as the clerks charge only Rp4000 to wrap and bind your box, with a plastic cover sewn on tightly and securely.

UPS, Jl. Raya Sesetan 118, tel. (0361) 232720, provides package and document delivery to more than 180 countries with electronic tracking capability. For rates, see the postal section in the Introduction.

For packaging and forwarding bulk shipments overseas, use **PT Khatulistiwa Mandiri,** Komplek

Perkantoran, Benoa Port, tel. (0361) 226897, fax 226897; or **Global Putra International Group,** Jl. Raya Sesetan 200 B, tel. (0361) 232835 or 237657. These companies offer full container, bulk cargo, air and sea freight, customs services, and parcel and courier service. There are scores of other cargo shipping companies in Sanur and the Kuta area. Allow about three days to arrange to send a container.

There are several banks to choose from at the eastern end of Jl. Gajah Mada. You'll get quick and continuous service (no break for lunch) at **Bank Negara Indonesia 1946** at Jl. Gajah Mada 20, tel. (0361) 227321. **Bank Duta,** Jl. Hayam Wuruk 165, tel. (0361) 226578, accepts Visa and MasterCard; open Mon.-Fri. 0800-1200, Saturday 0800-1100. **BCA,** Jl. Hasannudin 58, tel. (0361) 431012, also accepts plastic, open Mon.-Fri. 0800-1400, Saturday 0800-1200. One of the best banks for telegraphic transfers is **Bank Bumi Daya,** Jl. Veteran 12, tel. (0361) 231073, which will also cash most kinds of traveler's checks. **Bank Ekspor-Impor,** Jl. Udayana 11, tel. (0361) 234784, cashes Thomas Cook traveler's checks and is reliable for wire transfers. Get cash advances with your Visa card at the branch of the **Lippo Bank;** the main office is at Jl. Thamrin 77, tel. (0361) 422176. There are at least three **money-changers** at the airport, open until 2000 or later. Find an **ATM** at Bank Bali near the telephone office on Jl. Diponegoro where it intersects with Jl. Teuku Umar.

Police and Legal Services
For traffic problems, contact the **police head-quarters** on Jl. Supratman near the stadium, Polda Nusra, tel. (0361) 227711. Open Mon.-Sat. 0800-1200. Police stations are at Jl. Diponegoro 10, tel. (0361) 234928; Jl. Gunung Agung, tel. (0361) 234928; and on Jl. A. Yani, tel. (0361) 225456. For emergencies, call police at tel. 110.

Going by the title *notaris,* there are many lawyers in the Denpasar area. Start with **Amir Sjarifudin,** Jl. Veteran 11 A, tel. (0361) 235126, or **Francisca Teresa,** Jl. Patimura 7, tel. (0361) 227110.

Gay and Lesbian Resource
For information on gay and lesbian travel in Bali, call or write: **Gaya Dewata,** c/o Yayasan Citra Usadha Indonesia, Jl. Belimbing Gang Y No. 4;

tel. (0361) 222620, fax 229487. Also serves as an AIDS education center and sells *GAYa Nusantara.*

Churches and Mosques
Find a **Seventh-Day Adventist** church on Jl. Surapati, **Pentecostal** services at 0800 at Jl. Kresna 19, an **Evangelical** house of worship on Jl. Melati, and the **Gereja Kristen Protestan** at Jl. Debes 6, tel. (0361) 223758, holding services in Indonesian at 0700 and 0900 each Sunday. Also in Denpasar are **Gereja Maranatha,** tel. (0361) 222591, and **Gereja Baithani,** tel. (0361) 232414.

Above the **St. Joseph Catholic Church,** Jl. Kepundung 2, off Jl. Surapati, are angels dressed as *legong* dancers. In a stone bas-relief of Christ, Pilate studies the scrolls by electric light while a motorbike sits in the background. Services are on Saturday at 1730, Sunday 0830 and 1730. The **Raya Mosque** and **Mesjid An Nur** are on the corner of Jl. Hasannudin and Jl. Sulawesi, and **Uchuwah Mosque** is down Jl. Surapati. **Mesjid Al-Hissan** is at Hotel Bali Beach.

GETTING AROUND

Denpasar is the travel hub of Bali. Here you can catch *bemo,* minibuses, and long-distance buses to every part of the island. Denpasar drivers are reckless and inconsiderate, with one foot on the accelerator at all times. Pedestrians take their lives in their hands crossing Denpasar's streets. There are more vehicles here per capita than even Jakarta, and if the sheer volume and cacophony of traffic don't get you, the oppressive heat and humidity will.

If you try to drive on your own, use a map. Tourists have spent hours circling the city's confusing pinwheel of one-way streets, trying to escape. You can obtain a local license for motorbiking or driving at the Denpasar Police Station on Jl. Supratman. It's far better, however, to get an International License before you reach Bali.

Bemo, Taxis, and Dokar
The minimum *bemo* or minibus fare to anywhere in Denpasar is Rp500 for the inner city, and Rp700 maximum for the rest of the place.

Denpasar now has metered taxis—yellow, with a sign reading Taxi. Still, drivers for **Praja Taxi,** tel. (0361) 751919 or 289090, may claim the meter is broken, or may take a route longer than necessary, so it's best to settle on a fare before climbing in. With the recent rise in gasoline prices, flagfall is now around Rp800. From the Matahari Shopping Center to the Denpasar Tourist Office the fare should run about Rp2000. Taxis from Denpasar to the airport cost about Rp12,000; to Kuta, Rp10,000; to Sanur, Rp8000. Don't tip.

The most expedient and least expensive way to get somewhere in Denpasar is to charter a three-wheeled *bemo*—a poor man's taxi—for about Rp2000 or Rp3000 for an average run. Or just flag down anything going in your direction—private cars, trucks, or motorcycles. Many drivers cruise for paying riders, charging Rp1000-1500 for a two- to five-km ride.

You'll find pony-drawn *dokar* outside Kereneng Station or just off Jl. Sulawesi beside the household market. They aren't allowed on main streets. *Dokar* charge tourists at least Rp1500 for a short ride. Capacity three Australians or four Indonesians.

Car and Motorcycle Rental
Jeeps with drivers can be rented through **Utama Motors,** tel. (0361) 222073, or **Bali Wisata,** tel. (0361) 224479, both on Jl. Imam Bonjol; or **Surya Agung Dewata Rent-a-Car,** Jl. Diponegoro 69, tel. (0361) 233448. You can also ask your hotel desk clerk or homestay owner. **Taman Sari Hotel,** Jl. Danau Buyan 31, tel. (0361) 288187, also rents out cars. Rent a motorcycle from **Koperasi Jasa Bakor Motor,** Kompleks Pertokoan and Terminal Tegal Sari 33 B, Jl. Imam Bonjol, tel. (0361) 226576.

You'll have to pay for parking almost everywhere in Denpasar; as soon as you start to turn the key, attendants appear out of nowhere to collect Rp200 per car, Rp100 per motorcycle.

GETTING AWAY

By *Bemo*
Four-wheeled *bemo* emanate from Denpasar's five *bemo* stations on the perimeter of the city to points all over the island. Go to the station closest to your destination. If you find yourself in the wrong station, there are three-wheeled *bemo* constantly going around in circles, zipping passengers back and forth between stations.

Denpasar is so big that in most cases you must pass through it on your way to someplace else. For example, if heading from Kuta to Sanur you must first get a *bemo* from Kuta to Tegal station (Rp800), then transfer to Kereneng where you board a another *bemo* to Sanur (Rp500).

From Kereneng, on the east edge of town off Jl. Kamboja, *bemo* serve Denpasar itself and the suburbs of Batubulan and Sanur for Rp500. From Tegal, in western Denpasar, *bemo* depart for Kuta, Legian, the airport, and Nusa Dua; from Ubung Station on Jl. Cokroaminoto in the north of town, *bemo* head west and north to Gilimanuk (Rp3000), Bedugal (Rp2500), Singaraja (Rp3000), and points east on Java. From the mother of all bus stations, Batubulan, east of town just before the village of Batubulan, big vans and minivans leave for every major tourist destination. From Suci, take *bemo* to Benoa Port, and Sanggaran. From Wangaya, *bemo* depart for the Sangeh Monkey Forest, Plaga, and Petang. *Bemo* arrive and leave Denpasar's stations in all directions until around 2000 (or in the high season, as late as 2200). If you plan on returning to Denpasar the same day, plan ahead because after nightfall the *bemo* of Kuta, Legian, Sanur, Ubud, and Singaraja are the only ones still running (at jacked-up prices) on the island.

Organized thieves sometimes work *bemo* traveling out of Denpasar. Beware of pairs of young men: one will get on carrying large parcels, which he uses to cloak his attempt to pick your pocket, moneybelt, or backpack; the other distracts you with friendly conversation in quite intelligible English.

By Bus
All night buses leaving the island depart from Ubung. You can catch an overnight ride to Yogyakarta for about Rp40,000; guard your possessions and don't fret about getting much sleep. The trip is very long and slow—about 30 hours.

Sample fares to Java: Probolinggo, 4 hours, Rp21,000; Surabaya, 6 hours, Rp21,000; Malang, 8 hours, Rp21,000; Semarang, 14 hours, Rp35,000; Bandung, 24 hours, Rp45,000; Jakarta/Bogor, 24 hours, Rp56,500; Lampung on Sumatra, 47 hours, Rp90,000. All buses—except to Yogyakarta—depart at 1830 and are equipped with toilets, a/c, reclining seats, and refreshments.

You can also try a bus/train combo. At least if you take the train, you won't get a flat tire (oh, maybe on the *the way* to the train). Sample fares: Probolinggo, Rp8500 economy, Rp12,000 second class; Surabaya, Rp7700, Rp12,000 second Class; Semarang, Rp17,000 economy, Rp64,500 second class, Rp64,500 executive class; Yogyakarta, Rp12,500 economy, Rp34,500 second class, Rp64,500 executive class; Bandung, Rp15,500 economy, Rp36,000 second class; Jakarta, Rp23,000 economy, Rp34,500 second class, Rp71,500 executive class. Departure times 1300 and 1600.

Travel Agencies and Airline Offices

Discounts are available, so check around. Try **ANTA Express**, Jl. Dewi Sartika, Kompleks Pertokoan Duta Permai Bl 1/H, tel. (0361) 235581; **Bali Tours and Travel**, Jl. Sri Kesari 51, tel. (0361) 287720; **Surya Jaya Tours**, Jl. Nangka 231 A/B, tel. (0361) 225253 or 35058; and **Vaya Tours**, Jl. Hayam Wuruk 124 A, tel. (0361) 223747 or 24449.

P.T. Nitour, Jl. Veteran 5, tel. (0361) 222849, offers full- and half-day tours to such destinations as Lombok, Baluran Game Reserve, and the classical ruins of Central Java. For Rp144,000 rafting trips, contact **Ayung River Rafting Company**, Jl. Diponegoro 150 B-29, tel. (0361) 224236. **Gapura Jaya Tours**, Jl. Hayam Wuruk 74, tel. (0361) 228460, is an efficient airline ticketing agency for Garuda and Merpati. **Astina Tours & Travel**, Jl. Hayam Wuruk 8 (within walking distance from Kereneng Station), tel. (0361) 223266 or 227464, fax 231740, sells terrifically priced Air New Zealand tickets to Singapore and other points in Southeast Asia. Open Mon.-Thurs. 0800-2000, Saturday 0800-1600, holidays and Sunday 0800-1300.

Garuda is at Jl. Melati 61, near the Kereneng bus station, tel. (0361) 225245. Find **Merpati** at Jl. Melati 59, tel. (0361) 222864 or 225841. Both are opposite the stadium, near each other, and have roughly the same business hours: Mon.-Fri. 0700-1600, Saturday until 1300, Sunday 0900-1300.

Use **Bouraq**, Jl. Sudirman 19 A, tel. (0361) 224656 or 223564, in front of Udayana University, for flights at very competitive prices to Nusatenggara, Sulawesi, and Kalimantan.

Many foreign airlines—**Thai, Qantas, Cathay Pacific**—maintain offices in the Bali Beach Hotel in Sanur. **UTA** is at Jl. Bypass Ngurah Rai, tel. (0361) 233341.

VICINITY OF DENPASAR

Visit the saltmaking flats at **Suwung**, where salt is gleaned from sand, dried in the sun, then mixed with water and poured through a wooden filter, leaving salt residue. On a good day a family can make five kilos. Look for the salt factories on the right side of Jl. Bypass on the way from Kuta to Sanur.

Kesiman

Visit this village, four km from Denpasar, to see the slender *prasada* **Pura Petilan**, built for a former prince, with its beautiful *candi bentar*. Every six months on a Sunday afternoon during *odalan*, watch the strange parade of *barong* and Rangda that ends with a dramatic reenactment of an historical battle. Head to Kesiman's stage, 500 meters from Pura Petilan, to see entertaining, high-quality *barong* dances performed daily.

Kesiman has some of the best examples of Badung's brick buildings, many of which now sadly giving way to the kitschy new-baroque style devouring the island. Check out one of Bali's most remarkable *kulkul* on Jl. Gianyar opposite the end of Jl. Abiankapas, a four-tiered drum tower constructed almost exclusively of carved brick, giving the structure an age-old, warm, and rustic feeling.

SANUR

A prosperous and historic resort area, Sanur is Indonesia's answer to Waikiki. It's nine km southeast of Denpasar and crowded with high-priced luxury hotels and clusters of serene bungalows in leafy compounds along the shoreline of a gentle, reef-sheltered lagoon. Guesthouses started appearing here as early as the 1940s and heralded the age of modern tourism on the island. Large hotel enclaves, shady lanes, trees, and coral walls give the village a parklike setting.

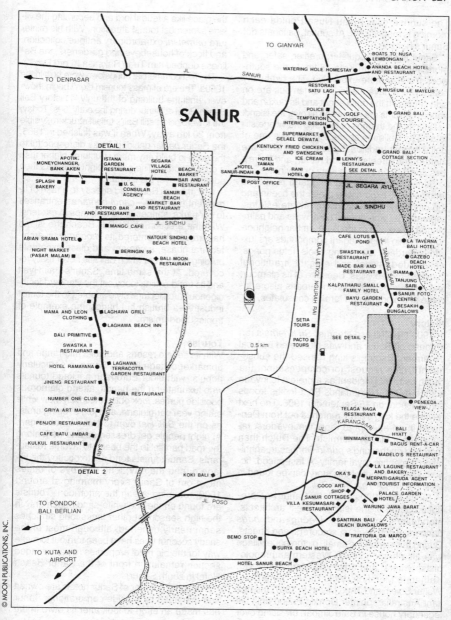

SANUR

TO GIANYAR

TO DENPASAR

JL. SANUR

DETAIL 1

APOTIK, MONEYCHANGER, BANK AKEN

SPLASH BAKERY

ISTANA GARDEN RESTAURANT

SEGARA VILLAGE HOTEL

U. S. CONSULAR AGENCY

SANUR BEACH MARKET BAR AND RESTAURANT

BEACH MARKET BAR AND RESTAURANT

BORNEO BAR AND RESTAURANT

MANGO CAFE

JL. SINDHU

ABIAN SRAMA HOTEL

NATOUR SINDHU BEACH HOTEL

NIGHT MARKET (PASAR MALAM)

BERINGIN 59

BALI MOON RESTAURANT

0   0.5 km

DETAIL 2

MAMA AND LEON CLOTHING

LAGHAWA GRILL

LAGHAWA BEACH INN

BALI PRIMITIVE

SWASTKA II RESTAURANT

HOTEL RAMAYANA

LAGHAWA TERRACOTTA GARDEN RESTAURANT

JINENG RESTAURANT

MIRA RESTAURANT

NUMBER ONE CLUB

GRIYA ART MARKET

PENJOR RESTAURANT

CAFE BATU JIMBAR

KULKUL RESTAURANT

JL. TANJUNG SARI

KOKI BALI

TO PONDOK BALI BERLIAN

TO KUTA AND AIRPORT

JL. POSO

BEMO STOP

SURYA BEACH HOTEL

HOTEL SANUR BEACH

© MOON PUBLICATIONS, INC.

BOATS TO NUSA LEMBONGAN

WATERING HOLE HOMESTAY

ANANDA BEACH HOTEL AND RESTAURANT

RESTORAN SATU LAGI

★ MUSEUM LE MAYEUR

POLICE

GOLF COURSE

GRAND BALI

TEMPTATION INTERIOR DESIGN

SUPERMARKET GELAEL DEWATA

KENTUCKY FRIED CHICKEN AND SWENSENS ICE CREAM

HOTEL TAMAN SARI

LENNY'S RESTAURANT SEE DETAIL 1

GRAND BALI COTTAGE SECTION

HOTEL SANUR-INDAH

RANI HOTEL

POST OFFICE

JL. SEGARA AYU

JL. SINDHU

JL. BAJA LETKOL NGURAH RAI

JL. TANJUNG SARI

CAFE LOTUS POND

LA TAVERNA BALI HOTEL

SWASTIKA I RESTAURANT

GAZEBO BEACH HOTEL

MADE BAR AND RESTAURANT

IRAMA

TANJUNG SARI

KALPATHARU SMALL FAMILY HOTEL

SANUR FOTO CENTRE

BAYU GARDEN RESTAURANT

BESAKIH BUNGALOWS

SETIA TOURS

SEE DETAIL 2

PACTO TOURS

PENEEDA VIEW

TELAGA NAGA RESTAURANT

BALI HYATT

JL. KARANGSARI

MINIMARKET

BAGUS RENT-A-CAR

MADELO'S RESTAURANT

LA LAGUNE RESTAURANT AND BAKERY

OKA'S

COCO ART SHOP

MERPATI GARUDA AGENT AND TOURIST INFORMATION

SANUR COTTAGES

PALACE GARDEN HOTEL

VILLA KESUMASARI RESTAURANT

WARUNG JAWA BARAT

SANTRIAN BALI BEACH BUNGALOWS

TRATTORIA DA MARCO

The sunrise over Pulau Nusa Penida each morning is magnificent. At sunset, sailboats dot Sanur's horizon.

Sanur is smaller, quieter, prettier, safer, and more sheltered than Kuta 15 km to the southwest. It's also more expensive. The big luxury hotels which have made Sanur famous are on side streets off the main street and its *dukun* and trance mediums are renowned all over the island.

Despite the throngs of tourists, the village still retains its Balinese character. Sanur is one of Bali's largest traditional villages; the trees are mature, the streets in good repair, and there's less construction than in Kuta or Lovina.

Sanur is the preferred long-term residence for those Bali expats who prefer the ocean and the city. The most exclusive private estates, separated by vine-draped coral walls and palm-fringed lanes, are in the Batu Jimbar neighborhood. Within these elegant compounds are luxurious gardens, swimming pools, lotus ponds, well-tended lawns, and elegant, traditional thatched-roofed villas. Because of its glamour, and snob appeal, the Sanur area is also a favorite of diplomats and foreign consulates.

History

In 1904 the Chinese steamer *Sri Koemala* ran aground off Sanur and was plundered by local fishermen. Badung's king refused the subsequent Dutch request for compensation; the Dutch used this incident as a pretext to invade southern Bali. Netherlands East Indies troops came ashore on 15 September 1906. The next day the the king's army marched out from Denpasar in an attempt to repel the invaders, resulting in a bloody skirmish. The Dutch then marched on the king's *puri* in Denpasar, annihilating the entire royal family. A fast-paced, fictionalized account of this story can be found in Vicki Baum's *A Tale from Bali.*

Since the 1920s and '30s Sanur has produced some of the island's finest architects, storytellers, musicians, *legong* and *baris* dancers, witch doctors, sorcerers, and priests. During this period the small, picturesque village was also home to such Western anthropologists, writers, and artists as Margaret Mead, Katherine Mershon, Vicki Baum, Jane Belo, Walter Spies, and Theo Meier. In 1967, the brilliant Australian painter Donald Friend built his legendary house in Batu Jimbar, presiding over

the place like a feudal lord and becoming the village's foremost tourist attraction. With his miniature *gamelan,* extraordinary antique collection, and flock of houseboys and gardeners, the Balinese dubbed him Tuan Raksasa ("Lord Devil").

The first commercial bungalows were built in the 1950s. The era of mass tourism didn't begin, however, until the building of the ugly, 11-story Bali Beach Hotel at Sanur during the early '60s. Today, the towerblock is still Bali's tallest structure, visible from 20 km away. When it was finished in 1965, the Sanur *banjar* decided it was disrespectful to the gods to build any more structures higher than a coconut palm. The palm height limit was then adopted all over the island.

Still, the Bali Beach led directly to a rash of irreverent practices—*candi bentar* as entrances to car parks, shrines used as lamps in gardens. With the erection of the Bali Beach the island had irreversibly entered its *modernisasi* architectural phase, a cement and glass expatriate building boom from which Bali has never really recovered. At the same time, Sanur's Bali Hyatt and its trend-setting lobby set the standard for indigenous architectural style adapted to the tourist industry—a brutish but handsome example of tropical modernism.

Tourism

With its sedate resorts and quiet mid-range and upmarket cottage hotels, Sanur is particularly popular with older European package tourists who luxuriate on the beach, attend glamorous poolside parties, look out at the lovely view while eating veal parmigiana, and join evening cruises on the *Bali Hai* over to Nusa Lembongan. At night people get dressed up and walk along the road parallel to the beach to favorite restaurants. Sanur tourists tend not to occupy the village during the day; long convoys of buses move out of Sanur every morning at around 1000, returning late in the afternoon. Tourists are found on the fine white-sand beach only in the high season; at other times long stretches seem nearly deserted, although most of the shady coconut trees have been torn out to make way for the big hotel properties (a palm-fringed section remains in front of the Sanur Beach Hotel in south Sanur).

Though a number of Sanur hotels are owned and managed by outside corporations, Sanur has made an effort to look after its own. In the

1970s and '80s, farsighted leaders established a village-owned cooperative that generates income for the benefit of the community. The co-op owns a beachside art market, filling station, and land in Denpasar and Kuta. Sanur also imposes a construction tax, the proceeds flowing to local government.

Although it has three discos, a bowling alley, cocktail lounges, and a wide variety of restaurants with international cuisine, Sanur's nightlife doesn't compare with Kuta's. Nor does Sanur have Kuta's noise, pollution, crime, or mosquitoes. The sellers are not as numerous—though they can be just as intolerable. Overall, Sanur has a more quaint, mellow, cosmopolitan feel than Kuta. The people of Sanur are full of pride and their behavior is more mannered than that of the people of Kuta who've become more sour and short as a result of the constant influence of poking, prying, bitching tourists. In Sanur the village atmosphere still survives. The people of Sanur chat with tourists, and there's no attempt at assimilation. The town *banjar* are cohesive and active, and the village's dozens of temples—squeezed tightly between art galleries, pubs, and hotel walls—go earnestly about their age-old business oblivious to tourists.

SIGHTS

Museum Le Mayeur

Also called the Ni Polok Museum, Box 7, Sanur, tel. (0361) 286164, formerly the home of Adrien Jean Le Mayeur Merpres (1908-1982), the Belgian impressionist painter who moved to Sanur in 1932 at the age of 52 and stayed for 26 years. Just 100 meters north of the Grand Bali Beach Hotel (take the lane to the right), smothered by buildings on all sides, the house is wedged between the Diwangkara Beach Hotel and the parking lot of the Grand Bali Beach Hotel. You can also reach the museum from the beach by taking the path off Jl. Hang Tuah in north Sanur. Open Tuesday, Wednesday, and Thursday from 0800 to 1600, Friday 0800-1330, Sunday 0800-1600; entrance fee Rp200 for adults, Rp100 children. Ni Polok's daughter guides you; she owns the adjacent Polok Art Shop.

Set in a lush tropical garden of hibiscus and bougainvillea and adorned with statues, the gallery contains 92 paintings captioned in English

and Indonesian, local artifacts, and some superb specimens of traditional Balinese carvings. Later works dramatically capture the people and scenes of Bali; earlier paintings, which depict Le Mayeur's extensive travels around Europe, tend to be in poor condition. Some paintings were executed on rough canvas made of woven palm leaves which Le Mayeur was forced to use during the Japanese occupation. The dark interior makes it difficult to view the works, but the stunning portraits and photographs of Ni Polok are the highlights of the museum.

Le Mayeur first settled in the village of Klandis, east of Denpasar, where he met Ni Polok, a star *legong* dancer and famed beauty. She agreed to model for Le Mayeur and became the subject of a number of his paintings, bringing him great success in exhibitions in Singapore. To the astonishment of the Balinese villagers who so feared the sea, the painter bought an isolated plot of land right on the beach at Sanur, where he built an elegant Balinese-style home. The artist painted during the day and at night entertained other gregarious travelers, providing them with huge Balinese feasts, dance performances, and the opportunity to purchase his paintings as a memento of their visit.

In 1935, Ni Polok and Le Mayeur were married. The couple lived in their lovely beach home until 1958, when they returned to Belgium so that he could be treated for cancer. Le Mayeur died the same year, without heirs, leaving his paintings to his wife. For many years Ni Polok managed the museum herself. She died in 1985 at the age of 85. The Indonesian government now looks after the house and collection.

Pura Belanjong

Southwest of Hotel Sanur Beach is one of Bali's most significant archaeological sites, an inscribed stone victory pillar erected by the Buddhist king Sri Kesari Varma in A.D. 914. Only partially deciphered, the inscription—in both Old Balinese and Sanskrit—refers to a military expedition against eastern Indonesia, where the Balinese once obtained their slaves. It's believed Kesari, a king of the Warmadewa dynasty, founded the Besakih sanctuary on the slopes of Gunung Agung.

The stone *prasasti*—Bali's oldest dated artifact—was discovered only in 1932. The great Dutch scholar Goris believed the Sanur pillar—

as well as the remains of prehistoric sanctuaries found along this coastal strip—proved an Indian colony settled the coast over 1,000 years ago. The volcanic stone's smooth 177-cm-high, 75-cm-diameter cylindrical body is crowned with a carved lotus cushion. Except at the top, most of the writing is indecipherable. The pillar lies behind Pura Belangjong, about a kilometer past the entrance to the Hotel Sanur Beach toward Suwungan.

SPORTS

There are generally more complete marine sports facilities in Sanur than in Kuta. Most of the dive outfits in Kuta and Nusa Dua have their main headquarters here. Surfboards (Rp15,000 per hour), windsurfing (Rp30,000 per hour), snorkel equipment (Rp6000 per hour), skin diving instruction, waterskiing (Rp60,000 per hour), jet skiing (Rp30,000 per 15 minutes), parasailing (once around Rp23,000), paddleboats (Rp8000 per hour), Balinese outriggers (Rp 12,000 per hour), speedboats (Rp70,000 per hour), glass-bottom boat rides (Rp23,000 per hour), and fishing excursions are all offered by water sports offices and fishermen right on the beach in front of the big hotels, or by freelancers cruising the beach.

Boating, Sailing, and Rafting

A good place to start is **Baruna,** which maintains offices in the Grand Bali Beach (tel. 0361-288511, ext. 1381), and the Sanur Beach (tel. 0361-288011). Baruna also maintains an office at Jl. Bypass 300 B, tel. (0361) 753820, fax 753809. The Bali Hyatt's leisure activities desk (tel. 0361-287777) sells luxury cruises, deep-sea fishing, and snorkeling adventures on their two fully equipped, diesel-powered speedboats for Rp690,000-920,000 full day (eight hours) or Rp460,000-690,000 half-day (four hours). A good outfit to contact is **Bali Camar Yacht Charter,** tel. (0361) 231591, which does full-day fishing expeditions for six people for around Rp1.5 million.

Traditional *prahu jukung* are more economical; they rent at a fixed rate of Rp20,000 per hour. One of the most exciting Sanur experiences is to rent one of the brightly painted motorized outriggers for a sail around the lagoon, beyond the reef to the port of Benoa, or to offshore islands such as Serangan (Rp115,000

return), and Nusa Lembongan or Nusa Penida (both Rp10,000 one way, Rp30,000 return).

Charter the *Wyeema,* a sturdy, 24-ton, 14-meter-long steel-hulled sailing yacht, for safe and comfortable sailing adventures. Marvel at the unpeopled islands, deserted beaches, and spectacular reef diving. The crew prepares delicious food. The specialty is a seven-day, six-night package to Komodo Island (Bali, Komodo, Sape, Bima, then return by air to Bali). This package may be extended to 12 days and 11 nights. Bookings: **Wyeema Adventure Sailing Surf N' Dive,** Jl. Pemamoran 12, Taman Sari, Sanur, tel. (0361) 287593, fax 31592.

Whereas Sobek runs hundreds of rafters a day down south-central Bali's Ayung River, **Bali Safari** (tel. 0361-221315, fax 232268) challenges you to Bali's most remote and swiftest river, the Telaga Waja, which starts in Muncan 17 km from Klungkung in east Bali—the Class IV river commercially rafted in Bali. Intense!

Diving and Snorkeling

At low tide, either wade out into the east-facing reef in front of the Bali Hyatt for almost a kilometer or rent a *jukung* to take you out five minutes farther to three- to 25-meter slopes and flat bottoms with some table- and trophy-shaped coral and sponges. Visibility is only around seven to 10 meters, dives range from two to 14 meters. Be careful here; currents can be ferocious. These reefs are inhabited by colorful fish in kaleidoscopic profusion as well as hundreds of sea urchins (wear foot covering). The ideal time to snorkel is a little past low tide when the tide is starting to flow; this brings clear water into the lagoon and the waves are not so high nor the current as strong. An ebbing tide also causes sediment to cloud the water. The usual cost for a single guide, including guide, tank, and weights, is Rp85,000. Snorkelers pay around Rp25,000 including fins and mask.

An efficient and well-managed dive outfit is **Oceania Dive Center,** Jl. Bypass Ngurah Rai 78, tel. (0361) 288652, fax 288652, which sells dive packages with a two person minimum. Also check out **Bali Diving Perdanda** (tel./fax 0361-288871), Jl. Duyung 10 just south of the Bali Hyatt, Semawang, for affordable dive tours and water sport activities. Other well-established dive outfits: **Bali Dive Sports Club,** Jl. D. Poso 38, tel. (0361) 288582, fax 287692; **Bali Marine**

Sports, Jl. Kesuma Sari, Semawang, in south Sanur (tel. 0361-288776) and at Jl. Bypass (tel./fax 287872); **Dive and Dives,** Jl. Bypass 23 (tel. 0361-288052, fax 289309); ENA Dive Center, Jl. Pangembak (tel./fax 0361-287945).

Rent flippers, mask, and snorkel for around Rp5000 per hour from any water sports center, the larger resort hotels, or on the beach itself. Rent such extras as wetsuits (Rp6000) and underwater cameras (Rp30,000) from specialized dive centers. A full-service water sports agent is **Graha Canti,** Jl. Kesumasari 9, Semawang, tel. (0361) 289601 or 288714. Another good outfit is **Kantor Jelati Willis,** on the beach where Jl. Segara ends in the sand. Men on the beach will offer to take you out in a in a glass-bottomed boat for Rp23,000 per person (minimum two people). For more on diving, see "Snorkeling and Scuba Diving" in the On the Road chapter.

Surfing and Swimming

Although Sanur's beach remains white and sandy, in front of La Taverna the shallow and weedy shore has been eaten away by lime removal; Semawang's beach, south of the main Sanur Beach, is nicer. At low tide, soupy water, pools, rocks, seaweed, and spiky sea urchins make swimming impossible; this is when the Balinese fish. At high tide the beach is completely nonexistent—the reason why many of the hotels have swimming pools. Day use of the pool at the Grand Bali Beach is Rp15,000 including towel, lawn chair, hamburger, and drink. From 0600 to 2000 you may also use the pool (for Rp5000) at the Puri Kelapa Hotel, tel. (0361) 286135, on the corner of Jl. Segara and Jl. D. Tamblingan.

Although the waves within the lagoon are tame, there's occasionally more dramatic surf—not all the time, but it happens—off the north beach off Alit's. In front of the Grand Bali Hotel is a decent right reef break; in front of the Beach Market is a fast left-hander. The only consistently good surf is two or three km out in the channel 1.5 km from in front of the Bali Hyatt; at high tide hire a parasailing boat to take you out and back for around Rp46,000.

For Rp25,000 per hour, utilizing special race boards, **Sanur Wind Surfing Centre** offers the resort's best service. The long board runs Rp20,000 per hour, fun board Rp30,000 per hour. Windsurfing lessons for beginners cost Rp30,000—including equipment and experienced instructor.

The center also offers surfing tours and rents Hobie Cats and paddle canoes. Office at Jl. Sekar Waru II, No. 1, Belanjong, Sanur, tel. (0361) 288976; more convenient beach counter on Jl. Duyung on the south side of the Bali Hyatt hotel next to Banjar Restaurant. July and August are the best time to windsurf.

Other Sports

All the big resort hotels have fitness centers that are available to nonguests (Rp12,500 per person) and tennis courts (Rp20,000 per hour). They also rent tennis racquets, shoes, and even partners if necessary. **The Grand Bali Beach Hotel** features a nine-hole seaside golf course that's all right for an easygoing round. Open to nonresidents, the greens fee is Rp65,000, club hire Rp25,000, caddy Rp6000, golf shoes Rp5000. To reserve, call the clubhouse at tel. (0361) 288511, ext. 1388. Hotel guests receive a 50% discount. Ten-pin bowling in the same hotel is Rp3500 per person per game.

Kite-flying is a distinctive event in Sanur. Sponsored by the local *banjar* in the windy, low-lying *sawah* behind the village, competitions take place from July through September. Teams dressed like samurai in white bandanas charge splashing through the rice paddies to keep the monstrous papier-mâché kites aloft. It takes two men to carry the heavy spool of nylon cord and up to six to get the 10-meter-long kite airborne. Once a kite is flying, the cord is tied to a tree. When there's wind, it's an unforgettable sight. Buy your own kites in varied sizes and shapes from local craft shops. The best is **Sederhaua,** Jl. Danau Buyan 73 in central Sanur, where you can help design your own kite for Rp15,000-25,000.

Corporate war games? **Bali Splat Mas** (tel. 0361-289073, fax 286845) pits participants with paintball making devices against each other on a 2.5-hectare strip of thickly forested land. The package cost of Rp100,000 includes all transfers, equipment, skirmish sessions, and training.

ACCOMMODATIONS

The beachfront is crowded with a whole string of expensive (Rp253,000-460,000) luxury hotels, some sprawling over vast areas abutting the ocean. Smaller, moderately priced, family-run, bungalow-style hotels (Rp115,000-230,000) offer more personalized attention, a more intimate atmosphere, air-conditioning, swimming pools, and are very good value. Cheaper still (Rp15,000-20,000) are the homestays with no sea view on the lanes running back from the main road. Accommodations differ tremendously in environs and services. Bookings are necessary in the high season, July-Aug. and Dec.-Jan.; during these periods the larger hotels frequently add a surcharge of 10-17% to your bill.

Guests in Sanur's upmarket establishments don't need to leave the hotel: everything is provided in the lobby, shops, kiosks, and restaurants, from international newspapers to film, painting exhibitions to taxi service. Here are poolside lunches, extensive gardens, buffet restaurants, room service, IDD telephones, tennis courts, massage rooms, saunas, first-class Western, European, and Asian cuisines. The price of bungalows and rooms increase the closer you get to the ocean. In these higher-priced places you could pay up to 21% extra in taxes.

Budget

Travelers are understandably put off staying in Sanur because of the high price of accommodation, but a growing number of homestays are now popping up in the *gang* running away from the beach off the northern end of the main road. Very basic rooms are often patched together in family compounds found behind the stores and shops along the main road. You're seldom more than a five-minute walk to a pool, such as the one at Santrian Beach Cottages, open to nonguests for Rp3000 or so. Don't forget to haggle for single occupancy and for any stay longer than one day!

A sweet and helpful Christian family runs **Prima Cottages** at Jl. Bumi Ayu 15 behind the Arena Restaurant, tel./fax (0361) 289153. It has an intimate atmosphere, is completely walled-in so you can't hear traffic, yet is only two blocks from the beach. Many places in this price range are like jail cells, but Prima's rooms are clean with private, Western-style bathrooms and mosquito nets. Cheaper rooms with fan Rp30,000, more expensive rooms with a/c Rp50,000, same price s or d; pool. Owned by Drs. Frans Nyoman Demung. **Yulia Homestay**, Jl. D. Tamblingan 38, behind Yulia Art Shop and diagonally opposite the Barong Disco, has cheap, clean rooms—large Rp25,000, small Rp20,000 s or d—set in a family compound. No break-

fast, but coffee and tea included in price; baths, fans, lending library. Eight rooms around a nice garden popular with travelers. Ask owner I Ketut Urip for a long-term discount. Two other basic but clean homestays nearby are the **Luisa** at Jl. Danau Toba 40 and the **Coco** at Jl. D. Tamblingan 40 (cheapest rooms in Sanur). In central Sanur, **Bah Wirasana**, Jl. D. Tamblingan 126, tel. (0361) 288632, fax 2885610, is an outstanding value with large terraced rooms around a garden and a swimming pool next door.

To the south on the main road of Jl. Tanjung Sari is the **Taman Agung Beach Inn,** tel. (0361) 288549 or 288006, fax 289161, a pleasant, easygoing place built around a well-maintained garden. Twenty-four rooms with bath and hot water. Rp55,000 s, Rp60,000 d, plus 15% tax and service. Without fan Rp44,000 s, Rp50,000 d plus 15%. Good but overpriced restaurant. Farther up and on the same side of the street and only five minutes from the beach is **Hotel Ramayana**, tel. (0361) 288429, with a/c rooms for Rp50,000; and the **Swaztika Bungalows,** tel. (0361) 288693, fax 287526, with bungalows for Rp50,000 s or d and unit rooms for Rp45,000 with a/c and hot water. Bungalows are all alone, units have neighbors.

Only a 15-minute walk from the beach and just down the street from the post office on busy Jl. Danau Buyan are three *losmen*-style guesthouses, **Hotel Rani, Hotel Taman Sari,** and **Hotel Sanur-Indah.** All provide more or less the same prices and services, with plain but adequate rooms in the Rp15,000-20,000 range; a/c rooms with hot water cost Rp50,000. The least together, tidy, and friendly of the three is Hotel Taman Sari, no. 31, tel. (0361) 288187. My personal favorite of the group, with the nicest rooms, a restaurant, and laundry service, is Hotel Rani, no. 33, tel. (0361) 288578, fax 288300. Rani has good service, is clean, and the "economic room" is only Rp19,500 s, Rp49,000 d, plus 10% tax. An a/c room with hot water and TV is Rp55,000 s, Rp57,000 d. *Bemo* heading to Denpasar pass by here.

Newly renovated and excellent value is **Pondok Wisata Bali Berlian,** Jl. Danau Tempe 9, tel. (0361) 287266, on the corner of Jl. Bypass and Jl. D. Tempe. Ten spacious a/c rooms, each with one single and one double bed, private bathroom/toilet with tub; five cheaper fan-cooled, motel-style rooms in front face rice fields over a stone wall. Room rates range from Rp16,000 (fan) to Rp30,000 (a/c). The small, very reasonably priced restaurant provides breakfast for Rp2000. The guesthouse is eight minutes from the beach. An excellent base for divers, with cleaning facilities for diving equipment. Bicycles and motorbikes for rent, a Praja taxi office close by, only two km from Serangan.

The well-run **Watering Hole Homestay** (Agung and Sue's), Jl. Hang Tuah, tel. (0361) 288289, has 12 rooms for Rp21,000-26,000 s or d (fan, fridge) surrounded by an interior garden. Four rooms are a/c, Rp35,000 s or d. Relatively cool and quiet for downtown Sanur. Their restaurant in front serves good Indo/Chinese food and nightly seafood specials—delectable frogs legs! The homestay features a bar that hosts a buffet with *legong* every Thursday night for Rp10,000. It's only 100 meters from the beach and is close to the landing place for boats to Pulau Lembongan.

Kalpataru Bar & Restaurant, Jl. D. Tamblingan 80, tel. (0361) 288457, fax 288457, is a small family hotel across the street from the Gazebo and Irama. Prices have been consistent for the past few years: Rp53,500 s, Rp64,500 d for rooms with a/c, hot water, shower *mandi*, and continental breakfast; Rp50,000 s or Rp53,000 d for rooms with fan. A light and airy hotel with a pool and a nice bonsai display. Friendly people. The restaurant serves pretty good Italian, Indonesian, Chinese, and seafood.

Abian Srama Inn, Jl. Bypass, tel. (0361) 288415, fax 288792, is a 10 minute walk from the beach, with nice rooms arranged in two facing blocks across a well-tended garden. Tariff as low as Rp25,000 s; Rp35,000 s, Rp42,000 d for rooms with fan, hot water, private bath, and hot water; Rp50,000 s, Rp60,000 d for a/c rooms with private bath and hot water. The hotel is well managed, quiet, clean, and close to the night market on a side street and features a restaurant, pool, and free airport transfer if you stay a week. Take in the *wayang kulit* for only Rp5000 every night from 1900 to 2100; order dishes from a set menu (restaurant tel. 0361-287658).

Ananda Beach Hotel, on Jl. Hang Tuah 43, near the Grand Bali, tel. (0361) 288327, has very clean and tidy rooms for Rp25,000-30,000 s and d. Balconies overlook the ocean. Two Rp15,000 rooms are almost always occupied. Located on the beach behind the restaurant of the same name. If coming from Denpasar, tell the driver

you want to get off at the Grand Bali Beach Hotel. For a beach hotel, incredibly good value.

Moderate

Highly recommended is the Bali-style **Laghawa Beach Inn**, Jl. D. Tamblingan 51, Batu Jimbar, Box 3557, Denpasar, tel. (0361) 288494, fax 289353, on the ocean side of the strip with the beach only 100 meters away. Rooms with a modern bathroom and hot water are Rp50,000 s; simple fan-cooled rooms Rp59,600 s, Rp71,000 d; a/c rooms Rp80,000 s, Rp110,000 d. Clientele is older European. Beautiful garden, pool, excellent food, safe, friendly staff—they even send their guests Christmas cards! Plastic accepted. Watch their shadow puppet theatre in the Grill Restaurant on Monday, Wednesday, and Saturday.

One of Sanur's top five moderately priced hotels, **Gazebo Beach Hotel**, Jl. D. Tamblingan 35, Box 3134, Denpasar, tel. (0361) 288212 or 289256, fax 288300, charges Rp94,000 s, Rp110,000 d for standard rooms, Rp117,000 s, Rp133,000 d for bungalows, Rp133,000 s, Rp154,000 d for studios. All rates include service and tax, but not breakfast. High-season surcharge: Rp35,000. Bargain. Book in advance Dec./Jan. and June-August. Credit cards accepted. The two-story bungalows—no. 12 is the best—are open downstairs to the outside except for screened-in *mandi* with big recessed tub; upstairs rooms have woven walls, with two walls of windows looking out over beautiful gardens. Great location, excellent service, sincere and friendly staff, TV, phone, well-kept gardens, nice pool, workout room (Rp5000 all day), close to a private beach area (like a cove, safe swimming). Restaurant prices are better than the restaurants on either side; good food. Continental breakfast Rp6000, American breakfast Rp8000, set lunch Rp8000, set dinner Rp15,000. Exchange books in the library; grab a copy of the *Jakarta Post* in the lobby. Free boat-snorkeling trip once a week, free videos and band in high season. Gazebo has bought out **Irama** and **Peneeda View** (tel. 0361-288425) with comparably priced rooms.

Santrian Beach Cottages, Jl. Tanjung Sari 47, Box 3055, Denpasar, tel. (0361) 288181, fax 288185, offers comfortable seaside traditional-style private a/c ricebarn-style bungalows or rooms on pathways meandering through large, lush gardens. Good sized pool. Garden-view rooms are Rp158,000 s, Rp163,000 d; sea-view rooms Rp170,000 s, Rp184,000 d; new superior rooms Rp195,000 and up. To all rates add 21% surcharge. Wide variety of dining and entertainment; friendly, warm, small, attractive family-operated hotel.

Less expensive, though showing its age, is **Alit's Beach Bungalows,** Jl. Hang Tuah 41, Box 3102, Denpasar, tel. (0361) 288560 or 288567, fax 288766. Great location at Sanur's north end next to the beach, yet also close to the road. Alit's has a/c Balinese-type bungalows with hot water and shower, and charges a reasonable Rp88,000 s, Rp94,000 d for standard, Rp96,000 s, Rp103,000 d for superior—don't bother with the higher priced, newer units. Set in large untidy gardens with tall trees and tacky statues, the complex includes restaurant, pool, squash and tennis courts, billiards, mini-golf, open stage, dance floor, TV lounge with nightly videos shown at 1900, barber and beauty shops, drugstore, conference hall. A long walk to central Sanur; catch a *bemo* next door.

Other options to consider are beachfront **Diwangkara,** Jl. Hang Tuah (tel. 0361-288577), which features terraced bungalows with all the comforts (a/c, hot water, TV) in attractive gardens with small pool, and the small, popular **Baruna Beach** on Jl. Sindhu (tel. 0361-288546, fax 289629) with very comfortable a/c bungalows with fridge. Good location.

Luxury

There are scores of first-class hotels with luxurious four-star properties as well as more intimate bungalow compounds at two-thirds to one-half the price. Be sure to book ahead in the peak tourist seasons.

Well-designed **Sativa Cottages,** Jl. D. Tamblingan 25, Box 3163, tel./fax (0361) 287881, is a good deal for the price—Rp170,000 s, Rp195,000 d. Standard Rp105,000 s, Rp170,000 d. Clean, quiet, professional operation. About 10 minutes south of the Grand Bali Beach Hotel is the older and popular **Segara Village Hotel,** Box 91, Denpasar, tel. (0361) 288407 or 288408, fax 289268, with rustic, beachfront a/c bungalows, aviaries, lush gardens, playground and rec room, gym, sauna, pool, sunken bar, and international restaurants. Standard rooms Rp92,000-115,000 per person, bungalows and suites run up to Rp253,000.

Just south of Segara Village, overlooking a quiet part of the lagoon, is three-star **Natour Sindhu Beach Hotel,** Jl. Danau Tondano 14, Box 181, tel./fax (0361) 288351 or 289268, with 59 bungalow-style rooms for Rp128,000 s, Rp154,000 d with pool view, Rp154,000 s, Rp175,000 d for sea view. Also suites for Rp175,000 s, Rp202,000 d. All prices include tax, service, and American breakfast. Meals in the open-air restaurant include lunch Rp20,000, dinner Rp25,000. Amenities include a fancy bar, children's playground, table tennis, billiards, pool, garden path to the beach, golf course, tennis courts, snorkeling, rafting, diving, art market, shopping, and nightlife within walking distance. Make reservations direct to the hotel or to Natour, Jl. Menteng Raya 7 B, Jakarta, tel. (0361) 343384 or 341325.

At the south end of Sanur's beach is top-grade, 200-room **Sanur Bali Travelodge,** Jl. Mertasari, Box 3476, Denpasar 80034, Bali, tel. (0361) 288833, fax 287303. Beachfront clusters of one and two-story thatched-roofed, cottage-style rooms are Rp230,000 s, Rp253,000-390,000 d in all seasons. In high season, add Rp45,000. Gracious and airy marble *wantilan*-style lobby, lovely gardens, two big pools, two good open-air restaurants, conference facilities—just the right balance of luxury and simplicity. Tune in on the "Balinese Cultural Night" on a moonlit open-air stage. European-trained chef, sports facilities, pool. The walk to the village is only four blocks down a pleasant small street that winds through a residential/hotel area; little traffic.

La Taverna Hotel, Jl. Tanjung Sari, Box 40, Denpasar, tel. (0361) 288497, fax 287126, consists of over 40 quiet, a/c, dark, thatched-roof and stucco bungalows stylishly decorated with art objects and *batik* and laid out like a *kampung.* Rates: Rp300,000 d garden standard, Rp370,000 d garden superior, Rp450,000 family unit, Rp530,000 d duplex suite. High season supplement Rp35,000. All rates subject to 21% tax and service. The hotel provides a pizzeria, bar, pool, and private beach. La Taverna is known for its amalgam of Balinese and Mediterranean architecture, verandas overlooking immaculate gardens, friendly service, and excellent Indonesian cuisine served in a beachside restaurant.

The sprawling 346-room **Hotel Sanur Beach,** Box 3279, Denpasar, tel. 0361-288011, fax 287566 or 287749, is a five-star, international-class hotel owned by Garuda. Located on a small, quiet side street, with a grand entrance of marble and cascading fountains, Sanur Beach offers standard rooms for Rp277,000 s, Rp330,000 d, Rp323,000 s, Rp346,000 d deluxe, Rp380,000 s, Rp460,000 d studios. Bungalow suites with marbled bathroom and private pool go for Rp920,000-2 million. All rates subject to 21% service and tax. Rooms vary: the "old" side has average 1960-ish accommodations (floral bedspreads, resin plastic chairs, etc.), but the 134 rooms in the new high-rise are something out of the Arabian Nights with gold gilt, hair dryers, and terrycloth bathrobes. Very good buffet breakfast. Disco, volleyball, tennis, badminton, putting green, pool, moneychanger, carving and painting gallery concessions, pools, friendly service. Enjoy drinks and snacks in the lounge or at Tirta Poolside Restaurant and Bar. Thai food is a specialty of the East West Restaurant, with light entertainment starting at 1930. Warung Seahorse is a romantic seafood restaurant on the hotel's beautiful tree-shaded beach.

The smaller, family-owned **Tanjung Sari**, JL. D. Tamblingan 41, Box 25, Denpasar, tel. (0361) 288441, fax 287930, between Besakih Bungalows and the Irama, has 29 elaborate, expensive, native-style bungalows with outside pavilions and sitting rooms, all impeccably furnished with antiques and set in an exotic, peaceful tropical garden. Tariffs range from US$220 to US$418. Along with the Oberoi of Seminyak, this hotel's construction in 1962 represented the glorious comeback of traditionalism in modern architecture. The hotel has been a favorite among celebrities and old Bali hands ever since it was built. Don't miss meeting Mr. Wawo-Runtu, a gracious and learned gentleman with impeccable bloodlines who is director of the Tanjung Sari Foundation which supports the dissemination of Balinese traditional knowledge.

The Tanjung Sari's sumptuous bungalows (Rp460,000 s or d, plus 21% tax and service) are set in their own private compound with gazebo, courtyard garden, and open-air bar. Restaurant, pool, and beach bar—a popular rendezvous spot—overlooks Sanur bay, with Gunung Agung in the background. A beautiful outdoor dining room is noted for its lavish *rijstaffel* (Rp67,500), exquisite dancing, and haunting *gamelan* music. The staff, dressed in graceful *sarung* and *kebaya,* dispenses slow

and dreamy service, but what the hotel lacks in snappiness it makes up for in style. The property's natural moss-covered coral walls, winding pathways, and junglelike atmosphere—completely in harmony with Bali's traditional culture—serve as a model for other hotels. Don't miss the dance rehearsals every Thursday and Sunday from 1400 to 1600 on the beachside *bale*—one of the best free things to do on Bali.

The **Grand Bali Beach Hotel,** P.O. Box 3275, Denpasar, tel. (0361) 288511, fax 287917, is the only skyscraper on the island. It's been rebuilt since the 20 January 1993 fire. How did the fire start? Four rumors abound: 1) divine punishment for the height; 2) torched for insurance purposes; 3) since it was built in 1965 with Japanese war reparations money, the place was cursed from the beginning; and 4) carpet installation people started it in the Qantas Airlines office while laying a new carpet (while heating glue with open fires). Once it started to burn, flames leapt all the way up to the top 11th floor; the fire department had equipment useful only for battling fires in one-story structures. All rooms were destroyed but for Room 327, reserved for the Goddess of the Southern Seas. Today there are 524 a/c rooms in a tower block, plus a low-rise garden wing and cottages. The Grand Bali features a staff of 1,000, three pools, massage, steambath, four restaurants, snack bar, karaoke bar, coffee shops, open air stage with *topeng* performances, *gamelan* orchestra, extensive grounds, children's play area, giant chess, bowling alley, shopping arcade, barber and beauty salon, indoor games room, free-form pool; the garden wing has two pools as well. The Grand Beach Bali offers an extensive range of water sports. There's a post office, banks, conference halls, tour offices, airport transfers, a fleet of buses. Bali's American Express, Garuda, Qantas, and Ansett offices are here; the brisk public places remind one of an airport terminal.

Rates: garden wing Rp265,000, Rp312,000 d; cottage Rp253,000 s, Rp300,000 d; tower wing deluxe Rp346,000 s, Rp370,000 d. Add 21% tax to all rates. Nonsmoking rooms available. The hotel grounds are immense; a shuttle service transports guests from one end of the property to the other. The hotel's Bali Seaside Cottages down the street appeal to those seeking a quieter, more natural environment.

Get an elegant sniff of the retro-Bali theme at Sanur's most beautiful luxury hotel, the big, flamboyant 390-room **Bali Hyatt**, Jl. D. Tamblingan, Box 392, Denpasar, tel. (0361) 288271 or 288361, fax 287693. For 17 years this hotel was the only show in town, the stylish trendsetter for all that followed. Today it must compete with the luxury resort hotels of Nusa Dua, not to mention another Hyatt. Sanur's Bali Hyatt, in contrast to the almost austere Grand Hyatt of Nusa Dua, has a mellow, aged feel to it. The friendly, relaxed, multilingual staff tend to be older than their counterparts at the Grand Hyatt—shuffling about in slippers before middle-aged paunches, they act completely themselves. Buses shuttle between the two hotels from 0700 to 2300.

The 36-acre complex, the biggest hotel property in Sanur, is made up of rooms in the main building (Rp380,000 s, Rp425,000 d; Regency Club rooms (Rp415,000 s, Rp495,000 d) and two-bedroom suites (Rp1.5 million). The rooms are furnished and traditionally decorated, and each day guests receive a fresh fruitbowl. Excellent breakfast buffet for Rp 22,000. Richly landscaped and well-established lawns, lotus ponds, magnificent pool, and justly famous gardens bursting with orchids, hibiscus, bougainvillea, and frangipani leading right to the beach. Rich woods grace the walls and arched ceiling of this "beached period cruise ship" with its enormous, handsome, open lobby. Activities include tennis, sailing, windsurfing, snorkeling, pleasure cruising, games, videos, and palm tree-climbing demonstrations. Private, 150-meter-long beach. Parents staying here may leave their children at Camp Sanur, a private club where they'll be entertained with a range of specially designed activities: arts, crafts, games, sports, Balinese dance.

FOOD

Sanur's restaurants offer a wide choice of high-quality food, but like most tourist enclaves you've got to really hunt for the good places. The restaurants along the main strip, Jl. D. Tamblingan and Jl. Tanjung Sari, are competitively priced, about equal to what comparative meals cost in Kuta or Ubud. But many of the restaurants lining these streets are filled with the same pedestrian bamboo furniture, the same cheap gingham tablecloths, the same Sundanese flute music, the same tiresome tourist menu. The fare offered is cheap enough and will fill you up, but that's about it. There are pizzerias, expresso cafes, dozens of hotels offering dinner performances, seafood and grill restaurants, *rijstaffel* and buffet restaurants galore, European, and ethnic Japanese and Korean restaurants. Nearly all the better restaurants offer free transport in the Sanur area. Few restaurants stay open past 2100.

Observe where the *bemo* drivers, waiters, and hotel workers eat; *warung* sustain Sanur's vast service staffs. Here you can sample inexpensive fresh fish and banana-leaf packets of *nasi campur*. Plenty of cheap eating and drinking *warung* face the beach at the end of Jl. Pantai Sindhu. Homesick Westerners can find sustenance at Swenson's and Kentucky Fried Chicken next to the big Gelael Dewata Supermarket on Jl. Bypass.

Markets
Visit **Sanur Food Market** on Jl. Tanjung Sari for snacks and Indonesian and Western meals from many different stalls. Good bakery here too. At **Pasar Sindu** buy inexpensive bananas, mangoes, apples, jackfruit, *salak*, papaya, and coconuts; open 0500 to 1100. The **pasar malam** is an even better bargain. Stalls offer Indonesian rice dishes for under Rp1000, sweet sugar- and nut-filled pancakes, delicious roasted corn to go. A smaller night market opens up at dusk on Jl. D. Buyan just before the post office.

You can also stay in your room and dine on real cheeses and wine purchased from the **Galael Dewata Supermarket,** tel. (0361) 288199, on Jl. Ngurah Rai Bypass. Prices are expensive for imported food but cheaper for staples, water, fruit drinks. Excellent ice cream parlor here too. From the intersection where Jl. Bypass meets Jl. Segara, walk north about 200 meters; it's on the left.

Budget
Cafeteria Sanur, on the left after the entrance to Sindu Market, is one of Sanur's best sit-down meal bargains. Not much ambience, with bright glitzy lights, but the food is good (*nasi campur* Rp2500). Big glass windows keep out the flies, noise, and dust. Open 0700-1000. **Bali Moon Restaurant,** Jl. D. Tamblingan 19, tel. (0361)

288486, near the Barong nightclub, serves Italian and European food in a garden setting on a high, thatched, open-air *bale.* Good food and attractive surroundings. The circular bar serves a full spectrum of exotic drinks. All prices subject to 15% tax and service. At **Hey Cafe,** Jl. D. Tamblingan beside the Wartel, you can sit outside, listen to live music, and enjoy well-prepared Indonesian food like *tempe* and curry dishes (Rp6000-12,000). Open 1930-midnight. Across the street is **Warung Lesse'an,** Jl. Danau Toba 10 B, tel. (0361) 286343, with gourmet food at tempting prices. Nice atmosphere. **Oka's,** tel. (0361) 288942 or 288630, recently underwent a facelift. Unique menu, open kitchens, live entertainment, and ice machines with a guarantee of 100% safe ice. Free return transport to any of the family's four restaurants (Oka's, Istana Garden, JJ, Bella). The **Legong Restaurant,** tel. (0361) 288066, is also known as a good place to eat.

Swastika Garden, tel. (0361) 288693, sits adjacent to the Swastika Bungalows and the Hotel Ramayana on Jl. D. Tamblingan in central Sanur. The name derives from *su* (goodness) and *asti* (to be); they serve delicious seafood, especially grilled prawns and fresh tuna, amid beautiful leafy gardens. Dances held twice weekly. Cheap cold beer. **Made's Bar & Restaurant,** Jl. Tanjung Sari 51, tel. (0361) 287515, is a popular tourist hangout opposite the Kalpataru Hotel. Much like a sidewalk tavern, in the off-season it's very low-key and casual but in the high season it's packed. Very good seafood, Indonesian, and Italian food.

Behind the Grand Bali Beach at Jl. Bypass 38, tel. (0361) 287975, is **Lenny's,** Sanur's first Chinese restaurant. Once known for superb seafood, it is now slammed by a reader complaining that "paying Rp40,000 for an oversized, tough, old lobster; a/c that didn't work; and soft rock blaring out of a karaoke machine is not my idea of a bargain." Open 1000-1100; *karoke* begins at 1800. Much better in the seafood department is **Resto Ming,** Jl. Mertasari in south Sanur, particularly their lobster dishes.

Donald's, tel. (0361) 289450, serves fabulous European-style dinners. You seldom pay more than Rp25,000 for two, including dessert and coffee. Try the grilled fish dinner (Rp7000) and the banana pancakes. Good bakery with croissants and bread; go early in the morning. Across

the street from Santrian Beach Cottages, open 0700-2200 or 2300. Across from Donald's is **Pualam International Restaurant,** Jl. Sanur Beach 37, tel. (0361) 288721. Excellent food and service. Count on Rp25,000 for a big meal for two. Great coffee; very European ambience. Kenny G in the background. Also noteworthy is the **Borneo Bar and Restaurant** on Jl. Pantai Sindhu, tel. (0361) 289291, offering the classic Western tourist menu of meat and fish dishes. Good and cheap.

A great breakfast place in south Sanur is **La Lagune** at Jl. D. Tamblingan 103, tel. (0361) 288893, open 0700-2200. Their cappuccinos and fresh-baked croissants are excellent. For an inexpensive lunch of *sate,* Chinese dishes, fresh fried fish, grilled lobster, *babi guling,* or other Indonesian dishes, try the unpretentious **Sanur Beach Market,** a village cooperative on the beach end of Jl. Segara next to the Segara Village Hotel. Set menu (Rp25,000) on Wednesday and Saturday nights during dance performances. Good food and reasonable prices. Open noon to 2200. Call (0361) 288574 for free transport.

Moderate

The **Cafe Batu Jimbar,** Jl. D. Tamblingan 152, tel. (0361) 287374, is one of several "health food" restaurants of Sanur with reliably tasty, wholesome, imaginative dishes, lavish desserts (chocolate fudge cheesecake Rp5500, baklava), and fresh baked bread. Wonderful salads (average Rp6000-8500), and real eggplant Parmesan (Rp5800). Other exotic dishes include spicy Thai chicken soup (Rp6800), French fries (Rp2800), gazpacho, and burritos (Rp7000). A substantial meal for two costs at least Rp25,000. Batu Jimbar's owner's brother supplies the restaurant with organic Western vegetables like asparagus and broccoli, cultivating around Pupuan in the mountains of Tabanan. Groceries like superb wholegrain bread, Torajan coffee, crunchy granola, homemade jellies, nuts, and fruit for sale in the small health food store behind the cashier. The restaurant is concealed behind a tall hedge opposite the SinBolan neon sign. The small enclave also contains an outstanding bookstore and an unusual Jenggala ceramics showroom. Be prepared for the New Age yupster atmosphere.

Folks at the **Lotus Pond,** tel. (0361) 289398, opposite Barong disco make their own bread, pasta, and cakes. Although the a la carte menu leans toward Mediterranean, the Balinese *bebek tutu* (Rp12,500) is brought all the way down from Ubud, where they make the best smoked duck on the island. The all-you-can-eat Balinese-style *rijstaffel* (Rp22,000) is justly praised. Pizzas baked in a traditional wood-fired oven—call and you can pick up your pie 15 minutes later. Under a magnificent airy *wantilan,* the restaurant is elegantly appointed with intricately carved Jepera doors and panels. Indulge in outrageous dessert in the lounge area.

There are also plenty of lunching possibilities while walking the beach. Eat authentic and much cheaper, though not as well-presented, Indonesian dishes in any *warung* down a side lane.

Indonesian

A good *padang*-style restaurant is **Beringin 59,** Jl. D. Tamblingan 5, tel. (0361) 288602. In south Sanur is popular, canteen-style **Jawa Barat,** Jl. Kesumasari 2, Banjar Semawang, tel. (0361) 286309, with very affordable Indonesian, European, and Chinese cuisine: grilled fish, chips, and vegetables Rp5000; *nasi goreng* Rp2000; *mie kuah* Rp1500; *kare ayam* Rp1500. Ice juices Rp1000, cold beer Rp2000, *es kelapa muda* Rp800. Jawa Barat is a favorite of drivers, *pegawi,* and hotel personnel, and one of the best places in town for genuine Indonesian dishes. Drive south of the Bali Hyatt one kilometer, and turn right at the statue toward Jl. Bypass; it's on the right. Open 0630-0200. *Selamat menikmati!* More authentic Indonesian *rumah makan* along the Bypass road.

RM Sari Laut, Jl. Kesumasari, tel. (0361) 289151, serves the best *nasi campur* in Sanur, as well as fresh seafood, and is frequented mostly by Indonesians. A fancier tourist restaurant, the **Penjor,** Batu Jimbar, tel. (0361) 288226 or 288731, is known for its Rp13,500 (with tax and service) set menu. Choice of six types of "rice table": Balinese, Indonesian, Chinese, Japanese, Korean, or seafood, the latter containing 300 grams of lobster. Balinese dances every other night.

For traditional Balinese festival dishes, as well as fresh Western and Chinese cuisine, go to the **Kul Kul Restaurant,** tel. (0361) 288038, near the Hyatt just south of Hotel Taman Agung and the Batu Jimbar Cafe. Established in 1974, Kul Kul is one of the oldest and most romantic restaurants in Sanur. Sit in one of the six-posted

pavilions and look out over the attractive garden courtyard dotted with antiques. Big portions of well-prepared Indonesian and Western food, Rp20,000 per person, are served on large offering trays *(dulung)* as a *tingklik* serenades in the background. Call first to see if there's a dance performance. Free transport.

Ethnic

Shima Japanese Restaurant, tel. (0361) 287712, is considered one of the best on the island. The manager is Japanese, and so is the cook. Japanese food is also served at the stylish and air-conditioned **Nan Ban Kan Sushi & Steak House,** Jl. D. Tamblingan 67. Though expensive, try **Kita,** Jl. D. Tamblingan 104, tel. (0361) 28815, for Japanese dishes such as tempura, yakitori, and sukiyaki. More reasonably priced is the excellent **Ryoshi's,** Jl. D. Tamblingan 150 (near Batu Jimbar Cafe).

Koki Bali, Jl. Bypass 9 X, tel. (0361) 287503, is a fully air-conditioned Korean seafood restaurant where you can also enjoy music, karaoke, and free movies. **Chong Gi Wa,** Jl. Tambaksari 6, tel./fax (0361) 287084, is a Korean restaurant and karaoke bar. A wide choice of high-priced authentic Thai cuisine is served at Sanur Beach Hotel's **East and West** restaurant in South Sanur. For reservations, call (0361) 288011, ext. 1744.

The **Trattoria Da Marco,** tel. (0361) 288996, in south Sanur serves excellent but pricey Italian food—a must is the spaghetti Viennese; also great minestrone soup, delicious fillet steaks, pizzas, and fine wines. Balinese sing Italian and Spanish songs with guitar accompaniment. Housed in the same building as the honorary Italian Consul. Open 1900-2300. Also in south Sanur is the small **Terrazza Martini,** Jl. Kesumasari, tel. (0361) 288371, with Italian-speaking staff and cheap, basic, very good food. Try the garlic spaghetti made with fresh garlic and the pasta prepared *al dente* (Rp6500). Most dishes are in the Rp6000-8000 range.

Nearly as good for pasta, as well as Indonesian buffet, is **La Taverna's,** tel. (0361) 288497, a pleasant beachside bar and restaurant in a tropical garden. One of Sanur's grand old establishments, with staff shuffling effortlessly and efficiently in a *tempo doeloe* rhythm. Superb seafood and Italian brick-oven pizzas. For a full dinner with wine, count on about Rp45,000 per person. Add 10% to all prices. Open 0700-2300.

Hotel Restaurants

The Hyatt, Sanur Beach, Grand Bali, and the very classy Tanjung Sari each contain a variety of premier restaurants with expensive Indonesian, Chinese, Italian, and Japanese menus; extravagant buffets; 24-hour coffee shops; beachside cafes. For fresh food at reasonable prices, try the **Laghawa Terracotta Garden Restaurant** at Jl. D. Tamblingan 51, tel. (0361) 287919. **Telaga Naga Restaurant,** Jl. D. Tamblingan, tel. (0361) 288271, ext. 85080 or 85006, operated by and across from the Bali Hyatt, offers high-quality Sichuan-style food on a picturesque wooden platform on stilts overlooking a carp-filled lotus pond and a garden of bridges and other pavilions. Tender smoked duck is the specialty. Average price Rp13,000-25,000, super service. Open 1200-1500, 1900-2200. **Kalpatharu Bar & Restaurant,** tel. (0361) 288461, is a good breakfast place open 0700-2400. Breakfast buffet Rp3950, American breakfast Rp3850, continental breakfast Rp2950.

Within the confines of the modernist Bali Hyatt enjoy al fresco dining in the terrace restaurant; excellent multinational breakfast buffet (Rp22,000). The outstanding **Omang Omang Grill** specializes in grilled seafood, while the **Cupak Bistro** offers European bistro-style cooking. **Cafe Wantilan** features an elegant setting complementing Rajalaya-style *rijstaffel* served by women in *kebaya* and *sarung*. The hotel's **Pizza Ria,** right on the beach, serves authentic Italian pizzas and pasta dishes. The Bali Hyatt is also the place for desserts; enjoy all the cakes you can eat for Rp9500.

The **Tanjung Sari Hotel restaurant** on Jl. Tanjung Sari, tel. (0361) 288441, south of La Taverna, is known for its pricey but genuine Indonesian and continental food prepared by a French chef. The open-air dining area is on an elevated terrace by the beach—an ineluctably romantic setting. Coffee, croissants, and fruit salad for two costs around Rp45,000, but the courteous, professional service and the immaculately presented and prepared food can't be beat. The *ikan pepes* is first class. On Saturday evening there's a splendid, colonial-style *rijstaffel* buffet for Rp67,500, accompanied on occasion by *pendet, topeng,* and *baris* dancing and *gamelan* music of a very high standard. At the nice seaside bar, ask for the legendary *arak bumbu:* cocktail from local rice liquor with a unique combination of spices. **Le Pirate,** facing the sea and attached to the Segara Village Hotel in central Sanur, is recommended for its outstanding Indian and Thai food plus very good pizza and pasta.

There's an excellent vegetarian restaurant on the first floor of Hotel Santai in Batu Jimbar at the south end of Jl. D. Tamblingan. Called the **Shanti,** this is the only true vegetarian restaurant in Sanur. Using mostly organically grown ingredients, the *urapan* (steamed vegetables with spicy sauce) is a favorite. Call for free pickup; closes at 2130. Get a table near the balcony and enjoy the delicious rice and vegetable dishes. Every Sunday from 1500 to 1800, a traditional English high tea is served in the Grand Bali Beach Hotel's 10th floor rooftop restaurant. High-class atmosphere, exquisitely presented. For Rp14,500 the treats include smoked salmon, fresh scones with thick whipped cream and homemade strawberry jam, watercress finger sandwiches, delicate French pastries, and a large selection of international teas. Sweeping views. For details, call (0361) 288511.

Baked Goods

Opposite the Batu Jimbar *bale* is **Choice Bakery & Coffee Shop,** Jl. D. Tamblingan 150, tel. (0361) 288401, selling fresh bread and croissants daily, specializing in health-oriented European food at prices half those charged at the Batu Jimbar Cafe next door. **Splash Bakery,** tel. (0361) 288186, on the corner of Jl. Bypass 100 and Jl. D. Buyan opposite the Biro Reklame Plastic Centre, is a perfect place for a quick breakfast. Very good prices: whole wheat bread Rp1500, fruit loaf Rp2000, a whole carrot cake Rp1000, dinner rolls Rp500 apiece, ham and cheese croissants Rp1200, fruit scones Rp1000, apple tarts Rp1000, all-meat pies and sausage rolls Rp2500. Australian-trained baker. Another bakery with a wide range of items—peanut bread, pineapple rolls, croissants—is the **La Lagune Restaurant & Cafe,** Jl. D. Tamblingan 103, tel. (0361) 288893.

ENTERTAINMENT AND EVENTS

Sanur's big hotels are some of the best places to see hour-long commercial cultural shows performed by professionals every day of the week. Keep your ears open and look for banners and fliers. Often you have to pay for dinner Rp45,000-80,000, and then you get to sit almost on top of the dancers. Book ahead. Or just stroll in, stand behind a chair, and watch (dress well). Another option is to visit nearby dance villages, Bona Denpasar or Batubulan, to see performances. Sanur's tour agencies sell tickets to these dance performances for Rp25,000-40,000 including roundtrip transport but it's cheaper to use public transport. First catch a *bemo* to Denpasar's Keveneng Terminal, then get another *bemo* to Batubulan (dances take place 0930-1030, Rp6000 entrance).

The **Sanur Beach Hotel**, tel. (0361) 288011, at the south end of the main drag, puts on a frog dance performance on Sunday, *legong* on Monday, and Ramayana ballet on Wednesday. Admission Rp47,000 with buffet or Rp10,000 without. Performances last from 1930 to 2330. **Oka's Restaurant** on Jl. D. Tamblingan in south Sanur also regularly stages frog dances.

From 1400 to 1800 every Thursday and Friday dance lessons are held on a *bale* in front of the Tanjung Sari Hotel; just sit on the beach and watch the teacher abuse her students.

A good place to hang out with the family is **Terrazza Martini** on Jl. Kesumasari (tel. 0361-288371). Swig a cold beer while taking in the view of the lagoon. Canoes rent from watersport businesses across the road. On weekends watch Balinese fly kites and bathe fully clothed on lovely Mertasari Beach stretching to the south. Open 1000-2200.

The **Abian Srama Hotel**, Jl. Bypass Ngurah Rai Sindhu, tel. (0361) 288415 or 828792, fax 288673, stages a *wayang kulit* every night (1900-2100) with three different set menus (Rp15,000-30,000). **Laghawa Beach Inn** also presents shadow puppet shows every Monday, Wednesday, and Saturday 1900-2000; call (0361) 288494 for reservations.

Watering Hole Homestay, tel. (0361) 288289, features a big Balinese all-you-can-eat buffet dinner with *legong* every Thursday night for Rp10,000. Reserve a table 24 hours in advance.

Independent restaurants outside the hotels put on buffet dinners and dances for around Rp35,000 per person. **Penjor Restaurant,** tel. (0361) 288226, on Jl. D. Tamblingan near the Bali Hyatt in central Sanur, stages "Bali Nights" with *legong* every Sunday night from 2015 to 2115; food and performance Rp13000-40,000

per person, the frog dance every Monday at 2015, the *joged* every Wednesday at 2015, and the *janger* every Friday at 2015. Other restaurants with dinner/dances include: **Kul Kul,** tel. (0361) 288038; **Swastika,** Jl. D. Tamblingan 124, tel. (0361) 288693. The latter presents a *legong* on Sunday and a frog dance performance on Thursday, both starting at 2030. A *kecak* dance is performed on an open-air stage under a giant *waringin* tree at Tanjung Bungkak from 1830 for Rp5000; get there on a Denpasar-bound *bemo* (Rp500, four km).

The Mango Cafe, Jl. D. Toba 13, tel. (0361) 288411, presents laser disc video movies each night at 2000; also very complete breakfast and dinner menus. Cheap, good, big servings of roast duck and other Balinese dishes. Bring your own compact video disc to **Sanur Beach Market & Restaurant,** tel. (0361) 288574, just off Jl. Pantai Sindhu, open 2100-0200; nice second floor bar overlooking the beach. Or just tune in a movie on your in-house video and tuck in by 2130.

If jazz is your interest try the Bali Hyatt's popular and sophisticated jazz bar **Grantung,** which serves tasty tapas-like Indonesian snacks. And you can't beat the twilight view from the Bali Hyatt's outdoor bar over the pool and sea.

Nightlife

Sanur is tamer than Kuta, and the nightlife starts and ends earlier. It's a 35-and-up tourist resort, not really the haunt of Australian/Euro all-night ragers. So if it's real nonstop frenzied action you want, go to Kuta where the drinks are cheaper and the music is faster.

Borneo Bar and Restaurant, Jl. Pantai Sindhu 11, tel. (0361) 289291, is a well-known pub with good-value Western menu. The **Trophy Club,** next to the Sindhu Beach Hotel, is another popular hangout. **LG Club Sehatku** at Jl. D. Tamblingan 23, tel. (0361) 287880, is a sauna, steam, shiatsu, and traditional massage spa south of the Bali Moon Restaurant. Get a voucher from the guard before opening (1100-2300) for the special Rp10,000 rate. The standard price for the sauna-spa-massage package is Rp62,100; VIP room Rp125,000. Sauna and spa alone Rp35,000, massage alone Rp35,000. All rates subject to 15.5% service charge and tax.

The huge, flashy **Barong Disco,** tel. (0361) 288888, is on Jl. D. Tamblingan next door to the Sehatku where, for Rp8,000 (Rp10,000 on

Saturday), you can enjoy its elaborate sound and light system from comfortable seats placed amphitheater-fashion around a large dance floor. In his flashing booth the disk jockey churns out a remorselessly loud wall of house music with lyrics emblazoned in red letters on an electronic sign. This place appeals to young Indonesians, yuppie couples from Denpasar, and the odd hooker or two. Black and chrome interior provides plenty of dark places. Open 2000-0300 on Saturday, or till 0200 the rest of the week.

Number One in Batu Jimbar at Jl. D. Tamblingan 138, tel./fax (0361) 288097, on the other side of the road, is also fun—lots of singles, a few prostitutes. Small dance floor. Dress casually, but no beachwear. Open 2100-0200, but only gets going around midnight. A happy hour every night 2200-2300 features half-priced drinks (draft beer Rp4000, mixed drinks Rp4400). Cover Rp10,000; add 10% to all prices. Ask about complimentary transportation for guests staying in Sanur. **Tiffany's Club,** Jl. Pantai Sindhu 12, tel. (0361) 288054, is a bit divey, a place where big German guys dance with diminutive Asian women—a pickup joint with loud music ideal for drinkers and smokers. Open 1100-0400 every night, Rp5000 cover. At the Segara Village Hotel, a live band starts playing in **Le Pirate** at 2000. Arrive early for an international dinner or just sit at the bar and take in the entertainment. Bali Hyatt's **Grantang Bar** is a sophisticated cocktail bar with live jazz every night but Wednesday from 2000 to 0100.

Banjar, right on the beach at the end of Jl. Duyung next to the Hyatt Hotel, is a small, fun venue with a good DJ playing reggae and worl beat to a young, mixed crowd. On the rooftop of the 10-story Grand Bali Beach Hotel is upmarket **Bali Hai Restaurant & Bar**—a live dance band plays nightly, except Sunday, while you enjoy a stunning view. The air-conditioned **Trophy Pub** features a genuine English pub atmosphere where locals and expats drink, play darts and pool, watch satellite TV, and enjoy good Western food. Live music nightly; tasty bar snacks.

The beachfront bar at the **Tanjung Sari** is a restful and scenic respite from Sanur's noisy restaurant bars; be sure to sample the pricy but wonderful *arak bumbu,* a bewitching and potent local rice liquor concocted with a combination of herbs and spices. Another relaxed scene is the small **Cocktail Bar** on Jl. D. Tamblingan in central Sanur, which looks out on the street life; happy hour 1700-1900.

Events

The village has eight full *gamelan* (you can often hear the sound of gongs drifting over the *kampung*), an infamous Black Barong, and the island's only a all-female *kris* dance. Sanur's temple festivals are famous for their color and grandeur. Public performances of authentic Balinese dances occur when a local business, *banjar,* or family celebrates an opening, temple anniversary, or tooth filing.

In this Brahman stronghold, rituals are assiduously tended and the people still practice religious events long ago abandoned in other parts of the island. These events the Balinese usually keep to themselves—tourists often miss an authentic and vibrant Balinese experience happening just over their hotel wall. The village's white- and black-sand beaches are sometimes the sites of religious ceremonies attended by people from all over southern Bali.

An unsual *odalan* is staged at the *pura dalem* nearly opposite the main gate of the Grand Bali Hotel. A long procession of girls carrying high offerings arrives in the late afternoon, followed by the cleansing of the temple's *pratima* and a performance by regimented and entranced *baris gede* dancers with long spears. When cholera season approaches in the wet season, the three-day **Karya Ngusaba Desa: Panangluk Marana** ("Ceremony to Safeguard the Village: The Containment of Death") sees offerings laid at all Sanur's temples. It's believed that long ago a cholera epidemic began in Sanur, raging over the whole of Bali, devastating the population.

SHOPPING

The shopping in Sanur village is good, but you have to bargain. Good quality T-shirts are Rp15,000, and there is almost as wide a variety of designer clothes, repro artifacts, leather goods, jewelry and books as is found in Kuta.

Scores of souvenir shops, fashion boutiques, and convenience stores line Sanur's main drag selling the usual tourist schlock. Exceptions are **Wayan Art Shop No. 1,** Jl. Sanur Beach 17 A, Semawang, for woodcarving, nameplates, Java dolls, small yogis, and bracelets. Good prices.

Konok Art Shop, Jl. Karang Sari, Gang No. 1, tel. (0361) 287320 or 287889, sells colorful *sarung* for only Rp8500. **Jenggala Pottery,** Jl. D. Tamblingan 152, carrying handsome ceramics, shares the same complex as Cafe Batu Jimbar. **Ra Basuki** on Jl. Belanjong, tel. (0361) 233230, sells Pejaten ceramics.

Also visit the exclusive showroom of **Linda Garland Designs** on Jl. Tanjung Sari, tel. (0361) 288072, for high-quality, high-priced Indonesian crafts, *batik* quilts, cushions, bedcovers, and bamboo furniture. For elegant apparel, tablecloths, wall-hangings, and stunning handwoven *ikat* fabrics, **Nogo,** Jl. D. Tamblingan 98, tel. (0361) 288765, fax 288557, offers items of interest. Located in south Sanur, its open 0800-2200. **Batik Gandy,** Jl. Bypass 146 X, tel. (0361) 289541, houses Sanur's widest *batik* selection, with ties, bags, pillowcases, bedcovers, paintings, and ready-to-wear clothes. **Putra Batik,** Jl. Sindhu 5 in north Sanur, has a mindnumbing selection of hand-dyed rayon batik *sarung*.

Yulia Art Shop, Jl. D. Tamblingan 38, tel. (0361) 288089, sells traditional paintings, woodcarvings, antiques, *batik* shirts and skirts, silver, and other souvenirs. At the end of Jl. Pantai Sindhu, take a right and go south to the Art Market (Pasar Seni) for garments, textiles, woodcarvings, masks, leather goods, jewelry, seashells, mobiles, *ikat* bags, and such distinctive folk crafts as large competition-class kites, and small handcrafted wooden sailing *prahu*. The place to go for reasonably priced gifts, this local cooperative donates all profits to the village foundation to run clinics, schools, and temples. Rest your feet at the pleasant open-air restaurant here, serving *nasi goreng, sate,* shrimp, fish, lobster, etc.

Klick, Jl. D. Tamblingan 49, is located inside the Trophy Pub Center at the entrance to the Sanur Beach Hotel in Belanjong in south Sanur. The most attractive items for sale in this gallery are the original hand-painted photographic prints by Swiss-born artist Pierre Poretti depicting Balinese daily life (Rp180,000 each), hand-painted cushions and postcards (set of 10, Rp15,000), gift boxes, and an excellent selection of magazines and books on Bali. Open daily 0900-2100. For elaborate handmade Balinese ceremonial parasols, head for **Dewi Sri Umbrellas,** Jl. D. Tamblingan 32 in central Sanur. Stretched over a mahogany frame and painted in traditional gold designs, they run Rp20,000-50,000.

Pisces, Jl. D. Tamblingan 105, tel. (0361) 289373, fax 288040, in Semawang, is just down the street from the Bali Hyatt near the La Lagune Restaurant. This shops deals in well-sewn, double reinforced black-and-white garments in unique designer cuts; prices from Rp18,000 for shorts and Rp25,000 for pants. These original and continentaly designed clothes are the creation of Kim and Made Patra. Only one exceptional painting gallery exists in Sanur, **Nata Ayu Contemporary Art Gallery** at the entrance of the Tanjung Sari Hotel. Operated by a father and son collaboration—Agus Setiawan Wawo Runtu, the manager of Tanjung Sari, and Wija Wawo Runtu, the founder of the Tanjung Sari Foundation. The Nata Ayu features the high-quality work of such notable artists as the mysterious Emiria Soenassa and the West Javanese artist Acep Zam Zam Noor.

Most ethnographic artifacts are available at their places of origin for a fraction of the prices charged in Sanur. Bean-beaded wall hangings that sell for Rp80,000 in Sumba cost Rp690,000 in Sanur, Sumbanese bone-carved betel nut containers running Rp14,000 are Rp80,000-140,000 in Sanur, and Kalimantan woodcarving purchased for Rp35,000 on Borneo sell for Rp700,000 here. **Asmat Arts,** Jl. D. Tamblingan 200, near Alita Restaurant, deals in "primitive arts made by 20th century Stone Age people"— statues, carvings, shields, and spears. from Irian Jaya, Flores, Java, Sumatra, and Bali. Several antique shops are on the north end of Jl. Tanjung Sari; hunt for unique textiles, baskets, tribal artifacts from the eastern islands, and reproductions of antique furniture. Cruise Jl. Bypass for antique and repro furniture; there are over a dozen dealers. Try **Tjek Lai** on Jl. Bypass near the Grand Bali Hotel for old wooden boxes and Chinese wedding beds. Bargain hard because Sanur is not the best place for antiques. Also check for antiques in the shopping arcades of the big hotels, especially the Bali Hyatt's. The **Trio Dewi Art Shop,** tel. (0361) 287029, in the Sanur Beach Hotel has some good stuff.

The largest and best plant nurseries on Bali are near Sanur on the road to Denpasar. **Sanur Tropical Bonsai,** Jl. D. Tamblingan 27, tel. (0361) 287475 or 289138, is down a small street almost to the beach next to a big house. Five gardeners take care of this large private horticultural enterprise, in which obsessive attention is paid to plants so they won't grow. Specimens are valued at from Rp30,000 to Rp15 million. Some Sentiggi *(pempis ajitula)* trees in the nursery are 500 years old. Founded in 1988. Open all day; Rp2000 entrance.

SERVICES

The majority of Sanur's tourist services are found along Jl. D. Tamblingan. Besides moneychangers, travel agencies, car and motorcycle rental offices, a million beauty salons, tailors, photo processing shops, minimarkets, kiosks, major airlines offices, telephone, fax, and telex services, Sanur has loads of packing and shipping companies to send home all your souvenirs.

Emergencies
A **police station,** tel. (0361) 288597, is on Jl. Bypass on the edge of the golf course. If you need an **ambulance,** call 118 or (0361) 27911. For **medical assistance,** there's a clinic in the Grand Bali Beach Hotel; call (0361) 288511 and ask for the clinic, open Mon.-Fri. 0700-0900, Saturday 0700-2000, Sunday and holidays 1000-1800; doctor on duty Mon.-Sat. 0800-1200. All the major hotels provide 24-hour medical service.

Money
American Express maintains an office in Pacto Ltd., Box 52, Sanur, tel. (0361) 288449, in the Grand Bali Beach Hotel, where you can purchase new checks with an Amex card or bank check, replace lost or stolen travelers checks, and collect mail. Letters held one month, then returned to sender. Open Mon.-Fri. 0830-1630, Saturday 0830-1230. A helpful office. A good place to change money is **P.T. Artha Moneychanger,** tel. (0361) 288965, beside the pool at the Grand Bali Beach; open 0800-1900.

Communications
The only business center in Sanur is the **Business & Communication Centre,** Jl. D. Tamblingan 89, tel. (0361) 281253 or 281254, fax 288191. Take advantage of the IDD, phone, and fax services, as well as secretarial support, translating, courier services, and real estate assistance.

For communications needs, go to the **Wartel,** tel. (0361) 286568, on the southeast corner of Jl. D. Tamblingan beside Hey Cafe. Here you can

make local, collect, and cash international calls from 0800 to 2200. There's another Wartel at the north end of Jl. Danau Toba on the corner of Jl. Segara. The Beach Market Bar and Restaurant on Jl. Segara Ayu has a card pay telephone in front. A great many of the hotels have IDD telephones hooked up in the rooms; an extremely convenient way to make international calls. For example, the Grand Bali Beach has a 24-hour Home Country Direct phone behind the first main porch on the right. Sanur's telephone code is 0361.

Sanur's **post office** is on the southern end of Jl. Danau Buyan, Banjar Taman, west of Jl. Bypass Ngurah Rai. Poste restante open Mon.-Thurs. 0800-1200 and 1300-1700, Friday 0800-1200 and 1330-1700, Saturday 0900-1100, and Sunday 0800-1200. Postal code 80228.

Postal agents are also found all over. One is just a few doors south of Cafe Batu Jimbar, next to Golden Bali Bar and Restaurant. It handles parcels and sells stamps, postcards, etc. If you'd like to receive mail, it's easiest to have it sent to your hotel. Most hotels offer postal services, sell stamps, and mail letters and postcards.

Consulates
There are a few consulates in the Sanur area. The **Australian Consulate** occupies Jl. Sanur 146, tel. (0361) 25997, open Mon.-Fri. 0800 to 1400. New Zealanders, Canadians, and Brits can also bring their problems there. The **U.S. Consulate,** tel. (0361) 288478, is on Jl. Segara Ayu; Margaret is very helpful and has a good attitude. Reach the **Japanese Consulate** at (0361) 25611. The consulate for Swedes and Finns is in the Segara Village Hotel, tel. (0361) 288407 or 288408.

Other Services
A good drugstore with English-speaking and knowledgable staff is located down from Alit's Bungalows. Find another pharmacy three buildings down from the Gazebo Beach Hotel—not as well stocked. The best massages in Sanur are provided by Susie at the Gazebo Beach Hotel, or find a masseuse on the beach for Rp8000 (30 minutes). You'll find just about everything—toiletries, Western, Japanese, and Indonesian food products—in the big **Gelael Dewata Supermarket** on Jl. Bypass. The store enjoys a steady, captive market so prices are high.

Try **Mercy Photo Studio,** Jl. D. Tamblingan 58, tel. (0361) 288603, for color, black and white, and slide film processing. A good place to order passport photos—one-day service, Rp900 for three, Rp2700 for 10. Laundromats include **Sharm Laundry Shop,** Jl. Tanjung Sari 12, tel. (0361) 756814, next to the night market.

The **Kika Book Shop** next to the Batu Jumbar Cafe at Jl. D. Tamblingan 152, tel. (0361) 287374, in central Sanur, offers a wide selection of books about Bali and Indonesia, novels in English, and varied international periodicals, postcards, and prints. On sale here is Made Wijaya's *Balinese Architecture—Towards an Encyclopedia.* De rigueur for the Bali traditionalist. Open 0900-2100, Sunday till 2000.

TRANSPORTATION

Bemo pick up fares along Sanur's five-km-long main road all day for Rp300. A *bemo* stop in the northern end of Sanur outside the entrance to the Grand Bali Beach compound at the intersection of Jl. Bypass and Jl. Hang Tuah. Another is outside the Trophy Pub Centre in southern Sanur near where Jl. D. Tamblingan meets Jl. Bypass. If you're heading into Denpasar, take one of the blue *bemo* to Kereneng Terminal or on to Tegal Terminal where you can board *bemo* to Kuta. Fare Rp600. The official yellow metered taxi fare to the airport is Rp12,000.

Shuttle buses also connect Sanur with all the popular tourist hubs, operating at least twice daily; sample fares: Rp12,500 to Lovina, Rp7500 to Ubud, Rp5000 to Kuta.

Charter *bemo* for short trips around Sanur for about Rp2000-3000, or simply walk anywhere within 10-15 minutes. It's also easy to hop on the back of an *ojek* motorcycle as a paying passenger by just flagging one down or approaching drivers you see with two helmets;all the way to Kuta costs Rp3000. Cars prowling Sanur's main street can be chartered into Denpasar for around Rp5000, to Kuta for Rp8000, to Ubud for Rp20,000. Bargain. Motorbikes rent for around Rp12,000 per day or Rp100,000 per week at Yulia Art Shop & Homestay, Jl. D. Tamblingan 38, tel. (0361) 288089, diagonally opposite the LG Club. Renting motorcycles from touts is less reliable but very easy. A few places rent bicycles for Rp4000 per day.

Numerous rental offices, travel agents, hotels, and shops along Jl. D. Tamblingan and on Jl. Tanjung Sari rent Suzuki Katanas, minibuses, Kijangs, and sedans for Rp60,000-130,000 per day; try first to strike up a good rental deal with your hotel manager. One place to try is Wirasana, Jl. D. Tamblingan 126, tel. (0361) 288706, and Jl. Ngurah Rai Bypass 545, tel. (0361) 286066, opposite the police station. One of the most dependable car rental businesses on the island is **Bali Car Rental** on Jl. Bypass, tel. (0361) 288550; automatic carry Rp10 million third-party liability insurance on all vehicles. Andre Reich, the owner, also maintains offices in Yogya, which allows you to drive your car to Yogya and vice versa. A 15% discount if you rent for a week, 25% for three weeks. **Norman's Rent A Car,** Jl. Sanur Beach, tel. (0361) 288830 or 288328, is another reliable agent for cars at reasonable prices.

Most foreign airlines serving Bali have their offices in the Grand Bali Beach Hotel in Sanur. Hours are generally Mon.-Fri. 0830-1630, with an hour off for lunch, plus Saturday mornings until noon. (Telephone numbers are listed in the Introduction.) Sempati, tel. (0361) 288824 or 281117, the domestic airline, is open 24 hours a day. Airport inquiries: tel. (0361) 751011.

Getting There
From Kuta to Sanur, take a *bemo* first to Terminal Tegal (Rp500) in Denpasar, then a dark blue *bemo* all the way to Sanur (Rp500). Or take a dark green *bemo* from Denpasar's Kereneng Terminal to Sanur (Rp600, 15 minutes). A two-km-long four-lane highway runs six km from the southeastern edge of Denpasar (Renon) to northern Sanur, dropping you off just north of the Grand Bali Beach compound, then continuing down Jl. D. Tamblingan. The official nonmetered taxi fare for the 20-minute drive from the airport to Sanur is Rp15,000; a metered taxi around Rp12,000. With or without prior booking, look for the name of your hotel on signs or vehicles at the airport for a free air-conditioned ride to Sanur. A different way to reach Sanur is to walk along the beach from Lebih, south of Gianyar. This involves crossing the mouths of several rather large rivers—exercise caution.

Getting Away
The Sanur Terminal is at the south end of Sanur near the Trophy Pub Centre at the end of Jl. D. Tamblingan. On Jl. Tanjung Sari, flag down a

blue or green public *bemo* heading northwest to Denpasar's Kereneng Station (Rp600) or a blue one heading south to Tegal Station (also Rp600). From here you get another *bemo* to Kuta for Rp600. Take yellow metered Praja taxis, tel. (0361) 289090 or 289191, for Rp10,000 to the Matahari Department Store in Denpasar; additional rupiah if going farther. Private cars or minibuses into Denpasar cost Rp20,000 first price.

If you have your own vehicle, drive the beautiful new superhighway via Batubulan in the direction of Ubud. This highway—perhaps the best on the island—makes Sanur a good base from which to explore the regencies of Bangli, Gianyar, and Klungkung.

Sanur village is also blessed with the majority of the head offices of international airlines serving Bali, most located in the Grand Bali, so it's easy to confirm or change your departure date here. Garuda's, tel. (0361) 287920, is open Mon.-Fri. 0800-1700, Satuday and Sunday 0900-1300. Reservation lines—tel. (0361) 227825, 235169, 234606, 234916, or 222788—open 24 hours. Also try Sempati Air, tel. (0361) 288823; **Singapore Airlines**, tel. (0361) 287940, ext. 1587, open Mon.-Fri. 0830-1300 and 1400-1630, Saturday 0830-1300; **Ansett,** tel. (0361) 289635-7.

Tour Companies

The biggest and busiest ticket agent in Sanur is **Tunas Indonesia Tours & Travel,** Jl. D. Tamblingan 107, tel. (0361) 288056, fax 828727. Merpati, Garuda, and Qantas tickets, as well as transport on all airlines flying from Bali. Inquire about packages to Gunung Bromo, Baluran Game Park, Yogya, and Komodo Island.

Daily air-conditioned coach tours are offered by **Santa Bali Tours & Travel,** Grand Bali Hotel Arcade, Sanur, tel. (0361) 287628 or 288057, fax 286825, to Bali's Art Villages (Rp20,000), Singaraja and Lake Bratan (Rp40,000), and Karangasem's east coast (Rp38,000). **Satriavi Tours & Travel,** Jl. D. Tamblingan 27 in Semawang (Sanur), tel. (0361) 287074, fax 287019, offers tours to Kintamani, Tanah Lot, and many other tourist sites. **Motive Bali Tours & Travel,** Jl. Bypass 21 XX, tel. (0361) 289018, sells a one-hour, four-passenger joy flight over Bali and its offshore islands for US$195 per person. Professional pilots and breathtaking scenery. Special charters available.

Meru Bicycle Day Trip

Iskander Wawo-Runtu (or simply Alexander), of the same family that owns Batu Jimbar Cafe, guides adventure tours on mountain bikes from his upland farm near Pupuan down to the sea for Rp140,000 per person. Explore the untouched side of Bali—beautiful rice fields, rainforests, rivers, ravines, small remote villages. Hotel pickup at 0700, finish between 1700 and 1800. Contact Alexander at the Tanjung Sari Hotel, Jl. D. Tamblingan 41, Sanur, tel. (0361) 288441, fax 287930, or at Cafe Batu Jimbar on Jl. D. Tamblingan, tel. (0361) 287374.

To Nusa Lembongan

Public ferries to Nusa Lembongan and Nusa Penida depart from the northern end of the beach in front of the Ananda Hotel & Restaurant. If standing facing the sea, the ticket office is 150 meters to the left after reaching the end of Jl. Hang Tuah. Ask for *stasiun bot.* The first boat leaves at around 0800. If you're small, big Balinese guys will carry you into the waves and put you aboard the bobbing *prahu.* The passage takes about an hour and costs a fixed Rp15,000, including surfboard.

VICINITY OF SANUR

Only 2.5 km south of the Grand Bali Hotel, just beyond the village of Kesiman, is an important place of remembrance, **Padanggalak.** From the beach enjoy fine views of the coastline and Sanur's "hotel row." It was on this beach that the Dutch forces which eventually subjugated the Balinese landed in 1906.

Padanggalak also commemorates a tragedy. A monument here is dedicated to the people who died in the crash of a Pan Am Boeing 707 that crashed into the side of Gunung Patas west of Singaraja on 22 April 1974. Visitors from 11 nations still come here to pay their respects to the dead.

Ayung Reptile Park (tel. 0361-286131 or 289212, fax 289211) is 10 minutes drive north of Sanur at the mouth of the Ayung River, in Singapadu, three km from the main highway at Celuk. Features many reptiles from the Indonesian archipelago. Performances are held twice daily at 0900 and 1700.

BENOA PORT AND SERANGAN ISLAND

BENOA PORT

A short boat ride from Benoa village at the Tanjung Peninsula's northern tip, or a relatively long trip by road around the cape via Jimbaran, takes you to the other side of Benoa Harbor to Benoa Port on the southern coast of Bali. For hundreds of years, reef-sheltered Labuhan Benoa was the entry point from the sea for all of south Bali. The accummulation of alluvium has long since rendered much of this natural harbor unnavigable, but a long causeway was built by the Dutch after their 1906 invasion. At the end are fuel tanks, a big wharf, dozens of moored vessels, warehouses, a lighthouse, fisheries, charter-boats offices, and a Pelni office.

Reach Benoa from Denpasar's Tegal Station by *bemo* for around Rp1000. A chartered *bemo* from Kuta will run Rp9000-12,000. If traveling by car, 10 km from Denpasar and just south of Pasangaran on the main Kuta/Sanur road, turn right and travel down a two-kilometer-long jetty (Jl. Pelabuhan) which stretches toward the northeast corner of the Bukit Peninsula.

Large cargo ships, fishing boats, oil tankers, cruise ships, private yachts, and intraisland *kapal layar* moor in this wide and shallow bay. The port is also the location of the Bali International Yacht Club, tel. (0361) 288391. If you'd like to crew on one of the visiting overseas yachts, hire a *jukung* to take you around to the different vessels; ask if there are any openings. Visiting oceangoing yachts usually arrive at this anchorage in the high season. If you get on as crew, give the captain your passport and he'll clear it with the harbormaster when he gets the Sailing Permit *(surat ijin belayar)*.

Catch the high-speed hydrofoil *Mabua Express* to Lombok. With its twin hulls and hightech design, this vessel will get you to Lembar in West Lombok quickly, comfortably, safely, and reliably. Enjoy stunning views while you luxuriate in a spacious air conditioned lounge with TV, video, and refreshments. Departs Benoa at 0830, arrives 1030; departs Lembar 1300, arrives back in Benoa 1500. Book through your travel agent, or call their offices directly, tel./fax (0361) 772370. The fare from Bali to Lombok is about Rp40,000; return about Rp35,000.

For the names and addresses of all the chartered yacht outfits operating fully equipped, luxury yachts out of this port to the island of Nusa Penida 24 km offshore, see the "Getting Around" section of the Introduction. These well-promoted companies will pick you up at your hotel for an early morning departure, arriving in a quiet bay off Nusa Lembongan two to two and a half hours later. These outings are especially popular with surfers who are able to paddle in to—not out to—the reef breaks off Nusa Lembongan. Late that afternoon you sail back to the mainland, enjoying the sunset en route. The price, which includes transfers, meals, and snorkeling gear is Rp161,000-173,000 per person (children half price).

SERANGAN ISLAND

Also known as Turtle Island or Pulau Sakenan, this dry, low-lying, 73-hectare, three-kilometer-long island formed on the sandbar at the entrance to Labuhan Benoa, only 250 meters off the southeast coast of Bali. The island's lovely, palm-lined southern beach is visible from the village of Benoa at the northern tip of the Tanjung Peninsula. At the northern end of Serangan are two villages, Pojok and, just 500 meters to the south, Dukuh, connected by a bridge over an inlet. Settled by Islamic Buginese from South Sulawesi, the villages are home to a Muslim mosque and a cemetery. Islanders—both Muslim and Hindu—live together harmoniously, selling shell artifacts to tourists, cultivating turtles, and growing maize, corn, and peanuts. There's only one *losmen* on the island, **Homestay Santap Sari**, located on the east coast near the *pura dalem*. They have six neat rooms with terraces, Rp15,000-25,000. Good *warung* serving seafood are found along the track leading to Pura Sakenan.

Unfortunately, Serangan has become a bit of a tourist trap. The island's main attraction seems to be a muddy pool inhabited by green-back turtles *(kura-kura),* 50 meters east of the Pojok jetty. Shops selling seashell and turtle-shell artifacts and cold drinks surround the pond. Despite its population of only 2,500, you'll likely be hounded by vendors, who try to sell you trays full of porcelain, Venus' combs, and tawny bishop's miters, as well as highly polished turtle shells. The latter you should buy only if you want to contribute to the extinction of these giant reptiles, now the focus of a worldwide conservation effort.

Green sea turtles *(Chelonia mydas)* are caught in the surrounding shallow coastal waters, or simply turned on their backs when they come ashore at night to lay eggs. First kept alive in bamboo pens, then fattened on seagrass or leaves, they're eventually slaughtered at Pegok on the outskirts of Denpasar. The meat is then sold to restaurants for turtle steaks and *sate,* or used as a vital ingredient in the Balinese ceremonial specialty, *lawar.* There used to be a balance between supply and demand on Bali, but now because of the voracious Balinese market hundreds of these magnificent wild animals must be imported from the eastern islands and Maluku. If you're fortunate, on a moonlit night you can watch them lay eggs on Serangan's beach. Eggs are now imported from West Java and buried in the sand so that tourists can see them hatch here. There's also a turtle egg hatchery on the island.

Sights

One kilometer south of Dukuh is Serangan's slender **Pura Sakenan,** a two-part sea temple, sacred to all south Bali. A feature of this seaside *pura* is its peculiar, graceful *bersayap*-style winged *candi bentar.* Inside is an obelisk to the rice goddesss, Dewi Sri. Legend has it Pura Sakenan was founded by the 10th century wanderer-priest Mpu Kuturan. It shares the same guardian statues and decorative designs as its contemporary, Pura Uluwatu, on the Bukit, and was constructed with the same material—hard coral stone. The more squarish **Pura Susunan Wadonan** contains pyramid-shaped *prasada*—Javanese *candi*-style, stepped shrines, but without the *cella.* The combination of *candi* and pre-

historic pre-Hindu stepped pyramid is seldom seen in Balinese temple architecture.

Events

It's best to visit the island at festival time. Once every 210 days, a **Turtle Festival** (Manis Kuningan) is held at the Pura Sakenan sea temple in the north of the island, one of Bali's eight most sacred public temples. For the two-day *odalan* festival, droves of people are ferried or wade across the sandbars bearing offerings to the sea gods. At the same time, towering giant puppets for the *barong landung* dance are carried by canoe in a water procession. A big colorful fair takes place outside the temple as throngs of people in all their finery stream in and out.

Getting There

The most common method is by motorized boat from Desa Suwung, about 1.5 km south of Sanur; you'll see the sign pointing to Serangan Island. There are no regular *bemo* but you can just charter one, Rp5000, from Sanur. Take a right turn off Jl. Bypass, then drive past shrimp farms and mangroves to the estuary where motorized longboats wait for passengers. The outrageous price is Rp25,000 (20 minutes); bargain the fare while waiting for other passengers to arrive to split the cost. The boat then negotiates the narrow and very shallow channel through the swamps. Once on the island, get to Pura Sakenan from the north by walking south over the bridge to the banjar of Dukuh. From Dukuh, follow the path that leads across the cement causeway over the lagoon then through a coconut grove.

From Tanjung Benoa, plan on about 20 minutes each way to cross the bay by *prahu motor,* and at least a half-day on the island. The fishermen ask as much as Rp30,000 first price, but will come down to Rp20,000. From Tanjung's tip, it's possible to walk across the mud to Pulau Serangan when the tide is low. Also, inquire at the water-sport centers in Tanjung, Sanur, Nusa Dua, and Kuta about day snorkeling excursions to coral formations off Serangan's east coast; these cost about Rp45,000 for a three- or four-hour excursion, including transport and equipment.

BADUNG REGENCY

Bali is divided into nine *kabupaten* (administrative districts, or regencies), based on the old post-Majapahit kingdoms; of these, Badung contains the neon-lit tourist swath of Legian, Kuta, and Nusa Dua. Badung also extends inland to the overtouristed monkey forest of Sangeh and on to the slopes of Gunung Catur (2,096 meters), high in the central mountains.

Badung has the island's highest prices and the poshest, most sophisticated hotels. Yet central and northern Badung are regions of fertile rice fields carved exquisitely out of hills and valleys, with small, densely settled villages surrounded by groves of coconut palms. Wealthy southern Bali's temple festivals, ceremonies, and dance performances are lavish and unending.

The drier, sparsely populated clubfoot shaped peninsula known as Bukit ("The Hill") is attached to the southernmost body of the island by a narrow isthmus. Here, high cliffs fall steeply into the Indian Ocean and surf pounds stretches of isolated coast; this is among the earth's top surfing spots. Although the soil is thin, water scarce, and the climate arid, Bukit is fast be-

coming an overflow residential area for the mushrooming population of Nusa Dua, Jimbaran, and Tanjung. Between Bukit and southern Bali's fertile plains is Ngurah Rai International Airport, which receives hordes of tourists from all over the world. The bulk of Bali's tourists visit the concentrated international beach enclaves of the south, taking day trips to sites all over the island.

History

Since it's the most accessible seaport in the southern part of the island, the Badung region has always been an important point of contact with the outside world. The Javanese Majapahit army came ashore at Kuta in 1343 to conquer Bali. The first Dutchmen landed on Bali at Kuta in 1597. In the 1830s an ambitious Danish trader, Mads Lange, established a thriving trading post at the same site.

Once ruled by the raja of Mengwi, Badung split from Tabanan in 1885. This historical event explains the regency's odd vertical shape—like an exclamation point—and accounts for Mengwi being included within its territory. The Pe-

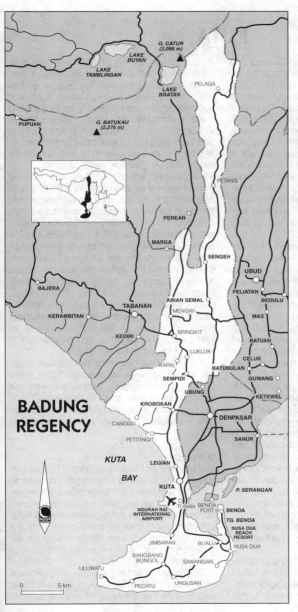

mecutan clan of Denpasar defeated Mengwi in 1891, but held sway only briefly, until the incursion of a new and increasingly powerful player, the Dutch. Though the Dutch subdued the northern part of the island in 1849, the fertile lava-rich lowlands of the south came under colonial rule only after prolonged resistance. Since the northern port of Singaraja was blocked by a central mountain range, all the trade of the south took place through the reef-sheltered port of Kuta, the only place ships could anchor and unload. This made it an irresistible target of Dutch expansion. One of the last areas of Indonesia to be occupied, Badung was pounded into submission in 1906, setting the stage for the conquest of all of southern Bali.

Since the establishment of the Ngurah Rai International Airport in Tuban in 1969, the provincial government of Bali has attempted to confine tourist development to the south. A whole generation of local residents have built *losmen* and restaurants in the south's tourist enclaves of Kuta and Sanur, and entrepreneurs from all over Indonesia flock here for money-making opportunities. Thousands of laborers from Java are also attracted to work on the new roads and hotels of the constantly expanding economic infrastructure. Thus Badung Regency is where Balinese culture has undergone the most radical and deepest changes.

KUTA

The tree in the middle of Bemo Corner, that struggled for years against pollution and the on-slaught of tourists, is dead. In late 1992, this solitary outpost of nature was finally cut down and replaced with a guardian statue. This event was part of a continuum that began in the 16th century, leading to today's rollicking honky-tonk tourist encrustation 10 km south of Denpasar on Bali's southwest coast. Kuta was just a sleepy fishing village on the way in from the airport when it was discovered by seasoned travelers in the late 1960s. Since then, tens of thousands of travelers, surfies, and package tourists have turned Kuta into a gigantic First World yuppie resort. If Sanur is Indonesia's Riviera, then Kuta is its Tijuana.

Kuta is essentially five kilometers of close-packed pubs, chic boutiques, tacky restaurants, juice bars, bookstores, supermarkets, surf shops, tie-dye T-shirt outlets, travel agencies, money-changers, beauty parlors, and blaring cassette shops. You can't walk 10 meters without encountering someone demanding you buy something. At night when the sun sets, Kuta Beach Road (Jl. Pantai Kuta) is an evil-smelling maze of bicycles, motorbikes, pedestrians, honking *bemo,* and cars plying their way through a smoggy layer of dust with thousands of milling people.

At least five of 10 visitors here are free-spending Australians—they're particularly in evidence during the Australian school vacation period of December and January. When you have restaurants serving Vegemite sandwiches and Toad in a Hole (hotdog in a bun), and a pub called Koala Blu, you know Australia isn't far away. Most never leave the Kuta area the whole time they're on Bali. Another hectic period is the July to August holiday season, when flights disgorge hordes of French, German, and Spanish tourists. There are also vast numbers of Japanese tourists of all ages. The streets can get so crowded during July and August you're forced to walk in the street.

In the 1830s, Kuta was a thriving slave market, attracting a wide variety of international lowlife, lepers, and black market practitioners. Some would say nothing has changed. Today Kuta's streets are full of Javanese foot peddlers, Madurese prostitutes, Surabaya transvestites, and ragged Bali Aga beggar women attended by their children. Garish signs and souvenir shops lend a tawdry air to the main roads, reaching far back into the village's narrow dirt lanes. Tenacious peddlers selling anything and everything pester sunbathers on the beach, and boys in dark glasses on motorcycles hustle tourists to buy "hashish" (a lie) or girls.

Fortunately, the cancer of Kuta is confined to this relatively small enclave. And if you accept it for what it is, Kuta can be a fun place to visit. Although rubbishy, cluttered, and increasingly crowded, the resort has undergone a rehabilitation of sorts since 1994 and 1995. Flower beds have been planted all along the beach now, trash cans are placed every 100 meters, the nettlesome admission charge to the beach has been discarded, and the beachfront food-stalls are now required to sell at fixed prices. Kuta's streets are regularly patroled, and the Kuta *banjar* consistently receives commendations. For a slice of Old Bali, visit the local food/small goods market on the intersection of Jl. Pantai Kuta and Jl. Raya Tuban.

Kuta offers cut-rate hedonism, nonstop nightlife, fancy restaurants, sophisticated hotels, some of Bali's best shopping, and surprisingly low prices for food (count on about Rp23,000-28,000 per day). Still one of the world's best-value hangouts and the island's liveliest and naughtiest spot.

Warnings

The local *banjar* have made a lot of headway in cleaning up crime and evicting predatory criminals, but rooms are still burglarized. It's imperative you find secure, well-guarded accommodations with bars on the windows. Always keep valuables more than an arm's reach from the windows. Watch out for children who gather around you and work in unison to pick your moneybelt or fannypack.

On the beach and in the lanes, drug peddlers may seem friendly, but four of five will cheat you. Even worse, they may be working with the

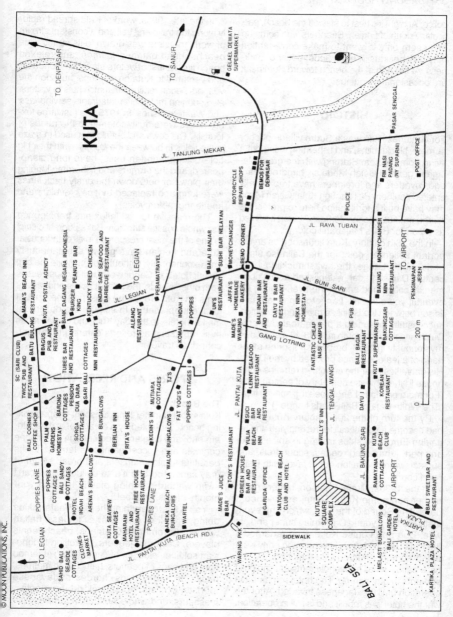

KUTA

TO SANUR

TO DENPASAR

GELAEL DEWATA SUPERMARKET

JL TANJUNG MEKAR

PASAR SENGGAL

POST OFFICE

RM NASI PADANG (NY SUPARNI)

BEMOS FOR DENPASAR

MOTORCYCLE REPAIR SHOPS

POLICE

JL RAYA TUBAN

TO AIRPORT

MONEYCHANGER

PENGINAPAN JESEN

BAKUNG MINI RESTAURANT

JL BUNI SARI

BAKUNGSARI COTTAGE

THE PUB

BALI BAGIA RESTAURANT

KUTA SUPERMARKET

KOREAN RESTAURANT

DAYU I

JL TENGAL WANGI

MAMA'S BEACH INN

KUTA POSTAL AGENCY

BATU BULONG RESTAURANT

BANK DAGANG NEGARA INDONESIA

BURGER KING

PEANUTS BAR

KENTUCKY FRIED CHICKEN

INDAH SARI SEAFOOD AND BARBECUE RESTAURANT

TO LEGIAN

JL. LEGIAN

PERAMATRAVEL

BALI BANJAR

SUSHI BAR NELAYAN

MONEYCHANGER

BEMO CORNER

BAGUS PUB AND RESTAURANT

TWICE PUB AND RESTAURANT

SC (SARI CLUB)

BALI CORNER COFFEE SHOP

ALEANG RESTAURANT

MINI RESTAURANT

KOMALA INDAH I

POPPIES

UN'S RESTAURANT

JAFFA'S HOMEMADE BAKERY

MADE'S WARUNG

BALI INDAH BAR AND RESTAURANT

DAYU II BAR AND RESTAURANT

ARKA NINI HOMESTAY

GANG LOTRING

FANTASTIC CHEAP NASI CAMPUR

PALM GARDENS HOMESTAY

POPPIES COTTAGES II

BALI SANDY COTTAGES

HOTEL INDAH BEACH

TUBES BAR AND RESTAURANT

BARONG COTTAGES

PENSION DUA DARA

SORGA COTTAGES

SARI BALI COTTAGES

MIMPI BUNGALOWS

BERLIAN INN

MUTIARA COTTAGES

TJ'S

POPPIES COTTAGES

POPPIES LANE II

SAHID BALI SEASIDE COTTAGES

CLOTHES MARKET

TO LEGIAN

KUTA SEAVIEW COTTAGES

MAHARANI HOTEL AND RESTAURANT

ARENA'S BUNGALOWS

KEDIN'S

RITA'S HOUSE

FAT YOGI'S

LA WALON BUNGALOWS

TREE HOUSE RESTAURANT

ANEKA BEACH BUNGALOWS

POPPIES LANE

WARTEL

MADE'S JUICE BAR

TONY'S RESTAURANT

GREEN HOUSE BAR AND RESTAURANT

GARUDA OFFICE

YULIA BEACH INN

SUCI BAR AND RESTAURANT

LENNY SEAFOOD RESTAURANT

JL. PANTAI KUTA

WILLY'S INN

JL. BAKUNG SARI

NATOUR KUTA BEACH CLUB AND HOTEL

KUTA SQUARE COMPLEX

RAMAYANA COTTAGES

KUTA BEACH CLUB

TO AIRPORT

JL. PANTAI KUTA (BEACH RD.)

WARUNG PKK

SIDEWALK

MELASTI BUNGALOWS

BALI GARDEN HOTEL

JL. KARTIKA PLAZA

BALI SWEETBAR AND RESTAURANT

KARTIKA PLAZA HOTEL

BALI SEA

200 m

0

© MOON PUBLICATIONS, INC.

police. At night it's best to stay off the beach, particularly north of Legian. Strangers who come up and seem only to want to make conversation may pick pockets or bags under cover of darkness. At the end of the beach toward Seminyak are occasional muggings.

HISTORY

For centuries Kuta was a Sudra village of poor farmers, blacksmiths, and fishermen eking out a living from the sea. Starting with the great Majapahit general Gajah Mada six hundred years ago, invaders and foreigners have traditionally entered southern Bali through Kuta. Gajah Mada may have built a fortification here to protect his rearguard; *kuta* means "fortress." Later, it served as a port for Bali's Majapahit colony.

In the 18th century, Kuta flourished as an important collection point for the Balinese slave trade. Mads Lange, the swashbuckling 19th-century Danish trader, established a vast commercial compound beside the river. During his eventful years in Bali, Lange often acted as a liaison between the Balinese rajas and the Dutch, successfully arranging a peace treaty after the Dutch attacked the south in 1848-49. Lange died mysteriously in 1856, probably poisoned at the hand of a jealous prince prodded by the Dutch. His grave lies near the crumbled remains of his house in the Chinese cemetary of central Kuta. (For more on Mads Lange, see the special topic "The White Raja of Bali: Mads Lange.")

By the turn of the 20th century Kuta village had become a port of call for resupplying and repairing European ships trading in spices. Like any port, it harbored rogues, scoundrels, and subjects who had fallen out of favor with Bali's royal courts.

In the 1930s, Muriel Pearson, better known by her pen name Ketut Tantri, established a hotel, The Sound of the Sea, which she eventually sold to a young Californian surfer and his wife, Bob and Louise Koke, who renamed it the Kuta Beach Hotel. This charming early Kuta establishment featured little thatched houses, brick patios, small household temples, and child servants in gay *sarung*. The hotel remained in operation until the Japanese invaded. After the war the hotel was rebuilt and is still in operation.

In the late 1960s, word of Kuta spread rapidly along the travelers' trail and a constant stream of world travelers was drawn to its sunny wide beach, cheap bamboo *losmen,* and relaxed beach life. At first travelers stayed in Denpasar and ventured to Kuta on day trips, but soon the villagers began renting out thatch huts to visitors, also opening makeshift restaurants serving *lassi* and Western dishes. In 1975, the first large luxury hotels were built, catering to the needs of tourists. The cows and buffalo that used to graze in the fields in between the *losmen,* with their big tick-tocking wooden bells, have long disappeared, and the farmers and fishermen lugging their plows or nets down the dusty back lanes were long ago replaced by tipsy revelers and sputtering motorcycles.

The massive tourist influx has transformed this whole coastal strip from Bali's poorest district to one of the most prosperous in all of Indonesia. Kuta and Legian have grown spontaneously and exponentially, without a plan. While the big, swank hotels of Sanur were built by businesses from other islands, the budget hotels and restaurants on Kuta are for the most part the work of local entrepreneurs. In spite of the dozen upmarket hotels, to this day Kuta and Legian retain their reputation as resorts catering to budget-conscious travelers.

SPORTS AND RECREATION

The Beach

Kuta's six-kilometer-long, crescent-shaped surfing beach, protected by a coral reef at its southern end, and long and wide enough for Frisbee contests and soccer games, is famous for its beautiful tropical sunsets and broad swath of gray sand. Too bad it's so polluted. You can't swim without catching plastic trash in your mouth, hands, and feet.

You'll see everything here—Western kids doing wheelies with BMXs, topless Italian women, Euromen in G-strings, beach-tennis players, California joggers, patrolling Indonesian soldiers, clusters of carts selling steamed corn and bags of peanuts, hefty Dutch matrons, packs of mangy dogs, hordes of Javanese tourists, cyclists, horseback riders, hippies, masseurs, and whole Australian families with

Whoopi Goldberg hairdos. Huge crowds gather at sunset, setting up tripods, reading novels, strumming guitars, swigging cold beer, tripping on magic mushrooms. Vendors, who may not venture beyond an official demarcation line, offer massages, drinks, souvenirs, and bikinis. Large sun umbrellas are for rent. Nude swimming and sunbathing, as well as motorcycle and surf buggy riding, are frowned upon by the local police. The beach is extremely crowded in August and December. For any semblance of seclusion you have to walk north for at least a kilometer past Legian.

Although Kuta's beach is inviting, watch the treacherous undertow and strong currents. Since 1958, over 100 tourists have drowned here. Always swim within the flag markers on the beach, keep near the crowds and lifeguards, and remain within the reef.

Surfing

Kuta became a hippie haven and surf paradise in the early '70s. The best waves are the left-handers out on Kuta Reef; the best surfing is from March to July. Kuta Reef is accessible by motorized outrigger from Jimbaran for about Rp30,000-40,000. Young Kuta cowboys tend to be real possessive about their waves, so make friends with them first. For surfing equipment, head for the dozen or so surf shops on Jl. Bakung Sari and Jl. Legian. Run by veteran surfers, these shops rent and sell surfboards, boogie boards, and such accessories as watersport wear and tide charts. These guys can also give you current information on the state of the surf. Surfboards can also be rented on the beach.

Scuba Diving

Wally Siagian, who gained world fame after the publication of Periplus Edition's best-selling *Underwater Indonesia* (1991), takes small groups on tours to his favorite dive sites. Wally specializes in night dives, spear fishing, and marine photography. Contact **Baruna Water Sports,** Jl. Bypass Ngurah Rai 300 B, Kuta, tel.

BEACH SAFETY: YOU COULD DROWN HERE

Don't be deceived by the crowds on the Kuta/Legian beach areas. Even though the beach here is quite dangerous, you still see people swimming exactly where they are not supposed to swim. It's common during the busy July/August period that as many as five people die or turn up missing over a six week period. During this same period, another four or five are pulled out of the dangerous undercurrents in front of Surya Restaurant and the Padma Hotel in Legian. If you extrapolate this over the course of a year, you get 40 fatalities a year due to drownings off Kuta and Legian.

There are certain facts that all tourists should be aware of when they arrive at Kuta. First, there are extremely strong undercurrents. Second, because Indonesia still does not have the resources that Australia, the U.S.A., or Japan, if you get pulled out to sea, well, it's basically you and the ocean, and if you are not Mark Spitz, the ocean will win. Between Kuta and Legian, there are only four lifeguards (beach security is trying to increase that number). Kuta is also not blessed with access to speedboats or helicopters that will come fish you out if you're unlucky enough to get pulled out to sea when the lifeguard is not looking your way.

Moreover, once it gets dark, there is no way that anyone can find you out in the endless black ocean. Indonesian authorities simply do not have access to the strong strobe lights necessary to conduct a search after dark. Furthermore, because the undercurrent is so strong, you could find yourself hundreds of meters out to sea before anyone even notices that you are missing. Aerial searches are not conducted and the few rubber boats on hand are no match for mother nature which certainly, as the search is going on, will be pulling you farther and farther out to sea. Kuta and Legian beach is not an episode out of Baywatch where being pulled out to sea is rewarded by mouth to mouth with Pamela Anderson.

While there are dangerous areas of the beach (especially between Surya Restaurant and the bungee jump), swimming on Kuta Beach does not have to be life threatening. The beach patrol, which puts up danger signs, knows what it's doing and swimmers who swim between the safe red and yellow flags have very little chance of encountering bad currents. People only die because they swim precisely where they are not supposed to swim.

(0361) 753809, fax 752779, the longest-established and best scuba dive operator on Bali. Another well respected operator is **Bali Dolphin** at the Bali Garden Hotel, Jl. Kartika, tel. (0361) 752725, ext. 139; these people can also arrange parasailing, fishing, jet skiing, and waterskiing activities.

North of Kuta

At low tide, bicycle rides or walks along the firm, moist sand are refreshing. Heading north of Kuta, you can ride for about seven kilometers. At this point either retrace your tracks or turn inland at the thatched roofs of Seminyak's Bali Oberoi and return to Kuta via Jl. Legian. Although the new tourist accommodations springing up north of Legian in Canggu and Pererean are bringing more people to previously isolated beaches, the crowds thin the farther north you get. If you're walking or riding northwest to Tanah Lot, you have to cross several rivers and stretches of deep black lava sand where the coast is rocky and unsuitable for swimming.

Along the beach to the northwest of Kuta, on the estuary of a lazy river, is the unusual temple of Pura Petitenget. Built entirely of white coral, this traditional temple was founded by one of the first Hindu-Javanese priests, Sanghyang Nirantha, on his journey along the beach to Uluwatu. After defeating a local *bhuta,* this Balinese-Hindu saint invited the people of the village of Krobokan to build a temple here to commemorate the place where the sacred books of India, the Vedas, were first brought to Bali. Pura Petitenget shares a common forecourt with the *subak* temple of Pura Ulun Tanjung. This was also the spot where the first Dutchman, Captain Cornelis de Houtman, set foot on Bali in 1596.

ACCOMMODATIONS

There are hundreds of *losmen,* beach inns, bungalows, cottages, and hotels here. Since the main roads Jl. Pantai Kuta and Jl. Legian are all built out, new accommodations appear down the lanes to either side of these roads. Each lane is actually a little neighborhood unto itself, with its own *warung,* shops, hotels, and strip of beach where the neighborhood gathers at sunset.

There are about 15 international-class (Rp210,000 and up) accommodations, 75 medium-priced (Rp75,000-160,000) accommodations, and about 350 budget joints with the cheapest class of rooms in the Rp40,000-80,000 range. In the low season (March-June), you can bargain prices down by as much as 20%. Don't get stuck paying Rp50,000 (plus tax) for a mosquito-ridden hole just because it's near the beach when a really together place like Dua Dara (Rp12,000 d) off Poppies Lane II is a much better value.

At the airport or along the road, Balinese owners, houseboys, and touts pitch *losmen* in person; some of these leads are worthwhile. Signs erected at the start of many lanes point the way to hidden accommodations. Avoid places along or near noisy, smelly, and polluted Jl. Panti Kuta and Jl. Legian; opt instead for accommodations in the back lanes nearer the beach or in the outskirts of Kuta. The villages north of Legian along the coast—Seminyak, Petitenget, Canggu—tend to be quieter and more easygoing, with lower prices and fewer peddlers. There are also many private, fan-cooled bungalows for rent in these villages; expect to pay about Rp20,000-30,000 per day. The drawbacks to staying here are lack of public transport to goods and services and the possibility of break-ins.

In the high season (July-Sept., December, January), hotels are booked solid so make reservations far in advance. There are so many places now and such intense competition that proprietors are often inclined to give a discount for stays of three or more days, so the inevitable first question is "How many nights?" Bargain. Following is a sample of the many accommodations available.

Budget

Kuta villagers created Indonesia's first budget seaside accommodations, which exist to this day—rows of concrete cells hastily erected in the family compound, with a basic *mandi* in back of each cubicle and a long, narrow veranda in front. Cheap bamboo furniture and spartan breakfast.

Maha Bharata in Banjar Pengabetan off Jl. Legian, tel. (0361) 752027, has clean rooms with toilet and *kamar mandi* for only Rp15,000 including breakfast (jaffles and tea). **Suci Bungalows,**

Jl. Pantai Kuta 65, tel. (0361) 753761, is also a good deal. Each room (Rp12,000 s, Rp15,000 d) has an overhead fan and private porch with bamboo chair facing a well-kept garden; light breakfast included in price. Good restaurant.

Relatively nice, with a secure inner courtyard, is **Puspa Beach Inn**, tel. (0361) 751988, on a lane off Jl. Bakung Sari. Rooms have fans, private bathrooms, and showers—a good deal in the heart of Kuta. A bit higher priced but still reasonable is **La Walon Bungalows** with pool; Rp40,000 d in high season, Rp37,800 d low season. The **Kuta Suci Bungalows**, tel. (0361) 52617, off Poppies Lane II, charges Rp30,000 s, Rp40,000 d per room. Basic but quiet and clean; two higher-priced cottages. Two minutes from the beach is **Yulia Beach Inn** on Jl. Pantai Kuta 43, tel. (0361) 751862, fax 751055. The 48 rooms start at Rp20,000 s, Rp25,000 d for fans and shared bath and rise to Rp45,000 s, Rp50,000 d for bungalows with fridge, a/c, private bath, and hot water. Also available are safety deposit boxes; postal and laundry service; car, motorbike, bicycle, and minibus hire; and daily tours starting at about Rp15,000 per person. The 16-room **Mama's Beach Inn**, tel. (0361) 751994 or 751512, is close to restaurants and clubs. From Jl. Legian, enter the lane beside Panin Bank. It's best suited for indestructible Aussie surfers who don't need a lot of sleep and like to stick with their own kind. Rates are Rp15,000 s, Rp20,000 d with cold shower, fan, no breakfast. Very conveniently located—maybe too much so, as street sounds intrude.

Bali Indra Village Resort behind Depot Viva, tel. (0361) 752167, has 15 air-conditioned rooms with TV and IDD for Rp80,500 s, Rp90,000 d, and a great swimming pool.

Close to the frenzy and very convenient is **Komala Indah I** on Poppies Lane I opposite Poppies Cottages and just before the turn to Gang Bedugul; Rp10,000 s, Rp15,000 d with fan and *mandi*. Around the corner (north) on Gang Bedugul are two cheap places: **Puri Agung** is a little ways down on the right, not that noisy, extremely central, yet only Rp15,000-20,000 s with fan. Opposite Puri Agung on the same lane is **Taman Ayu** with 15 ground floor rooms (Rp10,000 s, Rp15,000 d) clustered around a small compound.

Good value **Berlian Inn,** Poppies Lane I, tel. (0361) 751501, is quiet and close to the beach. Rooms with private bath, shower, hot water, fans, and bamboo decor go for Rp35,000 s, Rp46,000 d. With a/c, Rp51,000 s, Rp62,000 d. If heading for the beach, turn right into the lane just before the Tree House Restaurant.

Rita's House, in an alley between Poppies Lane I and Poppies Lane II, tel. (0361) 751760, is close to the beach and costs only Rp15,000 s, Rp20,000 d with fan, Rp25,000 s, Rp35,000 d with a/c, fan, and *mandi*. Quiet and away from the intense hustle, Rita's sets up tours, has parking, and can recommend *batik,* music, and painting teachers.

Mutiara, tel. (0361) 752091, has 15 two-unit cottages. Two are a/c (Rp75,000) and the rest are fan-cooled (Rp60,000) with twin beds, Western showers and toilets, hot water. Price includes breakfast. Plastic accepted. The pool is gorgeous and the central garden is nice and peaceful as it's set back from Poppies Lane. You'll seldom hear any noise except the roosters. The Mutiara can safely store your things while you travel. Also check out the **Sari Bali,** the owner's other hotel on the same lane, which offers poolside service. **Arena's Bungalows,** close to the beach on a lane off Poppies Lane, is clean, well-run, and quiet. Small bungalows are Rp25,000 s, Rp35,000 d. One of the best breakfasts in Indonesia: fresh fruit salad and wonderful jaffles. Free tea.

Maharani Hotel and Restaurant, tel. (0361) 751863, fax 752589, is a sterile, four-story hotel with pool. Rp138,000 s, Rp161,000 d for garden view, Rp207,000 s, Rp276,000 d for seaview; including breakfast, tax, and service. Half-hearted breakfast, not enough towels. Mediocre, but then again it's not that expensive for a hotel fronting the beach.

Many Rp15,000-plus places on Poppies Lane II are on the grungy side, both inside and out. An exception is the amazingly clean and tidy **Pension Dua Dara,** Segara Batu Bolong Lane, just off Poppies Lane II (entrance is opposite Twice Restaurant), tel. (0361) 754031. Each room (Rp10,000 s and Rp15,000 d) has bath, fan, and terrace. An incredible deal if you don't mind such inconveniences as no bathroom mirrors or towel-racks. Safety deposit boxes, free breakfast including coffee, toast, jaffle, and fruit salad, plus tea all day. The drinks are cheaper than in restaurants. Phone available. Caters mostly to young Australian surfers. **Palm Gardens Homestay,** tel. (0361) 752198, consists of clean brick cottages (Rp20,000 s, Rp25,000 d) with *mandi,* showers, nice private gardens, moneychanger, and tour service. Towels changed everyday, floors mopped, bathrooms cleaned. Several good restaurants nearby. Very private, little noise. Clean, safe, reasonably priced **Suji Bungalows,** tel./fax (0361) 752483, asks for its double bungalows Rp25,000 s, Rp35,000 d with fan, Rp33,000 s, Rp48,000 d for a/c. Pool, nice staff, and price includes breakfast. Recommended.

Bali Dwipa I, still a beautiful place with a courtyard full of wonderful flowers, is 700 meters from the beach. Three stories, best rooms on top floor (Rp15,000). The bathrooms are not completely enclosed, with flush toilets outside. The breakfast is not spectacular but you can have hot tea anytime. Cars and motorcycles for rent. Also check out **Bali Dwipa II,** down the lane toward the beach.

A great discovery is **Dewi Ratih Cottages,** tel. (0361) 751694, an inexpensive home away from home. On a side lane off Poppies Lane II, it's only 300 meters from Kuta Mall and 300 meters from the beach. They have only four cottages with 16 rooms for only Rp40,000-58,000 including breakfast, each with veranda, a/c, modern bath, hot water. The carved furniture was especially designed for the hotel. Beautiful gardens, swimming pool. An oasis of tranquility in the middle of madness. Bargain for longer stays. Call for reservations.

Sari Bali Cottages, tel. (0361) 753065, fax 752948, in central Kuta between Poppies Lane I and II, has 34 rooms, with a/c, private bath, and hot water, in an attractive garden for Rp54,000 s, Rp60,000 d. Fan-cooled rooms available for Rp33,000 s, Rp42,000 d. All prices include tax and service. Pool, open-air restaurant, bar. Easy access to the beach, plus a disco, supermarket, and pubs nearby.

The little lane of Gang Bena Sari comes closest to what Kuta was like in the old days. Halfway to Legian on the left-hand side, running between Jl. Legian and the ocean, Gang Bena Sari is diagonally across from the Mastapa Cottages. It has relatively sparse traffic, a great traveler's eatery (RM Panca Rasa), about five quieter *losmen*/homestays, and a *warung*. One of the quietest, prettiest *losmen* on Kuta is the **Lusa Inn** with spacious yard/garden, good security, and big rooms for only Rp25,000 s, Rp35,000 d. Also noteworthy is **Komala Indah II,** which has rooms with Asian toilets for Rp12,000 s, Rp15,000 d; newer rooms with Western flush toilets are Rp15,000 s, Rp25,000 d. Here you can live in a Balinese compound in a bungalow with shower, bath, sink, fan, mosquito nets, good beds, tile floors, and private garden. The place is clean, safe, quiet, private, and only a five-minute walk to either Jl. Legian or the beach. Free tea, jaffle breakfast. Nice boys run it.

Moderate

Medium-priced hotels have a/c, hot water, and pools, and many offer IDD telephones in the rooms. They do not, however, have the range of sports facilities and cultural activities of the luxury class hotels, though they do provide vehicles for rent and can take small groups of guests on personalized tours.

Pride of place goes to **Poppies,** Poppies Gong 1, Box 3378, Denpasar 80033, tel. (0361) 751059, fax 752364, which offers luxury, charm, privacy, and security in the heart of Kuta for Rp155,000 d, Rp145,000 s in 20 delightful Bali-style bungalows. Tax and service charge of 7.5% will be added to the rates. Cenik, the owner, started with just a *warung* on the beach. Poppies is peacefully enclosed in its own complex, a maze of stone paths meandering through lush gardens and lily ponds. Each unit has a/c, ceiling fans, fridges, hot water, baby cots; some have kitchens. Efficiently managed, Poppies provides complete room service, babysitters, safety deposit boxes, pool, free airport transfers, even parking. Book early as they have a steady and loyal clientele. Poppies runs another set of bungalows on Poppies Lane II, without pool, for Rp50,000 s, Rp120,000 d.

In 1973 **The Mastapa Garden Cottages** (Jl. Legian, Box 13, Denpasar, tel. 0361-751660, fax 755098) opened in the midst of a jungle. Within a decade, Kuta and Legian enveloped the cottages, now ideally located between Kuta and Legian. Its a/c rooms and bungalows, set way in from the street, surround a small, clean swimming pool and gardens. Enjoy home cooking in their upstairs restaurant (hearty banana pancakes, Hungarian goulash soup, tempura). Remarkably quiet and safe despite its eye-of-the-storm location, Mastapa is perfect for a few days' rest at reasonable rates: Rp80,000-105,000 s, Rp95,000-140,000 d. Higher-priced family units have TV, fridge, coffee and tea making supplies, and private rooftop terrace. All prices includes continental breakfast, but add 21% for service and taxes. Island tours, painting exhibitions, occasional Balinese dances in the inner courtyard, special buffets, childcare, fax, IDD, secretarial services, small conference facility, laundry, and luggage storage all available. About the best deal for the money in all of Kuta.

The Pendawa Inn, tel. (0361) 752387, in south Kuta lies down a lane across from the Kartika Plaza Hotel. A beautiful, well-kept garden, clean rooms with showers and Western toilets, friendly people. Tranquil and a bit away from the rush, it's about a five-minute walk to the beach and near a good, inexpensive restaurant, Puspa Ayu. Convenient because of its proximity to the airport. Rp40,000-80,000 (many classes); discounts for stays of a week or longer. Jimneys with a/c can be hired for about Rp60,000 per day.

Near Legian is **Wina Cottage,** tel. (0361) 751867, fax 751569, which offers 129 rooms around a tropical garden, with western style interiors. Prices vary; fan-cooled rooms run Rp60,000 s, Rp70,000 d, a/c studios Rp100,000 s, Rp110,000 d, and a/c deluxe units Rp140,000 s, Rp160,000 d. Amenities include private bath, hot water, wall-to-wall carpet, fridge, TV, tropical gardens, pool, videos in restaurant, drugstore, bar, safety deposit boxes, bicycles and motorbikes for rent, complimentary fruit basket every afternoon at 1400, free tea and ice water daily, free transport to and from the airport, shuttles to Kuta every hour from 0800-2100. Great value.

The 45-room **Hotel Ramayana** on Jl. Bakung Sari (Box 3334, Denpasar 80033, tel. 0361-751864, fax 751866) has rooms for Rp120,000-150,000, depending on whether you want fan or a/c. Add 21% tax and service. Food is above average, staff very polite, excellent service, tennis courts. Very central, only 200 meters from the beach and across the road from pubs and discos. Very good value.

Between the Kuta Beach Club and Yan's Travel Service on Jl. Bakung Sari is reasonable **Kuta Village Inn,** Box 3186, tel. (0361) 753052, fax 753051, very quiet, beautiful walled verdant backyard with pool. Three classes of rooms: Rp46,000 s, Rp60,000 d standard, fan only; Rp80,000 s, Rp100,000 d, deluxe, TV; Rp110,000 family rooms. All rooms have hot water. Just 200 meters away from the beach.

A good deal for Rp70,000-105,000 plus 15.5% tax and service is **Willy's Inn,** in the middle of Kuta at Jl. Tengal Wangi 18, tel. (0361) 751281. Willy's 26 rooms have antique furniture, tasteful art, verandas, and private open-air garden bathrooms under big mango trees—cheap, quaint, cool, quiet, beautiful, and full of character.

Popular **Barong Cottages** on Poppies Lane II, tel. (0361) 751804, has three-story rooms with two double beds, a/c, shower, and hot water for Rp47,500 s, Rp50,000 d. Rooms with fan are Rp40,000 s, Rp46,000 d. Price includes breakfast of toast, juice, coffee, and sliced fruit. Pool, gardens, restaurant, bar, nice views from each room's terrace.

Indah Beach Hotel, Poppies Lane II, tel. (0361) 753327, fax 752787, is a tranquil hideaway in the center of the bustle. A few minute's walk from the beach, this small and intimate hotel has outstanding service and a tropical decor. Rp60,000 s or d for standard rooms; Rp70,000 s or d for superior rooms. All rooms are air-conditioned and equipped with all the conveniences.

Modestly priced and quite comfortable **Fat Yogi Cottages,** Poppies Lane I, tel./fax (0361) 751665, has rooms with fan, shower, bathtub, and hot water for Rp38,000 s, Rp40,000 d including breakfast, but not including 15.5% tax and service. Facilities include pool, Italian restaurant, bar, laundry, and taxi service. Plastic accepted.

Jalan Pantai Kuta

Kuta Seaview Cottages (Box 3036, Denpasar, tel. 0361-751961, fax 751962) is on the beach, though few rooms in the three-story block actually have a view of the sea. In all there are 37 Balinese-style standard rooms, Rp100,000 s, Rp120,000 d, and cottages, Rp90,000 s, Rp100,000 d. Cottages are older than rooms. Prices include tax and service. There's a Chinese/European restaurant on the premises.

Newer **Aneka Beach Bungalows,** tel. (0361) 752892, fax 71777, is just across the road from the beach. Attractive, air-conditioned, thatch-roof bungalows cost Rp80,500 s, Rp92,000 d. Amenities include pool, karaoke screen, nice grounds.

Kuta Jaya Cottage (Jl. Pantai Kuta, Box 1093 TBB, tel. 0361-752308, fax 752309) costs Rp161,000 for standard rooms, Rp196,000 for superior, plus an additional 17.5% tax and service. The staff is courteous and grounds silent, even though it's in the middle of Kuta. Large swimming pool with sunken bar, and the beach is only a three-minute walk away. See the sunset from the 24-hour restaurant. Open-stage for cultural events, shopping arcade, photo center, drugstore, bank, and travel agency.

Bali Anggrek Inn (Box 435, Denpasar, tel. 0361-751265, fax 751766) has 151 rather ordinary rooms in four classes, with all the usual amenities. Their large pool, claimed to be the only above-the-ground one on Bali, has nice views over the beach.

Farther south, on Jl. Pantai Banjar Segara, is 100-room **Palm Beach Cottages,** tel. (0361) 751661-2, fax 752432, with pool, restaurant, disco, meeting rooms, and sea view from second- and third-floor rooms. Standard rooms (smaller, no balcony) are Rp50,000 s, Rp60,000 d, superior rooms are Rp120,000 s, Rp130,000 d. All rates subject to 15.5% tax and service. No charge for children under 12. Continental breakfast Rp8000, American Rp10,000, table d'hote dinner Rp18,000, Bali Night Buffet Dinner Rp20,000.

Luxury Class

Kuta boasts world-class resort hotels featuring every convenience. Many of these more expensive places deal only in dollars and may even find it difficult to figure out rupiah amounts!

Holiday Inn Bali Hai, Jl. Wana Segara 33, tel. (0361) 753035, fax 752527, is on the beach on three hectares of landscaped gardens, only a few minutes' walk from Kuta's center. Rates: standard Rp240,000 s or d; bungalows Rp360,000 s or d. Incorporates all the facilities and services one would expect from a Holiday Inn anywhere in the world.

The 32-room **Natour Kuta Beach Hotel,** Jl. Pantai Kuta, Box 393, Denpasar, tel. (0361) 751361, fax 751362, has quiet bungalows and lush gardens and overlooks the beach. Stan-

dard rooms are US$70 s, US$80 d, while junior suites run US$125. There's a very busy Garuda agent in the hotel. Natour also owns the venerable Bali Hotel in Denpasar, Bali's first hotel, established in 1927.

To the south along the beach, the **Bali Garden Hotel,** Box 1101, tel. (0361) 752725, fax 753851, under joint Japanese-Balinese ownership, is international-standard, pampering, and expensive (cheapest double room is US$106 s in the low season). Amenities include regular cultural performances, Japanese restaurant, tour desk, disco. Although the harmonious decor, the teakwood furnishings, colorful textiles, and pots of fresh flowers help, it doesn't measure up to the beauty of the Kartika Plaza and yet it costs about the same.

Support the greens? Four-star **Bali Dynasty Resort,** Jl. Kartika Plaza (Box 2047, Tuban 80361, tel. 0361-752403, fax 752402), is managed by the reliable and high-end Shangri-La International chain. This luxurious hotel supports a number of environmentally friendly policies like the installation of a sewage treatment plant and redirecting waste to the garden of fruit trees, herbs, and spices. They also use biodegradable chemicals in the kitchen and laundry. The Dynasty's Fun Pub is a relaxed venue with pool tables and a popular karaoke machine that can be used with a full, live band.

Five-star **Hotel Kartika Plaza** (Box 84, Denpasar, tel. 0361-751067, fax 752475) has 304 elegant rooms (US$110 s, US$120 d) plus 81 Balinese-style bungalows (US$115 s, US$125 d) set in a huge 12-hectare garden. The rooms are in the four-story wings that wrap around the giant pool and gardens. Standard bungalows are cozy, Bali-style, and have their own pool. Clearly in the splurge category—a pioneer up-market hotel on Kuta—it boasts an Olympic-size pool (open to the public for Rp2000) and an impressive full-size and well-equipped fitness center, including three clay tennis courts with instructors, massage rooms, weight room, and two jacuzzis. Kartika's breakfast buffet is US$12.50, lunch US$18.50, dinner US$23. Their subterranean, air-conditioned Bali Tavern has an exhibit of Blanco originals, a complete menu, and a happy hour 1700-2000. The air-conditioned Rejang Restaurant is a 24-hour coffee shop open seven days a week, and their new **Chi-Chi's Grill and Cantina** (tel. 0361-757937) specializes in Mexican and Tex-Mex cuisine. Each day of the week there's a buffet dinner (US$23) put on in the open-air theater featuring a different international cuisine, accompanied by a dazzling cultural performance. In their "Trip Around Asia" evening, visit night market stalls set up in the courtyard. The Kartika claims to have the most complete conference/convention center facilities on Bali, which can cater for up to 800. The hotel is near the airport, but you don't hear the planes. And it's only a 10-minute walk to Kuta. Worth the money.

Nearby and toward Kuta is another first-class resort, **Bintang Bali Hotel**, Jl. Kartika Plaza, Box 1068, Kuta, tel. (0361) 753292, fax 753288 or 753288, with 401 rooms and suites forming two wings, surrounded by a six-hectare garden that meets the white-sand beach. Though a blockish property, it boasts sophisticated restaurants with sumptuous buffets, bars, a piano lounge, disco with an "unrivaled lighting system," a karaoke Supper Club, swimming pool with waterfall, jacuzzi and cold dip, tennis court, gym, sauna, billiards, game room, massage, shopping arcade, conference facilties. Prices start at US$105 s, US$130 d, and climb to US$990 for the Presidential Suite.

Dead center to all the action, 200 meters from the beach but peacefully set back from Jl. Bakung Sari, is the **Kuta Beach Club**, Box 226, tel. (0361) 751261, fax 752896. Its 120 plushly furnished bungalows cost US$38 s, US$42 d. There's a pool and sundecks.

The big, upmarket 325-room **Sahid Bali Seaside Cottages** on Jl. Pantai Kuta, Box 1102, tel. (0361) 753855, fax 752019, part of the 14-hotel Sahid chain, is the only four-star hotel along Jl. Pantai Kuta. The tariff averages US$60 s, US$70 d for dependably predictable Motel 6-type rooms. If you're a nonsmoker, request the cottage section. The rooms stink of cigarette smoke. Its selling points are that it's right across from the beach, not so expensive, a mixture of Javanese and Balinese architecture, has beautiful, landscaped gardens, and has a nice lobby bar—the only hotel lobby where you can see the sea, particularly nice at sunset. Also a karaoke and live music room, children's playground, sports facilities, a 200-square-meter putting range, and the biggest pool on Kuta.

FOOD

Kuta's streets are lined with literally hundreds of restaurants serving a truly international, mind-boggling range of cuisine. They come in every size, price range, and degree of sophistication, serving Chinese, pseudo-Western, and Indonesian food, and all play the latest hit songs or videos. Don't leave without trying the seafood Kuta is famous for: succulent lobster, barbecued bluefish and mackerel, crab dishes, tuna steaks. Compared to Ubud or Candidasa, Kuta's food is not cheap. Lobsters here cost as much as Rp90,000. Ridiculously expensive jumbo shrimp are another favorite of free-spending tourists. An average meal is about Rp6000-7000, not including drinks. But its restaurants are as cheap as Singapore's, three times cheaper than New York's, and five times cheaper than Tokyo's. Look for fliers offering discounts of up to 50% at various restaurants. Some of Kuta's cheapest food is in the *pasar senggol* behind the post office.

On hotel row along Jl. Kartika Plaza is a whole series of restaurants that target hotel guests who balk at the Rp20,000 required for extravagant buffet breakfasts and dinners or hanker after a different dining experience than those offered in the monster hotels. One such opportunistic restaurant is **Bali Sunrise**, opposite the Kartika Plaza, where American and continental breakfasts are Rp6000 and Rp3500 respectively. Ask other travelers for the latest, best places to eat. Back-lane eateries are naturally quieter and less dusty and noisy than those in downtown Kuta and along Jl. Legian. Most of Kuta's restaurants close at around 2000.

Soups, Javanese *rujak tahu, nasi* and *mie goreng, pisang goreng,* wok stir-fries, steamed corn, steamed peanuts, and sweets are sold from carts that trundle down the main streets and back lanes of Kuta—heaps of food for under Rp2000.

Indonesian/Balinese Food

A multitude of *warung* are scattered throughout Kuta's side streets and alleys, most catering to the Indonesians who work in Kuta. Disappointing is the fact that not one restaurant in Kuta—with the possible exception of Made's Warung—exclusively serves up genuine Balinese food. On menus you see lots of mediocre *gado-gado* and *soto ayam* from Java, *gulai* from Madura, and Chinese *cap cay*, but no *lawar*. The **Ketupat Restaurant,** Jl. Legian 109, tel. (0361) 754209 or 754292, serves genuine Indonesian food, but it's a bit expensive.

Bali Seafood Market and Restaurants, tel. (0361) 753902, fax 754575, south of the Kartika Plaza and opposite the Santika Beach Hotel on Jl. Kartika Plaza, claims to serve Balinese seafood, but it's more Chinese-style. The fish is fresh, cooked just the way you want it. Phone for free transportation.

In the labyrinthine alleys, a few Balinese *warung* do survive, but these you really have to hunt down or hear about by word of mouth. One standout is on Jl. Tengal Wangi where a fantastic *nasi campur* is served for about Rp1000; walk down from Willy's and it's on the left just before Jl. Buni Sari. Catering as it does to locals, it could be closed early, the *ibu* could have run out of food, or she could have gone to a festival.

Spicy Lombok food is sold at **Rumah Makan Taliwang Bersaudera** on Jl. Imam Bonjol (the road to Denpasar), on the right-hand side about one kilometer up from Kentucky Fried Chicken. It's near the Lombok clay pot outlet. As is the case with most restaurants catering to Indonesians and not tourists, the row of restaurants here prepares decidedly better cuisine than 90% of Kuta's restaurants. A chicken dinner with vegetables and drink at the Taliwang will set you back about Rp7000.

The famous Dutch colonial *rijstaffel* dinner is served at the Mastapa Garden Hotel's (Jl. Legian, tel. 0361-751660) upstairs restaurant every Friday night.

Chinese Restaurants

With high customer turnover and international menus, the steaming, busy, open-fronted Chinese restaurants of Kuta specialize in seafood and barbecue dishes. After picking out your size or quantity of fish from ice trays in front, order the dish prepared either spicy or bland. The freshness of the food compensates for the lack of intimacy and personal attention. Reservations not necessary.

At big, lively, smoky, open, central, and crowded **Mini Restaurant,** opposite the disco on Jl. Legian, pay about Rp15,000 for a big fish that feeds two to three. Try such seafood dishes as the incomparable sweet and sour shrimp with rice, delicious crabs, or lobster. Mini is packed at night, so go early. Another Chinese seafood restaurant, **Bali Indah Bar and Restaurant** on Jl. Buni Sari, tel. (0361) 751937 or 752433, prepares sumptuous food in an authentic Chinese style. Across the street from the Mini is the slightly higher priced **Indah Sari,** where you can see seafood grilled on an open fire, then dine in a pleasing atmosphere of natural bamboo and old-fashioned *Casablanca* fans.

SC Restaurant, down from the Mini, is another perennially popular Chinese seafood restaurant, though, in my opinion, deluded by success and way overpriced. The *mie kuah udang,* for example, is depressingly ordinary—a ripoff at Rp4000!

On Jl. Pantai Kuta is another old favorite, **Lenny's,** tel. (0361) 752925, a good-quality seafood restaurant near the beach, but it's not for the impecunious: Rp15000-35,000 for a fish, while prawns run Rp12,000 and up. The frog legs are very good. Good service.

Plaza Bali Chinese Seafood Restaurant, tel. (0361) 754066, in the Bali Plaza serves outstanding seafood with prices to match. Authentic Asian food, not modified for Western tastes. Order the Special Fried Rice (Rp21,000) and a large, cold San Miguel (Rp6000) and you won't regret it. Dance and theatrical performances seven days a week.

One of the best budget restaurants on Kuta is **K Grand** at Jl. Legian 438, a little past Mastapa on the right toward Legian, with very reasonable Chinese-style food, although their fruit juices are kind of weak. Stick to the fish dinners. A whole fish and a *cap cai* for under Rp15,000 can easily feed two. A good restaurant but not as consistently good as RM Panca Rasa.

The small **RM Panca Rasa** (formerly El Dorado), on Gang Bena Sari (Gang Lusa Inn) off Jl. Legian, is an excellent traveler's eatery, serving a variety of international dishes—one of Kuta's best restaurants for the money. Especially popular for breakfast and with Hollanders since Chinese owner Tjipto Wiyono speaks Dutch. Known for a top-notch *nasi campur* (Rp2600) and wonderful iced fruit juices and *lasi* (Rp1400-2000). Open 0800-2000. Gang Bena Sari is about midway between Kuta and Legian on the left.

In the same budget category is **Viva's** (formerly Gemini) at Jl. Legian 135, tel. (0361) 751742. A poor man's Mini Restaurant, but much better value—the prices are unbelievable. Specializes in Chinese food and seafood. Everything on the menu is outstanding. Very clean, first-class service. Open 1000-1430 and 1800-2300.

In a Class of Their Own
The in-place is still age-old **Made's Warung,** tel. (0361) 751923, right on Jl. Pantai Kuta, two minutes' walk toward the beach from Bemo Corner, with great food and an inimitable atmosphere. For over 20 years, Made's has served excellent jaffles, smoked salmon on rye with cream cheese, chili, cappuccino, fresh-squeezed carrot juice, and absolutely top-class *nasi campur.* Dinner specialties include *gado-gado,* tuna fish with spicy Bali sauce, sushi deluxe, and *rijstaffel* (served on Saturday at 1700 only; get there early). Also European breakfast. A lively, crowded place and peerless venue for people-watching. Though every dish is good, the place isn't cheap; difficult to eat well here for less than Rp12,000-15,000. Open 0830-2400. Made's has a branch in Seminyak.

Some of the best Mexican food (actually Tex-Mex, with a touch of California) on Bali can be enjoyed in **TJ's,** tel. (0361) 751093, down Poppies Lane, halfway to the beach. Particularly prized are Jean's tacos and chips and salsa, but the varied, tantalizing menu also includes Chicken Fajitas (Rp11,500), Seafood Bahia (Rp10,000), famous Chocolate Diablo Cake (Rp3000), and chocolate mousse (Rp3500). Beef Fajitas are made with high quality fillet steak, and the flour tortillas are ground by hand then rolled with a beer bottle. Great wide wooden bar, too, with long drink menu, famous Jose Cuervo margaritas, free snacks, racy Latin music, and lots of conviviality in the evenings. Here you could meet anybody. Pray Woodruff is there.

Managed by Poppies, the **Kopi Pot,** Jl. Legian 82, tel. (0361) 752614, is one of the best places for vegetarian dishes. They also offer continental cooking, seafood, and the better known Indonesian dishes. Also well known for its steaks. Open daily until 2300. Relaxing, terraced garden setting; also an upstairs area away from the noise. Off-road parking. Look for fliers giving a 15% discount for meals over Rp20,000. Open 0800. **Aro-**ma's in south Legian is the other well-known vegetarian restaurant of the area.

The **Bebek Mas,** Jl. Kartika Plaza, tel./fax (0361) 752750, is an elegant gourmet restaurant done up in colonial style, in front of Melasti Beach Bungalows. It serves big portions of creative European-style food but for a moderate price. Very good French cuisine: the Chateaubriand steak (Rp26,000), cut right at your table, is enough for two people. A house specialty is the *bebek tutu.* Also recommended are the seafood salad, crab and grapefruit salad, and the Fettucini Señor Bianca.

The *menu du jour* is excellent, and each evening the restaurant spotlights different cuisine. On Thursday an authentic *rijstaffel* is presented by a whole line of waitresses in *tempo doeloe* to the accompaniment of a *joged* dance. If you have a group, the *rijstaffel* can be ordered on other days one day in advance. On Sunday a terribly touristy Frog Dance accompanies an Indonesian buffet (Rp16,500). No air-conditioning and many mosquitoes (they provide coils). After dinner, retire to the bar—a gathering place for Dutch and expats—and drink a special *arak*-spiked "Bali Coffee." They also sell a directory (Rp2000) of menus from some of Bali's best restaurants. Free transport to and from anyplace in Kuta (for Sanur Rp5000).

Poppies Lane I
Some of Kuta's best restaurants are on Poppies Lane I. **Poppies Restaurant,** tel. (0361) 751059, which plays the Ritz of Kuta, is in a delightful and romantic setting. In fact, it's worth eating there just to use the toilet. Unfortunately, prices are getting higher and service is getting poorer. This premier restaurant features above-average Western and Indonesian food, like fish chowder, seafood-avocado cocktail, shish kebabs, smoked marlin salad, curried vegetables, fresh fruit drinks, and a full wine list. Full bar. Add 10% tax and service. To get a table, eat there only for lunch, reserve ahead by calling, or arrive early in the evening, because it fills up fast with tourist groups.

Kedin's (look for the big yin-yang symbol on the back wall) is a classic traveler's eatery that serves up large portions of food in the Rp6000-10,000 range. Open early for breakfast at 0730, closes at 2000. Movies in the evenings. Another distinctive restaurant, just down from TJs, is **Fat Yogi,** tel./fax (0361) 751665. Besides their sought-after baked goods, they do delicious Italian (wood-fired pizza worth raving about) and French food. Because of their fresh baked bread and croissants, they are particularly popular at breakfast time.

Un's Cafe, Bar and Restaurant, tel. (0361) 752607, in a small lane off Poppies Lane I (the first left on the lane from Jl. Legian), has an Indo/Chinese/Euro menu. Run by an Indonesian lady with her Swiss husband. Nice atmosphere, music, comfortable chairs, big portions, reliably good food, though the service isn't the snappiest. Open 0800-1200. Expensive but worth it.

Poppies Lane II
There are dozens of small, fly-by-night Chinese, European, and seafood restaurants on Poppies Lane II, some of them quite good. An old standby is **Batu Bulong,** tel. (0361) 754365, of average quality, but very reasonably priced. A great place to look at all the errant activity is from the second floor of the **Twice Bar & Bakery,** tel. (0361) 751426. They serve a decent breakfast, with many choices, starting more or less at 0800 and closing at 1200. In particular, their croissants, Danish, and French bread are in high demand. Just off Poppies Lane II, the first lane on the right if going toward the beach, are six or seven very cheap places serving pizzas and Italian food—always full because their prices are so good.

All-You-Can-Eats
Recommended is the Saturday-night Indonesian feast at **Glory's Restaurant,** tel. (0361) 752512, in Legian for Rp9500. The food is excellent and it's a good chance to try those wonderful Balinese spices. The **Bali Bagia Bar & Restaurant,** tel. (0361) 751357 or 752757, on Jl. Bakung Sari (opposite the Agung Supermarket), serves some of the best steaks in Kuta. The "BB" on Saturday night offers free transport; reservations are recommended. Dinners start at 1900.

Ethnic Foods
If you get misty for home, many places offer milk shakes, steaks, ham and eggs, toast and Vegemite, peanut butter-and-honey sandwiches, and other worldly items. For example, the

menu at the **Jaya Pub Garden Restaurant** of Legian lists not only *sate* from Madura, but lasagne like in Napoli, steak *au poivre comme a Paris,* T-bone like in Texas, and *hutspot op z'n Hollands,* all prepared by a team of chefs experienced in Jakarta's ISO restaurants. At **Raja's** in Kuta Square, C.13-14-15, tel. (0361) 753117, a steak dinner can be enjoyed in a sidewalk cafe atmosphere. A nice sidewalk cafe for coffee is **Caddies,** Blok C 17, tel. (0361) 753308, specializing in Australian coffee with fresh milk.

Hotel restaurants generally offer better Western food than street restaurants. Some of Kuta's restaurants claim to serve such authentic Australian specialties as "vegetable pie" or burritos, but somehow the dish gets lost in the translation—it could end up as just a rolled pancake with spiced veggies inside. Brazilians can make up their own minds about **Warung Brasil Bali** on Jl. Benasari 10 X just past the intersection going to the beach, by sampling their *feijoada.* Nearby is probably Bali's best budget Thai restaurant, the **Pagoda** on Jl. Gang Benasari 15 (also open for breakfast).

With the coming of the Japanese in numbers, sushi bars have popped up. The small, air-conditioned **Sushi Bar Nelayan,** tel. (0361) 751386, on the other side of the street where Poppies Lane I meets Jl. Legian, is a top buy. The chef sells only fresh sushimi, sushi, and appetizers. Big portions of avocado tuna and Toco Octupus sashimi, miso soup, green tea. The best deal for sashimi lovers is The Orchid, 24 pieces (four pieces each of six kinds of fish) and the live lobster aquarium. The Kelapa is 12 pieces of mixed sushi. The Balinese sushi chef has 17 years experience. It's a wonder it's not full all the time. Open daily 1200-2400. Take out available. Only 40 meters from Bemo Corner.

For more elaborate fare, the **Yashi Japanese Restaurant** in Hotel Patra Jasa (formerly Pertamina Cottages), tel. (0361) 751161, in south Kuta is very good. They sell Japanese beer too. For Korean barbecue, seafood, *bulgogi, sam gae tang, doe jee sam kyub sal,* lobster with *yaki* sauce, and *gyaza musi,* the **Agung Korean House,** tel. (0361) 755130 or 751263, on the first floor (second floor to Americans) of the multistoried Kuta Supermarket building on Jl. Bakungsari is the place.

With the rise in value of the Italian lire, the latest craze are pizzerias that sell medium pizzas for Rp8000-12,000. **Lotus Tavern,** Jl. Wana Segara Rd. near Holiday Inn, tel. (0361) 753797, under Australian management with an Italian chef, is part of the well-run Cafe Lotus group. They specialize in oven-cooked pizzas, tagliolini, fettuccine, black pepper steak, and fresh seafood such as grilled seabass. Free pickup service.

Consistently good pizza is available from **Pizza Hut,** on the way to Denpasar at Jl. Imam Bonjol. For delivery to your hotel, call (0361) 751696 or 752144. Two of the best Italian restaurants, with surprisingly well-stocked wine cellars, are the remarkable and beautiful **Warisan** in Seminyak, and **Cafe Latino,** tel. (0361) 701880, on Jl. Ngurah Rai on the way to the airport.

For dedicated carnivores, there are now two **Mama's German Restaurants,** tel. (0361) 751805, on Jl. Legian specializing in steaks, famous homemade sausages, and "big soups from Mama's kettle." Under German management. This is one of the best places to eat an early breakfast because it's one of the very few places open 24 hours a day.

If you have a hopeless craving for American fast-food, the **Gelael Plaza** on the road to Denpasar (Jl. Imam Bonjol, near the gas station) has a Swenson's, Kentucky Fried Chicken, and Burger King. McDonald's now occupies the bottom floor of the big former Cinemex building on Jl. Legian.

Dinner Performances

A dazzling evening can be spent at the Kartika Plaza Beach Hotel's Legong and Rijstaffel Night. For Rp5300, dine on an authentic *rijstaffel,* which includes many of Indonesia's most delicious and renowned dishes such as *bihun goreng, oseng oseng sayuran, pepes ikan, rendang, sate campur, gado-gado,* and *perkedel kentang.* The excellent buffet is accompanied by sequences from Bali's most famous dances. Absolutely first class.

Also check out Sahid Bali Seaside Hotel's dinner shows for US$25 per person from 1930 to 1130. They feature clowns, door prizes, 30% off drinks, and serve up *13* different types of *satay.* To find out the show or make a reservation, call (0361) 753855, ext. 4088 or 4071.

Kuta Market

For good eating in an Indonesian environment at very good prices, head for Kuta Market (Pasar Senggol) in the north end of Kuta. See the sign at the start of Jl. Bakung Sari. Although most popular with locals, a few tourists have also discovered the Indonesian, Chinese, and Balinese eateries here. Available are tasty and traditional dishes such as Yogyanese-style Kalasan chicken, fresh fish in all sizes, steamed crab, sizzling *sate kambing,* and unmodified *nasi padang.* Food is as much as 25% cheaper than Kuta's restaurants, the place is almost untouristed, and the service is fast.

Baked Goods

New Bakery on Poppies Lane I serves donuts, fresh "brown" bread, and banana cake. If walking toward the beach down Jl. Pantai Kuta, on the right just before Made's Warung is **Jaffa's Homemade Bakery.** Righteous carrot cake, apple pie, croissants, and whole-wheat bread. Very handy and fast for pastries and snacks, **Galaxy Modern Bakery** on Jl. Legian, tel. (0361) 752249, opens 0900-2300.

Desserts and Drinks

An ancient Kuta fixture, **Aleang's** still has superb yogurt; the place looks brighter and cleaner nowadays. The **Kopi Pot,** Jl. Legian, tel. (0361) 752614, is known for its mouthwatering homemade desserts, cakes, and pies, and a wide variety of shakes, juices, coffees, and imported teas. Also praiseworthy is **Made's Warung** on Jl. Pantai Kuta: homemade ice cream, chocolate cake, and top-notch black rice pudding. At the beach end of the same street is **Made's Juice Shop,** also a long-standing favorite.

The best margaritas in Bali, using Jose Cuervo tequila, are served at **TJs** in Kuta and **Poco Loco** in Legian. Also well-prepared guacamole, nachos, seafood dishes, and tortilla soup. Strawberry daiquiris are also a specialty of TJs.

Another of Kuta's attractions is the *arak madu* served up at Made's Warung on Jl. Pantai Kuta in central Kuta. A blended drink, it consists of rice liquor with either honey or honey and lemon. Kuta's regulars have been drinking here from morning until late at night since the early 1970s when Made's was the only after-hours place in all of Kuta.

Magic Mushrooms

Perhaps half a dozen restaurants in Kuta and Legian prepare soups, omelettes, and pizzas spiked with magic mushrooms. In iced drinks, this nefarious beverage is mixed with a little lemon and honey. Though not openly advertised, dishes with hallucinogenic mushrooms can be recognized by the words "Magic" or "Special" written on the menu. Available in a variety of prices and strengths, they contain psilocybin, which may not take effect for one or two hours and may last four or five hours. Avoid driving, swimming, and hectic surroundings if you indulge.

ENTERTAINMENT AND NIGHTLIFE

Like any city, Kuta has it all. You have your choice of enclosed, air-conditioned places where you don't even feel like you're in Bali, huge dance halls with strobe lights, or open-air clubs facing the beach.

For at least two months (December and January) each year, Kuta is Asia's approximation of the United States' Palm Springs at Easter break. Get ready for a real scene, in which the tourists provide the richest source of entertainment for other tourists. Alcohol is served in copious quantities in scores of drinking establishments designed to entice the Australian collegian. You'll see pubs packed with beer-swilling Australians dressed in tank tops, shorts, and rubber thongs guzzling cans of Foster's Lager and eating meat pies while watching live broadcasts of Australian football matches on big screen monitors. Should the motto "rage with us!" appeal to you, you can join one of Kuta's organized "Pub Crawls," in which large groups of Australian revelers are transported by bus from pub to pub where they drink, ingest godawful food, and become more and more inebriated, until finally they're deposited semiconscious at the doors of their hotels in the middle of the morning. The promoter's advice: "Avoid Hangovers—Stay Drunk!"

The local rice beer, *tuak,* is served in bamboo mugs. Anytime after 2100 or 2200, you have to run the gauntlet of pimps, whores, and hashish sellers on Jl. Legian. Kuta really doesn't sleep until 0500 or even later, and even then you'll find a few Italians wandering around looking for cappuccino.

Watch out for notices and small posters announcing special events such as housewarming parties and full moon parties. If these parties are announced to the public, it means they are open to everyone—you just have to pay for drinks. Parties of the more commercial variety are also held occasionally at Zero Six in south Kuta near the Holiday Inn, Warisan in Seminyak, and even at private residences.

Gay men cruise the beach at night. There's no gay bar to speak of—every place is mixed now—but some bars are more gay than others. The gay scene is a lot healthier than it used to be as a tremendous effort has been put into AIDS prevention and education. You'll see anti-AIDS posters all over the island.

Movies

All the restaurants and bars showing movies have put Kuta's cinemas out of business. Most popular are American films, which usually start at 2100. New videos, before they are even released in the States, are shown on huge screens in bars and restaurants, drawing big loyal crowds of tourists every night. You watch a free movie, they earn money serving you drinks and food. A perennial favorite is the giant screen at **The Bounty,** tel. (0361) 754040, across from Depot Viva, where a large beer costs only Rp4000 during happy hour (1800-2000). No cover. Call to see what's playing.

A whole string of places in the heart of Kuta, such as Fat Yogi's and Kedin Inn, both on Poppies Lane I, show free films daily; most also serve meals and have a happy hour (1600-2100) with cocktails and large cheap Bintang.

Dances and Events

Kuta is an artificial tourist bubble, so most dances staged here—unless they accompany a ceremonial event—aren't the real thing. Major tourist hotels like Hotel Patra Jasa (formerly Pertamina Cottages) and the Oberoi present dances, which usually accompany dinner for US$20 and up. In Kuta, tickets are also sold for performances in other southern villages, which take place 0930-1100. If you have your own transport, tickets are cheaper at the venues themselves.

At **Plaza Bali,** Jl. Ngurah Rai in Tuban, tel. (0361) 753301, woodcarvers and silver craftsmen demonstrate their skill. There are also some nice restaurants in this complex, along with the Balinese Theatre, where traditional dance and music are performed nightly, free. Open 1000-2300 every day.

If your homestay or hotel is holding a traditional family ceremony, like a wedding or child's first birthday, it's customary for the owner to invite you. During the feast days Galungan and Kuningan, the temples of Kuta are just too clogged with tourists for the event to be any fun. Other religious holidays are less congested. For example, be in Kuta for the Melis high holy purification day before the Balinese New Year Nyepi. Enter a home behind those never-ending shops and you'll find that Bali still lives in Kuta.

Pubs, Clubs, and Discos

No less than 15 clubs operate in Kuta, Legian, and Seminyak, each with an atmosphere all its own. Most open late—2200 is when Kuta's nightlife really gets going—have no dress code, charge a Rp4000-10,000 cover (usually with one free, watered-down drink), and close anywhere from 0200 to 0400, officially 2400. The half-a-dozen most popular are within a few kilometers of each other, and some are next to the beach. Weekly events are advertised on fliers handed out on Jl. Legian.

The Swiss/German/Austrian crowd hangs out at the **Swiss Pub,** tel. (0361) 754719, on Jl. Legian, owned by Jon Zuercher who also owns the Swiss Restaurant in Legian. **A.J. Hackett Bungy Jump,** Jl. Double Six, boasts a happy hour that lasts all day long; call (0361) 730666 for free pickup. If you stand on Kuta Beach and look to the right you'll see a big white tower. That's them.

A good daytime place to look out on the street while enjoying a large, cold beer (only Rp4000) is the **Bali Purnama Beer Garden,** tel. (0361) 751898, on Jl. Legian near McDonald's. Small, open-air, very popular, friendly staff—but the food's not that good. **TJ's** on Poppies Lane I has a great bar and the food is good. **Made's Warung** on Jl. Pantai Kuta is always entertaining—something of the old days remains.

But the newest and biggest nightclub to hit the strip is **Club Gold** in the middle of Kuta on Jl. Legian, a multistory, air-conditioned dance club offering a line of cocktails and music played by international guest DJs. Decorated in red velvet

and chrome with comfortable booths, it has tucked-away alcoves and a members-only bar. French wines and champagne available by the glass. Open Tuesday, Friday, and Saturday until 0200. Depending on the entertainment, the cover charge runs Rp7500-10,000. Parking in rear. For details, call (0361) 752528.

Next door is two-story **Hard Rock Cafe,** Jl. Legian 204, tel. (0361) 755661 or 755662, fax 755664, with international pop music memorabilia. Drinks are expensive but regular live bands are a big draw. The music starts at 2300 and ends around 0200. Sunday night is jazz night.

With its traditional Balinese atmosphere, the **Gado Gado,** off Jl. Dhayna Pura in Legian, tel. (0361) 730955, is a relaxing al fresco beachfront disco that attracts a good mixture of older Indonesians, Westerners, and expats. Cover is Rp10,000, which includes a beer or soft drink. Open Tuesday, Wednesday, and Thursday 1130-0430.

Peanuts Disco 2 on Jl. Legian, tel. (0361) 754149, and the warm-up bars around it are down the short, noisy, littered street opposite the Mini Restaurant. Cover charge: Rp6000. Open 0800-0400. Lots of prostitution around the disco after 2300. The convivial **Warehouse,** in the same complex, obviously caters to the hearty as well.

Among Kuta's expat crowd, the thing to do is start out the evening at Made's Warung, watching the crowds until about 2300, then repair to a disco to dance the night away listening to live or recorded music at ear-splitting volume among a crush of tourists in garish tropical garb.

Others like to hang out at **The Strand, Goa 2001,** and **Cafe Luna** in Seminyak, all of which have sophisticated music, reasonably priced drinks, and imaginative hors d'oeuvres. Goa's is a good place to get in the mood before the discos start, and the volume and quality of the music allows you to talk. It's also slightly easier to find parking in Legian than in Kuta.

For live music, the **Jaya Pub,** Jl. Legian Kaja, opposite the start of Jl. Double Six, tel. (0361) 752973, uses the same musicians from the Jaya Pub in Jakarta. It's open 2100-0200, except Thursday and Saturday when it closes at 0230 or later. No cover charge, which makes it very good value if you want to listen to a band. Located in front, **Le Bistro** restaurant serves good food in a relaxing Balinese atmosphere; open until 2300.

Double Six, tel. (0361) 753366, is a huge place with different sections—even a Swenson's—tucked away on Jl. Double Six in Legian. Packed with exotic high-class people, the restaurant has very good salads, pastas, Italian dishes, and buffets when a show is running, and becomes a disco Monday, Friday, and Saturday from 1130-0430. Cover: Rp10,000 including a beer or soft drink.

Balinese Rastas dance to live reggae music at **Baruna's,** tel. (0361) 751565, a long-standing favorite of hardcore Australian party animals. Open 2300-0200. **Strand Bar** in Legian features art exhibits and a colonial plantation bar with superb drinks (the best vodka tonics), has no dancing, and is more geared to conversation. **Cafe Luna** in Seminyak, right across from the Goa, is very small, a place where everybody knows everybody and newcomers don't know what to do. The crowd is nearly 100% Western expats.

On Poppies Lane II behind the Sahid Bali Hotel is **Tubes,** tel. (0361) 753501, "The Surfers Bar and Restaurant." Here you'll find good vibes, pizza and fruit smoothies, a swimming pool, MTV, and movies playing at 1500 and 2000. During happy hour, 1700-1900, and nightly dancing, starting at 2000, spunky Japanese surf bunnies press their attentions on Kuta Cowboys, who by now speak very passable Japanese. Another hangout for the Beautiful People is the **Blue Ocean,** where the waves are first class and the sunsets, at times, enthralling.

The Sari Club, tel. (0361) 754901, on Jl. Legian is a popular open-air place to take in evening sights, but the food is overpriced. It attracts mainly a clientele bent on drinking themselves into oblivion—an environment of nonstop pounding music, loud conversation, and smoke. Facing the ocean, **Kuta Seaview Restaurant and Bar** on Jl. Pantai Kuta has a full bar and live music every night from 1900 until 2300, with no cover, tax, or service charge. Free pickup and dropoff if you call (0361) 751961. Free *arak* cocktail with every meal.

SHOPPING

Kuta has the largest concentration of shopping in Bali. Simply start at Bemo Corner at the south end of Jl. Legian and work your way north to Seminyak. It takes hours and hours of walking, including side trips into lanes and small shopping malls, in order to find the quality items interspersed among all the tourist kitsch.

The best buys are designer clothes, visors, straw hats, and either colorful cloth or rattan bags. Another great bargain are sunglasses, in every style imaginable, for Rp6000-10,000 (after bargaining); sunglasses are the only product for sale at **Mr. Sunny** on Jl. Legian. Bali dolls tagged with a name and description of name are all the rage—Rp21,000-25,000.

Pick up the latest tapes at numerous cassette shops for Rp9000-12,000; just ask, the clerks really know their music. A good place to start is **Kul-Kul** ("Castle of Music"), Jl. Bakung Sari, tel. (0361) 751523. Look for unique home furnishings at **C.V. Bali Lotus** at Jl. Pantai Kuta 10, near Bemo Corner (Box 3182, tel./fax 0361-752726). They have another shop in the Galleria in Nusa Dua (Blok A7 No. 1-6).

Imitation watches are cheaper in Kuta than anywhere else in Indonesia. Use your bargaining skills and know the prices (as little as Rp6000). Watches make good trading material in Lombok and Outer Islands, and they sell for big money in India. Don't be taken in by all the Gucci perfume. Once you open the bottle, the scent fades in a matter of minutes. Nothing like the original.

The general goods, three-floor **Gelael Dewata Supermarket,** Jl. Raya Kuta 105, tel. (0361) 751082, on the left before you enter Kuta from Denpasar (south of the gas station), sells a full range of cosmetics, toiletries, disposable diapers, imported foodstuffs, drinks, stationery, film, and clothing—what you'd expect from any supermarket/department store. They have a good bakery also. Expensive because it's in Kuta. It's cheaper to shop at **Loji I, Loji II,** tel. (0361) 751048, and **Alas Arum** supermarkets in Legian, which are smaller but well stocked for their size.

For a modern shopping experience, visit the 15,000-square-meter **Plaza Bali** on Jl. Ngurah Rai in Tuban, tel. (0361) 753301, which comprises an international duty-free store, souvenir shops, boutiques, galleries, restaurants, cocktail bar, cultural exhibits, drugstore, postal and international telephone service, car rental service, an overseas packing and shipping office, and secure parking. Open 1000-2300 every day, Plaza Bali is just a five-minute drive from the airport.

Vendors

The hustling on the beach can be horrific—a wild and open free market. If you decide to come to Kuta, you'd better get used to it. Your only defense is to joke around and try to have a good time. Roving vendors aggressively hawk giant polished sea turtle shells, hen-feather dusters, Sumba blankets, postcards, silver jewelry, cold beer, and wind chimes. Every craft and fakery from every workshop on Bali seems to eventually find its way to Kuta. Ninety-five percent of the items are mass-produced for tourist consumption. The silver articles may be silver-plated copper or brass, glass is sold as semiprecious stone, and horn and bone articles are passed off as ivory. Peddlers ask up to Rp20,000 for unbelievably bad paintings—acrylic on cloth—but they'll come down to Rp3000. It's all pure junk.

Women come up carrying baskets full of fabrics and garments; check carefully because the seams and zippers on clothing sold on the beach often give way in two or three days. Everything is bargainable. First prices are astronomical but soon the seller will offer a special price "only for you." After a few days, the sellers get to know you and you become friends. Don't buy anything for the first few days; talk to people and learn the prices.

Kids on the street trying to sell you stuff can be as pesky as flies. They also invade your space by touching you, getting in your way, and even picking your pocket. Kids will even pester you while you're getting a massage.

Shops

Some shops specialize in leather and silk, others in *batik* and designer fashions. Madonna shops sell lycra hats, belts, headbands, footwear, and dazzling sequined garments. Fixed-price places, like a few of the all-under-one-roof craft stores on the road to the airport, can give you a good idea of what certain items cost. Shop the side lanes for the best bargains; these shops don't get the swarms of people. Shops in the central Kuta cater to the mainstream tourist hordes.

Prices in Legian are generally lower than in Kuta, and the clerks are friendlier. Kuta shopkeepers sometimes get mad if you don't make an offer on something you've looked at. Good shops are hard to find in both ends of town. Because of the vast number of shops and the uneven quality and prices, shopping takes great patience—hours of it. Shop in the evening when it's cooler.

Clothes

Kuta and Legian, along with Thailand, are the fashion capitals of Southeast Asia. Indonesian, Italian, French, Japanese, and American designers use native tie-dyeing and *ikat* techniques to turn out brilliantly original garments exported worldwide. The best buys produced in Kuta's back-lane sweatshops are beachwear—bikinis, bathing suits, boxer and Bermuda shorts, T-shirts, tank tops—in lightweight cotton and rayon. A decidedly Australian bias in the bold colors and zany designs. If you bargain vigorously, you can buy merchandise in the shops cheaper than from the vendors on the beach. Ask how much and begin your bargain at one-half the price asked. Stick to your price. A wise alternative, if you have the time, is to have clothes made to order by one of the many tailors.

A number of classy designer boutiques take American Express and have high, fixed prices, which vary according to the material used and originality of design. Stunning shirts are available for Rp25,000-30,000; *batik* sundresses Rp30,000; *batik* shirts made from old *sarung* Rp8000-12,000; jackets Rp45,000-75,000; dress trousers Rp50,000 and up; dresses Rp40,000-75,000; T-shirts Rp8000-15,000; *ikat* purses Rp2000-10,000; *sarung* Rp8000-15,000. All very eye-catching and continental, but watch the quality. Examine goods carefully.

Carmen Dixon Collections, Jl. Pura Puseh 22, Legian Kelod, tel. (0361) 751717, carries contemporary designer fashions, resort wear, and cocktail dresses. Really good buys. **Mr. Bali** (tel. 0361-751232 or 755605) on Jl. Legian carries modern, Euro-chic men's wear at moderate prices; if they don't have your size in inventory, try their other branches on Jl. Pantai Kuta and Jl. Bunisari.

Sundance on Poppies Lane I sells only one-of-a-kind T-shirts and shorts. **Noa'noa,** Jl. Pantai Kuta 44 G, carries just bikini and beach clothing; they have another shop on Jl. Legian Kelod. Some surprising bargains can be found in the huge, fixed-price **Wisnu Garment,** Jl. Legian (opposite Mastapa). Children's clothing is another good-value Kuta speciality. **Kuta Kidz,** between Bemo Corner and Made's Warung, is filled with kid's clothes. **Hop On Pop,** Jl. Pantai Kuta 45 C, and **Bubbles** on Jl. Buni Sari, also specialize in kid's wear.

Kuta Square Complex

Housing the new Matahari Shopping Center and the Kuta Galleria, this mammoth complex at the beach end of Jl. Bakung Sari replaces the funky old Art Market that once occupied this site (and that had so much more character). Like any big city shopping complex, more than a hundred shops make up this extravagant emporium. Competition is fierce and the consumer is Lord, yet the shops high-priced and underpatronized, and parking is difficult. These microretailers deal in clothing and leisure wear, ethnic-exotic beach garb, arts and crafts, souvenirs, reproduced-antiques, carvings, *batik,* paintings, masks, textiles, mobiles, and bric-a-brac ad nauseam. Take a break and have a coffee in **Caddies Sidewalk Cafe** (Blok C 17, tel. 0361-753308) and look out on the passersby.

Jewelry and Antiques

Kuta offers a wide choice of jewelry, in both antique and contemporary designs. Famous goldsmiths established Kuta's **Banjar Pande Mas** in the 1890s; their extended families still include some exceptionally talented goldsmiths.

Silver is imported and ingeniously and meticulously worked into bracelets, pendants, and rings in local workshops. Beautifully designed silver set with stones is also available at, for example, **Suarti** on Poppies Lane II. Fine, custom-made jewelry is made by **Made Sundra** and **Nyoman Wanon** on Poppies Lane I.

Whole shops are devoted to seashell jewelry or painted dollar-a-pair attractive wooden earrings with dangling parrots, fish, cats, or stars. Try **Lisa Shop** at Jl. Pura Bagus Taruna 7, tel. (0361) 755508. For beads (Rp17,000 and up per strand), the place to go is **David Shop,** Jl. Legian Tengah 471, fax (0361) 752003. Also check out **Kencana,** Jl. Legian 357, tel. (0361) 751590, fax 751801, for original beads.

One of the largest and most complete stores

for bronze decorative objects in Indonesia is the **Golden Buffalo House of Bronze,** Jl. Legian Tengah 412, tel. (0361) 755936, fax 752013. They can create any kind of design.

Genuine antiques and tribal artifacts are ridiculously expensive, the starting prices so high you don't even feel like bargaining: Sumba blankets Rp450,000; Dayak baby carriers with handmade brass bells and colored beads Rp250,000-350,000. Kuta's fake antiques are products of inspired genius. If a woodcarving is claimed to be 50 years old but costs only Rp150,000, it isn't 50 years old. It may have been artificially aged by burial in the earth or exposure to the elements.

Nogo Bali Ikat Centre, tel. (0361) 754335, across from the Kopi Pot on Jl. Legian, specializes in textiles, carvings, and paintings. This chain of shops is best known for *endek.* Designer Lily Coskuner shied away from the wildly mixed colors favored by the Balinese, limiting combinations to varying shades of one or two colors in a single pattern. Nogo sells jackets (Rp150,000), slacks (Rp75,000), dresses (Rp120,000), and sashes, as well as lengths of *endek* for Rp15,000 per meter. Also check the mother-of-pearl and seashell buttons at Rp1000-4000 apiece and beautiful ties for Rp20,000. Another excellent shop for *ikat,* with good quality and good prices, is **Bobby Collection,** Jl. Legian Kaja 448, tel./fax (0361) 756049.

Leather

Leather is really big now, with scores of shops in Kuta. Leather jackets for as little as Rp200,000 if you bargain. Some are even interwoven with rattan designs. Very unusual chic leather belts, multicolored and studded, cost Rp30,000-100,000 for a nice one. Again, for the best prices, work the back lanes and make sure that the sewing and stitching is first rate.

Large leather bags go for around Rp80,000-150,000, small ones Rp40,000-75,000. Start by checking out **Sito Leather,** on the right if coming from Bemo Corner but before Perama Travel, just down the lane past Hotel Lingga. They sell nice leather jackets for around Rp200,000. Better buys than leather are the cheap tie-dye or *batik* cloth beach bags, in a million colors and patterns, sold just about everywhere.

Bookstores

Along Jl. Pantai Kuta and Jl. Legian are at least six secondhand bookstores with used paperbacks in all languages; most will buy back books at half the price. Don't throw away any books or even magazines as they can always be sold or exchanged, and new books are expensive. The largest selection of new hardcover books in English on Indonesia is the **Bookshop** on the corner of Jl. Legian and Jl. Benasari; also carries all the top international newspapers and magazines (if they're not banned).

English, German, and French daily newspapers are also available in shops such as **Kerta Book Store** (tel. 0361-751001) on Jl. Pantai Kuta up toward the beach from Made's Warung on the left, which sells used books, guides, and magazines. They will barter.

The **Bookshop,** also on Jl. Legian halfway between Kuta and Legian (diagonally across from Mastapa's on the corner of Jl. Legian and Jl. Benasari), has the best selection of new English-language books and periodicals about Indonesia in the Kuta/Legian area. Even newspapers like *The Australian,* banned in Indonesia, can be bought here. Also current issues of *Time, Newsweek,* and *Herald Tribune*

SERVICES

With banks, moneychangers, physicians, pharmacies, ambulance service (tel. 118 or 0361-27911), a police station (Jl. Raya Kuta, across from Bank Duta, tel. 0361-751598), a fire station (tel. 0361-25113), a post office, postal agencies, a market, cinemas, photo-processing shops, ticket agencies, Kuta is almost completely self-contained. There is even an Alcoholics Anonymous which holds a morning meeting in the coffee shop at the Dhyana Pura Hotel on Jl. Dhyana Pura in Seminyak four times weekly. Call (0361) 731047 for info.

The well-run **Badung Tourist Office,** Jl. Bakung Sari 1 (tel. 0361-751419), is a short walk from Bemo Corner. Walk down Jl. Buni Sari until it ends at Jl. Bakung Sari; the office is on the left. These guys can handle almost any question. Open Mon.-Sat. 0700-1700. They have a branch office (tel. 0361-751011) at the airport; open 0800-1800. A government tourist office is on the second floor of the Mastapa Garden Hotel on Jl. Legian.

Post and Shipping

The postal agent on Jl. Legian sells stamps and aerograms at the official price. Other services include registered post and do-it-yourself poste restante service, with dictionaries, phrase books, stationery supplies, and picture postcards for sale. There are other poste restante services at postal agents on Jl. Padma and Jl. Melasti in Legian. Parcel rates at these postal agencies are the same as official government rates but they charge high fees for packaging: Rp5000 for parcels weighing one to three kg, Rp7000 for three to five kg, Rp10,000 for five to 10 kg. Denpasar's *kantor paket pos,* on the corner of Jl. Teuku Umar and Jl. Diponegoro, tel. (0361) 223568, employs packagers who charge a bit less. For larger shipments, Kuta's international freight forwarding companies pack, arrange transport, and insure goods to Europe, the U.S., and Australia. Expect to pay a minimum of Rp367,500. Reliable **Alpha Cargo** (tel. 0361-752872 or 752873) will come to your hotel, pack and list in your presence, and transport to their office. Also check out **PT Nominasi Travel and Cargo Agent** on Jl. Legian (tel./fax 0361-751467). Beware of all those hidden charges like the cryptic "Archaeological Certificate," which can easily exceed the cost of shipping itself. Best to personally oversee the whole process.

Kuta's small **Kantor Pos** (GPO Kuta, Jl. Raya Tuban, Kuta, Denpasar, Bali 80361, tel. 0361-754012) is down a small lane off Jl. Kaya Kuta, opposite the elementary school. Open Mon.-Thurs. 0800-1400, Friday 0800-1100, Saturday 0800-1400. Here you may also have poste restante letters sent (Rp60 per letter pickup). This post office and **Ida's Postal Agent** (tel. 0361-751574, open Mon.-Sat. 0800-2000) on Jl. Legian across from the Sari Club at the intersection of Poppies Lane II and Jl. Legian are more convenient places to pick up mail than Denpasar's main post office way out in Renon. There are a number of other postal agents, open during business hours, that weigh letters and sell stamps.

Telephone

As a general rule, any hotel that charges Rp60,000 or more per day will offer IDD telephone calls. Hotels charge around Rp20,350 for a three minute international call, Rp6050 for each minute of an international telex, Rp13,000 per fax page—a great deal if you have lots to say—and Rp1000 to receive a fax.

A **Wartel** is at Universal across the street from the Mastapa Cottages, and a telephone office, with IDD capability, is at the airport. Telephone cards can be bought at the reception desks of many hotels. Public **Home Country Direct** telephones are found at the airport, on Jl. Legian next to Peanuts Disco, and in the lobby of the Natour Kuta Bead on Jl. Pantai Kuta; another one is near the intersection of Jl. Legian and Jl. Melasti. Kuta's telephone code is 0361.

Moneychangers

Opening at about 0800 or 0900, moneychangers are esconced in every other doorway along Jl. Legian and Jl. Pantai Kuta. They generally give quicker service, offer better rates, and stay open longer than banks. But one service banks do offer is a safety deposit box where you can leave valuables while traveling. Moneychangers are open as late as 2200 and change traveler's checks in five minutes. You have to present your passport and fill out a short form. For cash, no form needed.

Several cordial, efficient moneychangers are near the crossroads of Jl. Legian and Jl. Pantai Kuta (Bemo Corner). Try **Artha Yoga Utama** (tel. 0361-751445) situated where Jl. Bakung Sari meets Jl. Raya Kuta, the road to the airport, and **Krishna Moneychanger,** Jl. Legian (tel. 0361-51053), near Bank Danamon and the entrance to Poppies Lane II.

Banks ordinarily close 1400-1600 on weekdays and open only on Saturday mornings. For the best rates, try **Bank Duta,** Jl. Raya Kuta 57 (tel. 0361-753134), which has a 24-hour ATM and accepts Visa and MasterCard.

Photography

Instant photo processing and printing is now cheap and convenient not only in Kuta but all over Bali. Most places offer half-day service. Since these photo centers do so much business, new rolls of film are stocked regularly.

P.T. Modern Putraindonesia (tel. 0361-753194), opposite Geleal Supermarket, is a huge Fuji print processing outlet that does

blowups, without frames: 50 by 60 cm prints Rp28,000, 40 by 50 prints Rp19,000, 35 by 43 prints Rp14,500. Opposite Hotel Kartika Plaza is a big Kodak processing lab. **Bali Fotografie Centrum (BFC)** on Jl. Raya Kuta (Jl. Airport) has photo supplies and fast slide processing and framing. Many Kuta photo shops send their slide film to be processed there.

Church Services

Should you feel the need to do penance after a hard Saturday night, Kuta has several churches: **Catholic,** St. Francis Xavier, Jl. Kartika Plaza, tel. (0361) 751144, Sunday mass begins at 0800; **Pentecostal,** Gareja Pantekosta, Jl. Raya Kuta 18, tel. (0361) 751504, services 1000 and 1800; **Ecclesiastical** *(eklesia),* Jl. Ngurah Rai, tel. (0361) 553674, services Sunday at 0900 and 1800.

Massage

Platoons of masseuses—licensed for business but lacking professional training—with conical hats, yellow T-shirts, and incredibly strong hands, cruise the beach for customers. Using coconut oil, the majority give competent, thorough rubdowns. Go in the morning to get the best price, and agree on the price first. Don't pay more than about Rp10,000—they'll say their usual price is Rp35,000—for a 40-minute massage. Sometimes halfway through your massage, they'll demand more money. Special prices are given if you have a massage from the same masseuse every day. Try several until you find one you like and remember her number. Older women are usually better than the young ones, giving traditional massages using *lulur* paste from Java. You can also get massages at many hotels—Mastapa has an excellent masseuse—or at traditional Indonesian salons such as Selamat Datang at the Kulkul Beach Resort (tel. 0361-752520) on Jl. Pantai Kuta, which also offers hair and skin care and steam baths.

Beauty Salon

Numerous beauty salons all around the Kuta/Legian area offer the gamut of beauty services from simple haircuts to "computerized" facials to eyeline and eyebrow tattoos. Watch for their sandwich-board signs.

Recommended are **Ratu Ayu Salon,** Mastapa Garden Cottages, Jl. Legian (tel. 0361-751660), **Bravo Salon,** Jl. Raya Kuta 105, Block 4-5 (tel. 0361-754096 or 754097), just 500 meters north of Gelael Supermarket. **Eva,** Jl. Pantai Kuta (tel. 0361-751828), near Bemo Corner, offers haircuts with shampoo for ladies and gents for only Rp8500. You can also have your hair plaited Afro-style on the beach for Rp10,000 after bargaining, but to have your whole head of hair plaited is painful. Just get a token strand or two done so they'll leave you alone.

Health and Fitness
Doctors are on call at **Kuta Clinic,** Jl. Kaya Kuta 100 X, tel. (0361) 753268. Or make an appointment with **Dr. Tjok Gde Subamia,** who has an office on Jl. Raya Bypass Kuta, tel. (0361) 751315 or 753008. The closest clinic outside of Kuta is the excellent **Nusa Dua Clinic,** Jl. Pratama 81 A-B, tel. (0361) 71324, with 24-hour service, doctors on call, and an ambulance.

If you crave a real workout, the equipment and professional assistance at the **Fitness and Relaxation Centre,** tel. (0361) 751067, at the Kartika Plaza Hotel is top-notch. Open Mon.-Sun. 0600-2000, with an entrance fee of Rp10,000 per person per day. Fee includes use of gymnasium, pools, squash courts, lockers, showers, whirlpool baths, steam sauna, dry sauna, lounge, game room, aerobic classes, and mini-golf. A great deal for five bucks.

Odds and Ends
There's a whole slew of **vision shops** in Kuta where you may choose from a variety of fashion eyewear and contact lenses as well as avail yourself of free professional eye examinations. On Poppies Lane II, there are several **laundry services,** and Hotel Patra Jasa (formerly Pert- amina Cottages) to the south in Tuban does dry cleaning.

Take advantage of Bali Travel Service's **left luggage** service for only Rp500 per piece per day; their office is located in the modern a/c building on Jl. Benasri opposite Mastapa Cottages. The airport charges Rp2000 per piece per day.

TRANSPORTATION

The crossroads of Jl. Pantai Kuta and Jl. Legian, the exact center of Kuta, is Bemo Corner, called *perempatan* in Indonesian. An intricate network of small lanes run from Jl. Legian west to the beach. Most of these can barely if at all accommodate cars; motorcyclists riding down some of the narrowest force pedestrians literally against the wall.

Getting There and Around
A taxi from the airport costs Rp6000. The problem is the airport taxis won't go into Kuta's small lanes and often dump tourists out to schlep their bags sweating and cursing to their hotels. To avoid this, get out of the taxi on the main street outside the airport, then transfer to a metered blue/yellow Praja, tel. (0361) 751919 or 752299. Or walk out the airport gate and hire a *bemo* for Rp500 to the start of Jl. Pantai Kuta. Get to Kuta from Denpasar by boarding a *bemo* from Stasiun Tegal in southern Denpasar (Rp600). *Bemo* from Denpasar travel only one direction—Denpasar to Kuta, then to Legian via one-way Jl. Pantai Kuta, then back through Kuta down Jl. Legian before returning to Denpasar. Stay on the *bemo* until you're closest to your destination.

Professional motorcycle taxis will give you a ride anytime to anywhere, but most commonly from Legian to Kuta and vice versa if you're willing to pay around Rp2000. Depends on if it's

the busy season and/or how much they need the money. You can find them anywhere; they sleep on their bikes at night. Late at night, *dokar* are available for, say, Rp5000 from Peanuts to the Bintang Bali Hotel. *Bemo* leave as soon as they fill up, and once you pay your fare you can get off anywhere you want. Bear in mind that public *bemo* prices soar between 1900-2100, and ratchet up again around 2200 when you'll probably have to private charter.

Getting Away

A thick and endless stream of motorcycles, *bemo,* cars, vans, and buses travel to Legian via the beachfront road, Jl. Pantai Kuta. *Bemo* from Denpasar's Tegal station (Rp600) stop very briefly at Bemo Corner to let out passengers, then travel down traffic-snarled Jl. Pantai Kuta and the beachfront road to Legian. *Bemo* from Kuta to Legian are Rp500 before 1800; then drivers begin asking as much as Rp5000. After 2200, *bemo* become scarce and those that are available charge exorbitant fares. It costs at least Rp2000 to ride on the back of a motorcycle from Kuta to Legian, or around Rp3500 by taxi.

To Denpasar, get a *bemo* by walking down from Bemo Corner in the direction of Denpasar to Jl. Kaya Kuta, just where it turns in front of Kuta Market. From there head to Tegal station (eight km, 12-15 minutes) in southern Denpasar, then walk to downtown Denpasar in about 10 minutes, or hop on a three-wheeled *bajai* for Rp300. *Bemo* into Denpasar start getting scarce around 1900, after which you may be assessed a "surcharge." To get to Sanur you must travel via Tegal, transfer to Kereneng, then get on a *bemo* to Sanur. To Candidasa, take a *bemo* to Tegal, then Kereneng, then Batubulan, then a minibus to Amlapura, alighting at Candidasa en route. Sometimes the minibus only goes as far as Klungkung, at which point you have to change to another for Amlapura. To get to Ubud, go first to Tegal, transfer to Kereneng, then transfer again to Batubulan, then board a final *bemo* to Ubud. To Singaraja and Lovina, take a *bemo* first to Tegal, then to Kereneng, then to Ubung station, then to the north coast. ·

The heat, congestion, and time-consuming changes required to get to Ubud, Candidasa, or Sanur by public transport convince many people to charter a *bemo* direct. Don't worry

about finding charters; they'll find you. You'll pass motorcycle, minibus, and *bemo* drivers soliciting fares by shouting *"Transpor!"* and *"Charter!"* every 10 paces. To take you and all your stuff from Kuta to the airport in Tuban, they'll first ask Rp10,000. Just laugh at them—the going charter rate is Rp4000-5000. Unlicensed *bemo* can't enter the airport and must drop you off at the gate, where you have to walk 300 meters to the domestic terminal, or 600 meters to the international terminal. Taxis to Denpasar cost around Rp8000.

The shuttle to the airport leaves anytime for Rp8000. Sanur shuttles costs Rp5000 (see Ubud shuttles below for departure times). Shuttles for Padangbai and Candidasa run at 0530, 1300, and 1600 for Rp12,000; to Lovina at 0830, 1300, and 1600 for Rp15,000; to Ubud at 0530, 0830, 1000, 1300, and 1600 for Rp9000; to Bedugul at 1230 for Rp10,000; to Lembongan at 0700 for Rp32,000; to Senggigi (Lombok) at 0530, 1000, and 1300 for Rp22,500; to Gunung Meno (Lombok) at 0530 for Rp32,500; to Gunung Trawangan at 0530 for Rp33,500.

You'll see shuttles advertised on sandwich boards in the doorways of almost any kind of business, but it's best to leave it to professionals. A good, reliable company is **Perama** on Jl. Legian, on the left about five minutes walk north from Bemo Corner. Your seat is reserved via a 24-hour radio telephone, and their shuttles link Ubud, Sanur, the airport, and Kuta.

Rentals

Sturdy bicycles rent for about Rp3000-4000 per day or Rp10,000-12,000 per week; you must pay in advance and sign a contract. Motorcycles rent for Rp12,000-15,000 per day from your *losmen*, hotel, or just about anyone else you might run into. Take note that there's a row of motorcycle repair shops on the north side of the Jl. Pantai Kuta and Jl. Raya Tuban intersection. See the Introduction's Getting Around chapter for information on procedures, licenses, and other fees for renting motorcycles.

You can rent cars from literally hundreds of agencies in Kuta, although you could get a better deal per diem if you go through your hotel proprietor. Expect to pay at least Rp60,000 per day (three-day minimum) for a sedan, at least Rp50,000 for a Kijang, or Rp35,000-40,000 for a Jimney. A driver is Rp10,000-15,000 per day extra. For prices and availability of models, call: **Indah Jaya Car Rental** (tel. 0361-754467); **Bali Car Rental Service,** Jl. Ngurah Rai Bypass (tel. 0361-288539); **CV Wisata Motor Co.** (tel. 0361-751474) on Jl. Imam Bonjol.

If you plan to use Kuta as a base, its traffic, confusing one-way streets, and paucity of parking make using a car here trying.

Travel Agencies
To leave Bali, see the "From Bali" section of the Introduction, plus the Padangbai and Tanjung Benoa sections. Kuta's agents offer airline tickets to just about anywhere at pretty good prices, but for long-haul airfares you can do much better in Singapore or Bangkok.

Agencies also rent cars, bicycles, and motorbikes, offer tours, sell long-distance bus, train, and ferry tickets to the islands east and west of Bali, confirm flights (Rp2500 fee), and change money, dispense postage stamps, and sell books. One such all-in-one agent located toward Legian is **Easyway,** Jl. Benasari 7. Another is **Bali Baris Ceria,** Jl. Raya Kuta 106 C (tel. 0361-755633).

Also get an idea of what's available from **Perama Tourist Service** on Jl. Legian 16, tel. (0361) 751551, fax 751170. This excellent travel/transport company runs handy shuttle services to the main tourist areas of Bali. For flight reservations and confirmations, hotel tour desks will charge Rp2500. Or you can simply call Garuda (tel. 0361-224664) direct.

Garuda has an office in the Natour Kuta Beach Hotel, Jl. Pantai Kuta 1 (tel. 0361-751179), open Mon.-Fri. 0730-1600, Saturday and Sunday 0900-1300. The line can be annoyingly long, so get there early. **Air New Zealand**'s office is at the Kartika Plaza Beach Hotel on Jl. Kartika Plaza (tel. 0361-753593, fax 753592). A **Singapore Airlines** office is at the airport (tel. 0361-751011, ext. 2119).

Tours
Signboards and bulletin boards advertise tours everywhere you turn. Tours start as low as Rp15,000 (non a/c, eight to 10 people) all the way up to Rp60,000 (longer tours, a/c buses, fewer people). On the **Singaraja Tour** (eight hours) you visit Bedugul, Ulandanu Temple,

Gitgit, Singaraja, Sangsit, Kubutambahan, and Air Sanih. **The Besakih Tour** (eight hours) takes you to Batubulan, Celuk, Batuan, Mas, Gianyar, Klungkung, Kerta Gosa, Bukit Jambul, Pura Besakih. On the **Cremation Tour,** 12-15 people are transported by *bemo* to the event, look around, snap hundreds of exposures, then are driven back home, all within three hours.

Other tours include two- to five-day trips with overnight accommodations to Java, Lombok, Komodo, Sulawesi, and even Irian Jaya. One takes you on a climb up Gunung Bromo's crater for around Rp250,000, a bargain as the roundtrip is over 700 km and you get a wonderful glimpse of East Java. You even see surfing trips advertised to Grajagan on the Blangbangan Peninsula, East Java, at around Rp69,000 per day, or one-day snorkeling trips in south Bali for around Rp30,000.

Land/sea adventures to Komodo Island are being advertised around Kuta by Perama Travel (Jl. Legian 16, tel. 0361-751-551 or 751875). Tours depart every Sunday, Wednesday, and Friday, and the cost is only Rp100,000 per person. Day 1: Lombok countryside (Sweta, Loyok, Rungkang, Pringasela, Jurit, Labuhan Lombok, Camping Resort Perama). Day 2: reef exploration (Medang Island), then night-sailing to Komodo. Day 3: sightseeing Bima one morning, photo safari to Komodo.

VICINITY OF KUTA

North of Kuta
At low tide, bicycle rides or walks along the firm, moist sand are refreshing. Heading north of Kuta, you can ride for about seven kilometers before the sand changes and will no longer support a bicycle. At this point either retrace your tracks, or turn inland at the thatched roofs of Seminyak's Bali Oberoi and return to Kuta via Jl. Legian.

The Oberoi is no longer the last tourist bastion, beyond which few people besides the occasional fisherman are seen. Although the new tourist accommodations springing up north of Legian in Petitingit, Batubelig, Canggu, and Pererean bring more and more people to previously isolated beaches, the crowds thin the farther north you get. If you're walking or riding northwest all the way to Tanah Lot, you have to cross several rivers and stretches of deep black lava sand where the coast is rocky and not suitable for swimming.

If you walk north far enough (about 2.5 hours), you'll run into the sacred sea temple of Pura Petitenget, which is made completely of white coral. Founded by one of the first Javano-Hindu holy men to visit Bali, Sanghyang Niaratha. For more detail, see the section on Petitingit under "North of Legian."

Tuban

South of Kuta by the airport, Tuban is where all the rascals and *maling* (thieves) used to live, where outsiders outnumber the locals. If you meet transvestites, prostitutes, and pimps on Kuta, Tuban is where they usually live. With its mosque, branch government offices like immigration and customs in front of the airport, *padang* restaurants, and Java-style *kampung*, Tuban has a pan-Indonesian flavor.

Essentially, Tuban is a base for the service community serving the massive tourist infrastructure of southern Bali. The centerpiece for the whole neighborhood is a giant, alabaster white statue of Gatotkaca in the heat of battle. He was the only ancient Hindu god who could fly, thus his portrait is appropriately situated near Bali's airport, which is just down the road 1.5 kilometers west. The Bali government maintains a branch tourist information office (tel. 0361-51011) at the airport; open 0800-1800. There's also a branch immigration office (tel. 0361-751038) on Jl. I Gusti Ngurah Rai (the road to the airport) in Tuban.

Tuban's six seaside, international-class hotel properties are among the most exclusive on the island. The stretch of beach here is narrower and quieter than Kuta's, and just as beautiful. Access to the airport, Kuta, and Denpasar is quick, cheap, and easy.

The tourist promoters of Tuban have in fact disassociated themselves from Kuta's unsavory reputation. They are marketing their slice of Bali's southwest coast as a separate, more "remote," alluring, and tranquil destination with a sunset beach, a full range of hotels, and plenty of places to shop and dine.

Accommodations: Technically, Tuban extends from the Hotel Patra Jasa (formerly Pertamina Cottages) by the airport to the Kartika Plaza Hotel near Jl. Bakung Sari, but for con-venience, only hotels in the southerly section of Tuban are included here.

The neighborhood's least expensive is the **Palm Beach Hotel,** Jl. Pantai Banjar Segara (tel. 0361-751661, fax 752432), just north of the Bali Holiday Inn. Rp115,000-138,000, including tax, service, and breakfast. Pool, nice garden, dart board, chess, standby vehicle for rent, free transfers to and from the airport. Quiet, homey, secure, away from traffic pollution. From the hotel it's only a few minutes' walk to the beach, five minutes' walk to the main road, a handy five minutes' drive to the airport, and a 10 minutes' walk to Kuta.

Alit's Kuta Bungalows (Jl. Puri Gerenceng, Box 3102, Denpasar, tel. 0361-751968 or 751969, fax 288766) charges Rp69,000 s, Rp80,500 d for Balinese-style air-conditioned bungalows, shower, hot water, terrace, pool, restaurant, and bar. Located 500 meters from the post office and the airport, and one kilometer from the beach. Alit's is a welcome place to stay if you arrive on Bali late, hot, tired, and grungy, and want trouble-free accommodations quickly.

More upscale is international-class, beachfront **Santika Beach Hotel** (Jl. Kartika Plaza, Box 1008, Tuban, tel. 0361-751267, fax 751260) with 168 Bali-style rooms for Rp230,000 s or d in a three-story complex with two pools, tennis courts, restaurant, and bar. Also two-room family units facing a kid's playground, Rp368,000. Rooms have all the conveniences one would expect from a four-star hotel. Located just south of the Kartika Plaza Hotel.

In a class by itself, sprawling over 10 hectares, is handsome **Hotel Patra Jasa**—formerly Pertamina Cottages—(Jl. Kuta Beach, Box 121, Denpasar, tel. 0361-751161), the first five-star hotel on Bali and the southernmost hotel of Tuban. Not your usual U-shaped configuration, this government-owned hotel feels like a thinly populated assembly of private homes. There are 206 modern, two-room, red-brick cottages in all. Rack rates range Rp287,500-345,000 per day for the suites, Rp1.8 million per day for the villas. Though comparable accommodations can be found for less, the isolation is splendid with closed-circuit TV, fresh flowers daily, shopping arcade, open-air stage, two restaurants (one of them Japanese), bars, convention facilities, tennis courts, pool, badminton, three-hole golf course. Evening open-air buffet entertainment is a response to European business. Meals and guests are conveyed through the grounds on a minibus. The hotel is more oriented toward Asian package tourists and Indonesian business. Employees greet you with the Hindu gesture of peace. With the number of Caucasians arriving, a few much-appreciated nonsmoking rooms have come in.

In spite of Pertamina being only a five-minute drive from the airport, it's wonderfully quiet with only the sound from the ground's aviaries waking you in the morning. A major draw are the gardens—maintained at Rp11.5 million per month—which makes for a very quick, soft landing when arriving in Bali.

Shopping, Food, and Entertainment: One wild shop in Tuban, **Bali Walet** (Jl. Raya Tuban 2 B-C, tel. 0361-751930) carries bird's nest, dried sea products, Indonesian snacks, and other native products. **Bali Opal Center,** Jl. Raya Tuban 2 (tel. 0361-752761, fax 751930), carries some dazzling amethyst, blue sapphires, opals, amber, agates, and other expensive and high-quality stones and gems.

On a more familial note, dine, relax, and enjoy the twitter and beauty of exotic birds in Bali's first and only bird park restaurant at Jl. Ksatria 2, Tuban. A variety of Indonesian, Chinese, and European food is offered in *lesehan*-style huts, or eat in the main dining room facing the beautiful, bird-filled garden. For reservations and free shuttle, call (0361) 755833. **Rupah Makan Minang,** Jl. Raya Tuban (tel. 0361-755568), op-

posite the spectacular statue of Gatotkaca, offers Padang-style food to the many Indonesian transients of the area.

Waterbom Park (Jl. Kartika Plaza, tel. 0361-755676, fax 753517) is a three-and-a-half-hectare park offering 600 meters of exciting water slides, jungle rides, water race tracks, and a lazy 250-meter twisting rafting river. Open 0900-1800. Also restaurants, beautifully landscaped gardens, tubing, pools, restaurant, sunken bars, underwater music. Admission is Rp15,000 for children five to 12 years old, Rp8000 for children under five years old. Accepts Visa, MasterCard. Only a five-minute walk from Bemo Corner toward the airport.

Very popular with the locals is **BB's Discoteque** in the Bintang Bali Hotel (Jl. Kartika Plaza, tel. 0361-753292), a high-tech disco playing the very latest sounds. Also check out the **Taipan Karaoke** with its authentic and stylish Japanese nightclub interior, and the live jazz band at the **Alun Alun Lounge.**

On the beach near Tuban's Holiday Inn is **Zero Six,** a huge open venue with a live band. The **Fun Pub** in the Dynasty Hotel has pool tables, a very popular karaoke, happy hour, snacks, and frequent party nights. For more traditional entertainment, **Kuta Seafood Restaurant and Theatre** (Jl. Kartika Plaza 92 X) presents live performances of dances and music to accompany their fresh seafood dinners. Open daily 1100-2100, shows start nightly from 1900 to 2100. For reservations, call (0361) 755807.

LEGIAN

This once dusty, poor seaside village is now just an extension of Kuta, though with slightly more chic energy. Legian offers good music, outstanding food, both luxury and budget hotels, sophisticated fashion boutiques, banks, souvenir markets, and *arja, barong, kecak,* and Ramayana performances at least every other day. It even has its own bungee jump company now, **Adrenalin,** which offers a 50-meter human slingshot for US$50; book at tel. (0361) 757841. From Denpasar, Legian is Rp600 by *bemo,* or a two-km walk from Kuta Beach on a congested sidewalk beside a busy road running south. It's more pleasant to walk via the beach, then cut in at Jl. Padma.

ACCOMMODATIONS

No lack of accommodations in and around Legian. The northern section features unique, relaxed places surrounded by spacious gardens and coconut palms, with only the sound of birds, insects, and geckos. Nowhere, however, will you escape the 15.5% tax and service charge.

Budget
The inexpensive **Janji Inn** Banjar Legian Kelod, tel. (0361) 752389, in a quiet coconut grove off Gang Uluwatu, offers eight large, well-appointed rooms with *mandi* for Rp10,000 s, Rp15,000 d. Good security, free breakfast, tea all day, nice people. A welcome oasis not far from the madding crowd. **Wisata Beach Inn** (tel. 0361-752216), a short walk from the beach behind Glory's Restaurant, has very nice, quiet, two-room bungalows in a garden setting for only Rp10,000 s, just Rp9000 per day if you stay a week. Cheap, comfortable **Surya Dewata Beach Cottages** (tel. 0361-753776) is a small complex of little bungalows with 24-hour security down a small alleyway off Jl. Padma Utara; the path is very dark at night. A kitchen is available for preparing meals. For something closer to the beach, try the 10-room **Sri Beach Inn** (tel. 0361-755897), Rp8000 s, Rp12,000 d, light breakfast included. Set in the middle of a beau-

tiful and well-maintained orchid garden, the place is run by Wayan Tampa, who speaks better than average English and employs tireless houseboys.

On Jl. Padma is 90-room **Legian Village Hotel** (tel. 0361-751182 or 752455, fax 752455) with nicely appointed air-conditioned rooms, hot water, laundry service, pool, restaurant, and bar for only Rp30,000-55,000 s, Rp35,000-60,000 d, including continental Breakfast but not tax and service. A supplement is charged in the high season. Credit cards accepted. Only a couple blocks from the beach (five minutes on foot).

Considerably upgraded **Oka Melati Hotel,** on Jl. Padma, tel. (0361) 755894, has patio and upstairs rooms with balconies, each with wrought iron table and chairs. Rooms are simply but pleasantly furnished and include *mandi.* Features include an attractive courtyard with palms, a well-staffed front desk with fax, birdcages, and a lovely roof garden from which to view the sun's rising and setting. They'll keep your passport and valuables in a locked compartment. Price varies on length of stay and one's negotiating abilities. Mr. Oka and Mr. Ida, the managers, are very helpful. Directly across the street is another hotel with pool that you may use. Mr. Oka owns a small clothing store *cum* bookstore up the street.

Next door and on the same windy street as the Kuta Palace Hotel, the relaxing and attractive **Orchid Garden Cottages** (Jl. Pura Bagus Taruna 525, Box 3379, Legian Kaja Kuta, tel. 0361-751802, fax 752852) has 23 rooms on a 900-sq-m property. Low season rates, all subject to 15% tax and service, are Rp20,000 for room with fan, Rp40,000 for air-conditioned room. Hot water, attached bathrooms, but no breakfast. Rates in the high season go up by about Rp20,000. Clean rooms, beautiful garden, good atmosphere. Ayub, Putu, and their three daughters, plus a staff of 14 from all over Indonesia, really look after you. They all call you by name and bring you hot tea or water all day long. The hotel also has a small store, offers film processing, souvenirs, laundry, and tour service. The restaurant has a very complete menu and

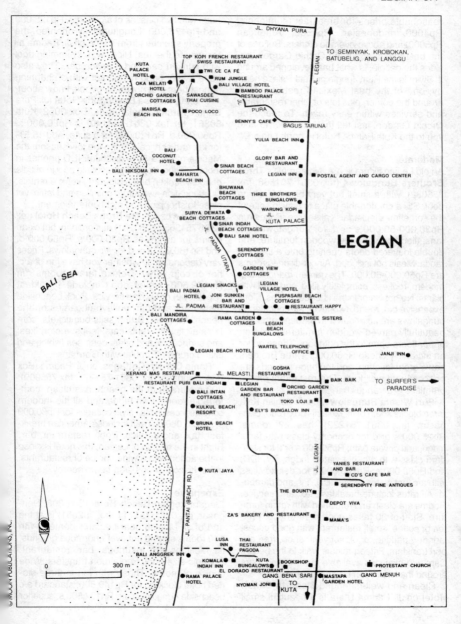

LEGIAN

TO SEMINYAK, KROBOKAN,
BATUBELIG, AND LANGGU

JL. DHYANA PURA

KUTA
PALACE
HOTEL

Top Kopi French Restaurant
Swiss Restaurant
TWI CE CA FÉ
OKA MELATI
HOTEL
RUM JUNGLE
BALI VILLAGE HOTEL
ORCHID GARDEN
COTTAGES
BAMBOO PALACE
RESTAURANT
SAWASDEE
THAI CUISINE
MABISA
BEACH INN
POCO LOCO
PURA
BENNY'S CAFE
BAGUS TARUNA

YULIA BEACH INN

BALI
COCONUT
HOTEL
GLORY BAR AND
RESTAURANT
BALI NIKSOMA INN
SINAR BEACH
COTTAGES
LEGIAN INN
POSTAL AGENT AND CARGO CENTER
MAHARTA
BEACH INN
BHUWANA
BEACH
COTTAGES
THREE BROTHERS
BUNGALOWS
WARUNG KOPI
JL.
KUTA PALACE
SURYA DEWATA
BEACH COTTAGES
SINAR INDAH
BEACH COTTAGES
BALI SANI HOTEL

BALI SEA

SERENDIPITY
COTTAGES

GARDEN VIEW
COTTAGES
LEGIAN SNACKS
JONI SUNKEN
BAR AND
RESTAURANT
LEGIAN
VILLAGE HOTEL
PUSPASARI BEACH
COTTAGES
RESTAURANT HAPPY
BALI PADMA
HOTEL
JL. PADMA
BALI MANDIRA
COTTAGES
THREE SISTERS
RAMA GARDEN
COTTAGES
LEGIAN
BEACH
BUNGALOWS

JL. PADMA UTARA

LEGIAN BEACH HOTEL
WARTEL TELEPHONE
OFFICE
JANJI INN
KERANG MAS RESTAURANT
JL. MELASTI
GOSHA
RESTAURANT
RESTAURANT PURI BALI INDAH
LEGIAN
GARDEN BAR
AND RESTAURANT
BAIK BAIK
TO SURFER'S
PARADISE
BALI INTAN
COTTAGES
ORCHID GARDEN
RESTAURANT
KULKUL BEACH
RESORT
TOKO LOJI II
ELY'S BUNGALOW INN
MADE'S BAR AND RESTAURANT
BRUNA BEACH
HOTEL

JL. PANTAI (BEACH RD.)

KUTA JAYA

YANIES RESTAURANT
AND BAR
CD'S CAFE BAR
SERENDIPITY FINE ANTIQUES
THE BOUNTY
DEPOT VIVA
ZA'S BAKERY AND RESTAURANT
MAMA'S

0   300 m

JL. LEGIAN

LUSA
INN
THAI
RESTAURANT
PAGODA
BALI ANGGREK INN
KOMALA
INDAH INN
EL DORADO RESTAURANT
KUTA
BUNGALOWS
BOOKSHOP
PROTESTANT CHURCH
RAMA PALACE
HOTEL
NYOMAN JONI
GANG BENA SARI
MASTAPA
GARDEN HOTEL
GANG MENUH
TO
KUTA

© MOON PUBLICATIONS, INC.

reasonable prices for breakfast (continental Rp4000, Indonesian Rp4500, American Rp5000) and above-average dinners. But one of the best things about the Orchid Garden, besides the people, is what has developed around it. Swim in the Rum Jungle or Kuta Palace nearby, one of the best Mexican restaurants is around the corner, plus lots of other restaurants and services within easy reach. To reach the Orchid Garden, just tell the taxi driver to take you to the Kuta Palace Hotel in north Legian.

Moderate

An old Legian fixture is A.A. Ngurah Alit's **Three Brothers Bungalows** (tel. 0361-751566, fax 756082), with a small but very nice swimming pool. Still a comfortable place to stay in spite of the sometimes lackadaisical service. Prices run Rp30,000-50,000 s or d, for bungalows with fans, tiled floors, ornate wooden furniture, and double louvered doors opening onto a tiled veranda. Meals not included. Air-conditioned rooms are Rp50,000-60,000. The garden *mandi* is big, modern, roofless, completely tiled, and filled with plants. No hot water in the cheaper rooms. More expensive big, round, two-level, air-conditioned bungalows are luxurious with garden baths and beautifully carved wooden furniture, some on upper floors open to the outdoors. These go for an incredibly cheap Rp60,000. Three Brothers has a great location, and the huge grounds are peaceful and well kept. The restaurant on the premises is a tranquil hangout.

Puri Wisata Bungalows, on Jl. Legian Kaja three blocks south of Jl. Melasti (Box 1060, Denpasar, tel. 0361-751222), has 22 rooms. Rp25,000 s or d for economy class with fans, fridge, and private bath; Rp50,000 s or d for standard class with a/c, hot water, fridge, TV, IDD; and Rp80,000 s, Rp100,000 d for deluxe class with a/c, hot water, fridge, IDD, TV, and parabola. All rates include breakfast, tax, and service. Rooms are clean and furnished with rattan furniture. Staff of 30 takes good care of you. Free tea or coffee, small restaurant with good prices, laundry, parking, pool, souvenir shop, free airport transfers. Fifteen-minute walk to the beach. Cars and minivans available for rent, and tours around the island can be arranged.

Clean and well-managed **Maharta Beach Hotel** on Jl. Padma Utara is a beautiful small hotel with two classes of a/c rooms, Rp125,000 and Rp175,000. Longitudinally oriented, the property stretches from a lane off Jl. Padma all the way to the sea. Nice lawn, swimming pool with sunken bar, and a beach bar. They also have a very good restuarant with a charming atmosphere that not many people know about.

Friendly **Mabisa Beach Side Hotel** (Jl. Pura Bagus Taruna, Legian Kaja, Box 2052, Kuta 80361, tel./fax 0361-754140) is Rp50,000 s, Rp60,000 d, Rp120,000 for a suite. Add 15.5% for tax and service. During the low season, the Mabisa offers a 50% discount. IDD phones in room, parking, tropical garden, big pool in middle of hotel, sunken bar, restaurant, vehicle rentals. Quiet location away from pollution and taffic, yet close to shopping and night entertainment.

Near the beach, the **Bruna Beach Hotel** (tel. 0361-751565 or 753201) has ordinary but clean rooms for as low as Rp30,000 s, Rp50,000 d, and Rp160,000 s or d for a/c bungalows. Prices vary depending on whether you have fan or a/c, hot or cold water. Deluxe family rooms run Rp172,500. Rates don't include breakfast (Rp10,000) or tax and service. Pool, beachside restaurant and bar, volleyball games on the beach, TV room. Bruna sells bus tickets, confirms air tickets, rents cars, jeeps, motorbikes, and surfboards, and offers deep-sea fishing and island cruises. Popular with Germans.

Rama Garden Cottages, on Jl. Padma (Box 334, Denpasar, tel. 0361-751971, fax 755909), 200 meters from the beach, has clean, comfortable rooms with fridge and all the modern conveniences in Bali-style cottages for Rp80,000 s, Rp120,000 d. Tariff includes American breakfast, tax, and service. Pool, restaurant, bar. Right in the middle of Legian, this hotel is close to the action with a wide choice of restaurants, pubs, discos, shops, and *bemo* nearby.

Expensive

Elegant **Legian Beach Hotel** (Box 308, Denpasar, tel. 0361-751711, fax 752651) is at the end of Jl. Melasti near Legian's center. With 140 rooms spread out over enormous grounds, its facilities are luxurious: bar, restaurant, Olympic-size pool, free airport transfers. Wide choice of rooms. Those with fan in three-storied hotel block go for Rp149,500, standard a/c beachside bungalows are Rp172,500 s, superior bungalows are Rp207,000 (doubles are Rp23,000 more), plus 21% tax and service.

Near the beach on Jl. Padma, the 96-room **Bali Mandira Cottages** (Box 1003, Denpasar, tel. 0361-751381, fax 752377) charges Rp172,500 s, Rp195,500 d (plus 20% tax and service) with a/c, hot water, IDD, sound system, lush courtyard gardens, pool, tennis and squash courts, bar, restaurant, and nice view of the ocean. Friendly service.

In northern Legian with plenty of shade, **Kuta Palace Hotel**, Jl. Pura Bagus Teruna (Box 244, Denpasar, tel. 0361-751433), has 281 rooms for Rp180,000 s, Rp200,000-300,000 d. Open-air theater, lots of sports and entertainment, and a marked-off beach.

Modernly designed and furnished, tropical-style **Bali Coconut Hotel** (Jl. Padma Utara, tel. 0361-754121, fax 754121) has a/c, telephone, fridge, satellite dish, video program, hot water, and snappy service. Restaurant and karaoke bar, coffee shop. Rates, subject to 15.5% tax and service, are Rp90,000 s, Rp100,000 d, with high-season supplement of Rp20,000 (20 Dec.-10 Jan.). It's only a short walk down a private alley to the beach.

On Jl. Pantai Kuta is the small but special **Kulkul Beach Resort** (Box 3097, Denpasar 80030, tel. 0361-752520, fax 752519) with 18 thatch-roof bungalows comprising 50 rooms, some with open-air baths, for Rp290,000. Standard garden view rooms are Rp195,500, superior garden view rooms are Rp218,500. To all prices, add 21% tax and service. The Kulkul at first doesn't impress you with its grandeur, but its services are comparable to those offered in a three-star hotel (though it doesn't have a business center) and the staff and management are attentive. Designed by a Balinese architect, the Kulkul maintains a quaint, rustic feel that appeals to a younger clientele. On the premises is the popular Kaktus Biru mexican restaurant (terrific music though), a karaoke bar, a traditional beauty salon, and a tour and travel desk. Rehana will give you a tour of the hotel. One drawback is the Kulkul is next to the Baruna Night Club, which pulsates with raucous music until at least 2300 most nights of the week.

The **Kuta Jaya Cottage** on Jl. Raya Pantai Kuta (tel. 0361-752308, fax 752309) is self-contained with a shopping arcade, photo center,

doctor on call, drugstore, bank, travel agency (cars for rent), postal and dry-cleaning service, and an open-air stage for performances. It has 135 rooms for Rp195,500-218,500, a nice garden, clean interiors, and a peaceful atmosphere.

Long-Term

There are dozens of self-contained complexes with bungalows well-suited for long-term rental. They come with complete kitchen, private garden, hot water, cassette stereo, maid and laundry service, good security. Each unit sleeps four or more people, starting around Rp35,000 per day (not including tax) and heading way up for posher units. They can be a great deal for large groups. Bargain for an even better monthly rate.

Homestays, rooms in out-of-the-way beachfront hotels, and private villa rentals are also available north of Legian in Seminyak, Petitinget, Berawa Beach, and Canggu. See "Private Villa Rentals" under "Accommodations" in the Introduction.

FOOD

To save money, shop at **Loji II Supermarket** (tel. 0361-751048) and cook yourself. For home-cooked meals **Warung Murah**, Jl. Legian (tel. 0361-752028), on the left about one-half km from Legian toward Seminyak, sells a classic Bali-style *nasi campur* with meat, egg, veggies, and *sambal* for around Rp2000. This once Balinese *warung,* now a full-fledged restaurant, closes around midnight.

A Singapore-style foodmart, **Matahari Legian Plaza,** Jl. Legian just up from the Mastapa Garden Hotel toward Kuta on the left, shares a complex with the wildly popular McDonald's. A coven of poorly patronized restaurants, the plaza's a bomb even on Saturday night because they're generally too ritzy and pricey. The only popular eatery of the bunch is **Warung Java,** which also has the best prices.

In Legian proper, medium-sized, upmarket **Gosha Restaurant,** Jl. Melasti (tel. 0361-751089), is one of the best restaurants in the area for seafood and European dishes. Offering a variety of food, the restaurant, constructed of bamboo with a thatch roof, is always crowded. Just as classy, in its own way, the restaurant at

Bruna Beach Hotel overlooks the beach, turning out delicious Indonesian and Western dishes.

Benny's Cafe I, Jl. Pura Bagus Taruna (Jl. Rum Jungle), Legian Kaja (down the on the left 100 meters before the bend in the road), is an above average breakfast place serving oatmeal bread, homemade cakes, and Aussie and Italian food. Benny Suhadi runs the restaurant, a neighborhood hotspot where you can sit in comfortable chairs, listen to electric harp, sample an original menu, and sip frothy cappucino while watching the panoply of humanity stream by.

Bamboo Palace, also on Jl. Pura Bagus Taruna, is a small restaurant and bar with good Indonesian and Western food, friendly staff, and warm, cozy atmosphere. The **Lido Restaurant and Pub** (tel. 0361-755343) on Jl. Melasti specializes in Chinese and European food.

Uncrowded **Orchid Garden Cottages,** Jl. Pura Bagus Taruna (tel. 0361-752852), has quite reasonable prices and a garrulous, homey atmosphere. They specialize in Chinese, Indonesian, and Balinese food and fish dishes with special sauces. One of the best desserts in Indonesia has to be their banana pancake heaped with fruit salad and topped with honey and yogurt (Rp6000). The restaurant entrance is covered in bougainvillea.

The small garden courtyard in the back of **Warung Kopi** (Jl. Legian Tengah 427, tel. 0361-753602) is a fine place to relax and enjoy generally very good and nutritious food. A lavish buffet is set up at 1900 every Wednesday night featuring the best dishes of India including curries and condiments. Call for a reservation, especially for large groups during prime time. The "special" breakfast of fruit salad, juice, two eggs, whole-wheat toast, jam, and Bali coffee is particularly popular. Extensive variety of desserts: cakes, chocolate mousse, black rice pudding, the to-die-for choco fudge pie. Reasonable prices, clean, nice atmosphere, reputable, and close to central Legian. Closes at midnight.

Also on Jl. Legian in Legian Kelod, halfway between Kuta and Legian, is award-winning **Za's Bakery and Restaurant** (Jl. Legian Kelod, tel. 0361-752973) known for its breakfast, brunch, seafood, and delightfully creative dishes. Try the flavorful fish soup with spicy tomato base and a thick slice of multi-grain bread. For breakfast, great juices, fruit, and divine yogurt,

homemade jams, toasted *muesli,* and fantastic baked goods. Also the cheapest margaritas on Bali (Rp5500). Fast, friendly service. A nice, cool place to stop for lunch while shopping.

Aroma's Cafe and Restaurant (Jl. Legian, tel. 0361-751003), a mostly vegetarian restaurant next to Za's, is above average, even exotic, though a bit expensive. Generous portions. They also have very good bread. The dining area is surrounded by a garden and fish pond.

Goa 2001 Restaurant (tel. 0361-730592 or 731178), just beyond Legian toward Seminyak on the right, is a popular eatery with Indian dishes and a sit-down sushi bar, as well as Indonesian, Italian, and German food. A limited menu, but what's on it is good (the environment is more noteworthy than the food). Tasty pumpkin soup, passable sushi, but their *gado-gado* is like a warm vegetable stew with peanut sauce poured over it. Meals with drink average Rp12,000-15,000.

Goa's isn't really popular as a dinner place but as a warmup spot before the discos open. Don't even bother going before 2300 when it starts to get packed with the Beautiful People lounging and drinking *arak madu* or exotic drinks from a three-page-long drink menu, while listening to a huge variety of superb music. You may even have to stand in line. A magnificent building with vaulted ceilings of ribbed bamboo and interlocking thatch, Goa's is elegant yet casual with a warm and inviting decor, nice sitting areas, always well-patronized, and the draught beer is always cold. A great spot to meet people—detractors call it a meat market—but it is indeniably one of Bali's best bars. Open from 1900 until about 0200.

Ethnic

A smashing success, **Poco Loco** (Jl. Padma Utara, across from Bali Niksoma, tel. 0361-756079) serves traditional, high-quality, and beautifully presented Mexican food. In a huge, posh, open-air building, with an upbeat atmosphere, they play cool, modern jazz on a great sound system. Tops on the menu are seafood combo fajitas, tostada with cabbage, enchilada, guacamole, burritos stuffed with seafood, salmon steaks. Don't miss the fantastic sangria, giant daiquiris, and awesome margaritas served up in their two bars. Made, one of God's smaller people, sells Cuervo Gold tequila shooters from his portable minibar. Great desserts too: "Very Muddy Mud Pie" and rich chocolate cake with homemade vanila ice cream. Punctual service, medium price range. Open for dinner from 1800 until about midnight.

New and trendy **Teras-La Terrazza,** on the third floor high above Jl. Legian (just before Jl. Double Six), is one of south Bali's best new restaurants, with a wonderful selection of grilled food, homemade pastas with delicious sauces, and sublime desserts. Recommended is the Brazilian Churasco platter for two featuring spit-roasted pork, chicken, beef, very good home-made sausages, and a full complement of side dishes—not bad for Rp30,000. Sit on the huge outdoor rooftop terrace or at the long bar tended by experienced bartenders and drink in the full moon. Check out the late night menu at the bar for a light and entertaining snack. Service is excellent. Nice bathrooms. Open 1900-0200 nightly.

The **Bali Rock Cafe** (tel. 0361-754466) in the combat zone on Jl. Melasti to the east of the Bali Intan Hotel puts on a "Big Bopper Burger Night" on Monday nights when you can eat as many hamburgers or veggie-burgers as you like from their big burger buffet. They also have "Homestay Roast Dinner Nights" on Sunday nights, "Pasta & Pizza Nights" on Wednesday nights, and Satay Bonanza Nights on Friday nights. Live music accompanies each free-for-all buffet.

A real find is **Pagoda Thai Bar and Restaurant,** Gang Benasari 15, a delightful, small Thai restaurant. The owner/hostess, Mama Eti, ran the famous Coffee House in Bukittinggi. Just family members work here to keep prices down. Particularly good seafood. Also a complete breakfast menu. No MSG. Nice atmosphere, nice music, nice family. Another Thai restaurant, with a very romantic atmosphere, is **Swasdee,** Jl. Pura Bagus Taruna (tel. 0361-232841).

The **Swiss Restaurant** (tel. 0361-751735), behind the Kuta Palace Hotel on Jl. Pura Bagus Taruna, is a Swiss oasis in the middle of Indonesia. Run by a Balinese woman and her Swiss husband, Jon Zurcher, who import wine from France, steak from New Zealand, and *bratwurst* and cheeses from Switzerland for the excellent fondue. Drop in on the Asia buffets every Saturday, "Bali Nights" every Thursday at 1930, plus daily *rijstaffel.* Also try the smoked fish, banana flambé, superb omelettes, champagne, wines,

cocktails. Jon, who also serves as the official Swiss Consul, can be recognized by his pipe and bare feet (even when climbing volcanoes!). He personally leads treks to places you'd never go alone. Ask to see his photo albums.

A traditional English self-service buffet brunch is presented every day between 1100-1300 at **The Bounty** (tel. 0361-754040) on Jl. Legian. It includes poached eggs, stewed tomatoes, mixed grill, croissants. In the shape of a rigged sailing ship, on the Bounty's upper deck restaurant, English dishes like steak and kidney pie are served. Or just have a drink in the Captain's Bar. Happy hours are 1800-2000 and 2200-2300.

Near the Bounty is **Mama's,** Jl. Legian 354, tel. (0361) 751805, specializing in German food such as *schweine braten mit rotkohl, fassbier,* and *gulasch-suppe.* Just like in the old country. The **Sari Rasa Restaurant** in the Maharta Beach Hotel on Jl. Padma serves excellent Austrian-style food and famous desserts like apple strudel and Palatschinkenala Esterhazy cakes at moderate prices. No one seems to know about it, yet it's first class.

The **Topi Koki** (tel./fax 0361-754243) on Jl. Pura Bagus Taruna opposite the Kuta Palace Hotel was Bali's first French restaurant (est. 1986). Authentic French cuisine, French TV by satellite, French video programs. Main dishes run around Rp8000-12,000, wine by the glass Rp5000. A dinner for two with drinks, appetizers, main course, dessert, and coffee will be around Rp60,000. Another French eatery is **Le Bistro,** Jl. Legian Kaja 2 (tel. 0361-730973), which specializes in Bouillabaisse escargots. This place is an offshoot of Jakarta's oldest French restaurant and the food *c'est magnifique!*

At the **Kurumaya** in the Bali Padma Hotel at Jl. Padma 1 (tel. 0361-752111), in central Legian, you may savor teppan yaki, tempura, shabu-shabu, and other traditional Japanese cuisines in a Japanese setting—a feast for both eyes and palate. Served up by new Japanese chef Ken Namba who worked at three premier Japanese restaurants in Los Angeles. Open 1900-2300. **Tanaya's Cafe,** Jl. Raya Legian 131 (tel. 0361-754362), is a Japanese steak house specializing in seafood barbecue, teriyaki steak bowl, beef bowl, and fried chicken. Open daily for breakfast, lunch, and dinner. Free transport in Kuta area.

Aussie Food

For international buffets, and Outback, American, Indonesian, or continental breakfasts, head for the **Glory Bar and Restaurant** on Jl. Legian (tel. 0361-751091, fax 753219). On Saturday nights Glory serves an excellent Indonesian/Chinese feast for Rp9500 (children half-price); also buffets Wednesday night. Free alcoholic drinks will served to buffet customers from 1900 to 2030. Or go to their Happy Harvey Hour, when popular cocktails are served by the jug. Plastic accepted. Open 0800-2400. Call Glory for bookings and for a free ride (Kuta area only).

Yanies, on corner of Jl. Legian and Jl. Melasti (tel. 0361-751292), also bills itself as "No. 1 for real Australian food." Started by an Australian and his Balinese wife in 1983, the place is very popular with Australians. The beer is cold. Also a fun place for kids because they have a pair of parrots and owls, and sell Bali dolls. Traditional thatched roof, garden setting. Open 1100-0400.

ENTERTAINMENT

The jazz bar at the **Poco Loco** (Jl. Padma Utara, across from Bali Niksoma, tel. 0361-756079) is also a fun, airy place to drink and hang out. Open 1800-2300 (no lunch). The Pub at the **Swiss Restaurant,** Jl. Pura Bagus Taruna (tel. 0361-754719), near Kuta Palace Hotel, jumps until it closes at 0300 or 0400. European crowd. One of the cheapest places to drink beer and watch the street crowds is **Loji II** open-air cafe and market; just Rp3000 for a large, cold *bir bintang.* Laid-back **Bruna Beach Bar,** next door (south side) to the Kulkul Hotel, features good local bands playing live reggae every night. Usually not that crowded and no cover charge.

Movies are shown in vast numbers of restaurants and bars all over Kuta and Legian, plus the latest world news, sports, music, and MTV videos. For example, at the **Bounty** (tel. 0361-754040) on Jl. Legian, movies are shown free every night at 2100, 2300, and 0100. Touts hand out fliers advertising films to be shown on a huge video screen that night, and some establishments even offer free transport for those staying in Kuta or Legian. The sailor-suited wait staff often becomes so absorbed in the movie that service slows to a crawl.

Dracula's Caberet Restaurant, two km north of Bemo Corner at Jl. Legian 494 (tel. 0361-751790), bills itself as the world's most outrageously funny caberet restaurant, complete with chains and rabbit traps, Igor, the three-foot, two-inch house hangman, a Chamber of Horrors, animated corpses, and over 200 sculptures ranging from tiny spiders to a giant Frankenstein. Feast on a sumptuous four-course meal, guzzle cocktails, and scream at the mad antics of the grotesque staff. Suitable for all ages. Dracula's doors open at 1900, and it turns into a disco after midnight. Bookings are handy.

One of the latest additions to the night scene is the **Bali Rock Cafe** (tel. 0361-754466) on Jl. Melasti near the Bali Intan. They boast international cuisine, friendly atmosphere, tranquil garden setting, ice cold imported beer, special meals and prices for children, an international chef, special buffet and party nights, starlight rock and roll dance floor, excellent hygienic standards. Open for lunch everyday at 1130. Lastly, there's a gigantic electronic arcade jammed with people inside the new **Matahari Legian Plaza,** Jl. Legian just up from the Mastapa Garden Hotel toward Kuta on the left.

SHOPPING

The shops along Jl. Legian in north Legian have more creative, unusual selections of clothes—and more realistic starting prices—than is generally the case in Kuta shops. If you're just starting out shopping, take a walk down Jl. Pura Bagus Taruna. The shops along this street have good selections, fair prices, and some of the best quality wares in the whole Kuta/Legian area—all self-contained on one windy side street. There are also several a/c, upscale shops behind glass windows. **Art Collection, Kembang Collection,** and **Kanuru,** are a few worth a look. For tribal Timorese arts and crafts, check out **Timor Arts** (Jl. Legian Tengah, tel. 0361-756018) and **Timor Art Shop** (Jl. Legian, tel. 0361-751537).

Run-of-the-mill clothes are also easy to find. Jalan Melasti, for example, is packed with cheap clothes shops and souvenir stalls selling everything from surfboard covers to *batik* patchwork quilts, from used books to sunglasses. In the shops where the clothing is actually made, they don't budge. If a dress costs Rp40,000, they might knock Rp5000 off—but don't count on it. You might as well shop in a fixed-price shop like **Baik Baik** (tel. 0361-751622), opposite the start of Jl. Melasti, which sells print shirts in bold colors, trendy men's pleated pants, and long-sleeved floral *batik* evening blouses for women incorporating some of the most original and za-niest designs on Bali. Arnold Schwarzenegger is an admirer of Baik Baik shirts and they export a lot of stylish products to Australia.

Also peruse **Mr. Bali** (tel. 0361-751232) for designer men's shirts, pleated Euro-pants, and safari shorts. The **Kidz Shop,** Banjar Legian Klod, specializes in made-to-order kid's clothing. Ni Wayan Kedi does good work. For ~~...~~

~~...~~ Indonesian cultured pearls, blue sapphires, rubies, emeralds, topaz, and aquamarines. The main shop (tel. 0361-71102 or 71112, ext. 3348) is in the Bali Hilton in Nusa Dua.

Sunglasses, hats, jewelry, seashells, and name plates are Zainol Arifin's specialties at **Zaz,** with two locations on Jl. Pura Bagus Taruna (nos. 9 and 506 in Hotel The Club). Also hand-made jewelry made-to-order. Legian has an excellent tape shop, **Lotus,** Jl. Legian 50 (tel. 0361-751532).

Leonard Karwelo's **Surya Prima Art Shop** on Jl. Pura Bagus Teruna deals in traditional *ikat* and antiques from Sumba, Flores, Timor, and Kalimantan. There are *many* shops selling very cheap *ikat* moneybelts and clothes. In fact, you'll fall in love with all the *ikat* around Legian and will want to go to Flores to see more for yourself. Jalan Tanjung Mekar is the shopping street in the Kuta area for furniture (mostly repros).

Kerta Book Store, Jl. Legian Tengah (tel. 0361-751001), is probably Legian's best store for new and used books, carrying novels in English and other languages at reasonable prices. On the corner of Jl. Legian and Jl. Benasari, diago-nally across from the Mastapa Inn, is another bookshop with the area's largest selection of new books in English, notably the Oxford Uni-versity Press "Oxford in Asia" series; also stocks English, American, and Australian.

...RVICES

...streets is an entire com-... cafes, restaurants, night-... vices, and craft shops. A ... e is located inside the ... down Jl. Benasari on ... permarket (tel. 0361-... tara is extremely well-... everything.

... **k Negara Indonesia** ... fety deposit boxes is ... utstanding bookshop ... iagonally across from ... To develop prints or ... ...ments, go to **Tia Photo** ...-751542) on Jl. Padma. Quick service, and they have a branch on Jl. Pura Bagus Taruna (same street as Kuta Palace Hotel).

Cafe Krakatoa (tel. 0361-752849, fax 752824), on Jl. Legian at the corner of Jl. Gado Gado, is also a business center where one can make international telephone calls, send and receive mail and faxes, type on electric or man-ual typewriters or computers. They also have a bulletin board.

Attend Sunday church service with Rev. Ketut Suyaga Ayub, S. Th., the manager of Orchid Garden Cottage (tel. 0361-752852). The **Legian Church,** on Gang Menuh off Jl. Legian, holds services at 1700. There's a **Protestant Church** (GKPB), tel. (0361) 224862, down the lane op-posite Gang Benasari (west of Mastapa Garden Hotel) with services by Preacher Sudira in English on Sunday at 1000. The Synod of Bali offers a tour; contact Wayan Sudira (tel. 0361-224862).

The **Kuta Fitness Center and Barbell Club** (KFC) on Jl. Tunjung Mekar 50 Q (tel. 0361-755448) charges Rp9000 for a one-time workout, Rp46,000 for one week, Rp86,500 for two weeks, Rp121,500 for three weeks, and Rp150,000 per month. Full member dues are Rp100,000. Open everyday 0800-0900 (except holidays). Aerobics programs are offered three days a week. **Milano** is a very popular traditional massage place opposite Jl. Melasti.

The Balinese **Jamu Traditional Salon** in the Kulkul Beach Resort (tel. 0361-752520) does facials, body soaks with flower and spice water, yogurt baths, and three different strengths of oil massages. Open 0900-2100. All treatments use 100% natural *jamu* products. Another traditional beauty salon, specializing in acne, hair care, and body massage, is the **Ratu Ayu** (tel. 0361-751660) in the Mastapa Garden Hotel on Jl. Legian. Open 0830-1900.

NORTH OF LEGIAN

SEMINYAK

The farther north you go from Legian, the less touristy and more mellow it becomes. Voyeur tourists from Java, who gawk at the European tourists and topless women, no longer target Kuta but now travel beyond Legian to Seminyak, which is like Legian five years ago. Get to Seminyak from Kuta by taxi for Rp5000. Though the recent appearance of luxury accommodations may eventually spell doom for the solitude of the northern beaches, right now Seminyak and points north are where you go to find relative tranquility. But keep your children away from the ocean in this area. The ferocious drop-off, in front of the Pesona Bali for example, is absolutely lethal.

Seminyak is where most Europeans and North Americans live who work in Bali's clothes/jewelry/handicraft export businesses, flying to Singapore every 60 days to renew their tourist visas. Many of these exporters live in rented bungalows far from the road amid rice fields, or lease property from a Balinese family to build their own thatched bungalow among the trees along the beach.

Accommodations

A big, clean, and comfortable place to get away from Legian yet enjoy nicely furnished bungalows, **Dhyana Pura** on Jl. Dhyana Pura (Box 1010, Interport Ngurah Rai, tel. 0361-731047, 731048, or 731049, fax 730683, e-mail intouch@denpasar.wasantara net.id) sits on four hectares of meticulously kept grounds near a romantic beach. Two types of rooms, old and new, have a/c, bathtubs, hot water, and cost Rp120,000. The older rooms have only fans and are a little tattered around the edges. Tariff includes continental breakfast in an attractive 24-hour restaurant and bar on a raised, open pavilion. Other strong points are the seaside pool and the open-air stage. The Dhyana Pura, with its big conference rooms and some dorm-style accommodations, is extremely well-suited for groups. Operated by a branch of the Bali Protestant Church, it is also a hotel training center for young Balinese Christians. They arrange Christian weddings, the couples outfitted in Balinese dress. From the hotel to Jl. Legian, there are about 10 good restaurants. The Dhyana Pura offers free shuttles into Legian and Kuta.

Next door, the **Raja Gardens** (Box 41, Kuta, tel./fax 0361-751494) is also very friendly, cheaper than the Dhyana Pura but without a/c and hot water, and it's not on the beach. Rp40,000 s, Rp50,000 d.

Puri Tjendana, on Jl. Dhyana Pura (Box 2037, Denpasar, tel. 0361-753574 or 753573, fax 753518), is a mammoth three-star international-style hotel and resort, like dozens of others along Bali's southern coast. Standard two-story bungalows are Rp150,000 s, Rp175,000 d; superior are Rp180,000 s, Rp200,000 d (with cooking facilities); suites are Rp350,000, plus 17.5% tax and service.

Legian Garden Cottage (tel. 0361-751876, fax 753405), at the end of Jl. Double Six, with lush gardens and big trees, has 22 cottage-style rooms for Rp75,000 s, Rp90,000 d. The three deluxe suites run Rp130,000, with TV and fridge in suites. No IDD connection, but calls can be put through hotel operator. Parking area. The grounds are patroled, bars on windows. The beach is only a three-minute walk, but it's also next to cliquey Double Six Disco, so it can be noisy at night. Blue Ocean Restaurant is nearby; other restaurants, pubs, and shops are within walking distance. Car rental and tour packages can be arranged.

Nusa di Nusa (off Jl. Dhyana Pura, Box 191, Denpasar, tel. 0361-751414) means "island in the island," which describes this serene, secluded hotel with a row of rice-barn shaped bungalows surrounded by tropical gardens. Rp60,000 s, Rp75,000 d with a/c, Rp50,000 s, Rp60,000 d with fan. Restaurant, pool, sunken bar, and snack bar on the beach. Rates subject to 15.5% tax and service. Also ask about the family houses available for monthly leasing. Facilities include kitchen, two or three bedrooms with private *mandi*, hot water, spacious living room.

For a little luxury, the **Bali Agung Village** (Jl. Dhyana Puri Sarinande, Box 2089, Kuta, tel. 0361-754267, fax 754269) in the rice fields near Bunga Seminyak is phenomenal. Separated by traditional Balinese compound walls, rooms have all the perks: TV, a/c, hot showers, private courtyard, garden terrace, luxurious bathroom, kitchen, fridge, room service. Tariff is Rp125,000 for a twin double bungalow, Rp325,000 for a villa. If you stay a few days, ask for a discount. Beautifully designed, the whole complex is small and cozy, very peaceful, and the decor is extremely tasteful. Good restaurant. Nice pool with swim-up bar. It's only a 500 meter walk to the beach and the Gado Gado.

Bali Subak Inn, on the same road, rents well-furnished a/c rooms for around Rp100,000. Swimming pool, laundry, tour desk, taxi counter, room service, and reasonably priced cafe attached. For a sweeping view of Kuta and Legian, take an elevator to the Sunset Bar at the top of the hotel, which is one of Kuta's highest buildings.

Designed to resemble a Balinese village, the spacious Indian-owned **Bali Oberoi** on Jl. Kayu Ayu (Box 351, Denpasar, tel. 0361-751061, fax 752791) has private, thatched-roof cottages, each with four a/c double rooms, on 35-acres of immaculate tree-filled grounds enclosed by a weathered stone wall. Designed by noted Australian architect Peter Muller, the Oberoi represented a radical new concept in hotel design when built in the early 1970s. One of the first ho-

tels on Bali to use traditional Balinese architecture for non-traditional purposes, it was built on a site once considered remote. Unfortunately, that was atop an ancient cemetery. Too advanced for its time, the hotel eventually went bankrupt, was put up for auction, sold for a ridiculously low price, and completely renovated. Today the property is an enclave of good taste, unobtrusive personal service, tranquility, and lovely splendor very much in theme with island life. Each villa has its own split-gate entrance; each room its own sumptuous garden bathroom with sunken bath partially open to the sky. The aesthetically pleasing bungalows start at US$225 (the ones facing the ocean are US$265). Deluxe (US$475) and presidential (US$650) villas have their own private pools and isolated beachfront. The five-star Oberoi is too exclusive for tour bookings. The Oberoi's open-air poolside Kura Kura is a first-class restaurant.

South of the Bali Oberoi on Jl. Dhyana Pura, the five-star **Bali Imperial** (Jl. Dhyana Pura, Box 384, Denpasar, tel. 0361-754545, fax 751545) looks like a gigantic ultra-modern Zen temple. The first hotel on Bali to be operated by a Japanese chain, it has 17 independent villas (US$150 and up per night) and exclusive maisonette suites (US$400-750) to attract Japanese upmarket clientele (80% of guests are Japanese). Built on 4.5 hectares of beachfront. Each bungalow has its own pool, jacuzzi, spacious bath. Embarrassingly devoted staff of 350, lush gardens, tranquil ponds, the last word in kitsch sculpture (a *kecak* dance in stone), restaurants serving Japanese, Balinese, and European cuisines, business services, shopping arcade, full recreational facilities, private beach. In Jakarta, reserve with Bali Imperial, Medco Building, Jl. Ampera Raya 20, Cilandak, Jakarta 12560, Box 757 JKS, tel. 7804766 ext. 505, fax 7804666.

Long-Term Stays: If you want to buy or rent real estate in the Seminyak/Legian/Kura area, contact **P.T. Bali In Touch,** Jl. Raya Seminyak 22, Seminyak (tel. 0361-731047, fax 730683). Also, Peter Rieger, a hard-working and conscientious property manager, has leads on hundreds of first-class holiday homes for rent or lease on Bali. He's available through **Private Villas Ltd.,** tel. (0361) 751546.

Your first choice for hotel-living should be **Lalu Village** (tel./fax 0361-752548), behind Alas Arum minimarket. Like living in your own full-service private villa in the middle of the rice fields, it's nine open-style bungalows nestled around the pool and gardens, featuring upstair master bedrooms, kitchen (caters to six people), lounge room, panorama windows, and breakfast balconies. The minimum area per villa is 200 square meters. Twenty-four-hour reception, phone and fax, babysitting and laundry, restaurant, room service, pool with built-in spa and children's pool, private parking, beach shuttle.

Another oasis of quiet and beauty is **Bunga Seminyak Cottage** (Jl. Camplung Tanduk, Seminyak, tel. 0361-751239, fax 752905) between the Nusa Di Nusa and the Dhyana Pura. Twelve elegant, thatched-roof rooms with private terraces within sound of the surf, marble bathrooms, hot water, self-adjusting a/c, telephone, color satelite TV, and tasteful *tempo doeloe*-style antiques in each room. Standard Rp100,000, cottage Rp150,000, superior Rp120,000. The best is Bungalow No. 3 at the end of the garden, beyond the main house. Guests commonly stay two to three months at a time. All rates include tax and service. No restaurant but your choice of continental or American breakfast. Pool, jacuzzi, postal service, laundry. The west end of this long, thin property faces the beach. Bicycles, motorbikes, and jeeps for rent. To get to there, go down Jl. Camplung Tanduk 800 meters toward the sea and turn left at the sign.

Food

The *warung* in Seminyak are much more reasonably priced than those in Kuta. There are several on the right as you head west past the Pesona Bali. The **Taman Sari** at the north end of Jl. Legian is owned by a German-Balinese couple. They specialize in a few authentic German dishes as well as some creative vegetarian dishes. Their formidable breakfast comes with whole-wheat bread, smoked ham, cheese, eggs, toast and jam, fruit, tea or coffee. If you want a pleasant, quiet atmosphere, this is it.

Ryoshi's (tel. 0361-261019) on Jl. Raya Seminyak 17 (between Jl. Double Six and Jl. Gado Gado) is a full a/c restaurant serving fresh, delicious sushi, tempura, and *robata* at surpris-

ingly low prices. Open everyday from 1200-2400. Clean, often crowded, take out also available. A late-night sushi bar is found in Goa 2001 almost opposite Ryoshi's.

Taj Mahal, Jl. Oberoi (tel. 0361-730525), bills itself as the only true Indian restaurant on Bali. Chef Jafar Dawood boasts that his fine ingredients, the secret of his success, are imported directly from India. Count on about Rp15,000 per person or Rp40,000 for three or four people for a meal of *tandoor, korma, naan, masala,* and curries. Extensive vegetarian section. Very comfortable and airy with a garden in back; enjoy the breeze coming in from the *sawah*. This very large place is located halfway down the road to the Oberoi Hotel on the left-hand side. Open 1900-2400 every night. With a little advance planning, they can easily accommodate a large party of 20 or so. Dance-party night every Wednesday at 1100; sometimes a DJ, other times live music. Also near the Oberai is the very chic **La Lucciola,** a beachfront open-air restaurant with an Italian flair, serving light Italian meals, trendy pizzas, polenta with pesto sauce, etc. Go for the sunset.

A very good Thai restaurant, the **Kin Khao** at Jl. Raya Seminyak 37 (fax 62-361-730824), is on the south side and about 150 meters from the Legian-side of Jl. Dhyana Pura. The chef/owner is from Thailand. Opens at noon and closes at 2100. Their menu is extensive.

Located in the middle of rice fields, **Warisan Resto** (tel. 0361-754710) has a romantic, candlelit atmosphere. Established in 1992 by three enterprising, astute women who wanted someplace out of the ordinary to go. You usually only hear about the Warisan, which means "heritage," by word of mouth. Its elegant nouvelle cuisine—avocado vinaigrette with blue cheese and walnuts, veal scallopini with prosciutto, sautéed baby lobsters, leg of lamb, tournedos artichoke hearts, and so on—is not really Italian but a continental, mixed-style. Dishes are beautifully presented and fine wines from California and France fill their racks. Count on about Rp50,000 per person for a full dinner. Opens every day at 1600. Tasteful art gallery and nice bar, the Aura, downstairs. Not a hustle-bustle place. To get there, turn right after the Oberoi turnoff and travel one km in the direction of Krobrokan. You'll see it on the left-hand side. It's about two km north of Legian. This is a sophisticated crowd, so dress accordingly. In the same class, while you're in the neighborhood, is the ultimate in hotel restaurant dining—the restaurant (not the coffee shop) in the Oberoi Hotel on Jl. Oberoi. A dinner for two without wine will cost around Rp200,000.

Another stylish eatery, **Cafe Seminyak** in the area above Jl. Double Six, with a color scheme reminiscent of Santa Fe, has indoor and outdoor seating, a comfortable bar, good music, and delicious Mexican food. Try the nachos and Key lime pie.

A great, casual place for Mexican food is **TJ's Cafe Seminyak** on Jl. Basangkasa, a few hundred meters beyond Jl. Dhyana Pura. You can't miss it because of the roomy dining patio in front. The guacamole, flauta, and chimichanga get very good grades, and their salsa top honors. Open for dinner only. Thursday is "Buffet Night." Friday is "Tequila Night." Very extensive bar menu, including cocktails and Corona in bottles. Good music, very clean, easy to find.

Cafe Krakatoa (tel. 0361-752849, fax 752824) on Jl. Raya Seminyak at the corner of Jl. Gado Gado, is a superb restaurant, especially for breakfast. Pricey but servings are generous. Here you can order "the best eggs benedict in S.E. Asia." Sunday brunch is 0900-1500, and on Sunday nights they lay out an outstanding buffet, complete with fine meats, bagels, lox, smoked salmon. Good service. Definitely caters to North American tastes. Watch CNN news by satellite mornings and afternoons, and the latest laser movies Mon.-Sat. at 2030. Kids Club matinee Saturday at 1530. Cafe Krakatoa also handles faxes, places telephone calls, and sends mail. Open Mon.-Sat. 0800-2330.

Next door to Krakatoa at Jl. Raya Seminyak 56 is **Temuku Bakery,** a health food store that carries freshly washed, organic salad lettuce, fresh herbs, homemade cakes, and excellent bread, including sourdough, raisin, and pumpernickel.

The **Alle Zoo** on Jl. Double Six, about halfway down on the right-hand side, across from the Blue Star, puts on a vegetarian buffet every Monday and Thursday evening starting at 1900 at a cost of only Rp4500. Get there on time because *lots* of people show up for this one.

In a hurry? **Pizzeria Rosticceria** on Jl. Dou-

ble Six sells authentic pizza by the slice for just Rp1500—served fresh, hot, and delicious. Or try one of their sandwiches served on homemade bread rolls with imported salami, prosciutto, and cheeses, freshly roasted beef, and cut salad. A range of desserts and great coffee available. They also do catering. A good place for real Indonesian food is **Warung Manja** (tel. 0361-756819) on Jl. Padma Utara, open 1800-2100. Free welcome drink and dessert.

Pica Pica (tel./fax 0361-751485), a little way down Jl. Dhyana Pura on the left (no. 7), is a Spanish *tapas* bar. Tapas, the name for an appetizer or light meal, is accompanied by Spanish drinks. The food is prepared by an expert "Tapiolo Gist." **El Mesón** is another Spanish restaurant at Jl. Raya Legian 80 A, Br. Pengabetan (tel. 0361-754261). Free transport in Kuta area.

A healthy alternative to the widespread bland and greasy Western food, the **Aladdin Restaurant** (Jl. Raya Seminyak, next to Golden Village 1), under a Casbah tent, offers the only Middle Eastern and Arabic cuisine *(halal)* on Bali. If you order *mezze,* you get to sample seven home-cooked dishes. Eat well for under Rp20,000. The owner moved from Canada, where he first established his business. Open everyday 1200-2400.

At **Gado Gado Restaurant,** Jl. Dhyana Pura (tel. 0361-730955), delicious Thai dishes are still the emphasis, but a mixture of grills, salads, and some nouvelle Western touches have been added, making it a menu offering great variety and excellent quality. Situated right on the beach, this is a clean, orderly, and romantic place to eat and socialize. A well-established crowd of expat residents meet here regularly for the sunset. Open for lunch and dinner, then it turns into a nightclub at midnight with lots of vendors.

Entertainment
The **A.J. Hackett Bungy Jump,** Jl. Pura Puseh, Legian Klod (tel./fax 0361-752658), offers free transport from Kuta and Sanur. Videos and photos of the horrific jump off a 45-meter tower are for sale after the event. Know that this enterprise has jumped over 500,000 clients without a mishap. Open 0900-2200.

Each night the fully air-conditioned **Jaya Pub,** Jl. Legian Kaja 2 (tel. 0361-730973), has live music (jazz, rock, oldies, country music) by the "Jaya Pub Band," the consummate entertainers "Hendrix and Lia" (the home band), and the "Surf Trio." The place is subject to spontaneous jam sessions in which visiting musicians, both amateur and professional, may join in. International menu. Happy hours are 1900-2000. Great atmosphere; Indonesians love it because it's air-conditioned and upmarket. Open until 0200.

Opposite the Jaya Pub, about 50 meters south of Goa 2001 is **Cafe Luna.** With a row of big motorcycles out front, and its humming crush of people, this is perhaps the trendiest late night hangout in south Bali; their motto is "to eat, drink and make noise." The street-front cafe is especially popular with Italians, expat entrepreneurs, and garment exporters, and is a little more expensive than most restaurants. Unequaled people-watching venue. Great interior and bar. Small menu of Italian dishes and cakes. It gets really crowded after 2000 and stays open until 0200; the kitchen closes at 0100.

Double Six (tel. 0361-753366) and the **Gado Gado** (tel. 0361-752255) alternate disco nights. There's no need to go to these nightclubs/pubs before midnight; after 0200 they are about the only places still open. Dine in their beachside pavilions at sunset or later—much later if you wish; they close at 0400. You can meet just about anyone in these clubs. The Italian food at Double Six is worth raving about, served until midnight. Also late-night pizzas. Located beside the A.J. Hackett Bungy Jump, you can eat to free entertainment—watching the screaming jumpers. On Sunday at sunset there's a live band, and the large pool is open to the public. On Monday, Friday, and Saturday nights, the club's first-class dance music draws big crowds. Cover charge is Rp15,000 on Saturday, Rp10,000 on Monday and Friday.

The **Strand Bar** on Jl. Double Six (five doors down from the Alle Zoo) exhibits art by local and Western artists on a monthly basis and sometimes hosts theatrical performances. Jazz on Thursday nights. Great cocktails; no cheap stuff. After the Strand closes, patrons go to the Blue Star to wile the night away.

On Sunday, Wednesday, and Friday a fish barbecue and live guitar are the draw at **Rum Jungle** (Br. Legian Kaja, tel. 0361-751992) on Jl. Pura Bagus Taruna off Jl. Legian, a secluded

and unique two-bar nightspot with a jungle hide-out atmosphere. Locals and tourists party here on a raised dance floor. Perfect for a beer, game of pool, or just hanging out watching CNN news. Also has a restaurant in front, a pool, and accommodations.

The **Balisani Suites,** on Jl. Batubelig (tel. 0361-752314) in Batubelig, puts on an occasional Asian buffet dinner with *legong* or the Ramayana Ballet poolside at 1930 for Rp30,000 per person. For reservations, call (0361) 754050, ext. 222. Also check out the program at **Warisan** (tel. 0361-754710), two km north of Legian, which puts on lively dress-up parties several times a month.

Shopping

Citra Batu Alam, Jl. Tanjung Mekar 27 A (Banjar Pelasa), tel./fax (0361) 738266, specializes in coral, fossils, minerals, eggs, old coins, and lapidary work. For pretty baubles, also check out **Ishmala Beadworks,** Golden Village 1, No. 16, 100 meters past Jl. Dhyana Pura (tel. 0361-752401).

Getting a lot of attention lately is the **Talismans of Power Gallery** on Jl. Raya Seminyak, a spectacular collection of ceremonial daggers, hand painted silk robes, crystal wands, gem-encrusted pill boxes, and unique silver and 22-carat gold jewelry. The creator of these spell-binding objects is the talented designer, internationally acclaimed ceramic sculptor, and white magician Jero Made Ariani. The eccentricity of the pieces appeal to a very select audience. Many of the rich and famous have acquired Jero's unusual and breathtakingly beautiful pieces—Cher, Kate Bush, Samantha Fox, Liza Minelli. Look for the shop with the black glass windows, which only increases the mystery that lies behind. Besides in the gallery, her work is also on display in the gift shops of Nusa Dua's Amanusa Hotel.

On the bottom floor of Warisan Resto is a very chic antique shop called the **Gallery,** which displays antiques, textiles, and curios to die for, and all in good condition.

Noteworthy are **Ikat Art,** Jl. Bakung Sari 12 (tel. 0361-752684 or 236722, fax 754959), for textiles, beads, and folk art from all over the archipelago; and **Homeboys,** with three locations on Jl. Legian at nos. 365 and 490, for technofashions and nice shirts. A small shop, **Biasa** (Jl. Raya Seminyak 39, tel. 0361-752945), owned by an American/Italian husband and wife team, creates very original unisex designs, makes clothes to order, and does a lot of wholesale.

Buy something to use and remember at **Dalung Village,** 3.5 km past Krobokan, which makes and sells ceramic products. Design your own, specify color, and pick the article(s) up a month later. Prices run Rp2,000 to Rp12,000. Near Dalung, in Banjar Tuka, you'll find **Father Shadeg,** an American who became an Indonesian citizen. He has one of the largest book collections on Baliana in the world.

Services
A **Bali Government Tourist Office** is on Jl. Bena Sari. Open 0700-1400, closed Saturday and Sunday. Personnel are reasonably well informed, but there's a shortage of handouts. A less orthodox but just as reliable source of information is Jon Zuercher at the Swiss Restaurant. The address is Jl. Pura Bagus Taruna (tel. 0361-751735), near the Kuta Palace Hotel. This is also the office of the Swiss Consular Agency.

For postal services, go to **Ida's Postal Agent** (tel. 0361-730092) at the start of the road to Seminyak after Legian. A convenient postal/shipping agent, **PT Yasa Utama International** (tel. 0361-752883, fax 222535), opposite Glory Restaurant. They sell stamps, postcards, mail parcels, clear customs, forward cargo, pack, truck, warehouse, handle export details. Another reputable Legian freight/mail handler is **Mangu Putra,** Jl. Benasari 7 (tel. 0361-225661).

The **Protestant Church** (Gereja Kristen Protestan) on Jl. Tanjung Mekar, Gang Menuh, Banjar Plasa, holds a service every Sunday morning at 1000. Refreshments served at conclusion of service so you have an opportunity to meet fellow Christians. If heading north on Jl. Legian, take the first right after the Mastapa and walk 500 meters; the church is on the left. Their phone is (0361) 754255.

For both men and women, **Bodyworks** offers massage and beauty treatments dispensed by professionals: manicures and pedicures (Rp11,000), full traditional massage and body exfoliation (a two-hour treat for Rp32,000), flowered herbal baths, and a hair cream bath that includes a head and neck massage (Rp17,500). A very pleasing environment with soothing music and colors. Open 1000-2200. For appointments, call tel. (0361) 751454.

The minimarket **Alas Arum,** Jl. Raya Seminyak (tel. 0361-751705 or 753133, fax 752214), has the largest stock of groceries, canned goods and beverages, toiletries, hardware, and household goods in the area—essentials for the expat resident. Lots of imported items. Also baked goods, tapes, appliances. Prices are much higher than in the Denpasar supermarkets, but you're paying for the convenience.

North of Seminyak
A few kilometers beyond Seminyak is Krobokan; the *puri* here contains over 75 temples. Tucked away in the village itself, next to rice fields, is moderately priced **Taman Ayu Cottage,** Jl. Petitingit (tel. 0361-730111 or 730112, fax 730113). From Krobokan, take the back road via Gaji north to Sempidi—rural Bali at its best. To do a complete loop, turn east from Krobokan to Denpasar, then back to Kuta.

A string of small fishing villages stretches along the coast north of Seminyak, each with at least one large and several smaller hotels. The isolation of these hotels is at the same time their drawback and chief asset. The drawback is you need transportation to get there and away. This is somewhat resolved by the hotels' free shuttle service to and from Legian and Kuta up to six times a day; metered taxis can also be called from the lobbies. Their asset is they're close enough to the nightlife, shopping, and services of Legian and Kuta, yet far enough away so that all the activity and noise won't disturb you.

PETITINGIT

On the estuary of a lazy river, along the beach northwest of Kuta, is unusual **Pura Petitenget** (*tenget* means "holy ground"). Built entirely of white coral, this traditional temple was founded by one of the first Hindu-Javanese priests, Sanghyang Niaratha, on his journey along the beach to Uluwatu in ancient times. After defeating a local *bhuta,* this Balinese-Hindu saint invited the people of the village of Krobokan to build a temple here to commemorate the place the sacred books of India, the Vedas, were first brought to Bali. Pura Petitenget shares a common forecourt with the *subak* temple of Pura Ulun Tanjung. By a bizarre coincidence, this was also the spot where the first Dutchman, Captain Cornelis de Houtman, set foot on Bali in 1596.

Accommodations

A few kilometers beyond the private road to the Oberoi—about where the rice fields start—is the three-star **Pesona Bali Beach Hotel and Cottages** on Jl. Kayu Ayu (Box 1085, Denpasar, tel. 0361-753914, fax 753915). Popular with European tour operators for its 69 rooms (US$70-200), seven bungalows (US$110-180), big pool, coffee shop, game room, and lobby in the shape of a huge *bale banjar*. The restaurant serves a continental breakfast for Rp14,500, American breakfast for Rp16,000, lunch Rp25,000, dinner Rp30,000, and a mind-boggling once-weekly *rijstaffel* for Rp25,000 (make reservations by asking for ext. 238). All prices subject to 21% tax and service. The strength of the Pesona is its isolation. There are only a few *warung* and practically no shops nearby. The famous Petitenget temple is just a 10-minute walk north on the road.

Safely cushioned from the Legian/Kuta scene is two-star, villa-style **Puri Ratih** (Jl. Puri Ratih, Petitinget, Krobokan, Box 1114, Tuban, tel. 0361-751546, fax 751549), winner of the "RCI Design Award." This property features eight individual, self-contained, *wantilan*-style bungalows, which resemble private homes and incorporate every modern convenience. Junior suites, 50-square-meters with second-floor bedrooms and outdoor terrace; deluxe lanais, 75-square-meters; lanai suites, full-size kitchen and upstairs study; and luxurious villas, 180-square-meters and sleeps six. Prices fluctuate with the season. The norm is US$288-320 in the high season.

The Puri Ratih has a very exclusive feel to it. They don't accept groups; its charm is its small hotel atmosphere. Even when the hotel is full you seldom see other people unless you're sharing the main pool. All bungalows are spacious, with a/c, outdoor living and dining areas, Bali-style bath, original paintings, color TV, electronic safes. Some have kitchenettes and fridge. An ocean view restaurant, library, squash court, and pools with water spouting from Balinese

statues complete the facilities. The nearest places to eat are a small *warung* and the **Agape Seafood Restaurant** up the road. The latter has lousy food and is always empty. Most guests just eat on the verandas of their bungalows. Go for the basil chicken or *sate lilit* (minced spiced seafood)—both excellent.

BATUBELIG

All the hotels in this neighborhood are luxury amid seclusion. A prime example is **Balisani Hotel** (Jl. Padma Utara, tel. 0361-752314 or 754050, fax 754055), on the same quiet and out-of-the-way road as the Rama Garden Cottages. Competitively priced for its class, this small, alluringly designed hotel has a sort of faded, crumbling charm to it—like a poor man's version of a Nusa Dua hotel. Standard rooms are Rp100,000 s, Rp110,000 d, cottages, with king-size bed, are Rp140,000, and two-story villas Rp160,000. High season supplement: Rp25,000. Rates do include tax and service charge. TV, intermittent hot water, working sauna, attractive grounds, nice swimming pool next to the ocean, swim-up bar, small gym, massage service, clothes and souvenir shops, business center, moneychanger, barbecue dance nights. Their restaurant looks over the pool. Very good and varied breakfast and mostly Western menu, but slow, dreamy service. Water sports, including surfing, can be easily arranged, but no swimming in the sea out front as the undertow is too treacherous. You'll need either their taxi or shuttle services, which run from 0900-2100 five times daily, as Legian is five km and Kuta eight km away.

A significant discovery is **Batubelig Beach Bungalows** (Jl. Batubelig, Krobokan, Box 2022, tel. 0361-730078), just 300 meters from the beach. This small, quiet accommodations charges only Rp30,000 for any of three twin-bed or double-bed traditional bungalows. Units have open-air bathrooms, fans, mini-kitchens, and cute yards. A pleasant cafe offers a simple breakfast of fruit salad, toast, butter, jam, and coffee or tea for Rp4000. Quite near the Balisani Hotel, so you can use all their facilities. The **Chandra Car Rental** is also nearby (tel. 0361-750078). A taxi from Batubelig costs

Rp7000 to Legian or Rp4000 to Goa 2001.

Just north of the Kuta Jaya, the large **Bali Intan Cottages** (Jl. Melasti 1, Box 1002, Denpasar, tel. 0361-751770, fax 751891) is the area's closest upmarket hotel to Kuta and caters to an almost strictly European clientele. It has 164 rooms with private balconies in two-story blocks for US$90 s, US$120 d, plus family suites for US$200. Everything is expensive because everything has a surcharge, telephone, meals, Rp7000 for a large Bintang. The big, sprawling complex has a grand *wantilan*-style lobby, restaurants, coffee shops, bars, pools, walkways, pavilions with gardens interspersed, and two rows of under-patronized souvenir shops with bored saleswomen sitting outside. Plus there are many facilities for the fitness-minded—table tennis, tennis and squash courts, seaside pool. Like dozens of other hotels of its type, but it has the edge because of its superb location between the Bali Sani and the Puri Ratih.

CANGGU

Pronounced "chan-GOO," the name is derived from the Samprangan Chronicles—part-myth, part-history—which relates stories of ancient Balinese kings. About three km north of Petitinggit, Canggu, the name of the village two km inland, is coastal Bali at its best. Known for sunbathing and surfing, Canggu is for those looking for a quiet beach. The few people hawking wares—12 at most—are slightly better behaved than at Kuta. Life is easy and relaxing. The waves here are big, though. Don't swim during high tide, and you must be a good swimmer to swim any other time.

Fishermen here still use the beach and sea for their livlihood. Take a walk to the north and you'll run into some important and attractive sea temples and more fishing villages where life goes on relatively undisturbed. Cremation ceremonies can sometimes be seen right in front of the hotels, which just doesn't happen anymore in Kuta or Sanur. Also, lots of wildlife, thousands of birds and butterflies, Roman Polanski has a house just down the beach, on Sunday morning dancers train on the street—onlookers welcome—and traditional temple ceremonies are ongoing.

Accommodations and Food

There are only three hotels along Berawa Beach; in order of rank, they are the Dewata Beach Hotel, the Legong Keraton Beach Cottages, and the Bolare. The Bolare and the Legong Keraton get Dewata's overflow. Travel agents don't send people here because they think Canggu is too far away from Kuta and Denpasar. Good!

The hotels' staffs are relatively callow rural youth who live in nearby Canggu village, thus the hotels have a warm and personal touch. As far as development is concerned, the hotels are *all* that's here. From their front you see the ocean and from their back you see rice fields.

As far as food is concerned, you're pretty much forced to eat in the hotels as there aren't any competing restaurants around. Not only do you have to pay for food but also a punishing 15-21% tax and service. There's only one *warung* at the beginning of the road to the Dewata and Bolare. It starts serving coffee and *nasi campur* at 0900, but has a droll, depressing, unkempt atmosphere and the *warung* dogs bark at you at night when you go for a stroll.

Between Legian and Canggu, the best thing about the small 21-room **Bolare Beach Bungalows** (Box 256, Denpasar 80001, tel./fax 730258) is its location on a white beach, surrounded by coconut palms and rice fields. The hotel's Bali-style bungalows are equipped with a/c, private bath, hot water, shower, spacious patio, and your own garden. Tariff is Rp100,000 s, Rp140,000 d; suites are Rp150,000. Rooms are a little damp-smelling, and the hotel isn't as snappy, clean, and well-managed as the Dewata Beach next door, but it's lower in price. Prices don't include 15.5% tax and service or breakfast.

The Bolare offers great sunsets from the beach bar at the small pool and occasional cultural shows. Hotel shop, travel agency, car rental service, library, launderette, doctor on call, drugstore, safety deposit box, and restaurant. Breakfast is Rp12,000, seafood, Asian, and Western meals are Rp4000-15,000. Only two shuttles per day, 0900 and 1900. A specialty of the Bolare is marrying Westerners, which costs US$1000 and includes lunch, dinner, all particulars for four people, traditional Balinese costuming, travel to Tanah Lot for a photograph, photo album, champagne, and priestly blessings. They've already married more than 100 couples, and the majority of guests are honeymooners.

The very quiet, 20-room **Legong Keraton Beach Cottages** (Box 617, Kuta, tel. 0361-730280, fax 730285) is a cheaper version of the Dewata, but more in tune with the island's rhythm and decor—*alang-alang*-thatched-roofed bungalows no taller than a palm tree, authentic Balinese furniture, woodworking, coral masonry, tile verandas. Beautiful tropical landscape, nice beachfront lawn, private beach, clear blue pool, sunken bar. Rather high-priced Balinese, Asian, and European specialties available in the delightful open-air restaurant. Hotel shuttle service operates only on Wednesday and Saturday (dropoff 1000, pickup 1600). All other times it costs Rp17,000 for dropoffs and pickups. It's a five-minute walk to the beach (good for surfing), or a 45-minute ride to the airport (free transfer), and 60 minutes to Denpasar. It doesn't have TVs or newspapers like the Dewata, but rooms do have full a/c, bath, shower, hot water, fridge, and IDD phones. It always runs below capacity (35%). Rates are Rp130,000-200,000 s or d, the super deluxe cottages with two bathrooms and jacuzzis being the most expensive. All prices subject to 15.5% tax and service, but continental breakfast included. All credit cards accepted.

The best of the Berawa Beach hotels, and perhaps Bali's most remote four-star beach hotel, is the **Dewata Beach Hotel**, one of the 3,400 Best Western hotels world-wide. The hotel staff is made up of 300 employees, for the most part disarmingly shy boys and girls from Canggu. Even the general manager is laid-back; sit and have a chat with him at the bar. Dewata is divided into the main building and the cottages. The two executive suites in the main building, at Rp345,000 per day, are much better value than the single rooms in most of Bali's most luxurious hotels. There's a view of the sea and you have your own private terrace. The furniture is Western. There are 25 cottages (116 rooms) in an immaculate, thriving, and tranquil garden—except in the morning when it's alive with chattering birds. They use no pesticides and grow vegetables for the restaurant. The hotel has a 24-hour coffee shop. Canggusari Restaurant serves an Asian buffet breakfast and the Khayangan has a European breakfast menu, both catering to differing tastes. No MSG. The food is not brilliant but okay. The winners on the menu are the pasta dishes and *sate campur* presented at your table in a brazier. To all prices add 21% tax and service. The Dewata has three bars, one of them *karaoke,* a kids' playground, tennis courts. Shuttle service six times daily to Kuta; for partygoers the last pickup from Kuta is at 0230!

Transportation

From Kuta, Canggu is about a 1.5-hour walk at low tide or a 20-minute drive (16 km). To get into Denpasar, you don't have to go to the time and trouble of going via Kuta. Just take one of the hotel shuttles two km from Canggu to Krobokan village, then a microlet 12 km (Rp500) further into Stasiun Gunung Agung in Denpasar from where you can hitch a *bemo* into city center.

Canggu makes a good base from which to explore coastal or inland Bali. Distances: 20 km to Sanur, 26 km to airport, 36 km to Nusa Dua, 38 km to Ubud. A beautiful 34-km-long road winds through villages to Tanah Lot. You can also walk north to Tanah Lot through a completely natural area in a little less than two hours during low tide (five days before the full moon) if you start out by 1400.

If you get stuck in Kuta/Legian, it'll cost you Rp15,000 to get back to Canggu. If it's low tide, reach Canggu by motorbike or bicycle along the beach. Or take a *bemo* down Jl. Legian toward Krobokan, then turn west toward Berawa Beach. The most convenient way to reach Berawa's hotels is by taxi.

NORTH OF DENPASAR

Near Sempidi, north of Denpasar on the road to Kapal, are beautifully decorated *pura desa* and *pura dalem.* Sempidi's *pura puseh* is known for its very colorful *odalan.* Also visit the cut-rock cave **Goa Krebing Langit** on the east bank of the river between Sempidi and Lukluk. Lukluk's *pura dalem* is worth a visit; its decoratively painted bas-reliefs portray mischievous village scenes as well as mythological themes.

Kapal

Sixteen kilometers north of Denpasar on the main road northwest to Tabanan (get a *bemo* from Ubung station) lies Kapal, a ceramics center that produces folksy, gaudily painted red clay articles as well as temple ornamentation and motifs used all over Bali. Stores lining the main street sell everyday, primitive-style ware including vases, *satay* holders, bowls, ashtrays, drinking flasks, plates, and lamp bases.

All the pieces are thrown on foot-operated potter's wheels. The prices are good, but the ware is brittle because it is unglazed and not very well fired. The best ceramic shop is **Jati Agung.** Though small, it carries better stuff than even the government ceramics research center in Suwung near Nusa Dua. Find Chinese-style handmade plates, cups and pots—very original designs.

Kapal's numerous roadside shops are also the place to buy gray, volcanic-stone statuary of mythological demons, gnomes, deer, and religious figures such as a brightly painted Buddha statue, all used for embellishing family gardens and shrines. Also sold are such common architectural motifs as balustrades, wall cappings, curlicues, and cornerstones.

While in Kapal, visit the unusually decorated and intricately carved **Pura Sada,** 200 meters south of the main road (turn in at sign near market). Dating from the Majapahit period, this originally was an old dynastic sanctuary for the Mengwi royalty. Destroyed by the 1917 quake, the original building was restored in 1948-49 by the Archaeological Service with the help of the villagers. The split gateway and the 16-meter-high tiered tower inside the *pura* are constructed much like the *candi* of Java.

As on Javanese *candi,* there is a small niche in front for visiting deities during temple celebrations. A big tree stands in the center. Along with a few of the sculptures, only the restored *candi bentar,* with its finely carved decoration and detailed *kala*-head, is truly ancient. The split-gate leads to the main courtyard where you'll find another gate to the west leading to the inner court. Here are 16 shrines and 54 stone seats—similar to megalithic ancestral shrines—which commemorate followers of the king who died at sea. The temple is dedicated to Ratu Sakti Jayengrat, the "Divine World Conqueror."

Mengwi

Sixteen kilometers northwest of Denpasar, Mengwi is Rp600 by minibus from Denpasar's

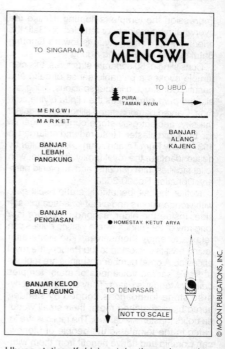

© MOON PUBLICATIONS, INC.

Ubung station. If driving, take the main road to Tabanan through Kapal to the Mengwi turnoff, then proceed north. This quiet town is important as the former seat of a long dynasty of kings; its large temple belongs to the group of Bali state or "national" temples. Since its beginnings in 1634 under Raja I Gusti Agung Anom until its demise in 1891, Mengwi was a separate kingdom that extended its political power as far as Blambangan, East Java. The dynasty was ultimately defeated by the neighboring Balinese kingdoms of Badung and Tabanan.

The elegant **Pura Taman Ayun** is the second largest temple complex on Bali, and one of the island's most beautiful shrines. This trim, impressive garden complex lies only one-half km east of the main highway (turn in at the market), accessible by a long walkway. The original structure dates from around 1740 when ruler Cokorda Munggu built what was to be his state temple on high ground. It's partly surrounded by a wide moat with lotuses, which gives the impression the temple is floating. Unlike the overwhelming majority of temples on Bali, the orientation of Taman Ayun is toward Gunung Batukau and not Gunung Agung.

Consisting of 50 separate structures, this clan temple evokes a palpable sense of calm and beauty. Constructed in four spacious, rising levels, the *pura* symbolizes the Hindu divine cosmos. Carved demons stand silhouetted against the sky; ancient gray stone contrasts against the brick-red plaster. Restored and enlarged in 1937, today Pura Taman Ayun is looked after by descendants of the royal family. It's clean, with toilet facilities, trim gardens, and an orchid nursery. Donation Rp500-2000.

Notice the tall, beautifully crafted split gate with wooden doors and a half *kala*-face to each side. Inside the older, second courtyard is a long row of 29 shrines where visiting deities can relax and enjoy themselves. The stone altar facing east is dedicated to Ibu Paibon, the royal ancestor. A great number of shrines are replicas of Bali's sacred volcanoes or major temples built by Mengwi's rulers. They sit on moss-covered stone foundations, topped by slender, tiered black-thatched roofs, their small wooden doors masterfully carved. The replicas are located in the temple so the people of Mengwi can worship and derive benefit from them without the expense and trouble of traveling to the originals. Uluwatu, for example, is symbolized by the 11-tiered *meru* in the far right-hand corner. This inner court also displays a superbly carved stone *trimurti padmasana* (three-god throne). To the left are various *bale* for visitors, dancers, priests, and musicians. Climb the small tower in the lower southwest corner of the complex for the best view of the temple, moat, and surroundings.

There's a lot going on in and around this complex. Hire a little boat and tour the sanctuary from the moat. Pavilions display paintings for sale as well as postcards, textiles, terra-cotta figurines, and fashions. Before the entrance is a huge *wantilan* where cockfights, *barong* dances, and other cultural events are staged. Farther on is a big collection of orchids; on the banks of the moat grow fruit trees and perfumed flowering *cempaka* and frangipani. Visit Pura Taman Ayun when the three-day *odalan* occurs; watch hundreds of women file over the bridge into the courtyard carrying high, multicolored offerings. The temple filled with people, music, dance, and processions is a magnificent sight.

The Mandala Wisata ("Museum of Cremation"), near the Taman Ayun temple, contains palm-woven offerings. Climb on the small raft pulled by ropes for a ride across the moat to the rather high-priced and touristy Royal Garden Restaurant. Visit only if tour buses aren't parked out front. The Indo/Chinese food is delicious and the view over the moat and the tall *meru* towers superb. Or eat more cheaply and authentically in the market or at the *bemo*/bus station.

Accommodations

A very nice homestay, the only one in town, lies south of the temple in Banjar Alang Kajeng. The owner, I Ketut Arya, is informative and helpful; six rooms at Rp8000 s, Rp10,000 d, breakfast included, other meals for around Rp1000. Ketut is quite willing to show his guests around Mengwi, Tanah Lot, the Monkey Forest of Sangeh, the cattle market, or take them on a walk through the rice fields and perhaps even arrange for them to participate in a religious event.

Vicinity of Mengwi

On the main road south to Kapal, just before town, is a strikingly painted *pura puseh* with relief panels on the outside wall portraying scenes from the Ramayana; also check out the long *bale gede.* Once every three days a *pasar hewan* is held in Bringkit, 1.5 km north of Kapal; see the *pura dalem* nearby that receives unusually high offerings.

It is time-consuming to take public transport from Mengwi east to Ubud through all the country towns. In Abian Semal, the road from Mengwi meets the main road from Denpasar to Sangeh. Two km before Sangeh is the village of Blahkiuh whose claim to notoriety is a particularly large and holy *waringin* tree just east of the intersection.

Sangeh

Travel fifteen kilometers beyond Mengwi on the road to Gunung Catur, Rp1000 by *bemo* from Wangaya station in Denpasar to Sangeh's parking lot, filled with Super-Kijangs and Suzuki Katanas and surrounded by a big souvenir shop scene. Here, under towering 30-meter-tall trees, is the holy Monkey Forest, with three clans of sacred, very aggressive monkeys crawling over lichen-covered Bukit Sari ("Nectar of the Mountains") Temple. Built by the royal family of Mengwi in the 17th century, the temple is dedicated to the god Vishnu and was initially used as a place of meditation. Restored in 1973, today it functions primarily as a *subak* temple where offerings to agricultural deities are made. Notice the old statue of Vishnu's mount Garuda, and the relief of a Japanese shooting at an airplane.

Legend says the monkey general Hanuman seized the giant cosmic mountain Mahameru in order to deal the evil demon Rawana a death blow. A piece of mountain with monkeys still clinging to it fell on Sangeh and there they live to this day. There are 10 hectares of *pala* (nutmeg) trees here, a species not native to Bali; their presence has never been explained, thus contributing to the mystery of the place. Another puzzle is that no monkey bodies or skeletons are ever found.

Buy a bag of peanuts and watch for the King of the Monkeys; also watch out for monkey claws and teeth (carry a stick). Don't get too close to their young and hang on to your glasses, cameras, and hats, and for God's sake don't go with money sticking out of your pockets. These descendants of Hanuman's warriors will grab at any protrusion and won't return a thing unless you divert them with a stick, peanuts, or a banana. Pestering peddlers and begging children are even worse.

Between the tour buses, absorb some of the quiet and serenity of Sangeh's magnificent forest. Walk down the pathway by the river gorge in back. From Sangeh, take a rocky side road that crosses over to Mengwi. From Sangeh an unpaved path leads through the rice fields to Ubud. A poor road leads from Sangeh to Ubud.

North of Sangeh is the rugged Petang district, with lots of fresh air, coffee, cloves, vanilla, and chocolate. Beyond, climb up to Pelaga through rice fields, vegetable gardens, bamboo stands, and more plantations.

THE BUKIT PENINSULA

Bukit ("Hill"), a lemon-shaped peninsula at the southernmost extremity of the island, is a dry, rocky land. Oval-shaped and about eight kilometers from north to south, 17 kilometers from east to west, with a maximum elevation of 200 meters, Bukit offers limestone caves, temples perched on the edge of dizzying cliffs, stretches of immaculate isolated beaches, and a dramatic coastline pounded by Bali's most challenging surf. This 100-square-kilometer tableland of stunted bush and prickly pear cactus once lay at the bottom of the sea but now sits 100-200 meters above sea level, its sides in the south rising 100 meters straight up. For years the Dutch called this curious windswept geographic feature Tafelhoek, the "Tableland." Bukit might once have been a separate island that eventually attached itself to the mainland. It shares climate, topography, and geology with Nusa Penida, a small island off Bali's southeast coast. Standing out in stark contrast to the lush, alluvial plains of southern Bali, the barren, underpopulated Bukit plateau has no streams and the land cannot be artificially irrigated. On the clifftops of the un-

developed west and south coasts are remains of ancient sea temples. Inland, stone blocks are mined from karst quarries.

There's a drastic difference between the dry season (May-Sept.) and the rainy season (Oct.-April). During the dry, few crops grow, there's almost no surface water, the area is denuded of vegetation, and the concrete water cisterns are empty. In the wet season (average 65 rainy days per year), rice, manioc, sorghum, corn, soybeans, peanuts, beans, coconuts, bananas, oranges, and flowering trees grow out of the thin layer of topsoil. Extensive erosion has created caves and deep cracks in the rocky earth. When the Nusa Dua complex was started, 14 deep bore holes had to be drilled and a water treatment plant built to provide the resort with a source of potable water.

With the building of the spectacular Bali Cliff Hotel, the peninsula made the transition from copra and lime to tourists and surfers. Today Bukit's flat, far eastern corner is the ritzy beach resort of Nusa Dua with its dozen or so four- and five-star hotels strung out along an idyllic,

BUKIT
PENINSULA

TELUK JIMBARAN

BENOA HARBOR

SUWUNG MANGROVE SWAMPS

TANJUNG BENOA

NUSA DUA

BUALU

SEE "TANJUNG - NUSA DUA" MAP

SEAWEED FARM

PURA GEGER

JL. DARMAWANGSA

BEMO TERMINAL

BALI EDELWEISS (AUSTRIAN RESTAURANT)

SAWANGAN

PURA KARANG BONA

KAMPIAL

TV TOWER

PURA TEGEH SARI

TV TOWER

UNGUSAN

SATELLITE DISH

PURA BATU PAGEH

JIMBARAN

PURA MUAYA

PURA GUAGONG

TV TOWER

(163 m)

YOUTH HOSTEL

PURA SARIN BUANA

PUNCAK PESONA RESTAURANT

SALAKAN

BONGOL

BAKUNG

PURA MASUKA

BALI CLIFF HOTEL

TELUK SAIT

GUA PETENG

G. INGAS (203 m)

PURA BALANGAN

BALANGAN

CENGILING

BINGIN

PAK RODA'S WARUNG

PAK LOTENG'S MASSAGE

CEPLUK SILVER

MICROWAVE STATION

PECATU

(184 m)

PADANG PADANG

BANGKET

SULUBAN

PURA ULUWATU

(125 m)

© MOON PUBLICATIONS, INC.

2 km

0

five-kilometer-long stretch of palm-lined, white-sand beach.

History

Bukit has played an important role in Balinese mythology. Legend tells how the gods created Bali by taking a piece of land from Java, then shaping the island to make it hospitable to human beings. They created the high mountains of Batukau in the west, Agung in the east, and Bukit in the south.

In ancient times, Bukit was considered a dangerous area where great herds of wild *banteng* and water buffalo roamed, driven south by population pressure. Bukit served as hunting grounds for pheasant, wild boar, and deer for the rajas of Denpasar and Mengwi; cattle still graze there. So inhospitable is this land that criminals, political enemies, and debtors were once banished here.

SURFING BUKIT

Since the early 1970s, Bukit has been a popular destination for surfers, beachcombers, seekers of solitude, and budget travelers. It boasts some of southeast Asia's best surfing beaches, and is considered among the top ten surfing spots in the world. Be prepared for huge breakers, which can dwarf those of Kuta and Sanur. A bonus is the dramatic backdrop of sheer cliffs which start at the northwest corner of Bukit and extend all the way around to just south of Nusa Dua.

Go early in the morning to catch the best waves. The best time to surf is the dry season from April through October. Strong winds during the wet season make surfing impossible. There are no official accommodations, and only one *losmen* at Bingin. But if the surf is really good, surfers customarily crash on the beach or at one of the full-service beachside *warung*. Bukit *warung* rent surfboards (Rp5000) and sell Indonesian *nasi campur* and simple Western meals, iced drinks, and a bed for the night. The best *nasi campur* is at **Warung Widari** in Pecatu; only Rp1000.

It costs little or nothing to surf. At most spots, the surfer need only pay a "board carrier" Rp10,000 or so. This work provides employment to local youths; there's even an official Board Carrier Association. Motorbike drivers will transport surfers and boards to the beach for Rp10,000-15,000. Drop in at the **Surf Information Warung** in Bongol and ask for Hank; he runs a *warung* at Balangan and provides guide services to all of Bukit's surfing spots.

Balangan

This long, beautiful, white-sand surfing (left-hander) beach, accessible by four-wheel drive or motorbike, lies six km northwest of Bongol. From Balangan's parking lot, it's a 10-minute walk to the beach—hard to find, as there's no sign. Six *warung* here. **Hank's Hangout,** which sells simple meals like fried rice, is right on the beach. A cave temple also sits on the beach. Walk up to Lookout Point for a grand panorama over Bukit and the airport.

Bingin

A great place for surfing (hollow left-hander) and relaxing. From the main highway in Pecatu, take the dirt road to Bingin; this is the same pretty, shady country road you take to Padang Padang. On the way, refresh yourself with a cold drink or *nasi campur* at **Pak Roda's Warung** at the turnoff to Bingin; from this *warung* to the homestay the road is seriously rutted. **Homestay Wayan,** just below the parking lot at Bingin, has three rooms (Rp15,000 s, Rp20,000 d), a living room for guests, small restaurant, veranda, and a nice garden. There's a river below the homestay, and you can take fresh showers thanks to the homestay's water tank. From the homestay it's a 10-minute walk to the beach.

Padang Padang

From the parking lot, it's a short walk to the caves where you start surfing; really nice beach here too. There are at least 10 *warung* at Padang Padang selling jaffles, noodle soup, cold drinks, and the like. Ketut Sugi's *warung* has the best selection. Kelly's Bar is also okay.

On the road to Padang Padang there are two places of note. **Pak Loteng** gives massages and administers traditional herbs. The other is **Cepluk Silver,** which produces made-to-order Gianyar-style silver.

Suluban

Called Ulu by surfers, this is the most famous—and crowded—surfing spot on the island. Waves sometimes reach eight meters in height with straight-line swells. Purportedly one of the best left-handers in the world, for daredevils and goofy-footers only. A footpath, which starts 200 meters before Pura Uluwatu's parking lot, leads down to the beach; look for the sign Suluban Beach 2 km. Boys will offer to carry your surfboard and equipment for the 45-minute trip. Motorbikes will take you most of the way down, but this is a narrow, dangerous path so drive cautiously if you're on your own. From the covered motorcycle parking area at the end of the trail, climb down to the large sea cave at the bottom of the cliff, which opens to the ocean.

There are some other isolated and lovely beaches for surfing, sunbathing, and swimming to the southeast and east of Uluwatu. One such beach, with outstanding surf, is Nyang Nyang; the turn is about 2.5 km inland.

Bali Cliff Resort

The first major hotel built on Bukit is set high above the crashing surf of the Indian Ocean just south of Ungusan, 25 minutes from Ngurah Rai Airport. Seven people died in the hotel's construction—they are considered *tumbal,* which means that they are more than sacrifices, they are offerings. It's said President Suharto's son Bambang invested in this new, five-star hotel. The only hotel on Bali offering views of both the sunrise and sunset, its 200 beautifully appointed rooms range from superior (Rp360,000) to executive (Rp925,000) to various classes of luxu-

rious suites (Rp945,000-Rp4 million). Special features include an elaborate laser/video entertainment program, in-house doctor, bank, Japanese restaurant, pizzeria, outdoor stage, and art market. The Olympic-size pool comes right up to the edge of a 75-meter-high cliff, water cascading down its face. A "travelator" (outdoor elevator) lowers guests to the beach; decent surfing nearby. A walkway from the hotel leads to the sacred cave temple of Pura Batu Pageh. Call (0361) 771992 for reservations (really not necessary as it runs at only 30% capacity).

PURA ULUWATU

On the south coast of Bali is a whole series of sea temples—Tanah Lot, Pura Sekenan, Pura Rambut Siwi, Pura Petitenget, and Pura Uluwatu. All pay homage to the guardian spirits of the sea, but none is more spectacular than Uluwatu.

This well-maintained temple, one of the *sadkahyangan* group of the holiest temples of Bali, is the least overwhelmed by tourism and commercialism because of its remote location on the southwestern tip of Bukit.

For years entrance was forbidden to anyone but the prince of Badung. He visited right up until his death at the hands of the Dutch in the *puputan* of 1906. Administered now by a royal family in Denpasar, Uluwatu actually belongs to the Balinese people, but is particularly sacred to fishermen, who come here to pray to

Uluwatu

the sea goddess Dewi Laut. Legend has it the temple is actually a ship turned to stone. The full name of the temple is Pura Luhur Uluwatu, which roughly translates as "The Temple Above the Stone," an accurate description as this temple perches on a cliff overhanging the Indian Ocean 90 meters below.

At the end of a beautiful country road, Uluwatu may be reached by public *bemo* from Kuta or Tegal station in Denpasar. From Kuta, it'll cost Rp12,000-15,000 (20 km) to charter a vehicle, though it's faster if you take a motorbike. From the parking lot, walk 300 meters down a path to the temple (open 0700-1900). Get there early in the morning for a quiet hour before the tourists start arriving. Contribute a donation for temple upkeep and take a sash, or *sarung,* if you're wearing shorts. For some obscure reason, visitors are prohibited from wearing black-and-white checkered cloths or red hibiscus.

Warning: Beware of mischievous resident monkeys who snatch unguarded items. Don't wear a hat, scarf, sunglasses, shoulder purse, dangling earrings, carry food or anything else that can be yanked from you. Positive reinforcement (food) is used to encourage the monkeys to keep on stealing.

Layout and Construction
Walk up the 71 steps through a strikingly simple limestone entrance to the rectangular outer courtyard. All three courtyards—representing the spiritual, earthly, and demonic realms—are surrounded by hard weathered coral which has enabled the temple to survive for centuries and gives it a brilliant white appearance. Towering over the middle courtyard is an enormous arched *kala* gate flanked by Ganesha guardians, reminiscent of East Javanese temple architecture.

From the center of the northwest wall is a beautiful view of the sheer cliffs and ocean below. Descend down into the outermost courtyard—from there you can see the tip of East Java 50 km away. As white breakers crash against the rocks below, watch sea turtles swim in a hundred shades of churning blue-green sea water; wide-winged white frigate birds soar against the sky, moving to and from nests in the cliffs.

When the temple is bathed in gold at sunset, streams of jeeps, cars, and buses head to Uluwatu for the spectacular view. Since the temple is so small, it can get very crowded. While here, refresh yourself with an *es kelapa muda* (Rp1500), sold at stands on a shady slope off the parking lot. Served with a straw and a spoon to scoop the soft gooey meat from the coconut—one of Asia's greatest pleasures.

JIMBARAN AND VICINITY

On the west side of Bukit's narrow isthmus is one of Bali's finest and cleanest white-sand beaches, curving for five km from just south of the airport to the jutting cliffs of eastern Bukit. The warm water is suitable for swimming and bodysurfing, but not for surfing; large waves don't break here because an unbroken coral reef, which only small *prahu* can transverse, blocks the entrance to Jimbaran Bay. In the middle of the isthmus is Jimbaran, the principal town of Bukit. This fishing village is making the jarring metamorphosis into an upscale tourist resort. Some of the hotels have planted Balinese rice fields *inside* the hotel complex.

Because the main road from Sanur to Nusa Dua passes east along Benoa Harbor, it's impossible to see unspoilt Jimbaran Bay from the highway. Its lovely calm beach has only relatively recently been developed for tourists. With not much to do in Jimbaran village, the multitudes of Swiss, Germans, and Austrians who fill the hotels along the strip seem content to enjoy poolside games, lounge at sunken bars, play pool and table tennis, eat Wiener schnitzel in open-air restaurants, and sunbathe their robust frames on Jimbaran's white-sand beaches bereft of itinerant vendors.

(To learn more about Jimbaran, get ahold of Fred Eiseman's book *The Story of Jimbaran,* the first published account of Jimbaran. Copies are available for US$20 from the author who can be be reached at Jl. Bukit Permai 8 A, Jimbaran, Tuban, Badung, Bali 80361, Indonesia.)

Accommodations
Besides several first-class and medium-priced hotel properties, there's not much to choose from. In the budget category, **Puri Bambu Bungalows,** Jl. Bangracikan, tel. (0361) 701377, fax 701468, on the west side of Jl. Ulu Watu,

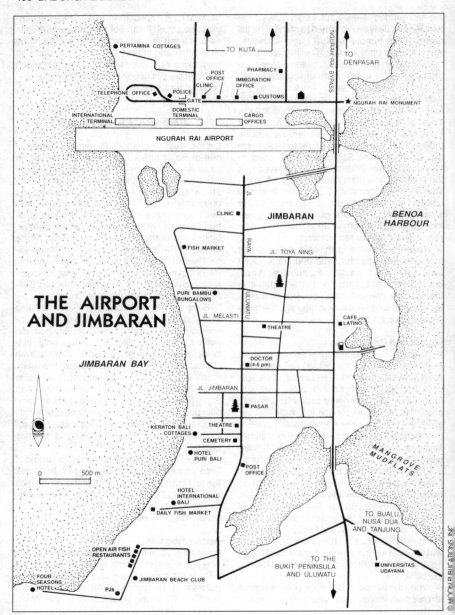

THE AIRPORT AND JIMBARAN

PERTAMINA COTTAGES

TO KUTA

NGURAH RAI BYPASS

TO DENPASAR

POST OFFICE

PHARMACY

IMMIGRATION OFFICE

TELEPHONE OFFICE

POLICE GATE

CLINIC

CUSTOMS

★ NGURAH RAI MONUMENT

INTERNATIONAL TERMINAL

DOMESTIC TERMINAL

CARGO OFFICES

NGURAH RAI AIRPORT

BENOA HARBOUR

CLINIC

JIMBARAN

JL. RAYA ULUWATU

JL. TOYA NING

FISH MARKET

PURI BAMBU BUNGALOWS

JL. MELASTI

CAFE LATINO

THEATRE

JIMBARAN BAY

DOCTOR (4-6 pm)

JL. JIMBARAN

PASAR

KERATON BALI COTTAGES

THEATRE

CEMETERY

HOTEL PURI BALI

MANGROVE MUDFLATS

POST OFFICE

0   500 m

HOTEL INTERNATIONAL BALI

DAILY FISH MARKET

TO BUALU, NUSA DUA AND TANJUNG

OPEN AIR FISH RESTAURANTS

FOUR SEASONS HOTEL

PJs

JIMBARAN BEACH CLUB

TO THE BUKIT PENINSULA AND ULUWATU

UNIVERSITAS UDAYANA

© MOON PUBLICATIONS INC

charges Rp127,000 s, Rp150,000 d for standard rooms, Rp150,000 s, Rp173,000 d for superior, Rp173,000 s, Rp207,000 d for deluxe. Up to 20% off in the low season. Pool, restaurant, bar, free pickup from airport, and free shuttle into Kuta from 1000 to 1800. Across the road and south of the Keraton Bali Cottages is **Puri Indra Prasta**, Jl. Ulu Watu 28A, tel. (0361) 701552, with clean, comfortable rooms, restaurant, bar, and swimming pool. At Rp35,000-45,000, including breakfast, this is Jimbaran's least expensive hotel. Near the beach, small **Hotel Puri Bali**, tel. (0361) 752225 or 752226, offers 41 modern air-conditioned rooms and good service for Rp300,000 s or d including tax, service charge, breakfast, and dinner. Many types of international food. Free shuttle to Kuta three times a day.

The **Pansea Puri Bali**, on Jl. Uluwatu, tel. (0361) 752605, fax 752220, is an upmarket, modern hotel. Choose from a variety of air-conditioned rooms and 33 charming thatched bungalows, Rp215,000-350,000. Rooms have open garden bathrooms, original paintings, fresh flowers, ornately carved doors, broad cool patios, nice chairs. Grounds have hardsurface tennis court, indoor games, toddler's pool, swim-up bar, and two restaurants that serve elaborate nightly buffets around the pool to live entertainment. Lots of privacy. Shuttle service can be arranged.

With rooms from Rp127,000, the 99-room **Keraton Bali Cottages**, Jl. Mrajapati, Box 2023, Kuta, tel. (0361) 701961, fax 701991, incorporates fine Balinese architecture and landscaping. Every Wednesday night from 1930 to 2030 there's either a Ramayana, *kecak* fire dance, *joget*, or *legong* on the grounds, Rp46,000 per person. Built in 1990, large, superior rooms are Rp253,000. Looks like a village of condos, in a palm-shaded tropical garden decorated with mythical stone statues, very self-contained, snappy service, happy guests. Open-air stage, tennis courts, two restaurants. From the Keraton Bali's second-floor cocktail lounge you can look irreverently right into the the village's *pura dalem* without even craning your neck. Don't miss the Barbecue Night at the hotel's **Blue Moon Restaurant** every Friday night at 2000 when guests dance to live music on the beach. Farther south and a bit out of the way on a small road to the west is **Jimbaran Beach Club**, tel. (0361) 701120, which primarily caters to tour groups; Rp75,000 s, Rp92,000 d. The **Hotel Intercontinental Bali**, tel. (0361) 701888, opened in 1993 and has 1,000 rooms—the largest hotel on Bali. Rates: garden view Rp426,000 s or d, sea view Rp449,000 s or d. Add Rp46,000 in the high season.

The **Four Seasons**, tel. (0361) 701010, is perhaps the most traditional resort on Bali—the Amandari idea taken to its ultimate conclusion. The gorgeous grounds were designed by famed landscape architect Made Wijaya (Michael White) of Sanur, who designed David Bowie's home in the Caribbean. Rates start at Rp780,000 for a one-bedroom villa and increase to Rp3.6 million for a two-bedroom royal villa. Rates are higher during the Christmas holidays. A larger hotel than the Amandari, its 147 villas (Rp690,000) are actually separate bungalows, each with an extravagant 200 square feet of indoor and open-air living space (big enough for six), a private plunge pool, secluded sundeck, and an astonishing three to nine employees assigned to each. The staff's language and people skills are very high. Dining in its three restaurants is varied and sophisticated.

Food

Eat cheaply at Jimbaran's main street *warung* or at the market on market days, but the most exciting, yet relatively undiscovered places to eat nowadays are the row of 20 or so smoky, open-air *warung* on the beach beside the Jimbaran Market (half km north of PJ's)—delicious grilled fish served in simple little huts. Probably the best of the lot is **Warung Ramayana**, where two people eat very well for Rp15,000 including dessert. The fresh fish comes with special spices, different *sambals*, tomato salad. Super popular at sunset time, so go early.

A very casual but more expensive beachside restaurant, with a stunning and romantic location, is **PJs**, where you can indulge in delicious Tex-Mex, vegetarian, and seafood dishes. Knockout lobster nachos is the most expensive at Rp56,000. Try the crisp, inspiring wood-fired pizzas with toppings such as margarita and tandoori chicken and spinach, or smoked salmon and cream cheese. Also good is their Firecracker Rice with spicy prawns (Rp24,000). Lots of light meals. Sunday brunch. Pull on ice-cold draught beer or one of their creative cocktails while listening to live jazz. Open 1100-2200 everyday.

In beautiful gardens with overhanging bougainvillea, **Cafe Layar,** tel. (0361) 701872, overlooks the beach and some brilliant sunsets. Their specialty is Indonesian-style freshly grilled seafood. The chairs are huge and comfortable. Open for lunch, dinner, and sunset drinks. **Little Indonesia,** Jl. Uluwatu 108, serves authentic Indonesian and Balinese food. Open for lunch and dinner. Call or fax (0361) 701763 for pickup service.

Also pleasant is to stroll along the beach where open-air hotel restaurants provide meals and drinks under umbrellas for at least Rp23,000. Among these higher-priced hotel restaurants, the **Singaraja** in the Inter-Continental stands out. They serve French favorites with a touch of Balinese spice: Lobster Consommé with ginger, chili, and star anise; duck with a flavorful risotto; folle salad with shredded fried suckling pig. Call (0361) 701888 for reservations.

From Jimbaran

From Jimbaran, it's only 10 minutes to the airport, 20 minutes to the Galleria in Nusa Dua, and 40 minutes to Denpasar. To enter the heart of the Bukit, head south on the old road from the airport. On the way, see beautiful yet simple Pura Ulunsiwi with its multiroofed *meru, kori* entrance, and *candi bentar.* West of town early in the morning fishing boats pull up on shore and women with buckets balanced on their heads line up to unload fish, then walk to the cooperative to weigh, sort, and sell. By midmorning the catch is in and the work done.

BUALU

About 3.5 km beyond Kampial is Bualu, once a sleepy dusty fishing village, but transformed since the start of the Nusa Dua resort project into a scruffy, bustling service and bedroom community. Not really attractive—an untidy hodgepodge of makeshift shops, car rental shops, tour agencies, beauty salons, tailors, and small restaurants sprawling in all directions. Bualu stands in vivid contrast to the immaculate lawns, gardens, and grand hotel properties of the exclusive resort next door. Bualu is where Nusa Dua guests can step out and experience "the real Indonesia."

In the southern part of the village is another exit out of Nusa Dua, Jl. Pantai Mengiat—a useful street with many services. This garish, Kutaish street, which starts on the other side of the roundabout opposite the entrance to Nusa Dua's Hilton, is more pleasant to walk along than Jl. Pramata, which heads north up the Tanjung Peninsula.

Food

The best place to eat for the money is the **Amanda Food Center,** just a six-minute walk west of the Tragia Supermarket. A Singapore-style food park with class, Amanda caters to the tastes of the vast and multiethnic Indonesian service community. Especially good for lunch. Go around to any of the 31 reasonably priced individual stalls serving Padang and Solonese food—many of the traditional foods of Indonesia, as well as European dishes. After you've made your choices, the food is brought over to your table. Great smells, squeaky clean, roofed, like a cafeteria with an upbeat atmosphere. Three times the value of Kuta. Live music seven days a week, starting at 1900.

Along this strip are a number of restaurants that do their main business at night. **Edelweiss** is operated by Austrian Otto King who was for many years Executive Chef of the Nusa Dua Beach Hotel. Outstanding Austrian and international dishes, especially the filet steak (Rp26,000) which is served on a hot stone platter and comes with dipping sauces and a potato/tomato salad. Main courses are around Rp15,000-22,000.

The **Rumah Makan Beringin** has a giddy assortment of *nasi padang* dishes, even late in the day. No nonsense food. The newer, flashier **Nusa Dua Grill** is across the street from a big car and motorbike rental place near the Bank Rakyat Indonesia.

Next door to the Tragia Supermarket is the overpriced **Tragia Restaurant,** tel. (0361) 772408, which serves mediocre Indonesian, Chinese, and European food. Their specialties are Sirloin Steaks Maitre d' Hotel (Rp15,000), T-bone Steak Cafe de Paris (Rp12,500), banana splits (Rp6500), and other pretentious stuff.

Just behind the row of souvenir stalls on Jl. Ngurah Rai Bypass is the **Novi Restaurant,** serving Westernized dishes at inflated prices.

Terminal Bualu with lots of *warung* is a good place to eat. Check out the old market next to the Sentral Theatre. Later, this area turns into a night market selling *nasi kuning, soto,* and *ayam bakar.* In front of the Tragia Supermarket is **Papa Bob's Donuts,** with pizza by the slice (Rp2000). Inside the Tragia is a very good bakery (delicious Danish) and lots of snacks. On Jl. Pantai Mengiat you'll find a whole row of seafood restaurants—the **Koki Bali, Maschere, Galliano** (Italian and Chinese food), and **Ming Garden. Ulam Restaurant** serves traditional Balinese seafood; lobster Rp29,000, Indonesian dishes Rp8000. Across the street is another lobster house, **Ulam II.**

Shopping

Bualu is a more pleasant shopping experience than Kuta. You can take your time, and the vendors are more polite. Though the crafts and souvenirs are identical to those found in all of Bali's tourist centers, the selection isn't as large. In the art market visit the *batik* painter Surarta. A few classier, pricier boutiques are found on Jl. Pantai Mengiat in south Bualu. Just west of the post office is the pride of Bualu, refreshingly air-conditioned **Tragia Supermarket,** tel. (0361) 772-70, open 0830-2000, which is convenient for those staying in Nusa Dua or Tanjung. The big building in the center houses the supermarket (first floor), a department store (second floor), and arts and crafts (third floor). Because of the proximity to Nusa Dua, prices are higher than Tragia's Denpasar counterparts. Shuttle buses from hotels in the Nusa Dua area will take you there. Open daily 0900-2000.

Services

Not only food and accommodations, but laundry, taxis, and other services tend to be more expensive in Bualu, Tanjung, and Nusa Dua than in other tourist areas. The *kantor pos* is just east of Tragia Supermarket. The moneychanger, **PT Batuan Indah,** is located on the Nusa Dua side of the Tragia complex, while **Panih Bank** is on the other side.

Transportation

It's a pleasant one-kilometer walk from Nusa Dua's big hotels to downtown Bualu. The Nusa Dua shuttle bus runs to the Tragia Supermarket

regularly. Up the street from the Tragia is Terminal Bualu, where you can catch blue Isuzu to Denpasar (Rp1000) or Kuta (Rp750). You can also hop on a green *bemo* for Tanjung Benoa; it passes all the hotels and restaurants of the east coast strip.

Diagonally across from the Amanda Food Center is a **Wartel** which accepts faxes and sells long-distance bus tickets to Denpasar, Yogyakarta, Semarang, Bandung, and Jakarta. Taxis to the airport are now Rp15,000. From Bualu's main intersection, a road leads south to Sawangan, another travels north to Tanjung Benoa, and yet another heads east to Nusa Dua.

NUSA DUA

The most luxurious hotels on Bali are located in this beach enclave on the east end of Bukit, 27 kilometers south of Denpasar. Named after two raised headlands connected to the east coast by sandspits (Nusa Dua means "Two Islands"), this full-scale, totally self-contained tourist resort has its own parks, roads, golf course, deepwater wells, sewer system, fire station, police, telephone exchange, banks, emergency clinic, mall, travel and tour agencies, and airline offices. The resort may be divided into south Nusa Dua, where the big international hotels are concentrated, and north Nusa Dua (Tanjung), which includes Club Med, the Bali Tropic Palace, Mirage, and Puri Joma.

A key element in the island's overall tourism plan and the most ambitious resort project in Indonesia's history, Nusa Dua has become a showcase for the government's policy of limiting the growth of tourism elsewhere on Bali to protect Balinese culture from tourism's negative impact. This policy, in the end, didn't really work because hotels and mini-resorts proliferated all over the island unchecked right through the 1970s and 1980s. Only in 1990 did the provincial government finally impose a ban on construction of additional hotels.

Kuta, Sanur, and Ubud—Bali's oldest tourist areas—grew spontaneously, and limits have since been placed on their expansion. In 1971, it was decided that only at Nusa Dua would further luxury hotel development be permitted. The area was chosen because of its breathtaking

TANJUNG NUSA DUA

SRIWIJAYA RESORT RESTAURANT

TANJUNG BENOA

POLICE

MEKAR SARI SEASPORTS

BMR (WATER SPORTS)
BENOA BEHARI SEASPORTS
TONNY MARINDO SEASPORTS

GRAND MIRAGE

MIRAGE

NYOMAN BALI

NUSA DUA
MEDICAL SERVICE

PURI JOMA

BALI
TROPIC
PALACE

BALI INDAH
CAR RENTAL

NUKA SARI
RESTAURANT

CLUB MED

NUSA DUA BEACH HOTEL

PUBLIC TELEPHONE

NUSA INDAH HOTEL

GRAND HYATT

TO AIRPORT AND KUTA

JL. NGURAH RAI BYPASS

WARTEL

NUSA DUA

SHERATON LAGOON

MELIA
BALI SOL

PAON MAS AND PUTRI DUYUNG

GOLF
COURSE

WALL

TO UNGUSAN AND ULUWATU

JL. PANTAI MENGIAT

HOTEL BUALU

HILTON HOTEL

AMANUSA

0   1 km

© MOON PUBLICATIONS, INC.

location, its proximity to the airport, and the fact that its relative isolation from Bali's population centers would cause minimum impact. With help from the World Bank and private developers, and with foreign consultants drawing up the plans, ground was broken for the multimillion dollar project in 1973.

The resort was long stalled by the reluctance of developers to invest. The fate of sacred seaside temples and the relocation and re-employment of fishermen and farmers were other thorny issues. The first project, the Bualu Hotel, opened in 1979 as a training ground for the BPLP (Tourism and Hotel School). In 1982 Garuda Indonesia opened a five-star property there. By 1993 the area had reached the provincial government's goal of nine four- and five-star hotels with a total of 2,700 rooms and a capacity of nearly 200,000.

With Bali's average hotel occupancy rate in the tourist season at 80-85%, more than half of Bali's tourists now stay in international-standard accommodations typified by the Nusa Dua hotels. Nusa Dua today gets the lion's share of government marketing resources because it has absorbed a gigantic portion of the government tourism infrastructure expenditures.

The enclave is a completely artificial instant Bali, with little spiritual connection to the rest of Bali or with the Balinese. No one actually *lives* in Nusa Dua; people only work or visit there. The haven of Nusa Dua offers a decidedly serene environment for those who want to get away from Bali. Walk down the hotel corridors to experience a spacious, make-believe, gloriously landscaped world—exactly what the guests want. Here, you won't get malaria, cocks won't wake you in the morning, you can drink water from the tap, there are no beggars or foot peddlers, and the service is at all times friendly and attentive. So safe are the confines of this big tourist compound, with its grandiose, floodlit split-gate entrances guarded by police posts, that Nusa Dua is vying with Jakarta as Indonesia's largest convention center for international conferences and trade fairs.

Water Sports

Nusa Dua's beach hotels front a three-kilometer-long white sand beach with gentle waves and not a rock in sight. However, barriers constructed to create a protected swimming environment have moved the surf quite a distance from shore. There's an excellent lagoon, and in the rocky outcroppings to the south are spectacular blowholes, natural waterspouts created when waves blow up through fissures in the coral.

For surfers, the right-hander in front of Club Med is a lark; park in the lot south of Club Med. Another right-hander, at high tide only, is found between the two headlands south of the Nusa Dua Beach Hotel. Also, rights and lefts up to two meters high peel off Nusa Dua channel, but watch the strong riptide. Take a *prahu* (Rp5000) about one km offshore to ride swells in three different directions. Beware of strong winds.

Shopping

Nusa Dua's newest shopping center is **Galleria,** tel. (0361) 771662—the largest on Bali and, at 3.5 hectares, one of the biggest in Indonesia. Opened in 1993, it's laid out like a Western mall. Here, tourists are made to feel comfortable browsing in air-conditioned shops among familiar surroundings while paying familiar prices. As long as you have money, Galleria offers something for everyone. Even though prices are supposed to be fixed, some stores will negotiate.

The Tantra Gallery exhibits exceptional Ubud artists including Yan Tino (oils), Made Nusa (oils on canvas), and Wayang Pundah (watercolors). The shops selling men's and women's fashion apparel are laid out like Macy's in the States. Though clean and well displayed, the prices are twice as much as the States. **The Keris Gallery,** tel. (0361) 771303 or 771304, is Bali's largest department store—like a huge Nordstrom or Filene's—carrying silks, handicrafts, traditional *batik,* Sumatra pearls, and Euro-style clothing from the collections of Yves Saint Laurent, Etienne Aigner, Kenzo, and Paloma Picasso. Open daily 0900-2000.

Country Interior features a stunning selection of folk art and home furnishings from Java and Lombok. Probably the nicest shop in the Galleria for tasteful decorator items is **Stiff Gallery.** Displayed attractively on its sand floor are beautifully glazed teapots, basketry from Java, and many other folk items. A showroom for both shops is at Jl. Gatot Subroto 128A, Denpasar, tel. (0361) 234029.

The place to shop for designer clothes is **Uluwatu Boutique** next to the Jaansan Cafe and opposite the Duty Free center. The collection is dominated by white rayon dresses with intricate embroidery. There are also beautiful light cotton dresses with soft colored patterns and a range of printed cotton fabric. Superb quality.

Folk Art Antiques carries such eye-catching stuff as an ornate blowgun from Kalimantan (Rp173,000) and other Outer Island tribal artifacts. The **Duty Free Shop**, tel. (0361) 772205, carries leading world labels from Hermez to Harley Davidson with prices to match, as well as exclusive lines of locally manufactured products.

Accommodations

With property values running Rp75 million per hectare and up, you won't find any *losmen,* homestays, or even intermediate accommodations here, although nearby Tanjung has a few moderately priced hotels. Nusa Dua now contains over a dozen luxury, international-class four- and five-star hotels with 50 to 1,000 rooms. Like gigantic adult amusement parks, each of these palatial hotel properties is located on park land adorned with stone sculpture, fountains, velvety grass, ornamental plants, and acres of palms and flowering trees. After entering the cool, open lobby, you're greeted with the delicate sounds of *gamelan* or *rindik,* then invariably handed a fresh-fruit drink and an ice cold face towel. From that moment on, staff performance is embarrassingly personalized.

Services include taxis, telex, fax, laundry, and tour and tourist information counters. There are indoor shopping arcades, convention facilities, restaurants, discos, and beauty salons. There are Javanese singers crooning in piano bars, as well as regular music and dance performances in open-air amphitheaters, fashion shows, and arts and crafts demos. Cremation ceremonies are advertised on easels in plush lobbies; comprehensive sports programs include snorkeling and windsurfing from private beachfronts. All these deluxe accommodations have at least two and sometimes three swimming pools, with beach and pool games, squash, tennis, bicycling, volleyball, and aerobics classes offered all day long. Plush guest rooms are air-conditioned, have all the modern conveniences including color TVs, in-house video and

music programming, minibars, safes, IDD phones, marble-tiled bathrooms, fresh toiletries and towels daily, bathrobes, and private balconies. The cheapest five-star hotel rooms go for around Rp157,000 (suites Rp1-4.2 million), while rooms on four-star properties are Rp157,000 and up. Always expect 21% tax and service charge, and even a Rp21,000-31,500 high-season surcharge. To see the exteriors of all the hotels, take the Rp1000 open shuttle bus that drives the loop between Bualu's Tragia Supermarket and each of the big hotels.

The smallest, oldest, but newly remodeled **Hotel Bualu Village,** Box 6, Nusa Dua, tel. (0361) 771310, fax 771313, was the former hands-on training site for the government's Hotel and Tourism Training Center (BPLP) next door. It's the only Nusa Dua hotel not facing the oceanfront, but is cheaper and quite peaceful. Simple rooms in modern two-story blocks, Rp159,000 s, Rp182,000 d. Add 21% tax and service. Set amid elaborate grounds, with a bar, the Kolak Restaurant, and two swimming pools. The beach is 700 meters away but *dokar* take you there free. Great childcare and sports facilities—jogging track, PADI-certified scuba diving instruction, and even horseback riding.

The massive, U-shaped **Putri Bali Hotel,** Box 1, Denpasar 80363, tel. (0361) 71020, fax 71139, is built on nearly 11 hectares of impressively landscaped grounds. Its 425 rooms rent for Rp253,000 s, Rp288,000 d; the 41 suites and 22 cottages are Rp437,000 to Rp1.2 million. The Putri Bali's exterior is shaped like a staircase, with most rooms facing the sea. Enjoy drinks at the sunken bar or take in *jegog, kecak, legong, barong, kris,* or the frog dance performances. It features extensive business facilities, two restaurants, bars, disco, fitness center, billiards, darts, and a video game room. Free diving demos, beachfront soccer, volleyball. A specialty is water sports.

The 388-room **Melia Bali,** Box 1048, Tuban, tel. (0361) 771510, fax 771360, is owned by Spain's leading hotel chain and caters to package tours from Europe as well as conferences. Rooms are Rp189,000-199,500 s, Rp315,000-1.2 million d. Meeting rooms with complete audiovisual equipment accommodate 40 to 500. This graceful, attractive hotel is noted for its fine cuisine, particularly the Asian dishes at the Lotus

Restaurant. Enjoy entertainment at any of several piano bars. Discos, shops, health center, kid's playground, library, three tennis courts, jogging track, beautiful open-air theater. See the 1,200-square-meter lagoon-style swimming pool with three islets.

The 450-room **Nusa Dua Beach Hotel,** Box 1028, tel. (0361) 71210, fax 71229, is run by Aerowisata, a subsidiary of Garuda Indonesia. Beyond the magnificent *candi bentar* and within the four-story hotel are four restaurants, two bars, a coffee shop, and a disco. All the principal styles of Balinese village architecture are represented: *puri, bale banjar,* and *kulkul.* Almost three-quarters of the guests are domestic tourists, incentive travelers, or conference attendees—impressive business services. Rooms are Rp189,000-252,000 s, Rp210,000-315,000 d. The jogging track, tennis and squash courts, and a huge swimming pool are surrounded by 8.5 hectares of lush park land under hundreds of graceful palms. With its long beachfront, marine sports abound. Guests may receive instruction and use equipment for scuba, snorkeling, boating, and waterskiing, then take a sauna or massage at the hotel's fully equipped gym.

Club Med, Box 7, Nusa Dua, tel. (0361) 71521, accommodates 700 in three- and four-story Balinese-style bungalows geared toward packaged stays for families and couples. A highly organized nonstop sports program is part of the Rp210,000 per person daily tariff: sailing, windsurfing, snorkeling, tennis, aerobics, yoga, volleyball, badminton, and archery. Emphasis is given to arts and crafts like *batik* and kite-making. Entertainment includes regular performances of Balinese theater, periodic talent contests, arts festivals. The environment can be raucous—announcements blare over squawk boxes, noisy crowds leave the small pool dirty—but the food is very good and the sports facilities first class. The rooms, though spartan, are comfortable. The majority of guests are Japanese and Australian. Extraordinary security; nonguests are not allowed to walk along the beach.

The breathtaking US$170 million **Grand Hyatt,** Box 53, Nusa Dua, tel. (0361) 71234, fax 72038, is one of Asia's classiest hotels. Inspired by the design of the Tirtagangga water palace, its four "villages" are linked by simulated ponds, gardens, and pools. Its environs and rooms (11 categories Rp315,000-12 million) are decorated with millions of dollars worth of original art. The staff of over 500 responds to your needs instantaneously. Fine restaurants; breakfast buffet is Rp31,500. The swimming pool is a continuous inland "lagoon" that flows beneath footbridges, by sparkling waterfalls and water slides. The Grand Hyatt is recreation oriented: snorkeling (Rp65,100 per hour), windsurfing (Rp16,800 per hour), and kayak flotation (Rp10,500 per hour). Or take the "Archaeological Tour" (Rp65,100). Forty percent of the clientele is European. Use your Hyatt Gold Passport in the Bali Hyatt in Sanur. For reservations, call (800) 233-1234 in the United States..

The 537-room **Bali Hilton,** Box 46, Nusa Dua 80361, tel. (0361) 771102 or 771112, fax 771199, provides more Westernized holiday facilities than the Hyatt. Rooms, Rp300,000 s, Rp345,000 d, have individually controlled air conditioning, color cable and satellite TV, private balcony. There are cottages as well as luxury suites, Rp910,000 to Rp4.3 million, all built around 11.5 hectares of quiet gardens and a huge maze-like lagoon—in the middle of which is the swimming pool—that stretches all the way to a beautiful 300-meter-wide beach. Next door is an 18-hole golf course. The Hilton has lounges, a cafe, disco, Japanese restaurant, seafood barbecue, poolside snackbar, theme theater, grand ballroom, games room, children's play center, fitness center, sauna, whirlpool, squash and tennis courts, and a full range of water sports.

The U-shaped, 400-room **Nusa Indah,** Box 36, tel. (0361) 71565, fax 71908, overlooks the beach. Nice gardens, four restaurants, and extensive convention facilities—in fact, the largest in Indonesia, with 2,000-person capacity and simultaneous translation service.

The 276-room **Sheraton Lagoon,** Box 2044, Kuta 80361, tel. (0361) 71327, fax 71326, consists of four-story room blocks with attractive terra-cotta roofs on one side of the complex, with food and beverage facilities, the lobby, and other public areas on the other side. Ultra-personalized services include special check-in, complimentary coffee, tea, and American breakfast, round-the-clock butler service in the suites, and "daily surprise." Rates are about the same as the Grand Hyatt's—Rp346,500-378,000 s, Rp409,500-430,500 d, suites Rp463,000-3.7 million. The Sheraton boasts the largest free-form pool on Bali; on the beach are pedal boats. Great views of the sea from the open-air Cascade Bar, while the Cafe Lagoon Coffeeshop overlooks the "lagoon" meandering through seven hectares of landscaped grounds. A spacious outdoor amphitheater hosts cultural performances.

The opulent **Amanusa Resort,** Box 33, Nusa Dua, tel. (0361) 772333, fax 772335, sits on a grassy knoll overlooking the Bali Golf and Country Club, commanding spectacular views of the ocean and Gunung Agung. The most expensive hotel in Nusa Dua, the Amanusa offers 35 freestanding luxury suites (Rp630,000-1.4 million) linked to the public facilities by pathways. Special features: sunken baths, queen-size four-poster beds, walled private courtyard, suites with private pools, two restaurants, a library, cruise boats, floodlit tennis courts, massage and beauty salons, free airport transfers. More family-oriented than Bali's other Aman hotels; kids really like the enormous pool. The last word in luxury vacation living.

Food

The **Tragia Convenience Store,** tel. (0361) 772170, in the Galleria sells a limited selection of drinks, snacks, fruit, and dairy products; it also has a bakery/coffee shop where a loaf of whole-wheat bread costs Rp4000. Open daily 0900-2000. Take a shuttle to Tragia from any of the Nusa Dua hotels. Nowhere, except for the minimarket and snack outlets of Galleria, can you get a cold beer in Nusa Dua for less than Rp5000.

The gourmet, high-priced, high-quality restaurants in the hotels serve international, European, Chinese, Balinese, and Indonesian cuisine. The Grand Hyatt's **Salsa Verde** restaurant is said to be one of the best Italian restaurants on the island—complete with a traditional Old World pizza oven. Open for lunch 1200, dinner 1800-2230. Superb seven-course French dinners are served at the elegant **Pavilion Restaurant** in the Melia Bali Sol. The five-star Sheraton Nusa Dua's **Ikan Restaurant** is known for its large selection of delicious grilled seafood with tangy sauces and marinades. Indonesians swear the Indonesian dishes take them back to the *warung* of the past. Amanusa Hotel's Italian restaurant is superb. Dine on the terrace with the magnificent view or in the intimate, the-

atrical, black-and-white dining room. Choose from a mouthwatering variety of appetizers and antipastos, homemade pastas, and robust main courses of veal, lamb, duck, and seafood. After dinner, stop for an *aperitif* in the open-air, starlit cocktail lounge off the lobby.

Outside the hotels, the Galleria has a few outstanding—but pricey—restaurants. Every Monday night at 2000, the **Paon Mas** features a *rijstaffel* buffet for Rp26,000, plus 21% tax; tel. (0361) 771981 for reservations. Next door is the **Putri Duyung,** tel. (0361) 772051, with a wide choice of fresh seafood; open for lunch and dinner 1100-2300.

Highly praised by the Japanese themselves is **Matsuri** (formerly Chikara Tei) in the Galleria, Block B14, tel. (0361) 772267. This authentic, glamorous restaurant is adorned with typical Japanese wall decorations, flags, and lanterns. Great food, atmosphere, and service. Focus on the grilled dishes and the teppanyaki. Several VIP rooms with exquisite interiors. Once weekly there are *legong* dancers, other nights Batak singers. Open 1100-2200. Free transport in the Nusa Dua, Tanjung Benoa, and Jimbaran areas. The best Mexican food in Nusa Dua is served up at **Poco Loco,** Jl. Pantai Mengiat 12, tel. (0361) 773923, a real taste sensation, large portions, and awesome frozen margaritas.

Also in the Galleria is **Jansan Cafe et Pub,** Block B1, tel. (0361) 772628, only a five-minute walk from the Bali Sol, Grand Hyatt, and the Sheraton, and facing Nusa Dua Lagoon. Fillet o' Fish with lemon-tequila sauce, the New Orleans King Prawn salad, Mom's garlic bread, and their famous tropical cocktails are the best. **Kura Kura,** also in the Galleria, Block D3, tel. (0361) 773278, is known for fresh seafood, pasta, and juicy ribs. The bar is claimed to be world famous for its piña colada.

Beyond the Nusa Dua barricades altogether, though not far to walk, is Jl. Pantai Mengiat in the southern part of Bualu, the supply base for Nusa Dua. On this street are the popular seafood restaurants **Koki Bali, Mascheri, Ming Garden,** and **Ulam I and II.** Lobster is the big item here. Look for all-inclusive specials advertised on signboards placed on the sidewalk outside the restaurants. Call the Ming, tel. (0361) 772125, or the Ulam, tel. (0361) 771590, for free transport from your hotel. The long-established Ulam is frequently recommended by hotel managers.

For those who want to go on a little Sunday outing, spend it at the **Bali Cliff Hotel** on the Bukit Peninsula. Their new brunch—an extravagant and delicious international buffet—is getting rave reviews. It features everything from barbecue steak and lobster to a variety of pastas and extensive salad and dessert bars. A dip in their breathtaking swimming pool is included in the price of brunch. Served in the Coffee Shop, brunch takes place from 1100 to 1500 every Sunday and costs Rp40,000. Book by calling tel. (0361) 771992.

Services

A clinic, **Nusa Dua Medical Service,** tel. (0361) 771324, is across from the Galleria; there are several other clinics in Tanjung. An interdenominational church service is held each Sunday at 1800 in the Melia Bali Sol Hotel. Most hotel rooms have IDD telephone service and card-operated telephones are common. The Galleria complex contains a **postal agent,** an **American Express** office (tel. 0361-773334, open 0830-1630), several **banks,** and a **Garuda** check-in center and ticket office (tel. 0361-771444, open 0800-1900).

Transportation

A smart new highway whisks arrivals the 10 kilometers from the airport to Nusa Dua in about 20 minutes. Public *bemo* leave Kuta for Nusa Dua (Rp1000) from the intersection of Jl. Pantai Kuta and the road to the airport. From Tegal station in Denpasar, take a *bemo* (Rp1000).

The resort offers easy access to Denpasar (25 minutes). There's a Garuda Airlines counter in Building A2 in the Galleria, tel. (0361) 71444 or 71342, where tickets can be reconfirmed, luggage checked in, and boarding passes obtained. Open Mon.-Fri. 0800-1900, Sunday and holidays 0900-1900. Extremely convenient. Taxis from Nusa Dua to the airport charge a fixed Rp15,000. Shuttle buses leave each hotel every hour or so for Bualu, the shopping center just outside the gates of Nusa Dua. Or just walk. It's agreeable sauntering around this parklike ghetto. The manicured scenery and luxuriant tropical vegetation is a delight, and you don't have the traffic, noise, fumes, dirt, and street vendors typical of other tourist areas of Bali. There are even sidewalks.

Taxi drivers in Nusa Dua are ruthless; there aren't that many of them and they have you captive on the big hotel properties. The only way to get cheaper fares is to walk from your hotel out to the main road, where you still might be quoted the same rip-off fares. Coming back from Kuta it's cheaper. Alternatively, charter a vehicle from an agent in Bualu for around Rp50,000-55,000 per day. Avis Rental Car has offices at Club Med (tel. 0361-71521) and the Nusa Dua Beach Hotel (tel. 0361-71220).

Vicinity of Nusa Dua

Visit the **Kuburan Katolik** (Catholic Cemetery) of Bualu. Northeast of Bualu are the extensive mudflats of Suwung, which extend for about seven km to Jimbaran; bridges cross over swampier sections. A commercial seaweed farm is located two km south of Nusa Dua. A road leads south to the small farming community of Sawangan; large banyan-like *bunut* trees in the town's center. **Pura Geger,** a temple dedicated to agricultural deities, is a short distance east of town on a rocky promontory. A track leads two km south to remote Pura Karang Bona, which also looks out over the sea.

TANJUNG

Three km north of Nusa Dua, the five-km-long peninsula of Tanjung Benoa points toward Benoa Harbor like a long finger. This once sleepy expanse of coconut palms and shallow beach has been transformed into a growing resort area with luxury hotels, dive agents, restaurants, and open-air cafes. Tanjung doesn't have the same feeling of sterile isolation as neighboring Nusa Dua. It's Nusa Dua's wild side. The rhythm of the peninsula is more like Costa Brava in the late '70s than the frantic pace of a modern Balinese resort. New hotels, shops, and restaurants are constantly being built, affording tourists plenty of options and all the conveniences, but there's not nearly the level of traffic, congestion, crime, and vice that plagues Kuta.

A nice place for evening strolls is the relatively quiet village of Benoa on the peninsula's tip. For hundreds of years this was an embarkation point for ferries crossing over to Suwungan; the overland journey to the main part of Bali via Jimbaran was too arduous and time-consuming. Offshore are foreigner's yachts along with smaller Indonesian vessels, Navy boats, and traditional Bugis *prahu*. Sit and drink a cold beer while watching the village life at the Sriwijaya Resort Restaurant. More romantic is to walk along the beach southeast of Benoa, past rows of *jukung* pulled up on shore. In Benoa village is a Bugis *kampung* with its small *mesjid*. Don't miss the large, garish Chinese Buddhist *klenteng* picturesquely sited looking out to Benoa Harbor. The annex of this local temple contains bronze icons salvaged from the shipwreck of a Chinese vessel in the 15th century. Recently renovated, the Ratu Cina shrine in the local *pura dalem* shows the long history of Chinese contact. Occasional *gong* or *legong* dances are held at the temple.

Recreation

Tanjung is popular with marine sports enthusiasts. Tourists enjoy parasailing, water scooters, scuba, snorkeling, waterskiing, glass-bottom boats, reef fishing, trawling, power boating, and banana boat rides. The intensive training for parasailing takes all of 12 seconds. It costs Rp25,000 for two to three minutes in the air—a blast. The best spot for parasailing is in front of the Mirage Hotel because the water is flatter.

Beluga, Jl. Segara Windu, Tanjung Benoa, tel. (0361) 771146 or 771-721, has a submarine—yes, submarine—moored in front of the restaurant. With a 36-person capacity, the submarine provides tours of the reef to the northeast of Tanjung, Rp196,000 per person for one hour. Leaves around 1100.

There are dozens of water sport clubs and shops, like **Jalayasa Seasports and Pub,** tel. (0361) 771963, **Tonny Marindo Seasports,** tel. (0361) 771694, and **Rai Restaruant,** tel. (0361) 772012. Because of all the boating activity, the water near the shore doesn't offer the best visibility for snorkeling.

The reef lies about 200 meters off the northeastern end of the peninsula—easy to reach, with a gentle current and a surprising variety of fish and scattered outcrops of coral. The dives are perfect for beginners. When the tide's in, you

board the dive agent's *prahu motor* for the five minute trip. Visibility is about 10-15 meters along a gradual downslope.

Accommodations

It all begins just a half kilometer north of the entrance to northern Nusa Dua's Club Med. If you're staying for a while, look for the many *rumah disewakan* (house for rent) signs on village lanes. The upmarket hotels on this strip have all the usual tourist features: a/c, private terraces or balconies, minibars, fridges, IDD telephones, sound systems, color TVs, 24-hour room service.

The **Bali Tropic Palace Hotel,** Jl. Pratama 34 A, Box 41, Nusa Dua 80361, tel. (0361) 772130 or 772107, fax 772131, is like a small version of a Nusa Dua hotel. It has 108 lavishly appointed cottages. With garden view Rp300,000 s, Rp345,000 d; also junior suite for Rp575,000, deluxe suite Rp805,000. Rates not including 21% tax and service. Two restaurants, pizzeria, two bars, butterfly-shaped swimming pool, and private beach. American buffet breakfast Rp23,000, set lunch Rp34,500, dinner Rp46,000, dinner with show Rp57,500. Serene atmosphere.

Small but high-class **Puri Joma** (Jl. Pratama 40, Terora, Nusa Dua 80361, tel./fax 0361-771634) offers 10 Bali-style bungalows decorated with stone carvings and traditional golden painted doors. Idyllic, safe, and relaxing garden. Nice quiet rooms have air conditioning, IDD telephones, fridge, and no TV. Enjoy the breezy, scenic beachfront seafood restaurant, swim in the modern pool. Only Rp103,500 s, Rp126,500 d. Lower prices during the off-season. Discounts for stays of more than seven days. Puri Joma can arrange the rental of a *prahu motor* for around Rp23,000 per hour.

Small, little-known, and far from overcrowded tourist sites, the **Bali Royal,** Jl. Pratama, tel. (0361) 771039, fax 771885, has only 15 rooms among gardens and lily ponds. Superior rooms are Rp218,500 s, Rp322,000 d; suites are Rp414,000, with direct access to the beach. Distinctive yet comfortable furniture. Bathrooms have jacuzzis and little gardens. Though it has a Balinese touch, the property is operated, with great efficiency, by Mr. Stefan Neumann, an Austrian. Excellent international and Indonesian food. Caters particularly to golfers, as the management is well-connected to the Nusa Dua Golf Club. Free airport transfers. Absolutely first class all around.

Grand Mirage Hotel and Resort, Box 145, Nusa Dua, tel. (0361) 772147, fax 772156, the most luxurious hotel on the Tanjung pro- vides 288 deluxe ocean-view suites from Rp334,000 to Rp1.9 million (high-season sup- plement: Rp46,000). American breakfast Rp32,200, lunch Rp48,300, dinner Rp62,100, buffet dinner Rp74,000. All rates subject to 21% service and tax. Features a Chinese restaurant, seafood restaurant, ice cream parlor, lounges, bars, disco pub, open-air theater, shuttle ser- vice, children's playground, tours-and-travel desk, free-shaped pool, a thalassotherapy cen- ter, tennis courts, audio-visual function room for 80 people, plus a whole range of water sports, and a golf course only five minutes away.

North of the Mirage on Jl. Pratama, the quiet and clean **Rasa Sayang Beach Inn,** tel. (0361) 771643, has 19 rooms. Upstairs rooms Rp20,000 s, Rp25,000 d for rooms with fans, Rp32,000 s, Rp40,000 d for air-conditioned rooms (including breakfast, tax, and service).

The cheapest accommodation on Tanjung— and very central—is **Hasan Homestay,** tel. (0361) 772456, which has a *losmen*-style row of 10 rooms with baths, fan, and Kuta-type break- fast for Rp25,000 s or d. Only full during the high season. No meals, but big, cold beers are only Rp4000.

Food

A number of seafood specialty restaurants have opened up on both sides of Jl. Pratama just south of Benoa village. All have a weary same- ness and are 50-90% empty except in July, Au- gust, and December. Those on the beach offer good views of the Nusa Penida cliffs. Most have full bars, and offer fare at prices about 10% high- er than Kuta. Menus are generally too Western.

The most touristy is **Rai Seafood Restau- rant,** tel. (0361) 772012, at the end of Jl. Prata- ma on the right. They specialize in lobster, fish, and Balinese *rijstaffel;* their *soto madura* (Rp4000) is authentic. Open 0800-2300 for breakfast, lunch, and dinner. "Theme Night" en- tertainment is put on from 2100 to 2200 three days a week; on Monday it's a cockfight demo,

Wednesday *legong,* and Saturday *barong* and Monkey Dance. Free transport from Nusa Dua.

The very large and empty **Beluga Restau- rant,** Jl. Segara Windu, Tanjung Benoa, tel. (0361) 771997, around the corner from the Rai seems to be perpetually waiting for July and August. This is the only eatery in the area that serves *rijstaffel* in the original style, served by young and lovely Indonesian girls.

The Dalang Restaurant and Bar, tel. (0361) 771540, provides the promised view, but meals, especially the "Western" cuisine, are pricey, skimpy, and uninspired—what Balinese think Western food should taste like. A *legong* dance is staged at 2000 Tuesday and Friday nights; ask about free transport to and from Nusa Dua. In the same building is a moneychanger, mini- market, stamps for sale, and letterbox.

A half dozen restaurants along Jl. Pratama, packed every night, draw business away from Tanjung's higher-priced restaurants. The clean and reasonably priced **Nusa Sari Restaurant,** Jl. Pratama 151 B, tel. (0361) 771701, near the car rental place of the same name, has excellent Balinese food and the portions are generous. Though they serve European food too, it's best to stick with the Balinese items on the menu— the *nasi campur* is especially tasty.

A *nasi campur* place, **Puri Panca Setia** is op- posite the Grand Mirage Hotel (don't confuse this with the Mirage Hotel). **Warung Jakarta,** also on the strip past Puri Joma heading north, has great *nasi campur* (Rp1200), Betawi-style *gado-gado* with mixed corn kernels (Rp800). Un- beatable prices for genuine Javanese cuisine.

Bali Gonsaga, tel. (0361) 773642 is a tourist restaurant specializing in Italian food. Heading north on Jl. Pramata, it's just before the turnoff to Club Med and the Nusa Indah Hotel. Dishes are Rp8000-10,000. Open 1800-2300. Also at the start of Jl. Pramata are a number of small *warung makan* and street vendors selling less expensive and more genuine food.

Services

There are well-stocked shops and *warung* up and down the Tanjung strip. A public telephone (accepts cards) is at the lower, Bualu-end of Jl. Pratama; see the blue sign between Warung Karina and the bank. A small shop opposite the Grand Mirage offers laundry service.

Getting There

If you're coming from Bualu, the start of Jl. Pratama leading to Benoa village (no sign) looks like the entrance to a crowded, noisy, dusty, Javanese *kampung*. Green minibuses run up and down narrow Tanjung until sunset; Rp300 for foreigners. If you're still in Bualu after dark and want to get back to your hotel, find a taxi (Rp4000-5000).

Per day rental car prices are relatively stable: Rp42,000 or so for a Jimney, about Rp52,500 for a *kijang*. **Bali Indah,** Jl. Pramata 51 B, tel. (0361) 71701, rents Suzuki Katanas for Rp35,000 (plus insurance). Also an authorized moneychanger with reasonable rates. **CV Puri Sarana,** which rents cars, is just before the Mirage Hotel. All the water sport agencies handle car rentals.

Because of speeding traffic, the narrow road, and the absence of sidewalks, walking Jl. Pramata is unnerving and potentially dangerous. From Nusa Dua you can walk 1.5 hours on the beach north to Tanjung Benoa. Another approach is by boat; boats shuttle back and forth all day long if the tide is right (Rp5000 per person). From the beach in Benoa village, boatmen will take you across to Pulau Serangan for Rp30,000. It's cheaper to take one of the many small *prahu* from Desa Suwungan; take a right off Jl. Bypass on the way from Kuta to Sanur.

BOB RACE

GIANYAR REGENCY

Culturally, Gianyar is the oldest and richest region on Bali. The town Gianyar (elev. 125 meters) is the regency's administrative capital, but Ubud is the cultural capital, and most populous town. Consisting of 244 *desa,* 504 *banjar,* 2,732 temples, and a population of around 350,000, the regency of Gianyar stretches from the southern undeveloped coastline into the cool, fresh hills and mountains to a point over 800 meters above sea level. The northern border lies only three kilometers away from Gunung Batur's active crater. Rivers run from the crater's lake through the valleys, hills, and terraced fields. One, the **Ayung,** is the island's longest river.

History
Around Bedulu-Pejeng lies a 10-kilometer-long strip of earth known as The Land Between the Rivers. The Elephant Cave hermitage at Bedulu, the royal tombs at Gunung Kawi, rock carvings at Yeh Pulu, and the Moon of Pejeng bronze drum—some of Bali's holiest sites—are found there. It's through this region the legendary rivers Petanu and Pakrisan flow. The Pakrisan is particularly rich in historic remains, having "magically" cut through rock cliffs and giant boulders. Its *candi,* monasteries, meditation

cells, sacred watering places, shrine compounds, and Bronze Age statuettes, rock inscriptions, and bronze plates, all point to the existence of a once-powerful kingdom where religion, architecture, technology, and art flourished 400-600 years ago. The irrigation tunnels north of Gianyar, the terracing of the slopes, and the intricate rice field system are products of this kingdom. Many Balinese have no knowledge of the pre-Hindu kingdom, believing the masterpieces in rock were carved by the thumbnails of Kebo Iwo, a mythical giant.

Great mythological battles took place here between the gods and the evil King Mayadanawa of Bedulu. Details of these ancient conflicts have been passed down not only in spoken folk tales but also recorded in Bali's epic poem, the Usana Bali, composed in the mid-16th century during the golden age of Middle Javanese literature. These stories depict the coming of Hinduism and the end of old customs. Historians surmise the evil king may have simply been a rebel leader who opposed the Hinduism on Bali.

The sacred bathing place Tirta Empul was created by the gods to revive the dead warriors of this mythic conflict. Blood running from the

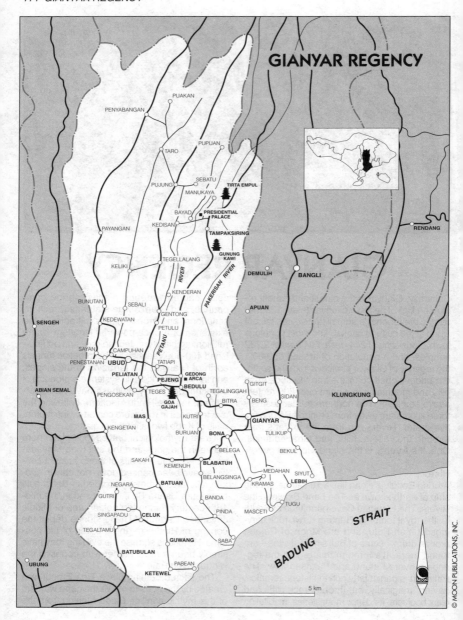

bodies of the dead changed into the Petanu ("The Cursed One") and for over 1,000 years its waters weren't used for drinking, bathing, or irrigation. At last, in 1928, the curse was lifted in a special ceremony. Because of the curse, no ancient monuments are found along the banks of the Petanu (the Goa Gajah complex is not an exception; it's on one of Petanu's tributaries). The victory of the gods over the forces of evil is celebrated annually in the Galungan festival.

Prior to the 18th century, the region now called Gianyar was divided among the kingdoms of Klungkung, Bangli, Mengwi, and Badung. By the late 18th century, the raja of Klungkung had lost much of his prestige and power after suffering defeat at the hands of the armies of Karangasem. This left a power vacuum that was filled by the ambitious and ruthless *punggawa* of the village of Gianyar, a distant relative of the Dewa Agung of Gelgel (Klungkung). By deceit, poisonings, and war, this first raja of Gianyar emerged as the ruler of a new rajadom. His control extended over a vast area, including neighboring states. He took the name Dewa Manggis ("Sweet God") after the village in Klungkung where he was born.

A confused series of wars between the kingdoms of southern Bali in the latter 19th century accelerated Dutch involvement in the area. Because the sons of Dewa Manggis were pitted against the allied states of Badung, Bangli, and Klungkung, they sought help from the Dutch in the 1880s. Since the Dutch were heavily engaged in the Aceh Wars during that time, they couldn't lend assistance and the Dewa Manggis and his family were captured. A second appeal was made in 1899 by Dewa Gede Raka that proved successful. In 1900 the colonial army was sent to protect Gianyar, and this meant automatic annexation as a Regentschaap.

In the early part of this century, as the Dutch struggled to subdue the rest of southern Bali, Dewa Gede Raka's successors flourished because of their special status. Agung Ngurah Agung (1892-1960), considered one of the most flamboyant and autocratic of Balinese raja, ruled from 1912 until 1943, when the Japanese forced him into exile in Lombok. His son, Anak Agung, an accomplished linguist, became a prominent diplomat and statesman in the post-war republican government, serving as the Minister of the Interior and Ambassador to Belgium and France. He was imprisoned by Sukarno from 1962 to 1966, then under Suharto served as Ambassador to Austria.

Tourism began in the regency in the 1930s when Tjokorda Agung Sukawati, of the old Sukawati line, established his *puri* in Ubud as the center of a renaissance in Balinese arts. In 1935 he sponsored the painter's cooperative Pita Maha, inviting foreign artists, musicians, anthropologists, and writers to stay at his palace. Among his first guests were the artists Walter Spies and Rudolf Bonnet, who influenced Balinese painting, and the first "Baliologists," Colin McPhee, Jane Belo, Miguel Covarrubias, Gregory Bateson, and Margaret Mead, who significantly influenced the way the West looked upon Bali.

The presence of foreigners in turn attracted more visitors, and a travelers' hostel opened in Campuan in 1937 (site of present-day Hotel Tjampuan). In the 1950s international tourism increased when dances and music recitals were staged, art shops opened, hotels built, antiquities excavated, and museums established. Although taking up only seven percent of the island's total land area, today Gianyar is Bali's most important region for cultural tourism.

Economy

More than half the population of this primarily rural region is directly involved in the tourism industry, while roughly the other half grow rice, sweet potatoes, and soybeans. The plantation districts of Payangan and Tegallalang also grow coconuts, lychees, cloves, and vanilla. Sukawati District grows tobacco, while Bali's best-quality coffee is harvested during August and September around the upland village of Taro. The villagers of Kramas and Ketewel on the south coast fish for a living, and the regency's freshwater ponds produce about 130 tons of fish each year.

Gianyar is the heartland of Bali's crafts production, where the weaving, plaiting, and wood- and stonecarving industries are major employers. The Technical High School in Guang gives instruction in sculpture and carving; Celuk is an important center for silversmiths and goldsmiths; Batubulan for stonecarving; Mas, Ubud, and Batuan for painting and woodcarving. Sukawati is known for its puppet sculptors, Pujung and

Sebatu produce expressive wooden statues and wooden jewelry, Bona is the center for bamboo furniture and a thriving tourist-oriented performance venue, and the artisans of Tampaksiring carve tusk and bone.

The Arts

The agricultural wealth of these densely populated plains, sometimes referred to as the Balinese "Valley of Culture," has always provided the nobility with the means to develop the arts. The villages of Blahbatuh, Batuan, Sukawati, Bona, and Ubud are preeminent centers for music, dance, drama, woodcarving, and other artistic activity. With its flourishing culture, its impressive handicrafts, warm climate, and monumental antiquities built as far back as two hundred years before Christ, Gianyar Regency is the traditional heart of Bali, the main focus of tourist interest on the island.

SOUTHERN GIANYAR REGENCY

BATUBULAN AND VICINITY

Batubulan ("Moon Stone") is only 10 kilometers up the "tourist corridor" from Denpasar and 17 kilometers before Gianyar. Batubulan and the neighboring villages of Celuk and Singapadu are heavily involved in handicrafts, music, and dance.

In Batubulan the headquarters of **SESRI** (High School of Indonesian Fine Arts) and **SMKI** (High School of Indonesian Performing Arts) welcome tourists to watch dance classes in the cool of the mornings. The director of SMKI is I Nyoman Sumandhi, an accomplished dancer, *dalang,* and musician, who received his Master's from Wesleyan University, Connecticut, following coursework at KOKAR and UCLA. After graduation SESRI and SMKI students are expected to return to their villages to teach. A great number continue their studies at ASTI (The Academy of Indonesian Dance and Music) in Denpasar, a tertiary institute of performing arts.

Arts and Crafts

Renowned for its decorative and fanciful stonecarving, Batubulan has sculptures and bas-reliefs adorning temples, houses, yards, public buildings, hotels, restaurants, bridges, and crossroads all over the island. Visit the many shaded outdoor workshops along the main road where child artisans chip away at stone blocks to liberate the heroes, gods, demons, Buddhas, and curious beasts of Bali's rich syncretic mythology.

Though a surprisingly soft carving medium, *paras,* gray volcanic stone or soapstone, is costly and cumbersome to ship. Thus, stone sculpture is seldom bought by tourists and therefore remains contained to the archipelago. Most of Batubulan's customers are Balinese who use standing statues as guardian figures for family shrines, courtyards, and doors. Semi-religious statuary also serves a civic function as guardians for government buildings.

Don't miss the workshops of I Made Sura and I Made Leceg on the main road. Shops also carry a wide variety of other crafts, antiques, and furniture—chests, trunks, carved door frames, bamboo sofas with big pillows. For old *topeng,* wooden friezes, mirror frames, and other antiques, try **Kadek's Antique Store.** For woven textiles and *batik,* **Galuh Artshop** on the main road is the place. For quality arts and crafts from Bali and beyond, visit **Satya** in Banjar Tegeha, tel. (0361) 298032; also *barong* and *kris* dances at 0930 every morning.

Pura Puseh

The talent of the local stone sculptors grace the gate of Batubulan's **Pura Puseh,** only 175 meters east of the main road, where Hindu deities and mammoth elephants are next to statues of meditating *bodhisattvas* with Balinese facial features. Those familiar with Indo-Javanese art will instantly recall the well-known statue of *Vishnu* from Belahan, East Java, King Airlangga's portrait statue. The *pura*'s gateway is even reminiscent of South Indian gateways. However, the sculptures aren't old but copies of statues in library books borrowed from the Archaeological Service. This temple is dedicated to the village founder, who is worshipped with the gods who own the ground. A particularly strong barong mask lives here; people say they can even hear it shuffling around in its guarded storage shrine now and then.

Performances

Except for the war years and Nyepi each year, dances have been held in this village almost continually since 1936. Batubulan's first dance troupe, **Denjalan Barong,** was established in 1970 and has performed the *barong* drama every morning since. The **Puri Agung** and **Tegaltamu** groups were formed in the 1980s. Altered and abbreviated for tourist consumption, these are basically recreational, popular, commercialized performances imbued with a certain languor born of playing day after day and year in year out. Nevertheless, they are vastly entertaining and always come as a surprise to the initiate. The clowns, monsters, monkeys, and pantomines are first-rate.

Batubulan is the original home of the enthralling *kecak* monkey dance, created in 1928 by the painter Walter Spies for the German film director Baron von Plessen, who was producing the first feature film on Bali, *The Isle of Demons* (1931). The story goes that while the two were watching a performance of *sanghyang dedari,* one dancer spontaneously leapt onto the stage and assumed the *baris* posture. This gave Spies the idea of combining the chorus of the trance dance with the gestures of the formalized war dance. Spies even re-scored an original *gamelan* composition for that stunning film, causing him great disappointment when it was never used.

Today, a total of four dance venues with rising rows of bamboo seats have been set up with almost continuous weekday performances. One airy theater is out in the rice fields—a really inspiring setting. *Barong* and *kris* dances are performed 0930 for busloads of domestic and foreign tourists. Rp5000 entrance. On another stage every Saturday night the *tari kecak* and *sanghyang* are performed. This is actually a medley of popular dances but features a *kuda kepang* firewalker and two tiny *sanghyang dedari* dancers.

Ketewel

South of Sukawati and 18 kilometers southeast of Gianyar, this is one of Bali's largest, fully co-operative villages, with 14 *banjar* and around 1,500 heads of household. As in many of these "Old Bali" villages on the slopes of Gunung Batur, the headman is also the spiritual leader, decides legal matters, and oversees the village temple *(pura puseh).* The village possesses a remarkable set of extremely *sakti* female masks that are used in an archaic form of the *legong* dance, the *legong bededari,* first conceptualized in the late 19th century by a priest of Ketewel who had seen two angels in a dream.

The houses, temples, and public structures of Ketewel are fine examples of the slender, spare, and beautiful south Gianyar style of architecture, their stonemasons, woodcarvers, and gardeners being respected all over southern Bali. Sights include the handsome *wantilan* and the grand **Pura Peyogaan Agung,** whose scale and craftsmanship is equal to any of the island's state temples. Check out the inner courtyard during the biannual *odalan* when the ghostlike Ratu Dedari mask dance is staged.

Also see Ketewel's **Pura Beji** holy water temple fed by a mountain spring, as are the communal baths. From Ketewel's T-junction, the road to the east leads to the beach at **Pabean** where purification ceremonies are held at sacred **Pura Segara** sea temple. On the same road, in the southern part of the village, is the cemetery and death temple with a view of the sea. From the same T-junction, the road to the south leads after two kilometers to Gumicik, a village with a nice beach.

Celuk

A gold- and silverworking center just beyond Batubulan, noted for its delicately detailed work and fine filigree-style silver pieces produced with the simplest of handtools. Wayan Kardana and Wayan Kawi have earned solid reputations as skilled artisans, but at least 1,700 silver- and goldsmiths out of perhaps 2,500 on the whole island live and work in the cottage industries of Celuk. A skill passed down from father to son.

The classier showrooms are on the south side of town, where prices are usually given in U.S. dollars and credit cards accepted, practices that reveal who their clientele are. Tourists pull into these shops in buses usually between 1000 and 1130 (after the *kris* dance in Batubu-lan), inundate a shop owned by the brother-in-law of the bus driver, then just as suddenly as they came they're gone again in a cloud of dust. Avoid the shops during these hours as it's too difficult to haggle prices down to a realistic level. The display rooms claim fixed prices, but bargaining is usually acceptable—nay, necessary. Sample starting prices for original designs: earrings with red coral inset, Rp15,000-20,000; beaten silver necklaces, Rp30,000-40,000; large silver tray with embossing, Rp150,000; dragon bracelets, Rp60,000-125,000. The smaller silver workshops in the back of the village are cheaper. If heading toward Sukawati, turn down either of the small lanes on the left; just follow the tap-tapping of the small family compounds. These workshops are always willing to fill special orders and are quite capable of designing modern jewelry, particularly if you provide a prototype from which they can work. They also offer their own contemporary designs suited to European and American tastes. Some pieces combine silver and gold. Request to view the craftsmen, jewelers, and apprentices—numbering from one to 35—at work in the rear of the building.

Semadi Gallery, Keraton Collection, Celuk Silver, and **Widiartha Art Shop** have reasonable prices, but it's difficult to recommend any one place because about 45 crafts shops line both sides of the street, each with thousands of chains, garnet-studded rings, armbands, earrings, earclips, hairpins, fancy butterfly brooches, pendants, pill boxes, coffee sets, trays, bowls, plus a wide variety of paintings, woodcarvings (Rp25,000 for a small ebony statue), masks, puppets, and no shortage of other souvenirs like statues, textiles, basketry. Expect to pay Rp230,000 for a painting you can buy in a small gallery in Ubud for Rp69,000. **Bali Souvenir Artshop** sells original articles—amber beads, bracelets—different from the usual tourist pap found in the other shops. Another unusual *toko* is **Suardana Gold and Silver Jewelry,** tel. (0361) 298011, run by I Ketut Suardana. The prices in these shops are better than Kuta or Denpasar.

Stay in **Dharma Samadhi Accommodations and Silversmith,** only 200 meters from the main road. Don't plan to eat in Celuk; move on to Sukawati where the food is better and cheaper and where there's a large marketplace. Four kilometers west of Celuk is **Tegaltamu** (19 km

southeast of Gianyar) where artisans from tender age to old carve stone images of gods and demons. Leaving Celuk east, but before reaching the concrete bridge alongside the old suspension bridge, take the smaller road to the right which runs through the villages of Guang and Ketewel. **Guang** is well known for its Garuda statues made of black ebony or brown *sabo* wood. A technical high school in this village trains students to sculpt and carve.

Singapadu

Only one and a half kilometers northwest of Celuk is Singapadu (from *singha-padu* meaning "two lions"). In the center of the village sits a huge banyan tree and a *pura desa*. Next to the temple is the main *puri*, home of an old ally of the ruler of Sukawati who together with his leige lord defeated the Kingdom of Mengwi in the 19th century.

Singapadu today is known primarily for its consummate maskmakers, notably I Wayan Tangguh, Cokorda Raka Tisnu, I Wayan Teguh, Nyoman Juala, and I Wayan Tedun. Expect to spend from Rp75,000 to Rp150,000 for a mask at any of these masters' workshops, the price depending on the style and type of wood used (see "Maskmaking" under "Arts and Crafts" in the Introduction).

Tedun's son, Made Hartawan, and Ketut Muja and Wayan Pugeg also do high-caliber work. They sell *topeng* at good prices, perfect for souvenir purchases. In Teguh's workshop is a large collection of all the principle characters in Balinese *topeng* theater, some of the finest specimens on the island. *Barong* masks are still made in Singapadu's palace. A conscientious silversmith is Cakra of **Gala Silver** in Banjar Seseh, tel./fax (0361) 298374.

Singapadu is also renowned for its *gong saron,* an archaic and somber seven-tone *gamelan* played only at funerals. It's found only in Banjars Seseh and Apuan. Singapadu's sacred ensemble *gamelan luang* is a rare mixture of bronze and bamboo instruments.

Gala Silver, Banjar Seseh Singapadu, tel. (0361) 298374, is a clean, well-organized silver business with better prices than most. The owner speaks excellent English, is willing to work on something unusual, and can ship. Singapadu is also noteworthy for its accomplished *barong* performers, in Banjar Sungguan, and *arja* singers and dancers.

SUKAWATI

A large crafts village northeast of Celuk, 14 kilometers southwest of Gianyar, and 15 kilometers northeast of Denpasar. Many Chinese have settled here, so Sukawati is a flourishing market town, now nearly indistinguishable from neighboring Batuan. Also the home of I Wayang Wija, one of Bali's top *dalang*. A produce market, with cheap coffee, takes place every morning in the town center. Park in the Art Market parking lot on the highway (Jl. Raya Sukawati) for Rp300, then walk around.

An excellent little place to eat is **Depot Selecta Sukawati,** a Chinese-run *warung* beside the Art Market where the Balinese themselves eat. Good, inexpensive dishes: Chinese omelettes, *mie kuah* (Rp2000), Chicken *nasi campur* (Rp2500), iced drinks. Its easy to meet people there.

During the village's *odalan*, there are up to three processions per day (one for each *banjar*) for four days in a row in which girls in long trailing dresses walk from Sukawati's striking temples to a nearby holy spring.

History
Sukawati was a center of power and arts during the Dalem dynasty in the early part of the 18th century. Legend has it the town came under the spell of Ki Balian Batur, an evil sorcerer. In his attempts to defend the kingdom, the raja of Mengwi sought assistance from I Dewa Agung Anom, the son of Dewa Agung of Klungkung. Using powerful weapons from the court at Klungkung, they soundly defeated the wicked man. Ki Balian Batur's name lives on in the name of the nearby hamlet of Rangkan ("Place of the Evildoer").

I Dewa Agung Anom set about establishing a kingdom along the lines of the grandiose Majapahit of East Java, bringing from Klungkung a whole company of high-bred dancers and musicians who entertained the raja on the lavish grounds and gardens of his palace. So sweet and intoxicating were the sounds of the *gamelan* wafting from the great gilded *bale* that the populace gave the palace the name *sukahatine,*

meaning "my heart's delight," which eventually evolved into Sukawati.

Although I Dewa Agung Anom's reign was long, who was to succeed him was eventually thrown into question. Tormented that his sons were ill-suited to rule, he declared that when he died whichever son dare take the corpse's tongue into his mouth would inherit the kingdom. Upon his death, the raja's body became so decomposed that none of his sons were willing to perform the repulsive task. However, when a close relative, the raja of Gianyar, stepped forward and took the hideous tongue into his mouth, the corpse immediately shrank to normal size and began to give off a pleasant aroma.

Soon after, the disgraced heirs of the kingdom were defeated in war by the armies of Gianyar, and the palace was abandoned. But Sukawati's royal legacy explains why the village still sponsors preeminent dance and *topeng* troupes and is the home of famous *tukang prada* (makers of gold painted umbrellas and costumes) and *tukang wadah* (builders of cremation towers). Sukawati has also been credited with creating the modern form of *legong,* which features two prepubescent girls.

Temples
Sukawati's complex of temples is only rivaled by Besakih. **Pura Penataran Agung** in the center of Sukawati is sacred to members of the royal houses of the surrounding areas since it was the highest ranking. Destroyed in the 1917 quake, the temple has since been rebuilt to a smaller scale. Next door, in **Pura Kawitan Dalem Sukawati,** check out the panel carvings of *Tantri* fables. In the northeast part of town is **Pura Desa** with its huge *candi bentar*.

Dalang and *Wayang Kulit*
Sukawati's 25 or so *dalang* and their troupes regularly win the island's Grand Puppeteer title, because, it is said, of the potent *taksu* shrine in Sukawati's *pura dale* before which the shadow puppeteers appeal for power. On Bali, the status of *dalang* is almost equal to that of priests. The town's most renowned are I Wayang Nartha, I Wayan Wija, Ganjreng, and the brilliant *gender wayang* performer I Wayang Loceng, who is an expert in all aspects of shadow puppetry *(pewayangan)*.

Shops all over Bali sell souvenir-quality *wayang kulit,* but in Sukawati you can buy the real thing. Wija, the popular *dalang* who lives in Banjar Babakan has developed a theater based on the *Tantri* fables, having created an utterly original set of leather animal puppets. In this neighborhood's puppeteer workshops prices range Rp15,000 to Rp45,000 depending on the size, quality, and complexity of the carved, punched, and brightly painted *wayang kulit,* made from high-grade cow or buffalo hide.

Handicrafts

Ata baskets (called *ato* here) show the same detail and quality yet are offered at cheaper starting prices than in Tengenan, where they are supposedly made (shopowners here say, simply, that *ata* come from Karangasem). **Kios Adi Putra,** Jl. Raya Sukawati, on the north side of *Pasar Sukawesi,* has a wide selection of these extraordinarily durable baskets. *Copot* baskets from Lombok start at Rp9000. Also sold are large, attractively patterned *lontar*-palm baskets tinted with natural brown, black, and white dyes (Rp5000-15,000), which are used by market women to carry goods.

Sukawati also produces woven bamboo baskets, bamboo bird cages, colorfully painted woodcarvings, miniature *jukung* (Rp3000), and ornate long-handled temple umbrellas. Sukawati is also the windchime-making capital of Bali.

For first-class, fairly priced, custom-made gold- and silversmithing, visit I Nyoman Sadia at Jl. Sarsan Wayan Pugig 5, just off the main road in Banjar Babakan in the north end of town. Nyoman takes one or two weeks for delivery. At the *bale banjar* on the left side of the road, turn right down a steep hill, then east 200 meters down an unpaved road. His workshop is on the left.

Sukawati Art Market

Opposite the *pasar* is the two-story Art Market (also called Pasar Seni), a crowded warren's nest of stalls selling woodcarvings, textiles, clothes (attractive *batik* shirts for only Rp4000-6000), curios, paintings, stone statues, dance costumes, and temple accessories like gilded umbrellas and bamboo flutes. A lot of flimsy junk and cheap souvenirs, so when bargaining keep your sense of humor. The prices are already very good. To save money, art shop owners and hawkers from all over Bali come here to buy articles in their original state then finish them.

Vicinity of Sukawati

North of the market, after the police station, is a side road to the left that leads to **Puaya,** about one kilometer from the main road, a production center for *wayang kulit* made from hide, *topeng* masks, traditionally painted dance costumes and theater ornaments, and dolls made of old Chinese coins.

A muddy but still satisfying walk in the rainy season is from Sukawati's 14-kilometers milestone, near the *pasar.* Take the dirt road east to **Banjar Delod Pangkung,** a traditional village of walled compounds and small thatched shrines. From here continue east to the village of **Banjar Babakan,** famous for its puppetmasters.

East beyond the *banjar* the path leads through a cold, dark bamboo forest. Carry on over the bamboo bridge spanning the Tukad Palak River, over another bamboo bridge, then past bathing places, fields of *alang-alang,* peaceful *subak* temples, and a rice hulling station until you reach the amazing 20-meter-high **Tegenungan Waterfall.** After the hike, bathe in the public bath of **Pura Musen,** the river temple of the *desa* of Belangsinga. The path ends up in **Belangsinga** where you pick up the asphalt road to Blahbatu between Denpasar and Gianyar.

Finally, there's an almost deserted beach, **Purnama,** only four kilometers off the main road, where no one will ask you where you come from or if you want to buy anything. Get there by either walking or hiring a ride on the back of a motorcycle (Rp3000 one-way). This beach has jet-black sand and is perfect for sunbathing.

BATUAN

An old Buddhist-Brahman village 13 kilometers southwest of Gianyar and 18 kilometers northeast of Denpasar. The name *batuan* ("stone") probably refers to an ancient time in the town's history when a circle of plinths was constructed as a ceremonial meeting place for ancestral worship. Opposite the *wantilan,* **Pura Puseh,** dating from the 11th century, has some fine carvings. The village's *pura dalem,* predictably, contains a fearsome statue of Rangda. In Batuan's main temple, **Pura Desa Batuan,** is an inscription dating from 1022. It's believed that Batuan's **Pura Gede Mecaling** was built on the site of the palace of the blackfaced, incestuous demon Jero Gede Mecaling, held in respect and awe by Balinese everywhere.

History

Batuan's golden age was from the early 1600s to the early 1700s when the royal family of Gusti Ngurah Batulepang controlled most of southern Bali. Their power was eclipsed when a splinter court of the Klungkung royal family established themselves in nearby Sukawati in the early 1800s. All that remains of the Batulepang kingdom is a small temple honoring Gusti Batulepang on the site of his former palace. Because of royal patronage by **Anak Agung Gede Oka** (1860-1947), Batuan became a very active center for woodcarving and the fine arts in the early part of this century.

Drama and *Gamelan Gambuh*

Batuan is celebrated for its dancers. Students from around the world visit this village to learn *baris* and *topeng* in the homes of several *topeng* dance masters, namely I Made Jimat and I Ketut Kantor. Kantor is the son of the late dancemaster I Nyoman Kakul who excelled in performing the *gambuh* repertoire, *arja* operettas, as well as the masked *wayang topeng.*

During Batuan's elaborate, colorful *odalan* celebrations, exquisitely poised old women perform the offering dance *(mendet)* and episodes from old Javanese stories in the courtyard of the village's main temple to the accompaniment of a superb *gamelan* ensemble, Bali's oldest extant orchestra. This stately *gamelan* consists of just a *rebab,* drums, and one-meter-long, ghostly sounding bamboo flutes.

Painting

Like the painters of Kamasan near Klungkung, Batuan artists had a long tradition of painting in the *wayang*-style until the 1930s when some of its artists came under the tutelage of Spies, Bonnet, and other influential Pita Maha members. Two brothers, I Patera and I Ngendon, were the first to adopt the principles of human anatomy taught by Bonnet and to introduce themes of

daily life into their early black and white ink drawings. Dewa Ketut Baru was another accomplished practitioner of distinctive China-ink drawings.

Batuan painters, many of them also dancers and musicians, developed a naive vitality using short, dynamic figures dotting their landscapes. Reds, browns, and blacks were the dominant colors used by these early painters. By contrast, Ubud's painters used tall and glamorous figures. The best paintings of the Batuan school of the 1930s are in the Puri Lukisan Museum of Ubud. That same attention to detail and magical atmosphere are retained in contemporary painting.

The most important exponents of the Batuan style today are Ida Bagus Putu Gede (son of Ida Bagus Togog), Made Tubuh, and Wayan Rajin. The painter I Made Budi (b. 1932) is noted for his colorful and ribald depictions of past tourists. Budi's home is near the schoolhouse.

Galleries and Art Shops

Batuan is a good place to shop for *patung* (statuary) and carved wooden panels, doors, furniture, screens, and reliefs. Numerous shops line the highway. Also check out the masks of Dewa Cita, son of the celebrated maskmaker Dewa Putu Bebes, Dewa Mandra of Batuan, and Made Regug of Negara, a hamlet one kilometer east of Batuan.

Owned by the family of I Patera and I Ngendon, **Dewata Art,** tel. (0361) 298426, displays a large selection of handwoven textiles, paintings, and woodcarvings. Coffee tables with fantastic erotic carvings sell for Rp9.2 million. The carving technique is demonstrated out front. Reasonable prices.

Gelombang Gold and Silversmith on the main road employs 20 experienced gold and silversmiths. Good export-quality, uniquely designed jewelry at competitive prices, ranging from plain gold rings to intricate gold brooches set with precious stones. Also traditional Balinese style cutlery sets. Special orders accepted.

The painter **Dewa Ketut Rai,** Banjar Tengah, practices a wide variety of styles. Dozens of young apprentices work in the courtyard outlining paintings. Their strong point are miniatures, very original and fine work, not the same old schlock of rice paddies and bare-breasted women. Pieces sell at widely differing prices. A valuable insight into Balinese painting *as a business.*

BLAHBATUH AND VICINITY

Four kilometers east of the Sakah turnoff to Ubud on the main Denpasar-Gianyar highway, or seven kilometers west of Gianyar. Blahbatuh District is known for the number of reservoirs where freshwater fish are raised. While in town, visit the orchid nurseries and the remarkable **Pura Gaduh** at the top of a steep stairway shaded by overhanging trees, rebuilt after the 1917 earthquake. The massive stone head is of the fearsome mythical giant, Kebo Iwo, believed to have carved with his fingernails a wealth of ancient stone monuments on Bali. He served the last Balinese king, Bedulu, an unrelenting despot with the head of a boar who was finally toppled by Gajah Mada in the Majapahit invasion of 1343. Though dating from the 14th century, the temple's statuary doesn't resemble Hindu-Javanese iconography of the time; it might be a native Balinese creation.

Blahbatuh is a minor kingdom founded by Gusti Ngurah Jelantik, prime minister of Gelgel, leader of a famous military expedition against Java in the early 17th century. During the campaign, booty was amassed and brought back to Bali, including 21 extraordinary portrait masks of important Majapahit personages. Said to be the prototypes of all Balinese dance-drama masks, these *topeng* have for over 600 years been kept in rather dilapidated **Pura Penataran Topeng** near Blahbatu's *puri*. These mysterious and powerful totems are only seen during the temple's *odalan* festival.

Blahbatuh is an important junction town from where you can head up to historic Gunung Kawi via Kutri, proceed to Bangli and the spectacular Batur region, or head for Klungkung, Rendang, and Besakih. About one kilometer to the west of the town's crossroads is a small road to **Belangsinga** village, the location of a waterfall on the Petanu River known as Srog Srogan or Air Terjun Tegenungan. It is reputed to be a place of healing. Don't go on Sunday, but on the night of the full moon when *pedanda* come to pray at the nearby Pura Merta Jiwa ("water of immortality").

The village of **Belaga**, one kilometer east between Blahbatuh and Bona, is noted for its bamboo artisans who craft mostly implements and furniture using "black" and natural bamboo.

Pieces can be broken down for shipping. On the road between Blahbatuh and Bona, take the small road south to **Kramas Beach** with its sweeping panoramas over the Indian Ocean.

Gongmaker

About 500 meters north of Blahbatuh's main crossroads in Blahbatu Kaja, a small road leads east (turn at the *balai banjar*) to **Banjar Babakan,** about 150 meters down on the left. Ask for **Kerajinan Gong Sidha Karya,** the home and workplace of Bali's only surviving gongmaker, I Made Gabeleran, a world authority on bronze casting and Balinese instrument-making. Gongsmiths are held in high esteem on Bali, having formed a caste of their own. A must-see for lovers of *gamelan,* this *pabrik gong* is bigger than it looks, at least five rooms given over to the production of musical instruments. All kinds of Balinese musical instruments—*gangsa, trompong, kendang* drum, tiny bells—are forged here. In the rear of the factory, scenes from the Ramayana are ornately carved and then painted in red and gold on stands, frames, and cases of jackfruit wood made by local woodcarvers. These carvers are amazingly fast; two working from either end are able to carve a whole *gangsa* in a day.

Metal components of the xylophone-like instruments are cast from a mixture of tin and copper. Using an ancient method, this alloy is then poured by squatting, bare-chested smiths into banana tree molds, which burst into flame as the metal sets. Casting is done every Saturday and Sunday to give student apprentices a chance to learn the technique, but on any day you might see a red-hot bronze disk taken from a roaring charcoal fire stoked by hand bellows and then hammered into a *kempli* gong on a hand-held anvil. Tuning the instruments to a pair of bamboo tuning forks is achieved by laboriously filing the metal. Each *gamelan* is tuned slightly differently so that the ensemble's unique character can emerge when played.

This workshop's capacity is about five or six *gamelan* sets per year. A complete *gong kebyar* sells for around Rp25 million. Large gongs 75 cm round and weighing 205 kg cost Rp1.5 million, small (40 cm, 4 kg) gongs are Rp300,000, bell sets Rp150,000, *kempur* Rp800,000, *rebab* Rp200,000, *cengceng* Rp150,000, and xylophonic-like *gangsa* Rp550,000-800,000. You're welcome to sound the gongs.

Kutri

Opposite Blahbatuh's *pura* is the road leading straight to Kutri (five kilometers). About 400 meters south of the village is **Pura Pedarman** (or Pura Durga Kutri) the *pura puseh* of Kutri, lying at the bottom of the hill of Bukit Dharma. It was built in honor of King Airlangga's mother, Gunapriadarmapatni (Mahendradatta), a Javanese princess who married Udayana, a prince from the Warmadewa dynasty, at the end of the 10th century. She came to Bali to rule until her death in 1006. This royal widow-sorceress cursed and plagued her own son's kingdom. Scholars speculate that she is the historical origin of the witch-queen Rangda. Possibly the queen was cremated on this hill, her ashes then taken to Gunung Kawi where a tomb dedicated to her was carved out of the riverbank.

In the temple's inner sanctum in the small, white shrine on the right are several statues of Durga. From the lower temple, climb the steep stone steps to the summit of Bukit Dharma through a forest of banyan trees gripping huge volcanic boulders. At the top is a sanctuary with an 11th-century stone frieze of Durga standing on a *nandi* (bull), possessed by a demon while she delivers the death-blow to the animal. Though well-worn, her face is still arresting. She carries all the trappings of almost unlimited supernatural power: javelin, shield, bow and arrow, winged conch shell, flaming sharp-edged disk *(chakra),* and flask containing *amerta.* With its fine classic Indian lines, this relief is considered one of the most finely wrought sculptures left from the early Pejeng Kingdom.

Vicinity of Kutri: North of Kutri, **Tegallinggah,** a complex of unfinished hewn-rock cloisters, niches, pavilions, and *candi* that has the appearance of a mini Gunung Kawi was abandoned because of an earthquake or some other natural disaster. When it was discovered by Krijgsman in the 1920s, most of the facades and niches had already collapsed. Excavation and restoration began in the 1950s. You'll need a guide because the access is difficult. South of Kutri is the small village of **Buruan,** the home of well-known sculptors and dancers. In the *banjar* of **Bangun Liman** to the west, the *pura desa,*

pura puseh, and the *pura dalem* have been built all in a row; usually these temples are in different locations in the village. Down on the riverbanks, to the west of Bangun Liman, troupes of wild monkeys live in a natural habitat.

Kemenuh

A major carving center about nine kilometers southwest of Gianyar, Kemenuh is known for its huge Garuda statues and other mythic figures up to three meters tall (either painted or unpainted). The so-called "driftwood carvings" of Kemenuh, if you can find them, are unique. Most of the carvings are done inside family compounds; the only advertisements are small signs on the compound gates. Visit **Bali Budaya, Ida Bagus Marka,** and **Ida Bagus Komang Menaka,** three spacious shops. A wide range of woodcarvings, from fine art to functional pieces, can also be seen at **Gallery Marka** in Br. Sumampan, P.O. Box 277, Denpasar 80001, tel. (0361) 235775, fax 87073. Over the years I.B. Marka has acquired the best work from the best artists. High prices. Also see the *pura dalem* of Kemenuh for its intricate and beautiful carvings.

Sakah

Heading west from Kemenuh, you'll see on the left just before reaching the Sakah crossroads a big *ganggahan* tree (similar to a *waringan*) supporting a sign directing the visitor to **Pura Canggi,** 500 meters from the Denpasar-Gianyar Highway. This 14th-century temple, in the shape of a *meru,* features curious inverted ornaments on its eaves, vase-shaped decorations resembling Chinese lanterns—an altogether peculiar Majapahit-period specimen. The Canggi gateway was only brought to the attention of the Archaeological Service in 1921. It's thought that prior to the great 1917 earthquake three gateways existed. The extant one is located between the *pura*'s first and second courtyards. Note the ram and bulls to each side of the entrance. The structure was restored in 1949-51; the shape of the gate's original roof is unknown. Near the gate are several ancient statues as well as *yoni* fragments. The villagers have added a second gateway *(kori agung)* in the modern style, which seems out of place.

In the village of Sakah itself is a similar gateway, **Pura Yeh Tiba,** also guarded by stone animals (elephants in the back, bulls in front). The date carved in the gateway is depicted in pictures: *candrasengkala,* meaning "moon-eye bow and arrow elephant," or 1336. Sakah is where the road to Klungkung and Ubud branches; you make your connection here when taking a *bemo* farther east.

The gigantic **baby statue** in the middle of the crossroads at Sakah is made from 45,000 kg of sandstone and represents the beginning of life.

MAS

An affluent center for the arts 20 kilometers northeast of Denpasar, Rp600 from Terminal Kereneng, and only five kilometers south of Ubud, Rp400 by *bemo*. Historically, the Brahmanic village of Mas (which means "gold") is thought to be where the wandering high priest Niratha finally settled. Niratha emigrated from East Java in the 15th century and founded temples all over the island. The majority of Bali's Brahmans today claim descent from this venerated Hindu sage.

Beautiful **Pura Taman Pule,** on the east side of town behind the soccer field, only 100 meters from the road, is believed to be built on the original site of Niratha's hermitage *(griya).* Note the temple's ornately carved wooden doors overlaid with gold leaf; woodcarving in temples isn't common.

The *kecak* dance is regularly staged in Mas, and during the three-day **Kuningan** festival the ancient *wayang wong* drama plays in Pura Taman Pule's umbrella-studded courtyard along with a huge outdoor fair, colorful processions with high offerings, and dancing and theater day and night. In the early morning one of the largest and most frenetic cockfights in Bali is held in a nearby arena.

Accommodations and Food
Stay in enormously pleasant **Taman Harum Cottages,** Box 216, Denpasar 80001, owned by the famous woodcarver Ida Bagus Tantra. Located behind the Tantra Gallery in the southern outskirts of Mas, this very high-level homestay costs US$45-50 (honeymoon suite US$75). Lots of great art in the large rooms; cultural programs are also offered. The only restaurant is **Puri Rasa** (Indonesian-Chinese food) down the

street from the Puri Rasa Gallery, but you can eat noodle soup with meatballs (Rp1000) and *rujak* (Rp500) at any of the *pedagang kaki lima.* The *warung* sell small snacks for Rp100.

Woodcarving
One could say that modern Balinese woodcarving had its origins in Mas. Formerly, carvings were done only by priests for religious purposes and featured exclusively characters from the Mahabarata and Ramayana. During the 1930s, the themes became more realistic and commercialized, depicting such mundane subjects as animals, farmers, villages.

Several old masters who made Balinese woodcarving famous throughout the world in the 1930s are still alive and working today in Mas. Their work is carried on by their families in traditional family compounds with carved doors and pillars, impeccably decorated and maintained, themelves fine examples of gorgeous Old Bali art and architecture.

They carve everything in Mas—weeping Buddhas, fishermen, Vishnu and Garuda figures, rice goddesses, yogi, roosters, herons, deer, prancing horses, key rings, chess pieces, and fruit trees *(pulusan).* Most master carvers are in fact designers, who make the original model or motif which is then copied by a young team of apprentices. Pieces don't leave the studio without approval. Typically, Mas carvings are smooth, unpainted, and made of the high-quality wood, but carvers also shape gnarly driftwood and tree roots into lizards, turtles, tortoises, abstract faces, fishheads. If you can't find what you're looking for, ask to see the inventory in back. Look for detail: fingernails, toenails, fingers, muscle delineation, even hair. An artist signs and dates his important pieces. Telling the clerks you want to buy goods for export to America or Europe will drop prices. For the best prices, comb the workshops in the back lanes of Mas and not in the overpriced retail shops along the main road. One of the newest phenomena in modern maskmaking are the works of **Garfield Pop Art and Cat and Masks** off the main road. The largest and most expensive shops are on the edges of Mas, where big turnaround driveways accommodate tour buses carrying hundreds of tourists (commissions are paid to drivers and tour leaders). Prices are in U.S. dollars.

Wiryati's Art and Handicraft Collection, tel. (0361) 975542, is a wholesale shop selling attractive painted statues of cats, tigers, and other animals quite cheaply. Individual pieces cost Rp3000-5000, while sets of three are Rp7500-15,000. Other artshops to visit are Ketut Roja's **Siadja and Son** and **Adil Artshop** featuring the works of Ida Bagus Taman.

Ever since Ida Bagus Tilem (1936-1994) was chosen to represent Indonesia at the 1964 World's Fair in New York, his work has been sought by collectors worldwide. The internationally acclaimed artist seems to have inherited considerable talent from his father, Ida Bagus Njana (1912-1985), a great innovator of carving styles in the 1960s, some say the inventor of modern Balinese carving. Njana came up with the statues with elongated torsos. Both Tilem's and the work of his father are exhibited in a large, fashionable, multilevel, multiroom gallery/atelier in Mas. Open 0930-1730.

To view this high-priced collection is to take in at one glance all aspects of traditional life on Bali—a lifetime of carving! In the back room is a very rare collection of old ivory, mostly from Sumatra, including an elaborately carved tusk, and wonderful old Balinese *topeng* (not for sale). In the downstairs courtyard is Tilem's collection of old Balinese religious carvings and statues.

Maskmaking

Some of Bali's most famous maskmakers work in home industries down the back lanes of Mas. You'll see the carvers' signs on the compound gates. Most produce wall hangings, not true masks. With some exceptions, the Balinese would seldom buy them for use in performances. Many of the more established maskmakers teach maskmaking for around Rp5000 per lesson. Each specializes in different kinds of masks. Prices range from Rp30,000 to Rp150,000, depending on size, color, and complexity. Better prices later in the day. **I.B. Sutarja** retails his masterpieces for Rp2.3 million but the masks by his 12 children are much cheaper.

Ida Bagus Oka of **Oka Travelyan Mask Makers** carves faces and figures with African, Oceanic, Northwest American Indian motifs. The phantasmagoric, traditional masks of **Ida Bagus Anom** are in high demand by *topeng* players and pantomines all over Bali. Anom offers a three week east-west *topeng* dance mask workshop (about Rp10,000 per day) and gives lectures and demos to groups on the maskmaking process. **Sadana,** Anom's brother, carves surrealistic statuary and fantastical masks.

Learning maskmaking from his grandfather from the age of six, **I Wayan Muka** (b. 1962), the head of Banjar Batan Ancak, is another original and skilled maskmaker with a sound reputation as a teacher. In his studio are two enormous masks, wide as a tree trunk, commissioned by President Suharto. These 1.5-meter-high masks took one and a half years to make. Ask for one of his very entertaining demos. His prices range Rp40,000-200,000. Visa and MasterCard accepted. Open 0800-1700, tel. (0361) 974530.

UBUD

Ubud lies 36 km from the resorts on the southern coast. The name for this royal village is derived from the Balinese word *ubad* (medicine), the moniker of a herb with healing properties which grows along the nearby Oos River. If you aren't interested in overpriced tourist hype but want comfortable accommodations at good prices, a central location, and all the facilities in a less hurried rural environment than the south, the Ubud area is for you. Despite the bumper-to-bumper traffic, too many loud motorcycles, and thousands of tourists during Bali's peak tourist seasons, when it's difficult to find a parking space, Ubud still shows glimpses of its basically rural character.

However, this may not be your first impression. When you first arrive, you might get the feeling there are more visitors than Balinese. With its hundreds of art galleries, studios, and souvenir shops, and the flurry and congestion around the two-story market on the main road, Ubud looks like a big commercial scene—totally disenchanting. A monster, Sarinah-style department store, with crafts from all over Indonesia, has gone up on Monkey Forest Road. Development is so frenetic now that shops,

UBUD

TAMAN INDAH HOMESTAY

SAMBAHAN

JUNJUNGAN

ANANDA COTTEGES

KETUT'S PLACE

CAMPUAN

KUTAH

BUMBU
MUMBUL'S GARDEN TERRACE CAFE

HAN SNEL
PURI LUKISAN
MUMBUL INN
GRIYA
LOTUS CAFE
PURI SAREN

SENIWATI WOMAN'S GALLERY

SHADANA VEGETARIAN RESTAURANT

GANESHA BOOKSHOP

POLICE

PENESTANAN

TJAMPUHAN HOTEL
MIRO'S
ARY'S WARUNG
ARY'S BOOKSHOP
BEGGAR'S BUSH

NOMAD RESTAURANT
SANAK

JL. UBUD RAYA

OKA KARTINI

BLANCO'S
MURNI'S
PRINGGA JUWITA WATER GARDEN COTTAGES
TJANDERI'S
WIDIANA'S HOUSE
GANDRA ACCOMMODATIONS

POST OFFICE

PELIATAN DANCE VENUE

JL. SRIWEDARI

JL. PADANGTEGAL

MATAHARI PENSION

PIZZA ROMA

OKA WATI'S SUNSET BUNGALOWS
MERTA HOUSE

RONA ACCOMMODATION

NICK'S PENSION

PANDE HOMESTAY

BENDI'S

SOCCER FIELD

IBU MASIH SUNGALOWS

WARSI'S HOUSE
CAFE BALI
JATI HOMESTAY

MANDALA BUNGALOWS
MUDITA INN

UBUD VILLAGE HOTEL
FROG POND INN

JL. HANOMAN

CAFE WAYAN RESTAURANT AND BAKERY

S. WOS

ARTINI GUESTHOUSE II

CAPPUCCINO ITALIAN RESTAURANT

MONKEY FOREST RD.

UBUD

ARTINI II

PERTIWI BUNGALOWS
DEWI SRI BUNGALOWS

NYOMAN KARSA BUNGALOWS
KURA KURA

MONKEY FOREST
JATI INN II

JL. COK GEDE RAI

AGUNG RAI GALLERY

ALAM INDAH
KUBUKU'S RESTAURANT

PELIATAN

NYUHKUNING

AGUNG RAKA BUNGALOWS
ARMA COMPLEX

BALI BREEZE BUNGALOWS
KOKOKAN RESTAURANT

PENGOSEKAN

SITI HOMESTAY

NOT TO SCALE

© MOON PUBLICATIONS, INC.

homestays, hotels, and restaurants ring the soccer field. The Menara has been taken down—the end of an era—and a Kuta-style glitzy restaurant put up in its place.

But not all development is bad. By spring of 1995, the paving of Monkey Forest Road was finally completed. A smooth blacktop road with sidewalks, which greatly reduces the dust, now leads from the center of Ubud all the way to Monkey Forest; new public trash cans dot the street and potted plants embellish the storefronts.

The village now seems to be growing toward Padangtegal, with new busineses opening up every month. The newest area to develop is Jl. Sukma. Some years ago it was just a sleepy dirt road with homes, a few *losmen,* and shops, but now it's paved all the way from the main road to the junction with the highway to Gianyar, cluttered with scores of accommodations, shops, and new restaurants. A moratorium on building new hotels, decreed by the local government in 1995, will help the situation enormously.

One of the most unpleasant things about Ubud is the pushy dance ticket hawkers. Those selling various modes of transportation are also rude and constantly hassle tourists. Also, try to avoid being in Ubud in August. After the first of September, the number of tourists crops dramatically.

The town and its surrounding collection of villages offer the best value accommodations on Bali, and certainly the best food. In the immediate outskirts, as little as 100 meters from the main road, traditional culture and the demands of the tourist industry coexist to some degree. Culture goes on in spite of the influx of tourists and their dollars, and much of the town is touristy without being tacky. It's classier than Kuta, with upper middle-class tourists and young travelers in the majority. Even the mangy dogs of Ubud are now so used to tourists that they no longer bark and keep you awake at night.

Although new tourist services are being added constantly, part of the Ubud area's charm is that these villages have a very spotty power supply, with electricity at a premium. A flashlight is definitely needed to wend your way safely at night along the rutted, muddy back lanes. Also make sure your door and windows are secure; thievery is worst on the Monkey Forest Road.

The air here is pungent—it smells of earth, river, and rainforest. Ubud is higher (300 meters) and cooler than the south, with delightful fresh air and fewer flies and mosquitoes. The stars over Ubud almost crowd out the sky they're so bright, and during the day the heavens are crowned with fluffy cumulus and wispy cirrus clouds. Wandering around in the crisp night air is pleasant and safe.

Candidasa, Denpasar, and the airport are all only an hour's drive from Ubud, and beautiful landscapes and historical sites—Pujung, Gunung Kawi, Goa Gadjah, Tirta Empul, Yeh Pulu—are within easy reach. You can enjoy dozens of scenic nature walks around the village—pick any lane and just keep on walking. The best time is at dawn. Just east of Ubud is Bali's former capital, Pejeng, the center of the Balinese Holy Land and home to the highest concentration of antiquities on the island.

Culturally speaking, Ubud is to Bali what Yogyakarta is to Java. Ever since the German painter Walter Spies made his home here in the 1930s, Ubud has been a haven for both native and European artists. In an area of 10 square km in and around this village live Bali's most accomplished dancers, musicians, painters, and carvers. Temple festivals, celebrations, and performing arts—baby's first haircut, dance rehearsals, even an occasional cremation—are offered somewhere in the area every day of the week. Ubud is also the expat capital of Bali. A permanent Western community resides here because cultural and natural attributes make it the ideal place for those who wish to stay for any length of time on Bali. It has the best restaurants and cafes on the island and long-term accommodations are plentiful, low-cost, and comfortable. From your *losmen* or homestay family you can learn how to make a bamboo mouth harp, study painting, maskmaking, and *gamelan,* or learn the art of the *dalang.*

History

The royal village of Ubud grew to prosperity in the fertile land between rivers in the 19th century, ruled by feudal lords who paid allegiance to the raja of Gianyar. Foremost among them were the greatly respected Sukawati family of the *satriya* caste, who at one time controlled most of the surrounding districts. The Sukawatis learned to successfully work within the Dutch colonial system through their membership in the Volksraad, the People's Council based in Batavia, and they became politically powerful on Bali by intermarrying with other aristocratic families of Mengwi and Gianyar. The eldest son of the king, Tjokorda Raka Sukawati (1910-1978) was an ultraconservative who worked closely with the Dutch.

The prince was one of the earliest sponsors of such Western artists as Walter Spies, who arrived on Bali in 1925 with a letter of introduction from his former patron, the sultan of Yogyakarta. This influential European artist built a house in Campuan, attracting celebrities from around the world. Ubud thus established its reputation as the flourishing cultural center of Bali, an image virtually guaranteed with the arrival of the artistic genius I Gusti Nyoman Lempad (1860-1978) who fled Bedulu in 1890 to escape the wrath of an oppressive lord.

In 1930s and '40s, Ubud's role as the epicenter of Balinese culture was further enhanced by the arrival of foreign painters (Bonnet), anthropologists (Mead, Bateson), and writers and musicologists (Covarrubias and McPhee), and the rise of Balinese painters and sculptures (Bagus Nyana, I Cokot), as well as architects, *lontar* experts, and literati. In the early days, when tourists in Ubud commissioned a dance troupe from another area, it made the locals so agitated they quickly learned the dance and music themselves. Mass tourism became, in effect, a new kind of patronage, a powerful incentive for performers to try out new ideas. The tiny village received electricity in 1976 and a telephone system in 1987.

SIGHTS

Ubud's main palace, **Puri Saren,** lies on the northeast corner of the town's main crossroads facing the two-story *pasar,* and at Jl. Hanoman 47 there's a beautiful temple. But Ubud's best-known landmark is busy, newly paved Monkey Forest Road, a tacky one-way thoroughfare recalling the hippie era. You can reach it either from the road beside Ubud's market or from Peliatan via Pengosekan. Because of congestion, the walk down Monkey Forest Road is only pleasant at night; in the daytime it's buzzing with automobiles, motorbikes, and small trucks.

All the *bale* are giving way to souvenir stalls, and the road is giving way to the blight of mass tourism.

This is one of my favorite places to watch both monkeys and people. It could be subtitled "Tourist Forest." Feeding time brings the monkeys down out of the trees at 1000 and 1600 when they are fed potatoes. Made, one of the feeders, has been caring for the monkeys for the past 15 years, and knows the individual monkeys. He is also a painter and later showed me some of his work, for 75% below the gallery prices, after negotiating.

The sign says "Do Not Feed the Monkeys" yet they sell peanuts and bananas. As Made showed me, the secret to enjoying the monkeys, without getting hurt or robbed, is this. You sit quietly and let them come to you. Put away all extra food, zip purses shut, lock down cameras, or they will search you. Before you go, take off any jewelry and paraphernalia that you don't need—they'll gladly take possession of earrings and necklaces. Then either hand the food to them or simply lay it in the palm of your hand.

I spent long stretches with the monkeys. They would perch on my lap, draping a warm furry arm on my shoulder while they munched and watched everything. They don't care to be petted at all. Unwary tourists can get scratched or bit by treating these creatures as pets. They are wild animals with all the dignity and free will that implies. If you take the cement path up the hill just inside the lower gate, you will see a temporary burial ground for those bodies awaiting cremation.

—ALAN R. JANSEN

The Monkey Forest

At the south end of Monkey Forest Road is the Monkey Forest, with a beautiful small, cavelike *pura dalem* embraced by roots and a holy spring inhabited by a band of irascible gray monkeys. The *pura dalem* on a hill around the corner (right fork) contains well-executed statues of Rangda devouring children. The temple has been given a face-lift—new entrance, an explanation in Balinese and English, more attractive walkways. It's fairly small and peaceful with no persistent hawkers. Give a donation.

Vendors sell bags of *kacang* (Rp500) for the monkeys, but if you carry no food they'll leave you alone. The simians are definitely habituated to people. The tour buses from the south tend to arrive in the early afternoons, a time to avoid. On the other hand, tourist-watching can be more fascinating than monkey-watching. Refresh yourself at the cold-water springs just before the forest or in *warung* beyond (Rp500 for an iced drink). A path beside the great banyan tree leads down to the bathing place inside a remnant of the dipterocarp forest that once covered all of Bali.

The Monkey Forest Road loops around to a fork; the left branch leads to Pengosekan's many woodcarving and clothing stores while the right leads to the small village of **Nyuhkuning,** another center for woodcarving.

Puri Lukisan

Meaning "Palace of Paintings," this is Ubud's art museum in the middle of Ubud at the north end of Jalan Ubud Raya. The complex is situated in a garden with serene rice paddies and water buffaloes out the back windows. Spanning the years between the 1930s and the present, this museum houses one of the island's finest selections of modern paintings, drawings, and sculptures (Bali Museum in Denpasar specializes mainly in traditional art). The museum was founded in 1956 by Tjokorde Gede Agung Sukawati, the raja of Ubud and a patron of the arts, and Rudolph Bonnet (1895-1979), a Dutchman who devoted much of his life to studying and preserving the unique quality of Balinese painting.

The mission of Puri Lukisan is to develop and set standards for local art, to educate and stimulate young artists, and to record for posterity unvulgarized Balinese art before the tourist indus-

Ubud has a special charm. You will see all sorts of people of all ages and nations wandering the streets every day but still the Balinese way of life seems largely unchanged. You'll see people giving customary offerings to the gods each morning, stop for a chat with the local farmers or villagers, try any of a myriad of beautiful walks around the area, spend the morning in the wonderful local market where true bargains abound, or just explore the craft and art workshops up and down the local streets. Don't pay for an aircon room here—you won't need it. The climate is cooler and, while still warm and humid in the day, it is very comfortable at night.

—Senior Farr

try finished it off for good. It's establishment was the first deliberate attempt to separate the arts from communal religious life. Thus Puri Lukisan is a monument or a tomb, whichever way you want to look at it.

During the frenzied activity of the 1930s, young painters broke away from the traditional formalistic paintings of mythological scenes and Hindu epic stories. It was in Ubud where Balinese artists first started painting village scenes, markets, funerals, and landscapes. Some artists even incorporated Hondas and transistor radios in scenes along jungle paths. The old style was combined with a new realism, discarding many rigid rules, and setting natural figures against natural backgrounds. This naturalism is still the preferred style and is exemplified in the works in Puri Lukisan.

The museum consists of three large buildings set in exquisite gardens of fountains, flowering shrubs, statues, and lotus ponds befitting a palace. Choose a nice place to sit and relax. Bring a pair of binoculars as the garden is a superb ornithological sanctuary; observe oriental white-eyes feeding on berries in the trees. At present the permanent collection is housed in two buildings containing hundreds of sculptures and paintings displayed in chronological order, covering the whole evolution into modern idiom (1930s through 1970s) with paintings of dances, temples, feasts, rice harvests, *wayang* stories, and Balinese folklore. Included are painters I Gusti Lempad, Ida Bagus Gelgel, Dewa Batuan, Ida Bagus Made, Ida Bagus Nadera, as well as sculptures of I Wayan Pendet, I Nyoman Cokot, I Bagus Nyana, I Mangku Tama, and I Ketut Tjedeng. The garden's many sculptures treat traditional subjects in modern style. The third building is operated by a local painters' cooperative. Here you'll get an overview of all the different stylistic trends in Balinese art, though the naive expressionist Young Artists School predominates. Some works in the cooperative are for sale and prices are negotiable; if you see an artist you like, note his name and village and visit his private gallery. Use the works in this museum as standards of excellence by which to judge the paintings in Ubud's hundreds of galleries and studios.

Tragically, since Tjokorde Sukawati's and Bonnet's deaths, the works in Puri Lukisan's permanent exhibits have fallen into serious disrepair. Because of the lack of air-conditioning in this humid, tropical climate, the paintings are steadily and progressively deteriorating to the point where green fungus could be seen under the glass *eating* away at the canvases.

By 1996 the laborious restoration of both paintings and buildings was still underway. Though much work remains ahead, the lighting has improved, some paintings have been tastefully reframed, and identifying labels are in the making. Meanwhile, the spacious, cool, and enchanting garden alone is worth the Rp1500 admission. Open daily 0800-1600. For more information, call (0361) 975136, fax 975137.

Pura Saraswati
The seat of Ubud's royal Sukawati family in central Ubud. Enter the complex from the main gateway on J1. Raya or through Cafe Lotus where you walk around the rear of a *raksasa* statue. Inside are numerous *bale,* some storing *barong* masks, some housing shrines. I Gusti Nyoman Lempad was invited here by the raja in 1898 and commissioned to build a water palace, ponds, and a garden to be dedicated to Saraswati, the Hindu goddess of art and learning. Note the exquisitely carved sandstone *naga,* florals, wall panels, and cosmic turtles, some by the master himself.

Puri Saren Agung
Also known as the Ubud palace, it's in the exact center of Ubud, 200 meters east of Pura Saraswati and opposite the corner of J1. Raya Ubud and J1. Monkey Forest. This remarkably intact and elegant palace—now doubling as a hotel—was once the seat of the Sukawatis, the ruling family of Ubud, from the late 19th century to the end of the war for independence. Visitors are welcome in the ornate inner courtyards of the *puri* to see the ornate thatched *bale* furnished with Dutch-era armchairs and to inspect numerous colonial-era photographs of the extended royal clan. Each night high-quality dance performances are staged against a torchlit backdrop in the outer courtyard.

Lempad's Home and Studio
The great artisan, carver, painter, and traditional architect I Gusti Nyoman Lempad (1862-1978) lived in this house for most of his very long and productive life. The building, located on main street, still belongs to his family and is now open to the public (daily 0800-1800) as a gallery and showroom for painters working in the Lempad-style. Little remains of the great artist's personal possessions and only two of Lempad's ink drawings are displayed; go to Puri Lukisan and the Neka Museum to see some of his most important extant works.

ACCOMMODATIONS

The Ubud area offers the largest selection of inland accommodations on Bali, suiting everyone's tastes and budget. Even the upscale places are a bargain. There are over 300 homestays and *losmen,* most inside family compounds, so you'll have plenty of choice and plenty of bargaining power. The majority are "illegal" meaning they don't pay taxes and operate without a license. These inexpensive inns open and close practically overnight.

The Ubud area now has six international-standard accommodations: Banyan Tree Hotel,

> *In August, Ubud was packed, the Balinese pushy and rude, intercepting us at all times to sell us things. Awful! We left after two days.*
>
> —JANE SARRON

Amandari, Kupu Kupu Barong, Ulun Ubud, Villa Cahaya Dewata, and Ubud Village. There are 80-odd places on the Monkey Forest Road alone. Jalan Hanoman, Jl. Kajeng, and Jl. Banjartegal are also full of homestays and upscale accommodations. And the frenzied building goes on everywhere. **Jalan Tebesaya** has exploded; 80% of this neighborhood has accommodations now.

Walk along the back lanes—Jl. Bisma, Jl. Gautama, Jl. Karna—off the main road in Ubud's various *kampung* to discover Ubud's cheapest, cleanest, quietest, and most picturesque *losmen* and homestays. You've got to look around; many places charge over Rp50,000 for terrible rooms. despite the multitude of tourists, it's still easy to find the perfect guesthouse—a lovely bungalow with gilded doors, shower, and porch facing a quiet, storybook garden, fresh *sawah* air, and far from the night howls of those dreaded Ubud dogs for only Rp8000-15,000. Because of the intense competition, in the off-season every accommodation gives a discount of at least 10% if you stay a week or more. Be sure to negotiate. Although you can find every class of accommodations all over the Ubud area, in July and August the village is flooded with French and German tourists and lodging is expensive and difficult to find.

Local boys, on commission from various homestays, will try and entice you with business cards, maps, and lower prices. Even if you're already staying in a place, they'll try to entice you away by offering you a cheaper price. Don't be quick to reject these—they could be good. Another source of possible accommodations is the board by Lotus Cafe. If you're not sure, just take a place for a night and go searching for your ideal homestay the next day.

Except for the higher priced hotels (Rp75,000 and up), breakfast is always included in the price, and the staff will bring you tea all day long. In the ritzier hotels, Western breakfasts cost at least Rp10,000. Most Rp8,000 to Rp15,000 places really knock themselves out serving you an extraordinary breakfast of fruit salad, banana pancakes, eggs, jaffles, tea or coffee—the best value in all of Bali. Only in the higher priced categories do Ubud accommodations offer pools, hot water, and air-conditioning. This class of hotel will invariably be able to arrange such recreational activities as transport to *gamelan* and cultural performances, whitewater rafting, pony-riding tours, birdwalks, trekking, volcano climbing, mountain bike riding. The following is only a sampling of Ubud's 300-plus accommodations—more are springing up in the rice paddies and in the hills north of town every week.

Budget

The average price for a small, tidy room in a family lodging is around Rp8000 s, Rp15,000 d. You share clean, Balinese-style bathrooms with the family or with other travelers. These low-end places don't normally have telephones, but you may store your baggage and souvenirs for free. An excellent example is **Alinda**, Jl. Hanoman 64 (opposite Dewi Sri Bungalows), with clean, new rooms with toilet, cold shower, and *mandi* for Rp12,000 d in the off-season, Rp15,000 d in the high season, including above average breakfast. The people are friendly. At Jl. Hanoman 55, near the end and opposite Three Brothers Restaurant, is **Rice Paddy Bungalows** with nice rooms, big beds, and hot water, making this an incredible deal for the price of Rp10,000 s, Rp20,000 d. **Adi Pension,** tel. (0361) 262853 or 975231, with only four rooms which have shower and fan, is very reasonably priced at Rp10,000 s, Rp15,000 d (breakfast included). An unusual homestay is **Arimurti & Sukadana Homestay,** Jl. Jembawan in Banjar Padantegal Kaja, Lorong Rinjani 4. Take the road beside the post office south, then turn left and follow a long, bamboo-shaded lane to this quiet and secluded cottage-like accommodation—like a treehouse in the jungle. The owner, Sukadana, is a primary school teacher and *wayang* puppeteer who teaches tourists the Balinese and Indonesian languages on the side. Doesn't get many guests because it's too far a walk from Ubud's *bemo* stop. Only Rp15,000 d with attached shower, toilet, and breakfast of *pisang goreng,* omelette, black rice pudding, hardboiled egg, tea or coffee all day.

On Jl. Sri Wedari you'll find several very reasonable and relatively quiet homestays. **Taman Cottages,** tel. (0361) 96477, after the bend in the road at the top of the hill, has four bungalows facing a lily pond, Rp20,000-30,000 s or d. Toward town, at no. 20, just before Taman Bunga Homestay, is **Ngurah Homestay** with three rooms at Rp15,000 d. Only 300 meters from Jl. Raya Ubud, **Taman Bunga Homestay** is near the rice fields and costs only Rp10,000 s, Rp15,000 d.

At **Arja Inn,** Jl. Kajeng 9, tel. (0361) 974425, you have your own open-air *mandi,* mosquito net, and comfy bed. Lovely family, very private—all for only Rp10,000 s, Rp15,000 d.

Dewi Putri House, Jl. Lapangan Bola (Soccer Field St.), Maruti Lane 8 (tel. 0361-96304), Ubud Kelod, has well-furnished bungalows, a beautiful garden, good breakfast. Owned by a painter. **Frog Pond Inn** gets consistently wonderful reviews. The owner is friendly and the rooms have billowy beds, clean white sheets, private *mandi* and toilet, and bottled water; surrounded by a tropical garden.

Gandra Accommodations, Jl. Karna 88, Ubud Kelod, 100 meters from Yuni's, charges only Rp8000-10,000 s, Rp10,000-13,000 d. Beautiful gardens, basic but clean rooms, great breakfast of fresh fruit and jaffles, free storage service, helpful family, nice garden. Dip into some of the old novels. One of the best accommodations for the price in Indonesia, yet only five minutes from Ubud's center. Walk down Monkey Forest Road 100 meters and turn left at the sign. A small shop sells blankets, clothes, and film at reasonable prices. Go out back entrance and take a right to **Warung Seroni,** a great budget place to eat.

Ibunda Inn, tel. (0361) 96252, central Monkey Forest Road in front of Yudit Restaurant has clean two-story bungalows, private bath downstairs, veranda, fan, screens, hot water, a garden, and breakfast—all for Rp15,000-25,000. **Indra Homestay,** Jl. Hanoman 26, Padangtegal 26, is quiet and cheap with *mandi* and shower in every room. Friendly atmosphere and just one km from Ubud's center.

One of the many small accommodations on Monkey Forest Road is **Jati's III Bungalows,** which lie down a small lane. Two-story rooms (Rp20,000-25,000) with hot water and ceiling fan overlook rice fields. Check out the others; **Pondok Alamanda, Putih Accommodations,** and **Sari Artha.**

Quiet **Kerta Accommodation,** tel. (0361) 96188, on Monkey Forest Road across from the soccer field, boasts beautiful sunsets. All rooms Rp20,000 (non-a/c) and Rp40,000 (a/c) with breakfast. Reduced rate for longer stays. The proprietor is very helpful in knowing local resources, guides, tours, and people. **Lecuk Inn** on Jl. Kajeng is a friendly place—nice bungalows, very quiet, storage, good security, facing a beautiful garden. It's run by Wayan and his younger sister Nyoman, who brings breakfast. Lower rates available for longer stays.

Matahari Cottage (Rp30,000 s, Rp40,000 d) is far from places to eat and there may be no other guests there at the time, but so what? It's eight Bali-style rooms have modern toilet, shower, tub, hot water, and it is close to a river. A quiet and safe place to stay. **Merta House,** Jl. Karna 96 (parallel with Monkey Forest Road), charges Rp8000-12,000 (all rooms the same). The smiling woman who runs this place is a real character; bargain with her.

Mimpi's Bungalows, Jl. Hanoman 60, Padangtegal (see the sign Friendly Place to Stay), is owned by an elegant man, Made Suarta, a dancer and painter of miniatures. The front looks really rustic but in the back are several spotless bungalows (Rp15,000 d).

At the bottom of the road on the right-hand side just before the Monkey Forest is the charming, peaceful, and secluded **Monkey Forest Hideaway,** tel. (0361) 975354, with spacious, airy rooms dramatically positioned over the river and forest, with romantic, old-fashioned beds. Rp25,000 without fan, Rp30,000 d with fan, and Rp50,000 d for a bigger room with fan, balcony, and hot water. Breakfast included in all prices, but add 10% for tax and service. Rooms in front are better than the shabby rooms in back. Friendly management. The small, cozy adjoining restaurant serves good food. Join the local children in the spring-fed swimming hole for a dip in the afternoons. The worst part about staying here is dodging traffic on the long, hectic walk up from the very bottom of Monkey Forest Road each day.

Mumbul Inn, tel. (0361) 975364, on Jl. Raya Ubud near Lotus Cafe has rooms upstairs with mosquito nets and hot water but no fans. Rooms downstairs have fans but no hot water for Rp25,000 d. Really airy, looking out over ravine, swarms of fireflies, and an amazing frog chorus at night. Nice people. The restaurant serves whole-wheat bread and inventive, nutritious meals. Pay just Rp2500 per day to swim in Puri Suraswati's pool next door.

Nick's Pension, tel. (0361) 975636, on Monkey Forest Road, 15 meters from Oka Wati's, is only Rp15,000 s or d for quite comfortable fan-cooled rooms, or Rp35,000 for a/c rooms with hot water and beautiful views over rice fields and the jungle-covered ravine. Good service, and considering its proximity to the town's center, it doesn't get much better than this.

Nyoman Warta Accommodations, Banjar Tebesaya 25, tel. (0361) 96220, offers some of the finest bungalows in the Ubud area for only Rp10,000 s, Rp12,000 d. You get coffee and tea all day long, as well as a nice breakfast of fruit salad, pancakes, and coffee. This is a clean, quiet, family business, run by very kind people. It lies about 200 meters from the center of Ubud down a small road near the cemetery.

Oka Homestay is tucked behind Pura Saren at Jl. Bingung 18. It's quiet, secure, small—just four rooms, each with *mandi,* shower, toilet. It's first and foremost a traditional family home. Oka speaks excellent English but he will patiently and cheerfully encourage your Bahasa. His wife is charming, speaks little English. The son is shy; the grandfather goes about his daily business save his gentle knowing smile. You feel like you're staying with friends—they always make time to chat, answer your questions, loan and help you dress up in *adat* clothing, and include you in family and community life and ceremonies. Breakfasts are sensational and often extra treats appear.

Pande Permai, on Jl. Monkey Forest, tel. (0361) 975436, is recommended highly. Built in 1990, it has clean rooms with hot showers overlooking a gorge and *sawah* with all the garden anyone could want. Quiet and peaceful with a pool. Rather than hearing dogs and roosters, it's birds and the river. Very nice people. The owner is the principal of a high school. A disadvantage is that the delicious breakfasts are served late (be sure to request an early breakfast if you want it). It's also on top of the hill on Monkey Forest Road so it's a bit of a walk to downtown Ubud. High season prices: Rp25,000 s, Rp30,000 d; in the low season they bargain easily to Rp20,000 s.

Panca Mustika, just opposite the night market, has five bungalows for Rp15,000 d. Perks include towels, soaps, and free tea. A central, friendly place and a good value for the money.

Pandawa, tel. (0361) 975698, on Monkey Forest Road by the record shop offers very clean, nice double rooms with *mandi,* full breakfast, and free tea.

Pelangi Bungalows on Jl. Arjuna (a lane running west of the Monkey Forest Road) rents bungalows for Rp20,000. Very quiet, in a beautiful garden, nice people, and breakfast is outstanding. Quiet **Puri Mertha Sari Bungalows,** Jl. Suweto 12 in Banjar Ubud Tengah, tel. (0361) 975183, has clean, spacious, comfortable (but no fan) rooms with private bath and breakfast for Rp20,000—it's only 200 meters from the tourist information office. The architecture is superb—intricate wall and pillar carvings under thatched roofs.

Putu's, Jl. Tebesaya 39, has four large bungalows in a family compound surrounded by nice gardens. Rooms are clean, safe, quiet, and airy with comfortable chairs on the outside. Very good breakfast includes homemade cakes. Ketut, Setia, and Putu treat you like royalty.

Rona's Accommodations & Book Exchange, Jl. Tebesaya 23, tel./fax (0361) 96229, is the ideal place to acclimate. Rona's is hardly ever empty, but when it is call for a free pickup in the Ubud area. The rooms, though basic, are excellent—comfortable, cleaned daily, and cheap at Rp10,000 s, Rp12,000 d. Price includes mosquito net, fan, towels, soap, toilet paper, spring beds, bamboo furniture, lamps, and private bath. Rona's also has Rp20,000 bungalows with showers (no hot water) and deluxe rooms for Rp30,000 with double bed, wardrobe, shower, flush toilet, and sink. Hosts Rona and Tracie make you feel really welcome. A wonderful crew helps out. The Indonesian food served in the restaurant is high quality and cheap, with a large and varied two-course breakfast and free tea or coffee all day. Luggage storage, security box, use of multilingual library are free. Also available: laundry service, moneychanger, dance and shuttle bus tickets, tour service.

I Made Sadia, tel. (0361) 975718, in Kampung Sari runs a homestay with views over rice fields; Rp10,000 s, Rp12,000 d. I Made is also the leader of the Ubud *legong* troupe. There are many nice homestays on Jl. Karna such as **Sania's Bungalows,** No. 7, tel. (0361) 975535, which is on the end nearest the market.

For a good breakfast and humble yet comfortable accommodations, head to **Seroni's Place;** follow the road just behind the marketplace for about 300 meters and you'll find it on the right. Painter **I Wayan Serathi** has a clean, quiet house at Jl. Jembawan 69; room with sitting area rents for Rp20,000.

Sudana Homestay, Jl. Goutama 11, tel. (0361) 975176, run by one of the friendliest families in Ubud, is in a traditional Ubud neighborhood not far from the town's center, just down from the Nomad Office on a small street between Jl. Hanoman and Monkey Forest Road. The homestay is basic (Rp8000 s, Rp12,000 d) with only two rooms carved out of an old banana house. Very clean, inside *mandi*, no fans, but an airy shared porch; fruit salad and jaffle breakfast, endless tea and coffee. A good place to learn and practice Indonesian and gain insight into local festivals.

Safe and relaxing **Taman Indah Homestay** is about 800 meters north of the main road on Jl. Sandat, just east of Jl. Hanoman and close to the main post office. Nice garden and beautiful view of rice fields. Three large, clean rooms are equipped with two beds, *batik* sheets, open-air bathrooms, toilet, shower, mosquito net, fan, cool tile floor, and a furnished private patio. All this and breakfast with unlimited coffee or tea for only Rp10,000 s, Rp15,000 d. Bapak Tantra is funny, kind, open-minded, open-hearted, and informative of Balinese life and specific needs of travelers. Laundry service, bike and motorbikes for rent.

At the start of Monkey Forest Road, on the left, is **Tjanderi's,** tel. (0361) 975054, a central, lively, long-established *losmen* with only five rooms with fan, bath, and toilet (Rp10,000 s, Rp12,000 d) or high bungalow rooms in the back for Rp12,000 s or d with inside *mandi*. Banana sweets in the morning and you can arrange for motorbike rental here. With her pleasant, easygoing manner, Tjanderi is liked by all—and she always remembers a face. Ask her about her two beautiful, secluded, sometimes-empty bungalows up in the rice paddies (Rp15,000 s, Rp25,000 d) with electricity, plumbing, hot water, a nice breeze, surrounded by a goldfish pond, and accessible by motorbike.

Villa Rasa Sayang on Monkey Forest Road boasts eight bungalows, two of which are suites (no. 1 is the best). A comfortable place with king-size bed, full bathroom, living room, and outdoor veranda. The hotel has an upstairs, open-air restaurant and pool with swim-up bar. The staff is most friendly. Use the on-site washing machine or have the staff do your laundry for a small fee.

Warsa Cafe & Bungalow at Jl. Jembangan 70, tel. (0361) 975590, is centrally located just 50 meters before Ubud Inn and across from the Meditation Shop. Rates: Rp8000-20,000. Large, new bungalows with private baths for Rp15,000 (talked down from Rp25,000); price includes an excellent breakfast but not the 10% tax. Tour, rental, and shuttle service available.

Warsi's House, tel. (0361) 975311, on Monkey Forest Road, has upstairs rooms for Rp35,000 overlooking the family compound and beautiful gardens. Rooms have fans, two double beds, Western toilet, hot shower with ventilator, inside tub with hot water, towels, and good security. Upstairs rooms have possibly the best view of the Monkey Forest. The room rate includes a large breakfast of banana pancakes, fresh fruit salad, tea or coffee; toast and eggs also available. Warsi is a sharp businesswoman who also owns a boutique. She likes to dress her guests up in traditional attire and take them to temple festivals. Tickets also available for dance performances.

Widiana's House, Jl. Karna 87, down a small alley behind Ubud's market at J1. Karna 87, has large, airy, clean bungalows with inside *mandi* nestled in a dense, shady, cool array of trees—very private yet extremely centrally located; Rp8000 s with breakfast. Recommended.

Yuni's House, tel. (0361) 975701, at Jl. Karna 84, offers really nice, quiet, private bungalows with clean *mandi*, tile floors, and showers for only Rp10,000 s, Rp12,000 d. Free pancake and bowl of fruit for breakfast. A good deal.

Moderate

Adi Cottages, tel. (0361) 262853, 975231, or 975459, fax 975231, on Monkey Forest Road near Ubud's center, has 12 rooms with modern toilet, hot water, bathtub, fan, and swimming pool. Rates are Rp50,000 s, Rp60,000 d. The owner, Ketut Koei, also owns three other accommodations. One of them, **Villa Tertanadi Guesthouse,** has much the same facilities as Adi Cottages but with beautiful views. In Desa Laplapan, a quiet area two km from Ubud, it has seven rooms big enough for small families (Rp80,000 s, Rp100,000 d, Rp200,000 for a family).

Artini II Guesthouse, tel. (0361) 975348, on Jl. Hanoman in Padangtegal Kelod, is in a beautiful, peaceful walled compound with 18 rooms and bungalows (Rp25,000-35,000) lined with bamboo matting. It features inside baths, hot/cold water, fans, bamboo frame beds, and porch facing a nice garden. **Artini I** has cheaper rooms at Rp17,000-22,000, but their breakfast is small and so-so.

Bali Ubud, not far from the Kubu Ku Restaurant on the road to Penestanan offers a crisp clean view from the middle of the rice paddies. Ten two-story bungalows rent for Rp80,000 apiece. Clean, new, tasteful, very comfortable, tightly run, nice environment, hot water. Walk into Penestanan easily; excellent for groups.

Dewi Sri Bungalows, Jl. Hanoman in Padangtegal, Box 23, Ubud 80571, tel. (0361) 975300, fax 975777, is a haven in the rice fields with three different classes of self-contained bungalows: standard Rp65,000s or d, second story Rp85,000, and suite Rp105,000. American or continental breakfast included. The duplexes are really nice, with private bedroom upstairs, relaxing open-air living area below, walled open-air bath, views of rice fields. Hot water, pool, attentive staff, coffee shop serving jaffles, fruit juices, lassies. A 10-minute walk from Jl. Raya, it's main draw is the antique exterior and interior. The **Fibra Inn** on Monkey Forest Road near the Ubud Palace, tel./fax (0361) 975451, has flowers, birds, nice breeze, and a pool. Standard Rp70,000 s, Rp85,000 d, deluxe Rp85,000 s, Rp95,000 d (including tax). All rooms built in traditional style with hot and cold water, fans, shower, bathtub, small garden. No charge for local calls. The staff is friendly and treats you like family. The **Grand Ubud** is a small hotel of about 30 rooms with private facilities and choice of fan or a/c for Rp40,000, including huge breakfast. Friendly staff, ideal location and lovely garden with pool. **Indraprastra Homestay,** Jl. Hanoman 40, Padangtegal, tel. (0361) 975599, offers four large guest rooms (Rp35,000 d) overlooking rice fields and gardens. The owner/proprietor, Mr. Rai Ardika, is a warm and gracious host who speaks excellent English and will make your stay pleasant. The homestay is in a quiet location, a short walk from the center of Ubud.

Sunset Bungalows, tel. (0361) 975345, fax 975120, in front of Kubu Ku's Restaurant, has two beautiful airy rooms right on the rice paddies, complete with Western bathrooms, hot water, and large beds. Tariff starts at only Rp38,000 d including breakfast. Indulge in the restaurant's magical environment where guests lounge on platforms watching the sun set over rice paddies while listening to a whole collection of elegant windchimes. The artist who runs it speaks English well. He serves vegetarian and Indian food prepared by a French meditation teacher.

Among the quietest places is **Masih Bungalows,** tel. (0361) 975062, on the Monkey Forest Rd. with bed, breakfast, fan, private bathroom and shower for Rp20,000-50,000. A newer place with the same proprietor is **Masih Accommodations,** about 20 meters beyond the football pitch off Monkey Forest Road. Prices for the six bungalows range from Rp15,000 s to Rp25,000 d; enormous upstairs rooms have pyramidal ceilings and magnificent bathrooms and verandas. Ibu Masih is a marvelous lady who will teach you dancing, talk to you about art, and make a royal tour of her guests each morning. Ibu Masih's personable homestay is just a 10-minute walk from Ubud's "downtown."

Oka Kartini's, tel. (0361) 975193, fax 975759, on Jl. Raya in Padangtegal on the left about 150 meters before the post office, as you're entering Ubud from Peliatan. Out of the busy center of Ubud with all its traffic and sellers, Oka's restful, Balinese-style bungalows, with intricately carved reliefs, and palm thatched roofs, surrounded by pool and gardens, are in the Rp65,000-85,000 range with hot showers; other rooms go for as little as Rp20,000. Oka worked for six years as a guide in the Puri Lukisan and is well informed about painting. She'll store your luggage while you travel around, find you a dance teacher, and is inclined to give out free treats to patrons whom she—and her small army of handsome sons—treat like honored guests. Public transport close at hand, or ask for airport transfer by private car (Rp42,000 for two). But the best part of staying here is the charm, grace, and liveliness of Oka's company.

Near the start of Monkey Forest Road is **Oka Wati's Sunset Bungalows**, Jl. Karna 1, P.O. Box 158, Ubud, tel. (0361) 96386, fax 975063 a superbly run, well-kept family operation. Three classes of accommodations: standard Rp52,500 s, Rp65,000 d, a suite Rp95,000 s, Rp115,000 d; plus 10% service charge. Newer Balinese-style rooms upstairs look over beautiful *sawah* and lily ponds with ceiling fans, big oval bathrooms, nice furnishings, bedside lights, balcony, and the restaurant only 30 meters away. All units have hot water. Oka Wati's knowledge of Ubud is an excellent resource. Her restaurant and new kitchen are very good; try the yummy chocolate cake served warm. Peaceful surroundings. Oka Wati's is down a *gang* off the top of Monkey Forest Road only a three-minute walk from Jl. Ubud Raya, the main road. You can arrange adventure rafting trips and tours to Kintamani and Besakih here. Bikes rent for Rp4500 per day. In June, July, or August, make reservations a month in advance for this popular place.

Pertiwi Bungalows, Monkey Forest Rd., tel. (0361) 975236, fax 975559, has eight standard rooms for Rp65,000 s, Rp75,000 d, 22 superior rooms for Rp75,000 s, Rp85,000 d, and eight deluxe rooms for Rp125,000 s, Rp175,000 d. Meals are extra: Rp6500 for continental breakfast, Rp7500 for American breakfast, Rp12,600 for lunch, Rp15,000 for dinner. All rates subject to 15.5% service and tax. Visa and MasterCard accepted. Rooms are very large in typical Balinese decor with peaked thatched roofs, bamboo wall matting, ceiling fans, ceramic tiles, and private baths with hot and cold water. Facilities include a fantastic pool, poolside bar, open-air pavilion restaurant, and parking lot. Staff is very helpful. If you want to be in the middle of the action, this is one of the best hotels on Monkey Forest Road.

The classy **Pringga Juwita Water Garden Cottages,** Jl. Bisma, tel. (0361) 95734, fax 975734, has 25 rooms in two different classes: standard for Rp80,000 s, Rp85,000 d; deluxe

Rp105,000 s, Rp115,000 d (plus 15.5% tax and service). You get the service, decor, and comfort of any of Ubud's six international-standard hotels at half the price. All rooms have hot water, private verandas, fans, Balinese-style furniture, woodwork finishing. The generous, high-quality breakfast (0700-1000) comes with endless whole-grain bread and homemade jam. The bungalows for Rp115,000, offering indoor-outdoor living, are the best deal, with luxuriant gardens, lotus ponds, jungle-enveloped swimming pool, and restaurant on leafy pavilion, plus conveniences including laundry and postal service, safety deposit box, bar service, car rental, airport transport, and IDD telephone and fax at reception desk. Credit cards accepted. Only about an eight-minute walk from Ubud's center, yet very quiet with only the sound of birds in the mornings. Ideal for small groups. **Puri Padi Hotel,** Box 55, Ubud, tel. (0361) 975010 or 975075, fax 975740, on Jl. Hanoman near Pengosekan, bills itself as an elite resort. Surrounded by rice fields, it features standard and deluxe bungalows with a/c, hot water, TV, minibar, pool, but no telephones in rooms. A lovely and quiet hotel for Rp180,000 d per night.

Ubud's oldest hotel, the **Puri Saren Agung** (tel. 0361-975057, fax 975137) was the former palace of Tjokorde Sukawati, the late raja of Ubud. When this *puri* burnt down in the 1950s, the raja had small guesthouses constructed and outfitted with Balinese antiques and Western conveniences—one of the first of Bali's accommodations to combine traditional and Western features. At one time the best paintings of Ubud could be seen in this *puri,* and it was once the custom for painters to bring their works to Tjokorde for approval before selling them. Peek in to see the fantastic carved wood panels and four-poster beds. Unfortunately, the fan-cooled, traditional bungalows have quite small rooms, impossible to secure (some windows have screens only, no bars), with atrocious plumbing. The best pavilion is Number Four as it shares a courtyard with the household of the current head of the family, Cokorda Putra Sukawati, and the family goes out of their way to be nice. Facilities-wise, you can probably do better for the US$40 (plus 15% tax and service) they ask. Very central.

Puri Saraswati Bungalows, Jl. Raya, tel./fax (0361) 975164, is next door to the Lotus Cafe and 250 meters from the Ubud market. Rates for the four standard rooms with cold water and fans are Rp45,000 s, Rp60,000 d. Thirteen superior rooms with hot and cold bath/shower, ceiling fan, go for Rp85,000 s, Rp110,000 d; breakfast included. All prices are subject to 10% tax. Though it's on the main road, the rooms are situated back in a peaceful, secluded garden of many trees and flowering plants, laid out in the manner of a nobleman's house. A majestic temple and big beautiful lotus pond now serve as the spectacular backdrop for the Lotus Cafe next to the hotel. Puri Saraswati i patroled through the night, and someone is in the office 24 hours a day. Front office phone or fax can be used by guests. Manager Anoushka Thompson confirms tickets, books performances, and arranges tours.

Han Snel's **Siti Bungalows**, Jl. Kajeng 3, tel. (0361) 975699, fax 975643, 150 meters up the lane next to the Lotus Cafe (Rp85,000-105,000, plus 15% tax and service) offers all the modern conveniences in the garden of the artist's home. One of Ubud's best-kept secrets, Snel offers one of the best rooms around for the price—solar-heated showers, away from traffic noise, nice garden, stylish verandas, and privacy. Just seven bungalows, so you'll be lucky to find one empty (reservations recommended). Meet the locals in the hotel bar where the eccentric, larger-than-life artist holds court every evening. Elegant restaurant.

Tebesari Homestay, Banjar Tebesaya 29, is about 500 meters south of Jl. Raya Ubud. Each room has private bath, Rp10,000 s, Rp12,000 d. Nice garden. The owner, Nyoman Sujana, is a high school teacher and producer of a weekly dance show at the Puri Dalem—he speaks excellent English. His wife Warti is a clothing designer whose shop sells beautiful patchwork clothes at good prices. Luxurious **Ubud Inn** on Monkey Forest Road, tel./fax (0361) 975188, has standard rooms for Rp70,000 s, Rp100,000 d, and Rp120,000 for family rooms with veranda. Paintings, carvings, and flowers adorn every room. Hot water, a/c, room service, high standard of cleanliness, nicely landscaped gardens, and good pool.

Ubud Village Hotel, south Monkey Forest Road, tel. (0361) 95571, fax 95069, is next to Cafe Wayan. Standard rooms are Rp100,000 s, Rp105,000 d; superior Rp115,000 s, Rp125,000 d; deluxe Rp150,000 s, Rp175,000 d. Breakfast is Rp5000-10,000 extra. Spacious rooms have separate garden entrance, full western-style bathroom with hot and cold water, ceiling fan, and views over rice fields. Friendly staff, pool with wet bar, entertainment, laundry service, IDD, restaurant with full Western menu, parking lot, airport transfers, and a multitude of art shops and other restaurants right outside your door. A brochure describing hotel-sponsored tours around Bali is available at the front desk.

Long-Term Stays

If it's real peace you require, consider staying in one of the villages around Ubud—Campuan, Penestanan, Kedewetan, Sayan, Peliatan, or Pengosekan—where you're almost assured of finding a secluded place out in the rice fields or over a jungle-filled ravine, as quiet as a convent and with the smell of fresh *sawah*. Work out a special per-day rate for a long-term stay in a hotel or with a family.

Whereas Europeans prefer Seminyak and other places along Bali's south coast for its marine recreation, North Americans prefer the Ubud area for its culture. Avail yourself of one of the real estate offices that have begun sprouting up (one is on Jl. Raya Ubud near Lempad Gallery, opposite Nomad's) which advertise fully furnished luxury homes for as much as Rp3 million per month. Expat business people build their fantasy castles in the surrounding hills for Rp10-20 million including permits and other legalities. There are no building codes on Bali. Prime Ubud land looking out over a gorge can cost up to Rp46 million per acre, though most just lease the land for 25 years.

FOOD

Half the fun of Ubud is finding new places to eat. Most of the best *warung* and restaurants are concentrated along Monkey Forest Road or the various other tracks and roads running adjacent to it. On request, almost any family-style homestay or *losmen* will cook up a wonderful Balinese dinner of smoked duck, fish cooked in leaves, steamed jackfruit with special sauce, plus other vegetable side dishes for around Rp20,000. In the morning you can buy huge

> *We took your advice and headed straight to Ubud once we landed in Bali. And were we ever glad! We loved it. What a romantic place, everything from the frogs croaking in the rice paddies, the monkeys down the street, the ballet every night, fun shopping, spiritual offerings left by the doorstep, fruit salad served with a red flower on top . . . it appealed to all the senses. I can see how days could melt into weeks and weeks into months, and this from a rather hyperactive person!*
>
> —P. JACKSON

portions of *nasi campur* (Rp1000) and black rice pudding (Rp500) to the side of Ubud's market. The best *babi guling* is served on market day every three days. In the late afternoons and evenings, treat yourself to *pisang goreng* from market vendors.

Budget Eateries

Warung Dewa on Jl. Sugriwa, one street to the east and parallel with Jl. Hanoman, is a superb eatery for the money, a real traveler's hangout with good food at rock-bottom prices. Rp1000 for a well-done *nasi goreng*. If heading down Jl. Hanoman look to the left just before reaching J1. Raya to find **Warung Padang.** One of the few *nasi padang* restaurants in Ubud, it serves generous portions of spicy, no-fooling-around Padang-style food. Choose from a number of chicken, beef, pork, vegetable, *tempeh,* and tofu dishes in the window, all Rp2000-3000. Open daily 0800-2100. If you're in a hurry, try **Warung Seroni,** Jl. Karna in front of Seroni's Bungalows, for great well-priced, home-cooked portions of food like traditional yellow rice for Rp2500, and tomato soup for Rp1000. Another find is **Three Brothers,** tel. (0361) 975525, near the end of Jl. Hanoman, on the left where it meets the end of the post office. This multilevel restaurant features Japanese-style tables and delicious food served in baskets. The grilled chicken *pepes bali* with rice and coconut wrapped in a banana leaf (Rp2500) beckons travelers fom afar.

Restaurants

Ubud's restaurants are clean and decent, but even in the best restaurants the food quality can be erratic. One nice service provided by many restaurants in Ubud is transport. Just ask and they'll send a car or some guy on a motorbike to fetch you and/or your group.

Pick your restaurant by its specialty. For Mexican food, go to **Kura Kura,** though their prices have gone up dramatically and their portions have shrunk. For barbecue go to **Griya;** for Japanese food, **Mumbul's;** Balinese village food aficionados should go to **Bendi's;** for Indian food **Bumbu.** For the best sandwiches go to the **Coffee Shop** (behind the Crackpot) with prices varying from Rp2600 to Rp3500 for a club sandwich with the works. For vegetarian food, **Shadana's** on Jl. Raya Ubud is one of the best.

The best restaurants have a good balance of food from east and west. Catering as they do to French and Italian tourists, restaurants have featured more international fare of late— Thai, vegetarian, pasta. The **Cappuccino Italian Restaurant** on Monkey Forest Road serves up pizza and homemade fettucine. Another restaurant with real Italian taste is **Apakabar Restaurant Bistro** on Jl. Dewi Sita (if going down Jl. Monkey Forest, take the first left just before the soccer field).

The best pizza in Ubud, prepared in a real pizza oven, is made by **Cafe Roma** on Jl. Sukma, about 300 meters from Jl. Raya—good spaghetti too. **Bridge Cafe** in Campuan also has great wood-oven pizzas (20 kinds). Ubud is so far from the sea that seafood is not the town's forte. **Murni's** (by the bridge) and **Lotus Cafe** have fresh grilled seafood specials two or three times weekly, but you never know when or for how long.

There are also lots more families traveling to Ubud now. At the **Gayatri Restaurant** a children's play area is provided upstairs so parents can enjoy a meal in peace. **Oka Wati's** and **Miro's** boasts Ubud's most romantic dinner setting. A few monstrosities have cropped up— like the **Menara Restaurant** on Jl. Raya—you wonder why the *banjar* ever let them build it. A great number of restaurants advertise their daily and evening specials on big sandwich boards set up on the sidewalk or street outside.

Jalan Raya Ubud

After the style of Made's Warung in Kuta, **Ary's Warung** has tables set up near the street. Incredible wine list, liqueurs, cocktails, and cappuccinos at pretty good prices, plus nutritious snacks and whole-wheat sandwiches such as hummus, BLTs, and granola. Delicious food including quite tasty vegetarian dishes. Great bathroom. Check out the old black-and-white photos of Bali and Java on the wall. Open until 0100. Ary's has now expanded upstairs next door and added a bar—nicer atmosphere, quieter. **Garden Roof Restaurant,** next to I Made Sadia Homestay and more or less opposite Griya, offers a wide variety of Indonesian and Western dishes. It's not cheap, but the food and service are good. Try the roasted chicken with fried potatoes and salad with a nice dressing (Rp4500). Also fruit juice and *brem.*

Some readers swear by it, others consider it overrated, but eating at **Lotus Cafe,** tel. (0361) 975660, on Jl. Raya near the tourist office is, unquestionably, an elegant experience. Recline on pillows and sip coffee in a gazebo on the edge of a breathtaking lotus pond with jazz music in the background. The homemade baked goods are excellent, but some readers report that the other dishes—daily specials, red pepper fettucine, vegetarian Indian dishes, smoked salmon—are expensive, mediocre, and skimpy. The winners are fresh carrot juice, rich cheesecakes, cheese samosas, high tea and cakes, chocolate brownies, and the Greek salad with feta cheese. Count on about Rp25,000 for dinner for three. For a place to hang out, Lotus Cafe is clean and friendly, with snappy service. Wander the gardens of Pura Saraswati which were developed by Rodolfo Giusti, the present owner; the pond was originally established by noted photographer Rio Helmi. Open 0800-2300; call for free pickup.

Casa Luna, tel. (0361) 975364, fax 96282, is a big three-story riverside restaurant (formerly Lilies) with a wonderful and refined (but a little expensive) selection of food. Really inventive dishes include black rice pudding with nutmeg ice cream (Rp3000), magnificent salads (around Rp3000), herb fettucine in fresh tomato-basil sauce (Rp4000), Moroccan chicken (Rp7500), and the best pumpkin soup and salads. Casa Luna is situated in an elevated *wantilan* with

colonial-style antique furniture—pure *tempoe doeloe.* Videos downstairs every night and live music Saturday night (*sitar,* flute, drums). The bakery in the foyer of the restaurant sells lovely croissants, whole-wheat bread (Rp4000 for large loaf, Rp2500 small), multi-grain and raisin muffins, scones (Rp1500), brownies, cookies, cheese, freshly made yogurt, and more. Also has a gallery and a bar with an inimitable multicultural atmosphere.

Mumbul's Garden Terrace Cafe, tel. (0361) 975364, just up from Lotus Cafe on the same side of street, features high-quality food at excellent prices. Definitely one of the most varied menus in town—an oasis in the desert of repetitive fare. Beautiful table settings, comfy chairs, very good service, with an airy view over a deep gulley. The menu has evolved from what people craved, resulting in an international array including Japanese and Thai dishes. Try the pork fillet in mustard sauce—delicious! Smoked duck available every Saturday night.

From Ubud's center, toward Padangtegal on the right, **Nomad Restaurant** stays open late and offers very good, expensive food and snacks like spicy guacamole with *krupuk* (Rp2000), seafood salad, and mango juice *(lassi).* A *gamelan* plays in the background; food is served by waiters and waitresses in traditional dress. Chic atmosphere, and the bar has the largest selection of beer, wine, and cocktails in Ubud—a perfect place for a nightcap.

A real sleeper is **Shadana Vegetarian Restaurant,** Jl. Raya Ubud, tel. (0361) 975630, specializing in superb and inexpensive homecooked vegetarian dishes like *tahu* burgers (Rp2500), vegetarian *sate kebab* (Rp2500), cheese, egg, and avocado jaffles (Rp2000), vegetable curries, artful *nasi campur,* and brown rice with *tempe* and fresh vegetables with a subtle sauce. Ask for the *sambal bali* hot sauce. Most people miss this small restaurant in central Ubud just opposite Jl. Hanoman east of Ubud's town center. And, unfortunately, it's shrinking, the tables gradually giving way to more lucrative clothes and souvenirs. *Please* patronize it. Open daily 0800-2100.

Ubud Restaurant is the place for Balinese food—*sate, lawar,* and sometimes *babi guling.* Try the very good vegetable omelette (Rp2000) and smoked duck dinner for two (Rp20,000).

Lastly, **Ryoshi's** (tel. 0361-976362), just west of Ary's, is moderately priced, accepts credit cards, and offers a huge variety of delicious Japanese food: *soba* noodles, *robata* grill, sushi, etc.

Monkey Forest Road

Opposite the soccer field on the Monkey Forest Road is open-air **Bendi's,** never a disappointment. The staff prepares simple and delicious Balinese village food such as ferns and grated coconut, chicken, vegetarian dishes, and an admirable *nasi campur* for only Rp2000. Close to Western-size portions are served. Count on dinner for two costing around Rp15,000. **Yogyakarta,** near the soccer field, has a special way of cooking grilled chicken—delicious. Half a chicken, french fries, and salad costs only Rp5000.

For backpackers, the **Monkey Forest Cafe** has cheap but excellent vegetarian food and a great *nasi campur* (Rp2000). If coming down Monkey Forest Road, turn left right after the soccer field and walk 20 meters through a corridor of shops—look for the menu board out front. Slow service, but nice view over rice paddies.

Cafe Bali, across from Warsi's on the far side of the football pitch, is an up-and-coming small restaurant with a variety of food at decent prices. The management is gentle, friendly, and kind, the premises clean and charming, and the Indonesian food and pizzas good. Try the corn *pacora,* veggie lasagna, or special duck. Three entrees and three sodas will set you back Rp10,000. Watch the fireflies at night.

Tjanderi's at the top of Monkey Forest Road is still going strong, laying out delicious, cheap, and generous meals—pizzas, scones, yogurt, coconut pie, and *gecok.* The cheese and vegetable tacos and banana-coconut tacos are acclaimed, and the vegetable soups are just as hearty as they were 20 years ago. Expect gregarious gatherings in the evenings as it's right on the main drag.

Ibu Rai's on Monkey Forest Road has a complete menu with pepper steak (Rp5000), chicken Cacciatore (Rp4000), pasta dishes (Rp3500), Balinese food (Bali Karangasem for Rp3500), Indonesian food, and special drinks like Tequila Mariachi (Rp3500). A good value and a pleasant atmosphere.

Ubud Dancer Restaurant, across from the soccer field, boasts a "watergarden" atmosphere with lots of unique touches such as Javanese buffalo-leather hanging lanterns, and a pollution-free environment with individual tables inside separate *bale.* Chinese and Balinese cuisine is served as well as seafood and steak. Waitresses wear traditional dress, and free Balinese dance performances are put on every Sunday night. Prices somewhat expensive, but worth it. **Yudit Restaurant, Bar & Bakery** is a pretty good restaurant with friendly and well-trained staff and free salad bar every night. During the busy season, five or six different salads are offered; they don't seem to mind if you just order soup and fill up on salads. German dishes such as *kaseshnitte* (Rp5000), sirloin steak with fries and veggies (Rp6500), and American hamburgers with coleslaw and fried potatoes (Rp5000) are other specialties. Not an extensive menu so it's easy to choose. The Black Forest Cake, and fresh croissants every morning are not to be missed. The management speaks English and is very helpful.

Elsewhere

The **Dirty Duck,** tel. (0361) 975489, also in Padangtegal at the end of Jl. Hanoman just before the fork to the Monkey Forest, has a nice atmosphere, uniformed staff, good music, gourmet menu, and looks out over rice fields and lily ponds. Sit on the floor or at tables. The vegetarian sandwiches are excellent (Rp7500 and up). Entrees, including bratwurst and pasta dishes, are Rp7000-10,000, and the crispy duck is expensive at Rp111,000. Open 1000-2230.

Bamboo Restaurant, on Jl. Dewi Shinta just off Monkey Forest Road at the north end of the soccer field, has friendly service, cushions on bamboo chairs, and reasonably priced, tasty food. The owner seems solicitous about her customer's satisifaction, the cleanliness of the establishment, and the quality of the food. Best for Balinese food and superb soups. The vegetarian platter (Rp3500) is a favorite.

Tutmak (tel. 0361-975754), Jl. Denisita (Jl. Shinta), west of Jl. Maruti, has the best organic salads, Middle Eastern plate, sandwiches, pasta, good veggie dishes, juices, desserts, assorted breads, and the best coffee in Ubud. Great music, local modern artists exhibited. A little secret place is **Balina,** on Jl. Kajeng on the opposite side of Gusti's (west); cheap, big portions, good food. Very good value. The Blue Marlin Fish Special is tops.

Kubu Ku Restaurant, 600 meters to the east of the Monkey Forest, serves Indian vegetarian food (*dahl*, curry, nice walnut tarts, salads) for about Rp5000 per entree. Also home-baked bread. With the soft musical clatter of its windchimes, this is a deliciously relaxing and romantic spot in the afternoon. Meet up here, sit crosslegged on big cushions at low tables, and sip coffee while looking out over expansive rice fields, lily ponds, gently swaying palms, and fluffy clouds in the distance. Located on connecting road between the end of Jl. Monkey Forest and Jl. Hanoman.

Miro's, tel. (0361) 96314, just off Jl. Raya Ubud and under new management, has a very romantic ambience (like dining in the middle of a temple) beautiful garden, waterfall, and an imaginative menu. Deserves more business than it gets (half empty on Saturday night!). Only lit by candles at night. Great breakfast menu includes Earl Grey tea in a pot (Rp2000), tropical fruit salad with yogurt (Rp4000), muesli with yogurt (Rp4000), "morning magic" of stewed prunes, yogurt, and muesli (Rp4500), whole meal or fresh bread with butter and jam (Rp1500), and jaffles (Rp3000). Tuna fish curry (Rp6500) is a sure bet, and the vegetable *mie goreng* (Rp4000) is well prepared. Outrageous desserts. Excellent iced watermelon juice (Rp2000). Open 0900-2000. To get there, do down Ubud's main street toward Campuan, then take a left at the sign after the SMP school.

Griya Barbecue & Restaurant, tel. (0361) 975428, opposite the lane next to the SMP school, specializes in barbecued chicken, pork, and beef. Check out the daily specials. If on, tuna with potatoes and mixed salad (Rp5000) is a winner. The restaurant in the **Monkey Forest Hideaway** at the bottom end of Monkey Forest Road does smoked chicken and *nasi kunyit* to perfection. A classy place to dine is **Han Snel's Garden Restaurant** with its Asian-Indonesian menu. Everyone raves about the dazzling mini-*rijstaffel* (Rp10,500 per person for seven dishes). The specialty of the house is steamed *bebek tutu* prepared with all the spices and served in sumptuous garden surroundings.

Oka Wati's, a little out of the town center off Monkey Forest Rd., has evolved into a delight-

ful, full-fledged restaurant in the emerald paddies. The establishment offers a winning combination of friendliness, reasonable prices, and excellent Western food including tuna sandwiches (Rp2500), scrambled eggs (Rp3000), famous red bean soup (Rp2000), and pasta dishes (Rp3750-4000). Or try exotics like beef mango (Rp6500) and cashew chicken (Rp6500), or the vegetarian swiss cheese *rosti* (Rp3500). Balinese ceremonial banquet dishes like *bebek tutu* (Rp25,000) or a whole suckling pig (Rp50,000) must be ordered 24 hours in advance. Just like she did in the early 1970s, Oka still makes excellent yogurt and banana sweets in the mornings.

Wayan's Cafe & Bakery is a hugely popular place to eat—perhaps Ubud's consistently best food. Nice atmosphere with low tables set under *bale* at different levels in a leafy garden. Recently interviewed and photographed for *Bon Apetit* magazine, Wayan herself is a nice, modest, hospitable, and generous woman. On top of the restaurant, she also caters lunch for 100-150 river rafters a day. Everyone raves about the cafe's homemade baked goods (whole-wheat bread) and the *ayam sate* (Rp2500) with a superb peanut sauce; also wonderful salads, pizza, "prawns a la ketut" (lots of garlic); the chicken curry and excellent daily specials (Rp10,000-12,000) are without peers. Scrumptious and genuine Balinese buffets are laid on every Saturday night for Rp17,000. Also great carrot juice and amazing desserts. Always crowded in the peak season, make reservations for the evening. The menu is so good, it's no problem dropping Rp30,000 for two.

Drinks

For pure entertainment, a mellow evening of *brem*-sipping is a real bargain. Don't pay the Rp2000 a glass at Cafe Lotus (view only; overpriced average food), Nomad's, or Murni's. Instead, buy a whole bottle for Rp2000 and order a big bowl of ice at a restaurant or *warung,* then just sit and watch the world go by. Some restaurants stay open until the wee hours on Saturday night if people are still drinking. You can sample fresh *tuak* early in the morning a few days a week at Pasar Ubud's market; look for the *tuak* vendors around the *sate*. The brilliant sculptor Wayan Cemul, whose workshop is on Hans

Snel's lane (Jl. Kajeng), makes some of the best rice wine on the island and sells it to restaurants such as Murni's in Campuan and TJs in Kuta. The best bar in the Ubud area is **Beggar's Bush** in Campuan.

Desserts and Baked Goods

Cafe Wayan and Casa Luna are the last word in desserts. The **Casa Luna** is the only place in town with frozen yogurt. **Cafe Lotus** is said to have the best chocolate cake on Bali. **Cafe Wayan's** Death by Chocolate cake is renowned; Wayan also serves an inimitable coconut pie. **Nomad's** serves near perfect apple strudel plus *gulek,* a Balinese concoction of boiled bananas and pineapples. At **Mumbul's** ice cream parlor, don't pass up the thick passion fruit shake with jackfruit ice cream and other delicious desserts. For a winning coconut pie (Rp1000), head for **Dewa Warung**, on Jl. Sugriwa (parallel and east of Jl. Hanoman).

Not that many restaurants are open for breakfast because most accommodations serve it as part of the price of a room, but street vendors do business long before most restaurants open at 0800. In the market early in the morning, get an ample serving of black rice pudding sprinkled with coconut and brown sugar syrup for Rp500—a healthy, filling breakfast. Every three days is the big market when there are lots of fruit stands selling crisp juicy apples from Java.

Many of Ubud's eating establishments now offer whole wheat bread (known as "brown bread"), Danish, and French bread. The bakery at Casa Luna offers very good brown bread. **Tino Drug Store,** tel. (0361) 975020, sells all kinds of baked goods at good prices (brown bread Rp1500, apple cake Rp1000). The ticket for a breakfast on the run, it's open 0800-2000.

SHOPPING

Ubud is a pleasant, enjoyable place to shop. Shopkeepers are easier to deal with than those in southern Bali; they give you more space, are more willing to haggle, and they don't jump all over you when you come into their shop. Prices are also cheaper than in the south. Ubud used to be known just for its galleries but now you can come here and buy all of your clothes,

souvenirs, and crafts as well. There are belt shops, pop-art shops, earrings shops, even *scarf* shops!

Ubud's main street and lanes are lined with a great variety of shops and kiosks, filled to bursting with woodcarvings, basketry, toy *gamelan* sets, originally designed jewelry, antiques, clothes, *batik,* bamboo windmills, and paintings. Purchase a good quality *ikat* at **Ibu Rai's** on Monkey Forest Road. Large round tablecloths with handpainted flowers can be bargained for as little as Rp40,000.

A picture framer, **I Gusti Made Gati**—old-fashioned, competent, cheap, and agreeable—is 50 meters up the street which runs left off Jl. Ubud Raya (if coming from Ubud's center), just short of the Neka Gallery. Look for the sign. I Gusti speaks some English and his son speaks a little more. His asking price for his most elaborate frames is Rp7500 per meter. His framing is not austere, but it goes well with the somewhat busy contemporary painting styles.

Because of recurring waves of free-spending visitors, the sellers can be a bit pushy at times, with extravagant first offers. In the market, especially, you have to bargain like a fishwife. The best time to shop is in the cool of the evenings. The majority of shops are open from 0900 to 2030 or 2100. A tip: for standard souvenirs go to Gianyar or Sukawati's *pasat seni* to shop. These towns are closer than Denpasar and have bigger art markets than Ubud's.

Ubud lies in the middle of the surrounding villages of Campuan, Penestanan, Peliatan, and Pengosekan, which have all more or less grown together. In these thriving craft villages live and work hundreds of painters, carvers, and weavers who create a surprising percentage of the wares sold in the island's galleries, art shops, and boutiques.

Pasar Ubud

Two-story **Pasar Ubud,** on the Jl. Raya in the middle of town, houses several hundred shops and stalls. This central market offers real low-end tourist clothes in booths upstairs as well as mostly tawdry handicrafts, fans, *batik* bags, fabrics, baskets, jewelry. Look in on I Nymoan Latin's shop behind the market with excellent *batik,* lengths of cloth, machine-woven *ikat,* and scarves at very affordable prices.

A quarter of these booths target the Balinese themselves with sandals, cheap belts, jackets, and white shirts—some nice things at reasonable prices. One woman spent Rp80,000 for four *batik sarung* and two tablecloths. You can buy produce and vegetables on the grounds and out back. Vanilla pods (Rp2500 for 20 sticks). A big lively crowded public market *(pasar)* takes place every three days, spilling over into the street as women come in from nearby and mountain villages to sell and buy livestock, hardware, fruit, vegetables, and other goods.

We have been sadly disappointed by the "quality" of tourists who have been infiltrating Ubud these past few years . . . drunkenness, loudness, rudeness, and total disrespect for the tradition is unforgivable in ANY culture.

—ELLEN B. MORROW

Bookshops

The largest selection of maps, guidebooks, new books, and expensive large format picture and culture books on Bali and Indonesia, as well as current issues of European, Asian, Australian, and American magazines and newspapers can be found at **Ary's Bookshop** opposite Puri Sakenan on J1. Raya. The *International Herald Tribune* (Rp3600) arrives after 1100. Open 0830-2030.

A few minutes away, at Monkey Forest Road 68, tel. (0361) 975359, is **Dewa House Book Shop.** Open 0800-2130, Dewa sells a fair selection of new and used books at the usual high prices. Books are bought back at half price. Also on Monkey Forest Road behind the soccer field is **Pondok Pekak,** a privately run lending library which stocks a good number of volumes on Bali and Indonesia and offers cheap lending fees and a 60-80% buy back rate. In Campuan, check out the small and tasteful selection of Oxford in Asia paperbacks in Murni's; the *Herald Tribune* (Rp3500) is also for sale.

Ganesha Bookshop, tel (0361) 976339, fax 96359, also on the main road (opposite the post office), is more user-friendly than Ary's Bookshop. Here you can buy a used book for Rp10,000, then sell it back for Rp5000. Anita, the Australian proprietor and her Balinese husband Ketut, are well-read and know their stock of new or used books which is categorized. Open 0830-1800 seven days a week. Anita is almost always there in the mornings. The closest thing to a metaphysical bookshop on Bali is the **Meditation Shop** (tel. 0361-976206) on Monkey Forest Rd., which sells multilingual spiritual and self-help literature and tapes. **Rona Bookshop,** part of Rona Losmen at J1. Tebasaya 23 in

Padangtegal, is another high-quality and well-stocked lending library and second-hand book shop with a buy back policy.

Clothes

Have a tailor make a shirt that you design, or have a seamstress make a *kebaya* to fit, Rp15,000 for the material, Rp5000 for the labor. A seamstresss works upstairs in the Ubud market. There are many stores on the main drag that sell unexceptional, touristy clothing and trinkets, but **Made Lastri's** produces clothing of good quality and design in unusual *batik* fabric. Lastri will make clothing to order if provided with a sample or pattern to work from. She needs only one day to create a simple skirt, a week for a jacket or full-length kimono robe. Buy fabric from the market and have a beautiful, lined robe made for about Rp35,000. Also check out **Tailor Astiti,** tel. (0361) 975061; the employees aren't fluent in English, but the shop's been in business for years. They will sew a suit, pair of slacks, *batik* pants, and vest for Rp35,000. Best dressmaker in Ubud.

Another very good shop, though relatively expensive, is **Bali Rosa,** fax (0361) 975162, Jl. Raya Ubud (opposite the start of the road up to Pringga Juwita), with a fine collection of Western fashion clothing designed by Nadine Thompson. Hand-painted silk and rayon print outfits with shoes to match are sold at fixed prices. They also sell small painted wooden jewelery and beadwork.

Kama Sutra, tel. (0361) 975315 on Monkey Forest Road next to Cafe Wayan, stands apart from the usual tourist schlock offered in many of Ubud's shops. Originals of above-average quality—silk scarves, sarongs, crepe and chiffon fabrics, and shirts—are sold at Western prices, but the garments are so unusual that somehow you don't mind paying (men's long-sleeved *batik* shirts are Rp200,000). Open 0900-1400. Browse awhile in **Mr. Bali** on Jl. Raya Ubud, for fairly well-made, trendy, and overpriced men's clothing.

On Monkey Forest Rd. is a women's clothing shop, **Balinka,** that makes high-quality, colorful clothes in cotton and rayon. The styles are simple, elegant, and very different from what's sold nearby. Some of the most original and fashionable clothes are found in **Neo Primitive** on Monkey Forest Rd. (left side, coming from town, right after Dian's Restaurant). Far superior to the ever-present *batik* and tie-dye.

PJ Collection, Banjar Tegallangtang, fax (0361) 975120, has a nice line of *batik* and contemporary hand-painted designs and cuts on cotton knit material. This retail, wholesale, and export business has fixed but reasonable prices: sleeveless tops for Rp5000 and lined pants for Rp25,000. **Puspa Shop** at the corner of the soccer field will make something for you, or do alterations on the spot. Good prices. Excellent selection of men's shirts and pants and women's dresses, blouses, and shorts for Rp12,000-40,000 first price. For an attractive made-to-order T-shirt collection, go to **Sama Sama Shop III** on Jl. Hanoman, tel. (0361) 975072, Padangtegal. Original hand-painted designs. Buy a nice quality *batik*-lined jacket at **Warsi's** for Rp35,000. Handsome cotton *batik sarung* cost around Rp12,000-15,000. Elsewhere, expect to pay Rp6000 for a machine-printed *batik sarung* and Rp15,000 for a *batik* outfit.

Miscellaneous

An excellent music shop, **Ubud Music and Photo Color Service Centre,** tel. (0361) 975362 is opposite Cafe Lotus on Jl. Raya Ubud, offering the most extensive tape collection in Ubud, including a very decent Indo-Javanese pop and classical music section. There's also a good choice of guidebooks, ice cream, perfume, toiletries, and film processing. Open 0900-2000. A branch, **Ubud Music II** (tel. 0361-975341), is on Monkey Forest Road. Another tape shop, **Remaja II,** is on Jl. Hanoman where you may also buy film. **Baliku** has an above-average selection of all types of music at reasonable prices, plus photo services. Located about halfway down Monkey Forest Rd. on the eastern side opposite Ubud Village Hotel. You'll pay about

Rp12,000 for processing and printing a 36-exposure roll of film, and about Rp8000 for a pre-recorded tape of fair quality.

Three hundred meters east of the Monkey Forest is **Kubu Ku Windchimes** for unusual and elegant tinkling, clapping, whirling noisemakers. Odds and ends like kitchen stools and clay figurines also for sale. **Genesha Bookshop,** Jl. Raya, tel. (0361) 96359, sells musical instruments, beads, jewelry, and other tasteful collectibles. Across the street on Jl. Raya you'll find **Pejaten Keramik,** an outlet for decorated greenware ceramics, ashtrays, candlesticks, small bowls, etc.

Maori, Jl. Raya Ubud 4, also specializes in music instruments and accessories. The owner Arif Hendrasto can be contacted by writing Box 173, Ubud, Bali 80571. Upscale **Murni's** in Campuan is one of the most fashionable antique shops in the Ubud area. Visit the village of **Nyuhkuning** southwest of Ubud, a woodcarving center since the 1930s. Other woodcarving villages north of Ubud are **Pujung, Sebatu, Taro,** and **Jati.** An outlet for unique Pejaten wheelthrown and decorated greenware ceramics is at **Pejaten Keramik** in Br. Taman (opposite Genesha Bookshop).

ARTS AND CRAFTS

Handicrafts

Artful and attractive carved and painted picture frames (around Rp20,000 for two) are found in a number of Ubud's shops and are a real good buy. Also unusual are big fish mobiles (about Rp50,000 for four). It's not hard to find shops with large collections of carvings and sculptures of all sizes, motifs, shapes, and ages. But if you're interested in woodcarvings, they sell for much cheaper in the little stalls behind the monkey temple. **Bali Bagus** (art studio), on Monkey Forest Road, is operated by a family of woodcarvers. They sell mirrors, picture frames, toy boxes, jewelry boxes, etc. The painter **I Wayan Suka** on Jl. Jembawan (the post office street) in Padangtegal sells baskets, mobiles, old Sanskrit calendars and chopsticks in boxes (19 pairs for Rp45,000).

PT Mondirama Bali (tel. 0361-96202, fax 96203) is a workshop producing some of Bali's finest iron and stained-glass creations for interior and garden decoration. Handmade by skilled Balinese craftsmen, their exclusive glass designs are handpainted, then fired in a kiln at 600° Centigrade. These unique works of art cannot be duplicated. Mondirama also customizes according to your specific design, color, and size and organizes packing, handling, and shipping. Visit their retail outlet in Andong daily from 0800 to 1900. Their wholesale factory is in Peliatan (Br. Tebesaya 72) where you can see the iron-making process firsthand. Open 0800-1200 and 1300-1600.

One of Indonesia's largest and most complete stores for bronze decorative objects is the **Golden Buffalo House of Bronze** on Monkey Forest Road (tel. 0361-96328, fax 752013) where artisans can create any kind of motif by designing a piece after one in their catalog or by creating a sample for your approval. **Wora,** Jl. Monkey Forest, has a stunning collection of *ikat* clothes from Nusatenggara (Rp35,000-1 million).

Jewelry

Unique items are earrings, bracelets, hair clips, brooches. Buy as many as three pairs of medium quality wooden earrings for Rp5000. Walk south from Warsi's and there's a shop (before the Frog Pond Inn) that has a great selection. **Mirah Silver** on Jl. Raya displays some beautifully designed rings, earrings, pendants, and necklaces, or try **Putra Silver** on the Monkey Forest Rd. which sells qualities of silver jewelry at good prices (no bargaining). Putra's wholesale office is in the Puri Agung in Peliatan. Also recommended is **Purpa Silver Gallery** on Monkey Forest Rd., tel. (0361) 975068, fax 975016. More than just a silver shop, Purpa has a very fine selection of contemporary and abstract art. **Art Gecko,** beside Rona's Accommodations at Jl. Tebesaya 23, carries a fascinating selection of reasonably priced jewelry and artifacts. **Suarti's** on Monkey Forest Road sells modern innovative jewelry at pretty good prices in spite of it being part of a chain.

Paintings

The Ubud area is noted for its painters. Signs point the way to studios all over town and there's also a massive array of galleries. It's more satisfying to buy directly from the painter and you may get a better price. Fame has not diminished the open nature, friendly demeanor, and hospitality of Ubud's painters, but you have to be dogged to find those working in a distinct style. The vast majority of paintings have a monotonous sameness to them—the same village and jungle scenes ad nauseam. Be prepared to look for days and not find anything original except for the colors and frame.

There's a painting and arts supply store called **Ud. Seni Warna** nearly opposite Oka Kartini's in Padangtegal. See the Painting section of the Introduction for biographical sketches of the foremost artists of Ubud. Also refer to *Perceptions of Paradise: Images of Bali in the Arts* by Garrett Kam, an invaluable and handsome reference work published by Museum Neka (1993) and costing Rp80,000 at the museum or Neka Art Gallery. In it, two dozen paintings and drawings representing over 50 years of creativity by artists of different cultural backgrounds are examined in their fuller Balinese contexts, in many cases supported by photos of ethnographic sources.

A commission is tacked onto the price if a painter puts his work in a gallery. Count on a good 50- by 70-cm painting costing around Rp500,000 minimum. Additionally, if you allow yourself to be led around to the art shops by locals, your driver will get 10% and your guide up to 15% of the price of a painting, so you could actually pay 25% more than you would if you negotiated directly with the painter. Don't forget the back-lane galleries. The same painting that would cost you Rp11 million in a high-class gallery may go for only Rp2 million in a lesser-known gallery.

Sanggar Seniwati

In Bali, women are not encouraged to be artists, as art is considered men's work. With all of their religious and family obligations, it's remarkable that Balinese women are able to produce art at all. To help publicize and support the efforts of women artists, the **Sanggar Seniwati** (Association of Women Artists) has been established.

At these premises, just up the road from **Seniwati Gallery,** is exhibition space for one-woman shows, studios for visiting artists, and a large open area for workshops and practice sessions (available on request). No studio or exhibition fee is charged, but visiting artists are asked to contribute their expertise to the organization. In this space also are held art lessons for talented Balinese schoolgirls aged from five to 12 years old, where they learn from senior Balinese women teachers the traditional Balinese painting styles.

Various other classes and workshops are held for visitors. Such luminous artists as **Kartika,** Affandi's daughter, have exhibited their work (she uses her palm as a palette!) here in 1992, followed by Judith Shelly, Yanuar Ernawati, Annie Ogie, Linda Kaun, Suzanne Vermaat. Topics covered in workshops have included art from trash, maskmaking, papermaking, portrait and self-portrait. For more information, contact Mary Northmore at Jl. Sriwedari 2 B (tel. 0361-975485, fax 975453), Banjar Taman, in the center of Ubud almost opposite Nomad's.

Noted Ubud Area Artists

I Bagus Made Poleng, in Tebasaya near Padangtegal, doesn't paint for the money. This eccentric Brahman only sells paintings when his village needs money for a religious festival. He deliberately starts with a high price—Rp6 million—so his paintings won't sell, then gets angry when they do.

A.A. Gd. Sobart, in Padangtegal, specializes in market scenes. He's more business-minded than I.B. Made Poleng. **Gusti Ketut Kobot** lives and works in Pengosekan and does paintings of harvests and paddy fields.

I Nyoman Meja is one of Bali's most successful artists. You'll see only a few of his works in Ubud's local galleries. His studio is in Taman near the Nomad Restaurant. He asks Rp5 million for an average painting and recently sold one of his works to a Japanese museum for the unheard-of price of Rp26 milion. Murjawan, in Kuto village near Ubud, is an experienced artist who paints in extreme detail. The quality of his work compares favorably with I.B. Made Poleng's, who is old and has a solid reputation.

I Bagus Nadra, in Tegallinggah, is a senior painter who enjoys painting *barong* dances, preferring larger paintings. **Guru Mirsa** and **Gugul,** both in Tebasaya, also do very good work (*barong* dances). **Sadia** in Penestanan paints in the Bonnet style. Pengosekan's **"Community of Artists"** includes **Barwo** and **Tujuh;** though

still young men, they are already producing high-quality work.

Noted European Artists

Ubud hosts a small European and Australian artist's colony: Australian Donald Friend, Dutch-born Han Snel, and the Catalan artist Antonio Blanco, whose specialty is erotic art and illustrated poetry. The paintings of these expat artists, who've devoted most of their professional lives to depicting Balinese life and culture, can be seen in the Neka or Agung Rai galleries, or in their home studios. One km through the rice fields beyond Campuan is Penestanan village where the Young Artists School developed under the influence of Balinese artist Cakra, and where Arie Smit, a Dutch-born artist who came to live in Ubud in 1956, lives. These compelling paintings, rendered in a naive, exuberant style and using strong primary chemical colors, often depict scenes from daily village life. The original "Young Artists" are now in their 50s, having been succeeded by a new generation of truly young "young artists" in their teens. Their paintings are much cheaper than those of the masters.

Galleries

In most of Ubud's art galleries at least five different contemporary styles are represented, with works by old veterans as well as brash young artists. Also on exhibit are modern forms such as Japanese-influenced screens. In many

---

ARTISTS OF BALI

1. Anak Agung Gede Sobrat
2. Antonio Blanco
3. Ida Bagus Nyana
4. Han Snel
5. Ida Bagus Made
6. I Gusti Nyoman Lempad
7. Ida Bagus Tilem
8. I Gusti Ketut Kobot
9. Arie Smit
10. I Gusti Made Deblog
11. Ida Bagus Made Wija
12. Rudolph Bonnet

of the galleries—even the big ones like Agung Rai in Peliatan and Neka Gallery in Ubud—you get a personal tour guide. Sometimes there are special exhibits or collections on loan from museums. Always ask to see the dealer's private collections, usually hidden away behind a locked door. Most galleries charge Rp500 to enter the showrooms; in some you may watch artists at work in the back.

The first and only one of its kind in Asia, the **Seniwati Gallery** is devoted to collecting, promoting, and encouraging the work of women artists who live and work in Bali, regardless of professional/educational level. Among the women artists the organization actively promotes is **Putu Suriati.** Early in life stricken by polio, Suriati has struggled against great odds, painting in painstaking detail in a dazzling range of colors. Other women artists involved here are **Tjok Istri Mas Astiti, Dewa Biang Raka, Ni Made Suciarmi**—the latter has over fifty years experience creating Kamasan paintings, the original Balinese works from which all others derive.

The Gallery now shows and sells works by over 40 women artists from Bali, Java, Sumatra, and overseas, of whom just over half are of Balinese origin. Information sheets are available on each artist. Only Western women married to Indonesian men may display their work here, in this way getting around the restriction against non-Indonesians working in Indonesia. The gallery recently held its first group show in the capital, Jakarta. The response was so favorable that a number of the organization's artists now have waiting lists for their work. Having already exhibited in London and Washington, a major one-year exhibition was put on in Australia in 1995/96.

For further information on Bali's nascent women's art movement, contact assistant director Mary Northmore, an Indonesian citizen of English origin, herself a noted patchwork artist and wife of Javanese artist Abdul Aziz. The Gallery and office are open daily 1000-1700, located just off Jl. Raya in Ubud at Jl. Sriwedari 2 B, Banjar Taman, Ubud, Gianyar (tel. 0361-

Rama and Sita Encounter Rawana's Sister Surpanakha, *by I. Gusti Lempad. Perhaps Bali's greatest artist of this century, Lempad achieved world fame for his sometimes risqué pen-and-ink drawings. He died at the age of 121. He is best remembered on Bali as a maker of barong masks, cremation towers, and stonecarvings in palaces and temples. Lempad's family still sells his paintings, but they keep the very best.*

975485, fax 975453). The Gallery publishes attractive full-color calendars, greeting cards, and prints picturing the works of women and girl painters, and sells these and other publications in its shop also at the above address.

At **I Gusti Nyoman Lempad's house** on Jl. Raya, on the north side of the road in the center of Ubud, his grandchildren carry on the painter's tradition, turning out some excellent work. Lempad, who died in 1978 at the extraordinary age of 116, originally painted in the traditional *wayang* style, evolving eventually toward an expressionistic, exaggerated stylization of the *wayang* figures. Toward the end of his life he developed a very distinctive sketching style using only black Chinese ink on paper. A few of these remarkable sketches are on display in the gallery, which feels more like a private home than a public exhibition hall. A visit gives you an insight into the traditional home of an upper-caste Balinese family. Open daily 0800-1800.

Han Snel's Gallery is back from the road, very quiet. A former Dutch soldier who deserted the colonial army after the War for Independence, Snel eventually married a Balinese woman and lives here today with his family. His style is abstract, with a stunning use of color. Han is now more a hobbyist painter; his most productive, provocative years are over. These days he turns out only three or four paintings a year. His gallery is well laid out, well lighted, and contains fine decorative works.

A must is the **Neka Gallery,** established in 1966 in Peliatan. Whereas Puri Lukisan represents only Balinese artists, the Neka Gallery exhibits painters from all over Indonesia, as well as expatriate artists who have lived and worked on Bali. The Neka Gallery in eastern Ubud in Padangtegal consists of five different buildings. Paintings cost Rp35,000-25 million; you can get a discount of 10-25%. Wayan Suteja Neka, the founder and international ambassador of Balinese art, no longer pays commissions to agents for taking tourists around to his gallery—he's so famous he doesn't have to. In 1982, the Neka Museum north of Campuan (about 2.5 km from Ubud on the main road) was formally opened. Affandi, Sujono, Sobart, Kebot, Ida Bagus Made, Lempad, and other famous artists are exhibited here in the most comprehensive collection of traditional and modern Balinese paintings on Bali. The art students of Bali's Udayana University must study the works in the Neka Museum to graduate. The museum exhibits and sells some of the highest-quality contemporary paintings found anywhere in Bali. The several hundred paintings range from impressionism to abstract expressionism, and each is neatly and thoroughly labeled in English (the museum guidebook is redundant). Open daily 0900-1700. Rp2500 admission.

Also visit the equally important **Agung Rai Gallery** in Peliatan and the **Agung Raka Gallery** just before Mas. These big commercial galleries, which feature Balinese, European, and Indonesian paintings, deal with international art connoisseurs and do a high-end, high-turnover trade in overseas markets. Acting as a virtual ambassador of the arts, Agung Rai even buys paintings in Europe and sells them here to Europeans (for more on this super gallery, see "Peliatan" under "Vicinity of Ubud").

Rudana Gallery (tel. 0361-975091, fax 975091), south of Teges (which is just south of Peliatan) on the right side, is a marvelous private collection put together over 14 years, comprising a great variety of painting styles—contempo-rary works by local artists as well as masterpieces by famous painters. The staff and guides will give you a tour of the gallery's 16 sections, nothing short of a comprehensive survey of Indonesia's art history. The artwork of Blanco, Bonnet, Donald Friend, Gunarsa, Basuki Abdulla, Dullah, and Affandi, as well as Kamasan epics, Batuan miniatures, and an eclectic array of paintings from around the archipelago, also make up the collection. In the traditional art room hang works by I Gusti Lempad, Ida Made, Wayan Djudjul, Kasta, and I Gusti Kobot. Modern work includes pieces by Wianta, Nidjara, and Soeporno.

ENTERTAINMENT AND WORKSHOPS

From the early 1920s, the royal family ensured that the most talented teachers of dance, music, and drama were brought to Ubud, both to entertain the king and to impart their knowledge to local performers. The brilliant ethnomusicologist Colin McPhee based himself here, assiduously conducting groundbreaking research and writing his classic *A House in Bali* (1944) about his prewar experiences in Ubud. Even earlier, the Dutch musicologist Jaap Kunst published *Music of Bali* (1925), in which he lauded the *gamelan* of neighboring Peliatan. Ubud and its satellite villages are still major dance centers where every night of the week up to five performances, as well as music recitals and dance classes are happening simultaneously. Since new troupes are being formed and new venues are opening constantly, the best is to get the very latest info on cultural performances from the tourist office on Ubud's main street, or wait for one of the touts selling tickets around the town's main crossroads.

There are no nightclubs to speak of—after you're expelled from Nomad's or the Bush, you're left alone on the streets with the howling dogs. The Beggar's Bush in Campuan is Ubud's only real bar. If you like the mature expat/Indonesian mix of clientele it offers, at **Han Snel's Restaurant** it's easy to meet people. His bar, next to elegant, overpriced **Siti Restaurant,** is unavoidably intimate, the drinks straight, and the off-color jokes mercifully short—a precious colonial bastion in today's Indonesia.

Dance and Music

The *kecak* and *barong* are the most spectacular and interesting—and most easily understood—of Balinese dances. People sell tickets in the streets—their commission is already included in the price, so helping them earn a living isn't costing you extra. Tickets are also available at the door. At only Rp5000, which sometimes includes transportation, the performances are a great value. These dance demonstrations are actually short demos of up to eight separate dances in one. Most start at 1930 or 2000 and last about 90 minutes. It's first come, first served, so get there early. Frequent camera flashes during the show are unnerving to both performers and spectators.

Because of its temple surroundings, the dances put on almost every night at **Puri Saren** by the Dadha Budaya dance troupe are outstanding. The *legong kraton* is staged each Monday and the *barong* every Wednesday night. Package tour operators drive clients here from Denpasar. The dancers are extremely talented, but the street noise can be distracting.

See children practice dance at the **Ubud Palace** on Sunday and Tuesday afternoons at 1500. It's free, fun, and fascinating to watch. Foreign kids can join in. At the Padangtegal stage every Thursday at 1900, a Ramayana ballet is staged by the Sekar Alit children's troupe. Performed on the same stage every Tuesday at 1930 are *legong* dance; every Saturday at 1930 see *legong* and *barong* dances. A children's *barong* dance is held every Sunday evening at 1030 in the Museum Puri Lukisan.

The huge **Gunung Sari** dance and music pavilion, in the *pura dalem* between Padangtegal and Peliatan, stages *legong* every Thursday and Saturday nights at 1930-2045. The performances of the Ciwa Ratri Dance & Classical Gamelan Gebyug at 1930 at the dance venue on Jl. Tebesaya are very popular. Audiences marvel at the dancers wearing big cowbells.

The **Gamelan Semara Ratih** ensemble in Banjar Kutuh, northeast of the post office, performs the best tourist *gamelan* every Tuesday night at 1930. The best tourist *gamelan* plays every Tuesday night at 1930 in Banjar Kutuh Kelod in north Ubud. Better than the Ubud Palace show, this *gamelan* is healthy, young, vibrant, and has a varied program. It is made up

> *In order to protect what is left of the natural environment to both sides of the road, and to keep it from becoming any tackier than it has already become, an ordinance should be passed turning the Monkey Forest Road into a walking street with traffic and supply vehicles allowed only for an hour or so in the mornings, no buildings erected not made of natural materials, no signs larger than a certain size and made of natural materials. Save what is left from becoming another Kuta!*
>
> —EDISON LINDQUIST

of dancers and musicians from all over, including many students, graduates, and teachers from STSI, the Bali Arts Academy in Denpasar. This group is new and still building a reputation with the show *The Spirit of Bali*. Semara Ratih also performs recent works by Nyoman Windha, a leading composer from the music and dance academy STSI, as well as other modern compositions and some classical dance pieces. Pak Windha was the founder of the group along with Agung Anom, the renowned *baris* dancer. This performance stands out from all the others for its freshly innovative, energetic, and extremely talented performers. *wayang* theater performance, *The Sacrifice of Bima,* takes place on Wednesday and Sunday from 2000 to 2100 (Rp5000) at Oka Kartini's on Jl. Raya in Padangtegal. This is an authentic shadow puppet show with a torch behind the screen; preceded by a short explanation. Upward of a third of the audience watches the skill of the *dalang* from behind the screen.

Courses and Workshops

Lots of courses—art, dance, music, healing, meditation—you see signs everywhere such as in restaurants along Jl. Raya Ubud. Also choose your family accommodations according to your interest, be it *wayang* theater, instrument-making, jewelry, or carving. The sign, Painter and

Homestay, for example, means that the *losmen* is owned or managed by a painter. If you stay with a dancer, (like Ibu Masih's on Monkey Forest Road), you'll be able to watch private *gabor, oleg,* and *tari tenun* dance lessons in the flowered courtyard. Guests are sometimes treated to special demonstrations. Another possibility is to stay with Ketut Madra of **Madra Homestay** who is a traditional *topeng* dancer (see "Peliatan" under "Vicinity of Ubud").

Infinitely patient I Nyoman Warsa at Pondok Bamboo (opposite Kubu Ku Windchimes) teaches the *gender* bamboo *tingklik* instrument for Rp5000 per hour. His son teaches music too. You'll find it's difficult to follow the rhythm and to count time, but don't despair. In the *ikat* shop next to Dian's Restaurant take lessons on the happy, galloping *klintik* for Rp5000 per hour. I Wayang Karta runs the **Nataraja Dance and Music School** and guesthouse at Jl. Sugriwa 20 in Padangtegal. Founded in 1987, this school specializes in teaching Balinese music and dance to non-Balinese. Informal methods have been developed which enable the student to progress quickly and efficiently, i.e., ear training, coordination excercises, learning the ornamentation, etc., so that they are able to master the basic dance, Pendet, in about 10 lessons at Rp7000 per lesson. Students of music are able to master particular songs within three lessons. There is no fixed timetable of classes. The school operates on the traditional *sanggar* system where the number and scheduling of classes are adapted to availability and what instruments or dance they want to learn. Inexpensive accommodations are available at a number of homestays near the school.

Balinese dance courses are also offered at **Dewi Sekar Ayu** on Jl. Hanoman. Walking away from Jl. Dewi Sita, where it intersects Jl. Hanoman, turn right and walk about 100 meters; Dewi Sekar Ayu will be on the left.

The ancient Indonesian self-defense system, Daya Putih, is taught at the **Daya Putih Study Centre,** Jl. Andong 1. This martial art discipline, which dates from the 13th century, is said to rejuvenate vitality and well-being, reduce stress and tension, improve memory and concentration, and awaken intuition. You may enroll in the regular program of two classes per week (each class is two hours) for one month or sign up for their intensive four or eight day program. All students must start at beginner's level. Call (0361) 975467 and ask about their free one hour introductory class. Taught by the Javanese painter and writer Madi Kertonegoro, the **Future Peace Art Gallery,** Jl. Tegalalang north of the Jl. Raya Ubud and Jl. Peliatan intersection (on the road to Petulu) is the venue for daily lessons in another traditional Indonesian self defense known as Daya Nurani Dewa Katon.

At the **Ganesha Bookshop** (tel./fax 0361-96359) on Ubud's main street opposite the post office, sign up for an informal introductory workshop in traditional Balinese music. No previous musical knowledge is necessary. Participants are given a brief history of the *gamelan* and are then invited to choose an instrument (drums, flute, cymbals, *rebab, gender wayang*) on which to learn some basic music. Instruments are provided and the tutors speak English. The workshop costs Rp15,000 per person and runs every Tuesday evening 1800-1930. Alternate times and group bookings available on request.

The **Meditation Shop,** on Monkey Forest Rd. (tel. 0361-976206), is the venue for silent meditation ("spiritual sharing") each day at 1800-1900. Short guided meditation also available. A free introductory course begins each Monday at 1900 (runs through Friday). The shop hosts lectures by spiritual teachers and sells metaphysical literature and tapes in English, French, German, Dutch, Cantonese, Japanese and Indonesian. Open daily 1700-2130. The Fibra Inn on Monkey Forest Rd. (tel. 0361-975451), offers meditation, dancing, *gamelan,* painting, and woodcarving courses.

At the Maspahit or **Crackpot** (tel. 0361-976698) on Monkey Forest Rd., you can learn *batik*-making. Make your own *batik* T-shirt, painting, *sarung,* or postcard with help and instruction from batikers. Create your own designs or use the ready-made design templates (hundreds to choose from). You can get into as much detail as you want and come and go as you please, no time limits. Adult T-shirt costs Rp25,000, child T-shirt Rp15,000, cushions Rp20,000-25,000, paintings Rp15,000-25,000. Organic dyes that change with the light are used. The Crackpot also has a book exchange service and a coffee shop where you can relax, read magazines and newspapers, play games, and enjoy the best sandwiches in town in a friendly atmosphere. Great place to leave your kid for the day. If heading south, it's about 100 meters beyond the soccer field on your left.

Learn Balinese cooking at **Casa Luna** on Wednesday morning. The course covers cooking techniques, Indonesian herbs and spices, alternative ingredients, and menu planning. Students try their hand at *sate base genep, sate lembat, lawar buncis,* sweet corn patties, peanut sauce *(bumbu kacang),* and *gado gado.* Each session costs Rp15,000, runs 2.5 hours (1100-1330), and includes a lunch and tea or coffee. Booking is essential as there's a five-person minimum. Classes can be arranged for the other days as well if minimum booking requirements are met.

To immerse yourself in Indonesian culture, **Sukadana,** in the middle of Jl. Jembawan on the left if coming from the post office, offers Balinese and Indonesian language courses. **Oka Wati's,** off Monkey Forest Rd., also gives lessons in Balinese and Indonesian.

SERVICES

The **police station** (tel. 0361-975316) is on Jl. Raya Andong. Head out of town toward Peliatan, then at the T-junction turn on the road north to Petulu; it's opposite the telecommunication center. Ubud has at least 20 **money-changers,** most open 0830-2000. On Ubud's main street and all the way down Monkey Forest Road are moneychangers, international freight forwarders, postal agents, film processing outlets, and travel agencies. A unique, locally managed, nongovernmental **tourist information center** (tel. 0361-96285), established by contributions from 12 *banjar* and the Indonesian Hotel and Restaurant Association, is on Ubud's main street across from the dance hall *bale* and only seconds from the main intersection in the exact center of Ubud. Staffed by at least three English-speaking Indonesians, this is a great place to find out what's going on. Dance schedules, shuttle bus costs and times, notices of ceremonies, emergency numbers, and trekking info is posted, and they also hand out a good map of Bali, sell tickets and organize transport to

dance and music performances, plus provide a convenient message board for travelers. Open daily 1000-2000.

Public bulletin/notice boards are found all around town, posting information about events happening around the island, details of transport costs, sightseeing tours, and other points of interests to tourists. It pays to check them each day. A useful one is at the Crackpot on Monkey Forest Road. Behind Ary's Book Store by Ary's Restaurant and diagonally across from Lotus Cafe, a printer will make you 100 single-color business cards for Rp12,000.

Tino Drug Store, tel. (0361) 975020, on Jl. Raya next to Casa Luna, is Ubud's best-stocked supermarket for anything from film, sunblock, groceries, canned goods, and beer to Corn Flakes, frozen pork chops and steaks, open 0800-2000. **Dewi Mas Market** (tel. 0361-975300) on Jl. Hanoman (just before the fork to the Monkey Forest) is a newer and brighter version. Open 0730-2000. Want to get married on Bali? I Nyoman Sujana can help make the arrangements. Make inquiries at Tebesari Homestay and Dressmaker, Banjar Tebesaya 29, in Peliatan.

There's now a Kodak photo processing shop called **Era Drug Store and Photo Color Service Centre,** tel. (0361) 975341 or 975362, at the start of Monkey Forest Rd.; a branch is down the road toward the Monkey Forest. **Segara,** near Nomad Restaurant, does photocopying and laminating, sells stationary, and offers binding service—the best service of it's kind in Ubud. A **laundry service** is advertised beside the sign to the Frog Pond Inn on Monkey Forest Road. **Ubud's Children Club,** Jl. Pengosekan 9, tel. (0361) 975320, is run by an Australian woman. Open 0800-1200, 1300-1600.

If your hotel doesn't have a swimming pool, for a small fee (Rp2000-3000) you can swim as a guest in a number of hotel pools—Puri Suaswati, Villa Rasa Sayang, Dewi Sri Bungalows, Fibra Inn, Grand Ubud, Oka Kartini's, Oka Wati's, Andong Inn, and Pertiwi's. The entrance to the pool at the Ubud Village Inn is Rp3000 but includes a drink, towel, and nice relaxing music.

Tourist Services
It's a harbinger of Ubud's maturity as a tourist center that agencies like **CV Three Brothers**

Wisata on Monkey Forest Road have arrived. These people do everything: car, motorbike, and pushbike rentals; insurance; packing and shipping; postal service, stamps, and parcel delivery; coach tours; shuttle bus tickets; moneychanging; cash for credit cards; bus tickets for Java; international and domestic air ticketing; importing/exporting; document clearance; hotel reservations; and laundry. Another full-service agency is **Surya International** on Jl. Raya, tel. (0361) 975133, fax 975120; staff will make hotel reservations for you for a fee.

Banks and Moneychangers

The Ubud branch of **Bank Duta**—Indonesia's best bank—offers the most services. It's near the major T-junction in north Peliatan just before Ubud. You can get a cash advance on your credit cards (Rp3000) and change traveler's checks here. Air-conditioned **Bank Danamon,** on Jl. Raya in the center of Ubud a little east of the town's main crossroads on the north side of the street, also does cash advances against your Visa card (open Mon.-Fri. 0800-1300). Another good bank is **BCI** beside Nyoman Communication Service. At least a dozen money changers are found along Monkey Forest Road and Jl. Raya. You don't have to look far for a moneychanger—virtually every shop in Ubud will change money. Look for the best rate.

Postal Services

There are postal agents all over Ubud where you can buy postcards and stamps or mail letters and parcels. **Rona's,** Jl. Tebesaya 23, sells stamps and posts letters. The poste restante service at Ubud's post office in Padangtegal is free, though not too reliable; it's better to have letters sent to a hotel. Large envelopes and packages are filed separately from the regular mail, and newly arrived mail doesn't even get sorted for a full day or two. The post office also offers *paket pos* service; first have your parcel inspected, wrapped by a *tukang bungkus* in a shop outside for Rp400-10,000, depending upon the size and material (Rp10,000 for a wooden box filled with protective foam). The post office is open Mon.-Sat. 0800-2000, Sunday 0800-1200. The postal code is 80571.

Book Exchanges and Lending Libraries

Rona's Accommodations and Book Exchange, Jl. Tebesaya 23, tel. (0361) 975120, has a library of over 2,000 books in English, German, French, Italian, Swedish, Norwegian, Danish, and Dutch. For guests, books are exchangeable one for one. For others, if you buy a book you get half its price refunded when you give it back, or you can trade two books for one. The **Crackpot** on Masapahit (tel. 0361-976698) also has a book exchange service. The **Library and Research Center** next to the football field rents books and has a reference library; tel. (0361) 976194, e-mail pondok@denpasar.wasantara.net.id. Run by a friendly American named Lori.

Telephone

From Ubud's center walk east to the T-intersection in north Peliatan, make a left, walk 200 meters north. On your left, just in front of the police station, you'll find the fully-computerized, efficient government telephone office Kantor Telcom. Here you can dial your home country direct by entering a booth and pressing the button marked with the country you want to call (choice of 20 countries). A call to the U.K., for example, can be made for Rp31,000 for three minutes, each additional minute Rp5000. Pay with Visa, an Indonesian telephone charge card, or call collect. Twenty-four hour **Home Country Direct** booths are also found at Ubud's main post office on Jl. Jembawan. Telephone cards can be bought at Kantor Telcom or at the tourist office on Jl. Raya. The telephone code for Ubud is 0361.

Although more expensive, another good convenient place to make international (IDD) calls via satellite is **Nomad's Telecommunications Center,** Jl. Raya Ubud 33 X, tel. (0361) 975520, fax 975115, which takes up the whole top floor of Bank Central Asia on Ubud's main street. Most other telecommunications businesses charge you for a minimum of three minutes but at Nomad's you pay only for the actual time you're on the phone. Collect calls must go through Denpasar and it could take anywhere from 30 to 90 minutes, depending on how busy they are. They also send and receive faxes. Open 24 hours. Nomad's runs another telephone office on Monkey Forest Road.

Ary's Travel Service, next to the Ubud Bookshop and beside the restaurant of the same name, offers a fast, efficient fax service (Rp10,000 to the U.S.), reconfirms tickets, offers a poste restante service, and allows you to leave messages for people. Very handy and central for people who don't have telephones. Open 0900-2100.

Freight Forwarding and Shipping
Dozens of reliable international air and sea freight forwarding companies are based in Ubud. These companies also provide container service, packing, custom clearance, guaranteed parcel delivery with insurance, and handicraft and garment exporting services. Check out **PT Sakura Citra Cargo,** Jl. Suweta 9, Ubud 80571 Gianyar, tel. (0361) 975070 or 975634, fax 975581, and **Ary's Travel Service,** Jl. Raya, tel./fax (0361) 975162 or 975523. **PT Purnama Cargo,** Jl. Jembawan 1 X (near Ubud's post office), P.O. Box 119, tel. (0361) 975033, will ship one container to Europe for about Rp630,000, less to the West Coast of the United States. Will wrap and prepare an average size box for sea shipment for Rp5000, not including postage. See manager I Wayan Rarem.

Beauty and Health
An indulgent treat for both men and women can be found at **Nur's Beauty Salon** at Jl. Hanoman 28. A friendly and professionally run operation. They specialize in using traditional products and *jamu* and their massage rooms are set in a peaceful garden. A full range of beauty treatments. The herbal bath is not to be missed—an hour and a half of pure relaxation for Rp42,000. You can spend the better part of the day at Nur's getting a manicure, pedicure, facial, massage, herbal bath, shampoo, trim, and style—for Rp95,000. Nur also offers two-hour body massages for both men and women. Another good beauty salon, **Marie's,** tel. (0361) 975622, Monkey Forest Road, does manicures and pedicures for Rp7500, wash and cut for Rp15,000, and facials, baths, and massages. Very friendly. **Salon Traditional Massage** on Jl. Hanoman offers face masks, cream baths, waxing, braids, beard trimming, and *jamu* treatments.

Ubud's best commercial masseuse is Dr. I Wayan Weda at **Mentari's Massage Service Center,** Jl. Hanoman 1 (tel. 0361-974001), right on the corner of Jl. Hanoman and Jl. Raya Ubud. Wayan offers relaxation massage, acupressure, and reflexology. If you have any doubts about the efficacy of the massage, read the dozens of testimonials on the bulletin board in front. The **Bodywork Centre,** Jl. Hanoman 25 (tel. 0361-975720), gives very deep massages for Rp20,000-40,000.

AA Meetings are hosted by the Mumbul Inn on Jl. Raya each week. Call (0361) 975364 for information. **Dr. Siada** holds consultations in his office opposite the market from 1700 to 2000, including Sunday. The bulletin board outside the tourist information office on Jl. Raya posts the addresses of other doctors and dentists, and there's a small clinic on Jl. Dewi Shinta just east of the soccer field.

Ubud has one small hospital, **Darma Usadha** on Jl. Abangan Tjampuhan (tel. 0361-975235), that's open 24 hours. It costs about Rp80,000 plus the price of drugs for a doctor to pay a house call to your bungalow or homestay. At **Ubud Sari Health Resort,** Jl. Kajeng 25 (200 meters from Jl. Raya Ubud), chiropractor Dr. James Taylor does excellent healing work. Beautiful environment—garden, ponds, jacuzzi, baths, massage, vegetarian restaurant, moderate, and takes credit cards. An extremely well-stocked drugstore, **Apotik Ubud Farma** (tel. 0361-974214), is located on the main road, Jl. Raya Ubud, just up from Genesha Bookstore on the right (if heading into Ubud's center). The pharmacist, Gidheo Winata, speaks good English (he worked in Germany), looks up all the medicines first, and even sends someone down to Denpasar to pick something up if he doesn't stock it. Nice guy. Open 0800-2100.

TRANSPORTATION

Getting There
From Kuta, get a public *bemo* first to Denpasar's Terminal Tegal (Rp600), then another *bemo* to Kereneng (Rp500), then another *bemo* to Batubulan (Rp500), then another *bemo* to Ubud (Rp1000). Getting to Ubud from Lovina Beach is awkward though tempting because the shuttle service is Rp12,000. If you take public transport, be sure to get off at Mengwi

and change *bemo* instead of going all the way into Denpasar.

Bemo arriving in Ubud turn left before the market on Jl. Hanoman, loop around by the soccer field, then turn right on Monkey Forest Road to finally stop in front of the market on Jl. Raya Ubud. If your accommodation lies in Padangtegal or the eastern edge of Ubud, ask the driver to drop you off before the central market. Shuttle buses usually drop you off near your accommodations, though Perama tends to unload its passengers at its office on the southern end of Jl. Hanoman, a full 10-minute walk from central Ubud. If heading to Campuan, Penestanan, Kedewetan, Saya, or any accommodation west of Ubud, take a *bemo* (Rp500) from the market.

Public Tansport from Ubud

Ubud's central location is ideal for tourists who visit Bali for only a week or so, as the town can be used as a handy base for trips around the island. You can reach almost any tourist site, get back the same day, and go to the theater that night. It's even possible in Ubud to arrange a seat on a bus from Denpasar to Yogyakarta. Book two days in advance; buses usually depart from the travel agency's office in Ubud.

The *bemo* stand is in the middle of town by the market. It's easy to board public transport out from 0500 right up until evening. Fares: Mas Rp600, Blahbatuh Rp600 (brown *bemo*), Gianyar Rp800 (turquoise and orange), Klungkung Rp800, Denpasar Rp1000. Blue *bemo* head for Sukawati and Payangan, other brown *bemo* serve Kintamani (via Tegalalang and Pujung). The *bemo* to Denpasar goes straight to the big Batubulan Station from where you can catch another *bemo* to Denpasar's Kereneng station near the city center within walking distance of the market and Merpati and Garuda offices. When returning to Ubud from Denpasar, remember the last *bemo* for Ubud leaves Terminal Blahbatu around 1800.

Going from Ubud to Kuta and Sanur is a bit complicated, taking four *bemo* and about two hours. First take one of the large brown vans from near Ubud's market to Batubulan (Rp800, 27 stops), then a cross-city *microlet* to Kereneng (Rp500), then another *bemo* to Tegal station, then another to Kuta. It's easier just to take

the shuttle bus (Rp5000), which drops you off at your door. Or just grab a microlet all the way to Sanur for Rp20,000. For western Bali, go to Batubulan first, then catch another *bemo*.

The Sakah Connection

For many destinations, you first have to go to the crossroads village of Sakah, seven km south. *Bemo* leave all the time for Sakah (Rp500). From Sakah connect with other *bemo* heading for Singaraja, 102 km; Gianyar, 10 km via Bedulu; Tampaksiring, 19 km; and Amlapura, 60 km via Gianyar with a stop in Candidasa. Sakah to Candidasa is normally Rp2000 but *bemo* drivers try to charge tourists Rp3000. Remember, if you want to head east or north from Sakah, there's no need to go all the way into Denpasar and get another *bemo* out. Just take a *bemo* to Gianyar, the junction town for the eastern and northern halves of the island. To the villages bordering Ubud, like Peliatan and Campuan, *bemo* cost only Rp500 from Ubud's center.

Shuttle Buses from Ubud

Take advantage of the express services in vans from Ubud to: Kuta/Sanur/airport for Rp7500 (one hour), departure times 0800, 1000, 1300, and 1730; Candidasa/Padangbai Rp8000, departure times 0630, 0800, and 1100; Kintamani Rp7500, departure time 1100; Lovina Rp12,000, departure time 1100. Shuttle buses also depart for Lombok: Mataram for Rp16,500, departure times 0630 and 1100; Senggigi Rp17,000, departure times 0630 and 1100; Gili Trawangan Rp22,500, departure time 0630. Book the day before. **Perama Tourist Service** at the southern end of Jl. Hanoman in Pengosekan, picks up passengers at all the better known accommodations on Monkey Forest Road. You can also buy Perama bus tickets at Rona's (tel. 0361-975120) on Jl. Tebesaya or at Purnama on Jl. Raya Ubud. **Nomad's,** with an office next to Nomad Restaurant (tel. 0361-975520) on Jl. Raya, and another on Monkey Forest Road just south of the soccer field is also a major shuttle operator.

The shuttle bus south usually drops people off at Sanur first, then drives on to the airport, then to Kuta. If you have something to do in

Sanur, you may stop over there and take another shuttle bus later in the day on the same ticket. There are two shuttle buses a day (40-50 minutes) to Denpasar's Terminal Ubung, one in the morning that connects with the bus to Jakarta and one in the afternoon that connects with the bus to Yogyakarta.

Travel Agencies
There are dozens of good travel agencies all over Ubud. A good one is **PT Cahaya Sakti Utama**, Jl. Raya 33, tel. (0361) 975520, 975721, or 975131, fax 975115. **PT Sapta Nugraha Kencana**, Jl. Hanoman 17, also gives service and the staff is knowledgeable. Sells plane and shuttle bus tickets, reconfirms tickets, and has been known to change flight departure times on tickets, charging you Rp5000, but saving you a trip to Denpasar.

Surya International on Jl. Raya, tel. (0361) 975133, fax 975120, opposite Puri Lukisan, confirms tickets on Garuda, Qantas, JAL, and MAS flights for Rp2500. Bus and shuttle tickets are available; also offers daily sightseeing tours to Bali, Lombok, and Java. Very handy location in Ubud's center.

Long-Distance Buses to Java
Although ultimately departing from Denpasar, in Ubud you can choose your seat and confirm your ticket. The bus to Surabaya leaves 1900, arrives 0700 the next day, Rp21,000; to Yogyakarta leaves 1530, arrives 0800, Rp24,000 non-a/c, Rp38,000 a/c; to Semarang leaves 1530, arrives 0800, Rp37,000; to Bandung leaves 0630, arrives 0800, Rp50,000; to Jakarta leaves 0630, arrives 0700 the next day, Rp56,500. Book two days in advance at any of Ubud's dozens of travel agencies, but you must cancel 24 hours in advance. Departure is from Denpasar's Ubung station. Get yourself there by *bemo* for Rp2000 via Batubulan or take a shuttle bus direct to Ubung for Rp12,000.

Vehicle Rental
If there are three or four of you, consider hiring a *bemo* for a day or two of leisurely sightseeing. Your hotel or *losmen* can almost always arrange car or motorcycle rentals. A decent four-wheel drive vehicle rents for about Rp50,000 per day including driver and insurance; a Suzuki jeep

without driver is Rp40,000 per day including insurance if you take it a week or more.

On Monkey Forest Road, **I Nyoman Hertia Car Rental**, tel. (0361) 975360, has a large fleet of cars to choose from. It costs about Rp30,000 to hire a taxi to the airport at 0430 or 0500 in the morning.

Pushbike and Motorcycle Rental
Pushbikes are one of the best ways to explore the Ubud area—you're able to cover more territory than if you walked. There are a number of bike rental places with big one-speed models that fit Western frames for Rp4000-5000 per day, or newer, fat-tired mountain bikes for Rp8000-10,000 per day. If you rent long-term (over a week), a bike costs only Rp3000-4000 per day. **Alit's** on Monkey Forest Rd., a little down from Tjanderi's on the right, has bicycles for Rp4000 per day; many mountain bikes to choose from. Near the Monkey Forest, **I Kt. Sudarsana Shop** rents new bikes with baskets for Rp4500 per day or Rp4000 per day for six to seven days.

It is very easy to cycle around Ubud, though it's difficult to stay on the right track, even with a Pathfinder map. It's also difficult not to end up on one of the crowded main roads. One warm-up ride is through Campuan to Keliki, then west to the main road and back to Ubud. This tour will take a leisurely three to four hours for nonathletic types and offers some brilliant views. Another *velo* outing is to Tampaksiring and Goa Gajah.

A good day tour is a ride from Ubud down the back roads via Kengetan to Denpasar, coasting almost the whole way. Watch those big lumbering tour buses. From Denpasar, put your bike on top of a *bemo* for the return trip to Ubud. Motorcycle rentals cost about Rp15,000 per day including insurance. Might as well go for a vehicle, which offers better protection and costs only Rp20,000-30,000 more. The nearest place to gas up is in Peliatan. It's not easy to find petrol in the Ubud area after 2000.

Tours
Many storefront travel agencies offer a comprehensive, well-priced range of organized or customized coach tours all over the island for Rp15,000-80,000, depending upon distance, carrier, and how many sights the tour takes in.

The agencies vary little in price and provide air-conditioned buses seating eight to 12 people. Tours to cremations make a mockery of the most important day in the life of a Balinese and amount to cultural pollution. Sample tours: the "Kintamani Volcano Tour" (Rp15,000), which includes Goa Gajah, Pejeng, Tampaksiring, Penelokan, Bangli, Gianyar, runs 0900-1700. The full-day "Besakih Mother Temple Tour" (Rp30,000) visits in Celuk, Bukit Jambul, Kusamba, Gianyar, and Taman Gili. The "Bedugal Tour" (Rp20,000) includes Mengwi, Alas Kedaton, and the Lake Bratan area.

Mutiara Tourist Service, Jl. Ubud Raya, tel. (0361) 975145, specializes in roundtrip sunrise tours of Mt. Batur, led by expert mountain trekker Jero Wijaya. You leave Ubud at 0230 for the base of the mountain. Don't forget good sneakers, T-shirt, long trousers, and camera. The price is about Rp75,000. If you're hale and hearty enough, Mutiara will also take you to climb Gunung Agung. Of great appeal to naturalists is **Bali Nature Walks,** tel. (0361) 975-678, opposite Paduna Indah Cottages in Penestanan. They specialize in overnight nature tours of the forests and hills of western Bali's Barat National Park.

Ibu Rai Trekking, Monkey Forest Road, Box 153, Ubud, 80571, tel. (0361) 975066 or 975579, fax 96472, organizes walking tours around Ubud every Tuesday, Thursday, Saturday, and Sunday. At 0800 meet at the Ibu Rai Restaurant, where a car will take you to Banjar Sala just outside Ubud, then you start walking through rice fields, river valleys, across bridges and streams, into tropical forest. At the end you visit the ancient temple of Pura Taman in the village of Umakuta where a traditional Balinese lunch awaits. Arrive back in Ubud around 1530. Cost: Rp25,000 per person.

Nomad's, tel. (0361) 975520 or 975131, sells a snorkeling day trip to Turtle Island for Rp20,000, starting at 0800 and returning by 2000 every day. Price includes transport and equipment. Book one day ahead. A very popular tour is Sobek's eight-km whitewater rafting trip down the Ayung River gorge near Ubud. The price of Rp130,000 includes transport to and from your hotel, all equipment, world class guides, stunning scenery, hot and cold showers, changing rooms, and an excellent meal. Also

ask about Sobek's Class IV wh... trip for Rp160,000 and the kaya... Rp115,000. Call them at (0361) 287...

The Pony Day Tour includes a/c tr... from your hotel to the stables in picture... Tabanan Regency, instruction in the basics... riding, catered lunch, and a guided circular tour on ponies of rice terraces, woodlands, river courses, and the beach—a nine-hour ride for Rp127,000 per person. Book at many hotels in the Ubud area or call the Campuan Tourist Service, tel. (0361) 975298, on Jl. Raya. If walking from Ubud's center, their office is at the bottom of the hill on the right, about 150 meters before the bridge. From Ubud you can also arrange for accommodation and tours to other areas of Indonesia. Ask Perama Tourist Service in Pengosekan, tel. (0361) 975120, about the "Land-Sea Adventure to Komodo Island" (Rp525,000), "Lombok Countryside Tour" (Rp200,000), and "Trekking Mt. Rinjani" (Rp300,000). The per person price includes transport and ferry ticket with no extra charge for stopovers.

If you want to do your own tour, a **one-day tour** taking in a wide cross section of Balinese country life and culture would be: Ubud-Pejeng (the Moon of Pejeng, bronze drum)-Gunung Kawi-Tampaksiring-Gunung Batur-Toyabungkah Hotsprings (on the lake)-through Jati to Sebatu-Gunung Kawi (another bath, cold)-Sebatu (better shopping than Tampaksiring)-Petulu (sunset and white herons)-Ubud.

Back Roads from Ubud

Ubud is a more convenient base than the south for exploring inland Bali. With your own *bemo* you can take the shortcut to Gianyar via Bedulu or travel north from Ubud via Campuan, Sayan, Kengetan to Sangeh—an infrequently traveled route with few public *bemo.* If heading south, take the quiet back road out of Ubud instead of the really busy main road via Mas. This country road, which starts at Banjar Tegal in Ubud, passes by a few art shops and through working agricultural villages, and emerges in Batuan. These narrow, paved back roads are ideal for mountain bikes. By the early-1990s, tour buses had begun to discover them and, although they're still a lot less traveled than the main roads, it's not as virgin an experience as it used to be.

s the 40-km trip via
angan, and Pung-
iter rim. This back
ed for all but six or
thousands of pot-
, making it an eas-
ar. The road inter-
............ad at Kalanganyar,
the village between Kintamani and Penelokan.
Another way up to Gunung Batur is Ubud-Peli-
atan-Goa Gajah-Bedulu-Pejeng-Tampaksiring-
Penelokan.

An even more adventurous route for a private vehicle is the one via Peliatan to Pujung
and Jasan. The surfaced mountain road that
passes through Pujung emerges onto the road
along the crater rim northwest of Penelokan.
Check out the woodcarving centers and art
shops of Tegallalang, Pujung, Jati, and Sebatu
on the way. Jati, where the great carver I Tjokot
lived, is just off the road beyond Tegallalang.
The Peliatan/Tegallalang/Pujung/Batur road is
much nicer than the one passing through Pejeng
and Tampaksiring.

Walks from Ubud

Go to Ubud to get close to the real Bali—a mystical land lying somewhere nearby. All around
this sprawling village are scenic rice fields,
forested gullies, deep river gorges, lush vegetation, half-overgrown shrines and grottos, beautiful and diversified landscapes, Tarzan pools,
moss-covered temples carved from rock hillsides, even a Monkey Forest. Wake with the
sun and set off on foot or bicycle down any of the
village's many lanes. Indispensable compan-
ions to bring along are Victor Mason's volume of
guided *Bali Birdwalks* (Insight Guides, 1992;
Rp12,500), the Pathfinder's trail map *Ubud and
Environs* (1992; Rp10,000), and bottled water.

Any track leading off Ubud's main road, Jl.
Raya, will do. The path will lead to pristine native
kampung with a contingent of yapping dogs.
You'll get an inside look at the enormously
durable community life of the Balinese. A walk
from Ubud to Kubuh, Tunjungun, Yeh Tengah,
Keliki, Campuan, and back to Ubud will take only
a day. Rest during the noonday heat, then set
off again in the late afternoon. Or just walk straight
to Keliki; the trail starts from beside the Pura
Campuan Batu Lebah in front of Murni's in Cam-

puan. This very nice two-hour walk up through a
river valley takes you by rice paddies and jungle with no vehicles or shops and few people.

Another, shorter walk north takes you over a
ridge between two river valleys to the small community of **Bangkiang Sidam,** only a 15 minutes
over open grassland from Ubud. Relax in **Klub
Kokos Cafe** (tel. 0361-975001, fax 974731) which
serves light food and drink in an unhurried, serene
atmosphere. Have a chat with Kirshna and Cathy
Sudharsana about the local area. Stay overnight
in one of their bungalows or walk farther north
and visit a half dozen painting galleries.

For total and instant immersion into Balinese
rice culture—really beautiful and only minutes
away—walk up through Ubud's *pura dalem* on
the east side of town, or pay to get in to the Puri
Lukisan. After taking in the exhibits, go around the
back of the last building and start walking north
along the gradually rising path between irrigation canals. This is as real as Bali gets, and you'll
probably be completely alone. You'll see pond
herons, rare Malay facewings, Javan mooniers,
white-bellied swiftlets, Troides Helena butterflies,
and Lucinea spiders. From the edge of the paddies, catch sight of the massive hotels of Nusa
Dua. Lie down in the irrigation ditches to stay
cool. Farther up is a *pura pujunganan* under a
frangipani. It is built of tuft and is in perfect al-
lignment with Ubud's *pura dalem* and Gunung
Batur. A bit farther still is a lush ravine.

To walk to Kintamani, leave Campuan at
0500 and walk steadily uphill through Sebali
and Keliki—you'll reach Kintamani around 1700
or 1800 the same day. Most of the mountains of
central Bali can be seen on this beautiful walk. If
it starts to get dark, stay on one of the village
platforms. It's a big event in the village when a
car or motorcycle drives by, or a westerner arrives on foot.

On the walk to Pejeng, you'll take in surpassing
views of rice fields. This is also a great cycling
and jogging road. East of Ubud at the T-junction,
go straight ahead instead of turning south to central Peliatan. This bituman road (Jl. Laplapan)
heads straight east to Tatiani (30 minutes). Cross
a river and ask the local boys in Tatiani to take you
to the waterfall. Farther on, in Pejeng Timor east
of the *kepala desa*'s office, is a temple with two
amazing reliefs with very deep dimensions and almost animated carvings of fish leaping from the

panel. In Pejeng, see the Moon of Pejeng, then walk south via Bedulu to visit the Musium Purbakala (Archaeological Museum) in Bedulu.

Victor Mason's Bali Birdwalks

This three-hour guided tour is not just for those who love birds but for anyone who appreciates natural productions—butterflies, trees, brilliant scenery. It combines exercise, nature, and cultural observations. Meet at 0900 in Victor's Bali-style restaurant and pub, Beggar's Bush by the bridge in Campuan. After a drink, the group sets out, getting back at around 1300 for lunch. The cost is Rp76,000 (10% goes to the Bali Bird Club), which includes the birdwalk, binocular use, lunch, bottled water, coffee, and tea.

The biggest draw is the inimitable humor, panache, and wit of Victor, your host, who has lived on Bali since 1970. With a torrent of excited exclamations in English, French, Balinese, and Indonesian, Victor really plays the part of the eccentric British ornithologists, a Sir Alfred Russell Wallace clone. He's started his vastly entertaining nature rambles in 1990; as the years go by, it's getting harder and harder to find good paths into the countryside, but Victor seems to know them all. He'll lead you into the exquisite gardens of Puri Lukisan, demonstrate how to paste a *cingke* leaf on your forehead to cool you down, teach you how to suck sweet nectar from a Cardinal's Hat or whistle birds up. Of the 100 species of native birds found around Ubud, you're bound to see 30 or so, as well as some quite abrupt alterations of habitat. The best way to go is barefoot. Sharp-eyed Sumadi is his able assistant. To make a reservation, call (0361) 975009.

VICINITY OF UBUD

CAMPUAN

A crossroads village one km west of Ubud. Walk down a road between huge green embankments, then cross the bridge over a deep river gully. The bridge 25 meters above the river is a vital link between Ubud and the villages of Campuan, Penestanan, Sanggingan, and Kedewatan to the west. The walk to and from Ubud has become quite hair-raising because of the traffic, but staying in a slower-paced village is incentive enough to brave it. Below the Campuan bridge flows the River Oos, which serves as a laundromat and bathing site. Down on the right side two branches of the river meet, a spiritual spot in Hindus. The word *campuan* actually means where two rivers meet, a corruption of *campuran* (as in *nasi campur*). On the spur in between is moss-covered 12th-century Pura Gunung Labuh, an agricultur-al and fertility temple. Bathe under pure mountain spring water pouring out of a bamboo spout.

History
Legend has it that a wandering Hindu priest named Rsi Markendya founded the temple of Pura Gunung Lebah in the 8th century at the confluence of Campuan's two rivers. Near this spot in 1906, Nieuwenkamp discovered a nine-by-one-by-two-meter hewn-rock cave supported by two columns. Characters were written on the roof, which had caved in during the 1917 earthquake. Ever since the German artist Walter Spies took up residence in the 1930s on the grounds of the present-day Hotel Tjampuan, the lush, tranquil beauty of the village has attracted famous painters, scholars, and celebrities from all over the globe. While here, Spies and Rudolph Bonnet made important contributions to modern Balinese art by coaching Balinese artists

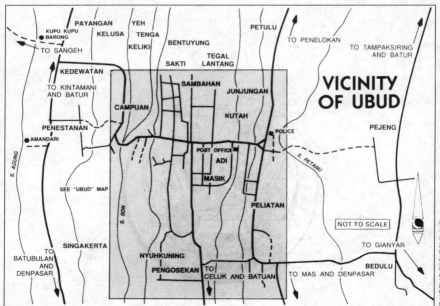

and providing them paints and canvases. These Europeans inspired the Balinese to forsake the rigid conventions of the traditional style and adopt some European painting techniques (see "Painting" in the Introduction).

Pura Gunung Lebah

This beautiful, tranquil, and impeccably maintained temple lies beside the river just north of the Campuan bridge, easily accessible from the Tjetjak Inn. The celebrated *batik* painter Nyoman Suradnya considers it the most important temple in the Ubud area. It was the site of the Penyegjeg Bhumi, the "Great Ceremony to Straighten the World" of October 1991, a ceremony held only once a century. An exciting discovery, the temple doesn't seem to be in anyone's maps or guides, so it has no sash-hawkers or other sellers lying in wait outside the front gate. Sit in the temple and listen to the river. You'll probably be the only person in the place.

Neka Museum

This nicely laid-out museum, one km north of Campuan, sits in a traditionally designed compound of four galleries containing the works of the greats of Balinese art. The museum portion, where works are not for sale, makes up only one small corner of the complex; the rest of the art is for sale. In the first gallery are exhibited the works of such well-known traditional Balinese painters as I Gusti Nyoman Lempad, a Balinese master who died at an amazing 121 years of age, Ida Bagus Made, Anak Agung Gde Sobrat, and Kebot. In the second gallery are the works of Nyoman Gunarsa, Abdul Aziz, Widayat, Abbas Dullah, and Affandi, modern, formally trained Indonesian artists who've worked on Bali. In the third gallery are the works of Walter Spies, Rudolph Bonnet, and Arie Smit, European artists who greatly influenced Balinese art. The works of other foreign painters who lived for extensive periods on Bali is displayed in the fourth gallery.

Besides these permanent exhibits, you can view paintings from an adjoining, continuously changing exhibit. In the small bookshop you can buy postcards of some of the gallery's best-known works and copies of the book *Perceptions of Paradise* (1993). Although a good variety of modern and traditional paintings are for sale, unfortunately there are no labels, no price list, and no information about the paintings. The Neka Museum was founded by Suteja Neka, who's collected works for this exhibit since 1966. Admission: Rp500.

Galleries

It's easy to strike up a rather rambling, enjoyable conversation with **Antonio Blanco,** an eccentric Catalonian artist who welcomes visitors to his home/gallery. He's an intriguing character on a big ego trip, which is great for business. Blanco calls his style renaissance; many of his paintings are bawdy and erotic, yet possess grace and rhythm, attractive colors, and lots of hidden meanings. Blanco paints in a pit below floor level so he can view his subjects at eye level. The steep driveway to Blanco's home is on the left immediately after the bridge on the way into Campuan from Ubud. Definitely worth a visit.

Accommodations

Family-operated **Ananda Cottages,** Box 205, Denpasar 80001, tel. (0361) 975376, fax 975375, has three classes of rooms: standard downstairs Rp69,000 s, Rp81,000 d; superior upstairs Rp81,000 s, Rp104,000 d, and family units Rp173,000. Add 15.5% tax and service. All rooms are big and comfortable with huge windows, hot and cold running water, Western baths, 24-hour room service, and veranda or terrace. Intercoms connect the rooms to front desk. An open-air restaurant serves European or Indonesian food. Nice surroundings and hospitable and friendly staff. Relax at the bar and take a swim or sunbathe in the natural cool and clean spring-fed pool. Recreational activities include badminton and jogging track nearby. The cottages are between the Campuan bridge and the Neka Museum, about 1.5 km from Ubud on the left, and face beautiful rice fields. Family-owned **Campuan Indah Homestay,** Jl. Raya Campuan, tel. (0361) 975087, charges Rp10,000 s, Rp20,000 d for rooms with bath, breakfast. They serve real Balinese food but you must order 24 hours in advance. *Kijang* for rent (Rp69,000 per day including insurance, Rp115,000 with driver). Ask the owner, I Gusti Nyoman Daria, who speaks good English, to take you to Keliki or down to the royal Gunung Lebah temple on the fork of the two tributaries of the River Oos—the oldest, biggest and most famous temple in the Ubud area.

Tjetjak Inn (or Cecak Inn), on the right as you're approaching Campuan, charges Rp35,000 s, Rp46,000 d (includes tax) for small, sparsely furnished bungalows overlooking the river. Breakfast is included, served either on your veranda or in the open-air restaurant. No phones in rooms. Close to the main Ubud-Campuan road, with a sweeping view, good vibrations, a nearby natural springs, and superb walking tracks in the vicinity. Call (0361) 975238 or fax 975052 for reservations, especially in July and August. **Made's and Uli Pering's Cottages,** a 20-minute walk uphill from the Tjetjak Inn, rent for Rp35,000 and look out over a magnificent ravine. For people who like to walk or meditate. Quiet, except for the sound of the rivers below. Negotiable seasonal rates.

Long a favorite of Jakarta-based expats, **Murni's Houses,** tel. (0361) 975165, lies below the restaurant by the same name; Rp104,000 d per day for an apartment and Rp173,000 per day for a private house (capacity eight people). Pool, maid service, and helpful staff. Each accommodation is whimsically decorated with Balinese paintings and hanging winged gods. From your veranda contemplate some of the area's most impressive examples of agricultural engineering. **Puri Sekar Ayu Bungalows,** Jl. Raya Campuan, tel. (0361) 975671, on the right on the road down to Campuan offers five bungalows on a hill. Rates are Rp51,000-69,000, with delicious breakfast included. Nice patio restaurant, peaceful surroundings.

On the slope of a green hill overlooking a deep gorge, the 26-room **Hotel Tjampuhan,** Jl. Raya Campuan, Box 198, Ubud 80571, tel. (0361) 975368 or 975369, fax 975137, is on the right, about 200 meters up after the bridge. The embodiment of the rustic charm architectural movement of the 1950s, with a decided air of neglect, the property is much bigger than it looks (some rooms are a 10-minute walk from the front desk). The rates are Rp109,000 s, Rp125,000 d, for standard, Agung rooms; Rp150,000 s, Rp184,000 d, for deluxe Raja rooms; all are subject to 15.5% tax and service. Sometimes booked out by package tour operators. Each large bungalow has its own bathroom with hot and cold water, jacuzzi-style bath, leaky toilet, shower, ceiling fan, and veranda,

but no in-room telephone. Don't get a room close to the noisy road. Spies and Bonnet lived here during the 1930s; in fact, you may sleep in Spies' old house. Facilities include a 1930s-style pool, immaculate tennis court (reportedly built for Woolworth heiress Barbara Hutton), badminton courts, bar, restaurant, and lots of exquisite privacy. Take a stroll through the scenic, rambling, and well-kept grounds.

Though Hotel Tjampuhan's restaurant is not so good, the breakfasts are okay, though late (0730). (Better American breakfasts can be had down the road at the Beggar's Bush or at the Bridge Cafe.) Nonguests may use the pool (Rp3000). Taxis always available and car, bicycle, and motorcycles for rent.

Also owned by Cokorda Putra Sukawati is Campuan's premier hotel, the high-priced **Pita Maha,** just short of the Campuan-Kedewetan line. Billed as a more Balinese version of Hotel Tjampuhan, the 20 luxurious units (Rp207,000 and up) plus four family units all have courtyards and extravagant stonework. Spread over different levels of hills, the hotel looks out over a deep river valley, rice fields, and mountains—a unique and romantic location.

Ulun Ubud Cottages, Box 3, Ubud, tel. (0361) 975024 or 975762, fax 975524, is actually in the outskirts of Campuan beyond the Neka Museum in Sanggingan, 2.5 km north. This top-class hotel boasts some truly distinct features: dramatic location with stunning views, fine performance and study spaces, good restaurant, bar, pool, and a variety of spacious traditional-style rooms with hot water, bath, shower, and antiques. Priced at Rp104,000 s, Rp127,000 d for standard rooms; Rp115,000 s, Rp150,000 d for studio bungalows; Rp253,000 twin, Rp207,000 triple for family units; Rp150,000 s, Rp207,000 d for suite rooms. All rates include breakfast, tax, and service. Clean, quiet, beautifully designed and decorated.

HILLTOP CAMPUAN

If you'll be staying in Ubud for three days, stay in one of the area's homestays. If you're staying for a month, rent one of the bungalows above the main road on the Penestanan side of Campuan. Pure country. The more picturesque and peaceful places—surrounded by rice paddies and overlooking gardens—are often under contract for months on end. On the higher levels of the village on a clear day you can see Gunung Agung towering in the distance. You're out of earshot of the main road and far away from Ubud's hustle, bustle, noise, and pollution.

Reach this peaceful area by taking the steep road to the left after the Campuan bridge, or the steep flight of steps on the left about 100 meters past Hotel Campuan. At the top of the stairway is **Warung Ibu Putu;** the names of a number of homestays and bungalows are found on signs at the entrance to walking lanes at the small intersection beyond, or people will be able to direct you. With its *warung,* restaurants, clusters of bungalows, lanes, swimming holes, and shops, it's an entirely self-contained community from which you never need venture. As it's uncertain where Campuan ends and Penestanan begins, just call it "Hilltop Campuan." Dotting the ridge are a dozen idyllic family-run homestays overlooking some of Bali's most beautiful *sawah,* only a few minutes walk from the road. These private compounds consist of two to five bungalows that rent long-term. There's almost always a waiting list, but in September it really slows down. Typically, on the bottom floor is a bathroom, a kitchen with cooking facilities, and an open-air living room. On the second floor you'll find a large bedroom and porch with great views of cascading terraces and forests. Outside are beautiful gardens and sometimes even a lotus pond. Security is usually more than adequate because family members are in residence nearly all the time, yet generally respectful of guest's private space. Also very quiet; closest motor vehicle access is at least 800 meters and there's no through traffic for motorcycles. Hilltop Campuan is only a 20-minute walk from Ubud, yet free from its noise and dust. There's usually a delightfully cool breeze from the south blowing through, keeping both the heat and the bugs down. Instead of paying Rp400,000 per day at Nusa Dua for make-believe Bali, see the real Bali in one of the many accommodations in this area for a fraction of the cost.

Accommodations

A wonderful place to stay is **Made Arta's,** three comfortable houses amid rice paddies, each costing Rp30,000 per day (up to four people). Made prepares a delicious breakfast every morning, speaks English well, and is a valuable source of local information, customs, and conversation. Climb the Penestanan steps and follow the path to the right. About 230 meters past Kori Agung, turn left on the path. Made Arta's is down 100 meters on the right. For reservations, write Arta Bungalows, Campuan, Ubud 80571, Bali, Indonesia.

Rent a whole house at isolated **I Nyoman Gelis Bungalows,** Box 143, Ubud. People often stay for months. As many as four people may share a bungalow. The price of Rp15,000-30,000, depending on the size of the bungalow, includes breakfast. Hot water. A bathing place is down the path below the homestay. To get there, walk up the Penestanan steps, go 400 meters past Ibu Putu's Warung, turn right at rock sign, then it's another 400 meters along a small stream to the next rock sign pointing to steps up to the homestay. The family offers beadwork instruction and private tours on request, and Nyoman gives great healing massages (Rp20,000 per hour).

Nearby **Melati Cottages,** Box 15, Ubud, tel. (0361) 975088, offers sumptuous, though a bit kitsch, quarters in a beautiful setting. Take a sharp left after Blanco's; at the top of the hill take the little path near Hotel Penestanan through the rice paddies. You'll see the sign. Its 12 bungalows (Rp23,0000-58,000 d) have traditional decor, hot water, ceiling fans, floor-to-ceiling glass walls, 360-degree views over *sawah,* wide wooden plank floors, life-size woodcarvings, a pool in the middle of rice paddies, and a library. Great breakfast. Numbers 1, 5, and 7 are the best (extra beds). Very quiet, good service, and well protected in an enclosed area. Nyoman Rata, the proprietor, will give you a ride to Ubud or pick you up at the airport. Visa/MasterCard accepted.

For **Made Bawa Bungalows,** take the stairs diagonally across from Hotel Tjampuhan, then take a right (you'll see the sign). Three beautiful thatched bungalows with refrigerator, stove, and coffee in the morning. The small ones are Rp15,000 while the two-story ones are Rp20,000. However, you may find the noise from the road bothersome.

Pugur's Bungalow, Box 10, Ubud, on the edge of the rice fields, lacks peace and quiet yet is close to restaurants and other conveniences. After Warung Ibu Put, take a left; it'll be on the right. Of the three bungalows, the front one has its own private garden. All have a well-equipped private kitchen; you can cook yourself or hire a Balinese cook for Rp100,000 per month. Very private. Beautiful views of Gunung Agung out one window and Gunung Batukau out the other. The owner, Pugur, studied with Arie Smit in 1963. He will probably invite you to his house for *kuningan.*

On the south side of Pugur's Bungalows is **Londa's,** which has three very nice bungalows at the same price as Pugur's. Nearby in the rice paddies is **Siddharta's,** an open-sided restaurant with accommodations. Friendly service, clean and attractive premises. Within easy walking distance, **Rasman's** rents lovely bungalows at a reasonable price that includes a delicious breakfast. Upon request, and for a fair price, they'll prepare a wonderful roast duck dinner with side dishes.

Sadri Homestay, near the "intersection" at the top of the stairs, has Balinese-style bungalows with big pavilions for Rp20,000 (no breakfast) or Rp22,000 (with breakfast). High up in the rice fields among flowering shrubs, the panorama is magnificent.

Food
Murni's Warung, tel. (0361) 975233, just before the bridge on the left if walking from Ubud, used to be highly recommended but lately it's considered generally overpriced for the food and service. It serves both Western and Indonesian food—chili con carne, sweet and sour pork, grilled fish, spring rolls, French fries—and is getting very *gucci* for the Euro-yuppies with drinks like sangria (Rp4500), gazpacho (Rp3000), and the Upper Elk Valley Authentic American Hamburger. Good reports, however, on their salads, Chinese meals, and desserts, as well as the fantastic coffee and ice-cold beer. It's clean and sits over the rushing river. Open 1030-2100 every day.

On the Campuan side of the bridge, **Beggar's Bush Bar and Restaurant,** tel. (0361) 975009, continues to enjoy a solid reputation for their excellent Western/Indonesian food and nice atmosphere. They have the best steak, spareribs, and baked potato in town, plus real Balinese food like *ayam takir* ("steamed running chicken") and *pecel paku* (ferns). An excellent introduction into Balinese cooking. Attractive prices.

On the other side of the road, the **Bridge Cafe,** tel. (0361) 975058, fax 975137, serves tasty food with no MSG. Above Rasman's, in the rice fields, is an excellent restaurant called **Kori Agung.** There are approximately eight tables with a beautiful view. Everything on the menu is fresh and well-prepared at moderate prices (a dinner for two, which includes appetizers, main dishes, desserts, and coffee, is about Rp46,000). The black rice pudding is some of the island's best.

Bali Restaurant, on the southerly road to Penestanan, is off and on. The old Bali Restaurant went bankrupt during a post-August thaw and the new one is under new management. The nightly specials could be good. Some people like the classier and slightly more expensive **Cafe Dewata** down the road. Although it's equally as uneven in food quality, the setting is airier and the menu more extensive. The service is good.

Entertainment
Laser disc videos are screened at **Coconut's,** but movies are not thoughtfully chosen—usually violent. Not only is this the clearest screen around but there's also a crystal-clear stereo system and pleasant dining area. Another place that shows big-screen movies is the **Bridge Cafe** near Campuan's suspension bridge. The person who picks the films has good taste. The food is good but expensive.

Beggar's Bush, on the right just after the bridge, captures the feeling of an English pub. Victor Mason's bar is named after a notorious 19th century tavern outside London. Truly cold draft beer is served at sensible prices (half pint Rp3000, full pint Rp5500); also try Beggar's Grog, a spiced *arak* from Karangasem brewed from a guarded family recipe. The Bush possesses a killer 1940s jazz and blues record collection. Balinese cowboys, regular irregulars, locals, police, and Brits love this sacred temple of low debauchery. The kitchen doesn't close until midnight to serve hungry late night revelers, many of whom are thankful for the free transport back to their hotels.

Shopping

Kunang-Kunang I in Campuan, tel. (0361) 975714, fax 975282, is an importer of stylish, collector-quality art objects, silver jewelry, textiles, pottery, musical instruments, furniture, and antiques from Lombok, Sumatra, Timor, and all the outlying islands—you name it, they've got it. Not a souvenir shop, this place displays expensive stuff in locked glass cases: contemporary jewelry, silver, precious stones, and some *ikat* pieces. The staff speaks good English. A branch, Kunang-Kunang II, tel. (0361) 975716, is on Jl. Raya in Ubud.

Daigo Yasugi sells Balinese art on T-shirts for Rp10,000-50,000. All are original works by Balinese painters living in Ubud—so original the other T-shirt makers copy his designs within a few days after they come out. His shirts are colorfast and fixed priced. Daigo can also make T-shirts to order. See his creations at the **Bali Art Co-op** on Jl. Raya, tel./fax (0361) 975087.

Services

Campuhan Tourist Service, Box 10, Ubud, tel./fax (0361) 975298, is the only travel agent in Campuan, handling faxes (Rp10,000 to the U.S.), airline ticketing and confirmations, hotel reservations, car rentals, moneychanging, and various tours.

Closer to Ubud's center, **Ary's Tourist Service Center,** Jl. Raya Ubud, tel. (0361) 96130, fax 975162, conducts tours at very good prices: the Bedugul Tour Rp22,500, Singaraja-Lovina Tour Rp27,500, Kintamani-Besakih Tour Rp22,500, East Part of Bali Tour Rp27,500, Uluwatu Tour Rp22,500. All tours leave at 0830 or 0900, require a minimum of three people, and the price does not include entrance fees. Special or private tours on request.

Telephone services are available at **Kori Agung Bungalows and Cafe,** which obviates visiting any of Ubud's telecommunications offices.

Walks from Campuan

The surrounding area is quite beautiful, and setting out for a walk is a good way to kill half a day. Generally speaking, the north is cleaner and less polluted than the south. To the west is the painter's village of Penestanan, an easy walk from Campuan. From here turn north and walk to Sayan where the rice terraces and views from the hills are magnificent. Get a reasonably early start for the best views and photo opportunities, as the mist and light provide tremendous ambience.

Sanginggan

There are many places to stay north of town, like in **Wisata Cottages** in the small village of Sanginggan a little past Campuan. The Wisata has Rp40,000 bungalows, which include a nice breakfast. Rooms are right on the edge of a dropoff to a ravine with the river below. The problem with this locale is that it's too dangerous to walk along the narrow road down to Campuan and back. There are deep ditches on both sides, into which you'll surely be forced to escape the roaring trucks. This road desperately needs a sidewalk.

PENESTANAN

From Campuan, Penestanan is at least five km by road via Kedewatan. However, a shortcut through rice fields lies about two km from the Campuan-Kedewatan road. After crossing the bridge in Campuan, bear right and after 200 meters turn left at the homestay signs and head up a steep flight of stone stairs. Continue on this path for one km to the main village of Penestanan. Just before the village, you cross a deep river gully. On the left, down a path, is a refreshing bathing, washing, and drinking spot with ancient stone statues. Along the way, there are several airy and extravagant private residences occupied by jet-setting expats and foreign-service personnel.

The School of Young Artists

The Dutch painter Arie Smit lived in this artists' village in the late 1960s and started the perennial School of Young Artists by teaching young Balinese artists European techniques. One of the best-selling painting styles on Bali, this school of "naive" painters has spawned hundreds of clones all over Bali. The Young Artists' paintings of dancers, market scenes, and rice harvests are characterized by bold colors, pronounced outlines, and an attractive harmony of form and color.

But, having been mass-produced to meet the demands of tourists, the new paintings this school is producing do not display the same strength of the earlier paintings. The technique has taken on a certain rigidity and the subject matter has become stultified (see "Painting" in the Introduction). This does not mean, though, that Penestanan's artists are not worthy of attention. The home of at least 40 artists sell their paintings at more down-to-earth prices compared to Ubud and many of its surrounding "art" hamlets.

Accommodations and Food

Reasonably priced **Penestanan Bungalows,** tel. (0361) 975803, is situated in magnificent rice fields. Negotiate a price of Rp35,000 per day for nice-sized rooms high up on the second floor with privacy, fantastic views, and hot water. Life here is altogether pleasant and extremely quiet. The place is half-full even in the high season, and even when the much more expensive Bali Ubud and Melati Bungalows nearby are nearly full. This is because you can't drive here.

In Penestanan Kelod, **Gerebig Bungalows,** Box 133, Ubud, has two single rooms (Rp16,000), two double rooms (Rp20,000), two standard bungalows with two double beds (Rp26,000), and one family-size bungalow (Rp40,000). The two-story bungalows are the nicest. All rooms and bungalows have private baths and showers, look out on rice fields, and face the sunset. Prices include breakfast, plus bananas and tea in the afternoon. The people who run it are the best part; the room service is a real advantage to staying here. Rooms are cleaned and supplied with fresh towels each day. To get to Gerebig, walk up the road by Blanco's house, past Cafe Dewata, across a small river, and take the path on the right (see sign) opposite a water temple. In all, it's about a 25-minute walk from Ubud's center, 10-minute walk from Penestanan village, and only five-minute walk to restaurants serving decent food.

SAYAN

Head west out of Penestanan until you hit a bigger road. This is the start of the village of Sayan, about seven km from Ubud. In the 1930s the Canadian-born composer and ethnographer Colin McPhee built a house here, hired a lazy houseboy and a querulous Madurese cook, and wrote his classic *A House in Bali*. Parallel with the road, but not visible from it, is one of the most spectacular views in all Bali—a deep, lush river valley formed by the fast-flowing Ayung River. A famous photographic subject, this scene is portrayed on many postcards. Take any of a number of paths to the west that lead through the trees and you'll come to the lip of the gorge. A number of private bungalows are available in the area—excellent value for those planning to spend three to four weeks.

Sayan Terraces, Box 6, Ubud 80771, tel. (0361) 975384, offers idyllic, quiet cottages for Rp35,000 s or d with free breakfast, hot water, and lovely porches overlooking the magnificent river valley. The owner/manager, I Wayan Ruma, is a kind and gentle man who'll pick you up at the airport if you write or call ahead. The *warung* next door has very good chicken *sate*.

Soak in the beauty of the Balinese countryside at **Taman Bebek,** tel./fax (0361) 975385 or 720507, an idyllic, self-contained retreat two km south of the Amandari on the Sayan-Ubud road. This luxury family-style homestay is on the northern side of Sayan Terraces, nestled in traditional Balinese gardens that plunge steeply into the gorge below. The four elegant and spacious one- or two-bedroom bungalows (Rp161,000-207,000), plus one presidential suite (Rp690,000), have phones, ceiling fans, kitchenettes, and large sitting areas furnished with Balinese woodcarvings and plush sofas. Laundry, transport, tour service, car park. Room service is available from **Cafe Sayan** on the road in front—the best *nasi campur* in Sayan. Add 21% tax and service. Book through PT Indosekar, Jl. Mertasari 40, Suwung Kangin, Denpasar 80224 (Box 3047, Denpasar 80001, tel./fax 0361-720507).

Bongkasa

The largest blooming banyan tree in the Malay Archipelago—100 meters across—is in Bongkasa, near Sayan. To get there from the Bale Banjar Kutuh in Sayan, walk 80 meters south and take a right on the footpath to Bongkasa. The trail leads past a temple, across bridges over an irrigation canal, then to the Ayung River. Continue north to the Pura Puseh of Bongkasa, an ornate temple built of brick surrounded by a spacious lawn. Walk on to stone steps that lead to the Tanggayuda *banjar* and on to Pura Desa Tenggayuda, where you'll see the tree. It's so large that from a distance it looks like a whole forest. The central bole has been entirely engulfed by a huge tangle of aerial roots and a mass of epiphytes. The tree is the habitat of a sizable population of birds, squirrels, and lizards. Proceed north to the sand-collecting gorge where laborers scoop sand from the bottom of the river using hand-operated pulleys, then haul the sand in buckets on their heads up the slope to the main road. From there it's collected by middlemen and sold for Rp4500 per cubic meter.

Begawan Giri
This small hamlet on the Sayan ridge is famous for its hot springs, Toya Mampeh, believed to have magical healing powers, within the confines of one of Bali's horticultural masterpieces, Begawan Giri. Established first as a private holiday home, Begawan Giri has grown into a complex of 11 luxurious, self-contained villas, each with its own garden. The designers have planted 1,500 trees, including teak, mahogany, tamarind, avocado, coconut, mango, durian, mangosteen, *nangka,* rambutan, as well as African tulip, flamboyant, champak, and other exotic ornamentals. The estate's spring-fed pools are stocked with fish; there's also a health spa, an amphitheater for dance performances, and sports facilities. Take the flight of stone steps down to the Ayung River, passing under moon orchids and drooping maidenhair ferns along the way. The sacred springs are about three-quarters of the way down.

Getting Away
The ambitious may continue on to Sangeh, a beautiful walk through rice fields, shadowy lanes, and palm plantations, crossing little canyons over split-bamboo bridges. If you take it easy, it requires about four hours. Just keep asking for

Sangeh; everybody knows the way. From Sangeh, take a *bemo* down to Denpasar (Rp800), then another *bemo* back up to Ubud again (Rp800)—a satisfying day trip.

KEDEWATAN

A small village in the foothills two km north of Sayan on the road to Kintamani via Payangan. At the T-junction the road to the east leads after about six km to Ubud, passing Neka Museum on the left and Ananda Cottages on the right. Take a swim or sunbathe on the black rocks along the river below by walking 25 meters south of the shrine, which is south of Kupu Kupu Barong Cottages. Then follow a winding path through terraces carved out of the hillside down to the river. Take a shower under one of the many chilly, natural springs. Another path starts north of Kupu Kupu Barong down a dramatic cliff face of switchbacks through rice fields and palms right to the edge of the foaming river. See the bat cave at the bottom of the gorge.

North of the T-junction is a *warung babi guling,* said to be the best in the area. This and several other Kedewatan *warung* are the last genuine *warung* in the whole Ubud area. The reasonably priced **Ubud Indah Garden** in Banjar Lungsiakan/Kedewatan serves good Indonesian and European food, has clean washrooms, and serves ice cubes made from boiled water. They also prepare Italian, Chinese, Japanese, Indian, Balinese, and seafood dishes. Friendly service. Open for breakfast, lunch, and dinner. The restaurant offers free transport to and from accommodations in the Ubud area. In Sayan Kutuh, visit the gallery of painter I Nyoman Weda, a particularly pleasant person.

Accommodations
Because of the unique and coveted location lining a precipice over a deep and fertile river valley, Kedewatan's accommodations tend to be very intimate, very exclusive, and very expensive. If you have to think about money, you probably can't afford it. These fine resorts typically offer delicious seclusion, spa bathrooms, gym facilities, flexible check-in/check-out, airport transfers, valet and tour services, courtesy shut-

tle buses into Ubud, even golf driving ranges. At least stop in these cool hillside hotels for a cup of tea or a glass of wine and enjoy the view with the rushing Ayung River 75-100 meters below.

Another of Bali's most exquisite hotel properties is the **Amandari,** tel. (0361) 975333, fax 975335, part of the Hong Kong-based Aman Resort group. This ultradeluxe two-million dollar hotel achieved world prominence in November 1990 when Mick Jagger and Jerry Hall married on the premises. Designed by Peter Muller, who also designed the Oberoi, the Amandari simulates a Balinese village with 27 walled garden suites—virtual house complexes. The cheapest bungalow rents for Rp690,000 per night, the most expensive at Rp1.6 million (plus 15.5% tax and service). Each fully tiled bungalow, with teak beams, rattan furniture, sliding floor-to-ceiling window walls, and sunken marble outdoor tubs, is connected by walkways leading to the resort facilities. On the grounds are lily ponds, a 29-by-nine-meter hillside pool in the shape of a rice terrace, and a tennis court. Both simplicity and elegance are the rule—no signs, no noise, no unnatural materials, no radios, no music, no telephones ringing. Free transport to and from the airport. Bikes and guides are available free of charge. Extraordinary security; sentinels in white tunics guard the grounds.

One of the area's premier accommodations is the **Kupu Kupu Barong,** Box 7, Ubud, Bali, tel. (0361) 975478, fax 975079, in Kedewatan, perched on the edge of a cliff above the impossibly green Ayung River. Out nearly every window of its 19 luxurious a/c bungalows are breathtaking views, in some ways superior to the Amandari's because you're closer to the river. Structures are built in traditional *lumbung* style, with thatch roofs, bath and shower, fridge, ceiling fans, separate entrances, and private balcony and terrace. Each unit is set at a different level amidst organic, leafy, extravagant gardens and pathways overgrown with bougainvillea and sprays of orchids. The property boasts three pools, a resort shop, and Balinese massage and whirlpool. Part of the complex is an excellent and spectacularly situated restaurant. Rajapala and Mahabarata dances are put on each evening. Rates (subject to 15.5% tax and service) begin at Rp710,000 and go up to Rp1.5 million for the Barong Suite with private pool. Tranquil Balinese exoticism.

Scenic **Cahaya Dewata Bungalows,** Box 59, Ubud 80571, tel./fax (0361) 975495, atop the same deep ravine, is a cheaper version of the Kupu Kupu Barong, costing "only" Rp138,000 s or d for standard rooms, Rp184,000 for suite with valley view, and Rp368,000 for the Agung Room with valley view. To all prices, add 17.5% tax and service. Bungalows, built on different levels of the hillside, are nicely appointed with veranda, solar-heated showers, kitchen, fridge. Pool. Local calls cost Rp3000 apiece. The Kupu Kupu Restaurant is expensive but worth it if you consider the surroundings. Excellent breakfast with whole-wheat toast and tofu/*tempe* scrambled eggs. Airport transfers are Rp45,000.

Completely self-contained **Puri Kamandalu** consists of 20 rooms combining classical Chinese and Indonesian motifs. Located right by a rafting river, you can take paths and walkways all the way down to the river. Great meditation place. Lowest priced bungalows with two-meter-long baths cost Rp368,000, 75-square-meter suites are Rp473,000.

Putra Ubara Homestay has four big, comfortable, cool, well-furnished rooms for Rp35,000 apiece, including breakfast and houseboy attendance. Off the road at the southern end of the Sayan chasm, the view over terraced *sawah* is less spectacular but also 30 times cheaper than the Amandari.

Vicinity of Kedewatan

Seven km beyond Kedewatan and about 13 km north of Ubud is Payangan, from where the road continues to climb toward the eastern mountains. You can also get to Payangan from Keliki. In **Keliki,** stay at the tranquil **Klub Kokos** (tel. 081-139-6218) run by Sudharsana and his Australian wife Cathy. Walk west via Keliki Kawan, noting its gargantuan banyan tree. After Klusa, cross over a river and end up in Payangan's marketplace. This is a nice, cool village with a busy fruit and vegetable *pasar* every three days, less commercialized than Ubud's market. The only place on Bali where litchi *(longan)* are cultivated; also in this region are vanilla, durian, pineapple, and coconut plantations.

NYUHKUNING

This village, renowned for its woodcarvers, lies beyond the Monkey Forest, removed from the hubbub of Ubud. Up till now relatively isolated, lately the area is starting to develop. Now there are dozens of woodcarving shops, a popular restaurant, and pockmarked paths leading to native-style homes rented out long term by Westerners. Nyuhkuning is also very popular with meditation and yoga groups. See the Widya Kusuma Woodcarving Museum in the middle of the paddies. Exhibited are 30 or so carvings dating from as far back as the 1950s. This is the first real effort to show the wide variety in Balinese carving. Open Tues.-Sun. 1000-1700; Rp500 admission.

Accommodations and Food

Stay in isolated, peaceful **River Garden Homestay**, with five rooms and two bungalows. Managed by an American, it's being developed as a healing spa. Peaceful **Alam Indala**, tel./fax (0361) 974629, consists of nine luxury bungalows, Rp92,000-207,000 per day, plus 15% tax and service. Located just before the village of Nyuhkuning, take the road to the right after the Monkey Forest. The architect has created here a stunning design, taking full advantage of the extraordinary views. Set back along the Campuan River Valley, the land all around is locked up from development. Some units are perfect for families and couples (10% discount for stays of 10 days or longer). There's a medium-size swimming pool with kids' pool. You hear no noise from the road, there's no TV, only a video player. Each room has fresh flowers, ceiling fans, a private bath, hot water, beautiful garden veranda, and looks out on lush gardens. Lunch and dinner menus prepared by Cafe Wayan. Laundry, dry cleaning service. Genuinely warm and attentive staff. You may use the hotel shuttle anytime (two or three vans available), and they'll also pick you up in Ubud. Airport transfers are Rp40,000. Mailing address: Box 165, Ubud, Bali, Indonesia.

You'll see a big fat yogi in front of Nyuhkuning's **The Blue Yogi 2** restaurant, next to the temple. It sells such Western dishes as tandoori chicken (Rp6500), muesli, and wholesome baked goods at fairly inexpensive prices. The **Blue Yogi 1**, tel./fax (0361) 91768, in Tegallalang has a similar menu. Located 9.5 km north of the Peliatan-Ubud crossroads at the beginning of Ubud, this restaurant makes for a very nice rest stop on the road north to Gunung Batur.

Environmental Bamboo Foundation

Nyuhkuning's most famous resident is the Queen of Bamboo, Irish-born Linda Garland, the passionate and visionary head of the **Environmental Bamboo Foundation**, Box 196, Ubud 80571, tel. (0361) 974027, fax 974029, a nonprofit organization that counts among its supporters rock stars, government ministers, U.S. senators, filmmakers, and famous writers. The purpose of the foundation is basically to accumulate and disperse knowledge to those in a position to replace degraded forests with bamboo—a symbol of both strength and flexibility.

Linda Garland's home, on a seven hectare tract of land south of the Campuan River, has become a power point and center of activity for the world-wide ecological movement. An interior designer by training, Linda arrived in Bali in 1974, founded the Bali International School, and opened a business manufacturing furniture made from big bamboo—to this day her trademark. In the late 1980s she worked on David Bowie's house in the Caribbean.

In 1994 the unique collection of structures Garland built was the feature of an article in *Architectural Digest*. This established her as a major international arbiter of taste in interior design. Her property consists of a series of open plains molded at different levels, merging naturally into adjacent rice fields and extending down to a river below. Buildings are constructed of bamboo with split bamboo floors and *alang-alang* thatched roof.

In 1995, the foundation sponsored the Fourth World Bamboo Conference. One thousand delegates from all over the world poured into tiny Nyuhkuning to participate in and conduct lectures, workshops, and discussions, and form networking groups in science, industry, the arts, and environmental issues. All this to celebrate this remarkable plant and the products it generates—perhaps the only hope of reforesting the earth quickly enough to save the forests and guard the topsoil.

Singakerta

From Nyuhkuning, it's an hour's walk (crossing en route a dizzying girder bridge over the Oos River) to Singakerta's *purah puseh,* with elaborate gargoyles on the gate and *kulkul* tower. From this temple walk about 50 meters west to Pura Gado, a strange temple which combines both stupa-like Buddhist and primitive Polynesian features. In Singakerta, some of Bali's best woodcarvers make their living. South of the village on a well-trod path is the extravagant Pura Penataran Agung next to a big *wantilan* tree. Refresh yourself in the picturesque bath behind the temple. Beyond, in the rice fields, is Goa Raksasa, a perfect meditation spot in a cove of hibiscus and poinciana bushes framing a Javanese-style *candi.*

PENGOSEKAN AND VICINITY

This artists' village of 70 painters lies about four km south of Ubud and one km west of Teges. A haven for painters since the 1930s, Pengosekan gained world notice in 1974 when Queen Elizabeth II visited Gina, an artist she admired. In those days it was a poor, isolated, dusty village cut off from Peliatan by a river which could be forded precariously only in the dry season. The Community of Artists, Bali's first artist's cooperative, was established here in 1979 under the direction of teacher turned artist Dewa Nyoman Batuan. Internal bickering broke up the co-op in 1985. Today you can still check out the amazing protest paintings of Dewa Nyoman Batuan at his gallery (tel. 0361-975321); his daughter will do the interpreting.

Pengosekan is peaceful yet within easy reach of restaurants and entertainment. Since it's about a 25-minute walk into Ubud, a bicycle or motorbike is handy if you're staying for any length of time. The village is only a 10-minute walk west from the main road at the corner in Banjar Kalah, where you can easily catch public transport in the direction of Ubud or Denpasar.

Desak Putu Warti Stretton, tel. (0361) 975647, is a Balinese master dancer-musician who provides individual and group instruction in English. She also arranges performances and leads private tours.

Accommodations

Agung Raka Bungalows, tel. (0361) 975757, fax 975546, is a collection of charming, elegant, and spacious bungalows on a quiet lane amid rice fields costing US$38 s, US$85 d. All rates include service and tax. One villa suite (US$120), with private entrance and kitchen, is surrounded by water-lily gardens. All have verandas, great outdoor *kamar mandi,* and plentiful hot water. The hotel has a pool, jacuzzi, parking, free transport to Ubud center, and the 16-seat open-air restaurant serves good Indonesian and continental food and a great breakfast. Friendly staff.

Bali Breeze Bungalows, Box 67, Ubud, 80671, tel. (0361) 975410, fax to Ary's (0361) 975546 or 976162, lies on the edge of the village with nice views of rice terraces: five two-story bungalows for Rp21,000-31,500 (one or two people), three family units for Rp52,500 (four people), breakfast included. Facilities include beautiful gardens, open lawns, table tennis, and badminton court. This very secure place features bars on the windows and night guards roaming the grounds. An informal, unpretentious, and comfortable place with lots of personalized service.

One of the hottest places right now is **Guci Guesthouse,** only 300 meters from the Community of Artists and 100 meters in from the road, in central Pengosekan. Super clean individual bungalows in a leafy garden feature ceiling fans, mosquito nets, and garden toilets. In the home of a painter, this is a marvelous and moderately priced place to stay.

Puri Padi is a weird place. There's CNN but no phones in the rooms, therefore no room service. You have to go up to the front desk to order something for your room. Also no menus in the restaurant. Heavenly quiet because it's far from the road. Taxi into town from here is Rp2000 unless you can snag something along the road (easy to do; Rp1000-2000).

Pondok Impian Bungalows on Jl. Raya Pengoskean, tel. (0361) 975253, is called a "village resort" by its owners. Rates: Rp58,000 s, Rp69,000 d for cool and tranquil bungalows, each with private bath, hot and cold water, and standing fan. In front is the restaurant furnished with antiques. The **Primitive Bar** serves International and Indonesian food 0630-2200.

Puri Indah Exclusive Villas, also on Jl. Pengosekan, tel. (0361) 975742, fax 975332, is a small hotel set amidst beautifully landscaped gardens overlooking a small river, palm forest, and rice terraces. Each individually decorated *pondok* features overhead fans, minibar, large modern bathroom with hot and cold water, and private terrace. Room rates: superior Rp126,000 s, Rp147,000 d; deluxe Rp252,000 s, Rp273,000 d; VIP deluxe Rp483,000 s or d. Family houses cost Rp252,000-420,000. All rates subject to 17.5% tax and service. Facilities include safe deposit boxes, beautiful pool, poolside bar open till midnight, restaurant, and complimentary transport to and from Ubud's main restaurants. Credit cards accepted.

Jati Homestay, Jl. Hanoman, offers beautiful rooms right on the rice paddies; Rp8000 s, Rp12,000 d, also one upstairs for Rp15,000 s or d. Can't beat the location. Run by the painter Mahardika, who is also a masterful *kebyar* player. Dinner fare includes delicious fish steamed in banana leaves with spices, great fried crispy noodles, and well-made rice wine. Gracious, serene accommodations are also provided by **Kebun Indah,** Jl. Padangtegal (tel. 0361-974629); features the wonderful food of Cafe Wayan.

Food and Entertainment

The elegant, open-sided **Kokokan Club** on Jl. Pengosekan, tel. (0361) 975742 or 96495, is rapidly becoming the place to be seen in Ubud. Located in front of Agung Rai's small hotel, Puri Indah, and adjacent to his large new museum, this is the first authentic Thai restaurant in the Ubud area, featuring dishes fragrantly spiced with lemongrass, lime, and mint. Order succulent seafood, innovative vegetarian dishes, mouthwatering cocktails, mixed drinks, fruit juices, wines and coffee, espresso, and cappuccino, all at reasonable prices (by Ubud standards). Open 1100-1400 for lunch, 1800-2000 for dinner. Every Saturday at 1930 is a special traditional Balinese buffet with smoked duck, prawns, seafood, chicken curry, vegetable, and salads—12 courses for Rp35,000 adult, Rp15,000 child under 15 years. Book a day ahead. Dinner is accompanied by live dance and drama; on alternate Saturdays hear live acoustic music and vocals. Free transportation in the Ubud area. Across from the Kokokan on Jl. Pengosekan is

Exiles for pastas, soups, Indonesian food. Nice garden setting; lots of expats.

Painting

Even during the 1930s, when Rudolph Bonnet was exerting a profound influence over Ubud area painters, the *wayang* style persisted in Pengosekan, most notably in the magnificent works of I Gusti Ketut Kobot. He painted classical puppet-like figures, but in a softer, more humanized, and naturalized style. Kobot was an active member of the Pita Maha Painter's Cooperative created by the cosmopolitan Ubud Prince Cokorda Gede Sukawati, Rudolf Bonnet, and Walter Spies in 1935. The group dissolved by the end of WW II. A post-Pita Maha painters' cooperative was established here in 1969 by brothers Dewa Nyoman Batuan and Dewa Mokoh. Known as the Community of Artists, these brothers and their colleagues rediscovered the hidden beauty of nature with delicate and graceful depictions of leaves, insects, birds, and legendary creatures. This phase became known eventually as the Pengosekan Style. They laboriously painted large canvases symbolic of Bali's myths. Each canvas looked like a detail of a larger painting or a colored photograph shot with a macro lens. The colors used were refined and muted, yet pleasingly matched, conveying a sweet and cheerful feeling.

Inspired by the Bali International Style of Irish designer Linda Garland, the commune's production in the 1980s concentrated on the more lucrative decorative arts, turning out partitions, screens, big parasols, tissue boxes, wooden fruit, toilet seats, children's furniture, floral mirror frames, small watercolor paintings, and other useful products—rendered with the same carving and fine drawing found in their less commercialized art. Strife and jealousy put an end to the cooperative by the mid-'80s. Now the thirty-some artists of the village produce work independently.

The brothers Barat and Kobot on the road to Padangtegal are the elders of the Pengosekan Style, still painting religious subjects. Just south is Sena, another advocate of the style. Under the banyan tree is Sana, known for his temple scenes and depictions of Hindu deities. Mangku Liyer, whose studio is behind Oka's Homestay, paints dark and mysterious phantasmagoria. In Batuan's studio, located just east of the bridge near Peliatan, you can see a large selection of carved furniture and flowers, paintings, and decorative parasols. Older brother Mokoh's paintings reflect his naughty sense of humor. Putralaya paints meticulous submarine landscapes. Gatra, at the southern end of the village, paints unearthly, moody scenes of nymphs and demons.

Plaiting and Carving

This village is also known for its basketry, a thriving cottage industry. The beautifully pleated *lontar*-palm basketry of Pengosekan and neighboring Nyuhkuning combines harmonious colors with utility: baskets that fit inside one another or ones shaped like a mangosteen or an egg. Opposite Pondok Impian Bungalows is a shop specializing in baskets of all shapes, sizes, and patterns. Wayan Ludra, whose workshop is in Pengosekan, produces attractive picture frames, boxes, trunks, chairs, and medicine cabinets. This family of woodcarvers owns an art studio on Monkey Forest Road, tel. (0361) 975271.

Teges

Just south of Peliatan, Teges is divided into two communities. Teges Kanginan, east of the main road, is renowned for its musicians, dancers, *wayang kulit* puppeteers, and teachers of the *kecak, kebyar,* and *legong,* as well as an accomplished children's gong orchestra and a beautiful, sweet *gamelan* of the *semar pegulingan* type. The people of Teges Kawan, west of the main road, are mainly sculptors who specialize in unusual giant woodcarvings like a whole eggplant tree with leaves, fruits, flowers, and branches. Stop in at the workshop of **I Wayan Pasti,** just north of the *bale banjar* of Teges Kawan. An architect by trade, Wayan also sculpts amazing cremation sarcophagi *(patulangan)* in the shape of creatures like bulls and winged lions as well as life-size deer and horses.

Good masked-dance performances, as well as boring *legong* and *baris* shows, are put on every Tuesday night at the main intersection in Banjar Teges. For special Balinese native foods, especially pork dishes, head for the **Warung Teges** run by Desak Putu. Sit down on a hard wood bench and eat with the *petani.* The crackling *babi guling* as well as chicken, *tempe,* vegetable, and *lawar* dishes are still the best in the area.

Nyoman Sumertha Fine Arts Gallery, Banjar Teges, tel. (0361) 975267, fax 975655, displays every style of Balinese painting: stylized puppets, pastoral scenes, young artists. A special section showcases the distinctive individualism of modern Indonesian painters. Talented artists demonstrate their skills on the spacious grounds.

PELIATAN

Just one and a half kilometers southeast of Ubud, Peliatan spreads out along a very busy kilometer-long throughfare from Ubud to the bend in the road at Teges. The Peliatan *puri* actually predates Ubud's but because of a 17th century argument between two princes, as chronicled in the *Babad Dalem Sukawati,* two separate courts were created—Puri Saren in Ubud and Puri Kaleran in Peliatan. The Ubud aristocracy still pays respects to their higher-ranking royal cousins in Puri Kaleren.

The village of Peliatan and its neighboring hamlets are known among the Balinese for their internationally famous *legong* troupes and fine *semar pegulingan* orchestra. In 1931, under the leadership of Anak Agung Gede Mandera, a Peliatan ensemble was the first to leave Bali and perform abroad, creating an international sensation in Paris. The same troupe of dancers and musicians took New York, London, and Las Vegas by storm in 1952 in a lavish tour organized by the British entreprenuer John Coast. Since the 1950s, Peliatan's *gong kebyar* group has dominated Bali's musical scene. In Ubud there are so many dance groups now it's difficult for individual groups to succeed financially, but in Peliatan there's ample opportunity to see both live dances and frequent rehearsals. With no less than 15 *gamelan* orchestras, Peliatan is a popular place for Westerners to study the performing arts.

Except—and this is a big exception—for the amount of traffic speeding down its long main street, Peliatan hasn't experienced the phenomenal growth that has afflicted Ubud. The village thus makes a good base if you don't want to see too many tourists. Because its relative isolation is conducive to studying, Peliatan makes an ideal language lab for learning Bahasa Indonesia or Balinese. For walkers, Peliatan is close to such historical attractions as Gajah Mada and Pejeng. Take off in any direction and you'll find something of interest. The lesser-known places can only be reached by foot or bicycle.

Accommodations

With about 15 pleasant, low-budget homestays and hotels in and around Peliatan, this village serves as an alternative to Ubud, especially when places in Ubud are too expensive or full in the peak season. Several accommodations are located just off the very busy and noisy main street, Jl. Cok Gede Rai, which runs right through town, but most lie down paths and lanes running into the surrounding countryside. Many rooms and bungalows are occupied semipermanently by Westerners studying dance and *gamelan*.

The **Andong Inn** is on the road from Peliatan to Petulu. In all, 11 rooms face a beautiful garden. The five Rp15,000 rooms without hot showers are the best deal; others with hot showers and bathtubs go for Rp35,000 s, Rp40,000 d including breakfast. Genuine Balinese food is served in the cafe. Very relaxing except for the humming of a nearby telephone tower. Run by level-headed Nyoman Adnyani Siada, who practices hairdressing and traditional cosmetics in the beauty salon in front. Her husband, Dr. Siada, holds consultations in his office opposite the Ubud market from 1700 to 2000 including Sunday.

Manuaba Inn, Br. Tebasaya 8 (on the border of Ubud), has rooms for Rp12,000 d. More expensive is **Dok Putu Putera Homestay,** Br. Tebesaya 30, a very nice, small, quiet place with only four rooms for Rp25,000 (each can hold three people). Price includes an enormous breakfast of fruit salad, tea or coffee, and a daily special of pancakes, waffles, or black rice pudding.

The **Gunung Merta Bungalow** is in Andong in north Peliatan by the police station, tel. (0361) 975463, fax 975120, a collection of eight comfortable rooms (Rp34,000-60,000 s or d) fashioned in traditional Balinese red and gray stone and set in a lovely tropical garden. Each room features a writing table, bamboo chairs, paintings, separate bathroom with tub, hot/cold shower, sink, flush toilet, and private patio. Rates include Indonesian, continental, or American breakfast. Amenities include a pool, IDD, fax, postal, transport and tour services, packing and shipping, and bicycle rental. Mr. Lilem, the owner, epitomizes Balinese hospitality, and possesses a broad knowledge of Bali and its people. The hotel's small size allows personalized attention.

Ibu Arsa Homestay, tel. (0361) 295817, in a walled-in compound under the banyan tree on the main road, offers three classes of rooms: a bungalow facing the family temple for Rp25,000, two small bungalows for Rp10,000 each, and two standard rooms for Rp5000 each. Price includes breakfast of your choice. All rooms are spotless with attractive bamboo furniture and Balinese-style squat toilets and *mandi*. There's no private sitting area, but guests can linger in the courtyard on bamboo couches and chairs or in the restaurant out front. The well-educated matriarch Ibu Arsa speaks excellent English. She and her family pamper guests and share all the local attractions and events with them. **Madra Homestay,** Banjar Kalah, tel. (0361) 975749, is a quiet place in the rice fields in a beautiful garden, only 150 meters from the main road. Graded by size, location, and type of bathroom, three classes of bamboo and thatch-roofed *pondok* are available: Rp10,000 and Rp15,000 for older rooms (popular with long-term residents), and Rp20,000 s, Rp25,000 d for rooms with shower, good breakfast included. All prices subject to 10% tax. An ideal location for study, relaxation, peace, and quiet, Madra's is strongly recommended for both the budget traveler and the student of Balinese culture. The staff works hard to keep the place tidy and the atmosphere friendly. There's no restaurant, but you can arrange to have meals prepared. Excellent security, storage service, parking. Make reservations at least one month in advance for June, July, and August by sending a fax care of Ary's Wisata Travel Service in Ubud, fax (0361) 975162.

Central Mandala Bungalows, tel. (0361) 975028, in the middle of town, is actually the site of the Puri Kaleran palace of the former raja of Peliatan. Clean rooms with fan, cupboards, big inside bathrooms, showers, and hot water for Rp25,000 s, Rp30,000 d. The grounds of the *puri* are large—a very private, enclosed environment. Mandala's has been taking in guests since 1962, when Helen and Frank Schreider wrote of their stay here in *The Drums of Tonkin*.

Students are always living in the compound. Ask to see the photo album. The Mandera Cafe (reasonable prices) is only open in the high season. **Puri Tirta Accommocations** (Rp35,000 s, Rp45,000 d for a/c bungalows) sits in the rice fields two km north of Peliatan and only 500 meters from Petulu's heronry. **Nyoman Astana's Bungalows,** Dusun Kalah, is a quiet, inexpensive place with nice garden, Balinese-style architecture, rooms with showers, and free transport for dinner in Ubud area. **Negara Accommodation,** a short walk down a *gang* off Jl. Cok Gede Rai, is one of the cheapest places to stay: Rp8000 s, Rp10,000 d with Indo-style *mandi* (untidy) for six basic rooms in family home. Price includes Balinese cakes, coffee, and tea in the morning. Good value, friendly, but not the tops on the comfort scale.

Away from the bustle of Ubud is relaxing **Pande Homestay,** on the main street, which charges Rp8000 s, Rp10,000 d, Rp15,000 s or d. The best rooms are the *gedong*-style house (for ceremonies, sleeping, weddings, cooking) in front, and the two rooms with bamboo walls in the back (also Rp12,000 s or d). The bathrooms are nice (you don't miss hot water). Outstanding breakfast includes fresh fruit salad, buttered toast with fried egg, black rice pudding with coconut milk, and tea or coffee. Pande, a former art student who started his homestay in 1985, is a kind and very informative man. Peliatan's all-woman gamelan *(gong wanita)* performs on the **Tirtasari Dance Stage** only 100 meters away.

The newly remodeled **Puri Agung Homestay** offers Balinese-style bungalows in five different classes, ranging from Rp6000-8000 s to Rp12,000-15,000 d. The more expensive feature living rooms, wardrobes, and small libraries. Bright, clean, spacious, peaceful. Cockatoos and parrots cackle in the attractive courtyard with its variety of trees and flowering plants. Since this has been the home of the old ruling clan of Peliatan for 12 generations, 16 different families live in 16 individual *kampung* within this large complex. Anom, the hostess, will regale you with tales of her dance troupe's tour of the world in the 1950s.

Travelers have written glowingly of **Siti Homestay,** Banjar Kalah, tel. (0361) 975599, which has six comfortable double rooms with attached *mandi* for only Rp8000 s, Rp10,000 d (larger

rooms), and one deluxe room for Rp15,000. Price includes a big, delicious breakfast. The proprietors, Wayan and Siti, are both school-teachers, and Wayan is articulate, well-informed, and speaks excellent English. Absolutely the top of the list for family homestays. Authentic Balinese atmosphere, quiet, pretty garden. The grounds are beautiful. Small bistro and cafe serving praiseworthy food. It's easy to get *bemo* on Jl. Peliatan one minute away, and Wayan can advise you about entertainment, best places to eat, celebrations, local transport, and good walks.

Food

Ageless **Ibu Arsa Restaurant,** tel. (0361) 975817, under the banyan tree on the main road, was Peliatan's first restaurant, offering excellent and inexpensive Balinese food since 1968. Noteworthy are *sayur bayam* (stewed spinach) for Rp1000, *gado-gado* for Rp1000, and *mie kuah* for Rp1500, plus European food including oatmeal, omelettes, and ham steak with pineapple. Desserts include lemon pancake (Rp800) and black rice pudding with fruit (Rp1500). Ibu Arsa also serves special orders if you ask a day in advance: stewed chicken in sauce, smoked duck or fried chicken for Rp20,000. *Bubur* and *lawar* stalls located nearby.

Near Ibu Arsa's is **Eka Wati,** which specializes in Chinese food. An excellent *gado-gado* is served at **Warung Jero Wati** south of Ibu Arsa's. **Warung Sate Madura** is just up the street from Siti Homestay in Banjar Kalah. Other fine restaurants are found along Jl. Padangtegal, the road north to Ubud.

Pande Homestay on Jl. Cok Gede Rai presents a smoked duck dinner for two served with rice and vegetables for only Rp18,000; order a day in advance. Next door is a very cheap *warung* serving *nasi goreng, sayur, ijo, ikan goreng, cap cai,* and *funghung hai.* You'll also find a bunch of excellent *warung* (try the Balinese-style *nasi campur*) near the T-junction east of Ubud where the road north leads to Petulu and the road south heads for Peliatan.

Mudita Inn, popular with travelers, cooks up huge *gado-gado,* freshly made from scratch for only Rp1500. Cheese omelettes with tomato are Rp1400, large cold Bintangs cost Rp3000, soft drinks Rp700. Mudita also offers soups, Balinese food, or lunch and dinner with two hours' notice. Open 0900-2200. Mudita is a guide and speaks good English. The kitchen staff of **Sita Homestay** in Banjar Kalah, tel. (0361) 975599, makes superb homemade yogurt that took two years to perfect. Their smoked duck dinner, prepared by the grandfather (who is nearing 100), is the absolute nectar of the gods.

Performances

The big draw is the only all-woman *gamelan* on Bali, the famous *gamelan pegulingan* Mekar Sari, which performs at the Tirtasari Dance Stage under Mrs. Anak Agung Raka Mas. Members range from little girls and teens to regal-looking white-haired matrons. The music accompanies a children's *legong* group performing fairy tales. Very professional, very good lighting, brilliant costuming. In addition, there's a stylized staff fighting dance *(baris tombok)* performed by four boys. This unique, spirited presentation takes place on Sunday night 1930-2100.

Legong and *kecak* tickets for performances in the Peliatan/Ubud area can be conveniently purchased at the centrally located Mudita Inn on the main street (Jl. Cok Gede Rai), tel. (0361) 975179. A sample of area performances: the tiny *legong* dancers, as well as the Mahabharata, every Tuesday 1930-2100 at Teges Kanginan; the *legong* with *barong* every Wednesday (same time) one km south of Pande Homestay at Banjar Teruna; and the *kecak* at Puri Kaleran in Mandala Bungalows at 1930-2030 every Thursday (over 200 performers, but it lasts but an hour). The **Kokokan Club** on Jl. Pengosekan, tel. (0361) 975742, in the nearby hamlet of Pengosekan presents a traditional Balinese buffet with live entertainment like *joged gudegan*, *barong buntut*, the frog dance, or even Western-style experimental theater, such as the black comedy *Shamlet* (a takeoff on *Hamlet*) by the Frequent Flyers. Dinner and show Rp35,000, show only Rp10,000; every Thursday at 2000.

Dance Instruction

Peliatan is one of the few places on Bali where dancers are still trained in the traditional manner. The instructor glides through the dance movements, mimicked by a brace of little girls, all synchronized perfectly to the beat of the *kenong*. Some instructors invite European pupils to join in.

Watch young Balinese students practice *gamelan* and dancing each day at around 1400 in the village *puri,* Puri Kaleran, otherwise known as Mandala Bungalows, tel. (0361) 975028, on Jl. Cok Gede Rai, the palace of the former raja. Anak Agung Raka, a daughter of Anak Agung Mandera, runs a dance school next to Puri Agung Homestay. She has many Japanese students and starts a new class every six months or so. The dance master Sang Ayu Ketut Muklin teaches dance to young trainees at Teges Kanginan.

Shopping

With art galleries lining its main street and the din of workshops in its back alleys, Peliatan is a major center for carving and painting. Some Peliatan specialties are the carved wooden fruit, flowers, ducks, fish, frogs, tiny birds in frames, and mobiles produced by young carvers. Carved horses, deer, and tigers are produced in Teges, a village to the south of Peliatan. Gifted carvers worth visiting are Nyoman Togog and I Wayan Pasti. The neighboring villages of Mas and Nyuhkuning have been centers for woodcarving since the 1930s.

Djujul, whose studio is down the street from the Dok Putu Putera Homestay, is a well-known painter who works only when he's inspired. Djujul usually has a work in progress so you're able to see a real master paint. It's cheaper to buy directly from him than from a gallery—expect about 25% off the gallery price of Rp2.1 million for a small painting. **Dewa Windia Handicraft** showroom and workshop in Peliatan (west of the banyan tree) sells napkin holders, mirror frames, miniature ducks, giant Garuda statues, and tropical fruit sculptures. A selection of attractive *sarung* sell for Rp10,000-12,000 at the bistro in Siti Homestay in Banjar Kalah, tel. (0361) 975599; also look for dresses and drawstring pants hand-tailored by Siti. Well-stocked groceries, dry goods, and appliance stores lie on the Teges end of town.

Banjar Kalah

This small hamlet is noted for its woodworking shops producing giant flowers, banana trees, small creatures, and fruits—an ideal place for those interested in wood handicrafts. Several *warung* and small restaurants here are popular with budget travelers. Drop in on toymaker I

Made Greriya, tel. (0361) 975241, who turns out educational toys, wooden animals, clever mobiles, puzzles, trees, flowers, and ducks. On the road west toward Pengosekan, which turns at the bend in the road to the east, is the workshop of Dewa Nyoman Batuan, who produces decorative boxes, handcarved mirror frames, and small cabinets.

Ketut Madra, in Madra Homestay, Banjar Kalah, tel. (0361) 975749, is a fine traditional-style painter of mythological themes. His style reflects classic Kamasan *wayang* models, but he has a unique sense of line and color that adds a very personal stamp to his work. Because of his popularity, his paintings must be ordered months in advance. Pak Madra is an active and competent *topeng* dancer, while his brother Pak Madri from nearby Pengosekan is a skilled *gamelan* musician. They have personally introduced many Westerners to the musical and dramatic arts, or guided them toward other appropriate teachers. Madra's homestay has long held a well-earned reputation for hosting groups of students of dance, music, painting, sculpture, *wayang,* and other traditional Balinese art forms.

Art Galleries
The painter, poet, writer, director, actor, musician, dancer, and choreographer Madi Kertonegoro, born in Ambarawa on Java, is a child of the Indonesian New Art Movement (Gerakan Seni Rupa Baru) and is reputed to be Indonesia's only antinuclear artist. His **Future Peace Art Gallery** is at Jl. Andong 1, tel. (0361) 975467, only 450 meters north of the T-junction at the northern end of Peliatan. You can't miss it; there's a big sign. Works on permanent display include landscapes, still lifes, portraiture, and experimental art. Examine some of the books Madi has written in the **Pustaka Bayu** bookshop next to his studio; also check out the 1991 video about him and the cassette tape of his band Wild Roots.

The **Agung Rai Gallery** lies beyond Peliatan but before Negara, one km south of Pande Homestay. One of the finest galleries on Bali, a mammoth art complex of thatch-roofed, traditional-style *bale,* each building houses a different school of Balinese art. Schoolboys, some only six years of age, are regularly invited to the gallery to practice line drawing and to make copies of paintings under the guidance of a senior artist. Works from this well-known gallery have been exhibited in Singapore, Holland, Germany, and Guam. Agung Rai established the gallery in 1978; he got his start in the art business by peddling his paintings to tourists on the hot sands of Kuta Beach in the early 1970s. At least as much an educational experience as Ubud's Puri Lukisan, these co-op showrooms give you a clear view of the scope and development of modern Balinese painting. See the marble-floored room filled with works costing up to Rp31.5 million. In the private collection in back are the haunting works of noted prewar Dutch, German, and Austrian artists who lived and worked on Bali, exerting a major influence on local painting styles. Agung's has the only Walter Spies painting on Bali, depicting Calonarang, plus an extraordinary Covarrubias showing Balinese dancers putting on makeup.

The **Agung Rai Museum of Art,** in back of Agung Rai's Kokokan Club in Pengosekan (see below), is one of the most dynamic cultural centers in southern Bali. Encompassing a hotel, performing stage, galleries, a fine restaurant/cafe/nightclub, conference center, and a well-stocked bookshop, it is now in the process of setting up a reference library and reading room. Address: ARMA, Ubud 80571, tel. (0361) 975742 or 976659, fax 974229, e-mail armaubud@denpasar.wasantara.net.id.

Services
Change money at Bakti Art Shop, Diana Express, Mudita Inn, Bank Duta, Bank Utama, and Bank BRI. **Wayan Sidhakarya** (Puri Saren Kangin 31, Peliatan) is a professional Bahasa Indonesia language instructor who works for the Experiment in International Living. He can be contacted through the Mudita Inn, tel. (0361) 975179. **I Wayan Paksa** of Siti Homestay, tel. (0361) 975599, in Banjar Kalah, is also an effective teacher of Indonesian, insisting upon good grammar and correct usage.

Rent bicycles from **Mudita Inn** on Jl. Cok Gede Rai, for an average daily rate of Rp2000 for one-gear bikes and Rp3000 for mountain bikes; 10% discount if you rent by the week. Bikes are also available (Rp3500 per day) from the Andong Inn.

Getting Away

A *bemo* to Ubud center, Petulu, or Mas costs Rp300, to Denpasar Rp700 (baggage extra). If traveling farther afield, catch a *bemo* (Rp300) down to the Sakah intersection on the main road between Denpasar and Amlapura. From Sakah, you can travel to most of the attractions to the north, west, and east. For Gunung Batur, go straight up via Pujung if you have your own vehicle. You can make it in a *bemo,* but since they're so rare it's faster to first get a *bemo* to the Sakah turnoff, then another *bemo* to Tampaksiring, then head on to Batur. Get an early start; head back from Penelokan no later than 1700. For Besakih, take a *bemo* to Sakah, then another one to Klungkung. Leave by 0800 so you can see Klungkung's Kerta Gosa en route.

North of Peliatan, an asphalt road with nice scenery leads into the mountains to the quiet, rural woodcarving villages of Jati, Pujung, and Sebatu. The famous woodcarver I Nyoman Tjokot came from the village of Jati, 15 km north of Ubud. His sons, Ketut Nongos Cokot and Made Dini, have carried on the family tradition, carving huge statues of Garuda and other mythological figures. Nongos's shop is in Teges at the crossroads of the roads east to Bedulu and west to Peliatan; Dini's shop is just west of the bridge before Goa Gajah, if coming from Teges.

Tegenungan

Relax and enjoy Balinese village surroundings twenty minutes south of Ubud by taxi. If traveling in your own vehicle, it's about six km south of Peliatan or 2.5 km south of the gas station, then turn right. Walk 300 meters from the main road through rice paddies and invigorate yourself at the **Waterfall Restaurant,** which affords outrageous 360-degree views or lush tropical paradise. Stand under the waterfall and receive the ultimate cold, clean water massage.

PETULU

A scenic area and bird sanctuary about an hour's walk up a gradual uphill road running north of Peliatan. Another approach is via the road by Coconut's in Ubud. As you approach Petulu, it feels like old Bali—the people aren't burned out on tourists yet. The population is 4,500, mostly farmers, and 15,000 herons.

Famous dancers, instructors, musicians, and wood- and stonecarvers live here, including dance master I Ketut Tutor, who teaches *baris;* I Ketut Tutur, a renowned *topeng* performer and teacher of dance; and I Wayan Gandra, a *gamelan* musician of international acclaim. On the road, especially near where the road to Petulu turns west off the main highway to Tampaksiring, are a number of shops selling woodcarvings in huge display rooms. The woodcarving village of Pujung lies 11 km north of Petulu.

From the roundabout in north Peliatan just before the entrance to Ubud, flag down a *bemo* (Rp300) heading toward Tampaksiring and get off at the start of the road west up to Petulu village, then walk 2.25 km to the heron-viewing site Petulu Gunung. In the northern part of the village are souvenir shops, a traditional bathing place, and a carved temple with water pouring from the mouths of stone animals.

The Heronry

Start this pleasant afternoon excursion so you arrive no later than 1700 to see the great flocks of thousands of large white herons (known collectively as *kokokan*) wheeling, drifting, sailing, landing in a number of tall palms and *bunut* trees to roost for the night. The next morning they fly north to the cool climes of Gunung Batur, where they feed for the day. It's an impressive sight, seeing flocks of herons shift trees. Considered sacred, plumed egrets, cattle egrets, and Javan pond herons may not be disturbed while they roost. Only if they fall to earth or become caught in a tree may they be captured and turned into a delectable sort of pâté wrapped in plantain leaf.

The birds began roosting here for the first time in 1966, just one month after an elaborate sacrificial ceremony petitioning for protection and blessings after the political butchering of thousands of "communists." Many Balinese believe the herons embody the souls of the dead come to reunify the people of Petulu. Twice a year on Saniscara Kliwon Landep the people of Petulu hold a special ceremony for these birds.

Accommodations and Food

The **Mudita Inn** has four rooms with showers and flush toilets for Rp25,000 d (a bargain during

PETULU

PURA
DESA

PURA
PUSEH SPRING
WATER

HERON
SANCTUARY

I NYOMAN KELINCED
(WOOD- AND STONECARVER)

I WAYAN REREH (TRADITIONAL PAINTER)

SINTRU (HANDCARVED PICTURE FRAMES)

I KETUT TUTUR (DANCE TEACHER)

I NYOMAN ADA
(HANDCARVED PICTURE FRAMES)

PURA
AGUNG

I MADE DANA
(TRADITIONAL PAINTER)

PETANU RIVER

PURA
TIYANG
SAKTI

PURA
PEMAKSAN

I WAYAN TUTUR
(TRADITIONAL PAINTER)

JENAYA BUDAYA
(T-SHIRT MAKERS)

NI LUH KAMIS
(WOODCARVER)

TO
PUJUNG

PURA
DALEM

RICE MILL

BEMO STOP

I WAYAN GANDRA
(GAMELAN MUSICIAN)

PAK WUK (TRADITIONAL
UMBRELLA MAKER)

BANYAN
TREE HOTEL

TO PELIATAN AND UBUD

NOT TO SCALE

© MOON PUBLICATIONS, INC.

the slow season). The **Puri Asri,** Box 37, Ubud 80571, fax (0361) 975120, a peaceful village house, lies just at the start of the smaller road up to Petulu from the main Peliatan-Tampaksiring road. Room rate is Rp40,000 d for any of five bungalows, hot water and breakfast included. Free jeep transport into Ubud for dinner. Quiet in spite of the location between two highways. Other places to stay along the Peliatan-Tampaksiring road are **Merpati Inn, Petulu Village Inn, Puri Thirta Accommodations,** and the **Loka Sari Guesthouse and Restaurant.**

Looking for the perfect environment for relaxation and rejuvenation? Five-star **Banyan Tree Kamandalu** (tel. 0361-975825, fax 975851) rents only 14 spacious traditional-style bungalows, Rp403,000 s or d, with private walled gardens, rich marble floors, two-meter-long baths, outdoor showers, fully stocked minibar, stereo, IDD phones, indigenous local textiles, ethnic artifacts, and a combination of classical Chinese and Indonesian motifs. There are also two luxu-

riously appointed suite villas, 75 square meters, Rp518,000. Brilliant location on a curving ridge overlooking deep Petanu River Valley to the east, terraced rice fields to the west, and the sea at Saba Bay. Villas have the best views. Completely self-contained; the hotel has its own water filtering system and generator. Very elegant, surface-tension, amoeba-shaped pool with swim-up bar (open 1000-2300). Service is dreamy, slow-paced. Treat yourself to an in-room massage, herbal facial, or a drink in the Cempaka Lounge. Food in the **Angsoka Restaurant,** open daily 0600-2300 is five-star quality and expensive, Rp35,000 breakfast, Rp58,000 dinner. Another highlight is their ground-level modern art gallery, which features paintings and sculptures of prominent Balinese and Indonesian artists—light years away from the mass art you encounter in Ubud. Laced with nature paths and viewing promontories, you can take paths all the way down to the river. Take free daily shuttles four km into Ubud center.

THE PEJENG AREA

With over 40 old temples in the region between the rivers Pakrisan and Petanu, the Pejeng area contains Bali's richest collection of antiquities—from the earliest known kettledrum and clay stupa to relatively modern Shivaite sculptures and rock-cut Buddhist sanctuaries and bathing places. Most antiquities are in the form of worn statues kept in important area temples. Because Balinese Prince Udayana married a Javanese princess, East Javanese cultural influences started to appear in Bali in the beginning of the 11th century and the language used in inscriptions changed from Old Balinese to Old Javanese.

The town of Pejeng, 48 km northeast of Denpasar, is named after an illustrious kingdom concentrated in the Bedulu-Pejeng area from the 9th century to the 14th century, when it fell to Majapahit invaders. Today it has a powerless but high-status *puri* (Pemahyun) and is full of Brahmans. Most visitors drive from Denpasar right through Bedulu and Pejeng on their way to Tampaksiring and Penelokan, sometimes stopping en route at the Gedong Arca archaeological offices in Bedulu. No accommodations or restaurants in Pejeng, but some good markets. From

Pejeng, take the wonderful walk to Manggis—lots of small villages, emerald green rice fields, and dense green forests.

The Moon of Pejeng

If heading north, Pura Panataran Sasih (*sasih* means "drum") is on the right side of the road after Gedong Arca, recognizable by its stone sculptures of wild boars and *naga*. The chief shrine of the 10th century Pejeng kingdom, this *pura* is linked to the Bali Aga mountain sanctuary of Penulisan north of Kintamani. Heading north from Bedulu, the temple is on the main road on your right just as you enter Pejeng.

Hanging in a high pavilion to the left, surrounded by a wooden fence, is a superb example of Bronze Age art, the sacred monumental bronze gong known as the Moon of Pejeng.

Considered a masterpiece of bronze-casting, this 186.5-cm-tall hourglass-shaped gong is thought to be the largest in the world cast in a single piece and the oldest surviving archaeological artifact on Bali.

Legend has it in the beginning of time, one of the Earth's 13 moons fell from heaven and landed in a tree. It was so bright it stopped the shameful work of a thief, who became so angry he climbed the tree and urinated on the heavenly object. With a loud boom the moon exploded, killing the thief and falling to earth as a gong. The fall caused it to crack and the urine colored it green. To this day no one dares touch the gong and daily offerings are made to it.

Other legends hold the gong is the wheel of the chariot of the moon or the earplug of the mythical giant Kebo Iwo or moon-goddess

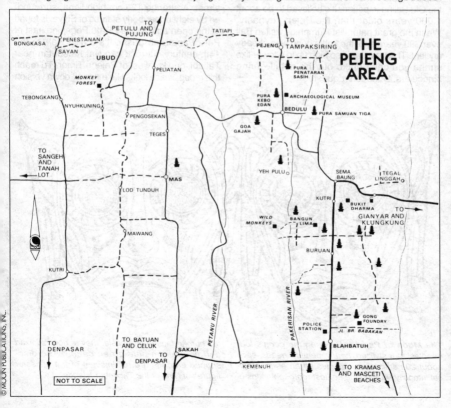

THE PEJENG AREA

NOT TO SCALE

© MOON PUBLICATIONS, INC.

Ratih. A highly revered object, the richly ornamented gong is believed by most Balinese to possess magic power. Its sounding surface measures 160 cm in diameter. The piece is thought to date from around 300 B.C., the beginning of the Indonesian Bronze Age. No one knows whether the gong originated in Bali or northern Vietnam. The gong could have been carried to insular Southeast Asia by royal personages fleeing the Chinese. Some scholars speculate it precedes the Mings, and may have been a gift from Kublai Khan to a raja of Bali. To support the theory that it originated in Bali, scholars point to the fact that ancient stone molds used in casting bronze have been found on the island.

The Pejeng gong has been on continuous display in the Pura Panataran Sasih ever since the Old Balinese period. It's believed to be about 1,000 years older than the Pejeng dynasty. When the great naturalist Rumphius visited Bali over 300 years ago, the kettle gong was already ancient. The treasure is so high up in a tower-like shrine you can't make out the detail—bring binoculars. Donation requested.

Museum Purbakala, 500 meters south of Pura Penataran Sasih (open Mon.-Thurs. 0700-1400, Friday 0700-1100, and Saturday 0700-1230; donation), is disappointing. Kept here are ancient commemorative statues of former kings and a well-weathered statue of Ganesha recovered from the Pakrisan River valley. Open pavilions in the complex contain an odd assortment of 10th- to 12th-century sculptures: commemorative statues of old rulers and a group of standing gods joined in prayer. The most interesting objects are the 10 or so massive sarcophagi in the back, dating from as far back as 300 B.C.

Getting Away
There are many archaeological odds and ends in this "Valley of the Kings" in the middle of Bali's rice belt; follow the directory on Pejeng's main street. A strange 120-cm-high linga, surrounded by eight upper-body statues of Shiva, is found in the open *bale* of Pura Ratu Pegening east of Pura Panataran Sasih. It's a nice walk to the 14th-century cut-rock *candi* at Kalebutan near Tatiapi, one km west of Pejeng Timor. To reach this group, which looks like a scaled down version

LOUISE FOOTE

The Moon of Pejang: *Between the gong's four handles, four stylized, nearly identical heads, each about 20 centimeters tall, give off an eerie, magical intensity. Among the earliest representations of* the human face in Indonesia, they're now oxidized and covered in blue-green patina. The disc-shaped earrings are reminiscent of the ancestor figures of Nias or the Tanimbar Islands.

of Gunung Kawi, start on the path from the second crossroads after the *puri* leading to Pejeng's graveyard. A landslide uncovered this *candi* in 1928; vegetation covered it again after the war and yet again in the 1950s. The 3.5-meter-high temple has been carved in relief from a two-meter-wide niche cut into solid rock. In 1951 a cloister with cut-rock niches and a courtyard were discovered on the other side of the ravine.

IMPORTANT TEMPLES OF THE PEJENG AREA

Pura Kebo Edan

South of Pejeng is Pura Kebo Edan ("Mad Buffalo Temple"). As you head north from Bedulu, you first pass the archaeological museum on the right; a bit farther on your left is Pura Kebo Edan. Small but historically significant, this temple features a huge statue under a wooden shelter. The figure goes by the local name of Bima. There is considerable conjecture about whether this horned and fanged giant, which probably dates from the 13th or 14th century, represents a demon or a god. Urs Ramseyer, in *The Art and Culture of Bali,* claims Pura Kebo Edan is probably a Balinese version of the East Javanese Singosari magic temples built on Java during the 12th century.

The 3.6-meter-high male dancing figure towers over the courtyard. Snakes curl around his ankles and wrists and he's endowed with a magnificent penis. On his head is an ornate mask and headdress. He stands on the bodies of a copulating couple. Legend says Bima wanted to have sex with the woman but his penis was too large for her. When he found her with a mortal, he crushed the man beneath his feet. The giant is flanked by a pair of lesser *raksasa* in threatening postures and decorated with skulls. In front are two reclining buffalo, one male and one female. The statue was restored in 1952.

Pura Puser Ing Jagat

A large, very old temple dating from 1329 with unique reliefs, thought to be the center of the old Pejeng kingdom. A major pilgrimage site, during the full moon this *pura* draws couples desiring children and people hoping to increase their healing powers. The temple is part of a legend about Bali's last indigenous king, Bedaulu, and his escape from the Majapahit army in 1343 through an underground tunnel to the bandit isle of Nusa Penida. In the *pura* is a stone that no one may ever move—it's believed to be the secret entrance to the tunnel.

See the four dancing mustachioed demons in Gedong Puser Tasik on the temple's east side—sneering expressions, bulging eyes, swinging penises, clubs in their right hands, conch shells in their left. This type of statuary, with figures on all four sides, is called *catuhkaya.*

Housed in a shrine behind the temple is the Pejeng Vessel, or Mandala Giri, a cylindrical stone vase entwined with serpents and portraying the churning of the sea of milk. The carvings on the bowl relate the story of nine gods, each corresponding to a different quarter of the compass. A chronogram dates the vessel from 1329.

South of Pura Puser Ing Jagat, **Pura Arjuna Metapa** ("Temple Where Arjuna Meditated"), comprises a small group of portrait statues of Arjuna and his ever-present, jocular companions/servants, Merdah and Twalen, heavenly nymphs who were sent by the gods to tempt him, as well as a large *kala*-head. The statues must have adorned temples and bathing places in the area.

Pura Pengukar Ukaran and Goa Garba

This walk to the Pakrisan River Valley, near the village of Sawangunung, is a total immersion into rural Bali in an area untrafficked by tourists. Start your walk by turning east at the intersection by the *pasar* just north of Pura Panataran Sasih. The small road bears to the right, then to the left. Walk for one km to the T-junction, turn left, then walk past the school to Pura Pengukur Ukuran. Below is Goa Garba.

Pura Pungukur Ukuran means "The Temple Where All Things Are Measured." Built by King Jayaprangus on the edge of a ravine at the end of the 12th century, the temple's inner courtyard contains numerous *bale,* pre-Hindu megaliths, carved stones, and an ornate shrine with linga. Out a side gateway take the flight of huge stone steps descending to Goa Garba ("The Womb") on the western bank of the Pakrisan River. A gouge on a boulder step is said to be the footprint of the giant Kebo Iwa himself.

In this small valley is a carved stone gateway, ancient disused bathing places (the king's on the left, the queen's on the right), and three meditation niches hewn out of the rock face, with slanting roofs and carvings decorating the wall above. Inscriptions in Kediri script above the hermitage cells are still legible; inside are a few pieces of ancient sculpture and pedestals.

BEDULU

A farming village south of Pejeng, Bedulu sits at the start of the road to Yeh Puluh, approximately 26 km north of Denpasar. If coming from Ubud, change *bemo* at Teges, en route passing Goa Gajah on the right. Bedulu was once the seat of the Old Balinese kingdom of Pejeng and the last indigenous dynasty to hold out against the mighty Majapahit Empire, which invaded Bali in 1343. After the invasion the Hinduization of Bali accelerated, culminating in the massive cultural migration to Bali of the Majapahit court in 1515.

Legend has it Bedulu's pre-Majapahit ruler, Sri Aji Asura Bumibanten, possessed supernatural strength and powers. At his command, he would have his head cut off and put back on again without any injury or pain. He got such a thrill out of this he had his servants decapitate him often. One day, however, during this neat parlor game the gods made his head to roll into a river, where it was carried away. His servants panicked and in desperation chopped the head off a wild boar that happened by and placed it on the neck stump of their master. Understandably, this caused the ruler some embarrassment, so he hid in a high tower out of sight of his subjects, forbidding anyone to look at him. A child discovered the secret and the bestial king became known as Dalem Bedulu, which means "He Who Changes Heads." A less theatrical explanation is that Bedulu comes from *bedaulu* which simply means "upstream."

Pura Samuan Tiga
Down a stony path about 100 meters east of the Bedulu crossroads is Pura Samuan Tiga ("Temple of the Meeting of Three Parties"), probably built by the great sage Mpu Kuturan. During the reign of King Udayana and Queen Dharmapatni (988-1011), religious sects were rife on

Bali, each with its own tenets and peculiar practices. Because this situation brought about instability and confusion, six holy men met at this temple to promote the Principle of the Hindu Trinity, unite all the sects, and establish basic island-wide customary law *(desa adat)*.

Museum Purbakala
A government archaeological museum two km north of Bedulu on the road to Gunung Kawi (ask for Musium Arkeologi). One of only five museums on Bali, it contains an embarrassingly scant and unlabeled collection of pre-Hindu artifacts: megaliths, bone ornaments, pottery, earthenware, stone axe heads, adzes, weapons, copper plate inscriptions from A.D. 885 and 903, untensils, bronze jewelry, Chinese ceramics, and Hindu statues and relics. Note the impressively decorated egg-shaped sarcophagus, hewn from a single block of stone, with a turtle and human features carved in high relief on its cover. These coffins, which contained bodies in the fetal position were used long before cremation was practiced on Bali. Small library. Open Mon.-Thurs. 0700-1400, Friday until 1300, Saturday until 1230, closed Sunday. Donation requested.

YEH PULU

A rarely visited carved cliff face about one km from Goa Gajah. Water is all-important to the Balinese culture and economy, and *yeh,* the Balinese word for "water" or "spring," occurs frequently in Balinese place-names. *Pulu* is the Balinese name for a stone water container.

To get there, start from the Bedulu crossroads. The road west to Ubud takes you by Goa Gajah, the road east leads to Pura Samuan Tiga, and the road south is the main road to Gianyar. On this road (Jl. Yeh Pulu) you'll see a sign after one km. Take a right, then a left, then a right again. This small road leads almost all the way to Yeh Pulu. Park in front of the small open *bale*. It's a nice cool 300-meter walk to the site, on a well-built walkway by an irrigation channel and bathing place. Village boys will volunteer to accompany you, although you don't need a guide. Pay an entrance of Rp1100, Rp500 for children. The old woman caretaker (pemangku) cleans and maintains the reliefs and a statue of Ganesha. For a donation, she'll tell you who's depicted on the reliefs, show you some worn-out carvings on the relief's northern side, and dispense holy water from a clear spring feeding a sacred pool filled with fish. Very calm surroundings, except when 20 tourists arrive by bus.

Lying between the Petanu and Pakrisan Rivers, the ruins of this unique late 14th-century high rock relief on a two-meter-high tuff wall lay buried for centuries under volcanic eruptions and vegetation, but its figures remained intact. Perhaps the most important and mysterious sculpture of the Middle Balinese Period, a 25-meter-long, life-sized frieze on the wall deviates radically from other carvings on Java or Bali. The carvings are enigmatic and naturalistically done, depicting not religious scenes but short vignettes from everyday village life. Stylized decorative leaves frame the work, and the chiseling is crude, earthy, almost homely, but with a primitive vigor and realism. When the site was excavated in 1925, water seepage from the rice fields above the rock wall damaged the figures. Measures have since been taken to prevent further decay.

Bernet Kempers pointed out in his book Monumental Bali (1977) that the relief represents stories from the life of Lord Krishna, one of Vishnu's incarnations. A hunting scene, for example, corresponds to the Hindu legend of Krishna defeating the bear Jambavat. The only deity directly represented is two-armed Ganesha, the elephant-headed son of Shiva, carved into his own niche to the far right.

Accommodations and Food

There's a whole little scene here, a cluster of drink and snack warung at the top of the pathway, an art gallery, and **Made's Cafe** looking out over rice fields. **Accommodations Ketut Lantur** asks Rp10,000 per person for an old set of rooms with Indonesian-style mandi, or Rp15,000 per person for a newer set of rooms facing the street. A quiet, laid-back place to stay, and the Lantur's prepare meals. (A nasi bubur stand, just up from Lantur's, opens up in the afternoon.) Buy delightful earthenware pottery made by traditional methods in his terracotta workshop.

Getting Away

Walk up to the main road to catch bemo to Ubud. Ketut, who lives 50 meters behind the warung, or any boy from the nearby kampung, will give you a fascinating tour of the surrounding countryside, including a rice temple (pura sawah) he claims is the only one of its kind on Bali. There's good swimming in a big river, a waterfall, beautiful rice terraces, and a nice place to view the sunset. Have him take you to the small bathing place 200 meters north of Yeh Pulu, with stylistic reliefs cut into the rock behind the two basins. These sites are not easy to find without a guide. Depending on the length of the tour, his age, and his performance, pay your guide Rp5000-10,000.

GOA GAJAH ("ELEPHANT CAVE")

This mysterious complex, two km east of the statue of the dancer in the Teges intersection, is probably the oldest excavated relic of ancient Balinese art. Epigraphs found at this site date Goa Gajah ("Elephant Cave") with certainty back to the 11th century, about the time of King Airlangga's reign in East Java. Until 1923 the site was known only to local people, and only in 1954 was an elaborate and extensive bathing place discovered nearby. Today it's a major tourist site.

The easily accessible man-made cave lies below the road between Peliatan and Bedulu, on the side of a steep ravine. It can be a restful place, especially when there aren't mobs of tour buses disgorging passengers onto the mammoth parking lot. It's best to visit Goa Gajah either in early morning or late afternoon to avoid the tour buses arriving from the southern resorts. Soft rindik music and lyrical flute melodies waft from two expensive tourist restaurants, **Puri Suling,** above the cave with a lovely location overlooking rice terraces, and **Sari Gading,** at the other end of the parking lot.

To get there, take a bemo from Ubud to Teges (Rp500, four km), then continue by bemo or walk two km in the direction of Bedulu. The road from Teges passes over the Petanu River just before reaching the cave. Once over this bridge you've entered the old kingdom of Pejeng, a long tongue of land between the Petanu and Pakrisan Rivers

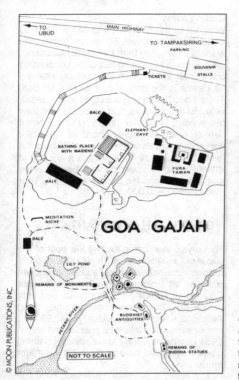

GOA GAJAH

NOT TO SCALE

© MOON PUBLICATIONS, INC.

strewn with Bali's most famous and treasured monuments and relics. If coming from the other direction, it's two kilometers from Bedulu.

You know you've arrived when you see the rows of tacky curio stands selling *batik,* leather goods, garments, carvings, baskets, and the usual tourist crap, plus fruit, snacks, and drinks. Parking fee Rp500. Entrance fee is Rp1100, Rp500 children, plus Rp500 for sash/*sarung* rental if your legs are uncovered. Open every day during daylight hours. A long flight of steps leads down to the site. It's possible to go on foot to Yeh Pulu from Goa Gajah, but the way along *sawah* dikes is a little tricky. Ask a local boy to guide you.

History

Goa Gajah is a curious name. Elephants have never inhabited Bali, and the many elephant motifs seen in Balinese art likely have artistic origins in India or Java. The old Javanese *lontar*-leaf chronicle, the Nagarakertagama (written in A.D. 1365), mentions that a high Buddhist official kept a hermitage at Lwa Gajah ("Elephant River"). This most likely refers to the Petanu River, which runs near the cave through a deep gorge. Perhaps the popular name "Elephant Cave" originated with early visitors who named the cave after the river. Other theories say the cave got its name from the statue inside of the elephant-god Ganesha, or the monster's head above the cave was mistakenly identified as an elephant's head. Legend has it the great hollowed-out boulder was the supernatural work of Kebo Iwo, the builder of Gunung Kawi and Yeh Pulu. Some have even suggested the monster head is in Kebo Iwo's image.

The decorations and interior plan of the cave are very similar to the hermit cells of East Java. Other hermitages with rock reliefs are found near Ubud (Goa Raksasa), on the River Oos (Jakut Paku), and in caves near Kapal. Archaeologists estimate Goa Gajah was built around A.D. 1022. Whether Goa Gajah was a hermitage for Buddhist or Hindu monks is uncertain. Both Buddhist and Hindu sculptures are inside and nearby. It's quite possible, given the intermingling between the two religions, that recluses of both sects sought peace and solitude at the site; a Shiva-Buddha belief system is found to this day among a small group of Brahman priests in eastern Bali. In any event, the 1954 excavation of a large bathing place in front of the cave proved the whole complex held an important place in the religious life of ancient Bali.

In modern times, Goa Gajah was first mentioned in 1923 in an Archaeological Service report filed in Singaraja by L. Heyting, a young Dutch civil servant who visited the site after hearing villagers speak of "a monster's head with elephant ears." The indefatigable Dutch artist Nieuwenkamp (1874-1950), during his fourth visit to Bali in 1925, also heard rumors of "a cave overshadowed by an enormous elephant's mouth" and reached the cave by automobile—the first tourist to do so. His subsequent visits proved once and for all that the head above the cave was that of a demon and not an elephant. But the name stuck.

The Facade

The cave was cut into a protruding rock wall, flat on top, with a flight of steps carved into the right side. It's been postulated the flat top was used by ascetics for meditation. The wall to either side of the entrance, curving slightly outward, is riotously decorated with stylized mountain scenery, forests, entangled leaves, rocks, ocean waves, animals, monsters, and phantom human shapes running in panic from the gaping mouth that forms the cave's entrance.

Directly over the entrance is the head of an enormous bulging-eyed demon that has mystified scholars and visitors alike. With its arched hairy eyebrows, long menacing fingernails, floppy ears, and long tusk-like fangs, it appears to be splitting and pushing the rock apart with its pudgy bare hands. Seeming to swallow everyone entering, this whole baroque facade appears to be set apart from the earthly civilized world of humans. The function of this carved goblin is to safeguard the heavenly character of the sanctuary. Balinese are quite comfortable with menacing, ugly faces on temples; they make the people feel safe from dangerous forces. Eerie monsters guarding hermit's caves, in the form of *kala*-heads, are also found in East Java. The figure may also represent Rangda, the widow-witch (its large earplugs are that of a woman's).

Another interpretation maintains the impressive head may represent Shiva Pasupati, who divided the cosmic mountain Mahameru into two parts, creating the rival mountains Agung and Batur as well as the split-gate *(candi bentar)*.

Yet another theory holds the head may represent Bima, son of Vishnu and Pertiwi, goddess of the soil. If this were the case, this would be the earliest representation extant of Bima, today a common sight guarding many of Bali's temples.

The Interior

The entrance of this hewn-rock cave, which opens to the south, is two meters high and one meter wide. The dark, musty interior is T-shaped. If you haven't brought a flashlight, a boy holding a candle, cigarette lighter, or oil lamp will take you inside. The grotto contains 15 niches cut out of its walls; these may have served as either meditation chambers or sleeping berths for ascetics. The niches prove the cave was not a temple.

In the cave's westernmost wing is a one-meter-high, four-armed statue of the elephant-god Ganesha holding an axe and broken tusk, symbols of his warlike nature, and a drinking vessel and beads, symbols of his wisdom. On the easternmost wing of the crossway are three 46.6-cm-high stone linga rising from a common base—distinctive features of a Shivaite sanctuary. Bits of statues, bases, and fragmented *raksasa* heads fill other niches. Notice the ancient graffiti on the wall to the right written in Old Javanese and probably dating from the second half of the 11th century.

The Bathing Place

In 1954, figurative torsos with waterspouts on their stomachs were found on either side of the entrance to the cave; it was surmised a bathing

Goa Gajah

S. MOONEY

place had to be nearby. In that same year a sunken, rock-bottomed courtyard of dressed stone was struck in front of the cave, and farther down the hill to the south a threefold flight of steps leading to the remnants of a former bathing place were unearthed. These were the most significant archaeological discoveries in post-WW II Bali.

Found were two distinct bathing partitions, one for men and one for women. Only the bases of six standing nymphs *(widadari),* three in each compartment, remained, but the upper portions of the statues previously found in front of the cave entrance fit perfectly. Today, the bathing place is fed by a pond, with water spouting from large, round urns held by the six Greek-looking statues. The elaborate carving and style of these divine female figures display Buddhist as well as Hindu religious symbols. The connection with Java is unmistakable: almost identical water nymphs grace the bathing places of Belahan on Gunung Penanggungan in East Java.

Goa Gajah's discoverer, Krijgsman, wanting the site accepted as a regular bathing place, took his daily bath there. The Balinese cheerfully joined in until leaders decided the ancient bathing pool was too holy a spot for such an earthly use.

Surrounding Antiquities

Other antiquities at the site cover a large time span. On a pavilion to the left of the cave are three ancient stone statues. One is an image of the Buddhist goddess Hariti, which may date from the Old Balinese Period (circa A.D. 1000). Originally a child-eating ogress worshipped in India, she converted to Buddhism and metamorphosed into a fertility goddess and child-protector. Hariti is always seen with a large number of lively children. On Bali, she, or any poor woman with many children, is known as Men Brayut; with her husband Pan Brayut, she lives on in the folk art of the island.

Other Buddhist figures are found by taking the stairway south of the bathing place down into a gorge that falls away to the Petanu River. Most tourists miss this well-kept, parklike hillside environment which, because of its serenity and beauty, is reminiscent of a Babylonian garden.

Across the rivulet and up a hill, sheltered in the remains of a small *candi* are two 9th-century Buddha statues sitting in the attitude of meditation *(dhyana-mudra).* Nearby are fragments of a once-enormous bas-relief of stupas, flowers, umbrellas, and *kalamakara* patterns once carved on the cliff face high above. Discovered in 1931, these broken sections had fallen and slid into the ravine. The relief is stylistically much different from the cave's carvings and is thought to be much older.

There are also two curious, five-meter-wide stones in the shape of a stupa with lotus flower motifs that once supported Buddha images. The arrangement of the stupa represents the superimposed heavens of the Buddhist religion. The Buddhist stupa, as well as the bas-relief fragments, date most likely from the reign of Kesari, a Buddhist king who ruled Bali during the Central Javanese Period (10th century). Buddhist antiquities indicate that Buddhism and Hinduism operated peacefully side by side at this site.

GIANYAR TOWN AND VICINITY

The small, bustling administrative center of Gianyar Regency, 23 km from Denpasar's Terminal Kereneng (Rp700 by *bemo*), Gianyar is important from a tourist point of view both as a *bemo* stop for those heading north to Kintamani or east to Klungkung and as a center for native Balinese *ikat* weaving (called *endek* in Balinese). It also has several jeweler's shops selling traditional gold jewelry and a large cockfighting arena *(wantilan).* Its *babi guling* stands and *joged* group are famous all over the island.

THE *PURI*

The old palace, visible through a gate, is in the middle of town facing the *alun-alun.* Still a private residence, prior permission is required to visit. First built in 1771 on the site of a priest's house, it barely survived a number of 19th-century wars, but was destroyed by the 1917 earthquake. Rebuilt in the 1920s, it's one of the few traditional and best preserved Balinese palaces still existing, and one of few still lived in by a royal family. Its spacious courtyards are decorated with stonework and carved wood pillars. Visit the western courtyard, with its two impressive gates and gilded *bale.* In the *alun-alun* stands a *waringin* tree, an all-important symbol of Balinese and Javanese royal courts.

During the wars of the 1880s, pressed by belligerent neighbors, Gianyar's raja, Dewa Manggis, agreed to pay liege homage to the Dewa Agung of Klungkung. Ultimately, the raja and his whole family were imprisoned. In 1889, two sons escaped from Klungkung and re-established their kingdom in the *puri.* Placing themselves under the protection of the Dutch, the kingdom was spared when the Dutch conquered the other southern Bali principalities. In the 20th century, the Gianyar royal line became administrators in the colonial government and after the war in 1950s and '60s, prominent republican leaders.

SHOPPING

The shops along the main street are not cheap, apparently the victims of tour buses, but still pretty good. There's a thriving "art market" everyday where you can bargain for just about any arts and crafts product made on the island, and a few that aren't.

A woodcarving training center is in Abianbase a few blocks from Gianyar's police station. Visit before 1200. Called **Sasana Hasta Karya,** it was set up in 1983 by the Denpasar Catholic church as an assistance program to unemployed youth. The carving follows Balinese traditional style with some thematic inspi-

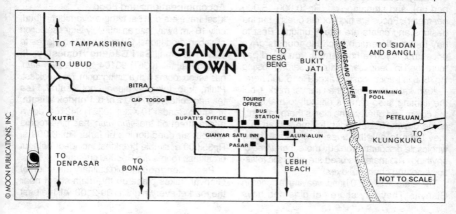

The Balinese ikat *weavers of Gianyar sit at their six-foot looms under the shade of their brick, mortar and stucco pavilions. The huge showroom up front overflows with their labors. The click-pause-clack of the shuttle cocks cuts a staccato rhythm in the humid air. As the tie-dyed weft threads fly through the white warp threads, a crisp pattern emerges in blue and white. One of the serene weavers blossoms into a smile as I say hello. She sits with her 15-month-baby quietly cradled in her lap. She chats with the other women—working, mothering and visiting as if it's perfectly ordinary to do three things at once, looking calm and radiant. She weaves a beautiful tapestry with the threads of her life.*

*—*Suzie Wolfer

ration from the Borobudur and Prambanan temples in Central Java.

Shop for your handwoven and hand-dyed textiles and *sarung* here. Just before entering town from Denpasar you'll find several textile shops and factories with showrooms selling *sarung*, colorfully decorated T-shirts, shirts (Rp30,000 and up), and stunning *ikat* (Rp10,000-15,000 per meter). Prices are high for the quality, but the designs and colors are utterly unique. Best to buy in the off-season because tourists drive prices up. If you're not careful, you could pay more than in Denpasar or Kuta; a *sarung* costing Rp7500 in Legian costs a fixed Rp15,000 here.

Kain ikat is cheaper in the Gianyar market, but the lighting is so dim it's difficult to make out the colors and quality. The clerks there can only come down 15% at most; for more than that they have to ask the boss. Always ask for a wholesale discount if you buy more than *three* of anything. The materials used are synthetic (plastic twine and chemical dyes).

There are at least 50 hand-weaving factories in Gianyar. They pay scores of girls and boys Rp60,000-70,000 per month. The kids work everyday but holidays 0800-1600; it takes about six hours to complete one *sarung*. The workers are too poor themselves to wear the *sarung* they make, but conditions have improved. Now they're given one free meal a day, plus free drinks.

Cap Togog, Jl. Astina Utara 11, tel. (0361) 93046 or 93443, fax 93442, is the largest (seven sweatshops) and oldest (1953) weaving factory in Gianyar. Open 0800-1630 every day. No women's clothes, but *endek* fabric is Rp17,000 per meter; lots of men's shirts starting at Rp30,000; silk *sarung*, Rp80,000. All fabrics made here. Colors won't run, as there is good quality control. The working looms are in the back where 300 people work. For discounts, see the manager Pande Nyoman Gede Maruta.

One of Gianyar's best known mills, **Cap Cili,** Ciung Wanara 7, Gianyar 80511, tel. (0361) 93409, fax 93724, is also one of Gianyar's largest and oldest (1960). They sell not only lengths of *endek* cloth (Rp10,000-12,500 per meter), but hand-painted *batik*, integrated garments, short-sleeve shirts (Rp17,500), long-sleeve shirts (Rp25,000), dresses (Rp20,000). Also purses (Rp5000), *sarung* (Rp10,000), swim trunks (Rp6000). Big display room, helpful clerks, owned by Pande Wayan Sira. Open 0800-1800 every day. Fixed prices. Also check out the **Bakti** and **Cap Putri Bali** weaving centers.

PRACTICALITIES

Accommodations and Food

Most travelers don't stay here overnight. Ubud, only 10 km away, has an infinitely larger selection of accommodations; Gianyar has two places to stay. The small **Sari Gadung Homestay,** Jl. Dalem Rai, tel. (0361) 93104, on the *alun-alun*, has seven rooms with a sitting room. No breakfast. Plain, drab, tolerably clean, cool, central. Free tea and coffee. Rp7000 s or d. **Pondok Wisata,** Jl. Anom Sandat 10 X, tel. (0361) 942164, down a little street off the *alun-alun*, has nine rooms without air conditioning or fans. Rp20,000 s, Rp35,000 d, simple breakfast included. Without breakfast, rooms are Rp5000 cheaper.

Pasar Senggol, the big culinary attraction of Gianyar, takes place on the main street near the market every night 1700-2100. All the best traditional dishes are found here: grilled chicken *(ayam kampung)*, rice mixed with sweet potatoes *(tepeng)*, and Balinese *kampung* sweets. Even the people from Denpasar drive all the way here because the night market has such a concentration of authentic Balinese village food without a touristy atmosphere.

Two **Warung Melati** serve the Balinese delicacy *babi guling*, roast piglet, on either side of the *stanplatz*. About Rp10,000 for two people. Get there early because by 1100 they're usually sold out. A *nasi padang* restaurant called the **Bundo Kandung** is on Jl. Kesatrian beside the cinema.

Information and Services
The poorly staffed **tourist office** for Gianyar District (Dinas Pariwisata Gianyar) is at Jl. Ngurah Rai 21 (Mon.-Fri. 0700-1700, tel. 0361-93401). It's easier to get info in Ubud. In rudimentary English they can only advise about the location of the various weaving factories. A **Wartel,** open 24 hours, is just to the west of the tourist office. Change money at **Bank Rakyat Indonesia,** 200 meters down the road in the town center by the palace; turn at the sign to Lebih.

Getting There and Away
Bemo heading east from Denpasar, from the south, and from the north are forced to pass through Gianyar; listen for the abbreviated *nyar!* Destinations, distances, and prices: Denpasar, 23 km, Rp700; Kutri, 10 km, Rp400; Bedulu, five km, Rp300; Sidan, three km, Rp300; Pejeng, 10 km, Rp400.

VICINITY OF GIANYAR

In **Bitra,** two km northwest of Gianyar, a famous death temple *(pura dalem)* sits under a big banyan tree beside a river. A state *pura* dedicated to the descendents of the throne of Dewa Manggis is found at **Beng,** three km northeast of Gianyar. **Kramas,** four km to the south, is a center for music and dance, particularly for its *arja* theatrical performers, as it was once the seat of 17th-century prince Gusti Agung Maruti.

Samprangan, two km to the east past the Sangsang River, was the site of a former royal palace of Javanese aristocrat **Kapakisan,** who was sent by general Gajah Mada to represent Majapahit interests in the area. The very old *pura dalem* that houses the sacral drinking bowl of Kapakisan's horse is behind the village *wantilan*. It's the only remnant of this *puri*. North of Gianyar is **Bukit Jati** ("Hill of Teak"). The teak trees disappeared decades ago, but there's a fine panorama from the temple of cascading rice fields.

Sidan
There are many beautiful temples in the Gianyar area, like the exquisitely carved temple near Sidan, a village three kilometers east of Gianyar town on the road to Bangli. A fine example of a *pura dalem*. At the *kulkul* tower, stone relief shows evildoers being tormented by devil giants, gates are flanked by deities of death, the temple's main motif, and the semi-divine Boma and Durga appear as the terrifying widow-witch Rangda. The *pura* is dedicated to Merajapati, the caretaker of the dead. It's believed the ashes of the great King Airlangga are interred here.

To get to Sidan, take a *bemo* for Rp300 from Gianyar in the direction of Bangli and get off at Peteluan. From Klungkung and Bangli it's also Rp300 by *bemo*. The *pura dalem* is only two kilometers north of Peteluan, the crossroads village leading up to Bangli. From this same crossroads, where you can change *bemo*, it's nine kilometers to Klungkung and 47 kilometers to Amlapura.

Lebih
In the coastal village of Lebih, three kilometers south of Gianyar, fishermen gather *nener* (tadpoles) to be sold to Javanese fishpond cultivators. On this road sits one of Bali's only Chinese temples. A large Chinese community once served as merchant middlemen between the Gianyar raja and his subjects. Many Chinese tradesmen took part in the construction of the *puri*, evidenced by the Chinese ornamentation on the roofs of the various *bale*.

A **pura segara** (sea temple) affords a good vantage point over Nusa Penida. Balinese all over the district bring the ashes of their dead here for the soul's final liberation in a ceremony known as *melasti*. Because of the undertow, swimming here is dangerous. The best beach in the area is at **Siyut,** 10 kilometers south (via

Tulikup and Bekul) of the main Gianyar-Klungkung road.

Bona and Vicinity

Many of the inhabitants of Bona, only three kilometers northeast of Blahbatuh on an asphalt road between Gianyar and Blahbatuh, are engaged in making good quality baskets, hats, sandals, wallets, handbags, fans, dolls, birds, flowers, and up to three-meter-tall Christmas trees made of dried *lontar* palm leaves. Plain and spotted bamboo chairs, beds, and tables, or plain or ornate wooden furniture can be ordered here.

Bona is also the venue of an extraordinary version of the modern *kecak,* the "fire dance," first performed here in the 1930s. It's a travesty of the *sanghyang dedari* trance dance performed with a male chorus accompaniment, at least six days a week from 1800 to 2000. Entrance is Rp5000, including transport from Ubud at 1700. Or buy tickets at the door. *Bemo* from Gianyar cost Rp300.

Visit the readymade *batik* and *ikat* outlet **Anoman Handicrafts Shop** up the road from Bona toward Gianyar. To see the *ikat* process, visit their weaving factory in **Beng.** There are also at least 50 weaving factories and dozens of showrooms in and around the town of Gianyar.

Saba and Masceti Beaches

Seven kilometers south of Gianyar, west of Lebih, and near the mouth of the Pakrisan River are the restful black- and gray-sand beaches of Saba and Masceti. If heading west from Gianyar, turn at the sign advertising the luxurious, never-opened Saba Bay Resort Hotel. A motorcyclist will take you down to Saba Beach for around Rp2000 (hitch another motorcycle or scooter back). For surfers there's a good right break over a sand and rock bottom. Once yearly, the people of Gianyar stage a huge rite here to placate the forces of disease and calamity.

At **Masceti,** 10 kilometers south of Bona via Medahan, is a much venerated sea temple, one of the nine that protect the south coast of Bali from the forces of the sea. From Medahan, follow the signs to the sea through rice terraces and you'll come to the impressive rough coral *candi bentar* that marks the entrance to the temple. An attractive lily pond lies to the east but the black-sand shore is marred by a hideously ornamented swimming pool and stage.

NORTHERN GIANYAR REGENCY

TAMPAKSIRING

A early center of Hinduism on Bali, Tampaksiring, just 14 kilometers northeast of Ubud, lies one kilometer south of the sacred bathing place Tirtha Empul, near the source of the Pakrisan River, and two kilometers upstream from monumental Gunung Kawi. Get there by *bemo* via Gianyar (Rp600). The weather is cool and it often rains lightly in the evenings.

Accommodations and Food

Because of the shortage of accommodations, most people just include Tampaksiring in a day trip from Ubud. The only place to stay in the area is **Gusti Homestay,** just 100 meters west of the main road, but it's a grotty dive (Rp5000 per person, no breakfast). If coming from the south it's on the left, behind the market in the middle of town. Gusti serves meals. A cheap and good place to eat is **Made's Warung.** The *warung* in front of Tirta Empul are okay for snacks and light refreshments. At the top of the stairs at Gunung Kawi enjoy *bubur sayur bayan* (porridge and vegetables) for only Rp500.

Tirta Empul

Situated in a valley in the northeast corner of Tampaksiring under a spectacular banyan tree, 37 km northeast of Denpasar at the end of a well-signposted road, the Tirta Empul temple and its 20 small sugar-palm thatched shrines are beautifully decorated and maintained. Savor the serene atmosphere of the complex, which is set against a backdrop of surviving forest. Even the souvenir shops outside the temple are neat and orderly. Tirta Empul is on nearly every tour group's itinerary of central Bali. Fleets of tour buses visit the site, which is open only during daylight hours. From the parking lot, visitors have to run the usual gauntlet of souvenir stands

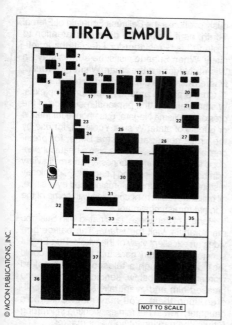

TIRTA EMPUL

NOT TO SCALE

© MOON PUBLICATIONS, INC.

up under the pools. The water is so clear plants growing at the bottom of the pool are clearly visible, as are a number of fish and a rather large eel. Because it's believed that from this spring bubbles the elixir of immortality, it's surrounded by a wall to prevent it from being profaned.

The Balinese use holy water as an essential part of almost every ritual. Their religion is in fact called Agama Tirta, or "The Religion of the Holy Water." Tirta Empul's water is looked upon as the holiest on Bali, widely thought to possess magical curative powers. The spring is believed to have been created by the god Indra, who pierced the Earth to tap *amerta,* the restoring waters that brought back to life his army, which was poisoned by the demon-king Mayadanava.

Events
Regular ceremonies are held at this sanctuary, particularly during Galungan, when dance clubs from the surrounding area bring their sacred *barong* masks to be purified by the spring's water.

An inscription in Old Balinese found in the village of Manukaya, north of Tirta Empul, states that two ponds were formed here in A.D. 962. When the badly worn inscription was finally deciphered by Sutterheim in 1969, it described in detail the ritual cleansing of a holy stone during the full moon of the fourth month in the Balinese calendar. For more than 1,000 years villagers from Manukaya carried a stone to the spring for purification rites on the precise day each year of Tirta Empul's founding, never knowing the origin or the reason, only that it was *adat.* Since none of the villagers then knew what the old inscription read, the date of the temple's founding must have been handed down orally through 33 generations of invasions, dynastic changes, and natural disasters.

Crafts
In the parking lot are 400 meters of stalls selling everything from bone and ivory carvings to coconut shell ornaments and chess sets. The best deals are the painted wooden jewelry and carved cow bone ornaments. The bone- and ivory-carving industry is centered around Manukaya.

The shop of **I Gusti Aji Meranggi** in Banjar Masangambu, 500 meters north of Tirta Empul,

to the temple compound, which you may enter after renting a sash (Rp500); entrance Rp1100. Seeking protective blessings and deliverance from illness, people journey from all over Bali to bathe in this sacred cleansing spring where terrifying *garuda* scowl down on naked bathers floating among the lily pads. Seeing it on a rainy day adds even more mystery to the site.

There's a large square altar dedicated to Batara Indra, and elaborate carvings adorn the lichen-covered walls surrounding the pools. Built under the rule of Sri Candrabhaya Singha Warmadewa in the 10th century, the complex was completely restored and given a new paint job in 1969. Tirta Empul conforms to the structure of most Balinese temples. It's divided into three main courtyards: the front, the middle, and the inner sanctum. Backing the outer courtyard are two rectangular bathing pools, one for men and one for women. According to tradition, each of the pool's 15 fountains has its own name and function: spiritual purification, cleansing from evil, antidote to poison. The gin-clear freshwater spring at a higher level is the source of the water that bubbles specializes in carvings of deer horn and ivory imported from Flores. Large, intricately carved tusks cost from two million rupiah, depending on the size and complexity of the carving. On the road up to Tampaksiring are numerous shops selling carvings from the workshops of Sebatu to the north, a busy woodcarving area.

This is also the area for Bali quilts, hand-painted fabrics quilted by machine, as well as colorful and cleverly designed bedcovers. Two or three km beyond Tampaksiring you'll see quilts flapping in the wind, draped on lines outside at least 12 shops specializing in color-rich—bordering on garish—quilts in a variety of sizes. A shop (actually a whole complex of shops) with a big selection is **Dewa Made Astina** right on the highway.

Prices run Rp75,000-250,000. You can usually bargain down from there. Dacron-filled quilts are nearly twice as expensive as foam-filled ones. Hand-painted cotton shirts and kimonos are also for sale. Every salesclerk asks for a dollar tip upon close of sale. **Gardana Art Collection,** beyond Tampaksiring in Kayuambua, also has a good selection. **Kesuma Nadi Shop** and the **Ketut Gisi Collection** across the street have pretty good prices.

Istana Tampaksiring

Two km north of Tampaksiring, the road branches to the right for Tirta Empul, while the left road climbs to a hilltop retreat built by Sukarno in 1954. Park for Rp500 and pay an entrance fee of Rp1000; open daily during daylight hours. With its large, well-kept lawns, this is a lovely place to walk. Since you can't enter any of the buildings, content yourself with looking in the windows.

This splendid presidential palace, its two main buildings connected by a footbridge, is a classic example of the first truly Indonesian national architectural style. The sprawling, one-story buildings, built along the lines of a Javanese *pendopo,* feature grooved plaster columns and the geometrically hardlined look of the art deco era. Sukarno is said to have designed the whole complex, a sort of ranch-house/social realism combo, an architectural amalgam he picked up during his engineering training at ITB in Bandung. Sukarno was half Balinese and he visited the island frequently, usually staying in this resthouse. The *istana* purposefully and incongru-

ously overlooks the Balinese Fountain of Eternal Youth, as if it were the dictator's intention to prolong his "President-for-Life" status indefinitely. When Suharto visits, he always stays in Wisma Negara rather than Wisma Merdeka, where Sukarno's ghost is said to roam.

On the palace grounds are four complexes: Wisma Merdeka, the personal residence of the president; Wisma Negara, guesthouse for friends or guests of state; Wisma Yudistira, for use by the press corps; and Wisma Bima, for presidential bodyguards. There's also a beautiful *pendopo* for dance performances and a small aviary with hornbills, eagles, and peacocks. Completely restored in 1957 and well-maintained ever since, all buildings are in mint condition with some of the original furnishings intact.

Hordes of Japanese, fascinated with Sukarno memorabilia, visit the *istana.* The palace provides an excellent view of the whole Tirta Empul sanctuary. The story goes that the dictator could look down through a telescope upon naked women bathing below, sending for those who pleased him and eventually siring a few children upon them. You may meet Sukarno's daughter, now in her thirties, working in Warung Bitar in the parking lot/souvenir market.

The Soviet Premier Khrushchev once watched a *topeng legong* dance on these palace grounds at a time (1965) when Sukarno's government had incurred debts of US$2.5 billion, half on loans for purchases of military equipment from Russia. After Sukarno was toppled in 1967, the palace became once again a government resthouse and museum, now open to the public.

Vicinity of Tampaksiring

Surrounded by large mossy trees, **Pura Gumang,** a 30-minute walk northeast of Munukaya, is an early Shivaite temple with a large gateway, huge linga and trident, carvings of mythical Hindu-Javanese sea monsters, and worn statue of Shiva's bull Nandi. **Pura Mengening,** a little west of Tirta Empul, is a sacred and picturesque spring under a large tree. The freestanding *candi* here, containing some ancient statues, is similar to those at Gunung Kawi. Atop a nearby hill is a venerable old *pura* which may have been dedicated to King Udayana. The connection between the three holy sites of Tirta Mancingan, Tirta Empul, and Gunung Kawi is obvious.

GUNUNG KAWI

Two kilometers south of Tampaksiring, on the banks of the upper course of the sacred Pakrisan River, Gunung Kawi ("Mountain of Poetry") lies in the heart of the archaeologically rich Pejeng area, a region where Hinduism first took hold on Bali. Gunung Kawi—open daily only during daylight hours—is one of the more impressive historical sites on Bali: a blinding green watery canyon where two rows of ancient blackened tombs have been hewn out of natural rock hillsides as royal memorials.

The whole complex is well swept and well maintained and should be visited in the cool mornings or late afternoons when few tourists are about. At the lookout on top of the long, steep stairway, look down upon overwhelming scenery: sunlit waterfalls and palm-studded rice terraces plunging to a deep ravine with a rushing river flowing through it all. The holy water of the river was meant to sanctify the site. Carved into niches on two facing cliffs, the somber and unembellished temples contain no interior chambers, only facades. Built in the late 11th century, the temples are remarkably well preserved. There are 10 temples in all. Across the gorge is an abandoned hermitage for the keepers of the tombs. All around flows holy water and steep-sided rock walls covered with dripping moss, all of which gives the site an elevated and venerated atmosphere.

History
Goa Gajah and these temples are the earliest known monuments of Balinese art. The Balinese knew of the Gunung Kawi *candi* long before they were "discovered" by H.T. Damte in 1920. Local lore says the legendary Kebo Iwo carved the ancient structures in one night with his fingernails—he's credited with carving nearly all the ancient monuments between the Pakrisan and Petanu Rivers.

Heavily weathered inscriptions etched over the sham doors of the *candi* date construction to the 11th century. The highly decorative script used here was in vogue during the East Javanese Kediri period. The Balinese usually prefer

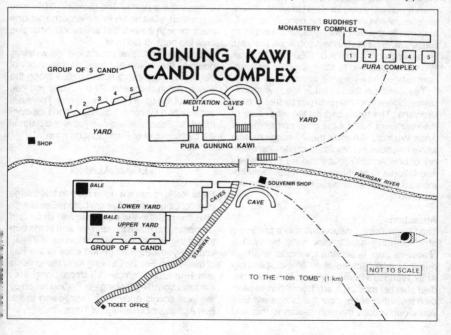

ornamentation to bulk, but not at Gunung Kawi, where the monolithic-style architecture obviously originates from Java. Urs Ramseyer observed that the tombs resemble Indian temples.

Stone monuments are rare on Bali, which only adds to the mystery surrounding the purpose of the structures. The structural difference between these and Javanese *candi* is that the impressively scaled Gunung Kawi monuments are not free-standing but are hewn in relief out of a solid rock hillside. Each *candi* is seven meters high and cut inside its own deep niche to provide protection. Further protection came from an erosion-resistant hard plaster coating that has long since vanished. Each group of *candi* rests on a common base accessible by a stone staircase. *Naga* gargoyle spouts once channeled water above the *candi* to anoint bathers and irrigate the fields.

There's little doubt each temple served as a memorial to deified royalty, as they're shaped like the burial towers found all over Central and East Java. The exact identity of the royal personages honored here is unknown. One very credible theory suggests the five *candi* in the main group were built for King Udayana, his Javanese queen Gunapriya, his concubine, his illustrious eldest son Erlangga who ruled over East Java, and his youngest son Anak Wungsu. Reigning over Bali from A.D. 1050 to 1077, Anak Wungsu is believed to have given up his kingdom to become a religious hermit.

The *candi* on the far left in the row of five, placed higher than the rest, may be that of King Udayana. The four *candi* on the other side of the river were built for the chief concubines of Anak Wungsu. Another theory suggests this whole mausoleum complex enshrines the memory of only Anak Wungsu and his royal wives and favorite concubines, who most likely immolated themelves to follow their sovereign into the afterlife.

Attractions

The "Tenth Tomb," discovered only a few years after Gunung Kawi's discovery by W.O.J. Nieuwenkamp, is either a memorial to a high priest or a high-caste state official, possibly Anak Wungsu's prime minister, Rakryan, who died after his master. A boy from the *toko oleh-oleh* (souvenir shop) near the bridge will take you along a path through *sawah* to this odd *candi* removed from the main complex. The one-km-long walk takes you by a small gateway hewn from rock. To the left of the Tenth Tomb are more niches.

To the right of the main ensemble of temples is a Buddhist monks' cloister *(patapan)* with five cells carved out of rock. In the confluence of the Oos River in Campuan, near Ubud, several other ascetic cells were also discovered, indicating the monastic tradition was entrenched in 11th-century Bali. Gunung Kawi's cloister inmates most likely were caretakers of the *candi*. There's a second hermitage near the main cloister, consisting of niches around a central courtyard, which might have served as sleeping quarters for visiting pilgrims.

Getting There and Away

From Tampaksiring, Gunung Kawi is a two-km walk south on the road to Pejeng, or take a *bemo* for Rp500. The small road to the tombs is on the left in Desa Panaka. From the main road, walk 600 meters to the ticket office—Rp1100 entrance, Rp300 parking—then walk through a fortress-like gateway and descend 315 stone steps that wind down into the gorge, at one point through a stretch of solid rock, emerging onto the bank of the river.

Souvenir and drink stands line the walkway down to the ravine but their presence is not cloying. During the descent, pause along the way to catch the views. At one point you can make out the tip of Pura Mengening. There are actually two Gunung Kawis, so don't be confused. In Sebatu village five km to the north is the bathing spot of Pura Gunung Kawi.

TEGALLALANG

From Keliki, there's a good road to this village north of Ubud, about five km before Sebatu. Or take the path on the right between Ubud and Campuan, go down to the river, and at the bottom of the ravine take the right fork up to Tegallalang—you'll be transported back to the Bali of the 1950s. For the Gunung Kawi monuments and Tirta Empul temple in Tampaksiring, take the road from Tegallalang via Pujung, or enjoy the very scenic drive from Tegallalang to the Bali Aga mountain village of Taro.

In northern Tegallalang, the **Blue Yogi Cafe,** tel. (0366) 91768, with its fabulous location just above the road, makes for a relaxing, breezy stop or place to stay while on the road north to Gunung Batur. Quite inventive menu: potato leek and Thai *tom yum* soup Rp3500, tandoori chicken Rp5800, vegetarian curry with real chutney and Indian-style cucumber salad Rp5100, great cake desserts. Nicely carved doorways and rice fields and mountains in the background. There are four comfortable two-story bungalows (Rp25,000 s or d) in the garden behind the restaurant, which are sometimes rented out to groups studying yoga. The farthest bungalow, with rice fields out both windows, is the best (but noisy servants' quarters next door).

The Tegallalang area is the place to buy woodcarvings—flowers, animals, birds—at better prices than in Ubud. Particularly known for superb *garuda* statues. Look in at the Bunga Mekar Art Shop, run by Ketut Tunas; it's cheaper and has more creative suns and moons than the shop next door. Few tourists ever visit these shops so you'll be received enthusiastically.

PUJUNG

A woodcarving village in the mountains five km north of Tegallalang. Between Tegallalang and Pujung are exquisite rice fields to the right side of the road. Coming from the south, 500 meters before turning right toward Sebatu, is a small shop selling handmade chess games starting at Rp30,000—a bit expensive, but beautiful work.

An even more spectacular road is from Gentong to Bayad. Heading east out of Ubud, turn left at the T-junction and travel northward toward Petulu. At Gentong turn right toward Kenderan. This road takes you through untraveled rice terrace landscapes all the way to Bayad; from here you can turn left to Pujung or right to Tampaksiring. Pujung village is divided into two *banjar,* Pujungklod and Pujungkaja. Visit the workshops of Anantaloga, Kresna Asih, Nyoman Pugra, Sri Sedana, Wayan Gede Artha, Wayang Nyungkal, and Wayang Tata, all specializing in different styles and sizes of *garuda* carvings, painted wooden banana trees, jewelry, and colored spirit boxes. Generally, the prices are better than in Mas or Kemenuh. The selection is immense, including some old woodcarvings, so take your time. Copies of old woodcarvings are a good deal. Always check for cracks; this can be a problem with cheap wood.

Leaving Pujung, travel another 20 km on the back road to Lake Batur. Just when you've had enough of this dirt road, Gunung Batur pops up. From Pujung, several roads head east to Tampaksiring; take the smaller one which bears left off the main road as it turns down to the *pasar.*

SEBATU

Two km east of Pujung, take the road opposite the road to Taro. On the way, stop and see the Duckman, the first Balinese sculptor to carve ducks on a commercial scale—he's quite famous now. The Sebatu area is the best place on Bali to buy small wooden crafts. There's a cluster of shops in the countryside selling painted wooden suns, moons, stars, flying goddesses, and animals for only Rp1000-4000 apiece.

See the huge elephants at the shop **Sedana Yogya.** In Telepud, Wayan Astika carves fanciful suns and moons in natural browns and black stains, as well as stools in the shape of striped cats (Rp6000-10,000). He and other carvers create made-to-order work as well. When the road goes down, turn right toward Sebatu. In a small valley before the village is the **Pura Gunung Kawi,** a bathing place with stone statues of maidens spouting water, carved stone *naga,* sacred golden carp, and lichen-covered ancient walls. The temple is in an exceptionally pretty spot against a backdrop of rich green foilage. At dusk small bats fill the air. Discreetly, have a look at the people having *mandi,* but don't take photos. The rectangular bathing place is separated into men's and women's sections.

Sebatu is a village of woodcarvers and musicians. In front of the temple are a few shops displaying a mass of wooden crafts. Look for sensual figures and exquisitely carved *garuda* statuary. Note the difference between the masks of Mas and those of Sebatu; the lines and colors of masks from Mas are pure, while those of Sebatu are more exuberant. Mas makes god's masks, Sebatu devil's masks. Bargain as much as possible; the sellers are receptive. Every three days the village *pasar* takes place in the area in front of the temple.

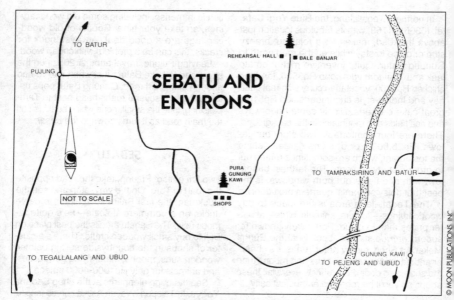

SEBATU AND ENVIRONS

TO BATUR

PUJUNG

REHEARSAL HALL ■ ■ BALE BANJAR

MOON

NOT TO SCALE

PURA
GUNUNG
KAWI

SHOPS

TO TAMPAKSIRING AND BATUR →

TO TEGALLALANG AND UBUD

GUNUNG KAWI
TO PEJENG AND UBUD

© MOON PUBLICATIONS, INC.

From the temple, the road continues to the peaceful village itself, which few tourists ever visit. It consists mainly of one street of houses decorated with plants and flowers. The village is very active in dance and music, renowned as much as Peliatan. It's home to a noted dance troupe that once toured the world. Ask to see the photos of Balinese in fur coats in London. Incredibly, this small village possesses three orchestras. Rehearsals take place at 2000 every night, except during harvest. This is an opportunity to see people performing without enduring the clicking of cameras and flashes. Travelers without their own transportation should be aware that *bemo* back to Ubud stop running around 1600 or 1700. From Sebatu, a small road before the temple leads to Tampaksiring and on to Gunung Batur.

TARO

Between Pujungklod and Pujungkaja, take the road northwest for six km to the small village of Taro. Set on a hillside and hidden behind a palm forest, Taro seems removed from the world. The village marks the exact center of Bali. This

area is known for its litchis, picturesque buff sandstone quarries, and unique architecture. These highlanders own the largest coffee plantation in the regency, a remnant of the big Chinese-owned estates of the last century. Taro domesticates the only hybrid breed of white cattle on the island. Since the locals believe this albino stock is holy, they are not used for work, may not be sold or eaten, and are strictly quarantined to keep the breed pure.

In Taro is the longest and one of the largest and most beautiful *bale agung* on Bali. This great pavilion, located in the village's *pura desa,* is the heart of the political and religious life of the community. Note the little bridge placed over a hole in front of the temple gate over which only the pure—gods and virgins—can pass.

According to legend, in the 8th century the itinerant priest Danghyang Markandeya visiting from his hermitage in East Java built Pura Gunung Raung with his entourage on the present-day site of Taro; they began breeding the white cattle before moving on to found Campuan's Pura Gunung Lebah and, according to some scholars, Pura Besakih on Gunung Agung in east Bali.

KLUNGKUNG REGENCY

Klungkung is the smallest regency on Bali, roughly divided between the fertile terraced slopes of the uplands, the coconut and banana groves of the narrow coastal strip, and the poor, arid, and sparsely populated islands of Nusa Penida, Nusa Lembongan, and Nusa Ceningan. Only Lembongan, the Kerta Gosa courthouse, and Goa Lawah are regularly visited by tourists.

History

From the 16th century until the beginning of this century, Klungkung was the royal capital of Bali, earned by a certain mystique rather than by its size and economic clout. From the 14th century to the 17th century, the Gelgel dynasty, governed from Gelgel, four km south of present-day Klungkung, played a major role in government and diplomacy, exerting a pervading influence over the whole island. This was the Golden Age of Bali, when dance, drama, music, and painting flourished.

The last Majapahit king, buckling under the onslaught of Islam on Java, fled Java to set up court in Gelgel around 1550. The Brahmans and Ksatriyas of the court commenced to divide Bali into a number of kingdoms, administered by relatives and generals. The Javanese-Hindu cul-

tural influence emanating from here laid the foundation for Bali's unique religion and society.

The greatest of the Gelgel dynasty kings was Batu Renggong, who called himself Dalem. After assuming the throne in 1550, he launched a military, political, and cultural renaissance, conquering Bali and sending roving bands of Balinese troops into large areas of East Java and the islands of Lombok and Sumbawa. Indonesia's first contact with Europeans occurred under Dalem's reign, when three Dutch ships put in near Kuta in 1597. Also dating from this critical era are the magnificent old courthouse, floating pavilion, and gardens of Klungkung. During Dalem's reign the Brahman priest Nirantha arrived on the island, assuming the position of the court high priest and exerting a considerable influence on arts and literature. Besakih became Bali's state temple and the abode of royal ancestors.

In the 17th century the brilliance of the Gelgel court began to flicker. Under the reign of Dalem di Made the dynasty steadily lost land, power, and status. Between 1650 and 1686 a power struggle broke out between two brothers over who was to succeed. Finally, an ambitious general, Gusti Agung Maruti, launched an attack

on Gelgel in 1686 and proclaimed himself raja. Dating from this critical era are the magnificent old courthouse, the "floating pavilion," and gardens which can still be seen in Klungkung.

The kings of Badung and Buleleng, refusing to accept Maruti's sovereignty, helped the rightful Majapahit descendant regain his throne in 1705. Five years later, for superstitious reasons, a new capital was built in Klungkung a few kilometers to the north. Klungkung's first king, Jambe, was the first to use the title Dewa Agung ("Great King"). The first major dynastic genealogy was compiled by this court in 1819. The Klungkung court also created new art forms, such as *arja* and the *geguritan* poetic form, and held elaborate state rituals to assert its status as Bali's spiritual capital.

The Dutch military campaign against Klungkung began in 1849. Troops landed at Padangbai and marched as far as Kusamba. Hearing the enemy's ranks were stricken by dysentery, the virgin queen Dewa Agung Istri Kanya launched a deadly night attack, inflicting heavy casualties on the Dutch and fatally wounding the Dutch commander. A peace settlement was negotiated by the wily Danish trader Mads Lange, and the next day the Dutch troops were ordered back to their ships.

Thus the conquest of south Bali was postponed for another 60 years. As a result of increasing conflicts in political and trade matters between the Balinese raja and the Dutch, a full scale Dutch invasion of the south was mounted in 1906, obliterating the royal houses of Denpasar and Tabanan. In April 1908 Dutch warships arrived from Batavia and both Klungkung and Gelgel were bombarded into submission. Dewa Agung Jambe and 300 of his relatives and followers chose collective suicide *(puputan)* over the colonial yoke. Clad in white and armed only with *kris*, the royal retinue marched straight into Dutch rifles. Dewa Agung was shot down and six of his wives stabbed themselves to death, falling over his body. When the smoke cleared, 108 Balinese had died without the loss of a single Dutch soldier. Today, across the road from the Kerta Gosa, a monument commemorates this ghastly event.

Economy

Once one of the most prosperous and fertile districts in all of Bali, 20% of Klungkung's arable land was destroyed in the 1963 eruption of Gunung Agung, which took 1,600 lives and drove 87,000 from their homes. Bali was unable to absorb the homeless, and many were resettled in *transmigrasi* areas of the Outer Islands. Farmers still eke out a subsistence living growing chilies, scraggly corn, and onions on gravelly land long since denuded of heartier vegetation.

The People

The people of Klungkung still claim a cultural and social superiority over other Balinese. One of every three Ksatriya priests hails from Klungkung. The area is home to the island's most strict and traditional caste rules. Klungkung nobles may use the formal Balinese language to speak down to everyone else. The regency's rigid class structure is evident in such societal extremes as the Resi Bhujangga sect of Takmung, a priestly class of Vishnu worshippers, and the *desa* of Anjingan, inhabited by dog eaters, scavengers, beggars, and corpse-robbers.

KLUNGKUNG

A historically important town 40 km from Denpasar (Rp2000 by minibus) and 13 km east of Gianyar (Rp500 by *bemo*), Klungkung was the seat of the Gelgel dynasty from 1710 until 1908. Most Balinese nobles are descended from Klungkung's raja, his family, or retinue. Until his death in 1965, the last Klungkung raja was regarded as the most exalted prince in Balinese aristocracy.

After the *puputan* of 1908 which wiped out the royal family, the Dutch controller took over Klungkung's affairs until 1929 when the heir to the throne returned. Throughout his life Ida Dewa Agung Geg, the last raja of Klunkung (1896-1965), bore the scars of the 1908 *puputan*, when he was stabbed in the side and shot in the knee. He was exiled to Lombok until 1929, then returned to Bali to occupy the old palace with his 40 wives and 100 children.

SIGHTS

Pura Taman Sari

You can reach Pura Taman Sari ("Flower Garden") by taking the road north to Besakih. After the police station, make a right at the small intersection and walk 300 meters until you see the sign announcing the temple. Built in the 17th century, this *pura* of *meru* towers, quiet ponds, and gardens is a welcome refuge from the noisy and polluted town.

The Taman Gili Palace Compound

Meaning literally "island garden," the Taman Gili complex consists of the Bale Kambang and the Kerta Gosa, set within an extensive garden enclosure and framed by a tall gateway to the west called the Pemedal Agung. These are all that remain of the Semara Pura Royal Palace after it was pounded by Dutch artillery, ending 200 years of rule in Bali by the lineal descendants of Majapahit. Open daily 0700-1800.

In 1710 the Dewa Agung himself, Gusti Sideman, took a personal hand in the design of his new *puri*. A great lover of the arts, he employed the realm's best carvers, carpenters, masons, and sculptors, working with only the very finest materials. The result was Bali's first and most opulent example of Hindu-Balinese court architecture. Indigenous forms blended with Ma-

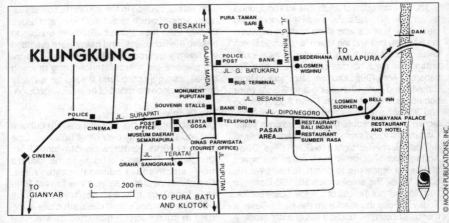

japahit motifs and techniques resulted in a unique complex, 150 meters on each side, built in the shape of a mandala—a microcosmic representation of the universe. Within the precincts of this "The Palace of the God of Love" (Semara Pura) were courtyards, gardens, and moats surrounding elegant pavilions, each serving a different function. In the northwest corner is a *kulkul* tower; on a side street to the west is the great stone gateway the Pemedal Agung, riddled with bullet holes during the *puputan.* Its main door, side doors, and arch are extensively carved; note the ridiculous-looking Dutchmen in top hats.

Pay the entrance fee of Rp1100 (Rp500 children) at the *loket* in the parking lot opposite the complex. Since the ceiling of the Kerta Gosa is high, it's a good idea to bring binoculars for more detailed study. Hire one of the wordy, vacuous, and virtually incomprehensible guides

Museum Daerah Semarapura

To the west of the Kerta Gosa is this small but functional museum (open Mon.-Fri. 0700-1700) you can visit on your ticket (Rp550 adults, Rp300 children) for Taman Gili. No English labels. The museum contains a number of old Dutch newspapers recounting firsthand the sickening *puputan*—fascinating examples of the hyperbole of the day. Exhibits also include the royal litter bearing the raja when the Dutch opened fire. Black-and-white photos of the raja

and his family, miniature cannon, ancient pounding stones, water jars.

Bale Kambang

One of the most important structures, built in the most sacred area of the compound, is open-air Bale Kambang, the Floating Pavilion. Surrounded by an artificial pond once covered in water lilies, this rectangular structure built in 1941 served as a reception pavilion for the raja's important visitors and a place of relaxation for Brahmanic judges.

The Bale Kambang was restored and enlarged by the Dutch in the early part of this century; note the whimsical statues of Dutchmen on both sides of the entrance. The date of the paintings on the ceiling is not known, but the last original work was completed, most likely, by the celebrated Kamasan artist Wayan Kayun in 1945. The paintings were last restored in 1983. Eight rows of paintings are decorated with symbols from Balinese astrology and scenes from the tale of Pan Brayut, concerning a poor couple with 18 children. Other paintings depict the legend of Sang Sutasoma, the wise old man of Balinese folk literature.

A striking status symbol of rajadom, the Bale Kambang is probably a descendant of Javanese three-tiered pagodas that served as water-locked meditation towers—remnants can be seen in the Taman Sari of Yogyakarta on Java. Architecturally, the Bale Kambang is related to the destroyed water palace at Ujung in Karangasem.

Kerta Gosa

The royal Court of Justice of the Gelgel dynasty lies at the beginning of the town center on the right, on the south side of Klungkung's main intersection. Located in the northeast corner of the Taman Gili complex, it's an elaborate open-sided pavilion reached by climbing a steep, short flight of brick steps with *naga* as balustrades.

In precolonial times the pavilion was a meeting place for the Dewa Agung and the princes and lords of the district, who assembled to discuss matters of state. From this high perch the raja and company could survey the entire palace compound, the town, and the surrounding land. It later became a courthouse where the king and his high priests sat in judgement. The supreme court of the land, the raja, with his Brahman judges and ministers, would hear cases of murder, political consipiracy, sacrilege, and breaches of caste rules. Summary justice was traditionally administered on the accused. Because of the severity of the sentences—mutilation was the most favored form of punishment—most cases were settled at the village level before a council of elders. Only the most important cases, beyond the jurisdiction of clan or village leaders, would be heard before this high court.

Although the 1908 fire destroyed most of the palace compound, the Kerta Gosa was officially reopened in 1909, designated as a court for cases involving *adat* law, as opposed to colonial law. It functioned as a court of justice until Indonesian independence in 1949.

The Dutch sponsored a renovation of the Kerta Gosa in 1920, remaining faithful to its

A panel from the ceiling murals of the former Gerta Gosa law court pavilion of Klungkung, painted in the wayang style, showing the unimaginable horrors that await sinners. The scene to the left shows the punishment being inflicted on a man who tried to seduce his best friend's wives and his own sister: his genitals are being burned by a demon with a torch. In the gory scene to the right, an enraged sow is savagely attacking a man who never married. Putting work above all human and spiritual values, he never had time for women, never married, and never had children—the most unpardonable sin of all. In vain, the man tries to tempt the sow away from his thigh by holding out nutmeg sprigs. These terrifying murals greatly influenced witnesses and defendants during hearings presided over by judges.

original design. In 1930 a group of master painters under the direction of Pan Seken completely replaced earlier, deteriorated paintings drawn on cloth. The only visual record of this group's work, applied directly on the wood of the ceiling, is a photograph taken by Walter Spies. The complex was again restored in 1960, when the Kerta Gosa's famous murals were repainted. The entire ceiling was replaced; new paintings by Pan Semaris (son of Pan Seken) depicting the story of Bima Swarga were rendered on asbestos sheeting. The last paintings, executed in 1989 to replace faded panels, are woefully inferior acrylic works. Carbon monoxide fumes, Bali's hot and humid climate, and the moisture of monsoon rains have exacted an irreversible toll on the superb 1960s work, in which no artificial dyes were used.

Meant to serve as a warning to evildoers and the guilty, every square centimeter of the walls and ceilings is covered in concentric murals painted in the traditional *wayang* style popular at the time the *puri* was constructed. The large, vaulted roof rests on carved columns, and the paintings ascend the pyramidal ceiling to a central gilded wood lotus surrounded by four fluttering doves. The various levels of heaven and hell are described through the story of Bima, the hero who journeys to the underworld to save the souls of his parents. Bima has a darker complexion than the other princes and is bereft of their winglike epaulets—he's relied upon for his strength, ferocity, and courage and has no need for such finery.

The scenes picture terrifying episodes defendants would meet after their deaths, before rebirth as dogs, snakes, or poisonous mushrooms. Thieves are boiled in oil in large copper kettles; souls are castrated, beaten, burned, and torn; birds peck out eyes; decapitated whores walk planks over seas of flames; unfortunates are sawn in half for disrespecting their parents; liars suffer clawing by tigers; women who underwent abortions have their breasts gnawed away by rats; miscreants are crushed by the elephant-king Gajahraja. All these lurid punishments are executed by fierce little demonic spirits called *buta* who work in the Kingdom of the Dead. They place wrongdoers under sword-trees which they then shake; they remove the intestines through

the anuses of those who farted in public. Old maids are chased by boars and poked with tusks; childless, promiscuous woman are forced to suckle a huge caterpillar.

Lawbreakers were obliged to attend their own trials. While relatives waited in the adjoining Bale Kambang, the accused would kneel before the all-powerful tribunal, their eyes taking in the horrendous punishments portrayed on the ceiling above. But if the wrongdoers lifted their eyes from the horrors of hell, they could perhaps find some comfort. Above hell's gruesome miseries and agonies shine the delights and beauty of heaven. The highest panels show pious souls attended by councils of divinities—the just rewards for those who lead good and honest lives.

PRACTICALITIES

Accommodations

Klungkung is not blessed with good places to stay—it's better to base yourself in Padangbai (15 km) with its much better selection of hotels and eateries, and do Klungkung on a day trip. **Graha Sanggraha** is located behind the tourist office near the mosque; Rp7000 per person, no meals. **Losmen Wishnu,** Jl. Gunung Rinjani 4, is a three-minute walk from the *terminal bis;* Rp6000 s or Rp8000 d. Rooms upstairs are better, with a balcony over the street. Central, but the place is noisy and bare-bones. Of late the odor of gasoline seems to permeate the place.

Losmen Sudihati, Jl. Diponegoro 125, is a 10-minute walk from the minibus station in the direction of Amlapura; Rp6000 s, Rp8000 d. Grubby and dark—okay in an emergency. Just around the corner, and in the same price range, is the **Bell Inn** (tel. 0366-22118). Down the road on the right on the edge of town, also toward Amlapura, is Klungkung's finest accommodation, **Ketut Oka Odean's Ramayana Palace Restaurant and Hotel,** Jl. Diponegoro 152, tel. (0366) 21044; Rp20,000 s, Rp35,000 d for any of three large, clean, well-furnished rooms. Five smaller rooms in back without *mandi* go for Rp8000 s, Rp10,000 d. Nice sitting areas on open pavilions in a flowery garden.

Food

The restaurant at the **Ramayana Hotel** serves Indo-Chinese food (*ayam goreng* Rp7000, omelette Rp2000), or eat at the **Sumber Rasa** at Jl. Nakula 5 across from the old *stanplatz*. Just a couple doors down is the Chinese-run **Bali Indah,** Jl. Nakula 1, tel. (0366) 21056—fairly clean, quite inexpensive, and only several minutes from the Kerta Gosa.

RM Sederhana, Jl. Gunung Rinjani 13, tel. (0366) 21524, is a Muslim restaurant next to Losmen Wishnu. Friendly service and cheap, local prices for delicious *sate kambing* (Rp4000), *gulai kambing* (Rp2500), and *sup ayam* (Rp2500). At dusk the bus terminal offers many *warung* serving delicious and inexpensive Balinese and Indonesian food—the best place to eat for the least money in town. The *sate* stalls are particularly good.

Shopping and Crafts

Klungkung is right on the interisland trade route and derives most of its wealth from commerce. Down some steps behind a row of shops to the east of the Kerta Gosa, right in the center of town, (past the stoplight if coming from Denpasar), is Klungkung's huge, covered, old-style Asian marketplace—the largest of its kind on Bali. This excellent *pasar* is divided into different sections—to the left is bamboo, in the back are food *warung,* to the front clothes. You'll also find spices, vegetables, fruits, flowers, sweet cakes, traditional implements, basketry, handmade housewares, *songket, ikat,* and jewelry. A real people's market. Prices are good; very crowded. Ponies, with tassles and bells on their foreheads, pull carts to and from the busy *pasar.*

Hard-sell vendors in the parking lot in front of the Kerta Gosa push souvenir-quality necklaces, fake coins, wooden sculpture, and cloth reproductions of the Court of Justice paintings (Rp25,000, first price). Along Klungkung's main street (Jl. Diponegoro) is a row of souvenir shops selling inexpensive woven *lontar* articles, gold

and silver jewelry, traditional *endek, songket, batik,* temple parasols, *wayang*-style paintings, carvings, and antiques. Find here also ceramics, old *selendang,* and clever reproductions sometimes not available in other parts of Bali.

Services

Klungkung features a row of general goods stores, a Bank Rakyat Indonesia, and a 24-hour Wartel office opposite the Kerta Gosa. Klungkung's telephone code is 0366. The tourist office (open Mon.-Fri. 0700-1700, tel. 0366-21448) is in front of Museum Daerah Semarapura on the grounds of Taman Gili. On the right as you approach Klungkung's first main intersection, there's also a gas station, an *apotik,* and good doctors. Working in the town's hospital (RSU) on Jl. Flamboyan is Dr. Julius Tanasale, tel. (0366) 21172, who studied in Thailand and specializes in tropical diseases.

Getting There and Away

From Denpasar's Terminal Kereneng, board a *bemo* to Klungkung for Rp2000. From Ubud, take a *bemo* to the Sakah intersection, then change to one for Klungkung (Rp2500 total). If coming from Candidasa (25 km) or Amlapura, make sure the *bemo* is heading straight to Klungkung; some stop and wait for ferry passengers in Padangbai. Klungkung's main *bemo* station (Terminal Kelod) is a transport hub for all *bemo* and minibuses except those heading for Besakih (21 km, Rp1000). The Besakih terminal is just north of Klungkung's main intersection.

Sample fares: Penelokan (Rp1200), Padangbai (Rp700), Amlapura (Rp1000), and Candidasa (Rp600). To Batubulan station in Denpasar it costs Rp2500 by minibus, Rp1250 by big bus. Transport out of Klungkung to Batubulan starts to wind down around 1900. After that, if you want to get back to Denpasar you have to charter (Rp20,000 and up). It can also be problematic to reach Besakih by public transport after 1500.

VICINITY OF KLUNGKUNG

At **Bukit Jambul,** eight km north of Klungkung and just north of Gembalan, the food in the restaurant is high-priced and low quality, but you can take in wide, unbroken, and breathtaking views of Klungkung Valley and Nusa Penida.

WEST OF KLUNGKUNG

Takmung
The highly revered temple of Pura Kentel Bumi ("The Temple of the Creation of the Earth") lies on the bend in the main road 10 km southwest of Klungkung, separated from the town by a wild, deep ravine. Takmung is the base for the priestly Resi Bhujangga sect that worships Lord Vishnu. North of Takmung is Aan, the home of high priest Pedanda Aan, who is often consulted each time it's necessary to determine the auspicious day to begin an important undertaking.

Tihingan
A *gong kembar* instrument-making factory near the village of Aan, Tihingan is an obligatory stop for lovers of *gamelan.* On the main road from Denpasar to Klungkung, take the turnoff at Salakan north to Tihingan (five km). You can also reach Tihingan from a road north of Sankanbuana, two km west of Klungkung (if coming from Klungkung, just keep straight ahead). The foundaries are on the right in the rice paddies; there's a sign out front.

There are a number of gongmakers in this village, employing over 100 people. The best known is the small factory run by I Ketut Lunga Yasa, whose father is a master player and instrument maker. This is a very warm and approachable family. Here they make smaller instruments— *gangsa, tawa-tawa, cengceng.* Gongs are forged on Sundays by men stripped to the waist wielding hammers against anvils set around a roaring fire pit in the ground. The pieces are then filed and polished the rest of the week. A *gender* goes for around Rp350,000, large gongs cost Rp800,000, *cengceng* around Rp50,000. These are not tourist souvenirs but actual musical instruments used in orchestras. Several showrooms (open 0700-

1500) are on the main street and the Tihingan smiths run a shop in Tohpati at the intersection of the Denpasar-Batubulan road and the Nusa Dua Highway.

While in Tihingan drop by the Puri Penetaran Pande in the village center, consecrated by the local *pande* gong. There's a magnificent *kulkul* tower supported by Rangda columns. In front of the temple is a stone statue of Twalen, the lovable clown of the Mahabharata. Under the *waringin* tree is a statue of the goddess of winds, who supplies the air for the bellows of foundaries.

Brickmaking is another cottage industry in the area (visit Penasan). Wander through the countryside and brickmakers will show you how bricks are formed in rectangular wooden molds, stacked to dry for seven days, then fit into a kiln and fired for a week using rice husks as fuel. Since the clay is dug out of the nearby topsoil, the brickmaker's factory looks like a house with a moat around it.

Museum Seni Lukis Klasik Bali
Near Tihingin, just beyond Takmung, the internationally acclaimed modern Balinese artist Nyoman Gunarsa has built this spacious three-story concrete museum (open daily except Monday 0900-1700, entrance Rp5000) devoted to 16th-19th century Balinese traditional paintings. Gunarsa has collected these rare classical paintings, many drawn on bark paper since 1982. The museum is also a center for dance, music, and the other fine arts of Bali, including embroidery, stone sculptures, carved doors, masks. Gunarsa's studio, itself within the building, is filled with old furniture, antique woodcarvings, impressionistic paintings, and traditional dance costumes. Born in 1944 in nearby Banda village, Gunarsa has twice been named the best painter in Indonesia by the Jakarta Arts Council and has put on one-man shows all over the world. His modern oil paintings of dancers and musicians now fetch up to Rp20 million apiece. Just take any public *bemo* west and get off at the giant Trimurti statue with the fake policeman at the base.

GELGEL AND VICINITY

This was once the seat of the old court of Gelgel, the capital of the kingdom of the same name which lasted almost 200 years from A.D. 1515. Founded by Javanese lords and priests, Gelgel was Bali's first unitary kingdom from which the other eight major Balinese kingdoms broke off. Gelgel reached its apogee during the reign of Batu Renggong in the late 16th century. In 1710 I Gusti Sideman moved his capital to the more strategic site of Klungkung, which controlled the road from Gianyar to Amlapura as well as the approach to Besakih, Bali's holiest temple.

Today, Gelgel is known for its pottery and beautiful handwoven ceremonial *songket.* Get here by simply turning south at the main crossroads by the Kerta Gosa in Klungkung and traveling three km, then taking a left one km to Gelgel. Except for the royal state temple of Pura Dasar and a few ruined gateways, nothing remains today of the noblest of all the Balinese rajadoms. Pura Dasar is entered through a huge outer courtyard. When the descendants of Gelgel's far-flung aristocracy arrive, this temple plays host to elaborate ceremonies on its large *bale* and *wantilan.* Try to make it here for the impressive *odalan.* Don't miss seeing the mysterious ancestral stones placed on a stone throne, and weathered Pura Nataran.

Not far away, to the east of Pura Dasar, is Gelgel Mosque, the most ancient mosque on Bali, established by Muslim immigrants who served the Dewa Agung during Bali's Golden Age. The story goes that when Muslim missionaries tried to convert the Dewa Agung, he balked at the circumcision requirement, and thus Bali remains Hindu to this day. Visitors are discouraged from entering the *mesjid,* which is smack in the center of the Muslim quarter, one of only several Islamic communities on Bali which have more of the feel of Java than of Bali (other old Muslim communities are at Kusamba in Klungkung, Sarenjawa in Karangasem, and Lovina in Buleleng).

The most significant temple in the neighborhood is Pura Jero Agung ("Great Palace Temple") built on the grounds of the former Gelgel *puri* to the west of Pura Dasar. Unusual and mysterious Pura Kuri Batu, in Jelantik village

northeast of Gelgel, features beautiful carved doors of solid stone. Who carved the doors and when no one knows. The villagers just say "the doors have always been here."

East of Gelgel is a large complex of *kuburan* and temples connected to the many noble families of Bali. North of the graveyards is Pura Dalem Gandamayu, thought to have once been the residence of the wandering Hindu priest Nirantha. One of the shrines in the temple is dedicated to the blacksmith clan; the other is kept by the descendants of Nirantha.

The nearby village of **Tangkas,** near the coast to the south, is known for its sacred *gamelan luang,* a rare and archaic ensemble combining both bamboo and bronze instruments. One km to the west of Tangkas is **Jumpai,** noted for its powerful *balian* and sacred *barong.* Visit the nearby beach of Klotok, frequent destination of pilgrims. To get there from Klungkung, take the road directly south past Gelgel until you hit the ocean.

KAMASAN AND VICINITY

Descendants of the Hindu-Javanese Majapahit court artisans still work in the villages surrounding Klungkung, practicing the same pro-

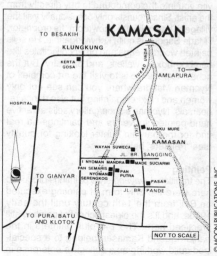

fessions as their ancestors of 25 generations ago. The coppersmith guild settled in Banjar Budaya (the western part of Semapura town), the ironsmiths in Klungkung and Kusamba, while the artists and silver- and goldsmiths established themselves in the hamlets of Banjar Jelantik and Banjar Sangging around the villages of Kamasan and Desa Tojan.

Originally a village of gold- and silversmiths who produced the crowns, body ornaments, and jewelry for the raja and his family, Kamasan later became known as a center for painters. Their art was devotional work *(ngayah)* for god or a leige lord, sent all over Bali to decorate *puri.*

When the Dutch arrived at the beginning of the century, Kamasan artists lost their royal patronage and the art of *wayang*-style painting nearly died. Kamasan underwent a resurgence when the Dutch commissioned the restoration of the Kerta Gosa paintings in the 1920s and 1930s. In the 1960s tourists and art and souvenir shops became an important source of revenue. High-ranking officials now commission works for their homes and offices.

Kamasan lies four km south of Klungkung. From Klungkung's main intersection, take a *bemo* (Rp300) down the hilly road in the direction of Klotok and ask to be dropped off at Kamasan. You know you've arrived when people start to invite you into the compound to buy directly from the artist. Since tourists only occasionally visit the village, it has only one showroom. Its proprietor, I Made Sondra, is quite knowledgeable. He sells painted wooden eggs and other collectibles like bamboo boxes, wallets, and basketry. But the richest experience is to visit the art complex of Nyoman Mandra where you can see not only women and children painting but also dance rehearsals. Nyoman's shop/gallery sells attractive hand-painted souvenirs and paintings—a real find for the bargain hunter looking for quality (see "Painters" below).

Painting

The traditional *wayang*-style paintings produced here were the only form of painting executed on Bali from the 14th century until the early 1920s, and it's the oldest school of painting still practiced here. The 140-plus painters in the *banjar* around Kamasan belong to a specialized guild working as a collective enterprise in home workshops and studios. Many of the best-known painters trace their lineage to I Gede Modara, a classical artist of the 18th century who enjoyed the patronage of the Dewa Agung.

As in the Kerta Gosa frescoes, the highly conservative, formalized Kamasan style imitates the two-dimensional shadow puppets, with faces drawn in three-quarters profile. The heroes and demons depicted are taken from the Ramayana, *Suthasoma, Pan Brayat,* and other Javanese and Bali-Hindu mythologies and literary classics. These characters are not really individuals but distinct, iconographic types. The village was once a lively center court for *dalang,* dancers, and musicians, all serving as inspiration for local painters.

It used to be paintings that depicted themes or characters that did not correspond to the accepted, cherished age-old values of the community risked severe criticism, but Kamasan's new patrons want painters to produce work with lighter themes. Kamasan painters also specialize in pictorial Balinese calendars costing Rp20,000 or less.

Kamasan paintings are actually colored drawings. Traditionally, rocks, leaves, soot, crushed limestone, bone, and other vegetable and mineral dyes produced yellow, blue, red, green, orange, caramel, dark ochre, and dark brown colors. Now poster paints are beginning to replace hand-pounded natural dyes. Cotton cloth is stretched, a layer of white rice flour starch applied, scenarios sketched from memory with charcoal, outlines drawn in with China ink, and the pigments filled in with a homemade, very fine bamboo paintbrush. Figures are usually colored orange. In the best pieces, look for figures set off by fluid and distinct black outlines. Colors are dabbed on the canvases before the black outlines, which are usually drawn by the master artist when finishing the piece. Colors should remain clear and separate without being muddied by overlapping. It takes about a month to finish a one-half-square-meter painting, including preparing the canvas and paints.

Because Kamasan lies outside the usual tourist routes, and because of the system of guide commissions that controls tourist marketing in Bali, these artists are unable to sell many paintings at a reasonable profit. The best of the Kamasan paintings are seriously undervalued and masterpieces can be purchased practically for the price of day labor and materials. The cheapest place to buy paintings is Banjar Sangging. The cloth paintings aren't usually framed and range in price from Rp100,000 to Rp750,000. Be generous; these fine traditional craftsmen are an endangered species.

Painters

The most famous and sought-after painter is **I Nyoman Mandra** (b. 1946), whose works are a favorite of international collectors and hang in European museums and galleries. Mandra is a delightful person and speaks so-so English. His students do amazing work as well, which you can observe in a government-sponsored school. Here, village children are trained to carry on this 500-year-old-tradition by imitating the master. Another well-known painter is **Mangku Mure** in Banjar Siku (the closest *kampung* to Klungkung), who sells his really big paintings for as high as 2.5 million rupiah. With Pan Semaris, Pak Mure directed the restoration of the Kerta Gosa paintings in 1960. **Ketut Rabeg** in Banjar Sangging is also considered a gifted artist. **Nyoman Serengkog**, a rare female practictioner in what used to be a male-dominated profession, is the wife of Pan Semaris and works in the adjoining *kampung*. **Ni Made Suciarmi** is another competent woman artist working in this style, see her work displayed in Ubud's Seniwati Women's Art Gallery.

PAKSABALI AND POINTS EAST

About a 10-minute drive east of Klungkung is the village of Paksabali, well known for the making of ceremonial parasols and flags. Be sure to catch the Dewa Mapalu ("Clashing of the Gods") festival celebrated at Pura Timbrah during Kuningan. Get to the temple by crossing the long suspension bridge, then taking the first asphalted road to the north; the temple's on the right side of the road. *Pratima* are carried on litters down a steep ravine for ritual bathing in the Unda River. When the bearers return, the *pratima* "refuse to go back" to the temple, so a wild free-for-all (or "god fight") ensues in which participants often fall into trance.

In Sampalan Tengah, the next village (one km) east of Paksabali, visit the *ikat* factory, which weaves designs on cotton (Rp12,500 per meter) or silk (Rp30,000 per meter). This village is also the home of Mangku Putu Cedet, Bali's preeminent traditional *undagi* (architect), his status equal to that of the island's highest ranking *dalang* or *pedanda*. Sadly, temples, ceremonial *bale*, and the occasional small Balinese-style boutique-hotel are the only opportunities left for the diversified talents of the *undagi*, his job having been largely taken over by modern-day building contractors and developers.

Three km after Sampalan Tengah, take the small paved road to the left and travel two km to the small *desa* of Dawan at the foot of Bukit Gunaksa in the foothills of Gunung Agung (in all, seven km southesast of Klungkung). Dawan is the home of Pedanda Gede Keniten, a direct descendant of the court priest of the Gelgel dynasty and a man believed to possess supernatural powers. The village lies in the middle of a *sawo*-growing area and is also renowned for its *tuak* and high-quality brown palm sugar. The adjoining village of Besang features a *pura* with the ancient *kawi* inscriptions under a soaring pagoda.

Kusamba

Take a *bemo* from Klungkung (Rp500) in the direction of Amlapura. On the descent, you'll come across gigantic lava beds, effluvia from Gunung Agung's 1963 eruption. Where the main road meets the sea, and where your nostrils meet the aroma of drying fish, about eight km east of Klungkung, is the working fishing village of Kusamba. On its sparkling, black-sand beach you can see many *jukung* in daily use. Turn south at the Y-junction in the center of town and drive about one km.

Upon Kuta's decline in the mid-1800s, Kusamba became southern Bali's busiest and most important entry port for agricultural products and slaves. It was also the center for a specialist clan of blacksmiths skilled at weapons-making. In 1849, Kusamba was the site of a pivotal fight between the Dutch and The Virgin Queen Istri Kanya; the Balinese emerged victorious and Istri Kanya has been a national heroine ever since.

The mixed and rather dour Hindu and Muslim population also mines sea salt, the other major industry of the area. Driving the coastal road east of Klungkung, you'll see small, brown, thatched, peculiarly shaped beach huts—salt-making factories. Across the road from Goa Lawah, three km east of Kusamba, they'll ask for money just to peer into one of the briny troughs; go farther up or down the coast to observe this centuries-old technique for free.

Wet, salt-rich black sand is first carried by yoked buckets from the sea and spread out on flat terraces along the beach. After drying, the sand is dumped in a large palmwood vat inside a hut. Next, seawater is leached through the sand, producing a clear, salty water which is then poured in hollowed-out coconut-log troughs set in low platforms in rows beside the huts. Under the sun's blazing heat most of the water evaporates, leaving a salt slush which is further processed into salt crystals. Weather permitting, the whole process takes two days. The salt panner can make three to five kilos of salt per day in the dry season. The coarse white sea salt, used in salting fish and not as table salt, is sold to distributors who in turn sell it in the markets of Klungkung, Amlapura, and Nusa Penida.

From Kusamba, *bemo* to Padangbai run Rp500; Denpasar Rp1000. Kusamba is also a port of embarkation for Nusa Penida. To Banjarbias Harbor it's about 500 meters from the main Klungkung-Amlapura road; for the old harbor, drive east through town past the market and take a right at the sign Dermaga Penyebarangan Kusamba. Motorized *prahu* require 45 minutes to 1.5 hours to reach the island of Nusa Lembongan or the landing stage at Toyapekeh on Nusa Penida. The fare for tourists for either of these destinations is Rp15,000 per person. The first boat, carrying sea salt, peanuts, fruit, and rice, leaves at around 0600. With enough passengers, a second boat departs in the afternoon. There are seldom any boats after 1600. The number of departures per day depends on weather, demand, cargo, and destination. These sprightly boats can carry up to 1.5 tons of cargo. They're also available for hire if you want to go snorkeling on the stunning coral reefs of Nusa Lembongan. The older harbor, on the beach in the village of Kusamba itself, also features boats to Toyapekeh, but they run less frequently.

Goa Lawah

The famous Bat Cave Goa Lawah lies just three km northeast of Kusamba and about nine km east of Klungkung on the left side of a dramatic road paralleling the sea with uninterrupted views of Nusa Penida. The holy cave begins at the foot of a rocky cliff and is said to extend all the way to the base of Gunung Agung. The ceiling is alive with thousands of fluttering, squeaking, vibrating, long-nosed fruit bats—an awesome sight. The wheeling, squealing bats are drawn again and again into the deep and dusky cavern; the noise is deafening.

A thick layer of slippery, sickly sweet bat droppings carpets the cave floor, through which bat-gorged pythons ooze in a state of surfeit. Bat excrement also covers the small shrines of a Shivaite temple guarding the cave's entrance. It's believed Pura Goa Lawah was founded in 1007 by the peripatetic holy man Empu Kuturan. The cave and temple, one of the great *sad-kahyangan* state temples of Bali, are both associated with religious rites surrounding death. The locals believe the cave harbors an enormous snake, Naga Basuki, the mythical sacred serpent of Gunung Agung and the caretaker of the earth's equilibrium. Homage is paid to this deity in the *pura*.

In 1904 the princes of Bali held a historic conference in this cave to plan action against the encroaching Dutch armies. Oral tradition says the cave leads by way of an underground river to Pura Goa ("Cave Temple") within the Besakih complex some 25 km away. A tale is told of how a prince of Mengwi actually entered the cave and emerged at Besakih, but his feat was never duplicated—entering the cave is now forbidden.

Today Goa Lawah is a real tourist trap. After alighting from the minibus, sellers of postcards and necklaces descend upon you; the parking lot is choked with *warung makanan* and souvenir stands. Watch for cheeky young girls who drape a shell necklace around your neck as a "welcome gift," then demand payment. Entrance fee Rp550. If traveling by public transport, don't arrive at Goa Lawah later than 1700; after that *bemo* to Klungkung or Denpasar (55 km) are scarce.

NUSA LEMBONGAN

A low, protected island about 11 km southeast of mainland Bali, measuring only four by three km and ringed with mangrove swamps, and palms and white sandy beaches. Inland the terrain is scrubby and very dry, with volcanic stone walls and processional avenues crisscrossing the small cactus-covered hills. Crops are meager, and the only fruit available is melon. All other food must be imported from the market in Denpasar or from the neighboring island of Nusa Penida.

The island is small enough to explore on foot, offering pristine beaches and coves, majestic views of Gunung Agung, unique Balinese architecture, and the friendliness of a simple country folk. With a lack of arable land and a severe shortage of tourist attractions, the island's economy is limited to its underwater wealth—seaweed. A secondary occupation is catering to visiting surfers. Between Nusa Lembongan and the adjacent island of Nusa Ceningan, the population is only 60,000.

There are just two villages on Nusa Lembongan—the large, spread-out administrative center of Desa Lembongan, and the village of Jungut Batu. Surfers and backpackers hang out in the latter—about 150 per month, for an average stay of three to five days. The only other visitors are European, Japanese, and Australian day-trippers on excursion boats. Jungut Batu offers the island's best accommodations and water sport opportunities. There's motorcycle traffic between the two villages and it's easy to get a lift.

Both villages are heavily involved in the cultivation of seaweed. Before government-supported commercial seafood production in 1980, the people of the island lived on maize, *singkong, ubi,* beans, and peanuts. Today most everyone is involved in one way or another with

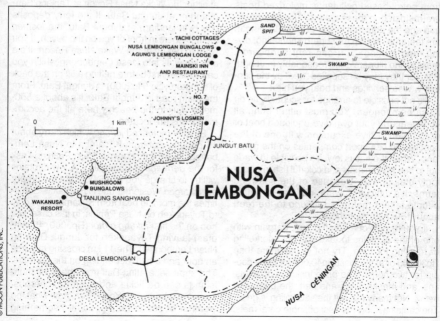

NUSA LEMBONGAN

TACHI COTTAGES
NUSA LEMBONGAN BUNGALOWS
AGUNG'S LEMBONGAN LODGE
MAINSKI INN AND RESTAURANT
NO. 7
JOHNNY'S LOSMEN
JUNGUT BATU
SAND SPIT
SWAMP
SWAMP
MUSHROOM BUNGALOWS
WAKANUSA RESORT
TANJUNG SANGHYANG
DESA LEMBONGAN
NUSA CENINGAN
0   1 km

© MOON PUBLICATIONS, INC.

cultivation of "sea vegetables," and the air is permeated with its smell.

Visit the seaweed gardens at low tide; they look like gigantic underwater botanical gardens. Two kinds are grown, the small red *pinusan* and the large green *kotoni*. Almost the entire crop is exported to Hong Kong for use in the cosmetics and food processing industries. After harvesting, gatherers leave a floating offering of rice and flowers that gently drifts away on the outgoing tide.

Life on Nusa Lembongan is very relaxing, with cool breezes, little traffic, no big hotels, no pollution, no stress, no photocopy machines, and hardly any telephones. Best of all, there are almost no *pedagang acung* (pushy vendors) and few thieves. Jungut Batu's charming "tree house" bungalow-style accommodations—with outdoor open-air *mandi*, rickety wooden furniture, sand-floor restaurants and offices—are reminiscent of Kuta Beach 20 years ago.

Water Sports

Since the seaweed gardens must be protected from petrol-based pollutants, motorized boats are restricted in these waters. Nusa Lembongan and the adjacent island of Nusa Ceningan are therefore known for superb snorkeling, diving, and surfing. You can rent surfboards, masks, and flippers quite reasonably in Jungut Batu, or they may be supplied "free" by the captain whose services and boat you hire.

It's not possible to arrange for scuba diving on Nusa Lembongan. You must either bring all your gear and your own dive-equipped boat or accompany a dive excursion with one of the specialized sea sport companies on the mainland. When the tide is low, it's possible to wade out to see reef animals and colorful fish in amazingly clear water. Because of the seaweed farms, it's difficult to wade out that far; most people take a motorized *jukung* to the reef, about 150 meters offshore.

If you're part of a small group, bargain with one of the captains to take you out snorkeling or trawling for tuna. Try not to pay more than Rp30,000 or at the most Rp40,000 for three people for two hours. The price includes snorkels, fins, and masks, lines and bait, the boat, and petrol. Not many fish but the snorkeling is great. The captains know the best offshore coral reefs.

Probably the best is Mushroom Bay, a small cover within easy reach of Jungutbatu, named after it's extensive mushroom coral.

Getting There

Public boats run from Kusamba and Padangbai, but the most popular point of embarkation is from Sanur, where *prahu motor* depart from in front of the Ananda Hotel (north of the Grand Bali Beach Hotel). Ask for *stasiun bot*. Buy your ticket in the small ticket office on the left at the end of Jl. Hangtua. It's Rp15,000 one-way for tourists and Rp3000 for locals. Boats usually leave only in the morning; in the afternoon the waves are too rough.

It's quite a trick to board. You run out to the boat between the waves while carrying your stuff on your head to keep it out of the waist-deep water, trying to climb aboard before the next big wave crashes over you. Sometimes help is required to push the boat over the sand and out to sea.

Sit in the back near the motors—you won't get as wet and you'll be first off the boat. You'll alight at either the Waka Nusa Resort at Tanjung Sanhyang or at Jungut Batu. If the ferry deposits you (wet landing) at Jungut Batu, the *losmen* are right there in front of you on the beach. If you want to get off at the Waka Nusa Resort, it's a one km walk into Desa Lembongan which you can explore first before getting a lift on the back of a motorcycle (Rp2000) to Jungut Batu. From the main road in Jungut Batu, it's about a 500-meter walk to the beach where all the accommodations are located.

Smaller motorized *jukung*, which carry about 15 people, sail from Kusamba to Nusa Lembongan. Turn right down Jl. Pasir Putih and ask for the *dermaga* in Banjarbias. A few captains will try to charge you Rp25,000, but the proper overcharged Westerner rate is Rp15,000. Sometimes the morning boat from Kusamba sails only to Toyapekeh on Nusa Penida; in this case, just hop on the first *jukung motor* (Rp3000, 45 minutes) leaving Toyapekeh for Jungut Batu on Nusa Lembongan. The 11 km crossing requires an hour and a half, depending on the currents. The strait separating Bali from these offshore islands can be fickle and even treacherous. Lives have been lost. You never know what the weather or sea will bring, so hire something substantial. Boats also leave when full from Padangbai (Rp4000, 1.5 hours).

One-way charters from Sanur or Kusamba cost around Rp60,000-75,000 to Nusa Lembongan or Nusa Penida. Per day the charter rate is Rp250,000, depending on the size and speed of the boat. If four or five people contribute to a charter, you can visit not only Nusa Lembongan but also Nusa Ceningan and Nusa Penida. The boatmen always want their money in advance, "to buy petrol."

Returning to Bali

The boats to Sanur leave Jungut Batu at 0400 or 0500. After 0600 it can prove expensive— Rp60,000 and up for a charter. Be prepared to get pretty wet even in a calm sea. Alternatively, you can grab a boat from Jungut Batu to Toyapekeh at around 0500; from there take the local boat to the mainlaind. Or climb aboard the speedy *Bali Hai* back to Sanur for Rp100,000; a small canoe will take you from Jungut Batu's beach out to the hydrofoil by 1400. The *Bali Hai* sails back to Sanur at around 1500. From Jungut Batu to Banjarbias in Kusamba, there's only one regular boat in the very early morning. The fare is a flat Rp15,000 per person—no bargaining. You could possibly find a seawood farmer in Jungut Batu who will take you across cheaper. Again, you may have to get yourself over to Toyapekeh on Nusa Penida to catch a boat.

Cruises to Nusa Lembongan

At least a dozen companies offer marine recreational tours to Nusa Lembongan. Craft range from slick high-tech specialized vessels to romantic tall ships. All pick up passengers early in the morning at Bali hotels, take them to Nusa Lembongan for two or three hours, feed them a lavish hot buffet lunch, then sail back to Bali into a tropical sunset.

A very elegant experience is the sleek catamaran *Wakalouka* (tel. 0361-261129, fax 261130; Rp145,000), boasting pool, oceanarium, glass-bottom boat, and barbecue seafood lunch. If it's swashbuckling you desire, take the gaff-rigged ketch *Golden Hawk* (Rp165,000), older than the Statue of Liberty and looking like something that sailed out of *Seven Years Before the Mast*. For a relaxing day excursion, and an extraordinary banquet, try the hydrofoil *Bali Hai*

(tel. 0366-234331, Rp150,000), which thunders and bounces in a straight line to Nusa Lembongan. The *Bali Hai* also offers a Hawaiianstyle "Sunset Dinner Cruise" for Rp75,000, departing at 1800 and returning at 2030. Bali Yacht Charters runs day cruises to Nusa Lembongan on the 47-foot sloop *Ocean Lady II* departing from Benoa Harbor at 0900 and returning at 1700. The Rp150,000 per person price—good value—includes all food and drinks, coral viewing, and island exploring. Call Dewi, Atik, or Captain Patrick, tel. (0366) 287739. Also, any major hotel on Bali carries brochures advertising day trips to Nusa Lembongan.

JUNGUT BATU

The island's only tourist-oriented beach inns, homestays, and restaurants are concentrated in this small seaside village which stretches for 1.5 km along the northwest coast. With just the sound of the waves, distant radios, crowing roosters, and an occasional motorbike, this is Bali at its best. The beer is cold and cheap and the clothing super casual—*sarung*, surf shorts, barefeet. There's not much to do except surf, snorkel, read, sleep, eat, drink, hang out. You go mad if you stay any longer than two weeks.

Come in January in the off-season—no one's here and the waves are really good. Jungut Batu is also one of the best places to take children on Bali. Nothing to do but play with the local children; there's a karate club for young ones, and during each full moon a festival and cockfights. Even in the busy tourist season. There's always lots of activity on the long beach or in the water—children flying kites, boats loading and unloading goods and passengers, seaweed gatherers walking and weaving between their gardens, no speeding motorboats or prowling hawkers like in Kuta. The sun sets right over Sanur's Bali Beach Hotel and at night lights twinkle all along the southeast coast of Bali.

Lining the beach are five eco-friendly bamboo surfer-style restaurants, several with TVs and videocassette players. Bring your CD player— lots of CDs, as well as books. If you bring your own tapes, they'll play them in the restaurants, though the blaring TVs and stereos seem out of place and drown the sound of wind and waves.

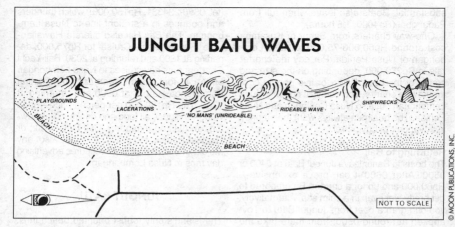

JUNGUT BATU WAVES

PLAYGROUNDS

LACERATIONS

'NO MANS' (UNRIDEABLE)

RIDEABLE WAVE

SHIPWRECKS

BEACH

BEACH

NOT TO SCALE

© MOON PUBLICATIONS, INC.

Also bring lots of cash, because there's no place here to change money. Also no telephone office.

A daily spectacle is the arrival of the luxury hydrofoil the *Bali Hai*. The ship moors for an hour at a wet dock off Jungut Batu, then used as a base by passengers who dive and snorkel within a roped-off area 200-300 meters from shore. Half the guests never leave the boat, remaining onboard in air-conditioned comfort, drinking and eating. The food is fantastic—shrimp, lobster, the finest wines.

From Jungut Batu walk to observe the island's birdlife. It's a hot but level three km walk (30 minutes) south to the main village of Desa Lembongan on the southern coast of the island. Take the stairs at the south end of the beach up into the hills; from there you get a fine view over Nusa Lembongan and the island of Nusa Penida. Tanjung Sanghyang is a 4.5 km walk west of Jungutbatu. Also explore the sandspit extending off the northwest coast.

Water Sports

Four of the best surf breaks in the world are off the Jungut Batu beach: Playground, Shipwreck, Lacerations, and Surgery. Why the foreboding names? Because you're surfing over deadly coral formations. If you slip and fall into these mushrooms of multicolored, razor-sharp coral, it's like jumping into a rubbish bin of broken glass. And there's only one doctor (in Desa Lembongan) on the whole island.

A surfer's typical day? Get up at sunrise, in the water by 0615, surf for two hours, eat breakfast and meet new people at Agung's until siesta time, snooze, arise and play cards, read, and the like. Some surfers warm up by paddling out to the breaks, but it's easier to charter a motorized *jukung* for Rp2000-3000. Catching one is as easy as catching a *bemo*. If you fork over Rp10,000, the *jukung* will wait in the channel a couple of hours.

Lacerations is a tubey right-hander with a name that speaks for itself. The tunnel waves are so big you can drive a bus through them. One of the best right-handers in the world, it's perfectly round with a perfectly calm channel in the middle. The tunnels occur only during high tide with the right sort of moon. **Surgery** is on the south side of the floating platform—a fast left-hander. A perfect right breaking over a coral reef grown over an old shipwreck is appropriately called **Shipwrecks.** From the beach you can see the prow of the ship sticking out of the ocean. This powerful right-hander, the most consistent wave on the island, ranges from a small mellow hot dog wave to a hairy stand-up tube. You can surf this break at any tide, but it usually fades at low tide. Watch the strong riptide. From the beach it's a long crawl—10-15 minutes (300 meters)—to Shipwrecks, but a *jukung* will take you out for Rp1500. **Playgrounds** is a left-hander, less consistent than Shipwrecks. It's a good fun wave that can get pretty scary at low tide, as the reef is sharp and the water shallow.

Dive tours to Nusa Lembongan can be arranged by the **Bali Adventure Club** at Tanjung Benoa, tel. (0366) 271767, **Baruna Watersports Bali,** tel. (0366) 751223-6, and **Oceania Dive Center** on Jl. Bypass in Sanur, tel. (0366) 288892, fax 288652. Surf tours to Lombok and Sumbawa can be organized at **Mainski Inn** in Jungut Batu. Rates are around Rp150,000 per person per day including transport, dive master, equipment, refreshments, and box lunch.

Accommodations

All accommodations face the beach—there's nothing between you, the crashing waves, and the setting sun. All water here tastes salty. Almost all accommodations feature generators (turned on only from 1830 to around 2300) and attached bathrooms. Places with two-story treehouse-style bungalows with upstairs verandas like the Nusa Lembongan Bungalows offer the best ventilation. Choose a bungalow with mosquito nets and screens on the windows. Few places have bars on the windows, just flimsy door locks, but thievery is kept to a minimum since everybody knows everybody. Ask for a lower per day price for extended stays or if the place doesn't have electricity. The tariff is less in the low season (Nov.-Feb.). The farther south you go, the cheaper the accommodations. Bobby's and No. 7 is only Rp5000 in the low season, and there's even a place between the police station and No. 7 that costs Rp3000 s, but it offers only grass huts with holes in the walls. Breezy atmosphere, no electricity. The Mainski Inn (Rp25,000) is Jungut Batu's most westernized, professionally run accommodations. Mellower and less expensive are "beach inns" and "beach bungalows" like the Nusa Lembongan Beach cottages. There are 10 places to stay in all, plus two in the village itself (be prepared for roosters).

Most remote is **Mushroom Beach Bungalows,** two coves and ridges south of Jungut Batu. It's almost too remote because you have to take a boat to Jungut Batu for a decent meal, unless you want to pay Rp20,000 for the smorgy at the nearby Waka Nusa Resort. Six rooms with double beds, wardrobe, and shower go for Rp25,000-30,000. Breakfast of tea, coffee, and toast; electricity from 1700 until 0700. Simple meals are served; remember, houseboys are

not known for their culinary skills. If there's fish, it's served. Great view over a private cove. Fifty meters away is a white-sand, pollution-free beach with offshore coral and fishlife. Very quiet and peaceful.

As soon as you get off the boat **Bobby's and No. 7** is on the right. This *losmen* is at the south end of the beach, farthest from the sunken ship. Nice people and nicely furnished rooms (Rp7000 s in the off-season, Rp15,000 s in July and August), breakfast included; good food. Garden. Staff will even help argue the price of the boat back to the mainland. **Johnny's,** south of Agung's and 50 meters from the beach, charges Rp7000 s. Indonesian-style *mandi*. A favorite of budget-surfers.

Agung's Lembongan Lodge and Restaurant offers four two-level bungalows big enough for a family, with electricity, WC, *mandi*, and porch for Rp15,000-30,000. Clean and pleasant, the clientele is mostly surfers. Agung's also has *losmen*-style rooms with two beds, bathrooms, and electricity for Rp8000-10,000 d. Good food. **Tarci Bungalows and Restaurant,** north of Agung's, has bungalows for Rp25,000. Each can hold up to four people. The four bungalows in front are split into upper (Rp15,000) and lower (Rp10,000) units. A single bungalow called **Eka Dharma** must rank as one of the best places to stay on the island. A very agreeable young man, a family member, oversees the bungalow. His name is I Nyoman Yudana; his seaweed storage barn and boat are next door. Nyoman will take you out snorkeling on his boat (Rp10,000), or you can go out when he and his brother tend their seaweed gardens. Facing Agung's with the water to your back, it's down the beach to the right about 150 meters.

Wayan Mandra is a former seaweed farmer who runs **Nusa Lembongan Bungalows** with his son I Wayan Adnyana; write to Jl. Hangtuah, Gang Mawar IX/9, Br. Batanpoh, Sanur. Eight bungalows renting for Rp20,000 s, Rp25,000 d in the middle of a coconut grove; the bungalows in the back are cheapest. Each two-story treehouse-style bungalow features a bath and sitting room, bamboo furniture, a skylight roof for cool breezes, a large double bed with clean sheets and mosquito net, and tea whenever you want it. In the rainy season (Dec.-Feb.) enjoy the nice garden. Wayan and his family treat you real good, on occasion even laying on young coconuts, *nasi campur,* or a fish dinner. Good security. An excellent deal.

Mainski Inn has nine spacious, double-story bungalows with nice upstairs rooms with thatched roofs, bamboo walls, and balconies open to the sea. Cost: Rp10,000 to Rp20,000, plus seven percent tax and service; rates go up in the busy season. Breakfast sometimes included. The most solid, well-built bungalows on the island, with big rooms, easy access to the path to the main road, and an outstanding second-story restaurant (videos in the evening). There's a good sound system—mostly loud disco and rap music—so bring tapes if you want your own music. The walls are covered with surfing decals. Peruse their bulletin board for information on island towns and surf safaris to Sumbawa.

Food
North of the main part of the village are a number of quite stylish beachfront tourist restaurants with luxurious oversized furniture. Kuta-style menus include Aussie jaffles, vegetable soups, Euro-breakfasts, delicious ice drinks, *gado-gado,* salads, and yogurt. Many items are unavailable, but the food is surprisingly good for such a remote area. The fresh fish, including lobster, are the best deals. If you go fishing or spearfishing and catch a reef fish or a lobster, the restaurants will cook it up for you. Suckling pig may be ordered in advance. Several *warung* in the village serve *nasi campur.*

No. 7 has the cheapest meals of any accommodation. With its tile floor and color TV, **Agung's** is one of the more popular places to eat. Certainly it's the most Westernized. Use the house binoculars to observe the surfers. The best place to view the sunset is Mainski Inn's upper-level restaurant. **Mainski's** has an unusual menu with lots of variety, and it changes every day. Try the killer vegetable pie (Rp3000)—great with an order of guacamole on top. Ask for the grilled tuna, the best dish. If you walk straight back from Mainski Inn to the main road, turn right to the pool hall and stroll 50 meters past; on the left is a *warung* with the coldest beer on the island. The restaurant in front of Tarci's has a full menu with good chili pizza. Small beers Rp1700, big ones Rp3500.

Shopping
Original woven articles are sold in the **Mermaid Shop** in the village. From 1100 to 1500 take a boat (Rp1500) out to the *Bali Hai* and shop in the big kiosk on the upper deck. Purchase film, batteries, shaving cream, razors, souvenirs, T-shirts, and coolers. This boat plugs you into the world; use your American Express card.

Services and Getting Around
A small post office is open 0800-1400; there's a larger post office in Sampalan on Nusa Penida. One doctor practices in Desa Lembongan. A dozen motorcycles are for rent at Rp10,000-15,000 per day. *Jukung motor* rent for around Rp10,000 per hour or Rp150,000 per day. A few bicycles rent for Rp5000 per day but they're so primitive you have to push them up hills. Get one with springs in the seats.

From Jungut Batu to Nusa Penida
A motorized ferry leaves at high tide at 0500 or 0530 and costs only Rp3000 per person (45 minutes). It's filled with people who shop for chicken, vegetables, and fruit in the market in Sampalan. Leaving Jungut Batu, you get a very picturesque tour of the bay: the adjacent ridges, beaches, and coves, the moored *Bali Hai,* the shipwreck, workers gathering seaweed from their farms. The channel separating Nusa Lembongan and Nusa Penida is unexpectedly deep, in some places over 120 meters. This early morning trip is beautiful, but it's possible to charter a trip later in the day for Rp15,000-20,000. It's about a 10-minute walk from Jungut Batu's beach inns to where the *jukung motor* picks up passengers for Nusa Penida.

DESA LEMBONGAN

With a population of around 4,000, Desa Lembongan is the largest village on the island. Its inhabitants also cultivate seaweed. Besides the temple high on a hill up a long flight of steps, about the only other *obyek wisata* in Desa Lembongan is the Underground House. Not really a house but a damp, cool, earthen cave with many passages, dips, tunnels, and exits. Watch your step and don't get lost in this rather forbidding labyrinth. The candle provided isn't really enough; you'll also need a flashlight. Built by the puppeteer Jero Mangku from 1961 until he died; they say the old man believed that he was cursed and wanted to hide. An eerie place. From Desa Lembongan, it's a one km walk northwest to Tanjung Sanghyang.

If you take the road north from Desa Lembongan, the mangroves thicken as the channel between Lembongan and Ceningan gradually narrows; where the land meets two temples face each other. A four-km track heads north past more swamps, salt vendors huts, and finally Pura Empuaji on the stunning northernmost point of the island. From this sacred temple take a right two km back to Jungut Batu.

TANJUNG SANGHYANG

Means "Beautiful Peninsula." The closest village to Desa Lembongan on the Bali side of the island. Very easygoing; a huge banyan tree dominates the beach. One *warung* near the beach serves *nasi campur* (Rp1000). The big attraction here, providing employment for the locals, is the **Waka Nusa Resort,** a tastefully designed, beautifully furnished facility with spectacular snorkeling and no vendors.

You approach this small, environmentally friendly resort on an environmentally friendly vessel—the club caters almost exclusively to patrons of the catamaran *Wakalouka.* When the ship pulls into port, this sleepy cove is transformed into a lively beach party; the centerpiece is a full seafood barbecue lunch buffet for Rp20,000 per person. Check out the four-tank aquarium—a taste of what you'll see yourself on a deep dive. A total fantasy world set in palm trees, with a nice white-sand beach out front facing a small cove where a small native fishing fleet bobs at anchor.

The Waka Nusa Resort is the *Wakalouka*'s only destination. The tour starts in Benoa, runs down the Sanur Reef, then turns east to Nusa Lembongan and moors off the beach. No other day-resort package offers such a class act. Guests may handline tuna over the rail, watch dolphin, swim in the pool, drink in the lounge,

frolic or lay on the beach, snorkel any of three reefs. The *Wakalouka,* a Learjet of the water, takes no more than 40 passengers at Rp154,000 apiece.

Combining luxury and simplicity, the Waka Nusa Resort's very limited number of bungalows offer big beds, private bathrooms, natural ventilation, *alang-alang* roofs, sundeck, and private verandas and gardens. The resort also maintains a Toyota to run guests to the villages, the local temple, or seaweed farms. For reservations call (0366) 261129 or 261130, or contact PT Tourdevco in Benoa (tel. 0366-231591 or 231592).

NUSA CENINGAN

The small, neighboring isle of Nusa Ceningan can be reached by boat (Rp5000) from Desa Lembongan or by simply walking out to it across the narrow, shallow 200 meter wide channel at low tide. The sea between the two islands is filled with seaweed gardens, so take a guide so you don't cause damage. The four-by-one-km island, with a limestone and chalky landscape and a 100-meter-high hill in the center, only has one village and no places to stay. It does offer great surfing, sandy beaches, and lazuli and cobalt-blue coral pools filled with starfish.

Immaculate snorkeling and scuba diving, with superior visibility and infinite small sealife, is possible in the calm, warm, crystal-clear channel between the two islands. Off the temple is a surf break which can jump in size quickly, as the waves come straight in from deep water onto a shallow ledge. The best way to get out to the breaks and around the indefinite channel between the two islands is to hire an outrigger: Rp10,000 for two to three hours.

The Balinese spearfish here, using homemade wooden spears. They even spear two-inch fish. Watch the sharks in this area. A Balinese was killed off Nusa Ceningan in 1988. He'd speared a sea turtle and was dragging it bleeding through the water when he was attacked. His headless corpse was found two days later. A dangerous sport.

NUSA PENIDA

Rarely visited by tourists, the towering southern seacliffs of the mysterious and foreboding island of Nusa Penida are clearly visible from Sanur Beach. The district capital is Sampalan, the island's principal town about 18 km from the island of Bali. There's only one other town of any size—Toyapekeh—and about 15 villages scattered along the coasts and in the acorched and inhospitable highland interior of the island.

Because of its mountains, Nusa Penida gets more rain, produces more crops, and is therefore better off economically than Nusa Lembongan or Nusa Ceningan. Nusa Penida and its satellite islands offer fine swimming, surfing, snorkeling, scuba diving, and sunbathing, also dramatic walks, unspoilt scenery, deep caves, and delightful, friendly villages. Not an island rich in elaborate temples, dance and drama performances, or the plastic arts, Nusa Penida is like a Balinese outpost transplanted to some alien shore. It's off the map, metaphorically speaking.

Radio communication between Klungkung and Sampalan wasn't established until 1985. The island has one hospital and one post and telegraph office. Generator-supplied electricity—and TV reception—exist only in the Sampalan area. The highlands, with its rough beauty, crude dwellings, and backward inhabitants, feel like the interior of Sumbawa. The roads are generally good, though there's very little traffic. People are easy to meet and talk to. The island is cooler than the mainland, there's less pollution, and the air seems to circulate more freely. Sampalan and Toyapekeh have the only official accommodations. Rice, fish, and vegetables are the main staples in the island's *warung*. Most visitors stay in Jungut Batu on Nusa Lembongan and come over to Nusa Penida island on day trips.

Land and Climate
The body of water separating the three islands from Bali—Nusa Penida, Lembongan, and Ceningan—roughly marks the division between Asia and Oceania. As the Balinese say, "Here the tigers end."

Though the Badung Strait that separates the islands and the main island of Bali is more than 100 meters deep, the trench in the Lombok Strait between Nusa Penida and Lombok is even deeper. Here the sea plunges to depths of over 300 meters just four km off Nusa Penida's east coast. The main island, nearly rectangular—22 by 16 km—with a total area of 203 square km, is basically a giant slab of limestone seabed uplifted out of the ocean. In its center is a stepped, rocky plateau—clearly seen as you approach the coast by boat from Bali—very similar in terrain and geology to the Bukit Peninsula of south Bali. A string of low, beautiful, palm-fringed, silvery white sandy beaches are found along the north, northwest, and northeast coasts, fringed with coral gardens. With waves crashing against sheer cliffs up to 230 meters high, Nusa Penida's southeastern and southwestern coastlines, which face the Indian Ocean, are rugged and magnificent. You can drive to within several hundred meters, hike to the top, then walk down steep paths to springs emerging at the foot of the cliffs just above the sea.

Flora and Fauna
No native vegetation here. The island's few uncultivated patches are mostly imported weeds and grass. In stark contrast to Bali, Nusa Penida is a dry, hostile land of arid hills, big cacti, low trees, patches of green, small flowers, thorny bush, shallow soil, and no running surface water. The few animals who live—or rather, survive—on Nusa Penida include birds, snakes, and *kra*. Walter Spies, in a trip to the island during the 1930s, discovered unusual copper-colored bats that derive their color from algae which grow in their hollow hair.

Birdlife—like white cockatoos—is more Australian than Asian. White cockatoos inhabit Nusa Penida. Other rare species, like the white-tailed tropicbird and the white-bellied sea eagle, breed in the spectacular cliffs of the southeast coast. The island is also the home of the exceedingly rare Rothchild's mynah and a breed of cock much prized as an offering in exorcistic rituals.

History

Once known as the Siberia of Bali, Nusa Penida was formerly a penitentiary island of banishment for criminals, undesirables, and political agitators fleeing the harsh and unyielding reign of the Gelgel dynasty. The inhabitants were overwhelmingly of the Sudra caste, with few Ksatriya and Brahmana among them. In Balinese mythology, the island is the home of the fanged giant Jero Gede Macaling, who periodically sends his invisible henchmen to southeastern Bali via the beach at Lebih, spreading plagues, famines, droughts, and rats. The word *caling* means "fang" and those dying of cholera on Bali are said to be *"ambil Macaling"* ("taken by Macaling"). Mainlanders attempt to chase the demons away by means of exorcistic trance dance-dramas such as the *sanghyang dedari*.

Although I Macaling has his own temple, Pura Dalem Penataran Ped near Desa Ped on the northeast coast, no cult images of this god of pestilence exist and he is spoken of only in hushed tones. The Balinese are loath to even utter his name, preferring to refer to him simply by the honorific title Beliau. In exchange for prescribed devotional rituals, I Macaling is expected to protect the people.

Economy

The level of chalk content in Nusa Penida's soil makes it impenetrable to water; lacking water for rice, the people grow only maize, sweet potato, cassava, soybeans, peanuts, mangoes, *sawo bali,* tobacco, and grass for cows. *Tegelan* rice is grown in the Tanglad area once a year. Except for seaweed off the coasts and coconut and cashew plantations in coastal areas, agricultural crops grown on the mostly dry, mountainous terrain are for domestic consumption, not for export.

All garden terraces are faced with the island's most abundant material—stone. Nusa Penida is literally covered in terraces supported by small coral stones. The government periodically sponsors *transmigrasi* programs to resettle the inhabitants in South Sulawesi. In an attempt to stem the devastating runoff and irrigate unproductive land, lined rain-catchment tanks and reservoirs have been built with the help of overseas aid programs. Concrete cisterns, a few wells drilled in the low coastal regions, and springs at the foot of cliffs in the south are the only sources of water during the long dry season.

There is no manufacturing or even cottage industry, save for a few women weaving *ikat,* and everything on the island is imported from Bali—motorcycles, cows, generators, most of the island's rice, even earth moving equipment.

Nusa Penida's most lucrative export is edible seaweed, grown in submarine pens along the northwest and northeast coasts, off Nusa Lembongan and in the channel between Nusa Lembongan and Nusa Ceningan. After drying on the beach and along the roads the seaweed is exported to Hong Kong for processing into agar, a thickening agent used in cooking, and carrageenan used in cosmetics and in crackers, sauces, condiments, and other food products. There's a big difference between the traditional, poor, cassava dependent, rural hill villagers of the arid interior and the more prosperous seaweed-farming villagers of the coast, which have become market dependent and can at least fish for their protein. The average seaweed farmer earns about Rp200,000 per month.

A small-scale fishing industry catches mostly sardines and Bali's largest and most succulent lobsters. On the south coast fishermen descend paths to the sea, where they fish from platforms protruding from the sheer cliff walls.

The People

The island's lack of infrastructure, meager resources, and harsh living conditions account for Nusa Penida's relatively small population of 47,000. The bulk are Hindu. Toyapekeh is the only part-Islamic village, consisting of a mixture of Sasak, Bugis, Malay, and Javanese settlers whose ancestors migrated hundreds of years ago.

Nusa Peniders are commonly thought to possess knowledge of black magic and are given wide berth by other Balinese. Most speak or understand a little Indonesian, but use their own peculiar vernacular of Old Balinese sprinkled with many words borrowed from Lombok. They have their own *adat,* dances, puppetry, weaving arts, and architecture. The dour and cheerless people of the central plateau live in austere one-room huts built of jagged limestone blocks, surrounded by rustic stables, storage sheds, the family shrine *(sanggah),* and terraced dry fields.

Most festivals and religious events are devoted to appeasing, deceiving, or exorcising the black-faced demon-king Jero Gede Mencaling and his white-skinned wife Jero Luh. Personified in giant puppets *(barong landung),* these terrifying deities dance and strut through village streets at festival times. Another popular exorcistic dance is *sanghyang jaran,* held during times of catastrophe in the Sakti area of west Nusa Penida.

Dance costumes, body ornaments, and gestures are less elaborate than on Bali. In Cemulik (near Sakti) and Pelilit (in the southeast), the *gandrung* is performed on Purnama, Tilem, and Kajeng Kliwon. In this dance two adolescent boys dress as women. The group *baris gede* dance is staged during *odalan* at Batunuggul, and the archaic *baris pati* is performed in graveyards during cremations, and the *baris jangkang* is occasionally trotted out to welcome officials to Sekartaji.

Water Sports

As a dive and snorkeling locale, Nusa Penida is at least as spectacular as Bunaken in North Sulawesi. But it's a long and expensive ride, and, once there, cold, strong, unpredictable swells and currents up to four or more knots make conditions challenging and even hazardous. Not the place for beginners. No dive operators exist on Nusa Penida so finding a well-organized dive outfit on Bali, a knowledgeable guide with plenty of experience in the area, a reliable craft, skilled boatmen, and a good engine are all necessities. The best dive sites, in the channel between Nusa Penida and Nusa Ceningan, are close together and you can move to alternate locations as conditions dictate.

Two of the most convenient sites lie off the *dermaga* east of Toyapekeh. Fish life, particularly pelagics, tuna, jacks, and reef sharks, are common; manta rays collect on the southwest end of the island. The variety of coral along the drop-offs and steep slopes is incredibly rich, but because of deep upwellings the water can be uncomfortably cold, dropping to below 19° C during the Balinese winter. Visibility, up to 15 meters, is quite good.

Crafts

Nusa Penida's weaving style is called *tenun Bali ikat cagcag,* or by the local names *cepuk* or *capuk.* Goods are woven by hand on backstrap

looms in the plateau villages of Tanglad and Karang. Distinctive blood-red, brown, and yellow traditional cloths with plaid and rough checkered designs are worn by participants in lifecycle ceremonies. The per meter price depends on the quality of the material and the intricacy of the design. A three-meter-long, one-meter-wide fabric usually sells for roughly Rp40,000. Nyoman at Bungalow Pemda in Sampalan sells cloth for only Rp6000 per meter. Clothes are also hung in Sampalan's **Kios Dew,** a few shops in Toyapekeh, and in the souvenir shops of Klungkung.

Getting There

Kusamba is a small Muslim fishing village on the southeast coast of Bali, a six-km *bemo* ride east of Klungkung (Rp600). Turn in at Jl. Pasir Putih east of 1.5 km east of the town of Kusamba and walk 500 meters to Banjarbias, where you'll see small, bullish outboard-powered outriggers taking on cargo. Boats usually leave twice daily (Rp15,000 for Westerners), but only when there are enough passengers. Another departure point, preferred by Nusa Penida residents, is from Kampung Kusamba about 100 meters from the *pasar.* These motorized outriggers carry passengers to, among other places, Toyapekeh on Nusa Penida. Make sure you're on the right boat. The charge for Westerners is also Rp15,000 one way and the 10-km passage takes 45 minutes to one hour, depending on the wind and the choppiness of the water. When you arrive in Toyapekeh, there are frequent *bemo* to Sampalan (Rp500, nine km). To charter a boat from Kusamba to any point on Nusa Penida's north coast costs Rp100,000-150,000 roundtrip. Boats must return to Kusamba by 1400.

From Padangbai the charge is the same. Buy your ticket in the *loket* to the north of the main Lombok ferry ticket office. The first express ferry departs at around 0630, but you have to wait for it to fill up. And you might wait awhile, what with its 45-passenger capacity. The crossing takes just 30 minutes, docking at Buyuk just east of Toyapekeh. From there you can hop a *bemo* east into Sampalan (Rp500, five km). From Jungut Batu on the northwest coast of the neighboring island of Nusa Lembongan, small *jukung motor* shoot over to Nusa Penida for Rp3000 per person (45 minutes). Landing at the charming fishing village of Toyapekeh, you have the option of spending the night in **Losmen Tenang** or going on into Sampalan.

Prahu sail from Sanur to Toyapekeh (25 km, 1.25 hours, Rp15,000) very early in the morning. Check out the day cruises offered by Bali International Yacht Club, tel. (0361) 288391, in Sanur; Bali Intai Tours and Travel, tel. (0361) 752005 or 752985 in Tuban; and many other outfits that visit the south coast of Nusa Penida. These cruises charge around Rp160,000 per person, which includes free transport to the boat, drinks, packed lunch or Indonesian buffet, and fishing and snorkeling equipment.

Getting Around

Roads cover the island; good roads run from Toyapekeh to Sampalan and on to Karangsari, and from Toyapekeh to Klumpu. The roads from Klumpu to Batumadeg, Tanglad, and Pejukutan are winding and bumpy but asphalted and traversable. Because of the island's rocky, undulating topography, only motorcycles, trucks, or tough canopied *bemo* can manage the bumpy, dusty roads of the outlying areas.

Bemo run irregularly between the main villages, connecting north coast towns and inland settlements. From Sampalan, *bemo* begin carrying passengers out to the villages early in the morning, but by the afternoon the terminal is all but empty.

The best way to get around quickly is by motorcycle. As soon as you get off the boat at Buyuk or wander into the Sampalan terminal you'll be approached by motorcycle owners or drivers. You can either drive or be driven. It's cheaper to drive yourself, though the drivers know all the best places, can introduce you to people, and speak better Indonesian. It's Rp20,000 for a motorcycle and driver for just a few hours; for that price don't accept anything less than six hours. Expect a per diem price reduction if you take the motorbike for more than a day. Or wait a few days to meet someone, and convince a newfound local friend to drive you around for free (give a "donation" to his younger siblings afterwards). Make sure your rental agreement makes it clear who pays for gas and oil. Try to negotiate a free dropoff at your embarkation point back to Bali or Nusa Lembongan. Two good, cautious drivers are

recommended: Nyoman Soma Arsana, who can be contacted by telephone through the *kantor camat* (tel. 0366-231-885), and Made Latoni, at Banjar Sental Kawan, Desa Ped.

You can charter a whole *bemo* for Rp50,000-75,000 per day; inquire at Toko Elektronik. You may also opt for an hourly rate, though drivers will demand at least Rp15,000 per hour. At Mentigi harbor, it's Rp75,000 for a small, two-engine boat; Rp100,000 for a larger one.

Getting Away

Take boats to Padangbai (30 minutes) and Sanur (1.25 hours) from Buyuk, one km east of Toyapekeh. Get there by 0700 to buy your ticket (Rp15,000) at the Departemen Perhubungan office near the pier. Each boat holds about 30 people. If there are enough passengers, a boat sometimes leaves for Padangbai in the afternoon. From Mentigi Harbor, one km west of Sampalan, hire boats to Banjarbias, then a *bemo* into Kusamba where other *bemo* pass by to Amlapura or Klungkung. The cost is Rp15,000. The Balinese operate an organized transport cartel that fixes all fares at Rp15,000 to and from Bali—and there's really no way around it if your skin is white. To their credit, most boats offer life-jackets, hard wooden benches, and double 85 hp outboards.

SAMPALAN

The largest settlement and Nusa Penida's administrative center, Sampalan is a long town around one narrow, tree-lined street crammed with shops selling food, necessities, agricultural tools, and cheap clothing. Don't miss the *pasar* north of the *bemo* terminal—traditional, classic, an example of a Bali gone by. Sampalan is a study of a growing "Outer Island Bali" urban culture, a delightful little town with just enough places to sleep, eat, snack, and drink. Warung Ceper and Kios Dewi boast color TVs to keep you connected to civilization. Because of its friendly, relaxed air, good transport services, and close proximity to the island's finest attractions, Sampalan is your best base on the island, with beautiful views across the Badung Strait to Bali; at night, try to guess which town belongs to which set of lights.

Sampalan's *pura dalem,* near the football field and cemetery, has a six-meter-high *candi bentar* adorned with menacing Bhouma statues and a fearsome Rangda.

Accommodations and Food

Bungalow Pemda, the government resthouse, is in the east part of town, a 10-minute walk from Pasar Sampalan and the *bemo* terminal. The bungalows, opposite a soccer field and only 50 meters from the police post, face a beach lined with *jukung.* Very convenient location. Five units, each containing two rooms with bathroom, cost Rp5000 s, Rp8000 d. The beds are too small and narrow, the place could be cleaner, and the mosquitoes are bad, but what do you want for two bucks? Ask to see the houseboy's private collection of *cepuk* (Penida cloth).

You can try to stay in cleaner rooms with local families. Ask the *bemo* drivers to drop you off at Made Latoni's house (Banjar Sental Kawan, Desa Ped, Nusa Penida). It is the red and white building on J1. Segara across from the bank about 100 meters west of the bemo terminal. He can arrange accommodations in one of several private homes for Rp10,000-15,000 per night. For Rp20,000 per day, Made offers motorcycle guide service.

On the road are small *warung* which serve *nasi campur, nasi goreng, mie goreng* (Rp2000), and cold drinks. Down Jl. Nusa Indah toward the terminal is **Kios Dewi**—neat, clean, well-lit, a good place to hang out at night. Another, cheaper place 100 meters farther toward the village is **Warung Ceper** (Jl. Nusa Indah 54), offering local foods like *lawar, urab, ayam kampung,* and veggies. A knockout *kampung*-style *nasi campur* with all the fixings is only Rp1500, though the food is generally gone by 1800. Great value, though there's no compromise with the fiery spice.

Services

Toko Anda on Jl. Nusa Indah between Kios Dewi and Warung Ceper is a very complete shop offering groceries, stationery supplies, color print film, snacks, ice cream, and cosmetics. **Toko Elektronik** in the bus terminal sells radios, watches, tapes, sunglasses, and calculators. There's also a bank, post office, clinic, telephone office, photo studio, and billiard hall.

Getting Away

It's easy to find *bemo* or a minibus east to Toyapekeh (Rp500, nine km). When full, *bemo* leave for Sewana to the southeast, usually starting at around 0900 (Rp500, eight km). The *bemo* fare to Klumpu is Rp1500, Tanglad Rp3000.

TOYAPEKEH

Means "Salt Water." A small, attractive Hindu coastal village nine km east of Sampalan, with the island's only mosque, inhabited by fishermen and seaweed farmers. This is the main market town of northwest Nusa Penida, yet it is peaceful, with an attractive white-sand beach. When the boat from Nusa Lembongan pulls in on the beach, *bemo* are waiting to take passengers to Sampalan (Rp500).

Stay at **Losmen Tenang,** right on the beach next to where the *bemo* wait. Price Rp6000 s, Rp10,000 d for four clean rooms with *mandi.* Order simple meals there or from a few simple *warung* on the main road. East of town is a nice beach. Motorized *jukung* from Toyapekeh to Jungut Batu on Nusa Lembongan cost Rp3000, and leave only in the mornings because of the tides. You disembark in front of the main surfer strip.

Pura Dalem Penataran Ped

From Toyapekeh minibus stand, ride or walk four km northeast down a tree-lined road along the sea to this temple in Desa Ped near Sentalo. On the way, you'll pass the landing stage of **Buyuk** on the left. The temple is about 50 meters from the beach, north of the main road to Sampalan. Built almost entirely of volcanic sandstone, limestone blocks, and patchwork cement, with rough *paras* carvings, guardian statues, and the leering face of Bhoma looming over the gate, it's architecturally very homely and sinister-looking. One of Bali's holy *sadkahyangan* temples, this rather crude and poorly maintained *pura* is considered magically powerful. It's the destination of devout pilgrims from all over Bali who seek to ward off evil and sickness by praying to the sorcerer and destroyer of evil Ratu Gede Macaling, a spirit who occupies a lofty place in the Hindu-Buddhist pantheon. Beyond the outer west wall of the temple is a shrine dedicated to that terrifying protective deity, where worshippers place their offerings. Pura Dalem Penataran Ped's *odalan,* which takes place on Buda Cemeng Kelawu, lasts three days and features entertainment and an open-air market. Every three years on the fourth full moon a big crowded, noisy *usuba* festival takes place.

AROUND THE ISLAND

Circumvent the whole island by starting from Sampalan and heading first to Toyapekeh, then Penida, Batumadeg, Tanglad, Sewana, Karangsari, and back to Sampalan. Traveling by rented motorcycle or *bemo* you can make it in four days: one day in the Sampalan-Toyapekeh region; another spent exploring the southwest coast; the third day touring Batumadeg, Debuluh, and Tanglad; the fourth wandering in the Sewana and Karangsari areas. From Toyapekeh, the road climbs a hill for three km southwest to **Sebunibus.** A bit south of Sebunibus the road branches west two km to **Sakti.** From there, a new road winds through barren country and over a hill to Penida, in all about 17 km from Toyapekeh.

The seacoast village of Penida is nestled at the bottom of a valley filled with coconut palms, surrounded by a peaceful woods. This pretty village offers a short beach and nice scenery but has only one *warung* and no place to stay. Rent a *jukung* and visit the Shark Cave offshore. In 1994 a pipe carrying fresh water and a new road to the village were put in. An Australian planning to build a homestay and a *berbintang* hotel is is the permit-acquisition stage.

The road east from Sebunibus leads to Klumpu (225 meters), a small, red-roofed village about 15 km southeast of Sakti. One-half km east of Klumpu, a paved road takes you north to the coastal road between Toyapekeh and Sampalan. The Klumpu area features the island's best indigenous architecture.

From Klumpu, the road heads south and then southwest to Batumadeg, passing Bukit Mundi, Nusa Penida's highest point and the dwelling place of Dewi Rohini, the female aspect of Shiva. Climb Bukit Mundi from Batumadeg up through grassy ridges; there's a temple in a small patch of forest on the western slope. On the way down pass through the small village of Ratug.

The first tourist didn't reach Batumadeg until 1977. Today there are some *warung,* a few shops, and *bemo* connections. From Sebuluh Waterfall (elev. 300 meters) near Batumadeg take the steep path between high stone walls two km down to the sea. The road southwest from Batumadeg ends in **Debuluh;** from here a path leads down to yellowish sea cliffs. All along the coastline you can stand on spectacular promontories and watch the dazzling green sea 200 meters below. Offshore, rock pinnacles eroded from the cliffs shoot straight up for hundreds of meters completely surrounded by water.

Another road from Batumadeg takes you across a plateau for seven km to **Batukandik,** which possesses "male" and "female" shrines. This unique temple also has a prehistoric stone altar: a heavily eroded woman with enormous breasts supports a stone throne on her head, two roosters standing on her shoulders. The Holy Forest of Sahab hides a temple, said to be the exit of a mythical tunnel connecting Bali with Nusa Penida; the hole apparently starts in Pejeng.

Tanglad

This stark, rolling country feels a million miles from Bali. From Batukandik a bumpy road takes you along a gently rising and falling ridge four kilometers to the cool, 400-meter-high village of Tanglad; from Klumpu turn right and climb the hill 10 km. You can catch a *bemo* to Tanglad (Rp3000, 25 km) from Sampalan at 0800 or 0900, after the market. Along the way glimpse both the northern and southern coasts of the island.

Tanglad is a very traditional, preindustrial, rocky mountain village of steep-roofed stone houses sprawling across hills, inhabited by bare-breasted, betel-chewing, middle-aged women. Of a population of 2,000, sixty are weavers. *Capuk* cloth costs Rp6000-10,000 per meter here. You'll be shown "antique" pieces for Rp50,000, woven with handspun cotton 15-20 years ago. The rough designs and crude techniques are light years away from the sophisticated *ikat* designs of Sumba and Flores.

Small *warung* serve noodle soup and very strong coffee. The only entertainment is two billiard tables in the town *bale.* In the temple on the village common, see the throne of the sun-god Surya in a sculptural style reminiscent of East Java's Candi Sukuh. From Tanglad, head north to Pejukutan. Take the road south to Sekar-taji, or visit the traditional houses of Pelilit on the south coast.

The East Coast

The nicest part of the island. If you see nothing else on Nusa Penida, see this. This undiscovered coastal strip lacks the laid-back quality of Nusa Lembongan's Jungut Batu but offers full Bali culture. If you can spend only a short time on Nusa Penida, just start walking south from Batu Malapan. *Bemo* leave Sampalan for Batu Malapan when full; Rp500 is the correct fare.

This stretch of coast is even more scenic than the east coast of Karangasem. Sewana and Karangsari villages are lovely, as are the adjacent offshore sea gardens. Here, industrious women use inflated inner tubes to move heavy baskets of seaweed. Long lines of bright *jukung* pull up on shore. At the side of the road are mats covered in drying seaweed.

From Tanglad, it's nine km northeast to the small fishing/seaweed village of Sewana. From Pejukutan, the road north leads down to the sea. The high cliffs of the southern part of the island give way to open beach and seaweed gardens. The village starts as soon as you come down the mountain, as the road levels out. Walk this beautiful coastal road; if you've rented a motorcycle, have the driver wait for you three km up the road at Gua Karangsari.

To the south of Sewana are several pago-dalike temples, including the island's second most important, **Pura Batu Madau,** and **Pura Batu Kuning** on the beach. **Malibu Point,** with stunning visibility of up to 20 meters, is a favorite scuba diving spot with an excellent variety of fish, including pelagic, tuna, and manta ray, as well as hawksbill turtles. With a current of up to four knots conditions can be fierce, and the water is cold.

Gua Karangsari

Northwest 3.5 km from Sewana and about five km southeast of Sampalan, within sound of the ocean, is an immense limestone cave known by the locals as Gua Giri Putri. Hindus worship at the holy spring inside. The entrance lies 150 meters up a steep stairway. Climb down through a small opening, crouch under a low ceiling, then descend into tremendously deep, vaulted grottos—still and silent except for the squeaking of bats, which grows louder the deeper you go. Tradition has it the cave leads eventually to Pura Puser Ing Jagat in Pejeng.

Some of the branch tunnels lead to openings; at the far end of the cave is a breathtaking view of fertile rolling hills and green mango groves. The main shaft rises to a small lake. The villagers will provide you with a big lamp for Rp2000. Without their assistance, entrance should be free. For safety's sake, bring a friend. Besides the bats and some birds, there's a certain species of crab found in this cave. During Galungan, a torchlit procession of women bearing offerings visits the underground lake.

BOB RACE

BANGLI REGENCY

Stretching north to south in central-eastern Bali, Bangli is the only landlocked regency on the island. Only tiny Klungkung has fewer people than Bangli's population of 180,000, divided into 187 community groups in 73 villages.

With its rugged, overgrown hillocks, wooded ravines, and steeply tiered gardens leading up to immense volcanic craters, the regency encompasses some of the most superb natural scenery on the island. The roads north from Bangli or Tampaksiring climb gradually, the air becomes cooler, and upland crops such as peanuts begin to replace rice. North of Bangli, the road meanders through eerie forests of giant bamboo, finally emerging on one of Bali's most dramatic vistas: the huge 10-km-wide basin of Lake Batur, with the smoldering black cone of Gunung Batur behind it.

The region offers mineral hot springs, volcano-climbing, boat tours of beautiful Lake Batur, unique archaeological sites, venerated temples, the mountain towns of Penelokan and Kintamani, and the Bali Aga village of Trunyan. Isolated corners of the mountainous Bangli region are home to a number of aboriginal, pre-Majapahit communities, ethnically and culturally distinct from the Balinese mainstream. These mountain folk don't believe in priests, holy water, or cremation. They speak archaic dialects, expose their dead to the elements, uphold a fine stonecarving tradition, and practice an archaic, non-Javanized form of Hinduism.

Tourism is not well developed in Bangli, with the exception of the Penelokan/Kintamani area, a favorite lunch stop for tour buses which take in the sights and return to Sanur or Nusa Dua in a single day. Most independent travelers visit the regency on a fast roundtrip from the south, or climb the Batur volcano one morning on their way to Lovina, heading back down via Bedugul and Lake Bratan in the western range. This despite the fact the Batur area really deserves three or four days.

The region's higher altitudes are quite cold at night, so bring warm clothes and shoes. Make certain your accommodations provide dry blankets and firewood. Visit the mountains in the morning because by the afternoon the volcano and lake are shrouded in clouds and fog. Thievery is just as much a problem here as in the madcap alleys of Kuta, so watch your gear.

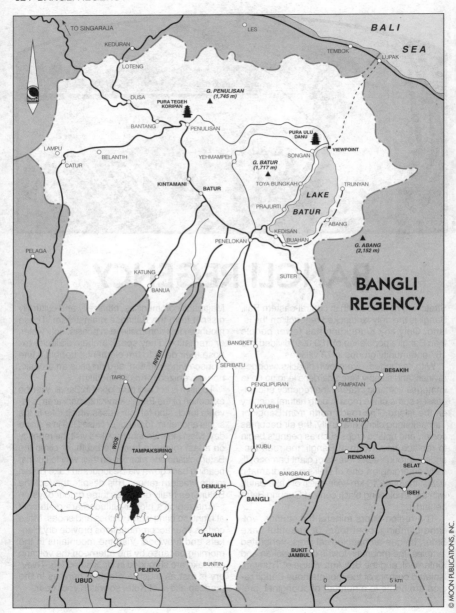

BALI SEA

TO SINGARAJA

KEDURAN
LOTENG
LES
TEMBOK
LUPAK

DUSA
PURA TEGEH
KORIPAN
G. PENULISAN
(1,745 m)
PURA ULU
DANU
VIEWPOINT

BANTANG
PENULISAN
SONGAN

LAMPU
YEHMAMPEH
G. BATUR
(1,717 m)
TRUNYAN

CATUR
BELANTIH
KINTAMANI
BATUR
TOYA BUNGKAH
LAKE
BATUR

PRAJURTI
KEDISAN
ABANG

PELAGA
PENELOKAN
BUAHAN
G. ABANG
(2,152 m)

KATUNG
SUTER

BANUA
BANGLI
REGENCY

BANGKET

RIVER
SERIBATU
BESAKIH

TARO
PENGLIPURAN
PAMPATAN

KAYUBIHI
MENANGA

WOS
KUBU
RENDANG

TAMPAKSIRING
SELAT

BANGBANG
ISEH

DEMULIH
BANGLI

APUAN
BUKIT
JAMBUL

BUNTIN

PEJENG

UBUD

0   5 km

© MOON PUBLICATIONS, INC.

History

This regency was born of cruelty, incest, betrayal, and murder. In Bali, where legend and history are so intertwined, the history of Bangli reads like a story from one of the *Panji* tales. In the 18th century, the ruthless king Dewa Rai of Taman married his cousin, Dewa Ayu from the Bangli Denbancingah family, and immediately began plotting to overthrow his uncle, the ruler of Nyalian. Dewa Rai adopted Dewa Gede Tangkeban, the son of the ruler of Nyalian, but the son fell in love and had an affair with his adoptive father's wife, the queen. She persuaded her lover to turn Dewa Rai's dissatisfied subjects against their despised king. After Dewa Rai was murdered in the courtyard of the Puri Agung of Bangli, Dewa Gede Tangkeban married his stepmother and became king of Bangli. Since this marriage was not sanctioned by the religious *adat* of the time, seven generations of rulers were cursed with bad luck.

In the 18th and 19th centuries, a time when maritime trade was paramount, only those kingdoms with ports were economically and politically powerful. To trade, Bangli was forced to transport its goods through other territories, paying heavy tribute to their sovereigns. Bangli's luck changed in 1849 when its king Dewa Gede Tangkeban II was appointed by the Dutch to rule the northern regency of Buleleng. This vast area came under Dutch control after Buleleng's King Gusti Ketut Jilantik committed *puputan*. This confederation was of great advantage to Bangli—it was then able to gain access to the sea. Buleleng could also benefit as it was able to irrigate its rice fields with Bangli water. But the union was short lived. In 1854, Buleleng rebelled against Bangli. No matter; in 1882, all of northern Bali came under direct Dutch colonial administration.

Bangli first became known to the Western world when a German doctor, Gregor Krause (1883-1959), was appointed to the Dutch hospital here from 1912 to 1914. An avid photographer and amateur ethnologist, Krause took over 4,000 photos during his tenure. Four hundred of them, together with his reports on Balinese cultural life, were published in Germany in 1922 and distributed worldwide. The book's effect on Europe, having just emerged from four years of war and still struggling with poverty, was electric. The majority of photos were shot in Bangli and constitute an invaluable historic record of the time—the *puri,* aristocratic life, raja and princesses in ceremonial attire, royal *topeng* dancers.

Another famous literary personality, Scottish-born Muriel Pearson, under the pen name Ketut Tantri, wrote *Revolt in Paradise,* a fascinating tale of her life in Bali and Java from 1932 to 1947. Inspired by the early Hollywood film *The Last Paradise,* she came to Bali, settling first in Denpasar. Soon growing restless, she drove inland in search of the real Bali. Her car ran out of gas in front of the Puri Denpasar in Bangli. The raja of the time invited her into the palace and eventually she became his quasi-adopted daughter. He gave her the name Ketut Tantri, *ketut* meaning fourth-born child. She wore traditional clothes and at the raja's suggestion dyed her red hair black—only *leyak* have red hair on Bali.

Economy

Traveling through Bangli regency even 10 years ago you could easily forget which century you were in. But by the mid-1990s the region seemed to be waking from a long sleep. Today, the streets are clean and the economy is growing, with many new shops and supermarkets rising to meet local demand. Agricultural products are still the most important source of revenue for this relatively remote regency. The broad plain in the south, consisting mostly of rice fields, lies about 100 meters above sea level; the higher elevations above Bangli town mark the dividing line between the two agricultural zones of the regency. Here you begin to see plots of corn, sweet potatoes, cassava, cabbages, peanuts, coffee, tobacco, and vanilla, as well as *salak,* passion fruit, citrus, and clove plantations. This mountainous district is also known for its decorative plants, particularly orchids and unusual ferns.

Events

Bangli's temple festivals are known for their stunning offerings. Ceremonies often last all night, and the dances are more traditional than in the south. Here, the dancers fall into a real trance. This is usually the only district where you can see a genuine *sanghyang dedari* (exorcistic dance).

The highlight of your stay here may be stumbling upon a *gamelan* competition. Only in the Bangli area can you still find the powerful, deep, and reverberating *gong gde,* a huge ensemble of *calung, jegogan, trompong, gong,* big drums, half a dozen *saron*-style *gangsa,* and large *cengceng.* In feudal times, the *gong gde* was perhaps the most important symbol of a court's opulence. Rare, streamlined versions of this archaic 50-musician orchestra can be found outside Bangli town in Demulih and Sulahan, and in Kintamani's Pura Batur.

The *balian* of Bangli are renowned for their supernatural powers, for their practice of the science of black magic *(pengiwa),* and for their ability to heal psychically through the medium of trance. Those patients the *balian* are unable to treat are sent to Bangli's lunatic asylum.

BANGLI AND VICINITY

A friendly, scenic town in the cool, sloping, rich farmlands of central Bali, Bangli is an hour's drive (40 km) northeast of Denpasar. Bangli dates back to A.D. 1204; a document tells of a sacrifice of a black ox and a feast held in that year at its great state temple, **Pura Kehen.** An offshoot of the early Gelgel dynasty, the ancient kingdom of Bangli became Bali's most powerful upland court in the second half of the 19th century, largely as a reaction to the Dutch presence in Bule-

BANGLI

TO PENELOKAN
PURA KEHEN
JAYA GIRI HOMESTAY
SASANA BUDAYA ARTS CENTER
PURA MANTIK TIRTHA
PURA DALEM PURWA
POLICE
TO BESAKIH AND SIDEMBUNUT
POST OFFICE
TO TAMPAKSIRING
BANK BPD
JL. NUSANTARA
PURA DALEM
JL. KUSUMAYUDA CUNGKUB
PUBLIC HOSPITAL
MENTAL HOSPITAL
BANK RAKYAT INDONESIA
ARTHA SASTRA INN
BEMO
JL. NANGKA
PASAR MALAM TERMINAL
PASAR
JL. LET ANOM
JL. BRIGEN NGURAH RAI
TELEPHONE OFFICE
TOURIST OFFICE
POLICE
PETROL STATION
PURA DALEM PENUNGGEKAN
JL. MERDEKA
TO GIANYAR AND DENPASAR
STATUE
NOT TO SCALE

© MOON PUBLICATIONS, INC.

leng. Bangli's prominence, however, never eclipsed the grandeur of the lowland courts, and its influence was not deeply felt in island politics.

Bangli today is perhaps the quietest and most easygoing of all the regency capitals. Dominated by one-story buildings, the town is spread out for some distance along the highway. Neat and trim concrete administration buildings and houses are surrounded by gardens and near-empty streets; no souvenir shops, tourist restaurants, or nightlife. You often have the whole town to yourself.

Travelers use Bangli as a transit stop halfway between Denpasar and Penelokan—between the mountains and the shore—spending several days here taking in Pura Kehen and the town's surroundings. Lying on the slopes of Gunung Batur, Bangli has one of the most temperate climates on Bali. When skies are clear, the town offers superb views of the still-active volcano.

To other Balinese the town has a certain stigma because of its dubious distinction as the site of one of Bali's only two mental hospitals. Established by the Dutch, this was the first facility of its kind on the island. The town is still the subject of fierce barbs, and the Balinese look at you askance when you say you're going to Bangli. Poor mental health is not the problem here that it is in the West, as the island's unending rituals and dramas tend to release pent-up emotions legally and safely.

SIGHTS

Eight royal *puri* were once situated around the main crossroads of town, but now only Puri Denpasar (the present Artha Sastra Inn) is open to the public. This was the original palace of Bangli's last raja and is now occupied by the raja's descendants. Note the sculptures of lions and bodhisattvas inspired by early photographs of Borobudur, and the remarkable painted mural and frieze in the *bale loji* depicting Chinese life in Bangli during the last century—many shops in the town market are still Chinese-owned. The mural is in bad shape but you can still make out detail. Also worth seeing is the 100-year-old *bale kulkul,* about a five-minute walk. This well-preserved three-story pagoda-like structure with coconut tree columns once functioned as an alarm/signal tower to warn or call for an assembly. From the top tower hang two *kulkul,* one male and one female.

Pura Kehen

Thousands visit this lovely old terraced temple, 1.5 km northeast of the town center—the largest and most sacred temple in the regency. To get there, follow the road to Penelokan, then turn right at the T-junction and walk 300 meters. Approaching it through surrounding woodland and coconut

PURA KEHEN

JEROAN (INNER SANCTUARY)

MERU TOWER

PADMASANA

CANDI BENTAR

ABA TENGAH (MIDDLE COURTYARD)

CANDI BENTAR

BANYAN TREE

JABAAN (FORECOURT)

MAIN GATE

TERRACES   TERRACES

0   10 m

© MOON PUBLICATIONS, INC.

groves, Pura Kehen has the appearance of a full-scale *wayang* performance in the middle of a breathtaking rice paddy. Brave the usual crush of vendors, some very aggressive (children accost tourists with flowers, asking for money).

One of the finest and most dramatic temples of its kind, Pura Kehen was founded in the early 11th century by Sri Brahma Kemuti Ketu as a state temple. Kehen is derived from the word *kuren,* meaning "household" or "hearth"; the temple is under the protection of Brahma, the Lord of Fire. Below the first long flight of steps is Pura Penyimpenan ("Temple of Safekeeping"), an old temple containing an ancient collection of historical *lontar* and inscribed *prastasis.* Here, a 9th century bronze plate alludes in Sanskrit to a dedication ceremony held here in honor of Hyang Api (Brahma), which even predates the official founding of the temple in 1206.

Pura Kehen's large layout, as well as the temple's high platforms and megalithic stone construction, betrays a link with the animistic terraced mountain sanctuaries dating from the earliest periods of Balinese history. Like Besakih, Pura Kehen was built on eight terraces on the southern slope of the hill. Each of the three main terraces is connected to the one above by a flight of stairs. The first five terraces make up the outer courtyards *(jabaan),* the sixth and seventh are middle courtyards *(jaba tengah),* while the eighth is the sacred inner courtyard *(jeroan).* Steep stairs lead to Pura Kehen's splendid gateway, the *pamedal agung,* known as "the great exit." Above it are the splayed hands and hideous face of a *kala-makara* demon who prevents malevolent spirits from entering the sacred grounds. *Wayang kulit*-like stone statues on pedestals depicting characters from the Ramayana line both sides of the 38 steps leading up to the main entrance. The forecourt and middle courtyard are shaded by a venerable old *waringin* tree with a *kulkul* in its branches. The courtyard's walls are inlaid with chipped Chinese porcelain plates, the balustrades of the steps decorated with ornamental carvings.

The inner sanctuary contains a shrine of 11 tapering *meru* roofs, resting places for the visiting mountain gods. The 11-tier *meru,* dedicated to Siwa, is the highest honor that can be offered. In the northeastern corner of this courtyard is a very unusual *padmasana,* a three-throned shrine of the holy Hindu triad. Go around the back and check out the superb carvings. Ornamentation on the highest temple is so overdone and uncontrolled it's rare even for Bali—a stirring testament to the virtuosity of Bangli's stonecarvers.

EVENTS

During the *odalan* temple festival, beginning in the afternoon, high offerings are carried up the long stairway to Bangli's Pura Kehen. At night, this temple anniversary is also celebrated with the sacred *rejang* dance. Even bigger than the state temple's *odalan* is Bangli's *ngusaba* ceremony. Unusual dance forms practiced in the Bangli area include various archaic forms of *baris* typical of Bali's mountain regions: *baris presi* (eight men with leather shields), *baris dadap* (men with shields made of *dadap* wood), and *baris jojor* (eight men in line with spears).

Besides temple festival days, Bangli's main event is market day, when you'll see products like sweet potatoes, peanuts, and spices not found in the south. The *pasar* is south of the Artha Sastra Inn. Dances and *wayang kulit* are sometimes staged in the town's *bale banjar* every *hari raya*, but not with the lavishness or regularity of Gianyar. A resident *dalang*, Dewa Made Rai Mesi, lives just 700 meters from the Artha Sastra Inn.

The **Sasana Budaya Art Center,** one of the largest cultural complexes on Bali, is about one km northwest of the town center, just around the corner from Pura Kehen. Here you can see *gamelan* and theater performances (*kecak, wayang* forms), *baris* dances, and art exhibits. Obtain a schedule of events from the local tourist office (see below). Tourist dances—the fire dance, *kecak,* and ballet—are performed nearly every day in Bona, 13 km southwest of Bangli (Rp5000). Buy tickets 15 minutes before show time at 1900.

ACCOMMODATIONS AND FOOD

The **Artha Sastra Inn,** Jl. Merdeka 5, tel. (0366) 91179, an original raja's palace, has seen better days. Still, the potted plants and palace court architecture gives this place a unique feel. You can sleep in the bed of the last king of Bangli and participate in the ritual life of a *triwangsa* family. The Inn is ideally located in the center of Bangli near the bus station—traffic noise from this busy intersection can be bothersome. Coming into town from Denpasar, the palace complex is on the right. The inn is managed by an obviously overworked adolescent boy. Funky, decaying rooms with *kamar mandi* outside are Rp8000 s, Rp15,000 d. Slightly less run-down are the five larger rooms in the interior of the *puri,* with inside *mandi* costing Rp15,000 s, Rp20,000 d. These are adapted from traditional Balinese *bale* and feature ancient carved doors and antique furniture. Prices include breakfast of banana or pineapple pancakes. Inexpensive menu, but the food is not that great.

The newer **Bangli Hotel,** Jl. Rambutan 1, tel./fax (0366) 91419, offers 15 rooms with attached bathrooms at Rp25,000 per. Clean and acceptable rooms, fresh mountain air, breakfast, small restaurant, tax and service not included. Good value. Doctor available. Ask for the traditional healing massage. Reservations direct or to Box 56, Nusa Dua 80361, Bali.

Inexpensive, spartan rooms are also available in two homestays: **Jaya Giri** at J1. Sriwijaya 6 nearly opposite Pura Kehen, and **Catur Aduyana** on the other side of town adjacent to the soccer field (J1. Lettulil 2, tel. 0366-91244).

The *pasar malam* to the east of the bus station serves cheap, delicious meals; *cap cay goreng* with rice for Rp1500, *ayam goreng* with vegetables for Rp4000. Or dine at several *warung makanan kecil* around the bus station; get there early as they stay open no later than 2100.

SERVICES AND TRANSPORTATION

Services

You'll find many shops in the local market south of the Artha Sastra Inn where you can buy the necessities of life. Though it takes up a whole block, it's not much of a market. The **tourist office** is at Jl. Brigjen. Ngurah Rai 24 (open Mon.-Fri. 0730-1700, tel. 0366-91537) but is of minimal use—just a pamphlet or two, with lackluster service. Change cash but not traveler's checks at **Bank Pembangunan Daerah** (open 0730-1400) by the Trimurti statue, or use a bank in Gianyar, 13 km and Rp500 by *bemo* to the south-west. There's a pay **telephone** in front of the Artha Sastra Inn, or go to the 24-hour **Wartel** just north of the tourist office.

Getting There and Away
Blue public *bemo* from Denpasar's Terminal Kereneng cost Rp1000 (40 km). From the town of Gianyar *bemo* cost Rp500 (13 km); from Kintamani Rp700. If coming from Klungkung (19 km, Rp500), you may have to change *bemo* in Peteluan or simply board a Singaraja-bound *bemo* and get off in Bangli. Magnificent views on the way up.

From the *bemo*/bus station opposite the Artha Sastra Inn in Bangli, get rides to Gianyar (13 km, Rp500), Penelokan, (26 km north, Rp600), Kintamani (33 km, Rp700), Tampaksiring (22 km), and Denpasar's Batubulan Station (40 km, Rp1000).

Bangli lies on the border between central and eastern Bali and it's easy to reach Besakih (21 km) from here on a lovely meandering surfaced road which runs by impressive rice terraces and along fast, clear, cold rivers at the bottom of deep ravines. The road emerges at Bangbang on the main Klungkung-Besakih road; from Bangbang turn south two km to enjoy the majestic vantage point from 300-seat Bukit Jambul Garden Restaurant. Sample a selection of Indonesian, European, and Chinese dishes while gazing out at the clove plantations stretched before you.

From Bukit Jambul, head north to Besakih via Rendang (12 km). *Bemo* run from Bangli direct to Rendang for Rp500, or take a *bemo* to Bangbang for Rp400 and walk a little. From Rendang, you can head east to Selat, then turn south on the postcard-scenic road to Klungkung via Iseh and Sideman. About an eight-hour trip via motorbike; too many changes if you take public transport.

VICINITY OF BANGLI

For starters, try a nice walk through *sawah* to the east, bringing you to Pura Dalem Cungkub. Dewa at the Artha Sastra Inn takes guests to this temple. An even bigger temple lies to the west—Pura Delem Purwa, in an area that looks like the surroundings of Ubud.

South of Bangli
One-half km south of Bangli toward Gianyar is **Pura Dalem Pengungekan,** a temple of the dead. Detailed outside panels show scene after vivid scene of unimaginable and grotesque horrors heaped upon pleading evildoers—impaled by arrows, boiled alive, devoured by demons, strung up from trees, roasted over flames. The central shrine, completed in 1995, depicts the stories of Ganesha, Siwa, Uma, and Raksasa. Bukit Jati is a scenic hill south of Bangli with 360-degree views; take a *bemo* first to Guliang, then walk 500 meters to the top, the site of several temples. Not generally known to tourists, **Pura Tirta Harum** ("Temple of the Fragrant Spring") is a royal temple six km south of Bangli, about an hour's walk up a long uphill path. It's believed the ancestor of the present-day dynasty of Bangli was born in a small thatched-roof building here. Enter through the *candi bentar.* Pura Tirta Harum derived its name from a nearby holy spring. An important *odalan* takes place here, attended by all castes.

In Bunutin, seven km south of Bangli, turn east off the main road. Overlooking a large lake, red-bricked **Pura Langgar** is designed along Islamic lines with a two-tiered roof, four central pillars, and four gateways in the direction of the four winds. The legend goes that, during the 17th century, a local Hindu prince fell gravely ill. Seeking a cure, a *dukun* was consulted; he advised the family to build a temple in honor of an Islamic ancestor of the prince, I Dewa Mas Wili, who joined the Gelgel court after immigrating from East Java's Blambangan peninsula. In accordance with the *dukun's* wishes, a beautiful mosque-like temple was built on the shore of a lake graced with palm trees and water-lilies. Today, both Muslims and Hindus worship at Pura Langgar and descendants of the prince's family still abstain from eating pork in deference to their ancestor. Three km farther south of Bunutin is the *pura dalem* at **Sidan,** very possibly the most grotesque temple of the dead on Bali, literally covered in gruesome carvings depicting the consequences of an evil life.

West of Bangli
Catch a bemo in front of the hospital toward Tampaksiring. After about one km, on the south

side of the main road, is the lake-fed spring of **Tirta Empul,** located at the bottom of a big ravine. Take the long flight of steps down to the springs. About two km farther west, after the school, you'll see the signpost and the track to the right to Bukit Demulih ("Hill of No Return"). If you continue straight up the wooded ridge, you'll reach Penelokan. Perched on top of Bukit Demulih is the small temple of Penataran Kentel Gumi. From the hilltop, you can see the Balinese Pyrenees, a range of nine mountains named after the nipple-like *trompong* percussion plates in the *gamelan* orchestra.

Also visible is Pura Kehen, under a giant banyan tree north of Bangli; the whole Bukit Peninsula to the south; and the ugly box of the Bali Beach Hotel along the east coast at Sanur. **Apuan** is a five-km walk south of Bukit Demulih, or take a bemo (Rp500) from Bangli. The house of the *kepala desa* here, with its gold-leaf decoration, is as beautiful as a king's palace.

Sulahan village, six km west, is known for its basketry and wonderful old *gong gde,* given to the village by the prince of the ranking court of Bangli. This venerable orchestra, which most likely dates from the 18th century and today is known as Gong Gde Sekar Sandat, once belonged to the kingdom of Klungkung. When the Dutch defeated that court in the 1908 *puputan,* they repaid the loyalty of the raja of Bangli by presenting him with this *gamelan.* It was first cast in an amalgam of gold and bronze, which made it very durable. Before the advent of the *gong kebyar,* this powerful class of *gamelan,* with its deep melancholy tolling and unusual melody, was once widespread on Bali. It is rarely heard today.

North of Bangli
The largest bamboo forest on Bali is in Kubu, four km north of Bangli on the road to Penglipuran. The sound of the wind blowing through the bamboo strikes some as eerie, but it can be quite relaxing when you grow used to it. The locals believe the bamboo took root from bamboo sticks used in the making of camp shelters and *pikulan* abandoned by the all-conquering army of Panji Sakti in the early 17th century. The most famous aboriginal village in the regency is Trunyan on the northeast shore of Lake Batur; few people know about **Kajubii,** eight km north of Bangli. Like most archaic Bali Aga villages, Kajubii is surrounded by a protective wall. Here the children are considered more important than the old people; looked upon as servants of God.

Eleven km north of Bangli, in Kubu District, is **Penglipuran,** a much-ballyhooed "undiscovered" village of 164 families which looks like a well-groomed stage set from pre-Javano-Hindu Bali—neat as a pin and set against a backdrop of great natural beauty. Though it's not really "undiscovered" (note the parking lot for tour buses), a visit nevertheless provides a valuable glimpse into Bali's past. Every highland village in Bali once had this unique street plan. The original outer walls of each compound form two unbroken walls on either side of the long street, sloping gradually north to south. A *pura penataran* and a *pura dalem* lie at the north end. Each compound has retained the old-style domestic gateway. If you're invited into a household, give the oldest woman at least Rp1000. Sit in the town *warung* and chat with the people, the best thing about visiting Penglipuran.

NORTHERN BANGLI REGENCY

PENELOKAN

Its name means "Place to Look." From Denpasar's Terminal Kereneng, Penelokan is 56 km and Rp3000 by *bemo.* This cool, 1,450-meter-high village perches on the rim of a caldera looking out over the sacred, blackened, smoking volcano of Gunung Batur and Lake Batur, an all-important water catchment for south central Bali's agricultural wealth. Sometimes the lake's colors change from glassy blue to platinum, a perfect mirror of the sky and mountains.

Get here by 0800 or 0900, before the clouds move in. Better yet, wake up early to catch the sunrise. In August and September the sunrise is too high, coming up over the middle of the peak, but in June and July it rises to the left of the peak in a golden yellow. At night see the moon sail over the volcano.

Though not a particularly attractive village—the roads untidy, the corrugated tin-roofed buildings decrepit, the vegetation sparse—views here are magnificent. In the mornings you can see not only all the surrounding mountains, but also Gunung Agung to the east, and sometimes even the sea and beyond to Gunung Rinjani on Lombok from here. Penelokan has a high, fresh climate, and reasonable *losmen*. There are some invigorating walks across the mountains, and along the road the views of Lake Batur, 300 meters below Penelokan, are unequaled. On the debit side, its vendors and street hustlers are rude and unscrupulous. There's also an admission charge for entering Penelokan—Rp1000 for a four-wheel vehicle plus Rp1050 per person and Rp200 per motorcycle. Pay at checkpoints when approaching from either the south or north; keep the ticket so you don't have to pay again if you leave and then return. To get down to the lake, public *bemo* drivers charge Rp1000 one-way. If driving yourself, make sure you have good brakes before descending this extremely steep, hairpin road.

Warnings

The Penelokan/Kintamani area has one of the worst reputations in all of Indonesia for money-hungry, aggressive people. The many food peddlers, who have no alternative livelihood, hound tourists mercilessly. Beware of road sellers who pull the big switch—substituting a low-quality item for the high-quality piece you agreed to buy. Try not to show even the slightest interest in the wares pushed by the clutch of vendors on the street or outside of the restaurants. If you stop and start bargaining a crowd of pushy, grabbing people will surround you, sticking items in your face. They really come out in numbers when the tourist buses start rolling into Penelokan from the southern resorts around 1030 or 1100. Don't stop when people on the road try to flag you down to sell you tours or boat rides across the lake. They may reach for the ignition key, or say your oil is leaking or they smell gas or you need air in your tires—all lies. One reader reports that this happened to him five times within three kilometers. Don't leave your motorbike unattended. Bystanders may steal a part, then offer their help—for an inflated price—when you can't start it.

Bemo drivers mercilessly hassle women travelers, and have been known to threaten physical violence during price disputes. By the mid-'80s the situation had become so grim the government stepped in and made all the hawkers get licenses and wear identity badges; the authorities also implemented fixed prices on local transport. Now the situation has improved somewhat, though freelancers offering transport deals are still a big problem. One scam perpetrated by *bemo* drivers involves offering to take you down the hill to accommodations in Kedisan. Even though the driver will insist the service is included in the price of the hotel, he'll ultimately charge you Rp2000 per person. Segara Bungalows has been known to employ this trickery. Motorcycle drivers offering offer to take you down to the lake won't accept anything less than Rp5000. Some *bemo* drivers want Rp8000 for a charter down to the lake. Just laugh and start walking. Someone will come along and offer to take you for the standard fare of Rp1000, or just hitchhike tourists or anyone else who happens along.

Accommodations

From Penelokan's *losmen* you'll discover one of the the town's most pleasant activities is just sitting and gazing at the mountain and lake. You'd pay a lot for the view, though, if you stay in the generally overpriced, damp, run-down, and very basic *losmen* here. Penelokan does not yet have any good-value, comfortable, reasonable accommodations. Power outages are a fact of life. Be prepared for cold, damp evenings and nights when bracing fog creeps over the crater's edge. Except for the most bare-bones places, blankets are provided with your room. You'll need them.

As Penelokan accommodations go, **Lakeview Homestay,** tel. (0362) 223464, is above average, though it doesn't really have the right to call itself a homestay. Its 20 tiny Rp15,000 rooms with communal *mandi*, Rp40,000 bungalows and Rp55,000 "superior" rooms with private baths are damp and smelly. The free breakfast is okay. Facilities include showers, hot water on request, safety deposit box, laundry service, and bar. But even with the 20% discount for guests (ask for the yellow menu, not the black one), the restaurant is overpriced—Rp8500 for *nasi goreng,* Rp4700 for a large beer, Rp2500 for a pot of coffee. The restaurant is expanding to seat 100 people, the owners hoping to lure the occupants of the tour buses. And it is a fine place to admire the 11 km expanse of the crater. The management can arrange for a guide to take you up Gunung Batur. Make reservations at (0361) 232023 in Denpasar. the homestay is located at the bend in the road just after the toll gate if approaching from the south.

Below and behind Lakeview, check out the **Caldera Batur Bungalows** with a good restaurant and clean rooms with private bath and bamboo beds (Rp15,000). For the money it's one of the best budget places in Penelokan. Sitting on its own promontory, **Losmen Gunawan** lies to the north, 250 meters past the road down to Kedisan on the right. The most expensive rooms with baths, which can hold a family of three or four, sit directly over the volcano and cost a steep Rp50,000 d (no bargaining). A word of advice—check your room first. The blankets could be soiled, the water barely a trickle, the shower and toilet leak, with dirt in the corners and no towels, soap, toilet paper, or hot water. Demand a nice room.

Economy rooms are Rp25,000 s or d, with a small table, two beds, cold showers, and no views. These smaller boxlike rooms, however, are warmer, desirable during Penelokan's chilly nights. Large, uncarpeted rooms with big bathrooms cost Rp35,000. The tariff includes a decent breakfast (banana pancake, tea, and fruit salad), and a buffet lunch is laid out each day for Rp12,500. Sit in the little gazebo. Telephone and baggage storage services available.

Another option is to stay up the road in Kintamani, only a 10-minute (Rp300) *bemo* ride north. Mellower, but not as close to the lake, without the views. Yet another possibility—perhaps the most desirable for the budget traveler—is to stay right down on the lakeshore in either Toya Bungkah or Kedisan. These villages are more relaxed, with inexpensive eateries. The locals are a couple notches friendlier, and it should cost only Rp1000 to go up and down the hill by *bemo.*

Food

A major drawback to staying anywhere in the Batur area is the poor food. There is a critical shortage of good eating *warung,* though the fruit stands opposite the road to Kedisan sell *jeruk,* passion fruit, and other exotic fruit. For less costly fare, try the *nasi campur* at a few local flyblown *warung* (**Warung Makan Ani Asih** or **Warung Makan Sederhana**) for as little as Rp1500-2000, though they tend to be bland. Request for *be jahir,* a small, lip-smacking variety of lake fish. Toyah Bungkah has the best budget restaurants in the area.

Then there are the big, sprawling tourist establishments. A string of expensive restaurants—the **Puri Selera,** Kintamani Restaurant, Danau Batur, **The Caldera,** Batur Indah, and the 400-seat **Batur Garden**—are found along the road north to Kintamani, with buffets in the Rp12,000-17,500 range. These restaurants, which serve MSG-laced pseudo Indonesian/Chinese food and Western bar drinks, cater mostly to tour groups. Open only for lunch, the **Kintamani Restaurant**'s (tel. 0361-88282) buffet costs about Rp14,500 per person. Meals at **Danau Batur,** one km up the road, are also delicious.

Between Penelokan and Kintamani on the volcano side of the road are several cheaper alternatives—**Puncak, Gong Dewata, Gunungsari,** and the **Mutiara Cafe**—with views just as nice as those offered by big tourist restaurants. The best of the lot is probably the **Ramana** on the right about 350 meters past Penelokan on the road to Kintamani; the sweeping views are free. **Gunawan**'s has an assorted menu including fresh fish dishes such as *ikan goreng a la Batur,* or "Bali Island Noodle," with secret ingredients. Some items wildly expensive (cheese sandwich Rp7000!). They kick you out of the toilets and the restaurant at 2130 after you're finished eating—no reading or writing allowed. **Lakeview Restaurant & Homestay,** tel. (0362) 223464, open for dinner, specializes in lake fish.

Shopping and Services

The shops along the road include some bargain buys. Chess sets sold in Kuta for Rp30,000 go for Rp20,000 here (no bargaining). Bone shell bracelets cost only Rp500. The shop owners are friendlier than the vendors on foot. The local tourist office (open daily 0900-1500, tel. 0362-23370) is nearly opposite the road down to the lake; scan the bulletin boards for info on charters, guides working the area, and accommodations. A post office located between Penelokan and Kintamani handles parcels; open 0800-1600. A postal agent is located next to the police post, about a five-minute walk north of the market. Change money at the branch of **Bank Rankyat Indonesia** about 200 meters up the road to Kintamani. The Selera Restaurant also changes at poorer rates.

Getting There
The most popular way to reach this mountain area is on the highway out of Denpasar by *bemo* from Batubulan station (Rp2000). *Bemo* pick up more passengers in Bangli, then head straight up to Penelokan. Or take a *bemo* from Batubulan first to Bangli (Rp1500), then on to Penelokan (Rp1000) on an excellent, paved, steadily rising road. The road north to Bangli and Penelokan begins at the crossroads town of Peteluan, just east of Gianyar. There you can always find public transport during the day for a ride up to Penelokan. From Singaraja in the north, a minibus costs Rp2500.

Another approach, via Rendang and Menanga, is described (in reverse) in the "Getting Away" section, below. This road emerges at the southernmost point of the crater rim. Take a moment to enjoy the fantastic view—no hassle from sellers or anyone else. Farther up the road you'll have plenty of unwanted company.

The majority of tour groups stop at Goa Gajah, Gunung Kawi, and Tampaksiring's Tirta Empul before they arrive in Penelokan in the late morning. These tours on air-conditioned buses are advertised all over Bali; a lunch at one of Penelokan's swank restaurants is usually thrown in. If traveling on public transport, from Ubud you must first go to Gianyar (Rp800), then to Penelokan. Or from Ubud take a *bemo* first to Sakah (Rp500), then flag down a minibus heading for Singaraja; get off at Penelokan.

There are also some unfrequented back-road approaches to Penelokan from Ubud. Try the narrow, potholed road through Tegallalang, Sebatu, and Pujung. This road offers nicer landscapes than the one through Tampaksiring. Even wilder is the road from Ubud via Payangan; drive a 100cc (or more) motorcycle through the deep upland interior of Bali. On the way you'll experience variegated scenery, bamboo

forests, and remote, hilly, pre-Hindu walled villages. To walk from Ubud via Payangan takes about 12 hours. The higher you ascend the more changes you'll encounter. The aboriginal natives of the Gunung Batur region even look different from the people of the coasts—darker, shorter, more wiry. In few other places is there a folk as stony-eyed as these.

Getting Away
Even getting out of this place is a hassle: men come out of nowhere to claim you promised them you'd go in their car. To get to Lovina, you could end up paying Rp25,000 for a private taxi. Too much maybe, but it's a quick way out. Neither is it easy finding direct transport to Ubud. The closest place one can easily reach is Bangli; then you have to get another *bemo* to Gianyar, another to Sakah, and another to Ubud. Regular *bemo* travel between Kintamani and Batubulan (Rp3000); they may stop in Ubud en route. The *bemo* drivers of Penelokan have established a monopoly on transport down to the shore of Lake Batur. *Bemo* travel as far as Songan on the western side of the lake and Abang on the eastern side but you generally have to bargain like mad to achieve a fair price for any points beyond Toya Bungkah and Buahan.

VICINITY OF PENELOKAN

An exciting, fun ride is to take a bicycle up to Penelokan on top of a *bemo*, then freewheel it all the way back down to the southern coast. From Penelokan, you can hike around the crater rim to the rainforest on top of Gunung Abang (2,152 meters) in about five hours, eating raspberries along the way to quench your thirst.

From Penelokan to Besakih, travel southeast over a fascinating road via Suter and Pempatan running high above the lake across the foothills of Gunung Agung. Move through remote villages; not many tourists take this route and the Balinese are surprised to see you. A little before Rendang (14 km south of Penelokan) at Menanga is the turnoff to Besakih.

There's a wonderful garden in Desa Teman, one km south of Seribatu, owned by Nyoman Tangun. See loving cultivation of *salak, cengkeh, apokat, coklat, ananas, kopi, nanas,* durian, mango, mangosteen, papaya, white and black pepper, ginger, and *kunyit*. Nyoman sells packets of spices (Rp2000 for six vanilla pods) plus fruits, cold drinks, and snacks in the back. Nice view over a river valley. Farther south is Quilt Alley.

In the highland jungle, among the slippery ravines and steep hills between Gunung Batur and Gunung Catur, are the Bali Aga villages of Selulung, Batukaang, and Catur. See remains of primitive pre-Hindu monuments, lichen-covered stone statues, small Polynesian-style megalithic pyramids. In these mountaineer Bali Aga villages, the *bale agung* (council house) is the heart of the political and religious life of the community. The longest council house on Bali is in Taro southwest of and downhill from Penelokan near Jati on the road to Ubud.

Climbing Gunung Abang

This old 2,152-meter-high volcano ("Red Mountain"), on the eastern side of the crater southeast of Penelokan, is the highest point on Batur's outer crater. Climbing it is demanding but easier than climbing Gunung Batur. The trailhead lies about six km southeast of Penelokan. From below Lakeview Homestay, drive or walk down the Penelokan-Suter-Rendang road around the rim east for five km (no public *bemo* on this route). Go one km past the turn south to Suter until you see several *warung*. Continue on this trail to a temple, then head down a steep incline for another one km. Walk straight along the rim of the caldera up through a slippery and muddy thick scrub forest. At the top is *Pura Puncak Tuluk Biyu,* surrounded by trees. About halfway up you'll pass another temple, **Pura Manu Kaya,** then after an hour you'll reach the windy, misty summit. The view is sensational. If you have a guide, descend down the other side of Gunung Abang on a track that emerges just above **Songan,** one of the nicest places to stay on the lake. The descent to Songan is much longer than the one on the Suter side of the mountain. The climb up and back from the trailhead takes about four or five hours, depending on the season.

BATUR

A mountain village, Batur is north of Penelokan on the western rim of the crater, with no distinguishable border separating it from Kintamani. The newcomer on the ridge, Batur until 1926 was a prosperous village located at the foot of Gunung Batur. In 1917, the volcano erupted and buried most of the village in lava. This cataclysm took the lives of 1,000 people, destroying 65,000 homes and 2,500 temples. Miraculously, the molten lava stopped short at the gateway of Batur's village temple. The survivors looked upon this good fortune as an auspicious sign from the gods, and thus rebuilt their village in the same location.

Nine years later the volcano erupted again. This time the village as well as the temple were completely buried under 30 meters of lava, but only one life was lost—an old woman who died of fright. Only a high shrine to the goddess of the sea was spared destruction. Finally getting the message, the community relocated high on the crater rim. With help from Dutch engineers, the villagers dismantled the surviving shrine and transported it piece by piece up the flank of the crater on the backs of horses and laborers. Once reassembled, the ancient dark stone shrine was incorporated in a new brick-and-stone temple, Pura Ulun Danu Batur ("Head of the Lake") with obvious Indian influences.

This is one of the most significant religious complexes on Bali. Lake Batur is the source of dozens of underground springs which help regulate the flow of water for the farmlands and sacred pools throughout the whole south-central region. Farmers from all over the island pay homage here to Ida Batari Dewi Ulun Danu, the life-sustaining and highly venerated goddess of the lake, who supplies the 37 rivers, tributaries, dams, and irrigation canals between here and the sea with water. The temple's high priest is an important advisor on agricultural and water-use issues. In times of drought or crop failure, elaborate rituals are performed to secure help and blessing from the goddess of the lake. In the temple is housed a grand old *gong gede,* which accompanies the sacred dances of *baris gede* and the ceremonial *rejang* dance for women in a major 11 day *odalan* that usually takes place in March.

The nine-temple complex, with its impressive tall gateway, contains a maze of 285 shrines and pavilions dedicated to the deities of water, agriculture, holy springs, and arts and crafts. The largest temple, Pura Penataran Agung

Batur, consists of five spacious well-swept black-gravel courtyards filled with rows of thatched-roof *meru* towers. The 11-roofed *meru* in the inner courtyard is dedicated to Dewi Danu, the goddes of the lake. In the northwest corner, the Chinese-style shrine honors the patron saint of commerce and the storekeeper of the gods, Ida Ayu Subandar. This practice dates back to Javano-Hindu times when each king employed a harbormaster who was most often Chinese. See the solid gold bell in the *bale gedung,* the storage place for valuable temple artifacts.

KINTAMANI

A windblown market town strung out along the highway north, 68 km (1.5 hours) from Denpasar's Batubulan Station (Rp2500 by *bemo*) and 52 km from Singaraja (Rp2500 by *bemo*), and Rp500 by *bemo* (10 minutes, eight km) north of Penelokan. *Bemo* from Bangli or Gianyar leave for Kintamani more often than from anywhere else. Kintamani is a cool, fresh retreat, bring warm clothes, as it's cold at night (1,500 meters above sea level). The fog comes rolling into Kintamani early, transforming it into a ghost town of howling *anjing,* so you'd best settle in before nightfall. The coldest months are July and August; lots of rain from October to March. Get up early to watch a superb sunrise.

Though the views are not as good, most travelers prefer to stay here instead of Penelokan. With its weather-beaten wooden and concrete buildings, and rusty corrugated iron roofs, the place has the feel of a frontier town. There are fewer annoying locals and you're treated with slightly more respect. Still, Kintamani has more barking dogs per square meter than any other place on Bali. The town boasts the world's finest specimens of the famous Bali Dog, now registered with the AKC. The Bali Dog is commonly white and the puppies roll up into furry puffballs. A particularly endearing characteristic of this breed is its habit of following you for upwards of a kilometer, barking in fits and starts the whole way, triggering mass barking frenzies in dozens of other dogs which linger on long after you're gone.

There's a busy market every third morning along the highway in the north part of town, right in front of Losmen Miranda. Because it's located along the main pass between north and south Bali, mountain people come into Kintamani from the surrounding villages to trade. Traditional and turbaned, these rustics are seldom without their *parang.* This damp climate encourages a variety of fruits and vegetables unknown elsewhere on the island: peanuts, cabbages, passion fruit, citrus, flowers, coffee beans, and Bali's best *kritik* (cassava chips). This spectacle of local color and produce is over by 1100.

The temples of the area look out over the crater. People come from all over the island to pray here, especially during *odalan.* A grand old *gong gde,* one of only three on Bali, plays for the ceremony. Its heavy somber tolling harkens back to a Bali now forever part of the past. Hear it on a moonlit night. Additionally, *sanghyang* trance dances, seldom seen in other parts of Bali, are practiced here but are often closed to tourists.

Accommodations

Most *losmen* are located on the main street, Jl. Pasar Kintamani, each offering cold, cubicle-like, damp-smelling rooms. This environment is somewhat alleviated by a crackling log fire at night—order the wood earlier in the day. Though in July and August there are many visitors, Kintamani's accommodations are generally not full. Bargain if business is slow.

Kintamani's best budget hotel is small, friendly, family-run **Losmen Miranda** in the upper end of town. Six rooms: Rp6000 s and Rp10,000 d with *mandi,* Rp8000 d without *mandi.* Services include free baggage storage, hot water at no charge, and a log fire. This clean, well-kept hotel and its good food are excellent value. Nothing glamorous but no bugs in the bed, and bars on the windows. The owner, Made Senter, works as a guide. *Warung* and stores nearby sell most anything you need.

Between Puri Astina and the market, **Losmen Sasaka** has four rooms with hot water, bath, and showers for Rp25,000 d, including breakfast. Meals available at reasonable prices. The market is just south of this *losmen.* In the south end of town, about 4.5 km north of Penelokan, **Superman Inn** offers small unpretentious rooms with breakfast and *mandi* for Rp10,000 s, Rp20,000 d. Bargain. Run by Kintamani's hippest, youngest hotelier, I Made

Rubin, this *losmen* is the best place in Kintamani to eat cheap.

The most northerly accommodation, about 800 meters in from the road past a little village, is **Puri Astina,** tel. (0362) 975254, the classiest and quietest place in town at Rp30,000 d (no bargaining) for six front rooms with views; four bargain rooms go for Rp15,000 d. A clean, friendly place with a big sitting room, private baths with hot water, showers, Western toilets, and an expensive and rather cheerless restaurant with tourist menu (Rp2500 for soup, Rp8000 for Johnny Walker). Beautiful floor-to-ceiling views of three volcanoes and the lake—worth rising at 0500 for. Postal service. Ask the owner Agus Sartono to arrange horseback riding and experienced guides for trekking or climbs up Gunung Batur (the path starts here). To get to Puri Astina, watch for the big sign just north of Kintamani's market before the radio tower. Don't confuse Puri Astina with **Astina Inn,** which has minimalist bath, no view, and costs Rp12,000-20,000.

Food

There are *warung makanan* up from Puri Astina in the market. **Losmen Miranda** has a pretty good fully Westernized 28-item breakfast and dinner menu, including fried noodles (Rp2000), veggie omelettes (Rp1750), black rice pudding (Rp2000), and vegetables, eggs, and sauce (Rp3000). Miranda claims to have the best pancakes (Rp2500) on Bali—banana inside, coconut on top.

A number of eateries are located on the left-hand side of the road if heading toward Penelokan. Some big fancy tourist restaurants on the right overlook lovely gardens to Lake Batur. Tour buses dump hundreds of Japanese, Taiwanese, and Korean passengers at the 400-seat **Batur Garden,** which serves only lunch—Chinese and Indonesian dishes plus Western bar drinks.

Buy export quality Robusta powdered coffee at **P.T. Perkebunan** in north Kintamani for Rp1600 (250 grams). This plantation office, at the six-km Penelokan marker, is a branch of the head office in Jember, East Java.

Getting Away

From Kintamani to Penelokan by *bemo* is Rp500, to Singaraja by bus is Rp2500 (1.5 hours), to Denpasar by bus is Rp2500 (1.5 hours). The Denpasar-Singaraja bus passes in front of Losmen Miranda. Ask Made Senter, the helpful owner, about his coffee and coconut plantation tours.

For Gunung Batur, it's possible to start your climb from Kintamani at 0600 and return by 1200. Expert local guides, available through the hotels, will lead you down the old bridle path that drops steeply from the lip of the outer crater, then climbs up and over the rim of the inner crater before descending into the innermost crater. It's only about a 45 minute hike to the rim of the inner crater, then another 1.5 hours to the top of Gunung Batur. All the guidebooks recommend **Gede's Trekking,** on Kintamani's main street near the market, for tours in almost any direction. **Made Senter** also offers guide services up Batur. Guides will ask Rp20,000 for one or two people, Rp40,000 for groups of more than two, but may accept as little as Rp25,000 for as many as six people. Depends on the demand. Or ask for detailed directions (Losmen Miranda has a map). Be prepared for hard going on Gunung Batur's ascent and the descent to Toya Bungkah. Catch a *bemo* back from Toya Bungkah, but leave by 1300 or you may have to charter (Rp6000 and up to Penelokan).

There are lots of other good walks in the area—to Gunung Abang, Gunung Agung, and the sea. The more people, the cheaper the guide rate. The track down to Ubud begins just south of Kintamani in Kubupenelokan, next to the Batur Garden. It can be negotiated by motorcycle or bicycle. Travel past walled-in villages and wild mountain scenery, bouncing into Ubud about three hours later.

PENULISAN

Penulisan means "Place of Writing." You'll find this site eight km north of Kintamani at a left bend on one of Bali's prettiest roads. Take the soaring, 333 high-stepped stairs covered in slippery green mold up to lonely **Pura Tegeh Koripan,** almost invariably covered in mist. Entrance is Rp1000.

Spectacularly situated on the outer edge of the Batur crater, this remote temple is the highest (1,745 meters) and perhaps oldest on the island. On Bali, high places are considered sacred—where the gods dwell. Archaeological evidence indicates the existence of a sanctuary here as early as 1500 B.C., 2,000 years before the arrival of Hinduism. This *pura* was the highest structure on Bali until the Perumtel station was built on the opposite knoll. Now it shares that distinction with an ugly TV tower.

Dedicated to the god of the mountains, Sanghyang Grinatha, a manifestation of Shiva, it's lowland counterpart is Pejeng's **Pura Pusering Jagat,** a temple for the gods of the plains. Penulisan is believed to have been the mountain sanctuary of the kings of the Pejeng dynasty. Today, people in the surrounding villages worship here; it's also visited by pilgrims from all over Bali. In the highest courtyard under a number of austere open *bale* are a whole row of linga and yoni, fragments of sculptures, finely wrought headless stone statues, and pagan phallic symbols and prehistoric divinities dating from the 9th century and before. The highest point of the temple, the tall Panerajon shrine, is a representation of the Hindu mythic mountain Mahameru. The pyramidal form of the complex, the site's 11 rising terraces, and its large megalithic stones are all typical of the arrangement of archaic Indonesian mountain sanctuaries.

Scholars conjecture the standing portrait statues of a king and queen with the inscription Batari Mandul and Anak Wungsu dated Saka year 999 (A.D. 1077), may represent King Udayana (d. 1011) and his consort Gunapriya—the source of the legend of *Calonarong.* Another theory is that the royal personage is the Chinese Buddhist princess Subandar. Since *mandul* means "childless," it's been surmised the princess became infertile as a result of a curse hurled by a Shivaite priest. This might explain why the shrine is visited and faithfully maintained by Bali's Chinese.

Not visited by a European until 1885, for years outsiders were forcibly prevented from entering this temple by armed natives. The famous archaeologist Nieuwenkamp tried to visit Pura Tegeh Koripan in 1904 but was warned against it by Dutch authorities. It wasn't until 1948 that the ruler of Bangli allowed the Netherlands Indies Archaeological Service to carry out some technical renovations. Since then, the site has been in an almost continual state of restoration. Because of the high, mist-laden elevation, the statuary and reliefs are in a pretty decrepit state.

Very early in the morning is the quietest and most pleasant time to visit. Surrounded by mountains, caressed with a cooling breeze, on the rare clear day you can see half the island from the highest terrace—all the way to the Indian Ocean in the south and Singaraja and the gleaming Java Sea to the north. Sometimes you can even see the deep purple volcanoes of East Java. Just below the temple is the village of Sukawana, the highest on Bali.

Vicinity of Penulisan

From the village of Sukawana, to the east of the stairway up to Pura Penulisan, take the high road that follows the northern rim of the outer crater from where you can take in the wild and rugged beauty of the crater. The road plunges to Pinggan on the crater's north side, then curves southeast to Songan. Through pine forests and coffee, clove, and citrus plantations the road north of Penulisan winds down to the ocean at Kubutambahan, 47 km away. From there you can either head west to Singaraja and Lovina or east to Tirtagangga and Amlapura. Down the road from Penulisan, toward Kubutambahan, is Desa Adat Loteng, where local *banjar* keep a traditional trinity temple.

Between Penulisan and Bantang, turn on the rough mountain road west through isolated Old Bali villages on the slopes of Gunung Catur. **Belantih** consists of two long, broad, east-west avenues that serve as communal living rooms. These flat avenues, sectioned off by gradual shifts in levels, reflect ancient class groupings. Lined with family dwellings, the aboriginal-style houses contain just a kitchen, sleeping rooms, and a *sanggah* house temple. Houses are constructed of wood with bamboo tile roofs, effective at keeping the occupants warm through the cold nights. A *pemakssan* ancestor temple lies just north of the village and another temple in south Bali style sits at the western end of the main avenue. Belantih's rustic, rough-hewn dwellings and its unusual layout make it a must for anthropologists. The road, which runs along the watershed between the north and the south of the island, takes you through Lampu and Catur, eventually leading to Pelaga in Badung Regency.

LAKE BATUR REGION

The crescent-shaped crater lake of Batur, 1,031 meters above sea level, is seven and a half km long, with a maximum width of two and a half km, and a depth of between 65 and 70 meters. The western side is barren lava rock while the eastern side is lined with trees. The average height of the huge outer rim is around 1,300 meters. Though there are no suface river outlets, the waters of the lake feed underground rivers which emerge as holy springs in the southern part of the island.

Eight villages huddle along its shores: the ancient Bali Aga settlements of Seked, Prajurti, Kedisan, Buahan, Abang, Trunyan, and Songan, and the newer village of Toya Bungkah. These small fishing settlements are characterized by their archaic layout and unusual, fully enclosed, pavilion-style, single-family houses—steep bamboo shingle roofs, low eaves, and walls of clay, mud, brick, woven bamboo matting, or wooden planks. Fish provide most of the protein for these lake dwellers.

After your three-km corkscrew descent from Penelokan down to the lake (Rp1000 by *bemo,* or walk it in 45 minutes), turn left and journey two km on the northwest side of the lake through a strange moonlike landscape. Rivers of black lava, a layer of gravelly volcanic ash, sparse scrub, a few onion fields, and scattered houses now occupy an area where villages stood before

the 1926 and 1963 eruptions. After seven km, this switchback, undulating road arrives in Toya Bungkah. The road down from Penelokan ends at an intersection—to the left is the way to Toya Bungkah and to the right is Pelabuhan Kedisan for boats to Trunyan and the villages of Buahan and Abang.

KEDISAN

The fishing and farming village of Kedisan, the community almost directly beneath Penelokan (three km), has foodstalls, *pasar* area, extensive gardens (oranges, corn, peanuts), souvenir shops, *bemo* terminal, a big parking lot, ticket office, and boat landing. The weather is exceedingly mild and enjoyable. Few mosquitoes but some flies due to the extensive gardens. No telephone or fax machines. There are a number of accommodations, several in attractive settings only minutes from the water. These are the best places to stay if you plan to take a boat trip across the lake. The lake is clean and nice to swim in. Sometimes a bit noisy with dogs at night and cocks in the morning. Always park your vehicle within your hotel grounds, where it will be safe. At night restaurants are convivial meeting places.

The big drawback of Kedisan's accommodations is the swarm of peddlers demanding you

Lake Batur

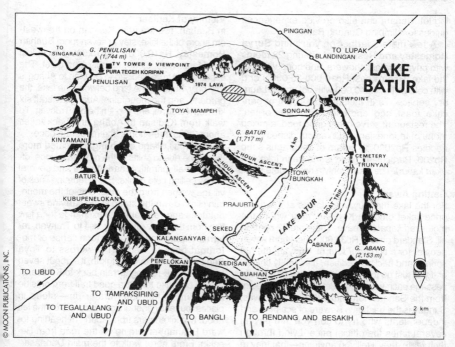

© MOON PUBLICATIONS, INC.

buy *sarung*, shorts, and paintings. They flash you large, sad eyes, show you their guestbooks filled with signatures of satisfied tourists who've bought from them before. Don't fall for it unless you want to buy mass-produced and tacky merchandise and encourage obnoxious behavior in so doing. Kedisan is also full of people trying to get you to pay them to guide you up the mountain. Again, don't do it; you don't need a guide. If you feel you must employ someone, choose I Wayan Pineh, a legendary figure who works out of Surya Homestay. Ask him about the 1963 eruption, when he led a geologist safely away from a fountain of hot lava. His knowledge of the region's volcanoes is extensive and his friendly character and exceptional skills make him the undisputed king of volcano guides.

Accommodations

Cheapest is **Segara Bungalows** near the ferry terminal and close to the road, next to the bar/restaurant and shops. Turn right after de-

scending from Penelokan and reaching the road along the lakeshore. Five basic rooms with *mandi* cost Rp8000 s, Rp10,000 d. The restaurant offers the standard menu, though it would be nice if someone taught them the basics of cooking; it's a shame a chicken has to die to be covered in such a vile sauce. North along the western side of the lake toward Seked village is **Segara Homestay,** separated from the lake by peanut and cabbage fields. The 33 rooms start at Rp30,000 s for bargain rooms with *mandi* and go up to Rp65,000 for larger rooms. Clean with big comfortable beds, fans, bathtubs, shower, hot water. In some rooms the hotel water exudes fumes—dangerous. Have the roomboy try it out first. The staff is helpful and friendly—the hotel has good vibes. A buffet is offered each night in a nice dining area; people from most of the surrounding hotels come here to eat. The restaurant also serves Indonesian and Balinese food, as well as margaritas and other mixed drinks. Another appreciated feature is the big, secure parking lot. Segara can also provide experienced guides for climbing Gunung Batur.

A few meters farther on you'll find **Surya Homestay and Restaurant** offering 22 rooms with private baths, showers, and good views of the lake. Rooms cost Rp10,000-25,000 s or d with cold water; Rp40,000 with hot water. Laundry service. Tariff includes breakfast of pancake, toast, egg, and choice of coffee or tea. The restaurant serves very good food, a mixed menu of Indonesian and Western dishes (fried noodles Rp2000, to cream of asparagus soup Rp200. Particularly good is the fresh lake fish *(ikan kapur)*. The lake is only a two-minute walk.

Getting Away

For the lake trip, buy your tickets at the fixed-price ticket office in Kedisan, near where the motorized *kapal bot* leave. There are 82 boats in all. Standard price is Rp35,000 (maximum seven people) for a two-hour tour of Trunyan, the hot springs and back to Kedisan. It's slightly cheaper if you just go to Trunyan and back (20-minute passage each way). This ferry is only 500 meters from the Segara Homestay. If you like crowds, Sunday is the best day. Beware of scalpers and independents who try to con you into paying several times the official price. Lying through their teeth, they'll tell you anything—that they're cheaper, that the government boats no longer operate, and so forth. They're also inclined to renegotiating the price halfway across the lake or once they have you captive in Trunyan.

A self-propelled dugout canoe is probably not a viable alternative, even though it's much cheaper at Rp10,000, unless you're prepared to paddle a hell of a long way across water that could get very rough should the wind come up. Don't try to paddle across unless you're very strong and race kayaks for a living. No matter what kind of boat you take or no matter when you leave, take jeans and a jumper or freeze your ass off.

Yet another alternative involves no boat across to Trunyan—walk it. Take a *bemo* (Rp500) or ride your motorbike from Penelokan to Buahan; from there it's about a one-hour (seven-km) hike along the well-maintained lakeshore path to Trunyan. A longer hike runs from Kedisan north to Toya Mempeh, looping around southeast to Songan, then back to Kedisan via Toya Bungkah.

Vicinity of Kedisan

In Buahan, two km from Kedisan on the western shore of the lake, stay at seven-room **Buahan Homestay,** Rp10,000 s, Rp15,000 d including breakfast—nice, clean, friendly, and quiet. The asphalt road from Kedisan to Buahan to Abang is roly-poly, hugging the land between the lake, the gardens, and the mountains. Abang is about six km from Kedisan, and two km before Trunyan. To walk from Kedisan to Abang and back takes about 2.5 to three hours at a moderate pace.

The small village of **Abang,** relocated more than once due to shifts of the mountain slope, offers a small, primitive marketplace and several shops selling cold drinks. Every morning lines of village women from the other side of the mountain climb down the steep slope carrying sweet potatoes and vegetables to exchange for a few fish from the lake. After your visit to Trunyan, return to Abang and negotiate for a canoe or motorboat back to Kedisan or across to Toya Bungkah. From Toya Bungkah, it's about seven km along hair-raising terrain back to Kedisan.

You can also take the good trail from outside Abang up to the outer crater rim—steep in places, but easy enough to handle. It's on the left about two kilometers from Abang (if heading toward Buahan) emerging on the road from Besakih. From here, walk to the main Denpasar-Kintamani road, a beautiful stroll above the lake. It's an hour's walk from Segara Hotel to the turnoff path up the mountain, then another hour to the main Denpasar-Kintamani highway. Inquire after guides in Abang or at a Kedisan hotel.

TRUNYAN

Bali's best-known Bali Aga village (pop. 600) nestles under a precipitous crater wall on the eastern shore of Lake Batur. You can walk to Trunyan from Buahan or travel by boat across the lake from Toya Bungkah, taking a motorized boat or canoe from Kedisan. Boats seating seven people leave when full from Kedisan's pier and cost Rp5100 per person; charter boats cost Rp36,000-43,000 for a maximum of seven people.

The Bali Aga are the island's oldest inhabitants, aboriginals who lived here long before the Majapahit invasion in the 14th century. The first direct evidence of Indic influence on Bali dates from an early copper plate, inscribed A.D. 882-914, referring to the founding of a temple to Batara Da Tonta in Trunyan. His title, Batara, indicates that the Bali Aga's most important ancestor figure was incorporated into the Hindu religion.

Legend has it the village was established on the spot where an ancient *taru menyan* tree stood—thus the town's name. It is said that in ancient times the lake goddess Dewi Danu was lured down from heaven by the lovely scent of this tree. The *taru menyan* is the lair of underworld spirits distracted only by corpses, which may explain the people's practice of neither burying nor cremating the dead.

Today Trunyan is a real tourist trap, and you may not get to experience much more than villagers clamoring for money. Still, the setting is spectacular—green mountain backdrop and deep blue lake, mist-shrouded Gunung Batur rising up dramatically on the other side. A path from Trunyan zigzags up the inside face of the crater wall on the southeast slope of Gunung Abang.

Culturally and ethnically outside the mainstream, Trunyan provides evidence of how Bali's earliest people lived. The inbred inhabitants are mostly fishermen, their harsh expressions mirroring a harsh life. Women wearing warm red *kain* pound *padi* in giant stone mortars. Although they plant cabbage, onions, and corn in plots near the lakeshore, the Bali Aga have no rice fields. Since ancient times they've relied on begging to supplement their meager diet. Much of the village—houses, walls, alleyways—has been cut crudely out of volcanic rock. Without trees and gardens, their homes present a bleak impression, unlike any other village on Bali. Modern Indonesia is now making heavy inroads, with the construction of new brick, concrete, and zinc-roofed buildings. Except for a massive 1,100-year-old milkwood tree in the center of the village, there's little sense any longer of Trunyan being an old village. The few traditional architectural oddities include special boys' and girls' clubhouses *(bale truna* and *bale daha),* a pavilion where married women meet *(bale loh),* and a great wooden ferris wheel put in motion during ceremonial occasions. The giant contraption is revolved by foot power. Trunyan's *bale agung,* where married men sit in council, is one of the largest traditional buildings on Bali.

In contrast to the Bali Aga village of Tengenan with its numerous craftspeople, old interesting buildings, and streets where you are free to stroll and look, visitors to Trunyan are not made to feel welcome. Except for the temple, which seems to take up half the village, you don't really see the ancient ways of the Bali Aga, and there are a lot of hustlers around. A guide will attach himself to you and expect a fee of at least Rp5000. Most visitors just get out of the boat, pay Rp5000 for stepping ashore, go up to a temple (also Rp5000) which Westerners are not allowed to enter, then march right back down to the boat again for a trip to the cemetery (another Rp5000) in Kuburan which is around a rocky point a little north of Trunyan and only accessible by boat.

Pura Pancering Jagat

Trunyan's old temple, Pura Pancering Jagat ("Temple of the Navel of the World"), stands under a massive banyan tree. Unusual architecture abounds in this austere *pura*—a fossilized relic of aboriginal Balinese society. The Bali Aga never came fully under Javano-Balinese domination, and the Polynesian features found in their temples are not seen elsewhere on Bali. One must cross over a symbolic little bridge *(titi gonggang)* before entering. Hidden away in a seven-tiered tower inside is Bali's largest statue, the megalithic-style Ratu Gede Pancering Jagat, the powerful patron guardian of the village. Known locally as Da Tonta, this unique 3.5-meter-high stone and clay statue, adorned with ornaments, is considered very ancient, and many magic powers are attributed to it. Every three years virgin boys ceremoniously clean and paint the surface of the colossus with a mixture of water, chalk, and honey. You won't be able to see this august statue, as it's jealously guarded by the villagers. Only they, and only during rituals, may gaze it.

The Kuburan

The Bali Aga prefer exposing their dead in the open air rather than cremating them. Valuable land cannot be given over to the burial of the dead. After complicated rituals, the naked body is first wrapped in white cloth, then placed in a shallow pit, protected from scavengers by a triangular bamboo fence and roof. Those who have committed suicide or who have died of horrible disfiguring diseases are buried.

The eerie cemetery, full of skulls and bones and bush, might have a fresh rotting body in it. Those selling boat-trip tickets might accost you in Kedisan, screaming "A new body at Trunyan!" Bizarre. Curiously, there is no stench of decomposing flesh—because, it is said the bodies are placed near a *taru menyan* tree, which smells of incense. But with the scavengers, the maggots, the scattered bones, the cans, plastic, bottles, and other garbage, you may wonder why on earth should you pay to see such a morbid sight.

TOYA BUNGKAH

Lying on the western shore of Lake Batur, along the roller-coaster road from Kedisan to Songan, the resort village of Toya Bungkah features an invigorating hot springs, massive cinemascopic views, and a black-sand beach. Many travelers choose to stay in Toya Bungkah rather than Kedisan because the latter has too many Bali Aga while the former is more a mixture of Balinese and Javanese. Watch your gear in both places—lotsa thieves.

Toya Bungkah gets busy only during July and August, otherwise there's little traffic or motorboat noise. Just roosters crowing, flies buzzing, children playing, and pool balls socking. There are worse places to stay for a few days. Free of city lights, at night the stars are brilliant and the air fresh, filled with the sound of generators supplying power to the restaurants and color TVs. Electricity only comes on from 0630 to 2400. *Bemo* run in front of most hotels and it's a very easy matter to get to and from the village to Penelokan, eight km distant.

Just before the village is a tollbooth where you're hit with another irritating entrance fee: Rp1050 per person, Rp1000 per vehicle, Rp200 per motorcycle. Keep your entrance ticket so you can reenter each day. Popular tourist activities include bathing in the lake, fishing (Rp1000 for bamboo poles and worms), touring the lake via motorized boat (Rp40,000 per hour with boatman), visiting Trunyan and/or the cemetery on the other side of the lake, walking along the scenic shore, getting up at 0400 to climb Gunung Batur, or simply hanging out and en-

joying the view and the cool air. At least five small open-air pool halls liven up the evening and somewhat occupy the many shiftless young men of the village. Although Toya Bungkah presents fewer hassles than other Batur communities, the males can be pretty aggressive to single women.

Hot Springs
This sulfurous hot springs is known to soothe muscle aches and pains, as well as cure rheumatism and skin diseases. The volcanically heated water bubbles up from under the lake in several places among the lava rocks. The water is not really that hot, though it becomes warmer as the day progresses. A private hot springs lies north of Amertha's. Admission fee of Rp300 just to look, Rp1000 for hot-tub style baths. Facilities include changing room and toilet. Bring your own towel. Signs ask patrons not to wash clothes, shampoo, or wear shoes in the bathing area. Be warned, the pool is untidy and unappealing, not that private, and swarming with vendors.

The public *air panas* is on the other side of Amertha's and free. However, since villagers wash their clothes and cows in these shallow pools, and there's lots of litter around, you don't always feel like bathing here. After a long, relaxing dunk, swim Finnish-style from the mineral pools straight into the chilly lake. Very therapeutic, especially fresh from a hike up Gunung Batur.

The Art Center
Also called the **Balai Seni Toya Bungkah.** Above the *air panas* is a retreat for the study of the arts, including a dance academy and amphitheater. Rooms and bungalows spread out among nice peaceful gardens (see "Accommodations," below). If you stay here, you can watch the dances and an occasional *wayang kulit* for free. Good selection of books available to guests, with the emphasis on painting, from Dyer to the Fauvists. If no visiting study group is in town, the center seems virtually deserted; no one can provide any information on anything other than the rooms and restaurant. When an event is going on, the place is bustling.

The center (tel. 0362-7802719) was established in 1971 by Sutan Takdir Alisjahbana, a

North Sumatran novelist, philosopher, and painter. Known as "The Father of the Indonesian Language," Alisjahbana played a pivotal role in developing Bahasa Indonesia as a tool for sophisticated intellectual and technical usage. The old professor now spends but a few days a month here; the rest of the year he's in Denpasar or Jakarta.

Accommodations

Toya Bungkah contains about 15 *losmen*, most lining the road and surrounded by neatly landscaped gardens. Look around before you settle on one. Except for the Art Center, all offer quite plain rooms for Rp8000 s, Rp10,000 or Rp12,000 d, which includes toilet, shower, and front veranda. Unlike other budget accommodations on Bali, breakfast is sometimes not included in the price; inquire first. Most *losmen* are located in the west end of the village. If the room doesn't offer a view of the lake, you could probably bargain it down to Rp6000 s, Rp8000 d. Whatever the price, insist upon clean bed linen and a towel or threaten to move to another *losmen*. Try to avoid places close to the road, as hikers set out at 0400 accompanied by a chorus of dogs; sputtering motorcycles and *bemo* start up in earnest at around 0500.

Darma Putra Homestay & Restaurant has 10 rooms and two bungalows with comfortable beds, bathroom, and shower for Rp7500 s, Rp12,000 d; bungalows are Rp20,000 d breakfast included. The owner, I Ketut Narsa, provides good information on trekking and guides. Behind Marini's Restaurant are three nice bungalows run by I Nyoman Mertha; Rp12,000 s, Rp20,000 d (includes breakfast) with nice views and clean tile floors. Fairly quiet, near restaurants. The very reasonable **Awangga** is just past the Art Center and about 75 meters from the Toya Bungkah-Songan road. Small rooms without showers overlook the lower baths of the hot springs and cost Rp8000 s, Rp10,000 d, Rp15,000 s and Rp25,000 d with hot water. Four bungalows with hot showers run Rp25,000 d. Quiet, enclosed courtyard. Jero Wijaya provides great information as well as maps of the crater area.

Another good place is **Arlina's,** tel. (0362) 51165, past the Art Center on the bend of the road, charging Rp10,000-15,000 for economy rooms with one bed, Rp30,000 for rooms with two beds (hot water, separate reading lights). Also included: excellent breakfast, small verandas, phantasmagoric grotto-like *mandi*, shower, and the clearest and most unobstructed views of the lake. Join the card-playing guides in front of the *losmen* and banter with them over their "fee" for taking you up Gunung Batur. Arlina's also rents bicycles, motorbikes, and cars with drivers. **Tirta Yatra,** right on the lake, wants Rp8000 s or Rp12,000 d for very basic rooms—virtual cells separated by bamboo mats. Outhouse in the back. This is like camping, so bring your own soap, drinking water, and sleeping bag. Rooms have a squat toilet, no shower, oil lamp lighting. A fine cheap restaurant overlooks the lake. Despite the noise from children, roosters, dogs, and the nearby road, **Nyoman Pangus Homestay & Warung** opposite Arlina's is often full because it's the best known. Located right in the village center, Nyoman asks Rp10,000, Rp12,000, and Rp15,000 s or d for clean rooms (no breakfast) in the back with bath, shower, and laundry facilities. More expensive rooms have hot water. A friendly, gentle man eager to please; an okay place to stay.

Behind Nyoman Pangus Homestay is **Mawa Bungalows.** The service-oriented owner charges Rp6000 s and Rp8000 d for rooms in front, Rp10,000 s and Rp15,000 d for rooms in back. Laundry service. **Asri Inn,** tel. (0362) 753645, fax (0361) 754784 in Denpasar, charges Rp15,000 d with *mandi*. Separate bungalow for Rp20,000 d. Nice location, though perhaps too central. **Amertha's Accommodations** is right on the lake, overlooking the hot springs. Bungalows for Rp20,000 and Rp25,000 s or d face the lake with private garden bath, walls of volcanic rock, and open verandas. Other, smaller rooms go for Rp12,000 and Rp15,000 s or d. All four classes of rooms have private *mandi*. Since it's very close to the hot springs, hot water is pumped up for showers. Wide parking lot and good restaurant.

More secluded than Toya Bungkah's other *losmen*, the **Art Center** has more expensive rooms, each with *mandi*, European toilet. Standard rooms with hot water cost Rp15,000 s, Rp18,500 d. The suites in front go for Rp18,000 s, Rp26,000 d—very nice, they look out over landscaped gardens, near the lake, with attached *mandi* with bathtub and shower. Family bungalows (capacity four or five) are Rp50,000. The Art Center is often booked by groups. Performances take place when hotel guests charter a dance troupe. The restaurant services American breakfast for Rp7000; lunch Rp8000, dinner Rp10,000. The other high-priced hotel, newly built, is the *Puri Bening Hayato Hotel* right beside the lake. Huge restaurant which serves tour group-type food.

Food

There's an abundance of small restaurants and shabby small *warung* that offer the usual tourist fare at cheap prices. Most come with great views of the lake, many specialize in grilled lake fish, small and bony but tasty.

The **Marini Bar & Restaurant,** attached to Amertha's and almost hanging over the hot springs, with beautiful views from the veranda, is the best place to eat. The resort's best grilled fish, but some dishes—like the vegetables—tend to be greasy. The **Art Center Restaurant** asks higher prices than any other eatery (fruit salad Rp2000), but the food is well prepared. **Under the Volcano Restaurant** is also a good place to eat, and even stocks cold beer. Though the menu's claim to "The Best Fried Fish In The World" is clearly an exaggeratio, the fresh lake fish is indeed excellent. Daily specials, stunning views of Gunung Batur. Only Rp2500 for three fish, grilled to perfection by an excellent cook. Owner Nyoman Mawa buys fish twice daily; the chicken run around out back until you order them.

Services

No telephones. The only official travel agent in town is **CV Jero Wijaya Tourist Service,** Box 01, Kintamani, Bali 80652, a privately run tourist office that changes money and sells a number of tours—Sunrise Breakfast at the Top (three hours), Bicycling Around the Lake (four hours), and Younger Batur Crater (six hours). After each outing, which range in price from Rp10,000 to Rp50,000, the driver picks you up in the company van and drives you back in air-conditioned comfort. In Ubud, the Jero agent is **Mutiara Tourist Service,** Jl. Raya Ubud, tel. (0361) 975145.

The shop in **Under The Volcano** sells toiletries, mosquito coils, some aspirin. Owner Nyoman Mawa is the closest thing to a tourist information bureau in the village.

Getting There

From Penelokan, there's a good paved road via Seked and Prajurti. Since Toya Bungkah gets little traffic, *bemo* drivers first want Rp1500; when you get in, the price suddenly skyrockets to Rp15,000, eventually falling to Rp8000. Just wait until a public *bemo* comes along and pay Rp1000. Alternatively, you can hitch a ride down to the crater from a tourist or a truck, then walk to Toya Bungkah from Kedisan in an hour. Or take a boat from Kedisan.

Getting Away

Hop on a *bemo* up to Penelokan (Rp1000); they leave from 0400 to 1300. From Penelokan regular buses leave for Singaraja and Denpasar. Public transport is always more frequent in the morning. After 1300, the *bemo* are more infrequent; you may have to charter (Rp6000 and up) or accept an outrageous price. Have your *losmen* or hotel owner make return transportation arrangements for you (bring this up before you take a room). Or hitch a ride with a construction truck for around Rp2000 to Penelokan. With a five-person minimum, you can arrange 1030 and 1200 shuttle service with Jero Wijaya Tourist Service to Ubud, Rp8000; Kuta, Rp17,500; Lovina, Rp12,500; Candidasa, Rp12,500. Some of the *losmen* also provide shuttle services. Ask Nyoman Mawa at **Under the Volcano,** who can also arrange treks. The short trek starts at 0400, returns at 0800, and costs Rp30,000; a lengthier journey commences at 0400, returns at 1200, and runs Rp60,000. Fees include breakfast. A tour of the volcano area costs Rp80,000 and requires 10 hours; at the end a car waits for you in Toya Mampeh to return you to Toya Bungkah.

At Toya Bungkah's tiny harbor and concrete pier, boatmen ask Rp10,000 up front for a rowboat across the lake to Trunyan's Bali Aga cemetery; you row. You'll die if you row by yourself, then they'll go through your pockets for the Rp5000 to see the cemetery. Motorized boats to the boneyard cost Rp40,000 for up to seven people. Not worth it.

Vicinity of Toya Bungkah

Walk north to **Tirta,** where there's only one *losmen.* The proprietors are desparate for guests. Take the path from Awangga to the north, crossing over black lava rocks; newer lava flows are along the way. Four km in the other direction, toward Kedisan, you'll see a sign pointing toward **Pura Jati,** a Vishnu temple on the lake shore with *exquisitely* decorated shrines and entrance gates.

Many travelers arrive in Toya Bungkah in the afternoon, stay the night, rise early to climb Gunung Batur, then descend from the mountain and reach Kedisan via Prajurti and Seked by midday. Houseboys and "professional guides" everywhere in Toya Bungkah are available for the climb. A guide will approach you with a "thank you" book for their guide services, informing you the fee is Rp50,000 per person roundtrip. then may "lower" the price to Rp30,000. In fact, the fair price for a guide for one person is Rp10,000-15,000. The final price depends on the age and experience of the guide, the size of the group, your bargaining power, and supply and demand.

SONGAN

From Toya Bungkah, walk one hour or drive the single-lane, surfaced road to Songan on the northeast corner of the outer crater, 12 km from Penelokan. Songan is also accessible by boat from Kedisan and Toya Bungkah. This is the largest village on the lake, with a population of around 5,000. The people make their living from fishing and cultivating the flatland beyond the village. The remote hamlet has only one *losmen,* **Restiti Homestay & Restaurant,** with simple rooms with bath for Rp12,000; it's located on the road to the temple 200 meters beyond the village. There are no *bemo* to Songan but you can get rides on gravel trucks; the drivers ask for lots of rupiah but are happy with Rp2000; some travelers wrangle free rides. Many sulfur wells and natural springs in the area. If you need to go back up to Penelokan in your own vehicle, gas up here.

Turn right at Songan and travel to the end of the road to reach beautifully situated Pura Ulun Danu (not to be confused with Pura Ulun Danu in Batur village on the western rim of the crater). Since the headwaters of Lake Batur are considered holy throughout the whole eastern half of Bali, a ritual drowning of live animals occurs here every 10 years in honor of Dewi Danu, the goddess of the lake. In 1994 two buffalo, a pig, a goat, a goose, and a chicken, adorned with gold, *kepeng,* and other decoration, were taken out into the middle of the lake and drowned with solemn grandeur. The floor of the lake is no doubt littered with incalculable wealth from the millennia of ceremonies since it's believed Pura Danu Danu was built on the site of a pre-Majapahit temple.

From the temple, climb 15 minutes up to the remote viewpoint on the crater rim; you can see Bali's east coast. It's a 12 km walk on an old trade road to Lupak on the Amlapura-Tianyar-Tejakula-Singaraja highway running northeast along the east coast. Walking downhill over streams and through little villages and beautiful forest areas, it's about a five- or six-hour hike. Take water, as the more you descend, the hotter and more barren it becomes. The path ends in the middle of Lupak's small local market. Turn left on the highway and catch a blue *bemo* to Lovina for around Rp3500.

Right behind Pura Ulun Danu, a small footpath climbs up to the rim of the outer crater. The right path then winds up to Gunung Agang, passing above Trunyan—an arduous climb. The path to the left leads down to the traditional village of Blandingan from where a path will take you back to Songan.

GUNUNG BATUR

After Agung, Batur is the most sacred mountain on Bali. Most often the mountain's only sign of life is an occasional wisp of smoke that drifts across its lava-blackened slopes. But when this 1,717-meter volcano erupts, it glows red, bellows, and throws out rocks and showers of volcanic debris. If you arrive in Penelokan at night, you'll awaken to an unforgettable sight. The next morning, the mist will lift from the shining lake and roll across the crater like a mammoth white and gray curtain. When the weather is clear there are also spectacular views of Gunung Batur's smoking cone.

Sitting in the middle of an old volcanic basin inside a gigantic caldera, smoldering Gunung Batur rises 686 meters above Lake Batur. The crescent-shaped lake takes up about one-third of the basin's total area. Measuring 13.8 km by 11 km, this is one of the largest and most beautiful calderas in the world. The crater's outer walls, about 30,000 years old, range from 1,267 meters to 2,153 meters above sea level. There are actually two calderas; the floor of one lies 120-300 meters lower than the floor of the other. Plan on a full day to explore both of them.

History

Like Krakatoa, Batur was initially formed in the shape of a sharply pointed cone over 3,500 meters above sea level. A terrific explosion blew the point off the cone, atomized a large portion of the volcano, and collapsed the bulk of the mountain into the magma chamber which was emptied by the initial cataclysm.

Before the present caldera was born, Penelokan and Kintamani lay on the western slope of the "first" Gunung Batur. Now Penelokan and Kintamani are spread out along the top of the caldera's outer crater rim. The present younger, smaller volcano—of the effusive rather than explosive type—gradually grew out of the crater floor over a period of hundreds of thousands of years.

Batur erupted in 1917, destroying 65,000 homes, 2,500 temples, and 1,372 people. Its last major eruption was in 1926, when the village below was covered in lava. In 1959 a crack in the lakebed emitted poisonous gases, coloring the water green and killing all the fish. There was further activity in 1963 during the Gunung Agung

catastrophe, when lava spilled down Batur's southeastern flank. The lava flows from those eruptions can still be seen beside the lake. In August 1994, one of Batur's lower peaks began belching smoke and debris. In Kedisan you could hear the mountain rumble, and from any vantage point the volcano glowed red. Climbers were prohibited from ascending the peak and people all over Bali complained of throat ailments, coughing, and congestion—Batur belched NO_3 and sulphuric acid up to 450 times a day.

Guides

Guides will approach you everywhere, offering their services for a starting price of Rp30,000. They'll eventually settle on Rp15,000 for two or three people. For six people, most guides won't accept anything less than Rp25,000 or 30,000. Guides you meet in your *losmen* tend to charge too much. You can easily find a guide if you arrive at the trailhead at 0330. They'll come out of the dark and offer to lead you for as little as Rp10,000.

Although you don't really need a guide, the fellow can help you find your way out of the clouds that can envelop the slopes of Gunung Batur without warning. If you decide to hire a guide, choose a younger man or boy; it's a difficult ascent. It's unnerving to hike up the mountain sweating and gasping for breath while your nimble guide scrambles up playing the flute, puffing away on cigarettes, and wearing only plastic thongs!

The guides in Toya Bungkah offer three different climbs. The short one, up and back for the

sacred Gunung Batur

sunrise, is Rp25,000-30,000 (four hours). The medium one involves a walk around Batur's three caters, a visit to the bat cave, and a breakfast of eggs boiled by volcanic steam for Rp30,000-40,000 (five hours). The third option is the more interesting tour. Here you get the volcanically boiled eggs with banana and bread, the sunrise, a hike down to the other side of Gunung Batur, plus a trip to the "lucky temple" (Pura Bukit Mentik) three km beyond Toya Mampeh, where lava stopped just meters before the gateway. From the other side of Batur you can see two other volcanoes. For this tour they ask Rp60,000-70,000 (all day). All these prices apply to a group (maximum four people) and reflect first offers only.

At least six guides work in Toya Bungkah. Consider I Nyoman Toto ("Charlie"), whom you'll meet sooner or later if you hang around Amertha's. Nyoman Mertha works in Marini's in the village center opposite Under the Volcano. He's very bright, has studied university level history and geography, and speaks good English. Ketut Lanus, a pleasant and honest man, also leads tours. Jero Wijaya (Toya Bungkah, Box 01, Kintamani 80652) is very knowledgeable about the volcanic history of the area. Your *losmen* can also arrange for a guide.

Approaches

You can attempt the climb from many different directions. As a rule, always take the widest, most obvious and worn path, not necessarily the most direct.

The easiest approach is from the northwest, beginning at Toya Mampeh. This climb, by way of the volcano's back door, can also begin from the west at Kintamani. Guides here ask Rp25,000 for one to two people plus around Rp5000 for each additional person. If you start on the path from Puri Astina at 0630, you can climb the volcano, rest in the hot springs, and grab a *bemo* back to Kintamani by 1200 or 1300. You can also hire horses in Kintamani, more difficult to arrange in Penelokan, Kedisan, or Toya Bungkah.

It's also possible to ascend the volcano directly from Kedisan, though this is an unrelentingly steep climb. Simply walk 20 minutes out of town in the direction of the mountain and follow signs on the left directing you to the trail. Don't be alarmed when the trail branches off; they all lead to the same place. Just keep walking uphill.

You can also start from the northeast. Drive or walk seven km on the good road west from Toya Bungkah to Toya Mampeh; on the way climb up through the lava fields on the volcano's northern side, a product of a 1974 eruption. This new track, circling the base of Gunung Batur, allows vehicles to ascend to within a 30-minute walk of the mountain's largest and highest crater, Batur I. To get there from Toya Bungkah, take the road northeast toward Songan, then turn left after about three km. Follow this road for about two km to a track on the left, which then climbs another two km to a parking area at Serongga.

One of two "tourist" approaches starts from Pura Jati. In this lakeside village, about three km southwest of Toya Bungkah, a big sign marks the start of the trail. Two shadeless hours up and 1.5 hours down. Or go up from Pura Jati but descend via Toya Bungkah, passing through a beautiful pine forest. As your reward, soak in the *air panas* in Toya Bungkah.

The hike from Toya Bungkah is the most popular. If you start at 0400, you'll make it to the peak of Gunung Batur in time for the sunrise. The climbs from Toya Bungkah and Pura Jati end in exactly the same spot, so ascend one way and descend the other. From Penelokan take a *bemo* to Toya Bungkah (Rp1000) or the boat from Kedisan. From Toya Bungkah, walk the gully with the rocky entrance behind the WC on the other side of Under the Volcano's parking lot (follow the sign). The path veers to the left; just keep going up. Half the climb is through a man-made eucalyptus forest. A group of locals—men with sodas in a bucket and would-be boy guides—will follow any tourist who takes this path. Sometimes they block the trail with plywood barriers, hoping to confuse you or force you to hire them. Ignore this behavior. Take the same trail down. Runoffs may lead to cliff edges and deadends and you may have to backtrack.

Climbing It

Though a strenuous ascent, Gunung Batur is the easiest Bali volcano to climb—you can drive to the base and you don't have to struggle through vegetation. Regardless of your approach, tackle the mountain only in good weather. It's coolest when overcast, but the climb is not recommended in the rainy season (Nov.-March). No matter the weather, make sure you have sturdy shoes; it's slippery near the top. Wear long pants and a warm sweater, windbreaker, or sweatshirt. Start up the scoria- and pumice-strewn slope by at least 0600. Take sunscreen and water to prevent sunburn and heatstroke.

As you start your ascent locals try to sell you drinks. When you say you don't need any, they'll accompany you anyway. As you get higher and higher you grow more and more thirsty. When you finally reach the top you realize you've bought all their drinks without really intending to. So bring your own food and water (two liters) or be prepared to pay for the most expensive drinks on Bali—Rp3000 for a soda and Rp2500 for a plastic bottle of water. It always amazes people when they find three *warung* on top of Batur's north crater, serving pancakes or jaffles (Rp2000) and reasonable tea and coffee (Rp500-700).

As you climb, the towering mountain is frequently hidden by dense fog and mist, revealing the summit momentarily, then surrounding it again. The way is well trodden, well marked, and well maintained, but if you get lost don't expect anyone to show you the way without exacting payment. And, unless you're a very experienced mountaineer, be sure to hire a guide at Rp10,000-15,000 if you intend to tackle Batur in the dark.

The Summit
There could be 100 people on the summit, but this is likely to occur only in the tourist season.

Most tourists are guided to the sandy top of the middle crater. The topmost crater to the north is another hour's climb, along a narrow rim only one meter wide, and the view isn't as fine. At the top there's a small shrine to Vishnu. See the sun slowly lighting the whole lake, catch glimpses of Gunung Rinjani on Lombok to the east. Peer into the volcano's steaming core and sit awhile on warm rocks. Take in the sweeping panorama across the shimmering waters of the lake, spot the rivers of lava diverted by huge boulders. Look for relatively recent, all-black lava flows, lava tubes, and parasitic cones. From the southern rim take the trail down inside the crater to the bat cave. If you intend to stay in the Batur region for just a day, get down in Toya Bungkah by 1300 or you may have to spend a lot of money chartering a *bemo* up to Penelokan. Allow time to bathe in the cool lake or in Toya Bungkah's hot springs below—just what you need.

Note: With your own transport, the four-hour up-and-back climb can be made in a single day from Denpasar or Ubud. If you leave Ubud at 0630, it takes just an hour to drive to Lake Batur via Penelokan, then start climbing by 0800 and you're back down to the lake by noon. (Don't pay more than Rp30,000 one-way for a chartered *bemo* from Ubud to Penelokan.) If you leave Ubud at 0300, you get to the base of the mountain at around 0400 and arrive at the summit just in time for the sunset.

BOB RACE

KARANGASEM REGENCY

With mighty Gunung Agung dominating the landscape, this regency's scenery is some of the most spectacular on the island. Karangasem is Bali's most traditional region, with rustic villages, hospitable people, and unique festivals. The 861-square-km regency is one of the most untouristed on Bali, removed from the frenzy of development. This is the only area of Bali where a number of archaic dance and musical forms are still regularly practiced and where the High Balinese language is still in common use.

In the "closed" village of Tenganan near Candidasa, unusual customs have been jealously guarded for centuries. Its pre-Hindu architecture is simple yet gracious; one of the most handsome buildings in all Bali is Tenganan's 12-poster *bale gede*. The mountain villages of Karangasem often incorporate a very distinctive, sturdy, volcanic-stone architecture found nowhere else on Bali. The villages of Selat, Iseh, and Rendang offer fine architecture as well as magnificent views.

On the southern slope of Gunung Agung is Besakih, the Mother Temple of Bali. From the village of Putung, perched on a steep cliff above the sea, one can clearly view Gunung Rinjani on the island of Lombok to the east. The ferry to Lombok leaves daily from the small port of Padangbai on the southeast coast, where accommodations are cheap and plentiful and local restaurants serve freshly caught seafood. In Manggis village is perhaps Bali's most dynamic hotel, the Amankila, an opulent palace built on the side of a mountain overlooking the ocean.

For marinelife enthusiasts, snorkeling and scuba diving off the coast in and around the beach resorts of Balina and Candidasa, as well as near Amed northeast of Tirtagangga, is a profound experience. One of the premier dive spots on the whole island is Tulamben in the northeast corner of the regency.

If you want to spend some time in Karangasem, the best place to base yourself is Padangbai—where the ferries for Lombok depart—or the tourist enclave of Candidasa. Starting in Klungkung, drive along a scenic road past Kusamba, Goa Lawah, Padangbai, then Candidasa. As soon as you get past Klungkung, the traffic thins, the pace slows, and the countryside opens up into dry stretches. The monsoons don't start until November, and toward the end of the dry season Karangasem's inhabitants are desperate for rain.

For a complete loop of the district, travel from Klungkung to Candidasa and Amlapura, then head west across the foothills of Gunung Agung to Rendang via Sibetan and Selat. From Rendang, visit Besakih to the northeast, then continue west on a little-used road to Bangli or south to Klungkung. Fares from Denpasar's Terminal Kereneng: Klungkung, Rp600; Padangbai, Rp1500; Candidasa, Rp1500; Besakih, Rp1800; Amlapura, Rp2500.

The Land

The undulating irrigated rice fields of Karangasem are dotted with fruit trees, corn, papaya, durian, and banana. In the arid northeast grow groundnuts, grapes, and cacao; coffee and cloves are the cash crops in the mountain regions. Rising from the sculptured rice fields in some areas are large, rocky, knoblike outcroppings, remnants of a previous volcanic age. Now covered with tropical vegetation, each knob is usually home to a small temple. Banana and coconut plantations along the coast are broken by small villages where people make their living from fishing, sea salt processing, and coral gathering.

KARANGASEM REGENCY

© MOON PUBLICATIONS, INC.

The hard work of reclaiming the land after Gunung Agung's great eruption of 1963 is complete, though remnants of the devastation are still visible in cracked buildings and fields strewn with volcanic debris.

History

After the 16th-century collapse of the Majapahit Empire, the royal *kraton* in Gelgel dominated Bali. In the 17th century the court of Karangasem rose to challenge Gelgel, becoming not only a powerful political force but a thriving center of the arts. In 1678 Karangasem conquered the island of Lombok, colonizing the western rice-growing portion of the isle. Tables turned in 1849 when the Dutch landed 4,000 Lombok troops in Karangasem; Lombok ruled the region until 1894, when Karangasem came under full Dutch control. To govern the regency the Dutch appointed one of the most cryptic figures in Balinese history, Gusti Gede Jelantik. His son, Raja Anak Agung Gede Jelantik, served as governor of east Bali from 1902 until Indonesian independence in 1945, when all of Indonesia's aristocracy lost their authority. See faded photos of the old raja and his family on the facade of the Maskerdam reception hall in Puri Kangin, Amlapura.

GUNUNG AGUNG

This sacred mountain is to the Balinese what Olympus was to the ancient Greeks—the Cosmic Mountain. The Balinese, who consider this volcano "the Navel of the World," always sleep with their heads toward Agung. The mystical Balinese believe the mountain was raised by the gods as a vantage point to view the unceasing pageant of life below. To them, it is a central, heavenly point of reference, the geographical and religious center of the world. With an elevation of 3,014 meters, the foot of the mountain stretches northeast right to the sea. To the southeast its slope is blocked by a line of small extinct volcanoes; to the northwest Agung is separated from Gunung Batur by a narrow valley.

When you fly into Bali, you'll see the shadowy outline of the giant blue-black mountain dominating the landscape. Early in the morning its conical peak can be seen poking through the clouds from almost any part of Bali. Whether in the bright sunshine or moonlight, a stream of clouds on the crest always trails off in the wind. From the summit, you can see Pura Besakih, Gunung Rinjani on Lombok to the east, and Singaraja and the whole north coast.

The gods rest above the mountain summit, and when they come down to visit the island they reside in Bali's holiest temple complex, Besakih, six km below the crater. When the gods are displeased, Agung showers the land with stone and ruin. Its feathery heights are the source of life-giving rivers and volcanic ash which irrigate and enrich the island's rice fields. The lower portions of the mountain are heavily forested, and farmed up to about 1,000 meters.

History

A major eruption in 1350 so fertilized the land around Besakih that year after year it has yielded enough rice to not only supply the needs of the complex but also defray the costs of the unending ceremonies staged in the mountain's honor. Agung's most recent eruption occurred in the closing years of the turbulent Sukarno regime, in 1963. The cataclysm began during the greatest of Balinese ceremonies, Eka Dasa Rudra, an exorcism of evil staged only once every 100 years. Except for minor activity in 1808 and 1843, this was the first time the sacred volcano had blown since 1350.

Many people looked upon the disaster as a divine condemnation of the ill-fated Sukarno regime, and the subsequent failure of crops, uprooting of villages, and forced evacuation of 86,000 people contributed substantially to the communal clashes and massacres during the so-called purge of Indonesian "communists" in 1966. Because empty land for the evacuees was no longer available on Bali, the consequences of overpopulation became acute for the first time in the island's history. No longer could farmers move temporarily to another part of the island, later returning to a land covered in fresh, fertile ash. Thousands were instead resettled in *transmigrasi* camps in central Sulawesi.

Few scars remain today. Until well into the 1970s the countryside northeast of Klungkung was blackened by lava streams, but the region is now replanted with fields and gardens. Remnants of the massive eruption are still visible in the Tianyar and Kubu areas on the northeast coast, the least populated region of Karangasem. Agung remains semi-active, and volcanologists in Rendang and Batulompeh continue to keep a wary eye on it.

CLIMBING THE MOUNTAIN

In the dry season, between April and October, the fit and adventuresome can attempt the ascent of Gunung Agung. It's exhausting, and can be downright dangerous. Climbers have become lost, never to be found. Don't climb alone, and bring a flashlight, water, warm clothes, an umbrella (a necessity), and trail food. Because of sharp grass, long pants are also a good idea. Good hiking shoes with nonslip soles are a must for the final steep scramble over loose scree to the summit. Since there are innumerable trails leading skyward, particularly in the early part of the climb, you should have a guide. The cost depends on the number of people in your group. Some guides will carry your pack; some will furnish food and water.

From Besakih Temple

The most popular route begins on the trail to the right of Pura Besakih, from Pura Pengubengan, the farthest temple in the Besakih complex. This is a difficult six-km climb to Agung's usually cloudy peak. If a religious festival is in progress, you may not be permitted to climb. Leave no later than 0630 if you don't want clouds to obscure the view from the top. If you want to catch the sunrise from the top, start no later than 0200. After climbing about 1.5 km past some houses, you come upon a *meru* temple at about 1,200 meters, where it's possible to sleep. From this point on, the slippery path through thick vegetation suddenly grows steeper; after two more hours it becomes steeper still. After three hours, the terrain changes from humid jungle to a slope of bare, rubbly volcanic debris and slick rock. Just before the tree line camp overnight at the holy spring of Tirta Mas. In the morning climb the last two hours to the sum-

mit. For the final assault you must literally crawl, scramble, and pull yourself up through a lava field. By sunrise you'll reach the windy two-meter-wide summit ridge, a frightening place with icy wind and thin air—a place where people are not meant to linger. Camp on broad ledges sheltered by large slabs of rock. Allow at least four hours to get back down.

From Muncan

The southern approach to the summit, the other popular starting point, is four km east of Rendang. As you enter Muncan village from the east you'll see a blue sign reading Mountain Guide Available/For Hire to Mt. Agung. The guide, I Ketut Uriada (in Dusun Pemuhunan), is a guru in the school a short distance away. Stay in Ketut's home for Rp5000, plus Rp2000 for meals. Ketut asks Rp30,000-50,000, depending on the size of group, plus vehicle charter (Rp50,000 roundtrip) to Pura Pasar Agung. Start by flashlight no later than 0300; under normal conditions you'll return to Muncan in the evening while it's still light.

From Sebudi

A third well-worn route starts above the small 900-meters-high village of Sebudi on the southern slopes of Agung, about 2,100 meters below the summit. This is an easier and shorter route up Agung than from Besakih. Take a car or *bemo* (Rp500) from Rendang to the small agricultural village of **Selat** (elev. 500 meters), four km east of Muncan. Let the police in Selat know your route (Rp3000 fee); check in with them again when you get back. At the start of the village (coming from Putung) is **Puri Agung Cottage** with nine rooms (Rp20,000-40,000), used mostly by BLKP students. The front and most expensive room over the street is poor value. No breakfast included in price, just coffee or tea.

From Selat, allow several hours for the five-km drive north on a rocky lava road to Sebudi, where you can view a monument to the 1963 eruption. The "road" ends about four km beyond Sebudi in the *desa* of **Sorga,** the farthest point you can reach by motorcycle or four-wheel-drive vehicle. It's possible to leave your transport and other gear with the local people; you might also spend the night here. This trailhead is also your last chance to hire a guide for the rest of the way up the mountain—well worth the price since trails are so poorly marked. Fit climbers can complete the whole ascent in a single day. If you begin the climb from Sebudi by 0730, stop for lunch two-thirds of the way up at around 1200, you'll reach the summit at 1330. Head down by 1430 so you can arrive in Sorga by 1730 for the drive back to Selat.

From Sorga you walk about an hour along streambeds to **Sangkawasa;** it's possible to stay the night here in Pura Pasar Agung, a small temple built on the last level area before the really steep part of the climb. See the *pemangku* and don't forget to make a donation (Rp5000) for a safe climb. Next come boulders and a dense pine stand. The trail is not well defined and you'll learn now to appreciate your guide. In an hour you reach a small, stony valley with a spring, the last chance for water. At 2,000 meters you leave the tree line and at 3,000 meters you can peer into the 500-meter-deep crater through a gap in the fragile wall. Since standing on the volcano's crumbling edge is madness, lie flat and hang over the sharp rim to look down on steam, smoke, and multihued rocks while breathing in a strong whiff of sulfur.

With an outer wall-to-wall diameter of 625 by 425 meters, a crater floor of 250 by 125 meters, and an elevation of 2,700 meters, this scarred crater is impressive. The summit, out of sight and to the west, is only about 20 meters higher than the edge of the crater—another 20-minute hike. Take a good look before you forsake this hostile environment of bitter cold and icy winds. Resist gravity's pull when slipping and sliding over loose volcanic rubble on your way back down; descending too fast is dangerous. A sturdy staff is an invaluable aid.

BESAKIH

Bali's oldest, largest, most impressive and austere temple complex sits one-third the way up the slopes of Gunung Agung. Besakih, actually consisting of three temple compounds, is the Mother Temple of Bali and the most important of the island's *sad-kahyangan* religious shrines. It's Bali's supreme holy place, the essence of all Bali's 20,000 temples, a symbol of religious unity, and the only temple that serves all Balinese.

Even though it's touristy, it's still spectacular—good energy!

Get an early start so you arrive about 0800, before the tourist hordes, when the top of the massive volcano behind Besakih is clear. Plan to leave before early afternoon rains. From Besakih, head down the hill to Pesaban, south of Rendang to the west, to the **Garden Restaurant** at Bukit Jambul for its afternoon Indo/Chinese buffet (Rp12,000). Look out over rice terraces all the way to the sea. Outside the restaurant, tour buses clog the highway. Or pause at the beautiful Kuri Agung restaurant about one km south of Besakih temple. A huge place with expensive views and great food at reasonable prices.

If you want to stay overnight in the Besakih area, on the road between Menanga and Desakih is the **Arca Valley Restaurant and Homestay**, Rp 15,000-20,000 for spartan rooms, or ask around for homestays at the shops and stalls on the road up from the parking lot to the temple. Eat reasonably well at the Arca Valley or at RM Mawar in Menanga.

History

Besakih was built on a terraced site where prehistoric rites, ceremonies, and feasts once took place. Perhaps it was here where the spirit of the great, angry mountain, which loomed menacingly above the island, received pagan sacrifices. Certain timeworn megaliths in some of the *bale* are reminiscent of old Indo-Polynesian structures.

Hindu theologians claim the temple was founded by the 8th century missionary Danghyang Markandeye, a priest credited with introducing the tradition of daily offerings *(bebali)* and the concept of a single god. His son, Empu Sang Kulputih, was the temple's first high priest.

The first record of the temple's existence is a chronogram dated A.D. 1007, possibly describing the death ritual for King Udayana's queen, Mahendradatta. This inscription also reveals that Besakih was used as a Buddhist sanctuary. Lontar books dating from the Majapahit Kingdom indicate Besakih's significance during the 14th century, and several 15th-century wood tablets refer to state support of Besakih, confirming its preeminence.

Besakih's central Pura Penataran Agung, the largest on the island, functioned as a funeral temple for the Gelgel dynasty's deified kings

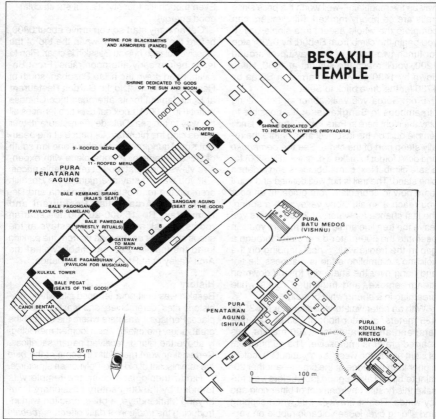

BESAKIH TEMPLE

SHRINE FOR BLACKSMITHS AND ARMORERS (PANDE)

SHRINE DEDICATED TO GODS OF THE SUN AND MOON

11 - ROOFED MERU

SHRINE DEDICATED TO HEAVENLY NYMPHS (WIDYADARA)

9 - ROOFED MERU

11 - ROOFED MERU

PURA PENATARAN AGUNG

BALE KEMBANG SIRANG (RAJA'S SEAT)

BALE PAGONGAN (PAVILION FOR GAMELAN)

SANGGAR AGUNG (SEAT OF THE GODS)

BALE PAWEDAN (PRIESTLY RITUALS)

GATEWAY TO MAIN COURTYARD

8

BALE PAGAMBUHAN (PAVILION FOR MUSICIANS)

KULKUL TOWER

BALE PEGAT (SEATS OF THE GODS)

CANDI BENTAR

0   25 m

MOON

PURA BATU MEDOG (VISHNU)

PURA PENATARAN AGUNG (SHIVA)

PURA KIDULING KRETEG (BRAHMA)

0   100 m

MOON

© MOON PUBLICATIONS, INC.

and as the central state temple for the entire island. Gelgel rulers are today enshrined in their own temple here, the Padharman Dalem. For centuries worship at Besakih was the exclusive privilege of rajas, not commoners, and the difficult trek here in former times reinforced the ardor of the devotional act.

The great 1917 earthquake destroyed the temple complex, but it was subsequently restored by the Dutch to its original form (only two structures survived this quake). Besakih was again heavily damaged on 17 March 1963 by a Gunung Agung eruption. The complex has since been extensively restored and now encom-

passes a mix of old and new buildings. Because it is a state shrine, the provincial and national governments pay for its upkeep.

Layout and Design

Besakih is a very complex architectural structure venerating the holy Hindu trinity. Via a series of long stairways, the temple group ascends parallel ridges toward Gunung Agung, the honored birthplace of Bali's deities, tantamount to heaven. The temple is continually enlarged as municipalities, regencies, and wealthy honored Brahman families add more shrines. In fact, each caste and kin group, as well as various sects, artisan guilds, and aristocratic families, maintains its own temple inside the complex. About 22 separate sanctuaries contain a befuddling array of over 60 temples and 200 distinct structures (a map is posted at the top of the road leading from the parking lot). Given the Balinese passion for covering surfaces with carving or paint, it's remarkable most of Besakih's sanctuaries are constructed simply of wood.

The sun-god (Bhatara Surya), the god of the sea (Ratu Waruna), and every major figure in the Balinese pantheon is represented here. Each of the island's nine regencies also maintains its own temple within this complex. Curiously, the small, relatively inconsequential rajadoms like Blahbutuh and Sukawati are assigned proportionally large sections, while major regencies like Badung and Gianyar are meagerly represented. The historical importance of the *negara* of Gelgel is evident, however, by its assignment to the innermost, central courtyard.

Beyond a great unadorned split gate, a broad terrace leads to a *gapura,* which opens onto 50 black, slender, pagodalike *meru* temples. The more roofs, the higher-ranking the god or deified ancestor to whom the *meru* is dedicated. Long flights of stone steps lead to the main central temple, Pura Penataran Agung, which consists of six rising terraces built on a slope, all connected by gateways. In the third inner court of the central temple is the *sanggar agung,* a beautifully decorated 17th-century triple lotus stone throne representing the divine triad. This is the ritual center of Besakih. Through the clear, fresh air of the topmost terrace, over 900 meters above sea level, is an unsurpassed view over spectacular rice terraces. Behind, thick white clouds hover over Gunung Agung.

Besakih's three main temples, which stretch for over a kilometer, are Pura Penataran Agung (in the symbolic center), dedicated to the paramount god Shiva, or Sanghyang Widhi Wasa; Pura Kiduling Kreteg, honoring Brahma; and Pura Batu Medog, dedicated to Vishnu. The longitudinal axis of this complex points directly *kaja,* toward Gunung Agung's peak to the northeast.

Farther up the mountain is another compound, Pura Gelap, the "Thunderbolt Temple." Highest, in the pine forests of Agung's southwest slope, is austere Pura Pengabengan.

Ceremonies and Events

Because so many gods, regencies, and old Bali clans are represented here, there's always something going on. About 70 rituals are held regularly at Besakih's different shrines, with banners representing each god hung on or near the temple and long lines of women walking up the terraces, their heads piled high with offerings.

A visit to the sanctuaries of Besakih is a special pilgrimage each Balinese must undertake periodically. They return with holy water for use in ceremonies back home. A visit to Besakih is also required to properly consecrate the soul of a dead relative as a family god in the house temple.

Each of Besakih's temples has its own *odalan,* and on the full moon of the 10th lunar month, vast crowds pack the entire compound to celebrate the visit of the gods *(turun kabeh);* this rite also commemorates Besakih's founding. During Galungan, enormous throngs of pilgrims turn Besakih into a hive of activity. An important islandwide Water Opening ceremony also occurs here, long-nailed priests dramatically gesticulating, sprinkling holy water, ringing tinkling bells.

The most majestic event is held only once every 100 years, the spectacular **Eka Desa Rudra,** a purification ceremony in which harmony and balance in people and nature are restored in all 11 directions. The rite last occurred in March 1963, some 16 years before the proper date, apparently because Sukarno wished to impress a convention of travel agents. Midway through the opulent ceremony, Gunung Agung began to shower the whole area with ash and smoke, finally exploding in its most violent eruption in 600 years. Earthquakes toppled temples, hot ash ignited thatched roofs, volcanic debris rained upon the earth. As the molten lava moved toward them, Hindu priests prayed frantically, hoping to appease the angry gods, assuring worshippers they had nothing to fear. In the end, 1,600 Balinese were killed and 86,000 left homeless. The Balinese don't take such extraordinary coincidences lightly; the catastrophe was attributed to the wrath of the god Shiva in his most evil aspect as Rudra. It ultimately became a damning judgment on the entire Sukarno era. Miraculously, the flaming lava flowed around Besakih, sparing most of the temple, though shrouding it with black ash for months.

The ceremony was held again in 1979, this time on a Saka year and with all the proper officiations. The sacrifice of an elephant, a tiger, an eagle, and 77 other animals seemed to do the trick—Eka Desa Rudra was completed without incident, and Besakih reestablished its place as the principal Hindu sanctuary in Indonesia.

Services
There's a tourist office on a corner of the parking lot that doesn't dispense much literature but adroitly answers questions. You'll also find a small post office, Wartel, and Bank Rakyat Indonesia (terrible rates) in the parking lot.

Warnings
Bring your change purse, as every device imaginable to separate tourists from their rupiah is in full operation here. One reader reports declining to rent a *sarung* offered for a preposterous Rp5000—you can *buy* a *sarung* for Rp8000. Little children approach quite sweetly, lay a flower in your lap, then demand money. The merits of the site are nearly outweighed by the swarms of hawkers, touts, beggars, and vendors. First they sting you for parking (Rp300), then when you sign the guestbook you're pestered for an inflated donation (Rp10,000-30,000 but just give Rp500), then they hit you for a ticket (Rp1100) to the temple grounds. Arrive as early as possible to experience the temple at its best (open 0800-1700).

Getting There
Besakih is about a two-hour (61 km) drive northeast of Denpasar, or one hour (18 km) northeast of Klungkung. On holidays take a *bemo* or minibus directly from the small terminal just north of Klungkung (Rp1000). At other times take one first from Klungkung via Rendang to Menanga (Rp750), then another up the steep six-km climb (Rp500) to the Besakih parking lot. Or get a *bemo* to Rendang (Rp600), then travel another nine km up the road to Besakih.

If you're coming from the north, take it slow over the potholed road from Penelokan, which begins along the route to Abang. From the Besakih parking lot, walk 600 meters past souvenir stalls, drink stands, and pay toilets (or ride on the back of a motorcycle, Rp2000 if you bargain) to the start of the stairway up to the main sanctuary. The walk is a steady gradual grade.

Even though it's a place for Hindu ancestor worship, non-Hindus may still enter the temple itself if they bring an offering or pay for an offering (Rp1000). You may also walk around the entire complex. There are a number of vantage points where you can peer inside and try to guess what's going on. Well-informed and friendly students will volunteer themselves as guides. About Rp2000 is adequate, but always agree on a price beforehand. After 1400, it may be difficult to find a public *bemo* back down to Klungkung.

THE EAST COAST

PADANGBAI

A tiny, charmingly scruffy port of transit for the neighboring island of Lombok and beyond, Padangbai is northeast of Gianyar (29 km), Kuta (62 km), and Denpasar (56 km). One of the most relaxed beaches on Bali, the port faces the Bali Strait and Nusa Penida. From Denpasar, take a bus from Batubulan (Rp1500) or Amlapura (Rp700); from Klungkung take a *bemo* (Rp1000). Or just hop on any bus out of Batubulan heading for Amlapura, get off at the turnoff to Padangbai, then hitch a ride down to the port.

As many as 100 travelers (mostly Europeans) may be staying in this small port village at any given time. About half are either leaving for or arriving from Lombok; the other half are just just hanging out. Listen to endless tales of travels through Indonesia's Southeast Islands; play soccer with the local children; sometimes there's dancing on the beach at night. The big craft item in Padangbai is miniature *jukung* (Rp1500 small, Rp2500 large), though they aren't even made here—Padangbai merchants buy them from the Sukawati Art Market.

Everything is within walking distance of the ferry offices, jetty, and parking lot. The waterfront is lined with *warung* and restaurants serving implausibly cheap, fresh seafood dinners. Drawn up on the rather dirty white-sand beach along this sheltered bay are dozens of painted outriggers with dolphin-head bows. A much nicer beach is a short walk north over the hills/temples. Accommodations are inexpensive and there's a good variety. Prices rise during August and December by at least 25%. Vendors sell watches, toy *jukung*, paintings, and sunglasses; a few shops sell clothing at inflated prices.

A ferry arrives from and departs to Lombok about every two hours, transforming Padangbai into a loud, jostling port jammed with buses, trucks, *bemo,* cars, and milling passengers. Private sailing yachts from Singapore and Australia moor in the landing stage, and cruise ships stop in the perfect pearl-shaped bay about once a week. The whole street leading to the pier is crammed with gaudy souvenir and clothing shops and stalls, the proprietors barking of their wares to the wandering passengers.

Accommodations

Part of Padangbai's charm is its inns and restaurants run by humble fisherfolk turned overnight entrepreneurs. Though the land is potentially very valuable, there are no international chains or fancy beach inns here. The accommodations opposite the beach have a quiet rhythm, and you get some of the best "included" breakfasts in Indonesia. Most places rent snorkeling equipment, change money, and sell miniature *prahu.* Get your room as early in the day as possible; accommodations fill up fast with travelers going to and from Lombok. The latest gimmick in Padangbai is "sweet water" showers—since water from most of the village wells is salty, this means the establishment offers salt-free water.

Probably the cheapest place to stay is **Marco's**—only Rp5000 s w/breakfast, full of interesting travelers, and right on the beach. Perhaps the best value is the clean, three-story **Pantai Ayu Homestay,** characterized by brightly painted doors built into the side of a hill. Downstairs rooms go for Rp10,000 s, Rp15,000 d, while the tariff for the six upstairs rooms is Rp15,000 s, Rp20,000 d. Corner *kamar* no. 4 is the best. All rooms with *mandi.* The top floor features a restaurant serving Padangbai's only homemade ice cream, including exotic flavors like nutmeg. Cool breezes. The only drawback to Pantai Ayu is that it's 300 meters from the beach.

In the center of town on Jl. Pelabuhan (tel. 0366-35393) near the harbor gate and close to the Perama office is the town's original **Hotel Madya,** not luxurious but okay. Rooms without *mandi* run Rp6000 d; the most expensive of the 31 rooms costs Rp10,000 d with *mandi.* Those facing the street are the noisiest, but from the balcony, you can watch life on the street. No meals, safety deposit box, frequented by Indonesian traders. The **Serangan Beach Inn** is a nice, central place with eight rooms at Rp15,000 each. A beautiful rooftop open-air lounge looking out over the harbor.

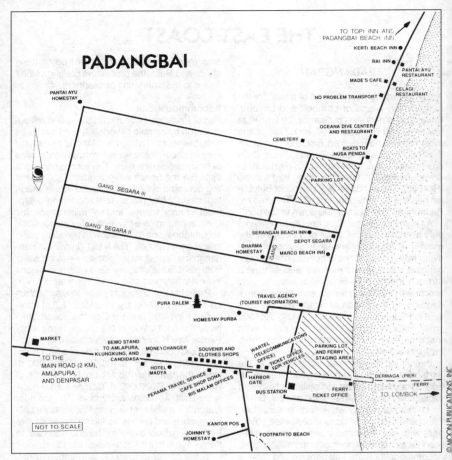

PADANGBAI

TO TOPI INN AND
PADANGBAI BEACH INN

KERTI BEACH INN ●

RAI INN ●

PANTAI AYU
RESTAURANT

MADE'S CAFE ●

CELAGI
RESTAURANT

NO PROBLEM TRANSPORT ●

PANTAI AYU
HOMESTAY ●

OCEANA DIVE CENTER
AND RESTAURANT

CEMETERY ■

BOATS TO
NUSA PENIDA ■

PARKING LOT

GANG SEGARA III

GANG SEGARA II

SERANGAN BEACH INN ●

DEPOT SEGARA ●

DHARMA
HOMESTAY ●

MARCO BEACH INN ●

GANG

PURA DALEM ■

TRAVEL AGENCY
(TOURIST INFORMATION) ■

HOMESTAY PURBA ■

MARKET ■

BEMO STAND
TO AMLAPURA,
KLUNGKUNG, AND
CANDIDASA

MONEYCHANGER ●

SOUVENIR AND
CLOTHES SHOPS

WARTEL
(TELECOMMUNICATIONS)
OFFICE

PARKING LOT
AND FERRY
STAGING AREA

TICKET OFFICE
FOR VEHICLES

TO THE
MAIN ROAD (2 KM),
AMLAPURA,
AND DENPASAR

HOTEL
MADYA ●

DERMAGA (PIER)

FERRY

PERAMA TRAVEL SERVICE

CAFE SHOP DONA

BIS MALAM OFFICES

HARBOR
GATE

BUS STATION ■

FERRY
TICKET OFFICE

TO LOMBOK

KANTOR POS ■

NOT TO SCALE

JOHNNY'S
HOMESTAY ●

FOOTPATH TO BEACH

© MOON PUBLICATIONS, INC.

Johnny's Homestay lies behind the post office. Rooms are secure but overpriced, with *mandi* and small fans. Johnny, an ex-cook with the colonial KPM steamship line, is a real character, as are his singing pet birds. **Dharma Homestay,** on a small lane just off the beach, has 10 rooms: five new rooms with *mandi* for Rp10,000 s, Rp15,000 d; five old ones for Rp5000 s, Rp8000 d.

Owned by Nyoman and Poppi Chin, the rambling **Topi Inn and Restaurant** on Jl. Silayukti at the north end of the beach is a large chalet-like wooden building with five rooms running Rp7000

s, Rp10,000 d with breakfast. The dormitory, which sleeps 20-29, just might be the cheapest accommodation on Bali (Rp3000 per person) with a genuine "backpacker's atmosphere" in the great open veranda upstairs. Fresh-water showers, baggage storage service. Sit upstairs, facing a steady breeze, looking out over a beach lined with *jukung,* sampling the unusual, international food—the yogurt is about the richest on the island.

Though the **Padangbai Beach Inn,** 500 meters east of town, offers Sulawesi-style bungalows for Rp15,000, the compound is poorly cared for, with dirty rooms, no fans, rats, showers crawling with green slime, and open exposure to thieves. Supplied mosquito nets, though. One of the best places for the money (depending upon your bargaining skills) is **Kerti Beach Bungalows;** each bungalow is situated under a palm tree with a nice sea view. Rp12,000 s, Rp15,000 d, Rp20,000 t with breakfast. The cheaper single-story units include some of the most ample windows of any budget bungalow on the islands, with curtains for privacy. Close the louvers near the door to prevent pilfering.

Farther south is comparably priced **Rai Inn,** very near the beach and opposite the Pantai Ayu Restaurant. The service hasn't kept up with expanded accommodations, now 10 two- or three-bed rooms, Rp13,000 s, and 25 rice-barn bungalows, Rp27,000—all with fans. Although basically well designed with a very relaxing restaurant pavilion in front, the place looks a little ragged around the edges despite a show of pretty flowers. Helpful staff. Breakfast (0700-1100) isn't bad.

Food

Padangbai is known for unbelievably cheap food—whole platters of seafood (snapper, marlin, barracuda, prawns) and salad for around Rp4000. The best value eating is in the many *warung* and cafes along the waterfront and beach. The three restaurants in one continuous building up from Pantai Ayu are all outstanding. Travelers also gravitate to the *rumah makan* catering to Westerners located between Marco Beach Inn and the bus station, right on the beach. A Sasak Muslim community of 50 families lives around the mosque near the dock; several *warung* serving Islam-style meals are here.

One of the top restaurants in town is Ibu Komang's **Pantai Ayu** ("Tropical Seafood") on Jl. Silayukti on the beach next to colorful *jukung*. Since it opened in 1988, sweet and warm Ibu has taken very good care of her customers, passing the *krupuk* jar regularly. Enjoy great curries, unbeatable salads, hot chips, and hamburgers; all meals in the Rp1000-3000 range. Open 0700-2000. Ibu's is also the place to buy toy boats, earrings, or postcards, borrow paperbacks from the lending library, rent snorkeling equipment (Rp2000) or a car, and mail letters. A

real traveler's haven—she even gives massages. Pantai Ayu has been destroyed by high winds and waves several times. Ibu keeps on going.

At the north edge of town is **Topi's** sand-floor restaurant. Lunch here on a huge plate of whole grilled fish and vegetable side dishes for only Rp2500, or choose pizza (Rp2500), muesli (Rp2500), yogurt, or lasagna. Although the food is very average to not so good, Topi's has perhaps the closest to a health food menu in Padangbai. Best offering is the huge plate of grilled tuna with carrots, cabbage, cucumbers, new potatoes, and French fries for Rp4000. At **Cafe Shop Dona** you can enjoy good *nasi campur* (Rp2000), cold drinks, and snacks. Next door is **Warung Java,** but the *nasi campur* is better at Cafe Shop Dona.

Services

At least three moneychangers here; rates slightly lower than in Kuta. At *kantor telepon* make calls to anywhere in the world; three minutes to Denpasar costs about Rp3000. A small *kantor pos* is just around the corner from Warung Java. Padangbai's postal code is 80872.

Getting Away

Travel and transport services sell tickets to all over Bali and to the neighboring island of Lombok. Arriving from Lombok, a line of *bemo* waits in the main car park at the end of the jetty to take passengers to all the major points on Bali. For Klungkung (blue or white, Rp700), Candidasa (Rp500), and Amlapura (orange Rp800), walk 100 meters from the harbor gate to catch *bemo*—blue for Klungkung, orange for Amlapura and Candidasa. For Batubulan direct it's Rp1500, or go first to Klungkung, then another Rp700 into Batubulan. After 1800, it's difficult to find a *bemo*, unless you walk out to the main road and flag one down. Bus tickets to Probolinggo (East Java) run Rp20,000; Surabaya, Rp25,000; Malang, Rp20,000; Yogya, Rp35,000.

Padangbai has at least six travel agents. **Perama** in the Sri Artha Inn sells tours and shuttle bus service to: Ubud, Rp7500; Lovina, Rp15,000; Sanur/Kuta/Airport, Rp10,000; Kintamani, Rp15,000; and express bus (reclining seats, 22 hours) tickets to Mataram and Bangsal in western Lombok for Rp38,000. An ultra-fast catamaran to Bangsal, roundtrip, is Rp20,000.

Another place to buy tickets is **Pantai Ayu Restaurant;** shuttle service to Mataram (Lombok) Rp10,000; Sengiggi Rp10,000; Bangsal Rp15,000; Gili Meno Rp20,000, Gili Trawangan. The shuttle bus to Sengiggi is worth the extra Rp2000.

For a break from the languor of Padangbai's beach life, take a boat over to Nusa Penida. Fiberglass speedboats depart from near the large parking area next to the pier (Rp3000); another way to reach Penida, or Nusa Lembongan, is from Kusamba village to the southwest. See Nusa Penida's beautiful east coast—you won't regret it.

The ferry ticket office is near the pier, under the Cepebri sign. A ferry for Lombok departs every two hours from 0200 to 2000. For the popular and crowded 0800 ferry, buy your ticket at 0700. Economy Rp4800, first class (a/c) Rp9000 between Padangbai and Lembar, a four-hour crossing. The ticket office for passenger cars (Rp59,200), motorcycles (Rp30,800), and push-bikes (Rp800) is just after the harbor gate heading toward the concrete *dermaga*. On board the ferry, keep a sharp eye on your stuff.

Vicinity of Padangbai

The area offers varied and exciting hiking. Hidden coves a short distance down the coast; the hills behind the bay present gorgeous views of Nusa Penida across the Bali Strait. Climb the paved road at the bay's northeast corner above the port to visit the headland on which perches Pura Silayukti, once a hermitage of the 11th-century Javanese priest Empu Kuturan, Erlangga's contemporary who purportedly introduced the caste system to Bali. Pura Telagamas is nearby, and Pura Tanjungsari is about 100 meters farther along the headland. Watch fishing boats chug out at night and return with their catch in the morning. To tag along, get to the beach by 0400 and bargain down the asking prices of Rp20,000 per person or Rp40,000 for up to three persons. Or head farther up the coast to Balina, where fishermen take tourists out for less. Surfers should check out the excellent right-hander on a big swell off the west point of the harbor.

Beaches

Yuo can sunbathe on the beach stretching north of the Pantai Ayu Restaurant, though the water is too polluted for swimming. A 15-minute walk over a grassy hill will bring you to quiet, sandy, beautiful Pantai Kecil in the quiet palm-lined village of Biastugal. Walk along the seawall, following it until you see a big tree; Then take the flight of stairs, walk on the road past a temple on a bluff, and descend to the small, uncrowded white beach. One of the three tiny *warung* here puts on beach parties in the busy season. To the southwest are more gray-sand beaches. The idyllic beach to the north, on Blue Lagoon Bay, is a longer walk, but has better snorkeling because of shallower water (but not the best swimming); the variety of fish and the hard coral outcrops on the sandy bottom are outstanding. Several places in Padangbai rent snorkeling equipment.

Diving in Amuk Bay

At least three dive spots are found off Padangbai, all a 10-15 minute *jukung* ride out into Amuk Bay. The water is cold; use a wetsuit. Pura Jepun, only 50 meters from shore, is a mixed reef with a flat, sandy bottom and a visibility of 10-12 meters, teeming with a great variety of fish, including some stingrays. On the way to Pura Jepun you'll pass a lighthouse on the north point of Padangbai Bay, then the rocky headland marking the entrance to Blue Lagoon Bay, with its brilliant white-sand beach and 25-meter-dropoff. Charter a boat from Padangbai for around Rp35,000 for two hours. South of Padangbai's harbor is Tanjung Bungsil, where the sloping bottom flattens out at between nine to 10 meters and the fish are numerous and varied.

BALINA BEACH

About five km beyond the turnoff to Padangbai, and after the village of Manggis, is a small steel bridge. About 500 meters beyond, turn right down a small lane to Buitan village. This is the heart of Balina, a simple, quiet resort with scant sellers, few tourists, a nice wide black sandy beach, tame waves, no treacherous currents, and seldom the sputter of a motorbike.

Though similar to Beach Inn-style complexes found all over Candidasa, Sanur, and Kuta, this simple, quiet resort is in the middle of a fishing village. All the amenities of Candidasa are accessible by *bemo* four km to the northeast, while the urban center of Amlapura lies 18 km to the northeast, and the metropolis Denpasar is a 1.5 hour's drive.

Water Sports

Balina is known for its diving excursions in a marine reserve offshore. If you reach the beach by late afternoon, you can go night fishing with local fishermen using laterns. The **Balina Diving Centre** has an impressive team of five instructors supervised by a PADI Open Water dive master; he can also arrange fishing and outrigger sailing trips. Dive trips, instruction, and snorkeling are offered every day starting at 0900. Minimum two people, except for the three-person minimum to Nusa Penida and Menjangan. Snorkeling and scuba diving rates, including transport, instruction, equipment, lunch, and tax, depend on the destination. Sample per person rates: Rp15,000 snorkeling/Rp85,000 diving Blue Lagoon; Rp45,000 snorkeling/Rp150,000 diving, Nusa Penida; Rp55,000 snorkeling/Rp180,000 diving, Pulau Menjangan. Snorkeling (Rp25,000) and diving (Rp115,000) at Tulamben, a stunning shipwreck 40 km northwest of Balina; same rate for Cemeluk, near Amed to the northwest. Diving Pulau Kambing, off Balina, costs Rp115,000 for two dives. Strong and dangerous undercurrents at the south end of the island can carry you up to 500 meters out of your way. Sharks frequent the area; a few foreigners have gone down here and never come up.

Accommodations and Food

The best midmarket place to stay is 34-room **Puri Buitan,** east of the Balina Beach Bungalows on one of east Bali's most beautiful, safe beaches. Definitely worth the price if you're looking for easy living—nicely furnished rooms with hot water, swimming pool, great snorkeling, shuttle service to Ubud (Rp5000), plus the personal attention of proprietor I Made Patera. Puri Buitan's motel-style units are clean and tidy: Rp65,000 s, Rp75,500 d for fan-cooled rooms; Rp85,000 s, Rp90,000 d for a/c rooms; Rp140,000 s, Rp160,000 d for deluxe a/c seaview rooms. Add 15.5% tax and service. The restaurant overlooking the pool has a full menu of so-so food reflecting heavy Italian patronage. Also snacks and toiletries. Remain connected to the real world via the international telecommunications office

in front of Puri Buitan. Guests can easily walk up the road and grab a *bemo* to Candidasa to get something to eat. Contact Box 444, Denpasar 80001, tel. (0361) 41021 or 41022.

More upmarket is the 58-room **Serai Hotel** (tel. 0363-41011, fax 41015) on a secluded beach amidst a beautiful coconut grove. Rates: US$110-140, depending on the season. Although designed by the same architect who designed the Amankila, this hotel appeals to a younger, upwardly mobile set. The low-rise Western architecture blends well with natural surroundings and typical Balinese pavilion-style public areas. What sets the Serai apart from other Balinese establishments is that it's under Australian management who understand better what guests require.

The **Nelayan Villages** (or **Balina Beach Bungalows,** Box 301, Denpasar, tel. 0361-41002 or 41005, fax 41001) offers accommodations with private verandas and baths set amidst palms and rice fields. Forty-one Balinese-style bungalows range from small two-bed units for Rp33,000 s, Rp42,000 d, up to Rp140,000 for family units (best views). Extra 15.5% for tax and service. Prices include continental breakfast; credit cards honored, postal service, moneychanger, safe deposit boxes, good parking, pool, gazebo bar, luncheon service, "Bali Night Dinner" with barbecue. Ideal for the sports-minded, as the Balina Diving Center maintains its office here. Drawbacks: expensive, terrible restaurant meals, and they don't smile much. At the nearby **Java Restaurant** the food is somewhat better and certainly more reasonably priced; also runs a small homestay. Fishing families will offer you drab rooms in the *kampung* for Rp10,000 s or d (first price). At the opposite end of the scale, Balina's most conspicuously upmarket hotel is the **Mandra Alila,** with 80 rooms at Rp200,000 per night. The luxurious beachside **Serai Hotel,** tel. (0366) 41011, fax 41015, built in the imposing Pacific Rim architectural style, is in the same class. Although the rooms are motel-style, they are spacious and well appointed. The swimming pool is near the beach under coconut palms.

Nearby accommodations include **Sunrise Bungalows,** tel. (0366) 41008, in Buitan, consisting of 10 bungalows in the Rp12,000-25,000 range. The nicest rooms, at Rp25,000 per person, are on the second floor in the back, with lots of windows overlooking palms and garden foilage, with the bay in the distance. Beach between two concrete jetties with good snorkeling. Full time security; small restaurant. Ketut has a car, speaks good English, possesses a wealth of information, and caters to a regular and devoted clientele. Mailing address Box 287, Denpasar 80001, Bali.

To the west is the even more isolated **Ampel Bungalows** in Manggis village—beautiful seascapes, nice gardens, restaurant. For Rp15,000 you get a simple, clean room (no hot water or electricity) and an exceptional view. The verandas are lit, with oil lamps provided in the evenings. There are no nearby restaurants, but proprietor Wayan Pastika Adijaya willingly arranges transport to the closest in Candidasa or Balina Beach. To get there go past Manggis and the turnoff to Amankila, where the road winds down to the coastal flats heading to Candidasa; the turn to Ampel is 300 meters before the bridge (see sign on right, if coming from Manggis), about one km before Balina Beach. Any *bemo* driver can find the place.

Hotelier Adrian Zecha's **Amankila** is another world. Only about two km from Padangbai, heading north past the stone mangosteen monument, is this spectacular resort palace, set on a high cliff facing the Bali Strait. The 400-meter-long "restricted access" salt and pepper beach lies below an old temple spotlighted at night. Built in a luxuriant grove of frangipani, palms, and other local mature trees, some 35 spacious suites, linked by walkways to the restaurants, pools, and beach. All are exceptionally well designed, with extreme attention to detail. The structures may look heavy and blocky (someone wrote that they were looking for the graffiti!) but are actually ecologically correct, built to preserve and encourage drainage via natural waterways and streams. No TVs, as guests are expected to relax in an atmosphere combining unobtrusive luxury with informality. Enormous areas are dedicated to public space, including a "staircase" of three pools at different levels; seven suites come with their own pools. Visit the decadently elegant Library Museum, the sumptuous Beach Club with its thin 45-meter-long pool in the midst of a coconut plantation. Nonguests may frequent the Beach Club and

the beach for a day for Rp45,000. Nice little restaurant (superb fish and chips) and the best lap pool on Bali. Barbecue every Tuesday and Friday night for Rp90,000 per person; *kecak* dances are held Wednesday, *baris* on Saturday. Room rates Rp700,000-2.5 million. Reservations c/o Amanusa, Nusa Dua, Bali, tel. (0363) 41333, fax 41555.

Getting Away
The man at **Kios Melati,** just up from the Puri Buitan, rents vehicles for Rp50,000 per day. You may also charter vehicles for the airport, Kuta, or Nusa Dua (Rp40,000). In the high season, a shuttle service may be in operation with shared rides to Ubud, Sanur, Kuta, and the airport for Rp10,000. For much cheaper public transport, go up to the main road and flag down a *bemo*. Kios Melati also develops film in one day.

The area west of Balina around **Manggis** is really picturesque, with the sea on one side and mountains on the other. Walk 1.5 hours through woods and gardens to **Ngis** via Manggis; **Tenganan** is a two-hour walk from Ngis.

CANDIDASA

A tidy, well-kept, three-km-long European (mostly Italian, French, and Scandinavian) tourist retreat and water sports center on the southeast coast where the local people are nonaggressive and the hotel owners eager to please. Attracting refugees from the frenetic southern honeypots, Candidasa is the type of place where you think you'll stay two days but end up staying a week. Best in the off-season, when its quietude and small-village air are godsent. One of the smallest resort areas on Bali; the rhythm is noticeably more laid-back than Kuta, Lovina, or Sanur. Tenganan, a traditional village nearby, exerts its influence—many Candidasa businesses are owned by Tenganan people. The Italian influence is heavy—hotels bear Italian names, and many Italian dishes dot the town's restaurant menus.

As recently as the mid-'70s vendors and *warung* were the only businesses in Candidasa, serving meditating travelers staying at the Hindu Gandi Asrama. From these first enterprises sprang the sprawling resort of Candidasa, which now stretches toward Balina Beach to the southwest. Today three-story hotels, huge souvenir shops, and full-size supermarkets occupy the town, but without watch-sellers, big tour buses, and other attendant blights of mass tourism. Candidasa is only really busy in July and August and a little bit in December; other times the place is dead and its denizens depressed.

For many visitors, Candidasa is the perfect blend, everything one would want in a seaside resort—reasonable accommodations, variegated dining, interesting sea sports, warm-water bathing, tranquil nights. Most of the Balinese here aren't after anything. A slow and friendly place, where you can pass the hours with locals on the streets and beaches, or find someone to take you fishing, snorkeling, or gambling. Walk, read, soak up the sun, and let the crickets and crashing surf lull you to sleep each night. Candidasa isn't going to change in a hurry. The only threat to Candidasa's repose is the large oil depot at Labuhan Amuk on the west end of the bay, raising concerns about encroaching pollution in the surrounding waters.

Candidasa also makes an excellent base for trips to all over east Bali: Tirtagangga, Kusamba, Goa Lawah, Klungkung, Bangli, and eastern mountain towns like Putung and Iseh. For a scenic land tour, rent bicycles or simply walk the gorgeous hill country above town. Visit nearby Tenganan to shop, and for a fascinating look at the ancient rituals of a traditional society.

Sights

Coral gathering off the coast over two decades ago destroyed the reef—it no longer protects the shore, and the sea swept away much of the sand. Since Candidasa's beach is so narrow, it accommodates few vendors. There is a tide, just like on a normal beach. At high tide predatory waves pound the seawall, chasing beachcombers to higher ground. At low tide, the beach west of the lagoon is only eight meters wide and you can walk as far as 50 meters on the shelf

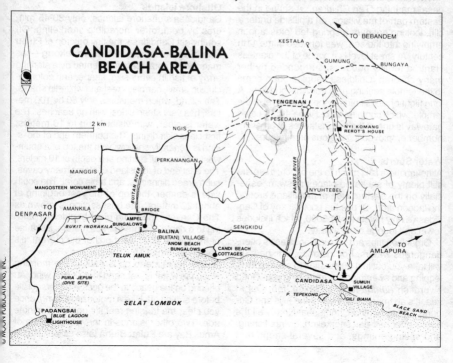

CANDIDASA-BALINA BEACH AREA

(wear sneakers) and observe rock pools and reef life. During all but the rainy season, the water is crystal clear. Cement walkways and sitting pavilions surround the inland lagoon at the east end of town—the beautiful lagoon, with its tepid water, is also the village bath. The community's fresh water is handpumped from wells.

To prevent further erosion, huge horrendous T-shaped concrete breakwaters were built. Because the currents caused by these stone piers are unpredictable, swimming is not advisable. If there's no pool where you're staying, you can use a pool at any of the ritzier hotels for around Rp6000. Sunbathing is best on the seawall. Take in views of the rocky Batu Manggar islet offshore, the lighthouse off Padangbai's headland, the looming island of Nusa Penida, and neighboring Lombok. Watch the wind and rain chase fishing craft across the sea. On calm days you can swim out past where the waves break, over the fringing reef about one-quarter km.

The name Candidasa is derived from "Cilidasa" meaning "Ten Children." A shrine in the eastern part of the village, on a hillside under a cliff, looking out over a spring-fed lotus lagoon emptying into the sea, was founded in the 11th century. At street level is a statue of the giantess Hariti, a fertility goddess, surrounded by her many children. Childless couples often come to the temple seeking help from this goddess. A long flight of steps leads to the upper level of the temple, which contains an old linga. Its 10-tiered gateway is one of the few instances of an even-number employed in religious architecture.

Water Sports

Although there isn't much to the beach, there are still plenty of sheltered places to swim, especially on the eastern side of the village around the lagoon area. Or use the pools at any of Candidasa's ritzy hotels for Rp6000, which includes towel and lounge chair all day.

Organized trips are best in Candidasa's often-dangerous waters. For instance, a fisherman will take you out just 30 minutes to see dolphins leaping and swimming—*surrounding* you. Good swordfish *(lumba-lumba)* fishing, too. Out at sea, it's an impressive view of the hills and Gunung Agung behind Candidasa. Nearly all the hotels offer half-day snorkeling, diving, fishing, and sailing outings, and several shops rent

masks and flippers. Underwater sports provide beautiful views of coral and psychedelic fish; starting price is around Rp30,000 for two hours (always ascertain if equipment is included in the price). Beware of currents and don't depend on Candidasa fishermen as lifeguards—they can't swim!

There are three dive shops in Candidasa where you can rent dive tanks, snorkels, and wetsuits. **Stingray Dive Center,** tel./fax (0366) 41063, is the cheapest; the equipment is okay but not too new. Stingray also offers two dives and a boat trip to Nusa Penida for Rp135,000. **Paris Diving,** east of Stingray, and **Baruna Diving,** Puri Bagus Beach Hotel, tel. (0366) 753820, offer the same trip for Rp47,000 more. Baruna seems most professional. Inquire at the Friendship Shop about **Dive Paradise** dive tours to Tulamben (Rp75,000, one dive), Pulau Tepekong (Rp145,000, two dives), and Nusa Penida (Rp190,000, two dives). Minimum two people.

Offshore Islands

Candidasa's offshore islands, only 30-45 minutes by boat, offer incredible snorkeling. Off southwest Candidasa, the tiny outcrop of **Pulau Kambing**—also called **Pulau Tepekong**—has magnificent coral reefs frequented by a startling array of fish in every size, shape, and color, including small, harmless reef and white-tip sharks. The island, which measures only 50 by 100 meters, has very steep sides, with no beaches. The water is clear, with visibility up to 10 meters; first-class skin diving. The northern end of the island is generally shallow, with the top of a southwest sloping wall starting at a depth of 10 meters. The east end of the island contains many caves, submerged pinnacles, and table coral. The south side is deeper, the top of the reef begining at about 22 meters. The best section is known as The Canyon, lined with giant boulders, plunging to a depth of more than 30 meters. Because of the strong downward pull of the current, it's been nicknamed The Toilet.

The best time to go is early in the morning when the water is clear and there's little wind. An offering on the beach to the gods is a prerequisite before setting off. Hire a motorized *jukung;* once you clear the fringing reef it's only a 15 minute ride. Two other islands in the western side of Amuk Bay are **Pulau Biaha** (also called Likuan) and **Gili Mimpang** (also Batu Tiga or Three Rocks)—both present difficult conditions to even experienced divers. There are sharks around, the water is cold, the underwater currents are strong and unpredictable, and waves crashing into the islands create an undertow. Best to go only with professional divers who've been there before. Excellent snorkeling in the vicinity.

One of the best-kept secrets of eastern Bali is brilliant *Pasir Putih,* 500-meter-long white-sand beach to the northeast. Ask a fisherman in Sumuh village (east of Candidasa) to take you there for Rp30,000 (two hours), or take a *bemo* to Perasi where a path leads past *sawah* to the coast. After 2.5 kilometers, you reach a small temple where the path forks. The left takes you to several black-sand beaches, while the right takes you down through coconut groves to Pasir Putih. Great views of rocky headlands and off-shore islands.

Accommodations

Ten years ago this small village had only a few thatched huts and one private homestay. Today it boasts over 60 accommodations, with more sprouting monthly. Tourist digs are everywhere. Largely a budget resort, big, expensive hotels just wouldn't make it here. Prices and services are generally comparable to Lovina, with bottom-end homestays at about Rp12,000 (first price) and luxurious bungalows for Rp185,000 per night in the high season. Most places include the same simple breakfast of one hard-boiled egg (or jaffles), bananas, and coffee or tea. Accommodations across the road tend to be cheaper than those close to or facing the sea. Most lie south along the main village road, though a growing number cluster along the seven-km stretch from Candidasa west to Manggis. A number of other quiet accommodations are spread out under coconut palms east of town center on Forest Road, which ends at the sea. Remember if you stay too far out of town, you'll probably need to rely on expensive hotel transport, as public transport stops at dusk.

Prices, which normally average 12,000-15,000 d for a basic bungalow, go up at least 25% in August. Top-of-the-line beachfront bungalows, with private *mandi* and luxurious bamboo verandas, go for Rp40,000-80,000, while new first-class hotels run Rp115,000-200,000. Try for a deal at one of the more uptown hotels during the off-seasons. When the manager presents you with the usual, ridiculously priced tariff, denounce the Rp180,000 figure as *"terlalu mahal"* and turn to leave. He'll probably drag you back, and five minutes later you'll be inside a palatial room with ocean view for Rp60,000.

Take note that Homestay Kelapa is now the shuttle bus station for "downtown" Candidasa. A brilliant move—now the place gets everybody. Touts hanging around the homestay do not necessarily represent the best in Candidasa Accommodations.

Budget: Clean, quiet **Dutha Seaside Cottages** is a nice, family place at the north end of the village—run like a large commune. Dutha has its own beachfront, with cool breezes, good swimming, and a beautiful view. Rooms in a two-story building run Rp8000 s, Rp10,000 d; a row of bungalows rent for Rp12,000-20,000. Tariff includes breakfast, or just go in the kitchen and make your own tea or coffee. Frequent parties and Balinese feasts. Made, the owner/manager, is a real character—portly, smiling, animated. Contact him at tel. (0361) 93296 in Blahbatuh or tel. (0361) 93061 in Gianyar, or just show up. A real traveler's place. The people at **Homestay Lilaberata,** on the other hand, show almost a complete disregard for their guests. This dirty, run-down dive in the middle of the strip is tolerable only if you clean your room thoroughly, both inside and out. Staff burn trash in the yard, giving off thick toxic fumes and a horrendous stench. See the rubbish heaps and rats in the garden.

Up the road toward Balina is **Homestay Ayodya,** with nicely furnished rooms for Rp14,000 s, Rp100,000 per month. The owner is the richest man in Candidasa—he holds title to most of the hills behind the village. Loves his 20 fighting cocks and employs a special boy to take care of them. This guy can lose Rp4 million in a cockfight and come home with a smile on his face. The dive operation Grace Divepro, tel. (0366) 34992, maintains an office here.

The rooms at **Homestay Agung** cost only Rp8000, and the people are very kind, but each night the disco in the restaurant nearby cranks up really loud music. Quieter is **Homestay Segara Wangi,** with attractive, well-kept gardens facing the sea. A friendly place with good breakfast, the bungalows are new and clean. If there are few tourists around, the front desk will accept Rp12,000 for a bungalow with double bed and private *mandi*. You may end up staying for days. **Homestay Kelapa Mas,** tel. (0366) 41947, next door to Homestay Ida, is cheaper and less touristy than most places. It's clean, quiet, well serviced, and almost always full. Stunning seaside location in a banana and coconut grove. The bamboo bungalows range from Rp15,000 to Rp35,000; the indoor *mandi*, almost the same size as the room itself (tiny), consists of a spigot shower high on the wall and a squat toilet. All rooms are linked by tidy concrete paths bordered by neatly clipped hedges. The thatch and brick cottages facing the sea are best.

Agung Bungalows is a great place to stay, starting at Rp10,000 for nice clean bungalows with fan, private bathrooms, and breakfast—very good value, good people. Contact Mr. Supadnya, manager, at tel. (0361) 355-535 in Denpasar. The **Dewa Berata,** east of Agung's, has comfortable bungalows for three people at Rp40,000. The seaside is right next to the pool. Quiet and friendly **Nani Beach Inn,** near the Ramayana, has bungalows with *mandi* for Rp15,000 d, which includes a good breakfast. Very close to the beach. **Losmen Geringsing** is one of the more comfortable low-priced *losmen,* with ornate brick-and-bamboo bungalows facing the beach for Rp15,000 d.

Luxury: Candidasa's first-class hotels tend to be on the wings of the central downtown strip. Located on oceanfront property amid palms, most of these accommodations feature European toilets and showers, hot water, lush gardens, air conditioning, full-size swimming pools, garden bathrooms, refrigerators, minibars, gift shops, and restaurants with magnificent views over the Lombok Strait and offshore islands. All offer sea sports, airport transfers, big dish TVs, extravagant buffet dinners, and continental, Indonesian, and American breakfasts. All accept credit cards and offer laundry, postal, massage, tour, and moneychanging services. The "best" are several kilometers from Candidasa, with nothing else in the vicinity. Like German prison camps with German food. This may be exactly what some people want; others will feel like trapped animals.

Nirwana Cottages, Sengkidu, Amlapura 80871, tel. (0366) 41136, fax 41543, has a superb location, nice rooms, pool, and wholesome home-cooked food. Ten traditional, well-appointed, one-story cottages go for Rp95,000-125,000. Close to the water, Nirwana is clean, private, and low-key, with Japanese baths, spring mattresses, and very personalized service. Eat bratwurst in the pleasant seaside restaurant; ask about the "Easy Rider" facilities whereby you can do Indonesia by camper van. Also in Sengkidu is **Ida Beach Village,** tel. (0366) 41118 or 41119, fax 41041, consisting of 17 thatched *lumbung*-style air-conditioned bungalows set in their own compound, surrounded by a garden and courtyard. All mod cons—hot water, bath, telephone, air conditioning, and fan. Tariff Rp125,000 per night for standard units. Facilities include restaurant, bar, swimming pool.

Centrally located **Candidasa Beach Bungalows II,** tel. (0366) 51205, is a big two-story hotel with an open-air bar and food. Despite its packed-in feeling, real Balinese breezes blow here, and the rooms are attractive and spacious. Breakfast, especially the banana pancakes, is excellent. All rooms have fans, air conditioning, hot water, Western-style bath, fridge, TV, and cost Rp65,000 s, Rp75,000-85,000 d. The elegant **Watergarden,** tel. (0366) 41540, fax 41164, offers 12 luxurious Balinese-style, fan-cooled cottages with thatched roofs and marble floors overlooking lily ponds stocked with koi. A virtual aquatic park laid out on gradually rising terraces. The well-designed bungalows are Rp150,000 d plus 15.5% tax and service, with adjustable ceiling fans, comfortable beds, and large wooden-decked verandas. Enjoy the natural gardens of coconut palms and lush frangipani and bougainvillea surrounding a large free-form swimming pool with waterfall—a lovely setting for evening barbecues and *gamelan* performances. Room service, IDD, laundry, ironing, safety deposit, library, flight reconfirmation, mountain bikes, tour and transport service. Dine on European and Indonesian cuisine, guzzle exotic cocktails at attached TJs. Peter Warren, the Australian manager, is hypnotic.

Tinarella Beach Hotel, in Samuh, tel. (0366) 33971, provides real comfort at reasonable rates, Rp35,000 s, Rp45,000 d, plus 15% service and tax. All rooms Balinese-style with private bathrooms, spacious gardens, large swimming pool, poolside bar, restaurant, water sports, taxi service, IDD, fax. Lovely view of the beach. Relaxing, clean, and comfortable **Puri Bagus Beach Hotel** is tucked away amid the palms in Samuh at the end of Forest Road: 50 well-designed, spacious bungalows for Rp140,000 s, Rp145,000 d. Higher rates for nine units and two suites facing the ocean. Terrace verandas, but beware of slippery tiles after it rains. Good 24-hour security, an unobtrusive, friendly staff. The floating pavilion is perfect for meditation, the pool good for diving. Buffet-style dinner (Rp30,000), Indonesian or American-style breakfast (Rp15,000, with whole-wheat bread!) in breezy second-story restaurant. Coral reef out front. For diving, **Baruna** has a desk here. Reservations: Jl. Bypass I Gusti Ngurah Rai 300 B, Box 419, Denpasar 80001, tel. (0361) 51223, fax 52779, or call direct to the hotel at (0366) 35238 or 35291, fax 35666.

Candidasa Bungalows II, Box 10, Amlapura, tel. (0366) 35536, fax 35537, in the center of town offers spacious bungalows for Rp115,000, with swimming pool and a restaurant right on the beach. The property has an air of abandon in the off-season, when it's overstaffed and underpatronized.

Out of Town: To get away from the crowds, head a few kilometers off the main drag to **Kubu Bali Bungalows,** tel. (0366) 35531 or 35532, high above the restaurant of the same name. Built in dramatic amphitheater-style, this Rp150,000-and-up hotel sits on a ridge overlooking the entire area. Beautiful, small, retro-rococo villas with brass coach lamps, smoked glass, antique carvings, and tame monkeys.

Sengkidu, five minutes southwest of Candidasa, is a tidy little tourist village consisting of cafes, souvenir shops, and bike rental joints—like a sane Kuta. **Anom Beach Bungalows** asks Rp25,000 for one of eight bungalows with fan, double bed, shower, and bountiful breakfast. Excellent restaurant overlooking a white-sand beach. Rent snorkeling equipment for brilliant views of coral gardens just 20 meters offshore inhabited by triggerfish and rays. Also check out **Homestay Dwi Utama** (Rp7000s, Rp10,000 d) with four rooms facing the ocean. High-class **Candi Beach Cottages** on the white sands of Mendire Beach charges Rp130,000-200,000 for luxurious rooms. Amenities include two bars, two restaurants, water sports, pool, tennis courts, fitness room, game room, spa, occasional *barong* dances, tour service, and free shuttle into town.

Flamboyant, on the other side of the bridge toward Balina, is a decent walk from town. They charge a fair price (Rp15,000), owners willing to bargain. A strip of bungalows leading to the beach with clean rooms, attentive staff, and okay breakfast. **Bayu Peeneda Bungalows** charges Rp30,000 for a nice bungalow with very good breakfast and wonderful ocean panorama. The meals are very good (Rp15,000 for two) and the sea spray provides a natural aerosol.

Uncrowded, six-room **Ida Cottages** is in the eastern part of town just before the lagoon. One of the first accommodations in Candidasa, Ida's charges Rp30,000-40,000 for beautiful bamboo-and-thatch traditional bungalows in a spacious coconut grove; also some rooms in two-story unit. No hot water. The only place in Candidasa proper you can rent a little home with lots of privacy. A great spot. **Rama Ocean View Bungalows and Resort Hotel,** Box 120, Amlapura 80801, tel. (0361) 233974 or 233975, fax 233975), lies 1.5 km southwest of town. A Holiday Inn-style resort hotel offering serenity, security, and the personal touch of a small hotel with the services of a larger one. The large air-conditioned rooms with beautiful garden bathrooms are normally Rp170,000 but may be much cheaper in the low season. Second-story rooms with stunning views. Facilities include video and TV, oceanfront swimming pool, tennis courts, fitness and massage center, sauna, conference room, large and pleasant dining area. Outstanding restaurant with *padi bali* and homemade yogurt, croissants, and bread; the honey/pineapple/banana pancakes can't be beat. Buffets by request. Great place for families. Easy 15-minute walk into the village.

Ashram Candi Dasa

A religious community—the only Gandian ashram in Indonesia—was founded in the mid-1970s by Ibu Gedong Bagoes Oka, the widow of a Balinese Hindu leader and former deputy governor of Bali. In daily pujas and lectures, Ibu teaches the Vedic scriptures, the Balinese religion, faith-healing, and the pacifist philosophy of Gandhi. The first arrivals were travelers seeking a quieter alternative than the pell-mell and frenetic development gripping southern Bali in the '70s. Today, Vedic chants still emanate from this beachfront ashram, heard above the pounding waves and music blaring from ghetto boxes and restaurants. Simple cottages facing the sea are rented out (Rp20,000 per person, including three vegetarian meals per day), providing the main source of revenue for the ashram and an elementary school that Ibu Oka runs for the village children. Guests are free to worship, meditate, work, and study as little or as much as they want with the several dozen young Balinese and Westerners who make up the permanent Ashram community. It's recommended that you book at least three months in advance, tel. (0366) 41108.

Food

Dinner is the big social event around here. Candidasa's imposing eateries, many set back from the road in big pavilions among the palms, offer the usual Kuta formula menus—generally speaking poor food—but with a Mediterranean twist. Pasta or German dishes always included. There are even several authentic Italian restaurants.

Seafood is fresh, cheap, and abundant. The fish dinners are the best buy, particularly the bream caught everyday by local fishermen and sold to the town's *warung* and restaurants. Find dozens of small, quaint, friendly *warung*, some with spectacular settings on the seawall. Most of Candidasa's restaurants will organize traditional dances if you have enough people, but even during the low season you can catch the occasional show once or twice a week.

Authentic and cheap is **Kelapa Mas,** with very good veggie soup (Rp1000) and grilled salmon with chips and veggies (Rp4000). Family-run **Arie's Restaurant,** in the west end of town, is a good bet for budget Western, Balinese, and Chinese food. The fish dinners are good value; also try the *gado-gado* and the fish curry with vegetables. Besides the food, Arie's offers a free bulletin board, provides daily English newspapers, rents life jackets and binoculars, sells children's furniture, and organizes fishing trips.

Cafe Lily used to be Candidasa's premier gourmet restaurant but the British owner has gone back to Australia, and the place has really fallen down—the food is terrible. The first and still one of the best restaurants in Candidasa is the candle-lit **Pandan Restaurant** on the beach—try the fantastic grilled fish with vegetable salad in a very romantic setting. Every second night an amazing smorgasbord (Rp12,000, with free beer). Highly recommended. Fan-cooled and well-posted **Raja's Restaurant & Bar** boasts such international cuisine as tuna cakes, kebab, sausages, apple pie, and margaritas. Nightly videos at 1930. **Baliku** is an artistically designed restaurant right on the ocean, next to Cafe Toke. A great spot to sit and take in the scenery, enjoy excellent Singapore crab, seafood, and continental European food. The cheapest soup is Rp3000 *plus* 10% tax for approximately four spoonfuls. Cafe Toko next door is a small seafront restaurant with an extensive menu offering seafood, pasta, pizzas. Friendly staff, high prices.

Probably the best place for Western food is **TJs,** tel./fax (0366) 35540, by The Watergarden. Homemade bread, stuffed baked potatoes, lots of salads, delectable grilled fish, and, authentic Balinese-style *nasi campur* with *urab* and not much oil. This is the place to be on Friday and Saturday nights for the barbecue buffet—salad bar, great spare ribs, chicken, and beef, only Rp15,000 per person including dessert. Super deal. Order French wines, Irish coffee, and almost anything long or short from the very extensive drink menu. TJs is also a popular place for cakes and "Ekspresso." Definitely try the coconut pie. Nice atmosphere.

Kubu Bali, tel. (0363) 41532, fax 41531, in the center of Candidasa, is an elegant, open-air restaurant featuring seafood: sweet shrimp and sauce Rp10,000, *sate campur* Rp7500, plain green vegetables with sauce Rp2000. Good desserts, especially the ice cream. Watch all the action in the open kitchen where flames shoot up around the wok. East of the village is **Mandara Giri Pizzeria,** the best Italian restaurant in Candidasa. Extremely good and inexpensive crab with cognac, pizza with seafood, outstanding spaghetti and lasagna.

Entertainment

See *barong, topeng,* and *legong* dances at **Pandan Harum** Tuesday and Saturday at 2100 for

Rp4000. During the tourist season performances are also staged at the Candidasa Beach Hotel and other upscale accommodations. If you like a lot of noise and high-priced drinks head to the **Tirta Nadi** where local bands play most nights of the week. The best bar scene, though, is **TJ's;** try their famous jumbo margaritas. Happy hour 1800-2000. You can also stay up late drinking and listening to high-volume music at the **Beer Garden** (no cover); all the gigolos hang out here.

For recent movies, **Raja's** has a huge monitor for videos, or see them on laser disc at **Molly's Garden Restaurant** (around 1930). Molly's also serves bar-quality food; since the British owner returned home the place has fallen on hard times. Try to focus on your snack while the screams from horror videos split the evening air.

Shopping

Candidasa shopkeepers display plenty of authentic Balinese crafts and textiles; they don't hassle you as they do in other places on Bali. *Ata* baskets and offering trays of *ata* vines from Candidasa's hillsides are an important home industry in the area. They're sturdy enough to last 100 years; the smartly decorated ones start at Rp30,000.

Across the street from the Candidasa Beach Bungalows II is Chinese-run **Asri,** a combination film developing/grocery/crafts store with fixed prices and computerized check out. Some readers report engaging in 90% of their Bali souvenir/gift shopping here. No pressure and reasonable prices. Buy cosmetics, medicine, stamps, tapes, film, snacks, simple clothes here. **Eddy's Market** makes the best photocopies in town, offers complete photo service, changes money, and stocks an outstanding collection of photo supplies. Plus groceries, books on Indonesian art and culture, and Candidasa's most complete postcard selection.

Tanteri's Ceramic is a showroom for remarkable Pejaten pottery, a unique variety of glazed stoneware, produced exclusively in Pejaten village. Purchase vases, soap dishes, cups, bowls, and plates with either a mat or shiny finish. The seaside village of **Jasi,** north of Bugbug, provides earthenware bowls and water jars. Attached to Chez Lily is a high-quality gift shop selling fine art and ceramics: *rebab* (Rp80,000), masks, antiques, clothes, handmade knives (Rp45,000).

A small bookstore without a name sits opposite Wiratha's Homestay. The owner, Aliep, sells used and new books in six languages for around Rp5000; an Irving Stone costs Rp8000. Open 0900 to 2000. Also check out the selection of books at Homestay Kelapa Mas.

Services

Candidasa has at least 10 moneychangers (similar rates as Kuta), two Wartels, lending libraries, bookstores, several doctors, a pharmacy, laundry and massage services, a postal agent, several big convenience markets, and a number of travel agencies, tour operators, and dive shops. The cost of basic provisions in shops and supermarkets is usually much cheaper than elsewhere on the island. The telephone code for Candidasa is 0366.

A reliable **bike rental** shop is **Kubu Bali Rental,** tel. (0366) 35532, charging Rp3000 per day for mountain bikes, Rp2000 for ordinary bikes. By the week Rp500 per day cheaper. **Motorbikes** (200 cc) rent for Rp10,000 per day without insurance, Rp15,000 with insurance. You can also rent motorcycles unofficially from the locals, avoiding all the red tape. **Car rental** runs Rp25,000 for 12 hours, Rp22,500 for a three-day minimum. **Saputra Rental,** tel. (0366) 41083, near the Tengenan turnoff, is also recommended. The nearest gas stations are just before the Tirtagangga turnoff and right after the turnoff to Padangbai.

At least 15 **tour operators** maintain offices in Candidasa, and all the hotels staff tour desks. Your hotel can arrange an English-, Japanese-, or German-speaking guide. The fancy hotels charge astronomical prices for **fax service;** Ayodya Homestay is cheaper. Of the two **Wartel,** the best known is at the Kubu Bali. If the wait is too long at Kubu's, go down to Asri Market. No public telephone in Candidasa accepts cards. The **postal agent** at Asri (open 0800 to 2000) sells stamps and provides poste restante (letters should be addressed to Asri Shop, Box 135, Candidasa, Karangasem, Bali). Asri also offers package parcels in a big 10-kg box for Rp5000. If staff can break off looking at the TV long enough, they may serve you. At a small shack southwest of town, on the same road as Rama Seaview Beach Bungalows, is a **laundry service,** Monalisa, about one-third cheaper than the hotels. Another *tukang cuci* (Wayang Resiyani) works near the temple; ask for her in one of the nearby *warung*. She charges Rp300-500 per piece, including ironing and washing. At the hotels, steel-fingered masseurs come around asking Rp6000 for one-hour massages.

Getting There and Away

From Klungkung or Padangbai take a *bemo* headed for Amlapura. If traveling from Denpasar, first take a minibus to Batubulan Station (a foreigner with luggage pays Rp1000), then catch another minibus to Candidasa (another Rp1500—many stops along the way). Regular shuttles run from Kuta for around Rp10,000. Both long-distance and local *minibuses* and *bemo* travel constantly up and down the coastal road between Amlapura and Klungkung from 0500 to 1900. Sample fares: Padangbai, Rp700; Amlapura, Rp700; Goa Lawah, Rp700; Klungkung, Rp1000; Denpasar, Rp1500; Singaraja Rp3000.

Shuttle buses to Ubud leave five times daily for Rp10,000; to Sanur, Kuta, and the airport, 0930 and 1000 for Rp10,000; to Kintamani, only at 0800 for Rp15,000; and for Lovina, 0800 and 1200 for Rp18,000.

Candidasa is about 2.5 hours from Bali's airport. Virtually all the better hotels in Candidasa offer private transfers to and from the airport, Kuta, Nusa Dua, Tanjung Benoa, or Ubud for around Rp30,000 one way (minimum two people).

MG International Ticketing, midtown, sells air and shuttle bus tickets, rents bikes and cars, and changes money. Buy long-distance bus tickets to Java here, too. MG is useful as an agent for such international airlines as SIA, MAS, UTA, KLM, Pan Am, JAL, Thai, and Qantas. **Perama Tours** near Arie's Restaurant has very good prices for tickets and offers tours around east Bali (from Rp20,000 per person), car rentals, and other tourist services.

On the western corner of the lagoon, across the road, is **No Problem Transport,** tel. (0366) 29110, for changing money, postal service, tours, shuttles, and international bookings. The only problem with No Problem is you must call Denpasar (Rp6000) to confirm your international ticket purchases.

Vicinity of Candidasa

Candidasa is an ideal point of departure for day excursions. Consult the guestbook at Arie's for the best hikes. Climb the rolling hills behind Candidasa for hidden valleys with wild monkeys, snakes, kingfishers, and superb panoramas. There are villages up there with no roads to them; wear a hat as there's little shade. Some of the paths are confusing, so it's best to take a guide.

Take the path opposite Homestay Kelapa Mas for the two-and-a-half-hour, five-km walk to Tenganan; once you reach the top of the hill, follow the ridge trail before dropping down into Tenganan. Go in the back way via stone steps. Another trail starts at Warung Srijati near the lagoon; at the top of the mountain take the trail to the left over some smaller hills to reach Tenganan.

See the sunset from the fishing village east of Candidasa, reached by walking around the headland when the tide is out. The beaches to the east are wider and offer perfect swimming for children. You can also reach a nice stretch of beach by taking the track from the Puri Bagus Hotel at the end of Forest Road, passing the Bung Putri, then ascending 200 meters to the top of cliffs where you descend to a deserted black-sand beach. There's another superb beach to the northeast at Jasi.

Drive to Besakih via Iseh and Sidemen; go all the way to Ubud on back roads only. In the other direction, toward Amlapura, the road climbs to **Pura Gamang Pass,** which affords beautiful views before dropping down to a rift valley with luscious landscapes just before the village of **Bugbug.** The people here collect coral for processing in beach limeburners in the making of cement. The entire area is covered with a layer of fine lime power, as if dusted with powdered sugar. Don't miss the *abuang taruna* dance of unmarried boys dressed in white and gold with *kris* and headdress. Takes place during the full moon of the first month in the Balinese calendar.

TENGANAN

This is an original pre-Hindu Balinese settlement, long a stronghold of native traditions, about halfway between Padangbai and Amlapura (67 km northeast of Denpasar). At the end of an asphalt country road up a narrow valley,

Tenganan is far removed from the Javano-Balinese regions of Bali. Like Trunyan on Lake Batur to the northwest, this small village is inhabited by the Bali Aga, aboriginal Balinese who settled the island long before the influx of immigrants from the decaying 16th-century Majapahit Empire. It might appear to be a stage-managed tourist site but is actually a living, breathing village—the home of farmers, artists, and craftspeople.

The lowland people of Tenganan have preserved their culture and way of life through the conviction they're descended from gods. They practice a religion based on tenets dating from the kingdom of Bedulu, established before the Hindus arrived. Tenganian origins can be traced back to the holy text Usana Bali, which states they must tend their consecrated land to honor the royal descendants of their creator, Batara Indra.

TENGANAN

NOT TO SCALE

© MOON PUBLICATIONS, INC.

Though Tenganan is today Hindu, it is also unmistakably Polynesian.

Except for such visual blights as the row of green power poles down the center of the village's unique pebbled avenues, Tenganan is a living museum in which people live and work frozen in a 17th-century lifestyle, practicing their own architecture, kinship system, religion, dance, and music. Signs of the 20th century are a public telephone just inside the entrance, TV antennas on bamboo poles piercing the thatch rooftops, the motorcycles parked outside the compounds, and the occasional tinny sound of a cassette recorder or radio.

Inhabited by a sort of "royalty" of proud villagers, Tenganan is one of the most conservative Bali Aga villages on the island, and perhaps the only one with a completely communal society. All village property and large tracts of the surrounding land belong to the whole community in a sort of "village republic." Most of these rich ricelands (over 1,000 hectares) are leased to and worked by sharecroppers from other villages, who receive half the harvest. This leaves Tenganians free for such artistic pursuits as weaving, dancing, music, and ritual fighting. Tenganan villagers are among the wealthiest on Bali.

About 106 families with a total of 49 children live in Tenganan—a significant drop from the estimated 700 at the turn of the century. A council of married people decides the legal, economic, and ritual affairs of the village (village headman Mangku Widia will provide details on Tenganian *adat*). The village customary law prohibits divorce or polygamy, and until recently only those who married within the village were allowed to remain within its walls; others were banished to a section east of the village called Banjar Pande. By the 1980s, this custom resulted in Tenganan achieving less than zero population growth, a result of inbreeding. Mandates from the gods were recently reinterpreted, allowing villagers who marry outside the clan to stay, provided the spouse undergoes a mock cremation ritual from which he or she is brought back as a Tenganian.

Architecture

Tenganan is an architectural wonder, one of the few places on Bali with a pre-Hindu South

Seas pagan feel. Here you'll see ancient court-yard walls, pavilion temples, magnificent community halls, and old high-based longhouses, all built in a powerful, very masculine, crude "aristocratic" style. These extraordinary structures come straight from the island's casteless prehistory. Note the number of homes with dog doors built into the stone facade.

Scholars theorize Tenganan's classical linear village layout, walled mountain-style court-yard dwellings, and ceremonial longhouses suggest the village was once located farther up the valley. Village legends of landslides and sudden evacuations lend credence to this theory.

Longhouses are actually the equivalent of southern Bali's *bale banjar* where meetings, weddings, and banquets take place and where the village *gamelan* is stored. Longhouses are still widespread in a number of isolated, animist, agricultural societies on Kalimantan and Sumatra.

Layout

The most striking feature of this 700-year-old walled village is its layout, totally different from any other community on Bali. Rectangular in shape (250-by-500 meters, about six hectares or 15 acres), Tenganan shares many characteristics with primitive villages on Nias and Sumba. Today there are three broad parallel avenues running along the same axis as Gunung Agung and the sea, lined with walled living compounds of nearly identical floor plans. The eastern street, which tourists rarely visit, is accessed through the lower parking lot. There are also three streets running east to west. The wide, stone-paved north-south streets, which serve as village commons, rise uphill in tiers so the rain flows down, providing drainage. Each level is connected by steep cobbled ramps. The only entrance to this fortresslike village is through four tall gates placed at each of the cardinal points (prior to Indonesian independence, Tenganan was surrounded by a high wall). The main entrance is the south, home to the highest concentration of souvenir stalls.

Villagers live in brick and mortar longhouses. Handsome ceremonial pavilions and giant grain storehouses run down the center of the widest avenue. There are also open kitchens and *bale*, administration buildings, the *kulkul*, an elementary school, *wantilan*, and a playing field, all arranged in a long neat row. Pigs wander peacefully and water buffalo graze on the lawns. At the south end is the long *bale agung*, site of all important village events and discussions; here you may see half the men in the village watching TV. In back of the village is a black *atap*-roofed temple, Pura Jero, set under banyan trees. Well to the north of the village, also under a huge *waringin* tree, is *pura puseh* (temple of origins). Here also is the village cemetery. Don't miss **Tenganan Tukad,** a smaller version of Tenganan to the east; amazing ceremonies.

Village Life

Much of it revolves around souvenir selling. The people have completely adapted to the tourist economy; nowadays tables selling palm leaf books are set up at intervals the whole length of the main street. Nearly every home seems to hold a display room or *bale.* The young men are cool dudes who speak American- or British-accented English while feigning an air of boyish innocence; cunning traders and bargainers, the people are friendly yet dignified. You're invited to take tea and photos of women weaving wide temple belts on rhythmical backstrap looms. The walled village's quiet somnolent air is accentuated by the lack of vehicular traffic except for the occasional motorcycle. There are no accommodations for tourists; the nearest hotels are in Candidasa. Morning is proclaimed at Tenganan by 21 low drumbeats at around 0600 and curfew is loudly announced at 2000 when all visitors must leave.

Events

Most rituals take place early in the morning. A famous celebration in May or June each year is the three-day **Udaba Sambah.** At this time one of the area's five primitive Ferris wheels is erected. The unmarried girls of the village sit on chairs and the giant wooden contraption is revolved by foot power for hours on end. For the past several years, however, the ceremony has not been held because of a shortage of young marriageable girls. The high point of Udaba Sambah is the killing of a black water buffalo, preceded by a ritual trance fight *(makara-kare)* between young men who attack each other with prickly pandanus leaf whips. These theatrical contests can last for three days and incorpote more than 100 participants. The duels, similar to the *peresean* whip fights of Lombok, are staged to the intense martial sounds of *kare* music. Blood is usually drawn because the fighters are only protected by plaited bamboo shields. During the festival the streets of Tenganan throng with people from all over Bali. Wayan Suwirta at the Nuri Arts Shop has a photo album of the ceremony.

Kawin pandan is also practiced here once yearly: a young man throws a flower over a wall and must marry whoever catches it. *Rejang* is a formal and sedate ritual offering dance, originally performed by virgin boys and girls. In this quiet, hypnotic dance, girls in three rows wear magnificent costumes and colorful sashes, their hair adorned with blossoms of hammered gold. It's accompanied by the slow, haunting *gamelan* music found only in Bali Aga villages.

Music

The xylophonic *rindik* is made of bamboo tubes suspended in a wooden frame. Played for dancing and entertainment rather than ceremonies, the *rindik* is part of the small village folk band and often serves as background music in tourist hotels and restaurants. The instrument can play a rich repertoire of music. There are two types, each tuned differently: *lanang* (higher, or "left") and *wadong* (lower, or "right"). They're cheap, light, easy to make, and cost around Rp35,000. The Gaguron Shop and House of Music carry *rindik* in both carved and plain frames. Don't buy a packaged instrument without first checking that it's not broken or rotten; don't take one off Bali or it will definitely become the latter.

The unique *gong selonding* is an archaic orchestra consisting of instruments with up to 40 tuned iron sound bars suspended on leather straps over resonators. This unusual orchestra is peculiar to the ancient, cloistered, conservative villages of eastern Bali. Quite different from Bali's Javanized Gong Kebyar, which uses bronze keys, the *selonding*'s resonant iron bars are more meditative and deeper. Tenganan's own *gong selonding* is so sacred that until recently it was locked away in the southernmost boys' assembly house. Taping and photos were prohibited, and no outsider could touch it, else the whole *gamelan* require reconsecration in an elaborate purification rite. Now you can buy a cassette of *The Best of Gamelan/Selongding Tenganan* in music shops throughout Bali. A full-size replica of this orchestra is displayed in the Basel Museum of Anthropology in Switzerland.

Tenganan's musicians also fashion and play *genggong* instruments. Inquire about lessons; around Rp10,000 per hour.

Kamben Gringsing

Tenganan is the only place in all of Indonesia that produces double-*ikat* textiles. In this difficult traditional technique, both the warp and weft threads are dyed before the fabric is woven. Reddish, dark brown, blue-black, and tan backgrounds, once dyed in human blood, are used to highlight intricate whitish and yellow designs of *wayang* puppet figures, rosettes, lines, and checks. Great care is taken to ensure that even tension is applied throughout so the patterns will match exactly.

Rather loosely woven, these *kamben gringsing* (or "flaming cloths") are used only in rites of passage or for ceremonial purposes: weddings, toothfilings, covering the dead, or during a child's first haircut. It's thought the *sarung*-length cloths can immunize the wearer against illness; small pieces for wrapping around the wrist are sold for this purpose.

No longer is it the custom to teach all village daughters this craft. Only about six families still know all the double-*ikat* processes (coloring, tying, dyeing), and only about 15 people still weave *gringsing* on small makeshift breast-looms. A good place to learn about double-*ikat* is Indigo Art Shop.

Because they are not worked on full time and because the coloring process is so involved, it can take up to seven years to complete a fine piece of *gringsing* and they're generally only sold upon the death of the owner. The really precious *gringsing*, prized by serious textile collectors, cost Rp7 million-10 million. Wayan Pura of the Dewi Sri Shop can show you some specimens; others are displayed in Jakarta's Textile Museum. Less *alus*, newer *gringsing* cost "only" Rp400,000 to Rp750,000—preposterous, as they're often tatty, dull-colored, and less than a meter long! You simply can't buy the perfect ones anymore. Like the people who make them, the magic cloths are disappearing.

Lontar Books

Lontar are palm leafs on which intricate drawings have been etched, usually depicting scenes from the Hindu epics. I Wayang Muditadnana makes about one five-page *lontar* book per month, which he sells mostly to tourists for Rp100,000 and up. On holy days or upon request he can be heard reading passages from his books. I Made Pasek is another *lontar* carver in the village. He, too, spends about a month inscribing one palm-leaf book with miniature Ramayana scenes and stories. A third artist, I Nyoman Widiana, asks Rp100,000 for his seven-page wordbooks. He also sells lesser quality *lontar* made by his students. Most cheap (Rp10,000) versions sold on the street are of low quality. The finer, antique, superbly etched works can fetch Rp500,000.

Ata Baskets

Ata baskets are a good buy, so sturdy they're said to last 100 years. They're made from a vine collected from the hills behind Tenganan. Basketry has been developed into a fine art on Lombok too, but baskets there are made from rattan. *Ata* is much stronger than rattan, as it's water, heat, and insect resistant. They come in all shapes and sizes, and cost from Rp5000 to Rp250,000; those with black woven designs are more difficult to make and cost more. An average-size basket takes two to three weeks to make, worked on by both men and women when it's too hot or rainy to work the fields.

A friendly place to purchase these traditional baskets, woven right on the premises by the whole family, is Inengah Kedep's on the main street. These are the finest *ata* baskets, "bowls," boxes, plaques, and even backpacks on the island; take time to linger and you'll learn a lot Inengah may even, eventually, bargain a bit. If you're really serious about buying, ask to see the baskets in the back room. Another reasonably priced shop for woven goods is **Mertha Shop** run by I Nyoman Setiawan.

Shops

Tenganan is a fantastic place to shop—both for local and Gianyar crafts, as well as fine textiles from the eastern islands. Many vendors have a good eye, ask reasonable prices, and don't hassle you to buy. The craft shops on the outside of Tenganan's southern entrance carry handsome tasseled shawls, *ata* baskets, offering trays, wickerwork, woven reeds, betel nut containers, and a good variety of woven eastern isle textiles. Watch for imitation Sumba blankets, carving from Gianyar, and other crafts which may be bought cheaper in Denpasar's Pasar Badung or in the villages of origin. You'll get a better price in the off-season (February to May), and in the morning before the tour buses start arriving and prices skyrocket.

Gagaron, located through the entrance gate from the parking lot in the lower part of the village, is a good place to start. The owner sells smallish *gringsing* for Rp350,000 to Rp400,000, as well as an extensive collection of *kain ikat,* antiques, palm-leaf books, woodcarvings, and bronze. *Rindik* cost Rp35,000 and can be disassembled and packaged to go. Ask the owner's nephew, I Komang Sika, to demonstrate how they're played. To make sure the notes ring true, have them break down and wrap a *rindik* you've personally played.

Art Shop Dewi Sri is on the right on the top parking lot. Large selection of new bronze pieces, single and double *ikat,* and *ata* goods. At **House of Music And Gamelan Centre,** toward the top of the village (fifth terrace), I Nyoman Gunawan makes distinctive nine-piece Tenganan-style *gong selonding.* He also sells gongs (Rp300,000), *rebab* (Rp150,000), carved *rindik* (Rp150,000), and tapes (Rp6000). The best place to buy the more elaborate xylophone-type musical instruments.

Getting There and Away

Tenganan is three km off the main road between Klungkung and Amlapura, just before Candidasa, and 17 km southwest of Amlapura. Catch a *bemo* from Klungkung or Padangbai to the Tenganan turnoff, then mount the back of one of the 15 or so waiting *ojek* motorcycles (Rp1000, after negotiations) and travel up through a tunnel of banana trees and bamboo. You can also stay in Candidasa—no accommodations in Tenganan—then early in the morning walk from the main road up to Tenganan. The turnoff is on the west side of the village, then it's about another five kilometers up the hill through thick forests—a great walk. Or hitch a minibus, *oplet,* truck, or anything else headed your way. Another option is to rent a bicycle in

Candidasa; it's a nice, though uphill, ride. The road ends at the southern entrance gate to Tenganan where you'll be asked for a donation. Foodstalls, inside and out, sell cold drinks and snacks. It's best not to arrive between 1100 and 1400 when the small village and parking lot are deluged with tourist.

Another way to reach this traditional village is to follow the road on top of the hill behind Candidasa in a northerly direction; a two-and-a-half-hour walk. Stop for boiled water and fruit at Nyi Komang Rerot's house along the way. If you walk into the hills beyond Tenganan, the road turns to the northeast. Check out the panorama from the *pura* in Gumang, the highest point overlooking a deep valley. In Tenganan, ask about the footpath to Tirtagangga.

AMLAPURA

At one time Amlapura was the seat of one of the richest kingdoms of Bali, tracing its origins back to the kings of southern Cambodia, and in more recent times directly to the 16th century Balinese prime minister known as Batan Jeruk. In the late 17th century, during the waning days of the Gelgel dynasty, this rajadom rose to the pinnacle of its power. In the 19th century, the kingdom owed its wealth mainly to the fact that its raja cooperated with the Dutch invaders, thus saving his title and autonomy.

Lying at the foot of the holy mountain Gunung Agung, Amlapura is today the capital of Karangasem Regency. Originally known as Karangasem, the name was changed to mislead evil spirits and prevent them from burying the town under tons of volcanic ash.

During Gunung Agung's monthlong eruption in 1963, massive lava streams devastated almost all of eastern Bali. Although the lava did not reach the town itself, the accompanying whirlwinds and earthquakes destroyed many buildings. The town was cut off for three years after the eruption, isolating this formerly prosperous trading community from the rest of Bali. To the visitor, Amlapura still has a sleepy air about it, although the city is the commercial and administrative center of east Bali.

Amlapura is the smallest of Bali's *ibukota* (regency capitals), with only about 30,000 people.

Shops shut down for the afternoon and open again at 1700; restaurants close early at night. Every three days there's a good open market.

Change money—but not traveler's checks—at Amlapura's Bank Rakyat Indonesia, or more easily in Candidasa. Telephone calls can be made at Amlapura's 24-hour, seven-days-a-week Wartel office; *bemo* pass it (see the tall signal tower) on their long loop into town, ending up at last in the *pasar*/termina. The post office is near the two hotels. If you drive in Amlapura, watch out for a lot of unmarked one-way streets. The nearest gas station is in Subugan, just west of town.

There's a **kantor pariwisata** on Jl. Diponegoro, open Mon.-Fri. 0730-1700, but it's obvious they get very few visitors.

Puri Kanginan

Of Amlapura's four palaces, each facing the cardinal points, the most famous is that of the last raja, Anak Agung Anglurah Ketut. Built early this century, Puri Kanginan is a big complex, surrounded by a thick red-brick wall. Enter through an elaborate three-tiered pagoda-style entrance. Inside, an air of slow decay prevails. The fountains have stopped spouting and dragons and serpents sit stonily with wide-open mouths, yet it's a functioning *puri* with connecting walkways over pools and compounds set aside for the royal family.

A combination of European, Chinese, and Balinese architecture and interior design were used in this *puri*'s construction. The Bale Amsterdam is the island's best known example of Balinese experimentation with the formal Dutch architectural style. Some of the deteriorating furniture in the palace's Maskerdam reception building was donated by Queen Wilhelmina of Holland. The largest and most striking pavilion is Bale London, with flourishing Edwardian decorations and a long veranda. It was given this curious name because its furniture is decorated with what the raja thought to be the British royal crest.

Over the *bale* entrance is a widely reproduced 1939 photo of the moustachioed raja, shot at a time when the district was granted limited self-rule by the Dutch. The king's own pavilion has all his clothes and belongings preserved under lock and key. Also see the traditional, ornate toothfiling *bale*.

As the raja had nine recognized wives, many families—as many as 150 people—still live inside the palace. Among the residents is the raja's grandson, painter Anak Agung Ardana, who produces bright colored cubist-style paintings. Several women occupants still weave gold-brocaded *songket*.

Princess Mirah and her American husband "Gipper," run **Bali Fabrications,** tel. (0366) 21496, fax 21074, which produces neo-modern ethnic *batik* designs and children's clothing emblazoned, for example, with the skulls of the Grateful Dead. Their showroom in the U.S. is at 1190 E. Napa St., Sonoma, CA 95476, tel. (707) 996-1445.

Since it's difficult to determine which buildings are occupied or sacred, it's best to let the eager children guide you. The *puri* is open to tourists for Rp550 admission (open 0800-1700) plus another Rp200 for a single-page info sheet explaining the pictures on the main building. Overnight guests sometimes accepted; Rp70,000 tariff includes breakfast, Balinese *rijstaffel*, drinks, laundry. Write in advance to the old raja's grandson, Anak Agung Ketut Rai, c/o Puri Agung, Amlapura. Guests may dine on a *bale* over a lily pond and are also admitted to scheduled palace celebrations.

Below the palace is a Muslim village, home to the descendants of the raja's slaves imported from Lombok. As if in revenge, these Sasaks besiege the palace daily with their blaring mosque loudspeakers. If coming from the town's center, take the road to the left just before the *puri* to the small water palace and a memorial statue from Queen Wilhelmina.

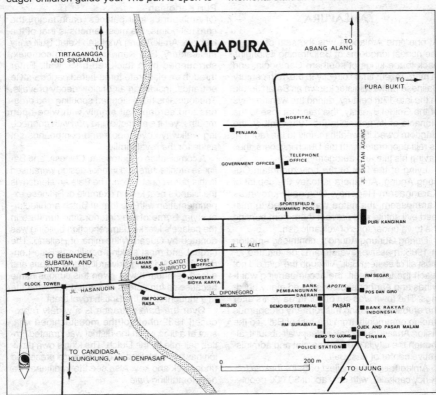

Accommodations and Food

Most travelers prefer to stay at more idyllic **Tirta-gangga** or **Abian Soan,** both about five km from town. On the road to Rendang is **Losmen Kembang Ramaja.** If you want to stay in Amlapura, there are two *losmen* close together at the town's entrance. Friendly **Losmen Lahar Mas,** Jl. Gatot Subroto 1, tel. (0366) 21345, on the left just as you're entering town, charges Rp10,000 s or d with *mandi* and breakfast. The Rp8000 s or d rooms around a large courtyard are better, more enclosed. Discount of Rp500 if you stay four days or longer. A better place to stay than the run-down, smelly **Homestay Sidya Karya,** on the right at the beginning of Jl. Gatot Subroto 8 (tel. 0366-21143). Ten rooms for Rp8000 s, Rp10000 d with breakfast of eggs and *roti* with marmalade. Can be noisy, as traffic streams by outside. The *pasar* and the bus, *bemo,* and minibus stations are all about a one-km walk from these *losmen.*

There's a *rumah makan* called **Pojok Rasa** nearby—*nasi goreng* and *cap cay,* Rp1500. Many *warung* around the *stasiun bis,* serve Javanese- and Balinese-style *nasi campur* on banana leaves, *sate,* and *martabak.* The **Sumber Rasa** on J1. Gajah Mada on the way to Puri Agung serves a worthy selection of soups, noodles, and rice dishes.

A little gem is **RM Surabaya** on Jl. Kesatrian: really cheap, high-quality *soto ayam, cap cay goreng, es campur,* **hot** *gado-gado,* wonderful *es jus nipis, es campur,* all Rp1500-3000. Open 0900-2100, and crowded every night. Extremely good value. There's also a *pasar malam* on Jl. Gajah Madah. Karangasem is the fruit-growing area of Bali—look for fresh papaya, pineapple, *belimbing, jambu,* and bananas.

Getting Away

About 20 big new buses leave Amlapura for Batubulan every day; the Balinese price is Rp2000. At about 1600 the buses go back to their villages so you have to be lucky to catch one headed to Batubulan or Klungkung after around 1700. At this time of day, it's best to hire an *ojek,* usually found near the bus/*bemo* terminal; Rp3000 to Candidasa. Minibuses or *bemo* to Candidasa and Padangbai (orange, 20 minutes), Selat and Muncan (green), Tirtagangga, Rp500 (seven km, 20 minutes); Klungkung, Rp1000 (38 km, one hour); Den-

pasar, Rp2000 (two and a half hours, 78 km); Singaraja, Rp2500 (three and a half hours).

Bemo also travel all the way to Singaraja's Penarukan Terminal along the northeast coast via Culik and Tianyar over a paved road with unusual scenery. Starting at 0400 at the turnoff in the town's outskirts, they run up until around 1600. The trip takes about 2.5 hours. Sit on the left for a better view of the rugged, brooding northern side of Gunung Agung. A good road and new bridges now cross over volcanic washouts and black lava flows along the way. Bicyclists without low gears may want to throw their bikes on top of a minibus up the big hill between Tirtagangga and Culik. Sweeping views of terraced rice fields as you come down into Culik.

VICINITY OF AMLAPURA

At the eastern extremity of the island is Gunung Seraya (1,174 meters), which was blanketed by a thick layer of black lava from Gunung Agung's 1963 eruption. Climb to its double peak in about six hours from the village of Ngis, eight km north of Amlapura. For an all-encompassing slow but cheap roundtrip of the regency, from Amlapura's bus terminal take a *bemo* to Rendang via Sibetan, Duda, and Muncan, then head down a very picutesque road to Klungkung and back to Amlapura. Public transport ply this route but taking your own vehicle will avoid lots of waiting time.

An untraveled inland road with magnificent views and lava fields starts at Subaga and eventually meets the Klungkung-Besakih road at Rendang. Between Selat and Rendang you travel over a scenic paved road winding through a section of *sawah* that looks like a natural amphitheater.

East Bali is the home of the juicy, delicious, sweet-sour *salak,* a brown snake-skinned fruit that grows on the stunted palms of plantations on the slopes of Gunung Agung. The markets that rotate between the towns of Rendang, Selat, and Bebandem are a lively sight, full of fresh produce, street vendors, and artisans turning out handmade farm implements.

Ujung

Four km south of Amlapura, this small coastal fishing village is the site of a majestic old mock

European-style water palace surrounded by a moat—a mini Taj Mahal laid out like the Hanging Gardens of Babylon. Reached easily by *bemo* (Rp500) from the station near Amlapura's *pasar, ojek* (Rp1000), or *dokar* (Rp2000 one-way, Rp5000 roundtrip). Or just start walking along the road that winds through Sawah southeast of town.

Formally opened in 1921, this extensive complex of pavilions, portals, gardens, statues, fountains, canals, and artificial lakes was occupied by the last raja of Karangasem. An avenue of Frangipani and mango trees leads into the complex. In your imagination take the decayed grandeur of ruins crowned with tufted grass, and uprooting plants and reconstruct the king's massive central palace. The stained-glass bungalow with arched, lead-light windows was a curio glittering with bits of mirror and studded with gaudily painted concrete animals gazing out over the ocean.

This same raja, Anak Agung Anglurah, who obviously had a water fetish, also built the Tirtagangga bathing pools six km northwest of Amlapura, and another small complex of soothing pools at Jungutan near Bebandem. Unfortunately, most of Ujung's buildings and moats did not survive the eruptions and earthquakes of 1963 and 1979. No evidence at all of restoration work supposedly long underway by now. All the better; this elegantly crumbling and desolate attraction should not be missed.

Take the track down to the black-sand beach 500 meters beyond, with graceful *prahu* lining the beach and good swimming. Or fish in the palace ponds with a pole borrowed from one of the boys. No official accommodations here, but you could possibly stay with fishing families up on the hill. From here the road climbs up to Seraya, a small market town at the foot of Gunung Seraya (see below).

Bukit Kangin, up a side road to the left just before Ujung, is a Grecian-style temple built to honor the dynasty's royal founder. Nice view. Several villages hold a festival here during the full moon of the fifth month of the Balinese calendar. Ujung Tengah is a beautiful spot overlooking Ujung. Look for the signs just before you reach Ujung, and follow the road to its end. You'll see foundations of a structure the raja used for rest and meditation. A plaque on the wall bears a 1927 inscription from Queen Wilhelmena. The large cow to the front spills water into a Garuda 10 meters below; there's another statue 20 meters beneath that.

The Road to Amed
Only opened since 1990, this incredible 30-km-long road is one of the wildest and most unvisited on Bali—little traffic, no telephone wires. It follows a tortuous route through arid hills high above the coast. Buy fresh *ikan awan* in Seraya village at the start. See cattle washed in streams, sweeping panoramas of the Bali Strait, isolated farmlets, grape arbors, and villages of Hindu fishermen with long unbroken lines of *jukung* with multicolored sails pulled up on the beach after the night's catch.

It's second and third gear nearly all the way, but the steeply undulating road is fairly well maintained, crawling through one of the poorest districts of Bali. The inhabitants here raise goats and grow small ears of corn, peanuts, and sweet potatoes. The road finally drops down to the fishing and salt-making village of Amed. From Amed, either return to Amlapura via Culik and Tirtagangga or head north along the coastal road to Singaraja via Tulamben.

Abian Soan
In the rice paddies just off the road on the northern edge of the village of Abian Soan, five km west of Amlapura on the road to Bebandem (three km east of Bebandem), is **Homestay Lila.** It can be difficult to find; only a small sign on a post showing the way. Located on the edge of a small ravine, these small, quaint, non-air conditioned, no-fan little cottages cost Rp7500 s, Rp12,000 d with sinks, bathrooms, verandas, and continental breakfast. The best deal for a family is the whole-house compound, complete with kitchen, oven, and sewing machine for only Rp15,000 per day. All the buildings have electricity; a nice garden of fruit trees out front. Small waterfall nearby. Beautiful scenery: mornings provide the clearest view of Gunung Agung. At 0500 see the sunrise over Gunung Rinjani on Lombok. Order meals through owner Nyoman Lali, he'll hop upon his moped to pick up *cap cay* and *nasi goreng* in Amlapura (45 minutes roundtrip). Or shop in Bebandem or Amlapura and cook yourself. From the homestay walk half

an hour to Bukit Kusambi, and it's a Rp300 three-km *bemo* ride to Karangasem.

Bebandem

Nine km west of Amalpura. Every three days there's a big cattle market *(pasar hewan)* here where you can mingle with the *petani* amidst the market smells of dirt, dung, coffee, cloves, and cattle. Arrive by 0800 to see the action, shop, and enjoy Balinese drinks. The market reaches its peak of activity at 0800 or 0900, depending on the season.

Unless it's a long distance, farmers walk their cattle to the Bebandem market; you'll see them strung out all along the Subaga-Rendang road before the dawn. With their long necks, soulful eyes, and fine rusty brown coats, Balinese cattle resemble overgrown deer. Bali's special breed *(bos benteng)* is found only on this island and no crossbreeding is allowed. Cattle are raised for many purposes: as beasts of burden, for export, for ceremonial purposes, and for meat. The Balinese farmer will only reluctantly sell his cow if he needs money for a ceremony.

This is no public auction; deals are struck between owners. Cattle are sold according to weight; only after a per kilo price is agreed upon is the beast weighed and the price adjusted accordingly—usually Rp300,000 for a small cow, Rp800,000 for a large ruminant. One section of the market is devoted to pigs (Rp15,000 for a suckling, Rp50,000 for a mid-sized pig). There are baskets of bobbing chickens, pigeons, and ducks.

To entice farmers and their families, all downtown Bebandem is crowded with stalls selling hand-forged knives, cockfighting spurs, farm tools, impressive daggers, irresistible snacks, *cendol* stands, tonics to increase virility, trinkets, rings and baubles for the children, sunglasses, pop posters, *kain,* cassette tapes, and bright, eye-catching clothing. See ironsmiths forging inexpensive *padi* sickles using hand-pumped billows in the open workshops opposite the *pasar hewan.* Sit in one of the *warung makan* near the terminal and look out on the panoply of market life. This is a lovely area; go the back way via Asak to the main Klungkung-Amlapura highway. From Bebandem, it's Rp500 by *bemo* (nine km) to Amlapura, Rp800 to Rendang.

Just west of Bebandem you'll see a sign on a side road leading to **Tirta Telaga Tista** in the village of Jungutan (north of Sibetan). After one km turn left at the monument, then make another left after 500 meters. This *pura* is an island temple in the middle of an artificial pool under frangipani trees. A serene and little-visited agricultural temple with hills behind and *sawah* stretching to all sides.

Sibetan

The attractive drive to Sibetan winds through palm-leaf fenced rice fields, flowering teak, fragrant clove trees, and plenty of snakeskin-like *salak.* Since 1950 Sibetan has been the *salak* center of Bali, hundreds of hectares planted of this low, thorny palm. The area *salak*s are known for their crisp, sweet taste, somewhere between apples and strawberries. Price depends on grade, ranging from Rp600 to Rp1000 per kg.

It requires three to four years of intensive tending for the three-meter-high trees to bear fruit. Pruning plants that have grown too tall and heaping soil around the stalk improves productivity. Planted among coconuts to provide shade, each plant yields from 40 to 50 fruit annually. Since the trees are planted close together, harvesters must crouch between the thorny branches to reach the fruit. The main season for *salak* is December through February. From October through November, trees bear smaller fruits, called *gadon,* which are more expensive because they're available so early in the season.

Putung

Located 11 km west of Bebandem, 20 km west of Amlapura, and 68 from Denpasar. This miniature tourist resort is famous for *salak* grown on area plantations. The accommodations lie at the terminus of a dead-end road. Enjoy the cool fresh air; it doesn't warm up until noon. An ideal place for meditation. Very quiet, these grandiose surroundings will nourish your soul.

From Amlapura, take a *bemo* to Bebandem (Rp500), another Rp400 *bemo* to the turnoff in Duda village, then walk or hitch 2.5 km to the **Putung Country Club.** Here are five *lumbung*-style rooms for Rp15,000 to Rp20,000 s, others from Rp20,000 to Rp25,000 d (without breakfast). Each bungalow comes with a good foam mattress, closets, veranda, downstairs *mandi* and sitting room, loft bedroom with large picture windows. Rooms 4 and 5, with adjoining doors, are perfect for a family (Rp40,000 for both).

Although plain and basic, what you're paying for is the knockout view. The bungalows sit on the edge of a high cliff over a deep chasm—no *padi*, just jungle falling sharply away to the sea 700 meters below. This area, it is said, is a favorite haunt of *leyak* who hover over the nearby hills and cliffs. The restaurant serves Balinese/Indonesian meals for Rp2000-10,000. In the off-season you'll probably have the whole place to yourself.

Several nice walks in the area. From Putung, take the seven-km-long path via Bakung through gardens and forests down to the coast to Manggis, six km west of Candidasa. Or head west along the road to Rendang, then spectacular terraced rice fields follow the land's dramatic contours to the coast. If you turn south at Duda, you can reach Klungkung via Sidemen.

Selat

A village surrounded by lovely rice terraces rising to Gunung Agung. During festivals, Selat builds a huge *barong*, requiring up to 20 men to lift it, made entirely of fruits, vegetables, and rice. From Selat, take the country road southwest via Sideman, which comes out just east of Klungkung. Just beyond Selat is the village of **Padangaji**, known for its *gambuh* troupe; this classical dance-drama is now rarely performed on Bali. Four km west of Selat, in the peaceful village of **Muncan,** a special ceremony called **Makanplengan** is held the day after Nyepi—large costumed figures simulate copulation. Feast on Balinese specialties or European and Chinese cuisine, meanwhile enjoying the scenery from **Bukit Jambul Garden Restaurant** in **Pesaban,** south of Rendang to the west.

The 900-meter-high village of **Sebudi,** five km north of Selat, is the favored starting point for the five-km southern assault on Gunung Agung. Sebudi is also the location of the very imposing **Pura Pasar Agung** ("Temple of the Agung Market"). The road to the *pura* climbs precipitously up through stands of bamboo and salak plantations to the parking lot where you take the 500 steps up to the 1,200-meter-high terraced temple with Gunung Agung towering above. An ethereal and dramatic spot.

Iseh

Three km south of Selat amid bamboo, coffee, and clove trees sits Iseh, a serene mountain village of rice, sweet potatoes, and onions. Approached on a beautiful untrafficked back road from Klungkung, with panoramas of *sawah* and hilltop temples.

In 1963, Anna Mathews lived beneath Gunung Agung as the volcano erupted, vividly capturing the terrifying experience in her powerful *The Night of the Purnama*. Walter Spies, seeking release from his life of notoriety in Campuan, bought an Iseh mountain hut in 1932. In this land of deep ravines, tier after tier of luminous rice fields, and incomparable views of the navel of the world, Spies created some of his most haunting paintings: *Sawahlandschaft mit G. Agung* (*"View across the Sawah to G. Agung,"* 1937) and *Iseh im Morgenlicht* (*"Iseh in Morning Light,"* 1938). After Spies died in 1942, the Swiss painter Theo Meier later lived in the same house. Now the house and the cabins behind it belong to the family that owns Homestay Sideman; you can rent the cabins and occasionally the house itself (Rp75,000).

Sidemen

The Swiss ethnomusicologist Ernst Schlager (1900-64) and ethnologist Dr. Urs. Ramseyer lived and worked for many years in the Sideman area, southwest of Iseh. Presently, a Swiss charitable foundation has established a special school here devoted to propagating and strengthening traditional Balinese culture. With 120 students, the school's curriculum includes the study of *adat*, crafts, music, dance, painting, water divination, calendrical traditions, the Balinese language, traditional penmanship, literature, and the Bali-Hindu religion. Visit also the weaving factory Pertenunan Pelangi opposite Sideman Homestay. There are several workshops and outlets where you can purchase expensive silk *kain songket* interwoven with designs of gold and silver thread, as well as distinctive Sideman-style *endek* garments. This beautiful area is also known for its scholarly healers, *balian usaba*. Here also is enacted the *barong ketek*, a dance drama concerning a highly esteemed mythical lion. This magical creature also serves a curative function—*tirta* from his beard is prescribed by area *balian* to clients ill or enduring ill fortune.

Sidemen Homestay (tel. 0366-21811) has one of the nicest locations on Bali: 14 comfortable bungalows with fans, fine food (four-course dinners), good service, and superb views. Climb the many steps to enjoy a drink at the bar, with Gunung Agung rearing up behind you. See also Sanur Beach; at night lights sparkle all along the coast. In the vast expanse of *sawah* in front is a wonderful collection of ragged, multicolored scarecrows.

Still, the Rp92,000-115,000 charge is an astonishing sum (though guests seem willing to pay it). No air conditioning, *kelambu,* hot water, nor Visa, but the rooms are nicely furnished, the beds decent, and the ambience peaceful. Good library of Balinesian books in all languages. Ibu Putu also runs **Subak Tabola Inn** (tel. 0366-23015) that lies in the middle of *padi bali,* three km from the main road at the end of a walking track; nice gardens, pool, and basic meals served.

Alternatives? Two km from Sideman Homestay in Desa Tabola is **Homestay Patal**, a better deal: with six spacious, quiet, and well-kept bungalows at Rp115,000 per night, set in a well-tended garden high on a hillside, half a km from the road. Also check out the American Emerald Star's **Tirta Sari**; luxury accommodations, meditation center, many sacred rocks in the area.

Reach Sidemen by traveling west on the scenic road from Amlapura through Bebandem, Putung, and Iseh, or by waiting for a *bemo* at the turn at Satria (or Sampalan Tenah) northeast of Klungkung, then traveling 12 km through the hills. Stand in front of Sidemen's market for a lift out of town in either direction.

TIRTAGANGGA

Seven km northwest of Amlapura (20 minutes, Rp500 by orange *bemo*); the turnoff is just one-half km beyond the bridge after leaving Amlapura. One of the prettiest places in Bali, Tirtagangga ("Water of the Ganges") is a well-maintained pool complex built by the last raja of Karangasem, Raja Anak Agung Anglurah Ketut, in 1947 with corvee labor on the site of a sacred spring emerging from under a banyan tree. The site of a small water temple, these formal,

almost Italianate-style water gardens were only one of the old raja's weekend retreats; the others lie in Ujung, and at Jungutan.

With its shallow pools and channels, pleasant cool weather (500 meters above sea level), few mosquitoes, great beauty, quiet star-filled nights, and birds chirping over the constant sound of splashing water, Tirtagangga is perfect for relaxation. Sitting on the slopes of Gunung Agung, the open-air palace's fabled water basins, fountains, bizarre statues, and figures have been repeatedly damaged by earthquakes. Locals and the government are involved in a seemingly ceaseless restoration project. Open daily 0700-1800, entrance is Rp1100; cameras Rp1000 (all day).

It's a sublime experience to swim laps in big flower-strewn pools filled from freshwater mountain streams. Pools are drained on Monday mornings, but are completely filled again by afternoon. It costs Rp2000 adults, Rp500 children to use the higher 45-meter-long pool and Rp1000 to use the lower pool; you can come and go all day. The water is spine-tingling cold, so wait until noon to plunge in. After 1800 swimming is free of charge, but the water is too cold.

The local moneychanger and Good Karma have poor rates for banknotes (they don't change traveler's checks); for other services, go to Amlapura. Get the excellent map (Rp500) of local hikes at Nyoman Budiarsa's woodcarving ship; Nyoman organizes sightseeing

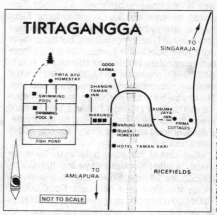

TIRTAGANGGA

TO SINGARAJA

TIRTA AYU HOMESTAY

GOOD KARMA

DHANGIN TAMAN INN

SWIMMING POOL A

SWIMMING POOL B

WARUNGS

KUSUMA JAYA INN

PRIMA COTTAGES

WARUNG RIJASA

RIJASA HOMESTAY

FISH POND

HOTEL TAMAN SARI

TO AMLAPURA

RICEFIELDS

NOT TO SCALE

trips and walking tours. Tirtagangga also makes the best base for exploring the splendid northeast coast.

Accommodations

During the busy tourist season, Tirtagangga's seven hotels fill up quickly. **Dhangin Taman Inn** rents 13 dingy, crowded, very basic rooms varying in price from Rp13,000 to Rp23,000 s or d, depending on size, view, sitting area, and bath. Recent reports of bugs, dirt, burned-out lights. The place seems to be going downhill.

Tirta Ayu Homestay, tel. (0366) 21697, consists of four bungalows at different angles around a garden, right inside the water palace on a small hill. Owned by the king's descendants, it costs Rp35,000 d for bungalows that includes toilet, shower, fan, pool admission, and breakfast. The tariff includes free admission to the pools of the water palace. Laundry service extra. Charming place to stay; nice lawn for yoga. New two-story, Balinese-style bungalows for Rp130,000 per night.

Outside the palace complex and across the road is **Taman Sari Inn.** Here are 25 cool, rustic rooms in adobe bungalows for Rp7000 s, Rp8000 d including breakfast. Double beds, big bathrooms, showers, picture windows looking out on a vast expanse of rice fields with the sea beyond. The two front rooms are the quietest—a best buy. Some rooms in back are even lower in price. The hotel compound is landscaped with bright flowers, ornamental bridges, fish ponds, streams, and tiny Christmas lights. Electricity is on only from 1700 to 0700, and there are too many ants and mosquitoes, but the price is right. Next door to the Taman Sari is the simple but immaculate **Homestay Rijasa** (tel. 0363-21873) with rooms for Rp13,000 s, Rp15,000 d including complimentary breakfast and tea. Rooms here are cleaner, nicer, and newer than Taman Sari's or Dhangin Taman's, with 24-hour electricity. Small library, laundry, no telephone. Excellent food next door in the *warung* of the same name.

Just east of the water palace, up 99 steep steps, is quiet **Kusuma Jaya Inn** (tel. 0363-21250). Its 18 bungalows, built in a semi-arc along the side of a hill, cost Rp20,000 s, Rp30,000 d for basic bungalows or Rp40,000 for larger deluxe rooms with huge beds, nice mat-tresses, fans, and big open-air bathrooms. You can sometimes bargain the rates lower. Superb 180-degree views (especially at sunrise and sunset) take in the glittering sea in front and Gunung Agung. Service is excellent, the food is well-prepared and reasonable. The imprisoned house porcupine is depressing. Around the bend find **Prima Cottages** (tel. 0363-21316). Though its five rooms are small, they're very comfortable. Nice atmosphere, less expensive than the Kusuma Jaya. Great restaurant where people gather in the evenings to play guitar.

Food

Tirtagangga's ground-level accommodations all offer restaurants serving fresh fish taken right from the pools for Rp3000. All feature filling, nutritious *nasi goreng;* special order Balinese dishes. **Tirta Ayu** has average food but a great view. At sunset climb the "stairway to heaven" to **Kusuma Jaya** or **Prima** for spectacular views and okay Indo-Chinese food.

Stalls at the head of the road are cheaper, with surprisingly good *nasi campur* (Rp2000); also cold drinks, fried peanuts, fruits, and *bubur.* **Rice Terrace Cafe** is down the hill from the Kusuma Jaya—take the road to the left if coming from Amlapura. Especially nice salads; highly recommended.

For great music, good food, and a convivial atmosphere try **Good Karma**, operated by an amiable former clove and vanilla farmer who calls himself Baba ("The King"). "Come for Talking and Joking with Baba for Good Karma" states the sign. "Where the hippies hang out." Decent tourist menu; great music. Ask Baba about his five rental cottages up the coast in Selang—an awesome location.

Getting Away

It's easy to get *bemo* into Amlapura (Rp500, 20 minutes); they run until 1700. For Singaraja, buses call on Tirtagangga starting at around 0900, doing the 92-km three-hour run for Rp2500. Red *bemo* also pass from 0400 to 1600 (Rp3000, three to four hours). Get the hotel boys to wake you up. To visit Kintamani from here, take the *bemo* to Kubutambahan (Rp2000, three hours), then go south one hour to Kintamani (Rp1000). For Candidasa, it's Rp750 by *bemo.*

This sparsely populated area lends itself to some dramatic photographs. Just before Culik there's an explosion of vegetation; you can smell it coming. After Culik, not much grows except poinciana, stunted palm trees, *kapok,* and cacti.

VICINITY OF TIRTAGANGGA

This area has fantastic scenery. It's a nice walk following the water source of the pools; take a dip in the pool when you return. Climb the hill in back of the water palace for about 1.5 km to the village, where locals host the occasional secret cockfight. Come back via the winding road through the valley: see coconut palms, brilliant rice fields, the distant sea, with Bali's biggest and most sacred mountain towering above. Three km west of Tirtagangga is Puncak Sari with a panorama over rice fields; bring binoculars.

Another superlative walk is the path leading uphill to Tanahlingis and Ababi. **Tanahlingis** is known for a choral group peculiar to Karangasem that rhythmically imitates *gamelan* instruments; **Ababi**'s attraction is a big washing place with walls of brick in a dry riverbed. From the *warung* look down on an immemorial scene of men, women, children, and cows as they wash, chat, and fetch water. A major agriculture ceremony is held at the end of the dry season each year. Also worth seeing is the Chinese cemetery, one km beyond Tirtagangga on the right.

Tanaharon

Make the hike up this miniature Gunung Agung. Turn left at Abang about three km after Tirtagangga and follow it for 10 km. It's 45 minutes to the top from where the asphalt ends beyond Pidpid; the roundtrip walk from Tirtagangga takes five hours. A battle with the Dutch is commemorated by a monument here. Nice lookout points over steep ravines.

Budahkling

In this colony on the slopes of Gunung Agung live two castes of Mahayana Buddhists who've retained pre-Hindu feasting traditions. Balinese come here to ask for the services of Brahmana priests. Also living in the region are descendants of a gold- and silversmiths guild that served the princely Karangasem court prior to WW II. Villagers here make *kain songket* and sell small *selendang* for Rp15,000, *sarung* for Rp50,000, large *kain* for up to Rp150,000.

Abianjero

Southeast of Ngis, this village is known for its particularly talented architects, painters, dancers, musicians, and wood- and stonecarvers. Visit the home of Made Kantor, a versatile traditional painter and architect. His younger brother Sujana and son Sudarsa are talented painters in the Pita Maha tradition.

Bukit Lempuyang

To get to Bali's easternmost hill and the site of an important temple, take an *ojek* from Bajo (Rp2000) to the parking lot about halfway up, then walk to Pura Lempuyang at Abang. About eight km from the main highway (see sign pointing the way to the temple) is a tollgate (Rp500 per person); from where the road ends, it's about a one-km walk to the first small temple, Pura Telagamas. From there it's 4,000 steps to the top through a forest. Start early before it gets too hot. If you go in the afternoon, the mountain is covered with clouds. On clearer mornings you'll see not only Gunung Agung but all the way to the islands of Nusa Penida and Lembongan. During festival times, public *bemo* run to the end of the road but on other days *bemo* run only from Abang to Ngis Tista, from where you must start walking (2.5 km). This is one of six major *sad kahyangan* spiritual points on Bali, right up there in stature with Ulu Watu, Besakih. The whole way up to the sacred site is littered with plastic and trash from drink containers.

THE LOST COAST

This undeveloped northeastern strip of coast offers some of Bali's best snorkeling, some of the island's most splendidly located self-contained dive *losmen,* quiet unpeopled beaches, and Bali's largest concentration of traditional *jukung.* Here you can finally find peace and quiet, enjoy great food, inexpensive accommodations, some massage, very few hawkers, and one or two boat trip guys who leave you alone after asking. This area is a big highlight but getting crowded quick.

On a beautiful bay is the solitary village of **Amed;** visit the fish market early in the morning when the tuna come in (both Rp2000 and Rp3000 sizes). The road south from Amed via Cemeluk, Lipah, Bunatan, and Selang is paved but very narrow, with Hindu fishing settlements hugging the shore all the way south to Ujung. A poor, very dry part of Bali, the area's farmers grow soybeans, corn, peanuts, *ubi kayu,* and corn rather than rice. Arid hills inland are terraced in *ladeng* supported by stone walls. This is an exhausting 2.5 hour trip on a motorbike with many curves and very steep ups-and-downs: taking your own car is definitely more comfortable, more expedient, but even more slow-going.

Europeans snorkelers and divers have discovered the coastline southeast of Amed. Snorkeling off the black-sand beaches here is said by some to be superior to Tulamben, the variety and numbers of fish are perhaps the best on Bali. The snorkeling begins just east of town, where the currents are calm year-round, visibility is 10-20 meters, and the hard coastal reefs are superb. Dive along the reef wall to see schools of cardinal fish, triggerfish, black snappers, pyramid butterflies, bannerfish, and damselfish among the sand slopes, table corals, big fan gorgonians, and magnificent staghorn *Acropora* and *Dendronephthya* trees, dense growths of sponges, crinoids, and sea fans—all within 20 meters of the shore.

Accommodations

Three places to stay on this coast are real escapes, perhaps fulfilling most people's popular paradisical visions of Bali. Six km southeast of Amed is isolated **Lipah village** (pop. 70) with a very good coral reef starting about 15-20 meters off shore. **Kusumajaya Beach Inn** is a barren place with brick bungalows; not yet worth considering. The next accommodations, on the west end of the bay, is the class act of the area, Kuchit and Gillian's **Hidden Paradise Cottages,** tel. (0366) 431273, rooms with fan for Rp69,000 d, Rp92,000 with air conditioning, and spacious, beautiful suites are Rp150,000 d (plus 11.5% for tax and service). Breakfast for two included; pool, laundry service, safety deposit box, library, children's playground, great pool, mountain bikes (Rp5000 per day), a whole wall of snorkeling gear (Rp5000 for 12 hours). The restaurant out front serves good seafood dinners for under Rp5000.

More upscale is **Coral View Villas** (Box 121, Amlapura, tel. 0361-431273, fax 0363-21044 or 0361-423820) between Hidden Paradise and Vienna Beach with bungalows for Rp50,000 to a/c suites for Rp55,000; hot water, bright outdoor bathrooms, beautiful pool and grounds, beachfront restaurant, excellent but expensive dive facility. Credit cards accepted.

Farther south (about 10 km from Culik) in grape-growing Bunutan is I Wayan Utama's pristine 10-bungalow **Vienna Beach;** (Rp25,000 s or d) plus three rooms in back by the parking lot for Rp20,000 s or d. A two-story furnished bamboo house goes for Rp50,000; Rp30,000 for just the upstairs. Very nice location in a leafy garden at the end of a small fishing village. Good service, safety deposit box, generator for 24-hour electricity, fresh well-water showers, laundry, and a nice, wide beach under trees. Reservations: I Wayan Utama, Box 112, Amlapura 80801. The restaurant serves good, honest, straightforward food—the kitchen may be out of menu items like *tahu,* as staff must drive drive to Amlapura each day to shop and may not get back by mealtime. Local *warung* sell snacks but no rice; you'll have to eat at the *losmen.* The villagers are sweet natured; they approach on the beach almost apologetically. Get a massage (Rp5000) with coconut oil while lying on a bamboo bed in a fishermen's hut. Rent snorkeling gear for Rp4000 per day. Fishermen will take you out to the reef in a *jukung* for Rp10,000-12,000. It doesn't get much better than this.

The most southerly accommodations are at **Good Karma Homestay** in Selang, Bunutan township. Ten simple, clean, rice-barn style bungalows go for Rp25,000-Rp40,000 d, including breakfast of *pisang goreng* and banana pancakes. Food average, service slow, prices a little high. Just the sound of the waves (except when you have noisy neighbors). Only basic services: no telephone, cold showers, generator power, laundry, cold beer, nice beach—all you need. Baba is obsessed with accumulating good karma, thus he's an inestimable host. Snorkeling starts just five to 10 meters from Good Karma, or you can hire one of the *jukung* in front for Rp5000-6000 per hour to travel farther from shore, or even better, to Vienna Beach. The fishermen go fishing at 0500 and return at 0900. There's a chance the place may be booked.

Getting There

Take a *bemo* from Tirtagangga 10 km to the turnoff at Culik (Rp500). Ocassionally, public *bemo* are available from Culik to Amed but most likely you'll have to hire one of the six to seven *ojek* waiting there to take you three km down to the coast to Amed (Rp1000), or all the way to accommodations at Hidden Paradise (Rp1500), Vienna (Rp1500), or Good Karma (Rp2000). From Amed, hitch a ride or catch an infrequent *bemo* two km down the coast to the fishing community of **Cemeluk,** consisting of just 20 families. You'll pass a long stretch of sea salt processing plants resembling stacked railroad ties. From Amlapura, public *bemo* sometimes run to Seraya, but seldom farther. Though the coastal road from Amlapura to Culik is only 42 km, you need to allow a full day to explore this area with your own vehicle.

TULAMBEN

Bali's parched northeast coastal road is one of the few stretches on Bali where rural life is largely unaffected by tourism. The only intrusion of Western culture are the makeshift bamboo pool halls frequented by young men of the village. On the drive to Singaraja you pass by villages of waving people, temple festivals, banana and coconut plantations, and subsistence farmers eking out a living gathering sea salt and coral. Beautiful tiered rice fields give way to a dry, barren country ravaged by massive black rivers of volcanic rubble from Agung's 1963 eruption.

The small fishing village of Tulamben lies along this hot, dry coast, 10 km west of Culik, 23 km from Tirtagangga, and 95 km from Denpasar. Due to its proximity to some of the island's best diving, it has attracted snorkelers and scuba divers from all over the world. Tulamben Beach is peppered with black rocks that scald your feet in the noonday sun. There's not much to do here but dive, eat, read, sleep, and stroll down the village street in the cool of the evening.

As yet, none of the hotels have swimming pools, and generator-powered electricity is only on from 1800 to 2300 (if someone wants an ice juice, Paradise Bungalows starts up the generator!), and even water stops then.

All the *losmen* here cater mostly to divers, so don't expect fancy services or facilities. As yet, none have swimming pools, and generator-powered electricity is only on from 1800 to 2300. Bargain if the accommodation is not full. If you stay at least three nights, most hotels will give you a 10% discount in the low season. No discounts available in busy season. There's a country doctor in Kubu, as well as a post office and small *warung* selling simple food, snacks, and fruit. Out on the ocean you can sometimes see dolphins and jumping *pasuh*. Besides the dining rooms at each of the four accommodations, there's a cute little restaurant between Paradise Palm Beach Bungalows and Bali Timur Bungalows, appropriately known as the Fish Restaurant.

Diving and Snorkeling

Tulamben is considered by many the premier dive spot on Bali. The best months for diving are July and August, but even in the rainy season the diving can be very satisfying. The numerous dive operators in Kuta, Bali, and Lovina bring large groups of enthusiasts here. Hardcore divers end up staying for days. A large variety of big fish is accessible right out in front of most accommodations; many of the fish are so tame, they'll eat bananas right out of your hand.

Rent snorkeling gear from any of the accommodations in the village for Rp3000; if you're not a hotel guest it's Rp4000. **Paradise Palm Beach Bungalows** offers 40-minute dives for Rp70,000 or two dives for Rp110,000 (three hours in all), including gear and an excellent guide, and gives a 10% discount on dive equipment for guests. A government forestry official will ask a Rp500 fee per person per day from anyone who is snorkeling or diving off the coast.

A sunken American Liberty ship, torpedoed by the Japanese in 1942, is the big diving attraction. This eerie ghost lies about a kilometer to the west of the main hotels, only 40-50 meters from the beach. Swim straight out from the white toilet block on the beach 100 meters north of Ganda Mayu Bungalows; it doesn't take much strength to reach it. The broken steel ship stretches in two pieces for over 100 meters along a steep sandy slope, its length almost parallel to shore. The top is only three meters below the surface, the bottom about 30 meters down. Visibility is 12-15 meters, and the wreck is within easy snorkeling distance from the shore. Large encrusted holes in the hull and deck allow exploration of the interior of the wreck. Plenty of soft corals, sponges, hydrozoans, and gorgonians. It's estimated 400 species of reef fish inhabit the wreck, as well as 100 species of surface organisms. A large coral outcropping lies 100 meters away to the east, and in the ocean off the eastern end of the beach is a great coral wall with overhangs, big gorgonians, and basket sponges.

Avoid diving in late June to August and from December to January when waves are highest. During the dive season, there can be as many as 60 people swarming over this popular site. If you overnight in Tulamben and go out early (before 1000) in the morning or late in the afternoon, you can avoid the crowds. Kal Muller, the author of *Underwater Indonesia,* writes that a full moon night dive on the wreck "is among the most memorable dives you'll ever make."

Accommodations and Food

Dewa Nyoman Chandra's **Paradise Palm Beach Bungalows** is the oldest and most pleasant budget accommodation in the area. Make reservations at Friendship Shop, tel. (0366) 29052 in Candidasa, or write Box 111, Amlapura 80811, Bali. Seventeen rooms: Rp25,000 s, Rp40,000 d; also a Rp20,000 s or d set of rooms. If you stay for three or more nights, ask for a discount. The most expensive rooms are the four facing the beach. Very nice, large rooms surrounded by a lush garden. The restaurant (0700-2400) is good: fish curry (Rp3500), *tahu campur* with vegetables (Rp2000), jaffles (Rp1500 to Rp1800), *ikan laut* (about Rp2000, depending on size), and drinks. A small kiosk sells snacks, cookies, toiletries, and clothing; the dive shop has batteries, film, snorkeling equipment, and books. Used book library; laundry service costs Rp500 for a T-shirt, Rp1000 for long pants.

East of the Paradise is the neglected-looking **Bali Timur Bungalows** with six rather forbidding cinderblock "bungalows" for Rp10,000 s, Rp12,000 d. Price includes breakfast of pancake, fruit salad, or omelette. The **Ganda Mayu Bungalows and Restaurant** has two big rooms for Rp15,000 s, Rp25,000 d and two small rooms for Rp10,000 s, Rp15,000 d, all facing the beach. Good parking, impressive menu, staffed solely by young men. This dive *losmen* is the closest (300 meters) to the shipwreck.

At the top end is the **Mimpi Resort** on the beach on the Tirtagangga side (east) of town. Make reservations through Bali Marine Sport on Jl. Ngurah Rai, Blanjong, Sanur (see manager, Ena Partha). Rooms are Rp190,000 (fan) to Rp210,000, including breakfast. Very private, eco-friendly, very large, and beautiful swimming pool.

Transportation

From Candidasa, reach Tulamben by *bemo* via Amlapura (Rp1400). From Singaraja (70 km to the west) it's Rp2000 by Isuzu van. Paradise Palm Beach Bungalows provides transport to the airport (up to four people), as well as a tour service. If you call from Candidasa, the Paradise will send a vehicle to pick you up (Rp30,000 per person, up to four people). Motorbikes and *jukung* (Rp5000 per hour) also for rent.

BOB RACE

BULELENG REGENCY

This sprawling, 1,370-square-km regency offers mountain hikes, rustic villages, waterfalls, hot springs, untouched marine and forest reserves, silversmiths, beach resorts of glistening black sand, a secluded coastline bordering a placid sea, and distinctive temples seething with baroque carved figures. The south end stretches across the foothills of Bali's central volcanoes while the whole north's coastal plain faces the Java Sea. This largest of Bali regencies touches all but one of the island's other regencies. The capital, Singaraja, has a cosmopolitan air with many ethnic and religious minorities existing in harmony.

Because of Buleleng's geographic isolation from the densely populated south, it has developed distinct cultural differences in architecture, dance, and art. The district was absent from early maps of Bali—Cornelis de Houtman's 1597 map of the island showed only the land south of the central east-west mountain range. Today the fleets of tour buses seldom venture over the mountain passes, and consequently there are fewer beggars, touts, and professional hasslers plaguing the region.

In the mid-1800s the European maritime powers established their presence on Bali here.

Buleleng women were ordered to adopt the *kebaya* (Malay blouse) by the Dutch commandant "to protect the morals of the Dutch soldiers"; previously, the *kebaya* had served as a badge of prostitution. From 1854, until the international airport opened at Tuban in 1962 Buleleng had much greater contact with the outside world than the south. Singaraja was the administrative center for the whole of Nusatenggara from Indonesian independence until 1958.

History
During the 14th century northern Bali came under the rule of the Javanese nobles of east Bali's Gelgel dynasty. In 1584 the legendary Panji Sakti built a palace called Puri Sukasada where Singaraja is today, extending his rule all the way to east Java. Panji Sakti broke with the overlords of the south and established a powerful maritime kingdom, which survived through 12 generations and into the mid-19th century. In 1814, while Sir Stamford Raffles was busy founding Singapore, a British force spent several months here.

Alarmed at the increasing involvement of the English in the region, the Dutch were next on the scene. Determined to grab all the islands of the Indies for themselves, the Dutch in 1846 sent

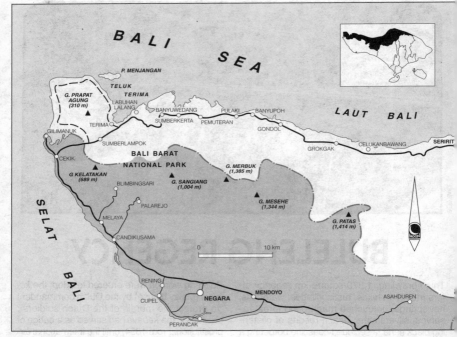

ashore a military expedition to capture Singaraja, then known as Buleleng. The attack ended in a stalemate and a shaky treaty was signed with the ruling princes.

Two years later, the troops of Prince Gusti Ketut Jelantik lured a Dutch force to the town of Jagaraga, killing 264 Hollanders and mercenaries while losing 2,000 of their own men. In 1849, a much larger and better equipped Dutch engaged the Balinese; a Dutch general was killed and Jelantik committed suicide by poison. Although the Balinese were extraordinarily brave, they were no match for the repeating rifles and modern howitzers of the Dutch. Another truce led to the 1855 separation of Buleleng from Jembrana, and the regency became the first on the island to fall under the direct political control of the empire-building Dutch.

Singaraja became the district's capital in 1882, and served as a major transshipment point for Nusatenggara throughout the colonial period. The descendants of the local regent became

bureaucratic officials in the employ of the Dutch. Feudal rule came to an end here a full 60 years prior to colonization of the more bucolic south. Even today northern Bali retains an anachronistic European air, the caste system ignored and the social order centering more on the family than on the communalized, institutionalized agricultural *banjar* of the south. Because of their strong egalitarian spirit, the cosmopolitan and well-mannered people of Buleleng are considered *kasar* by other Balinese.

In 1945 Anak Agung Panji Tisna, an 11th generation descendant of the Gelgel dynasty, became the first Balinese king to convert to Christianity. Tisna was the son of Anak Agung Putu Jelantik, who wrote much of Buleleng's history on *lontar*. His new faith, coupled with the perception that he was more artist and writer than ruler, drove Tisna to resign as raja in 1947; he was replaced by his brother. When Tisna died in 1978 he became the first Balinese king to be buried and not cremated.

BULELENG REGENCY

© MOON PUBLICATIONS, INC.

Economy

The regency is an important cattle export center and a major coffee, vanilla, nutmeg, cocoa, and clove-growing district. Since Buleleng's climate is drier than that of the south, Indian corn, copra, and fruits such as mangoes, mangosteen, bananas, passion fruit, and avocados can be grown here. The latest cash crop is red grapes, the sweetest in all Bali, cultivated on bamboo frames in the hills overlooking the coast. The island's best and stinkiest durian come from Bestala near Munduk Village. Several shrimp cultivation farms lie west of Lovina.

Singaraja, Buleleng's capital, has been an important educational and cultural center since the Dutch were here; the education faculty of Denpasar's Udayana University is based here. Tourism is a nascent but burgeoning industry. Though not as culturally rich as the classical southern half of the island, tourists are attracted to Buleleng's cheaper prices and stretch of relatively quiet beaches, dotted with inexpen-

sive accommodations and restaurants. Shallow reefs offshore offer some of the island's most accessible snorkeling and dolphin-watching opportunities.

Architecture

The temple architecture of northern Bali differs considerably from the stiff classical lines carved of gray sandstone in south Bali. The soft pink *paras* quarried near Singaraja allow northern sculptors more exuberance. Because the stone ages so quickly, carving is an art form kept constantly alive. In the north, stones are chosen for their color, white or brown, and are often painted.

Homeowners here paint their own *pura paibon* to deified ancestors and saints. These temples are more prevalent in the northern mountain villages than in the south.

Though the interior layout is basically the same as in South Bali temples, small shrines are replaced by one or two large pedestals containing houses for the deities placed in the in-

woodcarving in the style of northern Bali

nermost courtyard and built of elaborately carved tiered stone and covered by a single roof. Frequently, this flamelike pedestal supports a throne of the sun god.

Steep flights of narrow steps lead to airy thrones and shrines, scale is exaggerated, and the tall, dynamic, flowing *candi bentar* are covered with spiky, flame-like shapes, arabesques, and spirals studded with *leyak,* supernatural beings, and sea creatures. On the earthy, whimsical, cartoonlike bas reliefs of Buleleng, you'll see baroque gone wild—images of plump Dutchmen cramped into a motorcar, men drinking beer and cranking cars, people copulating in the bushes, men riding bicycles composed of leaves and flowers.

Getting There

Reach Buleleng by crossing Bali's central mountain range on one of the island's two main roads, both of which pass crater lakes and offer spectacular scenery. If you have your own transport, take the fastest route to Singaraja from Denpasar via Bedugul, then return to Denpasar via Kintamani, a roundtrip covering most of Bali's mountainous backbone. Also approach Buleleng from Gilimanuk along the northwest coast and from Amlapura along the scantily populated northeast coast. A third northbound road from Denpasar crosses the mountains (Gunung Batukau and Gunung Catur) through the coffee-growing district of Pupuan, offering impressive, hair-raising views.

SINGARAJA

A small seaport and the capital of Buleleng featuring tree-lined avenues, quiet residential perimeters, a wide market street, rows of bright Chinese shops, and horse-drawn carts amidst frenetic traffic. Singaraja is reminiscent of Java; traders from all over Asia have called at the port of Buleleng since the 10th century, trading arms, opium, and *kepang* for fresh water, food, livestock, and slaves. Each group has greatly impacted the cultural life of the city.

Singaraja means "lion king," a name commemorating a palace built in 1604 by Raja Panji Sakti. The Dutch fought the powerful raja at a fierce battle in the nearby village of Jagaraga, finally taking control of the northern Buleleng re-

gion in 1849. By 1882, Singaraja was the administrative center, principal harbor, and trading center for Bali and all the islands to the east.

Bali's road system wasn't constructed until the 1920s, when the first trickle of tourists began arriving in Singaraja's harbor on KPM steamers. Tours described in prewar travel books start in Singaraja. Small groups of tourists were chauffeured from the wharf over the mountains to southern Bali's "native districts," then quite an arduous journey.

During WW II, after the Japanese successfully occupied Indonesia, they established there headquarters in Singaraja. When the Dutch returned to Bali after WW II, they transfered their administrative offices to Denpasar because of its proximity to the new airport and much greater population density.

With a present population of more than 550,000 people, Singaraja is Bali's second largest city. It's cleaner, less polluted, less congested, and more attractive and relaxing than Denpasar. The influence of non-Balinese—Chinese, Bugis, Javanese, Malays, Indians, Arabs—is more noticeable in Singaraja than in other parts of Bali, as this city has been a marketplace for the Java sea trade economy for over a thousand years.

SIGHTS

The only part of the city that has retained its original character is the densely packed merchant's quarter south of the harbor. Many imposing residences and examples of European architecture still stand, reminders of Singaraja's former grandeur as the Dutch capital of Bali and all the islands to the east. A number of these white-painted colonial edifices can be found along Jl. Ngurah Rai, heading south from the harbor up to the winged lion statue, where Jl.

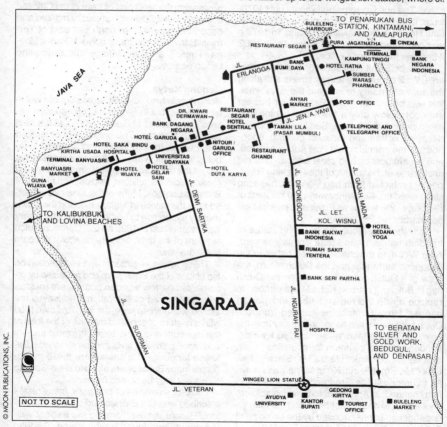

Ngurah Rai meets Jl. Pahlawan. In Indonesian called Tugu Singa Amabara Raja, the lion symbolizes the dynamic spirit of the people of Buleleng and serves as the regency's coat of arms.

At the top of Jl. Ngurah Rai is the **Kantor Bupati,** once the official residence of the Dutch "Resident" (a sort of governor). After independence it was used as the Indonesian Governor's office when Singaraja was the capital of Nusatenggara. In 1958, Nusatenggara was divided into three provinces—Bali, Nusa Tenggara Timur, Nusa Tenggara Barat—and the island's capital was moved from Singaraja to Denpasar. The building remained vacant until 1970, when it was used as the headquarters of the Fifth Regional Defensive Command. In 1977 it was converted into the Hotel Singaraja; in 1982 it became the mayor's office.

Enjoy beautiful sunsets over the old harbor area. Walk through the narrow streets and along the seawall and try to imagine the days when this was one of the Dutch East Indies' busiest entrepôts. Now only a few small fishing and cargo *prahu* bob offshore. See abandoned and decaying coffee and tobacco *gudang,* shophouses, the crumbling old Port Authority office, and an antique arched steel bridge. This old anchorage at the mouth of the Buleleng River, poorly protected from bad weather, has long since silted up. Celukanbawang, 40 km west of Singaraja, now serves as Buleleng's principle export harbor.

Near the waterfront, the haunting statue of freedom fighter Ketut Merta points seaward. After WW II, in the chaotic period between the Japanese surrender and the Dutch return, the crew of a Dutch patrol boat hoisted the Dutch flag in Buleleng Harbor; Ketut Merta climbed to replace it with the red-and-white Indonesian banner. He was machine-gunned from the Dutch boat the minute he stepped away from the pole. During the Indonesian struggle for independence it was common for guerrillas to use nicknames like Pak Hitam ("Mr. Black"), Pak Cilik ("Mr. Small"), etc. Ketut Merta was known as I Lontong, ("Mr. Steamed Rice"). Nothing has changed: in April 1995 Indonesian soldiers shot a man to death after he raised the Irian independence banner, moved by the same spirit that inspired heroic "Mr. Steamed Rice" 50 years previously. A shrine commemorating I Lontong

is located around the corner opposite the Chinese temple.

The huge Hindu temple **Pura Jagatnatha** is on Jl. Pramuka; in the evenings the local *gamelan* rehearses in the first courtyard. Singaraja's *pura dalem,* on Jl. Gajah Mada below the cemetery, contains a wall of incredible phantasmagoric reliefs depicting Balinese heaven and hell and the dire consequences of earthly sins. See miscreants with their tongues pulled out, arms sawed off, boiled, beaten, and stabbed. A large Chinese *klenteng* in the eastern part of the city houses priceless vases and tapestries. In the west part of town is the Chinese cemetery Bukit Suci with unusually marked and decorated graves; turn north just east of Terminal Banyuasri and travel down Jl. Pantai Lingga. There's a fishing village and swimming beach nearby.

Gedong Kirtya
Holy objects are ordinarily stored out of sight in high places, but in Singaraja you can view sacred *lontar* books at Gedong Kirtya at the east end of Jl. Veteran. The only library of its kind in the world, the 3,000-odd *lontar* stored in labeled tin boxes in this small nondescript archive record the literature, mythology, magic formulas, medical science, folklore, religion, and history of Bali and Lombok. Many of the *lontar* were looted from the palace in Mataram during the Dutch military expedition to Lombok 1894. The library was established in 1928 by L.J. Caron, a Dutch resident of the time; pictograms above the gate show the year.

These miniature pictures and texts etched on the blades of the *lontar* palm and protected by ornamented narrow wooden boards, are masterpieces of the art of illustration. The leaves are etched with a sharp knife, the incisions then filled with a mixture of soot and oil. One of the jobs of the museum is to transliterate the most ancient and rarest palm-leaf texts into the romanized Balinese language. So sacred are these manuscripts many Balinese are afraid to enter Gedong Kirtya lest they be cursed by spirits.

Look for examples of *prasastis,* metal plates inscribed with Old Balinese edicts from the Pejeng-Bedulu dynasty, among the earliest written documents found on the island. Gedung Kirtya also contains rare Dutch and English books, a complete collection of traditional Balinese calendars dating back to 1935, and an extensive archive of Balinese "scriptures"—actually high-quality copies; the originals remain with *dukun* and rajas' families. Near the institute are the royal temples **Puri Kawan** directly behind the library, and **Puri Kanginan** to the northeast. Open 0800 to 1400. Closes 1100 Friday, 1200 Saturday. Leave a donation. For more information call (0362) 22645.

ACCOMMODATIONS

Most Singaraja hotels cater to Indonesian business or *pegawi*. If you're staying longer than a day, it's more pleasant to stay six kilometers away at Lovina Beach than in the city itself. In Singaraja the budget hotel with the most character is **Hotel Ratna** on Jl. Imam Bonjolioz, Rp8000 s. There are also some Rp10,000 d rooms in front, while Rp15,500 d rooms feature *kamar mandi*. The upstairs rooms in back are quietest.

Most of Singaraja's hotels are conveniently located on Jl. Jen. A. Yani, heading west out of town. **Hotel Garuda**, at no. 76, tel. (0362) 22191, charges Rp10,000 s, Rp12,500 d with breakfast. Lots to choose from two sets of rooms, but no personality. On the other end of the scale, with personality *plus*, is **Tresna Homestay**, J1. Gajeh Mada 95 (tel. 0362-21816). The rooms at **Hotel Duta Karya**, tel. (0362) 21467, next to the Nitour/Garuda office on Jl. Jen A. Yani, have fans, intercoms, and sinks for Rp12,000 s, Rp15,500 d with bath; five air-conditioned rooms go for twice as much. Breakfast includes toast with egg and Bali coffee. Nice courtyard. A cafeteria serving Chinese seafood and Muslim dishes is only 100 meters away. More central **Hotel Sentral**, at no. 48, tel. (0362) 21896, is Rp9000 s, Rp12,000 d with fan, inside *mandi,* and breakfast; air-conditioned rooms run Rp25,500 s, Rp35,000 d. Twenty-six rooms in all. **Hotel Cendrawasih**, next door to the Sentral, seems to be full all the time at rates of Rp8000 s, Rp12,000 d. Clean, well-run **Hotel Sedana Yoga**, Jl. Gajah Mada 136, tel. (0362) 21715, asks Rp10,500 s, Rp15,000 d for rooms with fans, and Rp25,000 s, Rp35,500 d for air-conditioned rooms. Breakfast included. For the price, the most pleasant of any Singaraja hotel.

Hotel Gelar Sari, at Jl. Jen. A. Yani 87, tel. (0362) 21495, charges Rp10,000 s, Rp15,500 d. All bathrooms outside rooms. Only coffee and tea, no breakfast. Laundry service. Clean and adequate for the price, though a bit far from town. The **Saka Bindu**, also on Jl. Jen. A. Yani nearly across the street from the Gelasari, tel. (0362) 21719, wants only Rp8000 but is dumpy and riven with mosquitoes. Rooms with *kamar kecil* and *mandi* outside.

The newest, most comfortable accommodations is upmarket **Hotel Wijaya**, Jl. Jend. Sudirman 74, tel. (0362) 21915, featuring rooms with fan for Rp18,000 s, Rp22,000 d; or Rp42,000 s, Rp45,000 d for air-conditioned rooms. Breakfast, tax, and service included in price. Suite rooms cost Rp65,000 s, Rp70,000 d with color TV, telephone, fridge, private bath, and hot water. Credit cards accepted. Restaurant in front, courteous staff. Convenient location near Banyuasri Station.

FOOD

For strong north Bali coffee, try **Agus Mahardika** in Hotel Ratna, Jl. Imam Bonjolioz 100-102 (tel. 0362-21396 or 21851). Good, inexpensive eating near Banyuasri Station at **Pasar Anyar,** which opens at 1800 *(es campur, soto, bakwan, sate kambing)* in the Jalan Durian area. More expensive restaurants are located in the shopping complex Taman Lila (Pasar Mumbul) on Jl. A. Yani within walking distance of the big downtown intersection. Try **Restaurant Ghandi,** tel. (0362) 21163, for high-quality Chinese dishes—*mie,* prawns, lobster, pigeon—the shrimp vermicelli soup (Rp2500) is outstanding. Next door is the older and popular **Restaurant Kartika,** tel. (0362) 41296, for Chinese, Balinese, Indonesian, and seafood dishes. Order specials like *bebek tutu* a day ahead or choose from a reasonably priced menu (Rp4000-5000). Adequate parking. In the same complex is **Nurhayat Warung Muslim,** Jl. Jen. A. Yani 25 B. Other noteworthy restaurants along J1. Jen. A. Yani: **Avina** at no. 53; **Cafeteria** at no. 55; **Kantin** at 55 B.

An uncommonly good Chinese eatery is **Restaurant Segar I** on Jl. Erlangga near the harbor. Though very plain, almost open to the street, it serves a great *nasi campur* with lots of shrimp for Rp3000; Indonesian food too. **Restaurant Segar II** is on Jl. Jen. A. Yani within an easy walk of Pasar Mumbul; the two Segars, owned by the same family, are considered the best restaurants in the city.

SHOPPING

People are friendlier, laugh easier, and are more willing to bargain in this relatively untouristed city, but the craftsmanship doesn't compare with the variety and ingenuity of southern work. This artistic atrophy may be attributed to the long period of Dutch subjugation, as well as the dilution of culture due to heavy migration of non-Balinese peoples brought in to work the plantations and the docks of the north.

Take cash when you shop, as few places accept credit cards or traveler's checks. The souvenir shop **Tresna**, Jl. Gajah Mada 95, tel. (0362) 21816, sells antiques, *kain tenun,* and carvings. The city's retail shops, concentrated along Jl. Jen. A. Yani, are getting bigger, cleaner, with better selections. Self-service shops have arrived too, and in most you don't have to bargain. For almost any type of tropical fruit visit **Buleleng Market** just south of Jl. Semeru at the east end of Jl. Veteran. Each night until 2100 or so, depending on reliability of electricity, this market transforms into a dimly lit, lively *pasar malam.* **Indra Jaya Bookstore**, Jl. Diponegoro 30 (tel. 0362-22331) has a small collection of English-language books. One km east of Singaraja is the small pottery village of Banyuning which turns out unglazed urns, vases, roof tiles, and other pottery.

Textiles

A major weaving factory is **Berdikari** at Jl. Dewi Sartika 42 (open 0800-1900, tel. 0362-22217), specializing in the reproduction of ancient, finely detailed Buleleng silk *ikat* sold for sky-high prices. **Perusahan Puri Nadiputri**, on Jl. Veteran behind the Gedong Kirtya, sells distinctive handwoven silk and cotton *sarung* or *kain;* open 0800-1600. There are looms in practically every home in this *kampung,* set in the former *puri* compound. In 1960 the *puri* owed the bank so much money that it was forced to foreclose, and the bank sold the property to the government;

you can still see the old walls of the compound. Another place to buy *endek, ikat,* colorfast *sarung,* and gold-threaded *songket* is **Poh Bergong;** from Singaraja head for Penarukan, then turn south toward Jinengdalem and Poh Bergong. Retailers buy here at wholesale prices.

SERVICES

Most government offices are located near the junction of Jl. Veteran, Jl. Ngurah Rai, and Jl. Pahlawan, about one km inland from the harbor. Road distances in north Bali are measured from this point, where the Winged Lion statue sits.

The **tourist information office**, Jl. Veteran 23, tel. (0362) 61141, is near the Gedung Kirtya, about 100 meters back from the road; you'll see the sign from Jl. Veteran. From Banyuasri station, take a yellow *bemo.* The friendly staff may have a few pamphlets and maps of Buleleng and Singaraja. Open Mon.-Fri. 0700-1700, Saturday until 1230. Office chief Nyoman Suwela speaks excellent English. He is an unabashed promoter of Buleleng and infects all with his enthusiasm. The *kantor polisi,* tel. 110, is on Jl. Pramuka at the north end of Jl. Ngurah Rai, and the **post office** is at Jl. Gajah Mada 158 (where J1. Gajah Mada intersects with the eastern end of J1. Jen. A. Yani). Poste restante address, Kantor Pos, Poste Restante, Jl. Gajah Mada 156, Singaraja 81113. Open Mon.-Sat. 0700-1700.

At the official telephone office, called **Wartel Kopegtel**, where you can also receive and place faxes and make international telephone calls, is right next to the post office at Jl. Gajah Mada 154. Open 24 hours. Singaraja's telephone code is 0362. **Change money** at Bank Central Asia, tel. (0362) 23761, on the south side of Jl. Jen. A Yani (on the right if approaching from Banyuasri Terminal). Here you can get cash from Visa or MasterCard for a Rp5000 charge. Open Mon.-Fri. 0800-1400, Saturday 0800-1130. Also check rates at BDN, Jl. Jen. A. Yani, tel. (0362) 41344; Bank Bumi Daya, Jl. Erlangga 14, tel. (0362) 41245, open Mon.-Fri. 0800-1500, Saturday 0800-1130; and BRI, Jl. Ngurah Rai 14.

Nitour Tour & Travel, Jl. Jen. A. Yani 59, tel. (0362) 22691, is Singaraja's main agent for Garuda, Merpati, and Bouraq. Open Mon.-Sat. 0800-1400. Note that this agent cannot reliably confirm bookings on flights out of Bali; contact directly the main Garuda office in Sanur for confirmation by telephoning (0361) 288243.

Doctor Kwari Darmawan, tel. (0362) 21721, across the street from the Nitour Office, has a good reputation; open 0630-1900. **Rumah Sakit Umum,** on Jl. Njurah Rai (tel. 0362-22046), offers well-equipped medical facilities. For more serious injuries or illnesses, go to **Kertha Usada Hospital,** a private hospital at Jl. Jen. A. Yani 108, tel. (0362) 41396; also has a dentist. A well-stocked pharmacy is **Sumber Waras;** right past the bridge on the left if coming into town from the east. **Wijaya Kusuma Apotik,** Jl. Ngurah Rai 23, tel. (0362) 22890, is a 24-hour pharmacy. Several other pharmacies are located on Jl. Diponegoro.

TRANSPORTATION

Getting There
Board a minibus from Kintamani (Rp2000) or Denpasar (Rp3000) to Singaraja via Bedugul. Go through a hair-raising mountain pass, descend from a point 1,200 meters above sea level, and there it is. Another route is via Kintamani in the mountains through Kubutambahan on the north coast. Singaraja is also on the shuttle bus route. If traveling to Lovina from Karangasem, you arrive first at Penarukan Terminal then take a *bemo* into Singaraja or across town to Banyuasri Terminal, then another to Lovina.

Getting Around
Bemo constantly circulate between Terminal Banyuasri, Pasar Anyar, and Terminal Penarukan. The official "anywhere in the city" price is Rp500. *Bemo* from Banyuasri to Sangket are yellow, Sangket to Banyuasri red, Penarukan to Sangket blue, Penarukan to Banyuasri green or brown. *Bemo* are scarce after 1800. *Dokar* will also take you anywhere in town for Rp500-1000 (negotiate price before climbing in) emanating from Pasar Anyar, the night market.

Getting Away
Singaraja's Terminal Banyuasri is on Jl. Jen. A. Yani in the west side of town, serving such western destinations as Lovina (Rp500), Seririt (Rp1750), Gilimanuk (Rp2500), as well as Java.

To reach Labu⸢...⸣
gan) or Negara, ⸢...⸣
then take the m⸢...⸣
Minibuses leave B⸢...⸣
Pupuan, a mind-blo⸢...⸣

The quickest way t⸢...⸣
the bus station, Termi⸢...⸣
Sukasada) at the south ⸢...⸣
here minibuses for Denpa⸢...⸣ leave
about every 30 minutes f⸢...⸣ny morning to
around 1800; a two-hour trip. Denpasar-bound minibuses can even be found after 1800, but they'll charge Rp3500 instead of the usual Rp3000. Buses leave here also for Bedugul/Lake Bratan (Rp1500) and Gigit Waterfall (Rp1000).

The terminal Penarukan, tel. (0362) 61334, is on Jl. Supratman three km east of Singaraja, serving such eastern destinations as Amlapura and Kintamani. Penarukan Station offers a proper covered waiting area, and swarms with Isuzu vans and colts. Catch a ride to Tejakula, Rp1000; Sanih Beach, Rp1000; Amlapura, Rp3000; Padangbai, Rp4000; Kintamani, Rp3000 (infrequent after 1200, so get an early start); Klungkung via Penelokan, Rp3000; Batubulan, Rp3000.

By motorcycle or car, it takes about 2.5 to three hours to reach Amlapura. Direct buses travel to Surabaya (Rp20,000) from either Singaraja or Lovina; if you're in a hurry to get to Java, you can hop the first thing going to Gilimanuk, where you can connect with long-distance buses for destinations including Yogyakarta or Jakarta. Check out the long-distance night bus companies **Cakrawala,** Jl. Surapati 124, tel. (0362) 41791 or 21925, and **Puspasari,** tel. (0362) 41698. Ticket offices *(loket)* are found around the Taman Lila complex on Jl. Jen. A. Yani. **Lovena,** near Banyuasri Station, sells big *malam* tickets to Surabaya (Rp20,000) and Yogyakarta (Rp40,000). Also catch shuttle buses to Denpasar, Kintamani, Ubud, and Kuta (Rp12,500) which depart from **Perama Tourist Service,** tel. (0362) 21161, just before the bridge to Lovina.

SOUTH OF SINGARAJA

Beratan and Vicinity
Take a *bemo* from Banyuasri Station (Rp500) to the *kampung* of Beratan, where silver and gold-

...gly fashion temple accou-
...s, vases, brooches in the shape
...ckos, and seagulls (Rp9000-12,000),
... bracelets (Rp35,000), and rings at a
...ction of Celuk's cost. In the nearby village of
Jinang Dalem Balinese buy *ikat* and gold- and
silver-inlaid *songket* cloth used in ceremonial
dress (Rp150,000). **Nagasepaha** village, about
five km south of Singaraja, is known for unique
wayang kaca, used as coverings for offerings.

At **Panji**, 10 km south, the Bhuwana Kerta
Monument honors heroes of the Indonesian
struggle against the Dutch. In the 16th century,
Raja Panji Sakti, founder of the kingdom of Buleleng, was born in this village. Nearby is a cave
once home to *raksasa*. The *megoak goakas* is
unique to Panji region. These twisting mountain roads, overlooking steep banana canyon
plantations, will refresh you after the steaming
heat of the lowlands.

Gitgit
Eleven kilometers south of Singaraja, off the
dramatic road to Bedugul, is Bali's most spectacular waterfall, easily accessible at the end
of a 500 meter walk past numerous pushy textile
and souvenir sellers and peaceful rice fields.
Pull into the parking lot, cross the street, then
pay a small donation, Rp550. Enter a narrow
concrete path between a cement building on
the left and compound on the right. Open daily
0800-1730.

A fascinating walk for botanists, wind through
coffee trees, timber-sized bamboos, and a riot of
temperate zone "house plants"—King Kongs
compared to the dracena and philodendron of
the West. The path levels out among irrigated
rice fields and at the falls are a restaurant,
warung makan, souvenir shops, and toilets.
Cool off with a swim in the lagoonlike pool at
the foot of the powerful, mist-shrouded, free-
fall 45-meter falls. Even in the dry season the
water volume is stupendous. A beautiful little
pavilion with benches offers a great place to
rest. From here, take the rocky path down to
the river's edge.

You could do a lot worse than the **Giggit
Hotel & Restaurant** opposite the path to the
air terjun; clean rooms Rp25,000 s, Rp35,000 d,
deluxe rooms Rp45,000 s, Rp55,000 d. Tariff includes Indonesian, European, or continental

breakfast. Almost always empty. Take in the
sweeping panorama over the north coast and
the Bali Sea. Meals also available in **Mini
Restaurant** across the street.

DANAU TAMBLINGAN AND VICINITY

A trip to Danau Buyan and smaller Danau Tamblingan has the feel of a mini-archaeological ex-
pediton. Both are contained within one vast
caldera; a rugged area lying between 500 and
1,500 meters above sea level. Because of the
scarcity of public transport, the trip is best accomplished with a chartered vehicle or motorcycle.

There are two approaches. West of Singaraja, turn south at Seririt and follow the asphalt
road to Munduk, which then runs east along the
tranquil northern shores of Danau Tamblingan
and Danau Buyan. For an easier approach, head
south on the main highway out of Singaraja.
About eight km before Bedugul, bear right and
ride along a ridge for five km through the village

house shrine, Lake Tamblingan

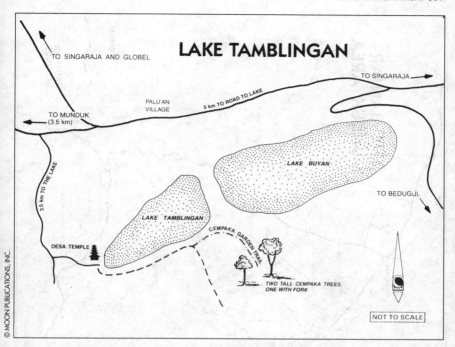

LAKE TAMBLINGAN

TO SINGARAJA AND GLOBEL

PALU'AN VILLAGE

5 km TO ROAD TO LAKE

TO SINGARAJA

TO MUNDUK (3.5 km)

3.5 km TO THE LAKE

LAKE BUYAN

TO BEDUGUL

LAKE TAMBLINGAN

CEMPAKA GARDEN TRAIL

DESA TEMPLE

TWO TALL CEMPAKA TREES, ONE WITH FORK

NOT TO SCALE

© MOON PUBLICATIONS, INC.

of Palu'an. Just before entering Munduk, turn left and bump along a dirt road for 3.5 km down to Lake Tamblingan. Ask for directions periodically, and pause to smell the fields of hydrangeas and coffee plants and hear the sounds of an almost primeval upland rainforest.

When you reach the lake, turn right just before the house and travel one kilometer on a road full of butterflies and morning glories. At the house ask for Komang, who can lead you. The road is drivable, but at the end you'll have to park and walk 500 meters down a wide trail to the archaeological site. Look for the old lichen-covered grindstones under a forked *cempaka* tree. The stones themselves are not such a big deal, but the trip there is an adventure, the serene lake is surrounded by beautiful peaks, and there are no ticket takers or tourists.

Munduk

At 800 meters above sea level, this hilly town in Bali's central mountains offers a delightfully fresh climate, lying amid the great natural beauty of coffee, cocao, clove, vanilla, and tobacco gardens. Munduk is the largest of a series of mountain villages that includes Gobleng, Gesing, and Umejero. To reach Munduk from isolated Danau Tamblingan, go back to the main road and take a left, then travel 3.5 km. On the way, you'll pass a waterfall 500 meters from the road. Munduk is approximately 30 km from Lovina.

Munduk is blessed with a number of safe, comfortable accommodations in a unique setting. **Puri Lumbung Cottage** ("Rice Storage Barn Palace") has five traditional raised cottages made completely of thatch, matting, and wood, nicely furnished, in immaculate condition. Located on the side of a mountain, the cottage affords magnificent views of rice terraces and *cengke* plantations. Each bungalow sleeps two and has its own water, electricity, and *mandi*.

One of the first environment-friendly and community development-oriented accommodations on the island, Puri Lumbung is part of a Balinese

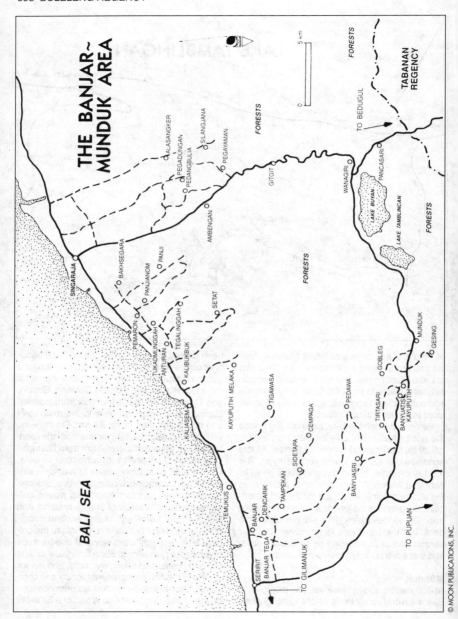

THE BANJAR~
MUNDUK AREA

5 km

FORESTS

TABANAN
REGENCY

TO BEDUGUL

FORESTS

FORESTS

ALASANGKER
PEGADUNGAN
PEDANGBULIA
SILANGJANA
PEGAYAMAN

GITGIT

WANAGIRI

LAKE BUYAN
PANCASARI
LAKE TAMBLINGAN

AMBENGAN

FORESTS

BAKHSEGARA
PANJANOM
PANJI

SINGARAJA

SETAT

MUNDUK
GESING

PEMARON
TUKADMUNGGAH
TEGALINGGAH
ANTURAN
KALIBUKBUK

GOBLEG

KALIASEM

KAYUPUTIH MELAKA
TIGAWASA

TIRTASARI
BANYUATIS
KAYUPUTIH

BALI SEA

CEMPAGA
PEDAWA

SIDETAPA
BANYUASRI

TEMUKUS
BANJAR
DENCARIK
TAMPEKAN

SERIRIT
BANJAR TEGA

TO PUPUAN

TO GILIMANUK

© MOON PUBLICATIONS, INC.

project to involve tourists in the everyday lives of Balinese natives. The hotel also serves as a training facility for students and locals in the tourism industry who are seeking to stop the migration of local youths attracted by jobs in the south of the island. The staff are incredibly hospitable.

In the hotel restaurant, **Warung Kopi,** partake of traditional home-cooked meals. Ask the kitchen to cook only Indonesian/Balinese food. The *ares ayam* (Balinese soup with boiled banana stem and chicken) for Rp2250 gets high marks, but the *cap cay* is too Westernized and rather bland. Intriguing Balinese desserts. After, relax with a cup of fresh-brewed coffee in a high pavilion with a beautiful view.

Too bad the private bungalows are so expensive. Peak season rates (15 Dec.-15 Jan.) are Rp80,000 s, Rp90,000 d; off-season rates Rp70,000 s, Rp80,000 d. Tariff includes government tax, service, and traditional Balinese breakfast. Guests who stay four nights receive a fifth night free. Transport to Munduk arranged once your reservations are placed with BPLP Nusa Dua, Box 2, Nusa Dua, tel. (0361) 437071 or 772078. The management of Puri Lumbung can also arrange for rooms in simple, less expensive, but attractive homestays in the area—Meme Surung, Mekel Ragi, and Guru Ratna.

This mountainous region is one of the few truly undiscovered regions of Bali. From Munduk walk 30 minutes to one of the highest waterfalls on Bali. Or try bicycle touring or horseback riding; hike to **Gunung Lesong** (four hours roundtrip) canoe or fish on Danau Tamblingan, learn to paint or handcraft bamboo *bungbung;* fly a kite; play *megangsing* (a village game using wooden tops); watch villagers process sugar palm and coconut oil; study white magic under a *balian;* cook in a village kitchen. No extravagant, tourist oriented dances; local events may include bloodless cockfights and cow races in rice paddies.

EASTERN BULELENG

Buleleng Timor is known for its rustic farming villages and elaborate temples in which every square inch is covered in curves, arabesques, spirals, flames, and floral ornamentation hewn from volcanic rock. The Balinese have a fondness for caricature, masterfully represented in the bas reliefs of Buleleng's temples. Scenes include corpulent Europeans, Dutch steamers under attack by sea monsters, and aircraft falling from the sky. Demon hands and heads emerge from the carving, as if three-dimensional figures were imprisoned in stone. All the main sights of east Buleleng lie fairly close to each other, are well served by public *bemo,* and make excellent day trips from either Singaraja or Lovina.

SANGSIT

Eight kilometers east of Singaraja (Rp500 by *bemo* from Penarukan station) lies Sangsit's main attraction, the brilliant **Pura Beji,** dedicated to the goddess of wet rice and fertility, Dewi Sri. Located about 500 meters down a cactus-lined side road to the sea; look for the small sign on the left side of the road. This extraordinarily lavish *subok* temple, one of the oldest in north Bali, was built in the 15th-century on the site of a well. Though a bit commercialized, it presents a perfect example of the northern rococo style of temple carving, with a strange off-angle symmetry.

Built of easily carved soft pink sandstone, the *pura* swarms with carved demons and stone vegetation. The temple's spellbinding gateway is composed of *naga*-snakes, imaginary beasts, devils, and *leyak* guardians overseeing tiny doors. In the temple's spacious inner courtyard you'll see gnarly old *kamboja* trees, wooden statues, and a throne of the sun-god.

Near Pura Beji, 400 meters to the northeast, is Sangsit's *pura dalem,* which contains relief panels illustrating the Balinese philosophy of *karma pala. Karma* means action or deed, *pala* result. On the panels you'll see the punishment awaiting a man who has committed adultery, and ghastly tortures meted out on childless women and other miscreants.

Accommodations and Food
The large and elaborate **Berdikari Cottages,** Sangsit, Buleleng 81171, tel. (0362) 25195,

rarely fills its rooms as few traveling the north coast choose to stay in such a remote location. Tariff including breakfast: Rp25,000 for economy rooms with foam mattress, shower, and dressing table; Rp50,000-70,000 for intermediate rooms including spring bed, shower, hot water, and cupboard; and Rp125,000 for luxury rooms containing air conditioning, spring bed, bathtub, shower, and hot water. No room phones, guests charged for local calls. Big parking area. The lush gardens are bird-filled and extensive, 2.3 hectares in all, with mango, bananas, oranges, pineapples, starfruit, and coconut. A restaurant with a skeletal staff; sometimes unable to come up with much on the menu.

Still, Berdikari has it's advantages. It's perfect for a meditating Buddhist or a reclusive novelist. Good security, clean, quiet, and lots of privacy. Staff celebrates guest birthdays and honeymoons. At the **Gunung Cekar Temple,** just 500 meters from the hotel, you can catch religious festivals and the rare, once-a-year Bukaka Ceremony. Berdikari's owner, I Made Pasek Sudarsana, will help you rent vehicles. Dive up to 22 meters on Rongke Reef in front of the hotel.

JAGARAGA

Heading east from Singaraja turn right (south) at the end of Sangsit village on the road to Sawan; Jagaraga is four kilometers and Sawan is two kilometers farther. From Singaraja's Penarukan station *bemo* go direct to Sawan so visit Sawan first then just walk down to Jagaraga. The villages on the steep inland slopes of Buleleng are of ancient origin. Inscriptions dating from the 10th century tell of pirate raids, earthquakes, and volcanic eruptions. Jagaraga was the stronghold of Gusti Ketut Jelantik and his army, who defied two large and well-armed expeditions in 1846 and 1848 before falling to a superior Dutch infantry and artillery force. This 16 August 1849 battle was known as Puputan Jagaraga; nearly the entire village was wiped out. Today Jagaraga is home to one of north Bali's best *legong* troupes.

Jagaraga's architecturally extravagant **pura dalem,** one km north of the village, is dedicated to Durga. It features carved comic-strip panels of cyclists, Balinese flying kites, dog fighting air-

planes, fishermen hooking a whale, a Dutch steamer, long-nosed Dutchmen in a Model-T Ford held up by a bandit with a horse pistol, and mammoth fish swallowing a canoe. Incredibly flamboyant statues of Rangda the witch, and the dazed mother, Pan Brayut, buried under a pile of children. The detail of the vintage cars is wonderful, with mudguards, lamps, carburetors, and doors all portrayed. Stone owls, roosters, bats, tigers, and crabs cling to the walls. Donation Rp1000.

A number of temples are found on this road, all featuring effusive, cunning, and mischievous carvings; ask the locals. A fantastic ride, with archaic villages surrounded by vegetation not found anywhere else on Bali. Reach by *bemo* (Rp750, 13 km) from Singaraja's Stasiun Penarukan.

SAWAN

Take a *bemo* (Rp1000) from Singaraja's Stasiun Penarukan to the turnoff, then from the main road grab another *bemo* (Rp500) or *ojek* (Rp500) via Menyali to reach this small village 16 km southeast of Singaraja. Sawan is the proud owner of a fine bamboo *gamelan angklung;* visit Sawan's *pasar malam* and the small hilltop temple surrounded by large trees.

Bronze gongs are made here; say "gong" to any local and you'll be taken down a lane where the gongsmiths *(pande gong)* cast instruments and carve frames and stands. At Sida Karya 10 workers under the supervision of I Made Widandra create *gender, ganggsa,* and *cengceng* daily from 0600 to 1600. Widandra provides a very complete explanation in rapid, intelligible English of the entire process. Check out the photos on the poster in the display room. The *slendro*-scale *klintik* (Rp60,000) here are of higher quality than those made in Tenganan. Please leave a donation if you don't buy anything. Widandra's cousin Gede is the other gongmaker of the village.

BUNGKULAN

Two km east of Sangsit and 12 km east of Singaraja (Rp500 by *bemo*) is Bungkulan, with

I Made Widandra at his craft

10,000 inhabitants and 13 *banjar* with three temples each. Though unaffected by tourism, there's always an event worth seeing, with 13 *odalan* and one or more annual celebrations per temple. Bungkulan's very old, worn **Pura Sari Pemerajan Agung** is perched on the highest hill overlooking the village. Inside are hand-carved statuary and a fine old *kulkul* with a carved human head on top. The temple's age is uncertain; there are records of a renovation in 1778.

The village is quite active, with a market held every day. Take an early morning swim in the river and watch children doing washing, men and boys taking the family cow to water, and women diving for sand which they carry up the bank in baskets on their heads.

Bungkulan is well positioned for day trips to Les Waterfall, Banjar, Lovina, Yeh Sanih, and Gitgit, as well as the temples of Sangsit, Jagaraga, and Kubutambahan. Or walk half an hour to the hot black-sand beach lined with fishing boats.

KUBUTAMBAHAN

Reach this important crossroads town by *bemo* (Rp1000) 12 km from Singaraja's Penarukan station. Find Kubutambahan where the north coast road intersects the road to the main highway south; from here it is 41 km to Kintamani, five km to Air Sanih, 84 km to Amlapura, 12 km to Singaraja, and 108 km to Denpasar. If coming

from Amalapuna, about 5.5 km before the town is **Air Sanih** with a number of hotels, several restaurants, and a dive site.

The unusual **Pura Meduwe Karang,** the "Temple of the Owner of the Land," is about one km beyond the Kintamani turnoff. This important district temple is dedicated to Ibu Pertiwi "Mother Earth," worshipped to ensure successful fertilization of crops grown on dry, unirrigated land such as coconuts, coffee, and corn. One of northern Bali's largest temples, its terraced entrance recalls some of Europe's stately baroque gardens. Steps lead past 34 stone figures from the Ramayana to a big, peaceful, nearly empty courtyard. More steps lead to an inner section containing a huge stone pyramidlike base flanked by two *bale* reserved for offerings.

The temple's carvings show ghouls, noblemen, home scenes, soft porn, and a riot of leaves and tendrils. One pedestal shows a horrifying rendition of Durga, another a large figure resembling Christ at the Last Supper. The centerpiece depicts a battle scene from the Ramayana. On the northern wall of the innermost shrine is a famous one-meter-high relief of a Dutch official riding a floral bicycle, a reproduction of a 1904 carving destroyed by an earthquake. The cyclist is W.O.J. Nieuwenkamp, a famous Dutch landscape and portrait artist who rode his bike around Bali in the early 1900s, painting as he went. During restoration the bicycle was born anew with lotus-flower spokes; even Nieuwenkamp's *sarung* and the bush in the background feature floral patterns. Between his feet and the wheels is a rat and small dog; Nieuwenkamp's initials and moustache, however, are gone. To view this wonderment, ask for the key, then leave your donation in the shop opposite.

Next to Pura Meduwe Karang is a small *warung* that sells possibly the best black rice pudding (Rp500) on Bali. Fantastic coffee, too.

On the corner of the road to Kintamani is **Pura Bale Agung;** 200 meters away is the *pura dalem.* In the early days it was common practice to paint temples; Kubutambahan's beautiful **Pura Maksan** has been painted in just the last few years.

YEH SANIH

To reach the quiet beach resort of Yeh Sanih catch a minibus (Rp1000, 17 km) from Singaraja's Penarukan station. This shady seaside spot offers an idyllic black-sand beach—a bit rocky, but the swimming is good. Enjoy wooden *bale* for sunning.

Yeh Sanih's main attraction is an enclosed natural swimming pool of clear, fresh, cool water welling up from an underground spring. Known by the locals as a recreation site since the early '30s, the water is believed to come from Lake Batur in the mountains—the temple near the pool is thus dedicated to Lord Vishnu. Cool sea breezes, tall trees, and the nice panorama over the Bali Strait make for a serene setting. Changing rooms. Entrance Rp500. Open 0700-1900.

On holidays this retreat could be stampeded by screeching schoolchildren, and it's also subject to groups of package tourists at any time. But on weekdays the place may be virtually empty. It's not a scene like Lovina; there are fewer sellers and hustlers. Many tourists pass through, but few stay.

Visit the *pura* on the hill, **Pura Taman Manik Mas.** In the mornings take a swim in the ocean—more like a lake than a sea. Not a soul on the beach to bother you. Quite passable snorkeling 500 meters out; another good snorkeling spot one km away. The nearest **Agen Pos & Telephone** is in Kubutambahan five km west. If you want nightlife go to Lovina, but remember the last *bemo* back to Yeh Sanih from Singaraja's Penarukan terminal leaves at around

1900. There's a small bus station, **Tempak Parkir Roda Empat Air Sanih,** with drink stands and toilet.

Accommodations and Food

Within Yeh Sanih's gorgeous pool complex is two-story **Puri Sanih Bungalows I** (tel. 0362-22490). The inflexible owner has recently upped the price to Rp30,000 for units with fans, mosquito nets, fresh flowers, and breakfast. What used to be quaint at Rp20,000 now looks run-down at Rp30,000. The rooms on the other side of the pool are in need of repair. The manager thinks the louder you yell, the better you manage; the employees do what they have to, but with no heart. Their restaurant serves up European and Indonesian food that is expensive and is barely edible. To the east, with the freshwater pool in between, is nicer **Puri Sanih Bungalows II,** tel. (0362) 22990, overlooking lily ponds and extensive gardens. Comfortable, spotlessly clean bungalows with sliding doors and private baths facing the ocean. Rates Rp20,000 s, Rp35,000 d in low season, Rp25,000 s, Rp40,200 d, in the high season. The row of rooms farthest away from the ocean are Rp20,000, Rp15,000 per day if you pay one month up front. Nice breakfast pavilion; eat lunch and dinner at one of the *warung.* No disturbances in this parklike setting, just the chirping birds.

Above the pool, up 33 steep steps, is pleasant **Puri Rena Bar & Restaurant.** Open 0700-2300, serving Indonesian, Chinese, and Balinese cuisine. You pay for the view, though—*gado gado* is Rp2500, while a vendor down the road charges Rp500. Puri Rena has four small budget rooms available for around Rp10,000 s (after bargaining). This hotel organizes excursions to local festivities, provides travel information, and is planning a center to give guests an inside look at Balinese culture. The **Tara Beach Inn,** about 500 meters east, charges Rp10,000 s, Rp15,000 d. Manager Putu Astawa can arrange for snorkeling, diving, fishing, and sailing excursions. He rents pushbikes, motorcycles, boats, canoes, and floats. Enjoy hot and cold drinks in the Tara Pub.

Those considering longer stays should know that when you sit down at any of the *warung* here people will approach to ask if you'd like to rent a room—could be anything from a bamboo fisherman's hut on the beach to a space in a private home above the village. Also lots of Rooms for Rent signs on the highway. Ask around; expect to pay about Rp150,000 per month.

Eat inexpensively at *warung* across the road from the pool. **Warung Seger** offers good *Bali asli nasi campur* (Rp1000), *nasi goreng* (Rp1500), and one of the best *sop ayam* (Rp1500) around. Try the *warung* next door for more *asli* food (*nasi campur,* Rp1500).

Vicinity of Yeh Sanih

Walk south up the mountain halfway to Kintamani. A good paved road along the northeast coast, sentineled by old, gnarled trees, leads to Amlapura. The road hangs over clifftops passing sandy coves sheltering fishing *jukung*—one of Bali's most picturesque journeys, with uninterrupted views of the island's highest peak. East of Yeh Sanih 1.5 km toward Amlapura is **Antara Bungalows & Refreshment;** Rp9000 for room and simple breakfast. Not in good condition; **Puri Sanih Bungalows** is better.

For elegant dining—real silverware, gracious service, table linen—head two km east of Yeh Sanih to the superlative **Apilan Restaurant** in Desa Bukti for wonderful French cuisine including homemade breads and cakes. Lunch is only Rp10,000 per person; a three-course romantic candlelight dinner is Rp15,000. Apilan rents a cottage for Rp25,000 per night s or d. If you're a guest, meals are available any time, otherwise the place is open Fri.-Sun. for lunch and dinner or by special request. No tax or service charge. The whole building is made of coconut palm by products—floor, roof, and walls. One km from Desa Bukti and three km east of Yeh Sanih is **Air Sanih Seaside Cottage;** Rp5000 s for any of four bungalows. Nice place, very quiet, close to the beach, a good-natured family takes care of you. Price doesn't include breakfast, but coffee and tea are available. Perfect if you want to be alone.

Seven km east of Yeh Sanih is the ancient temple Pura Pondok Batu ("Pile of Stones") perched on a small rock face and surrounded by hills, valleys, and twisted frangipani trees. It's said the wandering Javanese priest Nirantha sat on one of the temple's stones and composed poetry. Inside the temple is a well-crafted but eroded statue of Durga. Nearby on the beach at low tide is a freshwater springs frequented by locals, the water bubbling up from the sand and running into the sea.

SEMBIRAN

One of Bali's oldest traditional villages, Sembiran lies 30 km east of Singaraja. Like many of Bali's *asli* villages, Sembiran is located high in the hills off the main coastal road. From Terminal Penarukan take a *bemo* to Desa Pacung (Rp500), then catch a ride on a motorcycle the rest of the way (Rp1000). The winding four-km-long asphalt road to Sembiran is surfaced but extremely steep. This lovely country road, passes beautiful hills, valleys, and gnarly 20-meter-high *sonokeling* trees (rosewood). As you approach the village, there's a giant *kemit* tree, the base said to have been a place where corpses were laid out in ancient times. From the top, look down on the Java Sea.

With a population of 6,000 people, this is a Bali Aga village, where old traditions are not all forgotten. People speak with a distinct intonation and use a few Balinese words differently (for example, "rude" is considered "refined"). The caste system is not strictly observed. There are toothfiling ceremonies, but they are not as important or elaborate as in the south. Also, many of the typical Balinese time-marker ceremonies are not observed here. The Sembiranese have two Days of Silence (Nyepi) per year instead of the single day observed by the rest of the island. Marriage is by proposal, not elopement, nor are partners arranged by parents. There are 20 *pura* in Sembiran, 17 containing megalithic artifacts and carved stones.

Before 1951 Sembiran villagers wrapped their dead in cloth and laid them out on bamboo platforms exposed to the elements. If wild animals did not carry them away, the bodies were dumped onto the rocks. In 1951 they tried to burn their dead like the rest of the Balinese, but since the proper offerings were not carried out, inexplicable sicknesses occurred and many people died. The Sembiranese returned to laying out corpses until 1961, when they again began to burn their dead, this time observing the proper ceremonies. Nothing untowards has happened since.

This unique village of corrugated iron roofs gets about five or six tourists per week. From here you can take in the whole northern shore, as well as hundreds of hectares of terraced cornfields marching down the valley. Other crops grown include bananas, coffee, jackfruit, and papaya. In the *warung* near the market share tea and snacks with the friendly villagers, a number of whom speak Indonesian. No organized accommodations, but you can stay in homes. No telephones, but plenty of televisions. No curios shops.

To leave, take the road out the back way to Tajun on the main north-south road. This is a windy, rocky, only partially paved road through one of Bali's most undeveloped agricultural areas. Traverse rolling hills, profusions of foilage, hidden valleys, poor *desa*—about as wild as Bali gets.

TEJAKULA AND VICINITY

The fishing and farming village of Tejakula lies seven km east of Yeh Sanih, (Rp1500 by *bemo,* and 32 km east of the Terminal Penarukan in Singaraja. About 100 meters south of the main road, Tejakula's well-maintained bathing place is an elaborate fortlike structure, with water gushing into separate sections for *pria* and *wanita.* It was originally built to wash down horses and cattle—once the largest citrus growing area in Bali, Tejakula horses were used to pull carts filled with harvested oranges—but is now used solely for the human animal.

Tejakula boasts one of the finest *kulkul* towers on Bali. Typical of the style found in north Bali villages, it's brilliantly carved with Panji cycle legends and *wayang* characters. Also in the village is a unique *gamelan* called Gong Tejakula, a *kampung* of gold- and silversmiths called Banjar Pande.

The highest waterfall on Bali is in **Desa Les,** five km east of Tejakula (34 km east of Singaraja). There's no road to the falls, just a path through rice fields. Ask directions from the villagers in Desa Les; about a half-hour walk. Just one cascade, and the water can be quite frigid. One of the few unisex communal *mandi* on the island is found in Les. Also near Tejakula, at **Bondalem,** is a heat-conversion plant where surface seawater is evaporated into a vapor driving a turbine that generates 160 kilowatts of electricity. Nice view of the seacoast farther on at Culik.

SEMBIRENTENG

East of Tejakula in the village of Geratek, on Bali's northeastern coast, is a highly recommended dive facility, **Alam Anda** ("Your Nature"), perhaps the best dive/snorkel base on Bali. Dive on a dreamy reef, stretching along 135 meters of the coastline and lying 15-35 meters from your front door. Beyond is even deeper—a very sharp shelf. No waves, no undercurrent, the locale extremely safe for children and beginners.

Soft tourism at its best; the German owner, Uwe Siegriedsen, works to conserve the natural surroundings. Everything is built of natural materials—palm trunks, wood, bamboo. Uwe doesn't like to bargain and he doesn't like to do business with travel agents. The village regards hotel guests as *theirs;* travelers receive lots of invitations to homes and events and are generally integrated into the daily life of the village. Daily excursions offered to those who want to see the sights.

The nine bungalows of Alam Anda are family-style units, each accommodating up to five people. No air conditioning or hot water. Cost Rp60,000 d, Rp10,000 for each extra person. The veranda comes with a double bed which can be rigged with a mosquito net. Inside are bamboo furniture and double beds with nets. The Chinese/Indonesian food is very good—no Western food.

The dive shop offers the finest in equipment, very clean and well-maintained. Reasonable prices—perhaps the cheapest diving on Bali. Lunch, soft drinks, transportation, and guide are extra, government tax included. For dives to Amed and Menjangan a boat is included in the price. If you bring your own tanks, you receive a 10% discount. Most excursions require a minimum of two people. The Balinese dive master Kadek is outstanding and speaks good English. Since the entire area is under protection, the stock of fish has increased enormously in recent years and the condition of the coral is pristine.

For the Alam Anda reef, 15 meters to the front, Rp50,000 for one dive, Rp70,000 for two dives, Rp90,000 three. For the Tulamben wreck, (25 km distant), Rp65,000 one dive, Rp85,000 for two; for Ahmed, Rp70,000 for one dive, Rp90,000 for two. Menjangan Island, Rp85,000 for one dive, Rp110,000 for two (four people minimum). The CMAS Certificate—as good as PADI—involves seven dives, including Tulamben for Rp540,000.

Take the northern coastal road to Tejakula, then head east 15 km to Sembirenteng. After two more kilometers, you arrive in Geretek, home to Alam Anda. For reservations, contact Piketravel, c/o Nyumpene, Jl. Legian Tengah 436 N, Legian, tel./fax (0361) 752296. In Germany, the address is Piketravel, Ostersielzug 8, 25840 Friedrichstadt, fax 0049-4881-1200.

LOVINA BEACH

This area has a lot to offer, not the least of which is its distance from the southern honeypots. The beach is better than Candidasa's and the uphill areas inland are some of the prettiest on Bali. To get there, flag down a *bemo* (Rp500) from Singaraja anywhere on Jl. Jen. A. Yani, which turns into Jl. Seririt heading west out of town.

Actually, Lovina Beach was the first seaside resort to appear in the mid-'70s, taking its name from a restaurant that operated from 1953 to 1960 where Permata Cottages is today. Anak Agung Panji Tisna, the ruler of northern Bali, named this stretch of coast after the English word "love" in 1953. He is buried today not far from the first hotel he founded, Tasik Madu, "Sea of Honey." The few *losmen* that existed in the sleepy early 1970s were demolished in a 1976 earthquake.

The resort began anew and during the 1980s, new *losmen* and beach inns appeared. Lovina has since become the generic term for a whole line of six small villages and palm-fringed beaches that it has, touristically speaking, devoured. From east to west, these include: Pemaron, Tukadmungga, Anturan, Kalibuk strip, Kaliasem, and Temukus. The strip starts at about the six km mark west of Singaraja to about five km past Kaliasem. Kalibukbuk has the highest concentration while the fishing villages of Anturan and Temukus are less densely packed with restaurants and accommodations and thus are quieter.

Generally, the restaurants, stores, and services are on the inland side of the road, with accommodations to the north. Most are only a short walk from the beach or main road. Services include myriad moneychangers, convenience stores, used bookshops, bank, postal agent, Perumtel office, and vehicle rentals.

Though not as scenic as the southern coastline, Lovina attracts refugees fleeing the ripoffs, frenetic pace, and drunken Aussies of Kuta. It's about as far away (100 km) and as completely opposite Kuta and Sanur as you'll find—no flash menus, no surfies, few motorbikes, little music, few dogs, comparatively cheap. True, there is some prostitution, the north shore is not immune to thieves, and assertive, long-haired gigolos prey on female travelers.

Just a few years ago, you could easily live on about Rp12,000 a day. Today, the tourist economy makes accommodations and food less than the super-bargains they once were. Lovina keeps growing and changing, with prices rising and falling as demand changes.

In Lovina, enjoying beautiful sunsets involves simply walking out on your veranda. You can dive and swim safely in glass-clear water off the eight-kilometer-long unbroken black-sand beaches, find good trekking paths, temples, and hot sulphur pools in the hills, and use centrally located Lovina as a base for day trips to Tulamben Barat National Park, Pulau Menjangan, Yeh Sanih, and the lakes and volcanoes of the central mountain range. Bring anti-mosquito weapons (nets and repellent) as the beasties can get pretty bad in the rainy season.

If you time your visit for Independence Day (17 August) you can see Sapi Gerumbunjan (*kerbau* races) on a track near Kaliasem. The only other place this hair-raising event is held is in Negara in Jembrana District.

Vendor Overkill

Granted, the Lovina Beach strip is still not as overrun with tourists as the southern beaches. But, like Kuta, it's no longer Bali. In recent years, local entrepreneurs competing for tourist money have appeared en masse. Vendors will run from all directions the minute you alight from a *bemo* or park your car, asking if you'd like to rent a room, attend a buffet, see the dolphins, go snorkeling. Children beg, or ask to practice their Eng-

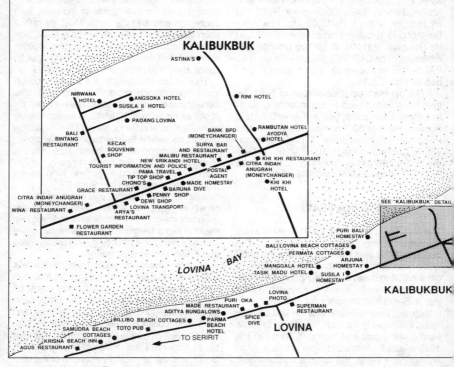

KALIBUKBUK

ASTINA'S •

NIRWANA HOTEL

• ANGSOKA HOTEL
• SUSILA II HOTEL
• PADANG LOVINA

• RINI HOTEL

BALI BINTANG RESTAURANT

KECAK SOUVENIR SHOP

BANK BPD (MONEYCHANGER)

SURYA BAR AND RESTAURANT

• RAMBUTAN HOTEL
AYODYA HOTEL

MALIBU RESTAURANT
NEW SRIKANDI HOTEL
TOURIST INFORMATION AND POLICE
PAMA TRAVEL
TIP TOP SHOP
CHONO'S

POSTAL AGENT

MADE HOMESTAY

KHI KHI RESTAURANT

CITRA INDAH ANUGRAH (MONEYCHANGER)

KHI KHI HOTEL

GRACE RESTAURANT

CITRA INDAH ANUGRAH (MONEYCHANGER)
WINA RESTAURANT

PENNY SHOP
DEWI SHOP
LOVINA TRANSPORT
ARYA'S RESTAURANT

BARUNA DIVE

■ FLOWER GARDEN RESTAURANT

SEE "KALIBUKBUK" DETAIL

PURI BALI HOMESTAY •

BALI LOVINA BEACH COTTAGES •
PERMATA COTTAGES •

LOVINA BAY

MANGGALA HOTEL •
TASIK MADU HOTEL •

ARJUNA HOMESTAY •

SUSILA I HOMESTAY •

KALIBUKBUK

MADE RESTAURANT
ADITYA BUNGALOWS

PURI OKA

LOVINA PHOTO

SUPERMAN RESTAURANT

BILLIBO BEACH COTTAGES •

SAMUDRA BEACH COTTAGES
KRISNA BEACH INN
AGUS RESTAURANT

TOTO PUB

PARMA BEACH HOTEL

SPICE DIVE

TO SERIRIT

LOVINA

lish. On the beach, pushy hawkers offer dance tickets, massages, fruit, *sarung,* cigarettes, coconuts, magic mushrooms. Lovina sellers are more familiar and more likely to joke than Kuta's all-business vendors, but they're just as persistent and will hassle you even when you're lying on the beach with your eyes closed.

What to do? Deal with a limited number of the pests. Buy a few *batik* from X, go snorkeling with Y, buy a pineapple from Z—someone else approaches you, say you already have your own supplies. Other vendors usually accept this and will leave you alone.

Women need to be especially wary of Lovina's underhanded beach boys. There are dreadful tales of the scams used to part Western women from massive amounts of money. Women—or anyone for that matter—who wish to totally avoid vendors and beach boys should hang out at the

lovely pools at Angsoka Cottages. Here, sellers are not allowed on the grounds.

Entertainment

Kuta-like nightlife spots on the north coast include the **Malibu Bar, Restaurant & Disco** in Kalibukbuk next to the New Srikandi, a meeting place for singles and travelers. Eat dinner while watching a big-screen movie (starts at 1910), followed by live singers or Balinese reggae music—the same tunes night after night. The disco serves every kind of drink imaginable, and the menu consists of Western tourist dishes. Malibu will pick you up if you call (tel. 0362-41671); stays open til the wee hours. The other "downtown" nightclub, the open-air **Wina Restaurant** on the northwest corner of Jl. Seririt and the road to Nirwana, also features big screen movies, bar, pool table, and live music until midnight, but has

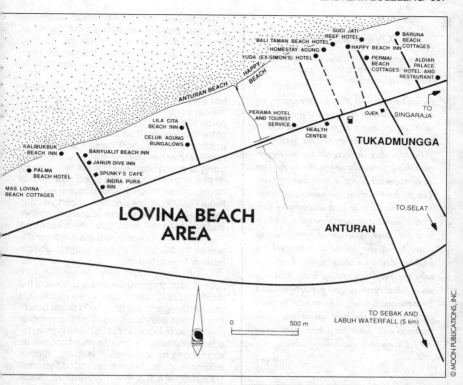

Map labels: SUCI JATI REEF HOTEL, BARUNA BEACH COTTAGES, BALI TAMAN BEACH HOTEL, HOMESTAY AGUNG, HAPPY BEACH INN, PERMAI BEACH COTTAGES, ALDIAN PALACE HOTEL AND RESTAURANT, YUDA (EX-SIMON'S) HOTEL, HAPPY BEACH, ANTURAN BEACH, PERAMA HOTEL AND TOURIST SERVICE, LILA CITA BEACH INN, CELUK AGUNG BUNGALOWS, HEALTH CENTER, OJEK, TO SINGARAJA, TUKADMUNGGA, KALIBUKBUK BEACH INN, BANYUALIT BEACH INN, JANUR DIVE INN, PALMA BEACH HOTEL, SPUNKY'S CAFE, INDRA PURA INN, MAS LOVINA BEACH COTTAGES, **LOVINA BEACH AREA**, **ANTURAN**, TO SELAT, TO SEBAK AND LABUH WATERFALL (5 km), 0 500 m, © MOON PUBLICATIONS, INC.

really expensive, lousy Chinese-style food. **Made's Warung** is a favorite gathering spot with an interesting but slightly expensive menu. **Toto Pub** in Lovina, run by Jro Sriasih, is another popular hangout so close to the water it's in danger of being swallowed by the sea.

Recreation
Laze on the beach and watch the sky turn red, yellow, and orange as the sun sinks behind the towering volcanoes of Java, which appear on the horizon rising purple from the ocean. At night fishing fleets head out in their *jukung*, luring fish into nets with kerosene pressure lanterns swaying and glowing yellow all along the water front. For Rp5000 you can join them for a two- or three-hour late afternoon trip. Or hire a freelancer and go out on a sailing excursion, with sailor, for Rp15,000.

The bay is great for swimming: Lovina's warm sea laps lazily at the gray-sand shore during the dry season, quite tame compared to the volatile southern coasts. Although a little dirty, the wide expanses of sand are good for sunning (especially at Kalibukbuk), and beach masseurs are available for Rp5000.

For a reef so close to the beach, the snorkeling, diving, and boat fishing are above average. The docile sea and the shallow lagoon make this coast ideal for beginners and young divers to safely explore the specialized marine communities of plant and animals which live in the intertidal zone. The Palmas Hotel has a nice pool where nonguests may swim for Rp5000.

You don't need to venture far for good snorkeling, but the best spots are two to three km from shore where the sea is shallow. The best dive sites lie closer to Singaraja, where the reef

THE LOVINA DOLPHIN TRIP

One reader took his family on the trip, after a high recommendation from a tourist from Chicago. He writes:

For our Rp30,000, they put the four of us on one boat and took us out a couple of miles before dawn to the grounds where these poor creatures try to have breakfast. Wherever they surface, all the outriggers rush them, for all the world like the hustlers at Kintamani when a tour bus arrives. The porpoises, of course, sound and eventually surface a mile or so away where they have a moment or two (depending on how well they have outwitted the boatmen) of peace before the flotilla of outriggers are beating down on them again. I wonder why the porpoises put up with it, and I imagine they soon will depart just as I trust the tourists will. The one saving grace of the trip was the gorgeous sunrise as we motored out. That must have been what the Chicago lady was talking about.

—SAM POST

juts farther out from the beach. Rent a motorless outrigger (Rp5000 low season, Rp8000 high season) to take you out; you can see fascinating reef life right from the boat just by sticking your head underwater.

When snorkeling you'll feel as if you're swimming inside an aquarium with moray eels, tropical fish, and pastel corals. As the offshore water is over your head, use the boat as your island. Wear sneakers, and watch out for the sharp coral, sea urchins, and catfishlike fish with poisonous spines. Get used to wearing your mask in shallow water before venturing out deeper waters. Start early before the water gets cloudy: the sand is so dark it can be difficult to see the bottom. In Feburary or March no snorkeling or dolphin trips are offered due to heavy rain and dirty water.

The skippers wait on the beach for customers; they may provide snorkeling gear. Count on Rp15,000 for a two-hour snorkeling trip. You can rent *prahu* from the hotels, or simply swim out to the reef. Snorkeling gear rents for Rp5000 for two or three hours.

An experience with mixed reviews is "Breakfast with the Dolphins." It's easy to buy a ticket the day before from boys on the beach; the average price is Rp10,000 per person, the length of the tour varying from 2.5 to three hours, depending on season, boat, captain, and luck. Determine in advance how many hours you're going to spend snorkeling versus hours spent dolphin-chasing. If you don't, you may end up having to bargain on the boat, paying an additional Rp5000 to see dolphins. When you buy your ticket, give the vendor your room number and someone will wake you with a knock on your door 15 minutes before the predawn departure for the 30- to 60-minute trip to dolphin territory (one to two km).

Dolphin-watching is very competitive, with dozens of boats going out at dawn. Most of the motorized boats can fit four to six people; big wooden outriggers can carry up to seven people and are less likely to pitch and roll than smaller craft. If you're lucky (about 75% of the time) for a few miraculous moments your boat will be surrounded by hundreds of leaping, flipping, blowing dolphins. Sometimes you find yourself in the midst of 500 or even 1000 dolphins. Watch for different species, particularly the large, slow swimmers that can weigh up to a ton. In any event you'll get a boat ride, tea and *pisang goreng* breakfast, and snorkeling on the return trip. Don't let the boatman go in before the agreed upon time.

A good place to obtain diving information and arrange trips is **Spice Dive** (tel./fax 0362-23305) which has an office in Arya's restaurant in Kalibukbuk. Staff is conscientious, honest, experienced, and properly qualified. See the photo albums of various dive locations (Lovina reef, Tulamben, Menjangan). Scuba (PADI) certification courses, at all levels, are also offered. **Baruna** (tel. 0362-23775), on the main road in Kalibukbuk, rents snorkeling gear by the hour (Rp1500), offers surf canoes (Rp2500), and sponsors cruises to see dolphins (Rp8000 per person), snorkeling trips (Rp5000 per person), and Sunset Cruises (Rp4000 per person), but no courses. Make reservations at your hotel. **Perama Tourist Service,** tel. (0362) 21161, in Anturan, also organizes marine excursions.

Permai Dive Sports, tel. (0362) 23471, Permai Hotel, Tukadmungga, offers a dive trip to Pulau Menjangan to the west, one of the best dive and snorkeling spots in Indonesia. In the off-season Permai may offer a dive to Menjangan for Rp125,000 per person plus one night's free accommodation. The beginner's course includes two dives, all equipment, guide, transport, food, and drink, for Rp160,000. Also check out **Barrakuda** (tel. 0362-22385) in the Bali Lovina Beach Cottages for CMAS courses.

Made Utama Jaya of **Khi Khi's,** tel. (0362) 21548, offers high-priced, quality half-day snorkeling and dolphin-viewing tours (includes transport, equipment, breakfast, lunch) for Rp30,000 per person. Using big *jukung* with outboard motors and sails, he sets out at 0530 from Banjar. Usually around 0900 you sight pods of dolphin, and by noon Pak Made is cooking the day's catch on the beach. After a native-style nap under a tree, caressed by sea breezes, you return to Lovina at 1300. The Cadillac of dolphin-watching outings. Khi Khi's also offers deep sea fishing tours (Rp40,000) and tuna fishing tours (Rp100,000).

Shopping and Services

Women, with stacks of *sarung* and blankets on their heads, sell their wares cheaper than in Lovina's shops, but you have to work on them. The **Air Brush T-Shirt Shop** sells some really unique garments and some funny postcards. Beach people offer magic mushrooms (Rp5000) but you hear of a lot of bad trips.

A little east of Arya's, across the road, is the **Tip Top Shop,** selling bus and shuttle bus tickets at good prices, snack foods, drinks, sundries, English newspapers, guidebooks, maps, medicine, waterproof cameras, cheap water, and clothes. Best prices in Lovina; it also has a telephone and a postal service (stamps, postcards). Open until 2300. Another useful retailer is the **Penny Shop,** opposite the street to Angsoka cottages. Extensive used book library, Fujichrome at Rp11,000 per roll, and one-day film processing. Also a cheap laundry service including ironing. A concentration of used book-

> *I thought the snorkeling at Menjangan Island was every bit as good as Australia's Great Barrier Reef. It only lacked the giant, sparkly clams, but it didn't have the tiny stinging jellyfish. A good enough trade-off!"*
>
> —JORGEN YOST

stores is along J1. Ketapang in Kalibukbuk. The best and cheapest supermarket is **Tiara Dewata,** Jl. Jen. A. Yani 192 A, Singaraja, tel. (0362) 23492. One km from the center of Singaraja and five km from Kalibukbuk (if heading into Singaraja). Extremely well-stocked groceries and dry goods. Open 0900-2200.

There's a very helpful **tourist office** on the beach side of the main Singaraja-Seririt road in Kalibukbuk; open Mon.-Thurs. 0700-1730, Friday 0700-1300, Saturday 0700-1730. A **clinic** lies south of the Lovina Beach Hotel in Kaliasem. The tourist office can recomment doctors. The police share the same builidng as the tourist office. Make international credit card **telephone calls** from the front desk of the big ritzy Palmas Hotel. Lovina has its share of **moneychangers,** several right on the main road. There's fax service and postal agents where you can send letters and parcels for the same prices charged by the post office. The **postal agent** (tel. 0362-41392) on the main drag is open 0800-1800. The only poste restante office is at the Perama office in Anturan (c/o Kantor Pos, Perama, Anturan, Lovina 81151, Singaraja, Bali. The **Wartel** (daily 0900-2300) is west of J1. Bina Ria in Kalibukbuk. The moneychanger at the Wartel is open 0800-1700; The moneychangers here offer rates about 10-15 rupiah lower than Denpasar's or Kuta's. The Perumtel office (tel. 0362-41101) on the beach side of the road in Temukus is open 0900-2300. Lovina's telephone code is 0362.

Accommodations

From the road, it appears Lovina hasn't changed much over the years. A great number of new accommodations, however, have crept in on lanes out of sight of the roadside hotels. In the low season, expect to pay Rp15,000 d for basic beachfront accommodations and around Rp80,000 for four-star luxury. You'll also be offered rooms for Rp6000-9000 including breakfast, but these will be rather old digs without a nice view of the sea or garden, usually facing the wall of the next bungalow.

There are two types of resort accommodations: the upstart, splash "beach inns" or resort hotels, which have sprouted up along the eastern beaches, and the venerable resorts of Kalibukbuk and Kaliasem that've been around for a while. Well-established, older places like the Rambutan and the Banyualit are more picturesque, offer more shade, and have more character than the newer hotels. Since these hotels are small, with but 10-15 rooms, they're able to provide friendly, personal service. A basic breakfast of toast, butter, jam, fruit salad, and coffee or tea is almost always included in the room rate.

The small street leading to the Banyualit is lined with seafood restaurants, garment and convenience shops, and different classes of hotels. It's less congested than most of Lovina, yet all you really need can be found on this street. If you stay in a hotel too near the main highway, mornings and at nights could be noisy. Closer to the beach is quieter; some units of the Kalibukbuk Beach Inn nearly touch the water. Mid-range accommodations—upscale but not four-star international—offer the most value for the dollar. For Rp45,000-90,000, they offer relative security, beautiful bungalows, nice gardens, full services (laundry, postal, safe-deposit boxes, free storage), phones and faxes, rooms cleaned daily, attractive restaurants with decent sound systems, free breakfast, stone and tile pools, cheap marine tours and snorkel gear rental—they even take plastic.

Reservations for the most popular accommodations are critical during the high season (July and August) and over the Christmas holidays, when rates rise Rp5000-10,000. Ask for a discount in the off-season, or if you're staying more than three days.

Food

In Lovina most social events involve food—which leans heavily to the mediocre side—and many accommodations woo the traveler with on-site, low-price restaurants, snack bars, cafes, or pubs. It's easy to find restaurants serving whole grilled tuna steak for around Rp4000. Magic mushrooms are served everywhere. Lovina's least expensive eateries are the beachside *warung* where the menu is limited but you can enjoy *lontong* with *sate* for Rp1000, fruit juices for Rp600, omelettes for Rp750-1000, soda for Rp700, and pancakes for Rp750-1000. In the high season you'll want to start out for dinner early, as the best restaurants are swamped and orders can take a while.

Competing restaurants try to outdo each other with huge buffets. Tables groan with curries, grilled meats, salads, noodle dishes, fruit. After dinner most eateries sweeten the deal with rather amateurish *regog* or *legong*. These buffets can be good deals, but pay attention to the menus—soy sauce and *krupuk* do not constitute an entree. Both the food and the performance cost Rp5000-9000, which must be one of the all-time bargains of Asia. The open-air **Rambutan Restaurant** in Kalibukbuk presents a *legong* and Balinese Banquet at 1930 every Sunday and Wednesday night featuring professional dancers performing traditional dances for only Rp6000. Also look for fliers advertising all-you-can-eats at the Puri Garden in Temukus and the Semina in Kalibukbuk. For more details on the eating scene, see the "Food" sections under the name of the villages below.

Getting There

On arriving from Kuta, the shuttle bus lets passengers off at Perama Tourist Service in Anturan, where passengers are taken to their hotels free of charge. The Perama shuttle leaves Kuta for Lovina at 0830 and 1600) (Rp13,500, 4.5 hours via Ubud). Public *bemo* from Denpasar's Ubung Terminal arrive at the Banyuasri station; from there hop on a *bemo* (Rp500) to Lovina. Tell the driver where you're staying and he'll drop you off as close as possible to it. If coming from Amlapura, the Isuzu bus arrives at Terminal Penarukan to the east of Singaraja; from there get a *bemo* through Singaraja (Rp500) to Banyuasri Station on the western edge of the city. From dawn to dusk *bemo* travel regularly from this station to Lovina (Rp800) on a road lined with huge trees and emerald-green rice paddies. If coming from Surabaya on a long-distance bus, ask the driver to let you off along the highway at either Lovina or Kalibubuk.

Shuttles and Rentals

Shuttles run to Ubud, Denpasar's Ubung Station, Sanur, Kuta, or the airport for Rp12,000-15,000. Shuttles leave for Kuta at 0700 and 1300 (2.5 hours). For four or five passengers, drivers offer service direct to Candidasa or Padangbai via the east coast for Rp20,000 per person. Or catch the shuttle to Kuta where you transfer to another shuttle heading for Candidasa for another Rp20,000 per person. Kuta is the transit point for shuttles to Senggigi or Mataram, Rp30,000 per person. Most hotels and homestays can arrange tickets and provide pickup service. Ask about Perama's "Stopover Service" offering southbound travelers up to two nights in scenic Bedugul at no charge. For guests, most Lovina hotels organize minibus tours of culture-rich Gianyar Regency; some rent cars. Jeeps rent for Rp35,000-40,000 per day, not including insurance; car rental is Rp60,000-190,000 per day. Motorcycles cost Rp12,000-15,000 for 12 hours, though good machines are hard to find. Scooters with automatic clutch cost around Rp10,000 per day, bicycles about Rp5000 for 12 hours, and mountain bikes Rp10,000 and up for 12 hours. Rent from virtually any homestay, hotel, or travel/tour agency.

Getting Away

Buses to Singaraja (Rp800) stop in front of Arya's. To Gilimanuk or Bedugul take a *bemo;* there's no shuttle service. If you're heading to western Bali or East Java, you don't have to go into Singaraja to catch a bus—buy tickets at Arya's or wherever buses to Surabaya stop to pick up passengers. Three travel services can be found in Anturan on the Singaraja side of the bridge. **Perama,** tel. (0362) 21161, sells direct bus tickets to Jakarta for Rp48,000. A dangerous ride of pure hell broken only by three meal stops. The bus leaves at 0630, arriving 28 hours later at 1000. The air conditioning usually doesn't work. Fares to: Probolinggo or Surabaya, Rp20,000; Yogyakarta, Rp38,000. Night buses leave for Java at 1900; you get into Probolinggo around 0300 and Surabaya about an hour later. Order air tickets from Perama,

too, brought back within 48 hours by shuttle from Denpasar. To reach Mt. Bromo in East Java take the public van-bus to Gilimanuk (Rp1750), a great scenic ride, then pay Rp300 for a *bemo* to the ferry, and Rp600 for the ferry to Java. From Ketapang it's only Rp3000 to to the Bromo turnoff, then Rp2500 to Cemoro Lawang on the outer crater rim.

PEMARON

Heading west from Singaraja, at about the 6.5 km mark, the first village you reach is Pemaron. This is a quiet section of coast with no shops or amenities but you can walk one kilometer down the beach to Anturan. Kalibukbuk is about two kilometers away by road. For sheer comfort, rest, and relaxation, the **Baruna Beach Cottages,** Box 149, Lovina Beach, Pemaron, tel. (0362) 23745 or 23746, fax 22252, set amidst landscaped gardens, can't be beat. Rooms in a two-story building or bungalows with Western toilets run from Rp40,000 to Rp110,000. Add 15.5% government tax and service. Try to make a reservation at least two weeks in advance. No phones or room service; wake-up calls come with a knock on the door—a nice touch, strictly person to person. Try to make a reservation at least two weeks in advance. Bats in the room, no extra charge. Ask to sleep in Mick Jagger's room. Few peddlers; American, Indonesian, or continental breakfast, lunch, or dinner Rp8800-23,000

To reach Baruna, take a *bemo* (Rp500) from Singaraja. A self-contained resort right on the beach, Baruna offers parking, a pool very near the beach, bar, boutique, cultural shows, sauna and massage services, sailing, windsurfing (Rp12,000/hour), diving, snorkeling (Rp3000), sunrise dolphin trips (Rp7000 per person), motorbike rental (Rp10,000 per day), and bicycle rental. Negotiate your return trip to Sanur for Rp55,000 plus driver's lunch and many stops.

TUKADMUNGGA

Accommodations offered in Tukadmungga are resortish, quiet, and attract fewer hawkers than the more congested beaches farther west. Though rooms may be spare, they're set back from the road and often surrounded by rice paddies. Upon entering Tukadmungga, the village just west of Pemaron about eight km west of Singaraja, head toward the sea and you'll come to **Permai Beach Cottages** on Happy Beach, tel. (0362) 23471, catering to water sport and dolphin enthusiasts. Rooms are Rp15,000 s, Rp35,000 d with air conditioning, fan, hot water, good ventilation, and shower. Also rooms for Rp50,000, breakfast included. The dive service to Lovina, Pulau Menjangan, Tulamben may include one night's free accommodation. Friendly people.

There are three restaurants and four accommodations at the end of the road to Happy Beach. From here, Lovina is four km. **Happy Beach Inn** is reasonably priced at Rp8000 s, Rp10,000 d for rooms with fans; cheaper rooms are Rp5000. Open-air *mandi.* The two bamboo rooms in the back of Happy's are the best, only Rp10,000. Ibu Ayu is a great cook; try her fish wrapped in banana leaves. She also serves black rice pudding with ginger and offers a big suckling pig and *nasi campur* with calamari (Rp2000)—real cheap, native cooking. This small cluster of accommodations makes a good base for snorkeling tours, and there's an amazing reef just off shore. Close by is the **Jati Reef Bungalows**, tel. (0362) 21952, with large four-room cottages among the rice paddies on the beach, smaller rooms in a two-story building, and a basic restaurant. Room prices are average, around Rp15,000. Facilities include private baths, safety deposit boxes, fans, laundry service, bar, motorbikes and bicycles for rent, and airport transfers. The owner of Suci Jati also owns **Yuda,** Box 151, tel. (0362) 41183, to the west. For Rp33,000-44,000, Yuda's rents 12 small, clean, raised cottages with thick mattresses, no hot water, no breakfast, hole-in-the-floor toilet, bamboo walls, and tiled roofs. Rooms are grouped around a restaurant pavilion with the waves only five meters away. Pay extra for private *mandi.* To the rear of Yuda's palm-filled compound is a view over *kerbau* working rice fields. Although the staff is friendly and the service good, beware of bugs, noisy children, loud TV, and conditions of general disrepair.

Farther west and close to the highway is the **Bali Taman Beach Hotel,** offering double rooms with air-conditioning, ceiling fan, bath in private garden, shower, TV, fridge, pool, and a Rp110,000-135,000 price tag. Nice restaurant overlooking the sea; good food; little shade.

Between Jati Reef and Yuda, down a narrow lane through rice fields, is basic 14-room **Sri Homestay.** Reservations are advised in July and August. Rates Rp13,000 for standard rooms, Rp20,000 for bungalows; breakfast included. No taxes or additional charges, though in August the rates may rise. Sri offers tours and vehicle, motorbike, or bicycle rental.

A very useful service is offered by **Perama Tourist Service** and **Agen Pos,** tel. (0362) 21161. The manager, Made Suartana, sells bus tickets and stamps. Toward Singaraja is a **health center.**

ANTURAN

In Anturan is **Homestay Agung,** a popular place for tired and hungry travelers. With bamboo-decorated rooms for only Rp8000 s, Rp15,000 d, Agung's is nearly always booked. Ask for the old mute Indonesian masseuse who gives unforgettable 45-minute massages for Rp5000. Walk down the beach at night for dinner.

Right on the water is **Lila Cita Beach Inn,** with plain second-floor rooms for Rp15,000 s, Rp20,000 d. Rooms with private outdoor *mandi* and flush toilets run Rp20,000 s, Rp25,000 d. Breakfast consists of any kind of pancake, toast, and fruit salad. Helpful staff, friendly atmosphere, quiet, superb snorkeling, and always the sound of the sea. In the evenings dine in the wide, second-story balcony which serves as the hotel lounge. In this area are several other homestays with basic bungalows but excellent locations: check out **Gede's** and **Mari's.**

On the same road as the Lila Cita and the Mandhara is peaceful, good value **Celuk Agung,** Box 191, Singaraja 81101, tel. (0362) 23039, fax 23379. Here are 16 comfortable Bali-style bungalows in three different classes, most with private bath, shower, hot water, IDD, satellite TV, and fridges. Prices range from Rp45,000 s, Rp57,000 d for standard (no air-conditioning), to Rp80,000 s, Rp90,000 d for medium and Rp110,000 s, Rp120,000 d for the five suites. Add 15% tax and service. Most of the hotel's grounds are devoted to gardens. Facilities include bar, reasonably priced restaurant, pool, tennis and badminton courts, laundry, safe-deposit boxes, and transport service. Nice views of rice fields and the sea.

BANYUALIT

If heading toward Singaraja, after the RRI Tower and Siwa Bungalows turn left on the small road leading to the beach. At the beach end of the road, on the right, is well-known **Janur's Dive Inn,** tel. (0362) 41056, offering nice double rooms for Rp8000 s, Rp10,000 d. Extravagant bathrooms, cheap good restaurant—pretty good value. The quiet **Banyualit Beach Inn,** Box 116, Singaraja 81101, tel. (0362) 41789, fax 41563, just up from Janur Dive Inn gets high marks for its concrete and traditional bunga-lows with clean and tidy rooms, *mandi* with plants, Western toilets, and bedside phones. One of the great bargains of Bali, room rates are Rp15,000 s, Rp55,000 d in three different classes, air-conditioned cottages also available. Extra bed: Rp15,000. Nice surroundings for strolling; an immaculate 1.24 hectare garden is filled with orchids and bougainvillea. Also a top-rated restaurant dispensing excellent food and chilled glasses of Bintang. Good security, ac-commodating staff; the receptionists are very efficient in organizing tours, transport, snorkeling, scuba, fishing, sailing, and dolphin watching. The beach is only a few meters away. All rates include service charge and government tax. Re-cently introduced is a cooking class, "Learn the Secrets of Balinese Cooking."

Down the same lane on the right toward the Banyualit is the family-oriented **Rambutan Beach Cottages,** Box 195, Kalibukbuk, tel. (0362) 23388, run by an English husband and Balinese wife team. Rates are Rp25,000 for budget rooms, Rp35,000 for rooms with ceiling fan, Rp40,000 for upstairs rooms with ceiling fan, and Rp50,000 for hot-water upstairs rooms with ceiling fan. Breakfast not included. Well-furnished upstairs rooms are spacious (five me-ters by five meters), cool, and soundproof, with veranda, balcony, decent lightbulbs, and electric mosquito coils. All rooms feature private bath with towels, soap, and toilet paper. English lan-guage newspapers delivered daily, many table and board games, children's playground. Big

restaurant (open 0700-2000) and chlorinated free-form freshwater pool. Near all the main restaurants and the beach and surrounded by a very large tropical garden of rambutan, coconut, and banana trees, this is an excellent place to stay. Try the **Sanary** Chinese and seafood restaurant across from the Rambutan. The swankiest hotel in this area is the **Padula Beach,** tel. (0362) 23775, fax 23659, with all the amenities you'd expect in this price range (Rp110,000-215,000)

KALIBUKBUK

Accommodations

The highest density of hotels and restaurants is found down Kalibukbuk's two roads to the sea, J1. Bina Ric and the smaller J1. Ketapang (starts opposite Khi-Khi Restaurant). The beach is widest along this strip. Look around before deciding on a place. The places close to the road are cheap but noisy. One of the cheapest (Rp8000 s, Rp10,000 d with breakfast) is the **Indra Pura Inn,** tel. (0362) 61560, near the Banyualit Beach Inn on J1. Ketapang. Another very reasonable *losmen,* down a small lane just before the Nirvana, is **Susila**—only Rp6000 s, Rp8000 d including breakfast. On the main road right in the main thicket of Lovina, only five min-utes to the beach, is the remarkable **Chono's,** tel. (0362) 23569, which rents clean, spacious rooms with good beds, large baths for Rp15,000-20,000. Fan rooms with shower and private toilet, Rp25,000 if towels provided. Sim-ple breakfast included in price. Transport, car rental, sightseeing and snorkeling tours, and laundry and baggage storage service. See the helpful manager, Mrs. Peni Darmadi, the one with the big smile. Located just five minutes from beach. Can be a bit noisy because it's next door to Malibu Bar & Restaurant. Nice restaurant upstairs with buffets and dances.

Just south of Angsoka Cottages is popular **Padang Lovina Seaside Cottages** (tel. 0362-23302) on JI. Binaria, only two minutes walk from the beach. Thirteen clean double rooms for Rp20,000 s, Rp30,000 d, all with tile floors, private baths, showers, ceiling fans, mosquito netting, and breakfast. Second-story rooms are cooler and breezier. One air-conditioned suite room for Rp25,000 s, Rp35,000 d. Large parking area and beautiful gardens. Also recommended is secure, quiet, well-kept **Rini Hotel & Restaurant,** tel. (0362) 23386, in the center of Kalibukbuk. Rates Rp20,000-25,000 for economy rooms, Rp30,000 for standard, Rp50,000 for superior (add five percent tax). Room number two in the highest demand. Bungalows are fully equipped with big beds, fan, mosquito net, shower, and veranda. Friendly service, good food, large garden. Located one minute from the beach, three minutes from the main road.

Spiffy and relaxing **Angsoka Cottages,** (tel. 0362-22841, fax 23023), but two minutes from the beach, offers a variety of rooms, ranging from cozy rice-barn units from Rp15,000 d to detached bungalows with a/c, inside *mandi,* hot water, and nice veranda for Rp60,000. Restaurant and bar, discreet and helpful staff, laundry service, IDD telephones, pleasant gardens, ample parking. Centrally located in the heart of Kalibukbuk. Appeals to the younger set; guests seem to particularly enjoy the attractive pool (open 0730-2000) with sunken bar surrounded by bamboo and *angsoka* flowers. The front desk books for shuttle service, marine excursions, and dolphin watching tours. Luxury accommodations at a budget price. Next to Angsoka's, just around the corner from the bus stop, is **Ray Beach Inn;** Rp10,000 for a double with clean *mandi.* Though meager breakast and leaky showers, it is a good value.

An established, friendly place 300 meters from the water is **Ayodya Accommodations** (tel. 0362-23803), within its own enclosed, restful, flower-filled compound. Rp8000 s, Rp10,000 d for traditional, clean *nipa* and bamboo huts. Rate includes breakfast. Each room is cool and spacious with a private reading-cum-dining area. Efficient food service, ample laundry facilities, good security. About 500 meters north of Ayodya is **Astina's,** Box 42, Singaraja 81151. Although the rooms tend to be a bit dark, the charge is only Rp7000 s, Rp8000 d for rooms with outside *mandi,* Rp12,000 s, Rp15,000 d for larger Bali-style bungalows with inside *mandi,* sink, shower, carved furniture, fan, and breakfast. Rates even cheaper in the off-season. Quiet, peaceful location with lush gardens under coconut palms—away from everything but only a short walk to anything.

Expect little English at the **Kalibukbuk Hotel.** Right on the beach, very clean and lovely; Rp12,500 d with private bath and breakfast. The food is overpriced and you receive teeny portions; just walk into town and eat well for Rp3000-4000.

The latest high-end Lovina accommodation is **Mas Lovina Beach Cottages,** a charming seaside resort of 10 maisonette type cottages (Rp230,000 and up), each with two twin upper floor air conditioned bedrooms and private bathrooms with hot and cold running water. On the ground floor find a living room with audio visual equipment and a dining room complete with fully equipped kitchen, refrigerator, and tableware. Tennis court and putting green, snorkeling, diving, and dolphin watching trips. Contact the manager, Mas Lovina Beach Cottages, Jl. Raya Kalibukbuk, Singaraja, Bali 81151, tel. (0362) 23237, fax 23236.

Food

Warung on the beach serve good food. As for restaurants, one of the best deals going is friendly **Superman.** You can frequent the place every night, trying different dishes each time, and all will be fantastic and abundant. Also provides useful information for travelers—how to reach destinations, *bemo* prices, and the like. Record your own experiences and recommendations, and review the comments of others. A little more expensive, but definitely worth it, is **Rumah Rumah Tamah** (tel. 0362-41149); very well-prepared vegetarian food with traditional Balinese dishes.

Surya Bar & Restaurant is cozy and attractive, with inexpensive, delicious food, particularly the fresh charcoal-grilled fish and chicken *sate.* Probably the best value in Lovina, with the finest *gado-gado.* The **Grace Restaurant,** across from Arya's, serves excellent Javanese-Indonesian style food and the view of the sunset from their open upstairs attracts many. Fresh seafood is their specialty. **Khi Khi's,** tel. (0362) 21548, serves fresh lobster or crab with choice of seven sauces, grilled fish steak (Rp7500), sweet-and-sour snapper (Rp4000), and special Thai soup (Rp4000). Most main dishes run around Rp6000. Ask first if the fish is frozen; it will take over an hour to cook if it is. Otherwise, fast service. A 30-minute dance in the evening is free and includes a complimentary dessert of rice cakes. The owner, Made, is quite a character. Try his home-brewed *arak* flavored with vanilla—it'll blow your mind. Open 0800. Made rents some Rp12,500-15,000 rooms in the back.

Open-air **Banyualit Restaurant** specializes in seafood, Indonesian dishes with a Chinese accent, and curries. One of the best restaurants in Lovina—even the *bupati* eats here. Complete menu, Western prices; eat beautifully for around Rp15,000 per person. Quieter than Khi Khi's, with no dust, no traffic. For excellent Balinese fish, head for **Spunky's Cafe** in Banyualit.

KALIASEM (LOVINA BEACH)

Accommodations
Susila Beach Inn has opened a branch on the beach next to the Angsoka called—you guessed it—**Susila Beach Inn II;** offering cozy bungalows with verandas, showers, toilets, and a fruit salad breakfast. Rates Rp9000 s, Rp10,000 d. Lovina's largest and oldest accommodation, **Nirwana Cottages**, tel. (0362) 22288, fax 21090, is 500 meters past the 11 km marker. The brick, bamboo, and thatch structures feature flush toilets, showers, and enclosed outdoor patios, but are not very well cared for. Five classes ranging from Rp15,000 for fan rooms to Rp50,000 d for two-story bungalows nos. 34-39. The best are back from the beach so no peddlers bother you, facing the hotel's spacious grounds, long walkways, and attractive lawns and gardens. Also cheaper double rooms for Rp20,000. Meager breakfast of fruit salad, and tea or coffee; restaurant service painfully slow; staff doesn't speak English; no swimming pool. No room phones, though there's a phone in the front office. Credit cards not accepted.

On the beach, very central, good restaurants within walking distance. Family-run, no-frills **Arjuna Homestay** is a good, small, budget hotel. Tucked away only 50 meters from the beach, the rooms cost Rp8000 d, including breakfast. Though very central (the Bali Ayu is north and Tasik Madu west), it is little known. A former homestay, the **Manggala Holiday Inn,** tel. (0362) 41371, just west of the Purnama, is the oldest *losmen* in town. Room prices only Rp10,000-20,000. Nearby "John's House," is

only Rp12,500 for a double room with *mandi* right on the beach. Be warned the breakfast here is horrible.

Thirty-room **Bali Lovina Beach Cottages,** tel./fax (0362) 41385, between Arjuna and Lovina Beach Hotel is pure luxury living: immaculate Bali-style cottages with bath, shower, and hot water for Rp100,000 s, Rp110,000 d superior rooms, Rp90,000 s, Rp100,00 d standard rooms, Rp70,000 s, Rp80,000 d fan rooms. All rates subject to 15.5% tax and service. Includes hearty breakfast. Restaurant, beautiful pool, poolside bar, beach access, very few beach hawkers. Water sports offered include sailing, snorkeling, fishing, canoeing, windsurfing, and dolphin-watching tours. Plastic accepted. Outside peak season bargain for half the rate. Lovina's most imposing, largest, and most expensive hotel is the **Palma Beach Hotel,** Jl. Raya Lovina, tel. (0362) 62362, 61775, or 61658, fax 61659, a quiet, luxury marine resort catering primarily to Swiss and German package tourists. Nineteen standard rooms go for Rp135,000 d; superior class rooms are more spacious, with open-air bathrooms, fridge, TV, and garden for Rp170,000 d. Live music (karaoke) weekly, coffee shop, restaurant serving Indian dishes, pizza and pasta. All prices subject to 15.5% tax and service fee. Recreation facilities include tennis court, large pool, open-air fitness center. Make reservations at the Denpasar office, Jl. Raya Puputan 17 X, tel. (0362) 25256, fax 25231. Watch for Palma business cards offering a 20% discount.

Quiet, family-run **Lovina Beach Hotel,** tel. (0362) 23473, was built on the site of Lovina's original hotel, founded by the late raja in 1953. Owner Anak Agung Ngurah Sentanu is the raja's grandson. The Lovina Beach offers convenience, friendly 24-hour service, good security, laundry and mailing service, and safe-deposit boxes. Rates for the three different classes of rooms are Rp60,000 for spacious a/c beachfront cottages, with large bathrooms, hot water, and verandas; Rp35,000 for beachfront cottages with ceiling fan; and Rp23,000 for rooms with garden view, shower, and fan. All prices include breakfast, tax, service. An excellent place for children; the restaurant right on the sea is a nice touch. Motorcycles rent for Rp12,000 per day, bicycles for Rp4000 per day. At **Hotel Puri Tasik Madu** ("Sea of Honey"), tel. (0362) 23376, prices start at Rp15,000; three a/c beachfront bungalows with inside *mandi* Rp35,000. The best value are the cheapest rooms. Good location on the beach side of the main road. Quiet and friendly staff; some of them are dynamite chess players.

West of the Tasik Madu is friendly 52-room **Aditya Bungalows,** Box 134, Singaraja 81101, tel. (0362) 41059, literally seven meters from the beach. Rp90,000 for very nice air conditioned deluxe rooms with hot water, private terrace, color TV, fridge, and sea view; Rp70,000 for air conditioned rooms with garden view; Rp50,000 for fan rooms with hot water; Rp40,000 for fan rooms with *mandi*. Rates include continental breakfast, add 15% government tax and service. The Aditya also runs a very efficient travel service. Older but well-kept (the sweeping never stops!) **Parma Beach Hotel,** tel. (0362) 23955, offers nice rooms looking out on gardens running down to the black-sand beach. Rates Rp15,000-25,000 in the low season, Rp18,000 s, Rp30,000 d in the high. Four different classes of rooms. Fine, reasonably priced kitchen, friendly staff. Breakfast of juice, banana pancake, fruit salad, toast, and coffee or tea included. Good security: bars on the windows and two *penjaga* posted beachside to keep out the riffraff.

The quiet **Bayu Kartika Beach Bungalows,** tel. (0362) 41055, is right on the beach, with comfortable beds, large ceiling fans, functional plumbing, and a decent place to eat. All rooms are clean with lovely garden bathrooms, hot water, and garden views. In the off-season try to negotiate a Rp20,000 per person rate. **Billibo Beach Cottages,** tel. (0362) 23498, the last place west in Lovina, has six clean cottages (Rp25,000) with screens on the windows, and reading lamps by the bed and on the veranda. Large, outdoor fenced-in area where people can't harass you. Great views of the ocean; not even a wall separates you from the private beach. People wait days for a cottage at Billibo's.

Food

The Lovina Beach Hotel's **Permata Restaurant,** serving Balinese, Indonesian, Chinese, and Western dishes, is right on the beach, flanked by a garden and fishpond. Specialties include *betutu bebek* (stuffed steamed duck), *babi guling, sate ayam, nasi goreng spesial,* and *gado-gado.* The pride of Permata is *nasi tumpeng,* true Balinese cuisine served on a *duleng* table, consisting of a mountain of rice encircled by *sate,* vegetables, curries, and *betutu.* Sit in the beachfront gazebo and watch the sunset.

Made's Warung, on the north side of the main road, offers a set menu with choice of starter, main meal, and great dessert for Rp10,000. No other restaurant serves salads as good. Prices are very competitive, live music every night and a happy hour. Made's does have its off-days, when the guacamole has no flavor, the chocolate mousse is flat, the music lousy, and the salads lack dressing.

Of the four restaurants on the south side of the main road, the hands-down favorite is **Arya's,** tel. (0362) 23797, where you'll find imaginative pasta dishes, grilled tuna fish dinner (Rp4000), a selection of vegetarian meals, and the best homemade desserts in Lovina including lemon meringue pie. Bills itself as the health food restaurant of Lovina. The service is so-so; the awful mixed green salad (Rp1500) comes with but one piece of lettuce, a slice of tomato, and tons of oil; and the avocado/shrimp cocktail is at best ordinary. Arya's strength is its breakfast with multigrain bread baked on the premises, homemade jams, *muesli,* and porridge. Free transport offered within a 10-km radius of Lovina.

Next to Aryas is the **Flower Garden Restaurant** offering items from a set menu for Rp7500-9500 in intimate surroundings. Some dishes are good, but portions are sometimes skimpy. If Made is cooking, count on a superb meal—dishes like guacamole and potato skins, cream of prawn soup, tuna wrapped in bamboo leaf. Try Made's Bali wine at your peril—not exactly vintage bordeaux. Balinese dancing starts at around 2000.

Three nights a week **Chono's** hosts an extravagant *rijstaffel* buffet. The meal—15 tasty dishes including rice wine, chocolate milk, peanuts, and fried *tempe*—is followed by Balinese dancing—all for Rp6000. Chono's also serves fresh seafood at very reasonable prices: fried calamari with garlic butter (Rp3000), grilled tuna (Rp3000), or snapper with choice of sauce (Rp3500). Relax in the comfortable, leafy restaurant and play chess, backgammon, scrabble, cards.

Manggala Holiday Inn, tel. (0362) 41371, serves a better than average fish in ginger and oyster sauce for Rp3000. The best breakfast buffet is put on by **Bali Apik** hidden away off J1. Bina Ria; open 0700-1100.

TEMUKUS

Temukus is the last village to the west, on the wings of Lovina. A convenient base for touring the Banjar area—just a short ride down the road. **Pondok Wisata Ayu's Restaurant,** tel. (0362) 21338, has five rather exposed, shadeless rooms for Rp15,000 s/d plus 10% tax and service. Not worth it—too hot. Across the road is **Agus Homestay,** nice rooms with fans, close to the sea for Rp10,000 s, Rp15,000 d (a drawback: close to the highway). Ten-room **Samudra Beach Cottages & Restaurant,** in an out-of-the-way setting one-half km west of Aditya on the road to Gilimanuk, charges Rp25,000-30,000 for a/c rooms with hot water just 10 meters from the beach. Continental breakfast in the breezy restaurant included in the price. A certain dreariness about the place, however. On the Kalibukbuk border is **Purnama,** a homestay on the beach side of the road. Rents rooms with partially outside bath for Rp10,000 s or d; less in the off-season. Breakfast included; only 100 meters from the beach.

Best of the lot is **Krisna Beach Inn,** tel. (0362) 24941, on Jl. Seririt about 13 km west of Singaraja. Eight plain but clean rooms for Rp10,000 s, Rp18,000 d in a U-shaped compound facing the ocean. The upper rooms receive breezes. Price includes simple breakfast; the open-air restaurant serves fresh seafood 0700-2200. Laundry service, swimming out front on a nice private beach, few sellers. Offshore there's a splendid coral reef. Quiet; just fishermen along here.

VICINITY OF LOVINA BEACH

From Lovina, walk to Singaraja along the beach in a couple of hours, crossing about six small rivers. A number of outstanding walks lead into the high country behind Lovina. From Kalibukbuk take the sealed road opposite Ayodya's Kayuputih, from here you can take the road west back down to the coast. Another loop starts at Banjar—take the steep road to Banyuseri, on a high plateau, five km from the coast. Continue five km through rice paddies east (left) along the ridge, to **Banjar Tega,** where you can get a lift on the back of a motorcycle to Banjar. You can also make this loop from the other direction.

From Seririt to Mayong (seven km) are many scenic rice fields and fields of cultivated grapevines. From Mayong, head east toward Kayuputih, Gobleg, and Munduk (known all over Bali for its durians and its mangosteens). The small, paved road from Mayong to the lakes climbs high into the mountains through a number of small villages. From Kayuputih walk to Banjar or continue on to Munduk; from there a track skirts the crater rim with superb views over lakes Tamblingan, Buyan, and Bratan. On a clear day you can see the Batukau range and sometimes all the way to the coast. This road gets a lot worse before it finally joins the Singaraja-Denpasar route north of the Bali Handara Country Club approximately 10 km north of Lake Bratan.

Waterfalls
From Lovina take a *bemo* (Rp500, one km) west to Temukus, or walk in 30 minutes from the bridge in Kaliasem. At the 14.5 km mark turn up the dirt road and you'll see a sign for **Air Terjun Singsing** ("Daybreak Waterfalls"). It's about a 500-meter walk with good eating stalls along the way. Boys will show you the way to the 12-meter-high falls, but will want Rp1000 once there. At the falls, swim in the pool below while cool, fresh water cascades over you. The falls only run in the wet; at other times farmers may block them off because they need the water. There's a bigger, better, more isolated waterfall known as Singsing Dua on a path to the east; swim here too.

To reach a third waterfall go back on the road to Singaraja to Anturan, then turn right up a steep side road. *Ojek* drivers sit at the start of the road and ask Rp1000 to deliver you to the falls. If driving yourself, park and follow the trail down to the river, then boulder-hop along the riverbed for about one kilometer. A beautiful falls and a nice place to swim.

Banjar

The starting point for sightseeing in the area. In the Banjar area are two villages, one a Muslim community called Banjar, the other is an authentic fishing village called Dencarik on the sea eight km to the west of Lovina; turn north at the intersection of Jl. Seririt and the road to Dencarik. No tourists, no hotels, no sellers—like Malaysia's Batu Ferringhi 20 years ago. Ask to share some fishermen's food with the villagers. Along this coast there are no plastic bottles in the water, which makes for superior snorkeling.

Buddhist Monastery

Go first to Dencarik village, about 18 km west of Singaraja on the highway to Seririt. From the highway where the *bemo* lets you off, walk two km; then, at the intersection just before the Banjar Tega market, turn left up the paved road. Climb another two km (40 minutes) to the hilltop monastery. Or take a *honda ojek* (Rp2000) all the way up the steep hill from the Banjar turnoff. Wear long pants or a *sarung* as you must be respectfully dressed. *Sarung* rent for Rp500. Entering the *vihara,* sign the guestbook and give a donation.

This storybook monastery, also known as Brahma Vihara Asrama, has a gleaming orange tile roof, Sukothai-style gold leaf Buddha images, *raksasa* door guardians, brightly painted stupa with Buddha eyes, and exuberant woodcarvings—a dazzling mix of Balinese Hindu and Buddhist components. Opened in 1970, it's the only Buddhist monastery on Bali. Tibet's Dalai Lama paid a visit in 1982, and Bali's Chinese make regular pilgrimages to this peaceful hillside ashram. Severely damaged in the July 1976 earthquake, it has since been completely restored.

The Theravadic *vipashana* breathing technique is practiced here, the aim to produce clear comprehension and mindfulness. The resident *bhikku* (Buddhist teacher) will guide you to equanimity. The *bhikku* is only here May-June, Aug.-Sept., and Dec.-January. Instruction in English only in September and April. All are welcome, but anyone visiting overnight is encouraged to write first. Several times a year students "speech fast," and no writing, reading, or talking is allowed. Quite comfortable, with plenty of good vegetarian food. If you eat, pay.

Note the panels depicting Buddha fables, a temple bell from Thailand, and a specimen of the *bo* tree of enlightenment. A number of books on Buddhism are for sale. The hall at the bottom is for prayer, the top building for meditation. Unsurpassed views over the north coast. At night, stars reflect in the rice paddies and fireflies fill the air.

The road continues past the monastery and up the mountain to the village of Pedawa. Walk from the monastery to the *air panas* on a small path in just 10 minutes, or drive by going back down the hill and taking the first left, then another left after the market. Drive 120 meters, then make another left and drive two kilometers.

Air Panas

A hot spring only a 10-minute walk from the monastery, if you take the shortcut. Or drive six km east of Lovina on Jl. Seririt, take a left and travel two km to the Banjar Tega market, then a further two km uphill. Motorcycle *ojek* drivers or *dokar* wait at this turnoff to Banjar to give you a lift, Rp1500. Fifty meters on the left after the market look for the Air Panas 1 KM sign and follow the forested road to the end. After cycling up the hill, the hot water will be a great relief. Arriving, it costs Rp500 to park and Rp1050 entrance (Rp500 child) but you can swim all day.

Surrounded by jungle and luxurious gardens, this is the perfect setting for a day's loafing. There are three pools of varying temperatures. Lay back in one big lovingly warm pool or another smaller pool of soft, green-yellow sulphur water, both filled by water pouring out of naga-shaped pipes from the hill and pool above. Wash and soap in the lowest. If it gets too hot, take a dip in the river. Neat and clean toilets, showers, and changing rooms available.

Stay at the moderately priced, nice-looking **Pondok Wisata Grya Sati Hotel and Restaurant** near the entrance. Overlooking the pool is the fairly reasonably priced Komala Tirta Restaurant with a full Indonesian/Western menu—*sop ayam* Rp2000, beef *sate* Rp4000, *gado-gado* Rp1500. Good, average food and a cool, relaxing place to sit, read, or write. Two *warung makan* serve up *nasi campur* (Rp500), snacks, fruit, cakes, and *es campur.* About 10 souvenir shops with very aggressive, hungry sellers selling Kuta-style garments lurk up the road. Buy your bathing suit here.

Open from 0800 to 1600, the complex is tidy and well maintained. No nude bathing, shampoo and soap permissible in a third pool off to the side. The pools could be peaceful, or crowded with a busload of tourists or screaming schoolkids. One-hundred meters upstream is another, smaller *air panas.*

Pedawa
From the Buddhist monastery in Banjar Tega it's a seven-km hike north to Pedawa, about 10 km inland from Banjar Tega. This is a big grape-growing area and you'll see vineyards stretching away from both sides of the road. Pedawa is a quiet, friendly town. Strike up a conversation with one of the shopowners.

At the T-junction, turn west, go past the public *mandi,* and stay on this sealed road for four km to Banyuseri through a country of peanuts, corn, and fruit gardens. From Banyuseri walk down to Banjar on the coast. In all, it's 13 km from Pedawa to Banjar on this route. If heading east from Pedawa, the good road ends here.

WEST BULELENG

From Lovina, travel the road west toward Gilimanuk through a relatively arid landscape of coconut groves and grape orchards. The administrative center of Buleleng Barat is the small market town of Seririt, 22 km west of Singaraja. At Seririt, turn inland for the road to Denpasar via Pupuan.

The Pupuan Area
Down the western side of the mountains just north of Pupuan are a few coffee growing villages. Not many visitors here; the children will shy away from you at first. They are very generous and warm people and will show you around the plantation and processing plant and offer you *kopi Bali.* The village of Pupan, 25 km south of Seririt on a north-south road, is the location of a 100-meter-high water-fall called **Blahmantung** which is only worth seeing at the height of the rainy season. The road up to the falls is very precipitous and bumpy; see the sign Sabah Hulu 1,450 meters at the side of the road in the southernmost outskirts of Pupuan. Farther down the mountain, beginning about 10 km south of Pupuan, are some of the island's most spectacular rice terraces. These works of art make incredible viewing around sunset. Watch the insane truck drivers on this road.

Seririt
Twelve km west of Kalibukbuk, where the road turns south on the dramatic ride to Pekutatan via Pupuan (two hours, 90 km). Stay at **Hotel Singasari** on Jl. Gajah Mada, tel. (0362) 111, past the bridge in the west end of town. Rates from Rp5000 for a basic single to Rp20,000 for an air conditioned double. Check out shops and foodstalls just north of the *bemo* stop. A good starting point is **Rumah Makan Sederhana** on Jl. Surapati near the mosque. From Seririt, take a *bemo* toward Pupuan, get off at Mayong, about 10 km southeast. From Mayong head east toward Kayuputih; from there you can walk back to Banjar or continue on to Munduk. In **Munduk,** Pan Wicarna makes *gong besar* and complete *gamelan* sets in a simple foundry next to his house.

From Munduk a track skirts the crater rim with superb views over Tamblingan and Buyan Lakes (a single lake before they were split by a landslide in 1818). This small but paved road finally joins the Singaraja-Denpasar road at a point approximately 20 km south of Singaraja and 10 km north of Lake Bratan, and is even passable in the rainy season. Another way to the south coast is to take the road south of Mayong to Pupuan, then through the mountains on a breathtaking road to Antosari, 16 km west of Tabanan on the Tabanan-Gilimanuk road.

Celukanbawang
Just off the main coastal road 40 km west of Singaraja, this port receives timber and cement from Kalimantan and Java; here you may catch Bugis schooners trading between Bali and Kalimantan. The port is also used by the oil company ARBN as a supply base for its offshore drilling explorations. In Celukanbawang stay, eat, drink, and watch movies at **Drupadi Indah Hotel & Restaurant.**

Lodging costs Rp10,000 d, or Rp13,000 d for larger rooms with bigger beds. *Mandi* inside both classes of rooms. Another okay place to eat is **Depot Muslim Abdullah** in the village.

Tanjung Gondol

About 30 km west of Seririt, or 35 km east Gilimanuk, just before the poor fishing village of Gondol, are the solitary sands of Tanjung Gondol. With rows of *jukung* and surrounded by a coconut plantation, this part of the coast is idyllic and peaceful, with no tourists and no facilities but plenty of good swimming and snorkeling. Coming from the east, or four km before Pulaki, start looking for this peninsula with a small temple on top of a small hill. The best area for viewing the extremely rare Bali mynah (or Bali starling) is the guardpost at Teluk Kelor near Gerokgak on the north coast of the Prapat Agung Peninsula. About 45 mynahs inhabit this savannah area with patches of monsoon forests. Reach them by motorboat from Labuan Lalang village; on your way, refresh yourself with a dive around Menjangan Island.

Pulaki

Pura Agung Pulaki, a large, dramatic temple only 25 metes from the sea, is situated 30 km west of Seririt (48 km west of Singaraja) near the grape-growing village of Banyupoh. Cliffs tower behind the temple surrounded by jungle and overrun by hordes of aggressive simians. Considered sacred, the macaques are well-fed by locals but always eager for tourist handouts.

This important temple commemorates the arrival of the Javanese saint-priest Nirantha to Bali in the early 16th century. It was completely restored with black stone gates and terraces in 1983 in a ceremony presided over by the governor of Bali and the *bupati* of Buleleng. *Pedanda* fanned out all over Java and Lombok to obtain holy water for use in the ceremony.

Legend has it a great village exists here, invisible but for its temple. It is said that when Nirantha lived in Gelgel he was forced to hide his daughter lest she be abducted by the king. He finally brought her to this remote place, rendering it invisible to keep her safe. To this day, the people who occupy the invisible village are known as *gamang* and are said to wander the countryside.

The parking lot is jammed with souvenir and food stalls. Also a handy stop for truck drivers headed to and from the ferry terminal at Gilimanuk. Time your arrival for the sunset at beautiful Pantai Gondol which offers clean white sand, coral reefs, and above-average snorkeling. There's a smaller, monkey-infested temple one-half km west of Pura Pulaki where a tunnel has been cut through large rocks hanging over the road.

One km past Pulaki and 500 meters off the road is an *air panas.* A more famous hot springs, known for the medicinal qualities of its mineral waters, is at Banyuwedang (entrance Rp450 adults, Rp250 children). It's 900 meters off the highway just before the entrance to Bali Barat National Park.

In a beautiful setting, only two km from **Banyupoh** at the end of a pretty country road, is Pura Melanting. Dedicated to the god of prosperity, this temple with its huge and ornately carved *candi bentar* is set impressively against a mountain. Zero tourists visit this site.

PEMUTERAN

Four km west of Pulaki, 15 km east of Labuhan Lalang, 28 km east of Gilimanuk, and about 40 km west of Lovina, this is one of the most idyllic resorts in all of Bali. The tidy, black-sand, scenic beach leads to some of the island's best snorkeling, with great dropoffs just one km offshore. Visit Chris Brown's turtle hatchery. At night, the fishing boats light their lamps out on the ocean.

Visit the home selling singing *perkutut* (doves). Take a *dokar*—Rp15,000 for three people for two hours—to Melanting Temple. Venture out to look for dolphins, Rp15,000 per person for three hours. From the small nearby fishing village you can rent *jukung* for Rp5000 per hour. Good fishing along this gorgeous, inviting coast with a dramatic backdrop of mountains. In two hours you can climb to the top of the mountains to the west from where you can view either the sunrise and sunset.

Beware of the Muslim mosque which blasts early morning prayers. Bring earplugs. These loudspeakers are all that keep this beautiful, reclusive place from becoming the perfect getaway.

Water Sports

Australian dive master and PADI instructor Chris Brown operates an eco-friendly dive and snorkel operation here (Reef Seen, Desa Pemuteran, Gerogak, Singaraja 81115, tel. 0362-92339, e-mail: reefseen@denpasar.wasantara.net.id) 100 meters east of Pondok Sari: Rp70,000 for a dive, Rp115,000 for dives, Rp75,000 for night dives. Credit cards accepted. Brown caters to underwater videomakers and photographers, and also offers equipment rental, repair, and service. As a teacher, he's competent and patient. Several nights a week he screens a video of the superlative dive sites in Bali. The "tickets" he sells to snorkelers (Rp200) are basically a way of familiarizing people with the rules: respect the reef and the community, don't stand on it, don't feed the fish, no nudity. Chris also gives back to the village, holding Balinese dance classes for kids with performances of five different dances on Saturday nights. Delightful.

Midday is high tide at Pemuteran. The Napoleon Reef is 1.5 km out; the soft coral like flowers blooming. There's a large shallow area with plenty of reef fish (damsel fish, silver fusiliers, blue dancers, snappers, etc.), as well as a dropoff with occasional manta rays. Modified dive *prahu* take you to the reef from the dive center. Great snorkeling too. Closer to the shore in front of Pondok Sari it's murkier and there's not as much fishlife as farther out, although you still see locals fishing near the beach.

Accommmodations and Food

One of Bali's nicest hotels is the 22-room **Pondok Sari,** Desa Pemuteran, Gerokgak, Singaraja, tel. (0362) 92623 or 288096, fax 286297. Five hundred meters from the main road, with clean and spacious bungalows set in a tropical garden. Simple but comfortable bamboo furniture, wardrobe and dresser, okay lighting, ceiling fans, mosquito nets, beautiful open-roofed *mandi,* verandas and chairs. Good room service, safety deposit box, guard at night, accepts credit cards. Rates: standard fan-cooled Rp75,000, deluxe a/c with garden view Rp105,000, deluxe a/c with ocean view Rp135,000, suites a/c with hot water Rp175,000. Breakfast not included here—a big negative.

The food in the small, charming, open-air restaurant is overpriced but quite good and the portions large: try jaffles (Rp3500), banana pancakes (Rp2500), or a nightly special like beef-steak (Rp7500) or fish (Rp9500). Open 0700-2400. Fifteen percent service and tax charged for both rooms and meals. Transfers available upon request.

The Pondok Sari stages a *joget bumbu* dance in the evenings either in the restaurant or near the temple. Dances are sometimes held simultaneously with a festive, crowded *pasar malam* featuring a *gamelan* ensemble. The hotel also rents snorkeling masks and fins for Rp5000 (three hours) and mountain bikes for Rp2000 per hour. Ask the manager about tours to Bali Barat National Park.

bungalow at Pondok Sari

The secluded, beachfront, eco-friendly **Taman Sari Resort,** 500 meters west of Pondok Sari, has 21 bungalows with ocean views, abundant gardens of indigenous plants, and plenty of quiet space for peaceful relaxation. Rates from Rp75,000 for fan rooms, Rp110,000-135,000 for deluxe a/c rooms, and Rp175,000 for suites with hot water. Walls not as paper-thin as Pondok Sari's. The open-air restaurant provides spectacular views of mountainous western Bali. Water sports, *dokar* rides, temple tours, sunset trips, and excursions to wild regions all offered. Bookings: tel (0362) 92623 or through Nagasari Tours in Sanur (tel. 0361-288096, fax 286297).

One km east of Pondok Sari is three-star **Matahari Beach Resort** (tel. 0362-92312, fax 92313) with very nice bungalows (US$160-350

d, plus 21% tax and service) but a strangely lifeless atmosphere. Art lessons, diving, and tours offered.

BALI BARAT NATIONAL PARK

The Land
The 76,312 hectare (777 square km) Taman Nasional Bali Barat, with its complex of habitats including forests and coral-fringed islands, is the wild side of Bali. Since Bali is such a densely populated, intensively cultivated island, very little of Bali's forests are left. To preserve a portion of the island as a wilderness zone, as a buffer against human settlements that border it, and as a resource for forest products, Bali

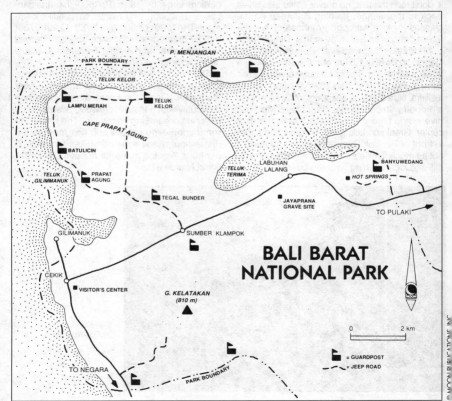

Barat National Park in Bali's western end was officially gazetted as one of Indonesia's 10 national parks in 1984. The park today encompasses 10% of Bali's total land area. If managed wisely, the tourism potential of its adjacent marine reserve is almost unlimited.

The park is managed by the Indonesian Forestry Service (PHPA), which limits and controls public access. Bali Barat National Park was initially established by the Dutch in 1941 to protect the endemic white starling of Bali (*Loucospar rothschildi*), and the last of the island's wild *banteng*. The Balinese subspecies of the Asian tiger may also have roamed the area, but by 1941 its existence was doubtful. Despite rumors to the contrary, the last animal was probably shot in the 1930s.

Though not nearly as rugged as the areas surrounding the higher mountains of eastern Bali, primary monsoon forests (about 50,000 hectares) are found along the watershed on the southern slopes of the mountains Sangiang, Merbuk, Musi, and Patas. None of these mountains, lying in the eastern and central areas of the park, are higher than 1,500 meters. Gunung Patas gained international notoriety in April 1974 when a Pan-Am 707 jet slammed into its side, killing all 107 people aboard.

The park's southern sector is watered by clear streams and traversed by footpaths that promise steep but relatively easy walking through forested hills. The park's northern sector is much drier than the south, the habitat of scrub acacia, palm savanahs, dense mangrove swamps, and unspoilt reefs.

On the way to the park from the east, immediately before the park's entrance on the right (21 km northeast of Cekik) is Banyuwedang Hotsprings, believed to posses curative powers. A well is the source of the sulphurous water; you bathe in a wooden shelter close to the mangroves. Entrance Rp400, children Rp250, shower Rp2000, insurance Rp50. From the highway walk or drive 900 meters to the gate, pay, then walk 100 meters to the springs.

Climate

The north coast of Bali is generally drier than the south, especially between May and November. The coast of Cape Prapat Agung is exposed to rainy season squalls, though the cape shelters Pulau Menjangan and Teluk Terima. At sea level, temperatures are high throughout the year. Hill temperatures inland vary according to elevation and tree cover.

Fauna

The park offers *rusa* deer, *kancil,* barking deer, long-tailed macaques, civets, monkeys, wild boars, and perhaps 30 or so *banteng (Bos javanicus)*—living ancestors of today's deer-like Balinese cattle. The park's profuse and beautiful birdlife includes the endangered Bali starling (popularly known as *jalak bali*) and sea and shore birds, the most conspicuous being brown boobies and lesser frigate birds. Two species of terns nest in large numbers on a sandy cay at the entrance of Teluk Lumpur ("Mud Bay"), while the boobies and frigates roost on **Pulau Burung** farther east.

An extremely rare species, Bali's only remaining endemic creature, the Bali starling (*jalak putih* in Indonesian) averages 23 cm in length and features black wingtips and tail, silky white feathers, and brilliant blue rings around its eyes. Not to be confused with the black-winged starling which has black wings and tail. It lives in groups of two or three in the acacia scrub and dry monsoon forests on the north coast of Cape Prapat Agung. A very shy and easily agitated bird, the *jalak putih* can fetch as much as US$1500 in the pet market. Using birds from zoos on Java for breeding, conservationists hope to increase the small number of birds surviving in the wild. To see live specimens, visit the Bali Starling Recovery Project in Tegal Bunder or at Teluk Kelor, north of Batu Licin, to the east. Get a *bemo* (Rp500 each way) from Labuhan Lalang to Sumberklampok, then turn right and walk two km to the Recovery Project at Tegal Bunder. When you come to some buildings, turn right and walk another 200 meters to the aviary. Take off your shoes and socks, walk down a hall, and look through the tiny windows of the aviary. The birds live in the trees and are fed from big buckets of bugs. There are only nine birds and perhaps 50 more in the jungle. Entrance fee is Rp2000.

Hawksbill turtles and 10-meter-long toothless whale sharks have been sighted along the reserve's north coast, and whales and dolphins migrate via Selat Bali between Java and Bali.

More like a forest than a jungle, the park offers exceptional walking and first-class panoramas. Day trips can be arranged by the PHPA office in Labuhan Lalang. Part of the walk is cross-country with no trails. At times you have to crawl through undergrowth and use paths frequented by wild ox and deer. Birds are everywhere—incredible surround sound.

An interesting walk is the 25-km-long track along the coast of Cape Prapat Agung (highest elev. 310 meters). This cape is cut off from the rest of the reserve by the main Singaraja-Gilimanuk road, as well as by settlements and coconut, teak, and eucalyptus plantations. Into this wilderness bring lots of water as it can get extremely hot. Make sure your guide is a good birdspotter (the park has 160 species) and bring binoculars.

Information and Permits
The best info on hiking and guides, a small exhibit, scale model of the park, and possibly even maps can be had from the park headquarters in Cekik, three km south of Gilimanuk at the junction of the road from Singaraja with the road from Denpasar. Dark green *bemo* from Denpasar's Ubung Station pass Cekik on their way to Gilimanuk. The park headquarters is open Mon.-Thurs. 0800-1400, Friday 0800-1100, and Saturday 0800-1200. The PHPA maintains a branch office at Labuhan Lalang (12 km east of Cekik) with a useful relief map of the park. Open 0800-1800.

You must have a permit, and be accompanied by a guide (Rp15,000 per hike) to enter the reserve plus the cost of vehicles or boats. One day permits (Rp2500) and guides are available at the park headquarters in Cekik and the ranger station at Labuhan Lalang, as well as the Department of Forestry (PHPA) office in Denpasar (Jl. Suwung 40, Box 320). You don't need a permit to drive through the park from Singaraja to Gilimanuk road; get to Labuhan Lalang by public *bemo* from Lovina for Rp2800.

The park entrance fee is Rp2500 per person per day, plus Rp2500 per vehicle per day. A guide costs Rp15,000—for all fees and guides, count on about Rp20,000 per day. A typical walk lasts five hours. Early or the late in the day is the best time to see wildlife. Dress like your guide: jeans and long sleeves for protection from thorns and snags. Take a lunch and sit quietly in the forest to hear the symphony.

Accommodations and Food
Undoubtedly, the best place to stay is **Pondok Sari** just before Pulaki to the east, or in Gilimanuk. There's a guesthouse (tel. 0365-40060) at park headquarters in Cekik (Jembrana), nice rooms, shared *mandi,* Rp10,000 per person. For a small charge you can spend the night in four guard posts on the Cape Prapat Agung peninsula—three on the west coast, one on the north. Facilities are very basic—beds, wood fire, and cooking pots. Bring all your own food and eating utensils. Yet another option is **Pondok Wisata Lestari,** a combination restaurant and losmen two km from Cekik on the way to Gilimanuk (Rp10,000 s, Rp15,000 d); food. There are also designated campgrounds east of Cekik. Be sure to let the rangers know you plan to stay overnight. For overnights, bring sleeping bag, mosquito net, all food and beverages. Camping equipment can be rented from the park forestry office at Labuhan Lalang.

In the middle of the complex at Labuhan Lalang, between the Taman Nasional Bali Barat offices and the sea, are two open-air restaurants with Western-oriented menus. Very rustic: lots of mosquitoes, incredible humidity, no fans. Cold beer served out of ice chests. Lots of locals hang out on weekend dates. The cafes rent snorkeling equipment—Rp5000 for fins, mask, and snorkel, or Rp2500 for fins only.

Jayaprana's Gravesite
Near Labuhan Lalang is the sacred grave of the folk hero Jayaprana, the foster son of treacherous king Anak Agung Gde Murka. In the 17th century, the king sent Jayaprana to Teluk Terima under the pretext of investigating wrecked ships plundered by pirates. His real motive was to steal Jayaprana's wife Layon Sari. During this royal mission, Jayaprana was ambushed and killed by the king's minister. Hearing the news, Layon Sari stabbed herself to death. The king then went insane, ran amok, and was killed by his subjects.

Jayaprana was finally given a proper cremation in 1949, an event accompanied by many strange, unexplained apparitions. The folk hero's grave (Rp1050 admission), with figures of the betrayed Brahman and his bride behind glass, is inside a temple after climbing 10 minutes up steep concrete steps from the south side of the road, one km west of Labuhan Lalang (12 km east of Cekik). About halfway up the stone stairway are splendid views of the old volcanoes of eastern Java, Gilimanuk Bay, and Pulau Menjangan.

The Marine Reserve

This unspoilt 6,600-hectare marine reserve includes the shores of the mountainous outcrop of land (Cape Prapat Agung) between Teluk Terima and Gilimanuk, and several bird islands in the bay near Gilimanuk, but is centered primarily on Pulau Menjangan and the excellent coral reefs surrounding it. Because it's a national park, both the number of boats and number of passengers visiting the island are controlled. A PHPA officer accompanies you on the boat; request one who speaks English.

Coral reefs are also found off the mainland. In fact, just out in front of **Labuhan Lalang,** the drop-off (gradual) is just five meters from the shore. Since these waters are protected, the snorkeling is superb. Go early in the morning when the water is clearest. Just drift along the coral wall; unbelievable. This dive site is particularly suited for beginner and intermediate divers.

It costs Rp60,000 for a four-hour snorkeling trip to Pulau Menjangan (maximum 10 people). In Labuhan Lalang you'll probably be able to find other tourists to share in the boat rental fees. Just hang out in the restaurant or parking lot until you gather enough people. For scuba diving, the boat costs the same (maximum six people with all their gear). Additional hours are Rp7500 extra. Prices are fixed, and one person costs the same as 10. From the jetty at Labuhan Lalang take one of the good-sized boats waiting for passengers. The passage takes about 30 minutes. You can rent snorkeling equipment from the PHPA office in Labuhan Lalang (Rp6000 per set), or hire in Lovina or Kuta before you go.

The 175-hectare sanctuary island of **Pulau Menjangan,** off the northwest coast at the western entrance to Teluk Terima, received its name ("Deer Island") from the wild Java deer that graze on its open savannahs. One of Bali's premier scuba diving and snorkeling locales, these reefs are frequented by species of fish of every size, shape, and color.

There's a great variety of underwater terrain, for the most part about two meters below the surface extending 100-150 meters offshore, with no dangerous currents or wind-generated waves to contend with. The soft coral walls around the island are almost vertical and extend to a depth of 35-60 meters. The unusually rugged surface of the reef is pockmarked with caves, grottoes, fissures, and hollows, and covered with giant gorgonians and barrel sponges. At 25-50 meters the visibility is crystal clear.

The spectacular 120-meter dropoffs and caves off Pulau Menjangan's south side are only surpassed by the particularly fine species of coral off its northern shores. Menjangan's northwestern end is the site of an old shipwreck, called the **Anker,** near a small pier and PHPA guardpost about 75 meters from shore. The 25-meter-long wreck lies on a sandy slope from seven meters to 45 meters underwater. This is an excellent spot for a soft coral, caves, fish, and other reef life.

There's a break in the wall on the east side; this is where all the boats come in. Boats land in the shallows, then after gearing up on the beach, divers start exploring along the edge of the underwater wall only one to five meters down. You'll find the fish are quite cheeky as the guides feed them regularly with leftover rice. Boats usually visit the same sites day after day; permanent mooring buoys are in place to prevent anchor damage to the coral. Guides allow sightseers to disembark so they can walk the short nature trail on the island and view the plantlife and wild deer; it starts near the jetty, leads east to a small shrine (15 minutes), and will take in all only about an hour. An onshore shelter for divers is on Pulau Menjangan's western end, but spending the night on the island isn't allowed. Much of the island is flat and very dry, the soil sandy with sparse vegetation, and some sections of the coast are fringed with mangroves. The only animals are a herd of barking deer, Java deer, the green-yellow mangrove white-eye, and few Bali starling.

Everyone in these waters should beware of tiny stinging jellyfish. You could end up with welts all over your torso; jellyfish get stuck in one-piece bathing suits. Within an hour the painful welts are gone. Lemon juice helps.

Organized Tours
Tunas Indonesia, Jl. D. Tamblingan 107, tel. (0361) 288450, and the travel office in the Hotel Bali Beach in Sanur, tel. (0361) 288056, offer two-day, one-night "Walking Safari Tours" of the park for Rp315,000 per person for two people. **Oceania,** Jl. Bypass Ngurah Rai 78, tel./fax (0361) 88652, in Kuta; **Aquanaut,** Jl. W.R. Supratman, Abiankapas Kaja, tel. (0361) 28562, fax 32872, in Denpasar; **Spice Dive,** tel. (0362) 41841, in Lovina; **Barrakuda,** tel./fax (0361) 33386, in Sanur; and **Stingray,** Puri Bali Homestay, tel./fax (0366) 35540, in Candidasa, are all popular dive companies with good equipment that offer marine tours to Pulau Menjangan and environs. They arrange everything—transportation, boat, PHPA permit—and arrive with

filled tanks, weights, box lunch waiting in the van. The boat operators themselves also serve as experienced guides to marine attractions. These dive outfits organize tours to not only Pulau Menjangan but also to Pulau Lembongan, Tulamben.

You can arrange one-day snorkeling/scuba diving excursions from the Kuta-Sanur-Denpasar area, but it's a long, hard day. Tours start at 0730, arrive 2.5 hours later, return at 1700, and cost an absolutely unbargainable Rp150,000-300,000. Since the roundtrip to Labuhan Lalang by van from Kuta takes at least six hours, eating up most of the day, it's better to spend the night near the park in Gilimanuk, Pemuteran, or Lovina. From the latter, Labuhan Lalang is Rp2800 by dark red public *bemo*. Dive tours operating out of Candidasa to Pulau Menjangan take even longer (five to six hours one way) and cost too much because of the distance.

BOB RACE

JEMBRANA REGENCY

The Balinese call this rugged, thinly populated region Pulaki, site of a lost invisible city condemned to one day sink beneath the sea. Except for a strip of coast, most of the district's 841,800-square-kilometers are mountainous, with impenetrable highlands said to harbor strange wild animals. The wilderness area of Bali Barat National Park—with its jungle fowl, boar, wild deer, Javan buffalo, and monkeys—falls almost wholly within Jembrana Regency (40% of the district's land area). So rugged are the lonely mountain forests of Jembrana that the villages are spread far apart. West of Pulukan no roads head north across the island.

Jembrana is the most heavily Javanized regency of Bali. Settlements with typical Javanese names like Palarejo are common in the area; in some instances the people have adopted Balinese *subak*-style irrigation practices. In a subtle gray area around Negara you can see where Java really starts. You begin to notice more mosques, *peci, nasi padang* restaurants, Javanese-style wooden *cikar* carts pulled by plodding water buffalo. The Balinese culture recedes to the east, almost as if the Balinese had relinquished this swath of island to the Javanese.

Jembrana is also home to Bali's strongest and most populous Christian communities.

Jembrana is the least populated regency of Bali. The population today is around 215,000, scattered throughout 51 villages, mostly situated along the main Denpasar-Gilimanuk coastal artery. Four of five inhabitants earn their income from farming or fishing. Drier and not as agriculturally rich as the rest of the island, revenues derive for the most part from huge coconut plantations along the coastal strip, ubiquitous rice fields, coffee plantations in the highlands near the border of Tabanan, and vanilla, cocoa, and cloves. One of the main fishing ports of Bali is Pengambengan, eight km southwest of Negara.

Jembrana is also the least visited part of Bali. Its isolation only came to an end with the Gilimanuk-Ketapang ferry in the 1930s. Today, most tourists speed through the region on buses, racing along the 134-km-long road from Denpasar to Gilimanuk. All Jembrana's hotels are located in Negara, Medewi, or the ferry terminal of Gilimanuk. Not even rudimentary English is widely spoken. Ample *bemo* and minibuses regularly service the district, *dokar* and *ojek* are available in the smaller towns and villages.

Other than exciting bull races held in the vicinity of Negara, in which buffalo thunder down racetracks at speeds of 80 kph, there's a dearth of historic sights and cultural performances. The regency does offer utterly unique dance and *gamelan* forms, isolated, stunning sea temples, challenging surf, and a heavily trafficked 71-km-long stretch of highway paralleling a coast lined with rocky, black-sand beaches pounded by high surf.

Flora
Besides the mangrove and *nipah* palms of the region, the *buyuk* grows in the saltwater marshes of the Perancak River. This plant prevents shore erosion and provides habitat for fish, birds, and monkeys. The people of Jembrana use the leaves of the *buyuk* as roofing material. The leaves are resistant to sunlight, helping to keep the interior of homes comfortable when it is hot, and retain heat when it is cold.

History
The present channel between eastern Java and Bali's northwestern tip was exposed as dry land during the Pleistocene epoch about 20,000 years ago. This enabled settlement by early human beings; Jembrana, in fact, was the first place people lived on Bali. During WW II, pottery fragments,

basalt pebble-tools, and neolithic adzes were found at Cekik, south of Gilimanuk. The remains of a burial site of 100 people were also discovered.

A Balinese chronicle records that the region came under the jurisdiction of the Gelgel dynasty in the 15th century. Two princes were sent by the king to civilize the wild western wilderness, establishing separate courts near present-day Gilimanuk and Negara. The princes vied with each other over who could develop the most prosperous kingdom, their rivalry eventually erupting into a full civil war which destroyed both courts. Jembrana then slipped again into anonymity until 1803, when another court developed in present-day Negara. When the Dutch subjugated Buleleng Regency to the north in 1849, they assumed control of Jembrana.

Neither wealthy nor powerful, Jembrana never played an important role in Balinese politics. Because of its close proximity to Java, Jembrana was visited early by Chinese, Javanese, and Buginese traders who leased land from the local lords for planting cash crops. The Dutch and other Europeans established huge plantations of cotton, cacao, coconuts, and tobacco in the regency as early as 1860. Coffee land grants were still awarded to Chinese merchant princes in the late 19th century. Sparsely populated Jembrana has also

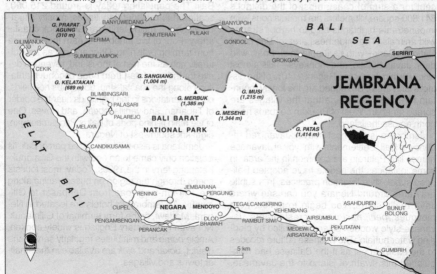

been settled by transmigrants from Java and other parts of Bali, particularly after the devastating eruption of Gunung Agung in 1963.

Arts and Crafts

The most famous painter in the regency is I Gusti Putu Windya Anaya, who can be found in his home-studio in the village of Yeh Embang. Jembrana's traditional handloom weaving centers are Sangkaragung and Dauh Waru near Negara, producing *songket* and *endek* for formal occasions. The best woodcarvers and sculptors work in Pendem village near Negara. Look for silverware and gold jewelry in Dauh Waru. Bamboo artifacts such as lamp covers, bags, and baskets are the specialty of Pulukan near Melaya in western Jembrana, while *lontar* palm leaf handicrafts are produced in Gilimanuk. To see a traditional blacksmith at work, visit the village of Batu Agung near Negara.

Dance and Music

Bamboo has been the mainstay of music-making here since the beginning of recorded time. The intriguing and sonorous *gamelan jegog* ensemble of Jembrana, created by Kiyang Gelinduh in 1912, consists of 14 instruments made of giant bamboo tubes that play a reverberating, low-pitched melody. Likened to the sound of deep, roaring thunder, these instruments formerly functioned as a means of calling people for cooperative village work. So large are these natural resonating tubes, the musicians must sit on top, striking the swaying bamboo beneath them with heavy mallets. The *gamelan jegog* accompanies Jembrana's traditional *leko*-style dances. In his book *Balinese Music,* Michael Tanzer describes the tubes "stretching to an incredible three meters in length, with circumferences of 60-65 centimeters."

It's best to hear the orchestra during a village celebration, or you can commission a performance for around Rp175,000 by contacting Ida Bagus Raka Negara in Tegalcangkring, a village that traditionally produces the finest *jegog* players and instrument makers. Also check at the Office of Education and Culture in Negara.

The largest version of *jegog* is the *jegog mebarung,* in which two *gamelan* compete with one another, accompanied by *kendang, rebana, kecak,* and *tawa tawa.* Sets of *jegog* instruments are displayed both at **STSI,** the Institute of Arts

and Dance, tel. (0361) 72361, on Jl. Nusa Indah in Abiankapas (near Denpasar), and at Sangkar Agung, a private museum three km east of Negara near the village of Pangintukadaya.

For *jegog* music visit the villages of Moding near Melaya and Yeh Kuning on the way to Perancak. The Grand Hyatt Hotel of Nusa Dua features a mighty *gamelan jegog* during their *pasar malam.*

Other musical forms in Jembrana show distinct folk influences from Java and Madura. Examples include the daring *cabang* (knife dance), the *jegog* dance, and *pencak silat. Sewa gati* is a "seated opera" found in the village of Berangbang five km north of Negara. The *leko* from Pendem village stars two female dancers dressed in classical *legong* garments. *Kendang mebarung* is a duel between two one-meter-wide drums *(kendang)* accompanied by a set of *angklung. Genggong,* from Penyaringin village (near Mendoyo), emulates the sound of frogs. The resonant *bumbung gebyog* employs lengths of bamboo in varying pitches, playing harmonious interlocking rhythms. It accompanies such dance dramas as Goak Ngajang Sebun ("Crow Building its Nest"). Derived from the pounding of newly harvested *padi,* it's perhaps the only music on Bali created by women.

Bull Races

Negara is famous for its thrilling water buffalo races *(mekepung),* introduced by Madurese migrants to celebrate the end of the rice harvest. The competitive races take place on erratic tracks outside Negara, beginning about 0800 before the heat makes the big bulls sluggish. Mostly locals attend this festive event—there's lots of rooting and cheering, and the betting is frantic. It's possible to attend rehearsals, trials, and competitions, and even to commission a bull race.

There are also year-round races held for tourists every two weeks, usually every second Thursday at 1500 on a special track near Perancak, 10 km south of Negara. Though the course length and rules are identical to the real thing, the competition last only an hour. To see a race, contact Peanuts, tel. (0361) 75259, in Kuta; it costs Rp20,000 entrance at the event or you can join a tour for Rp55,000 which takes in the race, lunch at Lalang Linggah, Pura Rambut Siwi and a tour of the pathetic zoo next to the racetrack.

Only the island's handsomest, sleekest water buffaloes are chosen to compete. Teams are divided into two clubs, the Eastern Division (east of the Ijo Gading River) and the Western Division (west of the river). Look for the red banners of the east, and the green flags of the west. Organized by the regional government, trials are usually held in the dry season on the second and third Sundays in September and October. The Bupati's Cup occurs on the Sunday before Indonesian Independence Day in the town square in Negara. The even more prestigious Governor's Cup takes place on a Sunday in October. The dates and places are different each year, so get current information from Negara's Department of Tourism on Jl. Setia Budhi behind *kantor bupati*.

Before the race the bull's horns are painted and around their necks are placed decorated harnesses and silk ribbons. After teams are paraded before the crowd of spectators, their ornaments are stripped off and the beasts teamed with their brightly clad jockeys. Each pair of bulls pulls a small two-wheeled cart (a modified *cikar*) manned by a precariously balanced jockey over a two-km-long stretch of back road converted to a racecourse. To gain speed, the jockeys twist the bulls' tails and lash their backs with whips. Entrants are judged not only for speed, but are also awarded points for strength, color, and style. These heavy, awkward looking, normally docile animals can reach speeds of up to 60 kph. The winning bulls are used for stud and fetch up to twice the market value when sold.

A variation of the *mekepung* is the *megembeng,* in which a pair of bulls is harnessed together and decorated with elaborate ornaments. Huge wooden bells *(gembeng)* are hung around their necks, making a distinctive sound as the bulls race across the field dragging the colorfully dressed jockeys behind them on skids. The only other places traditional bull races are held are on the home island of Madura off the northeast coast of Java and near Singaraja in Buleleng Regency on Bali's north coast.

MEDEWI

Twenty-four km east of Negara, and 72 km (Rp2500 by *bemo*) west of Denpasar on the main Gilimanuk-Denpasar road is the small, peaceful seaside resort of Medewi, offering an excellent sand-and-rock bottom surfing beach. Formerly this area was a thick forest of thorny trees; the Balinese name for the thorny forest was *alas meduwi.* The forest was cleared and settled in 1912 and rice fields and coconut plantations planted. Today, Medewi gets about 700 visitors a month. Pura Rambut Siwi, six km farther west, is the main tourist site of the area.

Coming from Negara, as you're heading downhill in the eastern edge of the village of Pulukan, turn right before the bridge and drive or walk down the asphalt road to the turn-around area just before the sea. This headland offers constant, cool sea breezes, a public toilet, fishing *jukung* in the mornings, soft sunsets, the perfect dark shape of Java's Gunung Ijeu, and the twinkling lights of Banyuwangi in East Java far in the distance. Brown-sand Pantai Medewi is very quiet, with no dogs and few roosters, only the sound of the waves. Up on the main road, catch *bemo* to Negara (Rp1500) or Tabanan (Rp2000). Medewi is Rp1000 and 25 km west of Balian.

Surfing

The very rocky, flat shoreline along this coast provides little sand to lie on. The surfing in front of Medewi's beach is known for the length of the ride. Paddle out from Medewi Beach Cottage and try the high, rolling, uninterrupted, left-point break, its peak finishing in the river's mouth. It's easier to get out there in low tide with booties. Or reach the surf via the river to the west—a long paddle. One can also rent *jukung* for Rp10,000 to take you out for a couple of hours. During the full moon, the waves are best at midtide. Lately, Medewi has become popular with Japanese surfers. Another little-known surfing beach is Selabih to the east.

Accommodations

Three accommodations sit at the end of a tarred road. The best is the **Tim Jaya Hotel** which has rooms and *lumbung*-style bungalows (Rp10,000-25,000) with inside *mandi.* Run by friendly houseboys, everything works—electricity, plumbing, showers, fans. Rooms are nicely furnished with good mattresses and clean bed linen. The bungalows are situated in a grassy yard that slopes down to the beach.

One hundred meters east along the beach is a *warung* run by I Gede Suyasa where you can order tea, coffee, snacks, and *nasi campur.* Behind his *warung,* in his homestay Gede rents two rooms in two raised bamboo bungalows for Rp15,000 s, Rp20,000 d; less in the low season, with common *mandi.* Another homestay, **Ketut's,** charges Rp10,000 d.

Across the road still farther to the east from the Nirwana is first-class **Medewi Beach Cottages,** Box 26, Negara 82217, Bali, tel. (0365) 40029, or fax 41555; Rp88,000 s, Rp100,000 d for standard units, or Rp120,000 s, Rp138,000 d for ocean view suites with air conditioning, satellite TV, refrigerator, terrace, private bath, and hot water. Rooms with garden views are Rp88,000 s, Rp100,000 d. Amenities include a pool, well-designed grounds and gardens, ample parking, bar, and restaurant with fairly high prices—Rp9000 for Indonesian or American breakfasts, Rp23,000 for lunch or dinner. All prices subject to 15.5% government tax and service. Major credit cards accepted. Good folks work here. A romantic spot for honeymooners. Every Sunday night there's a *joged bumbung* folk dance in the garden of the Medewi Beach Cottages starting at 2000. Free for guests of all of Medewi's hotels; just buy drinks and food. Bamboo *gamelan* accompanies this dance.

Food
One can eat cheaply. Boys come around selling lobsters for Rp25,000-30,000 per kilo (two to five lobsters per kg, depending on size). Gede will cook them for you in his *warung;* he also offers soup and an entree for only Rp2000-5000. The *warung* at Tin Jaya has an outstanding traveler's menu serving tasty fish dishes, jaffles for the Australian contingent, and the Indonesian standards. Check out the *warung* (good *gado-gado*) on the main road. The best eating for the money is at Chinese-style **BMC Hotel and Restaurant,** a 10-minute walk along the highway from Medewi Beach. Go toward Denpasar on the main road. It's a little ways up on the left after you cross the bridge. Try the superb *mie kuah ayam* (Rp2500) and *sate* (rabbit *sate!*) served by friendly and beguiling waitresses. Sometimes offers shrimp. The BMC Hotel also rents rooms: most are pretty sub-standard; the few good ones go for around Rp25,000 d.

VICINITY OF MEDEWI

Rambut Siwi Temple
On the south side of a deserted stretch of the Gilimanuk-Denpasar highway between the villages of Yeh Embang and Yeh Sumbul, 17 km east of Negara, is a shrine and several *warung* selling fruit and flowers. Here is the start of the one-km narrow asphalt road to Pura Rambut Siwi, the regency's most important temple. A *pemangku* blesses truck drivers who don't have time to pray at the main temple. At the end of the road is a parking area, garden, toilet, pavilion, and *warung* selling fresh local fruit. At the carved gateway travelers are blessed, asked to make a donation, then given a sash to wear before proceeding into the red brick and stone temple complex through a side entrance.

Its name means "Worship of the Hair" in reference to the 16th-century Hindu priest Sanghyang Nirantha. The priest stopped in the village of Yeh Embang in 1546, leaving a symbolic gift of his hair as a gesture of esteem for the devout villagers. View the panorama of rice fields from the pavilion north of the complex, walk through the temple, then descend to the long narrow black-sand beach below. Walk east down the beach and take the stairway back up to the small road which leads again out to the main highway.

Special because of its simplicity and natural location, this beautiful clifftop sea temple is shaded by frangipani and *cempaka* trees and hugged on two sides by *sawah.* Except during festivals, it's very peaceful here. The temple anniversary occurs every six months, when worshippers arrive from all over the island to ask blessings for safety and prosperity. Like all temples, Rambut Siwi consists of three principal enclosures. The entrance is guarded by beautifully carved wild boars and *naga;* the structures are of aged red brick and stone. Inside are shrines to Saraswati (symbolized by a goose) and the rice goddess. To the side of the gate to the second courtyard, note the *pedanda* being swallowed by a snake. An impressive *candi bentar* on the southern wall opens onto the cliff with the surf lapping below. Since 1988 the Bali government has been shoring up the more precariously perched buildings threatened by the sea.

Flanking the main temple is **Pura Penataran** 100 meters to the east on the rocks up a winding stone stairway. This is the original temple, believed to be the site where Nirantha first prayed, and since 1993 the site of a permanent painting exhibition. See small Pura Melanting at the top of another stairway to the west. Dedicated to the goddess of prosperity, Dewi Melanting; merchants often pray at this shrine. Under an overhanging rock is the sacred five-chambered cave Goa Harimau ("Cave of the Tiger God") and the holy spring Goa Tirta ("Holy Water Cave"), where priests obtain holy water, salt-free in spite of its proximity to the ocean.

Pura Prancak

If you continue west you come the sea temple **Pura Prancak** which commemorates Nirantha's first landing on Bali to begin his teachings of the Hindu doctrine which lasted until his ascension (death) in 1550. Carved of white stone, the *pura* overlooks the slow-moving Prancak River about 150 meters to the south. Nice beach, too. To reach the temple, turn left off the highway at the village of Tegalcangkring seven km west of Rambut Siwi. After one and a half kilometers you reach an intersection with a monument. Turn right and travel nine km down a narrow back road to the sea. The temple lies on the right just before the road turns south, in all about 10 km southeast of Negara.

The Pekutatan-Pupuan Road

About 20 km east of Negara (86 km west of Denpasar), Pekutatan is where you climb steeply up from the coast to the upland village of Pupuan, then head northwest. If heading west, this is the last road north before reaching **Cekik,** three km southeast of Gilimanuk. If entering Jembrana from Siririt, enjoy sweeping views of Java and the Bali Strait to the west.

On the narrow twisting Pekutatan-Pupuan road, in the village of Manggissari, you'll ride through the gnarly tendrils of a wild *bunut* tree (similar to a *waringan* tree) at Bunut Bolong. The base is hollow and the hole big enough for a bus. The tree is very old; it is said that when the settlement of Manggissari was founded in 1928, the *bunut* was already there.

Farther on is a clove plantation; the coconut, cocoa, rubber, and clove plantations in the villages of Pulukan, Ashaduren, and Manggissari are all worth visiting. You'll pass fragrant spices laid out on mats by the roadside. See the historic Hindu temple of Bujangga Sakti, then wind down through fantastic rice terraces and coffee-growing country to Pupuan. Another popular scenic route north via Pupuan is from Antosari, also on the Denpasar-Gilimanuk road, Rp2000 by *bemo* from Denpasar.

NEGARA

Since 1803 the capital and main town of Jembrana Regency, Negara is 33 km southeast of Gilimanuk and about 100 km west of Denpasar. During the revolution, Negara's *raja-puri* was a center of fierce republicanism. The wide streets, the inhabitants faces, the wail of the mosques, the businesses all have an unmistakable feel of Java—Javanese and Buginese have settled here since the 19th century. Lately, Negara has been spiffed up with a new civic center, a big Honda dealership, and new monuments as centerpieces to new roundabouts. Yet, Negara hasn't lost its market town charm. It is perhaps best known for the *mekepung* (bull races) held between July and October, a sport introduced by Madurese agricultural migrants.

Take a *bemo* from Tabanan (Rp1500) or from Denpasar's Ubung station (Rp2000) to travel on one of Bali's busiest roads, through rolling paddy fields with mountains on the right and the sea on the left. If you want the journey to go faster, take a night bus. The downtown consists of two main parallel one-way streets. Along the four-lane bypass road Jl. Surapati in the north are the government buildings and the telephone office. The southern street, Jl. Ngurah Rai, is home to a gas station, bus station, post office, market, and shophouses.

For most tourists, Negara is little more than a pitstop on the long road from Gunung Bromo to Denpasar. The town sits inland and not on the coast, so it's not so attractive to tourists. It's a great place to practice Indonesian with the friendly inhabitants—it's also cheap. While a coffee in Kuta costs Rp1500, here it's only Rp400. The city telephone code is 0365.

Accommodations
Decrepit-looking **Hotel Ana** is a Javanese-style business hotel with 23 budget rooms for Rp4000 s, Rp6000 d or Rp6000-8000 s with *mandi.* Set in from the main street at Jl. Ngurah Rai 75, tel. (0365) 41063. No restaurant, and no fan (could be muggy), but very central. Mix with the Indonesians. Cute, garish **Hotel Tis** lies downtown on Jl. Srikandi, tel. (0365) 41034, by the river. Nine rooms go for Rp10,000 d, Rp15,000 t; Rp25,000 for rooms on top. Attached is a restaurant serving Javanese-style food like *ayam goreng.* **Losmen Intaran,** Jl. Ngurah Rai 73, tel. (0365) 41073, is another inexpensive downtown hotel. **Hotel Tjogading,** Jl. Diponegoro 5, tel. (0365) 23, is a typical small traders hotel far from downtown. Nearly across the street is the more expensive **Hotel & Rumah Makan Taman Sari,** Jl. Diponegoro 18, tel. (0365) 41154. A short distance away is **Penginapan Indra Loka,** the cheapest of the three. No sense staying in any of these, as the 25 rooms of the vastly superior Wira Pada are excellent value. At Jl. Ngurah Rai 107, tel. (0365) 41161, is Negara's best accommodation, **Hotel Wira Pada,** behind the restaurant of the same name. The tariff is Rp12,500 for quiet back rooms with *mandi* and fans to Rp20,000 for front rooms with showers. Breakfast included. The hotel's 10 spacious rooms with air conditioning and porch are a pretty good deal. Plenty of parking, moneychanger, secure, above average restaurant, and a minibus for rent at Rp100,000 per day.

Accommodations out of Town: The new Bali-style **Penginapan Segara Mandala,** Jl. Sudirman 34, tel. (0365) 41839, is opposite the *kantor bupati.* It has three units with two rooms each, equipped with bath and fan. Tariff is Rp7500 s or d. Kind of a lonely, sterile-feeling place. About 1.5 km from Negara down the main highway toward Denpasar is a sign pointing to the **Cahaya Matahari Bungalows** in Desa Batuagung. The homestay lies about one km up this country road. Ask one of the guys hanging out on the corner to give you a lift on the back of his motorcycle for Rp600-800, or wait for an infrequent *bemo.* Nice view up here 100 meters above sea level. Surrounded by *sawah,* each bungalow has twin beds, Asian toilet, shower, art on the walls, clock, electricity, and porch. The tariff of Rp15,000 s, Rp20,000 d includes breakfast and

free tea and coffee served all day. You can order a day's meals for two for Rp30,000; single meal is Rp15,000 for two. Also several small local *warung.* Except for the loud radio, this is a pleasant place run by a nice family. To book, contact Wayan Tony Villa Indah in Ubud, tel./fax (0361) 975490. It's a seven km walk to a waterfall in the hills behind the homestay.

Food
The food served in the *warung* is very Java-oriented. Try one of the many pan-Indonesian *warung* in the bus station. The clean **Wira Pada Restaurant,** Jl. Ngurah Rai 107, tel. (0365) 161, serves cheap Chinese-style *nasi campur* (Rp2000) and fantastic *cap cay* (Rp2500, but specify if you don't want chicken liver—enough for two people. The *udang goreng* (Rp6000) is among the best on Bali! Also try the great grilled fish or chicken (Rp3000-5000), fried prawns (Rp6000), or *es stroop* (Rp500).

A half-km down Jl. Ngurah Rai toward Denpasar is the "100% halal" **Rumah Makan Puas** where you can enjoy classic Javanese entrees such as *nasi plecing, nasi lele, Rawon Jawa, gado-gado,* and *pepes ikan.* Choose from an array of Javanese desserts like *soda gembira* or *es buah.* Standard prices. A smaller Javanese eatery, **Rumah Makan Caterina,** Jl. Pahlawan 17, tel. (0365) 41325, specializes in homemade *sambal* and Javanese dishes like *soto ayam* and *nasi rawon;* the *es caterina* is not so great. The foodstalls of the *pasar malam* open up at night around the *bemo* station.

The Padang-style restaurant **Papin** is five km east of town. On the other side of town on road to Gilimanuk is **Rumah Makan Miranda,** Jl. Gatot Kaca 39, tel. (0365) 41195, a real gem with delicious Balinese food. A classic *nasi campur* with tea costs only Rp1500.

Services
The **tourist office** is located within the Pecangakan Civic Centre, Jl. Setia Budhi 1, tel. (0365) 41060. A competent guide who works in this office is Ketut Lanus Sumatra, Jl. Abimanui 15, tel. (0365) 41441. The only bank with an authorized moneychanger is **Bank Pembangunan Daerah Bali,** Jl. Srikandi, tel. (0365) 41066. For medical attention, go to the **RSU,** Jl. Abimanui 6, tel. (0365) 41006; also **Poliklinik Kerta Yasa,** Jl. Ngurah

Rai 143, tel. (0365) 41248; or **Poliklinik Darma Sentana,** Jl. Ngurah Rai 151, tel. (0365) 41656. **Apotik Karya Farma** is a big pharmacy at Jl. Rama 16.

Transportation
By *bemo* it's Rp2500 from Negara to Tabanan, Rp1000 to Gilimanuk, Rp3000 to Denpasar. All *bemo* traveling the Denpasar-Gilimanuk road pass through Negara's center, stopping at the *bemo* terminal 100 meters north of the J1. Ngurah Rai roundabout. Here's where you can buy long-distance bus tickets to Java. Next door to Penginapan Indra Loka is an office selling bus tickets to Malang, Jakarta, Bandung, and Bogor, as well as Pelni ship tickets on the *Kerinci, Kabuna,* and *Umsini.* The agent in **Rumah Makan Puas** on the eastern end of J1. Ngurah Rai also sells long-distance bus tickets.

Vicinity of Negara
Negara's population has a noticeably strong Javanese, Madurese, and Sulawesi element. Muslim Buginese settlers from southern Sulawesi founded the town of **Loloan Timur** in 1653. Here, the sea-faring Bugis culture is most obvious in the oblong two-level wooden dwellings built on high piles. This architecture is found in no other village on Bali.

Visit the busy fishing port of **Pengambengan,** 10 km southwest of Negara; motorized *prahu* pulled up on the beach, sardine canning facilities, prawn-breeding ponds. The secluded beach at **Candikusuma,** 12 km west of Negara, boasts excellent bathing and swimming. Legend says a holy well here, marked by a triangular-shaped monument, was the bathing place of Nirantha's wife. Another beach, **Pantai Rening,** 10 km west of Negara, features black sand, sea cliffs, and a dramatic view of the mountains of East Java. Swim and windsurf at the beach in the village of **Dlod Brawah** about four km south of Mendoyo, 11 km east of Negara. The sand is said to be of great benefit to those suffering from rheumatism. A good road to the beach brings you to a parking area, toilet, and *mekepung* arena. Crowded on Sunday and holidays. Up the side of a mountain, 20 km inland from Negara at **Asahduren,** is a large clove plantation.

THE MELAYA AREA

Blimbingsari and Palasari
For many years after conquering southern Bali in 1908, officials of the Netherlands East Indies attempted to bar Christian missionary activity on Bali. The Dutch wanted no interference in the well-integrated religious life of the Balinese, who oftentimes opposed—sometimes violently—Christian proselytizing. But in the 1930s the government relaxed its hands-off policy.

With the tacit consent of the Dutch Resident, a Chinese missionary named Tsang was sent to Bali in 1929 by the American Christian and Missionary Alliance to work among the Balinese Chinese. Tsang soon began to win converts, first among the Balinese wives of the Chinese, then among Balinese of the lower castes. He promised the Balinese freedom from taxes and corvee work gangs if they converted. By the mid-1930s, several hundred converts had been exiled from their own villages. The swelling numbers of new Christians soon caused unemployment and housing problems in Denpasar.

Meanwhile back in Holland, missionary groups protested that an American fundamentalist church was allowed to establish itself on Balinese soil. Under pressure, the Resident expelled Tsang and allowed Netherlands-based Protestant and Catholic churches access to Bali. The 1930s were a period of worldwide economic recession and a time of unrest on Bali. The number of converts steadily increased throughout the thirties. In 1939, to relieve the tensions between Christian and Hindu Balinese, Christian agricultural communities were constructed in a part of Bali nobody wanted—the sparsely populated, malarial swamps of western Bali, 25 km northwest of Negara.

Blimbingsari (pop. 1,900), a big Protestant community, was hacked out of the jungle in the form of a cross in 1939. The Blimbingsari church features a high, sweeping roof with three distinct tiers representing the island's mountains. Christian congregations from all over Bali consider this striking church with its graceful Balinese lines their "Navel Church." Even though the total culture of Bali is an *adat* system subordinated to all-powerful religious beliefs, at times it seems that the culture is even stronger than the religion. For example, the island's churches of all denominations, are decorated with typical Balinese motifs, incorporate the standard Balinese architectural features of split gateways and *kulkul* towers to summon worshippers, and practice and teach classical Balinese music and dance, but with biblical stories and characters rather than those of the Hindu epics.

Blimbingsari, only 10 minutes inland by road from Melaya and 30 km northwest of Negara, is one of the best kept villages on Bali, the rice production one of the highest in Indonesia. A number of families put up visitors; ask the *kepala desa,* a nice young man. For breakfast eat *pisang goreng,* Bali cookies, and coffee or tea. Families also offer lunch or dinner, or you can eat in a *warung.* Give a donation—Rp15,000 would be a fair amount. Visit people making *tuak* and processing copra, or swim in nearby Grogogan Dam.

The Catholic community of Palasari (pop. 1,700), five km to the southeast, has the largest Catholic church in eastern Indonesia, with a parish of over 700. Unfortunately, both Blimbingsari and Palasari are dying villages because all the young people are leaving. The roads to both villages are terrible; to get to either, hire one of the *ojek* that cluster around the corner of the turn-off roads and the main Denpasar-Gilimanuk highway.

The Palasari Dam
Located in a mountainous area in the village of Palarejo near Ekasari, 26 km northwest of Negara, this dam was built to prevent floods, provide a source of water for irrigation, and as a fish breeding pond and place of recreation, bringing great economic benefit to an impoverished area. The high elevation assures breezes and a cool temperature. *Prahu* for fishing and paddling about are for rent, and there are a few scenic walking trails. The dam is a beautiful 20 minutes drive on a bad road from Blimbingsari through the hills and fields of *ladang.*

GILIMANUK

This ferry port at Bali's westernmost tip—88 km from Singaraja and 134 km from Denpasar—links Bali with East Java across a narrow strait, Selat Bali. Looming up purple through the haze to the west are three of Java's most easterly volcanoes. Much of Bali's imports and exports, and most of its domestic tourists, pass through this point. Except as an around-the-clock ferry terminus, Gilimanuk has little to offer tourists, who usually alight the ferry or landing barges from Java and shoot straight through to Denpasar or Lovina. But with its basic no-frills services and amenities, Gilimanuk is a friendly little town for stopovers, for resting up.

History
The strait that separates Java and Bali, less than three km wide and only 60 meters in depth, is said to have been formed by some mythical king who, hoping to excommunicate his son, gouged a line with his finger along the ground. Then the earth parted and the waters of the Indian Ocean and the Java Sea rushed in, separating Bali from Java.

It was an easy matter for neolithic humans hunting in the primeval wilderness of East Java to cross this narrow strait. During WW II, stone adzes and pottery fragments were discovered just two km south of Gilimanuk at Cekik. Over time, about 100 burial places were excavated—containing funerary objects, simple tools, earthenware vessels, and sacrificed animals—demonstrating that this was Bali's earliest human settlement discovered to date. See these neolithic artifacts in the Bali Museum in Denpasar, the Archaeological Museum in Pejeng, the archaeological project at Sanglah, and at Gilimanuk's Museum of Ancient Life north of the Bay of Gilimanuk.

Gilimanuk shows a greater influence from Islamic Java than other parts of Bali. In fact, it was from Java that Balinese revolutionaries derived their material and ideological sustenance in their fight to oust the Dutch. In Cekik a war memorial commemorates landing operations by the Indonesian army, navy, and police on Bali from April to July 1946. Boarding a large number of outrigger canoes under cover of darkness, Indonesian irregular troops set off from Banyuwangi in East Java and landed at three points— Melaya, Candikusama, and Cupel—along Bali's southwest coast. The republic's first sea conflict took place during these operations, and fierce land battles erupted as the Indonesians came ashore. Many lost their lives. The survivors fled to the hills, where they joined units from earlier landings and engaged in guerrilla warfare.

Accommodations

There are plenty of places to stay. Cheapest are the **Kartika Candra** and **Homestay Gili Sari** (Rp8000 per person, no breakfast), both on the main street in the east side of town across from a mosque loudspeaker. **Pondok Asih** charges only Rp10,000 d for clean rooms with private bathrooms and tea and biscuits in the morning. The young employees are very helpful and very interested in female guests but harmless and just bored. Gilimanuk's best hotel, only 500 meters from the ferry, is the **Nusantara Dua,** facing a quiet mangrove-fringed beach with a lovely view of the mountains of Taman Nasional Bali Barat. Attractive and peaceful grounds with rooms for Rp10,000 s to Rp20,000, depending on room and bed size. Also a row of dark, depressing *losmen*-style rooms with squat toilets for a budget Rp8000; no breakfast. Bungalows with attached garden *mandi* farther down the beach run Rp25,000 s or d. More central but noisier **Penginapan Putra Sesana,** on the road toward Denpasar, has 11 small, tight rooms for Rp10,000 s, Rp15,000 d. No fan, small Indo-style toilets; restaurant.

Food

There's a long row of *warung, rumah makan,* and *kaki lima* by the ferry terminal where you can also buy fresh seasonal fruit. Several *nasi padang* restaurants are right across from the terminal; a good one is **Rumah Makan Meriah.** The **Rumah Makan Bakungan** on Jl. Gilimanuk, a half km down from the Putra Sesana, is the town's best restaurant. Order from the English menu if you can't read Indonesian. Particularly good is the *gado-gado* and *ayam kecap* (Rp3500).

Services

Visit the friendly staff at the **Government Tourist Information Centre** on Jl. Muhara beside Hotel Nusantara to pick up their map and brochure. I Ketut Lanus Sumatra is a fount of information on Jembrana, speaks quite good English, and can arrange almost anything. The town now has a **Wartel;** change money in the bank across from the *bemo* terminal or at Nirwana Homestay opposite.

Transportation

Take *dokar* or one of the Hondas clustering around the terminal to anywhere in town for Rp500-1000, or rent a motorcycle for Rp4000 per hour. From Gilimanuk's *bemo* station, *bemo* head out regularly to Denpasar until 2200 (Rp4000, two hours, 134 km). Dark red *bemo* also travel regularly to Singaraja via Lovina until around 1800 (Rp3500, 88 km). Less crowded minibuses travel to Singaraja/Lovina for Rp4000 or to Denpasar's Ubung for Rp4500.

Crossing from Gilimanuk over the Bali Strait to Ketapang on the Java side takes only 30 minutes and costs Rp450 deck class, Rp650 for the more comfortable lounge. Bicycles are Rp950, motorcycles Rp1800, cars Rp7500. Ferries depart 24 hours a day every 20 minutes during the day and about every 30 minutes at night; the crossing takes only 30 minutes including loading and docking time. Watch for pickpockets. The coffee in the *ekonomi* class lounge is terrible. Buses to Surabaya (Rp3500, five hours) wait for passengers on the Java side. Agents all over Bali will sell you a ticket to any point on Java that includes the ferry crossing. In Banyuwangi, eight km south of Ketapang, is a major bus terminal if you miss out on a cross-Java bus at Ketapang.

If there's room, you can also board one on the Gilimanuk side. Or hitch (politely) the lorry drivers or tourists driving their own cars. Another ferry terminal is 2.5 kilometers before the main ferry terminal if you're coming into town from the Denpasar side; motorcyclists will take you to the bus station (Rp500).

The Northern Route

Consider a different approach by heading up Bali's north coast road, visiting some of the island's most serene beach accommodations. The road between Gilimanuk and Singaraja (88 km) is also very scenic bicycling country, mostly flat with only a couple of hills. Not as much traffic as on the Gilimanuk-Denpasar road.

The lagoons and extensive mangrove swamps north of Gilimanuk harbor an unusual variety of wildlife. Pulau Menjangan, off Bali's northwest coast, is famous for its snorkeling and scuba diving. This marine reserve is part of **Bali Barat National Park,** the last wilderness area on Bali. Access to the park is easiest from Labuhan Lalang, about 25 km northeast of Gilimanuk. Three km south of Gilimanuk in Cekik is the park headquarters. For details on the park see "Buleleng Regency."

BOB RACE

TABANAN REGENCY

Tabanan is one of Indonesia's richest rice-growing districts, with paddies stretching from the coast to as high as 700 meters on the lower slopes of the imposing Gunung Batukau volcano (elev. 2,276 meters), the second highest mountain on Bali. Every temple in Tabanan contains a shrine venerating this mountain's spirit, Mahadewa. Tabanan's other major summits are Sangiyang (2,093 meters) and Pohen (2,063 meters).

Three labor-intensive crops of the new high-yield rice are grown each year, with soybeans planted in between to rejuvenate the soil. The *subak* of Tabanan average seven to eight tons of rice per hectare, making the inhabitants some of the most productive rice growers in all Indonesia. Besides rice, there are crops of coconuts, cacao, groundnuts, and tropical fruits. The area around Pupuan is Bali's principal coffee growing district. The regency's higher climes are alpine, with mountain streams, moss, prehistoric tree ferns, wildflowers, creepers, orchids, leeches, butterflies, birds, and screaming monkeys. Lake Bratan in the middle of the regency's cool central highlands was formed by the volcano Gunung

Catur, now inactive. The area is green, opulent, and peaceful, the people generally friendly. As you leave Tabanan's southern plains and drive north to Bedugul on Lake Bratan, the cooler landscape changes from tiers of gentle rice fields to gardens of onions, cabbages, and papaya. Thatched palm huts give way to sturdy cottages made of wood, tile, and stone to withstand the heavy rains. In the southern villages, the kitchen is separated from the other buildings of the family compound, but in these cold mountain villages people often cook in the same building where they sleep and live.

For the traveler, Tabanan Regency offers remote mountain villages with fresh, crisp air; picturesque hill resorts; overflowing fruit, vegetable, and flower markets; austere lakeside temples; premier montane hiking; one of world's finest golf courses; a 30-km-long strip of unspoilt black-sand beaches; and perhaps Bali's most famous and photographed temple, the island sanctuary of Tanah Lot.

Tabanan is targeted as the next big tourist area. Why? The region is far from the bustle of city life, hawkers, and everyday hassles. Its attractions are accessible on day trips from Denpasar or Kuta, or tourists can stay within the regency—new accommodations are built as soon as electricity and water became available. There are ambitious plans for the regency's isolated coastline, and a new road is under construction connecting Kuta and the mammoth Bali Nirwana Resort in Tanah Lot. Balinese fiercely resisted this US$200 million property sited next to one of the island's most sacred temples—an angry anti-development march in Denpasar was quelled violently by police—but in the end the resort rose and opened in 1995.

History

The regency has a lively history. Records indicate it came under the suzerainty of King Airlangga in 1037. When Majapahit invaded Bali in A.D. 1343, the territory was allotted to one of Gajah Mada's field generals, Arya Kenceng. Tabanan's classical period was in the 17th century and included the founding of the main *puri* by Raja Singasana. Tabanan, Mengwi, and Penebel were almost constantly at war until 1891 when Mengwi was defeated by the princes of Tabanan and Badung. Through a series of court intrigues, assassinations, truces, and marriages, the prin-

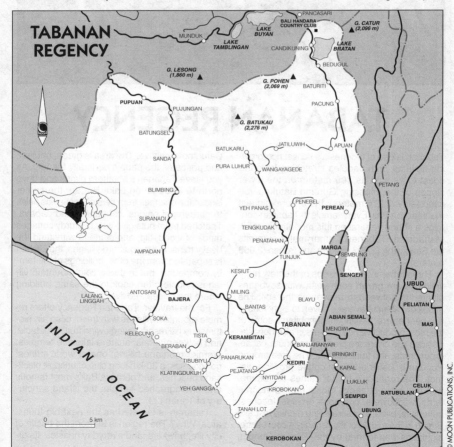

cipal houses of the district—Kaleren and Krambitan—were formed in the 19th century. When the Dutch conquered Bali in the early 20th century, they captured the king and crown prince (who committed suicide while in captivity), sacked the Tabanan palace, and exiled most of the surviving royalty to Lombok. The Dutch controller's office was established right in front of Puri Kaleran, but it was the outcaste marriage of a high-ranking princess that finished the kingdom for good. Since the rajadom had not entered into an agreement with the Dutch, the heirs lost their titles and lands, which were parceled out to the regency's *banjar.* Some historians believe this early redistribution of land to the peasants accounts for Tabanan's prosperous rice economy today. In 1929, the Dutch reorganized Bali's kingdoms into eight regencies, restoring the raja's titles and authority, a status that lasted until 1950, when Sukarno abolished Indonesia's royalty with the stroke of a pen.

The Arts

Although the rajas of Tabanan's royal houses lost political power in the early 1900s, they continued to support the arts. Their palaces have long been famous for *gamelan,* dance, and drama groups. The regency's most famous native son was I Ketut Mario, the consummate dancer and choreographer who dominated Bali's performing arts in the 1920s and '30s. The solo *kebyar* dance, which he created, is still widely performed. In the seated version, the dancer not only exhibits his skill as a graceful contortionist but also his mastery of the music, parodying every nuance and mood of the *gamelan* rhythm. Tabanan's large concert hall, Gedung Mario, built in 1973, is named after this genius. Commemorative performances are held there each year in his honor.

The Chinese-Balinese painter and *batik* artist Kay It was one of Bali's most promising and unique painters until his sudden death in 1977 at age 39. Born to a family of shopkeepers in Tabanan, It's brilliant, modern, impressionist painting style was full of life and movement. He was also a master of clay and ceramics, which he learned from the villagers of Pejaten. Today you can see its ceramics and tall totem poles on the grounds of the Bali Hyatt Hotel in Sanur. Its continuing influence can also be seen in the designs of household ceramics for sale in the markets of Bali. View his paintings at the Art Center in Abiankapas in Denpasar and at the Neka Gallery in Ubud.

Events

A genuine Balinese feast is put on for tourists about three times monthly in Krambitan's Puri Anyar. Every year a purification ceremony *(melasti)* occurs several days before Nyepi, and every five years a much grander exorcism is held in which thousands of youngsters march from Gunung Batukau to the sea. Don't miss the splendid *odalan* every 210 days at Tanah Lot, when dances are performed on the beach below Beraban village opposite the offshore temple.

Beaches

It seems that every side road in Tabanan ends in a deserted, steep, beautiful black-sand beach. Enjoy stunning views of the sea with the mountains and rice terraces behind—no dogs, no tourists, not even a fisherman. Drawbacks, if you're not a surfer, are the three-meter-high waves and lethal undertows. French and Italian joint venture companies plan to develop the best of these beaches; hotels have already gone up at Yeh Gangga, Beraban, Kelating, and Soka. Big waves crash over black sand at Kedungu Beach, west of Tanah Lot. Nice views, beautiful rice terraces, and a Japanese golf course nearby. Thirteen km from Tabanan is long, wide Kelating Beach, with big rolling waves and beautiful panoramas.

Pasut Beach, near Sungai Ho and Pura Segara, is a quiet beach lying 14 km southwest of Tabanan. The Ho River is navigable by small sampan. Northwest of Pasut (24 km from Tabanan) is Beraban Beach, which offers excellent budget accommodations. Even more isolated, with great views and rice terraces, is Kelecung Beach west of Beraban. The most westerly of Tabanan's beaches is Soka, between Antosari and Lalang Linggah. The rocks said to be the pot and old kitchen of Kebo Iwa, the legendary figure who carved Gunung Kawi.

SOUTHERN TABANAN REGENCY

TABANAN

The regency's capital as well as the commercial and arts center. Lying in the heart of Bali's thriving rice belt, Tabanan's town center is bustling with small industries and many Chinese-owned shops. East- and westbound traffic streams in and out of this medium-sized town on several one-way streets.

Visit **Puri Tabanan,** the ornate traditional residence of the raja and the seat of a powerful kingdom from the 17th to 20th centuries. The Kingdom of Tabanan consisted of a large number of rich and powerful *jero* and *puri*—the most influential were the rival houses of Puri Anom and Puri Kaleran. During the 1945-48 period of violent political turmoil on Bali, Tabanan swarmed with anti-Dutch activities. On the edge of town is the **Pancaka Tirta Cemetery,** where Republicans killed in the conflict are buried.

Prior to 1989 Tabanan was a dirty shophouse town, but when the new *bupati* was elected that year new buildings and a new market were built. There's now a supermarket, gardens and sidewalks beautify the roadways, and an efficient waste disposal system is in place. The town has even won prizes for cleanliness; some say it's the best-organized town on Bali. Today the place is booming, attracting even lawyers and a notary republic.

Though seldom visited by tourists and not known as an art center, Tabanan is actually rich in dance and art traditions. There are classical poetry *(kakawin)* clubs, it's been a woodcarving center since the 19th century, and the town is home to a famous *gamelan* and the much acclaimed dance troupe Rama Dewa. Five km east of Tabanan in the village of Abiantuwung the dance masters *(sarjana senitari)* of the **Sanggar Tari Warhatnala** ("School of Dance") train Balinese and foreign dancers. If coming from Denpasar, the school is on the right (16 km from Denpasar). See the sign by a big *pura* and *waringan* tree. Contact director I Gusti Ngurah Supartha, a well-known choreographer and musician.

Gedung Marya

Named after I Ketut Mario, Bali's preeminent choreographer and dance master of the 1920s and '30s who singlehandedly created the *kebyar* and *terompong,* this building is in front of the Puri Tabanan. Dances are staged here only in June during the art fair *(pesta seni)* and for Independence Day celebrations on 17 August. During the fair you may see the *kebyar, arja, wayang kulit,* and *lomba-lomba* festival.

Accommodations

There are few hotels in Tabanan. Since the selection is limited and substandard, it's best to push through and stay outside the city in more agreeable seaside accommodations at Yeh Gangga, Tibubiyu, or Balian Beach. If you have to stay, on the east side of town is **Hotel Sederhana,** Jl. Saha Dewa, tel. (0361) 811708, right across from the police station; Rp8000 s, Rp12,000 d. Clean and quiet. Opposite the *bupati* office is the trader's hotel **Taruna Jaya,** Jl. Dharma Wanasa 1, about the same price as the Sederhana. If coming from Denpasar, turn left at the Rumah Sakit, east of the *bupati* office.

Food

Eat bargain meals in the *pasar senggol* (open 1700-2400) east of Gedung Marya. Also good, simple food at Terminal Pesiapan, Tabanan's bus/*bemo* station. One of the best *nasi padang* restaurants around is the **Murah Meriah** in the bus station. People from all over Bali associate Tabanan with a spinachlike vegetable called *gondo* (or *sayur pelecing*); try a dish in the *pasar senggol.* Tabanan is also a good place to buy *brem.* In the *nasi padang* restaurant **Pura Bulia,** Jl. Gajah Mada 45, a quite good *nasi campur* is served. Reflecting Javanese influence, there's another Muslim restaurant as well. **Taliwang Bersaudara** on Jl. Gatot Subroto specializes in *ayam goreng, ayam pangang,* and other Sasak dishes. On the other side of the road is the Indonesian restaurant **Taman Senggulan,** which is famed for its baked fish. **Toko Makanan Sedia,** on the main street Jl. Gajah Mada, is a small Chinese restaurant with tasty food.

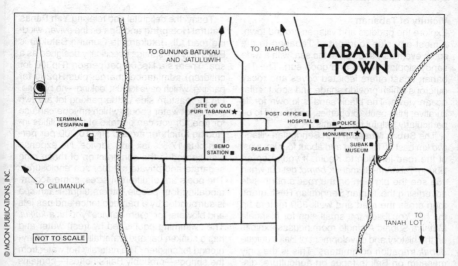

Shopping
Tabanan is one of the best and cheapest places on Bali to shop for everyday articles. The big market for the whole regency is in the middle of Tabanan, selling even exotic items like avocados. This busy *pasar* is neater and cleaner than most markets, and the sellers don't hassle you. Shop here for clothes, shoes, *krupuk,* and household and electronic goods. Also for sale are *sarung,* ceremonial clothes, and temple umbrellas. **Toko Swardana,** Jl. Gajah Mada 41, tel. (0361) 811249, has a beautiful collection of reasonably priced clocks, watches, alarm clocks, perfume, and sunglasses. Check out the supermarket **Nanushka Utama Pusat Perbelanjaan,** about three km before Tabanan on the way from Kediri. About 1.5 km from Tabanan on the road to Kediri is **Miranda Fashion Clothing Store.**

Services
The **tourist information office** is on Jl. Gunung Agung, tel. (0361) 811602, on the east side of Gedung Marya; see Pak Ketut Suaba. **Change money** at the BPD Bank, which accepts traveler's checks at fair rates, on the main street Jl. Gajah Mada. For **phone calls** to Australia, Europe, and the U.S., try the telephone and telegraph substation (Perumtel Telekommunikasi) on Jl. Anggrek in a new Balinese-style building. Tabanan has a big **hospital**—including an optometrist—on the main road coming into town from Denpasar.

Getting There
From Denpasar, take a *bemo* from Ubung station (Rp800) or follow the main highway west toward Negara through the villages of Sempidi, Lukluk, and Kapac, arriving in Tabanan after 20 km. Or take a *bemo* from Denpasar's Ubung station heading to Gilimanuk and get off in the town center.

Getting Away
The Tabanan bus station (Terminal Pesiapan) is on the west side of town. From this terminal big Isuzu vans head for Mengwi, Rp500; Denpasar, Rp800; Bedugul, Rp2000; Negara, Rp1750; and Gilimanuk, Rp2500. All *bis malam* leave from Terminal Pesiapan; arrive one hour before departure. A bus ticket office is in Warung Ani, Jl. Gajah Mada 128. If coming from Gilimanuk, the office is before the row of shops on the left. Long-distance bus ticket fares are Jakarta, Rp56,500 (departs 0700, 24 hours); Bandung, Rp50,000 (0700); Bogor, (0700); Surabaya, Rp21,000 (1900); Malang, Rp21,000 (1800); Yogyakarta, Rp38,000 (1530). Another *bis malam* office is east of Bank Republic Indonesia.

Vicinity of Tabanan

Explore the paddies and villages around town. Almost any side road out of Tabanan to the south eventually ends up at the sea, with a wide sandy sloping beach and good surf. The Tabanan coast offers isolated coves and rocky outcrops which provide shade and spectacular ocean views. The black sand is known for its curative, therapeutic properties, and is said to be particularly helpful for arthritis.

The **Subak Museum** is in Senggulan village two km east of Tabanan and about four km west of the road junction to Kediri. If you're on an Ubung-Tabanan-Gilimanuk *bemo,* get out when you see the big sign on the road's north side advertising the Taman Senggulan Restaurant, then cross the road and walk 350 meters up the hill. You'll see the small sign for Mandala Mathika Subak. A single room houses exhibits on the history and development of Bali's unique *subak* irrigation committees. This is the only museum on Bali to focus on agriculture, displaying farming implements for cutting, cleaning, and pounding rice; tools for leveling land, ploughing, weeding, and digging water tunnels; various fish traps; tweezers for catching eels; wooden nets used to catch dragonflies; a miniature kitchen with utensils used for cooking rice; a scale model of a farming *kampung;* and old-style structures. Open daily 0730-1830, closed Sunday. By donation.

NORTH OF TABANAN

Yeh Panas

The holy spring of Yeh Panas Penetahan, about 12 km north of Tabanan. Japanese soldiers stationed in Tabanan used to visit this spring during the war to refresh themselves in its hot, pungent, sulphurous mineral waters. They widened the track to the spring, and built small bathing sheds. In the 1960s luxury tourist villas were constructed at the best vantage points around the spring, but the project lacked financing and the buildings were abandoned. The shells were soon occupied by invisible spirits *(memedi);* the voices of women were heard wimpering in the night. To discourage these new occupants from settling in permanently, the remaining structures were used to shelter pigs and cattle.

Today, the delightful and relaxing **Yeh Panas Natural Hotspring and Spa** on the sylvan winding road (Jl. Batukaru) to Gunung Batukau is Bali's only hot springs specifically designed as a spa. There's a Rp500 per person (Rp300 for children) admittance charge, plus Rp250 for parking, which pays for just looking—no bathing. On the eastern side of the parking lot are two public hot water spouts which anyone can use for free. Or you can partake of the facilities including lunch for around Rp110,000 per person plus 17.5% tax and service. No expense was spared in the construction of these nine separate and private outdoor spa enclosures. The pools are of different sizes, some accommodating four people, others eight. Each spa is surrounded by a bamboo fence and has jets and blowers; for "room service" you hit a *kulkul.* The swimming pool is fed by fresh water and has a sunken bar and waterfall. There's a playground for children. The naturally hot water from the springs—probably Bali's hottest—contains sulphur, potassium, sodium, and small percentages of minerals, with no additives except an occasional dose of chlorine. The water, it is said, will relieve itching and heal skin diseases.

The comfortable restaurant, overlooking the rushing river, serves expensive drinks (Rp5000 for a large Bintang), and Western, Indonesian, and Chinese food, pizza, and pasta. For more information and reservations, contact Varianusa, Jl. Raya Kuta 15 X, Denpasar, tel. (0361) 262356.

Marga

The **Margarana Monument** in Marga is 15 km northeast of Tabanan. This memorial park honors a regiment of guerrilla fighters killed here by a Dutch ground attack and aerial bombardment shortly after WW II. The Dutch far outnumbered the Balinese, many of whom were armed only with sharpened bamboo poles. The engagement was a shattering defeat for the Balinese resistance movement, killing many of its original leaders. So many high caste cadre lost their lives that the battle marked the beginning of much heavier participation of lower-caste guerrillas. The aristocratic leader of this futile stand was 29-year-old Lt. Col. I Gusti Ngurah Rai; Denpasar's airport is named after him. The Battle of Marga was joined after the Indonesians refused a Dutch demand for surrender. After a series of clashes in Tabanan, Rai's platoon set out on a long march to Gunung Agung, seeking to draw attention away from a landing on Jembrana of Republican troops from Java. The ploy was discovered by the Dutch, who attacked and annhilated the Balinese force at Marga on 20 November 1946 with the aid of a B-25 bomber. In all, 96 Balinese guerrillas were killed.

The Margarana ("Battle of Marga") monument was built in 1954. In the middle is a 17-meter-tall, eight-roofed monument shaped like a Javanese *candi*, designed to symbolize the unity of the fallen revolutionaries in their fight for freedom.

A strange, eerie feeling permeates this place. The memorial stones of 1,372 men and women, Muslims, Hindus, and Christians, who died on Bali fighting Dutch forces lie in a cemetery here, including 11 Japanese soldiers who defected to the Indonesian side. Christian tombstones bear the cross, Muslims the half moon, Balinese the swastika. The monument is inscribed with the text of a famous letter Rai wrote to a Dutch officer, pledging to give his life for the revolution.

Marga is not a regular tourist stop, there will probably be few people here, but it is worth a visit. Every 20 November, a Hero's Day Ceremony is held here with a reenactment of the "Long March." Attended by *pemuda,* scouts, and soldiers, this eight-hour march to Denpasar lasts from evening to the early morning. Visit the small museum on the grounds (open 0800-1200) exhibiting uniforms, weapons, documents, photos, battle plans, and remnants of the battle.

KEDIRI AND VICINITY

Alas Kedaton

Four km north of Kediri in Kukuh village is a temple surrounded by a lovely, state-owned sacred forest with cool, peaceful walking paths. In and around the temple cavort more than 700 friendly monkeys, while *kalong* hang from the treetops. This monkey forest is smaller than Sangeh's, and the monkeys seem better behaved. At least three families live completely separated from one another in the forest.

On the way to the temple from the parking lot, you'll pass through an art market. The custom now is for a young girl to escort you (tip her

Rp500) and help you feed the monkeys. These girls will tell you that they'll get in trouble with the boss if you don't stop by their shop and buy something on the way out. Just laugh and do it. Near Alas Kedaton in the vicinity of Sangeh is Carangsari village, a miniature Ubud with *losmen,* restaurants, and *warung.* Beautiful rice fields.

Kediri

Four km south of Tabanan in Kediri is the site of one of Bali's largest cattle markets. Amid a din of human and animal sounds and pungent smells, game cocks, potbellied swine, lumbering oxen, squealing geese, squawking ducks, and soft golden-brown cattle are sold and traded. Other equally animated and exciting cattle markets are held in Bringkit near Kapal and Bebandem near Tirtagangga.

In Kediri's *puri* is a particularly honored historical relic, the magic *kris* of the Javanese priest Nirantha. Known as Jaramenara, this holy object was left with the village headman as a token of Nirantha's gratitude just before the saint went off to Ulu Watu and his final transcendence. Every Kuningan festival the *kris* is removed and washed in a special ceremony.

All Ubung (Denpasar)-Gilimanuk *bemo* pass through Kediri (Rp1000, 30 minutes). The town's *bemo* terminal is at the junction where the road branches right for Tabanan and Gilimanuk and left for Tanah Lot (12 km to the southwest).

Pejaten

Just four km southwest of Kediri (12 km south of Tabanan) is this small and friendly pottery village of one-story thatch compounds squeezed between two rivers, covering an area of 1.5 square km. Untouched by the modern world, Pejatan has long been known as a center for hand-decorated, wheel-thrown pottery and ceramic roof tiles. The red clay was traditionally mined on village land until it began to run out in the early '80s. In 1985 the villagers started experimenting with high temperature porcelain, and within a few years Pejetan was turning out not only washbasins and pots but porcelain dinner sets, elegant bowls, delicate animal figurines, and open lattice-work filigree vases. High-fired porcelain is much less fragile than traditional terra-cotta. Before long, the ceramic pieces were in high demand at Bali hotels, restaurants, and shops.

Roof tile-making, however, remains the primary economic activity of about 90% of the town's 4,000 inhabitants. Widely used by the island's building trade, these dull red terra-cotta tiles with reliefs of gods, goddesses, and *wayang* heroes are patterned after a style first introduced by the painter Kay It. Check out the fanciful ornaments, called *jambangan,* popularly used to decorate the apex of thatched roofed houses. Pejaten's humorous, grotesque standing clay figures—inspired by the stories of the Ramayana and Mahabharata—decorate gardens and walls all over Bali. A big, jolly, clownish terra-cotta fat man goes for Rp50,000, weighs about 15 kg, but is quite fragile since the sculpture isn't high-fired. You'll also see huge 80-cm unglazed earthen water jars for about the same price. Clay is imported from the Malang area of East Java.

Smoke from dozens of coconut husk-fueled brick kilns billows from the yards of the village *kampung.* Any ceramic worker will lead you to one of dozens of workshops. There are only two retail display rooms, open daily 0800-1800, about one-half km from one another. At **Tanteri Ceramic's,** tel. (0361) 91897, work can be seen in their showrooms in Pejaten and Candidasa and in the **Griya Art Market** in Sanur. Tanteri's makes the best tiles. Pejaten's other showroom is **Pejaten Keramic** (ask to see additional inventory in adjoining building). This outfit has its works displayed in Ubud.

The best pieces are the glazed Chinese-style ceramics with beautiful ornamentation. Look for unique animal shapes—fish, lizards, frogs, turtles, monkeys—which climb out of sugar bowls, lidded bowls, teapots, stopped perfume jars, soap dishes, ashtrays, cups, covered clay glasses, and napkin holders. Colors are flat, pastel shades of gray-green celadon, light blue, or ivory. Order a whole dinner set for six to 12 people, made specifically to your design. As you browse in the showrooms, you realize that prices aren't that cheap: Rp5000-10,000 for simple pieces, Rp45,000 and up for more involved work. And don't expect startling artistic merit—craftspeople in Europe, Australia, and the States are just as original and charge about the same price. These are more curios than art pieces. On hand are factory-produced sure sellers which are duplicated over and over again. Look for the unusual.

Seven km north of Tanah Lot, Pejetan is easily reached on a narrow, beautiful country road west of the main west-to-east road. Just follow the signs. An even more scenic way is the nine-km back-country road from Krambitan. Head east, cross over the bridge in the dip, then turn right at the intersection to Pejetan via Seronggo (a popular fishing spot), Curah, Sudirmara, Bedha (a large agricultural temple), then Pejetan. Be ready to stop for festivals and ceremonies on the way. After Pejaten, go six km southwest to Tanah Lot for the sunset.

YEH GANGGA

On the beach six km from Tanah Lot is Yeh Gangga ("Holy Water"). Four two-room bungalows and one bungalow with four rooms are offered by **Yeh Gangga Beach Bungalows** (formerly Bali Wisata). Each room is well furnished, with two beds, fridge, and fan. No air conditioning, but it's breezy. Some bungalows have kitchens. Tariff is Rp40,000-60,000 d, breakfast included. The owners are conscientious, knowledgeable hosts with exemplary attitudes on local culture. The hotel caters mostly to a European clientele. Javanese-style food at reasonable prices is served in the hotel's small dining room (order dinner in the morning), or try the delicious *nasi bubur* (Rp500) in one of the *warung* in the village. A spring on the property provides fresh water for the hotel. Watch CNN in the restaurant each evening at 1900, or browse in the library. Free pickup from the airport. For bookings, write Box 131, Tabanan 82101, or fax (0361) 261354.

The best thing about Yeh Gangga is the location. The bungalows overlook rice fields, cacti, picturesque offshore rocks, and empty Yeh Gangga Beach, where religious processions frequently end. Borrow the hotel's dinghy and explore along the river. You can't swim in the ocean here because the riptide is too dangerous. The hotel has a nice, unchlorinated pool and bathhouse. The whole area is untouristed, and the government won't allow any more hotels to be built here. You can arrange a car from the village. Occasional *bemo* run from the village 10 km northeast to Tabanan via the hamlet of Geybug.

To Tanah Lot

It's a six km walk (one hour, 20 minutes) southeast along the shore to Tanah Lot. Leave early in the morning so you can cross the river at low tide, then walk along the beach to a cliff where there's a small temple complex that's even more beautiful than Tanah Lot. Descend to the beach again, totally deserted for about one km. On the next cliff, after a few small stores, turn left and follow the stone path to the end of the street, then right, and follow the path parallel to the ocean. Cross a creek, climb a hill, cross a river, and you arrive in Tanah Lot, missing the parking lot, stores, restaurants, entrance fee, and donation. For more walks and bicycle rides in the area, refer to Yeh Gangga Beach Bungalows' photo album and information booklet.

TANAH LOT

Like a delicate Chinese painting, this small, pagoda-like temple 13 km southwest of Tabanan sits on a huge eroded outcropping of rock offshore. Tanah Lot ("Sea Temple of the Earth") is only one of a whole series of splendid sea temples on the south coast of Bali, all paying homage to the guardian spirits of the sea. So that these spirits may be constantly propitiated, allowing pilgrims to walk between them, each temple is visible from the next along the entire southern coastline. On crystal-clear days from Tanah Lot you can just make out Pura Uluwatu.

Legend has it that the temple was built by one of the last Brahman priests to arrive in Bali from Java, Sanghyang Nirantha, a man remembered for his successful efforts in strengthening the religious beliefs of the populace and for founding several of Bali's most dramatic 16th century *sad sanghyang* temples. At that time, the area's holy leader, Bendesa Beraben, jealous when his followers joined the newcomer, ordered the Hindu saint to leave. Using his magical powers, Nirantha left by simply moving the rock upon which Tanah Lot is built from the land into the sea, changing his scarf into the sacred snakes that still guard the temple. Later, Bendesa Beraben converted wholeheartedly to Nirantha's teachings.

Incomparably situated off a black volcanic sand shore, Tanah Lot is one of the most photographed and sketched temples in Asia. Watch the hypnotic sunset from the park opposite the temple, its oddly shaped rock silhouetted against a blood-red sky. Tanah Lot is actually only one reason to come here; this relaxing nearby park is another. Follow the paths to the cliff-top temples in the vicinity—Pura Batu Bolong, Pura Batu Mejan, Beji Taman Sari, Pura Enjung Galuh. There are many vantage points from which to view Tanah Lot, the best from Pura Enjung Galuh on a bluff just west of Tanah Lot.

The whole site is well-maintained; commercial activities are in keeping with its peaceful isolation, charm and holiness. The tacky souvenir stands are outside the park. A favorite of the multitude of domestic tourists who visit Tanah Lot are the scores of poisonous snakes *(ular suci)* sleeping in sandy holes just above the waterline along the beach. When the tide is out, they slither into the temple. The locals believe these snakes guard the sanctuary from intruders, and great care must be taken by all who visit the temple not to disturb or anger them. The snakes are the property of the temple's guardian spirit.

Big crowds come to pray here even though the structures that make up the Tanah Lot complex are actually quite unremarkable, consisting of just two pavilions and two black thatched-roof *meru* shrines—one with seven-tiers, dedicated to Sanghyang Widi Wasa, and the other with three-tiers, dedicated to Nirantha. Like all Bali temples, Pura Tanah Lot celebrates *odalan* once every 210 days; the birthday falls close to the festivals of Galungan and Kuningan, when ancestor spirits are invited to visit their family shrines. Four days after Kuningan, Hindus from all over Bali come laden with rice cakes, fruit, carved palm leaf, and holy water to pray to the Hindu gods and goddesses. Women bear towers of votive offerings on their heads, waiting until low tide to safely walk over a concrete-reinforced walkway and up rock-cut steps to the solitary temple. At high tide, when the walkway is submerged, the incoming waves can get pretty ferocious.

Fees are required to park your vehicle and walk through a gauntlet of souvenir stalls onto the rocky beach opposite the temple (Rp550).

Only Hindu devotees may actually climb the temple stairway and enter the grounds. Time your arrival for low tide, which is around noon at times of the full moon. From Tanah Lot a beautiful panorama unfolds as headlands jut out into the sea and heavy surf pounds the rock, throwing spumes of spray high into the sunlit air. To prevent further erosion around the south side of the temple base, unsightly concrete tetrapods have been lowered into the sea by helicopters to help "protect" the temple.

Accommodations and Food

Tanah Lot has enough amenities—postal agent, telcom office, minimarts, moneychanger, restaurants, accommodations—to make for a very comfortable sojourn. During the day, escape from the tourist throngs clambering over the temple by sightseeing elsewhere in Tabanan Regency, returning at night to have the place to yourself, mingling with the small service population of friendly Balinese delighted you came to the temple to stay a few days.

The closest accommodations to the temple is **Mutiara Tanah Lot,** tel. (0361) 812939, fax 22672, with eight bungalows facing the sea. Half with air conditioning (Rp92,000 s or d), the other half have fans (Rp80,000 s or d). Price includes breakfast, tax, and service. The restaurant presents a pricey tourist menu. A breezy, quiet, and meditative place to stay. A big complex near the art market is **Dewi Sinta Cottages,** Box 8, Tabanan 82171, tel. (0361) 812933, which charges Rp50,000 for deluxe, air-conditioned family rooms. The seven non-air-conditioned standard rooms for Rp32,000 are a better deal. Plain but undeniably quiet. Most rooms have private baths, hot water, and shady veranda overlooking *sawah.* Amenities include safe-deposit boxes, nice grounds, *wantilan*-style convention hall, sometimes *kecak* performances at night. See the assistant manager, I Ketut Sudiartana. The **Tanah Lot Losmen** (Rp10,000 s) is at the entrance of the village opposite the police post. Another *losmen,* without a name, is located on the other side of the market; only Rp10,000 s or d, bargained down from Rp25,000. The rooms are pedestrian with Indonesian-style, floor-level toilets and no shower, but the place faces the ocean and is incredibly clean. No meals available, but free tea or coffee. On the main road coming into town on the left are a group of drab little fan-cooled bungalows (Rp15,000-20,000) set back from the road behind an art gallery; look for the sign that just says Losmen. There is plenty of cheap, semitourist places to eat like **Warung Made;** cheapest of all are the *warung* in the *bemo* station/parking lot. **The Dewi Sinta** and **Mutiara** restaurants are more expensive but still affordable.

New on the scene—some would call it an ugly and irreverent blight on the scene—is the US$200 million, 121-hectare **Bali Nirwana Resort,** tel. (0361) 5705021, fax 4705030. Complete with 156 five-star luxury Rp655,000 villas, championship golf course, thalassotherapy spa, racquet sports center, and shopping complex. Basic units start at Rp200,000.

Getting There and Away

The most scenic way to reach Tanah Lot is to walk at low tide six hours (14 km one way) up and back from Kuta. Wear a bathing suit, as the rivermouths along the way can be forded. Time your arrival for Tanah Lot's spectacular sunset. You can also reach the temple by driving from Denpasar toward Tabanan and Negara, then taking a left (southwest) at Kediri's stoplight down a side road that leads after nine km to Tanah Lot's parking lot. Tanah Lot is about an hour's drive and 31 km to the northwest of Denpasar.

Most of the travel agents in Bali's major resorts include Tanah Lot as an almost de rigueur stop. Minibuses and *bemo* depart Denpasar's Ubung Station for Kediri (Rp1000, 30 minutes), from where you take *bemo* onward to Tanah Lot (Rp600, nine km, 30 minutes). *Bemo* departures slow down in the afternoons, so if you want to arrive by sunset you might have to consider alternate transport. When you're ready to return to Denpasar or Kuta, don't wait too long after 1600 to get a *bemo* back to Kediri so you can connect with another *bemo* to Denpasar. Otherwise you might have to charter a ride on the back of a motorbike, or walk. If you're staying overnight at Tanah Lot, be aware there are no public *bemo* until 1100. Just start walking and someone will pick you up, for a fee, of course. It takes about three hours to return to Kuta by public transport.

Vicinity of Tanah Lot

Within walking distance is a serene beach to the west called **Pantai Nyanyi,** with black sand, big waves, and beautiful views, especially during the full moon. About 13 km from Tabanan. About an hour's walk away, **Kedungu** and **Yeh Gang-ga** are nice beaches along a jagged coastline northwest of Tanah Lot toward Negara.

KRAMBITAN DISTRICT

Six km west of Tabanan is Krambitan, a small district located in a prosperous agricultural region. Terraced rice fields surround the district's villages. If you hear of any ceremonies taking place in the countryside, drop everything and go out to see them.

The main village is Krambitan, about eight km southwest of Tabanan (Rp500 by *bemo*). Though it lacks an inexpensive *losmen,* this village makes an excellent base from which to visit Tanah Lot, Mengwi, Pejaten, Alas Kedaton, Gunung Batukau, and Bedugul. Five km to the south of Krambitan village are the black-sand beaches of Pasut and Klating. Located on either side of the mouths of two rivers, these beaches are clean and graced with native *jukung.*

Krambitan Village

Not by accident is the name Krambitan derived from the Sanskrit *karawitan,* which means "art, music, and dance." This small, attractive village is renowned for its classical literature, *legong* dancing, *wayang*-style painting, stone- and woodcarving, and a *tektekan* orchestra believed to have magical powers.

The painters of the village belong to a school begun by Gusti Wayang Kopang and I Macong in the 1930s. The style is similar to that of Kamasan except that the teeth and the costumes are depicted differently. Ask the friendly villagers the way to the unique **Luhur Ulun Desa** temple dating from the neolithic period.

Krambitan was the seat of a branch of one of the old ruling *triwangsa* houses of Tabanan, the legendary court of Arya Kenceng. The village still contains old-style residences, as well as two treasure-filled 17th century gilded palaces, Puri Gede and Puri Anyar, lovingly restored by the family of the *puri.* Cultural programs and dinners have

been presented here since 1967. Identical twin grandsons—Anak Agung Ngurah Oka Silagunadha or "Pak Oka" and Anak Agung Rai Giri Gunadhi or "Pak Rai"—of the late king preside over the palaces. The two princes are the ninth generation of royalty to occupy the palace, with Pak Oka designated as head of family because his birth preceded his brother's by 30 minutes. Inside the *puri* traditional dancing and arts are kept very much alive. The *puri* also arranges special tourist events such as traditional-style dinner parties accompanied by *legong, tektekan,* and *joged* performances. Overnight guests are welcome in Puri Anyar, *gamelan* lessons can be arranged, and you are invited to join the village's *lontar*-reading or kite-flying clubs.

Puri Anyar

Inside the royal compound are peaceful gardens, pavilions with unusual gold-plated carvings, and many charming traditional buildings filled with well-preserved antiques and art objects. In perfect harmony with this setting, Pak Oka maintains an unmistakable royal bearing. Ask him to show you his "celebrity" corner in the family living quarters; on the wall are framed photographs of Pak Oka with all the distinguished guests who've visited the palace—King Hussein, Prince Bartiel of Sweden, Kurt Waldheim, Mick Jagger, David Bowie, and that of a famous *kabuki* dancer.

The *bale gong* (concert hall) in front of the *puri* houses art work, the royal orchestra, and an impressive collection of musical instruments, *kris,* and sacred masks. On the right as you enter the *puri* is a courtyard containing the family shrines, embedded with Chinese and Dutch porcelain and tiles. One rare blue Delft piece dates from the Napoleonic period; Bonaparte can be seen on horseback.

Tektekan

Not actually a dance but a procession of men carrying bamboo split drums and giant cowbells around their necks, this classical, very old orchestra is played to exorcize malignant spirits when an epidemic, serious drought, or pestilence befalls the village. The ceremony accompanies the Calon Arang, a legend dating from the 10th century in Java. Puri Anyar's *tektekan* is made of bamboo, whereas the typical Balinese *kebyar gong* is made of bronze. This unique ensemble marches through the village only on the day before the Balinese New Year, whenever an exorcism is required, on certain auspicious days, or by special order of the raja when a tourist bus arrives. The drama must be accompanied by blood sacrifices (a small chicken or duck) at both the beginning and end.

Puri Night

Your inestimable host Pak Oka puts on monster banquets for as many as 300 Dutch cruise passengers, or big groups of Italians, French, or Germans who really lap it up. This magical evening begins with *tektekan* dancers carrying enormous tick-tocking cowbells and lighted torches greeting buses full of astonished European tourists. Behind the men are lines of maidens performing a welcoming dance.

The guests are then invited into the second open-air courtyard to seat themselves around the central *cempaka* tree at candlelit tables with young coconut leaf settings. Delicious Indo-Chinese food is brought in by a procession of servers. This buffet dinner (pay extra for beer) is the ultimate dining experience for those who like Balinese food served in the traditional manner. After dinner, the guests are invited to dance the *joged.* What follows is one of the most mesmerizing *kris* dances on the island, a version of the Calon Arang legend performed to the beat of hypnotically tuned bamboo tubes. To drive away the demons, some of the players become entranced, arm themselves with *kris,* and attack Rangda. The last part of the dance can be so dangerous no one is allowed to use a flash for fear of snapping the dancers out of their deep state of trance. Half the village is there looking on.

Taking place about three times a month, this special event is usually reserved for private parties only. With permission, individuals may attend a large, already-booked Puri Night paying separately, or commission a private performance with dinner. For more information, contact Pak Oka at tel. (0361) 812774 or Mr. Ajus Erawan, Jl. Anyelir 23, Denpasar, tel./fax (0361) 233774.

Accommodations

Treat yourself to an amazing stay in one of 12 rooms (including four princely rooms) in the maze of **Puri Anyar,** a fully functioning Balinese palace. The full-board tariff is Rp175,000 for a whole bungalow, or Rp46,000 for one room in a bungalow with garden *mandi,* hot water, fan, and a big four-poster bed. One ornate, gold-leaf decorated bungalow is called the royal pavilion and features a bathroom with a cascading waterfall. Breakfast is included, lunch is Rp16,000, dinner Rp25,000. Pak Rai may take you kite-flying on the beach with a packed lunch, or you can jog in the countryside north and west of Krambitan. For bookings, contact Pak Rai at his office at Jl. Surapati 7, tel. (0361) 812668. Book in advance with a tour agent or through the tourist office in Denpasar. If they're full, you can still attend a Puri Night.

Vicinity of Krambitan

One km to the west of Krambitan is **Tista,** a village renowned for its unique version of the *legong—legong leko,* which is only danced around Tabanan. In this social dance, two tiny *leko* dancers wearing *legong* dress and headdresses are accompanied by the melodies of the *janger.*

Unusual and slightly incongruous is Penyalin's, a Chippendale furniture factory located close to where the road to Krambitan leaves the main road to Gilimanuk. The showroom features tables, chairs with velvet cushions, rolltop writing desks. The pieces are mostly carved by hand, though there is some routing work; high prices.

Two km south of Krambitan is **Panarukan,** a village known for its many fine wood and stone sculptors and a smaller version of *tektekan.* Visit the studio of Panarukan's most famous native son, the modern painter Ajin Ida Putu Cegeg. Only two km beyond Panarukan is the wide and empty black-sand beach of **Klatingdukuh,** offering fine views of the coast. Follow the road about nine km southwest of Krambitan to wide, quiet, black-sand **Pasut Beach** with waves up to three meters high. At the beach, turn southeast and walk 20 km to Tanah Lot.

Tibubiyu

The ceremonies in the tidy traditional village of Tibubiyu, four km beyond Krambitan, are almost unceasing. As in days of old, performances take place right on the street. *Tektekan* dances can be arranged for groups of eight or more. Tibubiyu consists of 300 families who grow rice and vegetables. This village doesn't even have an eating *warung,* only one small stall that sells cigarettes, salt, coffee, drinks, and batteries; no newspapers or telephones. The market takes place daily at 0500.

BeeBees Restaurant and Bungalows is undoubtedly one of the best traveler's hotels on Bali. Run by Australian artist Barbara Miller and partner Dewa Made Suamba Negara, these six rustic yet comfortable *lumbung*-style thatched bungalows with garden bathrooms are set in an attractive compound. The tariff is Rp32,000 s, Rp40,000 d, including a breakfast of coffee, fruit, and toast. Book directly through BeeBees, Tibubiyu, Krambitan, Tabanan 82161; Denpasar fax (0361) 36021.

Bee Bee's open-air restaurant looks out over a broad expanse of rice fields stretching to the sea. The menu offers most Indonesian standard meals plus Western breakfasts. Its strength, though, are the delicious Balinese entrees like *tum* and *gundo.* Try the Village Combination (Rp2000), a vegetarian *nasi campur.* The drink list includes small bottles of Balinese *brem* (Rp2000), ginger tea (Rp800), and brandy coffee (Rp1000). Check the blackboard for three-course daily specials (Rp8000), usually pork or chicken. Not a place for pub-crawlers; this is the gentle side of Bali. Groups of painters attend painting workshops here. There's always a cooling breeze, and in the evenings you often need a jacket. A bucket of hot water is offered to guests at shower time. Ask the Queen Bee to fetch Pak Guru Rasin, who gives superb traditional massages (Rp5000). Laundry service available. Airport transfers arranged on request, Rp40,000 for a chartered *bemo,* 46 km, 1.5 hours. The village *bemo* driver often comes by BeeBees early in the morning to see if anyone wants to go to Denpasar.

Getting Away: Take local *bemo* on the main street of the village to Ubung Station in Denpasar (Rp2000) or Tabanan (Rp1000). From Bee Bees, follow the path through rice fields (10-minute walk) to the well-formed beach—fine, glistening, diamond dust black sand, with really high surf and not a structure or vendor in sight.

LALANG LINGGAH

Beautiful, unspoilt **Balian Beach Bungalows** lies near the village of Lalang Linggah, 50 km west of Denpasar on Bali's main south coast highway. Situated in a six-acre coconut plantation beside the estuary of the Balian River and within 500 meters of the Indian Ocean, this tranquil area offers excellent river swimming, surfing, miles of uninhabited coastline, fishing villages, and friendly, unaffected locals. The complex has 24-hour electricity, a small bar and restaurant, superb gardens overlooking Bali's biggest river, and a helpful staff. One of the most peaceful *losmen* on Bali. For reservations, call (0361) 234138, ext. 2842.

The Balian offers a range of accommodations, from dormitory-style bunk beds to bungalows supported on piles. The tariff includes simple breakfast. In the *losmen* block (Rp15,000 s, Rp20,000 d), each room has its own *mandi* and WC; each pair of rooms—one overlooking the river, the other the valley behind—shares a balcony. Another stilted bungalow overlooking the river is Rp25,000 s, Rp40,000 d. The Balai Gede (nicknamed Honeymoon Suite) is a traditional building with a huge platform bed. It affords the best view across the river and down to the sea (Rp40,000 s or d). Other similarly priced units face the sea. One two-room suite for Rp50,000 is suitable for a large family. Plastic accepted. Enjoy Western/Indonesian fare at the Balian's inviting restaurant. Or try **Made's Warung** one km west; reach it from the road at the small *desa* of Surabrata (take a left at the surfboard). Made uses all the surfie four-letter words, a great place to hang out while enjoying jaffles, noodles, and cold soda.

The Balian is not for ragers or low-budget travelers. Some comments in the guestbook: "Big Waves, No Babes!" and "Watch out for bats in your room!" Most of the guests appreciate the quiet, the lack of even one seller on one of the best beaches on Bali just a 10-minute walk away, and the simple beauty of the surroundings. The locale is noticeably cooler as it gets sea breezes all day, which helps keep the mosquitoes down. Though the area is too rough to swim in, the Balian River turns into a blue lagoon in the dry season and offers clean, re-freshing swimming.

Visit the small village on the coast at the mouth of the river; the inhabitants make salt and collect rocks. Also visit the fishing village at one end of the bay. If you venture around the point, you'll find a multitude of caves, tunnels, and small bays. Explore the area on foot or rent a mountain bike at the Balian.

All *bemo* from Denpasar's Ubung station pass by Lalang Linggah (Rp1500, 1.5 hours). All buses from Java to Denpasar pass the front gate; ask the driver to stop just over the bridge

on the Balian River. Or take advantage of the shuttle leaving Kuta from Sea Water Sport on Jl. Legian opposite the Bounty every Wednes-day and Sunday at 1400 (Rp5000). From Lov-ina, catch a *bemo* to Seririt and on to Pupuan, then continue south around Gunung Batukau to Antosari or Pulukan, both on the main Den-pasar-Gilimanuk highway. Lalang Linggah is 10 km west of Antosari and 20 km east of Pu-lukan. Take the Balian's transport service, or a public *bemo* into Tabanan (Rp1000, 29 km), Negara (Rp1000, 55 km), or Gilimanuk (Rp2000).

NORTHERN TABANAN REGENCY

The western uplands of Gunung Batukau are famous for their magnificent landscapes. From Wongaya Gede, take the narrow mountain road leading east to 700-meter-high Jatuluwih (27 km north of Tabanan town) with a peculiar tem-ple embellished with gargoyle-like creatures—mindful of Chinese temples. Fine views from Jatuluwih, Apuan, and Pacung, and the slopes of Gunung Batukau, Bali's second-highest mountain. Pause awhile in the **Sari Restaurant** at the scenic viewpoint in Jatuluwih. The temples Pura Natar Sari in Apuan and Pura Bukit Kem-bar in Pacung are known for their *barong* dances during the temple *odalan;* check with one of the tourist offices about times.

From these heights you can take in the whole of southern Bali to the coast, as well as the mountain range extending to the island's heav-ily forested western tip. Get to Jatuluwih early or you'll be above the clouds; it also tends to rain in the afternoons. If the scenic but rough road through steeply terraced rice fields hasn't been rendered impassable by heavy rains, reach Jat-uluwih directly from Pura Luhur.

The farmers of Jatuluwih cultivate a special variety of rice called *padi bali,* which grows up to 120 cm in height. The rice is fluffier and more fragrant than the new "miracle rice" varieties more recently introduced. *Padi bali* can only be harvested twice a year whereas the new types of rice yield three crops a year. No accommoda-tions in Jatuluwih; neither are there sellers.

On the way south to Tabanan town visit the *pura puseh* in Penebel. The phallic linga and vagi-

nal yoni in the *bale* west of the gate to the inner courtyard, represent Shiva and his consort Uma. While in the Penebel area stay in super **Taman Sari Bungalow & Coffee House,** tel. (0361) 812898, in Dukuh village. Tariff Rp35,000 s or d, including breakfast. Facilities include restaurant, fishing pool, and local and international telephone service. Clean, nice gardens, and right next to a rambutan orchard that slopes down to a river. Ask manager I Made Rumadi about treks and jeep tours around Bali and Lombok.

Perean

On the road north from Mengwi to Bedugul take the turnoff west to the village of Perean, about 30 km from Denpasar. Balinese *meru* are almost al-ways made entirely of wood, but in the com-pound of the grand old temple here, **Pura Yeh Gangga,** the body and foundation consist of stone. On three sides of the *pura* are niches, on the fourth is a mock door with a stone carving in the shape of a lock. Porcelain plates are em-bedded in the sides of the temple; steps from the *meru's* east side lead up to a narrow terrace. Pura Yeh Gangga is crowned with a seven-tiered thatch roof.

Dating from A.D. 1334, and first taken note of by the Dutch Archaeological Service only in 1920, the remains of three other small build-ings have also been found. The simple temple compound is surrounded by a wall broken by a *candi bentar.* Inscribed stones discovered in the vicinity bear the dates A.D. 1339 and 1429. On the opposite side of the river are several hewn-rock caves, and to the east are the hot springs, Yeh Gangga ("Water of the Ganges"), that gave Perean's temple its name.

Pupuan

Difficult to reach and seldom visited, beautiful **Bangsing Waterfall** lies in Pujungan village near Pupuan. If coming from Denpasar, the way to the falls starts down a small alley in Pujungan. Drive 10 minutes to the teahouse 500 meters before the *air terjun,* then walk in and swim in the pool beneath the falls, which is quite deep in the middle.

The coffee-growing region of Pupuan is on the spectacularly panoramic road north from Antosari to Seririt, the island's most westerly north-south road. On the way, stop in at Pura Makori in Blimbing village (32 km from Tabanan and 55 km from Denpasar) which consists of a number of stones hidden in the forest. With clean, fresh air, an ideal site for meditation.

At Pupuan, the road turns west and follows the mountain ridge, passing through clove, cacao, and coffee plantations. Since there's not a decent restaurant on the whole trip, take along some fruit and drinks for a picnic.

GUNUNG BATUKAU

Except for Bali Barat National Park, the pristine rainforest covering 2,275-meter-high Gunung Batukau is the only wilderness region left on this densely populated island. Known locally as Coconut Shell Mountain, this inactive volcano is the most westerly of Bali's three highest summits and completely dominates the regency of Tabanan. On Batukau's slopes is Pura Luhur, one of the island's national *sad-kahyangan* temples, seldom visited by tourists because of its remote location in the middle of a montane forest.

To climb Gunung Batukau, hire a guide for Rp50,000 in Wangaya Gede village two km south of Pura Luhur. From the outer courtyard of the temple, walk 200 meters to a small river, then cross the bridge and turn north up the steep trail through a thick, damp, slippery forest to the top. Only birdsong is audible and only the trail visible during the five to six hour climb. Though climbing it in one go is possible, most climbers rent a tent from their guide and spend the night near the top.

The view from Gunung Batukau's overgrown summit is blocked by trees. A small temple of roofless stone shrines is on the top. Don't attempt this climb in the rainy season, and don't even try to reach Pura Luhur by road if you don't have a sturdy vehicle with a cooling system in good working order. If you're on a motorbike, you're going to get wet.

Pura Luhur Batukau

A unique, sacred mountain sanctuary and royal temple near the peak of Gunung Batukau, 23 km north of Tabanan, built to venerate deities of mountains and lakes. All the regencies of Bali maintain temples at the temple of Besakih except for the Tabanan princes, who have their ancestral temples here. Pura Luhur served as the state temple for all of western Bali when Tabanan was an independent kingdom, and even today every temple in western Bali has a shrine dedicated to it. When the archaeologist Hooykaas visited the site in the 1920s, he discovered a number of large upright linga, so it's presumed this place has served as a sanctuary since prehistoric times. Legend says the temple was founded by the Hindu sage Kuturan who proselytized on Bali in the 11th century. This date was corroborated in 1925 when Goris discovered statues in a nearby bathing place similar to those found at 11th century Goa Gajah. Legend has it that in 1604 the temple was attacked and partially destroyed by the raja of Buleleng, but his troops were beaten back by millions of bees unleashed by the protective spirits of the temple. Pura Luhur was not rebuilt until 1959, even though pilgrims had continued to worship in the rubble.

The temple lies in a solitary clearing 1,300 meters above sea level, set amidst a garden of flowering frangipani and hibiscus, with a gigantic, uninhabited, humid tropical forest all around it. The site is often cool and has the highest rainfall on Bali. Not a very large complex, it consists of a main enclosure to the north, plus two smaller temple complexes tucked away in the forest.

Within the complex are a number of symbolically distinct shrines, each representing a different Tabanan dynasty. Many of the shrines have been newly renovated, so the place has lost a bit of its charm. One of the few temples of its type on Bali, Pura Luhur is known as a *pura taman,* which means it has a bathing place and is maintained by a king. Note Pura Luhur's seven-tiered *meru,* similar in shape to a Thai stupa, dedicated to the god Mahadewa who presides over Gunung Batukau. The shrine also exalts Di Made, a ruler of Gelgel A.D. 1164-1686.

A few meters east of the temple are steps leading past lichen-covered statues and demons down to a square artificial pool with a tiny island in the middle, a symbolic microcosm of the Hindu Mount Meru.

On the isle are two *bale,* one dedicated to Gunung Batukau and the other to the deity of the three lakes—Tamblingan, Buyan, and Bratan—which stand within its catchment area. Nearby is a small temple and sacred *air panas* bubbling up from a riverbank. Several paths lead off into the forest, the domain of cicadas and frogs.

If you get to Pura Lunur in the late afternoon you'll probably have the place all to yourself. If there's a ceremony going on, spend the whole day. Thousands of pilgrims journey to this remote *pura* during Umanis Galungan, (the day after Galungan). Regional water-opening rites are also held here; *subak* heads, *pemangku,* and *klian* carry small containers of its holy water back to their *subak* to bless similar ceremonies.

Getting There and Away

Public *bemo* only go to Pura Luhur on festival days but you can reach Jatuluwih (via Penebel) by *bemo* from where you can bargain with the driver to take you up to the temple. Board Jatuluwih-bound *bemo* from Tabanan's Tawakilang bemo station, two km north of Tabanan's center, leaving about every hour until noon. If driving yourself, first turn right a bit west of Tabanan and travel north on a steep narrow road up the southern slopes through lovely rice terraces and untouristed villages. Three km before the mid-sized market town of Penebel a turnoff west takes you to the hot springs of Yeh Panas, then on to Wangaya Gede, a village just two km south of Pura Luhur, and finally to the *desa* of Batukaru where Pura Luhur Batukau is located. Pura Luhur can also be reached from the main Mengwi-Bedugul road by taking the road east to Marga. These cool, jungled uplands have sublime landscapes, with green moss everywhere.

BEDUGUL AND THE LAKE BRATAN AREA

A small, friendly lakeside resort in the middle of the central highlands southwest of Gunung Catur, an hour's drive (48 km) from Denpasar on the main road north (30 km) to Singaraja. Bedugul is the name given to a whole string of villages along the lake's western shore. With its comfortable accommodations, wonderful fresh fruit and vegetables, lakeside views, blankets of fog, beautiful mystical quality, and an average temperature of 18-24° Centigrade, Bedugul has been a popular weekend retreat since Dutch times. It's a welcome change from Bali's tropical humidity. Few tourists stop here. If you time your arrival for the late afternoon, you can practically have Ulun Danu Temple and the botanical gardens to yourself. Bedugul has a huge Muslim population; loudspeaker chanting starts blasting from the mosque at 0430.

Serene Lake Bratan fills the ancient crater of long-inactive volcano Gunung Catur, which towers over the lake. Over 1,200 meters above sea level, Bedugul is nearly as cool as the Gunung Batur region only 20 impassable kilometers directly to the east. The cool ride up to this valley through terraced mountain vegetable gardens of cabbage, onion, and papaya is even more scenic than the ride to Penelokan.

Bedugul is a bit more relaxing and quieter—especially in the hot season—than Penelokan where there are too many grabby sellers. Like Penelokan, however, the locals seem to be spoiled by the loads of package tourists (especially Japanese), and Bedugul is a strangely expensive place. It's cheaper to stay in Lovina and charter a car or rent a motorcycle for a day trip.

The first entrance on the right as you near the top of the mountain is 100% commercial. In fact, there are so many domestic tourists swarming around touristy Hotel Bedugul that sitting quietly on the shore of the lake is impossible. Guides are available at the hotel, but their English needs a lot of work.

Across the lake are three 25-meter-deep caves (Goa Jepang) dug out by Indonesian slave laborers for the Japanese during the war.

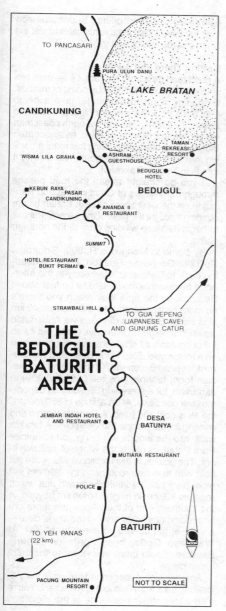

THE BEDUGUL~ BATURITI AREA

NOT TO SCALE

It is said that after the caves were constructed the workers were all shot. The caves are accessible from the rim trail to Gunung Catur. You can walk there from Taman Rekreasi in about 45 minutes.

Don't pass up the beautiful hikes along the exquisitely cultivated lakeshore and through the steep, jungle-covered rolling hills and pine forests surrounding the lake. Bedugul and the mountains around it start to cloud over in the afternoon. Overcast skies or rain cause the area to become severely cold (down to 11° C at night), so bring a sweater. A lovely *desa* called Kembangmerta, on the other side of the lake from Hotel Bedugul, is two km from the main road or just one km from Ulun Danu Temple. Dotting this whole hillside are holiday homes of rich Balinese.

Water Sports

It's really crowded here on holidays and weekends and during the vacation season, 20 December to 5 January. At other times, the lake is a quiet refuge nearly devoid of tourists both domestic and foreign. Along the pier in front of Hotel Bedugul are moored boats of every size and description. Powerboats stand ready to pull water-skiers and parasailors around the lake, or you may hire a small *prahu* (Rp5000 per hour) and paddle around the placid waters under shady trees, and glide through reflections of steep mountain slopes and fleecy clouds. Lake swimming is chilly, but early in the day when the sun's out the waterskiing on the lake's glassy surface is primo enough to attract international competitions.

In front of Hotel Bedugul is the **Taman Rekreasi** complex, admission Rp500, plus parking fee. Here you can rent parasailing (Rp20,000 for 15 minutes) and waterskiing (Rp25,000 for training, tows and use of jumping ramp) equipment. Motorboats rent for Rp20,000 per person (30 minutes, capacity four people), covered boats Rp20,500 per person for a tour of the lake, capacity eight people, and jet skis (Rp20,000 for 15 minutes). Paddleboats (Rp12,000) and wooden *prahu* are also available from private operators for paddling across to the temple; bargain intensely. Join the children fishing for minnows from the shore; fishing poles and bait cost Rp500 per day.

Accommodations

Don't settle for the limited selection and high prices in just the market village of Bedugul. Check out accommodations in each of the different communities of the area—Pancasari, Candikuning, Bedugul, Pacung. It's a spread out area and it helps to know where you're going.

Three km south of Candikuning in Bedugul village at the junction of the road to Taman Rekreasi is basic, 10-room **Strawbali Hill,** tel. (0362) 23467. Ten *losmen*-style rooms with private *mandi* and cold water for Rp15,000 single rooms, Rp20,000 twins (breakfast included) are packed into a small compound. Tasty Indonesian food served, as well as Western dishes like salads, chicken, omelettes, and pancakes. Good value, with prices geared to budget travelers.

Hotel Bedugul (tel. 0362-226593), on the lake's southern shore, seems to have absorbed all the adjacent, less expensive hotels. This enables the place to get away with charging Rp80,000-104,000 for rather decrepit motel-style lakeside rooms. There are also 36 bungalows facing the lake (Rp70,000-115,000) with TV, private *mandi,* and hot water, breakfast included. All prices subject to 15.5% tax and service. Patronized by rich Chinese, Jakartans, and Japanese, who seem to be the only ones able to afford the waterside restaurant (lunch buffet Rp12,000). The quality of the expensive Chinese-Indonesian food is not that high. A wide range of water sports is offered. A scene for people who like people.

Between Candikuning and Bedugul is the **Mini-Bali,** appropriately named for its six tiny Rp15,000 rooms, small beds, and the truly mini portions served in its restaurant. One Rp20,000 room has a private *mandi.* Spartan yet clean.

Food

Owing to the temperate climate and heavy rainfall in these mountains, Bedugul offers a giddy selection of European and Asian produce grown on the area's fertile mountain slopes. Bedugul supplies the southern population centers and hotel resorts with most of its vegetables and succulent fruits. The *warung* near the trailhead up to Gunung Catur serve delicious *gado-gado,* fried vegetables, and *nasi goreng.* Bargain. Bedugul also features several grocery stores and lots of fruit vendors. The tourist restaurant, **Bukit Permai,** tel. (0362) 223662 and 223663,

right off the main road, offers a stupendous view over the lake. Most restaurants cater to just the lunch crowds and close by 2000.

Getting There and Away

A good road runs from Singaraja's western bus station to Bedugul, Rp2000 by *bemo* or minibus. If heading north to Singaraja, take a *bemo* (Rp2500) from Denpasar's Ubung Station to Bedugul—a faster route to the north coast than via Kintamani. Bands of dark, heavy-coated monkeys are often seen along this road. If coming into Bedugul from the south, the first right turn is to **Taman Rekreasi.**

If you go straight ahead the road passes through the villages of Candikuning and Pancasari on the west shore of Lake Bratan before climbing throught the pass of the water at Puncak to begin its steep winding drop to the northern plains.

By *bemo* to Mengwi is Rp800; Singaraja, Rp2000; Denpasar, Rp2500. If you're heading back to Denpasar, start early in the afternoon because *bemo* tend to fill up fast above Bedugul; by the time they reach you there's no more seating room. At the Denpasar 40 km sign below Baturiti, a dirt road via Apuan and Jatiluwih emerges at Wangaya Gede, but it's so full of boulders it'll shake the guts out of anyone on a motorcycle. Stop in the **Soka Sari Restaurant** (serving European, Chinese and Indonesian food, reservations tel. 0361-235909) in **Jatiluwih,** for a sweeping 360-degree panorama over rice fields. At an altitude of 850 meters, the air is cool and fresh. A Rangda temple and parking lot are beside the viewpoint. A two km walk into the woods will bring you to unique **Pura Petali,** as old as the village of Jatiluwih itself. The houses in this traditional village are still built with thatched roofs, and the farmers still work *padi bali,* traditionally grown rice which reaches 120 cm in height. Three km beyond, in the southern end of the village, are more unobstructed rice fields and—if the sky is clear—a view of the curved southern tip of Bali. At **Wangaya Gede,** head north for Gunung Batukau. South takes you down to the cultivated plains.

Another nice experience is to walk the 25-km-long track from Bedugul to Kintamani. You're also within striking distance of the mountain area or Munduk; just head north by road to Gig-git, then turn east. Stop in at pristine **Danau Tamblingan** en route.

Pura Puncak Mangu

This remote temple is located on the rim of the caldera above Lake Bratan. What the temple on top of Gunung Abang is to the people of the Gunung Batur region, this temple is to the people of Bedugul. Though it's one of the sacred *sad-kahyangan* temples of Bali, it's difficult to access and little known. If you're in reasonably good shape, the six-km hike along the north-eastern edge of Lake Bratan requires about 2.25 hours of hard climbing through a canopied rainforest. Bring water. Ask at the ranger station about a guide (Rp10,000-15,000)—you'll need one, especially if you intend to take the steep and arduous path down to the lakeshore.

Reach the trailhead by turning right off the main road at the Y before Bedugul; the well-marked path starts by the ranger guardpost just as the small road turns left 180 degrees to Bedugul's lakeshore recreation complex. Register at the guardpost, then walk past the trash pile. Get used to the trash. Left by Indonesian tour groups and schoolchildren, plastic bottles and discarded wrappers litter the trail all the way to the summit.

The first segment of the trail is gradual, winding through bean and cabbage patches, then it climbs through a dank *lantana* and pandanus forest with glimpses of the lake down below. You really start to climb as the mist sets in—up one steep hill, then a saddle before an even steeper section where you must pull yourself up by the roots of trees up through a slippery, muddy slope. The last 500 meters is pure torture.

At the top is a flat shady area, inhabited by gray monkeys; gaps in the dense forest provide stupendous views of Gunung Batur and Gunung Abang to the east and the mountains of west Bali to the west. Ancient Pura Puncak Mangu, built by Mengwi's first raja, is a simple, peaceful temple with a *padmasana,* shrine, a linga, some nice reliefs, and two *meru.* Camping is allowed under the temple's several *bale.* Unless a festival is going on, it's unlikely that any-one will be there.

On your return, after about one and a half km (45 minutes) there's a path to the right—marked by plastic bottles—that is very steep, slippery, and scrabbly, with loose dirt jungle weeds, scratchy vines, leading straight down for 700 meters to the lakeshore. This trek is im-possible in the rainy season. There's also a path from the back of the temple that leads down the other side of the mountain and emerges on the main road above Pancasari, but you'll definitely need a guide for this.

From the bottom, walk three km past grazing cows and thriving market gardens of cabbages, carrots, parsley, scallions, and potatoes. See Goa Jepang on the way. The path soon turns into a small road which leads to a village on the north shore, your vehicle can meet you here or you can flag down transport on the highway one kilometer farther north.

Baturiti

A village five km south of Bedugul, with breath-taking views and wonderful fresh air. Market every three days. Both accommodations and food are less expensive here than in Bedugul. The lookout restaurants of Baturiti are the only places to stop on the twisting mountain road between Bedugul and Mengwi.

The **Pacung Hotel & Restaurant,** tel. (0361) 262460 or (0368) 21043, overlooks the valley four km south of Baturiti just before Pacung. With a lovely setting, good service, and small pool, it's expensive at Rp138,000 per bunga-low with private baths, hot water, fridge, TV, and in-house video. Suite bungalows cost Rp160,000. The best of the best in the area. The restaurant offers well-prepared Indonesian and Chinese dishes (Rp4000-5000), freshwater fish, and a Westernized buffet (Rp12,000) from 1200 to 1500. Add 15.5% to all prices. About one km south of Candikuning market in Baturiti is the **Bukit Mungsu Indah Hotel,** (tel. 0361-23662 or 23663) with 13 cottages on a hill look-ing south toward the lowlands. Standard rooms are Rp40,000-55,000, superior Rp55,000-60,000 with TV, fireplace; basic breakfast in-cluded. The best rooms face the Kebun Raya botanical gardens. Cheaper rooms are smaller and have no TV. In the mornings you can see the surrounding mountains.

The **Green Valley Homestay & Restaurant,** about two km south of Candikuning market, has fantastic views, taking in Gunung Agung and rice fields to the sea. In addition to the lunchtime buffet for Rp11,000 food is available a la carte (drivers eat free). More of a small hotel than a homestay, Green Valley has rooms for Rp20,000-40,000 with TV and hot showers. The owner, Ida Bagus Wiryana, also owns restaurants in Lovina and Candidasa. Mr. Wiryana is studying for the priesthood and he is definitely a good Samaritan.

Pacung Cottages & Restaurant, tel. (0361) 25824, fax 37638, just south of Baturiti in Pacung village, is a pleasant rest stop. Rates are Rp127,000-150,000 s, Rp138,00-160,000 d, suites are Rp138,000-160,000 (subject to 15.5% tax and service). Rooms are carpeted, with private baths, hot water, and balconies. The bar and restaurant serves international cuisine (too Westernized). Amenities include 24-hour room service, heated pool, conference room, gift shop, dry cleaning, and ample parking.

Candikuning
Two km north of Bedugul, extending along the road on the west side of Lake Bratan, are the Muslim lakeside villages of Candikuning I and Candikuning II, settled by Javanese, Madurese, and Islamic Sasaks from Lombok. A Wartel is opposite the market. This is a popular fishing spot.

Be sure to visit the colorful fruit/vegetable/spice/flower market, Pasar Candikuning, north of the turn to Hotel Bedugul; in front is a statue of an ear of corn standing on a fat cabbage. Buy luscious passion fruit, jackfruit, wild strawberries, mangoes, pomegranates, and such temperate and tropical vegetables as carrots, potatoes, corn, and year-round asparagus. Try to visit during the strawberry season. This area supplies vegetables to not only the Denpasar area but also exports to other islands like Java.

PROHIBITED TO ENTER THE TEMPLE WITHOUT DECENT DRESS AND SCARF AROUND YOUR WAIST. AND FOR WOMAN HAVING MENSTRUATION

S. MOONEY

Starting prices are high: Rp3000 for a kilo of apples, Rp5000 for a bunch of vanilla pods. Don't believe them when they say they're selling saffron—this is the name for *nasi kuning* coloring and flavoring, for which they want Rp1000. Be prepared to bargain vigorously. In the back is the fresh flower market, with tier upon tier of potted ferns, hydrangeas, begonias, *cempaka,* canna lilies, and beautiful wild mountain orchids. You'll find the widest variety of ornamental plants August to September.

The Ulun Danu Temple Complex
On a small promontory jutting out from the western shore of the lake is this peaceful half-Hindu, half-Buddhist temple complex built by the raja of Mengwi in 1633. Lake Bratan is looked upon as the source of irrigation water for the southern districts, and the *subuk* shrine here is the focus of island-wide ceremonies meant to ensure a steady and continued supply of water. Periodically the temple is flooded by the rising lake, reclaimed again and again.

Turn in from the main north-south highway and into the parking lot, which faces the usual row of gaudy souvenir shops. Admission Rp500, open 0700-1800 daily. The **Ulun Danu Restaurant,** inside the well-kept temple grounds overlooking the lake, sells a big, delicious buffet Indo-Chinese-Balinese lunch for Rp12,500. From the restaurant, walk under the canopy of a huge banyan tree past a satiny lawn and gorgeous gardens with trumpet-flower trees and gladiolas—a scene of placid beauty. Observe the Buddhist stupa with intricate carvings on the left, then enter the main temple Pura Teratai Bang dominated by a seven-tiered *meru* tower. The goddess of food and drink is revered at the smaller Pura Dalem Purwa. Farther on is Pura Ulun Danu Bratan floating out on the lake with its elegant 11-roofed *meru* dedicated to Vishnu, it's seven-roofed *meru* dedicated to Brahma, and its three-roofed *meru* housing a linga to Shiva. There are also two smaller shrines. This is Bali's most important irrigation temple, the destination of pilgrims from all over the island who come to worship Dewi Danu, the water goddess.

During the first half of the '90s, Ulu Danu had few pushy sellers, lots of native Balinese, and occasional busloads of tourists. It still gets lots of Balinese, but starting in 1996 the tour companies started to include the temple in their itineraries. The site is no longer as peaceful as it was: many vendors, lots of buses, speedboats, and so on. Better to go in the late afternoon.

You can also approach Pura Ulun Danu from the lake. Any number of boatmen around Hotel Bedugul will take you there for Rp20,000 or so. From the temple, walk around the shore of the lake. If you lose interest halfway, you can always hire a canoe to take you across to Pura Ulun Danu or Bedugul.

Kebun Raya Eka Karya

The start of the 2.5-km-long road up to Bali's sprawling botanical gardens, arboretum, and mountain orchid collection lies just 200 meters south of the Candikuning market. Founded in 1959, the park is dedicated to the study of the mountain flora of eastern Indonesia. Open Mon.-Fri. 0700-1630, Sat.-Sun. 0800-1630. Entrance Rp1100 (free for Balinese), auto parking Rp500, motorcycles Rp150. Study the map at the entrance. Benches, sitting pavilions, three temples, herbarium, cafeterias, and clean restrooms all provided inside the park. It's a one-km walk from the parking lot up to the study office at the top (north) of the gardens; the office library is open Mon.-Thurs. 0700-1400, Friday 0700-1100, Saturday 0700-1230. Interested botanists should contact the office beforehand by writing Cabang Belai Kebun Raya, Eka Karya Bali, Candikuning, Baturiti, Tabanan 82191, Bali.

A branch of the Bogor Botanical Gardens in West Java, this extensive 130-hectare park is situated on the hilly lower slopes of 2,065-meter-high Gunung Pohen ("tree mountain") to the west at 1,200-1,450 meters elevation. The tallest tree in the garden's collection is the Geseng pine tree (Casuarina junghuniana Miq). Featured are a collection of 500 varieties of orchids and 668 species of local and imported trees.

Also expect to see lilies, poinsettas, bougainvillea, bamboo, palms, and such rare species as *Podocarpus imbricatus* and *Pinanga Javana*. The plants are meticulously arranged in family and species order, specimens are labeled in Latin while park signs are in Indonesian.

Like a huge, beautifully landscaped, cool, green, inviting country estate, this is a superb place for a picnic or shady stroll. If you're looking for peace and solitude, avoid the weekends. An excellent eight-km undulating footpath at the garden's north side leads through the foothills of Gunung Tapak at the north end of the valley. The path comes out on the main road in Pancasari.

Accommodations and Food: On the road to the botanical gardens, at Rp15,000, the very basic **Mawar Indah** is highway robbery. The best food around is at the **Bogi Sari** on the main road; cheap, basic, good.

Ananda, a small clean *losmen* just across from the Candikuning market on the main road. At Rp20,000 with breakfast, this is a "Best Buy." Also not a bad deal is **Lila Graha,** tel. (0362) 23848, high on a hill looking out over Ulun Datu Temple and the lake, though the barbed wire installed for security reasons makes the backyard look like a concentration camp. An old Dutch wooden villa built in 1935, bungalows were added in 1970. The 15 rooms cost Rp25,000-35,000 with suites running Rp65,000. Same price during busy season; rates include breakfast. The bungalows on the side of the hill are more private and nicer but noisier. Restaurant. Around the lakeside north of Bedugul, almost opposite the road up to the Lila Graha, is **Ashram Guesthouse** (tel. 0362-22439) which caters primarily to groups. Bungalows spread out over a whole hillside next to the lake with gardens, stepping-stone paths, tennis court. The tariff is Rp30,000-70,000 for rooms with hot water, bathtub, spring beds, and terrace. The smaller Rp30,000 rooms come with cold water, no shower, no bathtub. The Ashram has two restaurants, one a delightful open-air pavilion looking out over the lake, the other in the middle of the attractive hillside garden.

In Candikuning Market, eat cheaply at **Warung Nasi Era** and **Warung Nasi Sari Sedana,** which sell inexpensive *nasi campur* for Rp2000. Or in the market buy the steamed corn on the cob, and sweet rice wrapped in coconut leaves. Try fresh lake fish and Indonesian food across the road at **Ananda.** Next door is **Ayam Goreng Jogya,** specializing in *ayam goreng.* Several doors away is **Ananda II** for Chinese food. Don't forget marvelous **Warung Ibu Hadi** on the road to the botanical gardens. One of the nicest venues for tea and dessert is the open-air patio of the **Ulum Danu Restaurant** on the lake on the south side of the Ulun Danu temple complex; good and cheap *warung* are also found in the temple parking lot.

Pancasari

A vegetable-growing and service community of Pancasari, north of Bedugul, is actually located in Buleleng Regency just over the border separating it from Bangli Regency. The **Lake Buyan Recreation Area** is on the left as you enter Pancasari from the south. There's a very scenic walk around the south side of the lake, up over the saddle, then on to Lake Tamblingan to the road around the northern side of the lakes back to Pancasari.

The family-oriented **Pancasari Inn & Restaurant**, tel. (0362) 21148, is north of Bedugul just before the Bali Handara Country Club turnoff. Though better value than the Hotel Bedugul, their high-season starting price is Rp115,000 for rooms (two per bungalow) with private bath and hot water. Furnished suites with kitchens and fireplaces at Rp160,000 are ideal for families. Extra bed Rp27,000. All rates subject to 15.5% tax and service; continental breakfast included. In the low season, the tariff could drop as low as Rp50,000 s. Room and laundry service, tennis court, children's playground, kiosk. Located in the heart of town, just five minutes from the market. The restaurant is pricey—not good value. Good views when it's not foggy. Overlooking Lake Buyan is **Bali Lake Buyan Cottages**, Desa Pancasari, Sukasada, Buleleng, tel. (0362) 21351 or 23739, fax 21388. Close to the post office, just down from the market, and 200 meters up from the main road. Consisting of just nine elegant cottages, each with two twin bedrooms, private bathrooms with hot water, spacious living room with fireplace, and dining room complete with kitchenette. Tennis court and putting green; five-minute drive from the Kosaido Country Club.

The **Bali Handara Kosaido Country Club** is just north of the lake, six km from Bedugul. Enter this internationally known hotel through Bali's largest split gate. Built in the early 1970s by the state-run Pertamina oil company, the Bali Handara is sterile and lacking charm, frequented most by golfers, particularly the Japanese. The buildings and grounds themselves remind one of an institution, and the cottages look like something from a California Highway rest stop. The clubhouse has become worn around the edges, but the club's cool, 1,142-meter-high, 6,400-meter-long, year-round 18-hole championship golf course is world-class. Masterfully designed by Peter Thomson & Associates of Australia, it's a worthy enough venue to host international golf tournaments. With tall trees and beds of flowers in riotous colors separating the fairways, the lawn virtually flown in from California, the Bali Handara is considered one of the most beautiful golf courses in Asia. It's also the only course in the world sited inside a volcanic crater. Greens fees are Rp196,000 per 18 holes or Rp108,000 for nine holes, 25% less if you stay in the hotel. The caddy fee for 18 holes is Rp14,000, and a half set of clubs rents for Rp57,000, shoe rental Rp16,000, driving range Rp10,000, a one-hour video analysis Rp230,000. There are also tennis courts (Rp14,000 per hour), a pro shop, health club, massage parlor (Rp28,000, 45 minutes), sauna and fitness center (Rp12,000), and Japanese traditional bath.

Rooms and suites with baths, adjustable heaters, and satellite TV rent from Rp196,000 to Rp800,000; Bali-style luxury bungalows with fireplaces from Rp147,000 to Rp425,000. All rates subject to 15.5% service and tax. Upscale **Kamandalu Restaurant** offers international cuisine with a novel touch. There's also a snack bar, karaoke bar, and a full bar in the lobby, visit to take in the magnificent view over the golf course, Lake Buyan, and lush mountains beyond—definitely worth the high priced coffee or beer. Reservations: Box 324, Denpasar, tel. (0362) 22646, fax 23048. All major cards accepted. Hope that the place isn't booked up by some big international petroleum company from Jakarta.

BAHASA INDONESIA

Any seasoned traveler will tell you the ability to speak the language of your host country will have a huge effect on the quality of your experience there. It's not necessary to commit to memory hundreds of complicated sentences. A basic grasp of such simple, everyday phrases as "Good morning," "Thank you," and variations of the theme "I want to eat/sleep" are enough to explain what you want, make friends, find your way, learn correct prices, and generally make your stay more enjoyable. You'll be amazed at how much you can say with only a 500-word vocabulary.

Don't worry about grammar and sentence construction at first. Just concentrate on memorizing the most important commonly used words and phrases in this appendix, all selected specifically for their value to travelers. Your emphasis should be on effective, speedy communication. The most important phrase in this section is *"Saya belum lancar di Bahasa Indonesia"* ("I'm not yet fluent in Indonesian"). Say this first, then ask your questions. If you don't first admit your ignorance, any inquiry is likely to produce an outpouring of verbiage impossible to comprehend.

At first, Indonesian might appear extremely simple. It's a nontonal language with no tense suffixes or prefixes, no case genders or definite articles, no declensions, no conjugations, not even a verb "to be." In actuality, however, the very lack of obvious rules makes it difficult to speak the language correctly or express yourself in a natural way. To speak enough Indonesian to get by is easy—easier than English. But to speak Indonesian well is another matter; it's as difficult and sophisticated as any of the world's great languages. But the surprised expressions and smiles of those you address will be your reward. *Selamat belajar!*

SPELLING

Bahasa Indonesia is written in Latin script and consists of 21 letters. Spelling is strictly pho-netic; small children after a very few years of schooling can read adult literature aloud to their grandparents. In 1972 Indonesia simplified its spelling, making revisions in the language to conform to Malay, though pronunciation remains the same. Sometimes the old spelling is used on road signs and maps, and in publications and dictionaries.

In the "new" spelling, every "j" becomes "y" (as in "yarn"), every "dj" changes to "j" (as in "jam"), every "tj" to "c" (as in "chair"), "ch" to "kh," "nj" to "ny," and "sj" to "sy." To make matters even more confusing, there are spelling variations everywhere you go, depending on the island or even the district of the island. Words from other major languages of Indonesia have also influenced Bahasa Indonesian. Many Javanese words change "o" for "a" when translated into Indonesian; Diponegoro becomes Dipanegara and Solo becomes Sala. Some Indonesians spell *tolong* (please) as *tulang*.

Until about 1947, Indonesian words on signs, maps, and other materials were transcribed using Dutch sounds—e.g., Bandoeng (Bandung) and Boekoe (Buku). Occasionally you'll still come across these archaic spellings.

GREETINGS

Selamat may be used in conjunction with almost any action word. Together they form a phrase which translates as "May your (action) be prosperous, blessed!" Thus, *"Selamat tinggal"* means literally "May your remaining be prosperous"; *"Selamat tidur"* means "Sleep well"; *"Selamat bekerja"* means "Enjoy your work." By itself, *"Selamat"* means "Congratulations" or "Good luck" (literally, "Health"). *"Asalamu alaikum"* (literally, "Peace be unto you") is a greeting used before entering someone's house in Muslim areas; the reply is *"Walaikum salam"* ("And unto you, peace").

Good morning/Good afternoon/Good night
  Selamat pagi/Selamat siang/Selamat malam

Where are you going? (a common greeting)
Mau kemana? or *Pergi ke mana?*

I'm taking a walk. (a common answer)
Jalan-jalan.

please/go right ahead
silahkan

Come in please. Please sit down.
Silahkan masuk. Silahkan duduk.

Hot today, isn't it? It will rain soon.
Panas sekali, ya? Sebentar lagi (hari) mau hujan.

It's a beautiful day, isn't it? Nice day, isn't it?
Harinya indah, ya? Harinya enak, ya?

Nice view, isn't it?
Pemandangannya indah sekali, ya?

pleased/be happy
senang

Thank you/Excuse me (Pardon me)
Terima kasih/Ma'af

Bon appetit! This food is delicious.
Selamat makan! Makanan ini nikmat sekali.

Happy Hari Raya! Merry Christmas! Happy New Year!
Selamat Hari Raya! Selamat Hari Natal! Selamat Tahun Baru!

Thanks for the invitation.
Terima kasih atas undangan anda.

Have a good trip.
Selamat berjalan.

Welcome (literally, "Good fortune on arrival").
Selamat datang.

very interesting/very beautiful (of buildings, monuments)
sangat menarik/bagus sekali

INTRODUCTIONS

How are you?/What's new?
Apa kabar?

Fine, thanks, and you?
Kabar baik, terima kasih, dan Tuan?

Don't be shy.
Jangan malu-malu.

Do you know Mr. Ali?
Apakah saudara kenal Tuan Ali?

I'm glad to meet you. (literally, "Good fortune on meeting.")
Saya senang bertemu dengan anda.

I want you to meet my father/mother.
Saya perkenalkan anda dengan ayah/ibu saya.

This is Mrs. Ahmad.
Ini Nyonya Ahmad.

Hello, what's your name? My name is Mohammad.
Halo, siapa namamu? Nama saya Mohammad.

Do you know Mr. Panggabean? I know him well.
Saudara kenal Tuan Panggabean? Saya kenal baik dia.

Are you Mr. Jones? Where are you from?
Apa saudara bernama Jones? Dari mana asal anda?

I'm from New York. Here is my card.
Saya berasal dari New York. Ini kartu saya.

May I offer you something to drink or eat?
Anda ingin minuman atau makanan?

Perhaps no. Are you sure?
Mungkin tidak. Apakah anda pasti?

You are very hospitable. It's very kind of you.
Anda sangat ramah tamah. Anda baik sekali.

Excuse me. Come again.
Permisi (asking for permission to leave).
Silahkan datang lagi.

DO YOU SPEAK INDONESIAN?

Can you speak Indonesian?
Dapatkah anda berbahasa Bahasa Indonesia?

I don't speak Indonesian.
Saya tidak bicara Bahasa Indonesia.

Please speak slowly.
Tolong bicara pelan-pelan.

Yes, a little. Just enough to make myself understood.
Ya, sedikit. Hanya cukup untuk dimengerti.

Where did you learn it? I learned it by myself.
Tuan belajarnya dimana? Saya belajar sendiri.

Your Indonesian is fluent. Your pronunciation is good.
Bahasa Indonesia anda lancar. Ucapan kata-kata anda baik.

How long have you been studying Indonesian?
Sudah berapa lama anda belajar Bahasa Indonesia?

Do you speak English? May I practice my English with you?
Apa saudara dapat bicara Bahasa Inggeris? Boleh saya praktek Bahasa Inggeris pada anda?

I'm very sorry. Perhaps another time.
Ma'af sekali. Mungkin lain waktu.

What is the name for this? What does this word mean?
Apa namanya ini? Apa arti kata ini?

What do you call this? What is this (that) called in Indonesian?
Ini namanya apa? Apa namanya ini (itu) dalam Bahasa Indonesia?

How do you spell it? How do you pronounce it?
Bagaimana mengejanya? Bagaimana mengucapannya?

What did he (she) say? Please repeat. Say it again.
Apa katanya? Coba ulangi lagi. Sekali lagi.

I understand. I don't understand.
Saya mengerti. Saya kurang mengerti.

What is *pembangunan* in English?
Apakah arti "pembangunan" dalam Bahasa Inggeris?

How do you translate *jam karet* into English?
Bagaimana terjemahan "jam karet" dalam Bahasa Inggeris?

CONVERSATION

Where are you from? I'm from the U.S.A.
Anda berasl dari negara mana? Saya berasal dari U.S.A.

My nationality is Australian/American/Dutch.
Saya berkebangsaan Australi/orang Amerika/orang Belanda.

How old are you? I'm twenty years old.
Umur berapa anda? Saya berumur duapuluh tahun.

Are you a tourist? What's your address?
Adakah anda seorang wisatawan? Dimana alamat anda?

When did you arrive here? How long have you been here?
Kapan anda tiba disini? Sudah berapa lama anda disini?

I've just arrived in Indonesia.
Saya baru datang di Indonesia.

Have you ever been here before? Where are you going?
Apakah anda sudah pernah kemari sebelum ini? Mau kemana?

Will you stay long in Indonesia? No, just a couple of months.
Anda akan tinggal lama di Indonesia? Tidak, hanya beberapa bulan.

Have you already been to Bali? Yes, already.
Sudah pernah ke Bali? Ya, sudah.

No, I've never been to Torajaland.
Belum, saya belum pernah ke Tanatoraja.

How do you like the climate of Indonesia? The climate is wonderful!
Bagaimana tentang iklim Indonesia? Iklimnya baik sekali!

Do you smoke? May I have a light (for a cigarette)?
Anda suka merokok? Boleh saya minta korek api?

What's your ocupation?
Apakah pekerjaan anda?

I'm a businessman. I go to school.
Saya adalah seorang pengusaha. Saya seorang pelajar.

My occupation is artist/sailor/teacher/writer.
Pekerjaan saya seniman/pelaut/guru/penulis.

What's your religion? I'm a Christian/Jew/Muslim.
Agama apa anda? Saya orang Kristen/orang Jahudi/orang Islam.

Are you married? Yes, I am. Not yet. Do you have children?
Apa anda sudah kawin? Ya, sudah. Belum. Sudah punya anak?

Do you like Indonesian cooking?
Apakah anda suka makanan Indonesia.

Yes, but some dishes are too hot for me.
Ya, tetapi sebagian masakan pedas bagi saya.

Will you be free this evening?
Anda tidak akan sibuk malam nanti?

Would you like to come to my house?
Maukah anda datang ke rumah saya?

Where shall we meet? Let's meet in front of . . .
Dimana kita akan jumpa? Kita jumpa saja di depan . . .

Okay, no problem. I'm sorry, I can't.
Baiklah, tidak ada masalah. Ma'af, saya tak dapat.

USEFUL PHRASES

yes
ya (Dutch spelling and pronunciation)

no
tidak (with an adjective or verb) or *bukan* (with a noun)

this, that
ini, itu (after the noun)

I do not have . . .
Saya tidak punya . . .

There is . . . There is not . . .
Ada . . . Tidak ada . . .

Yes, you're right.
Ya, anda benar.

It seems wrong. It's not necessary.
Rupanya salah. Ini tidak penting.

In my opinion. That's right.
Saya rasa or *saya kira* or *menurut saya. Itu betul* or *Itu benar.*

As much as possible.
Sebanyak mungkin.

I'm tired/hungry/thirsty.
Saya lelah/lapar/haus.

I want . . . Do you want . . .? I'm looking for . . .
Say mau . . . Anda mau . . .? Saya mencari . . .

I'm interested (in) . . . to like . . .
Saya tertarik . . . suka . . .

I need . . . I like . . . I hope so.
Saya perlu . . . Saya suka . . . Saya harap begitu.

I want to borrow . . . Do you have . . .?
Saya mau pinjam . . . Anda punya . . .?

Don't . . . I don't like that . . . I don't want . . .
Jangan . . . Saya tidak suka itu . . . Saya tidak mau . . .

I like Indonesia. Fine, okay.
Saya suka Indonesia. Baik.

I know. I don't know.
Saya tahu. Saya tidak tahu.

I think so. I don't think so.
Saya kira begitu. Saya kira tidak begitu.

I have . . . Of course.
Saya punya . . . Tentu saja.

an expression of surprise or pain
Aduh!

in the future . . . in that manner . . .
in this manner . . .
pada masa yang akan datang . . . begitu . . . begini . . .

Yes, you're right. You're wrong.
Ya, anda benar. Anda salah.

It's possible. It's not possible. To be able.
Mungkin. Tidak mungkin. Bisa or *dapat* (may) or *boleh*

I'm glad to hear it.
Saya senang mendengarnya.

Thanks for the gift. It's very kind of you.
Terima kasih atas hadiah anda. Anda baik hati sekali.

Excuse me for being late. Excuse me for interrupting.
Ma'afkan, saya terlambat. Ma'afkan, saya mengganggu.

Excuse me for a moment. May I be excused?
Ma'afkan saya sebentar. Bolehkah saya tidak ikutserta?

I beg your pardon.
Saya mohon ma'af. or *Ma'afkan saya.*

Excuse me, what did you say?
Ma'af, apa yang anda katakan?
I'm sorry, I can't help you.
Ma'af, saya tidak dapat menolong anda.

ACCOMMODATIONS

Where's a hotel? Where's a *losmen?*
Dimana ada hotel? Dimana ada losmen?

Which is the best hotel/*losmen?*
Hotel/losmen mana yang terbaik?

Please recommend a good first-class hotel.
Tunjukkan lah hotel kelas satu yang baik.

I want a quiet, small hotel.
Saya ingin hotel yang tenang dan kecil.

That hotel is near the town square, far from the airport.
Hotel itu terletak dekat alun-alun, jauh dari lapangan terbang.

Please take me to Wisma Borobudur.
Tolong antar saya ke Wisma Borobudur.

Do you have a room available? Sorry, there aren't any rooms.
Ada kamar kosong? Ma'af, tidak ada.

Can I have a room for one night?
Bisakah saya dapat kamar untuk semalam?

We have a reservation. We want to reserve a room.
Kami telah memesan kamar. Saya ingin memesan kamar.

How long are you staying?
Berapa lama anda akan tinggal disini?

I will stay two days. On Tuesday I travel to Malang.
Saya akan tinggal dua hari. Hari selasa saya terus ke Malang.

One or two people? I'm alone.
Untuk satu atau dua orang? Saya sendiri.

Single, please. Two (three) of us, one room.
Untuk satu orang. Dua (tiga) orang, satu kamar.

One room, two beds. Clean and tidy.
Kamar dengan dua tempat tidur. Bersih dan rapih.

Have you a room with a private bath?
Apa ada kamar yang pakai kamar mandi tersendiri?

hot and cold water
air panas dan dingin

How much for one night? One person?
Berapa harga satu malam? Satu orang?

What is the rate per day? Week? Month?
Berapa taripnya sehari? Minggu? Bulan?

Does the price include breakfast? It includes three daily meals.
Apakah sewanya termasuk makan pagi? Termasuk tiga kali makan.

What time do I have to check out?
Jam berapa harus saya keluar?

May I see the room first? What's my room number?
Bolehkah saya melihat kamarnya dulu? Nomor berapa kamar saya?

I'm leaving tomorrow midday.
Saya berangkat besok tengah hari.

Here is the key to your room. It's unlocked.
Ini kunci kamar anda. Tidak dikunci.

Is it safe here? First floor. Second floor.
Amankah disini? Lantai pertama. Lantai kedua.

Is there a bathroom on this floor? Where's the toilet?
Apa ada kamar mandi di lantai ini? Dimana WCnya?

Please spray my room. It has mosquitoes.
Tolong semprot kamar saya. Ada nyamuk didalam.

The mattress is too hard. I want to change rooms.
> *Kasurnya terlalu keras. Saya mau ganti kamar.*

I want a better room/cheaper room.
> *Saya minta kamar yang lebih baik/kamar yang lebih murah*

larger room/smaller room/quiet room
> *kamar yang lebih besar/kamar yang lebih kecil/kamar yang tenang*

Have you anything cheaper? Have you anything better?
> *Adakah yang lebih murah? Adakah yang lebih baik?*

I'll take this one. It'll do.
> *Saya ambil yang ini. Boleh juga.*

Please put out the light, I want to sleep.
> *Tolong padamkan lampunya, saya mau tidur.*

Please turn down the radio, it's loud.
> *Pelankan radio itu, suaranya terlalu keras.*

Just ring for service. May I have . . . ?
> *Telpon saja untuk pelayanan. Bolehkah saya minta . . . ?*

I want another pillow. Another blanket.
> *Saya ingin bantal lagi. Satu selimut lagi.*

Dutch wife/hot water/ice/ice water
> *bantal guling/air panas/es/es batu*

Please clean my room.
> *Tolong bersihkan kamar saya.*

to make a bed
> *membereskan tempat tidur*

soap/toilet paper/towel
> *sabun/kertas toilet/handuk*

I want to speak to the manager.
> *Saya mau bicara dengan pengurus.*

May I deposit my passport/luggage with you?
> *Boleh saya titip paspor/barang saya dengan anda?*

May I use your telephone?
> *Bolehkah saya meminjam telpon?*

Is there a message for me? I'm sorry, you were out.
> *Ada pesan untuk saya? Ma'af, anda sedang tidak ada disini.*

I need a porter. Will you please fetch my suitcases.
> *Saya memerlukan seorang portir. Tolong ambil kopor-kopor saya.*

Please call a taxi.
> *Tolong panggilkan taxi.*

Can I have breakfast in my room?
> *Bisakah saya makan pagi di kamar?*

Please send my breakfast up.
> *Tolong kirimkan makan pagi saya keatas.*

Is there someone who washes clothes? Please wash these clothes.
> *Ada orang yang mencuci pakaian? Tolong cucikan pakaian ini.*

Can I have them back tomorrow? Yes, all these are mine.
> *Apakah bisa selesai besok? Ya, ini semua punya saya.*

Please wake me up at 0600/before sunrise/very early.
> *Harap bangunkan saya pukul enam pagi/subuh/pagi-pagi.*

Don't wake me up.
> *Jangan bangunkan saya.*

I want to check out now. Give me my bill, please.
> *Saya mau keluar sekarang. Saya minta rekening saya.*

I will return next week.
> *Saya akan kembali minggu yang akan datang.*

Can you store my things for five days?
> *Bisakah anda menyimpan barang-barang saya untuk lima hari?*

AT THE RESTAURANT/MARKET

I'm hungry. I'm going to go to a downtown restaurant.
> *Saya lapar. Saya akan pergi ke restoran di pusat kota.*

Where's a good restuarant?
> *Restoran mana yang baik?*

Can we stop for lunch/dinner?
> *Dapatkah kita berhenti untuk makan siang/makan malam.*

Let's have lunch. Who'll join me?
Mari kita makan siang. Siapa ikut saya?

This is the best foodstall here.
Ini warung yang terbaik disini.

I'm a vegetarian, I don't eat any meat. Vegetables only.
Saya seorang vegetaris, saya tidak makan daging-dagingan. Sayur saja.

I want Indonesian food.
Saya mau makanan Indonesia.

What time is breakfast? It's served at seven o'clock.
Jam berapa waktu makan pagi? Makan pagi dihidangkan pada pukul tujuh.

Waiter! I want a table for five people.
Pelayan! Saya ingin meja untuk lima orang.

I'm sorry, this table is reserved.
Ma'af, meja ini sudah dipesan.

Give me tea instead of coffee.
Berilah saya teh untuk gantinya kopi.

Do you take sugar and milk?
Anda pakai gula dan susu?

Is this water drinkable? No, it's not drinkable.
Apa air ini bisa diminum? Tidak, itu tak bisa diminum.

I'm thirsty. Please get me a glass of ice water.
Saya haus. Tolong ambil segelas air es.

Please give me some hot water. I want boiled water (for drinking).
Tolong beri saya air panas. Saya minta air matang (untuk minum).

May I see the menu? What's the specialty in this restaurant?
Boleh saya lihat daftar makanan? Apa keistimewaan rumah makan ini?

We're in a hurry, please bring our orders quickly.
Kami terburu-buru, tolong cepatkan pesanan kami.

When will it be ready? What's the price?
Kapan siapnya? Berapa harganya?

That's too expensive. Have you got Indonesian dishes?
Itu terlalu mahal. Apakah anda menyajikan makanan Indonesia?

Let's have some *sate*. Don't make it too spicy!
Mari kita makan sate. Jangan terlalu pedas!

What is that/this? I'd like another helping. Is there more?
Apa itu/ini? Saya mau tambah lagi. Ada lagi?

Please bring us some hot chili sauce. Bring me coffee.
Bawakan lah kami sambal. Bawakan untuk saya kopi.

Bring me another glass. What do you have for dessert?
Ambilkan untuk saya gelas yang lain. Apa yang anda punyai untuk makanan perwei mulut?

I have had enough. I want a banana.
Saya sudah kenyang. Saya ingin pisang.

I want to wash my hands. Where's the toilet?
Saya mau cuci tangan. Dimana kamar kecil?

Good. Waiter, please bring me the bill.
Bagus. Bung, saya minta nota.

Can you change a 10,000-rupiah bill?
Bisakah anda menukar sepuluh ribu rupiah uang kertas?

at the same time/each person/if there is any/finished
pada waktu yang sama/setiap orang/kalau ada/habis

to like very much/really delicious/Enjoy your meal!
suka sekali/enak sekali/Selamat makan!

a little/too little/a little more
sedikit/terlalu sedikit/sedikit lagi

fresh/clean/dirty/to taste
segar/bersih/kotor/mencicipi, merasa

lukewarm/hot/underdone/well done
hangat/panas/mentah/matang

cold/hot (temperature)/hot (spicy)
dingin/panas/pedas

to cook/one serving/forbidden (for Muslims)
memasak/satu porsi/haram

to boil/to fry/to slice/to squeeze (fruit)
merebus/menggoreng/mengiris/memeras

salty/sour/vinegar/sweet/honey/bitter (or plain)
asin/asam/cuka/manis/madu/pahit

plastic bag/bottled drinking water
tas plastik/botol air minum

fork/spoon/knife/glass/plate/bowl/cup
garpu/sendok/pisau/gelas/piring/mangkok/cangkir

rice (after cooking)/rice noodles/sticky white rice
nasi/bakmi/ketan

beans/fermented white soybeans/soybean curd/shrimp paste
buncis/tempe/tahu/terasi

soup/noodle soup/curried chicken/fried rice/fried noodles
sup/mie kuah/ayam kari/nasi goreng/mie goreng

fish/prawns/squid/crab/carp/lobster/eel
ikan/udang/cumi/kepiting/ikan mas/udang karang/belut

meat/liver/heart/beefsteak/water buffalo/frog legs
daging/hati/jantung/bistik/daging kerbau/kaki kodok

beef/chicken/lamb/mutton/pork
daging sapi/daging ayam/daging domba/daging kambing/daging babi

vegetables/tomato/onion/cabbage/corn/potato/sweet potato/carrots/avocado
sayur/tomat/bawang/kol/jagung/kentang/ubi/wortel/apokat

salt/ginger/chili/cinnamon/pepper/cloves/garlic/lemon
garam/jahe/cabe/kayu manis/merica/cengkeh/bawang putih/jeruk

beer/rice wine/water/cordial/ice/orange juice/soda water
bir/tuak/air/strop/es/air jeruk/air soda

bread/toast/cake/cracker/spring rolls
roti/roti bakar/kue/biskuit/lumpia

butter/cheese/cream/milk/ice cream
mentega/keju/kepala susu/susu/es krim

egg/fried egg/omelette/boiled egg/soft-boiled egg
telur/telur mata sapi/telur dadar/telur rebus/telur setengah matang

snacks/peanuts/candy/shrimp chips
makanan kecil/kacang tanah/gula-gula/krupuk udang

Where can I buy fruit? Where's the market?
Dimana saya bisa beli buah-buahan? Pasar dimana?

apple/coconut/citrus fruit/papaya/pineapple/banana fritters
apel/kelapa/jeruk/papaya/nanas/pisang goreng

to pick out good ones/ripe/remove the skin
pilih yang baik/matang/kupas

How does one eat this? Peel it and then you can eat it as is.
Bagaimana cara makannya? Dikupas, lalu bisa dimakan begitu saja.

TRANSPORTATION

What are the tourist places I should visit?
Apa nama tempat pariwisata yang harus saya kunjungi?

There are two caves near the hot springs.
Ada dua gua dekat sumber air panas.

Is it safe to swim here?
Aman berenang disini?

Where do you want to go?
Anda mau pergi ke mana?

I want to go to Yogyakarta.
Saya mau pergi ke Yogyakarta.

When are you leaving?
Kapan anda berangkat?

I depart tommorrow/today.
Saya berangkat besok/hari ini.

not sure/not certain
belum tentu/belum pasti

I'm worn out.
Saya agak capai.

How far is it from here? Is it near?
Berapa jauh dari sini. Dekat?

Far from here. This way/that way. Which way?
Jauh dari sini. Kesini/kesana. Kemana?

Turn left at the corner.
Belok ke kiri di prapatan.

Go straight ahead and then turn to the left/right.
Jalan terus dan kemudian belok kekiri/kekanan.

Go back to the intersection, then follow the sign.
Kembali kepersimpangan jalan, lalu ikuti tanda arah.

My address is . . ./I live on Melati Street.
Alamat saya . . ./Saya tinggal di Jalan Melati.

Straight ahead. On the right. On the left.
Terus. Disebelah kanan. Disebelah kiri.

Cross here. Wait here. Stop here.
Di sini menyeberang. Tunggulah disini. Berhenti disini.

to back up or go backwards/to go forward or advance
mundur/maju
To search for. Where can I find a post office?
Mencari. Kantor pos dimana?

Please show me the way to the highway.
Tolong tunjukkan ke jalan raya.

I want to find this address. I am lost.
Saya mau mendapat alamat ini. Saya tersesat.

Please show me on this map.
Tolong tunjukkan dipeta ini.

What is the name of this street?
Apa nama jalan ini?

What town does this road lead to?
Jalan ini menuju kekota apa?

Where can I catch a . . . ? Where can I rent a . . . ?
Dimana saya akan naik . . . ? Dimana bisa menyewa . . . ?

How many kilometers is it to Rantepao?
Berapa kilometer ke Rantepao?

What's the best route to follow?
Jalan mana yang terbaik?

This road is under repair.
Jalan ini sedang diperbaiki.

This road is very slippery. Look out.
Jalan ini sangat licin. Hati-hati.

My car has broken down. Where can I find a mechanic?
Mobil saya mogok. Dimana saya bisa dapat seorang montir?

I have a flat tire. Will you please repair the tire?
Ban saya kempis. Harap perbaiki ponpa itu?

What's wrong with the engine? Switch off the engine.
Apa yang rusak pada mesin ini? Berhentikah mesin.

The engine won't start. Is there enough gasoline?
Mesin ini mogok. Apakah bensinnya cukup?

Fill it up please. Check the oil.
Tolong diisi penuh. Periksa olinya.

at the bus/train station.
di stasiun bis/stasiun kereta api.

Where is the ticket window?
Dimana ada loket?

How long does it take from here to Bogor?
Berapa lama perjalanan dari sini ke Bogor?

Where's the airport?
Dimana lapangan terbang?

How much does a taxi to the airport cost?
Berapa tarip taxi kepelabuhan udara?

Please help me with my luggage.
Bung, tolong bawakan barang-barang saya.

There are three pieces.
Semuanya ada tiga barang.

Where is the passport and customs checkpoint?
Dimana tempat pemeriksaan paspor dan barang?

Which gate do I go to for the plane for Singapore?
Saya harus pergi kepintu mana untuk naik pesawat ke Singapura?

When is the next flight?
Jam berapa ada penerbangan berikutnya?

When is the next flight to Jambi?
Kapan ada penerbangan lagi ke Jambi?

At what time does the plane for Ambon leave?
> *Jam berapa pesawat terbang ke Ambon berangkat?*

Is there a nonstop flight between Jakarta and Samarinda?
> *Apakah ada pesawat langsung antara Jakarta dan Samarinda?*

What's the fare to Solo?
> *Berapa ongkosnya ke Solo?*

I want a single/return ticket.
> *Saya mau beli karcis sejalan/pulang pergi.*

Stewardess, are we near Kupang?
> *Pramugari, apakah kita sudah dekat dengan Kupang?*

Where is the railway station?
> *Dimana stasiun kereta api?*

Where is the railway information desk?
> *Dimana tempat bertanya?*

Where is the baggage room?
> *Dimana kamar bagasi?*

I want a ticket to Bandung. What's the fare?
> *Saya mau beli karcis ke Bandung. Berapa ongkosnya?*

Which class do you want? First class or second class?
> *Kelas berapa yang anda mau? Kelas satu atau kelas dua?*

How much is a first class roundtrip ticket to Bogor?
> *Berapa harga karcis kelas satu pulang-pergi ke Bogor?*

Is it half price for a child?
> *Apakah anak-anak setengah harga?*

I want to reserve two seats to Bandung on Monday.
> *Saya mau pesan dua kursi untuk ke Bandung pada hari senin.*

What time is the first train for Banyuwangi?
> *Jam berapa kereta-api pertama menuju Banyuwangi?*

Is this seat taken? Sorry, already full.
> *Apakah kursi ini kosong? Ma'af, sudah ada orang.*

There's room for one more. Take a seat, please.
> *Ada tempat untuk satu orang lagi. Silahkan duduk.*

How long does the train stop here?
> *Berapa lama kereta-api berhenti disini?*

What time does the train arrive?
> *Jam berapa kereta api datang?*

Does this train go to . . . ?
> *Apakah kereta api ini ke . . . ?*

We will arrive in Cilacap at around noon.
> *Kita akan sampai di Cilacap kira-kira tengah hari.*

time of arrival
> *waktu kedatangan* or *jam datang*

What time will the ship be sailing?
> *Jam berapa kapal ini akan berangkat?*

Where do I get the boat to Balikpapan?
> *Darimanakah dapat saya naik kapal ke Balikpapan?*

Perhaps on Monday.
> *Barangkali hari senin.*

Which class are you traveling?
> *Perjalanan anda di kelas berapa?*

First class (or cabin)/Economy class
> *Kelas satu/Kelas ekonomi*

It's time to go on board.
> *Sekarang ini waktu untuk naik ke kapal.*

to take a *becak*/call a *becak*
> *naik becak* or *berbecak/panggil becak*

turn to the right/left
> *belok ke kanan/kiri*

What is the *becak* fare there?
> *Berapa ongkos becak ke sana?*

Don't pay more than 1500 rupiah.
> *Jangan bayar lebih dari seribu limaratus rupiah.*

Driver, take me to Losmen Matahari.
> *Bung, bawa saya ke Losmen Matahari.*

Two thousand! How is it possible nowadays, sir!
> *Duaribu! Mana bisa sekarang ini, Pak!*

All right, make it one thousand.
> *Ayo, satu ribu!*

What time will the bus leave? Let's get on the bus.
> *Jam berapa bis ini akan berangkat? Mari kita naik bis.*

Are there buses that go there? How long from here to there?
> *Apa ada bis yang ke sana? Berapa lama dari sini kesana?*

Which bus will take us downtown?
> *Bis yang mana yang akan ke kota?*

Does this bus go directly to Bukittinggi?
> *Apakah bis ini pergi langsung ke Bukittinggi?*

Are there any empty seats? No standing room!
> *Ada tempat duduk yang kosong? Tak ada tempat untuk berdiri!*

Where shall we get off? Let's get off the bus here!
> *Dimana kita akan turun? Kita turun disini!*

At the next stop, please let me off.
> *Saya akan berhenti dipemberhentian berikut.*

Do we need to take a taxi? We have to take a taxi.
> *Perlu kita naik taksi? Kita harus naik taksi.*

call a taxi/please get me a taxi
> *panggil taksi/tolong panggilkan saya taksi*

Where is the taxi stand? Is this taxi taken?
> *Dimana tempat taksi? Apakah taksi ini ada yang pakai?*

How much is this taxi per hour? That taxi has a meter.
> *Berapa sewa taksi ini per jam? Taksi itu pakai meter.*

Taxi! To the airport!/Drive me to . . .
> *Taksi! Ke lapangan terbang!/Antar saya ke . . .*

Take me to a cheap/expensive hotel.
> *Antarkan saya kehotel yang murah/mahal.*

I want to see the city. Please drive me around for sightseeing.
> *Saya ingin melihat kota. Tolong antar saya berkeliling lihat-lihat kota.*

Drive a bit faster. I'm in a hurry.
> *Cepat sedikit. Saya buru-buru.*

Please slow down. Please drive more slowly.
> *Kurangi kecepatan. Jalan pelan-pelan saja.*

Stop here. What's the fare, driver?
> *Berhenti disini. Berapa ongkosnya, Bung?*

STREET SIGNS

Parking—*Parkir*

No parking—*Dilarang parkir*

Cross here—*Menyeberang di sini*

Women/Men—*Wanita/Laki-laki*

Keep Out—*Dilarang Masuk*

Entrance—*Pintu Masuk*

Exit—*Pintu Keluar*

Caution—*Awas/Hati-hati*

Open/Closed—*Buka/Tutup*

Danger—*Bahaya*

Waiting Room—*Ruang Tunggu*

Information—*Penerangan*

Up/Down—*Naik/Turun*

Push/Pull—*Dorong/Tarik*

Police—*Polisi*

Police Station—*Kantor Polisi*

Headquarters—*Kantor Pusat*

Branch—*Cabang*

RECREATION AND SIGHTSEEING

Where's the theater/movie house/music hall?
> *Dimana gedung sandiwara/gedung bioskop/gedung musik?*

What kind of play (movie) would you like to see?
> *Sandiwara (film) apa yang anda suka?*

What's on at the Jakarta Theatre tonight? What's showing?
> *Film apa di Jakarta Theatre malam ini? Film apa yang diputar?*

Is there a matinee today? What's the admission?
> *Adakah matinee hari ini? Berapa harga karcisnya?*

Please reserve two tickets for Friday.
Saya mau pesan dua karcis untuk hari Jumat.

What time does it start? It will start at 1800.
Jam berapa mulainya? Mulainya jam 6 sore.

Let's sit in the first row. This is a good seat.
Mari kita duduk dibaris depan. Disini baik juga.

Sorry, all tickets have been sold out. Sorry, the house is full.
Ma'af, karcis sudah habis terjual. Ma'af, kami sudah penuh.

Where can we go to dance? Is there a discotheque in this hotel?
Dimana kita bisa berdansa? Ada diskotik di hotel ini?

I'd like to dance to live music. Is there a nightclub here?
Saya suka berdansa dengen diiringi band. Ada kelab-malam disini?

Would you like to dance?
Maukah anda berdansa?

Is there a lot to interest tourists around here?
Apakah disini banyak pemandangan yang menarik untuk turis?

What is there to see around here?
Pemandangan apa yang bisa dilihat di daerah ini?

Is there a tourist office near here?
Apakah ada kantor pariwisata di sekitar ini?

What's the fare for a roundtrip to the Loksado area?
Berapa ongkos pulang-pergi ke daerah Loksado?

What will we see on that trip?
Apa saja yang akan dilihat di perjalanan itu?

What shall we bring on the trip?
Apa saja yang harus kita bawa?

How much do you charge per hour? What's included in the price?
Berapa taripnya sejam? Termasuk apa saja itu?

What time does the bus leave? What time do we get back?
Jam berapa bisnya berangkat? Jam berapa kita kembali?

I want a guide who speaks English.
Saya ingin seorang petunjuk-jalan yang bisa bicara Bahasa Inggeris.

Is it all right to take photographs?
Bolehkah memotret?

What's that building? Where can I see good paintings?
Gedung apa itu? Dimanakah saya bisa melihat lukisan-lukisan yang baik?

Is there a cave near here? Where's the waterfall?
Ada gua dekat sini? Dimana air terjun?

I want to climb to the peak of that volcano.
Saya mau naik kepuncak gunung itu.

From where can one start the climb? From a village to the north.
Dari mana bisa berangkat? Dari desa ke utara.

How long (time) to the top?
Berapa lama keatas?

Is it safe to swim here? Yes, it's shallow here.
Aman berenang disini? Ya, disini dangkal.

Don't swim too far. It's very calm. Rough. Deep. Dangerous.
Jangan berenang terlalu jauh. Tenang sekali. Berombak. Dalam. Bahaya.

There's a bathing spot on the river.
Di sungai itu ada tempat pemandian.

I only want to sunbathe. Is there a quieter beach?
Saya hanya mau berjemur. Ada pantai yang lebih sepi?

I'm a good swimmer. I like big waves and white sand.
Saya perenang yang baik. Saya suka ombak besar dan pasir putih.

I want to hire a mat/sailboat/tent.
Saya mau menyewa tikar/perahu layar/tenda.

May I go fishing? What time is high/low tide?
> *Bolehkah saya memancing? Jam berapa air pasang/surut?*

Note: Banners on buildings, stretched out over streets, and hanging from fences and walls announce current and upcoming events, performances, dramas, and movies. Checking banners is one of the best ways to keep abreast of the events in a town or city.

concert/solo concert/recital
> *konser/konser tunggal/pertunjukan*

theater/play/movie/art exhibition
> *teater/sandiwara, drama/bioskop/pameran lukisan*

SHOPPING

I want to buy . . . Where can I buy . . .?
> *Saya mau beli . . . Dimana saya bisa beli . . .?*

Where's the shopping center in this town? How do I get there?
> *Dimanakah pusat pertokoan di kota ini? Naik apa saya pergi kesana?*

Do you sell arts and crafts here? May I see some *batik*?
> *Tuan ada menjual barang kesenian dan kerajinan tangan di sini? Boleh saya lihat batik?*

I'd like to buy silver crafts.
> *Saya mau membeli barang-barang kerajinan perak.*

I'm just looking around.
> *Saya hanya melihat-lihat.*

I'd like to look at blouses. Which one (do you) want?
> *Saya ingin melihat-lihat blus. Mau yang mana?*

Do you have many kinds? I only want this one.
> *Punya banyak macam? Saya hanya mau yang ini.*

Do you have it in other colors?
> *Apakah ini ada warna yang lain?*

I prefer something of better quality. These are better.
> *Saya lebih suka kwalitas yang lebih baik. Ini lebih baik.*

I want one which is new. Can you show me something else?
> *Saya mau yang baru. Tolong tunjukkan yang lainnya?*

May I try on this dress? Where is the fitting room?
> *Boleh saya mencoba rok? Dimana kamar pasnya?*

Will it fade/shrink? Where are these goods made?
> *Ini bisa luntur/menyusut? Barang-barang ini dibuat dimana?*

Those are bad. Same or different? Is there enough?
> *Itu jelek. Sama atau lain? Apakah cukup?*

What is the price of this? May I bargain?
> *Ini berapa harganya? Boleh ditawar?*

That's too expensive. Do you have a cheaper one?
> *Itu terlalu mahal. Ada yang lebih murah?*

Can you come down in price? No, the price is fixed.
> *Bisa saudara kurangkan harganya? Tidak, ini harga pasti.*

When will it be ready? Can you deliver it to my hotel?
> *Kapan selesainya? Bisa anda antarkan kehotel saya?*

I'll take it with me.
> *Saya akan membawanya sendiri.*

How much is it altogether? May I have a receipt, please?
> *Berapa jumlah semuanya? Boleh saya minta tanda terimanya?*

Please wrap this with thick paper.
> *Tolong bungkuskan dengan kertas yang tebal.*

Let's go to the market.
> *Mari, kita pergi ke pasar.*

What is this? What are you making?
> *Apakah ini? Sedang bikin apa disini?*

Do you sell mosquito nets? Yes (there is), sir.
> *Jual kelambu? Ada, Tuan.*

How much is this mosquito net?
Berapa harga kelambu ini?

Six thousand-five hundred rupiah, sir.
Enamribu limaratus rupiah, Tuan.

Don't give me a crazy price! I've seen some that are cheaper.
Jangan beri harga gila! Saya pernah lihat ada yang lebih murah.

I'll come back later.
Saya akan kembali lagi.

I can only pay five and a half thousand.
Saya hanya bisa bayar lima ribu limaratus rupiah.

If you want it for five thousand rupiah, just take it.
Kalau Tuan mau lima ribu rupiah, ambil saja.

Last price. It's up to you.
Harga akhir. Terserah Tuan.

Here is four and a half thousand rupiah. Is it enough?
Ini empat ribu limaratus rupiah. Cukup?

Please wrap it up for me. Please make a very strong package.
Tolong bungkuskan. Tolong bungkuskan yang kuat sekali.

for sale/to pick out/to point out
untuk dijual/memilih/menunjukkan

cheap/expensive/to make a profit
murah/mahal/membuat untung

to pay/to pay cash
membayer/membayar kontan

there is/there is not/as much again
ada/tidak ada/sekali lagi

big and little/little (not much)/same
besar dan kecil/sedikit/sama

on top of/in front of
diatas/dimuka or *didepan*

maker or doer/merchant or shopkeeper/antique dealer
tukang/pedagang, penjual/pedagang antik

AT THE BANK

Where's a bank? Where's the nearest bank?
Dimana bank? Dimanakah bank yang terdekat?

What time does the bank open?
Jam berapa bank buka?

Where can I cash traveler's checks?
Dimana boleh saya menguangkan cek perjalanan turis?

Is there a wire transfer for me?
Ada kiriman uang untuk saya?

I'm sorry, it hasn't arrived yet.
Ma'af, belum datang.

Please contact the Jakarta branch for me.
Tolong hubungi cabang Jakarta untuk saya.

I want to change some American dollars.
Saya mau menukar dolar Amerika.

What's the exchange rate for the dollar?
Berapa kurs uang dolar?

Two thousand one hundred rupiah for one dollar.
Duaribu seratus rupiah untuk satu dollar.

Give me five thousand rupiah notes.
Beri saya uang lima ribuan.

I want to change this into small money.
Saya ingin tukar ini uang kecil.

AT THE POST OFFICE

I'm looking for the post office.
Saya sedang mencari kantor pos.

Where can I mail this? Do not fold!
Dimana saya dapat mengirimkan ini? Jangan dilipat!

Please post this letter/parcel for me.
Tolong poskan surat/bungkusan ini untuk saya.

I want to send this letter via regular mail/airmail.
Saya mau mengirim surat ini biasa/pos udara.

I want to register this letter.
Saya mau surat ini tercatat.

This is a special-delivery letter.
Ini adalah surat kilat.

Airmail to New York is Rp1800.
Pos udara untuk New York Rp1800.

Please weigh this letter/packet.
Tolong timbang surat/paket ini.

Please give me postage stamps/aerograms/postcards.
Saya mau beli perangko/warkatpos udara/kartu pos.

This package is overweight.
Paket ini terlalu berat.

Do you want a return receipt?
Tuan ingin surat tanda terima?

To tie with nylon string/to wrap with paper/scotch tape
mengikat dengan tali/bungkus dengan kertas/pita plastik

TELEPHONE

May I use the telephone?
Bolehkah meminjan telpon anda?

I want to make a long-distance call.
Saya ingin menelpon untuk interlokal.

ow much is a long-distance call to . . .?
Berapa ongkos interlokal ke . . .?

Can I dial direct?
Dapatkah saya menelpon langsung?

What number are you calling?
Anda minta nomor berapa?

the line is busy/out of order
telponnya sedang bicara/telpon ini rusak

hold the line/there's no answer
tunggu sebentar/tidak ada jawaban

He's not in. Who's speaking?
Ia tak ada di tempat. Siapakah ini?

Is this telephone directory still new?
Buku telpon ini masih baru?

wrong number/the line was interrupted
salah sambung/hubungan telpon terganggu

May I speak with . . . ?/Wait a minute.
Boleh saya bicara dengan . . . ?/Tunggu sebentar.

I want to speak to Mr. Sujono.
Saya mau bicara dengan Tuan Sujono.

PHOTOGRAPHY

May I take photographs here?
Bolehkah saya mengambil foto disini?

I have a camera. Photography prohibited.
Saya punya tustel (fototustel). Dilarang memotret.

Where is the nearest photo studio?
Dimanakah foto studio yang terdekat?

Where can I get photographic materials?
Dimana saya bisa memperoleh bahan-bahan fotografi?

Can I buy a roll of film? Please develop this film.
Dapatkah saya membeli satu rol film? Tolonglah cuci film ini.

I want to have my photo taken.
Saya ingin difoto.

I want to have this film developed and printed.
Saya mau mencuci dan mencetak film ini.

Can you enlarge this photo? I want this size.
Dapatkah anda memperbesar foto ini? Saya mau ukuran ini.

Let me have a proof, please.
Coba lihat contohnya.

When will it be ready? Can you make it earlier?
Kapan selesainya? Bisa lebih cepat?

What type of paper do you use (to print film)?
Kertas produksi apa yang anda pakai (untuk mencetak film)?

NUMBERS AND AMOUNTS

0—*nol*

1—*satu*

2—*dua*

3—*tiga*

4—*empat*

5—*lima*

6—*enam*

7—*tujuh*

8—*delapan*

9—*sembilan*

10—*sepuluh*

11—*sebelas*

12—*duabelas*

15—*limabelas*

20—*duapuluh*

30—*tigapuluh*

40—*limapuluh*

100—*seratus*

200—*duaratus*

500—*limaratus*

1,000—*seribu*

3,000—*tigaribu*

10,000—*sepuluh ribu*

100,000—*seratus ribu*

268—*duaratus enampuluh delapan*

150—*seratus limapuluh*

307—*tigaratus tujuh*

537—*limaratus tigapuluh tujuh*

11,347—*sebelas ribu tiga ratus empatpuluh tujuh*

first—*pertama, kesatu*

second—*kedua*

third—*ketiga*

fourth—*keempat*

fifth—*kelima*

sixth—*keenam*

seventh—*ketujuh*

eighth—*kedelapan*

ninth—*kesembilan*

tenth—*kesepuluh*

eleventh—*kesebelas*

twelfth—*keduabelas*

one-half—*setengah*

one-quarter—*seperempat*

three-quarters—*tigaperempat*

1.5—*satu setengah*

2.5%—*dua setengah persen*

one-third—*sepertiga*

two-thirds—*dua pertiga*

one-fifth—*seperlima*

one-tenth—*sepersepuluh*

divide—*bagi*

multiply—*kali*

to slice—*iris, potong*

one slice—*satu iris, sepotong*

a dozen—*duabelas/satu lusin*

to cut—*potong*

number—*nomor*

total/quantity—*jumlah*

to add—*tambah*

to subtract—*kurang*

more (quantity)—*lagi*

approximately—*kira-kira*

how many/much—*berapa*

many/much—*banyak*

too—*terlalu*

too many—*terlalu banyak*

few—*sedikit*

enough—*cukup*

a handful—*segenggam*

a spoonful—*satu sendok penuh*

fix two slices (pieces) of meat—*bikin dua iris (potong) daging*

buy four fish—*beli empat ekor ikan*

I need five eggs.—*Saya perlu lima biji telur.*

I need five shirts.—*Saya perlu lima helai baju.*

sheets of/paper/cloth—*helai/kertas/kain*

three sheets of paper—*tiga lembar kertas*

TIME, SEASONS, MEASUREMENTS, COLORS

What time is it?
Jam berapa?

I was 10 minutes late.
Saya terlambat sepuluh menit.

How long? It takes only 10 minutes.
Berapa lama? Itu hanya sepuluh menit.

When? What time does it start?
Kapan? Jam berapa mulai?

earlier/already/ago/recently
tadi/sudah/yang lalu/baru-baru ini

now/once again/just now
sekarang/sekali lagi/baru saja

immediately/quick
segera/cepat

later/afterwards
nanti/kemudian or *sesudah*

to be late/already late (in the day)
terlambat/hari sudah siang

not yet/nearly finished
belum/hampir habis

a few hours/a few minutes ago
beberapa jam/beberapa menit yang lalu

just a moment longer
sebentar lagi or *segera*

It's not going to happen/it won't come about
tidak jadi/tidak akan terjadi

very flexible schedule; "rubber time"
jam karet

When did you leave Sydney?
Kapan anda meninggalkan Sydney?

I arrived here only yesterday.
Saya sampai disini kemarin.

many times/just this once
sering kali/baru sekali ini

for the first time
untuk pertama kali

I saw him a week ago.
Saya ketemu dia seminggu yang lalu.

I left San Francisco two months ago.
Saya pergi dari San Francisco dua bulan yang lalu.

0500-0700 (5-7 a.m.)
pagi pagi

0700-1200 (7 a.m.-noon)
pagi

1200-1500 (noon-3 p.m.)
siang

1500-1900 (3-7 p.m.)
sore

1900-0500 (7 p.m.-5 a.m.)
malam

today/yesterday/the day before yesterday
hari ini/kemarin/kemarin dulu

tomorrow/the day after tomorrow/tomorrow morning
besok/besok lusa/besok pagi

two more days/in the daytime
dua hari lagi/di siang hari

next month
bulan yang akan datang or *bulan depan*

day off/everyday/nowadays
hari libur/tiap hari/sekarang ini or *sahat ini*

midday/later in the afternoon
tengah hari/nanti sore

last night/tonight/the whole night/midnight
tadi malam/malam ini/semalam suntuk/tengah malam

thirty minutes
tigapuluh menit

second
detik

hour/o'clock
jam/pukul

past or after
lewat

quarter past five
jam lima lewat seperempat

six-thirty
setengah tujuh

just seven o'clock
tepat pukul tujuh

It's seven-ten.
Sekarang pukul tujuh lewat sepuluh menit.

quarter to eight
jam delapan kurang seperempat

twenty to nine
jam sembilan kurang duapuluh menit

It's eleven-thirty.
Jam setengah duabelas.

week/last week/next week
minggu/minggu yang lalu/minggu depan

once a week/in a week
seminggu sekali/seminggu lagi

Monday/Tuesday/Wednesday
Hari Senin/Hari Selasa/Hari Rabu

Thursday/Friday/Saturday/Sunday
Hari Kamis/Hari Jum'at/Hari Sabtu/Hari Minggu

What day is today? Monday morning.
Hari ini hari apa? Senin pagi.

Tomorrow is Tuesday.
Besok hari Selasa.

It's Friday, the twenty-second.
Ini hari Jum'at, tanggal duapuluh dua.

Yesterday was Sunday.
Kemarin hari Minggu.

January/February/March/April
Januari/Februari/Maret/April

May/June/July/August
Mei/Juni/Juli/Agustus

September/October/November/December
September/Oktober/Nopember/Desember

What date is today?
Tanggal berapa hari ini? or *Tanggal berapa sekarang?*

It's the sixteenth of July.
Hari ini tanggal enambelas Juli.

hat date was it yesterday?
Kemarin tanggal berapa?

Do you have a calendar?
Apa saudara punya tanggalan?

17 May 1941
Tujuhbelas Mei, sembilanbelas empatpuluh satu.

this year/for years and years
tahun ini/bertahun-tahun

season/dry season/hot season/rainy season
musim/musim kemarau/musim panas/musim hujan

wind/humid/nice day/beautiful weather
angin/lembab/hari bagus/cuaca bagus

lear/cloudy/cool/hot/foggy
terang/mendung/sejuk/panas/berkabut

measurement/distance
ukuran/jarak

to weigh/width/length
timbang/lebarnya/panjangnya

to measure (for size)/to measure (for volume)
mengukur/menakar

depth/height/bigger than that
dalamnya/tingginya/lebih besar dari itu

black/white/yellow/red/blue/green/brown/orange
hitam/putih/kuning/merah/biru/hijau/coklat/oranje

HEALTH

Where is the nearest drugstore? Hospital?
Dimanakah apotik (toko obat) yang terdekat? Rumah sakit?

What's your ailment? I need medicine for diarrhea.
Sakit apa? Saya perlu obat untuk berak-berak.

Do you have something for an upset stomach? Insect bites?
Apakah ada obat untuk gangguan perut? Gigitan serangga?

My throat is very sore. Can you make up this prescription?
Tenggorokan saya sakit sekali. Tolong buatkan resep ini?

"enter wind" (to catch a cold or flu)/dry cough/itching
masuk angin/batuk kering/gatal

I have a splitting headache/stomachache/sore eye/disease
Saya pusing sekali/sakit perut/sakit mata/penyakit

earache/toothache/backache/stomach cramp
sakit telinga/sakit gigi/sakit punggung/kejang perut mules

infection/malaria/cough (n.)/cough (v.)
infeksi/malaria/batuk-batuk/batuk

healthy/seriously sick
sehat/sakit keras

broken arm/broken leg
lengan patah/kaki patah

I don't sleep well. I have a cough/fever.
Tidur saya tidak nyenyak. Saya batuk/demam.

take medicine/take a pill
minum obat/minum pil

How many pills shall I take a day? Three times daily.
Berapa tablet harus saya makan sehari? Tiga kali sehari.

Take three teaspoons before/after meals.
Minumlah tiga sendok teh sebelum/sesudah makan.

on getting up/on going to bed/sleepy
waktu bangun tidur/jika mau tidur/ngantuk

I'm sick. I want to see a doctor.
Saya sakit. Saya mau pergi ke dokter.

Where is there a doctor who speaks English?
Dimana ada dokter yang bisa berbicara Bahasa Inggeris?

doctor's consulting hours/patient
jam bicara/pasien

Please call a doctor. That wound/cut needs dressing.
Tolong panggilkan dokter. Luka itu perlu dibalut.

How long have you had this cold? About a week.
Sudah berapa lama anda menderita masuk angin? Kurang lebih satu minggu.

You're very pale. Is your temperature still high?
Anda pucat. Apakah suhu badan anda masih tinggi?

Where's the pain? How's your appetite?
Dibagian mana yang anda rasakan sakit? Bagaimana nafsu makan anda?

I'll write you a prescription.
Saya akan menuliskan resep untuk anda.

Wash the cut in boiled water.
Basuh luka itu dengan air panas.

medicine/alcohol/antiseptic cream/aspirin
obat/alkohol/krem antiseptik/aspirin

bandage/plasters/cotton/injection
perban/plester/kapas/suntikan

cough medcine/laxative/ointment/powder
obat batuk/obat peluntur/salep/bedak

sedative/sleeping pill/talcum powder/tranquilizer
obat untuk meredakan sakit/obat tidur/bedak talek/obat penenang

urine specimen/stool specimen
contoh buang air kecil/contoh buang air besar

to rub (with salve)
menggosok

TROUBLES, DIFFICULTIES, HASSLES

Indonesia is not a violent environment and you very seldom hear of muggings, rapes, or fights. But due to its huge population base, there is an element of the population who are ill-bred and rude (*kasar,* in Indonesian). If anyone is ever bothering you or touching you indecently, it's usually enough to say *"Jangan begitu, itu tidak baik"* ("Don't act like that, it's not nice"). This is sufficiently firm, yet polite, and will cover most unpleasant situations.

Please help me for a moment. I've missed the train.
Tolonglah saya sebentar. Saya ketinggalan kereta api.

I've been robbed. I've been held up. What a pity!
Saya baru dirampok. Saya baru di todong. Kasihan!

My money has been stolen. Our bags are missing.
Uang saya dicuri orang. Barang-barang kami hilang.

I've lost my passport. All my IDs are gone.
Paspor saya hilang. Semua pengenalan saya hilang.

Where's the police station? Please call the police.
> *Dimana kantor polisi? Tolong panggilkan polisi.*

Can I speak with the manager? I am angry.
> *Bisakah saya bicara dengan pengurus? Saya marah.*

Let's talk over the problem with . . .
> *Marilah, kita bicarakan persoalan ini dengan . . .*

Is there anybody here who speaks English?
> *Ada yang bisa berbahasa Inggeris disini?*

Is there a translator here?
> *Ada penterjemah disini?*

Where's the information desk? Where's the moneychanger?
> *Dimana "information desk?" Dimana tempat menukar uang?*

Don't be angry with me. Don't be ill-mannered.
> *Janganlah marah kepada saya. Jangan kurang ajar.*

Don't do that. Absolutely not!
> *Jangan bikin itu. Sama sekali tidak!*

Don't talk nonsense! Don't bother me!
> *Jangan omong kosong! Jangan ganggu saya!*

Excuse me, I must be going now.
> *Ma'af, saya harus pergi sekarang.*

I want to go away from here.
> *Saya ingin pergi dari sini.*

Will you please leave me alone? Please go away. Go away!
> *Sudikah anda membiarkan saya sendiri? Pergilah. Pergi!*

Be patient, please! Don't disturb me. Leave her alone.
> *Sabarlah sebentar! Jangan ganggu saya. Jangan ganggu dia.*

What's the matter? Be careful of him.
> *Ada apa? Hati-hati sama dia.*

His manners are very vulgar. He's ill-mannered (impolite/rude).
> *Dia tidak sopan. Dia kurang ajar.*

Never mind. That's all right. Forget it!
> *Tidak apa-apa. Itu tak mengapa. Lupakan saja!*

GLOSSARY

aben—cremation, cremation ceremony

abuang—ritual dances

acar—pickle salad

adat—traditional law or custom. Unwritten, recognized rules of behavior and conduct covering such matters as taboos, inheritance rights, ownership of land, cooking, eating, courtship, ceremonies of birth, marriage, and death, times and methods of sowing rice, building houses, praying for rain. *Adat* is the real law of the land, the oldest and most respected.

Agama Hindu Bali—the Hindu-Balinese religion

agung—great, big

Airlangga—an East Javanese hermit-king who ruled from A.D. 1019-1049 during the Golden Age of Indonesian history

air panas—literally means "hot springs," but could also be a medicinal springs or health spa

air terjun—waterfall

aling-aling—a solid wall behind the entrance gate to a family compound or temple which prevents demons and other malevolent spirits from entering (demons can only travel straight lines)

alun-alun—the main town square, playing field, and/or town park where public meetings, festivals, and sporting events take place. This large expanse of lawn—the "town common"— usually faces local government offices, the post office, police station, banks, schools.

alus—see halus

amerta—the elixir of life

Anak Agung—an honorable title given to members of the princely Ksatriya class

angklung—a portable rattle instrument made from hollow bamboo tubes that produces a single pitch when shaken. Not common on Bali

ani-ani—traditional hand-held blade used in harvesting rice

apokat—avocado

arak—distilled, colorless, fiery palm or rice brandy distilled from *tuak;* the fermented milk of the coconut or *lontar* palm

areca—the tall, thin betel nut palm tree that produces betel nuts which are used in offerings and in a chewing quid

arja—a refined form of folk operetta which utilizes sung dialogue. Themes derive from Hindu, Arabic, Chinese, and Balinese sources and usually contain a goodly portion of melodrama and romance sung in Old Javanese meter.

Arjuna—one of the five Pandawa brothers in the Mahabharata, a model of physical prowess, self-mastery, and loyalty

Arjuna Wiwaha—a play composed by Mpu Kanwa in A.D. 1035. One of its more famous scenes describes the hero Arjuna meditating in the Himalayas to gain strength. To test him, Shiva sends heavenly nymphs to dance near him, but his concentration holds.

ASEAN—Association of South East Asian Nations (Singapore, Thailand, Malaysia, Indonesia, Philippines). This political/economic/military organization was founded to check the tide of communism in Southeast Asia in 1968.

atap—roof, often using *ijuk* fiber

ayam panggang—baked or roasted chicken

babad—called *gunungan* on Java. Meaning "the story," this is the triangular symbol of the *wayang* theater which is set in the middle of the stage or screen when the shadow play begins and ends. It could also be the link that connects the different parts of the play. The *babad* represents the world cosmic order, harmony and peace with nature, and the "Tree of Life." By its motions or the angle in which it is set, it shows the mood of the next scene.

babi guling—spit-roast suckling pig, a famous Balinese delicacy

bade—cremation or funeral tower

Badung—the old pre-colonial era name for present-day Denpasar

bagus—splendid, magnificent; also used in the title of Brahmana-caste men, as in Ida Bagus

Bahasa Indonesia—the national language of Indonesia

bale—open-air pavilion, platform, elevated area, small building, or shelter, usually within the house compound, on which is often placed a bed or couch

bale agung—a large pavilion, used as a council house for the village elders, often in a temple.

bale banjar—headquarters of the village ward, the meeting place of the *banjar* where community events and activities are organized, and the storage and rehearsal place for the *gamelan*

bale gede—the reception hall or guest pavilion in a wealthy Balinese *puri*

bale kulkul—*see kulkul*

Bali Aga—aboriginal, pre-Hindu inhabitants of the non-Javanized villages of Bali, the native "original" Balinese who resisted the religious and cultural influence of the Javanese Majapahit empire. Also refers to the religion still practiced in some of the villages of the northern mountainous areas of Bali.

balian—the local witch doctor, folk doctor, shaman, black magic advocate, diviner, conjuror, herbalist, druggist. He or she could be a traditional village faith healer who uses incantations, a ritual specialist who has knowledge of the occult and employs simple prayers or amulets, or a spiritual leader of great prestige who takes no part in community ritual. In Indonesian, *dukun*.

banjar—the local village council, the community extension of the house and family, and the basic local political unit

bantal guling—bolster, the "Dutch

babad

baris *dancer*

Wife." A sausage-shaped pillow which you wrap your legs around while sleeping in the tropics

banten—general term for ritual offerings

banyan—a fig or *waringan* tree with writhing arteries which spread out 10-15 meters. Also Buddha's bo tree under which he received enlightenment. Its sturdy trunk, umbrella-shaped crown and cool shade symbolize physical protection and divine blessing. The banyan is believed to never die, replenishing itself from seedlings which drop from its branches. It may never be cut down for powerful spirits may dwell in it.

Bapak—literally "father." A respectful form of address when talking to or referring to a headman, leader, male teacher, department head, boss, or any older man. Often shortened to *Pak* as in Pak Suadi

baris—any of a number of ritual male drill dances that are based on the movements and gestures of a warrior. Characterized by the dancer wearing a pointed helmet

barong—a ferocious but benevolent and protective creature, usually taking the shape of a mythical dragon, who battles the evil witch Rangda; or the sacred animal mask, worn by two men, with moveable lower jaws, elaborate headdress, twitching tail, long shaggy body

barong dance—the most violent and dramatic of Balinese tourist dances. Two demonic characters, Rangda and the *barong,* feature in this mythological story. Also called the "*kris* dance"

barong landung—large, tall puppets representing humanlike creatures, supported by a man who carries the puppet's clothing and mask on a wooden frame over his head. This dance play is staged in an annual festival on Serangan Island

Baruna—god of the sea

Batavia—the former name for the Indonesian city of Jakarta

batik—a traditional way of decorating cloth by the wax-resist or "negative" painting method. The cloth is first coated with hot wax, then dyed; the wax is then melted, leaving the waxed part uncolored. Repeated waxings and dyeings creates a cloth with beautiful patterns and designs.

Batu Renggong—Javano-Balinese ruler of Gelgel

Bayu—god of wind or of the air

bebek—duck

Bedulu—the legendary, semidemonic last ruler of the Pejeng dynasty, defeated by Gajah Mada in A.D. 1343. Also the name of a small town in Gianyar Regency.

belimbing—starfruit

bemo—a small, privately owned, four-wheeled covered pickup truck with bench seats used for public transport

betel—the slightly narcotic nut of the areca palm, chewed together with the leaf of the *sirih* vine, *damar* gum, and lime paste

Bharta-yuddha—a poem masterpiece begun by the court poet Mpu Sedah in A.D. 1157. The poem describes a tremendous 18-day epic battle in Indian mythology between two family groups, the five Pandava brothers (the Five Senses of Man) pitted against hundreds of their evil cousins, the Korawas. The most popular stories and figures in the Balinese *wayang* plays of today are based directly on this involved Javanized story.

Bhatara—a title used to address a deity or honored deceased person or ancestor

bhikku (female: *bhikksuni*)—the Pali form for "religious hermit." On Bali, it means "Hindu or Buddhist teacher."

Bhima—*see* Bima

Bhoma—*see* Boma

bhuta—*see* buta

Bima—a warrior-lover of the Hindu Mahabharata epic who figures largely in *wayang kulit* productions. One of the five Pandava brothers, the biggest and the baddest, this black-headed giant hero is a symbol of superhuman strength and courage.

bis malam—special, fast, more expensive buses which travel long distances at night to and from Bali and Java

blimbing—the starfruit (*Averrhoa carambola*). A crispy, watery, thirst-quenching sour fruit. Usually yellow, but there are white and green varieties too. With a knife, peel off the fibrous periphery of the star lines and eat the meat. The more yellow the *blimbing,* the sweeter it will be.

Boma (or **Bhoma**)—the son of the earth and the forest, most often represented by a leering, fanged face carved above the entrance to a cave or a temple's inner courtyard, it's purpose being to prevent malevolent spirits from entering

boreh—a mixture of roots and leaves used as a poultice

Bouraq—an Indonesian airline which flies to many out-of-the-way places on Sulawesi, Kalimantan, Nusatenggara, Ambon, Ternate, and the Philippines.

Brahma—the four-headed Hindu God of Creation who gave birth to the Hindu castes; head of the Hindu Trinity. Brahma appears in white robes and rides a goose. Once thought to be the greatest and most revered of all the Hindu gods because he set the universe in motion, he faded in importance with the rise of Shiva and Vishnu. Brahma was seldom worshipped in Indonesia.

Brahmana (or **Brahman**)—the priestly and learned caste, the highest of Bali's four aristocratic castes with the title Ida Bagus.

breadfruit—related to figs, this massive fruit (weighing up to 20 kg), which grows all over Indonesia and Polynesia, must be cooked before eating. Breadfruit wood is easily worked and its inner bark was once used to make *tapa* cloth.

brem—wine made from fermented sticky white rice and black rice; tastes a bit like sweet sherry and should be served cold

bubur—porridge

Buginese—*see* Bugis

Bugis—a seafaring folk of southwest Sulawesi; also called Buginese

bukit—a hill or hilly area; also the name of the arid peninsula separated from southern Bali by a narrow isthmus

bupati—a local government district officer in one of Bali's nine *kabupaten* or regencies, appointed by the minister of internal affairs. The Dutch called them "regents" and governed through them. In the larger towns the *bupati*'s function can be compared to the position of mayor, e.g., the *bupati* of Denpasar.

buta (or *bhuta*)—a demon or malevolent spirit which can cause sickness or accidents to humans

cak—*see kecak*

calon arang—a dance drama which narrates a story from a 12th-century East Javanese kingdom—the struggle of King Airlangga to save his kingdom from destruction by the widow-witch, Rangda; usually accompanied by *gamelan pelegongan*

camat—civilian assistant head of a regency *(kecamatan),* the second in command after the *bupati*. Each *kabupaten* has 50 *kecamatan* under a *camat.*

candi—a Hindu or Buddhist tomb-temple. The term is commonly applied to all ancient monuments and ruins on Java and Sumatra, irrespective of their particular purpose or religion.

candi bentar—a topless split gateway, frequently the entrance to the outer courtyard of a temple

cap cai—Indonesian vegetable and/or meat chop suey

cempaka—small shrub

cengceng—a set of small cymbals used in most *gamelan*

ciku—a sweet, soft fruit, shaped like an egg, brown outside and in. To eat it, the skin must be sliced off. You'll find that its smooth flesh almost melts in your mouth. Be careful of the smooth doe-eyed stones inside.

cili—a palm-leaf decorative motif, usually the stylized figure of a beautiful young girl. This symbol for wealth and fertility, a representation of Dewi Sri, is an important and ubiquitous element of native decorative art.

Cokorda—a title applied to the male rulers of the princely Ksatriya caste, title of paramount lord

condong—nurse, attendant, or lady-in-waiting to a noblewoman or heroine in a dance drama. Most often seen in the *legong kraton* dances

controleur—In colonial times, the Dutch *controleur* stood at the head of the native administration who wielded power through subordinate native officials.

copra—coconut meat pried loose from the shell and dried in the sun until it looks like soles of shoes, curled by the heat and tinged with mold. Coconut oil, which is extracted from it, is used in such products as cooking oil, beauty lotion, soap, nitroglycerin.

dagang—young girls who run refreshment stands in the villages and towns of Bali

dalang—the *wayang* puppeteer who either manipulates the *wayang kulit* puppets and speaks the words, or narrates a plot for live actors. He is the playwright, producer, directer, singer, mystic scholar, and poet who cues the *gamelan,* philosophizes, jokes, impersonates.

Dalem—one of the four grotesque *panasar* characters in Balinese *wayang; see also* panasar

dalem (or *dalam*)—lit. "within," "deep," or "inner." Used to refer to a paramount lord, his residence, his court, or his family. The Pura Dalem, commonly translated as the Temple of Death, is dedicated to Durga, goddess of death, as well as to Dewi Sri, the goddess of rice. Dalem is also the main character, the virtuous king, in *wayang topeng.*

danau—lake, as in Danau Batur

candi bentar

Dang Hyang Nirartha—a Hindu priest from Majapahit (East Java) who arrived in Bali at the time of the reign of Dalem Waturenggong (A.D. 1546-1551).

Daya—high-caste title for a Brahmana woman

dedari—heavenly nymphs, angels

dermaga—pier

desa—a small, independent agrarian village consisting of a central square, houses, grain-storage sheds, community meeting places, market, temples, *waringan* tree, alarm drum tower, rice fields, community fishponds, forests. Also a general term for rural settlements and their life-ways, as in *di desa*, "in the countryside."

dewa—generic word for god or any benign supernatural spirit

Dewa Agung—"Great Lord." The hereditary title of members of the highest-ranking royal family of Bali who resided in Klungkung, once regarded as kings for the whole of Bali.

Dewa Manggis—the title of the raja of Gianyar

dewi—divinity, goddess

Dewi Danau—goddess of the lake

Dewi Sri—goddess of rice and fruits of the earth. From the time of rice-planting to the harvesting, ceremonies are held all over Bali in honor of this old, indigenous, animistic spirit of the rice and of fertility in general. She is the focal point of a whole complex of rituals, playing a major role in the Hinduized popular religion of the Balinese.

dharma—religious duty

Dinas Pariwisata—the Tourist Information Office

dodol—a sticky sweet concoction made of coconut milk, nuts, and dried palm sugar wrapped in bamboo leaves.

dokar—a light, two-wheeled pony cart, usually with two seats for four to six passengers, popular as transport to and from market in Denpasar and as tourist transportation in Kuta/Legian.

double *ikat*—*see* ikat

Drama Gong—a theater form developed in the 1960s, evolved from *arja,* which portrays contemporary stories

duku—ping-pong-ball-sized fruits, sweet with a sour tinge. Each wedge of the translucent white flesh is enclosed in a light brown shell, containing a greenish hard center which might taste bitter if you took too deep a bite. To open, just squeeze.

Durga—consort and evil counterpart of Shiva, the goddess of death and destruction

durian—The outside of this malodorous fruit *(Durio zibethinus)* is spiked like a mace. The inside consists of three or four compartments where the cream-colored fruit surrounds large pods. Suck the mushy custard-like pulp from the pods. The taste is indescribable. Tastes like vanilla ice cream with onions, Camembert cheese and nectarines, brandied eggnog with radishes, and other such wild combinations. Definitely an acquired taste.

Eka Desa Rudra—an island-wide series of purification ceremonies which takes place on the last day of the Saka calendar every 100 years, most recently in 1979

empu—a *kris*-maker or smith

endek—Balinese *ikat*

Erlangga—*see Airlangga*

es—ice; could also mean sweet frozen fruit-flavored water on a stick

es buah—a mixture of fruit with shaved ice and/or sweetened condensed milk, coconut, *bubur,* and chocolate syrup

es jus—a combination of fruit, crushed ice, and sweet syrup mixed in a blender. Some spike their *es jus* with liquor.

gabor—women's ceremonial dance with offerings

gado-gado—a dish of mixed steamed green beans, soy beans, potatoes, cabbage, and bean sprouts and covered in a rich tangy peanut sauce. Of Javanese origin, it is now found all over Indonesia.

Gajah Mada—Javanese prime minister and general of the Majapahit empire, which conquered Bali in

Durga

A.D. 1343 and introduced Majapahit culture and institutions

Galungan—Bali's most important cycle of rituals, occurring every 30 weeks, celebrating the new year of the *wuku* or *oton* 210-day calendar. The 10-day holiday, which celebrates the creation of the universe, is time of fun, family reunions, prayers, and offerings, when the ancestral spirits come down to visit the island for a week.

gambang—ritual musical ensemble

gambuh—a Javano-Balinese dance drama performed in the inner temple, the oldest genre of Balinese court theater. Episodes are based mainly on legendary versions of the East Javanese history of Panji, a princely figure similar to Arjuna and known in Bali as Malat.

gamelan—a generic term for any number of Balinese percussion-type orchestras first developed on Java. Made up mainly of bronze and wooden xylophones shaped like discs, cylinders, keys, or bulbous hollow bowls beaten with hammers, sometimes accompanied by a chorus of singers, drums, bamboo flutes, and bronze gongs.

gamelan gambang—a very old seven-tone ritual orchestra using two metal *saron* and four wooden-keyed instruments

gamelan gandrung—a bamboo ensemble used to accompany processions and street dances

gamelan gender wayang—a four-piece ensemble, tuned to *slendro* scale, which accompanies *wayang* theater

gamelan gong gede—the largest *gamelan*, used in the courts during Bali's feudal era

gamelan gong kebyar—the most multipurpose and popular modern Balinese concert orchestra, tuned to the five-toned scale and consisting of up to 25 instruments. Characterized by sudden changes in rhythm and embellishments. *See also* kendang, reyong, gong, kempur, gangsa, suling, *and* cengceng.

gamelan pelegongan—a *gamelan* ensemble, tuned to the five-tone scale, which accompanies *legong kraton*

Ganesha—in Hindu mythology, the fat-bellied, elephant-headed son of Shiva and Parvati; the household god, the god of learning and prosperity. Beloved Ganesha is worshipped before every major undertaking to assure success.

gang—alleyway, small lane, path, or street

gangsa—pairs of floating bronze-keyed middle-register metallophones in three sizes (*gangsa kantil, gangsa pamade,* and *gangsa jegogan*) over bamboo tube resonators which play ornamental parts

gapura—gate, gateway, portal

Garuda—a legendary bird, like a combination eagle and supernatural roc. Garuda, the mount of Vishnu, tried to rescue Sita midflight during her abduction by the devil-king Rawana, but died in the attempt. You see this episode from the Ramayana enacted often in *wayang* shows. Garuda is a common motif in Balinese art, and the bird is as well the official modern emblem of the Indonesian Republic. Garuda is also the name of the government-run international airlines.

Garuda

gecko—a lizard found in Balinese houses which makes intermittent, hiccup-like sounds varying in number to which the superstitious Balinese attach meanings and omens

gede—large, big, great; also, eldest son. In elevated speech, used as a status-elevating form of address for objects or actions, as in *Karya Gede* ("Grand Work").

Gelgel—a Balinese kingdom of the 15th to 17th centuries based near Klungkung

gender—a type of *gangsa* instrument played by two round mallets, its keys suspended over bamboo resonators, which plays the basic *gamelan* melody in the *slendro* scale

genggong—the Balinese jew's harp

geria—an elaborate resident of a Brahman

geringsing—*see gringsing*

Goa Gadjah—the Elephant Cave, near Bedulu

gong—large suspended gongs, usually made of bronze, used in *gamelan gong*. Also the name of a multipurpose musical ensemble *gong gede*—a full *kebyar*-type *gamelan* orchestra

gotong royong—a traditional village practice of mutual cooperation through group work, usually in planting, irrigation, and harvesting. This form of village socialism or community service is at work in all of Indonesia.

gringsing—a rare double *ikat* weaving design, the so-called "flaming cloth," made only in Tenganan village of Karangasem Regency. Segments of both the warp and the weft threads are bound and dyed before the weaving begins. Believed to have magical properties and the ability to protect the wearer from illness.

griya—a Brahmana compound, residence, or household

guling—to roll, turn

gunung—mountain. Gunung Agung means "Mount Agung."

guru—teacher or spiritual advisor

Gusti—the title of the Wesya caste, third-highest ranking in the Balinese caste system and the lowest of the nobility

halus—a term used to describe the most refined cultural traits and behavior in real life as well as in characters in the *wayang* theater forms; all gestures, judgments, behaviors, or temperaments which are smooth, polished, gracious, civilized, pure, polite, noble, subtle, graceful, civilized, sophisticated, exquisite, perfect. Opposed to *kasar,* which means all things coarse, blunt, impolite.

Hanuman—the white monkey-general of the monkey army, an ally of Rama, who plays a major role on the side of good in the Ramayana epic in his efforts to recapture Sita, Rama's wife, from the evil King Rawana. An extremely popular hero of Balinese children.

hewan—cattle, livestock

homestay—small, family-run accommodations

honda sikap—riding on the back of a motorcycle as a paying passenger

I—"Mr."; for women, "Ni"

Ibu—mother. A deferential or affectionate title used when addressing any married woman such as a landlady, washerwoman, or *warung* proprietor.

Ida—"he" when addressing a person of the Triwangsa castes

Ida Bagus—honorable title for male members of the Brahmana caste

ider-ider—long, narrow, painted cloth friezes in the traditional *wayang* style which are hung along temple or *bale* eaves during festivals. Usually made of *prada* cloth decorated with gold leaf.

ijuk—black palm fiber widely used for roofing, primarily in temples but more and more in swank tourist hotels. *Duk* in Balinese

ikan mas—goldfish or carp, a restaurant delicacy in Indonesia served baked, fried, or in a tangy soup

ikat—a tie-dye technique used in decorating fabrics in which ancient iconography is used. The threads are tightly bound to prevent them from absorbing the color when they're dipped into the dye bath. By changing the wrappings after dyeing, various colors and patterns can be applied to the unwoven threads, resulting in a highly unusual and colorful overall design. *Ikat* is applied to either the warp or the weft. In southern Bali, *ikat* of the weft is preferred. On the very rare *gringsing* cloths of Tenganan, east Bali, both the warp and the weft threads are tied to predetermined patterns before weaving.

imigrasi—the immigration department or office

Indra—king of the gods in Hinduism; god of the rain and thunder

istana—palace or castle. Usually precedes a proper name, as in Istana Bogor.

jaba—the first (or front or "outer"), secular temple courtyard, and the general term for the world outside Bali. Also used to describe the Sudra caste, the fourth caste below the Triwangsa three-caste system.

jaba tengah—the central temple courtyard

jaffle—an Australian, filled toasted sandwich, either sweet or non-sweet, made with a jaffle iron. Very popular in tourist restaurants all over Bali

jaja—multicolored rice cakes, Balinese "cookies"; in Indonesian, *jajan*

jalan—street

jambu-air—the rose apple *(Syzygium jambos)*. A juicy, pink, light-green, or white bell-shaped fruit about the size of a large strawberry. The whole fruit is edible and quite refreshing, though tasteless. First break it apart by squeezing it between the palms of the hands and then dipping the pieces into a mixture of soy sauce, sugar, and sliced red chilies.

jamu—traditional Indonesian herbal medicine made from a mixture of roots, barks, and grasses, usually steeped in hot water and drunk. Other *jamu* are applied directly on the skin or simply eaten.

janger—a modern social dance involving a dozen or so young men and women who sing in chorus, accompanied by a *gong batel;* many variations

jauk—a violent solo pantomime mask dance of a demonic warrior wearing a tall, pagodalike helmet

jeroan—the inner and the most sacred temple courtyard

jeruk—this term is applicable to all citrus fruits. In some parts of Indonesia it means an orange, but in other parts, a lemon. *Jeruk Bali* is the local variety, somewhat larger than a grapefruit—sweet, closest to taste to an orange, but not as juicy as an orange or grapefruit.

joged—social, not religious, dancing. Based on the Calonarang, in this recently developed and socially sanctioned flirtation dance a solo young woman, accompanied by a *bungbung* orchestra, entices men of any age to match their skill with her within a circle formed by onlookers.

joget—see joged

jukung—the Balinese native outrigger sailboat *(prahu)*. Often built entirely without metal or nails, a *jukung* shows a high level of traditional technology.

juru kunci—caretaker and/or "keeper of the shrine." You must go to this man for the keys to let you into the temple, monument, museum, historical site, etc. A *juru kunci* sometimes produces a guestbook and asks for a donation.

kabupaten—a regency of a province. The province of Bali is divided into nine *kabupaten* (Badung, Bangli, Buleleng, Denpasar, Gianyar, Jembrana, Karangasem, Klungkung, and Tabanan). The office or residence of the head of a regency is called Kantor Kabupaten and the head is called *bupati*.

kain—a length of material, about 2.75 meters long and 1.2 meters wide, worn by men and women from the waist down on special occasions. Also may refer to specific textiles used in sacred ceremonies, such as *kain gringsing* and *kain prada*.

kain poleng—a black-and-white checked cloth used by the Balinese as protective garb against evil influences. Its pattern is believed to convey magic power.

kain prada—cloths with gold-leaf ornamentation

kaja—north, toward the mountains, represented by the color black and the god Vishnu. A heavenly, lucky, and positive direction. The other cardinal directions are: *kelod, kangin,* and *kauh*.

kala—literally "badness" or "evil," but in the figurative sense the demon himself, the son of Shiva and Uma, who invisibly causes evil. This ground spirit, a symbol of courseness and malice, haunts desolate places like the seashores, deep forests, dangerous parts of villages such as the cemetary or the crossroads. A *kala*-head is the carved stone head of a monster over temple gates and recesses to ward off demonic forces by magic means; looks like a stylized lion's head.

kala

kamar mandi—bathroom, washroom. A cement, palm, or bamboo bathroom with a large cement tub in it from which you throw water over yourself with a dipper, elephant-fashion. The tub is not meant to be jumped into and its water is not for drinking.

kamboja—the frangipani tree

kampung—a village, neighborhood, or living compound in a town or city, usually densely settled

kanari—small nuts found in coastal areas that are used for baking bread or biscuits and in making cooking oil

kangin—the direction of the rising sun (east), represented by the color white and the god Iswara

kantor—office

Kantor Camat—office of the *camat*

Kantor Kabupaten—*bupati*'s (regent's or mayor's) residence or office

Kantor Parawisata—the Tourist Office

karma—a Hindu belief that our destiny will be determined by the sum total of all our actions, good and bad, in all preceding lives.

kasar—a term used to describe rough, uncivilized, ungracious, unfit, impolite, coarse, blunt traits or attributes in objects, people, or skills. Also could mean in poor taste, inappropriate. Includes things like poorly played music, stupid jokes, cheap pieces of cloth, blotchy paintings; *see also* halus

kauh—direction of the setting sun (west)

Kawi—The classical literary language of early Javanese and Balinese poetry (*kawi* means "poet"), classical literature, and religious texts. Nine out of 10 words in it are Sanskrit. This language is very rich, flowery, and archaic, well suited for singing, chanting, and musical meter. Kawi is now kept more alive and best preserved on Bali rather than on Java.

kawitan—a sacred, ancestral object

kayan—a motif, often a tree, that precedes the *wayang kulit* play

kebaya—a delicate Chinese long-sleeved blouse with shaped bodice, hand-embroidered edges, and typically made of cotton. Worn by Balinese and Indonesian women.

kebyar—an abbreviation of *gamelan gong kebyar;* see also gamelan gong kebyar

kebyar duduk—a freestyle dance, created by Mario of Tabanan in the 1920s, performed completely in the sitting position

kecak—a seated men's dance drama taken from a climactic episode of the Ramayana. Often called the "monkey dance" because of its characteristic interlocking staccato chorus ("chaka, chaka, chaka") and percussive vocals, with the dancers' arms shooting up and bodies contorting. Invented during the 1930s to accompany certain trance dances, today the *kecak* is performed only for tourists.

kecamatan—subdistrict, the administrative unit that falls within the *kabupaten.*

Kediri—a town in East Java; also the name of an East Javanese dynasty (A.D. 1049-1222) known mainly for its poetry

kelapa—the general Indonesian word for both the coconut tree and the coconut fruit. The coconut has a wide variety of uses: food, drink, oil, wood, leaves for thatching, fiber for matting, its shells made into water vessels and dippers.

kelod—south, toward the south, downstream, in the direction of the sea. This direction is demonical, unlucky, negative. It is represented by the color red and the god Brahma.

kemban—the long, narrow standard women's breast- or shoulder cloth, neckerchief, or shawl. Worn folded or wound, two and a half meters long by 100 cm wide, made of *endek* or *batik,* it does not require any tailoring or fasteners. The *kemban* could be used as a sling for carrying babies and burdens on the back, or as a cushion for a heavy basket on the head, but is generally thrown over one shoulder or wrapped around the head for warmth or fashion.

kempli—small horizontal gong, either suspended or hand-held, that keeps up a steady beat

kempur—a pair of medium-sized gongs mounted on a stand

kendang—a double-headed cylindrical drum played on the lap with both hands by the *gamelan gong* leader; the Balinese word for drum

kepala desa—village leader or headman

kepeng—small lead or bronze Chinese coins with a hole in the center used in offerings and as decoration in rituals. In the 19th and early 20th centuries the *kepeng* was the most widespread form of "cash" used on Bali, worth a fraction of a Dutch cent and the smallest coin in use. Also used in weight measurement.

kepuh—a large tree (*Bombax malabaricum*), related to the *kapok,* most often found in cemeteries

keramat—a place, a tree, or anything that is regarded as sacred or in possesion of supernatural powers

keshatriya—see Ksatriya

Ketut—name prefix for fourth- and eighth-born children of the Wesya and Sudra castes

kijang—a large, powerful jeep which can be rented on Bali for Rp60,000-70,000 per day

klenteng—a Chinese word that has been transformed into an Indonesian word, a common term for Chinese temples throughout the island of Java

kliang (or klian)—government-appointed headman of a *banjar*

kolintang—wooden xyloponic orchestra

kopi—coffee

Korawas—cousins and bitter enemies of the Pandawas in the Mahabharata tale

kori agung—the large, elaborately carved gate that leads from the *jaba tengah* to the *jeroan* of a temple

kramat—see keramat

kraton—a small walled and fortified palace city or court. Derived in part from India, the *kraton* was the supreme center of religious worship in the Hindu-Javanese system of rule.

kendang

kretek—Indonesian clove-flavored cigarettes, named after the sound they make when smoked. Like smoking a dessert.

kris—a double-edged dagger. Designed for thrusting, its blade twists and winds like a snake. Simultaneously a weapon, an ornament, a cultic object, a symbol of masculine strength, and perhaps the finest example of Balinese metalcrafts.

Krishna—a dark-skinned Hindu god of human form, the eighth incarnation of the god Vishnu, but worshipped by the masses in his own right. Krishna is a popular hero in the Bhagavad Gita who could lift elephants at four years of age; he later became a magnificent warrior and a great lover.

krupuk—fried prawn or fish crisps; Indonesian bread. Looks like a giant misshapen cracker.

Ksatriya—the old ruling princely class, above the Wesya but below the Brahmana castes, from which most higher lords are drawn; the soldier caste

kulkul—an alarm tower (*bale kulkul*) housing a slit-drum made of a hollowed tree trunk which gives signals, sounds the alarm, or calls people to meetings

Kuningan—the Balinese "All Saint's Day." A cycle of rites which celebrate the culmination of the 10-day period that begins with Galungan. The family's deified ancestors are invit-

KULKUL DRUM BEATS

Number of Beats	Meanings
• • • • • •	*rampuk kampak* (bandits)
• • • • •	*kecurian royokoyo* (theft of cattle)
• • • •	*bencana alam* (natural catastrophe)
• • • —• • •	*kembakaran* (fire)
• •—• •	*pencurian barang* (theft of personal property)
• • • • • •	*menemukan mayat, caruk, atau gantang* (a death, murder, manslaughter, or suicide)

ed to come down from heaven to visit and be entertained. Most ceremonies take place around family temples in the privacy of the house compound.

Korawas—cousins and bitter enemies of the Pandawas in the Mahabharata epic

ladang—nonirrigated slash and burn fields which grow such crops as rice, corn, and sweet potatoes

lahar—lava or mud emitted from active volcanoes

lamak—tapestry-like woven palm-leaf altar hangings, up to several meters long and ornamented with colored cutouts, used to decorate shrines and for offering rituals

langse—traditional painted tapestries or curtains hung during temple festivals

latihan—practice, rehearsal

lawar—a special food offering—a sort of tartar—made of finely chopped raw meat, blood, vegetables, grated coconut, and other spices, eaten in connection with religious ceremonies and festivals.

legong—a highly stylized classical dance performed by two prepubescent girls or women, often preluded by a dance by the *condong*. There are many variations including an abbreviated version performed for tourists.

leko—a style of *gamelan* played in Jembrana Regency. The name is derived from the *legong kraton* classical dance.

lemper—snack made of steamed glutinous rice with meat or other stuffing and wrapped in a banana leaf

leyak—a roaming evil spirit or sorcerer that haunts dark, lonely places, roads at night, and graveyards. Through knowledge of black magic, these spirits can assume any supernatural shape. They devour the entrails of babies and corpses, cast spells, drink blood from the necks of sleeping people, and can manifest as an animal or ball of fire. Rangda is queen of all the *leyak*.

liana—a species of tropical vine whose strong fibers are used in binding

linga—a Hindu religious symbol in the form of an upright, phallus-shaped, stone column—a symbol of virility and manliness, of divine kingship. It is the emblem of Shiva and of male potency. Yoni is the female counterpart.

LIPI—Lembaga Ilmu Pengetahra Indonesia. A government association based in Jakarta which approves or disapproves a foreign academic's or student's application for study or research in Indonesia.

lombok—chili

longsat—a small round fruit with a yellowish-white skin and sweet white meat

lontar—a species of life-giving palm tree (*Corypha gebanga*), providing food, shelter, utensils, and ornaments. Its fanlike leaves are plaited into sacks, fishing nets, food covers, baskets, etc. Much Balinese literature, history, and sacred texts have been inscribed over the years on dried strips of this palm, cut evenly and shaped like rulers about 25 mm wide and 300 mm long. The leaves are then fitted between two boards bound by a cord that passes through a hole in the center of each leaf to make a "book."

lontong—glutinous rice wrapped in pandanus leaves

losmen—rooms to let. Cheaper than hotels, *losmen* are often family-run inns using traditional native-style structures.

lurah—village headman

Made—name prefix for second- and sixth-born children of the lower caste

Mahabharata—a Hindu myth containing 100,000 couplets—the longest epic poem in the world. This is the legend of the descendants of the Hindu gods, reaching its climax in a tremendous 18-day battle between the five Pandawa brothers and their cousins, the Korawas, in the mythical state of Bharat during the Vedic Age in India (1500-500 B.C.). The battle makes up less than a quarter of the poem, the remainder consisting of Vedic philosophy, ethics, military science, fairy tales, legendary history, cosmology, and statecraft. Translated in the Middle Ages into the high language of Kawi, this Indian masterpiece plays a gigantic part in Balinese literature, art, and theater.

Mahameru—in Hindu mythology, a legendary mountain located in the center of the earth, at the top of which is heaven (*suarga*)

Majapahit—an ancient East Javanese empire which held power over much of Indonesia from A.D. 1292-1478, finally dissolved by Islamic princes around A.D. 1520. The mightiest indigenous kingdom in Indonesia's history, Majapahit's influence had a profound effect on the art, culture, and political organization on Bali.

malam—night

Malat—the Balinese version of the Panji cycle

mamadik—traditional arranged marriage

mandi—to take a bath or to bathe. Also could mean "bathing ritual"; *see also* kamar mandi

mangga—the mango fruit (genus *Eugenia*). The easiest way to eat it is to slice it in half lengthwise and scoop out the delicious pulp with a spoon.

mangosteen—a round purple-black skinned fruit with a whorl of green sepals on the top. Inside, white, sweet-sour juicy segments huddle together in a ball. Be careful of the rind because it stains. *Manggis* in Balinese.

mantra—chanted magic formula of Hindu derivation. In Balinese theater, sacred mantras serve to guide deities or ancestors downward onto the stage.

mapadik—marriage by request or familial arrangement

mekepung—bull races staged in the Negara area of Jembrana Regency of east Bali.

Melasti—This religious procession, a time for casting out evil, takes place the day before Nyepi. Animal sacrifices are made, then *pratimas* are carried to the holy springs or the sea for a symbolic washing. At this time, little boys all over Bali raise general pandemonium to scare away evil spirits. Also called *melis*.

mendet—a sacred dance of offerings inside a temple

Merdah—one of the four grotesque *panasar* characters in Balinese *wayang; see also* panasar

Merpati—the Indonesian government-run airline which mainly operates domestic flights, offering the most extensive network of any of the domestic airlines

meru—a multiroofed pagoda or shrine made of black thatch found only on Bali. Also the symbol of the Buddhist mountain-of-heaven, Mahameru, the *axis mundi* of the world and abode of the gods. The legend of this sacred mountain, represented on Bali by Gunung Agung, originates in India.

meru towers

mie—noodles

mie goreng—fried noodles with meat and/or vegetables

moksa—a Hindu term meaning "oneness with the godhead"

Mpu—an ancient title for a Hindu priest or sage, still used on Java

mudra—sacred ritual hand gestures of Hindu or Buddhist origin that accompany mantras in rituals

murah—cheap, inexpensive

naga—a Hindu mythical crowned serpent or dragon charged with magic powers. Most snake symbols encountered on Bali are derived from this legendary creature. To augment its power, the blade of the *kris* resembles a *naga*.

nangka—jackfruit (*Artocarpus heterophyllus*). A sweet, refreshing, fibrous, segmented fruit weighing up to 20 kilos. On the tree it hangs like a heavy green water-bag. Upon cutting open the thick, tough outer layer, the golden-yellow pulpy fruit is juicy and chewy at the same time. Semi-hard *nangka* wood is used to carve drums and instrumental frames.

nasi campur—a combination of eggs, vegetables, meat, or fish and sauce on top of a heap of steamed rice, a good bargain meal all over Indonesia

nasi padang—rice with many side dishes, usually quite spicy-hot. This style of cooking originated in West Sumatra but is now found everywhere in Indonesia.

nasi putih—cooked white rice

negera—state, realm, capital, court, town. A general term for urban political authority and all the social privileges that go with it

ngerorod (or *ngrorod*)—marriage by elopement in which the bridegroom's friends "steal" the bride with her tacit consent. Much more common than *mamadik*, the traditional arranged marriage

Ngurah—a common title of the Wesya caste

Nini Pantun—Rice Mother; *see also Dewi Sri*

nipah—a palm *(Nypa fruticans)* whose foilage is used for roof thatching, basketry, etc.

Nyepi—the Balinese New Year according to the Javanese *caka* calendar. An annual day of silence, stillness, prayer, meditation, and fasting in order to delude evil spirits into thinking that all mankind has deserted the island so that they will also leave. On this day there is no traffic, at night no lamps are permitted, and people refrain from all activities.

Nyoman—name prefix for the third- and seventh-born children of lower castes

odalan—a three-day-long temple festival, which often includes music and dance performances, celebrating the date the temple was founded. Takes place every 210 days, when the gods descend from heaven to receive blessings from the temple congregation. This is the easiest ceremony to visit on Bali because *odalan* anniversaries follow a fixed and regular schedule.

ojek—to ride on a motorbike pillion seat; *see also* honda sikap

oleg tambulilingan—a dance depicting the story of two bumblebees in a flower garden; first choreographed by Mario in the early 1950s

oton—a Balinese year of 210 days

padi—rice in the husk growing in the field

padmasana—the high, open-seated lotus throne dedicated to Surya, the sun-god, considered the chief seat of the gods when they descend. In southern Bali located in the north-east corner of a temple, in northern Bali located in the southeast corner of a temple.

Pagerwesi—a festival day during which special offerings are made to ward off any ill-fortune or illness which might strike family.

Pak—the term of respect for a grown man (from *bapak,* meaning "father" or "Mr.")

pala—fresh raw nutmeg

palegongan—the type of *gamelan* accompanying the *legong* dance

pamangku—*see* pemangku

panasar—scholar-servants or clowns that give comic relief in numerous Balinese stories. They translate the high-bred Kawi of the aristocrats into colloquial Balinese, adding their own irreverent comments and jokes while doing so. The *panasar*—Twalen, Merdah, Delem, and Sangut—are the equivalent to the medieval court jesters of Europe. With their ridiculous paunches, short legs, flat noses, and flabby breasts, they are a distinctive and hilarious Balinese addition the Hindu epics.

Panca Sila—a Sanskrit phrase meaning "The Five Principles." This political philosophy was put forth in 1945 by Sukarno to provide a constitutional basis for the new Indonesian Republic. The principles are: belief in one of the four great universal religions, nationalism, Indonesian-style "guided" democracy, humanitarianism, and a just and prosperous society. Surmounted by a proud eagle, the Panca Sila plaque can be seen at the entrance archways of even the smallest villages the width and breadth of Indonesia. These principles are meant to be a point of social and political reference, a touchstone for the state, and national education is aimed at producing citizens who are morally responsible to the Five Principles.

pandanus—leaves of a species of tree native to Indonesia which are used in building, making utensils, wrapping, or for clothing. *Pandan* in Indonesian.

Pandawa—a family whose five brothers (Arjuna, Bima, Yudistra, Nakala, and Sahadewa) are the main protaganists in the age-old Hindu epic, the Mahabharata. In the story, these semidivine heroes defeat their 100 cousins, the Korawas.

pande—the clan of smiths—magically powerful artisans who can handle with impunity such dangerous, holy elements as fire and iron. *Pande besi* is an ironsmith, *pande mas* is a goldsmith.

pantai—beach

parang—chopping knife, machete, cleaver

paras—soft, ashy, light gray, volcanic sandstone (tuff) quarried on the banks of rivers, the principal material for stonecarving

pariwisata—tourism. A *pariwisatawan* is a "tourist."

pasanggrahan—government lodge, resthouse, or forestry hut which might accept travelers for a modest price or for free.

pasar—market

pasar hewan—cattle or livestock market

pasar malam—a festive, noisy fair held at night

pasar senggol—a market set up with dozens of stalls selling goods and hot and cold meals and snacks

patih—a minister to the old rajas

pawpaw—papaya *(Carica papaya)*

pedagang kaki lima—foot peddlers with carts, "vendors with five feet"

pedanda (or *padanda*)—a Shivaite or Buddhist high priest, male or female, of the Bali-Hindu religion, belonging to the Brahmana caste

pegawai—a white-collar worker, functionary, staff member, or employee, most often a civil servant or government official

pegulingan—a lighter, minor orchestra, especially for *legong*

Pelni—the state shipping line of Indonesia, with an extensive inter-island network

pelog—the seven-tone tone system used in Java and Bali. Unlike the *slendro* tuning system, it features many semi-tone derivatives.

pemaksan—a voluntary worship group; a congregation responsible for the temple's upkeep and for preparing offerings

pemangku (or *pamangku*)—a non-Brahmana curator and guardian of a temple. These lay priests, who officiate at everyday temple rituals, are of a lower station and more humble than *pedanda*. Most are men.

pemuda—young people. The term also has political overtones as it was used to describe young fervant revolutionaries during Indonesia's 1945-49 struggle for independence.

pencak silat—the Indonesian national self-defense art, both a lethal fighting skill and a graceful style of dance

pendet—a traditional welcoming dance with offerings, inviting the gods to descend, performed by young girls in the inner courtyard of a temple

penjaga—guard or watchman to a temple site, building, bank, residence, hotel, etc.

penjor—eight-meter-high bamboo poles, festooned with bamboo decorations, which arch over roadways or pathways during Galungan or other important occasions. Whenever you see this fertility symbol, it means there's some sort of celebration or ceremony about to happen or being held nearby.

perbekel—a lesser government official responsible for the ceremonial and military mobilization of members of a certain number of *banjar*. In former times, the *perbekel* was the agent and tax-collector for Bali's feudal lords.

pikulan—a stout carrying pole which rests in grooves in the shoulders of a laborer or a peddler on the move. Cans, wares, bricks, water, and other burdens are suspended from each end of this strong, flexible pole.

pisang—banana; *pisang goreng* is fried banana or banana fritters. Indigenous to Bali are *pisang bali,* pink and easy to peel.

Pita Maha Association—a painter's cooperative created in 1935 by Cokorda Gede Agung Sukawati of Ubud with the assistance of Walter Spies and Rudolph Bonnet.

plangi—a tie-dye technique for decorating cloth practiced in the eastern districts of Bali. In this very attractive process, the motifs are first drawn or stamped on the fabric, then the figures are sketched in outline by using a tacking thread. When the threads are pulled tight small loops come up. When the fabric is dipped into the dye vat, the areas that were covered with the string don't absorb the dye, forming a design according to the pattern stitched. Many colors and a broad range of shades can be applied on the one fabric. This technique probably reached Indonesia by way of India.

pomelo—*citrus decumana*, like a large grapefruit

pondok—small one-room huts

post restante—a postal service in which a post office holds mail for a limited period of time (usually a month) until the addressee claims it

prahu—a small, swift, strong, all-wooden sailing boat or outrigger of Malay origin used for fishing

prasasti—ancient royal edicts and memorials inscribed on stone, bronze, or other types of metallic plates

pratima—small stone figures which portray religious personages. These serve as receptacles or vehicles for deified ancestors or the various manifestations of gods during their visits to earth.

pria—man, male

punggawa—the title of indigenous regents, usually a relative of the raja, who were appointed by the Dutch

puputan—literally "the end." A ritualized fight to the death, a military suicide or sacrifice charge

pura—a terraced temple consisting of three tiers enclosed by walls. A gateway, often lavishly decorated and sculpted, leads to the enclosed terraces. The third terrace is usually the most sacred, wherein are recesses for offerings, shrines, and *meru*-roofed structures. A *pura* could also be a temporary offering place for invisible deities and ancestors.

pura bale agung—the great council temple, dedicated to enhancing the fertility of the land and people

pura dalem—the temple of the dead, dedicated to appeasing the spirits of the local uncremated dead. Always situated on the village outskirts in the *kelod* end of the village near the cemetery and the rice fields.

pura desa—the village or secular temple used for everyday worship, dedicated to the deities which protect the *desa* in its day-to-day life. Usually located in the middle of the village and used in all public celebrations.

pura panataran—state temple dedicated to perpetuating the unity and prosperity of the *negara; see also* sad-kahyangan.

pura puseh—the temple of origin, the "navel" temple, dedicated to commemorating the village's first settlers and temple founder. Usually located in the *kaja* end of the village. This temple is the most important social and religious link between the villagers and those of nearby communities which at one time broke away from the mother village.

pura subak—temple dedicated to the irrigation deities

puri—the residence and household of a noble family and its court; a dwelling place for descendants of a local lord of the Ksatriya or Wesya caste.

purnama—full moon

pusaka—sacred family heirlooms passed down from generation to generation, imbued with magic qualities

puskemas—health clinic, often staffed with paramedics and nurses but seldom with a doctor

raja—a Sanskrit-derived term meaning prince, lord, or king, the social title of one of Bali's eight hereditary pre-Dutch traditional noble rulers

raksasa—a mythical giant from Hindu mythology. Sculptures and reliefs of *raksasa* figures are often seen guarding entrances to temples, erected on either side of the gates. Fierce, moustached, armed with a large club, with long canine teeth sticking out through the cheeks like wild boar's teeth, this demon wards off evil forces. *See also* kala

Ramayana—an Indian epic containing 18 books and 24,000 verses divided into 500 songs, all about an Aryan king of the Vedic age. The hero Rama (Vishnu reincarnated) defeats the wicked King Rawana of Ceylon, who has stolen his consort and who is generally troubling the world. This story is known throughout Southeast Asia and all over Indonesia wherever Hindu culture penetrated. The Ramayana provides the story line for nearly all Balinese theater as well as inspiring much of its art: fabric design, painting, sculpture, etc. Written over 2,000 years ago, this epic is as old as Homer's *Iliad,* and it has also incorporated the same legend: the abduction of a great beauty followed by a terrible war to rescue her.

rambutan—a hairy lychee-like, red-skinned ping-pong-ball-sized fruit *(Nephelium lappaceum)* with sweet white juicy meat; tastes like a big, sweet grape

Rangda—the famous evil widow, the legendary queen of the witches in the Balinese Calonarang dance drama, the nemesis of the *barong.* Rangda, who wears an immense, leering, frightening mask, huge white fangs, long sharp nails, flowing hair, and out-thrust tongue, is much feared for her very real and dangerous magical power. Yet this old heroine is not entirely evil as she guards the temples and protects the village from demons.

rattan—a long, slender, tough pliable climbing palm *(genera Calamus* and *Daemonorops),* with long slender tough stems, from which handicrafts and wickerwork furniture are made. *Rotan* in Indonesian.

Rawana—the evil ruler of Sri Lanka who captures Rama's wife Sita and is defeated and killed by Hanuman and his monkey army

rebab—a one- or two-stringed heart-shaped bowed lute of Arab-Persian origin. The instrument's primary function is to anticipate the main notes of the melody. Also found in Central and East Java.

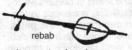
rebab

rebana—tambourine

regency—one of nine administrative districts into which Bali is divided, each governed by a *bupati*

regent—a Dutch term denoting the governor of a regency. During the 20th century, regents were gradually divested of their independent power and many of their feudal privileges, though they still retained great social authority and much of their wealth.

rejang—an ancient ceremonial purification dance performed only by young unmarried girls, usually in a temple

reyong—a gong-chime with 12 small bossed gongs resting on cords in a long, low wooden frame and played in interlocking ornamental figurations by pairs of musicians seated behind it on the ground.

rijsttafel—means literally "rice table" in Dutch. A tropical smorgasbord, an elaborate banquet specialty. Though the food is Indonesian, the way of presenting it is Dutch. Boiled rice is the base with 20-40 individual spicy side dishes: meat, fish, eggs, and vegetables in various curries and sauces, dried pickled fruit and fresh fruit, tasty small dried fish, dried coconuts and nuts, and on and on. Plan to overeat.

rindik—*see* tingklik

ringgit—during Dutch colonial rule, a silver coin worth two and a half guilders. The term is still used on Bali by old people.

rumah makan—a native-style Indonesian restaurant

rumah makan padang—a native-style restaurant where the diner is presented with an assortment of dishes, from which he selects those he wants. The diner is charged for each dish tasted. What is not touched is not charged.

rumah sakit—hospital or clinic

rupiah—the Indonesian monetary unit; US$1 equals approximately Rp2100

sad-kahyangan—eight (some claim six) special state temples of Bali dedicated to the prosperity of the island and its people as a whole. These important temples include Besakih, Uluwatu, Goa Lawah, Batukau, Pusering Jagat, Kehen, Taman Ayun, Lempuyang Luhur. All Balinese pay tribute to these "national" temples which are related to Bali's principle mountain sanctuaries: Gunung Agung, Gunung Batur, and Gunung Batukau.

sajen—offerings

saka calendar—the Hindu-Balinese lunar calendar of 12 months, each ending in a new moon, *tilem*

sakti (or *sekti*)—magical or mystical powers; a deity's, animal's, or object's spiritual energy or charisma

salak—a pear-shaped, plum-sized soury fruit with a brown snake-like skin; comes from a palm tree. To avoid tartness, peel the inner membrane before eating.

sandratari—*see* sendratari

sambal—a hot spicy chili sauce whose basic ingredients are fresh chilies, garlic, sugar, salt, vinegar, and onions

sanggah—small family temple, house shrine, or any type of shrine

sangging—artisans who have mastered the arts of drawing, painting, decorating, and sculpture

sanghyang—a protective deity, an honorific title for a god. Also ritual dances, the source dance from which a great number of modern-day dances are derived. The most famous and rarest is the *sanghyang dedari*, a trance dance of "heavenly nymphs" in which two untrained young girls who embody the spirits of deities dance in unison on top of mens' shoulders.

Sanghyang Widhi—the all-powerful deity in the Balinese religion; the godhead. All Hindu gods and spirits, including Vishnu, Shiva, Brahma, and Dewi Sri are manifestations of the cosmic force of Sanhyang Widhi.

Sangut—one of the four grotesque *panasar* characters in Balinese *wayang; see also* panasar

santan—coconut milk or cream

Sanghyang Widhi

Saraswati—goddess of learning, science, literature, and wisdom, and wife of Brahma. Each *oton* (210 days), elaborate offerings are made and ceremonies held in her honor for books, particularly the sacred *lontar* palm-leaf books. No one is supposed to read on her festival day, Hari Raya Saraswati. Students flock to Pura Jagat Natha in Denpasar.

sari—flower; essence of an offering

saron—any metallophone with thick bronze slabs held in place by posts and laid over a trough. Found in four main sizes, the instrument is beaten with a hard mallet *(panggul)*.

sarung—a *kain* with both ends sewn together, used by men, women, and children. Worn with a tight sheathlike effect, the slack of this long, loose tubular-shaped step-in skirt is folded and tucked in. Can also be used to carry fruit or children, or worn as a jacket or raincoat by wrapping it around the shoulders.

sate—a national dish much like kebab found throughout the Arab world. Chicken, beef, mutton, seafood, pork, or entrails are threaded on thin bamboo skewers and grilled over a charcoal fire. After roasting, *sate* is often served with a sharp peanut sauce, a small plate of raw onions, and some *lombok*.

satria—*see* Ksatriya

sawah—flooded irrigated fields of stalk rice; deep mud artificially constructed (often terraced) and continuously cultivated with rice

sawo—a fruit, the sapodilla plum, shaped like a potato but has the texture and flavor of sweet bread

sebel—a state of ritual pollution of an individual, family, temple, or village. Being spiritually fouled or unclean weakens the spirit of a place or thing.

sekaha—any organized group with a specific social function, usually that of a music or dance club or association; also spelled *seka* or *sekehe*

selonding—a ritual musical ensemble

semangka—watermelon

semar pegulingan—a traditional type of *gamelan*

sembah—prayer or gesture of reverence to a god, lord, superior; a bow with clasped hands

sendratari—From *seni* (art) and *tari* (dance). In this lavish dance play, using a variety of music and dance steps, a narrator *(juru tandak)* sits in the *gamelan* and relates stories from the Ramayana and Mahabharata epics.

Shiva—in the Hindu galaxy of gods Shiva is one of the mightiest, the Destroyer of the

World—identified with the sun. Shiva is the most venerated of Bali's gods, the one you really have to worry about because he can hurt you. Shiva's emblem is the phallus (linga).

singha—winged lion, a common sculptural motif

Singosari—an ancient, ruthless Javanese dynasty whose official faith was a Buddhist-Shivaite syncretism. Though it ruled for only 71 years (A.D. 1222-1293), Singosari initiated a new sculptural style in its temple reliefs, the so-called *wayang kulit* style.

sirih—the leaf of a species of slightly narcotic pepper. These scarlet seeds, when combined with betel nut and lime, are chewed mostly by older people all over Indonesia; the teeth become rust-colored after years of chewing. Chewed in Indonesia for over 2,500 years, *sirih* could also serve important ritual functions in restoring harmony and peace between individuals or within a community. On Bali, only a diminishing number of old people still chew *sirih*.

sirsak—*see zirzak*

Sita—wife of Rama, the chief heroine of the Ramayana who is captured by Rawana and forced to live in his palace in Sri Lanka and is finally rescued by Rama and Hanuman

Siwa—*see Shiva*

slendang (or *selendang*)—waist sash worn at temple festivals and religious ceremonies

slendro—the five-toned tuning system used in Java and Bali which, unlike the *pelog* system, has no semitone intervals. Based on the division of the octave into five equal parts, there are three main *slendro* modes.

songket—a fabric with gold or silver weft threads handwoven by the floating-weft technique. *Sarung songket* is traditional wear for high-caste Balinese bridegrooms.

soto—a spicy soup found all over Indonesia. Served with rice or *lontong,* soybean sprouts, chicken, mutton, or beef, and garnished with fried or green onions. *Soto ayam* is Javanese chicken broth.

Sri—*see Dewi Sri*

Sriwijaya—a trading empire, based in southeast Sumatra, which flourished between the 8th and 9th centuries and controlled large areas of the Indonesian archipelago and the Malayan Peninsula.

stupa—a bell-shaped burial place for the remains or relics of Buddha or one of his disciples, or of Buddhists

subak—the village water board or cooperative which controls the flow of water, irrigation, canal building, drainage, maintenance. This basic local cultivation association also settles disputes and polices the dams.

suci—ritually clean, pure, consecrated

Sudra—the term used to designate those Balinese outside the Triwangsa caste system. These "commoners" are the lowest of Bali's castes, originally meant to serve the other three. They make up about nine-tenths of the population. The Indian term Sudra is hardly ever used; Jaba is much more widely used.

suling—bamboo flute

sunguhu—a low-caste priest who performs rituals similar to that of Brahman priests but whose office is limited to the propitiation of evil spirits

Surya—the sun or the sun-god, identified with Lord Shiva. The word is also used to designate the high caste patrons of a low caste family.

suttee—ritual immolation of a Hindu widow on her husband's funeral pyre, a practice which died out in the last century on Bali

syahbandar—the harbormaster who works in every port in Indonesia where ships call. See him about ships and boats to anywhere, when they are expected to arrive or depart, and how much you may expect to pay for your passage.

taksu—describes a dancer's charisma and power while performing; also the name of the shrine that gives one *taksu*

taman—ornamental garden, most often with a pond

Tantri—stories of Hindu origin. In the Balinese *Tantri* tales, Tantri is the name of the woman who tells stories to the king.

tapel—mask. The Indonesian word is *topeng*.

tari lepas—a short freestyle modern dance

tegalan—a dry (not irrigated) field near *sawah* used for vegetables and other secondary crops

tektekan—a *gamelan* type orchestra unique to the village of Krambitan in Tabanan in which wooden clappers and bamboo split drums are used in processions

tempat penitipan barang—boxes or spaces used to store luggage safely

tempe—a protein-rich cake made from fermented soybeans

tenget—magical, dangerous, mysterious; a supernaturally charged place or object

teruna—a boys' organization or clubhouse

tilem—the new moon; the beginning of the Balinese month; *see also* purnama

tingklik—an instrument consisting of bamboo tubes suspended in a wooden frame; also known as *rindik*

tirtha—holy water

topeng—mask; *see also* wayang topeng

toya tirtha—*see* tirtha

transmigrasi—a government resettlement program aimed at relocating Javanese and Balinese individuals, families, or communities to the Outer Islands to set up farming colonies under government sponsorship and supervision

trisakti—the holy Hindu trinity: Brahma, Shiva, and Vishnu

Triwangsa—a term used to describe the three highest Balinese castes (Brahmana, Ksatriya, and Wesya), traditionally placed above the Sudra caste. The aristocracy of Bali.

trompong—a row of small tuned gongs with protruding knobs arranged on a long frame on which a solo melody is played by one musician using two long sticks. Considered an old-fashioned instrument and not often seen in *gong kebyar*

tuak—sweet, bubbly rice or palm beer or toddy, pale pink or white in color, produced by fermenting the sap of the young flower stalk of a *lontar* palm

tukang—artisan, workman, craftsman, skilled laborer; one who does something (e.g., *tukang banten* is a specialist in preparing offerings)

tulisan Bali—Sanskrit-like characters of the Balinese language

tumpak wayang—holy day for artists

Twalen—one of the four grotesque *panasar* characters in Balinese *wayang; see also* panasar

udeng—traditional head-covering worn by men

usaba—harvest celebration or festival

Vedas—the four sacred books of the Aryans dating from about 1000 B.C. Of the four, the Rig Veda is the best known and is claimed to the oldest religious text in the world.

Vishnu—in the Hindu pantheon of gods, Vishnu functions as the guardian and preserver of the world. Vishnuism attached great value on the service and love of God, thereby achieving identity of existence with him. On Java, kings and other historical personages (such as Sukarno) were frequently regarded as incarnations of Vishnu. This Hindu god was personified symbolically in many creatures such as fish, tortoises, and in the Hindu epics in Krishna and Rama.

V.O.C.—Vereenigde Oost-Indische Campagnie, or United East India Company is a unique Dutch institution established in 1602 by the merger of a number of Dutch trading concerns with the aim of establishing a ruthless and nearly unbreakable monopoly of the spice trade.

wadah—funeral tower carried to cremations and containing the corpse or the effigy *(ukur)* of the deceased

wadon—a low-pitched pair of gongs or drums

wanita—woman

wantilan—an open pavilion used as a hall for members of a village or temple. The structure can also be used as a cockfighting arena.

waringan—*see* banyan

Wartel—Short for Warung Telekommikasi, a privately owned telecommunications center that sends and receives faxes, telexes, telegrams and—most importantly—offers international telephone service

warung—Usually a roofed, open-air structure where food and drinks are served. It will sell coffee, soft drinks, cigarettes, canned foods, snacks, and *sirih*, or often specialize in one or two types of food. The *warung* fulfills a social function roughly analogous to the French cafe or the Turkish coffeehouse. Although it can be just a small table or portable kitchen, nowadays a *warung* can also be an elaborate restaurant where only the rich can afford to eat.

Wayan—the name prefix for the first- and fifth-born children of the lower caste

wayang kulit—two-dimensional (flat) leather shadow puppets cut out of polished and gilded buffalo leather or goatskin

wayang-style—a style of Balinese painting adapted from the *wayang kulit* used for calendars, scrolls and *langse* for temples, and large rectangular works for palaces

wayang lemah—ritual *wayang* performances without the screen or lamp

wayang orang (or *wayang wong*)—traditional live human drama performed on a platform in a theater with actors and actresses wearing elaborate costuming with or without masks *(topeng)*. Displaying extraordinary control and discipline, dancers are made up to look like *wayang kulit* puppets, even simulating movements of the shadow figures and relying on the same stylized gestures to convey emotion.

wayang kulit

wayang topeng—live dance plays in which actors and actresses wear brightly colored, expressive wooden masks; up to 80 masks make up one complete set. Stories are usually based on the genealogical chronicles *(babad)* of the Balinese ruling families.

Wesya—the third-ranking—and lowest—caste in the Triwangsa system. This military and business caste is the most numerous of all Bali's aristocratic castes.

widyadhari—heavenly nymphs

Wong Majapahit—exiles who fled from the spread of Islam in Java in the 15th and 16th centuries. Also, a general code word for anything that occurred in the distant past. *See also Bali Aga.*

wuku—a period of seven days; 30 *wuku* make up the 210-day Balinese year

Yama—god of the underworld

yeh—water, river, waterway, or spring (as in Yeh Sanih)

YHA—Youth Hostel Association

yoni—a stylized vagina usually carved out of stone; the Hindu symbol of female life-giving force

zirzak—custard apple *(Annona squamosa)*. Rich, sweet-sour flavor, and creamy texture. Squeeze open and scoop out the flesh with a spoon. It's a bit of a chore separating the milky white meat from the numerous black seeds, but worth it. Though it tastes heavenly, don't overeat as too much will give you a bellyache.

BOOKLIST

ARCHITECTURE

Wijaya, Made. *Balinese Architecture: Towards an Encyclopedia, Vols. I and II.* Bali, 1980. The most extensive survey yet of Balinese architecture, written by a famous landscape architect who has lived the past 20 years on Bali.

ANTHROPOLOGY

Belo, Jane. *Transitional Balinese Culture.* New York: Columbia University Press, 1972. An anthology of articles including a study of how children are treated on Bali.

Geertz, Hildred, and Clifford Geertz. *Kinship in Bali.* Ithaca: University of Chicago Press, 1967. Two renowned anthropologists' study of Bali's involved social system.

Jensen, Gordon D., and Luh Ketut Suryani. *The Balinese People: A Reinvestigation of the Balinese Character.* Kuala Lumpur: Oxford University Press, 1993. Co-authored by a Balinese, this wonderful book takes a refreshing look at the Balinese character from a Balinese perspective. The authors scrutinize Mead and Bateman's conclusions of the 1930s, as documented in their *The Balinese Character* (1942), and overturn them one by one.

Jensen, Gordon D., and Luh Ketut Suryani. *Trance and Possession in Bali: A window on Western Multiple Personality, Possession Disorder, and Suicide.* Kuala Lumpur: Oxford University Press, 1993. The authors describe the psycho-social experiences of the Balinese in trance-possession states during traditional healing, dance, drama, and *gamelan* performances, as well as in several mental disorders.

Kertonegoro, Madi. *The Spirit Journey to the Bali Aga, Tenganan Pegringsingan.* Indonesia: Harkat Foundation, 1986. An unusual book which collects the traditions, ceremonies, and lost legends of Tenganan village, eastern Bali, the home of the "original" Balinese.

Lansing, J. Stephan. *The Three Worlds of Bali.* New York: Praiger Publishers, 1983. Contains an outstanding discussion of water temples and their function in a rice-growing culture.

State and Society in Bali: Historial, Textual and Anthropological Approaches. Edited by Hildred Geertz. Leiden: KTLV press, 1991. Seven interdisciplinary essays by eminent Baliologists analyze texts, temples, institutions, theater performances, and rituals in the context of the society as a whole. In contrast to previous Bali research, these studies put more emphasis on historical background and pay close attention to local Balinese perspectives.

Warren, Carol. *Adat and Dinas: Balinese Communities in the Indonesian State.* Kuala Lumpur: Oxford University Press, 1993. A carefully researched ethnographic work dealing with the relationship between the local communities in Bali and the Indonesian state. Warren is particularly elegant when she describes ways in which the *banjar* functions as a social, ritual, and administrative entity.

BIBLIOGRAPHY

Stuart-Fox, David. *Bibliography of Bali: Publications from 1920 to 1990.* Leiden: KTLV Press, 1995. Contains almost 8,000 titles of books, articles, and periodicals about Bali published in the last 70 years. Covers all fields of study (110 subject categories) and includes publications in Indonesian and foreign languages. Author index, corporate and project index, and subject index provide extensive and detailed access to the titles listed. The main libraries where the materials can be found are identified in the introduction.

ECONOMY

McCarthy, John. *Are Sweet Dreams Made of This?* Australia: IRIP, Norcote, 1995. A fascinating account of the impact of tourism on local Balinese communities. It looks sharply at Bali's tourism boom, tourist types, sex and AIDS, who benefits from tourism, and tourism's affect on Bali's culture and environment. A provocative must-read for all Balinists.

FOOD

von Holzen, Heinz, and Lother Arsana. *The Food of Bali: Authentic Recipes from the Island of the Gods.* Singapore: Periplus Editions, 1995. Real Balinese cooking is seldom served in hotels or restaurants. Includes an extensive introduction, the intricacies of preparing sauces and condiments, and easy-to-follow receipes and techniques for preparing unusual and traditional dishes.

GUIDEBOOKS

Bali: Island of the Gods. Edited by Eric Oey. Lincolnwood, IL: Passport Books, 1995. A complete guide with hundreds of pages of travel tips, articles on Balinese history, art and culture. Also includes 30 maps, scores of color photographs, information on how to get around, and where to get the best value for your money.

Baedeker Bali, 2nd edition. Edited by Alec Court. Baedeker, 1995. Includes hundreds of photographs and detailed maps to towns, sights, museums, galleries. Also offers A to Z listing of places to visit, hotel and restaurant recommendations, shopping, entertainment. Comes in durable plastic cover.

Beshra, Mark. *Eating Bali: The Complete Restaurant Guide.* Singapore: Times Books International, 1990. An honest source of information for the gourmand. Humorously evaluates over 200 restaurants in the island's six tourist areas. Restaurants are graded on their food, service, atmosphere, sanitation, and price. Includes maps, photos, plus a list of 59 restaurants to avoid. The information in this book, published in 1990, is only about 60% accurate now.

Black, Star, and Willard A. Hanna. *Insight Guides: Bali.* Boston: Houghton Mifflin, 1995. This fascinating photographic overview has been a classic from the day it first left the presses in 1970. The latest edition presents the history, culture, arts, dance and drama, and people of Bali. In the back there's an expanded section of detailed travel tips, food, hotels, special events, and other information. Since it tries to be an all-in-one guidebook—lavishly illustrated with art and photos—many visitors feel it is to heavy to lug around and they will buy it for its souvenir value *after* their trip.

Blackwood, Sir Robert. *Beautiful Bali.* Melbourne, Australia: Hampden Hall, 1970. An introduction to the island, its history, its places of interest, its people, their way of life, and their art forms. One of the earliest guidebooks to Bali. Illustrated.

Eiseman, Fred. B. Jr. *Bali and Lombok.* Prentice Hall Travel, 1993. User-friendly and handy-sized, this guide is packed with information on culture, sights, people, shopping, eating, accommodations, plus maps.

Fischer, Edith Andrea. *Bali: A World of its Own.* Self-published, Australia, 1991. Aimed at the cultural tourist, Fischer explains in a matter-of-fact, straightforward way Bali's history, legends, philosophy, people, and culture.

Hogan, Rae. *Guide to Bali.* Sydney, Australia: Paul Hamlyn, 1974. An excellent, very early guidebook—now serving as an historical document—containing color and black and white photographs, maps, and numerous illustrations. The first good guidebook to Bali.

Kooiker, Hunt. *Bali by Bicycle*. Arizona: Cosmic Dragon Publications, 1977. A concise booklet which describes how one can explore Bali by bicycle. With the help of two short *bemo* rides to scale the central mountains, one can accomplish a beautiful, mostly level or downhill 200-km circle trip of Bali by bicycle. Unfortunately out of print.

Muller, Kal. *Underwater Indonesia: A Guide to the World's Greatest Diving*. Singapore: Periplus Editions, 1992. The first dive guide available on the archipelago. Includes hundreds of beautiful color photographs of marine species found across some of the richest tropical waters in the world. Detailed maps show the location of drop-offs, wrecks, and coral gardens. All major sites on Bali are well covered, with complete information on how to get to dive spots. Listings of scuba operators, as well as prices and hotels, are found at the end of each geographical section.

Santosa, Silvio. *Bali Pathfinder*. Ubud: Bina Wisata Tourist Office, 1995. A detailed and well-illustrated booklet to the Ubud area. Very helpful map.

Wheeler, Tony, and James Lyon. *A Travel Survival Kit: Bali & Lombok*. Australia: Lonely Planet Publications, 1994. A popular travel guide to Bali and the neighboring island of Lombok. Excellent travel information with extensive restaurant listings, 49 maps, a 32-page color guide to arts and crafts, and an Indonesian language section and glossary.

Wijaya, Made. *Insight Pocket Guides: Bali*. Singapore: Apa Publications, 1995. Includes a brief historical and cultural introduction, practical and easy-to-follow itineraries, and the author's favorite restaurants and shops. A slim, handy guide recommended for a short stay.

HANDICRAFTS

Donald Friend's Bali. Sydney, Australia: Art Gallery of New South Wales, 1990. A catalog of an exhibition of Balinese art collected by Donald Friend during his 15 years in Bali, reflecting the artist's passion for the exotic and the unusual.

Eiseman, Fred. *Woodcarvings of Bali*. Periplus Editions, Singapore, 1988. An introduction to the centuries-old Balinese woodcarving tradition. Traces the history of the highly developed craft from the earliest Buddhist influences, the classical period of the 9th to 16th centuries, and finally Bali's modern period of experimentation. Exceptional coverage, with numerous excellent color photos of carvings and their artists. Even the trees and woods of Bali are included.

Hauser-Schaublin, Brigitta, Marie-Louise Nabholz-Kartaschoff, and Urs Ramseyer. *Textiles in Bali*. Swiss ethnologists chronicle the breadth of Bali's social classes, regional groupings, ceremonial and religious rituals as seen through the island's myriad woven arts—from simple *poleng* and *ikat* to more complicated *songket* and *gringsing*. The only reference work on the full range of Balinese textiles, covering the history, meaning, and production methods. Richly illustrated with beautiful photographs.

Ramseyer, Urs. *The Art and Culture of Bali*. Kuala Lumpur: Oxford University Press, 1986. This large format book explains the social, religious, and philosophical concepts that rule the lives of the Balinese and find their expression in their paintings, temples, folk art, ritual offerings, music, dance, and dramatic arts. Overwhelming detail and magnificently illustrated with photographs keyed to the text. Written by the former head of the Indonesian Collection at the Basle Museum of Ethnology, Switzerland. Ramseyer conducted his field research in east Bali and in villages around the foot of Gunung Agung, so his work has a bias to the cultural practices of that region of Bali.

HISTORY

Frederick, R. *An Account of the Island of Bali, Vol. 8 of the Journal of the Royal Asiatic Society of Great Britain and Ireland*. London:

Trubner and Co., 1876. One of the earliest accounts of Bali written by a Westerner.

Geertz, Clifford. *Negara: The Theater State in the 19th Century Bali.* Princeton, N.J.: Princeton University Press, 1980. A captivating account of the unbelievably intricate social conventions widespread on Bali during the last century. Get ready for some dense, sometimes marvelous reading in sociology.

Hann, Willard H. *Bali Profile: People, Events, Circumstances 1001-1976.* The most comprehensive and compassionate history of Bali yet published.

Kempers, A.J. Bernet. *Monumental Bali.* Singapore: Periplus Editions, 1995. An authoritative introduction and guide to Balinese archaeology, concentrating on the early period of the island's history but with many connections to later Balinese culture. Helps to understand the island's most famous monuments but also encourages the reader to descend into the depths of ravines in search of the lesser-known mysteries of prehistoric Bali. Dutch-born Kempers lived the first 50 years of his life (1906-56) in Indonesia and has made frequent expeditions between 1970 and 1984.

Koke, Louise G. *Our Hotel in Bali.* New Zealand: January Books, 1987. How two young Americans made a dream come true by opening one of the first Balinese-style tourist hotels on Kuta Beach in the 1930s. The architectural style they pioneered flourishes today as does the surfing they introduced to Bali. Their adventure lasted until the Japanese invasion in 1942.

Krause, Gregor. *Bali 1912.* New Zealand: January Books, 1988. More than 70 years ago a young German doctor working for the Dutch East Indies government took more than 4,000 photographs on Bali. In 1920, 400 of his photos accompanied by his own reports were published in Germany. This new selection of Krause's best work, including many black-and-white prints made from his original glass plates, offers a unique view of traditional Bali.

Vickers, Adrian. *Bali, A Paradise Created.* Australia: Penguin Books, 1989. Explores the history of the image-making process that has surrounded Bali since the 1930s. This book dispels the myth of a harmonious, exotic island, a paradigm first created by the Dutch and maintained by subsequent Indonesians administrators and Western writers. Vickers shows how the Balinese people are undergoing great confusion, change, hardship, and tension as they attempt to maintain their culture while their island is catapulted into the modern age.

INTRODUCTORY

Bali. Singapore: The Times Travel Library, Times Editions, 1987. Photos, local trivia, do-it-yourself walks and excursions, and detailed practical travel information.

Covarrubias, Miguel. *Island of Bali.* Kuala Lumpur: Oxford University Press, 1972. Written by a Mexican painter who lived and worked in Belahluan, Bali, for two years in the 1930s collecting material for this artistic and well-written classic of traditional Balinese culture, the scope of which makes fascinating reading. Covarrubias was one of the first to call what the Balinese were living and creating "art." He rendered the drawings, his wife shot the photographs.

Eiseman, Fred B., Jr. *Bali: Sekala & Niskala.* Scottsdale, Arizona: Fred B. Eisman Jr., 1986. A collection of three volumes of intriguing, extensive, and quirky articles and essays, each written in different lengths, styles, and degrees of scholarship. With nearly 30 years spent on the island, Eiseman writes with uncommon perspicacity on such wide-ranging topics as Balinese witchcraft and magic, cricket fighting, seaweed farming, and all the uses of the coconut.

Eiseman, Fred. B., Jr. *The Story of Jimbaran.* The first book published about Jimbaran, the strip of land between Tuban and Uluwatu. Copies are available for US$20 from the author who can be reached at Jl. Bukit Permai 8

A, Jimbaran, Tuban, Badung, Bali 80361, Indonesia.

Mabbett, Hugh. *In Praise of Kuta*. New Zealand: January Books, 1987. From slave port to fishing village, this is the story of Kuta Beach, today one of the most popular tourist resorts in the world. More than 50 exuberant full-color photos.

The Balinese. New Zealand: January Books, 1985. A well-written introduction to all elements of Balinese culture—from family and village life to cremation and religion, from music and dance to wildlife and the effects of tourism. Based on firsthand observation supported by impressive scholarship delivered in an unwaveringly objective style. Mabbet's book offers much more detail than the usual guidebook.

LANGUAGE

Almatsier, A.M. *How to Master Bahasa Indonesia*. Penerbit Djambatan, Jakarta, 1974. A very good short-term course for English-speaking foreigners. Sold all over Indonesia.

Almatsier, A.M. *The Easy Way to Master the Indonesian language*. Penerbit Djambatan, Jakarta, 1992. This widely available book is a lesson by lesson method of learning Indonesian. Designed especially for the long-term resident, it has chapters on everyday situations expats are likely to run into—To the Supermarket, Sports, Colloquial Expressions, etc.

Echols, John, and H. Shadily, *An English-Indonesian Dictionary*. Ithaca, New York: Cornell University Press, 1975. With 25,000 headwords, this is the only truly comprehensive modern English-Indonesian dictionary. Includes modern idioms and slang, many abbreviations, technical terms, cross-references, especially to irregular verb forms and noun plurals. Complements the authors' latest work (see below). This is the Big Artillery, the best available, the standard used by English speakers ever since the first edition was published in 1961.

Echols, John and H. Shadily, *An Indonesian-English Dictionary*. Ithaca, New York: Cornell University Press, 1989. A much-revised and much-expanded third edition of the authors' previous edition published in 1963. This comprehensive, well-balanced register of the Indonesian vocabulary contains all the main derivations and clear, accurate definitions. Where necessary, definitions are accompanied by simple sentences that illustrate usage. None better for the serious English-speaking student.

Everyday Indonesian Phrasebook & Dictionary. Singapore: Periplus Editions, 1995. An in-depth teach yourself book for people who want to master rudimentary Indonesian without spending too much time at it, focusing on practical usage and colloquial speech. Coverage of basic pronunciation, grammar, and conversation is followed by a handy dictionary listing the most commonly used words. Oey's book is also a useful guide to Indonesia's etiquette, body language, cultural dos and don'ts, though the black and white illustrations don't contribute much. Available in both the U.S. and Indonesia.

Indonesia Phrasebook. Australia: Lonely Planet Publications, 1995. If you memorize this little booklet, it'll serve you quite adequately for a 30-day-or-less stay.

Johns, Yohanni. *Bahasa Indonesia, Books One & Two*. Singapore: Periplus Editions, 1995. This two-volume set presents a graded course in Bahasa Indonesia developed at the Australian National University. Used by universities all over the world, it is particularly appreciated by those who wish to master the language through self-study at intermediate and advanced levels. An excellent, in-depth, and completely self-contained course, providing clear explanations of all the basic grammar, sample sentences and exercises, plus extensive notes on usage and etiquette.

Kramer, A.L.N. *Tuttle's Concise Indonesian Dictionary*. Rutland, Vermont: Charles E. Tuttle, 1993. This easy-to-use bilingual dictionary features 18,000 entries including colloquial usages, multiple definitions, clear, easy-to-read type, pronunciation aids. Sturdily cloth-bound for heavy travel, it's one of the best pocket dictionaries around.

Kwee, John B. *Teach Yourself Indonesian*. England: Hodder & Stoughton, 1992. Carefully graded, difficult lessons, with exercises and answers at the end of each chapter, take the student through pronunciation and word order, parts of speech and grammar, to the point where he or she will be able to take part in everyday conversation and read simple texts.

Pocket Dictionary: Indonesian-English/English-Indonesian. Singapore: Periplus Editions, 1995. A handy pocket bidirectional dictionary containing the 2,000 most commonly-used Balinese words, though the word "truck" is inexplicably ommitted.

Practical Balinese. Singapore: Periplus Editions, 1995. A communication guide aimed at tourists and travelers. With this book and a few hours practice you can begin to converse immediately. Convenient glossary included in the back.

Shadeg, N. *A Balinese Vocabulary*. Denpasar: Dharma Bakti, 1977. This pocket dictionary of 1,000 basic words and 3,000 basic sentences is now in its 7th edition.

Wolff, John U. *Say it in Indonesian*. New York: Dover Publications, 1983. Compiled by professional linguists, no other Indonesian-language phrasebook contains these features: 2,100 up-to-date practical entries, easy pronunciation transcription, every entry numbered and indexed, quick word substitution for every need, handy bilingual glossary. Very thorough.

Wolff, John U., Dede Oetomo, and Daniel Fietkeiwicz. *Beginning Indonesian Through Self Instruction, Books One, Two and Three*. Ithaca, New York: Cornell University Southeast Asian Program, 1992. The Indonesian language courses at U.C. Berkeley still use this classic coursebook in conjunction with accompanying tapes.

LITERATURE

Baum, Vicki. *A Tale From Bali*. Singapore: Oxford University Press, 1984. Embracing the tumultuous *puputan* years 1904 to 1906, this historical novel is a free rendering of actual events seen from the Balinese point of view. Also a remarkably vivid and melodramatic portrayal of the character of the Balinese, their traditional customs and way of life. First published in English in 1937 by the German author of the *Grand Hotel*.

Darling, Diana. *The Painted Alphabet*. Boston, Massachusetts: Houghton Mifflin, 1990. A novel based on the traditional story *Dukuh Siladri*, this is a vastly entertaining story told with warmth, humor, and wisdom.

The Haughty Toad & Other Tales. A bewitchingly eccentric children's book of Balinese fables, charmingly illustrated by members of Pengosekan's "Community of Artists."

Mahabharata and Ramayana. New York: Mentor/New American Library, 1976. This lively version of the two great Indian classics has been retold by William Buck.

Mason, Victor. *The Butterflies of Bali*. Singapore: Periplus Editions, 1992. A cultural thriller which delves into a secretive civilization where strange characters interact to create an evocative tale of adventure, mystery, and magical encounters.

Mathews, Anna. *The Night of Purnama*. London: The Travel Book Club, 1965. An account of the experiences of Denis and Anna Mathews in the remote village of Iseh on the slopes of Gunung Agung during the disastrous volcanic eruption of 1963.

Weise, Michael. *On the Edge of a Dream*. Michael Weise Productions, 4354 Laurel Canyon Blvd., Suite 234, Studio City, CA 91604. Part dreamscape, part travelogue, this is an enthralling semi-fictional story of two free-spirited adventurers traveling in search of the miraculous, at a time when Balinese society was poised on the brink of the modern tourist age.

MUSIC AND DANCE

Bandem, I Made, and de Boer, Fredrick. *Kaja and Kelod: Balinese Dance in Transition.* Kuala Lumpur: Oxford University Press, 1981. A survey of Balinese dance by the head of the STSI Dance Academy in Denpasar, co-authored by an eminent professor of theater studies at U.S.A.'s Wesleyan University and editor of the *Bali Arts & Culture Newsletter.*

Coast, John. *Dancers of Bali.* New York: G.P. Putnam's Sons, 1953. Fresh out of a Japanese prison camp, Coast toured Bali in a battered jeep, immersing himself in the study of Balinese music and dance. The author organized the first tour of Balinese dancers to visit America. Contains pictures and stories of Balinese performing artists during the 1950s.

Daniel, Ana *Bali: Behind the Mask* New York: Alfred A. Knopf, 1981. A rich, beautiful book that gives, in words and photos, a fascinating document of Bali, its people, and its complex tradition of dance. During several extended stays, the photographer/author studied with a man revered by the Balinese as the last of their great classical dancers, I Nyoman Kakul.

de Zoete, Beryl, and Walter Spies. *Dance and Drama in Bali.* Oxford in Asia, 1973. Working in collaboration, Spies and dance expert de Zoete compiled in the 1930s this first complete survey of Balinese dance, plays, and music. All of the book's brilliant black-and-white photos were taken by Spies, a longterm resident of Bali and creator of the *kecak* dance. A recognized, intelligently written classic.

Kartomi, Margaret J. *Musical Instruments of Indonesia.* Melbourne: Indonesian Arts Society, 1985. An excellent illustrated survey of the full range of musical instruments used in the many island regions of Indonesia, including Bali. Alphabetical format.

McPhee, Colin. *Music in Bali.* New Haven, Connecticut: Yale University Press, 1966. An early definitive classic in the literature of Balinese *gamelan* and musical life in the 1930s, combining ethnographic description with detailed analysis of instrumentation and repertoire.

Slattum, Judy. *Masks of Bali.* San Francisco: Chronicle Books, 1992. A very good introduction to Balinese *wayang topeng.* This beautiful picture book contains 50 stunning photographs of masks, the first mask history, explanations on the process of making ritual masks, and a discussion of the specific types and functions of making Balinese masks. Anyone who is shopping for a mask, or who already owns one, can find in this book the type of character it represents and which rituals it is used in. Photographs by Paul Schraub.

Tenzer, Michael. *Balinese Music.* Singapore: Periplus, 1991. The definitive introduction to more than a dozen different types of Balinese *gamelan* with color photos, a discography, descriptions of the instruments, and a guide to studying and hearing music on Bali. Written by an assistant professor of music at Yale University, this work is the most significant overview of Balinese music to have appeared since Colin McPhee's *Music in Bali* and is considerably more updated than de Beryl Zoete's and Walter Spies' *Dance and Drama in Bali.*

NATURAL PHENOMENON

Eiseman, Fred, and Margaret Eiseman. *Flowers of Bali.* Singapore: Periplus Editions, 1995. An introduction to more than 50 species of Bali's colorful and exotic blossoms. Each bloom is illustrated in full color. Also includes information on the cultural uses of flowers, physical descriptions, and concordances of Balinese, Indonesian and Latin names.

Eiseman, Fred, and Margaret Eiseman. *Fruits of Bali.* A feast of colors, tastes, and smells from Bali's cornucopia of mouthwatering fruits, with descriptions and photos of over 50 delicious fruit varieties. These range from the more familiar mango, guava, and papaya to the exotic durian, rambutan, and *salak*.

King, Ben F., and Edward C. Dickinson. *Birds of South-East Asia*. New York: The Stephen Greene Press, 1988. The only competent field manual to the birdlife of Bali and Indonesia.

Mason, Victor. *Bali Bird Walks*. Boston, Massachusetts: Houghton Mifflin, 1992. Essentially, a very British paean to the natural beauty of the Balinese countryside. The lyrical, humorous, and informative text takes you away from the usual touristic haunts into what the author calls "the realm of the faerie." Emphasis is also given to flowers, trees, mammals, insects, customs, rites, temples, and monuments. Though its use as a guide is limited, trails are graded in order of difficulty.

Mason, Victor. *Birds of Bali*. Singapore: Periplus Editions, 1995. Illustrations by Frank Jarvis. A comprehensive and richly illustrated introduction to 120 of Bali's most notable avian species. Each bird is portrayed in a striking watercolor, and a complete checklist of sighted species is appended, giving likely habitats as well as all the most convenient places for viewing birds.

Warren, William. *Balinese Gardens*. Singapore: Periplus Editions, 1995. A large-format book filled with information on Bali's physical landscape and Balinese conceptions of nature and the traditional house, temple, and palace gardens. Numerous superb photographs by Luca Invernezzi Tettoni show modern and traditional gardens.

PAINTING

Djelantik, A.A.M. *Balinese Paintings*. Singapore: Images of Asia Series, Oxford University Press, 1986. A concise primer of Balinese painting styles and techniques written by an authority on the subject for the non-specialist reader. The author also examines the intriguing period of transition in which Balinese art finds itself today. Although a thin volume, it is extensively illustrated.

Friend, Donald. *Donald Friend, 1915-1989: Retrospective*. Sydney, Australia: Art Gallery of New South Wales, 1990. The first published retrospective of one of the leading Australian artists of the modern era. Friend's greatest works were painted on Bali where he lived and worked between 1966 and 1980.

Kam, Garrett. *Perceptions of Paradise: Images of Bali in the Arts*. Ubud, Indonesia: Neka Museum, 1993. Not only a handsomely produced catalog of 22 paintings found in the collection of the Neka Museum, but a wide-ranging historical and cultural study of the whole Balinese artistic tradition. Kam uses the paintings and accompanying photographs as a window through which he interprets Bali's entire artistic life. The publisher, Suteja Neka, is a dynamic and enthusiastic patron of the arts.

Neka Museum: Guide to the Painting Collection. Bali, Indonesia: Neka Museum, 1986. An illustrated history of Balinese painting by Neka, a respected painter, collector, and gallery owner in Campuan, Bali. Contains full-color photos and black-and-white renditions of the works in Neka's collection, as well as biographies of Balinese and foreign painters.

Pucci, Idanna. *The Epic of Life*. New York: Alfred Van der Marck Editions, 1985. The extraordinary paintings in this large-format art book grace the ceiling of the Kerta Gosa Palace of Justice in Bali's former royal capital of Klungkung. Opposite each full-color reproduction is a vivid recounting of the section in the Hindu epic, the Mahabharata, which corresponds to the scene. An exhaustive and important study.

Rhodius, Hans, and John Darling, *Walter Spies and Balinese Art*. Published under the auspices of the Tropical Museum, Amsterdam, by Terra, Zutphen, 1980. A narrative portrait of the extraordinary life and work of Walter Spies, the Russian-born German artist who lived and worked in Bali from 1927 to 1940.

Willem G. Hofker, Painter of Bali. A helpful and carefully researched text. The plates bring home the style, poetry, and pathos of Hofker's beautiful paintings of women.

PHOTOGRAPHY BOOKS

Bali. Singapore: Times Editions, 1986. An attractive full-color photo essay of Balinese life and culture by three talented professional photographers.

Lueras, Leonard, and Ian R. Lloyd. *Bali: The Ultimate Island.* New York: St. Martin's Press, 1987. A spectacular coffee table book with historical black-and-white photos, everyday portraits, and coverage of contemporary arts and crafts, ceremonies, workers of the land, and commerce. Special features are a comprehensive discography-cassettography and a filmography.

Lueras, Leonard, and Rio Helmi. *Bali High: Paradise from the Air.* Singapore, Times Editions: 1990. In this book you see, from a new and elevated vantage point, beautiful color photographs of the volcanoes, towns, hamlets, ravines, terraces, rivers, temples, harbors, and beaches of Bali.

RELIGION

Bakker, F.L. *The Struggle of the Hindu Balinese Intellectuals.* VU University Press, 1993. An investigation of the recent developments in modern Hindu thinking in Indonesia since the country became independent and the leading role Balinese Hindus play in modern Indonesian Hinduism.

Belo, Jane. *Balinese Temple Festival.* Seattle: University of Washington Press, 1953. A guide through one of Bali's colorful festivals as observed by an astute and insightful anthropologist.

Hooykaas, C. *A Balinese Temple Festival.* The Hague: Martinus Nijhoff, 1977. A word-by-word and gesture-by-gesture explanation of a

temple festival which will be of interest to not only anthropologists and students of comparative religions but also to travelers.

TRAVELOGUES

Baranay, Inez. *The Edge of Bali.* Sydney: Angus & Robertson, 1992. This tale explores the culture of tourism on Bali through the experiences of three different tourists, unknown to each other and each with an entirely different agenda. An interesting evocation of the kinds of encounters one has within the Kuta-Ubud-Candidasa circuit.

Blair, Lawrence, with Lorne Blair. *Ring of Fire.* New York: Bantam Books, 1988. The story of two brothers who, for a period of 12 years starting in 1973, penetrated and filmed some of the most remote regions of Indonesia. The book is an adaptation from a film which became a four-part cycle which opened public television's "Adventure" series in May of 1988. Part two and three of the series take place on Bali.

Gorer, Geoffrey. *Bali and Angkor.* Singapore: Oxford University Press, 1986. A 1930s pleasure trip to Sumatra, Java, Bali, Thailand, and Cambodia. An observant travel writer analyzes the role art and religion play in the life of the Balinese. Gorer's writing has great style.

McPhee, Colin. *A House in Bali.* Singapore: Oxford University Press, 1985. This account of a young American composer and ethnomusicologist's stay in Bali prior to WW II is an amusing and sympathetic look at Balinese society and a rare look at the original importance of music in Balinese life. McPhee was significant not for his music but for his incisive role in reviving many dying *gamelan* traditions and his invaluable descriptions of the music of Bali during the 1930s.

Powell, Hickman. *The Last Paradise.* Singapore: Oxford University Press, 1986. An American journalist's "discovery" of Bali in the 1920s. A description of Bali's inhabitants, customs, and beliefs before the advent of modern tourism.

Simpson, Colin. *Bali and Beyond.* Sydney: Angus and Robertson, 1972. Simpson describes the dancing, music, and other arts, a cremation, and his chapter "The muddy-legged musician" conveys vividly the life of a typically cultured peasant who is a rice farmer by day and a *gamelan* musician by night. Includes 24 pages of color plates.

VIDEOS

Done Bali. Australia: SBS, 1994. While there have been many films which have expounded the Western image of Bali as an idyllic, creative, tropical holiday destination, Australian-made *Done Bali* looks behind the glamorous, romantic appearances to the island's traumatic past and its current, fragile present as it moves into the era of "five-star tourism." This beguiling film uses rare archival film footage to examine a range of the island's social and historical tragedies.

Lempad of Bali. New York: Mystic Fire Video, 1979. Directed by John Darling and Lorna Blair, co-director of *Ring of Fire.* This 60-minute color video captures some of the strength and genius of a remarkable artist famous throughout Europe in the 1920s for his remarkable religious and erotic art. Lempad died a fully conscious death (which he predicted, and to which he invited his family) at the age of 116.

Ring of Fire, Vol. Two. New York: Mystic Fire Video, 1988. A four-part film which chronicled the 10-year voyage of two filmmakers, brothers Lorne and Lawrence Blair, through Indonesia's exotic, mysterious Outer Islands. Volume Two ("Dance of the Warriors") in the series shows a mesmerizing segment of a Balinese *barong* dance.

INDEX

Italicized page numbers indicate information in charts, maps, or special topics.

ABOUT THE AUTHOR

KIETH GUNNAR

Bill Dalton was born in Waltham, Massachusetts. After a stint as a paramedic in the street battles of Santo Domingo and four years as a student of philosophy at the University of Copenhagen on the GI Bill, Dalton embarked on a seven-year journey through 81 countries, working as a letter sorter in Scandinavia, an apple-picker in Israel, a rum-runner in India, an English teacher in war-torn Cambodia, and a gardener in Australia. Dalton founded Moon Publications in a youth hostel in Queensland, Australia, in 1973, and has worked writing and publishing travel guides ever since. Though his travels have taken him around the world, he has a special interest in Southeast Asia. During the past 26 years, Dalton has explored over 100 of Indonesia's 17,000 islands, visiting the country at least 30 times and amassing a total of more than six years in the islands.

READER PROFILE

Knowing a bit about you and your travel experience will help me improve this book. I'll collect the results—including your picks for Bali's top-10 lists—and report my findings in the next edition. Include suggestions on guesthouses, restaurants, and transportation secrets that might help the next traveler. Use extra pages if necessary. Please send the following survey, plus your comments and recommendations, to:

Bill Dalton
Moon Travel Handbooks
P.O. Box 3040
Chico, CA 95927-3040
USA

1. Gender: ☐ male ☐ female

2. Age: ☐ under 25 ☐ 25-30 ☐ 31-35
☐ 36-40 ☐ 41-50 ☐ 51-65 ☐ 66+

3. Status: ☐ single ☐ married

4. Income: ☐ less than $15K ☐ $16-25K
☐ $26-40K ☐ $41-60K
☐ $61-90K ☐ $91K+

5. Occupation: _____

6. Education: ☐ high school
☐ college post-grad

7. Travel style: ☐ budget
☐ moderate ☐ luxury

8. Vacations: ☐ once yearly
☐ twice yearly ☐ 3+ yearly

9. Why do you travel?

10. What's best about traveling in Bali?

11. What's worst about traveling in Bali?

12. This journey:
Length of time: _____
Places on Bali visited: _____

Expenses:
a. Total: _____
b. Average daily expense: _____
c. Average hotel price: _____
d. Average meal price: _____
e. Total airfare: _____
f. Shopping expenses: _____

13. Favorites (also include a list of your least favorites):
a. Best regions of Bali (in order of preference):
b. Hotels and guesthouses (address, price, description):
c. Restaurants (address, price, favorite dishes):
d. Airline:
e. Cuisine:
f. Nightspots:
g. Cultural events:
h. Outdoor adventures:
i. Temples or historical sites:
j. Beaches:
k. People:
l. Travel moments:

14. This book:
a. Strongest points:
b. Weakest points:
c. How accurate did you find the information:
d. Favorite introduction section (history, government, etc.; none):
e. Suggestions for improvements:

Name: _____

Address: _____
_____
_____

Date of survey: _____

☐ Please give me a free subscription to Moon's newsletter, *Travel Matters*.

MOON TRAVEL HANDBOOKS
DISCOVER THE DIFFERENCE

Moon Travel Handbooks provide focused, comprehensive coverage of distinct destinations all over the world. Our goal is to give travelers all the background and practical information they'll need for an extraordinary travel experience.

Every Handbook begins with an in-depth essay about the land, the people, their history, art, politics, and social concerns—an entire bookcase of cultural insight and introductory information in one portable volume. We also provide accurate, up-to-date coverage of all the practicalities: language, currency, transportation, accommodations, food, and entertainment. And Moon's maps are legendary, covering not only cities and highways, but parks and trails that are often difficult to find in other sources.

Below are highlights of Moon's Asia and Pacific Travel Handbook series. Our complete list of Handbooks covering North America and Hawaii, Mexico, Central America and the Caribbean, and Asia and the Pacific, are listed on the order form on the accompanying pages. To purchase Moon Travel Handbooks, please check your local bookstore or order by phone: (800) 345-5473 Monday-Friday 8 a.m.-5 p.m. PST.

MOON OVER ASIA
THE ASIA AND THE PACIFIC TRAVEL HANDBOOK SERIES

"Moon guides are wittily written and warmly personal; what's more, they present a vivid, often raw vision of Asia without promotional overtones. They also touch on such topics as official corruption and racism, none of which rate a mention in the bone-dry, air-brushed, dry-cleaned version of Asia written up in the big U.S. guidebooks."
—*Far Eastern Economic Review*

AUSTRALIA HANDBOOK
by Marael Johnson, Andrew Hempstead, and Nadina Purdon, 913 pages, **$21.95**
Explore the "land down under" with Moon's *Australia Handbook*, providing comprehensive coverage of outdoor recreation, the hottest sights, and detailed travel practicalities.

BALI HANDBOOK
by Bill Dalton, 800 pages, **$19.95**
"This book is for the in-depth traveler, interested in history and art, willing to experiment with language and food and become immersed in the culture of Bali."

— *Great Expeditions*

BANGKOK HANDBOOK
by Michael Buckley, 221 pages, **$13.95**
"Helps make sense of this beguiling paradox of a city . . .
very entertaining reading."

—*The Vancouver Sun*

FIJI ISLANDS HANDBOOK
by David Stanley, 275 pages, **$13.95**
"If you want to encounter Fiji and not just ride through it, this book
is for you."

—*Great Expeditions*

HONG KONG HANDBOOK
by Kerry Moran, 347 pages, **$15.95**
"One of the most honest glimpses into Hong Kong the Peoples
Republic of China would like never to have seen."

—*TravelNews Asia*

INDONESIA HANDBOOK
by Bill Dalton, 1,351 pages, **$25.00**
"Looking for a fax machine in Palembang, a steak dinner on
Ambon or the best place to photograph Bugis prahus in Sulawesi?
Then buy this brick of a book, which contains a full kilogram of
detailed directions and advice."

—*Asia, Inc. Magazine*

"The classic guidebook to the archipelago."

—*Condé Nast Traveler*

JAPAN HANDBOOK
by J.D. Bisignani, 952 pages, **$22.50**
Winner: Lowell Thomas Gold Award, Society of American Travel
Writers
"The scope of this guide book is staggering, ranging from an
introduction to Japanese history and culture through to the best
spots for shopping for pottery in Mashie or silk pongee in
Kagoshima."

—*Golden Wing*

"More travel information on Japan than any other guidebook."

—*The Japan Times*

MICRONESIA HANDBOOK
by Neil Levy, 330 pages, **$14.95**
"Remarkably informative, fair-minded, sensible, and readable . . ."

—*The Journal of the Polynesian Society*

NEPAL HANDBOOK
by Kerry Moran, 428 pages, **$18.95**
Winner: Lowell Thomas Gold Award, Society of American
Travel Writers
"This is an excellent guidebook, exploring every aspect of the
country the visitor is likely to want to know about with both wit
and authority."

—*South China Morning Post*

NEW ZEALAND HANDBOOK
by Jane King, 544 pages, **$19.95**
"Far and away the best guide to New Zealand."

—*The Atlantic*

OUTBACK AUSTRALIA HANDBOOK
by Marael Johnson, 432 pages, **$18.95**
Winner: Lowell Thomas Silver Award, Society of American
Travel Writers
"Well designed, easy to read, and funny"

—*Buzzworm*

PAKISTAN HANDBOOK
by Isobel Shaw, 660 pages, **$19.95**
Pakistan Handbook guides travelers from the heights of the
Karakorams to the bazaars of Karachi, from sacred mosques in
Sind to the ceasefire line of Azad Kashmir. Includes a detailed
trekking guide with several itineraries for long and short treks
across the Hindu Kush, Karakorams, and Himalayas.

PHILIPPINES HANDBOOK
by Peter Harper and Laurie Fullerton, 638 pages, **$17.95**
"The most comprehensive travel guide done on the Philippines.
Excellent work."

—*Pacific Stars & Stripes*

PRACTICAL NOMAD
by Edward Hasbrouck, 500 pages, **$17.95**
The Practical Nomad is a planning guide for travelers
considering extended, multi-stop international trips, including
around-the-world journeys. This how-to handbook features
essential information on understanding airfares and ticketing,
working with a travel agent, and handling required
documentation such as passports and visas.

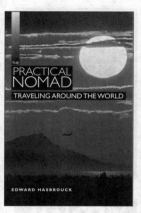

SINGAPORE HANDBOOK
by Carl Parkes, 300 pages, **$15.95**
The most comprehensive guide to the region available, replete
with insider information from a seasoned travel writer.

SOUTHEAST ASIA HANDBOOK
by Carl Parkes, 1,103 pages, **$21.95**
Winner: Lowell Thomas Bronze Award, Society of American
Travel Writers
"Plenty of information on sights and entertainment, also provides
a political, environmental and cultural context that will allow
visitors to begin to interpret what they see."

—*London Sunday Times*

MOONBELT

A new concept in moneybelts. Made of heavy-duty Cordura nylon, the Moonbelt offers maximum protection for your money and important papers. This pouch, designed for all-weather comfort, slips under your shirt or waistband, rendering it virtually undetectable and inaccessible to pickpockets. It features a one-inch high-test quick-release buckle so there's no more fumbling around for the strap or repeated adjustments. This handy plastic buckle opens and closes with a touch, but won't come undone until you want it to. Moonbelts accommodate traveler's checks, passports, cash, photos, etc. Size 5 x 9 inches. Available in black only. **$8.95**

MOON TRAVEL HANDBOOKS

NORTH AMERICA AND HAWAII

Alaska-Yukon Handbook (0897) $17.95
Alberta and the Northwest Territories Handbook (0463) $17.95
Arizona Traveler's Handbook (0714). $17.95
Atlantic Canada Handbook (0072) $17.95
Big Island of Hawaii Handbook (1001). $15.95
British Columbia Handbook (0145). $15.95
California Handbook (0803) $21.95
Colorado Handbook (0447) $18.95
Georgia Handbook (0390) $17.95
Hawaii Handbook (0005). $19.95
Honolulu-Waikiki Handbook (0587) $14.95
Idaho Handbook (0889). $18.95
Kauai Handbook (0919) $15.95
Maui Handbook (0579) $14.95
Montana Handbook (0498). $17.95
Nevada Handbook (0641) $16.95
New Mexico Handbook (0862). $15.95
New York Handbook (0811) $19.95
Northern California Handbook (3840) $19.95
Oregon Handbook (0102) $16.95
Road Trip USA (0366). $22.50
Southern California Handbook (1028) $19.95
Tennessee Handbook (0439) $17.95
Texas Handbook (0633) $17.95
Utah Handbook (0870) $17.95
Washington Handbook (0455). $19.95
Wisconsin Handbook (0927) $16.95
Wyoming Handbook (0854) $17.95

ASIA AND THE PACIFIC

Australia Handbook (0722) $21.95
Bali Handbook (0730). $19.95
Bangkok Handbook (0595) $13.95
Fiji Islands Handbook (0382) $13.95
Hong Kong Handbook (0560) $15.95
Indonesia Handbook (0625) $25.00
Japan Handbook (3700) $22.50

Micronesia Handbook (0773) $14.95
Nepal Handbook (0412) $18.95
New Zealand Handbook (0331) $19.95
Outback Australia Handbook (0471) $18.95
Pakistan Handbook (0692) $22.50
Philippines Handbook (0048) $17.95
Singapore Handbook (0781) $15.95
Southeast Asia Handbook (0021) $21.95
South Korea Handbook (0749) $19.95
South Pacific Handbook (0404) $22.95
Tahiti-Polynesia Handbook (0374) $13.95
Thailand Handbook (0420) $19.95
Tibet Handbook (3905) $30.00
Vietnam, Cambodia & Laos Handbook (0293) $18.95

MEXICO
Baja Handbook (0528) $15.95
Cabo Handbook (0285) $14.95
Cancún Handbook (0501) $13.95
Central Mexico Handbook (0234) $15.95
Mexico Handbook (0315) $21.95
Northern Mexico Handbook (0226) $16.95
Pacific Mexico Handbook (0978) $17.95
Puerto Vallarta Handbook (0986) $14.95
Yucatán Peninsula Handbook (0242) $15.95

CENTRAL AMERICA AND THE CARIBBEAN
Belize Handbook (0307) $15.95
Caribbean Handbook (0277) $16.95
Costa Rica Handbook (0358) $19.95
Cuba Handbook (0951) $19.95
Dominican Republic Handbook (0900) $16.95
Honduras Handbook (0994) $15.95
Jamaica Handbook (0706) $15.95
Virgin Islands Handbook (0935) $13.95

INTERNATIONAL
Egypt Handbook (3891) $18.95
Moon Handbook (0668) $10.00
Moscow-St. Petersburg Handbook (3913) $13.95
Staying Healthy in Asia, Africa, and Latin America (0269) $11.95
The Practical Nomad (0765) $17.95

WHERE TO BUY MOON TRAVEL HANDBOOKS

BOOKSTORES AND LIBRARIES: Moon Travel Handbooks are sold worldwide. Please contact our sales manager for a list of wholesalers and distributors in your area.

TRAVELERS: We would like to have Moon Travel Handbooks available throughout the world. Please ask your bookstore to write or call us for ordering information. If your bookstore will not order our guides for you, please contact us for a free catalog.

> Moon Publications, Inc.
> P.O. Box 3040
> Chico, CA 95927-3040 U.S.A.
> tel.: (800) 345-5473
> fax: (916) 345-6751
> e-mail: travel@moon.com

IMPORTANT ORDERING INFORMATION

PRICES: All prices are subject to change. We always ship the most current edition. We will let you know if there is a price increase on the book you order.

SHIPPING AND HANDLING OPTIONS: Domestic UPS or USPS first class (allow 10 working days for delivery): $3.50 for the first item, 50 cents for each additional item.

EXCEPTIONS: *Tibet Handbook, Mexico Handbook,* and *Indonesia Handbook* shipping $4.50; $1.00 for each additional *Tibet Handbook, Mexico Handbook,* or *Indonesia Handbook.*

Moonbelt shipping is $1.50 for one, 50 cents for each additional belt.

Add $2.00 for same-day handling.

UPS 2nd Day Air or Printed Airmail requires a special quote.

International Surface Bookrate 8-12 weeks delivery: $3.00 for the first item, $1.00 for each additional item. Note: Moon Publications cannot guarantee international surface bookrate shipping. Moon recommends sending international orders via air mail, which requires a special quote.

FOREIGN ORDERS: Orders that originate outside the U.S.A. must be paid for with an international money order, a check in U.S. currency drawn on a major U.S. bank based in the U.S.A., or Visa or MasterCard.

TELEPHONE ORDERS: We accept Visa or MasterCard payments. Minimum order is US$15. Call in your order: (800) 345-5473, 8 a.m.-5 p.m. Pacific standard time.

ORDER FORM

Prices are subject to change without notice. Be sure to call (800) 345-5473
8 a.m.–5 p.m. PST for current prices and editions, or for the
name of the bookstore nearest you that carries Moon Travel Handbooks.
(See important ordering information on preceding page.)

Name: _____ Date: _____

Street: _____

City: _____ Daytime Phone: _____

QUANTITY	TITLE	PRICE

Taxable Total_____

Sales Tax (7.25%) for California Residents_____

Shipping & Handling_____

TOTAL_____

Ship: ☐ UPS (no P.O. Boxes) ☐ 1st class ☐ International surface mail

Ship to: ☐ address above ☐ other _____

Make checks payable to: **MOON PUBLICATIONS, INC.**, P.O. Box 3040, Chico, CA 95927-3040 U.S.A.
We accept Visa and MasterCard. **To Order**: Call in your Visa or MasterCard number, or send a written order with your Visa or MasterCard number and expiration date clearly written.

Card Number: ☐ **Visa** ☐ **MasterCard**

☐ ☐ ☐ ☐ ☐ ☐ ☐ ☐ ☐ ☐ ☐ ☐ ☐ ☐ ☐ ☐

Exact Name on Card: _____

Expiration date: _____

Signature: _____

THE METRIC SYSTEM

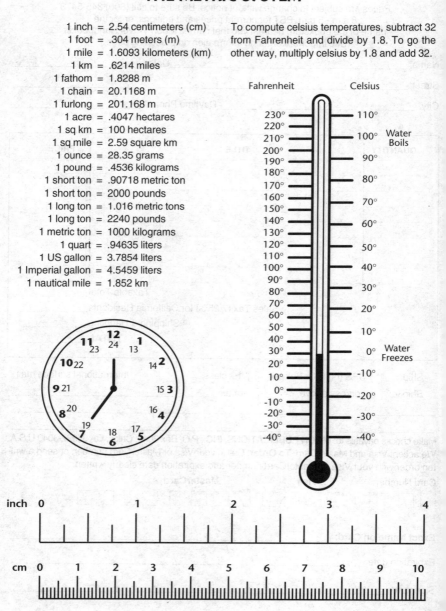

1 inch = 2.54 centimeters (cm)
1 foot = .304 meters (m)
1 mile = 1.6093 kilometers (km)
1 km = .6214 miles
1 fathom = 1.8288 m
1 chain = 20.1168 m
1 furlong = 201.168 m
1 acre = .4047 hectares
1 sq km = 100 hectares
1 sq mile = 2.59 square km
1 ounce = 28.35 grams
1 pound = .4536 kilograms
1 short ton = .90718 metric ton
1 short ton = 2000 pounds
1 long ton = 1.016 metric tons
1 long ton = 2240 pounds
1 metric ton = 1000 kilograms
1 quart = .94635 liters
1 US gallon = 3.7854 liters
1 Imperial gallon = 4.5459 liters
1 nautical mile = 1.852 km

To compute celsius temperatures, subtract 32 from Fahrenheit and divide by 1.8. To go the other way, multiply celsius by 1.8 and add 32.

Fahrenheit   Celsius

230°   110°
220°
210°   100°   Water Boils
200°
190°   90°
180°
170°   80°
160°
150°   70°
140°
130°   60°
120°
110°   50°
100°   40°
90°
80°   30°
70°
60°   20°
50°
40°   10°
30°   0°   Water Freezes
20°
10°   -10°
0°
-10°   -20°
-20°
-30°   -30°
-40°   -40°

inch 0   1   2   3   4

cm 0 1 2 3 4 5 6 7 8 9 10

INDONESIA

OVER 17,000 ISLANDS TO EXPLORE.

ONE AIRLINE TO TAKE YOU THERE.

Garuda Indonesia
THE AIRLINE OF INDONESIA

800 3 GARUDA
800 342-7832